The Oxford Dictionary of

Phrase,
Saying, and
Quotation

The Oxford Dictionary of

Phrase, Saying, and Quotation

SECOND EDITION

Edited by **Susan Ratcliffe**

OXFORD
UNIVERSITY PRESS

OXFORD

UNIVERSITY PRESS

Great Clarendon Street, Oxford OX2 6DP

Oxford University Press is a department of the University of Oxford.
It furthers the University's objective of excellence in research, scholarship,
and education by publishing worldwide in

Oxford New York

Auckland Bangkok Buenos Aires Cape Town Chennai
Dar es Salaam Delhi Hong Kong Istanbul Karachi Kolkata
Kuala Lumpur Madrid Melbourne Mexico City Mumbai Nairobi
São Paulo Shanghai Singapore Taipei Tokyo Toronto

with an associated company in Berlin

Published in the United States
by Oxford University Press Inc., New York

First published 1997
This second edition published 2002

British Library Cataloguing in Publication Data

Data available

Library of Congress Cataloging in Publication Data

Data available

ISBN 0-19-866269-6

10 9 8 7 6 5 4 3 2 1

Designed by Jane Stevenson
Typeset in Photina and Argo
by Interactive Sciences Ltd
Printed and bound in Great Britain
on acid-free paper by Biddles Ltd
www.biddles.co.uk

Project Team

Managing Editor	Elizabeth Knowles
Associate Editor	Susan Ratcliffe
Index Editor	Carolyn Garwes
Library Research	Ralph Bates Marie G. Diaz
Reading Programme	Verity Mason Helen Rappaport
Proof-reading	Kim Allen Fabia Claris Penny Trumble

We are grateful to Jean Harker and Richard Ramage for additional reading.

Contents

Preface to the Second Edition

As Edmund Burke tells us, 'Nothing in progression can rest in its original plan. We may as well think of rocking a grown man in the cradle of an infant'. The *Oxford Dictionary of Phrase, Saying, and Quotation* is a unique reference book which provides a means of access to aspects of our language more commonly separated, emphasising the links between individual remarks and fixed phrases and sayings. In this second edition we have focused more particularly on those links, adding new material and in many instances giving more detailed information on existing items.

Where sufficient fresh material has been available, new themes have been added. Topics such as **Computers and the Internet** ('The PC is the LSD of the '90's'), **Farming**, **Health and Fitness** ('Exercise is bunk'), **Management**, **The Paranormal** (*It's life, Jim, but not as we know it*), and **Photography** ('a moment of embarrassment and a lifetime of pleasure') make an appearance. In all themes, the order of the sections now reflects the importance of the phrases and sayings which distinguish this book from more conventional dictionaries of quotations.

Proverbs and sayings, which now appear at the beginning of each theme, have been enhanced by the introduction of many more modern sayings which have passed into the language, including advertising slogans such as . . . *But I know a man who can*, television catchphrases (*The truth is out there*), political sayings (*Don't ask, don't tell*), and even video games (*All your base are belong to us*). At the same time, more traditional sayings which still have a modern resonance have been added: *It is easier to build two chimneys than to maintain one* seems as true today as in the 16th century. Some modern sayings which sound ancient can indeed be traced back to much earlier forms: *I cried because I had no shoes, until I met a man who had no feet* derives from the 13th century Persian poet Sadi.

The information given on the proverbs and sayings has been greatly expanded. Glosses have been added to all but the clearest, explaining archaic or unusual usages or words, and indicating the circumstances in which the saying may be used. The historical aspect of the dictionary has been enhanced by adding an approximate date of first record for the proverbs (mid 17th century, early 19th century), though the reader should bear in mind that the proverb may well have been current long before, and indeed in many cases this first written appearance is of the form 'as has often been said'.

The phrase sections have been more closely linked to the rest of the book, by concentrating on phrases related to sayings or quotations, or with a history of some kind, and removing transparent idioms. So *like as two peas* has no story behind it, and has been removed, but *true blue* and *the Red Queen hypothesis*, which have interesting origins and links to quotations, have been added. We have been able to draw on the results of the reading programme for the *Oxford English Dictionary*, and this has brought to light many new items: modern sayings such as *Three strikes and you're out*, and older ones such as *Who goes home?*, old phrases such as *a poisoned chalice*, new ones such as *the triple-witching hour*, and others from all over the

English-speaking world: *Buckley's chance* and *stolen generation* from Australia, *Big Blue Machine* from Canada, *watchful waiting* and *bully pulpit* from the United States, and *Jedburgh justice* from Scotland.

The quotations sections have been extensively revised. The ongoing reading programme of Oxford Quotations Dictionaries has been of great assistance here, monitoring the arrival of new quotations and the re-emergence of old ones. Thus non-Western cultures are more widely represented: in **Education** Confucius tells us 'In education there should be no class distinction', and in **Duty and Responsibility** the Bhagavadgita says 'And do thy duty, even if it be humble, rather than another's, even if it be great. To die in one's duty is life: to live in another's is death'. More material of historical interest has been included (for example the Declaration of Arbroath under **Scotland**, James Cook's views of the inhabitants of **Australia**, and Lord Reith's 1926 view of standards in **Broadcasting**), and there are still many new quotations from the past to re-discover. Recent wars have revived Helmuth von Moltke's 'No plan survives first contact with the enemy' (and the medieval concept of a *just war*), while modern science is still unsure whether to agree with Plato that 'God is always doing geometry', and a recent Chancellor of the Exchequer has quoted Colbert, Louis XIV's Finance Minister, on **Taxes**: 'The art of taxation consists in so plucking the goose as to obtain the largest possible amount of feathers with the smallest possible amount of hissing'. More recent quotations include the science-fiction writer Arthur C. Clarke on the millennium at **Festivals and Celebrations**, actress Julia Roberts on **Fame**, and US politician Donald Rumsfeld's advice on **Advice**.

The new additions range from the traditional maxim to the current soundbite, from the flippant to the philosophical, and from the moral to the subversive. So **Murder** now includes James Bond's *licensed to kill*, the Koran's 'Whoso slays a soul not to retaliate for a soul slain, nor for corruption done in the land, shall be as if he had slain mankind altogether', and the poisoner Thomas Griffiths Wainewright's justification for his crime 'She had very thick ankles'. **Excellence and Mediocrity** begins with the sixteenth century Latin saying *Corruptio optimi pessima* [*Corruption of the best becomes the worst*], and ends with George W. Bush's encouraging words 'And to the C students, I say you, too, can be president of the United States'. In **Quantities and Qualities**, the astronomer Patrick Moore considers infinity, while the theologian St Augustine discusses the number six, and the traditional saying *The whole is more than the sum of the parts* is related to Aristotle's thoughts on the subject in **Causes and Consequences**.

While more than 20% of this second edition is new, and extensive material has been added to the existing sayings and phrases, any such book must inevitably depend very heavily on all the work done for the previous edition, and I should like to acknowledge that. Likewise, I am grateful to the many people who have contributed to the current text in various ways. In particular, my thanks go to Elizabeth Knowles, editor of the first edition and Managing Editor of Oxford Quotations Dictionaries, for her practical assistance in matters lexical and her manifold ideas and encouragement while editing this book. Working on such a varied and wide-ranging text has been fascinating and enlightening, and I hope the reader will find it equally interesting.

SUSAN RATCLIFFE

Oxford, 2002

Introduction to First Edition

The *Oxford Dictionary of Phrase, Saying, and Quotation* opens up an overall view of the central stock of our figurative language, by bringing together over 10,000 quotations, proverbs, and phrases, in a structure which at once allows access to individual items, and expresses the essential relationship between them.

Traditionally, dictionaries covering this aspect of the language have focused on the difference between the given categories. A dictionary of quotations, for example, is likely to establish its selection criteria on the definition of a quotation as 'a passage or remark quoted'; that is, a reference to something said by a particular person at a particular time. Such a definition by implication excludes the proverb, which we may define as 'a short pithy saying . . . held to embody a general truth', and the phrase 'a group of words (not a sentence) with a particular meaning'. However, even as we describe these categories, we are likely to think of exceptions to the rule. The most established proverbs, after all, come from the Old Testament book of *Proverbs*, and may thus be regarded as forming part of the wide range of biblical quotations. To take one verse as an example:

> Hope deferred maketh the heart sick: but when the desire cometh
> it is a tree of life.

This is a quotation; we derive from it the saying *Hope deferred makes the heart sick*, to set with other proverbial expressions about hope. One of these, recorded from the eighteenth century, is the comment (now often used ironically) *Hope springs eternal*, the source of which is a quotation from Pope's *Essay on Man*:

> Hope springs eternal in the human breast.
> Man never Is, but always To be blest.

The essential difference between a quotation and a proverb or saying is that a quotation is seen as something traceable back to a single utterance at a given instance (whether or not the precise time and place can now be identified); a proverb or saying embodies an essential truth, and as such is by implication capable of being coined by different people at different times. But it is also clear from these examples that there is a considerable degree of overlap, and that one can derive from the other.

It might be thought easier to make the case for confining phrases to a separate dictionary, but as soon as we begin looking at examples, the connection with the other two categories becomes clear. If we compare an unbreakable rule to *the law of the Medes and the Persians*, or say of an ominous sign that it is *the writing on the wall*, we are quoting directly from the biblical story in the Old Testament book of *Daniel* of Belshazzar's feast and the fall of Babylon. If we express the utter completeness of a loss in the words *at one fell swoop*, we are quoting Shakespeare, and if a cat catches a bird and we exclaim *Nature red in tooth and claw*, we are quoting Tennyson. The phrase deriving from the quotation is likely to have become so familiar that knowledge of its origin is submerged, but the links are there, and in this dictionary they can be seen. The links between proverbs and phrases can be even clearer, as in the relationship between *It is the last straw that breaks the camel's back* and *the final straw*.

With material brought together in this way, the reader need not feel that the item about which information is wanted has been excluded because of how it is regarded. You do not need to know whether *Dogs bark, but the caravan moves on* is a quotation or a proverb before looking for it here. Someone wanting an explanation of the term *weasel words* will be led by the keyword index to Theodore roosevelt's explanation of the term in the quotations for **Language**. Approaching from another angle, someone looking for an apt or pithy association associated with a particular topic can turn to a specific section in search of *winged words*.

The interrelation between quotations, sayings, and phrases is best seen when considering items dealing with the same subject, and so this dictionary is arranged by theme. From **Absence** and **Achievement**, through **Broadcasting**, **Chance and Luck**, **Festivals and Celebrations**, **Government**, **Human Nature**, **Science**, **The Seasons**, and **Towns and Cities**, to **Youth,** the theme titles have been chosen to reflect as wide a range of subjects as possible, while most accurately representing the actual evidence. Classification of items is by subject rather than keyword; Montaigne's 'When I play with my cat, who knows whether she isn't amusing herself with me more than I am with her' (*Essais*, 1580) and the proverbial *A cat has nine lives* are properly found at **Cats**, but *A cat may look at a king* can be used in many contexts, and illustrates **Equality**.

Themes may bring together apparently disparate aspects of a single topic. **Winning and Losing** offers views of competition in a variety of fields. 'One more such victory and we are lost', said Pyrrhus of his costly defeat of the Romans at Asculum in 279 BC, a comment which gives us the phrase *Pyrrhic victory*. 'What is our aim? . . . Victory, victory at all costs . . . for without victory there is no survival', asserted Winston Churchill in 1940. 'What's lost upon the roundabouts we pulls up on the swings', said Patrick Chalmers in 1912, using the fairground metaphor expressed in the proverb *What you lose on the swings you gain on the roundabouts*. The world of sport offers different perspectives on the same theme. 'When in doubt, win the trick' is advice attributed to Edmond Hoyle; Pierre de Coubertin, establishing the modern Olympic Games, put forward the view that 'The important thing in life is not the victory but the contest; the essential thing is not to have won but to have fought well.' This statement of the ideals of amateurism can be set against the golfer Nick Faldo's 1996 assessment of the situation when leading a championship field in wet weather, 'Of course I want to win it . . . I'm not here to have a good time, nor to keep warm and dry.'

Quotations are the heart of the book, as they are at the centre of this overview of language: the standard movement is from quotation to proverb and phrase. (Although at times a quotation may make deliberate allusion to a known saying. *Don't put all your eggs in one basket is traditional advice*—modified by Mark Twain in *Pudd'nhead Wilson* (1894) to 'Put all your eggs in the one basket, and—WATCH THAT BASKET.') Each section, therefore, opens with quotations which are chronologically arranged, a pattern which allows us to hear the different voices speak over the centuries. 'A venal city ripe to perish, if a buyer can be found' said Sallust of Rome

in the first century BC. 'All these men have their price', said Robert Walpole, of
fellow-parliamentarians in the eighteenth century. 'Youth's a stuff will not endure',
said William Shakespeare in 1601. Nearly 400 years later, we have Mary Quant's
comment on the early stages of life, 'Being young is greatly overestimated . . . Any
failure seems so total. Later on you realize you can have another go.'

Quotations for each theme are supported and enhanced by two further sections,
for the best-known and most interesting proverbs and phrases associated with that
theme. (For ease of use, and as specific dates are less significant in these groups,
items are arranged alphabetically: for further details, see the notes on How to Use
the Dictionary.) Coverage is intentionally selective: items have been chosen for their
intrinsic interest, with the aim of illuminating the stock of figurative language for a
given subject.

Proverbial sayings can come from any area of life. *Evil communications corrupt good
manners* was originally a warning from St Paul to the Corinthians about their
unsatisfactory mode of life. *April showers bring forth May flowers* and *Rain before seven,
shine before eleven* are among the traditional sayings of calendar and weather lore.
Your King and Country need you comes from a World War I recruiting poster. Modern
advertising has proved a fertile ground, with such items as *Go to work on an egg* and
more recently the Victoria and Albert's controversial *An ace caff with quite a nice
museum attached*. Catch-phrases also make their contribution, in a range including
Monty Python's *And now for something completely different* and the Nixon
administration's political assessment *It'll play in Peoria*.

As with quotations, it is possible to hear a variety of voices in the 'general truths'
which the proverbs express. Conflicting advice, centuries apart, is offered at
Advertising: if we accept that *Good wine needs no bush*, we are unlikely to believe that
It pays to advertise. At **Appearance**, the traditional view *The cowl does not make the
monk* can be set against the assertion from the world of computing, *What you see is
what you get* (the origin of the term *wysiwyg*). On the other hand, at **Causes and
Consequences**, the old and new speak with one voice, as *Good seed makes a good crop*
is matched with the terse assessment, *Garbage in, garbage out*.

Phrases, like proverbs, come from many sources, from the most traditional to
brand-new: we have already seen examples from the Bible and Shakespeare.
Classical references include *apple of discord, a sop to Cerberus, sow dragons' teeth*, and
Trojan horse. If we describe someone as behaving like a *dog in a manger* we are
making an allusion to one of Aesop's fables; the expression *Open Sesame* for an
apparently magical solution to an insoluble problem takes us back to the *Arabian
Nights* and the story of Ali Baba and the Forty Thieves. Modern politics has given us
clear blue water and *fudge and mudge*. Sometimes it is possible to guess that a phrase
may be emerging. The source-note to Norman Lamont's upbeat statement 'The
green shoots of economic spring are appearing once again' points out that this is
often quoted as 'The green shoots of recovery'; it seems probable that *green shoots of
recovery* will become an established allusive phrase.

Different allusions to the same story may take us far from the original. One of the
phrases at **Sleep** is the punning *the land of Nod*, a reference to the desolate land, 'east
of Eden', given to Cain after the murder of Abel. 'I am rather inclined to believe that
this is the land God gave to Cain,' said the sixteenth century explorer Jacques
Cartier, on discovering the bleak northern shore of Labrador (see **Canada**). At **Order
and Chaos**, we find the expression *raise Cain*.

It is, however, the interrelation between so many of the individual items which gives this book its particular identity. We may take as one example, the assessment made by Lord Randolph Churchill of the Irish political situation in 1886: 'I decided some time ago that if the G.O.M. [Gladstone] went for Home Rule, the Orange card would be the one to play.' *Play the—card*, deriving from this, has long been an established phrase, but both quotation and phrase were given a new twist by Robert Shapiro's assessment of the defence's conduct of the O. J. Simpson trial in 1995: 'Not only did we play the race card, we played it from the bottom of the deck.' These three items, quotation, phrase, and quotation, are included respectively at their appropriate themes; cross-references allow the reader to follow up the links between them.

Allusions are part of our linguistic stock-in-trade, and this dictionary allows the reader to find examples of both modification and source. ' "The question is," said Humpty-Dumpty, "which is to be master—that's all." ' This passage from Lewis Carroll's *Through the Looking-Glass* (1872) was quoted by the Labour politician Hartley Shawcross in a speech in the House of Commons in 1946, often summarized in the statement, 'We are the masters now'. The theme for **Power** finds room for both these items, and gives the reader explicit links between them.

It has been an object to provide explanations where these are helpful, and where the further material will be of interest to the reader. As the source-notes for quotations provide background information where this is illuminating, the source-notes for proverbs and phrases clarify words and references which may now be obscure or misleading; for example, the original meaning of *Do not spoil the ship for a ha'porth of tar*, and the comparison originally drawn in the phrase *like the clappers*.

'Figurative language' is a broad term, and inevitably some exclusions have been made. We have not treated direct allusions, although allusive references are properly here: there is no entry for *Judas*, but his identity is explained in the source-note for *Judas kiss*. We have avoided the strictly encyclopedic, although again the information is given where needed: the source-note to the phrase *eighth wonder of the world* explains the reference to the Seven Wonders of the ancient world. Slang as a category is regarded as generally outside the remit of this book, although there are exceptions: *couch potato* was felt to claim a place. We have sought to be consistent rather than rigid, while believing that the nature of the material makes some inconsistency inevitable. It is also inevitable that the creation of this text will render apparent gaps which were invisible before the book existed. We look forward to adding to the stock of material that we have brought together; meanwhile we hope that the text in its current state will allow the reader to share our pleasure and interest in watching the interplay of quotations, proverbs, and phrases.

ELIZABETH KNOWLES

Oxford, January 1997

How to Use the Dictionary

The sequence of entries is by alphabetical order of themes, from **Absence** and **Achievement** to **Writing** and **Youth**. Theme titles have been chosen to reflect as wide a range of subjects as possible, and related topics may be covered by a single theme, for example **Apology and Excuses** and **Ways and Means**. Linked opposites may also be grouped in a single antithetical theme, such as **Heaven and Hell**, **Trust and Treachery**, and **Winning and Losing**. A cross-reference from the second element of the pair, for example '**Losing** see **Winning and Losing**', appears in its appropriate place in the alphabetic sequence both in the main text and in the **List of Themes**.

Where themes are closely related, 'see also' references are given immediately following the theme title. The heading **Belief** is thus followed by the direction 'see also **Certainty and Doubt**, **Faith**', and **Danger** by 'see also **Caution**, **Courage**'.

Each theme may have up to three subdivisions: PROVERBS AND SAYINGS, PHRASES, and QUOTATIONS. In each of the first two of these items are ordered alphabetically, but with initial 'A' and 'The' ignored. Each saying appears in bold. Where the saying is proverbial, a note of the period when first found in written form (late 15th century, mid 18th century) is given, though where the saying has a more precise origin, such as an advertising slogan or a television catchphrase, a more exact date may be given. Where helpful a gloss is provided to explain the origin and usage of the saying. Phrases also appear in bold, followed by a brief definition text, as in '**crowning glory** a woman's hair'. In most cases, a note on the origin (for example an explanation of *Herod* for the phrase **out-Herod Herod**') follows the text.

Sayings, phrases, and quotations are numbered in a single sequence throughout each theme.

Cross-references are made between items in the same theme and to and from specific items in other themes. Cross-references between items in the same theme are expressed in the form 'see **12** above' or 'see **34** below'. Cross-references to specific items in other themes use a similar style, but identify the target theme: 'see **Excess** 6' or 'see **Marriage** 38'.

Index

The index provides the facility for finding individual quotations, sayings, and phrases by key word. Both the keywords and the entries following each keyword, including those in foreign languages, are in strict alphabetical order. Singular and plural nouns (with their possessive forms) are grouped separately.

References show the theme name, sometimes in a shortened form (**Festivals** for **Festivals and Celebrations**; **Seasons** for **The Seasons**) followed by the number of the item within the theme: **Science 7** therefore means the seventh item within the theme **Science**.

List of Themes

Absence
Achievement
Acting
Action and Inaction
Administration
Adversity
Advertising
Advice
Africa
Alcohol
Ambition
America
American Cities and States
Anger
Animals
Apology and Excuses
Appearance
Architecture
Argument
The Armed Forces
The Arts
Arts and Sciences
Australia

Beauty
Beginning
Behaviour
Belief
The Bible
Biography
Birds
Birth *see Pregnancy and Birth*
The Body
Books
Boredom
Borrowing *see Debt and Borrowing*
Britain
British Towns and Regions
Broadcasting
Business
Buying and Selling

Canada
Capitalism and Communism
Cats
Causes and Consequences
Caution
Celebrations *see Festivals and Celebrations*
Censorship
Certainty and Doubt
Chance and Luck
Change
Chaos *see Order and Chaos*
Character
Charity
Child Care
Children
Choice
The Christian Church
Christmas
The Cinema
Circumstance and Situation
Cities *see Towns and Cities*
Civilization *see Culture and Civilization*
Class
Clergy
Communism *see Capitalism and Communism*
Computers and the Internet
Conformity
Conscience
Consequences *see Causes and Consequences*
Consolation *see Sympathy and Consolation*
Constancy and Inconstancy
Conversation
Cooking and Eating
Cooperation
Corruption
Countries and Peoples
The Country and the Town
Courage
Courtship

Absence see also Meeting and Parting

1 Absence is the mother of disillusion.
American proverb, mid 20th century

2 Absence makes the heart grow fonder.
mid 19th century, meaning that affection for a person is strengthened by missing them; 1st century BC in Latin

3 He who is absent is always in the wrong.
late Middle English, meaning that someone who is not present cannot defend themselves from blame

4 A little absence does much good.
American proverb, mid 20th century

5 Out of sight, out of mind.
mid 13th century, meaning that someone who is not present is easily forgotten; see 9 below

PHRASES

6 gone with the wind gone completely, disappeared without trace.
*from Ernest Dowson (see **Memory** 17); subsequently popularized by the title of Margaret Mitchell's novel (1936) on the American Civil War*

7 Hamlet without the Prince a performance or event taking place without the principal actor or central figure.
from an account given in the Morning Post, *September 1775, of a theatrical company in which the actor who was to play the hero ran off with the innkeeper's daughter; when the play was announced, the audience was told 'the part of Hamlet to be left out, for that night.'*

QUOTATIONS

8 The Lord watch between me and thee, when we are absent one from another.
Bible: Genesis

9 Today the man is here; tomorrow he is gone. And when he is 'out of sight', quickly also is he out of mind.
Thomas à Kempis c.1380–1471: *De Imitatione Christi*; see 5 above

10 Absence diminishes commonplace passions and increases great ones, as the wind extinguishes candles and kindles fire.
Duc de la Rochefoucauld 1613–80: *Maximes* (1678)

11 I wish you could invent some means to make me at all happy without you. Every hour I am more and more concentrated in you; every thing else tastes like chaff in my mouth.
John Keats 1795–1821: letter to Fanny Brawne, August 1820

12 *Partir c'est mourir un peu,*
C'est mourir à ce qu'on aime:
On laisse un peu de soi-même
En toute heure et dans tout lieu.

To go away is to die a little, it is to die to that which one loves: everywhere and always, one leaves behind a part of oneself.
Edmond Haraucourt 1856–1941: 'Rondel de l'Adieu' (1891)

13 I am reduced to a thing that wants Virginia.
Vita Sackville-West 1892–1962: letter to Virginia Woolf, 21 January 1926

14 The more he looked inside the more Piglet wasn't there.
A. A. Milne 1882–1956: *The House at Pooh Corner* (1928)

15 The heart may think it knows better: the senses know that absence blots people out. We have really no absent friends.
Elizabeth Bowen 1899–1973: *Death of the Heart* (1938)

16 Where you used to be, there is a hole in the world, which I find myself constantly walking round in the daytime, and falling into at night. I miss you like hell.
Edna St Vincent Millay 1892–1950: Allen R. Macdougall (ed.) *Letters of Edna St Vincent Millay* (1952)

17 When I came back to Dublin, I was courtmartialled in my absence and sentenced to death in my absence, so I said they could shoot me in my absence.
Brendan Behan 1923–64: *Hostage* (1958)

18 Where were you in '62?
Anonymous: advertising slogan for *American Graffiti* (1973 film)

19 Most of what matters in your life takes place in your absence.
Salman Rushdie 1947– : *Midnight's Children* (1981)

Achievement see also Ambition, Effort, Problems and Solutions, Success and Failure

1 Didn't she [or he or they] do well?

catchphrase used by Bruce Forsyth in 'The Generation Game' on BBC Television, 1973 onwards

2 The difficult is done at once, the impossible takes a little longer.

slogan of the US Armed Forces; recorded earlier as a quotation by Charles Alexandre de Calonne (1734–1802) in the form 'Madam, if a thing is possible, consider it done; the impossible?—that will be done'

3 Palmam qui meruit, ferat.

Latin, Let him who has won it bear the palm, adopted by Lord Nelson (1758–1805) as his motto, from John Jortin Lusus Poetici (3rd ed., 1748) 'Ad Ventos'

4 Per ardua ad astra.

Latin, through struggle to the stars, motto of the Mulvany family, quoted and translated by Rider Haggard in The People of the Mist (1894), and still in use as motto of the RAF, having been approved by King George V in 1913

5 Seriously, though, he's doing a grand job!

catchphrase used by David Frost in 'That Was The Week That Was', on BBC Television, 1962–3

6 A sow may whistle, though it has an ill mouth for it.

early 19th century, meaning that someone not naturally suited to a task will perform it badly

7 Still achieving, still pursuing.

American proverb, mid 20th century; from Longfellow: see **Determination** 37

8 Whatever man has done, man may do.

mid 19th century, meaning that anything that has been achieved once can be achieved again

9 While the grass grows, the steed starves.

mid 14th century, meaning that by the time hopes or expectations can be satisfied, it may be too late

10 You cannot have your cake and eat it.

mid 16th century, meaning that you cannot have things both ways

11 The desire accomplished is sweet to the soul.
Bible: Proverbs

12 *Non omnia possumus omnes.*
We can't all do everything.
Virgil 70–19 BC: Eclogues

13 I have fought a good fight, I have finished my course, I have kept the faith.
Bible: II Timothy

14 None climbs so high as he who knows not whither he is going.
Oliver Cromwell 1599–1658: attributed

15 The General [Wolfe] . . . repeated nearly the whole of Gray's Elegy . . . adding, as he concluded, that he would prefer being the author of that poem to the glory of beating the French to-morrow.
James Wolfe 1727–59: J. Playfair Biographical Account of J. Robinson (1815)

16 The distance is nothing; it is only the first step that is difficult.
commenting on the legend that St Denis, carrying his head in his hands, walked two leagues
Mme Du Deffand 1697–1780: letter to Jean Le Rond d'Alembert, 7 July 1763; see **Beginning** 6

17 He has, indeed, done it very well; but it is a foolish thing well done.
on Goldsmith's apology in the London Chronicle for physically assaulting Thomas Evans, who had published a letter mocking Goldsmith
Samuel Johnson 1709–84: James Boswell Life of Johnson (1791) 3 April 1773

18 Now, gentlemen, let us do something today which the world may talk of hereafter.
Admiral Collingwood 1748–1810: before the Battle of Trafalgar, 21 October 1805; G. L. Newnham Collingwood (ed.) A Selection from the Correspondence of Lord Collingwood (1828)

19 *J'ai vécu.*
I survived.
when asked what he had done during the French Revolution
Emmanuel Joseph Sieyès 1748–1836: F. A. M. Mignet Notice historique sur la vie et les travaux de M. le Comte de Sieyès (1836)

20 That low man seeks a little thing to do,
Sees it and does it:
This high man, with a great thing to pursue,
Dies ere he knows it.

That low man goes on adding one to one,
His hundred's soon hit:
This high man, aiming at a million,
Misses an unit.
Robert Browning 1812–89: 'A Grammarian's
Funeral' (1855)

21 If a man write a better book, preach a
better sermon, or make a better mouse-
trap than his neighbour, tho' he build his
house in the woods, the world will make a
beaten path to his door.
Ralph Waldo Emerson 1803–82: attributed to
Emerson in Sarah S. B. Yule *Borrowings* (1889); Mrs
Yule states in *The Docket* February 1912 that she
copied this in her handbook from a lecture
delivered by Emerson; the quotation was the
occasion of a long controversy owing to Elbert
Hubbard's claim to its authorship

22 I struggled for forty-seven years, I
distinguished myself in every way I
possibly could. I never had a compliment
nor a 'Thank you', nor a single farthing. I
translated a doubtful book in my old age,
and I immediately made sixteen thousand
guineas.
Richard Burton 1821–90: Arthur Symons *Dramatis
Personae* (1923)

23 There are two tragedies in life. One is not
to get your heart's desire. The other is to
get it.
George Bernard Shaw 1856–1950: *Man and
Superman* (1903)

24 Because it's there.
on being asked why he wanted to climb Mount Everest
George Leigh Mallory 1886–1924: in *New York
Times* 18 March 1923

25 This very remarkable man
Commends a most practical plan:
You can do what you want
If you don't think you can't,
So don't think you can't think you can.
Charles Inge 1868–1957: 'On Monsieur Coué'
(1928); see **Medicine** 22

26 BETTER DROWNED THAN DUFFERS IF NOT
DUFFERS WONT DROWN.
Arthur Ransome 1884–1967: *Swallows and
Amazons* (1930)

27 Here is the answer which I will give to
President Roosevelt . . . Give us the tools
and we will finish the job.
Winston Churchill 1874–1965: radio broadcast, 9
February 1941

28 I could have had class. I could have been a
contender.
Budd Schulberg 1914– : *On the Waterfront* (1954
film); spoken by Marlon Brando

29 That's one small step for man, one giant
leap for mankind.
Neil Armstrong 1930– : in *New York Times* 21 July
1969; interference in the transmission obliterated
'a' between 'for' and 'man'

30 Where there is no risk there can be no
pride in achievement and consequently no
happiness.
Ray Kroc 1902–84: *Grinding It Out* (1977)

31 At the end of your life you will never regret
not having passed one more test, winning
one more verdict or not closing one more
deal. You will regret time not spent with a
husband, a child, a friend or a parent.
Barbara Bush 1925– : in *Washington Post* 2 June
1990

32 When people are put into positions slightly
above what they would expect, they're apt
to excel.
Richard Branson 1950– : in *Success* November
1992

33 The trouble with fulfilling your ambitions
is you think you will be transformed into
some sort of archangel and you're not.
You still have to wash your socks.
Louis de Bernières 1954– : in *Independent* 14
February 1999

Acting see also The Cinema, Shakespeare, The Theatre

PHRASES

1 **Anyone for tennis?**
*a typical entrance or exit line given to a young man in
a superficial drawing-room comedy*

PROVERBS AND SAYINGS

2 **sock and buskin** comedy and tragedy.
*the sock was a light shoe worn by comic actors on the
Greek and Roman stage, and the buskin a thick-soled
laced boot worn by Athenian tragic actors; see 5
below, **Theatre** 7*

QUOTATIONS

3 Be not too tame neither, but let your own discretion be your tutor: suit the action to the word, the word to the action; with this special observance, that you o'erstep not the modesty of nature; for anything so overdone is from the purpose of playing, whose end, both at the first and now, was and is, to hold, as 'twere, the mirror up to nature.
William Shakespeare 1564–1616: *Hamlet* (1601)

on attempting to paint two actors, David Garrick and Samuel Foote:
4 Rot them for a couple of rogues, they have everybody's faces but their own.
Thomas Gainsborough 1727–88: Allan Cunningham *The Lives of the Most Eminent Painters, Sculptors and Architects* (1829)

5 He was a critic upon operas, too
And knew all niceties of sock and buskin.
Lord Byron 1788–1824: *Beppo* (1817); see 2 above

6 To see him act, is like reading Shakespeare by flashes of lightning.
on Edmund Kean
Samuel Taylor Coleridge 1772–1834: *Table Talk* (1835) 27 April 1823

7 She ran the whole gamut of the emotions from A to B.
of Katharine Hepburn at a Broadway first night, 1933
Dorothy Parker 1893–1967: attributed

8 Don't put your daughter on the stage, Mrs Worthington,
Don't put your daughter on the stage.
Noël Coward 1899–1973: 'Mrs Worthington' (1935 song)

9 Actors are cattle.
Alfred Hitchcock 1899–1980: in *Saturday Evening Post* 22 May 1943

10 For an actress to be a success, she must have the face of a Venus, the brains of a Minerva, the grace of Terpsichore, the memory of a Macaulay, the figure of Juno, and the hide of a rhinoceros.
Ethel Barrymore 1879–1959: George Jean Nathan *The Theatre in the Fifties* (1953)

11 An actor is a kind of a guy who if you ain't talking about him ain't listening.
George Glass 1910–84: Bob Thomas *Brando* (1973); often quoted by Marlon Brando, 1956 onwards

12 Just say the lines and don't trip over the furniture.
advice on acting
Noël Coward 1899–1973: D. Richards *The Wit of Noël Coward* (1968)

13 Acting is a masochistic form of exhibitionism. It is not quite the occupation of an adult.
Laurence Olivier 1907–89: in *Time* 3 July 1978

14 You've got to perform in a role hundreds of times. In keeping it fresh one can become a large, madly humming, demented refrigerator.
Ralph Richardson 1902–83: in *Time* 21 August 1978

15 When I read 'Be real, don't get caught acting,' I thought, 'How the hell do you do that?'
Billy Connolly 1942– : John Miller *Judi Dench: With a Crack in Her Voice* (1998)

16 Let's not get too precious about it: actors are not heart surgeons or brain surgeons. We are just entertaining people.
Malcolm McDowell 1943– : in *Mail on Sunday* 14 May 2000

Action and Inaction see also Idleness, Words and Deeds

PROVERBS AND SAYINGS

1 Action is worry's worst enemy.
American proverb, mid 20th century

2 Action this day.
annotation as used by Winston Churchill at the Admiralty in 1940

3 Action without thought is like shooting without aim.
American proverb, mid 20th century

4 A barking dog never bites.
16th century, 13th century in French; meaning that noisy threats often do not presage real danger

5 If it ain't broke, don't fix it.
late 20th century, warning against interference with something that is working satisfactorily

6 If you want something done, ask a busy person.
late 20th century saying, implying that a busy person is most likely to have learned how to manage their time efficiently

7 It is as cheap sitting as standing.
mid 17th century, often used literally

8 Lookers-on see most of the game.
early 16th century, meaning that those who are not participating are able to take an overall view

9 The road to hell is paved with good intentions.
late 16th century; earlier forms of the proverb omit the first three words

10 Seek and ye shall find.
mid 16th century, meaning that an active search for something wanted is likely to be rewarded; see **Prayer 7**

11 When in doubt, do nowt.
mid 19th century, advising against taking action when one is unsure of one's ground

PHRASES

12 no peace for the wicked no rest or tranquillity for the speaker; incessant activity, responsibility, or work.
from the Bible (Isaiah); see **Sin 8**

QUOTATIONS

13 Nowher so bisy a man as he ther nas, And yet he semed bisier than he was.
Geoffrey Chaucer c.1343–1400: *The Canterbury Tales* 'The General Prologue'

14 Iron rusts from disuse; stagnant water loses its purity and in cold weather becomes frozen; even so does inaction sap the vigour of the mind.
Leonardo da Vinci 1452–1519: Edward McCurdy (ed. and trans.) *Leonardo da Vinci's Notebooks* (1906)

15 But men must know, that in this theatre of man's life it is reserved only for God and angels to be lookers on.
Francis Bacon 1561–1626: *The Advancement of Learning* (1605)

16 If it were done when 'tis done, then 'twere well
It were done quickly.
William Shakespeare 1564–1616: *Macbeth* (1606)

17 A first impulse was never a crime.
Pierre Corneille 1606–84: *Horace* (1640)

18 You have sat too long here for any good you have been doing. Depart, I say, and let us have done with you. In the name of God, go!
addressing the Rump Parliament, 20 April 1653; quoted by Leo Amery to Neville Chamberlain in the

House of Commons, 7 May 1940. Chamberlain resigned three days later
Oliver Cromwell 1599–1658: oral tradition

19 We have left undone those things which we ought to have done; And we have done those things which we ought not to have done; And there is no health in us.
The Book of Common Prayer 1662: *Morning Prayer* General Confession

20 They also serve who only stand and wait.
John Milton 1608–74: 'When I consider how my light is spent' (1673)

21 He who desires but acts not, breeds pestilence.
William Blake 1757–1827: *The Marriage of Heaven and Hell* (1790–3) 'Proverbs of Hell'

22 Think nothing done while aught remains to do.
Samuel Rogers 1763–1855: 'Human Life' (1819)

23 It is vain to say that human beings ought to be satisfied with tranquillity: they must have action; and they will make it if they cannot find it.
Charlotte Brontë 1816–55: *Jane Eyre* (1847)

24 Action is consolatory. It is the enemy of thought and the friend of flattering illusions.
Joseph Conrad 1857–1924: *Nostromo* (1904)

25 Under conditions of tyranny it is far easier to act than to think.
Hannah Arendt 1906–75: W. H. Auden *A Certain World* (1970)

26 The world can only be grasped by action, not by contemplation . . . The hand is the cutting edge of the mind.
Jacob Bronowski 1908–74: *The Ascent of Man* (1973)

27 I grew up in the Thirties with our unemployed father. He did not riot, he got on his bike and looked for work.
Norman Tebbit 1931– : speech at Conservative Party Conference, 15 October 1981

28 I do nothing, granted. But I see the hours pass—which is better than trying to fill them.
E. M. Cioran 1911–95: in *Guardian* 11 May 1993

29 Inertia can develop its own momentum.
Douglas Hurd 1930– : in *Mail on Sunday* 27 May 2001

Administration see also Management

1 **A committee is a group of the unwilling, chosen from the unfit, to do the unnecessary.**
20th century saying

2 **men in suits** bureaucrats, faceless administrators.
regarded as representatives of an organization rather than creative individuals; probably related to suit *a man who wears a business suit at work, a business executive*

3 **red tape** excessive bureaucracy or adherence to rules and formalities, especially in public business.
the expression refers to the reddish-pink tape which is commonly used for securing legal and official documents

4 For forms of government let fools contest; Whate'er is best administered is best.
Alexander Pope 1688–1744: *An Essay on Man* Epistle 3 (1733)

5 I have in general no very exalted opinion of the virtue of paper government.
Edmund Burke 1729–97: *On Conciliation with America* (1775)

6 If any man will draw up his case, and put his name at the foot of the first page, I will give him an immediate reply. Where he compels me to turn over the sheet, he must wait my leisure.
on appeals made by officers to the Navy Board
Lord Sandwich 1718–92: N. W. Wraxall *Memoirs* (1884) vol. 1

7 Whatever was required to be done, the Circumlocution Office was beforehand with all the public departments in the art of perceiving—HOW NOT TO DO IT.
Charles Dickens 1812–70: *Little Dorrit* (1857)

8 A place for everything and everything in its place.
Mrs Beeton 1836–65: *The Book of Household Management* (1861); often attributed to Samuel Smiles; see **Order** 2

9 It is an inevitable defect, that bureaucrats will care more for routine than for results.
Walter Bagehot 1826–77: *The English Constitution* (1867) 'On Changes of Ministry'

10 Sack the lot!
on overmanning and overspending within government departments
John Arbuthnot Fisher 1841–1920: letter to *The Times*, 2 September 1919

11 Where there is officialism every human relationship suffers.
E. M. Forster 1879–1970: *A Passage to India* (1924)

12 Let's find out what everyone is doing, And then stop everyone from doing it.
A. P. Herbert 1890–1971: 'Let's Stop Somebody from Doing Something!' (1930)

13 Oh for just
one
more conference
regarding the eradication of all
conferences!
Vladimir Mayakovsky 1893–1930: 'In Re Conferences'

14 Official dignity tends to increase in inverse ratio to the importance of the country in which the office is held.
Aldous Huxley 1894–1963: *Beyond the Mexique Bay* (1934)

15 In the case of nutrition and health, just as in the case of education, the gentleman in Whitehall really does know better what is good for people than the people know themselves.
Douglas Jay 1907–96: *The Socialist Case* (1939)

16 This island is made mainly of coal and surrounded by fish. Only an organizing genius could produce a shortage of coal and fish at the same time.
Aneurin Bevan 1897–1960: speech at Blackpool 24 May 1945

17 What is official
Is incontestable. It undercuts
The problematical world and sells us life
At a discount.
Christopher Fry 1907– : *The Lady's not for Burning* (1949)

18 By the time the civil service has finished drafting a document to give effect to a

principle, there may be little of the principle left.
Lord Reith 1889–1971: *Into the Wind* (1949)

19 Committee—a group of men who individually can do nothing but as a group decide that nothing can be done.
Fred Allen 1894–1956: attributed

20 Time spent on any item of the agenda will be in inverse proportion to the sum involved.
C. Northcote Parkinson 1909–93: *Parkinson's Law* (1958)

21 The Civil Service is profoundly deferential — 'Yes, Minister! No, Minister! If you wish it, Minister!'
Richard Crossman 1907–74: diary, 22 October 1964

22 In a hierarchy every employee tends to rise to his level of incompetence.
Laurence J. Peter 1919–90: *The Peter Principle* (1969); see **Management** 4

23 Guidelines for bureaucrats: (1) When in charge, ponder. (2) When in trouble, delegate. (3) When in doubt, mumble.
James H. Boren 1925– : in *New York Times* 8 November 1970

24 A memorandum is written not to inform the reader but to protect the writer.
Dean Acheson 1893–1971: in *Wall Street Journal* 8 September 1977

25 Back in the East you can't do much without the right papers, but *with* the right papers you can do *anything*. They *believe* in papers. Papers are power.
Tom Stoppard 1937– : *Neutral Ground* (1983)

26 I think it will be a clash between the political will and the administrative won't.
Jonathan Lynn 1943– and **Antony Jay** 1930– : *Yes Prime Minister* (1987) vol. 2

27 A camel is a horse designed by a committee.
Alec Issigonis 1906–88: attributed; in *Guardian* 14 January 1991 'Notes and Queries'

Adversity see also **Misfortunes**, **Suffering**

PROVERBS AND SAYINGS

1 Adversity makes strange bedfellows.
mid 19th century, meaning that shared difficulties may bring together very different people; see **Misfortune** 17

2 A dose of adversity is often as needful as a dose of medicine.
American proverb, mid 20th century

PHRASES

3 gall and wormwood a source of bitter mortification or vexation.
gall *bile, the secretion of the liver;* wormwood *an aromatic plant with a bitter taste; taken together as the type of something causing bitterness and grief*

4 the iron entered into his soul he became deeply and permanently affected by captivity or ill treatment.
from the Bible (Psalms), from Latin mistranslation of Hebrew for 'his person entered into the iron', i.e. fetters

5 light at the end of the tunnel a long-awaited sign that a period of hardship or adversity is nearing an end.
see **Optimism** 35

6 locust years years of poverty and hardship.
coined by Winston Churchill in his History of the Second World War (1948) to describe Britain in the 1930s; from the Bible (Joel) 'I will restore to you the years that the locust hath eaten'

7 a thorn in one's side a constant annoyance or problem, a source of continual trouble or annoyance.
from the Bible (Numbers) 'those which ye let remain of them shall be . . . thorns in your sides'

8 under the harrow in distress.
harrow *a heavy frame set with iron teeth or tines, drawn over ploughed land to break up clods and root up weeds;* see **Suffering** 21

QUOTATIONS

9 No stranger to trouble myself I am learning to care for the unhappy.
Virgil 70–19 BC: *Aeneid*

10 Sweet are the uses of adversity,
Which like the toad, ugly and venomous,
Wears yet a precious jewel in his head.
William Shakespeare 1564–1616: *As You Like It* (1599)

11 Prosperity doth best discover vice, but adversity doth best discover virtue.
Francis Bacon 1561–1626: *Essays* (1625) 'Of Adversity'

12 Adversity is sometimes hard upon a man; but for one man who can stand prosperity, there are a hundred that will stand adversity.
Thomas Carlyle 1795–1881: *On Heroes, Hero-Worship, and the Heroic* (1841)

13 But there, everything has its drawbacks, as the man said when his mother-in-law died, and they came down upon him for the funeral expenses.
Jerome K. Jerome 1859–1927: *Three Men in a Boat* (1889)

14 By trying we can easily learn to endure adversity. Another man's, I mean.
Mark Twain 1835–1910: *Following the Equator* (1897)

15 Adversity, if a man is set down to it by degrees, is more supportable with equanimity by most people than any great prosperity arrived at in a single lifetime.
Samuel Butler 1835–1902: *Way of All Flesh* (1903)

16 The heart *prefers* to move against the grain of circumstance; perversity is the soul's very life.
John Updike 1932– : *Assorted Prose* (1965) 'More Love in the Western World'

17 Life is not meant to be easy.
Malcolm Fraser 1930– : 5th Alfred Deakin lecture, 20 July 1971

18 A woman is like a teabag—only in hot water do you realise how strong she is.
Nancy Reagan 1923– : in *Observer* 29 March 1981

Advertising

PROVERBS AND SAYINGS

1 Any publicity is good publicity.
*early 20th century, meaning that it is always preferable to have attention focused on a name than to be unnoticed; see **Fame** 18*

2 Don't advertise what you can't fulfil.
American proverb, mid 20th century

3 Good wine needs no bush.
early 15th century, meaning that there is no need to advertise or boast about something of good quality as people will always discover its merits; a bunch of ivy was formerly the sign of a vintner's shop; see 17 below

4 It pays to advertise.
American proverb, mid 20th century

5 Let's run it up the flagpole and see if anyone salutes it.
recorded as an established expression in the 1960s, suggesting the testing of a new idea or product

PHRASES

6 proclaim from the housetops announce publicly, announce loudly.
from the Bible (Luke) 'that which ye have spoken in the ear in closets shall be proclaimed upon the housetops'

QUOTATIONS

7 Promise, large promise, is the soul of an advertisement.
Samuel Johnson 1709–84: in *The Idler* 20 January 1759

8 It is far easier to write ten passably effective sonnets, good enough to take in the not too enquiring critic, than one effective advertisement that will take in a few thousand of the uncritical buying public.
Aldous Huxley 1894–1963: *On the Margin* (1923) 'Advertisement'

9 Advertising may be described as the science of arresting human intelligence long enough to get money from it.
Stephen Leacock 1869–1944: *Garden of Folly* (1924) 'The Perfect Salesman'

10 Half the money I spend on advertising is wasted, and the trouble is I don't know which half.
Lord Leverhulme 1851–1925: David Ogilvy *Confessions of an Advertising Man* (1963)

11 Those who prefer their English sloppy have only themselves to thank if the advertisement writer uses his mastery of vocabulary and syntax to mislead their weak minds ... The moral of all this ... is that we have the kind of advertising we deserve.

Dorothy L. Sayers 1893–1957: in *Spectator* 19 November 1937

12 Advertising is the rattling of a stick inside a swill bucket.

George Orwell 1903–50: attributed

13 It is not necessary to advertise food to hungry people, fuel to cold people, or houses to the homeless.

J. K. Galbraith 1908– : *American Capitalism* (1952)

14 The hidden persuaders.

Vance Packard 1914–97: title of a study of the advertising industry (1957)

15 The consumer isn't a moron; she is your wife.

David Ogilvy 1911–99: *Confessions of an Advertising Man* (1963)

16 A good poster is a visual telegram.

A. M. Cassandre 1901–68: attributed

17 Good wine needs no bush,
And perhaps products that people really want need no hard-sell or soft-sell TV push.
Why not?
Look at pot.

Ogden Nash 1902–71: 'Most Doctors Recommend or Yours For Fast, Fast, Fast Relief' (1972); see 3 above

18 Society drives people crazy with lust and calls it advertising.

John Lahr 1941– : in *Guardian* 2 August 1989

Advice

PROVERBS AND SAYINGS

1 **Ask advice, but use your common sense.**
American proverb, mid 20th century

2 **Don't teach your grandmother to suck eggs.**
early 18th century; a caution against offering advice to the wise and experienced

3 **A fool may give a wise man counsel.**
mid 14th century, sometimes used as a warning against overconfidence in one's judgement

4 **Night brings counsel.**
late 16th century, sometimes used as a warning against taking a hasty action or decision

5 **A nod's as good as a wink to a blind horse.**
late 18th century, meaning that the slightest hint is enough to convey one's meaning in a particular case

6 **A word to the wise is enough.**
early 16th century, meaning that only a very brief warning is necessary to an intelligent person; earlier in Latin 'verbum sat sapienti [a word is sufficient to a wise man]'; see 10 below

PHRASES

7 **counsel of perfection** advice designed to guide one towards moral perfection, often seen as ideal but impracticable.
sometimes with reference to the Bible (Matthew), 'If thou wilt be perfect, go and sell all that thou hast, and give to the poor'

8 **Delphic oracle** the oracle of Apollo at Delphi in classical antiquity, where a priestess, the Pythia, acted as a medium through whom advice or prophecy was sought from the gods.
the characteristic riddling responses have given rise to the use of Delphic to mean deliberately obscure or ambiguous

9 **Miss Lonelyhearts** a journalist who gives advice in a newspaper or magazine to people who are lonely or in difficulties.
see 22 below

10 **a word to the wise** used to imply that further explanation of or comment on a statement or situation is unnecessary.
from the proverb: see 6 above

QUOTATIONS

11 A word spoken in due season, how good is it!
Bible: Proverbs

12 Who is this that darkeneth counsel by words without knowledge?
Bible: Job

13 Books will speak plain when counsellors blanch.
Francis Bacon 1561–1626: *Essays* (1625) 'Of Counsel'

14 Advice is seldom welcome; and those who want it the most always like it the least.
Lord Chesterfield 1694–1773: *Letters to his Son* (1774) 29 January 1748

15 In matters of religion and matrimony I never give any advice; because I will not have anybody's torments in this world or the next laid to my charge.
Lord Chesterfield 1694–1773: letter to Arthur Charles Stanhope, 12 October 1765

16 It was, perhaps, one of those cases in which advice is good or bad only as the event decides.
Jane Austen 1775–1817: *Persuasion* (1818)

17 Of all the horrid, hideous notes of woe, Sadder than owl-songs or the midnight blast, Is that portentous phrase, 'I told you so.'
Lord Byron 1788–1824: *Don Juan* (1819–24)

18 Get the advice of everybody whose advice is worth having—they are very few—and then do what you think best yourself.
Charles Stewart Parnell 1846–91: Conor Cruise O'Brien *Parnell* (1957)

19 I always pass on good advice. It is the only thing to do with it. It is never of any use to oneself.
Oscar Wilde 1854–1900: *An Ideal Husband* (1895)

20 It's the worst thing that can ever happen to you in all your life, and you've got to mind it . . . They'll come saying, 'Bear up—trust to time.' No, no; they're wrong. Mind it.
E. M. Forster 1879–1970: *The Longest Journey* (1907)

21 Well, if you knows of a better 'ole, go to it.
caption to a cartoon of Old Bill and a friend in a shellhole under fire
Bruce Bainsfather 1888–1959: *Fragments from France* (1915)

22 The Miss Lonelyhearts are the priests of twentieth-century America.
Nathaniel West 1903–40: *Miss Lonelyhearts* (1933); see 9 above

23 After all, when you seek advice from someone it's certainly not because you want them to give it. You just want them to be there while you talk to yourself.
Terry Pratchett 1948– : *Jingo* (1997)

24 Look for what's missing. Many advisers can tell a president how to improve what's proposed, or what's gone amiss. Few are able to see what isn't there.
Donald Rumsfeld 1932– : *Rumsfeld's Rules* (2001)

Africa

PROVERBS AND SAYINGS

1 Always something new out of Africa.
mid 16th century, from Pliny; see 6 below

PHRASES

2 the Dark Continent Africa.
referring to the time before it was fully explored by Europeans, first recorded in H. M. Stanley Through the Dark Continent *(1878)*

3 the Gold Coast a former name (until 1957) for Ghana.
so called because it was an important source of gold

4 the Slave Coast part of the west coast of Africa, between the Volta River and Mount Cameroon.
an area from which slaves were exported in the 16th–19th centuries

5 the white man's grave equatorial West Africa.
traditionally considered as being particularly unhealthy for whites

QUOTATIONS

6 *Semper aliquid novi Africam adferre.*
Africa always brings [us] something new.
Pliny the Elder AD 23–79: *Historia Naturalis*; see 1 above

7 We are . . . a nation of dancers, singers and poets.
of the Ibo people
Olaudah Equiano c.1745–c.1797: *Narrative of the Life of Olaudah Equiano* (1789)

8 Are you there . . . Africa of the millions of royal slaves, deported Africa, drifting continent, are you there? Slowly you vanish, you withdraw into the past, into the tales of castaways, colonial museums, the works of scholars.
Jean Genet 1910–86: *The Blacks* (1959)

9 The wind of change is blowing through this continent.
Harold Macmillan 1894–1986: speech at Cape Town, 3 February 1960

10 The shape of Africa resembles a revolver, and the Congo is the trigger.
Frantz Fanon 1925–61: attributed

11 I who have cursed
The drunken officer of British rule, how choose
Between this Africa and the English tongue I love?
Derek Walcott 1930– : 'A Far Cry From Africa' (1962)

12 I have dedicated my life to this struggle of the African people. I have fought against white domination, and I have fought against black domination. I have cherished the ideal of a democratic and free society in which all persons live together in harmony with equal opportunities. It is an ideal which I hope to live for, and to achieve.

But my lord, if needs be, it is an ideal for which I am prepared to die.
Nelson Mandela 1918– : speech at his trial in Pretoria, 20 April 1964, which he quoted on his release in Cape Town, 11 February 1990

13 Hopeless doomed continent! Only lies flourished here. Africa was swaddled in lies—the lies of an aborted European civilisation; the lies of liberation. Nothing but lies.
Shiva Naipaul 1945–85: *North of South* (1978)

14 I am a woman and a woman of Africa. I am a daughter of Nigeria and if she is in shame, I shall stay and mourn with her in shame.
Buchi Emecheta 1944– : *Destination Biafra* (1982)

15 Westerners have aggressive problem-solving minds; Africans experience people.
Kenneth Kaunda 1924– : attributed, 1990

Alcohol see also Drunkenness

PROVERBS AND SAYINGS

1 **Alcohol will preserve anything but a secret.**
American proverb, mid 20th century

2 **Don't ask a man to drink and drive.**
British road safety slogan, from 1964

3 **Guinness is good for you.**
reply universally given to researchers asking people why they drank Guinness; advertising slogan for Guinness, from c.1929

4 **Heineken refreshes the parts other beers cannot reach.**
slogan for Heineken lager, from 1975 onwards

5 **I'm only here for the beer.**
slogan for Double Diamond beer, 1971 onwards

6 **Let's get out of these wet clothes and into a dry Martini.**
line coined in the 1920s by Robert Benchley's press agent and adopted by Mae West in Every Day's a Holiday *(1937 film)*

PHRASES

7 **shaken, not stirred** popular summary of the directions for making the perfect martini given by James Bond
from Fleming; see 28 below

QUOTATIONS

8 Wine is a mocker, strong drink is raging.
Bible: Proverbs

9 No verse can give pleasure for long, nor last, that is written by drinkers of water.
Horace 65–8 BC: *Epistles*

10 Use a little wine for thy stomach's sake.
Bible: I Timothy

11 Let schoolmasters puzzle their brain,
With grammar, and nonsense, and learning,
Good liquor, I stoutly maintain,
Gives genius a better discerning.
Oliver Goldsmith 1728–74: *She Stoops to Conquer* (1773)

12 Claret is the liquor for boys; port, for men; but he who aspires to be a hero (smiling) must drink brandy.
Samuel Johnson 1709–84: James Boswell *Life of Johnson* (1791) 7 April 1779

13 Freedom and Whisky gang thegither!
Robert Burns 1759–96: 'The Author's Earnest Cry and Prayer' (1786)

14 O for a beaker full of the warm South,

Full of the true, the blushful Hippocrene,
With beaded bubbles winking at the brim,
And purple-stainèd mouth.
John Keats 1795–1821: 'Ode to a Nightingale' (1820)

15 Champagne certainly gives one werry
gentlemanly ideas, but for a continuance, I
don't know but I should prefer mild hale.
R. S. Surtees 1805–64: *Jorrocks's Jaunts and Jollities*
(1838)

16 Man wants but little drink below,
But wants that little strong.
Oliver Wendell Holmes 1809–94: 'A Song of other
Days' (1848); see **Life** 24

17 Your lips, on my own, when they printed
'Farewell',
Had never been soiled by the 'beverage of
hell';
But they come to me now with the
bacchanal sign,
And the lips that touch liquor must never
touch mine.
George W. Young 1846–1919: 'The Lips That Touch
Liquor Must Never Touch Mine' (c. 1870); also
attributed, in a different form, to Harriet A.
Glazebrook, 1874

18 Fifteen men on the dead man's chest
Yo-ho-ho, and a bottle of rum!
Drink and the devil had done for the rest—
Yo-ho-ho, and a bottle of rum!
Robert Louis Stevenson 1850–94: *Treasure Island*
(1883)

19 We drink one another's healths, and spoil
our own.
Jerome K. Jerome 1859–1927: *Idle Thoughts of an
Idle Fellow* (1886)

20 And malt does more than Milton can
To justify God's ways to man.
Ale, man, ale's the stuff to drink
For fellows whom it hurts to think.
A. E. Housman 1859–1936: *A Shropshire Lad* (1896);
see **Writing** 16

21 I'm only a beer teetotaller, not a
champagne teetotaller.
George Bernard Shaw 1856–1950: *Candida* (1898)

22 Our country has deliberately undertaken a
great social and economic experiment,
noble in motive and far-reaching in
purpose.
on the Eighteenth Amendment enacting Prohibition
Herbert Hoover 1874–1964: letter to Senator W. H.
Borah, 23 February 1928

23 Candy
Is dandy

But liquor
Is quicker.
Ogden Nash 1902–71: 'Reflections on Ice-breaking'
(1931)

24 Prohibition makes you want to cry into
your beer and denies you the beer to cry
into.
Don Marquis 1878–1937: *Sun Dial Time* (1936)

25 It's a naïve domestic Burgundy without
any breeding, but I think you'll be amused
by its presumption.
James Thurber 1894–1961: cartoon caption in *New
Yorker* 27 March 1937

26 Some weasel took the cork out of my
lunch.
W. C. Fields 1880–1946: *You Can't Cheat an Honest
Man* (1939 film)

27 A good general rule is to state that the
bouquet is better than the taste, and vice
versa.
on wine-tasting
Stephen Potter 1900–69: *One-Upmanship* (1952)

28 A medium Vodka dry Martini—with a slice
of lemon peel. Shaken and not stirred.
Ian Fleming 1908–64: *Dr No* (1958)

29 One reason why I don't drink is because I
wish to know when I am having a good
time.
Nancy Astor 1879–1964: in *Christian Herald* June
1960

30 A man shouldn't fool with booze until he's
fifty; then he's a damn fool if he doesn't.
William Faulkner 1897–1962: James M. Webb and
A. Wigfall Green *William Faulkner of Oxford* (1965)

31 I have taken more out of alcohol than
alcohol has taken out of me.
Winston Churchill 1874–1965: Quentin Reynolds
By Quentin Reynolds (1964)

32 I'd hate to be a teetotaller. Imagine getting
up in the morning and knowing that's as
good as you're going to feel all day.
Dean Martin 1917– : attributed; also attributed to
Jimmy Durante

33 Wine is for drinking and enjoying, talking
about it is deadly dull.
Jancis Robinson 1950– : in *Daily Mail* 19 October
1995

Ambition see also Achievement, Success and Failure

PROVERBS AND SAYINGS

1 Hasty climbers have sudden falls.

mid 15th century, meaning that the over-ambitious often fail to take necessary precautions

2 The higher the monkey climbs the more he shows his tail.

late 14th century, meaning that the further an unsuitable person is advanced, the more his inadequacies are apparent

3 It's ill waiting for dead men's shoes.

*mid 16th century, often used of a situation in which one is hoping for a position currently occupied by another; see **Possessions** 8*

4 Many go out for wool and come home shorn.

late 16th century, meaning that many who seek to better themselves or make themselves rich, end by losing what they already have

5 There is always room at the top.

*early 20th century; as a response to being advised against joining the overcrowded legal profession, it is also attributed to the American politician and lawyer Daniel Webster; see **Opportunity** 20*

QUOTATIONS

6 [I] had rather be first in a village than second at Rome.

Julius Caesar 100–44 BC: Francis Bacon *The Advancement of Learning*; based on Plutarch *Parallel Lives*

7 *Aut Caesar, aut nihil.*
Caesar or nothing.

Cesare Borgia 1476–1507: motto inscribed on his sword; John Leslie Garner *Caesar Borgia* (1912)

8 Who shoots at the mid-day sun, though he be sure he shall never hit the mark; yet as sure he is he shall shoot higher than who aims but at a bush.

Philip Sidney 1554–86: *Arcadia* ('New Arcadia', 1590)

9 When that the poor have cried, Caesar hath wept;
Ambition should be made of sterner stuff.

William Shakespeare 1564–1616: *Julius Caesar* (1599)

10 WALTER RALEGH: Fain would I climb, yet fear I to fall.

ELIZABETH: If thy heart fails thee, climb not at all.

Elizabeth I 1533–1603: lines written on a window-pane; Thomas Fuller *Worthies of England* (1662)

11 Cromwell, I charge thee, fling away ambition:
By that sin fell the angels.

William Shakespeare 1564–1616: *Henry VIII* (1613)

12 Ambition, in a private man a vice,
Is in a prince the virtue.

Philip Massinger 1583–1640: *The Bashful Lover* (1636)

13 Better to reign in hell, than serve in heaven.

John Milton 1608–74: *Paradise Lost* (1667)

14 My father was an eminent button maker . . . but I had a soul above buttons . . . I panted for a liberal profession.

George Colman, the Younger 1762–1836: *New Hay at the Old Market* (1795)

15 Well is it known that ambition can creep as well as soar.

Edmund Burke 1729–97: *Third Letter . . . on the Proposals for Peace with the Regicide Directory* (1797)

16 Before this time to-morrow I shall have gained a peerage, or Westminster Abbey.

Horatio, Lord Nelson 1758–1805: before the battle of the Nile, 1798; Robert Southey *Life of Nelson* (1813)

17 Remember that there is not one of you who does not carry in his cartridge-pouch the marshal's baton of the duke of Reggio; it is up to you to bring it forth.

Louis XVIII 1755–1824: speech to Saint-Cyr cadets, 9 August 1819

18 I had rather be right than be President.

Henry Clay 1777–1852: to Senator Preston of South Carolina, 1839; S. W. McCall *Life of Thomas Brackett Reed* (1914)

19 Ah, but a man's reach should exceed his grasp,
Or what's a heaven for?

Robert Browning 1812–89: 'Andrea del Sarto' (1855)

20 All ambitions are lawful except those which climb upwards on the miseries or credulities of mankind.

Joseph Conrad 1857–1924: *Some Reminiscences* (1912)

21 He is loyal to his own career but only
incidentally to anything or anyone else.
of Richard Crossman
Hugh Dalton 1887–1962: diary, 17 September 1941

22 Do you sincerely want to be rich?
stock question to salesmen
Bernard Cornfeld 1927– : Charles Raw et al. *Do You Sincerely Want to be Rich?* (1971)

23 Yo I'll tell you what I want, what I really
really want
so tell me what you want, what you really
really want.
The Spice Girls: 'Wannabe' (1996 song, with Matthew Rowbottom and Richard Stannard)

America see also **American Cities and States**

1 America is a tune. It must be sung together.
American proverb, mid 20th century

2 Good Americans when they die go to Paris.
mid 19th century; coinage attributed to Thomas Gold Appleton (1812–84)

3 It is a striking coincidence that the word American ends in can.
American proverb, mid 20th century

PHRASES

4 the Bird of Freedom the emblematic bald
eagle of the US.

5 founding father an American statesman at
the time of the Revolution, especially a
member of the Federal Constitutional
Convention of 1787.

6 Land of the Free the United States of
America.
from 'The Star-Spangled Banner': see 14 below

7 Old Glory the national flag of the United
States.
attributed to Captain William Driver (1803–86), who is reported to have said, 'I name thee Old Glory!', when saluting a new flag flown on his ship in 1831

8 the Stars and Bars the flag of the
Confederate States of America.
it had three bars, and a circle of eleven stars for the eleven states of the Confederacy

9 the Stars and Stripes the national flag of
the United States.
when first adopted in 1777 it contained 13 stripes and 13 stars, representing the 13 states of the Union; it now has 13 stripes and 50 stars

QUOTATIONS

10 We must consider that we shall be a city
upon a hill, the eyes of all people are on
us; so that if we shall deal falsely with our
God in this work we have undertaken, and
so cause Him to withdraw His present help
from us, we shall be made a story and a
byword through the world.
John Winthrop 1588–1649: *Christian Charity, A Model Hereof* (sermon, 1630)

11 Westward the course of empire takes its
way;
The first four acts already past,
A fifth shall close the drama with the day:
Time's noblest offspring is the last.
George Berkeley 1685–1753: 'On the Prospect of Planting Arts and Learning in America' (1752)

12 Then join hand in hand, brave Americans
all,—
By uniting we stand, by dividing we fall.
John Dickinson 1732–1808: 'The Liberty Song' (1768); see **Cooperation** 18

13 Where today are the Pequot? Where are
the Narragansett, the Mohican, the
Pokanoket, and many other once powerful
tribes of our people? They have vanished
before the avarice and oppression of the
white man, as snow before the summer
sun.
Tecumseh 1768–1813: Dee Brown *Bury My Heart at Wounded Knee* (1970)

14 'Tis the star-spangled banner; O long may
it wave
O'er the land of the free, and the home of
the brave!
Francis Scott Key 1779–1843: 'The Star-Spangled Banner' (1814); see 6 above

15 I called the New World into existence, to
redress the balance of the Old.
George Canning 1770–1827: speech on the affairs of Portugal, House of Commons, 12 December 1826

16 I have heard something said about
allegiance to the South. I know no South,

no North, no East, no West, to which I owe any allegiance . . . The Union, sir, is my country.

Henry Clay 1777–1852: speech in the US Senate, 1848

17 I was born an American; I will live an American; I shall die an American.

Daniel Webster 1782–1852: speech in the Senate on 'The Compromise Bill', 17 July 1850

18 Go West, young man, and grow up with the country.

Horace Greeley 1811–72: *Hints toward Reforms* (1850); see **Exploration** 7

19 The United States themselves are essentially the greatest poem.

Walt Whitman 1819–92: *Leaves of Grass* (1855)

20 A Star for every State, and a State for every Star.

Robert Charles Winthrop 1809–94: speech on Boston Common, 27 August 1862

21 What law have I broken? Is it wrong for me to love my own? Is it wicked for me because my skin is red? Because I am Sioux; because I was born where my fathers lived; because I would die for my people and my country?

Sitting Bull (Tatanka Iyotake) c.1831–90: to Major Brotherton, recorded July 1881; Gary C. Anderson *Sitting Bull* (1996)

22 Give me your tired, your poor, Your huddled masses yearning to breathe free.

inscription on the Statue of Liberty, New York
Emma Lazarus 1849–87: 'The New Colossus' (1883)

23 Isn't this a billion dollar country?

responding to a Democratic gibe about a 'million dollar Congress'
Charles Foster 1828–1904: at the 51st Congress, in *North American Review* March 1892; also attributed to Thomas B. Reed

24 America! America! God shed His grace on thee And crown thy good with brotherhood From sea to shining sea!

Katherine Lee Bates 1859–1929: 'America the Beautiful' (1893)

25 I'm a Yankee Doodle Dandy, A Yankee Doodle, do or die; A real live nephew of my Uncle Sam's, Born on the fourth of July.

George M. Cohan 1878–1942: 'Yankee Doodle Boy' (1904 song)

26 America is God's Crucible, the great Melting-Pot where all the races of Europe are melting and re-forming!

Israel Zangwill 1864–1926: *The Melting Pot* (1908)

27 The chief business of the American people is business.

Calvin Coolidge 1872–1933: speech in Washington, 17 January 1925

28 'next to of course god america i love you land of the pilgrims' and so forth oh say can you see by the dawn's early my country 'tis of centuries come and go

e. e. cummings 1894–1962: *is 5* (1926)

29 The American system of rugged individualism.

Herbert Hoover 1874–1964: speech in New York City, 22 October 1928

30 I pledge you, I pledge myself, to a new deal for the American people.

Franklin D. Roosevelt 1882–1945: speech to the Democratic Convention in Chicago, 2 July 1932, accepting the presidential nomination

31 In the United States there is more space where nobody is than where anybody is. That is what makes America what it is.

Gertrude Stein 1874–1946: *The Geographical History of America* (1936)

32 God bless America, Land that I love, Stand beside her and guide her Thru the night with a light from above. From the mountains to the prairies, To the oceans white with foam, God bless America, My home sweet home.

Irving Berlin 1888–1989: 'God Bless America' (1939 song)

33 Yes, America is gigantic, but a gigantic mistake.

Sigmund Freud 1856–1939: Peter Gay *Freud: A Life for Our Time* (1988)

34 This land is your land, this land is my land, From California to the New York Island. From the redwood forest to the Gulf Stream waters This land was made for you and me.

Woody Guthrie 1912–67: 'This Land is Your Land' (1956 song)

35 I like to be in America! O.K. by me in America! Ev'rything free in America

For a small fee in America!
Stephen Sondheim 1930– : 'America' (1957 song)

36 America is a nation created by all the hopeful wanderers of Europe, not out of geography and genetics, but out of purpose.
Theodore White 1915-86: *Making of the President* (1960)

37 The immense popularity of American movies abroad demonstrates that Europe is the unfinished negative of which America is the proof.
Mary McCarthy 1912-89: *On the Contrary* (1961)

38 The weakness of American civilization, and perhaps the chief reason why it creates so much discontent, is that it is so curiously abstract. It is a bloodless

extrapolation of a satisfying life . . . You dine off the advertisers 'sizzling' and not the meat of the steak.
J. B. Priestley 1894-1984: in *New Statesman* 10 December 1971

39 America is a vast conspiracy to make you happy.
John Updike 1932– : *Problems* (1980) 'How to love America and Leave it at the Same Time'

40 The microwave, the waste disposal, the orgasmic elasticity of the carpets, this soft resort-style civilization irresistibly evokes the end of the world.
Jean Baudrillard 1929– : *America* (1986)

41 God, guts and paranoia made America great.
Tom Holt 1961– : *Who's Afraid of Beowulf?* (1988)

American Cities and States

PHRASES

1 **the Aloha State** Hawaii.
aloha = *Hawaiian word used when greeting or parting from someone*

2 **the Bay State** Massachusetts.
the original colony was sited around Massachusetts Bay

3 **the Bear State** Arkansas.

4 **the Big Apple** New York City.

5 **the Buckeye State** Ohio.
where buckeye trees are abundant

6 **the Centennial State** Colorado.
admitted as a state in 1876, the centennial year of the United States

7 **City of the Angels** Los Angeles, California.

8 **City of Elms** New Haven, Connecticut.

9 **City of Magnificent Distances** Washington, DC.

10 **the Crescent City** New Orleans.
the city is built on a curve of the Mississippi

11 **the Diamond State** Delaware.
said to be so named because it was seen as small in size but of great importance

12 **the Empire City** New York.

13 **the Empire State** New York State.

14 **the Empire State of the South** Georgia.

15 **the Equality State** Wyoming.
the first state to give women the vote

16 **the Forest City** Cleveland, Ohio.

17 **the Garden State** New Jersey.

18 **the Golden State** California.

19 **the Gopher State** Minnesota.

20 **the Granite State** New Hampshire.

21 **the Great White Way** Broadway in New York City.
referring to the brilliant street illumination

22 **the Hawkeye State** Iowa.

23 **the Keystone State** Pennsylvania.
the seventh or central one of the original thirteen States

24 **Land of Enchantment** an informal name for New Mexico.

25 **the Lone Star State** Texas.

26 **the Magnolia State** Mississippi.
the state's emblem is the magnolia flower

27 **the Monumental City** the city of Baltimore, Maryland.
named after the Washington Monument

28 **Mother of Presidents** informal name for the state of Virginia and (later) Ohio.
Virginia was the birthplace of Washington, Jefferson, and Monroe, and Ohio the birthplace of Garfield and Taft

29 the North Star State Minnesota.
North Star the polestar

30 the Nutmeg State Connecticut.
the inhabitants of Connecticut reputedly passed off as the spice nutmeg-shaped pieces of wood; see **Deception** 9

31 the Old Dominion Virginia.

32 the Palmetto State South Carolina.

33 the Pelican State Louisiana.

34 the Prairie State Illinois.

35 the Prairie States Illinois, Wisconsin, Iowa, Minnesota, and other states to the south.

36 Quaker City Philadelphia.
founded by the Quaker William Penn in 1681

37 the Quaker State Pennsylvania.

38 Queen of the West Cincinnati, Ohio.

39 the Silver State Nevada.
referring to its silver mines

40 Soul City the Harlem area of New York city.
referring to the prevalence of soul music

41 the Sunflower State Kansas.
the sunflower is the state flower

42 the Tarheel State North Carolina.
with allusion to tar as a principal product of that state

43 the Treasure State Montana.
noted for its gold, silver, copper, and coal mines

44 the Turpentine State North Carolina.
from the quantity of turpentine obtained from its pine forests

45 the Volunteer State Tennessee.
from which large numbers volunteered for the Mexican War of 1847

46 the Windy City Chicago.

47 the Wolverine State Michigan.
where wolverines are found

QUOTATIONS

48 A very Italy, without its art.
of California
Oscar Wilde 1854–1900: letter to Norman Forbes-Robertson, 27 March 1882

49 A Boston man is the east wind made flesh.
Thomas Gold Appleton 1812–84: attributed

50 And this is good old Boston,
The home of the bean and the cod,

Where the Lowells talk to the Cabots
And the Cabots talk only to God.
John Collins Bossidy 1860–1928: verse spoken at Holy Cross College alumni dinner in Boston, Massachusetts, 1910

51 Hog Butcher for the World,
Tool Maker, Stacker of Wheat,
Player with Railroads and the Nation's
Freight Handler;
Stormy, husky, brawling,
City of the Big Shoulders.
Carl Sandburg 1878–1967: 'Chicago' (1916)

52 California is a fine place to live—if you happen to be an orange.
Fred Allen 1894–1956: *American Magazine* December 1945

53 New York, New York,—a helluva town,
The Bronx is up but the Battery's down.
Betty Comden 1919– and **Adolph Green** 1915– : 'New York, New York' (1945 song)

54 The state with the prettiest name,
the state that floats in brackish water,
held together by mangrove roots.
Elizabeth Bishop 1911–79: 'Florida' (1946)

55 Last week, I went to Philadelphia, but it was closed.
W. C. Fields 1880–1946: Richard J. Anobile *Godfrey Daniels* (1975)

56 A hundred times I have thought: New York is a catastrophe, and fifty times: it is a beautiful catastrophe.
Le Corbusier 1887–1965: *When the Cathedrals were White* (1947) 'The Fairy Catastrophe'

57 A big hard-boiled city with no more personality than a paper cup.
of Los Angeles
Raymond Chandler 1888–1959: *The Little Sister* (1949)

58 Hollywood is a place where people from Iowa mistake each other for stars.
Fred Allen 1894–1956: Maurice Zolotow *No People like Show People* (1951)

59 I left my heart in San Francisco
High on a hill it calls to me.
Douglas Cross: 'I Left My Heart in San Francisco' (1954 song)

60 This is Red Hook, not Sicily . . . This is the gullet of New York swallowing the tonnage of the world.
Arthur Miller 1915– : *A View from the Bridge* (1955)

61 Washington is a city of southern efficiency and northern charm.
John F. Kennedy 1917–63: Arthur M. Schlesinger Jr. *A Thousand Days* (1965)

62 New York makes one think of the collapse of civilization, about Sodom and Gomorrah, the end of the world. The end wouldn't come as a surprise here. Many people already bank on it.
Saul Bellow 1915– : *Mr Sammler's Planet* (1970)

63 I had forgotten just how flat and empty it [middle America] is. Stand on two phone books almost anywhere in Iowa and you get a view.
Bill Bryson 1951– : *The Lost Continent* (1989)

Anger

1 Anger improves nothing but the arch of a cat's back.
American proverb, mid 20th century

2 A little pot is soon hot.
mid 16th century, meaning that a small person quickly becomes angry or passionate

3 When angry count a hundred.
late 16th century, advising against precipitate response (the number proposed varies, and sometimes the advice is '. . . recite the alphabet'); see 10, 12, 14 below

4 A soft answer turneth away wrath.
Bible: Proverbs; see **Diplomacy** 1

5 *Ira furor brevis est.*
Anger is a short madness.
Horace 65–8 BC: *Epistles*

6 Be ye angry and sin not: let not the sun go down upon your wrath.
Bible: Ephesians; see **Forgiveness** 4

7 Anger makes dull men witty, but it keeps them poor.
Francis Bacon 1561–1626: 'Baconiana' (1859); often attributed to Queen Elizabeth I from a misreading of the text

8 Anger is never without an argument, but seldom with a good one.
Lord Halifax 1633–95: *Political, Moral, and Miscellaneous Thoughts and Reflections* (1750)

9 The tygers of wrath are wiser than the horses of instruction.
William Blake 1757–1827: *The Marriage of Heaven and Hell* (1790–3) 'Proverbs of Hell'

10 When angry, count ten before you speak; if very angry a hundred.
Thomas Jefferson 1743–1826: letter to Thomas Jefferson Smith, 21 February 1825; see 3 above, 12, 14 below

11 We boil at different degrees.
Ralph Waldo Emerson 1803–82: *Society and Solitude* (1870)

12 When angry, count four; when very angry, swear.
Mark Twain 1835–1910: *Pudd'nhead Wilson* (1894); see 3, 10 above, 14 below

13 It's my rule never to lose me temper till it would be dethrimental to keep it.
Sean O'Casey 1880–1964: *The Plough and the Stars* (1926)

14 When you get angry, they tell you, count to five before you reply. Why should I count to five? It's what happens *before* you count to five which makes life interesting.
David Hare 1947– : *The Secret Rapture* (1988); see 3, 12, 14 above

Animals see also Birds, Cats, Dogs

1 From beavers, bees should learn to mend their ways.
A bee works; a beaver works and plays.
American proverb, mid 20th century

2 A howlin' coyote ain't stealin' no chickens.
American proverb, mid 20th century

3 If you want to live and thrive, let the spider run alive.
mid 19th century; it was traditionally unlucky to harm a spider or a spider's web

4 One white foot, buy him; two white feet, try him; three white feet, look well about him; four white feet, go without him.

a horse-dealing proverb, categorizing features in a horse which are believed to be unlucky; recorded in various forms from the 15th century

5 Three things are not to be trusted; a cow's horn, a dog's tooth, and a horse's hoof.

late 14th century; meaning that one may be gored, bitten, or kicked without warning

PHRASES

6 the king of beasts the lion.

7 the lion's provider the jackal.

8 the little gentleman in black velvet the mole.

in a Jacobite toast, from the belief that the death of William III was caused by his horse's stumbling over a molehill

9 the ship of the desert the camel.

QUOTATIONS

10 There went in two and two unto Noah into the Ark, the male and the female.
Bible: Genesis

11 A righteous man regardeth the life of his beast: but the tender mercies of the wicked are cruel.
Bible: Proverbs

12 All breathing, existing, living, sentient creatures should not be slain, nor treated with violence, nor abused, nor tormented, nor driven away.
This is the pure, unchangeable, eternal law.
Jaina Sutras 6th century BC: *Ācārāṅga Sutra*

13 Nature's great masterpiece, an elephant, The only harmless great thing.
John Donne 1572–1631: 'The Progress of the Soul' (1601)

14 The serpent subtlest beast of all the field.
John Milton 1608–74: *Paradise Lost* (1667)

15 Old pond,
leap-splash—
a frog.
Matsuo Basho 1644–94: translated by Lucien Stryk

16 The question is not, Can they reason? nor, Can they talk? but, Can they suffer?
Jeremy Bentham 1748–1832: *Principles of Morals and Legislation* (1789)

17 Tyger Tyger, burning bright,

In the forests of the night;
What immortal hand or eye,
Could frame thy fearful symmetry?
William Blake 1757–1827: *Songs of Experience* (1794) 'The Tiger'

18 Animals, whom we have made our slaves, we do not like to consider our equal.
Charles Darwin 1809–82: Notebook B (1837–8)

19 All things bright and beautiful,
All creatures great and small,
All things wise and wonderful,
The Lord God made them all.
Cecil Frances Alexander 1818–95: 'All Things Bright and Beautiful' (1848)

20 I think I could turn and live with animals, they are so placid and self-contained,
I stand and look at them long and long.
They do not sweat and whine about their condition,
They do not lie awake in the dark and weep for their sins,
They do not make me sick discussing their duty to God,
Not one is dissatisfied, not one is demented with the mania of owning things.
Walt Whitman 1819–92: 'Song of Myself' (written 1855)

21 But I freely admit that the best of my fun I owe it to horse and hound.
George John Whyte-Melville 1821–78: 'The Good Grey Mare' (1933)

22 When people call this beast to mind,
They marvel more and more
At such a little tail behind,
So large a trunk before.
Hilaire Belloc 1870–1953: *A Bad Child's Book of Beasts* (1896) 'The Elephant'

23 With monstrous head and sickening cry
And ears like errant wings,
The devil's walking parody
On all four-footed things.
G. K. Chesterton 1874–1936: 'The Donkey' (1900)

24 All animals, except man, know that the principal business of life is to enjoy it—and they do enjoy it as much as man and other circumstances will allow.
Samuel Butler 1835–1902: *The Way of All Flesh* (1903)

25 'Twould ring the bells of Heaven
The wildest peal for years,
If Parson lost his senses
And people came to theirs,
And he and they together

Knelt down with angry prayers
For tamed and shabby tigers
And dancing dogs and bears,
And wretched, blind, pit ponies,
And little hunted hares.
Ralph Hodgson 1871–1962: 'Bells of Heaven' (1917)

26 The turtle lives 'twixt plated decks
Which practically conceal its sex.
I think it clever of the turtle
In such a fix to be so fertile.
Ogden Nash 1902–71: 'Autres Bêtes, Autres Moeurs'
(1931)

27 God in His wisdom made the fly
And then forgot to tell us why.
Ogden Nash 1902–71: 'The Fly' (1942)

28   Giraffes!—a People
Who live between the earth and skies,
Each in his lone religious steeple,
Keeping a light-house with his eyes.
Roy Campbell 1901–57: 'Dreaming Spires' (1946)

29 A four-legged friend, a four-legged friend,
He'll never let you down.
sung by Roy Rogers about his horse Trigger
J. Brooks: 'A Four Legged Friend' (1952 song)

30 Where in this wide world can man find
    nobility without pride,
Friendship without envy, or beauty
    without vanity?
Ronald Duncan 1914–82: 'In Praise of the Horse'
(1962)

31 I am fond of pigs. Dogs look up to us. Cats
look down on us. Pigs treat us as equals.
Winston Churchill 1874–1965: attributed; M.
Gilbert *Never Despair* (1988)

32 I hate a word like 'pets': it sounds so much
Like something with no living of its own.
Elizabeth Jennings 1926–2001: 'My Animals' (1966)

33 Whales play, in an amniotic paradise.
Their light minds shaped by buoyancy,
    unrestricted by gravity,
Somersaulting.
Like angels, or birds;
Like our own lives, in the womb.
Heathcote Williams 1941– : *Whale Nation* (1988)

34 If our history of bear-baiting, pit ponies
and ejected Christmas puppies can
honestly be called a great British love affair
with animals then the average praying
mantis and her husband are Darby and
Joan.
Stephen Fry 1957– : *Paperweight* (1992)

35 I'm not over-fond of animals. I am merely
astounded by them.
David Attenborough 1926– : in *Independent* 14
January 1995

36 It is part of the pathos of a pet, that it
always stands on the edge of the moral
dialogue, staring from beyond an
impassable barrier at the life which is now
everything to it, and which yet it cannot
comprehend.
Roger Scruton 1944– : *Animal Rights and Wrongs*
(1996)

Apology and Excuses

PROVERBS AND SAYINGS

1 **Apology is only egoism wrong side out.**
American proverb, mid 20th century

2 **A bad excuse is better than none.**
*mid 16th century, meaning that it is better to attempt
to give some kind of explanation, even a weak one*

3 **A bad workman blames his tools.**
*early 17th century, often used as a comment on
someone's excuses for their lack of success; late 13th
century in French*

4 **Don't make excuses, make good.**
American proverb, early 20th century

5 **He who excuses, accuses himself.**
*early 17th century, often used to mean that attempts
to excuse oneself show a guilty conscience*

6 **It is easy to find a stick to beat a dog.**
*mid 16th century; meaning that it is easy to find
reasons to criticize someone who is vulnerable; see*
Argument 19

7 **When you are in a hole, stop digging.**
*late 20th century saying, meaning that complicated
explanations and attempts to exculpate oneself often
make a bad situation worse; often associated with the
Labour politician Denis Healey*

PHRASES

8 **mea culpa** an acknowledgement of one's
guilt or responsibility for an error.
*Latin, literally '(through) my own fault': from the
prayer of confession in the Latin liturgy of the Church*

9 a sop to Cerberus something offered in propitiation.

Cerberus the three-headed watchdog of classical mythology which guarded the entrance of Hades; in the Aeneid, Aeneas was able to pass him safely by drugging him with a specially prepared cake

QUOTATIONS

10 Never make a defence or apology before you be accused.

Charles I 1600–49: letter to Lord Wentworth, 3 September 1636

11 A man should never be ashamed to own he has been in the wrong, which is but saying, in other words, that he is wiser to-day than he was yesterday.

Alexander Pope 1688–1744: *Miscellanies* (1727) vol. 2 'Thoughts on Various Subjects'

12 I think the noble young man has no business to make any apology. He is a gentleman, and none such should be asked to make an apology, because no gentleman could mean to give offence.

on the motion to expel Lord Edward Fitzgerald from the Irish Parliament, c.1796

Boyle Roche 1743–1807: Jonah Barrington *Personal Sketches and Recollections of his own Time* (1827)

13 Never complain and never explain.

Benjamin Disraeli 1804–81: J. Morley *Life of William Ewart Gladstone* (1903)

14 I have invented an invaluable permanent invalid called Bunbury, in order that I may be able to go down into the country whenever I choose.

Oscar Wilde 1854–1900: *The Importance of Being Earnest* (1899)

15 Never explain—your friends do not need it and your enemies will not believe you anyway.

Elbert Hubbard 1859–1915: *The Motto Book* (1907)

16 As I waited I thought that there's nothing like a confession to make one look mad; and that of all confessions a written one is the most detrimental all round. Never confess! Never, never!

Joseph Conrad 1857–1924: *Chance* (1913)

17 It is a good rule in life never to apologize. The right sort of people do not want apologies, and the wrong sort take a mean advantage of them.

P. G. Wodehouse 1881–1975: *The Man Upstairs* (1914)

18 Very sorry can't come. Lie follows by post.

telegraphed message to the Prince of Wales, on being summoned to dine at the eleventh hour

Lord Charles Beresford 1846–1919: Ralph Nevill *The World of Fashion 1837–1922* (1923)

19 Several excuses are always less convincing than one.

Aldous Huxley 1894–1963: *Point Counter Point* (1928)

20 This is the only country in the world where you step on somebody's foot and he apologises.

Keith Waterhouse 1929– : in *Independent* 1 April 2000

Appearance see also **The Body**

PROVERBS AND SAYINGS

1 All that glitters is not gold.

early 13th century, meaning that an attractive appearance is not necessarily evidence of intrinsic value

2 Appearances are deceptive.

mid 17th century, meaning that the outward form of something may not be a true guide to its real nature

3 A blind man's wife needs no paint.

mid 17th century, meaning that there is no point in making efforts that cannot be appreciated

4 A carpenter is known by his chips.

mid 16th century, meaning that the nature of a person's occupation or interest is demonstrated by the traces left behind

5 The cowl does not make the monk.

late 14th century, warning against judging nature and moral character by appearance

6 Distance lends enchantment to the view.

*late 18th century, from Campbell; see **The Country and the Town** 11*

7 A good horse cannot be of a bad colour.

early 17th century, meaning that colour is not an indicator of a horse's quality

8 Keep that schoolgirl complexion.

advertising slogan for Palmolive soap, from 1917

9 Merit in appearance is more often rewarded than merit itself.

American proverb, mid 20th century

10 Never choose your women or linen by candlelight.

late 16th century, warning against being deceived by apparent attractions seen in a poor light

11 What you see is what you get.

a late 20th century computing expression, from which the acronym wysiwyg derives. The expression is used generally to mean that the function and value of something can be deduced from its outward appearance; there are no hidden drawbacks or advantages

12 You can't tell a book by its cover.

early 20th century, meaning that outward appearance is not a guide to a person's real nature

QUOTATIONS

13 A merry heart maketh a cheerful countenance.
Bible: Proverbs

14 There's no art
To find the mind's construction in the face;
William Shakespeare 1564–1616: *Macbeth* (1606)

15 He was one of a lean body and visage, as if his eager soul, biting for anger at the clog of his body, desired to fret a passage through it.
Thomas Fuller 1608–61: *The Holy State and the Profane State* (1642) 'Life of the Duke of Alva'

16 Has he not a rogue's face? . . . a hanging-look to me . . . has a damned Tyburn-face, without the benefit o' the Clergy.
William Congreve 1670–1729: *Love for Love* (1695); see **Clergy** 5

17 An unforgiving eye, and a damned disinheriting countenance!
Richard Brinsley Sheridan 1751–1816: *The School for Scandal* (1777)

18 Like the silver plate on a coffin.
describing Robert Peel's smile
John Philpot Curran 1750–1817: quoted by Daniel O'Connell, House of Commons, 26 February 1835

19 The Lord prefers common-looking people. That is why he makes so many of them.
Abraham Lincoln 1809–65: attributed; James Morgan *Our Presidents* (1928)

20 It's as large as life, and twice as natural!
Lewis Carroll 1832–98: *Through the Looking-Glass* (1872)

21 She may very well pass for forty-three
In the dusk with a light behind her!
W. S. Gilbert 1836–1911: *Trial by Jury* (1875)

22 Most women are not so young as they are painted.
Max Beerbohm 1872–1956: *The Yellow Book* (1894)

23 You look rather rash my dear your colors dont quite match your face.
Daisy Ashford 1881–1972: *The Young Visiters* (1919)

24 The photograph is not quite true to my own notion of my gentleness and sweetness of nature, but neither perhaps is my external appearance.
A. E. Housman 1859–1936: letter 12 June 1922

25 In England and America a beard usually means that its owner would rather be considered venerable than virile; on the continent of Europe it often means that its owner makes a special claim to virility.
Rebecca West 1892–1983: *The Thinking Reed* (1936)

26 Men seldom make passes
At girls who wear glasses.
Dorothy Parker 1893–1967: 'News Item' (1937)

27 Sure, deck your lower limbs in pants;
Yours are the limbs, my sweeting.
You look divine as you advance—
Have you seen yourself retreating?
Ogden Nash 1902–71: 'What's the Use?' (1940)

28 At 50, everyone has the face he deserves.
George Orwell 1903–50: last words in his notebook, 17 April 1949

29 My face looks like a wedding cake left out in the rain.
W. H. Auden 1907–73: Humphrey Carpenter *W. H. Auden* (1981)

30 The most common error made in matters of appearance is the belief that one should disdain the superficial and let the true beauty of one's soul shine through. If there are places on one's body where this is a possibility, you are not attractive—you are leaking.
Fran Lebowitz 1946– : *Metropolitan Life* (1978)

31 No power on earth, however, can abolish the merciless class distinction between those who are physically desirable and the lonely, pallid, spotted, silent, unfancied majority.
John Mortimer 1923– : *Clinging to the Wreckage* (1982)

32 You can never be too rich or too thin.
Duchess of Windsor 1896–1986: attributed

33 I think your whole life shows in your face and you should be proud of that.
Lauren Bacall 1924– : in *Daily Telegraph* 2 March 1988

34 Being blonde is definitely a different state of mind. I can't really put my finger on it, but the artifice of being blonde has some incredible sort of sexual connotation.
Madonna 1958– : in *Rolling Stone* 23 March 1989

35 Anything which says it can magically take away your wrinkles is a scandalous lie.
Anita Roddick 1942– : in *Daily Telegraph* 19 October 2000

Architecture

PROVERBS AND SAYINGS

1 **In settling an island, the first building erected by a Spaniard will be a church; by a Frenchman, a fort; by a Dutchman, a warehouse; and by an Englishman, an alehouse.**
late 18th century saying

2 **It is easier to build two chimneys than to maintain one.**
mid 16th century

3 **No good building without a good foundation.**
late 15th century

PHRASES

4 **the Seven Wonders of the World** the seven most spectacular man-made structures of the ancient world.
traditionally they comprised the pyramids of Egypt, the Hanging Gardens of Babylon, the Mausoleum of Halicarnassus, the temple of Artemis at Ephesus in Asia Minor, the Colossus of Rhodes, the huge ivory and gold statue of Zeus at Olympia in the Peloponnese, and the Pharos of Alexandria (or in some lists, the walls of Babylon); see **Excellence** 6

QUOTATIONS

5 Well building hath three conditions. Commodity, firmness, and delight.
Henry Wotton 1568–1639: *Elements of Architecture* (1624)

6 Houses are built to live in and not to look on; therefore let use be preferred before uniformity, except where both may be had.
Francis Bacon 1561–1626: *Essays* (1625) 'Of Building'

7 Light (God's eldest daughter) is a principal beauty in building.
Thomas Fuller 1608–61: *The Holy State and the Profane State* (1642)

8 Architecture in general is frozen music.
Friedrich von Schelling 1775–1854: *Philosophie der Kunst* (1809)

9 As if St Paul's had come down and littered.
on Brighton Pavilion
Sydney Smith 1771–1845: Peter Virgin *Sydney Smith* (1994)

10 Form follows function.
Louis Henri Sullivan 1856–1924: *The Tall Office Building Artistically Considered* (1896); see **Beauty** 37

11 Remember that it is the glory of Gothic architecture that it can do *anything*.
John Ruskin 1819–1900: J. Mordaunt Crook *Dilemma of Style* (1987)

12 A house is a machine for living in.
Le Corbusier 1887–1965: *Vers une architecture* (1923)

13 Architecture, of all the arts, is the one which acts the most slowly, but the most surely, on the soul.
Ernest Dimnet: *What We Live By* (1932)

14 We shape our buildings, and afterwards our buildings shape us.
Winston Churchill 1874–1965: in the House of Commons, 28 October 1943

15 A bicycle shed is a building; Lincoln Cathedral is a piece of architecture. Nearly everything that encloses space on a scale sufficient for a human being to move in is a building; the term architecture applies

only to buildings designed with a view to
aesthetic appeal.
Nikolaus Pevsner 1902-83: *An Outline of European
Architecture* (1943)

16 Less is more.
Ludwig Mies van der Rohe 1886-1969: P. Johnson
Mies van der Rohe (1947); see **Excess** 6

17 The physician can bury his mistakes, but
the architect can only advise his client to
plant vines—so they should go as far as
possible from home to build their first
buildings.
Frank Lloyd Wright 1867-1959: in *New York Times*
4 October 1953

18 Architecture is the art of how to waste
space.
Philip Johnson 1906- : in *New York Times* 27
December 1964

19 God is in the details.
Ludwig Mies van der Rohe 1886-1969: attributed,
in *New York Times* 19 August 1969; see **Order** 1

20 Official designs are aggressively neuter,
The Puritan work of an eyeless computer.
John Betjeman 1906-84: 'The Newest Bath Guide'
(1974)

21 A monstrous carbuncle on the face of a
much-loved and elegant friend.
*on the proposed extension to the National Gallery,
London*
Prince Charles 1948- : speech to the Royal
Institute of British Architects, 30 May 1984

22 You should be able to read a building. It
should be what it does.
Richard Rogers 1933- : lecture, London, March
1990

23 Skyscrapers are as much a reality as
urbanization itself . . . What do we do if we
don't build high? Give up and live in
bunkers? And then what, fret about death
by nerve gas or germ warfare?
Norman Foster 1935- : in *Guardian* 15 September
2001

Argument see also Opinion

PROVERBS AND SAYINGS

1 Birds in their little nests agree.
*a nursery proverb, also used as a direction that young
children should not argue among themselves; from
Isaac Watts Divine Songs (1715)*

2 It takes two to make a quarrel.
*early 18th century, meaning that some responsibility
for a disagreement rests with each party to it; see 18
below*

**3 The more arguments you win, the less
friends you will have.**
American proverb, mid 20th century

**4 The only thing a heated argument ever
produced is coolness.**
American proverb, mid 20th century

**5 While two dogs are fighting for a bone, a
third runs away with it.**
*late 14th century, meaning that while the attention of
the disputants is on their quarrel, both may lose
possession of what they are fighting over to a third
party; see 7 below*

PHRASES

6 apple of discord a subject of dissension.
*from the golden apple inscribed 'for the fairest'
contended for by Hera, Athene, and Aphrodite; the
result of Paris's awarding the apple to Aphrodite was*

*that Hera through jealousy brought about the Trojan
War*

7 bone of contention a subject or issue over
which there is continuing disagreement.
*a bone thrown between two dogs as the type of
something which causes a quarrel; see 5 above*

QUOTATIONS

8 It is better to dwell in a corner of the
housetop, than with a brawling woman in
a wide house.
Bible: Proverbs

9 Give you a reason on compulsion! if
reasons were as plentiful as blackberries I
would give no man a reason upon
compulsion, I.
William Shakespeare 1564-1616: *Henry IV, Part 1*
(1597)

10 Our disputants put me in mind of the
skuttle fish, that when he is unable to
extricate himself, blackens all the water
about him, till he becomes invisible.
Joseph Addison 1672-1719: in *The Spectator* 5
September 1712

11 My uncle Toby would never offer to
answer this by any other kind of

argument, than that of whistling half a dozen bars of Lillabullero.
Laurence Sterne 1713-68: *Tristram Shandy* (1759-67)

12 There is no arguing with Johnson; for when his pistol misses fire, he knocks you down with the butt end of it.
Oliver Goldsmith 1728-74: James Boswell *Life of Johnson* (1791) 26 October 1769

13 I hate a fellow whom pride, or cowardice, or laziness drives into a corner, and who does nothing when he is there but sit and *growl*; let him come out as I do, and *bark*.
Samuel Johnson 1709-84: James Boswell *Life of Johnson* 10 October 1782

14 Who can refute a sneer?
William Paley 1743-1805: *Principles of Moral and Political Philosophy* (1785)

15 Persuasion is the resource of the feeble; and the feeble can seldom persuade.
Edward Gibbon 1737-94: *The Decline and Fall of the Roman Empire* (1776-88)

16 He never wants anything but what's right and fair; only when you come to settle what's right and fair, it's everything that he wants and nothing that you want. And that's his idea of a compromise. Give me the Brown compromise when I'm on his side.
Thomas Hughes 1822-96: *Tom Brown's Schooldays* (1857)

17 There is no good in arguing with the inevitable. The only argument available with an east wind is to put on your overcoat.
James Russell Lowell 1819-91: *Democracy and other Addresses* (1887)

18 It takes in reality only one to make a quarrel. It is useless for the sheep to pass resolutions in favour of vegetarianism, while the wolf remains of a different opinion.
William Ralph Inge 1860-1954: *Outspoken Essays: First Series* (1919) 'Patriotism'; see 2 above

19 Any stigma, as the old saying is, will serve to beat a dogma.
Philip Guedalla 1889-1944: *Masters and Men* (1923); see **Apology** 6

20 The argument of the broken window pane is the most valuable argument in modern politics.
Emmeline Pankhurst 1858-1928: George Dangerfield *The Strange Death of Liberal England* (1936)

21 Making noise is an effective means of opposition.
Joseph Goebbels 1897-1945: Ernest K. Bramsted *Goebbels and National Socialist Propaganda 1925-45* (1965)

22 The Catholic and the Communist are alike in assuming that an opponent cannot be both honest and intelligent.
George Orwell 1903-50: in *Polemic* January 1946

23 Get your tanks off my lawn, Hughie.
to the trade union leader Hugh Scanlon, at Chequers in June 1969
Harold Wilson 1916-95: Peter Jenkins *The Battle of Downing Street* (1970)

24 That happy sense of purpose people have when they are standing up for a principle they haven't really been knocked down for yet.
P. J. O'Rourke 1947- : *Give War a Chance* (1992)

25 Conflicts, like living organisms, had a natural lifespan. The trick was to know when to let them die.
Ian McEwan 1948- : *Enduring Love* (1998)

The Armed Forces see also Warfare, Wars, World War I, World War II

PROVERBS AND SAYINGS

1 The army knows how to gain a victory but not how to make proper use of it.
American proverb, mid 20th century

2 Daddy, what did you do in the Great War?
daughter to father in First World War recruiting poster

3 The first duty of a soldier is obedience.
mid 19th century

4 If it moves, salute it; if it doesn't move, pick it up; and if you can't pick it up, paint it.
1940s saying

5 Old soldiers never die.
early 20th century; see 37 below

6 One of our aircraft is missing.
*title of film (1941), an alteration of the customary
formula used by BBC news in the Second World War,
'One of our aircraft failed to return'*

**7 Providence is always on the side of the big
battalions.**
early 19th century; see **God** *20,* **Strength** *17,* **Warfare**
20

**8 A singing army and a singing people can't
be defeated.**
American proverb, mid 20th century

9 A willing foe and sea room.
naval toast in the time of Nelson

10 Your King and Country need you.
*1914 recruiting advertisement, showing Lord Kitchener
with pointing finger*

**11 Your soul may belong to God, but your ass
belongs to the army.**
American saying to new recruits, mid 20th century

PHRASES

12 the awkward squad a squad composed of
recruits and soldiers who need further
training.
*shortly before his death Robert Burns said, 'don't let
the awkward squad fire over my grave'*

13 the thin red line the British army.
*William Howard Russell said of the Russians charging
the British at Balaclava, 'They dashed on towards that
thin red line tipped with steel'; Russell's original
dispatch to The Times, 14 November 1854, reads 'That
thin red streak topped with a line of steel'; see* **The
Law** *12*

14 the wooden walls ships or shipping as a
defensive force.
*the Athenian statesman Themistocles interpreted the
Delphic oracle's reference to 'safety promised in a
wooden wall' as referring to the Greek ships with
which the decisive victory over the Persian fleet at
Salamis was achieved; see* **The Sea** *11*

QUOTATIONS

15 For a city consists in men, and not in walls
nor in ships empty of men.
*speech to the defeated Athenian army at Syracuse, 413
BC*
Nicias c.470–413 BC: Thucydides *History of the
Peloponnesian Wars*

16 Then a soldier,
Full of strange oaths, and bearded like the
pard,
Jealous in honour, sudden and quick in
quarrel,
Seeking the bubble reputation

Even in the cannon's mouth.
William Shakespeare 1564–1616: *As You Like It*
(1599)

17 I would rather have a plain russet-coated
captain that knows what he fights for, and
loves what he knows, than that which you
call 'a gentleman' and is nothing else.
Oliver Cromwell 1599–1658: letter to Sir William
Spring, September 1643

18 It is upon the navy under the good
Providence of God that the safety, honour,
and welfare of this realm do chiefly
depend.
Charles II 1630–85: 'Articles of War' preamble; Sir
Geoffrey Callender *The Naval Side of British History*
(1952); probably a modern paraphrase

19 Rascals, would you live for ever?
to hesitant Guards at Kolin, 18 June 1757
Frederick the Great 1712–86: attributed

20 Heart of oak are our ships,
Heart of oak are our men:
We always are ready;
Steady, boys, steady;
We'll fight and we'll conquer again and
again.
David Garrick 1717–79: 'Heart of Oak' (1759 song);
see **Character** 21

21 Every man thinks meanly of himself for not
having been a soldier, or not having been
at sea.
Samuel Johnson 1709–84: James Boswell *Life of
Samuel Johnson* (1791) 10 April 1778

22 Without a decisive naval force we can do
nothing definitive. And with it, everything
honorable and glorious.
George Washington 1732–99: to Lafayette, 15
November 1781

23 Some talk of Alexander, and some of
Hercules;
Of Hector and Lysander, and such great
names as these;
But of all the world's brave heroes, there's
none that can compare
With a tow, row, row, row, row, row, for
the British Grenadier.
Anonymous: 'The British Grenadiers' (traditional
song)

24 Who is the happy Warrior? Who is he
Whom every man in arms should wish to
be?
William Wordsworth 1770–1850: 'Character of
the Happy Warrior' (1807); see **35** below

25 As Lord Chesterfield said of the generals of his day, 'I only hope that when the enemy reads the list of their names, he trembles as I do.'

usually quoted as 'I don't know what effect these men will have upon the enemy, but, by God, they frighten me'

Duke of Wellington 1769–1852: letter, 29 August 1810

26 *La Garde meurt, mais ne se rend pas.*

The Guards die but do not surrender.

when called upon to surrender at Waterloo, 1815

Pierre, Baron de Cambronne 1770–1842: attributed to Cambronne, but later denied by him; H. Houssaye *La Garde meurt et ne se rend pas* (1907)

27 An army marches on its stomach.

Napoleon I 1769–1821: attributed, but probably condensed from a long passage in E. A. de Las Cases *Mémorial de Ste-Hélène* (1823) vol. 4, 14 November 1816; also attributed to Frederick the Great

28 Ours [our army] is composed of the scum of the earth—the mere scum of the earth.

Duke of Wellington 1769–1852: Philip Henry Stanhope *Notes of Conversations with the Duke of Wellington* (1888) 4 November 1831

29 *C'est magnifique, mais ce n'est pas la guerre.*

It is magnificent, but it is not war.

on the charge of the Light Brigade at Balaclava, 25 October 1854

Pierre Bosquet 1810–61: Cecil Woodham-Smith *The Reason Why* (1953)

30 Theirs not to make reply,
Theirs not to reason why,
Theirs but to do and die:
Into the valley of Death
Rode the six hundred.

Alfred, Lord Tennyson 1809–92: 'The Charge of the Light Brigade' (1854)

31 There is only one way for a young man to get on in the army. He must try and get killed in every way he possibly can!

Garnet Wolseley 1833–1913: in *Strand Magazine* May 1892; see **Satisfaction** 8

32 The 'eathen in 'is blindness must end where 'e began.
But the backbone of the Army is the non-commissioned man!

Rudyard Kipling 1865–1936: 'The 'Eathen' (1896); see **Religion** 20

33 You can always tell an old soldier by the inside of his holsters and cartridge boxes.

The young ones carry pistols and cartridges; the old ones, grub.

George Bernard Shaw 1856–1950: *Arms and the Man* (1898)

34 We're foot—slog—slog—slog—sloggin' over Africa!—
Foot—foot—foot—foot—sloggin' over Africa—
(Boots—boots—boots—boots—movin' up and down again!)
There's no discharge in the war!

Rudyard Kipling 1865–1936: 'Boots' (1903); the final line is from the Bible (Ecclesiastes)

35 I saw him stab
And stab again
A well-killed Boche.

This is the happy warrior,
This is he . . .

Herbert Read 1893–1968: 'The Happy Warrior' (1919); see 24 above

36 Nor law, nor duty bade me fight,
Nor public men, nor cheering crowds,
A lonely impulse of delight
Drove to this tumult in the clouds;
I balanced all, brought all to mind,
The years to come seemed waste of breath,
A waste of breath the years behind
In balance with this life, this death.

W. B. Yeats 1865–1939: 'An Irish Airman Foresees his Death' (1919)

37 Old soldiers never die,
They simply fade away.

J. Foley 1906–70: 'Old Soldiers Never Die' (1920 song); possibly a 'folk-song' from the First World War; see 5 above

38 I divide my officers into four classes as follows: the clever, the industrious, the lazy, and the stupid. Each officer always possesses two of these qualities. Those who are clever and industrious I appoint to the General Staff. Use can under certain circumstances be made of those who are stupid and lazy. The man who is clever and lazy qualifies for the highest leadership posts. He has the requisite and the mental clarity for difficult decisions. But whoever is stupid and industrious must be got rid of, for he is too dangerous.

Kurt von Hammerstein-Equord 1878–1943: attributed, c.1933; possibly apocryphal

39 You'll get no promotion this side of the ocean,
So cheer up, my lads, Bless 'em all!

Bless 'em all! Bless 'em all! The long and the short and the tall.
Jimmy Hughes and **Frank Lake**: 'Bless 'Em All' (1940 song)

40 I suppose every pilot knows that, knows that it cannot happen to him; even when he is taking off for the last time, when he will not return, he knows he cannot be killed.
Richard Hillary 1919–43: *The Last Enemy* (1942)

41 Naval tradition? Monstrous. Nothing but rum, sodomy, prayers, and the lash.
often quoted as, 'rum, sodomy, and the lash', as in Peter Gretton Former Naval Person *(1968)*
Winston Churchill 1874–1965: Harold Nicolson diary 17 August 1950

42 To save your world you asked this man to die:
Would this man, could he see you now, ask why?
W. H. Auden 1907–73: 'Epitaph for the Unknown Soldier' (1955)

43 In bombers named for girls, we burned

The cities we had learned about in school—
Till our lives wore out; our bodies lay among
The people we had killed and never seen.
When we lasted long enough they gave us medals;
When we died they said, 'Our casualties were low.'
Randall Jarrell 1914–65: 'Losses' (1963)

44 The sergeant is the army.
Dwight D. Eisenhower 1890–1969: attributed

45 I didn't fire him because he was a dumb son of a bitch, although he was, but that's not against the law for generals. If it was, half to three-quarters of them would be in jail.
of General MacArthur
Harry S. Truman 1884–1972: Merle Miller *Plain Speaking* (1974)

46 When I was in the military, they gave me a medal for killing two men and a discharge for loving one.
Leonard Matlovich d. 1988: attributed

The Arts see also **Acting, Arts and Sciences, Music, Painting and Drawing, Photography, Sculpture, Writing**

PROVERBS AND SAYINGS

1 **All arts are brothers; each is a light to the other.**
American proverb, mid 19th century

2 **Art is long and life is short.**
*late 14th century; originally from Hippocrates (see **Medicine** 7), comparing the difficulties encountered in learning the art of medicine or healing with the shortness of human life ('Art' is now commonly understood in the proverb in a less specific sense); see also **Education** 14*

3 **Art is power.**
*American proverb, mid 19th century; see **Knowledge** 5*

PHRASES

4 **ars gratia artis** art for art's sake.
Latin, taken as the motto of Metro-Goldwyn-Mayer film studios, and apparently intended to say 'Art is beholden to the artists'; see 9 below

5 **art for art's sake** used to convey the idea that the chief or only aim of a work of art is the self-expression of the individual artist

who creates it.
*associated with the Aesthetic movement of the 1880s; see 9 below, **Writers** 1*

QUOTATIONS

6 Painting is silent poetry, poetry is eloquent painting.
Simonides c.556–468 BC: Plutarch *Moralia*

7 The poet ranks far below the painter in the representation of visible things, and far below the musician in that of invisible things.
Leonardo da Vinci 1452–1519: Irma A. Richter (ed.) *Selections from the Notebooks of Leonardo da Vinci* (1952)

8 In art the best is good enough.
Johann Wolfgang von Goethe 1749–1832: *Italienische Reise* (1816–17) 3 March 1787

9 Art for art's sake, with no purpose, for any purpose perverts art. But art achieves a purpose which is not its own.
Benjamin Constant 1767–1834: diary 11 February 1804; see 4, 5 above, 15, 22 below

10 God help the Minister that meddles with art!
Lord Melbourne 1779–1848: Lord David Cecil *Lord M* (1954)

11 I believe the right question to ask, respecting all ornament, is simply this: Was it done with enjoyment—was the carver happy while he was about it?
John Ruskin 1819–1900: *Seven Lamps of Architecture* (1849)

12 The artist must be in his work as God is in creation, invisible and all-powerful; one must sense him everywhere but never see him.
Gustave Flaubert 1821–80: letter to Mademoiselle Leroyer de Chantepie, 18 March 1857

13 Art is a jealous mistress.
Ralph Waldo Emerson 1803–82: *The Conduct of Life* (1860)

14 Human life is a sad show, undoubtedly: ugly, heavy and complex. Art has no other end, for people of feeling, than to conjure away the burden and bitterness.
Gustave Flaubert 1821–80: letter to Amelie Bosquet, July 1864

15 Art for art's sake is an empty phrase. Art for the sake of the true, art for the sake of the good and the beautiful, that is the faith I am searching for.
George Sand 1804–76: letter to Alexandre Saint-Jean, 1872; see 9 above

16 Then a sentimental passion of a vegetable fashion must excite your languid spleen,
An attachment à la Plato for a bashful young potato, or a not too French French bean!
Though the Philistines may jostle, you will rank as an apostle in the high aesthetic band,
If you walk down Piccadilly with a poppy or a lily in your medieval hand.
W. S. Gilbert 1836–1911: *Patience* (1881); see **Writers** 1

17 All that I desire to point out is the general principle that Life imitates Art far more than Art imitates Life.
Oscar Wilde 1854–1900: *Intentions* (1891)

18 We know that the tail must wag the dog, for the horse is drawn by the cart;
But the Devil whoops, as he whooped of old: 'It's clever, but is it Art?'
Rudyard Kipling 1865–1936: 'The Conundrum of the Workshops' (1892)

19 We work in the dark—we do what we can—we give what we have. Our doubt is our passion and our passion is our task. The rest is the madness of art.
Henry James 1843–1916: 'The Middle Years' (short story, 1893)

20 I always said God was against art and I still believe it.
Edward Elgar 1857–1934: letter to A. J. Jaeger, 9 October 1900

21 The history of art is the history of revivals.
Samuel Butler 1835–1902: *Notebooks* (1912)

22 Art for Art's sake. Why not?
Art for Life's sake. Why not?
Art for Pleasure's sake. Why not?
What does it matter, as long as it is Art?
Paul Gauguin 1848–1903: formula for his work: Herbert Read *The Meaning of Art* (3rd ed., 1951); see 9 above

23 The true artist will let his wife starve, his children go barefoot, his mother drudge for his living at seventy, sooner than work at anything but his art.
George Bernard Shaw 1856–1950: *Man and Superman* (1903)

24 Life being all inclusion and confusion, and art being all discrimination and selection.
Henry James 1843–1916: *The Spoils of Poynton* (1909 ed.)

25 The artist, like the God of the creation, remains within or behind or beyond or above his handiwork, invisible, refined out of existence, indifferent, paring his fingernails.
James Joyce 1882–1941: *A Portrait of the Artist as a Young Man* (1916)

26 Art is vice. You don't marry it legitimately, you rape it.
Edgar Degas 1834–1917: Paul Lafond *Degas* (1918)

27 Another unsettling element in modern art is that common symptom of immaturity, the dread of doing what has been done before.
Edith Wharton 1862–1937: *The Writing of Fiction* (1925)

28 The artist is not a special kind of man, but every man is a special kind of artist.
Ananda Coomaraswamy 1877–1947: *Transformation of Nature in Art* (1934); see 36 below

29 The proletarian state must bring up thousands of excellent 'mechanics of culture', 'engineers of the soul'.
Maxim Gorky 1868–1936: speech at the Writers' Congress 1934; see 33 below

30 I suppose art is the only thing that can go on mattering once it has stopped hurting.
Elizabeth Bowen 1899–1973: *Heat of the Day* (1949)

31 Art is born of humiliation.
W. H. Auden 1907–73: Stephen Spender *World Within World* (1951)

32 Artists are the antennae of the race, but the bullet-headed many will never learn to trust their great artists.
Ezra Pound 1885–1972: *Literary Essays* (1954)

33 In free society art is not a weapon . . . Artists are not engineers of the soul.
John F. Kennedy 1917–63: speech at Amherst College, Mass., 26 October 1963; see 29 above

34 We all know that Art is not truth. Art is a lie that makes us realize truth.
Pablo Picasso 1881–1973: Dore Ashton *Picasso on Art* (1972)

35 An artist is someone who produces things that people don't need to have but that he — for *some reason* — thinks it would be a good idea to give them.
Andy Warhol 1927–87: *Philosophy of Andy Warhol (From A to B and Back Again)* (1975)

36 In the words of that old idiot and very bad artist Eric Gill, 'The artist is not a special kind of man; every man is a special kind of artist.' That's only possible if making mud pies counts as art.
Kingsley Amis 1922–95: lecture in Blackpool, October 1979; see 28 above

37 Do not imagine that Art is something which is designed to give gentle uplift and self-confidence. Art is not a *brassière*. At least, not in the English sense. But do not forget that *brassière* is the French for life-jacket.
Julian Barnes 1946– : *Flaubert's Parrot* (1984)

38 Art has to move you and design does not, unless it's a good design for a bus.
David Hockney 1937– : in *Guardian* 26 October 1988

39 All art, permanent or temporary, has a life in the immediate experience, but then has a life in the imagination.
Anish Kapoor 1954– : in *Sunday Times* 11 July 1999

Arts and Sciences

PHRASES

1 the nine Muses in classical mythology the nine goddesses, daughters of Zeus and Mnemosyne, who preside over the arts and sciences.

2 the two cultures the arts and the sciences.
from C. P. Snow The Two Cultures and the Scientific Revolution (1959)

QUOTATIONS

3 Histories make men wise; poets, witty; the mathematics, subtile; natural philosophy, deep; moral, grave; logic and rhetoric, able to contend.
Francis Bacon 1561–1626: *Essays* (1625) 'Of Studies'

4 Newton *was* a great man, but you must excuse me if I think that it would take many Newtons to make one Milton.
Samuel Taylor Coleridge 1772–1834: *Table Talk* (1835)

5 In science, read, by preference, the newest works; in literature, the oldest.
Edward Bulwer-Lytton 1803–73: *Caxtoniana* (1863) 'Hints on Mental Culture'

6 A contemporary poet has characterized this sense of the personality of art and of the impersonality of science in these words—'Art is myself; science is ourselves'
Claude Bernard 1813–78: *Introduction à l'Étude de la Médecin Experiméntale* (1865)

7 Poets do not go mad; but chess-players do. Mathematicians go mad, and cashiers; but creative artists very seldom. I am not, as will be seen, in any sense attacking logic: I only say that this danger does lie in logic, not in imagination.
G. K. Chesterton 1874–1936: *Orthodoxy* (1908)

8 Don't talk to me of your Archimedes' lever. He was an absent-minded person with a mathematical imagination. Mathematics commands all my respect, but I have no use for engines. Give me the right word and the right accent and I will move the world.

Joseph Conrad 1857–1924: *A Personal Record* (1919); see **Technology** 5

9 Even if I could be Shakespeare, I think I should still choose to be Faraday.

Aldous Huxley 1894–1963: in 1925, attributed; Walter M. Elsasser *Memoirs of a Physicist in the Atomic Age* (1978)

10 Every good poem, in fact, is a bridge built from the known, familiar side of life over into the unknown. Science too, is always making expeditions into the unknown. But this does not mean that science can supersede poetry. For poetry enlightens us in a different way from science; it speaks directly to our feelings or imagination. The findings of poetry are no more and no less true than science.

C. Day-Lewis 1904–72: *Poetry for You* (1944)

11 Art is meant to disturb, science reassures.

Georges Braque 1882–1963: *Le Jour et la nuit: Cahiers 1917–52*

12 I think it more important to know about the properties of chlorine than about the improprieties of Clodius; or about the behaviour of crystals than about the misbehaviour of Christina. Surely it is more important to know what a calorie is than what Caligula did; and anyhow what catalysts do is certainly more useful and less objectionable than what Catiline did.

Lord Cherwell 1886–1957: in *Chemistry and Industry* 1954

13 Science must begin with myths, and with the criticism of myths.

Karl Popper 1902–94: 'The Philosophy of Science'; C. A. Mace (ed.) *British Philosophy in the Mid-Century* (1957)

14 Once or twice I have been provoked and have asked the company how many of them could describe the Second Law of Thermodynamics. The response was cold: it was also negative. Yet I was asking something which is about the scientific

equivalent of: *Have you read a work of Shakespeare's?*

C. P. Snow 1905–80: *The Two Cultures* (1959); see **Physical Sciences** 3

15 The true men of action in our time, those who transform the world, are not the politicians and statesmen, but the scientists. Unfortunately poetry cannot celebrate them, because their deeds are concerned with things, not persons, and are, therefore, speechless. When I find myself in the company of scientists, I feel like a shabby curate who has strayed by mistake into a drawing room full of dukes.

W. H. Auden 1907–73: *The Dyer's Hand* (1963) 'The Poet and the City'

16 If a scientist were to cut his ear off, no one would take it as evidence of a heightened sensibility.

Peter Medawar 1915–87: 'J. B. S.' (1968)

17 Shakespeare would have grasped wave functions, Donne would have understood complementarity and relative time. They would have been excited. What richness! They would have plundered this new science for their imagery. And they would have educated their audiences too. But you 'arts' people, you're not only ignorant of these magnificent things, you're rather proud of knowing nothing.

Ian McEwan 1948– : *The Child in Time* (1987)

18 Scientists are explorers, philosophers are tourists.

Richard Feynman 1918–88: Christopher Sykes (ed.) *No Ordinary Genius* (1994)

19 If Watson and Crick had not discovered the nature of DNA, one can be virtually certain that other scientists would eventually have determined it. With art— whether painting, music or literature — it is quite different. If Shakespeare had not written *Hamlet*, no other playwright would have done so.

Lewis Wolpert 1929– : *The Unnatural Nature of Science* (1993)

Australia see also Towns and Cities

1 **Advance Australia.**

catchphrase used as a patriotic slogan or motto, mid 19th century onwards; see 15 below

2 **Australians wouldn't give a XXXX for anything else.**

advertising slogan for Castlemaine lager, 1986 onwards

3 Apple Island Tasmania, popularly identified as an apple-growing region.

4 Cabbage Garden the state of Victoria.

5 First Fleet the eleven British ships under the command of Arthur Phillip, first governor of New South Wales, which arrived in Australia in January 1788.

6 the Lucky Country Australia.
see 22 below

7 the Never Never Land the unpopulated northern part of the Northern Territory and Queensland; the desert country of the interior of Australia.

8 stolen generation the Aboriginal people forcibly removed from their families as children between the 1900s and the 1960s, to be brought up by white foster families or in institutions.
see 31 below

9 Top End (the northern part of) the Northern Territory of Australia.

10 From what I have said of the natives of New Holland, they may appear to some to be the most wretched people upon earth; but in reality they are far happier than we Europeans; being wholly unacquainted not only with the superfluous but the necessary conveniences so much sought after in Europe, they are happy in not knowing the use of them.
James Cook 1728–79: diary, August 1770

11 The loss of America what can repay? New colonies seek for at Botany Bay.
John Freeth c.1731–1808: 'Botany Bay' (1786)

12 True patriots we; for be it understood, We left our country for our country's good.
prologue, written for, but not recited at, the opening of the Playhouse, Sydney, New South Wales, 16 January 1796, when the actors were principally convicts
Henry Carter d. 1806: A. W. Jose and H. J. Carter (eds.) *The Australian Encyclopaedia* (1927); previously attributed to George Barrington (b. 1755)

13 I have been disappointed in all my expectations of Australia, except as to its wickedness; for it is far more wicked than I have conceived it possible for any place to be, or than it is possible for me to describe to you in England.
Henry Parkes 1815–95: letter, 1 May 1840 *An Emigrant's Home Letters* (1896)

14 Earth is here so kind, that just tickle her with a hoe and she laughs with a harvest.
Douglas Jerrold 1803–57: *The Wit and Opinions of Douglas Jerrold* (1859)

15 In joyful strains then let us sing Advance Australia fair.
the national anthem of Australia, which officially replaced 'God Save the Queen' in 1984; see 1 above
P. D. McCormick c.1834–1916: 'Advance Australia Fair' (c.1878 song)

16 The crimson thread of kinship runs through us all.
on Australian federation
Henry Parkes 1815–95: speech at banquet in Melbourne 6 February 1890; *The Federal Government of Australasia* (1890)

17 Once a jolly swagman camped by a billabong,
Under the shade of a coolibah tree;
And he sang as he watched and waited till his 'Billy' boiled:
'You'll come a-waltzing, Matilda, with me.'
'Banjo' Paterson 1864–1941: 'Waltzing Matilda' (1903 song)

18 Australia has a marvellous sky and air and blue clarity, and a hoary sort of land beneath it, like a Sleeping Princess on whom the dust of ages has settled.
D. H. Lawrence 1885–1930: letter to Jan Juta, 20 May 1922

19 And her five cities, like teeming sores, Each drains her: a vast parasite robber-state
Where second-hand Europeans pullulate Timidly on the edge of alien shores.
A. D. Hope 1907– : 'Australia' (1939)

20 What Great Britain calls the Far East is to us the near north.
Robert Gordon Menzies 1894–1978: in *Sydney Morning Herald* 27 April 1939

21 Above our writers—and other artists— looms the intimidating mass of Anglo-Saxon culture. Such a situation almost inevitably produces the characteristic Australian Cultural Cringe—appearing either as the Cringe Direct, or as the Cringe Inverted, in the attitude of the Blatant Blatherskite, the God's-Own-Country and

I'm-a-better-man-than-you-are Australian bore.

Arthur Angell Phillips 1900–85: *Meanjin* (1950) 'The Cultural Cringe'; see 29 below

22 Australia is a lucky country run mainly by second-rate people who share its luck.

Donald Richmond Horne 1921– : *The Lucky Country: Australia in the Sixties* (1964); see 6 above

23 In all directions stretched the great Australian Emptiness, in which the mind is the least of possessions.

Patrick White 1912–90: *The Vital Decade* (1968) 'The Prodigal Son'

24 Waiting for the Australian republic is like waiting for the other shoe to drop. We all know it is coming; according to one's convictions, the waiting is therefore either a sour and uncreative delaying operation or a sort of null interregnum in which all energies are frustrated.

Les Murray 1938– : 'The Coming Republic' in *Quadrant* April 1976

25 I wanted to know the true nature of the 'otherness' I had been born into. It was not a European thing. I wanted to paint the great purity and implacability of the landscape. I wanted a visual form of the 'otherness' of the thing not seen.

Sidney Nolan 1917–93: Elwyn Lynn *Sidney Nolan—Australia* (1979)

26 Australia is a huge rest home, where no unwelcome news is ever wafted on to the pages of the worst newspapers in the world.

Germaine Greer 1939– : in *Observer* 1 August 1982

27 Australia is the flattest, driest, ugliest place on earth. Only those who can be possessed by her can know what secret beauty she holds.

Eric Paul Willmot 1936– : *Australia The Last Experiment* (1987)

28 We wish no harm to England's native people. We are here to bring you good manners, refinement and an opportunity to make a *Koompartoo*, a fresh start.

planting an Aboriginal flag on the white cliffs of Dover and 'claiming' England for the Aboriginal people
Burnum Burnum 1936–97: on 26 January 1988, the year of Australia's bicentenary

29 Even as it [Great Britain] walked out on you and joined the Common Market, you were still looking for your MBEs and your knighthoods, and all the rest of the regalia that comes with it. You would take Australia right back down the time tunnel to the cultural cringe where you have always come from.

addressing Australian Conservative supporters of Great Britain
Paul Keating 1944– : on 27 February 1992; see 21 above

30 A broad school of Australian writing has based itself on the assumption that Australia not only has a history worth bothering about, but that all the history worth bothering about happened in Australia.

Clive James 1939– : *The Dreaming Swimmer* (1992)

31 I was so angry because they were denying they had done anything wrong, denying that a whole generation was stolen.

of official response to concerns about the 'stolen generation'
Cathy Freeman 1973– : interview in *Daily Telegraph* 16 July 2000; see 8 above

Beauty see also The Body

PROVERBS AND SAYINGS

1 **Beauty draws with a single hair.**

late 16th century, asserting the powerful attraction of a woman's beauty (often shown as outdoing great physical strength); see Strength 18, Women 23

2 **Beauty is a good letter of introduction.**

American proverb, mid 20th century; see 7 below

3 **Beauty is in the eye of the beholder.**

mid 18th century, meaning that beauty is not judged objectively, but according to the beholder's estimation

4 **Beauty is only skin deep.**

early 17th century, meaning that physical beauty is no guarantee of a good character or temperament; see 32 below

5 **Monday's child is fair of face.**

traditional rhyme, mid 19th century; see also Gifts 2, Sorrow 2, Travel 5, Work 6

6 **Please your eye and plague your heart.**

early 17th century, contrasting the pleasure given by the appearance of a beautiful person with the heartache they may cause

7 A beautiful face is a mute
recommendation.
Publilius Syrus: *Sententiae*; see 2 above

8 Consider the lilies of the field, how they
grow; they toil not, neither do they spin:
And yet I say unto you, That even
    Solomon in all his glory was not arrayed
    like one of these.
Bible: St Matthew

9 And she was fayr as is the rose in May.
Geoffrey Chaucer c.1343–1400: *The Legend of Good
Women* 'Cleopatra'

10 Was this the face that launched a
    thousand ships,
And burnt the topless towers of Ilium?
Sweet Helen, make me immortal with a
    kiss!
Christopher Marlowe 1564–93: *Doctor Faustus*
(1604)

11 Love built on beauty, soon as beauty, dies.
John Donne 1572–1631: *Elegies* 'The Anagram'
(c.1595)

12 O! she doth teach the torches to burn
    bright.
It seems she hangs upon the cheek of night
Like a rich jewel in an Ethiop's ear;
Beauty too rich for use, for earth too dear.
William Shakespeare 1564–1616: *Romeo and Juliet*
(1595)

13 There is no excellent beauty that hath not
some strangeness in the proportion.
Francis Bacon 1561–1626: *Essays* (1625) 'Of Beauty'

14 Beauty is the lover's gift.
William Congreve 1670–1729: *The Way of the
World* (1700)

15 The flowers anew, returning seasons
    bring;
But beauty faded has no second spring.
Ambrose Philips c.1675–1749: *The First Pastoral*
(1708)

16 Beauty is no quality in things themselves.
It exists merely in the mind which
contemplates them.
David Hume 1711–76: *Essays, Moral, Political, and
Literary* (ed. T. H. Green and T. H. Grose, 1875) 'Of
the Standard of Taste' (1757)

17 She walks in beauty, like the night
Of cloudless climes and starry skies;
And all that's best of dark and bright

Meet in her aspect and her eyes.
Lord Byron 1788–1824: 'She Walks in Beauty' (1815)

18 A thing of beauty is a joy for ever:
Its loveliness increases; it will never
Pass into nothingness.
John Keats 1795–1821: *Endymion* (1818); see **Men** 15

19 'Beauty is truth, truth beauty,'—that is all
Ye know on earth, and all ye need to
    know.
John Keats 1795–1821: 'Ode on a Grecian Urn'
(1820); see **Truth** 27

20 There is nothing ugly; *I never saw an ugly
thing in my life*: for let the form of an object
be what it may,—light, shade, and
perspective will always make it beautiful.
John Constable 1776–1837: C. R. Leslie *Memoirs of
the Life of John Constable* (1843)

21 Remember that the most beautiful things
in the world are the most useless; peacocks
and lilies for instance.
John Ruskin 1819–1900: *Stones of Venice* vol. 1 (1851)

22 If you get simple beauty and naught else,
You get about the best thing God invents.
Robert Browning 1812–89: 'Fra Lippo Lippi' (1855)

23 All things counter, original, spare,
    strange;
Whatever is fickle, freckled (who knows
    how?)
With swift, slow; sweet, sour; adazzle,
    dim;
He fathers-forth whose beauty is past
    change:
Praise him.
Gerard Manley Hopkins 1844–89: 'Pied Beauty'
(written 1877)

24 The awful thing is that beauty is
mysterious as well as terrible. God and
devil are fighting there, and the battlefield
is the heart of man.
Fedor Dostoevsky 1821–81: *The Brothers Karamazov*
(1879–80)

25 I have a left shoulder-blade that is a
miracle of loveliness. People come miles to
see it. My right elbow has a fascination
that few can resist.
W. S. Gilbert 1836–1911: *The Mikado* (1885)

26 When a woman isn't beautiful, people
always say, 'You have lovely eyes, you
have lovely hair.'
Anton Chekhov 1860–1904: *Uncle Vanya* (1897)

27 Beauty is all very well at first sight; but who ever looks at it when it has been in the house three days?
George Bernard Shaw 1856–1950: *Man and Superman* (1903)

28 I shall never get used to not being the most beautiful woman in the room. It was an intoxication to sweep in and know that every man had turned his head. It kept me in form.
Jennie Churchill 1854–1921: in 1914; Anita Leslie *Jennie* (1969)

29 A pretty girl is like a melody
That haunts you night and day.
Irving Berlin 1888–1989: 'A Pretty Girl is like a Melody' (1919 song)

30 He was afflicted by the thought that where Beauty was, nothing ever ran quite straight, which, no doubt, was why so many people looked on it as immoral.
John Galsworthy 1867–1933: *In Chancery* (1920)

31 Oh no, it wasn't the aeroplanes. It was Beauty killed the Beast.
James Creelman 1901–41 and **Ruth Rose**: *King Kong* (1933 film) final words

32 I'm tired of all this nonsense about beauty being only skin-deep. That's deep enough. What do you want—an adorable pancreas?
Jean Kerr 1923– : *The Snake has all the Lines* (1958); see 4 above

33 There are no ugly women, only lazy ones.
Helena Rubinstein 1882–1965: *My Life for Beauty* (1966)

34 Is it too much to ask that women be spared the daily struggle for superhuman beauty in order to offer it to the caresses of a subhumanly ugly mate?
Germaine Greer 1939– : *The Female Eunuch* (1970)

35 At some point in life the world's beauty becomes enough. You don't need to photograph, paint or even remember it. It is enough.
Toni Morrison 1931– : *Tar Baby* (1981)

36 The beauty myth moves for men as a mirage; its power lies in its ever-receding nature. When the gap is closed, the lover embraces only his own disillusion.
Naomi Wolf 1962– : *The Beauty Myth* (1990)

37 'Form follows profit' is the aesthetic principle of our times.
Richard Rogers 1933– : in *The Times* 13 February 1991; see **Architecture** 10

38 Beauty is handed out as undemocratically as inherited peerages, and beautiful people have done nothing to deserve their astonishing reward.
John Mortimer 1923– : in *Observer* 21 March 1999

Beginning see also **Change, Ending**

1 **Are you sitting comfortably? Then we'll begin.**
Julia Lang (1921–), introduction to stories on Listen with Mother, *BBC Radio programme for small children, 1950–82*

2 **First impressions are the most lasting.**
early 18th century

3 **The golden rule of life is, make a beginning.**
American proverb, mid 20th century

4 **A good beginning makes a good ending.**
early 14th century, meaning that getting things right at the outset is likely to ensure success

5 **It is easier to raise the Devil than to lay him.**
mid 17th century, sometimes used to mean that it is easier to start a process than to stop it

6 **It is the first step that is difficult.**
late 16th century; see **Achievement** 16

7 **It was a dark and stormy night.**
one variant of an opening line intended to convey a threatening and doom-laden atmosphere; in this form used by the novelist Edward Bulwer-Lytton (1803–73) in his novel Paul Clifford (1830)

8 **I've started so I'll finish.**
said by Magnus Magnusson when a contestant's time runs out while a question is being put, on Mastermind, *BBC television (1972–97)*

9 **The longest journey begins with a single step.**
late 20th century saying, often used to emphasize how important a single decision may be; ultimately derived from Lao Tzu: see 18 below

10 **The sooner begun, the sooner done.**
late 16th century; used as a warning against putting off a necessary but unwanted task

11 There is always a first time.

late 16th century

12 Well begun is half done.

early 15th century; emphasizing the importance of a successful beginning to the completion of a project

PHRASES

13 First Cause in philosophy, a supposed ultimate cause of all events, which does not itself have a cause, identified with God.

*see **God** 13*

14 fons et origo the source and origin.

Latin, earliest in fons et origo mali (mali *of evil*)

15 primum mobile an originator of an action or event, an initiator; an initial source of activity.

medieval Latin, literally 'first moving thing', in the medieval version of the Ptolemaic system, an outermost sphere supposed to revolve round the earth in twenty-four hours, carrying with it the inner spheres

16 vita nuova a fresh start or new direction in life, especially after some powerful emotional experience.

Italian = new life, a work by Dante describing his love for Beatrice

QUOTATIONS

17 In the beginning God created the heaven and the earth. And the earth was without form, and void; and darkness was upon the face of the deep. And the Spirit of God moved upon the face of the waters. And God said, Let there be light: and there was light.

Bible: Genesis

18 A tower of nine storeys begins with a heap of earth.
The journey of a thousand *li* starts from where one stands.

Lao Tzu c.604–c.531 BC: *Tao-te Ching*; see 9 above

19 Ere time and place were, time and place were not;
Where primitive nothing something straight begot;
Then all proceeded from the great united what.

John Wilmot, Lord Rochester 1647–80: 'Upon Nothing' (1680)

20 'Where shall I begin, please your Majesty?' he asked. 'Begin at the beginning,' the King said, gravely, 'and go on till you come to the end: then stop.'

Lewis Carroll 1832–98: *Alice's Adventures in Wonderland* (1865)

21 In my beginning is my end.

T. S. Eliot 1888–1965: *Four Quartets* 'East Coker' (1940); see **Ending** 6

22 when god decided to invent
everything he took one
breath bigger than a circustent
and everything began

e. e. cummings 1894–1962: *1 x 1* (1944) no. 26

23 All this will not be finished in the first 100 days. Nor will it be finished in the first 1,000 days, nor in the life of this Administration, nor even perhaps in our lifetime on this planet. But let us begin.

John F. Kennedy 1917–63: inaugural address, 20 January 1961

Behaviour see also **Manners, Words and Deeds**

PROVERBS AND SAYINGS

1 Be what you would seem to be.

late Middle English; earlier in classical sources

2 Cleanliness is next to godliness.

*late 18th century; next here means 'immediately following', as in serial order, and is now often used humorously to mean, 'the second most desirable quality possible'; see **Dress** 8*

3 Evil communications corrupt good manners.

early 15th century, meaning that proper conduct is harmfully influenced by false information or

knowledge; the saying is also used to assert the deleterious effect of bad example; see **Manners** 9

4 Good behaviour is the last refuge of mediocrity.

American proverb, mid 20th century

5 Handsome is as handsome does.

late 16th century; handsome here originally referred to chivalrous or genteel behaviour, although it is often popularly taken to refer to good looks

6 He is a good dog who goes to church.

early 19th century, meaning that good character is shown by moral custom and practice

7 When in Rome, do as the Romans do.
late 15th century, from St Ambrose; see 14 below

PHRASES

8 conduct unbecoming unsuitable or inappropriate behaviour.
from Articles of War (1872) 'Any officer who shall behave in a scandalous manner, unbecoming the character of an officer and a gentleman shall . . . be CASHIERED'; *the Naval Discipline Act, 10 August 1860 uses the words 'conduct unbecoming the character of an Officer'*

9 prunes and prisms (marked by) prim, mincing affectation of speech.
offered by Mrs General in Dickens's Little Dorrit *(1857) as a phrase giving 'a pretty form to the lips'*

10 the Queensberry Rules standard rules of polite or acceptable behaviour.
a code of rules drawn up in 1867 under the supervision of Sir John Sholto Douglas (1844–1900), eighth Marquis of Queensberry, to govern the sport of boxing in Great Britain; the standard rules of modern boxing

11 sweetness and light extreme (and uncharacteristic) mildness and reason in manner and behaviour.
from Swift (1704): see **Virtue** 26

12 to the manner born naturally fitted for some position or employment.
Shakespeare Hamlet: *see* **Custom** 9

QUOTATIONS

13 *O tempora, O mores!*
Oh, the times! Oh, the manners!
Cicero 106–43 BC: *In Catilinam*

14 When I go to Rome, I fast on Saturday, but here [Milan] I do not. Do you also follow the custom of whatever church you attend, if you do not want to give or receive scandal.
St Ambrose c.339–97: 'Letter 54 to Januarius' (AD c.400); see 7 above

15 This noble ensample to his sheep he yaf,
That first he wroghte, and afterward he taughte.
Geoffrey Chaucer c.1343–1400: *The Canterbury Tales* 'The General Prologue'

16 Careless she is with artful care,

Affecting to seem unaffected.
William Congreve 1670–1729: 'Amoret'

17 Take the tone of the company that you are in.
Lord Chesterfield 1694–1773: *Letters to his Son* (1774) 16 October 1747

18 They teach the morals of a whore, and the manners of a dancing master.
of the Letters *of Lord Chesterfield*
Samuel Johnson 1709–84: James Boswell *Life of Samuel Johnson* (1791) 1754

19 Always ding, dinging Dame Grundy into my ears—what will Mrs Grundy zay? What will Mrs Grundy think?
Thomas Morton c.1764–1838: *Speed the Plough* (1798); see **Morality** 7

20 May I ask whether these pleasing attentions proceed from the impulse of the moment, or are the result of previous study?
Jane Austen 1775–1817: *Pride and Prejudice* (1813)

21 There was a little girl
Who had a little curl
Right in the middle of her forehead,
When she was good
She was very, very good,
But when she was bad she was horrid.
composed for, and sung to, his second daughter while a babe in arms, c.1850
Henry Wadsworth Longfellow 1807–82: B. R. Tucker-Macchetta *The Home Life of Henry W. Longfellow* (1882)

22 He only does it to annoy,
Because he knows it teases.
Lewis Carroll 1832–98: *Alice's Adventures in Wonderland* (1865)

23 Go directly—see what she's doing, and tell her she mustn't.
Punch: 1872

24 Conduct is three-fourths of our life and its largest concern.
Matthew Arnold 1822–88: *Literature and Dogma* (1873)

25 Be a good animal, true to your instincts.
D. H. Lawrence 1885–1930: *The White Peacock* (1911)

26 Vulgarity has its uses. Vulgarity often cuts ice which refinement scrapes at vainly.
Max Beerbohm 1872–1956: letter 21 May 1921

27 Being tactful in audacity is knowing how
far one can go too far.
Jean Cocteau 1889–1963: *Le Rappel à l'ordre* (1926)

28 Private faces in public places
Are wiser and nicer
Than public faces in private places.
W. H. Auden 1907–73: *Orators* (1932)

29 I get too hungry for dinner at eight.
I like the theatre, but never come late.
I never bother with people I hate.

That's why the lady is a tramp.
Lorenz Hart 1895–1943: 'The Lady is a Tramp' (1937 song)

30 When people are on their best behaviour
they aren't always at their best.
Alan Bennett 1934– : *Dinner at Noon* (BBC television, 1988)

31 Already at four years of age I had begun to
apprehend that refinement was very often
an extenuating virtue; one that excused
and eclipsed almost every other
unappetizing trait.
Barry Humphries 1934– : *More Please* (1992)

Belief see also **Certainty and Doubt**, **Faith**

PROVERBS AND SAYINGS

**1 Believe nothing of what you hear, and only
half of what you see.**
*mid 19th century; a related Middle English saying
warns that you should not believe everything that is
said or that you hear*

2 A believer is a songless bird in a cage.
American proverb, late 19th century

3 Believing has a core of unbelieving.
American proverb, mid 19th century

**4 Pigs may fly, but they are very unlikely
birds.**
mid 19th century; see 7 below

5 Seeing is believing.
*early 17th century, meaning that acceptance of the
existence of something depends on actual
demonstration*

PHRASES

6 a doubting Thomas a person who refuses
to believe something without
incontrovertible proof; a sceptic.
from the story of the apostle Thomas, *who said that
he would not believe that Christ had risen again until
he had seen and touched his wounds; from the Bible
(John)*

7 pigs might fly an expression of ironical
disbelief
from the proverb: see 4 above

8 swallow a camel make no difficulty about
something incredible or unreasonable.
*from the Bible (Matthew) 'Ye blind guides, which
strain at a gnat, and swallow a camel'*

QUOTATIONS

9 It is convenient that there be gods, and, as
it is convenient, let us believe that there
are.
Ovid 43 BC–AD c.17: *Ars Amatoria*

10 Lord, I believe; help thou mine unbelief.
Bible: St Mark

11 Except ye see signs and wonders, ye will
not believe.
Bible: St John

12 *Certum est quia impossibile est.*
It is certain because it is impossible.
*often quoted as 'Credo quia impossibile [I believe
because it is impossible]'*
Tertullian AD c.160–c.225: *De Carne Christi*

13 Say to the unbelievers: 'You shall be
overthrown, and mustered into
Gehenna—
an evil cradling!'
The Koran: sura 3

14 'Twas God the word that spake it,
He took the bread and brake it;
And what the word did make it;
That I believe, and take it.
*answer on being asked her opinion of Christ's presence
in the Sacrament*
Elizabeth I 1533–1603: S. Clarke *The Marrow of
Ecclesiastical History* (1675)

15 For what a man would like to be true, that
he more readily believes.
Francis Bacon 1561–1626: *Novum Organum* (1620)

16 By night an atheist half believes a God.
Edward Young 1683–1765: *Night Thoughts* (1742–5)
'Night 5'

17 Truth, Sir, is a cow, that will yield such people [sceptics] no more milk, and so they are gone to milk the bull.
Samuel Johnson 1709–84: James Boswell *Life of Samuel Johnson* (1791) 21 July 1763

18 Confidence is a plant of slow growth in an aged bosom: youth is the season of credulity.
William Pitt, Earl of Chatham 1708–78: speech, House of Commons, 14 January 1766

19 Credulity is the man's weakness, but the child's strength.
Charles Lamb 1775–1834: *Essays of Elia* (1823) 'Witches, and Other Night-Fears'

20 *We can believe what we choose.* We are answerable for what we choose to believe.
John Henry Newman 1801–90: letter to Mrs William Froude, 27 June 1848

21 Why, sometimes I've believed as many as six impossible things before breakfast.
Lewis Carroll 1832–98: *Through the Looking-Glass* (1872)

22 I do not pretend to know where many ignorant men are sure — that is all that agnosticism means.
Clarence Darrow 1857–1938: speech at the trial of John Thomas Scopes, 15 July 1925

23 Of course not, but I am told it works even if you don't believe in it.
when asked whether he really believed a horseshoe hanging over his door would bring him luck, c.1930
Niels Bohr 1885–1962: A. Pais *Inward Bound* (1986)

24 The dust of exploded beliefs may make a fine sunset.
Geoffrey Madan 1895–1947: *Livre sans nom: Twelve Reflections* (privately printed 1934)

25 When men stop believing in God they don't believe in nothing; they believe in anything.
G. K. Chesterton 1874–1936: widely attributed, although not traced in his works

26 Man is a credulous animal, and must believe *something*; in the absence of good grounds for belief, he will be satisfied with bad ones.
Bertrand Russell 1872–1970: *Unpopular Essays* (1950) 'Outline of Intellectual Rubbish'

27 If it were an innocent, passive gullibility it would be excusable; but all too clearly, alas, it is an active willingness to be deceived.
Peter Medawar 1915–87: review of Teilhard de Chardin *The Phenomenon of Man* (1961)

28 I do not believe . . . I know.
Carl Gustav Jung 1875–1961: L. van der Post *Jung and the Story of our Time* (1976)

29 I confused things with their names: that is belief.
Jean-Paul Sartre 1905–80: *Les Mots* (1964)

30 No matter how I probe and prod
I cannot quite believe in God.
But oh! I hope to God that he
Unswervingly believes in me.
E. Y. Harburg 1898–1981: 'The Agnostic' (1965)

31 Of course, Behaviourism 'works'. So does torture. Give me a no-nonsense, down-to-earth behaviourist, a few drugs, and simple electrical appliances, and in six months I will have him reciting the Athanasian Creed in public.
W. H. Auden 1907–73: *A Certain World* (1970)

32 There is a lot to be said in the Decade of Evangelism for believing more and more in less and less.
John Yates 1925– : in *Gloucester Diocesan Gazette* August 1991

33 It is harder for some people to believe that God loves them than to believe that he exists.
Basil Hume 1923–99: in *Guardian* 18 June 1999

The Bible

PHRASES

1 **the Authorized Version** the King James Bible of 1611.
this translation became widely popular following its publication, and although in fact never officially 'authorized' it remained for centuries the Bible of every English-speaking country; see 5 below

2 **the Breeches Bible** the Geneva bible of 1560.
so named because the word breeches *is used in Genesis 3:7 for the garments made by Adam and Eve, rendered* aprons *in the King James bible*

3 **the Geneva Bible** the English translation first printed at Geneva in 1560.

4 the Great Bible the English version of the Bible by Coverdale (1539).

5 the King James Bible the 1611 English translation of the Bible.

ordered to be made by James I, and produced by about fifty scholars; see 1 above

6 the Printers' Bible a translation which has 'printers' where other translations have 'princes'.

as in Psalm 119 'Printers have persecuted me without a cause'

7 Sin On Bible an edition of 1716, the first English-language Bible to be printed in Ireland.

so named because John 5:14 reads 'sin on more' instead of 'sin no more'

8 the Treacle Bible a translation which has 'treacle' where other translations have 'balm'.

as in Jeremiah 8:22 'Is there no treacle in Gilead?'

9 the Vinegar Bible a 1717 Oxford edition of the Bible.

in which 'the parable of the vineyard' at Luke 20 read 'the parable of the vinegar'

10 the Wicked Bible an edition of 1631.

in which the seventh commandment was misprinted 'Thou shalt commit adultery'

QUOTATIONS

11 The devil can cite Scripture for his purpose.
William Shakespeare 1564–1616: *The Merchant of Venice* (1596-8); see **Quotations** 1

12 The pencil of the Holy Ghost hath laboured more in describing the afflictions of Job than the felicities of Solomon.
Francis Bacon 1561–1626: *Essays* (1625) 'Of Adversity'

13 *Scrutamini scripturas* [Let us look at the scriptures]. These two words have undone the world.
John Selden 1584–1654: *Table Talk* (1689) 'Bible Scripture'

14 We present you with this Book, the most valuable thing that this world affords. Here is wisdom; this is the royal Law; these are the lively Oracles of God.
Coronation Service 1689: The Presenting of the Holy Bible

15 The English Bible, a book which, if everything else in our language should perish, would alone suffice to show the whole extent of its beauty and power.
Lord Macaulay 1800–59: 'John Dryden' (1828)

16 There's a great text in Galatians,
Once you trip on it, entails
Twenty-nine distinct damnations,
One sure, if another fails.
Robert Browning 1812–89: 'Soliloquy of the Spanish Cloister' (1842)

17 We have used the Bible as if it was a constable's handbook—an opium-dose for keeping beasts of burden patient while they are being overloaded.
Charles Kingsley 1819–75: *Letters to the Chartists*

18 LORD ILLINGWORTH: The Book of Life begins with a man and a woman in a garden.
MRS ALLONBY: It ends with Revelations.
Oscar Wilde 1854–1900: *A Woman of No Importance* (1893)

19 An apology for the Devil: It must be remembered that we have only heard one side of the case. God has written all the books.
Samuel Butler 1835–1902: *Notebooks* (1912)

20 It ain't necessarily so,
It ain't necessarily so,
De t'ings dat yo' li'ble
To read in de Bible
It ain't necessarily so.
Du Bose Heyward 1885–1940 and **Ira Gershwin** 1896–1989: 'It ain't necessarily so' (1935)

21 I know of no book which has been a source of brutality and sadistic conduct, both public and private, that can compare with the Bible.
Reginald Paget 1908–90: in *Observer* 28 June 1964

22 There's a Bible on that shelf there. But I keep it next to Voltaire—poison and antidote.
Bertrand Russell 1872–1970: in *Kenneth Harris Talking To* (1971) 'Bertrand Russell'

23 Anyone who thinks that politics and religion don't mix is not reading the same Bible I am.
Desmond Tutu 1931– : attributed; David Rogers *Politics, Prayer and Parliament* (2000)

Biography

1 **lues Boswelliana** a biographer's tendency to magnify his or her subject, regarded as a disease.
from Latin lues *plague and the name of James Boswell (1740–95) as the friend and biographer of Samuel Johnson*

QUOTATIONS

2 Many brave men lived before Agamemnon's time; but they are all, unmourned and unknown, covered by the long night, because they lack their sacred poet.
Horace 65–8 BC: *Odes*; see **Reputation** 1

3 I am writing biography, not history, and the truth is that the most brilliant exploits often tell us nothing of the virtues or vices of the men who performed them, while on the other hand a chance remark or a joke may reveal far more of a man's character than the mere feat of winning battles in which thousands fall, or of marshalling great armies, or laying siege to cities.
Plutarch AD c.46–c.120: *Parallel Lives* 'Alexander'

4 Nobody can write the life of a man, but those who have eat and drunk and lived in social intercourse with him.
Samuel Johnson 1709–84: James Boswell *Life of Samuel Johnson* (1791) 31 March 1772

5 Lives of great men all remind us
We can make our lives sublime,
And, departing, leave behind us
Footprints on the sands of time.
Henry Wadsworth Longfellow 1807–82: 'A Psalm of Life' (1838)

6 A well-written Life is almost as rare as a well-spent one.
Thomas Carlyle 1795–1881: *Critical and Miscellaneous Essays* (1838) 'Jean Paul Friedrich Richter'

7 There is properly no history; only biography.
Ralph Waldo Emerson 1803–82: *Essays* (1841) 'History'

8 Then there is my noble and biographical friend who has added a new terror to death.
on Lord Campbell's Lives of the Lord Chancellors *being written without the consent of heirs or executors*
Charles Wetherell 1770–1846: Lord St Leonards *Misrepresentations in Campbell's Lives of Lyndhurst and Brougham* (1869); also attributed to Lord Lyndhurst (1772–1863)

refusing an offer to write his memoirs:
9 I should be trading on the blood of my men.
Robert E. Lee 1807–70: attributed, perhaps apocryphal

10 Every great man nowadays has his disciples, and it is always Judas who writes the biography.
Oscar Wilde 1854–1900: *Intentions* (1891) 'The Critic as Artist'

11 It is not a Life at all. It is a Reticence, in three volumes.
on J. W. Cross's Life of George Eliot
W. E. Gladstone 1809–98: E. F. Benson *As We Were* (1930)

12 The Art of Biography
Is different from Geography.
Geography is about Maps,
But Biography is about Chaps.
Edmund Clerihew Bentley 1875–1956: *Biography for Beginners* (1905)

13 And kept his heart a secret to the end
From all the picklocks of biographers.
of Robert E. Lee
Stephen Vincent Benét 1898–1943: *John Brown's Body* (1928)

14 Discretion is not the better part of biography.
Lytton Strachey 1880–1932: Michael Holroyd *Lytton Strachey* vol. 1 (1967)

15 Reformers are always finally neglected, while the memoirs of the frivolous will always eagerly be read.
Chips Channon 1897–1958: diary 7 July 1936

16 To write one's memoirs is to speak ill of everybody except oneself.
Henri Philippe Pétain 1856–1951: in *Observer* 26 May 1946

17 He made the books and he died.
his own 'sum and history of my life'
William Faulkner 1897–1962: letter to Malcolm Cowley, 11 February 1949

18 If you really want to hear about it, the first thing you'll probably want to know is where I was born, and what my lousy childhood was like, and how my parents were occupied and all before they had me, and all that David Copperfield kind of crap, but I don't feel like going into it.
J. D. Salinger 1919– : *Catcher in the Rye* (1951)

19 Only when one has lost all curiosity about the future has one reached the age to write an autobiography.
Evelyn Waugh 1903–66: *A Little Learning* (1964)

20 An autobiography is an obituary in serial form with the last instalment missing.
Quentin Crisp 1908–99: *The Naked Civil Servant* (1968)

21 I used to think I was an interesting person, but I must tell you how sobering a thought it is to realize your life's story fills about thirty-five pages and you have, actually, not much to say.
Roseanne Arnold 1953– : *Roseanne* (1990)

22 It's an excellent life of somebody else. But I've really lived inside myself, and she can't get in there.
on a biography of himself
Robertson Davies 1913–95: interview in *The Times* 4 April 1995

23 Nobody likes being written about in their lifetime, it's as though the FBI and the CIA were suddenly to splash your files in the paper.
Saul Bellow 1915– : in *Guardian* 10 September 1997

24 I feel, in writing this, that I have made myself smell of dead rat, and I am not sure how to get rid of the smell.
of a novel based on the life of her mother
Margaret Drabble 1939– : *The Peppered Moth* (2001)

Birds see also Animals

PROVERBS AND SAYINGS

1 A mockingbird has no voice of his own.
American proverb, mid 19th century; the mockingbird is noted for its mimicry of the calls and songs of other birds

2 One for sorrow; two for mirth; three for a wedding, four for a birth.
mid 19th century; a traditional rhyme found in a variety of forms, referring to the number of magpies seen on a particular occasion

3 The robin and the wren are God's cock and hen; the martin and the swallow are God's mate and marrow.
late 18th century (marrow means 'companion'); there was a traditional belief that the robin and the wren were sacred birds, and that to harm them in any way would be unlucky

PHRASES

4 the bird of Jove the eagle.

5 the bird of Juno the peacock.

6 Mother Carey's chicken the storm petrel.

QUOTATIONS

7 The silver swan, who, living had no note, When death approached unlocked her silent throat.
Orlando Gibbons 1583–1625: 'The Silver Swan' (1612 song)

8 While the cock with lively din Scatters the rear of darkness thin, And to the stack, or the barn door, Stoutly struts his dames before.
John Milton 1608–74: 'L'Allegro' (1645)

9 A robin red breast in a cage Puts all Heaven in a rage.
William Blake 1757–1827: 'Auguries of Innocence' (c.1803)

10 O blithe new-comer! I have heard, I hear thee and rejoice: O Cuckoo! Shall I call thee bird, Or but a wandering voice?
William Wordsworth 1770–1850: 'To the Cuckoo' (1807)

11 Hail to thee, blithe Spirit! Bird thou never wert, That from Heaven, or near it, Pourest thy full heart In profuse strains of unpremeditated art.
Percy Bysshe Shelley 1792–1822: 'To a Skylark' (1819)

12 Alone and warming his five wits,

The white owl in the belfry sits.
Alfred, Lord Tennyson 1809–92: 'Song—The Owl'
(1830)

13 That's the wise thrush; he sings each song
twice over,
Lest you should think he never could
recapture
The first fine careless rapture!
Robert Browning 1812–89: 'Home-Thoughts, from
Abroad' (1845)

14 I once had a sparrow alight upon my
shoulder for a moment while I was hoeing
in a village garden, and I felt that I was
more distinguished by that circumstance
than I should have been by any epaulette I
could have worn.
Henry David Thoreau 1817–62: *Walden* (1854)
'Winter Animals'

15 I caught this morning morning's minion,
kingdom of daylight's dauphin, dapple-
dawn-drawn Falcon.
Gerard Manley Hopkins 1844–89: 'The
Windhover' (written 1877)

16 At once a voice outburst among
The bleak twigs overhead
In a full-hearted evensong
Of joy illimited;
An aged thrush, frail, gaunt, and small,
In blast-beruffled plume,
Had chosen thus to fling his soul

Upon the growing gloom.
Thomas Hardy 1840–1928: 'The Darkling Thrush'
(1902)

17 It was the Rainbow gave thee birth,
And left thee all her lovely hues.
W. H. Davies 1871–1940: 'Kingfisher' (1910)

18 Oh, a wondrous bird is the pelican!
His beak holds more than his belican.
He takes in his beak
Food enough for a week.
But I'll be darned if I know how the
helican.
*usually quoted as, '. . . But I'm damned if I see how
the helican'*
Dixon Lanier Merritt 1879–1972: in *Nashville
Banner* 22 April 1913

19 The Ostrich roams the great Sahara.
Its mouth is wide, its neck is narra.
It has such long and lofty legs,
I'm glad it sits to lay its eggs.
Ogden Nash 1902–71: 'The Ostrich' (1957)

20 It took the whole of Creation
To produce my foot, my each feather:
Now I hold Creation in my foot.
Ted Hughes 1930–98: 'Hawk Roosting' (1960)

21 Blackbirds are the cellos of the deep farms.
Anne Stevenson 1933– : 'Green Mountain, Black
Mountain' (1982)

Birth see **Pregnancy and Birth**

The Body see also **Appearance**, **The Senses**

1 Cold hands, warm heart.
*early 20th century, meaning that the outward sign
may contradict the inward reality*

2 The eyes are the window of the soul.
*mid 16th century, meaning that it is in the eyes that a
person's true nature can be discerned*

3 The larger the body, the bigger the heart.
American proverb, mid 20th century

PHRASES

4 a boneless wonder a contortionist.
*see **People** 46*

5 crowning glory a woman's hair.
*the most beautiful feature or possession, the greatest
achievement; see 10 below*

6 Cupid's bow a particular shape of (the
upper edge of) the upper lip.
*referring to the double-curved bow traditionally
carried by Cupid*

7 lump of clay the human body regarded as
purely material, without a soul.

8 unruly member the tongue.
*after the Bible (James) 'the tongue is a little member
. . . the tongue can no man tame; it is an unruly evil'*

QUOTATIONS

9 I will give thanks unto thee, for I am fearfully and wonderfully made.
Bible: Psalm 139

10 Doth not even nature itself teach you, that if a man have long hair, it is a shame unto him?
But if a woman have long hair, it is a glory to her.
Bible: I Corinthians; see 5 above

11 He does smile his face into more lines than are in the new map with the augmentation of the Indies.
William Shakespeare 1564–1616: *Twelfth Night* (1601)

12 Raised by that curious engine, your white hand.
John Webster c.1580–c.1625: *The Duchess of Malfi* (1623)

13 Her feet beneath her petticoat,
Like little mice, stole in and out,
As if they feared the light.
John Suckling 1609–42: 'A Ballad upon a Wedding' (1646)

14 The hands are a sort of feet, which serve us in our passage towards Heaven, curiously distinguished into joints and fingers, and fit to be applied to any thing which reason can imagine or desire.
Thomas Traherne c.1637–74: *Meditations on the Six Days of Creation* (1717)

15 Why has not man a microscopic eye?
For this plain reason, man is not a fly.
Alexander Pope 1688–1744: *An Essay on Man* Epistle 1 (1733)

16 And our carcases, which are to rise again, are they worth raising? I hope, if mine is, that I shall have a better pair of legs than I have moved on these two-and-twenty years, or I shall be sadly behind in the squeeze into Paradise.
Lord Byron 1788–1824: letter 13 September 1811

17 I sing the body electric.
Walt Whitman 1819–92: title of poem (1855)

18 Our body is a machine for living. It is organized for that, it is its nature. Let life go on in it unhindered and let it defend itself, it will do more than if you paralyse it by encumbering it with remedies.
Leo Tolstoy 1828–1910: *War and Peace* (1865–9)

19 A large nose is in fact the sign of an affable man, good, courteous, witty, liberal, courageous, such as I am.
Edmond Rostand 1868–1918: *Cyrano de Bergerac* (1897)

20 An impersonal and scientific knowledge of the structure of our bodies is the surest safeguard against prurient curiosity and lascivious gloating.
Marie Stopes 1880–1958: *Married Love* (1918)

21 Anatomy is destiny.
Sigmund Freud 1856–1939: *Collected Writings* (1924)

22 There is more felicity on the far side of baldness than young men can possibly imagine.
Logan Pearsall Smith 1865–1946: *Afterthoughts* (1931)

23 Only God, my dear,
Could love you for yourself alone
And not your yellow hair.
W. B. Yeats 1865–1939: 'Anne Gregory' (1932)

24 This Englishwoman is so refined
She has no bosom and no behind.
Stevie Smith 1902–71: 'This Englishwoman' (1937)

25 Imprisoned in every fat man a thin one is wildly signalling to be let out.
Cyril Connolly 1903–74: *The Unquiet Grave* (1944)

26 I travel light; as light,
That is, as a man can travel who will
Still carry his body around because
Of its sentimental value.
Christopher Fry 1907– : *The Lady's not for Burning* (1949)

27 I came in here in all good faith to help my country. I don't mind giving a reasonable amount [of blood], but a pint . . . why that's very nearly an armful.
Ray Galton 1930– and **Alan Simpson** 1929– : *The Blood Donor* (1961 BBC television programme) words spoken by Tony Hancock

28 A woman watches her body uneasily, as though it were an unreliable ally in the battle for love.
Leonard Cohen 1934– : *The Favourite Game* (1963)

29 it's a sex object if you're pretty
and no love
or love and no sex if you're fat
Nikki Giovanni 1943– : 'Woman Poem' (1970)

30 My brain? It's my second favourite organ.
Woody Allen 1935– : *Sleeper* (1973 film, with Marshall Brickman)

31 Fat is a feminist issue.
Susie Orbach 1946– : title of book (1978)

32 The leg, a source of much delight,
which carries weight and governs height.
Ian Dury 1942–2000: 'The Body Song' (1981)

33 Entrails don't care for travel,
Entrails don't care for stress:
Entrails are better kept folded inside you
For outside, they make a mess.
Connie Bensley 1929– : 'Entrails' (1987)

34 I think with my hands. I just like
manipulation. I began to like it as a child
and it's continued to be a pleasure.
Dorothy Hodgkin 1910–94: Lewis Wolpert and
Alison Richards *A Passion for Science* (1988)

35 Modern body building is ritual, religion,
sport, art, and science, awash in Western
chemistry and mathematics. Defying
nature, it surpasses it.
Camille Paglia 1947– : *Sex, Art, and American
Culture* (1992)

36 You and I have been physically given two
hands and two legs and half-decent brains.
Some people have not been born like that
for a reason. The karma is working from
another lifetime.
Glenn Hoddle 1957– : in *The Times* 30 January 1999

Books see also **Fiction and Story-telling, Libraries, Reading, Writing**

PROVERBS AND SAYINGS

**1 A book is like a garden carried in the
pocket.**
American proverb, mid 20th century

2 A great book is a great evil.
*early 17th century, meaning that a long book is likely
to be verbose and badly written; a contraction of
Callimachus (c.305–c.240 BC) 'the great book is equal
to a great evil'*

**3 It is a tie between men to have read the
same book.**
American proverb, mid 19th century

QUOTATIONS

4 Of making many books there is no end;
and much study is a weariness of the flesh.
Bible: Ecclesiastes

5 Some books are to be tasted, others to be
swallowed, and some few to be chewed
and digested; that is, some books are to be
read only in parts; others to be read but
not curiously; and some few to be read
wholly, and with diligence and attention.
Some books also may be read by deputy,
and extracts made of them by others.
Francis Bacon 1561–1626: *Essays* (1625) 'Of Studies'

6 A good book is the precious lifeblood of a
master spirit, embalmed and treasured up
on purpose to a life beyond life.
John Milton 1608–74: *Areopagitica* (1644)

7 An empty book is like an infant's soul, in
which anything may be written. It is
capable of all things, but containeth
nothing.
Thomas Traherne c.1637–74: *Centuries of
Meditations*

8 I hate books; they only teach us to talk
about things we know nothing about.
Jean-Jacques Rousseau 1712–78: *Émile* (1762)

9 The reading or non-reading a book—will
never keep down a single petticoat.
Lord Byron 1788–1824: letter to Richard Hoppner,
29 October 1819

10 Your *borrowers of books*—those mutilators
of collections, spoilers of the symmetry of
shelves, and creators of odd volumes.
Charles Lamb 1775–1834: *Essays of Elia* (1823) 'The
Two Races of Men'

11 A good book is the best of friends, the same
to-day and for ever.
Martin Tupper 1810–89: *Proverbial Philosophy* Series
I (1838) 'Of Reading'

12 No furniture so charming as books.
Sydney Smith 1771–1845: Lady Holland *Memoir*
(1855)

13 Books are made not like children but like
pyramids . . . and they're just as useless!
and they stay in the desert! . . . Jackals piss
at their foot and the bourgeois climb up on
them.
Gustave Flaubert 1821–80: letter to Ernest
Feydeau, November/December 1857

14 'What is the use of a book', thought Alice, 'without pictures or conversations?'
Lewis Carroll 1832–98: *Alice's Adventures in Wonderland* (1865)

15 There is no such thing as a moral or an immoral book. Books are well written, or badly written.
Oscar Wilde 1854–1900: *The Picture of Dorian Gray* (1891)

16 '*Classic*'. A book which people praise and don't read.
Mark Twain 1835–1910: *Following the Equator* (1897)

17 All books are either dreams or swords,
You can cut, or you can drug, with words.
Amy Lowell 1874–1925: 'Sword Blades and Poppy Seed' (1914)

18 A bad book is as much of a labour to write as a good one; it comes as sincerely from the author's soul.
Aldous Huxley 1894–1963: *Point Counter Point* (1928)

19 A best-seller is the gilded tomb of a mediocre talent.
Logan Pearsall Smith 1865–1946: *Afterthoughts* (1931)

20 Books can not be killed by fire. People die, but books never die. No man and no force can abolish memory . . . In this war, we know, books are weapons. And it is a part of your dedication always to make them weapons for man's freedom.
Franklin D. Roosevelt 1882–1945: 'Message to the Booksellers of America' 6 May 1942

21 The principle of procrastinated rape is said to be the ruling one in all the great best-sellers.
V. S. Pritchett 1900– : *The Living Novel* (1946) 'Clarissa'

22 I suggest that the only books that influence us are those for which we are ready, and which have gone a little farther down our particular path than we have yet got ourselves.
E. M. Forster 1879–1970: *Two Cheers for Democracy* (1951)

23 Some books are undeservedly forgotten; none are undeservedly remembered.
W. H. Auden 1907–73: *The Dyer's Hand* (1963) 'Reading'

24 The possession of a book becomes a substitute for reading it.
Anthony Burgess 1917–93: in *New York Times Book Review* 4 December 1966

25 Long books, when read, are usually overpraised, because the reader wishes to convince others and himself that he has not wasted his time.
E. M. Forster 1879–1970: note from commonplace book; O. Stallybrass (ed.) *Aspects of the Novel and Related Writings* (1974)

26 The good of a book lies in its being read.
Umberto Eco 1932– : *The Name of the Rose* (1981)

27 Books say: she did this because. Life says: she did this. Books are where things are explained to you; life is where things aren't . . . Books make sense of life. The only problem is that the lives they make sense of are other people's lives, never your own.
Julian Barnes 1946– : *Flaubert's Parrot* (1984)

28 Russian literature saved my soul. When I was a young girl in school and I asked what is good and what is evil, no one in that corrupt system could show me.
Irina Ratushinskaya 1954– : in *Observer* 15 October 1989

29 Literature is the one place in any society where, within the secrecy of our own heads, we can hear *voices talking about everything in every possible way*.
Salman Rushdie 1947– : lecture 'Is Nothing Sacred' 6 February 1990

30 What literature can and should do is change the people who teach the people who don't read the books.
A. S. Byatt 1936– : interview in *Newsweek* 5 June 1995

31 The book is the greatest interactive medium of all time. You can underline it, write in the margins, fold down a page, skip ahead. And you can take it anywhere.
on taking over as head of Penguin Books
Michael Lynton: in *Daily Telegraph* 19 August 1996

Boredom

1 been there, done that used to express past experience of or familiarity with something, especially something now regarded as boring or unwelcome.
*see **Travel** 1*

2 The secret of being a bore . . . is to tell everything.
Voltaire 1694–1778: *Discours en vers sur l'homme* (1737)

3 He is not only dull in himself, but the cause of dullness in others.
on a law lord
Samuel Foote 1720–77: James Boswell *Life of Samuel Johnson* (1791) 1783

4 Society is now one polished horde,
Formed of two mighty tribes, the *Bores* and *Bored*.
Lord Byron 1788–1824: *Don Juan* (1819–24)

5 A desire for desires—boredom.
Leo Tolstoy 1828–1910: *Anna Karenina* (1873–6)

6 Boredom is . . . a vital problem for the moralist, since half the sins of mankind are caused by the fear of it.
Bertrand Russell 1872–1970: *The Conquest of Happiness* (1930)

7 Someone has somewhere commented on the fact that millions long for immortality who don't know what to do with themselves on a rainy Sunday afternoon.
Susan Ertz 1894–1985: *Anger in the Sky* (1943)

8 Nothing happens, nobody comes, nobody goes, it's awful!
Samuel Beckett 1906–89: *Waiting for Godot* (1955)

9 Nothing, like something, happens anywhere.
Philip Larkin 1922–85: 'I Remember, I Remember' (1955)

10 Small earthquake in Chile. Not many dead.
the words with which Cockburn claimed to have won a competition at The Times *for the dullest headline*
Claud Cockburn 1904–81: *In Time of Trouble* (1956)

11 Life, friends, is boring. We must not say so
. . .
And moreover my mother taught me as a boy
(repeatedly) 'Ever to confess you're bored means you have no
Inner Resources.' I conclude now I have no
inner resources, because I am heavy bored.
John Berryman 1914–72: *77 Dream Songs* (1964) no. 14

12 What's wrong with being a boring kind of guy?
during the campaign for the Republican nomination
George Bush 1924– : in *Daily Telegraph* 28 April 1988

Borrowing see **Debt and Borrowing**

Britain see also **England**

1 Cool Britannia Britain, perceived as a stylish and fashionable place.
especially (in the late 1990s) as represented by the international success of and interest in contemporary British art, popular music, film, and fashion; see 17 below

2 from Land's End to John o'Groats from one end of Britain to the other.
Land's End *a rocky promontory in SW Cornwall, which forms the westernmost point of England;* John o'Groats *a village at the extreme NE point of the Scottish mainland*

3 the Mother of Parliaments the British parliament.
*from Bright: see **Parliament** 19*

4 the red, white, and blue the Union flag of the United Kingdom.
the colours of the three crosses making up the Union flag, the red on white cross of St George (for England), the white on blue cross saltire of St Andrew (for Scotland), and the red on white cross saltire of St Patrick (for Ireland)

5 twist the lion's tail provoke the resentment of the British.

a lion as the symbol of the British Empire

6 Rule, Britannia, rule the waves;
Britons never will be slaves.

James Thomson 1700–48: *Alfred: a Masque* (1740)

7 It must be owned, that the Graces do not seem to be natives of Great Britain; and I doubt, the best of us here have more of rough than polished diamond.

Lord Chesterfield 1694–1773: *Letters to his Son* (1774) 18 November 1748

8 Born and educated in this country, I glory in the name of Briton.

George III 1738–1820: *The King's Speech on Opening the Session* 18 November 1760

9 He [the Briton] is a barbarian, and thinks that the customs of his tribe and island are the laws of nature.

George Bernard Shaw 1856–1950: *Caesar and Cleopatra* (1901)

10 Other nations use 'force'; we Britons alone use 'Might'.

Evelyn Waugh 1903–66: *Scoop* (1938)

11 The British nation is unique in this respect. They are the only people who like to be told how bad things are, who like to be told the worst.

Winston Churchill 1874–1965: speech in the House of Commons, 10 June 1941

12 Britain will be honoured by historians more for the way she disposed of an empire than for the way in which she acquired it.

Lord Harlech 1918–85: in *New York Times* 28 October 1962

13 Great Britain has lost an empire and has not yet found a role.

Dean Acheson 1893–1971: speech at the Military Academy, West Point, 5 December 1962

14 A soggy little island huffing and puffing to keep up with Western Europe.

John Updike 1932– : 'London Life' (written 1969)

15 [The Commonwealth] is a largely meaningless relic of Empire—like the smile on the face of the Cheshire Cat which remains when the cat has disappeared.

Nigel Lawson 1932– : attributed, 1993; see **Cats** 3

16 Fifty years on from now, Britain will still be the country of long shadows on county [cricket] grounds, warm beer, invincible green suburbs, dog lovers, and—as George Orwell said—old maids bicycling to Holy Communion through the morning mist.

John Major 1943– : speech to the Conservative Group for Europe, 22 April 1993; see **England** 28

17 When I think of Cool Britannia, I think of old people dying of hypothermia.

Tony Benn 1925– : at the Labour Party Conference, in *Daily Star* 30 September 1998; see 1 above

18 What you have within the UK is three small nations who've been under the cosh of the English.

Jack Straw 1946– : in *Sunday Times* 6 January 2000

19 Chicken Tikka Masala is now a true British national dish, not only because it is the most popular, but because it is a perfect illustration of the way Britain absorbs and adapts external influences. Chicken tikka is an Indian dish. The Masala sauce was added to satisfy the desire of British people to have their meat served in gravy.

Robin Cook 1946– : speech to Social Market Foundation, London, 19 April 2001

British Towns and Regions

1 Essex stiles, Kentish miles, Norfolk wiles, many a man beguiles.

traditional saying, early 17th century

2 From Hell, Hull, and Halifax, good Lord deliver us.

traditional saying, late 16th century

3 Glasgow's miles better.

slogan introduced by Provost Michael Kelly, 1980s

**4 Kirton was a borough town
When Exon was a vuzzy down.**

traditional saying, on the relative age of Crediton (Kirton) and Exeter (Exon)

5 Lincoln was, London is, and York shall be.

traditional saying, late 16th century, referring to which is the greatest city

**6 London Bridge is broken down
My fair lady.**

traditional nursery rhyme, early 18th century

7 May God in His mercy look down on Belfast.

traditional refrain; see 44 below

8 Northamptonshire for squires and spires.

traditional saying, late 19th century

9 Some places of Kent have health and no wealth, some wealth and no health, some health and wealth.

traditional saying, late 16th century, referring to the north and east of the county, Romney Marsh, and the Weald respectively

10 Sussex won't be druv.

early 20th century; asserting that Sussex people have minds of their own, and cannot be forced against their will (druv is a dialect version of drove, meaning driven)

11 What Manchester says today, the rest of England says tomorrow.

late 19th century, occurring in a variety of forms

12 Yorkshire born and Yorkshire bred, strong in the arm and weak in the head.

mid 19th century; the names of other (chiefly northern) English counties and towns are also used instead of Yorkshire

PHRASES

13 the Athens of the North Edinburgh.

alluding to its academic and intellectual traditions, and to the predominantly neoclassical style of architecture in its city centre

14 Auld Reekie Edinburgh.

literally 'Old Smoky'

15 the big Smoke London.

16 City of Bon-accord Aberdeen.

bon-accord in Scottish usage (from French) means 'good will, fellowship'

17 City of Dreaming Spires Oxford

deriving originally from Matthew Arnold's 'Thyrsis' (1866): 'And that sweet City with her dreaming Spires'; see Universities 27

18 the garden of England Kent; the Vale of Evesham.

19 the Granite City the city of Aberdeen, Scotland.

20 the great wen London, as the type of a large and overcrowded city.

from William Cobbett Rural Rides (1822) 'But what is to be the fate of the great wen of all?'

21 the land of the broad acres Yorkshire, NE England.

QUOTATIONS

22 London, thou art the flower of cities all!

Anonymous: 'London' (poem of unknown authorship, previously attributed to William Dunbar, c.1465–c.1530)

23 That shire which we the Heart of England well may call.

of Warwickshire

Michael Drayton 1563–1631: *Poly-Olbion* (1612–22)

24 When a man is tired of London, he is tired of life; for there is in London all that life can afford.

Samuel Johnson 1709–84: James Boswell *Life of Samuel Johnson* (1791) 20 September 1777; see 45 below

25 Earth has not anything to show more fair:
Dull would he be of soul who could pass by
A sight so touching in its majesty:
This City now doth like a garment wear
The beauty of the morning.

William Wordsworth 1770–1850: 'Composed upon Westminster Bridge' (1807)

26 *Was für Plunder!*
What rubbish!

of London as seen from the Monument in June 1814; often misquoted as 'Was für plündern [What a place to plunder]!'

Gebhard Lebrecht Blücher 1742–1819: Evelyn Princess Blücher *Memoirs of Prince Blücher* (1932)

27 One has no great hopes from Birmingham. I always say there is something direful in the sound.

Jane Austen 1775–1817: *Emma* (1816)

28 Oh! who can ever be tired of Bath?

Jane Austen 1775–1817: *Northanger Abbey* (1818)

29 It is from the midst of this putrid sewer that the greatest river of human industry springs up and carries fertility to the whole world. From this foul drain pure gold flows forth.

of Manchester

Alexis de Tocqueville 1805–59: *Voyage en Angleterre et en Irlande de 1835* 2 July 1835

30 Kent, sir—everybody knows Kent—apples, cherries, hops, and women.

Charles Dickens 1812–70: *Pickwick Papers* (1837)

31 Towery city and branchy between towers;
Cuckoo-echoing, bell-swarmèd, lark-charmèd, rook-racked, river-rounded.

Gerard Manley Hopkins 1844–89: 'Duns Scotus's Oxford' (written 1879)

32 St Andrews by the Northern sea,
A haunted town it is to me!
Andrew Lang 1844–1912: 'Almae Matres' (1884)

33 When Adam and Eve were dispossessed
Of the garden hard by Heaven,
They planted another one down in the
west,
'Twas Devon, glorious Devon!
Harold Edwin Boulton 1859–1935: 'Glorious
Devon' (1902)

34 God gives all men all earth to love,
But since man's heart is small,
Ordains for each one spot shall prove
Belovèd over all.
Each to his choice, and I rejoice
The lot has fallen to me
In a fair ground—in a fair ground—
Yea, Sussex by the sea!
Rudyard Kipling 1865–1936: 'Sussex' (1903)

35 The folk that live in Liverpool, their heart
is in their boots;
They go to hell like lambs, they do,
because the hooter hoots.
G. K. Chesterton 1874–1936: 'Me Heart' (1914)

36 For Cambridge people rarely smile,
Being urban, squat, and packed with guile.
Rupert Brooke 1887–1915: 'The Old Vicarage,
Grantchester' (1915)

37 I belong to Glasgow
Dear Old Glasgow town!
But what's the matter wi' Glasgow?
For it's going round and round.
I'm only a common old working chap,
As anyone can see,
But when I get a couple of drinks on a
Saturday,
Glasgow belongs to me.
Will Fyffe 1885–1947: 'I Belong to Glasgow' (1920
song)

38 Bugger Bognor.
*comment made either in 1929, when it was proposed
that the town be renamed Bognor Regis following the
king's convalescence there; or on his deathbed when
someone said 'Cheer up, your Majesty, you will soon
be at Bognor again.'; see* **Last Words** *27*
George V 1865–1936: Kenneth Rose *King George V*
(1983)

39 Very flat, Norfolk.
Noël Coward 1899–1973: *Private Lives* (1930)

40 If one wanted a rough-and-ready
generalization to express the difference
between a Glasgow man and an Edinburgh
man, one might say that every Edinburgh
man considers himself a little better than
his neighbour, and every Glasgow man
just as good as his neighbour.
Edwin Muir 1887–1959: *Scottish Journey* (1935)

41 London Pride has been handed down to us.
London Pride is a flower that's free.
London Pride means our own dear town to
us,
And our pride it for ever will be.
Noël Coward 1899–1973: 'London Pride' (1941
song)

42 Maybe it's because I'm a Londoner
That I love London so.
Hubert Gregg 1914– : 'Maybe It's Because I'm a
Londoner' (1947 song)

43 With the possible exceptions of Jerusalem
and Mecca, Belfast must be the most
religion-conscious city in the world.
Tyrone Guthrie 1900–71: *A Life in the Theatre* (1959)

44 O the bricks they will bleed and the rain it
will weep
And the damp Lagan fog lull the city to
sleep;
It's to hell with the future and live on the
past:
May the Lord in His mercy be kind to
Belfast.
Maurice James Craig 1919– : 'Ballad to a
Traditional Refrain' (1974); see 7 above

45 'A man who is tired of London is tired of
life'—no, I was tired of hunting for parking
places.
Paul Theroux 1941– : *The Kingdom by the Sea*
(1983); see 24 above

46 Try Manchester after midnight and you'll
think you've walked into the Book of
Revelations.
Howard Jacobson: *The Mighty Waltzer* (1999)

Broadcasting

1 Always turn the radio on before you listen to it.
American saying, mid 20th century

2 Nation shall speak peace unto nation.
motto of the BBC, adapted from the Bible (Isaiah) by Montague John Rendall (1862–1950); see **Peace** *7*

3 So much chewing gum for the eyes.
small boy's definition of certain television programmes, 1950s

PHRASES

4 couch potato a person who takes little or no exercise and watches a lot of television.
coined in the US from a pun on boob tube *as a slang expression for television; someone given to continuous viewing was a* boob tuber, *and the cartoonist Robert Armstrong drew the most familiar tuber, a potato, reclining on a couch watching TV*

QUOTATIONS

5 He who prides himself on giving what he thinks the public wants is often creating a fictitious demand for lower standards which he will then satisfy.
Lord Reith 1889–1971: memo to Crawford Committee 1926; Andrew Boyle *Only the Wind Will Listen* (1972)

6 *Television?* The word is half Greek, half Latin. No good can come of it.
C. P. Scott 1846–1932: Asa Briggs *The BBC: the First Fifty Years* (1985)

7 I hate television. I hate it as much as peanuts. But I can't stop eating peanuts.
Orson Welles 1915–85: in *New York Herald Tribune* 12 October 1956

8 When the politicians complain that TV turns their proceedings into a circus, it should be made plain that the circus was already there, and that TV has merely demonstrated that not all the performers are well trained.
Ed Murrow 1908–65: attributed, 1959

9 Radio and television . . . have succeeded in lifting the manufacture of banality out of the sphere of handicraft and placed it in that of a major industry.
Nathalie Sarraute 1902– : in *Times Literary Supplement* 10 June 1960

10 Like having your own licence to print money.
on the profitability of commercial television in Britain
Roy Thomson 1894–1976: R. Braddon *Roy Thomson* (1965)

11 It used to be that we in films were the lowest form of art. Now we have something to look down on.
of television
Billy Wilder 1906– : A. Madsen *Billy Wilder* (1968)

12 Television brought the brutality of war into the comfort of the living room. Vietnam was lost in the living rooms of America—not the battlefields of Vietnam.
Marshall McLuhan 1911–80: in *Montreal Gazette* 16 May 1975

13 Let's face it, there are no plain women on television.
Anna Ford 1943– : in *Observer* 23 September 1979

14 Television is simultaneously blamed, often by the same people, for worsening the world and for being powerless to change it.
Clive James 1939– : *Glued to the Box* (1981)

15 Television contracts the imagination and radio expands it.
Terry Wogan 1938– : attributed, 1984

16 Television . . . thrives on unreason, and unreason thrives on television . . . [It] strikes at the emotions rather than the intellect.
Robin Day 1923–2000: *Grand Inquisitor* (1989)

17 Television has made dictatorship impossible, but democracy unbearable.
Shimon Peres 1923– : at a Davos meeting, in *Financial Times* 31 January 1995

18 A terminal blight has hit the TV industry nipping fun in the bud and stunting our growth. This blight is management—the dreaded Four M's: male, middle class, middle-aged and mediocre.
Janet Street-Porter 1946– : MacTaggart Lecture, Edinburgh Television Festival, 25 August 1995

19 [Daytime television] is stupidvision— where most of the presenters look like they have to pretend to be stupid because they think their audience is . . . It patronises. It talks to the vacuum cleaner and the washing machine without much contact with the human brain.

Polly Toynbee 1946– : in *Daily Telegraph* 7 May 1996

20 In television a lot of the time I just shut up because the pictures are so powerful and

the sounds that go with them. I call it the art of writing silence.

Martin Bell 1938– : Anthony Clare *In the Psychiatrist's Chair III* (1998)

Business see also Buying and Selling

1 Business before pleasure.
mid 19th century, often used to encourage a course of action

2 Business goes where it is invited and stays where it is well-treated.
American proverb, mid 20th century

3 Business is like a car: it will not run by itself except downhill.
American proverb, mid 20th century

4 Business neglected is business lost.
North American proverb, mid 20th century

5 The customer is always right.
early 20th century; see 34 below

6 If you don't speculate, you can't accumulate.
mid 20th century; meaning that outlay (and some degree of risk) is necessary if real gain is to be achieved

7 I liked it so much, I bought the company!
advertising slogan for Remington Shavers, coined by owner Victor Kiam (1926–2001)

8 Keep your own shop and your shop will keep you.
early 17th century, recommending attention to what is essential to one's livelihood

9 Never knowingly undersold.
motto, from c.1920, of the John Lewis partnership

10 No cure, no pay.
late 19th century; known principally from its use on Lloyd's of London's Standard Form of Salvage Agreement

11 No penny, no paternoster.
early 16th century, meaning that if you want a thing you must pay for it (the reference is to priests insisting on being paid for performing services)

12 Pay beforehand was never well served.
late 16th century, meaning that payment in advance removes the incentive to finish the work

13 Pile it high, sell it cheap.
slogan coined by Jack Cohen (1898–1979), founder of the Tesco supermarket chain

14 Sell in May and go away.
stockmarket saying

15 There are tricks in every trade.
mid 17th century; meaning that the practice of every skill is likely to involve some trickery or dishonesty

16 Trade follows the flag.
late 19th century; meaning that commercial development is likely to follow military intervention

17 bear market a market in which share prices are falling encouraging selling.
in Stock Exchange usage, a bear is a person who sells shares hoping to buy them back again later at a lower price. The dealer is this kind of stock was known as the bearskin jobber, and it seems likely that the original phrase was 'sell the bearskin'; see **Optimism** 14. The associated bull is of later date, and may perhaps have been suggested by the existence of bear in this sense: see 19 below

18 blue-chip denoting companies or their shares considered to be a reliable investment, though less secure than gilt-edged stock.
US, early 20th century, from the blue chip used in gambling games, which usually has a high value

19 bull market a market in which share prices are rising, encouraging buying.
see 17 above

20 Chinese wall on the Stock Exchange, a prohibition against the passing of confidential information from one department of a financial institution to another.
alluding to the Great Wall of China, as an insurmountable barrier to understanding

21 the triple-witching hour in the US, informal name for the unpredictable final hour of trading on the US Stock Exchange before the simultaneous expiry of three different kinds of options.
a development of witching hour: see **Day and Night** 3

22 **a white knight** a welcome company bidding for a company facing an unwelcome takeover bid.
likened to a traditional figure of chivalry rescuing someone from danger

23 A merchant shall hardly keep himself from doing wrong.
Bible: Ecclesiasticus

24 They [corporations] cannot commit treason, nor be outlawed, nor excommunicate, for they have no souls.
Edward Coke 1552–1634: *The Reports of Sir Edward Coke* (1658) 'The case of Sutton's Hospital'; see 30 below

25 A Company for carrying on an undertaking of Great Advantage, but no one to know what it is.
Anonymous: Company Prospectus at the time of the South Sea Bubble (1711)

26 There is nothing more requisite in business than dispatch.
Joseph Addison 1672–1719: *The Drummer* (1716)

27 It is the nature of all greatness not to be exact; and great trade will always be attended with considerable abuses.
Edmund Burke 1729–97: *On American Taxation* (1775)

28 People of the same trade seldom meet together, even for merriment and diversion, but the conversation ends in a conspiracy against the public, or in some contrivance to raise prices.
Adam Smith 1723–90: *Wealth of Nations* (1776)

29 To found a great empire for the sole purpose of raising up a people of customers, may at first sight appear a project fit only for a nation of shopkeepers. It is, however, a project altogether unfit for a nation of shopkeepers; but extremely fit for a nation whose government is influenced by shopkeepers.
Adam Smith 1723–90: *Wealth of Nations* (1776); see **England** 14

30 Corporations have neither bodies to be punished, nor souls to be condemned, they therefore do as they like.
often quoted as 'Did you ever expect a corporation to have a conscience, when it has no soul to be damned, and no body to be kicked?'
Lord Thurlow 1731–1806: John Poynder *Literary Extracts* (1844); see 24 above

31 Here's the rule for bargains: 'Do other men, for they would do you.' That's the true business precept.
Charles Dickens 1812–70: *Martin Chuzzlewit* (1844)

32 The public be damned! I'm working for my stockholders.
William H. Vanderbilt 1821–85: comment to a news reporter, 2 October 1882

33 The growth of a large business is merely a survival of the fittest . . . The American beauty rose can be produced in the splendour and fragrance which bring cheer to its beholder only by sacrificing the early buds which grow up around it.
John D. Rockefeller 1839–1937: W. J. Ghent *Our Benevolent Feudalism* (1902); see **Life Sciences** 6

34 *Le client n'a jamais tort.*
The customer is never wrong.
César Ritz 1850–1918: R. Nevill and C. E. Jerningham *Piccadilly to Pall Mall* (1908); see 5 above

35 The best of all monopoly profits is a quiet life.
J. R. Hicks 1904– : *Econometrica* (1935)

36 NINOTCHKA: Why should you carry other people's bags?
PORTER: Well, that's my business, Madame.
NINOTCHKA: That's no business. That's social injustice.
PORTER: That depends on the tip.
Charles Brackett 1892–1969 and **Billy Wilder** 1906– : *Ninotchka* (1939 film, with Walter Reisch)

37 For a salesman, there is no rock bottom to the life . . . A salesman is got to dream, boy. It comes with the territory.
Arthur Miller 1915– : *Death of a Salesman* (1949)

38 How to succeed in business without really trying.
Shepherd Mead 1914– : title of book (1952)

39 For years I thought what was good for our country was good for General Motors and vice versa.
Charles E. Wilson 1890–1961: testimony to the Senate Armed Services Committee on his proposed nomination for Secretary of Defence, 15 January 1953

40 You cannot be a success in any business without believing that it is the greatest business in the world . . . You have to put your heart in the business and the business in your heart.
Thomas Watson Snr. 1874–1956: Robert Sobel *IBM: Colossus in Transition* (1981)

41 Consumer wants can have bizarre, frivolous, or even immoral origins, and an admirable case can still be made for a society that seeks to satisfy them. But the case cannot stand if it is the process of satisfying wants that creates the wants.
J. K. Galbraith 1908– : *The Affluent Society* (1958)

42 Accountants are the witch-doctors of the modern world and willing to turn their hands to any kind of magic.
Lord Justice Harman 1894–1970: speech, February 1964; A. Sampson *The New Anatomy of Britain* (1971)

43 Could Henry Ford produce the Book of Kells? Certainly not. He would quarrel initially with the advisability of such a project and then prove it was impossible.
Flann O'Brien 1911–66: *Myles Away from Dublin* (1990)

44 The most striking thing about modern industry is that it requires so much and accomplishes so little. Modern industry seems to be inefficient to a degree that surpasses one's ordinary powers of imagination. Its inefficiency therefore remains unnoticed.
E. F. Schumacher 1911–77: *Small is Beautiful* (1973)

45 In the factory we make cosmetics; in the store we sell hope.
Charles Revson 1906–75: A. Tobias *Fire and Ice* (1976)

46 The salary of the chief executive of the large corporation is not a market reward for achievement. It is frequently in the nature of a warm personal gesture by the individual to himself.
J. K. Galbraith 1908– : *Annals of an Abiding Liberal* (1979)

47 Deals are my art form. Other people paint beautifully on canvas or write wonderful poetry. I like making deals, preferably big deals. That's how I get my kicks.
Donald Trump 1946– : Donald Trump and Tony Schwartz *The Art of the Deal* (1987)

48 Nothing is illegal if one hundred well-placed business men decide to do it.
Andrew Young 1932– : Morris K. Udall *Too Funny to be President* (1988)

49 We even sell a pair of earrings for under £1, which is cheaper than a prawn sandwich from Marks & Spencers. But I have to say the earrings probably won't last as long.
Gerald Ratner 1949– : speech to the Institute of Directors, Albert Hall, 23 April 1991

50 We used to build civilizations. Now we build shopping malls.
Bill Bryson 1951– : *Neither Here Nor There* (1991)

51 I think that business practices would improve immeasurably if they were guided by 'feminine' principles—qualities like love and care and intuition.
Anita Roddick 1942– : *Body and Soul* (1991)

52 Only the paranoid survive.
dictum on which he has long run his company, the Intel Corporation
Andrew Grove 1936– : in *New York Times* 18 December 1994

Buying and Selling see also Business

PROVERBS AND SAYINGS

1 The buyer has need of a hundred eyes, the seller of but one.
mid 17th century, stressing the responsibility of a purchaser to examine goods on offer

2 Let the buyer beware.
early 16th century, warning that it is up to the buyer to establish the nature and value of a purchase before completing the transaction

3 You buy land, you buy stones; you buy meat, you buy bones.
late 17th century; meaning that every purchase has its drawbacks

QUOTATIONS

4 It is naught, it is naught, saith the buyer: but when he is gone his way, then he boasteth.
Bible: Proverbs

5 I have heard of a man who had a mind to sell his house, and therefore carried a piece of brick in his pocket, which he showed as a pattern to encourage purchasers.
Jonathan Swift 1667–1745: *The Drapier's Letters* (1724)

6 I often wonder what the Vintners buy
One half so precious as the Goods they sell.
Edward Fitzgerald 1809–83: *The Rubáiyát of Omar Khayyám* (1859)

7 Every one lives by selling something.
Robert Louis Stevenson 1850–94: *Across the Plains* (1892) 'Beggars'

8 The car, the furniture, the wife, the children—everything has to be disposable. Because you see the main thing today is—shopping.
Arthur Miller 1915– : *The Price* (1968)

9 The consumer, so it is said, is the king . . . each is a voter who uses his money as votes to get the things done that he wants done.
Paul A. Samuelson 1915– : *Economics* (8th ed., 1970)

10 In a consumer society there are inevitably two kinds of slaves: the prisoners of addiction and the prisoners of envy.
Ivan Illich 1926– : *Tools for Conviviality* (1973)

11 The source of status is no longer the ability to make things but simply the ability to purchase them.
Harry Braverman: *Labour and Monopoly Capital* (1974)

12 Buying is much more American than thinking and I'm as American as they come.
Andy Warhol 1927–87: *Philosophy of Andy Warhol (From A to B and Back Again)* (1975)

13 Women are people who shop. Shopping is the festival of the female oppressed.
Germaine Greer 1939– : in *Sunday Times* 23 July 2000

Canada

PROVERBS AND SAYINGS

1 The Mounties always get their man.
unofficial motto of the Royal Canadian Mounted Police

PHRASES

2 the land God gave to Cain a name for Labrador.
from Cartier (see 4 below), referring to Cain's banishment by God to a desolate land 'east of Eden'; see also **Murder** 7, **Order** 7, **Travel** 8

3 the Land of the Little Sticks the subarctic tundra region of northern Canada, characterized by its stunted vegetation.
Chinook stik wood, tree, forest

QUOTATIONS

4 I am rather inclined to believe that this is the land God gave to Cain.
on discovering the northern shore of the Gulf of St Lawrence in 1534
Jacques Cartier 1491–1557: *La Première Relation*

5 These two nations have been at war over a few acres of snow near Canada, and . . . they are spending on this fine struggle more than Canada itself is worth.
of the struggle between the French and the British for the control of colonial north Canada
Voltaire 1694–1778: *Candide* (1759)

6 Fair these broad meads, these hoary woods are grand;
But we are exiles from our fathers' land.
John Galt 1779–1839: 'Canadian Boat Song' (1829); translated from the Gaelic; attributed

7 I expected to find a contest between a government and a people: I found two nations warring in the bosom of a single state.
John George Lambton, Lord Durham 1792–1840: *Report of the Affairs of British North America* (1839)

8 Dusty, cobweb-covered, maimed, and set at naught,
Beauty crieth in an attic, and no man regardeth.
O God! O Montreal!
Samuel Butler 1835–1902: 'Psalm of Montreal' (1878)

9 The twentieth century belongs to Canada.
encapsulation of a view expressed in a speech to the Canadian Club of Ottawa, 18 January 1904, 'The nineteenth century was the century of the United States. I think we can claim that it is Canada that shall fill the twentieth century'
Wilfrid Laurier 1841–1919: popularly attributed in this form

10 *O Canada! Terre de nos aïeux,*
Ton front est ceint de fleurons glorieux!
Car ton bras sait porter l'épée,
Il sait porter la croix!

O Canada! Our home and native land!
True patriot love in all thy sons command.
With glowing hearts we see thee rise,
The True North strong and free!

Robert Stanley Weir 1856–1926: 'Oh Canada' (1908 song); French words written in 1880 by Adolphe-Basile Routhier (1839–1920)

11 If some countries have too much history, we have too much geography.

William Lyon Mackenzie King 1874–1950: speech on Canada as an international power, 18 June 1936

12 We French, we English, never lost our civil war,
   endure it still, a bloodless civil bore;
   no wounded lying about, no Whitman wanted.
   It's only by our lack of ghosts we're haunted.

Earle Birney 1904– : 'Can.Lit.' (1962)

13 Canada could have enjoyed:
   English government,
   French culture,
   and American know-how.
   Instead it ended up with:
   English know-how,
   French government,
   and American culture.

a similar (prose) summary has been attributed to Lester Pearson (1897–1972), 'Canada was supposed to get British government, French culture, and American know-how. Instead it got French government, American culture, and British know-how'

John Robert Colombo 1936– : 'O Canada' (1965)

14 Canada has, for practical purposes, no Atlantic seaboard. The traveller from Europe edges into it like a tiny Jonah entering an inconceivably large whale, slipping past the Straits of Belle Isle into the Gulf of St Lawrence, where five Canadian provinces surround him, for the most part invisible . . . To enter the United States is a matter of crossing an ocean; to enter Canada is a matter of being silently swallowed by an alien continent.

Northrop Frye 1912–91: 'Conclusion to a *Literary History of Canada*' (1965)

15 *Vive Le Québec Libre.*
   Long Live Free Quebec.

Charles de Gaulle 1890–1970: speech in Montreal, 24 July 1967

16 A Canadian is somebody who knows how to make love in a canoe.

Pierre Berton 1920– : in *The Canadian* 22 December 1973

17 Canadians are Americans with no Disneyland.

Margaret Mahy 1936– : *The Changeover* (1984)

18 I see Canada as a country torn between a very northern, rather extraordinary, mystical spirit which it fears and its desire to present itself to the world as a Scotch banker.

Robertson Davies 1913–95: *The Enthusiasms of Robertson Davies* (1990)

19 Our country is large in extent, small in population, which accounts for our fear of empty spaces, and also our need for them. Much of it is covered in water, which accounts for our interest in reflections, sudden vanishings, the dissolution of one thing into another. Much of it however is rock, which accounts for our belief in Fate.

Margaret Atwood 1939– : *Good Bones* (1992) 'Homelanding'

Capitalism and Communism see also **Class, Political Parties**

PROVERBS AND SAYINGS

1 **All power to the Soviets.**
slogan of workers in Petrograd, 1917

2 **Are you now or have you ever been a member of the Communist Party?**
formal question put to those appearing before the Committee on UnAmerican Activities during the McCarthy campaign of 1950–4 against alleged Communists in the US government and other institutions; the allusive form are you now or have you ever been? *derives from this*

3 **Better red than dead.**
slogan of nuclear disarmament campaigners, late 1950s

PHRASES

4 **the bamboo curtain** a political and economic barrier between China and non-Communist countries.
after iron curtain: *see 6 below*

5 dictatorship of the proletariat the Communist ideal of proletarian supremacy following the overthrow of capitalism and preceding the classless state.

6 the iron curtain a notional barrier to the passage of people and information between the Soviet bloc and the West.

in this specific sense from Churchill (see 20 below), but the figurative use of iron curtain (literally a fire-curtain in a theatre) is recorded earlier; see also 4 above

7 reds under the bed denoting an exaggerated fear of the presence and harmful influence of Communist sympathizers within a society or institution.

QUOTATIONS

8 The Riches and Goods of Christians are not common, as touching the right, title, and possession of the same, as certain Anabaptists do falsely boast.
The Book of Common Prayer 1662: *Articles of Religion* (1562)

9 In the first stone which he [the savage] flings at the wild animals he pursues, in the first stick that he seizes to strike down the fruit which hangs above his reach, we see the appropriation of one article for the purpose of aiding in the acquisition of another, and thus discover the origin of capital.
Robert Torrens 1780–1864: *An Essay on the Production of Wealth* (1821)

10 A spectre is haunting Europe—the spectre of Communism.
Karl Marx 1818–83 and **Friedrich Engels** 1820–95: *The Communist Manifesto* (1848)

11 What is a communist? One who hath yearnings
For equal division of unequal earnings.
Ebenezer Elliott 1781–1849: 'Epigram' (1850)

12 Communism is a Russian autocracy turned upside down.
Alexander Ivanovich Herzen 1812–70: *The Development of Revolutionary Ideas in Russia* (1851)

13 All I know is that I am not a Marxist.
Karl Marx 1818–83: attributed in a letter from Friedrich Engels to Conrad Schmidt, 5 August 1890

14 Imperialism is the monopoly stage of capitalism.
Lenin 1870–1924: *Imperialism as the Last Stage of Capitalism* (1916) 'Briefest possible definition of imperialism'

15 I have seen the future; and it works.
following a visit to the Soviet Union in 1919
Lincoln Steffens 1866–1936: *Letters* (1938)

16 Communism is Soviet power plus the electrification of the whole country.
Lenin 1870–1924: Report to 8th Congress, 1920

17 The State is an instrument in the hands of the ruling class, used to break the resistance of the adversaries of that class.
Joseph Stalin 1879–1953: *Foundations of Leninism* (1924)

18 Communism is like prohibition, it's a good idea but it won't work.
Will Rogers 1879–1935: in 1927; *Weekly Articles* (1981)

19 M is for Marx
And Movement of Masses
And Massing of Arses.
And Clashing of Classes.
Cyril Connolly 1903–74: 'Where Engels Fears to Tread' (1945)

20 From Stettin in the Baltic to Trieste in the Adriatic an iron curtain has descended across the Continent.
the expression 'iron curtain' previously had been applied by others to the Soviet Union or her sphere of influence
Winston Churchill 1874–1965: speech at Westminster College, Fulton, Missouri, 5 March 1946; see 6 above

21 Whether you like it or not, history is on our side. We will bury you.
Nikita Khrushchev 1894–1971: speech to Western diplomats in Moscow, 18 November 1956

22 Capitalism, it is said, is a system wherein man exploits man. And communism—is vice versa.
quoting 'a Polish intellectual'
Daniel Bell 1919– : *The End of Ideology* (1960)

23 Normally speaking, it may be said that the forces of a capitalist society, if left unchecked, tend to make the rich richer and the poor poorer and thus increase the gap between them.
Jawaharlal Nehru 1889–1964: 'Basic Approach' in Vincent Shean *Nehru . . .* (1960)

24 History suggests that capitalism is a necessary condition for political freedom. Clearly it is not a sufficient condition for it.
Milton Friedman 1912– : *Capitalism and Freedom* (1962)

25 Capitalism is using its money; we socialists throw it away.
Fidel Castro 1927– : in *Observer* 8 November 1964

26 Left wing, chicken wing, it's all the same to me.
Woody Guthrie 1912–67: Joe Klein *Woody Guthrie: a life* (1980)

27 In the service of the people we followed such a policy that socialism would not lose its human face.
Alexander Dubček 1921–92: in *Rudé Právo* 19 July 1968

28 The unpleasant and unacceptable face of capitalism.
on the Lonrho affair
Edward Heath 1916– : speech, House of Commons, 15 May 1973

29 It is as wholly wrong to blame Marx for what was done in his name, as it is to blame Jesus for what was done in his.
Tony Benn 1925– : Alan Freeman *The Benn Heresy* (1982)

30 The clock of communism has stopped striking. But its concrete building has not yet come crashing down. For that reason, instead of freeing ourselves, we must try to save ourselves being crushed by the rubble.
Alexander Solzhenitsyn 1918– : in *Komsomolskaya Pravda* 18 September 1990

31 Transformations in Eastern Europe seem to have been fuelled by people's desire to buy rather than their desire to vote, by dreams of purchasing rather than dreams of participating.
Rosabeth Moss Kanter 1943– : *World Class* (1995)

32 It would be simplistic to say that Divine Providence caused the fall of communism. It fell by itself as a consequence of its own mistakes and abuses. It fell by itself because of its own inherent weaknesses.
Pope John Paul II 1920– : Carl Bernstein and Marco Politi *His Holiness: John Paul II and the Hidden History of our Time* (1996)

33 Yes to the market economy, No to the market society.
Lionel Jospin 1937– : in *Independent* 16 September 1998

Cats see also **Animals**

1 **A cat has nine lives.**
traditional saying

2 **Touch not the cat but a glove.**
early 19th century Scottish proverb, but *meaning 'without'; the cat here is a wild cat*

PHRASES

3 **Cheshire cat** a cat depicted with a broad fixed grin.
as popularized through Lewis Carroll's Alice's Adventures in Wonderland (*1865*). *The origin is unknown, but it is said that* Cheshire *cheeses used to be marked with the face of a smiling cat; see* **Britain** 15, **God** 32

4 **fight like Kilkenny cats** two cats from Kilkenny in Ireland which, according to legend, fought until only their tails remained.

QUOTATIONS

5 When I play with my cat, who knows whether she isn't amusing herself with me more than I am with her?
Montaigne 1533–92: *Essais* (1580)

6 For I will consider my Cat Jeoffrey. . . .
For he counteracts the powers of darkness
  by his electrical skin and glaring eyes.
For he counteracts the Devil, who is death,
  by brisking about the life.
Christopher Smart 1722–71: *Jubilate Agno* (c.1758–63)

7 When I observed he was a fine cat, saying, 'Why yes, Sir, but I have had cats whom I liked better than this'; and then as if perceiving Hodge to be out of countenance, adding, 'but he is a very fine cat, a very fine cat indeed.'
Samuel Johnson 1709–84: James Boswell *Life of Samuel Johnson* (1791) 1783

8 Cruel, but composed and bland,
Dumb, inscrutable and grand,
So Tiberius might have sat,
Had Tiberius been a cat.
Matthew Arnold 1822–88: 'Poor Matthias' (1885)

9 He walked by himself, and all places were alike to him.
Rudyard Kipling 1865–1936: *Just So Stories* (1902) 'The Cat that Walked by Himself'

10 Cats, no less liquid than their shadows,
Offer no angles to the wind.
They slip, diminished, neat, through
  loopholes
Less than themselves.
A. S. J. Tessimond 1902–62: *Cats* (1934)

11 The Naming of Cats is a difficult matter,
It isn't just one of your holiday games;
You may think at first I'm as mad as a
  hatter
When I tell you, a cat must have THREE
  DIFFERENT NAMES.
T. S. Eliot 1888–1965: 'The Naming of Cats' (1939)

12 The trouble with a kitten is
THAT
Eventually it becomes a
CAT.
Ogden Nash 1902–71: 'The Kitten' (1940)

13 Cats seem to go on the principle that it
never does any harm to ask for what you
want.
Joseph Wood Krutch 1893–1970: *Twelve Seasons*
(1949)

14 Daylong this tomcat lies stretched flat
As an old rough mat, no mouth and no
  eyes,
Continual wars and wives are what
Have tattered his ears and battered his
  head.
Ted Hughes 1930–98: 'Esther's Tomcat' (1960)

15 If a fish is the movement of water
embodied, given shape, then cat is a
diagram and pattern of subtle air.
Doris Lessing 1919– : *Particularly Cats* (1967)

Causes and Consequences

PROVERBS AND SAYINGS

1 As you bake so shall you brew.
*late 16th century, meaning that as you begin, so shall
you proceed*

2 As you brew, so shall you bake.
*late 16th century, meaning that your circumstances
will be shaped by your own initial actions*

**3 As you make your bed, so you must lie
upon it.**
*late 16th century, meaning that as you begin, so shall
you proceed*

4 As you sow, so you reap.
*late 15th century, meaning that you will have to
endure the consequences of your actions; see 8, 15, 17
below*

5 Good seed makes a good crop.
*mid 16th century, meaning that something which has
a sound basis will do well*

6 Great oaks from little acorns grow.
*late 14th century, meaning that great results may
ensue from apparently small beginnings*

**7 The mother of mischief is no bigger than a
midge's wing.**
*early 17th century, meaning that the origin of
difficulties can be very small*

**8 They that sow the wind, shall reap the
whirlwind.**
*late 16th century, meaning that those who have
initiated a dangerous course must suffer the
consequences; see 4 above, 15, 17 below*

**9 Who won't be ruled by the rudder must be
ruled by the rock.**
*mid 17th century; meaning that a ship which is not
being steered on its course will run on to a rock*

PHRASES

10 the butterfly effect the effect of a very
small change in the initial conditions of a
system which makes a significant
difference to the outcome.
*from Lorenz: see **Chance** 35*

11 a grain of mustard seed a small thing
capable of vast development.
*from the great height attained by black mustard in
Palestine, as in the Bible (Matthew) 'a mustard seed
. . . indeed is the least of all seeds: but when it is
grown, it is the greatest among herbs'*

12 hoist with one's own petard ruined by
one's own devices against others.
*blown up by one's own bomb, after Shakespeare
Hamlet 'For 'tis the sport to have the engineer Hoist
with his own petar'; petar a petard, a small bomb
made of a metal or wooden box filled with powder,
used to blow in a door or to make a hole in a wall*

13 poetic justice the ideal justice in
distribution of rewards and punishments
supposed to befit a poem or other work of
imagination; well-deserved unforeseen
retribution or reward.
*from Pope The Dunciad 'Poetic Justice, with her lifted
scale'*

14 He that diggeth a pit shall fall into it.
Bible: Ecclesiastes

15 They have sown the wind, and they shall reap the whirlwind.
Bible: Hosea; see 8 above, 17 below

16 Whenever anything which has several parts is such that the whole is something over and above its parts, and not just the sum of them all, like a heap, then it always has some cause.
Aristotle 384–322 BC: *Metaphysica*; see **Quantities and Qualities** 10

17 Whatsoever a man soweth, that shall he also reap.
Bible: Galatians; see 4, 15 above

18 Who buys a minute's mirth to wail a week?
Or sells eternity to get a toy?
For one sweet grape who will the vine destroy?
William Shakespeare 1564–1616: *The Rape of Lucrece* (1594)

19 One leak will sink a ship, and one sin will destroy a sinner.
John Bunyan 1628–88: *The Pilgrim's Progress* (1684)

20 Whoever wills the end, wills also (so far as reason decides his conduct) the means in his power which are indispensably necessary thereto.
Immanuel Kant 1724–1804: *Fundamental Principles of the Metaphysics of Ethics* (1785)

21 Sow an act, and you reap a habit. Sow a habit and you reap a character. Sow a character, and you reap a destiny.
Charles Reade 1814–84: attributed; in *Notes and Queries* 17 October 1903

22 The present contains nothing more than the past, and what is found in the effect was already in the cause.
Henri Bergson 1859–1941: *L'Évolution créatrice* (1907)

23 The captain is in his bunk, drinking bottled ditch-water; and the crew is gambling in the forecastle. She will strike and sink and split. Do you think the laws of God will be suspended in favour of England because you were born in it?
George Bernard Shaw 1856–1950: *Heartbreak House* (1919)

24 As it will be in the future, it was at the birth of Man—

There are only four things certain since Social Progress began:
That the Dog returns to his Vomit and the Sow returns to her Mire,
And the burnt Fool's bandaged finger goes wabbling back to the Fire;
And that after this is accomplished, and the brave new world begins
When all men are paid for existing and no man must pay for his sins,
As surely as Water will wet us, as surely as Fire will burn,
The Gods of the Copybook Headings with terror and slaughter return!
Rudyard Kipling 1865–1936: 'The Gods of the Copybook Headings' (1919)

25 The English . . . are paralysed by fear. That is what thwarts and distorts the Anglo-Saxon existence . . . Nothing could be more lovely and fearless than Chaucer. But already Shakespeare is morbid with fear, fear of consequences. That is the strange phenomenon of the English Renaissance: this mystic terror of the consequences, the consequences of action.
D. H. Lawrence 1885–1930: *Phoenix* (1936)

26 You have broader considerations that might follow what you might call the 'falling domino' principle. You have a row of dominoes set up. You knock over the first one, and what will happen to the last one is that it will go over very quickly. So you have the beginning of a disintegration that would have the most profound influences.
Dwight D. Eisenhower 1890–1969: speech at press conference, 7 April 1954

27 The structure of a play is always the story of how the birds came home to roost.
Arthur Miller 1915– : in *Harper's Magazine* August 1958

28 Every positive value has its price in negative terms . . . The genius of Einstein leads to Hiroshima.
Pablo Picasso 1881–1973: F. Gilot and C. Lake *Life With Picasso* (1964)

29 I fear we have only awakened a sleeping giant, and his reaction will be terrible.
of the attack on Pearl Harbor
Larry Forrester et al.: *Tora! Tora! Tora!* (1970 film); said by the Japanese admiral Isoruko Yamamoto (1884–1943), although there is no evidence that Yamamoto used these words

30 If you wish to make an apple pie from scratch, you must first invent the universe.
Carl Sagan 1934–96: *Cosmos* (1980)

Caution see also **Danger**

PROVERBS AND SAYINGS

1 Better be safe than sorry.
mid 19th century, urging the wisdom of taking precautions

2 A bird in the hand is worth two in the bush.
mid 15th century, meaning that it is better to accept what one has than to try to get more and risk losing everything; see **Certainty** *4*

3 A cat in gloves catches no mice.
late 16th century, meaning that deliberate restraint and caution (or 'pussyfooting') often result in nothing being achieved

4 Caution is the parent of safety.
American proverb, early 18th century

5 Discretion is the better part of valour.
late 16th century, often used to explain caution, and sometimes with allusion to Shakespeare's 1 Henry IV *(1597), 'The better part of valour is discretion'*

6 Don't put all your eggs in one basket.
mid 17th century, meaning that you should not chance everything on a single venture, but spread the risk; see 28 below

7 Full cup, steady hand.
early 11th century, used especially to caution against spoiling a comfortable or otherwise enviable situation by careless action

8 He who fights and runs away, may live to fight another day.
mid 16th century

9 He who sups with the Devil should have a long spoon.
late 14th century, meaning that one should be cautious when dealing with dangerous persons

10 If you can't be good, be careful.
early 20th century, often used as a humorous warning. The same idea is found in 11th-century Latin, si non caste tamen caute

11 Let's be careful out there.
catchphrase from Hill Street Blues *(police procedural television series, 1981 onwards), written by Steven Bochco and Michael Kozoll*

12 Let sleeping dogs lie.
late 14th century, meaning that something which may be dangerous or difficult to handle is better left undisturbed

13 Let well alone.
late 16th century, often used as a warning against raising problems which will then be difficult to resolve

14 Look before you leap.
mid 14th century, used to advise caution before committing oneself to a course of action

15 The more you stir it [a turd] the worse it stinks.
mid 16th century; meaning that disturbance of something naturally unpleasant will only make it more disagreeable

16 Never trouble trouble till trouble troubles you.
late 19th century; another version of the advice that one should let well alone

17 Safe bind, safe find.
mid 16th century, meaning that something kept securely will be readily found again

18 Second thoughts are best.
late 16th century, meaning that it is dangerous to act on one's first impulse without due thought; see 25 below

19 A stitch in time saves nine.
early 18th century; meaning that a small but timely intervention will ensure against the need for much more substantial repair later

20 Stop-look-and-listen.
road safety slogan, current in the US from 1912

21 Those who play at bowls must look out for rubbers.
mid 18th century, meaning that one must beware of difficulties associated with a particular activity; a rubber here is an alteration of rub, an obstacle or impediment to the course of a bowl

QUOTATIONS

22 Happy is that city which in time of peace thinks of war.
inscription found in the armoury of Venice
Anonymous: Robert Burton *The Anatomy of Melancholy* (1621–51)

23 Beware of desperate steps. The darkest day (Live till tomorrow) will have passed away.
William Cowper 1731–1800: 'The Needless Alarm' (written c.1790)

24 Prudence is a rich, ugly, old maid courted by Incapacity.
William Blake 1757–1827: *The Marriage of Heaven and Hell* (1790–3) 'Proverbs of Hell'

25 Have no truck with first impulses for they are always generous ones.
Casimir, Comte de Montrond 1768–1843: attributed; Comte J. d'Estourmel *Derniers Souvenirs* (1860), where the alternative attribution to Talleyrand is denied; see 18 above

26 Tar-baby ain't sayin' nuthin', en Brer Fox, he lay low.
Joel Chandler Harris 1848–1908: *Uncle Remus and His Legends of the Old Plantation* (1881)

27 Prudence is a wooden Juggernaut, before whom Benjamin Franklin walks with the portly air of a high priest.
Robert Louis Stevenson 1850–94: *Virginibus Puerisque* (1881)

28 Put all your eggs in the one basket, and— WATCH THAT BASKET.
Mark Twain 1835–1910: *Pudd'nhead Wilson* (1894); see 6 above

29 Them that asks no questions isn't told a lie.
Watch the wall, my darling, while the Gentlemen go by!
Rudyard Kipling 1865–1936: 'A Smuggler's Song' (1906)

30 Of all forms of caution, caution in love is perhaps the most fatal to true happiness.
Bertrand Russell 1872–1970: *The Conquest of Happiness* (1930)

31 All the same, sir, I would put some of the colonies in your wife's name.
Joseph Herman Hertz 1872–1946: the Chief Rabbi to George VI, summer 1940; Chips Channon diary 3 June 1943

32 All the security around the American president is just to make sure the man who shoots him gets caught.
Norman Mailer 1923– : in *Sunday Telegraph* 4 March 1990

Celebrations   see Festivals and Celebrations

Censorship

PHRASES

1 blue-pencil censor or make cuts in a manuscript.
a blue 'lead' pencil was traditionally used for marking corrections and deletions; see **Culture** *26*

QUOTATIONS

2 If these writings of the Greeks agree with the book of God, they are useless and need not be preserved; if they disagree, they are pernicious and ought to be destroyed.
on burning the library of Alexandria, AD *c.641*
Caliph Omar d. 644: Edward Gibbon *The Decline and Fall of the Roman Empire* (1776–88)

3 As good almost kill a man as kill a good book: who kills a man kills a reasonable creature, God's image; but he who destroys a good book, kills reason itself, kills the image of God, as it were in the eye.
John Milton 1608–74: *Areopagitica* (1644)

4 I disapprove of what you say, but I will defend to the death your right to say it.
his attitude towards Helvétius following the burning of the latter's De l'esprit *in 1759*
Voltaire 1694–1778: attributed to Voltaire, the words are in fact S. G. Tallentyre's summary; *The Friends of Voltaire* (1907)

5 Wherever books will be burned, men also, in the end, are burned.
Heinrich Heine 1797–1856: *Almansor* (1823)

6 You have not converted a man, because you have silenced him.
Lord Morley 1838–1923: *On Compromise* (1874)

7 Assassination is the extreme form of censorship.
George Bernard Shaw 1856–1950: *The Showing-Up of Blanco Posnet* (1911)

8 We have long passed the Victorian Era when asterisks were followed after a certain interval by a baby.
W. Somerset Maugham 1874–1965: *The Constant Wife* (1926)

9 Everybody favours free speech in the slack moments when no axes are being ground.
Heywood Broun 1888–1939: in *New York World* 23 October 1926

10 God forbid that any book should be banned. The practice is as indefensible as infanticide.
Rebecca West 1892–1983: *The Strange Necessity* (1928)

11 Don't you see that the whole aim of Newspeak is to narrow the range of thought? In the end we shall make thoughtcrime literally impossible, because there will be no words in which to express it.
George Orwell 1903–50: *Nineteen Eighty-Four* (1949)

12 Those who want the Government to regulate matters of the mind and spirit are like men who are so afraid of being murdered that they commit suicide to avoid assassination.
Harry S. Truman 1884–1972: address at the National Archives, Washington, D.C., 15 December 1952

13 We are paid to have dirty minds.
on British Film Censors
John Trevelyan: in *Observer* 15 November 1959

14 Is it a book you would even wish your wife or your servants to read?
of D. H. Lawrence's Lady Chatterley's Lover
Mervyn Griffith-Jones 1909–79: speech for the prosecution at the Central Criminal Court, Old Bailey, 20 October 1960

15 It's red hot, mate. I hate to think of this sort of book getting into the wrong hands. As soon as I've finished this, I shall recommend they ban it.
Ray Galton 1930– and **Alan Simpson** 1929– : *The Missing Page* (1960 BBC television programme) words spoken by Tony Hancock

16 The state has no place in the nation's bedrooms.
Pierre Trudeau 1919–2000: interview, Ottawa, 22 December 1967

17 If decade after decade the truth cannot be told, each person's mind begins to roam irretrievably. One's fellow countrymen become harder to understand than Martians.
Alexander Solzhenitsyn 1918– : *Cancer Ward* (1968)

18 One does not put Voltaire in the Bastille.
Charles de Gaulle 1890–1970: when asked to arrest Sartre, in the 1960s; in *Encounter* June 1975

19 To portray only what you would like to be true is the beginning of censorship.
David Hare 1947– : *The History Plays* (1984)

20 The Khomeini cry for the execution of Rushdie is an infantile cry. From the beginning of time we have seen that. To murder the thinker does not murder the thought.
Arnold Wesker 1932– : in *Weekend Guardian* 3 June 1989

21 What is freedom of expression? Without the freedom to offend, it ceases to exist.
Salman Rushdie 1947– : in *Weekend Guardian* 10 February 1990

Certainty and Doubt see also **Belief, Faith, Indecision**

PROVERBS AND SAYINGS

1 Does she . . . or doesn't she?
advertising slogan for Clairol hair colouring, 1950s

2 Don't be vague, ask for Haig.
advertising slogan for Haig whisky, c.1936

3 Nothing is certain but death and taxes.
early 18th century, summarizing what in life is inevitable and inescapable; see **Pregnancy** *10,* **Taxes** *14*

PHRASES

4 a bird in the hand something certain (as implicitly contrasted with the prospect of a greater but less certain advantage).
from the proverb: see **Caution** *2*

5 Lombard Street to a China orange great wealth against one ordinary object, virtual certainty.
Lombard Street *a street in London, originally occupied by Lombard bankers and still containing many of the principal London banks; China orange taken as the type of something worthless*

6 How long halt ye between two opinions?
Bible: I Kings

7 O thou of little faith, wherefore didst thou doubt?
Bible: St Matthew

8 If a man will begin with certainties, he shall end in doubts; but if he will be content to begin with doubts, he shall end in certainties.
Francis Bacon 1561–1626: *The Advancement of Learning* (1605)

9 I beseech you, in the bowels of Christ, think it possible you may be mistaken.
Oliver Cromwell 1599–1658: letter to the General Assembly of the Kirk of Scotland, 3 August 1650

10 Negative Capability, that is when man is capable of being in uncertainties, mysteries, doubts, without any irritable reaching after fact and reason.
John Keats 1795–1821: letter to George and Thomas Keats, 21 December 1817

11 My deplorable mania for analysis exhausts me. I doubt everything, even my doubt.
Gustave Flaubert 1821–80: letter, 8–9 August 1846

12 I wish I was as cocksure of anything as Tom Macaulay is of everything.
Lord Melbourne 1779–1848: Lord Cowper's preface to *Lord Melbourne's Papers* (1889)

13 There lives more faith in honest doubt, Believe me, than in half the creeds.
Alfred, Lord Tennyson 1809–92: *In Memoriam A. H. H.* (1850)

14 Ah, what a dusty answer gets the soul When hot for certainties in this our life!
George Meredith 1828–1909: *Modern Love* (1862); see **Satisfaction** 9

15 Ten thousand difficulties do not make one doubt.
John Henry Newman 1801–90: *Apologia pro Vita Sua* (1864)

16 What, never?
No, never!
What, *never?*

Hardly ever!
W. S. Gilbert 1836–1911: *HMS Pinafore* (1878)

17 I am too much of a sceptic to deny the possibility of anything.
T. H. Huxley 1825–95: letter to Herbert Spencer, 22 March 1886

18 Oh! let us never, never doubt What nobody is sure about!
Hilaire Belloc 1870–1953: 'The Microbe' (1897)

19 Life is doubt, And faith without doubt is nothing but death.
Miguel de Unamuno 1864–1937: 'Salmo II' (1907)

20 I respect faith but doubt is what gets you an education.
Wilson Mizner 1876–1933: H. L. Mencken *A New Dictionary of Quotations* (1942)

21 My mind is not a bed to be made and re-made.
James Agate 1877–1947: *Ego 6* (1944) 9 June 1943

22 Human beings are perhaps never more frightening than when they are convinced beyond doubt that they are right.
Laurens van der Post 1906–96: *The Lost World of the Kalahari* (1958)

23 It was not the power of the Spaniards that destroyed the Aztec Empire but the disbelief of the Aztecs in themselves.
E. F. Schumacher 1911–77: *Roots of Economic Growth* (1962)

24 The trouble with the world is that the stupid are cocksure and the intelligent are full of doubt.
Bertrand Russell 1872–1970: attributed

25 When a Southern Irishman says 'Not an inch', he means no more than four or five inches, and certainly not, at any rate for the next five or six years. But when an Ulsterman says 'Not an inch', that's it: he means not the tiniest fraction of an inch, from now until the last syllable of recorded time. And when he says 'No Surrender' he means just that, no surrender, ever.
Tony Gray 1928– : *St Patrick's People* (1996); see **Defiance** 2

Chance and Luck

1 Accidents will happen (in the best-regulated families).

mid 18th century, meaning that the most orderly arrangements cannot prevent accidents from occurring

2 Blind chance sweeps the world along.

American proverb, mid 20th century

3 The devil looks after his own.

early 18th century, often used to comment on the good fortune of someone undeserving; see 4 below

4 The devil's children have the devil's luck.

late 17th century, commenting on the good fortune of someone undeserving; see 3 above

5 Diligence is the mother of good luck.

late 16th century, meaning that success results more from application and practice than from good fortune

6 Fools for luck.

mid 19th century, meaning that a foolish person is traditionally fortunate

7 It could be you.

advertising slogan for the British national lottery, 1994

8 It is better to be born lucky than rich.

mid 17th century, often with the implication that riches can be lost or spent, but that good luck gives one the capacity to improve one's fortunes

9 Lightning never strikes the same place twice.

mid 19th century, often used as an encouragement that a particular misfortune will not be repeated

10 Lucky at cards, unlucky in love.

mid 19th century, suggesting that good fortune in gambling is balanced by lack of success in love

11 Moses took a chance.

American proverb, mid 20th century, used to urge someone to take a risk

12 See a pin and pick it up, all the day you'll have good luck; see a pin and let it lie, bad luck you'll have all day.

mid 19th century, extolling the virtues of thrift in small matters

13 There is luck in odd numbers.

late 16th century

14 Third time lucky.

mid 19th century, reflecting the idea that three is a lucky number; often used to suggest making another effort after initial failure

15 Aladdin's lamp a talisman enabling the holder to gratify any wish.

*in the Arabian Nights, an old lamp found by Aladdin in a cave, which when rubbed brought a genie to obey his will; see **Wealth** 7*

16 Buckley's chance in Australia, a slim chance, no chance at all.

sometimes said to be from the name of William Buckley (died 1856), who, despite dire predictions as to his chances of survival, lived with the Aboriginals for many years

17 in the lap of the gods subject to fate.

*see **Fate** 10*

18 wheel of Fortune the wheel which Fortune is fabled to turn, as an emblem of mutability.

*see **Circumstance** 6*

19 Cast thy bread upon the waters: for thou shalt find it after many days.

Bible: Ecclesiastes; see **Future** 7

20   Fortune's a right whore:
If she give aught, she deals it in small parcels,
That she may take away all at one swoop.

John Webster c.1580–c.1625: *The White Devil* (1612)

21 What a world is this, and how does fortune banter us!

Henry St John, Lord Bolingbroke 1678–1751: letter to Jonathan Swift, 3 August 1714

22 Care and diligence bring luck.

Thomas Fuller 1654–1734: *Gnomologia* (1732)

23 The chapter of knowledge is a very short, but the chapter of accidents is a very long one.

Lord Chesterfield 1694–1773: letter to Solomon Dayrolles, 16 February 1753; see **Misfortunes** 8

24 O! many a shaft, at random sent,
Finds mark the archer little meant!
And many a word, at random spoken,
May soothe or wound a heart that's broken.

Sir Walter Scott 1771–1832: *The Lord of the Isles* (1813)

25 All you know about it [luck] for certain is that it's bound to change.
Bret Harte 1836–1902: *The Outcasts of Poker Flat* (1871)

26 The ball no question makes of Ayes and Noes,
But here or there as strikes the player goes.
Edward Fitzgerald 1809–83: *The Rubáiyát of Omar Khayyám* (4th ed., 1879)

27 Some folk want their luck buttered.
Thomas Hardy 1840–1928: *The Mayor of Casterbridge* (1886)

28 A throw of the dice will never eliminate chance.
Stéphane Mallarmé 1842–98: title of poem (1897)

29 There is much good luck in the world, but it is luck. We are none of us safe. We are children, playing or quarrelling on the line.
E. M. Forster 1879–1970: *The Longest Journey* (1907)

30 A million million spermatozoa,
All of them alive:
Out of their cataclysm but one poor Noah
Dare hope to survive.
And among that billion minus one
Might have chanced to be
Shakespeare, another Newton, a new Donne—
But the One was Me.
Aldous Huxley 1894–1963: 'Fifth Philosopher's Song' (1920)

31 At any rate, I am convinced that *He* [God] does not play dice.
often quoted as 'God does not play dice'
Albert Einstein 1879–1955: letter to Max Born, 4 December 1926

32 If an army of monkeys were strumming on typewriters they *might* write all the books in the British Museum.
Arthur Eddington 1882–1944: *The Nature of the Physical World* (1928); see **Computers** 17

33 now and then
there is a person born
who is so unlucky
that he runs into accidents
which started to happen
to somebody else.
Don Marquis 1878–1937: *archys life of mehitabel* (1933)

34 Mr Bond, they have a saying in Chicago: 'Once is happenstance. Twice is coincidence. The third time it's enemy action.'
Ian Fleming 1908–64: *Goldfinger* (1959)

35 Predictability: Does the flap of a butterfly's wings in Brazil set off a tornado in Texas?
Edward N. Lorenz: title of paper given to the American Association for the Advancement of Science, Washington, 29 December 1979; see **Causes** 10

36 What we call luck is the inner man externalized. We make things happen to us.
Robertson Davies 1913–95: *What's Bred in the Bone* (1985)

37 The chance of winning the lottery jackpot is less than that of being struck by lightning. I have never bought a ticket and plan to buy an insulating rubber helmet with the money I save. It will increase my life expectancy by precisely one fourteen-millionth.
Steve Jones 1944– : in *Independent on Sunday* 5 November 1995

Change see also Beginning, Ending, Progress

PROVERBS AND SAYINGS

1 And now for something completely different.
catchphrase popularized in Monty Python's Flying Circus (*BBC TV programme, 1969–74*)

2 Be sure you can better your condition before you make a change.
American proverb, mid 20th century

3 A change is as good as a rest.
late 19th century, suggesting that a change of activity can be refreshing

4 It is never too late to mend.
late 16th century, meaning that one can always try to improve

5 The leopard does not change his spots.
mid 16th century, meaning that a person cannot change their essential nature, from the Bible: see 19, 25 below

6 Never say never.
late 20th century saying, used as a warning against over-confidence that circumstances cannot change; see **Time** *2*

7 New brooms sweep clean.
mid 16th century, often used in the context of someone newly appointed to a post who is making changes in personnel and procedures

8 New lords, new laws.
mid 16th century, meaning that new authorities are likely to change existing rules

9 No more Mr Nice Guy.
mid 20th century, said to assert that one will no longer be amiable or cooperative

10 Other times, other manners.
late 16th century, used in resignation or consolation

11 Semper eadem.
Latin, ever the same, motto of Elizabeth I (1533–1603)

12 There are no birds in last year's nest.
early 17th century, meaning that circumstances have changed, and former opportunities are no longer there

13 Three removals are as bad as a fire.
mid 18th century; meaning that moving house is so disruptive and unsettling, that the effects of doing it three times are as destructive as a house fire

14 Times change and we with time.
late 16th century, meaning that we adapt in response to changes in the world around us

15 Variety is the spice of life.
late 18th century, originally with allusion to Cowper: see 35 below

16 You can't put new wine in old bottles.
early 20th century, often used in relation to the introduction of new ideas or practices; from the Bible (Matthew) 'Neither do men put new wine into old bottles: else the bottles break, and the wine runneth out, and the bottles perish'; see 23 below

PHRASES

17 be subdued to what one works in become reduced in capacity or ability to the standard of one's material.
in allusion to Shakespeare Sonnets: see **Circumstance** *15*

18 change horses in midstream change one's ideas or plans in the middle of a project or process.
also in proverbial form, 'Don't change horses in midstream'

19 change one's skin undergo a change of character regarded as fundamentally impossible.
probably originally with reference to the Bible (Jeremiah): see 5 above, 25 below

20 fresh fields and pastures new new areas of activity.
from a misquotation of Milton: see 30 below

21 the law of the Medes and Persians a rule which cannot be altered in any circumstances.
from the Bible (Daniel) 'The thing is true, according to the law of the Medes and Persians, which altereth not'

22 mover and shaker a person who influences events, a person who gets things done.
see **Musicians** *7*

23 new wine in old bottles something new or innovatory added to an existing or established system or organization.
from the proverb: see 16 above

24 sea change a profound or notable transformation.
from Shakespeare's Tempest: see **The Sea** *9*

QUOTATIONS

25 Can the Ethiopian change his skin, or the leopard his spots?
Bible: Jeremiah; see 5, 19 above

26 Everything flows and nothing stays . . .
You can't step twice into the same river.
Heraclitus c.540–c.480 BC: Plato *Cratylus*

27 Times go by turns, and chances change by course,
From foul to fair, from better hap to worse.
Robert Southwell c.1561–95: 'Times go by Turns' (1595)

28 Bless thee, Bottom! bless thee! thou art translated.
William Shakespeare 1564–1616: *A Midsummer Night's Dream* (1595-6)

29 He that will not apply new remedies must expect new evils; for time is the greatest innovator.
Francis Bacon 1561–1626: *Essays* (1625) 'Of Innovations'

30 At last he rose, and twitched his mantle blue:
Tomorrow to fresh woods, and pastures new.
John Milton 1608–74: 'Lycidas' (1638); see 20 above

31 When it is not necessary to change, it is necessary not to change.
Lucius Cary, Lord Falkland 1610–43: 'A Speech concerning Episcopacy' delivered in 1641

32 The world's a scene of changes, and to be
Constant, in Nature were inconstancy.
Abraham Cowley 1618-67: 'Inconstancy' (1647)

33 Change is not made without
inconvenience, even from worse to better.
Samuel Johnson 1709-84: *A Dictionary of the
English Language* (1755)

34 If we do not find anything pleasant, at
least we shall find something new.
Voltaire 1694-1778: *Candide* (1759)

35 Variety's the very spice of life,
That gives it all its flavour.
William Cowper 1731-1800: *The Task* (1785) bk. 2
'The Timepiece'; see 15 above

36 There is a certain relief in change, even
though it be from bad to worse . . . it is
often a comfort to shift one's position and
be bruised in a new place.
Washington Irving 1783-1859: *Tales of a Traveller*
(1824)

37 A foolish consistency is the hobgoblin of
little minds, adored by little statesmen and
philosophers and divines. With consistency
a great soul has simply nothing to do.
Ralph Waldo Emerson 1803-82: *Essays* (1841) 'Self-
Reliance'

38   Forward, forward let us range,
Let the great world spin for ever down the
ringing grooves of change.
Alfred, Lord Tennyson 1809-92: 'Locksley Hall'
(1842)

39 Change and decay in all around I see;
O Thou, who changest not, abide with me.
Henry Francis Lyte 1793-1847: 'Abide with Me'
(probably written in 1847)

40 *Plus ça change, plus c'est la même chose.*
The more things change, the more they
are the same.
Alphonse Karr 1808-90: *Les Guêpes* January 1849

41 There is in all change something at once
sordid and agreeable, which smacks of
infidelity and household removals. This is
sufficient to explain the French Revolution.
Charles Baudelaire 1821-67: *Journaux intimes*
(1887) 'Mon coeur mis à nu'

42 The old order changeth, yielding place to
new,
And God fulfils himself in many ways,
Lest one good custom should corrupt the
world.
Alfred, Lord Tennyson 1809-92: *Idylls of the King*
'The Passing of Arthur' (1869)

43 All conservatism is based upon the idea
that if you leave things alone you leave
them as they are. But you do not. If you
leave a thing alone you leave it to a torrent
of change.
G. K. Chesterton 1874-1936: *Orthodoxy* (1908)

44 Most of the change we think we see in life
Is due to truths being in and out of favour.
Robert Frost 1874-1963: 'The Black Cottage' (1914)

45 I write it out in a verse—
MacDonagh and MacBride
And Connolly and Pearse
Now and in time to be,
Wherever green is worn,
Are changed, changed utterly:
A terrible beauty is born.
W. B. Yeats 1865-1939: 'Easter, 1916' (1921)

46 Consistency is contrary to nature, contrary
to life. The only completely consistent
people are the dead.
Aldous Huxley 1894-1963: *Do What You Will* (1929)

47 Toto, I've a feeling we're not in Kansas
any more.
Noel Langley 1911-   et al.: *The Wizard of Oz* (1939
film)

48 God, give us the serenity to accept what
cannot be changed;
Give us the courage to change what
should be changed;
Give us the wisdom to distinguish one from
the other.
Reinhold Niebuhr 1892-1971: prayer said to have
been first published in 1951; Richard Wightman Fox
Reinhold Niebuhr (1985)

49 If we want things to stay as they are,
things will have to change.
Giuseppe di Lampedusa 1896-1957: *The Leopard*
(1957)

50 But catastrophes only encouraged
experiment.
As a rule, it was the fittest who perished,
the mis-fits,
forced by failure to emigrate to unsettled
niches, who
altered their structure and prospered.
W. H. Auden 1907-73: 'Unpredictable but
Providential (for Loren Eiseley)' (1976)

51 I sometimes sense the world is changing
almost too fast for its inhabitants, at least
for us older ones.
Elizabeth II 1926- : on a tour of Pakistan, 8
October 1997

Chaos see Order and Chaos

Character see also Human Nature

1 An ape's an ape, a varlet's a varlet, though they be clad in silk or scarlet.
mid 16th century, meaning that inward nature cannot be overcome by outward show

2 A bad penny always turns up.
mid 18th century, referring to the inevitable return of an unwanted or disreputable person

3 Better a good cow than a cow of a good kind.
early 20th century; meaning that good character is more important than distinguished lineage

4 Character is what we are; reputation is what others think we are.
American proverb, mid 20th century

5 The child is the father of the man.
early 19th century, asserting the unity of character from childhood to adult life; from Wordsworth, see **Children** *14*

6 Eagles don't catch flies.
mid 16th century, meaning that great or important persons do not concern themselves with trifling matters

7 It takes all sorts to make a world.
early 17th century, often used in recognition that a particular group may encompass a wide range of character and background

8 Like a fence, character cannot be strengthened by whitewash.
American proverb, mid 20th century

9 The man who is born in a stable is not a horse.
mid 19th century; sometimes attributed to the Duke of Wellington, who asserted that being born in Ireland did not make him Irish

10 Once a —, always a —.
early 17th century, meaning that a particular way of life produces traits that cannot be eradicated; see **Clergy** *4*

11 Still waters run deep.
early 15th century; now commonly used to assert that a placid exterior hides a passionate nature

12 A stream cannot rise above its source.
mid 17th century; used to suggest that a person's natural level is set by their ultimate origin

13 The tree is known by its fruit.
early 16th century, meaning that a person is judged by what they do and produce

14 There's many a good cock come out of a tattered bag.
late 19th century, meaning that something good may emerge from unpromising surroundings (the reference is to cockfighting)

15 What can you expect from a pig but a grunt.
mid 18th century, used rhetorically of coarse or boorish behaviour

16 What's bred in the bone will come out in the flesh.
late 15th century, meaning that inherent characteristics will in the end become apparent

17 When the going gets tough, the tough get going.
mid 20th century, meaning that pressure acts as a stimulus to the strong; often used by Joseph Kennedy (1888–1969) as an injunction to his children

18 You cannot dream yourself into a character, you must forge one out for yourself.
American proverb, mid 20th century

19 a curate's egg something of very mixed character, partly good and partly bad.
from the Punch cartoon: see **Satisfaction** *30*

20 feet of clay fundamental weakness in a person who has appeared to be of great merit.
from the Bible (Daniel) 'This image's head was of fine gold . . . his feet part of iron and part of clay'

21 heart of oak a person with a strong, courageous nature.
literally, the solid central part of the tree; see **Armed Forces** *20*

22 Jekyll-and-Hyde someone with violent and unpredictable changes of mood and personality.
from the central character of Robert Louis Stevenson's story The Strange Case of Dr Jekyll and Mr Hyde (1886). He discovers a drug which creates a separate personality (appearing in the character of Mr Hyde) into which Jekyll's evil impulses are channelled

23 a man for all seasons a person who is ready for any situation or contingency, or adaptable to any circumstance.
from Whittington on Thomas More: see **People** *26*

24 neither fish, nor flesh, nor good red herring of indefinite character.
from distinctions made by early religious dietary laws; see **Food** *7*

25 of shreds and patches made up of rags or scraps, patched together.
from Shakespeare Hamlet *'A King of shreds and patches'; see* **Singing** *9*

QUOTATIONS

26 A man's character is his fate.
Heraclitus c.540–c.480 BC: *On the Universe*

27 He was a verray, parfit gentil knyght.
Geoffrey Chaucer c.1343–1400: *The Canterbury Tales* 'The General Prologue'

28 Nature is often hidden, sometimes overcome, seldom extinguished.
Francis Bacon 1561–1626: *Essays* (1625) 'Of Nature in Men'

29 Youth, what man's age is like to be doth show;
We may our ends by our beginnings know.
John Denham 1615–69: 'Of Prudence' (1668)

30 It is not in the still calm of life, or the repose of a pacific station, that great characters are formed . . . Great necessities call out great virtues.
Abigail Adams 1744–1818: letter to John Quincy Adams, 19 January 1780

31 Talent develops in quiet places, character in the full current of human life.
Johann Wolfgang von Goethe 1749–1832: *Torquato Tasso* (1790)

32 Qualities too elevated often unfit a man for society. We don't take ingots with us to market; we take silver or small change.
Nicolas-Sébastien Chamfort 1741–94: *Maximes et Pensées* (1796)

33 I am not at all the sort of person you and I took me for.
Jane Carlyle 1801–66: letter to Thomas Carlyle, 7 May 1822

34 Affection beaming in one eye, and calculation shining out of the other.
Charles Dickens 1812–70: *Martin Chuzzlewit* (1844)

35 The great qualities, the imperious will, the rapid energy, the eager nature fit for a great crisis are not required—are impediments—in common times.
Walter Bagehot 1826–77: *The English Constitution* (1867)

36 Though I've belted you and flayed you,
By the livin' Gawd that made you,
You're a better man than I am, Gunga Din!
Rudyard Kipling 1865–1936: 'Gunga Din' (1892)

37 A man of great common sense and good taste, meaning thereby a man without originality or moral courage.
George Bernard Shaw 1856–1950: *Notes to Caesar and Cleopatra* (1901) 'Julius Caesar'

38 McKinley has no more backbone than a chocolate éclair!
Theodore Roosevelt 1858–1919: H. T. Peck *Twenty Years of the Republic* (1906)

39 If you can trust yourself when all men doubt you,
But make allowance for their doubting too;
If you can wait and not be tired by waiting,
Or being lied about, don't deal in lies,
Or being hated, don't give way to hating,
And yet don't look too good, nor talk too wise.
Rudyard Kipling 1865–1936: 'If—' (1910)

40 Slice him where you like, a hellhound is always a hellhound.
P. G. Wodehouse 1881–1975: *The Code of the Woosters* (1938)

41 It is the nature, and the advantage, of strong people that they can bring out the crucial questions and form a clear opinion about them. The weak always have to decide between alternatives that are not their own.
Dietrich Bonhoeffer 1906–45: *Widerstand und Ergebung* (Resistance and Submission, 1951)

42 There exists a great chasm between those, on one side, who relate everything to a single central vision . . . and, on the other side, those who pursue many ends, often unrelated and even contradictory . . . The first kind of intellectual and artistic personality belongs to the hedgehogs, the second to the foxes.
Isaiah Berlin 1909–97: *The Hedgehog and the Fox* (1953); see **Knowledge** 16

43 A thick skin is a gift from God.
Konrad Adenauer 1876–1967: in *New York Times* 30 December 1959

44 Underneath this flabby exterior is an enormous lack of character.
Oscar Levant 1906–72: *Memoirs of an Amnesiac* (1965)

45 We are all worms. But I do believe that I am a glow-worm.
Winston Churchill 1874–1965: Violet Bonham-Carter *Winston Churchill as I Knew Him* (1965)

46 Fame vaporizes, money goes with the wind, and all that's left is character.
O. J. Simpson 1947– : *Juice: O. J. Simpson's Life* (1977)

47 Those who stand for nothing fall for anything.
Alex Hamilton 1936– : 'Born Old' (radio broadcast), in *Listener* 9 November 1978

48 You can tell a lot about a fellow's character by his way of eating jellybeans.
Ronald Reagan 1911– : in *New York Times* 15 January 1981

49 Claudia's the sort of person who goes through life holding on to the sides.
Alice Thomas Ellis 1932– : *The Other Side of the Fire* (1983)

50 Nice guys, when we turn nasty, can make a terrible mess of it, usually because we've had so little practice, and have bottled it up for too long.
Matthew Parris 1949– : in *The Spectator* 27 February 1993

51 If you have bright plumage, people will take pot shots at you.
Alan Clark 1928–99: in *Independent* 25 June 1994

Charity see also Gifts

PROVERBS AND SAYINGS

1 Charity begins at home.
late 14th century, meaning that you should look first to needs in your immediate vicinity

2 Charity is not a bone you throw to a dog but a bone you share with a dog.
American proverb, mid 20th century, meaning that the recipient of one's charity should not be treated as an inferior

3 Give a man a fish, and you feed him for a day; show him how to catch fish, and you feed him for a lifetime.
mid 20th century saying, perhaps deriving from the Chinese proverb Who teaches me for a day is my father for a lifetime

4 Keep your own fish-guts for your own sea-maws.
Scottish proverb, early 18th century, meaning that any surplus product should be offered first to those in need who are closest to you

5 The roots of charity are always green.
American proverb, mid 20th century, meaning that true generosity constantly renews itself

PHRASES

6 blood out of a stone pity from the hardhearted or money from the impecunious or avaricious.
see Futility 5

7 a good Samaritan a charitable or helpful person.
from the Bible (Luke) 'A certain Samaritan . . . had compassion on him', in the parable of the man who fell among thieves, in which the succouring Samaritan had been preceded by a priest and a Levite, both of whom 'passed by on the other side'; see 12, 26 below

8 ladies who lunch women who organize and take part in fashionable lunches to raise funds for charitable projects.
from 'The Ladies who Lunch', 1970 song by Stephen Sondheim (1930–) 'A toast to that invincible bunch . . . Let's hear it for the ladies who lunch'

9 a ministering angel a kind-hearted person, especially a woman, who nurses or comforts others.
originally from Shakespeare Hamlet 'A ministering angel shall my sister be, When thou liest howling'; later reinforced by Scott: see Women 29

10 a widow's mite a person's modest contribution to a cause or charity, representing the most the giver can manage
from the Bible (Mark) in the parable of the poor widow who contributed two mites (coins of low value) to the treasury, and of whom Jesus said that 'this poor widow hath cast more in, than all they which have cast into the treasury', because she 'of her want did cast in all that she had'

QUOTATIONS

11 When thou doest alms, let not thy left hand know what thy right hand doeth.
Bible: St Matthew

12 He passed by on the other side.
Bible: St Luke; see 7 above

13 Friends, I have lost a day.
on reflecting that he had done nothing to help anybody all day
Titus AD 39–81: Suetonius *Lives of the Caesars* 'Titus'

14 Thy necessity is yet greater than mine.
on giving his water-bottle to a dying soldier on the battle-field of Zutphen, 1586; commonly quoted 'thy need is greater than mine'
Philip Sidney 1554–86: Fulke Greville *Life of Sir Philip Sidney* (1652)

15 'Tis not enough to help the feeble up, But to support him after.
William Shakespeare 1564–1616: *Timon of Athens* (c.1607)

16 Defer not charities till death; for certainly, if a man weigh it rightly, he that doth so is rather liberal of another man's than of his own.
Francis Bacon 1561–1626: *Essays* (1625) 'Of Riches'

17 For Charity is cold in the multitude of possessions, and the rich are covetous of their crumbs.
Christopher Smart 1722–71: *Jubilate Agno* (c.1758–63)

18 The living need charity more than the dead.
George Arnold 1834–65: 'The Jolly Old Pedagogue' (1866)

19 Much benevolence of the passive order may be traced to a disinclination to inflict pain upon oneself.
George Meredith 1828–1909: *Vittoria* (1866)

20 People often feed the hungry so that nothing may disturb their own enjoyment of a good meal.
W. Somerset Maugham 1874–1965: *A Writer's Notebook* (1949) written in 1896

21 Without trampling down twelve others You cannot help one poor man.
Bertolt Brecht 1898–1956: *The Good Woman of Setzuan* (1938)

22 I have always depended on the kindness of strangers.
Tennessee Williams 1911–83: *A Streetcar Named Desire* (1947)

23 Keeping books on charity is capitalist nonsense! I just use the money for the poor. I can't stop to count it.
Eva Perón 1919–52: Fleur Cowles *Bloody Precedent: the Peron Story* (1952)

24 Oh I am a cat that likes to Gallop about doing good.
Stevie Smith 1902–71: 'The Galloping Cat' (1972)

25 We ourselves feel that what we are doing is just a drop in the ocean. But if that drop was not in the ocean, I think the ocean would be less because of that missing drop. I do not agree with the big way of doing things.
Mother Teresa 1910–97: *A Gift for God* (1975)

26 No one would remember the Good Samaritan if he'd only had good intentions. He had money as well.
Margaret Thatcher 1925– : television interview, 6 January 1980; see 7 above

27 Feed the world
Let them know it's Christmas time again.
Bob Geldof 1954– and **Midge Ure** 1953– : 'Do They Know it's Christmas?' (1984 song)

28 Foreign aid is a system of taking money from poor people in rich countries and giving it to rich people in poor countries.
Lord Bauer 1915– : attributed

Child Care see also **Children, The Family, Parents**

PROVERBS AND SAYINGS

1 **The art of being a parent consists of sleeping when the baby isn't looking.**
American proverb, mid 20th century

2 **Spare the rod and spoil the child.**
*early 11th century, meaning that the result of not disciplining a child is to spoil it; see **Crime** 18*

QUOTATIONS

3 Train up a child in the way he should go: and when he is old, he will not depart from it.
Bible: Proverbs

4 Diogenes struck the father when the son swore.
Robert Burton 1577–1640: *The Anatomy of Melancholy* (1621–51)

5 Who ran to help me when I fell,
And would some pretty story tell,
Or kiss the place to make it well?
My Mother.
Ann Taylor 1782–1866 and **Jane Taylor** 1783–1824: 'My Mother' (1804)

6 There never was a child so lovely but his mother was glad to get asleep.
Ralph Waldo Emerson 1803–82: *Journal* 1836

7 Her bringing me up by hand, gave her no right to bring me up by jerks.
Charles Dickens 1812–70: *Great Expectations* (1861)

8 You will find as the children grow up that as a rule children are a bitter disappointment—their greatest object being to do precisely what their parents do not wish and have anxiously tried to prevent.
Queen Victoria 1819–1901: letter to the Crown Princess of Prussia, 5 January 1876

9 If there is anything that we wish to change in the child, we should first examine it and see whether it is not something that could better be changed in ourselves.
Carl Gustav Jung 1875–1961: 'Vom Werden der Persönlichkeit' (1932)

10 Oh, what a tangled web do parents weave When they think that their children are naïve.
Ogden Nash 1902–71: 'Baby, What Makes the Sky Blue' (1940); after Scott: see **Deception** 17

11 There is no finer investment for any community than putting milk into babies.
Winston Churchill 1874–1965: radio broadcast, 21 March 1943

12 Parentage is a very important profession, but no test of fitness for it is ever imposed in the interest of the children.
George Bernard Shaw 1856–1950: *Everybody's Political What's What?* (1944)

13 If you bungle raising your children I don't think whatever else you do well matters very much.
Jacqueline Kennedy Onassis 1929–94: Theodore C. Sorenson *Kennedy* (1965)

14 The art of dealing with children might be defined as *knowing what not to say.*
A. S. Neill 1883–1973: Jonathan Croall *Neill of Summerhill: The Permanent Rebel* (1983)

15 They fuck you up, your mum and dad.
They may not mean to, but they do.
They fill you with the faults they had
And add some extra, just for you.
Philip Larkin 1922–85: 'This Be The Verse' (1974)

16 The first child is made of glass, the second porcelain, the rest of rubber, steel, and granite.
Richard J. Needham 1939– : in *Toronto Globe and Mail* 25 January 1977

17 It is only in our advanced and synthetic civilization that mothers no longer sing to the babies they are carrying.
Yehudi Menuhin 1916–99: in *Observer* 4 January 1987

18 If I'm more of an influence to your son as a rapper than you are as a father . . . you got to look at yourself as a parent.
Ice Cube 1970– : in *Rolling Stone* 4 October 1990

19 I don't work that way . . . The very idea that all children want to be cuddled by a complete stranger, I find completely amazing.
on her work for Save the Children
Anne, Princess Royal 1950– : in *Daily Telegraph* 17 January 1998

20 Quality time? There's always another load of washing.
Julian Barnes 1946– : *Love, Etc.* (2000)

Children see also **The Family, Parents, Schools, Youth**

PROVERBS AND SAYINGS

1 Children should be seen and not heard.
early 15th century, originally applied specifically to (young) women

2 Children: one is one, two is fun, three is a houseful.
American proverb, mid 20th century

3 the young idea the child's mind.
*from Thomson: see **Teaching** 8*

QUOTATIONS

4 Like as the arrows in the hand of the giant: even so are the young children. Happy is the man that hath his quiver full of them: they shall not be ashamed when they speak with their enemies in the gate.
Bible: Psalm 127

5 Suffer the little children to come unto me, and forbid them not: for of such is the kingdom of God.
Bible: St Mark

6 A child is owed the greatest respect; if you ever have something disgraceful in mind, don't ignore your son's tender years.
Juvenal AD c.60–c.130: *Satires*

7 A child is not a vase to be filled, but a fire to be lit.
François Rabelais c.1494–c.1553: attributed

8 It should be noted that children at play are not playing about; their games should be seen as their most serious-minded activity.
Montaigne 1533–92: *Essais* (1580)

9 At first the infant,
Mewling and puking in the nurse's arms.
And then the whining schoolboy, with his satchel,
And shining morning face, creeping like snail
Unwillingly to school.
William Shakespeare 1564–1616: *As You Like It* (1599)

10 Children sweeten labours, but they make misfortunes more bitter.
Francis Bacon 1561–1626: *Essays* (1625) 'Of Parents and Children'

11 Men are generally more careful of the breed of their horses and dogs than of their children.
William Penn 1644–1718: *Some Fruits of Solitude* (1693)

12 Behold the child, by Nature's kindly law
Pleased with a rattle, tickled with a straw.
Alexander Pope 1688–1744: *An Essay on Man* Epistle 2 (1733)

13 Alas, regardless of their doom,

The little victims play!
No sense have they of ills to come,
Nor care beyond to-day.
Thomas Gray 1716–71: *Ode on a Distant Prospect of Eton College* (1747)

14 The Child is father of the Man;
And I could wish my days to be
Bound each to each by natural piety.
William Wordsworth 1770–1850: 'My heart leaps up when I behold' (1807); see **Character** 5

15 You are a human boy, my young friend. A human boy. O glorious to be a human boy!
. . .
O running stream of sparkling joy
To be a soaring human boy!
Charles Dickens 1812–70: *Bleak House* (1853)

16 Go practise if you please
With men and women: leave a child alone
For Christ's particular love's sake!
Robert Browning 1812–89: *The Ring and the Book* (1868–9)

17 Oh, for an hour of Herod!
*at the first night of J. M. Barrie's Peter Pan in 1904; see **Festivals** 28*
Anthony Hope 1863–1933: Denis Mackail *The Story of JMB* (1941)

18 Childhood is the kingdom where nobody dies.
Nobody that matters, that is.
Edna St Vincent Millay 1892–1950: 'Childhood is the Kingdom where Nobody dies' (1934)

19 There is no end to the violations committed by children on children, quietly talking alone.
Elizabeth Bowen 1899–1973: *The House in Paris* (1935)

20 There is always one moment in childhood when the door opens and lets the future in.
Graham Greene 1904–91: *The Power and the Glory* (1940)

21 The summer that I was ten—
Can it be there was only one
summer that I was ten? It must
have been a long one then.
May Swenson 1919–89: 'The Centaur' (1958)

22 Childhood is measured out by sounds and smells
And sights before the dark of reason grows.
John Betjeman 1906–84: *Summoned by Bells* (1960)

23 Literature is mostly about having sex and not much about having children. Life is the other way round.
David Lodge 1935- : *The British Museum is Falling Down* (1965)

24 A child becomes an adult when he realizes that he has a right not only to be right but also to be wrong.
Thomas Szasz 1920- : *The Second Sin* (1973)

25 Childhood is Last Chance Gulch for happiness. After that, you know too much.
Tom Stoppard 1937- : *Where Are They Now?* (1973)

26 For children, childhood is timeless. It's always the present. Everything is in the present tense. Of course they have memories. Of course, time shifts a little for them and Christmas comes round in the end. But they don't *feel* it.
Ian McEwan 1948- : *The Child in Time* (1987)

27 There is no such thing as other people's children.
Hillary Rodham Clinton 1947- : in *Newsweek* 15 January 1996

28 When I look back on my childhood I wonder how I managed to survive at all. It was, of course, a miserable childhood: the happy childhood is hardly worth your while. Worse than the ordinary miserable childhood is the miserable Irish childhood, and worse yet is the miserable Irish Catholic childhood.
Frank McCourt 1930- : *Angela's Ashes* (1996)

Choice see also **Indecision**

see also **Indecision**

PROVERBS AND SAYINGS

1 **Different strokes for different folks.**
late 20th century, meaning that different ways of doing something are appropriate for different people (the saying is of US origin, and strokes *here means, 'comforting gestures of approval')*

2 **A door must be either shut or open.**
mid 18th century, said of two mutually exclusive alternatives

3 **He that has a choice has trouble.**
American proverb, mid 20th century, meaning that choosing between two things or persons may cause difficulties

4 **Horses for courses.**
late 19th century, originally (in horse-racing) meaning that different horses are suited to different race-courses; now used more generally to mean that different people are suited to different roles

5 **No man can serve two masters.**
early 14th century; see **Money** *23*

6 **The obvious choice is usually a quick regret.**
American proverb, mid 20th century, meaning that selection on outward appearance alone soon disappoints

7 **Of two evils choose the less.**
late 14th century; see 11, 24 *below*

8 **Small choice in rotten apples.**
late 16th century, meaning that if all options are unpalatable there is little choice to be had

9 **You pays your money and you takes your choice.**
mid 19th century, said when there is little or nothing to choose between two options

PHRASES

10 **Hobson's choice** the option of taking what is offered or nothing; no choice.
from Hobson (1554–1631), a Cambridge carrier who gave his customers a choice between the next horse or none at all.

11 **the lesser of two evils** the less harmful of two evil things; the alternative that has fewer drawbacks.
see 7 *above,* 24 *below*

12 **Morton's fork** a situation in which there are two choices or alternatives whose consequences are equally unpleasant.
Morton *Archbishop of Canterbury and minister of Henry VII,* Morton's fork *the argument (used by Morton to extract loans) that the obviously rich must have money and the frugal must have savings*

QUOTATIONS

13 For many are called, but few are chosen.
Bible: St Matthew

14 To be, or not to be: that is the question.
William Shakespeare 1564–1616: *Hamlet* (1601)

15 How happy could I be with either,
Were t'other dear charmer away!
John Gay 1685-1732: *The Beggar's Opera* (1728)

16 From this day you must be a stranger to one of your parents.—Your mother will never see you again if you do *not* marry Mr Collins, and I will never see you again if you *do*.

Jane Austen 1775–1817: *Pride and Prejudice* (1813)

17 What man wants is simply *independent* choice, whatever that independence may cost and wherever it may lead.

Fedor Dostoevsky 1821–81: *Notes from Underground* (1864)

18 A woman can hardly ever choose . . . she is dependent on what happens to her. She must take meaner things, because only meaner things are within her reach.

George Eliot 1819–80: *Felix Holt* (1866)

19 White shall not neutralize the black, nor good
Compensate bad in man, absolve him so:
Life's business being just the terrible choice.

Robert Browning 1812–89: *The Ring and the Book* (1868–9)

20 Any customer can have a car painted any colour that he wants so long as it is black.
on the Model T Ford, 1909

Henry Ford 1863–1947: *My Life and Work* (with Samuel Crowther, 1922)

21 Two roads diverged in a wood, and I—
I took the one less travelled by,
And that has made all the difference.

Robert Frost 1874–1963: 'The Road Not Taken' (1916)

22 If it has to choose who is to be crucified, the crowd will always save Barabbas.

Jean Cocteau 1889–1963: *Le Rappel à l'ordre* (1926)

23 Many men would take the death-sentence without a whimper to escape the life-sentence which fate carries in her other hand.

T. E. Lawrence 1888–1935: *The Mint* (1955)

24 Between two evils, I always pick the one I never tried before.

Mae West 1892–1980: *Klondike Annie* (1936 film); see 7, 11 above

25 Whose finger do you want on the trigger?
headline alluding to the atom bomb, apropos the failure of both the Labour and Conservative parties to purge their leaders of proven failures
Anonymous: in *Daily Mirror* 21 September 1951

26 If one cannot catch the bird of paradise, better take a wet hen.

Nikita Khrushchev 1894–1971: in *Time* 6 January 1958

27 Which do you want? A whipping and no turnips or turnips and no whipping?

Toni Morrison 1931– : *The Bluest Eye* (1961)

28 Chips with everything.

Arnold Wesker 1932– : title of play (1962)

29 Was there ever in anyone's life span a point free in time, devoid of memory, a night when choice was any more than the sum of all the choices gone before?

Joan Didion 1934– : *Run River* (1963)

30 I'll make him an offer he can't refuse.

Mario Puzo 1920–99: *The Godfather* (1969)

31 There is no real alternative.
popularly encapsulated in the acronym TINA
Margaret Thatcher 1925– : speech at Conservative Women's Conference, 21 May 1980

32 A compromise in the sense that being bitten in half by a shark is a compromise with being swallowed whole.

P. J. O'Rourke 1947– : *Parliament of Whores* (1991)

The Christian Church see also Clergy, God, Religion

PROVERBS AND SAYINGS

1 The blood of the martyrs is the seed of the Church.
mid 16th century, meaning that persecution causes the Church to grow; see 15 below

2 Christ has no body now on earth but yours, no hands but yours, no feet but yours, yours are the eyes through which he looks compassion on this world, yours are the feet with which he is to go about doing good.
modern saying, often attributed to St Teresa of Ávila (1512–82), but not found in her writings

3 A church is God between four walls.
American proverb, mid 20th century

4 The church is an anvil which has worn out many hammers.
mid 19th century, meaning that the passive strength of Christianity will outlast aggression

5 The nearer the church, the farther from God.
early 14th century, sometimes used to indicate a lack of true spirituality where it is most likely to be found; see 18 below

6 Meat and mass never hindered man.
early 17th century, indicating human need for physical and spiritual sustenance

7 You can't build a church with stumbling-blocks.
American proverb, mid 20th century, meaning that members of a church need to work together in fellowship

PHRASES

8 God's Acre a churchyard.
German Gottesacker 'God's seed-field' in which the bodies of the dead are 'sown'; from the Bible (I Corinthians)

9 muscular Christianity Christian life characterized by cheerful physical activity or robust good works; Christianity without asceticism.
as described in the writings of Charles Kingsley; see 27 below

10 the Old Hundredth the traditional tune to which the hymn 'All people that on earth do dwell' is sung, and the hymn itself.
the hymn (which appears first in the Geneva Psalter of 1561) is an early metrical version of Psalm 100

11 the second Adam Jesus Christ.
*from the Bible (I Corinthians) 'The first man Adam was made a living soul; the last Adam was made a quickening spirit . . . The second man is the Lord from heaven'; see **Human Nature** 5*

12 the Sermon on the Mount the discourse in the Bible (Matthew) in which teachings of Jesus, including the Lord's Prayer and the Beatitudes, are presented.
*it is introduced by the words, 'he went up into a mountain . . . and taught them, saying'; see **Science and Religion** 13*

QUOTATIONS

13 Thou art Peter, and upon this rock I will build my church; and the gates of hell shall not prevail against it.
Bible: St Matthew

14 I am the way, the truth, and the life: no man cometh unto the Father, but by me.
Bible: St John; see also **Custom** 7

15 As often as we are mown down by you, the more we grow in numbers; the blood of Christians is the seed.
Tertullian AD c.160–c.225: *Apologeticus*; see 1 above

16 He cannot have God for his father who has not the church for his mother.
St Cyprian c. AD 200–258: *De Ecclesiae Catholicae Unitate*

17 *In hoc signo vinces.*
In this sign shalt thou conquer.
traditional form of Constantine's vision of the cross (AD 312)
Constantine the Great AD c.288–337: reported in Greek 'By this, conquer'; Eusebius *Life of Constantine*

18 Take heed of thinking, *The farther you go from the church of Rome, the nearer you are to God.*
Henry Wotton 1568–1639: Izaak Walton *Reliquiae Wottonianae* (1651); see 5 above

19 The papacy is not other than the ghost of the deceased Roman Empire, sitting crowned upon the grave thereof.
Thomas Hobbes 1588–1679: *Leviathan* (1651)

20   As some to church repair,
Not for the doctrine, but the music there.
Alexander Pope 1688–1744: *An Essay on Criticism* (1711)

21 The Gospel of Christ knows of no religion but social; no holiness but social holiness.
John Wesley 1703–91: *Hymns and Sacred Poems* (1739) preface

22 The Christian religion not only was at first attended with miracles, but even at this day cannot be believed by any reasonable person without one.
David Hume 1711–76: *An Enquiry Concerning Human Understanding* (1748)

23 Christians have burnt each other, quite persuaded
That all the Apostles would have done as they did.
Lord Byron 1788–1824: *Don Juan* (1819–24)

24 He who begins by loving Christianity better than Truth will proceed by loving his own sect or church better than Christianity, and end by loving himself better than all.
Samuel Taylor Coleridge 1772–1834: *Aids to Reflection* (1825)

25 He may be one of its [the Church's] buttresses, but certainly not one of its pillars, for he is never found within it.
of John Scott, Lord Eldon (1751–1838)
Anonymous: H. Twiss *Public and Private Life of Eldon* (1844); later attributed to Lord Melbourne

26 If the Church of England were to fail, it would be found in my parish.
John Keble 1792–1866: D. Newsome *The Parting of Friends* (1966)

27 His Christianity was muscular.
Benjamin Disraeli 1804–81: *Endymion* (1880); see 9 above

28 Scratch the Christian and you find the pagan—spoiled.
Israel Zangwill 1864–1926: *Children of the Ghetto* (1892)

29 The Christian ideal has not been tried and found wanting. It has been found difficult; and left untried.
G. K. Chesterton 1874–1936: *What's Wrong with the World* (1910)

30 The sinner is at the heart of Christianity . . . No one is as competent as the sinner in matters of Christianity. No one, except a saint.
Charles Péguy 1873–1914: *Basic Verities* (1943) 'Un Nouveau théologien . . . ' (1911)

31 The Church should go forward along the path of progress and be no longer satisfied only to represent the Conservative Party at prayer.
Maude Royden 1876–1956: address at Queen's Hall, London, 16 July 1917

32 Christianity is the most materialistic of all great religions.
William Temple 1881–1944: *Readings in St John's Gospel* vol. 1 (1939)

33 Perhaps it is no wonder that the women were first at the Cradle and last at the Cross. They had never known a man like this Man—there never has been such another . . . who never made arch jokes about them, never treated them either as 'The women, God help us', or 'The ladies, God bless them!'
Dorothy L. Sayers 1893–1957: *Unpopular Opinions* (1946)

34 A serious house on serious earth it is,
In whose blent air all our compulsions meet,
Are recognised, and robed as destinies.
Philip Larkin 1922–85: 'Church Going' (1955)

35 The two dangers which beset the Church of England are good music and bad preaching.
Lord Hugh Cecil 1869–1956: K. Rose *The Later Cecils* (1975)

36 The chief contribution of Protestantism to human thought is its massive proof that God is a bore.
H. L. Mencken 1880–1956: *Minority Report* (1956)

37 I want to throw open the windows of the Church so that we can see out and the people can see in.
Pope John XXIII 1881–1963: attributed

38 You have no idea how much nastier I would be if I was not a Catholic. Without supernatural aid I would hardly be a human being.
Evelyn Waugh 1903–66: Noel Annan *Our Age* (1990)

39 The Church can no longer contain the fizzy, explosive stuff that the true wine of the bottle ought to be.
Donald Soper 1903–98: in *Methodist Recorder* 18 January 1968

40 Our cathedrals are like abandoned computers now, but they used to be prayer factories once.
Lawrence Durrell 1912–90: in *Listener* 20 April 1978

41 We are an Easter people and Alleluia is our song.
Pope John Paul II 1920– : speech in Harlem, New York, 2 October 1979

42 The Catholic Church has never really come to terms with women. What I object to is being treated either as Madonnas or Mary Magdalenes.
Shirley Williams 1930– : in *Observer* 22 March 1981

43 If you're going to do a thing, you should do it thoroughly. If you're going to be a Christian, you may as well be a Catholic.
Muriel Spark 1918– : in *Independent* 2 August 1989

44 I see it as an elderly lady, who mutters away to herself in a corner, ignored most of the time.
on the Church of England
George Carey 1935– : in *Readers Digest* (British ed.) March 1991

45 We must recall that the Church is always 'one generation away from extinction.'
George Carey 1935– : Working Party Report *Youth A Part: Young People and the Church* (1996) foreword

46 To end cruelty! That's almost apocalyptic.
I don't mind *that* definition of Christianity.
Richard Holloway 1933– : in *Independent* 18
August 2001

Christmas

PROVERBS AND SAYINGS

1 Only — shopping days to Christmas.
the imminence of Christmas expressed in commercial terms

PHRASES

2 the twelve days of Christmas the
traditional period of Christmas festivities.
from Christmas Day to the Feast of the Epiphany

3 a white Christmas Christmas with snow on
the ground.
from Irving Berlin: see 14 below

QUOTATIONS

4 For unto us a child is born, unto us a son
is given: and the government shall be
upon his shoulder: and his name shall be
called Wonderful, Counsellor, The mighty
God, The everlasting Father, The Prince of
Peace.
Bible: Isaiah

5 She brought forth her firstborn son, and
wrapped him in swaddling clothes, and
laid him in a manger; because there was
no room for them in the inn.
Bible: St Luke

6 Welcome, all wonders in one sight!
Eternity shut in a span.
Richard Crashaw c.1612–49: 'Hymn of the Nativity'
(1652)

7 I have often thought, says Sir Roger, it
happens very well that Christmas should
fall out in the Middle of Winter.
Joseph Addison 1672–1719: *The Spectator* 8 January
1712

8 'Twas the night before Christmas, when all
through the house
Not a creature was stirring, not even a
mouse;
The stockings were hung by the chimney
with care,
In hopes that St Nicholas soon would be
there.
Clement C. Moore 1779–1863: 'A Visit from St
Nicholas' (December 1823)

9 'Bah,' said Scrooge. 'Humbug!'
Charles Dickens 1812–70: *A Christmas Carol* (1843)

10 Christmas won't be Christmas without any
presents.
Louisa May Alcott 1832–88: *Little Women* (1868–9)

11 It is Christmas Day in the Workhouse.
George R. Sims 1847–1922: 'In the
Workhouse—Christmas Day' (1879)

12 Yes, Virginia, there is a Santa Claus.
*replying to a letter from eight-year-old Virginia
O'Hanlon*
Francis Pharcellus Church 1839–1906: editorial in
New York *Sun*, 21 September 1897

13 The darkness drops again but now I know
That twenty centuries of stony sleep
Were vexed to nightmare by a rocking
cradle,
And what rough beast, its hour come
round at last,
Slouches towards Bethlehem to be born?
W. B. Yeats 1865–1939: 'The Second Coming' (1921)

14 I'm dreaming of a white Christmas,
Just like the ones I used to know,
Where the tree-tops glisten
And children listen
To hear sleigh bells in the snow.
Irving Berlin 1888–1989: 'White Christmas' (1942
song); see 3 above

15 And girls in slacks remember Dad,
And oafish louts remember Mum,
And sleepless children's hearts are glad,
And Christmas-morning bells say 'Come!'
John Betjeman 1906–84: 'Christmas' (1954)

16 Still xmas is a good time with all those
presents and good food and i hope it will
never die out or at any rate not until i am
grown up and hav to pay for it all.
Geoffrey Willans 1911–58 and **Ronald Searle**
1920– : *How To Be Topp* (1954)

17 Christmas is the Disneyfication of
Christianity.
Don Cupitt 1934– : in *Independent* 19 December
1996

The Cinema see also Acting, The Theatre

1 Come with me to the Casbah.
often attributed to Charles Boyer in the film Algiers
(1938), but not found there

2 Have gun, will travel.
*supposedly characteristic statement of a hired
gunman in a western; popularized as the title of an
American television series (1957–64)*

3 Play it again, Sam.
*popular misquotation of Humphrey Bogart in
Casablanca (1942), subsequently used as the title of a
play (1969) and film (1972) by Woody Allen*

4 You dirty rat.
*frequently attributed to James Cagney in a gangster
part, but not found in this precise form in any of his
films*

5 It is like writing history with lightning.
And my only regret is that it is all so
terribly true.
on seeing D. W. Griffith's film The Birth of a Nation
Woodrow Wilson 1856–1924: at the White House,
18 February 1915

6 The lunatics have taken charge of the
asylum.
*on the take-over of United Artists by Charles Chaplin,
Mary Pickford, Douglas Fairbanks and D. W. Griffith*
Richard Rowland c.1881–1947: Terry Ramsaye *A
Million and One Nights* (1926)

7 There is only one thing that can kill the
movies, and that is education.
Will Rogers 1879–1935: *Autobiography of Will
Rogers* (1949)

*on being asked which film he would like to see while
convalescing:*
8 Anything except that damned Mouse.
George V 1865–1936: George Lyttelton letter to
Rupert Hart-Davis, 12 November 1959

9 Bring on the empty horses!
said while directing the 1936 film The Charge of the
Light Brigade
Michael Curtiz 1888–1962: David Niven *Bring on
the Empty Horses* (1975)

10 If we'd had as many soldiers as that, we'd
have won the war!
on seeing the number of Confederate troops in Gone
with the Wind *at the 1939 premiere*
Margaret Mitchell 1900–49: W. G. Harris *Gable
and Lombard* (1976)

11 If my books had been any worse, I should
not have been invited to Hollywood, and if
they had been any better, I should not
have come.
Raymond Chandler 1888–1959: letter to Charles
W. Morton, 12 December 1945

12 JOE GILLIS: You used to be in pictures. You
used to be big.
NORMA DESMOND: I am big. It's the pictures
that got small.
Charles Brackett 1892–1969, **Billy Wilder** 1906– ,
and **D.M. Marshman Jr.**: *Sunset Boulevard* (1950
film)

13 The biggest electric train set any boy ever
had!
of the RKO studios
Orson Welles 1915–85: Peter Noble *The Fabulous
Orson Welles* (1956)

14 If I made Cinderella, the audience would
immediately be looking for a body in the
coach.
Alfred Hitchcock 1899–1980: in *Newsweek* 11 June
1956

15 Why should people go out and pay to see
bad movies when they can stay at home
and see bad television for nothing?
Sam Goldwyn 1882–1974: in *Observer* 9 September
1956

16 Above all, he taught us how to photograph
thought, not only by bringing the camera
close to a player's eyes, but by such
devices, novel and daring in their time, as
focusing it on a pair of hands clasped in
anguish or on some symbolic object that
mirrored what was in the player's mind.
of D. W. Griffith
Cecil B. de Mille 1881–1959: *The Autobiography of
Cecil B. DeMille* (1959)

17 Photography is truth. The cinema is truth
24 times per second.
Jean-Luc Godard 1930– : *Le Petit Soldat* (1960 film)

18 All I need to make a comedy is a park, a
policeman and a pretty girl.
Charlie Chaplin 1889–1977: *My Autobiography*
(1964)

19 The words 'Kiss Kiss Bang Bang' which I
saw on an Italian movie poster, are

perhaps the briefest statement imaginable of the basic appeal of movies.

Pauline Kael 1919– : *Kiss Kiss Bang Bang* (1968)

20 Pictures are for entertainment, messages should be delivered by Western Union.

Sam Goldwyn 1882–1974: Arthur Marx *Goldwyn* (1976)

21 [The camera] is so refined that it makes it possible for us to shed light on the human soul, to reveal it the more brutally and thereby add to our knowledge new dimensions of the 'real'.

Ingmar Bergman 1918– : in *New York Times* 22 January 1978

22 GEORGES FRANJU: Movies should have a beginning, a middle and an end.

JEAN-LUC GODARD: Certainly. But not necessarily in that order.

Jean-Luc Godard 1930– : in *Time* 14 September 1981

23 There are no rules in filmmaking. Only sins. And the cardinal sin is dullness.

Frank Capra 1897–1991: in *People* 16 September 1991

24 Sexuality is such a part of life, but sexuality in the movies—I have a hard time finding it.

Catherine Deneuve 1943– : in *Première* April 1993

25 If you gave him a good script, actors and technicians, Mickey Mouse could direct a movie.

Nicholas Hytner 1956– : in *Daily Telegraph* 24 February 1994

Circumstance and Situation

PROVERBS AND SAYINGS

1 **Circumstances alter cases.**

late 17th century, meaning that a general principle may be modified in the light of particular circumstances

2 **New circumstances, new controls.**

American proverb, mid 20th century

3 **One man's loss is another man's gain.**

early 16th century, often said by the gainer in self-congratulation

4 **There's a time and place for everything.**

early 16th century; often used as a warning against doing or saying something at a particular time or in a particular situation

5 **There's no great loss without some gain.**

mid 17th century, said in consolation or resignation

6 **The wheel has come full circle.**

the situation has returned to what it was in the past, as if completing a cycle, with reference to Shakespeare's King Lear 'The wheel is come full circle'; see Chance 18

PHRASES

7 **catch-22** a dilemma or difficult circumstance from which there is no escape because of mutually conflicting or dependent conditions.

from Joseph Heller's novel: see Madness 13

8 **on the horns of a dilemma** faced with a decision involving equally unfavourable alternatives.

dilemma in Rhetoric, a form of argument involving an adversary in the choice of two alternatives (the horns'), either of which is or appears to be equally unfavourable

9 **the plot thickens** the situation becomes more difficult and complex.

from George Villiers The Rehearsal (1671): see Theatre 8

10 **a square peg in a round hole** a person in a situation unsuited to his or her capacities or disposition, a misfit.

see 18 below

11 **swings and roundabouts** a state of affairs in which different actions result in no eventual gain or loss.

from the saying: see Winning 3

QUOTATIONS

12 Every honourable action has its proper time and season, or rather it is this propriety or observance which distinguishes an honourable action from its opposite.

Agesilaus 444–360 BC: Plutarch *Lives* 'Agesilaus'

13 But for the grace of God there goes John Bradford.

on seeing a group of criminals being led to their

execution; usually quoted as, 'There but for the grace of God go I'
John Bradford c.1510–55: in *Dictionary of National Biography* (1917–)

14 The time is out of joint; O cursèd spite,
That ever I was born to set it right!
William Shakespeare 1564–1616: *Hamlet* (1601)

15   My nature is subdued
To what it works in, like the dyer's hand.
William Shakespeare 1564–1616: sonnet 111; see **Change** 17

16 And, spite of Pride, in erring Reason's spite,
One truth is clear, 'Whatever IS, is RIGHT.'
Alexander Pope 1688–1744: *An Essay on Man* Epistle 1 (1733)

17 *No se puede mirar.*
One cannot look at this.
Goya 1746–1828: *The Disasters of War* (1863) title of etching

18 We shall generally find that the triangular person has got into the square hole, the oblong into the triangular, and a square person has squeezed himself into the round hole. The officer and the office, the doer and the thing done, seldom fit so exactly that we can say they were almost made for each other.
Sydney Smith 1771–1845: *Sketches of Moral Philosophy* (1849); see 10 above

19 For of all sad words of tongue or pen,
The saddest are these: 'It might have been!'
John Greenleaf Whittier 1807–92: 'Maud Muller' (1854); see 21 below

20 It was the best of times, it was the worst of times, it was the age of wisdom, it was the age of foolishness, it was the epoch of belief, it was the epoch of incredulity, it was the season of Light, it was the season of Darkness, it was the spring of hope, it was the winter of despair, we had everything before us, we had nothing before us, we were all going direct to Heaven, we were all going direct the other way.
Charles Dickens 1812–70: *A Tale of Two Cities* (1859)

21 If, of all words of tongue and pen,
The saddest are, 'It might have been,'
More sad are these we daily see:
'It is, but hadn't ought to be!'
Bret Harte 1836–1902: 'Mrs Judge Jenkins' (1867); see 19 above

22 We are so made, that we can only derive intense enjoyment from a contrast, and only very little from a state of things.
Sigmund Freud 1856–1939: *Civilization and its Discontents* (1930)

23 I love to feel events overlapping each other, crawling over one another like wet crabs in a basket.
Lawrence Durrell 1912–90: *Balthazar* (1958)

24 People should be taught what is, not what should be. All my humour is based on destruction and despair. If the whole world were tranquil, without disease and violence, I'd be standing in the breadline.
Lenny Bruce 1925–66: *The Essential Lenny Bruce* (1967)

25 Anyone who isn't confused doesn't really understand the situation.
on the Vietnam War
Ed Murrow 1908–65: Walter Bryan *The Improbable Irish* (1969)

26 The whole world seemed so unequal, so unfair. Some people were created with all the good things ready-made for them, others were just created like mistakes. God's mistakes.
Buchi Emecheta 1944– : *Second-Class Citizen* (1974)

Cities see Towns and Cities

Civilization see Culture and Civilization

Class see also Capitalism and Communism, Rank and Title

PROVERBS AND SAYINGS

1 **It takes three generations to make a gentleman.**

early 19th century; the idea that it took three generations before the possession of wealth conferred the status of gentleman occurs from the late 16th century

2 When Adam delved and Eve span, who was then the gentleman?
traditional rhyme from Richard Rolle (see 8 below), taken in this form by John Ball as the text of his revolutionary sermon on the outbreak of the Peasants' Revolt, 1381

PHRASES

3 Essex man derogatory term for a type of British Conservative voter in the late 1980s.
associated particularly with the county of Essex, and characterized as a brash, amoral, self-made young businessman, of right-wing views and few or no cultural or intellectual interests, devoted to the acquisition of goods and material wealth; see **Women** *10*

4 the gentlemen and the players
distinguishing between the amateur (gentlemen) and professional (players) players of cricket, and hence other sports.
figuratively, a player means a lower-class person

5 Islington person a middle-class, socially aware person with left-wing views.
characteristics supposedly typical of Islington residents, seen as a typical supporter of New Labour who, while rejecting the brash self-interest of Essex man, is nevertheless similarly insulated by material wealth from the harshest pressures of modern society

6 the many-headed monster an archaic term for the people, the populace.
after Horace Epistles *'The people are a many-headed beast'; see* **Theatre** *10*

7 Sloane Ranger a fashionable and conventional upper-class young woman, especially one living in London.
a play on Sloane Square, *London, and* Lone Ranger, *a fictitious cowboy hero; coined in 1975 in the magazine* Harpers & Queen

QUOTATIONS

8 When Adam dalfe and Eve spane
Go spire if thou may spede,
Where was than the pride of man
That now merres his mede?
Richard Rolle de Hampole *c.*1290–1349: G. G. Perry *Religious Pieces* (1914); see 2 above

9 I must have the gentleman to haul and draw with the mariner, and the mariner with the gentleman . . . I would know him, that would refuse to set his hand to a rope, but I know there is not any such here.
Francis Drake *c.*1540–96: J. S. Corbett *Drake and the Tudor Navy* (1898)

10 That in the captain's but a choleric word,
Which in the soldier is flat blasphemy.
William Shakespeare 1564–1616: *Measure for Measure* (1604)

11 He told me . . . that mine was the middle state, or what might be called the upper station of low life, which he had found by long experience was the best state in the world, the most suited to human happiness.
Daniel Defoe 1660–1731: *Robinson Crusoe* (1719)

12 O let us love our occupations,
Bless the squire and his relations,
Live upon our daily rations,
And always know our proper stations.
Charles Dickens 1812–70: *The Chimes* (1844) 'The Second Quarter'

13 The proletarians have nothing to lose but their chains. They have a world to win.
WORKING MEN OF ALL COUNTRIES, UNITE!
commonly rendered as 'Workers of the world, unite!'
Karl Marx 1818–83 and **Friedrich Engels** 1820–95: *The Communist Manifesto* (1848); see 25 below

14 The rich man in his castle,
The poor man at his gate,
God made them, high or lowly,
And ordered their estate.
Cecil Frances Alexander 1818–95: 'All Things Bright and Beautiful' (1848)

15 *Il faut épater le bourgeois.*
One must astonish the bourgeois.
Charles Baudelaire 1821–67: attributed; also attributed to Privat d'Anglemont (*c.*1820–59) in the form '*Je les ai épatés, les bourgeois* [I flabbergasted them, the bourgeois]'

16 The so called immorality of the lower classes is not to be named on the same day with that of the higher and highest. This is a thing which makes my blood boil, and they will pay for it.
Queen Victoria 1819–1901: letter to the Crown Princess of Prussia, 26 June 1872

17 All the world over, I will back the masses against the classes.
W. E. Gladstone 1809–98: speech in Liverpool, 28 June 1886

18 The bourgeois are other people.
Jules Renard 1864–1910: diary, 28 January 1890

19 Bourgeois . . . is an epithet which the riff-raff apply to what is respectable, and the aristocracy to what is decent.
Anthony Hope 1863–1933: *The Dolly Dialogues* (1894)

20 You may tempt the upper classes
With your villainous demi-tasses,
But; Heaven will protect a working-girl!
Edgar Smith 1857–1938: 'Heaven Will Protect the Working-Girl' (1909 song)

21 Dear me, I never knew that the lower classes had such white skins.

supposedly said when watching troops bathing during the First World War

Lord Curzon 1859–1925: K. Rose *Superior Person* (1969)

22 The bourgeois prefers comfort to pleasure, convenience to liberty, and a pleasant temperature to the deathly inner consuming fire.
Hermann Hesse 1877–1962: *Der Steppenwolf* (1927)

23 Civilization has made the peasantry its pack animal. The bourgeoisie in the long run only changed the form of the pack.
Leon Trotsky 1879–1940: *History of the Russian Revolution* (1933)

24 Finer things are for the finer folk
Thus society began
Caviar for peasants is a joke
It's too good for the average man.
Lorenz Hart 1895–1943: 'Too Good for the Average Man' (1936)

25 We of the sinking middle class . . . may sink without further struggles into the working class where we belong, and probably when we get there it will not be so dreadful as we feared, for, after all, we have nothing to lose but our aitches.
George Orwell 1903–50: *The Road to Wigan Pier* (1937); see 13 above

26 Ladies were ladies in those days; they did not do things themselves.
Gwen Raverat 1885–1957: *Period Piece* (1952)

27 Impotence and sodomy are socially O.K. but birth control is flagrantly middle-class.
Evelyn Waugh 1903–66: 'An Open Letter' in Nancy Mitford (ed.) *Noblesse Oblige* (1956)

28 I can't help feeling wary when I hear anything said about the masses. First you take their faces from 'em by calling 'em the masses and then you accuse 'em of not having any faces.
J. B. Priestley 1894–1984: *Saturn Over the Water* (1961)

29 Will the people in the cheaper seats clap your hands? All the rest of you, if you'll just rattle your jewellery.
John Lennon 1940–80: at the Royal Variety Performance, 4 November 1963

30 Edith Evans was savage as Lady Bracknell. You see, she came from a family of servants whom the Lady Bracknells of this world rang for to put a lump of coal on the fire. Her performance was pure revenge.
John Gielgud 1904–2000: John Mortimer *In Character* (1984)

31 The real solvent of class distinction is a proper measure of self-esteem—a kind of unselfconsciousness. Some people are at ease with themselves, so the world is at ease with them. My parents thought this kind of ease was produced by education . . . they didn't see that what disqualified them was temperament—just as, though educated up to the hilt, it disqualifies me. What keeps us in our place is embarrassment.
Alan Bennett 1934– : *Dinner at Noon* (BBC television, 1988)

32 The worst fault of the working classes is telling their children they're not going to succeed, saying: 'There is life, but it's not for you.'
John Mortimer 1923– : in *Daily Mail* 31 May 1988

33 I was born in the real world, not with a silver spoon in my mouth. If you plant a rose in the best soil it'll grow whatever you do. It's a lot harder growing in concrete, understand what I'm saying?
Vinnie Jones 1965– : in *Radio Times* 8 July 2000; see **Wealth** 8

Clergy see also The Christian Church

PROVERBS AND SAYINGS

1 Clergymen's sons always turn out badly.

late 19th century; the implication is that the weight of expectation on clergyman's children is often in itself damaging

2 Like people, like priest.

late 16th century; from the Bible (Hosea) 'And there shall be like people, like priest'

3 Nobody is born learned; bishops are made of men.
American proverb, mid 20th century

4 Once a priest, always a priest.
mid 19th century; see **Character** 10

see **Character** 10

PHRASES

5 benefit of clergy historically, exemption from ordinary courts of law because of membership of the clergy or (later) literacy or scholarship; exemption from the sentence for certain first offences because of literacy.
see **Appearance** 16

QUOTATIONS

6 A bishop then must be blameless, the husband of one wife, vigilant, sober, of good behaviour, given to hospitality, apt to teach;
Not given to wine, no striker, not greedy of filthy lucre; but patient, not a brawler, not covetous.
Bible: I Timothy; see **Money** 16

7 In old time we had treen chalices and golden priests, but now we have treen priests and golden chalices.
John Jewel 1522–71: *Certain Sermons Preached Before the Queen's Majesty* (1609)

8 A single life doth well with churchmen, for charity will hardly water the ground where it must first fill a pool.
Francis Bacon 1561–1626: *Essays* (1625) 'Of Marriage and the Single Life'

9 New *Presbyter* is but old *Priest* writ large.
John Milton 1608–74: 'On the New Forcers of Conscience under the Long Parliament' (1646)

10 And of all plagues with which mankind are curst,
Ecclesiastic tyranny's the worst.
Daniel Defoe 1660–1731: *The True-Born Englishman* (1701)

11 I look upon all the world as my parish.
John Wesley 1703–91: *Journal* 11 June 1739

12 In all ages of the world, priests have been enemies of liberty.
David Hume 1711–76: *Essays, Moral, Political, and Literary* (1875) 'Of the Parties of Great Britain' (1741–2)

13 They seem to know no medium between a mitre and a crown of martyrdom. If the clergy are not called to the latter, they

never deviate from the pursuit of the former. One would think their motto was, *Canterbury or Smithfield*.
Horace Walpole 1717–97: *Memoirs of the Reign of King George II* (1758)

14 I never saw, heard, nor read, that the clergy were beloved in any nation where Christianity was the religion of the country. Nothing can render them popular, but some degree of persecution.
Jonathan Swift 1667–1745: *Thoughts on Religion* (1765)

15 Men may call me a knave or a fool, a rascal, a scoundrel, and I am content; but they shall never by my consent call me a Bishop!
John Wesley 1703–91: Betty M. Jarboe *Wesley Quotations* (1990)

16 A Curate—there is something which excites compassion in the very name of a Curate!!!
Sydney Smith 1771–1845: 'Persecuting Bishops' in *Edinburgh Review* (1822)

17 *Merit*, indeed! . . . We are come to a pretty pass if they talk of *merit* for a bishopric.
John Fane, Lord Westmorland 1759–1841: Lady Salisbury's diary, 9 December 1835

18 As the French say, there are three sexes—men, women, and clergymen.
Sydney Smith 1771–1845: Lady Holland *Memoir* (1855)

19 How can a bishop marry? How can he flirt? The most he can say is, 'I will see you in the vestry after service.'
Sydney Smith 1771–1845: Lady Holland *Memoir* (1855)

20 Pray remember, Mr Dean, no dogma, no Dean.
Benjamin Disraeli 1804–81: W. Monypenny and G. Buckle *Life of Benjamin Disraeli* vol. 4 (1916)

21 I wouldn't take the Pope too seriously. He's a Pole first, a pope second, and maybe a Christian third.
Muriel Spark 1918– : in *International Herald Tribune* 29 May 1989

22 People have described me as a 'management bishop' but I say to my critics, 'Jesus was a management expert too.'
George Carey 1935– : in *Observer* 3 March 1991

23 Pastors need to start where people are and not where we think they should be.
Basil Hume 1923–99: in *Independent* 18 June 1999

Communism see **Capitalism and Communism**

Computers and the Internet

1 Do not fold, spindle or mutilate.
instruction on punched cards (1950s, and in differing forms from the 1930s)

2 Garbage in, garbage out.
mid 20th century; in computing, incorrect or faulty input will always cause poor output; see 9 below

3 It's not a bug, it's a feature.
late 20th century saying; bug an error in a computer program or system

4 No manager ever got fired for buying IBM.
IBM advertising slogan

5 To err is human but to really foul things up requires a computer.
*late 20th century saying; see **Mistakes** 5*

6 Moore's law the principle that a new type of microprocessor chip is released every 12 to 24 months, with each new version having approximately twice as many logical elements as its predecessor, and that this trend is likely to continue, resulting in an exponential rise in computing power per chip over a period of time.
an observation and prediction originally made in 1965 by Gordon Earle Moore (1929–)

7 Trojan horse a computing program that breaches the security of a computer system, especially by ostensibly functioning as part of a legitimate program, in order to erase, corrupt, or remove data.
*a hollow wooden statue of a horse in which the Greeks are said to have concealed themselves to enter Troy; see **Trust and Treachery** 15*

8 The Analytical Engine weaves algebraic patterns just as the Jacquard loom weaves flowers and leaves.
of Babbage's mechanical computer
Ada Lovelace 1815–52: Luigi Menabrea *Sketch of the Analytical Engine invented by Charles Babbage* (1843), translated and annotated by Ada Lovelace, Note A

9 His patience in explaining his machine in those days was really exemplary . . . A lady, to whom he had sacrificed some very precious time, on the supposition that she understood as much as she assumed to do, finished by saying, 'Now, Mr Babbage, there is only one thing that I want to know. If you put the question in wrong, will the answer come out right?'
of Charles Babbage (1791–1871), inventor of the mechanical computer; see 2 above
Harriet Martineau 1802–76: *Autobiography* (1877)

10 We used to have lots of questions to which there were no answers. Now with the computer there are lots of answers to which we haven't thought up the questions.
Peter Ustinov 1921– : in *Illustrated London News* 1 June 1968

11 Computers are composed of nothing more than logic gates stretched out to the horizon in a vast numerical irrigation system.
Stan Augarten: *State of the Art: A Photographic History of the Integrated Circuit* (1983)

12 A modern computer hovers between the obsolescent and the nonexistent.
Sydney Brenner 1927– : attributed in *Science* 5 January 1990

13 Computers are anti-Faraday machines. He said he couldn't understand anything until he could count it, while computers count everything and understand nothing.
Ralph Cornes: in *Guardian* 28 March 1991

14 The PC is the LSD of the '90s.
Timothy Leary 1920–96: remark made in the early 1990s; in *Guardian* 1 June 1996

15 On the Internet, nobody knows you're a dog.
Peter Steiner 1940– : cartoon caption in *New Yorker* 5 July 1993

16 The Internet is an elite organisation; most of the population of the world has never even made a phone call.
Noam Chomsky 1928– : in *Observer* 18 February 1996

17 We've all heard that a million monkeys banging on a million typewriters will eventually reproduce the entire works of Shakespeare. Now, thanks to the Internet, we know this is not true.
Robert Wilensky 1951– : in *Mail on Sunday* 16 February 1997; see **Chance** 32

18 Think what we would have missed if we had never . . . used a mobile phone or surfed the Net—or, to be honest, listened to other people talking about surfing the Net.
reflecting on developments in the past 50 years
Elizabeth II 1926– : in *Daily Telegraph* 21 November 1997

19 The symbol of the atomic age, which tended to centralise power, was a nucleus with electrons held in tight orbit; the symbol of the digital age is the Web, with countless centres of power all equally networked.
Walter Isaacson 1952– : in *Time* 29 December 1997

20 The Web is a tremendous grassroots revolution. All these people coming from very different directions achieved a change. There's a tremendous message of hope for humanity in that.
Tim Berners-Lee 1955– : in *Independent* 17 May 1999

21 Silicon Valley is the Florence of the late 20th century.
Francis Fukuyama 1952– : in *Independent* 19 June 1999

22 [The Internet is] a whining Californian mall rat, forever demanding that the real world be redefined to suit its whims.
Terry Pratchett 1948– : in *Bookseller* 15 September 2000

Conformity

PROVERBS AND SAYINGS

1 **Obey orders, if you break owners.**
late 18th century; the saying is nautical, and means that orders should be followed even if it is clear that they are wrong

PHRASES

2 **be all things to all men** be able to please everybody.
originally probably in allusion to the Bible (I Corinthians) 'I am made all things to all men'

3 **marching to a different drum** conforming to different principles and practices from those around one.
ultimately from Thoreau: see 8 below

QUOTATIONS

4 While we were talking came by several poor creatures carried by, by constables, for being at a conventicle . . . I would to God they would either conform, or be more wise, and not be catched!
Samuel Pepys 1633–1703: diary 7 August 1664

5 'It's always best on these occasions to do what the mob do.' 'But suppose there are two mobs?' suggested Mr Snodgrass. 'Shout with the largest,' replied Mr Pickwick.
Charles Dickens 1812–70: *Pickwick Papers* (1837)

6 Whoso would be a man must be a nonconformist.
Ralph Waldo Emerson 1803–82: *Essays* (1841) 'Self-Reliance'

7 Teach him to think for himself? Oh, my God, teach him rather to think like other people!
on her son's education
Mary Shelley 1797–1851: Matthew Arnold *Essays in Criticism* Second Series (1888) 'Shelley'

8 If a man does not keep pace with his companions, perhaps it is because he hears a different drummer. Let him step to the music which he hears, however measured or far away.
Henry David Thoreau 1817–62: *Walden* (1854); see 3 above

9 You cannot make a man by standing a sheep on its hind-legs. But by standing a flock of sheep in that position you can make a crowd of men.
Max Beerbohm 1872–1956: *Zuleika Dobson* (1911)

10 Imitation lies at the root of most human actions. A respectable person is one who conforms to custom. People are called good when they do as others do.
Anatole France 1844–1924: *Crainquebille* (1923)

11 The Party line is that there is no Party line.
Milovan Djilas 1911– : comment on reforms of the
Yugoslavian Communist Party, November 1952;
Fitzroy Maclean *Disputed Barricade* (1957)

12 These are the days when men of all social
disciplines and all political faiths seek the
comfortable and the accepted; when the
man of controversy is looked upon as a
disturbing influence; when originality is
taken to be a mark of instability; and
when, in minor modification of the
scriptural parable, the bland lead the
bland.
J. K. Galbraith 1908– : *The Affluent Society* (1958);
see **Leadership** 6

13 Never forget that only dead fish swim with
the stream.
Malcolm Muggeridge 1903–90: quoting a
supporter; in *Radio Times* 9 July 1964

14 Her exotic daydreams do not prevent her
from being small-town bourgeois at heart,
clinging to conventional ideas or
committing this or that conventional
violation of the conventional, adultery
being a most conventional way to rise
above the conventional.
Vladimir Nabokov 1899–1977: *Lectures on
Literature* (1980) 'Madame Bovary'

15 The Normal is the good smile in a child's
eyes—all right. It is also the dead stare in a
million adults. It both sustains and kills—
like a God. It is the Ordinary made
beautiful; it is also the Average made
lethal.
Peter Shaffer 1926– : *Equus* (1983 ed.)

16 To be like everyone else. Isn't that what
we all want in the end?
Carol Shields 1935– : *Larry's Party* (1997)

17 My parents were convinced that I would
one day become Mr Average, but almost
30 years on I am still an A1 freak.
Boy George 1961– : in *Independent on Sunday* 28
March 1999

Conscience see also **Forgiveness and Repentance**, **Sin**

PROVERBS AND SAYINGS

1 **Conscience gets a lot of credit that belongs
to cold feet.**
American proverb, mid 20th century

2 **Do right and fear no man.**
mid 15th century

3 **Evil doers are evil dreaders.**
*mid 16th century, meaning that someone engaged in
wrongdoing is likely to be nervous and suspicious of
others*

4 **A guilty conscience needs no accuser.**
*late 14th century, meaning that awareness of one's
own guilt has the same effect as an accusation*

5 **Let your conscience be your guide.**
American proverb, mid 20th century

6 **A quiet conscience sleeps in thunder.**
*late 16th century, meaning that someone with an
untroubled conscience will sleep undisturbed whatever
the noise*

PHRASES

7 **agenbite of inwit** remorse.
*used as a conscious archaism derived from James
Joyce's Ulysses; see 16 below*

8 **prick of conscience** compunction, remorse,
guilt.
*used as the title of a devotional treatise by the English
mystic Richard Rolle of Hampole (c.1290–1349)*

QUOTATIONS

9 Then I, however, showed again, by action,
not in word only, that I did not care a whit
for death . . . but that I did care with all
my might not to do anything unjust or
unholy.
*on being ordered by the Thirty Commissioners to take
part in the liquidation of Leon of Salamis*
Socrates 469–399 BC: Plato *Apology*

10 *O dignitosa coscienza e netta,
Come t'è picciol fallo amaro morso!*
O pure and noble conscience, how bitter a
sting to thee is a little fault!
Dante 1265–1321: *Divina Commedia* 'Purgatorio'

11 Every subject's duty is the king's; but
every subject's soul is his own.
William Shakespeare 1564–1616: *Henry V* (1599)

12 Thus conscience doth make cowards of us
all.
William Shakespeare 1564–1616: *Hamlet* (1601)

13 If I am obliged to bring religion into after-dinner toasts (which indeed does not seem quite the thing) I shall drink—to the Pope, if you please—still, to Conscience first, and to the Pope afterwards.
John Henry Newman 1801–90: *A Letter Addressed to the Duke of Norfolk . . .* (1875)

14 Conscience is thoroughly well-bred and soon leaves off talking to those who do not wish to hear it.
Samuel Butler 1835–1902: *Further Extracts from Notebooks* (1934)

15 Conscience: the inner voice which warns us that someone may be looking.
H. L. Mencken 1880–1956: *A Little Book in C major* (1916)

16 They wash and tub and scrub. Agenbite of inwit. Conscience.
James Joyce 1882–1941: *Ulysses* (1922); see 7 above

17 Most people sell their souls, and live with a good conscience on the proceeds.
Logan Pearsall Smith 1865–1946: *Afterthoughts* (1931)

18 Sufficient conscience to bother him, but not sufficient to keep him straight.
of Ramsay MacDonald
David Lloyd George 1863–1945: A. J. Sylvester *Life with Lloyd George* (1975)

19 I cannot and will not cut my conscience to fit this year's fashions.
Lillian Hellman 1905–84: letter to John S. Wood, 19 May 1952

Consequences see **Causes and Consequences**

Consolation see **Sympathy and Consolation**

Constancy and Inconstancy

PROVERBS AND SAYINGS

1 **Love me little, love me long.**
early 16th century, meaning that love of great intensity is unlikely to last

2 **Quickly come, quickly go.**
late 16th century

3 **A rolling stone gathers no moss.**
mid 14th century, used to imply that someone who does not settle down will not prosper, or form lasting ties

PHRASES

4 **true as Troilus** completely devoted.
alluding to Shakespeare Troilus and Cressida ' "As true as Troilus" shall crown up the verse'

QUOTATIONS

5 My true love hath my heart and I have his,
By just exchange one for the other giv'n;
I hold his dear, and mine he cannot miss,
There never was a better bargain driv'n.
Philip Sidney 1554–86: *Arcadia* (1581)

6 If I could pray to move, prayers would move me;
But I am constant as the northern star,
Of whose true-fixed and resting quality
There is no fellow in the firmament.
William Shakespeare 1564–1616: *Julius Caesar* (1599)

7   Why, I hold fate
Clasped in my fist, and could command the course
Of time's eternal motion, hadst thou been
One thought more steady than an ebbing sea.
John Ford 1586–after 1639: *'Tis Pity She's a Whore* (1633)

8 I loved thee once. I'll love no more,
Thine be the grief, as is the blame;
Thou art not what thou wast before,
What reason I should be the same?
Robert Aytoun 1570–1638: 'To an Inconstant Mistress'

9 Tell me no more of constancy,
that frivolous pretence,
Of cold age, narrow jealousy,
disease and want of sense.
John Wilmot, Lord Rochester 1647–80: 'Against Constancy' (1676)

10 An inconstant woman, tho' she has no chance to be very happy, can never be very unhappy.
John Gay 1685–1732: 'Polly' (1729)

11 No, the heart that has truly loved never
     forgets,
   But as truly loves on to the close,
   As the sunflower turns on her god, when
     he sets,
   The same look which she turned when he
     rose.
   Thomas Moore 1779–1852: 'Believe me, if all those
   endearing young charms' (1807)

12 Bright star, would I were steadfast as thou
     art—.
   John Keats 1795–1821: 'Bright star, would I were
   steadfast as thou art' (written 1819)

13 There is no infidelity when there has been
   no love.
   Honoré de Balzac 1799–1850: letter to Mme
   Hanska, August 1833; in *The Penguin Book of
   Infidelities* (1994)

14 'Yes,' I answered you last night;
   'No,' this morning, sir, I say.
   Colours seen by candlelight
   Will not look the same by day.
   Elizabeth Barrett Browning 1806–61: 'The Lady's
   Yes' (1844)

15 The shackles of an old love straitened him,
   His honour rooted in dishonour stood,
   And faith unfaithful kept him falsely true.
   Alfred, Lord Tennyson 1809–92: *Idylls of the King*
   'Lancelot and Elaine' (1859)

16 But I was desolate and sick of an old
     passion,
   Yea, all the time, because the dance was
     long:
   I have been faithful to thee, Cynara! in my
     fashion.
   Ernest Dowson 1867–1900: 'Non Sum Qualis Eram'
   (1896); also known as 'Cynara'; see 18 below;
   Memory 17

17 Sexual fidelity is more important in a
   homosexual relationship than in any
   other. In other relationships there are a
   variety of ties. But here, fidelity is the only
   bond.
   W. H. Auden 1907–73: Nicholas Jenkins (ed.) *Table
   Talk of W. H. Auden* (1990) 20 October 1947

18 But I'm always true to you, darlin', in my
     fashion.
   Yes I'm always true to you, darlin', in my
     way.
   Cole Porter 1891–1964: 'Always True to You in my
   Fashion' (1949 song); see 16 above

19 Your idea of fidelity is not having more
   than one man in bed at the same time.
   Frederic Raphael 1931– : *Darling* (1965)

20 You're . . . turning into a kind of serial
   monogamist.
   Richard Curtis 1956– : *Four Weddings and a Funeral*
   (1994 film)

Conversation see also **Gossip, Speech, Speeches**

PROVERBS AND SAYINGS

1 **It's good to talk.**
  advertising slogan for British Telecom, from 1994

PHRASES

2 **feast of reason** intellectual discussion.
  *from Pope 'The feast of reason and the flow of soul';
  see 3 below*

3 **flow of soul** genial conversation, as
  complementary to intellectual discussion.
  from Pope: see 2 above

4 **glittering generalities** platitudes, clichés,
  superficially convincing but empty
  phrases.
  *see **Human Rights** 10*

QUOTATIONS

5 I am not bound to please thee with my
  answer.
  William Shakespeare 1564–1616: *The Merchant of
  Venice* (1596–8)

6 Whilst he was cautious of his own words,
  (not putting forth too many, lest they
  should betray his thoughts) he made
  others talk until he had, as it were, sifted
  them, and known their most intimate
  designs.
  of Oliver Cromwell
  William Waller 1598–1668: Christopher Hill *God's
  Englishman* (1970)

7 JOHNSON: Well, we had a good talk.
  BOSWELL: Yes, Sir; you tossed and gored
    several persons.
  James Boswell 1740–95: *Life of Samuel Johnson*
  (1791) Summer 1768

8 Religion is by no means a proper subject of conversation in a mixed company.
Lord Chesterfield 1694-1773: *Letters . . . to his Godson and Successor* (1890) Letter 142

9 Questioning is not the mode of conversation among gentlemen. It is assuming a superiority.
Samuel Johnson 1709-84: James Boswell *Life of Samuel Johnson* (1791) 25 March 1776

10 He seems to have the particular talent of knowing more about what he is saying and with less pains than anybody else—his conversation is like a brilliant player of billiards, the strokes follow one another, piff, paff.
Georgiana, Duchess of Devonshire 1757-1806: E. Lascelles *Charles James Fox* (1936)

11 He talked on for ever; and you wished him to talk on for ever.
of Coleridge
William Hazlitt 1778-1830: *Lectures on the English Poets* (1818)

12 Two may talk and one may hear, but three cannot take part in a conversation of the most sincere and searching sort.
Ralph Waldo Emerson 1803-82: *Essays* (1841) 'Friendship'

13 The fun of talk is to find what a man really thinks, and then contrast it with the enormous lies he has been telling all dinner, and, perhaps, all his life.
Benjamin Disraeli 1804-81: *Lothair* (1870)

14 'The time has come,' the Walrus said,

'To talk of many things:
Of shoes—and ships—and sealing wax—
Of cabbages—and kings.
Lewis Carroll 1832-98: *Through the Looking-Glass* (1872)

15 It is the province of knowledge to speak and it is the privilege of wisdom to listen.
Oliver Wendell Holmes 1809-94: *The Poet at the Breakfast-Table* (1872)

16 He speaks to Me as if I was a public meeting.
of Gladstone
Queen Victoria 1819-1901: G. W. E. Russell *Collections and Recollections* (1898)

17 Although there exist many thousand subjects for elegant conversation, there are persons who cannot meet a cripple without talking about feet.
Ernest Bramah 1868-1942: *The Wallet of Kai Lung* (1900)

18 There is no such thing as conversation. It is an illusion. There are intersecting monologues, that is all.
Rebecca West 1892-1983: *There is No Conversation* (1935)

19 How time flies when you's doin' all the talking.
Harvey Fierstein 1954- : *Torch Song Trilogy* (1979)

20 The opposite of talking isn't listening. The opposite of talking is waiting.
Fran Lebowitz 1946- : *Social Studies* (1981)

Cooking and Eating see also Food and Drink, Greed

PROVERBS AND SAYINGS

1 After dinner rest a while, after supper walk a mile.
late 16th century; the implication is that dinner is a heavy meal, while supper is a light one

2 After meat, mustard.
late 16th century; traditional comment on some essential ingredient which is brought too late of be of use

3 All are not cooks who sport white caps and carry long knives.
American proverb, mid 20th century

4 A cook is no better than her stove.
American proverb, mid 20th century

5 Eat to live, not live to eat.
late 14th century, distinguishing between necessity and indulgence

6 Fingers were made before forks.
mid 18th century, commonly used as a polite excuse for eating with one's hands at table. The earlier variant 'God made hands before knives' is found in the mid 16th century

7 God sends meat, but the Devil sends cooks.
mid 16th century, meaning that anything which is in itself good or useful may be spoiled or perverted by the use to which it is put

8 Go to work on an egg.
advertising slogan for the British Egg Marketing Board, from 1957; perhaps written by Fay Weldon or Mary Gowing

9 Hunger is the best sauce.

early 16th century, meaning that food which is needed will be received most readily

10 We must eat a peck of dirt before we die.

mid 18th century, often used as a consolatory remark in literal contexts

11 You are what you eat.

mid 20th century; see 19, 30 below

PHRASES

12 Barmecide feast an illusory or imaginary feast.

from the name of a prince in the Arabian Nights, *who gave a beggar a feast consisting of ornate but empty dishes*

13 dine with Duke Humphrey in archaic usage, go without dinner, go hungry.

possibly originally associated with a part of Old St Paul's, wrongly believed to be the site of the tomb of Duke Humphrey of Gloucester, where people walked instead of dining

QUOTATIONS

14 You won't be surprised that diseases are innumerable—count the cooks.
Seneca c.4 BC–AD 65: *Epistles*

15 Now good digestion wait on appetite,
And health on both!
William Shakespeare 1564-1616: *Macbeth* (1606)

16 Strange to see how a good dinner and feasting reconciles everybody.
Samuel Pepys 1633-1703: diary 9 November 1665

17 I look upon it, that he who does not mind his belly will hardly mind anything else.
Samuel Johnson 1709-84: James Boswell *Life of Samuel Johnson* (1791) 5 August 1763

18 Some have meat and cannot eat,
Some cannot eat that want it:
But we have meat and we can eat,
Sae let the Lord be thankit.
Robert Burns 1759-96: 'The Kirkudbright Grace' (1790), also known as 'The Selkirk Grace'

19 Tell me what you eat and I will tell you what you are.
Anthelme Brillat-Savarin 1755-1826: *Physiologie du Goût* (1825); see 11 above, 30 below

20 Cooking is the most ancient of the arts, for Adam was born hungry.
Anthelme Brillat-Savarin 1755-1826: *Physiologie du Goût* (1825)

21 Anyone who tells a lie has not a pure heart, and cannot make a good soup.
Ludwig van Beethoven 1770-1827: Ludwig Nohl *Beethoven Depicted by his Contemporaries* (1880)

22 I'll fill hup the chinks wi' cheese.
R. S. Surtees 1805-64: *Handley Cross* (1843)

23 Let onion atoms lurk within the bowl,
And, scarce-suspected, animate the whole.
Sydney Smith 1771-1845: Lady Holland *Memoir* (1855) 'Receipt for a Salad'

24 Kissing don't last: cookery do!
George Meredith 1828-1909: *The Ordeal of Richard Feverel* (1859)

25 We each day dig our graves with our teeth.
Samuel Smiles 1812-1904: *Duty* (1880)

26 He sows hurry and reaps indigestion.
Robert Louis Stevenson 1850-94: *Virginibus Puerisque* (1881) 'An Apology for Idlers'

27 The healthy stomach is nothing if not conservative. Few radicals have good digestions.
Samuel Butler 1835-1902: *Notebooks* (1912)

28 The cook was a good cook, as cooks go; and as cooks go, she went.
Saki 1870-1916: *Reginald* (1904)

29 'Oh, my Friends, be warned by me,
That Breakfast, Dinner, Lunch, and Tea
Are all the Human Frame requires . . . '
With that, the Wretched Child expires.
Hilaire Belloc 1870-1953: *Cautionary Tales* (1907) 'Henry King'

30 It's a very odd thing—
As odd as can be—
That whatever Miss T eats
Turns into Miss T.
Walter de la Mare 1873-1956: 'Miss T' (1913); see 11, 19 above

31 Time for a little something.
A. A. Milne 1882-1956: *Winnie-the-Pooh* (1926)

32 Be content to remember that those who can make omelettes properly can do nothing else.
Hilaire Belloc 1870-1953: *A Conversation with a Cat* (1931)

33 Hot on Sunday,
Cold on Monday,
Hashed on Tuesday,
Minced on Wednesday,
Curried Thursday,
Broth on Friday,

Cottage pie Saturday.

Dorothy Hartley 1893–1985: *Food in England* (1954) 'Vicarage Mutton'

34 Gluttony is an emotional escape, a sign something is eating us.

Peter De Vries 1910–93: *Comfort Me With Apples* (1956)

35 Lunch? You gotta be kidding. Lunch is for wimps.

Stanley Weiser and **Oliver Stone** 1946– : *Wall Street* (1987 film)

36 It [bingeing] gives you a feeling of comfort. It's like having a pair of arms around you, but it's temporary. Then you're disgusted

at the bloatedness of your stomach, and then you bring it all up again.

Diana, Princess of Wales 1961–97: interview on *Panorama*, BBC1 TV, 20 November 1995

37 Her cooking is the missionary position of cooking. That is how everybody starts.

defending Delia Smith

Egon Ronay: in *Independent on Sunday* 1 November 1998

38 The difference between a chef and a cook is the difference between a wife and a prostitute. Cooks do meals for people they know and love. Chefs do it anonymously for anyone who's got the price.

A. A. Gill 1954– : in *Independent* 4 November 1998

Cooperation

PROVERBS AND SAYINGS

1 . . . But I know a man who can.

advertising slogan for the Automobile Association, 1980s

2 A chain is no stronger than its weakest link.

mid 19th century, often used when identifying a particular point of vulnerability; see **Strength and Weakness** *7*

3 Dog does not eat dog.

mid 16th century, meaning that people of the same profession should not attack each other

4 Every little helps.

early 17th century

5 Four eyes see more than two.

late 16th century, meaning that two people are more observant than one alone

6 Hawks will not pick out hawks' eyes.

late 16th century, meaning powerful people from the same group will not attack one another

7 If you don't believe in cooperation, watch what happens to a wagon when one wheel comes off.

American proverb, mid 20th century

8 If you think cooperation is unnecessary, just try running your car a while on three wheels.

American proverb, mid 20th century

9 It takes two to make a bargain.

late 16th century, often used to imply that both parties must be prepared to give some ground

10 It takes two to tango.

mid 20th century, meaning that a cooperative venture requires a contribution from both participants; from the 1952 song by Al Hoffman and Dick Manning

11 Little birds that can sing and won't sing must be made to sing.

late 17th century, meaning that those who refuse to obey or cooperate will be forced to do so

12 Many hands make light work.

mid 14th century, often used as an encouragement to join in with assistance

13 One good turn deserves another.

early 15th century

14 One hand washes the other.

late 16th century, referring to cooperation between two closely linked persons or organizations

15 There is honour among thieves.

early 19th century, sometimes used ironically

16 A trouble shared is a trouble halved.

mid 20th century; meaning that discussing a problem will lessen its impact

17 Union is strength.

mid 17th century; unity is a popular alternative for union, especially when used as a trade-union slogan

18 United we stand, divided we fall.

late 18th century, a watchword of the American Revolution; see **America** *12*

QUOTATIONS

19 The wolf also shall dwell with the lamb, and the leopard shall lie down with the kid; and the calf and the young lion and

the fatling together; and a little child shall lead them.
Bible: Isaiah; see 30 below

20 If a house be divided against itself, that house cannot stand.
Bible: St Mark

21 If someone claps his hand a sound arises. Listen to the sound of the single hand!
Hakuin 1686–1769: attributed

22 When bad men combine, the good must associate; else they will fall, one by one, an unpitied sacrifice in a contemptible struggle.
Edmund Burke 1729–97: *Thoughts on the Cause of the Present Discontents* (1770)

23 We must indeed all hang together, or, most assuredly, we shall all hang separately.
Benjamin Franklin 1706–90: at the signing of the Declaration of Independence, 4 July 1776; possibly not original

24 Now who will stand on either hand,
And keep the bridge with me?
Lord Macaulay 1800–59: 'Horatius' (1842)

25 All for one, one for all.
motto of the Three Musketeers
Alexandre Dumas 1802–70: *Les Trois Mousquetaires* (1844); see **Friendship** 7

26 Government and cooperation are in all things the laws of life; anarchy and competition the laws of death.
John Ruskin 1819–1900: *Unto this Last* (1862)

27 To my daughter Leonora without whose never-failing sympathy and encouragement this book would have been finished in half the time.
P. G. Wodehouse 1881–1975: *The Heart of a Goof* (1926) dedication

28 Why don't you do something to *help* me?
Stan Laurel 1890–1965: *Drivers' Licence Sketch* (1947 film); words spoken by Oliver Hardy

29 We must learn to live together as brothers or perish together as fools.
Martin Luther King 1929–68: speech at St Louis, 22 March 1964

30 The lion and the calf shall lie down together but the calf won't get much sleep.
Woody Allen 1935– : in *New Republic* 31 August 1974; see 19 above

31 'Solidarity' means taking care of the person standing next to you.
Lech Wałęsa 1943– : speech, Gdansk, Poland, May 1988

32 In a place where 'please' is pronounced 'I s'pose you couldn't'
it is rare to meet with any belief in help.
Les A. Murray 1938– : *The Boys Who Stole the Funeral* (1989)

Corruption

PROVERBS AND SAYINGS

1 Corruption will find a dozen alibis for its evil deeds.
American proverb, mid 20th century

2 Every man has his price.
mid 18th century, meaning that everyone is susceptible to the right bribe; see 11 below

3 A golden key can open any door.
late 16th century, meaning that any access is guaranteed if enough money is offered

4 The rotten apple injures its neighbour.
mid 14th century, often used to mean that one corrupt person in an organization is likely to affect others

PHRASES

5 itching palm avarice
originally with reference to Shakespeare; see 9 below

QUOTATIONS

6 A venal city ripe to perish, if a buyer can be found.
of Rome
Sallust 86–35 BC: *Jugurtha*

7 . . . *Omnia Romae*
Cum pretio.
Everything in Rome—at a price.
Juvenal AD c.60–c.130: *Satires*

8 If gold ruste, what shall iren do?
Geoffrey Chaucer c.1343–1400: *The Canterbury Tales* 'The General Prologue'

9 Let me tell you, Cassius, you yourself
Are much condemned to have an itching palm.
William Shakespeare 1564–1616: *Julius Caesar* (1599); see 5 above

10 Nothing to be done without a bribe I find,
in love as well as law.
Susannah Centlivre c.1669–1723: *The Perjured Husband* (1700)

11 All those men have their price.
of fellow parliamentarians
Robert Walpole 1676–1745: W. Coxe *Memoirs of Sir Robert Walpole* (1798); see 2 above

12 I am not worth purchasing, but such as I am, the King of Great Britain is not rich enough to do it.
replying to an offer from Governor George Johnstone of £10,000, and any office in the Colonies in the King's gift, if he were able successfully to promote a Union between Britain and America
Joseph Reed 1741–85: W. B. Read *Life and Correspondence of Joseph Reed* (1847)

13 But the jingling of the guinea helps the hurt that Honour feels.
Alfred, Lord Tennyson 1809–92: 'Locksley Hall' (1842)

14 It is always a temptation to a rich and lazy nation,
To puff and look important and to say:-
'Though we know we should defeat you, we have not the time to meet you,
We will therefore pay you cash to go away.'
And that is called paying the Dane-geld;
But we've proved it again and again,
That if once you have paid him the Dane-geld
You never get rid of the Dane.
Rudyard Kipling 1865–1936: 'What Dane-geld means' (1911)

15 When their lordships asked Bacon
How many bribes he had taken
He had at least the grace
To get very red in the face.
Edmund Clerihew Bentley 1875–1956: 'Bacon' (1939)

16 Men are more often bribed by their loyalties and ambitions than money.
Robert H. Jackson 1892–1954: dissenting opinion in *United States v. Wunderlich* 1951

17 I stuffed their mouths with gold.
on his handling of the consultants during the establishment of the National Health Service
Aneurin Bevan 1897–1960: Brian Abel-Smith *The Hospitals 1800–1948* (1964)

18 The flood of money that gushes into politics today is a pollution of democracy.
Theodore H. White 1915–86: in *Time* 19 November 1984

Countries and Peoples see also **Africa, America, Australia, Canada, England, France, International Relations, Ireland, Russia, Scotland, Towns and Cities, Wales**

PROVERBS AND SAYINGS

1 Every land has its own law.
Scottish proverb, early 17th century, used to emphasize the individuality of a nation or group

PHRASES

2 the Celestial Empire Imperial China.
translation of a Chinese honorific title

3 the children of Israel the Jewish people.
people whose descent is traditionally traced from the patriarch Jacob (also called Israel), each of whose twelve sons became the founder of a tribe

4 the chosen people the Jewish people.
the people specially favoured by God; compare the Bible (1 Peter) 'but ye are a chosen generation, a royal priesthood, an holy nation, a peculiar people'

5 the Holy Land a region on the eastern shores of the Mediterranean, in what is now Israel and Palestine, with religious significance for Judaism, Christianity, and Islam.
medieval Latin terra sancta, French la terre sainte, applied to the region with reference to its having been the scene of the Incarnation and also to the existing sacred sites there, especially the Holy Sepulchre at Jerusalem

6 the Land of the Long White Cloud New Zealand.

7 land of the midnight sun any of the most northerly European countries.
in which it never gets fully dark during the summer months

8 land of the rising sun Japan.
the Japanese name of the country is Nippon, literally 'rising sun'

9 the Lost Tribes Asher, Dan, Gad, Issachar, Levi, Manasseh, Naphtali, Reuben, Simeon, and Zebulun, ten of the twelve divisions of ancient Israel, each traditionally descended from one of the sons of Jacob.

the ten tribes of Israel taken away c.720 BC by Sargon II to captivity in Assyria, from which they are believed never to have returned, while the tribes of Benjamin and Judah remained

10 on which the sun never sets (of an empire, originally the Spanish and later the British) worldwide.

11 the sick man of Europe Turkey in the late 19th century.

originally with reference to the view expressed by Nicholas I, Russian Emperor from 1825, 'Turkey is a dying man. We may endeavour to keep him alive, but we shall not succeed. He will, he must die'

QUOTATIONS

12 The Netherlands have been for many years, as one may say, the very cockpit of Christendom.
James Howell c.1594–1666: *Instructions for Foreign Travel* (1642); see **Europe** 1

13 This agglomeration which was called and which still calls itself the Holy Roman Empire was neither holy, nor Roman, nor an empire.
Voltaire 1694–1778: *Essai sur l'histoire générale et sur les moeurs et l'esprit des nations* (1756)

14 She has made me in love with a cold climate, and frost and snow, with a northern moonlight.
on Mary Wollstonecraft's letters from Sweden and Norway
Robert Southey 1774–1843: letter to his brother Thomas, 28 April 1797

15 I look upon Switzerland as an inferior sort of Scotland.
Sydney Smith 1771–1845: letter to Lord Holland, 1815

16 The isles of Greece, the isles of Greece!
Where burning Sappho loved and sung,
Where grew the arts of war and peace,
Where Delos rose, and Phoebus sprung!
Eternal summer gilds them yet,
But all, except their sun, is set!
Lord Byron 1788–1824: *Don Juan* (1819–24)

17 Holland . . . lies so low they're only saved by being dammed.
Thomas Hood 1799–1845: *Up the Rhine* (1840)

18 A quiet, pilfering, unprotected race.
John Clare 1793–1864: 'The Gipsy Camp' (1841)

19 Some people . . . may be Rooshans, and others may be Prooshans; they are born so, and will please themselves. Them which is of other naturs thinks different.
Charles Dickens 1812–70: *Martin Chuzzlewit* (1844)

20 Except the blind forces of Nature, nothing moves in this world which is not Greek in its origin.
Henry Maine 1822–88: *Village Communities* (3rd ed., 1876)

21 I'm Charley's aunt from Brazil—where the nuts come from.
Brandon Thomas 1856–1914: *Charley's Aunt* (1892)

22 The traveller who has gone to Italy to study the tactile values of Giotto, or the corruption of the Papacy, may return remembering nothing but the blue sky and the men and women under it.
E. M. Forster 1879–1970: *Room with a View* (1908)

23 He is crazed with the spell of far Arabia,
They have stolen his wits away.
Walter de la Mare 1873–1956: 'Arabia' (1912)

24 Poor Mexico, so far from God and so close to the United States.
Porfirio Diaz 1830–1915: attributed

25 What cleanliness everywhere! You dare not throw your cigarette into the lake. No graffiti in the urinals. Switzerland is proud of this; but I believe this is just what she lacks: manure.
André Gide 1869–1951: diary, Lucerne, 10 August 1917

26 Nothing in India is identifiable, the mere asking of a question causes it to disappear or to merge in something else.
E. M. Forster 1879–1970: *A Passage to India* (1924)

27 Were I to . . . take a [Yugoslav] peasant by the shoulders and whisper to him, 'In your lifetime, have you known peace?' wait for his answer, shake his shoulders and transform him into his father, and ask him the same question, and transform him in turn into his father, I would never hear the word 'yes' if I carried my questioning of the dead back for a thousand years.
Rebecca West 1892–1983: *Black Lamb and Grey Falcon* (1940)

28 Latins are tenderly enthusiastic. In Brazil they throw flowers at you. In Argentina they throw themselves.
Marlene Dietrich 1901–92: in *Newsweek* 24 August 1959

29 A country is a piece of land surrounded on all sides by boundaries, usually unnatural.
Joseph Heller 1923-99: *Catch-22* (1961)

30 There are very few Eskimos, but millions of Whites, just like mosquitoes. It is something very special and wonderful to be an Eskimo—they are like the snow geese. If an Eskimo forgets his language and Eskimo ways, he will be nothing but just another mosquito.
Abraham Okpik d. 1997: attributed, 1966

31 Nothing and no one can destroy the Chinese people. They are relentless survivors. They are the oldest civilized people on earth. Their civilization passes through phases but its basic characteristics remain the same. They yield, they bend to the wind, but they do not break.
Pearl S. Buck 1892-1973: *China, Past and Present* (1972)

32 Whereas in England all is permitted that is not expressly prohibited, it has been said that in Germany all is prohibited unless expressly permitted and in France all is permitted that is expressly prohibited. In the European Common Market (as it then was) no-one knows what is permitted and it all costs more.
Robert Megarry 1910- : 'Law and Lawyers in a Permissive Society' (5th Riddell Lecture delivered in Lincoln's Inn Hall 22 March 1972); see **Europe** 2

33 India . . . is not a place that one can pick up and put down again as if nothing had happened. In a way it's not so much a country as an experience, and whether it turns out to be a good or a bad one depends, I suppose, on oneself.
Ruth Prawer Jhabvala 1927- : *Travellers* (1973)

34 It's where they commit suicide and the king rides a bicycle, Sweden.
Alan Bennett 1934- : *Enjoy* (1980)

35 In Turkey it was always 1952, in Malaysia 1937; Afghanistan was 1910 and Bolivia 1949. It is twenty years ago in the Soviet Union, ten in Norway, five in France. It is always last year in Australia and next week in Japan.
Paul Theroux 1941- : *The Kingdom by the Sea* (1983)

36 The Third World is an artificial construction of the West—an ideological empire on which the sun is always setting.
Shiva Naipaul 1945-85: *An Unfinished Journey* (1986); see **International Relations** 8

37 If you take Greece apart, in the end you will see remaining to you an olive tree, a vineyard and a ship. Which means: with just so much you can put her back together.
Odysseus Elytis 1911- : 'The Little Seafarer' (1988)

38 The Japanese are full of surprises, because the women are so refined and elegant and the men fundamentally so crude and tough.
Harold Acton 1904-94: Naim Attallah *Singular Encounters* (1990)

39 Why is politics making us unhappy, separating us, when we ourselves know who is good and who isn't? We mix with the good, not with the bad. And among the good there are Serbs and Croats and Muslims, just as there are among the bad. I simply don't understand it.
Zlata Filipovic 1980- : *Zlata's Diary: A Child's Life in Sarajevo* (1993) 19 November 1992

40 The forest is the spiritual, mystical heart of Germany, the engine and the ultimate metaphor of their literature, poetry and music.
A. A. Gill 1954- : in *Sunday Times* 11 July 1999

The Country and the Town see also Farming

PROVERBS AND SAYINGS

1 **An everyday story of country folk.**
traditional summary of the BBC's long-running radio soap opera The Archers

2 **God made the country and man made the town.**
mid 17th century, contrasting rural and urban life; in this form from Cowper: see 10 below

3 **You can take the boy out of the country but you can't take the country out of the boy.**
mid 20th century, meaning that even when a person moves away from the place they were brought up in, they retain its essential manners and customs

4 concrete jungle a city with a high density of large, unattractive, modern buildings and which is perceived as an unpleasant living environment.
after Morris: see 24 below

5 a country mouse a person from a rural area unfamiliar with urban life.
from one of Aesop's fables in which the country mouse *and the* town mouse *visit each other, and each in the end is convinced of the superiority of its own home; see 7 below*

6 rus in urbe an illusion of countryside created by a building or garden within a city; an urban building which has this effect.
*Latin, literally 'country in city', from Martial (*AD *c.40–c.104)*

7 a town mouse a person with an urban lifestyle unfamiliar with rural life.
see 5 above

8 As one who long in populous city pent,
Where houses thick and sewers annoy the air,
Forth issuing on a summer's morn to breathe
Among the pleasant villages and farms
Adjoined, from each thing met conceives delight.
John Milton 1608–74: *Paradise Lost* (1667)

9 God the first garden made, and the first city Cain.
Abraham Cowley 1618–67: 'The Garden' (1668); see 10 below

10 God made the country, and man made the town.
William Cowper 1731–1800: *The Task* (1785) bk. 1 'The Sofa'; see 2, 9 above

11 'Tis distance lends enchantment to the view,
And robes the mountain in its azure hue.
Thomas Campbell 1777–1844: *Pleasures of Hope* (1799); see **Appearance** 6

12 We do not look in great cities for our best morality.
Jane Austen 1775–1817: *Mansfield Park* (1814)

13 There is nothing good to be had in the country, or if there is, they will not let you have it.
William Hazlitt 1778–1830: *The Round Table* (1817) 'Observations on Mr Wordsworth's Poem *The Excursion*'

14 If you would be known, and not know, vegetate in a village; if you would know, and not be known, live in a city.
Charles Caleb Colton c.1780–1832: *Lacon* (1820)

15 I have no relish for the country; it is a kind of healthy grave.
Sydney Smith 1771–1845: letter to Miss G. Harcourt, 1838

16 Anybody can be good in the country.
Oscar Wilde 1854–1900: *The Picture of Dorian Gray* (1891)

17 It is my belief, Watson, founded upon my experience, that the lowest and vilest alleys in London do not present a more dreadful record of sin than does the smiling and beautiful countryside.
Arthur Conan Doyle 1859–1930: *The Adventures of Sherlock Holmes* (1892) 'The Copper Beeches'

18 Wiv a ladder and some glasses,
You could see to 'Ackney Marshes,
If it wasn't for the 'ouses in between.
Edgar Bateman and **George Le Brunn**: 'If it wasn't for the 'Ouses in between' (1894 song)

19 The materials of city planning are sky, space, trees, steel and cement in that order and in that hierarchy.
Le Corbusier 1887–1965: in *The Times* 1965

20 So *that's* what hay looks like.
said at Badminton House, where she was evacuated during the Second World War
Queen Mary 1867–1953: James Pope-Hennessy *Life of Queen Mary* (1959)

21 Slums may well be breeding-grounds of crime, but middle-class suburbs are incubators of apathy and delirium.
Cyril Connolly 1903–74: *The Unquiet Grave* (1944)

22 Oh, give me land, lots of land under starry skies above,
Don't fence me in.
Let me ride through the wide open country that I love,
Don't fence me in.
Cole Porter 1891–1964: 'Don't Fence Me In' (1944 song); see **Solitude** 20

23 The modern city is a place for banking and prostitution and very little else.
Frank Lloyd Wright 1867-1959: Robert C. Twombly *Frank Lloyd Wright* (1973)

24 Green belts should be the start of the countryside, not a ditch between Subtopias.
Hugh Gaitskell 1906-63: in *Observer* 1 January 1961

25 The city is not a concrete jungle, it is a human zoo.
Desmond Morris 1928- : *The Human Zoo* (1969); see 4 above

26 I come from suburbia . . . and I don't ever want to go back. It's the one place in the world that's further away than anywhere else.
Frederic Raphael 1931- : *The Glittering Prizes* (1976)

27 Villages, unlike towns, have always been ruled by conformism, isolation, petty surveillance, boredom and repetitive malicious gossip about the same families. Which is a precise enough description of the global spectacle's present vulgarity.
on the concept of the 'global village'
Guy Debord 1931-94: *Comments on the Society of the Spectacle* (1988); see **The Earth** 4, **Technology** 18

28 'You are a pretty urban sort of person though, wouldn't you say?'
'Only nor'nor'east,' I said. 'I know a fox from a fax-machine.'
Stephen Fry 1957- : *The Hippopotamus* (1994); see **Madness** 4

29 Judaism, Christianity and Islam all took root among nomads who had recently settled, and all three characterize nomadic traits—the shepherd, the pilgrim, the wanderer in the wilderness—as godly, and the life of the city as degenerate.
George Monbiot: *No Man's Land* (1994)

Courage see also Fear

PROVERBS AND SAYINGS

1 Attack is the best form of defence.
late 18th century (usually quoted as 'the best defence is a good offence' in the US)

2 A bully is always a coward.
early 19th century

3 Courage is fear that has said its prayers.
American proverb, mid 20th century

4 Courage without conduct is like a ship without ballast.
American proverb, mid 20th century

5 Don't cry before you're hurt.
mid 16th century, sometimes used as a warning against appealing for sympathy on the assumption of an unpleasant outcome

6 Faint heart never won fair lady.
mid 16th century, often used as an encouragement to action

7 Fortune favours the brave.
late 14th century, meaning that a person who acts bravely is likely to be successful; originally often with allusion to Terence Phormio 'Fortune assists the brave' and Virgil Aeneid 'Fortune assists the bold'

8 None but the brave deserve the fair.
late 17th century, from Dryden: see 17 below

9 You never know what you can do till you try.
early 19th century; often used as encouragement to the reluctant

PHRASES

10 grasp the nettle tackle a difficulty or danger with courage or boldness.
*see 18 below, **Danger** 22*

QUOTATIONS

11 The wicked flee when no man pursueth: but the righteous are bold as a lion.
Bible: Proverbs

12 Happiness depends on being free, and freedom depends on being courageous.
Thucydides c.455-c.400 BC: *History of the Peloponnesian War*

13 Cowards die many times before their deaths;
The valiant never taste of death but once.
William Shakespeare 1564-1616: *Julius Caesar* (1599); see **Fear** 1

14 Boldness be my friend!
Arm me, audacity.
William Shakespeare 1564-1616: *Cymbeline* (1609-10)

15 He either fears his fate too much,
Or his deserts are small,
That puts it not unto the touch
To win or lose it all.
James Graham, Marquess of Montrose 1612–50:
'My Dear and Only Love' (written *c.*1642)

16 For all men would be cowards if they
durst.
John Wilmot, Lord Rochester 1647–80: 'A Satire
against Mankind' (1679)

17 None but the brave deserves the fair.
John Dryden 1631–1700: *Alexander's Feast* (1697);
see 8 above

18 Tender-handed stroke a nettle,
And it stings you for your pains;
Grasp it like a man of mettle,
And it soft as silk remains.
Aaron Hill 1685–1750: 'Verses Written on a
Window in Scotland'; see 10 above, **Danger** 22

19 Perhaps those, who, trembling most,
maintain a dignity in their fate, are the
bravest: resolution on reflection is real
courage.
Horace Walpole 1717–97: *Memoirs of the Reign of
King George II* (1757)

20 My valour is certainly going!—it is
sneaking off!—I feel it oozing out as it
were at the palms of my hands!
Richard Brinsley Sheridan 1751–1816: *The Rivals*
(1775)

21 It is thus that mutual cowardice keeps us
in peace. Were one half of mankind brave
and one half cowards, the brave would be
always beating the cowards. Were all
brave, they would lead a very uneasy life;
all would be continually fighting: but
being all cowards, we go on very well.
Samuel Johnson 1709–84: James Boswell *Life of
Samuel Johnson* (1791) 28 April 1778

22 Boldness, and again boldness, and always
boldness!
Georges Jacques Danton 1759–94: speech to the
Legislative Committee of General Defence, 2
September 1792

23 As to moral courage, I have very rarely
met with two o'clock in the morning
courage: I mean instantaneous courage.
Napoleon I 1769–1821: E. A. de Las Cases *Mémorial
de Ste-Hélène* (1823) 4–5 December 1815

24 Was none who would be foremost
To lead such dire attack;
But those behind cried 'Forward!'

And those before cried 'Back!'
Lord Macaulay 1800–59: 'Horatius' (1842)

25 No coward soul is mine,
No trembler in the world's storm-troubled
sphere:
I see Heaven's glories shine,
And faith shines equal, arming me from
fear.
Emily Brontë 1818–48: 'No coward soul is mine'
(1846)

26 In the fell clutch of circumstance,
I have not winced nor cried aloud:
Under the bludgeonings of chance
My head is bloody, but unbowed.
W. E. Henley 1849–1903: 'Invictus. In Memoriam
R.T.H.B.' (1888)

27 Had we lived, I should have had a tale to
tell of the hardihood, endurance, and
courage of my companions which would
have stirred the heart of every Englishman.
These rough notes and our dead bodies
must tell the tale.
Robert Falcon Scott 1868–1912: 'Message to the
Public' in late editions of *The Times* 11 February 1913

28 Courage is the thing. All goes if courage
goes!
J. M. Barrie 1860–1937: Rectorial Address at St
Andrews, 3 May 1922

29 Grace under pressure.
*when asked what he meant by 'guts', in an interview
with Dorothy Parker*
Ernest Hemingway 1899–1961: in *New Yorker* 30
November 1929

30 Courage is rightly esteemed the first of
human qualities because as has been said,
it is the quality which guarantees all
others.
Winston Churchill 1874–1965: *Great
Contemporaries* (1932)

31 Cowardice, as distinguished from panic, is
almost always simply a lack of ability to
suspend the functioning of the
imagination.
Ernest Hemingway 1899–1961: *Men at War* (1942)

32 Morally, he was in the bravest of all
categories: he flinched, but he always
went on.
Roy Jenkins 1920– : W. T. Rodgers (ed.) *Hugh
Gaitskell 1906–63* (1964)

33 For every ten men who are willing to face
the guns of an enemy there is only one
willing to brave the disapproval of his
fellow, the censure of his colleagues, the

wrath of his society. Moral courage is a rarer commodity than bravery in battle or great intelligence.

Robert Kennedy 1925–68: speech in Cape Town, 7 June 1966

34 What's courage? Failure of planning, that's all.

David Hare 1947– : Bertolt Brecht *Mother Courage and her Children* (1995 version for the National Theatre)

Courtship see also Love

1 Can you make me a cambric shirt, Parsley, sage, rosemary, and thyme, Without any seam or needlework? And you shall be a true lover of mine.

traditional song

2 Happy's the wooing that is not long a-doing.

late 16th century, reflecting a traditional belief

QUOTATIONS

3 She is a woman, therefore may be wooed; She is a woman, therefore may be won.

William Shakespeare 1564–1616: *Titus Andronicus* (1590)

4 Why so pale and wan, fond lover? Prithee, why so pale? Will, when looking well can't move her, Looking ill prevail?

John Suckling 1609–42: *Aglaura* (1637)

5 Had we but world enough, and time, This coyness, lady, were no crime.

Andrew Marvell 1621–78: 'To His coy Mistress' (1681)

6 Courtship to marriage, as a very witty prologue to a very dull play.

William Congreve 1670–1729: *The Old Bachelor* (1693)

7 My only books Were woman's looks, And folly's all they've taught me.

Thomas Moore 1779–1852: 'The time I've lost in wooing' (1807)

8 There are very few of us who have heart enough to be really in love without encouragement. In nine cases out of ten, a woman had better show *more* affection than she feels.

Jane Austen 1775–1817: *Pride and Prejudice* (1813)

9 If you want to win her hand, Let the maiden understand

That she's not the only pebble on the beach.

Harry Braisted: 'You're Not the Only Pebble on the Beach' (1896 song)

10 Holding hands at midnight 'Neath a starry sky, Nice work if you can get it, And you can get it if you try.

Ira Gershwin 1896–1989: 'Nice Work If You Can Get It' (1937 song); see **Envy** 6

11 Wooing, so tiring.

Nancy Mitford 1904–73: *The Pursuit of Love* (1945)

12 A man chases a girl (until she catches him).

Irving Berlin 1888–1989: title of song (1949)

13 We've got to have We plot to have For it's so dreary not to have That certain thing called the Boy Friend.

Sandy Wilson 1924– : 'The Boyfriend' (1954 song)

14 Ten years of courtship is carrying celibacy to extremes.

Alan Bennett 1934– : *Habeas Corpus* (1973)

15 Woe betide the man who dares to pay a woman a compliment today . . . Forget the flowers, the chocolates, the soft word— rather woo her with a self-defence manual in one hand and a family planning leaflet in the other.

Alan Ayckbourn 1939– : *Round and Round the Garden* (1975)

16 Dating is a social engagement with the threat of sex at its conclusion.

P. J. O'Rourke 1947– : *Modern Manners* (1984)

17 Everyone knows that dating in your thirties is not the happy-go-lucky free-for-all it was when you were twenty-two.

Helen Fielding 1958– : *Bridget Jones's Diary* (1996)

18 If you want to get to know someone better, you shouldn't take them out for a candlelit dinner, you should watch them at work.

When they're full of concentration, only not concentrating on you.
Julian Barnes 1946– : *Love, etc.* (2000)

Creativity

1 If you don't make mistakes you don't make anything.
late 19th century; see **Mistakes** 19

2 the tenth Muse a spirit of inspiration.
a muse of inspiration imagined as added to the nine of classical mythology; see **Arts and Sciences** 1

3 Nothing can be created out of nothing.
Lucretius c.94–55 BC: *De Rerum Natura*

4 All things were made by him; and without him was not any thing made that was made.
Bible: St John

5 The whole, though it be long, stands almost complete and finished in my mind, so that I can survey it, like a fine picture or a beautiful statue, at a glance. Nor do I hear in my imagination the parts *successively*, but I hear them, as it were, all at once. What a delight this is I cannot tell!
on his method of composition
Wolfgang Amadeus Mozart 1756–91: letter, Edward Holmes *The Life of Mozart* (1845)

6 The urge for destruction is also a creative urge!
Michael Bakunin 1814–76: *Jahrbuch für Wissenschaft und Kunst* (1842) 'Die Reaktion in Deutschland' (under the pseudonym 'Jules Elysard')

7 Urge and urge and urge,
Always the procreant urge of the world.
Walt Whitman 1819–92: 'Song of Myself' (written 1855)

8 Birds build—but not I build; no, but strain,
Time's eunuch, and not breed one work that wakes.
Mine, O thou lord of life, send my roots rain.
Gerard Manley Hopkins 1844–89: 'Thou art indeed just, Lord' (written 1889)

9 Poems are made by fools like me,

But only God can make a tree.
Joyce Kilmer 1886–1918: 'Trees' (1914)

10 An artist has no need to express his thought directly in his work for the latter to reflect its quality; it has even been said that the highest praise of God consists in the denial of Him by the atheist who finds creation so perfect that it can dispense with a creator.
Marcel Proust 1871–1922: *Guermantes Way* (1921)

11 Like a piece of ice on a hot stove the poem must ride on its own melting. A poem may be worked over once it is in being, but may not be worried into being.
Robert Frost 1874–1963: *Collected Poems* (1939) 'The Figure a Poem Makes'

12 Think before you speak is criticism's motto; speak before you think creation's.
E. M. Forster 1879–1970: *Two Cheers for Democracy* (1951)

13 All men are creative but few are artists.
Paul Goodman 1911–72: *Growing up Absurd* (1961)

14 Why does my Muse only speak when she is unhappy?
She does not, I only listen when I am unhappy
When I am happy I live and despise writing
For my Muse this cannot but be dispiriting.
Stevie Smith 1902–71: 'My Muse' (1964)

15 Our current obsession with creativity is the result of our continued striving for immortality in an era when most people no longer believe in an after-life.
Arianna Stassinopoulos 1950– : *The Female Woman* (1973)

16 Creating is a harrowing business. I work in a state of anguish all year. I shut myself up, don't go out. It's a hard life, which is why I understand Proust so well; I have such an admiration for what he has written about the agony of creation.
Yves Saint Laurent 1936– : Nicholas Coleridge *The Fashion Conspiracy* (1988)

17 The worst crime is to leave a man's hands empty.

Men are born makers, with that primal
simplicity

In every maker since Adam.
Derek Walcott 1930– : *Omeros* (1990)

Cricket

1 barmy army a self-designation of (a group of) the supporters of a particular team, particularly a group of young, vociferous followers of the England cricket team.

2 break one's duck in cricket, score one's first run.
in allusion to the origin of duck for a score of 0, as resembling a duck's egg in shape

3 sticky wicket a cricket pitch that has been drying after rain and is difficult to bat on.
figuratively, a tricky or awkward situation

QUOTATIONS

4 It's more than a game. It's an institution.
of cricket
Thomas Hughes 1822–96: *Tom Brown's Schooldays* (1857)

5   In Affectionate Remembrance
of
ENGLISH CRICKET,
Which Died at The Oval
on
29th August, 1882.
Deeply lamented by a large circle of
sorrowing friends and acquaintances.
R. I. P.
N. B.—The body will be cremated and
the ashes taken to Australia.
following England's defeat by the Australians
Anonymous: in *Sporting Times* 2 September 1882

6 There's a breathless hush in the Close
to-night—
Ten to make and the match to win—
A bumping pitch and a blinding light,
An hour to play and the last man in.
Henry Newbolt 1862–1938: 'Vitaï Lampada' (1897);
see **Sports** 11

7 Then ye returned to your trinkets; then ye
contented your souls
With the flannelled fools at the wicket or
the muddied oafs at the goals.
Rudyard Kipling 1865–1936: 'The Islanders' (1903)

8 If everything else in this nation of ours
were lost but cricket—her Constitution
and the laws of England of Lord

Halsbury—it would be possible to reconstruct from the theory and practice of cricket all the eternal Englishness which has gone to the establishment of that Constitution and the laws aforesaid.
Neville Cardus 1889–1975: *Cricket* (1930)

9 Personally, I have always looked on cricket as organized loafing.
William Temple 1881–1944: attributed

10 It is hard to tell where the MCC ends and the Church of England begins.
J. B. Priestley 1894–1984: in *New Statesman* 20 July 1962

11 Cricket—a game which the English, not being a spiritual people, have invented in order to give themselves some conception of eternity.
Lord Mancroft 1914–87: *Bees in Some Bonnets* (1979)

12 Bowl fast, bowl faster. When you play Test cricket you don't give Englishmen an inch. Play it tough, all the way. Grind them into the dust.
Don Bradman 1908–2001: Jack Fingleton *Batting from Memory* (1981)

13 Cricket civilizes people and creates good gentlemen. I want everyone to play cricket in Zimbabwe; I want ours to be a nation of gentlemen.
Robert Mugabe 1924– : in *Sunday Times* 26 February 1984

14 I don't think I can be expected to take seriously any game which takes less than three days to reach its conclusion.
a cricket enthusiast on baseball
Tom Stoppard 1937– : in *Guardian* 24 December 1984

15 I couldn't bat for the length of time required to score 500. I'd get bored and fall over.
Denis Compton 1918– : in *Daily Telegraph* 27 June 1994

16 I have learnt to think of three words all the time—what, when and why. That means always knowing what I am going to bowl,

when I am going to bowl it and to be clear why I have chosen that option.
Shane Warne 1969– : *My Autobiography* (2001)

Crime and Punishment see also Guilt and Innocence, Justice, The Law, Murder

PROVERBS AND SAYINGS

1 A conservative is a liberal who's been mugged.
American saying, 1980s; see 51 below

2 Crime doesn't pay.
American proverb, early 20th century; a slogan of the FBI and the cartoon detective Dick Tracy

3 Crime must be concealed by crime.
American proverb, mid 20th century

4 Hang a thief when he's young, and he'll no' steal when he's old.
Scottish proverbial saying, early 19th century

5 If there were no receivers, there would be no thieves.
late 14th century

6 Ill gotten goods never thrive.
early 16th century, meaning something which is acquired dishonestly is unlikely to be the basis of lasting prosperity

7 Little thieves are hanged, but great ones escape.
mid 17th century, meaning that sufficient power and influence can ensure that a wrongdoer is not punished

8 Opportunity makes a thief.
early 13th century, often used to imply that the carelessness of the person who is robbed has contributed to the crime

9 Three strikes and you're out.
late 20th century, referring to legislation which provides that an offender's third felony is punishable by life imprisonment or other severe sentence; deriving from the terminology of baseball, in which a batter who has had three strikes, or three fair opportunities of hitting the ball, is out

10 When thieves fall out, honest men come by their own.
mid 16th century; meaning that it is through thieves quarrelling over their stolen goods that they are likely to be caught, and the goods recovered

PHRASES

11 cruel and unusual punishment punishment which is seen to exceed the bounds of what is regarded as an appropriate penal remedy for a civilized society.
from the Eighth Amendment (1791): see 26 below

12 dead-end kid a young slum-dwelling tough, a juvenile delinquent.
the Dead End Kids were the juvenile delinquents in the films Dead End (1937) and Angels with Dirty Faces (1938)

13 lash of scorpions an instrument of vengeance or repression.
a whip of torture made of knotted cords or armed with metal spikes, especially in allusion to the Bible (1 Kings): see 19 below

14 read the Riot Act reprimand or caution sternly.
the Riot Act, passed in 1715 and repealed in 1967, made it a felony for an assembly of more than twelve people to refuse to disperse after the reading of a specified portion of it by lawful authority

15 short sharp shock a form of corrective treatment for young offenders in which the deterrent value was seen in the harshness of the regime rather than the length of the sentence.
advocated by the Home Secretary, William Whitelaw, to the Conservative Party Conference in 1979; see 38 below

16 smite hip and thigh punish unsparingly.
originally referring to the Bible (Judges) 'He smote them hip and thigh with a mighty plague'

QUOTATIONS

17 I the Lord thy God am a jealous God, visiting the iniquity of the fathers upon the children unto the third and fourth generation of them that hate me.
'the sins of the fathers' in the Book of Common Prayer (1662)
Bible: Exodus; see **The Family** 28

18 He that spareth his rod hateth his son.
Bible: Proverbs; see **Child Care** 2

19 My father hath chastised you with whips, but I will chastise you with scorpions.
Bible: I Kings; see 13 above

20 This is the first of punishments, that no guilty man is acquitted if judged by himself.
Juvenal AD c.60–c.130: *Satires*

21 Severity breedeth fear, but roughness breedeth hate. Even reproofs from authority ought to be grave, and not taunting.
Francis Bacon 1561–1626: *Essays* (1625) 'Of Great Place'

22 I went out to Charing Cross, to see Major-general Harrison hanged, drawn, and quartered; which was done there, he looking as cheerful as any man could do in that condition.
Samuel Pepys 1633–1703: diary 13 October 1660

23 Hanging is too good for him, said Mr Cruelty.
John Bunyan 1628–88: *The Pilgrim's Progress* (1678)

24 Men are not hanged for stealing horses, but that horses may not be stolen.
Lord Halifax 1633–95: *Political, Moral, and Miscellaneous Thoughts and Reflections* (1750) 'Of Punishment'

25 All punishment is mischief: all punishment in itself is evil.
Jeremy Bentham 1748–1832: *Principles of Morals and Legislation* (1789)

26 Excessive bail shall not be required, nor excessive fines imposed, nor cruel and unusual punishment inflicted.
Constitution of the United States 1787: *Eighth Amendment* (1791); see 11 above

27 Lay then the axe to the root, and teach governments humanity. It is their sanguinary punishments which corrupt mankind.
Thomas Paine 1737–1809: *The Rights of Man* (1791)

28 Whenever the offence inspires less horror than the punishment, the rigour of penal law is obliged to give way to the common feelings of mankind.
Edward Gibbon 1737–94: attributed

29 As for rioting, the old Roman way of dealing with that is always the right one; flog the rank and file, and fling the ringleaders from the Tarpeian rock.
Thomas Arnold 1795–1842: letter written before 1828, quoted by Matthew Arnold in *Cornhill Magazine* August 1868

30 The Cardinal rose with a dignified look, He called for his candle, his bell and his book!

In holy anger, and pious grief, He solemnly cursed that rascally thief!
R. H. Barham 1788–1845: 'The Jackdaw of Rheims' (1840); see **The Supernatural** 2

31 Punishment is not for revenge, but to lessen crime and reform the criminal.
Elizabeth Fry 1780–1845: Rachel E. Cresswell and Katharine Fry *Memoir of the Life of Elizabeth Fry* (1848)

32 A clever theft was praiseworthy amongst the Spartans; and it is equally so amongst Christians, provided it be on a sufficiently large scale.
Herbert Spencer 1820–1903: *Social Statics* (1850)

33 The best of us being unfit to die, what an inexpressible absurdity to put the worst to death!
Nathaniel Hawthorne 1804–64: diary 13 October 1851

34 Better build schoolrooms for 'the boy', Than cells and gibbets for 'the man'.
Eliza Cook 1818–89: 'A Song for the Ragged Schools' (1853)

35 Thou shalt not steal; an empty feat, When it's so lucrative to cheat.
Arthur Hugh Clough 1819–61: 'The Latest Decalogue' (1862)

36 To crush, to annihilate a man utterly, to inflict on him the most terrible punishment so that the most ferocious murderer would shudder at it beforehand, one need only give him work of an absolutely, completely useless and irrational character.
Fedor Dostoevsky 1821–81: *House of the Dead* (1862)

37 The boy learns not to fear sin, but the *punishment* for it, and thus he learns to lie.
Charles Kingsley 1819–75: F. G. Kingsley *Charles Kingsley* (1877)

38 Awaiting the sensation of a short, sharp shock,
From a cheap and chippy chopper on a big black block.
W. S. Gilbert 1836–1911: *The Mikado* (1885); see 15 above

39 My object all sublime I shall achieve in time—
To let the punishment fit the crime—
The punishment fit the crime.
W. S. Gilbert 1836–1911: *The Mikado* (1885)

40 Singularity is almost invariably a clue. The more featureless and commonplace a crime is, the more difficult is it to bring it home.
Arthur Conan Doyle 1859–1930: *The Adventures of Sherlock Holmes* (1892) 'The Boscombe Valley Mystery'

41 Thieves respect property. They merely wish the property to become their property that they may more perfectly respect it.
G. K. Chesterton 1874–1936: *The Man who was Thursday* (1908)

42 For de little stealin' dey gits you in jail soon or late. For de big stealin' dey makes you Emperor and puts you in de Hall o' Fame when you croaks.
Eugene O'Neill 1888–1953: *The Emperor Jones* (1921)

43 Any one who has been to an English public school will always feel comparatively at home in prison. It is the people brought up in the gay intimacy of the slums, Paul learned, who find prison so soul-destroying.
Evelyn Waugh 1903–66: *Decline and Fall* (1928)

44 Once in the racket you're always in it.
Al Capone 1899–1947: in *Philadelphia Public Ledger* 18 May 1929

45 Major Strasser has been shot. Round up the usual suspects.
Julius J. Epstein 1909–2001 et al.: *Casablanca* (1942 film)

46 Crime isn't a disease, it's a symptom. Cops are like a doctor that gives you aspirin for a brain tumour.
Raymond Chandler 1888–1959: *The Long Good-Bye* (1953)

47 The fear of burglars is not only the fear of being robbed, but also the fear of a sudden and unexpected clutch out of the darkness.
Elias Canetti 1905–94: *Crowds and Power* (1960)

48 I hate victims who respect their executioners.
Jean-Paul Sartre 1905–80: *Les Séquestrés d'Altona* (1960)

49 The thoughts of a prisoner—they're not free either. They keep returning to the same things.
Alexander Solzhenitsyn 1918– : *One Day in the Life of Ivan Denisovich* (1962)

50 Jails and prisons are designed to break human beings, to convert the population into specimens in a zoo—obedient to our keepers, but dangerous to each other.
Angela Davis 1944– : *An Autobiography* (1974)

51 A liberal is a conservative who has been arrested.
Tom Wolfe 1931– : *The Bonfire of the Vanities* (1987); see 1 above

52 Society needs to condemn a little more and understand a little less.
John Major 1943– : interview with *Mail on Sunday* 21 February 1993

53 Labour is the party of law and order in Britain today. Tough on crime and tough on the causes of crime.
Tony Blair 1953– : speech at the Labour Party Conference, 30 September 1993

54 You can be a famous poisoner or a successful poisoner, but not both, and the same seems to apply to Great Train Robbers.
Clive Anderson 1952– : in *Mail on Sunday* 20 May 2001

Crises

PROVERBS AND SAYINGS

1 Duck and cover.
US advice in the event of a missile attack, c.1950; associated particularly with children's cartoon character 'Bert the Turtle'

2 Ohhh, I don't *believe* it!
catchphrase used by Victor Meldrew in One Foot in the Grave (BBC television series, 1989–2000), written by David Renwick

3 We won't make a drama out of a crisis.
advertising slogan for Commercial Union insurance

PHRASES

4 cross the Rubicon take a decisive or irrevocable step.
the Rubicon was a stream in North-East Italy which marked the ancient boundary with Cisalpine Gaul; by taking his army across it into Italy from his own province in 49 BC, Julius Caesar broke the law forbidding a general to lead an army out of his

province, and so committed himself to war against the Senate and Pompey; see 9 below

5 the Dunkirk spirit the refusal to surrender or despair in a time of crisis.

from the evacuation of the British Expeditionary Force from Dunkirk in 1940; see 20 below, **World War II** *9*

6 the final straw a slight addition to a burden or difficulty that makes it finally unbearable.

from the proverb: see **Excess** *3*

7 moment of truth a crisis, a turning-point; a testing situation.

Spanish el momento de la verdad the time of the final sword-thrust in a bullfight

8 the parting of the ways the moment at which a choice must be made.

after the Bible (Ezekiel) 'The king of Babylon stood at the parting of the ways'

QUOTATIONS

9 The die is cast.

at the crossing of the Rubicon (see 4 above); often quoted in Latin 'Iacta alea est' but originally spoken in Greek

Julius Caesar 100–44 BC: Suetonius *Lives of the Caesars* 'Divus Julius'; Plutarch *Parallel Lives* 'Pompey'

10 For it is your business, when the wall next door catches fire.

Horace 65–8 BC: *Epistles*

11 The illustrious bishop of Cambrai was of more worth than his chambermaid, and there are few of us that would hesitate to pronounce, if his palace were in flames, and the life of only one of them could be preserved, which of the two ought to be preferred.

William Godwin 1756–1836: *An Enquiry concerning the Principles of Political Justice* (1793)

12 Whatever might be the extent of the individual calamity, I do not consider it of a nature worthy to interrupt the proceedings on so great a national question.

on hearing that his theatre was on fire, during a debate on the campaign in Spain

Richard Brinsley Sheridan 1751–1816: speech, House of Commons 24 February 1809

13 We have the wolf by the ears; and we can neither hold him, nor safely let him go. Justice is in one scale, and self-preservation in the other.

on slavery

Thomas Jefferson 1743–1826: letter to John Holmes, 22 April 1820; see **Danger** 12

14 Swimming for his life, a man does not see much of the country through which the river winds.

W. E. Gladstone 1809–98: diary, 31 December 1868

15 If you can keep your head when all about you
Are losing theirs and blaming it on you . . .

Rudyard Kipling 1865–1936: 'If—' (1910); see 19 below

16 The British people have taken for themselves this motto—'Business carried on as usual during alterations on the map of Europe'.

Winston Churchill 1874–1965: speech at Guildhall, 9 November 1914

17 I felt as if I was walking with destiny, and that all my past life had been but a preparation for this hour and this trial.

on becoming Prime Minister

Winston Churchill 1874–1965: on 10 May 1940

18 Comin' in on a wing and a pray'r.

the contemporary comment of a war pilot, speaking from a disabled plane to ground control

Harold Adamson 1906–80: title of song (1943); see **Necessity** 15

19 As someone pointed out recently, if you can keep your head when all about you are losing theirs, it's just possible you haven't grasped the situation.

Jean Kerr 1923– : *Please Don't Eat the Daisies* (1957); see 15 above

20 I myself have always deprecated . . . in crisis after crisis, appeals to the Dunkirk spirit as an answer to our problems.

Harold Wilson 1916–95: in the House of Commons, 26 July 1961; see 5 above

21 We're eyeball to eyeball, and I think the other fellow just blinked.

on the Cuban missile crisis

Dean Rusk 1909– : comment, 24 October 1962; see **Defiance** 6

22 In bygone days, commanders were taught that when in doubt, they should march their troops towards the sound of gunfire. I intend to march my troops towards the sound of gunfire.

Jo Grimond 1913–93: speech at Liberal Party Annual Assembly, 14 September 1963

23 There cannot be a crisis next week. My schedule is already full.

Henry Kissinger 1923– : in *New York Times Magazine* 1 June 1969

24 Crisis? What Crisis?

headline summarizing James Callaghan's remark of 10 January 1979: 'I don't think other people in the world would share the view there is mounting chaos'
Anonymous: in *Sun* 11 January 1979

25 Don't panic.
Douglas Adams 1952–2001: *Hitch Hiker's Guide to the Galaxy* (1979)

26 We do not experience and thus we have no measure of the disasters we prevent.
J. K. Galbraith 1908– : *A Life in our Times* (1981)

Criticism see also **Likes and Dislikes**, **Taste**

1 The best place for criticism is in front of your mirror.
American proverb, mid 20th century, recommending that you judge yourself before others

2 Criticism is something you can avoid by saying nothing, doing nothing, and being nothing.
American proverb, mid 20th century, implying that abstaining from criticism will result in complete inaction

3 cast the first stone be the first to make an accusation, especially when not oneself guiltless.
with allusion to the Bible (John): see **Guilt** 7

4 Critics are like brushers of noblemen's clothes.
Henry Wotton 1568–1639: Francis Bacon *Apophthegms New and Old* (1625)

5 One should look long and carefully at oneself before one considers judging others.
Molière 1622–73: *Le Misanthrope* (1666)

6 How science dwindles, and how volumes swell,
How commentators each dark passage shun,
And hold their farthing candle to the sun.
Edward Young 1683–1765: *The Love of Fame* (1725–8)

7 Yet malice never was his aim;
He lashed the vice, but spared the name;
No individual could resent,
Where thousands equally were meant.
Jonathan Swift 1667–1745: 'Verses on the Death of Dr Swift' (1731)

8 You *may* abuse a tragedy, though you cannot write one. You may scold a carpenter who has made you a bad table, though you cannot make a table. It is not your trade to make tables.
on literary criticism
Samuel Johnson 1709–84: James Boswell *Life of Samuel Johnson* (1791) 25 June 1763

9 I have always suspected that the reading is right, which requires many words to prove it wrong; and the emendation wrong, that cannot without so much labour appear to be right.
Samuel Johnson 1709–84: *Plays of William Shakespeare . . .* (1765)

10 A man must serve his time to every trade
Save censure—critics all are ready made.
Lord Byron 1788–1824: *English Bards and Scotch Reviewers* (1809)

11 This will never do.
on Wordsworth's The Excursion *(1814)*
Francis, Lord Jeffrey 1773–1850: in *Edinburgh Review* November 1814

12 I never read a book before reviewing it; it prejudices a man so.
Sydney Smith 1771–1845: H. Pearson *The Smith of Smiths* (1934)

13 You know who the critics are? The men who have failed in literature and art.
Benjamin Disraeli 1804–81: *Lothair* (1870)

14 The good critic is he who relates the adventures of his soul in the midst of masterpieces.
Anatole France 1844–1924: *La Vie littéraire* (1888)

15 We must grant the artist his subject, his idea, his *donnée*: our criticism is applied only to what he makes of it.
Henry James 1843–1916: *Partial Portraits* (1888) 'Art of Fiction'

16 I am sitting in the smallest room of my house. I have your review before me. In a moment it will be behind me.
responding to a savage review by Rudolph Louis in Münchener Neueste Nachrichten, *7 February 1906*
Max Reger 1873–1916: Nicolas Slonimsky *Lexicon of Musical Invective* (1953)

17 She was one of the people who say 'I don't know anything about music really, but I know what I like.'
Max Beerbohm 1872–1956: *Zuleika Dobson* (1911)

18 People ask you for criticism, but they only want praise.
W. Somerset Maugham 1874–1965: *Of Human Bondage* (1915)

19 Never trust the artist. Trust the tale. The proper function of a critic is to save the tale from the artist who created it.
D. H. Lawrence 1885–1930: *Studies in Classic American Literature* (1923)

20 Parodies and caricatures are the most penetrating of criticisms.
Aldous Huxley 1894–1963: *Point Counter Point* (1928)

21 Remember, a statue has never been set up in honour of a critic!
Jean Sibelius 1865–1957: Bengt de Törne *Sibelius: A Close-Up* (1937)

22 Whom the gods wish to destroy they first call promising.
Cyril Connolly 1903–74: *Enemies of Promise* (1938); see **Madness** 1

23 When the reviews are bad I tell my staff that they can join me as I cry all the way to the bank.
Liberace 1919–87: *Autobiography* (1973); joke coined in the mid-1950s

24 Long experience has taught me that to be criticized is not always to be wrong.
speech at Lord Mayor's Guildhall banquet during the Suez crisis
Anthony Eden 1897–1977: in *Daily Herald* 10 November 1956

25 Interpretation is the revenge of the intellect upon art.
Susan Sontag 1933– : in *Evergreen Review* December 1964

26 A critic is a man who knows the way but can't drive the car.
Kenneth Tynan 1927–80: in *New York Times Magazine* 9 January 1966

27 *Il n'y a pas de hors-texte.*
There is nothing outside of the text.
Jacques Derrida 1930– : *Of Grammatology* (1967)

28 I doubt that art needed Ruskin any more than a moving train needs one of its passengers to shove it.
Tom Stoppard 1937– : in *Times Literary Supplement* 3 June 1977

29 No theoretician, no writer on art, however interesting he or she might be, could be as interesting as Picasso. A good writer on art may give you an insight to Picasso, but, after all, Picasso was there first.
David Hockney 1937– : Wendy O. Brown (ed.) *Hockney on Photography* (1988)

30 If you are not criticized, you may not be doing much.
Donald Rumsfeld 1932– : *Rumsfeld's Rules* (2001)

Cruelty

PROVERBS AND SAYINGS

1 **It takes 40 dumb animals to make a fur coat, but only one to wear it.**
slogan of an anti-fur campaign poster, 1980s, sometimes attributed to David Bailey (1938–)

PHRASES

2 **out-Herod Herod** behave with extreme cruelty or tyranny.
Herod *a blustering tyrant in miracle plays, representing Herod the ruler of Judaea at the time of Jesus' birth (see* **Festivals** *28); after Shakespeare*

Hamlet '*I would have such a fellow whipp'd for o'erdoing Termagant; it out-herods Herod*'

3 **Roman holiday** an event occasioning enjoyment or profit derived from the suffering or discomfort of others.
from Byron: see 8 below

QUOTATIONS

4 Boys throw stones at frogs for fun, but the frogs don't die for 'fun', but in sober earnest.
Bion c.325–c.255 BC: Plutarch *Moralia*

5 Strike him so that he can feel that he is dying.
Caligula AD 12–41: Suetonius *Lives of the Caesars* 'Gaius Caligula'

6 I must be cruel only to be kind.
William Shakespeare 1564–1616: *Hamlet* (1601); see 12 below

7 Man's inhumanity to man
Makes countless thousands mourn!
Robert Burns 1759–96: 'Man was made to Mourn' (1786)

8 *There* were his young barbarians all at play,
There was their Dacian mother—he, their sire,
Butchered to make a Roman holiday.
Lord Byron 1788–1824: *Childe Harold's Pilgrimage* (1812–18); see 3 above

9 Cruelty, like every other vice, requires no motive outside itself—it only requires opportunity.
George Eliot 1819–1880: *Scenes of Clerical Life* (1858)

10 With many women I doubt whether there be any more effectual way of touching their hearts than ill-using them and then confessing it. If you wish to get the sweetest fragrance from the herb at your feet, tread on it and bruise it.
Anthony Trollope 1815–82: *Miss Mackenzie* (1865)

11 The infliction of cruelty with a good conscience is a delight to moralists. That is why they invented Hell.
Bertrand Russell 1872–1970: *Sceptical Essays* (1928) 'On the Value of Scepticism'

12 Being cruel to be kind is just ordinary cruelty with an excuse made for it . . . And it is right that it should be more resented, as it is.
Ivy Compton-Burnett 1884–1969: *Daughters and Sons* (1937); see 6 above

13 The healthy man does not torture others— generally it is the tortured who turn into torturers.
Carl Gustav Jung 1875–1961: in *Du* May 1941

14 The wish to hurt, the momentary intoxication with pain, is the loophole through which the pervert climbs into the minds of ordinary men.
Jacob Bronowski 1908–74: *The Face of Violence* (1954)

15 Our language lacks words to express this offence, the demolition of a man.
of a year spent in Auschwitz
Primo Levi 1919–87: *If This is a Man* (1958)

16 Nothing there is in nature as thoughtlessly cruel as a small boy, unless it be a small girl.
John Steinbeck 1902–68: *America and Americans* (1966)

17 It is cruel to break people's legs, even if the statement is made by someone in the habit of breaking their arms.
Brigid Brophy 1929– : S. and R. Godlovitch and J. Harris (eds.) *Animals, Men and Morals* (1972)

Culture and Civilization

PROVERBS AND SAYINGS

1 An ace caff with quite a nice museum attached.
advertising slogan for the Victoria and Albert Museum, February 1989

PHRASES

2 the age of reason the late 17th and 18th centuries in western Europe, during which cultural life was characterized by faith in human reason; the enlightenment.

3 the end of civilization as we know it the complete collapse of ordered society.
supposedly a cinematic cliché, and actually used in the film Citizen Kane *(1941) 'a project which would mean the end of civilization as we know it'*

4 the golden age an idyllic past time of prosperity, happiness, and innocence; the period of a nation's greatest prosperity or literary and artistic merit.

5 the noble savage primitive man, conceived of in the manner of Rousseau as morally superior to civilized man.
see also 8 below

QUOTATIONS

6 Our love of what is beautiful does not lead to extravagance; our love of the things of the mind does not make us soft.
Pericles c.495–429 BC: funeral oration, Athens, 430 BC; Thucydides *History of the Peloponnesian War*

7 In the youth of a state arms do flourish; in the middle age of a state, learning; and then both of them together for a time; in the declining age of a state, mechanical arts and merchandise.
Francis Bacon 1561–1626: *Essays* (1625) 'Of Vicissitude of Things'

8 I am as free as nature first made man,
Ere the base laws of servitude began,
When wild in woods the noble savage ran.
John Dryden 1631–1700: *The Conquest of Granada* (1670); see 5 above

9 I must study politics and war that my sons may have liberty to study mathematics and philosophy. My sons ought to study mathematics and philosophy, geography, natural history, naval architecture, navigation, commerce, and agriculture, in order to give their children a right to study painting, poetry, music, architecture, statuary, tapestry, and porcelain.
John Adams 1735–1826: letter to Abigail Adams, 12 May 1780

10 If a nation expects to be ignorant and free, in a state of civilization, it expects what never was and never will be.
Thomas Jefferson 1743–1826: letter to Colonel Charles Yancey, 6 January 1816

11 The three great elements of modern civilization, Gunpowder, Printing, and the Protestant Religion.
Thomas Carlyle 1795–1881: *Critical and Miscellaneous Essays* (1838) 'The State of German Literature'; see **Inventions** 6

12 Philistinism!—We have not the expression in English. Perhaps we have not the word because we have so much of the thing.
Matthew Arnold 1822–88: *Essays in Criticism* First Series (1865) 'Heinrich Heine'

13 Civilized ages inherit the human nature which was victorious in barbarous ages, and that nature is, in many respects, not at all suited to civilized circumstances.
Walter Bagehot 1826–77: *Physics and Politics* (1872) 'The Age of Discussion'

14 What are we waiting for, gathered in the market-place?

The barbarians are to arrive today.
Constantine Cavafy 1863–1933: 'Waiting for the Barbarians' (1904)

15 Civilization advances by extending the number of important operations which we can perform without thinking about them.
Alfred North Whitehead 1861–1947: *Introduction to Mathematics* (1911)

16 Mrs Ballinger is one of the ladies who pursue Culture in bands, as though it were dangerous to meet it alone.
Edith Wharton 1862–1937: *Xingu and Other Stories* (1916)

17 All civilization has from time to time become a thin crust over a volcano of revolution.
Havelock Ellis 1859–1939: *Little Essays of Love and Virtue* (1922)

18 The nations which have put mankind and posterity most in their debt have been small states—Israel, Athens, Florence, Elizabethan England.
William Ralph Inge 1860–1954: *Outspoken Essays: Second Series* (1922) 'State, visible and invisible'

19 Cultured people are merely the glittering scum which floats upon the deep river of production.
on hearing his son Randolph criticize the lack of culture of the Calgary oil magnates, probably c.1929
Winston Churchill 1874–1965: Martin Gilbert *In Search of Churchill* (1994)

20 JOURNALIST: Mr Gandhi, what do you think of modern civilization?
GANDHI: That would be a good idea.
Mahatma Gandhi 1869–1948: on arriving in England in 1930; E. F. Schumacher *Good Work* (1979)

21 Whenever I hear the word culture . . . I release the safety-catch of my Browning!
often quoted: 'Whenever I hear the word culture, I reach for my pistol!'
Hanns Johst 1890–1978: *Schlageter* (1933); often attributed to Hermann Goering; see 26, 29 below

22 Culture may even be described simply as that which makes life worth living.
T. S. Eliot 1888–1965: *Notes Towards a Definition of Culture* (1948)

23 In Italy for thirty years under the Borgias they had warfare, terror, murder, bloodshed —they produced Michelangelo, Leonardo da Vinci and the Renaissance. In Switzerland they had brotherly love, five hundred years of democracy and peace and what did that produce . . . ? The cuckoo clock.

Orson Welles 1915–85: *The Third Man* (1949 film); words added by Welles to Graham Greene's script

24 Rousseau is the greatest militant lowbrow of history, a kind of guttersnipe of genius.

Isaiah Berlin 1909–97: *Freedom and Its Betrayal* (1952)

25 The soul of any civilization on earth has ever been and still is Art and Religion, but neither has ever been found in commerce, in government or the police.

Frank Lloyd Wright 1867–1959: *A Testament* (1957)

26 When politicians and civil servants hear the word 'culture' they feel for their blue pencils.

Lord Esher 1913– : speech, House of Lords, 2 March 1960; see 21 above, **Censorship** 1

27 'Sergeant Pepper'—a decisive moment in the history of Western Civilization.

Kenneth Tynan 1927–80: in 1967; Howard Elson *McCartney* (1986)

28 Sooner or later we must absorb Islam if our own culture is not to die of anaemia.

Basil Bunting 1900–85: Omar Pound *Arabic and Persian Poems* (1970) foreword

29 It is unlikely that the government reaches for a revolver when it hears the word culture. The more likely response is to search for a dictionary.

David Glencross 1936– : Royal Television Society conference on the future of television, 26–27 November 1988; see 21 above

30 If civilization had been left in female hands, we would still be living in grass huts.

Camille Paglia 1947– : *Sexual Personae* (1990)

31 A cultural Chernobyl.

of Euro Disney

Ariane Mnouchkine 1934– : in *Harper's Magazine* July 1992; see 32 below

32 Some refer to it as a cultural Chernobyl. I think of it as a cultural Stalingrad.

of Euro Disney

J. G. Ballard 1930– : in *Daily Telegraph* 2 July 1994; see 31 above

33 Popular culture is a contradiction in terms. If it's popular, it's not culture. If everyone loves it, it's not original.

Vivienne Westwood 1941– : in *Independent on Sunday* 8 November 1998

34 The culture of the 1990s can be summed up by Neighbours and football.

Spike Milligan 1918–2002: in *Sunday Times* 2 January 2000

35 Television today has replaced the theatre of the 20th century, the novels of the 19th, the Bible of the 17th, the folktales of the village, the bedtime stories parents told their children.

Jonathan Sacks 1948– : *Culture and Communications* (2001)

Custom and Habit

PROVERBS AND SAYINGS

1 **Custom is mummified by habit and glorified by law.**

American proverb, mid 20th century

2 **Old habits die hard.**

mid 18th century

3 **What is new cannot be true.**

mid 17th century, used to imply that innovation is less soundly based than custom which has been proved by experience

4 **You can't teach an old dog new tricks.**

mid 16th century; meaning that someone who is already set in their ways is not able to learn new ways of doing things

5 **You cannot shift an old tree without it dying.**

early 16th century; often used to suggest the risk involved in moving an elderly person who has lived in the same place for many years

PHRASES

6 **pass on the torch** pass on a tradition.

from Lucretius 'Some races increase, others are reduced, and in a short while the generations of living creatures are changed and like runners relay the torch of life'

QUOTATIONS

7 The Lord says in the gospel; 'I am the Truth'. He does not say 'I am custom'.

Therefore, when the truth is made manifest, custom must give way to truth.
Bishop Libosus of Vaga fl. 256 AD: St Augustine of Hippo *On Baptism*; see **The Christian Church** 14

8 *Consuetudo est altera natura.*
Habit is second nature.
Auctoritates Aristotelis: a compilation of medieval propositions

9 But to my mind,—though I am native here,
And to the manner born,—it is a custom More honoured in the breach than the observance.
William Shakespeare 1564-1616: *Hamlet* (1601); see **Behaviour** 12

10 Custom that is before all law, Nature that is above all art.
Samuel Daniel 1563-1619: *A Defence of Rhyme* (1603)

11 Custom, that unwritten law,
By which the people keep even kings in awe.
Charles D'Avenant 1656-1714: *Circe* (1677)

12 Actions receive their tincture from the times,
And as they change are virtues made or crimes.
Daniel Defoe 1660-1731: *A Hymn to the Pillory* (1703)

13 Custom reconciles us to everything.
Edmund Burke 1729-97: *On the Sublime and Beautiful* (1757)

14 The satirist may laugh, the philosopher may preach, but Reason herself will respect the prejudices and habits which have been consecrated by the experience of mankind.
Edward Gibbon 1737-94: *Memoirs of My Life* (1796)

15 Habit with him was all the test of truth,
'It must be right: I've done it from my youth.'
George Crabbe 1754-1832: *The Borough* (1810)

16 People wish to be settled: only as far as they are unsettled is there any hope for them.
Ralph Waldo Emerson 1803-82: *Essays* (1841) 'Circles'

17 The tradition of all the dead generations weighs like a nightmare on the brain of the living.
Karl Marx 1818-83: *The Eighteenth Brumaire of Louis Bonaparte* (1852)

18 Tradition means giving votes to the most obscure of all classes, our ancestors. It is the democracy of the dead.
G. K. Chesterton 1874-1936: *Orthodoxy* (1908)

19 Every public action, which is not customary, either is wrong, or, if it is right, is a dangerous precedent. It follows that nothing should ever be done for the first time.
Francis M. Cornford 1874-1943: *Microcosmographia Academica* (1908)

20 One can't carry one's father's corpse about everywhere.
Guillaume Apollinaire 1880-1918: *Les peintres cubistes* (1965) 'Méditations esthétiques: Sur la peinture'

21 Tradition is entirely different from habit, even from an excellent habit, since habit is by definition an unconscious acquisition and tends to become mechanical, whereas tradition results from a conscious and deliberate acceptance . . . Tradition presupposes the reality of what endures.
Igor Stravinsky 1882-1971: *Poetics of Music* (1947)

22 The air is full of our cries. (*He listens*) But habit is a great deadener.
Samuel Beckett 1906-89: *Waiting for Godot* (1955)

23 Routine, in an intelligent man, is a sign of ambition.
W. H. Auden 1907-73: 'The Life of That-There Poet' (1958)

24 I don't think you can make a conscious decision about tradition. I mean, you're either of it, or you're not. I don't think you belong to a tradition by aping it.
Harrison Birtwistle 1934- : Andrew Ford *Composer to Composer* (1993)

Cynicism   see **Disillusion and Cynicism**

Dance

1 **When you go to dance, take heed whom you take by the hand.**
early 17th century

2 **You need more than dancing shoes to be a dancer.**
American proverb, mid 20th century

PHRASES

3 **antic hay** an absurd dance.
from Marlowe; see 5 below

4 **trip the light fantastic** dance.
originally with allusion to Milton: see 8 below

QUOTATIONS

5 My men, like satyrs grazing on the lawns,
Shall with their goat feet dance an antic hay.
Christopher Marlowe 1564–93: *Edward II* (1593); see 3 above

6 This wondrous miracle did Love devise,
For dancing is love's proper exercise.
John Davies 1569–1626: 'Orchestra, or a Poem of Dancing' (1596)

7 A dance is a measured pace, as a verse is a measured speech.
Francis Bacon 1561–1626: *The Advancement of Learning* (1605)

8 Come, and trip it as ye go
On the light fantastic toe.
John Milton 1608–74: 'L'Allegro' (1645); see 4 above

9 On with the dance! let joy be unconfined;
No sleep till morn, when Youth and Pleasure meet
To chase the glowing Hours with flying feet.
Lord Byron 1788–1824: *Childe Harold's Pilgrimage* (1812–18)

10 Will you, won't you, will you, won't you, will you join the dance?
Lewis Carroll 1832–98: *Alice's Adventures in Wonderland* (1865)

11 I wish I could shimmy like my sister Kate,
She shivers like the jelly on a plate.
Armand J. Piron: *Shimmy like Kate* (1919 song)

12 O body swayed to music, O brightening glance
How can we know the dancer from the dance?
W. B. Yeats 1865–1939: 'Among School Children' (1928)

13 Heaven—I'm in Heaven—And my heart beats so that I can hardly speak;
And I seem to find the happiness I seek
When we're out together dancing cheek-to-cheek.
Irving Berlin 1888–1989: 'Cheek-to-Cheek' (1935 song)

14 There may be trouble ahead,
But while there's moonlight and music and love and romance,
Let's face the music and dance.
Irving Berlin 1888–1989: 'Let's Face the Music and Dance' (1936 song)

15 [Dancing is] a perpendicular expression of a horizontal desire.
George Bernard Shaw 1856–1950: in *New Statesman* 23 March 1962

16 The truest expression of a people is in its dances and its music. Bodies never lie.
Agnes de Mille 1908– : in *New York Times Magazine* 11 May 1975

17 Dance is the hidden language of the soul.
Martha Graham 1894–1991: *Blood Memory* (1991)

18 Line dancing is as sinful as any other type of dancing, with its sexual gestures and touching. It is an incitement to lust.
Ian Paisley 1926– : in *Mail on Sunday* 20 May 2001

Danger see also Caution, Courage

1 **Adventures are to the adventurous.**
mid 19th century, meaning that the person who wants exciting things to happen must take the initiative

2 **A common danger causes common action.**
American proverb, mid 20th century

3 Heaven protects children, sailors, and drunken men.

mid 19th century; often used (in a number of variant forms) to imply that someone unable to look after themselves has been undeservedly lucky

4 He who rides a tiger is afraid to dismount.

late 19th century, meaning that once a dangerous or troublesome venture is begun, the safest course is to carry it through to the end; see 17 below

5 If you play with fire you get burnt.

late 19th century, meaning that if you involve yourself with something potentially dangerous you are likely to be hurt

6 Just when you thought it was safe to go back in the water.

advertising copy for the film Jaws 2 (1978), featuring the return of the great white shark

7 Light the blue touch paper and retire immediately.

traditional instruction for lighting fireworks

8 The post of honour is the post of danger.

mid 16th century

9 Who dares wins.

motto of the British Special Air Service regiment, from 1942

10 bell the cat take the danger of a shared enterprise upon oneself.

from the fable in which mice proposed hanging a bell around a cat's neck so as to be warned of its approach

11 cry wolf raise repeated false alarms, so that a genuine cry for help goes unheeded.

from the fable of the shepherd boy who tricked people with false cries of 'Wolf!'

12 have a wolf by the ears be in a precarious situation; be in a predicament where any course of action presents problems.

see Crises 13

13 a lion in the way a danger or obstacle, especially an imaginary one.

from the Bible (Proverbs) 'The slothful man saith, There is a lion in the way'

14 the lion's mouth a place or situation of great peril.

with reference to the Bible (Psalms) 'Save me from the lion's mouth' and (2 Timothy) 'I was delivered out of the mouth of the lion'

15 a pad in the straw a lurking or hidden danger.

pad a toad, regarded as a venomous creature

16 pull the chestnuts out of the fire succeed in a hazardous undertaking on behalf of or through the agency of another.

in allusion to the fable of a monkey using a cat's paw to get roasting chestnuts from a fire; see Duty 3

17 ride a tiger take on a responsibility or embark on a course of action which subsequently cannot easily or safely be abandoned.

from the proverb: see 4 above

18 a snake in the grass a secret enemy, a lurking danger.

after Virgil Eclogues 'There's a snake hidden in the grass'

19 a sword of Damocles an imminent danger; a constant threat, especially in the midst of prosperity.

Damocles a legendary courtier who extravagantly praised the happiness of Dionysius I, ruler of Syracuse, and whom Dionysius feasted while a sword hung by a hair above him

20 the valley of the shadow of death a place or period of intense gloom or peril.

from the Bible (Psalms) 'Though I walk through the valley of the shadow of death, I will fear no evil'

21 I am escaped with the skin of my teeth.
Bible: Job

22 Out of this nettle, danger, we pluck this flower, safety.
William Shakespeare 1564–1616: *Henry IV, Part 1* (1597); see **Courage** 10

23 It is the bright day that brings forth the adder;
And that craves wary walking.
William Shakespeare 1564–1616: *Julius Caesar* (1599)

24 Our God and soldiers we alike adore
Ev'n at the brink of danger; not before:
After deliverance, both alike requited,
Our God's forgotten, and our soldiers slighted.
Francis Quarles 1592–1644: 'Of Common Devotion' (1632); see **Human Nature** 10

25 When there is no peril in the fight, there is no glory in the triumph.
Pierre Corneille 1606–84: *Le Cid* (1637)

26 Dangers by being despised grow great.
Edmund Burke 1729–97: speech on the Petition of the Unitarians, 11 May 1792

27 In skating over thin ice, our safety is in our speed.
Ralph Waldo Emerson 1803–82: *Essays* (1841) 'Prudence'

28 We took risks, we knew we took them; things have come out against us, and therefore we have no cause for complaint.
Robert Falcon Scott 1868–1912: 'The Last Message' in *Scott's Last Expedition* (1913)

29 My inclination to go by Air Express is confirmed by the crash they had yesterday, which will make them careful in the immediate future.
A. E. Housman 1859–1936: letter 17 August 1920

30 Anyone who expects to meet a lunatic brandishing a hatchet and instead finds a man hiding a revolver in his trouser pocket is bound to feel relieved. But that doesn't prevent a revolver from being more dangerous than a hatchet.
Leon Trotsky 1879–1940: in *Bulletin of the Opposition* 1933

31 Security is mostly a superstition. It does not exist in nature, nor do the children of men as a whole experience it. Avoiding danger is no safer in the long run than outright exposure. Life is either a daring adventure, or nothing.
Helen Keller 1880–1968: *The Open Door* (1957)

32 Security is when everything is settled, when nothing can happen to you; security is the denial of life.
Germaine Greer 1939– : *The Female Eunuch* (1970)

33 It is no good putting up notices saying 'Beware of the bull' because very rude things are sometimes written on them. I have found that one of the most effective notices is 'Beware of the Agapanthus'.
Lord Massereene and Ferrard 1914–93: speech on the Wildlife and Countryside Bill, House of Lords 16 December 1980

Day and Night

PROVERBS AND SAYINGS

1 The morning daylight appears plainer when you put out your candle.
American proverb

PHRASES

2 the watches of the night the night-time.
watch originally each of the three or four periods of time, during which a watch or guard was kept, into which the night was divided by the Jews and Romans

3 the witching hour midnight.
the time when witches are proverbially active; after Shakespeare: see 5 below; see also **Business** 21

QUOTATIONS

4 Night's candles are burnt out, and jocund day
Stands tiptoe on the misty mountain tops.
William Shakespeare 1564–1616: *Romeo and Juliet* (1595)

5 'Tis now the very witching time of night,
When churchyards yawn and hell itself breathes out
Contagion to this world.
William Shakespeare 1564–1616: *Hamlet* (1601); see 3 above

6 Lighten our darkness, we beseech thee, O Lord; and by thy great mercy defend us from all perils and dangers of this night.
The Book of Common Prayer 1662: *Evening Prayer*

7 Now came still evening on, and twilight grey
Had in her sober livery all things clad.
John Milton 1608–74: *Paradise Lost* (1667)

8 The curfew tolls the knell of parting day,
The lowing herd wind slowly o'er the lea,
The ploughman homeward plods his weary way,
And leaves the world to darkness and to me.
Thomas Gray 1716–71: *Elegy Written in a Country Churchyard* (1751)

9 The Sun's rim dips; the stars rush out;
At one stride comes the dark.
Samuel Taylor Coleridge 1772–1834: 'The Rime of the Ancient Mariner' (1798)

10 It is a beauteous evening, calm and free;
The holy time is quiet as a nun
Breathless with adoration.
William Wordsworth 1770–1850: 'It is a beauteous evening, calm and free' (1807)

11 The cares that infest the day
Shall fold their tents, like the Arabs,
And as silently steal away.
Henry Wadsworth Longfellow 1807–82: 'The Day is Done' (1844)

12 And ghastly through the drizzling rain
On the bald street breaks the blank day.
Alfred, Lord Tennyson 1809–92: *In Memoriam A. H. H.* (1850)

13 Awake! for Morning in the bowl of night
Has flung the stone that puts the stars to flight:
And Lo! the Hunter of the East has caught
The Sultan's turret in a noose of light.
Edward Fitzgerald 1809–83: *The Rubáiyát of Omar Khayyám* (1859)

14 There midnight's all a glimmer, and noon a purple glow,
And evening full of the linnet's wings.
W. B. Yeats 1865–1939: 'The Lake Isle of Innisfree' (1892)

15 Let us go then, you and I,
When the evening is spread out against the sky
Like a patient etherized upon a table.
T. S. Eliot 1888–1965: 'The Love Song of J. Alfred Prufrock' (1917); see **Poetry** 32

16 The winter evening settles down
With smell of steaks in passageways.
Six o'clock.

The burnt-out ends of smoky days.
T. S. Eliot 1888–1965: 'Preludes' (1917)

17 I have a horror of sunsets, they're so romantic, so operatic.
Marcel Proust 1871–1922: *Cities of the Plain* (1922)

18 I have been one acquainted with the night.
Robert Frost 1874–1963: 'Acquainted with the Night' (1928)

19 Morning has broken
Like the first morning,
Blackbird has spoken
Like the first bird.
Eleanor Farjeon 1881–1965: 'A Morning Song (for the First Day of Spring)' (1957)

20 I cannot walk through the suburbs in the solitude of the night without thinking that the night pleases us because it suppresses idle details, just as our memory does.
Jorge Luis Borges 1899–1986: *Labyrinths* (1962)

21 What are days for?
Days are where we live.
They come, they wake us
Time and time over.
They are to be happy in:
Where can we live but days?
Philip Larkin 1922–85: 'Days' (1964)

22 It's been a hard day's night.
John Lennon 1940–80 and **Paul McCartney** 1942– : 'A Hard Day's Night' (1964 song)

Death see also **Epitaphs, Last Words, Mourning and Loss, Murder, Suicide**

PROVERBS AND SAYINGS

1 **As a tree falls, so shall it lie.**
mid 16th century, meaning that one should not change from one's long established practices and customs because of approaching death; from the Bible (Ecclesiastes) 'in the place where the tree falleth, there let it lie.'

2 **Blessed are the dead that the rain rains on.**
early 17th century

3 **[Death is] nature's way of telling you to slow down.**
American life insurance saying, in Newsweek *25 April 1960*

4 **Death is the great leveller.**
early 18th century, meaning that all people will be equal in death, whatever their material prosperity

5 **Death pays all debts.**
early 17th century, meaning that the death of a person cancels out their obligations; see 30 below

6 **One funeral makes many.**
late 19th century, sometimes with the implication that attendance at a deathbed or funeral may have fatal consequences

7 **Stone-dead hath no fellow.**
mid 17th century; traditionally used by advocates of the death penalty, or to suggest that only when a dangerous person is dead can one be sure that they will cause no further trouble

8 **There is a remedy for everything except death.**
mid 15th century

9 **This ae nighte, this ae nighte,**
  —Every nighte and alle,
Fire and fleet and candle-lighte,

And Christe receive thy saule.

'Lyke-Wake Dirge', traditional ballad; fleet =
corruption of flet: see **The Home** 8

10 You can only die once.

mid 15th century, used to encourage someone in a
dangerous or difficult enterprise; see 26 below

11 Young men may die, but old men must die.

mid 16th century, meaning that death is inevitable for
all, and can at best be postponed until old age

PHRASES

12 beyond the veil in the unknown state of
being after death.

originally with reference to Tyndale 'Christ hath
brought us all in into the inner temple within the veil',
taken as referring to the next world

13 go the way of all flesh die.

alteration of the Bible (I Kings) 'I go the way of all the
earth' (Douay Bible 1609 'I enter into the way of all
flesh')

14 join the great majority die.

Edward Young The Revenge (1721) 'Death joins us to
the great majority'; see 23 below; **Elections** 11

15 the potter's field a burial place for paupers
or strangers.

in reference to the Bible (Matthew), of how the chief
priests and elders made use of the thirty pieces of
silver returned to them by Judas after the Crucifixion,
'And they took counsel, and bought with them the
potter's field, to bury strangers in'; see **Trust and
Treachery** 14

16 smite under the fifth rib stab to the heart,
kill.

originally with reference to the Bible (II Samuel) 'Abner
. . . smote him under the fifth rib'

QUOTATIONS

17 I would rather be tied to the soil as another
man's serf, even a poor man's, who hadn't
much to live on himself, than be King of all
these the dead and destroyed.
Homer: The Odyssey

18 For dust thou art, and unto dust shalt thou
return.
Bible: Genesis; see 38 below

19 If any man thinks he slays, and if another
thinks he is slain, neither knows the ways
of truth. The Eternal in man cannot kill:
the Eternal in man cannot die.
The Upanishads c.800–200 BC: Katha Upanishad

20 Death, therefore, the most awful of evils, is
nothing to us, seeing that, when we are
death is not come, and when death is
come, we are not.
Epicurus 341–271 BC: Diogenes Laertius Lives of
Eminent Philosophers

21 *Non omnis moriar.*
I shall not altogether die.
Horace 65–8 BC: Odes

22 O death, where is thy sting? O grave,
where is thy victory?
Bible: I Corinthians; see **World War I** 20

23 *Abiit ad plures.*
He's gone to join the majority [the dead].
Petronius d. AD 65: Satyricon; see 14 above;
Elections 11

24 Anyone can stop a man's life, but no one
his death; a thousand doors open on to it.
Seneca ('the Younger') c.4 BC–AD 65: Phoenissae;
see 33 below

25 Finally he paid the debt of nature.
Robert Fabyan d. 1513: The New Chronicles of
England and France (1516)

26 I care not; a man can die but once; we
owe God a death.
William Shakespeare 1564–1616: Henry IV, Part 2
(1597); see 10 above

27　　　　To die, to sleep;
To sleep: perchance to dream: ay, there's
the rub;
For in that sleep of death what dreams
may come
When we have shuffled off this mortal coil,
Must give us pause.
William Shakespeare 1564–1616: Hamlet (1601);
see **Lifestyles** 9, **Problems** 12

28 Nothing in his life
Became him like the leaving it.
William Shakespeare 1564–1616: Macbeth (1606)

29 Death be not proud, though some have
called thee
Mighty and dreadful, for thou art not so.
John Donne 1572–1631: Holy Sonnets (1609)

30 He that dies pays all debts.
William Shakespeare 1564–1616: The Tempest
(1611); see 5 above

31 O eloquent, just, and mighty Death! . . .
thou hast drawn together all the
farstretched greatness, all the pride,

cruelty, and ambition of man, and covered it all over with these two narrow words, *Hic jacet.*
Walter Ralegh c.1552–1618: *The History of the World* (1614); see **Epitaphs** 3

32 Only we die in earnest, that's no jest.
Walter Ralegh c.1552–1618: 'On the Life of Man'

33 I know death hath ten thousand several
   doors
   For men to take their exits.
John Webster c.1580–c.1625: *The Duchess of Malfi* (1623); see 24 above

34 Any man's death diminishes me, because I am involved in Mankind; And therefore never send to know for whom the bell tolls; it tolls for thee.
John Donne 1572–1631: *Devotions upon Emergent Occasions* (1624)

35 The long habit of living indisposeth us for dying.
Thomas Browne 1605–82: *Hydriotaphia* (Urn Burial, 1658)

36 We shall die alone.
Blaise Pascal 1623–62: *Pensées* (1670)

37 In the midst of life we are in death.
The Book of Common Prayer 1662: *The Burial of the Dead*; see **Debt** 19

38 Forasmuch as it hath pleased Almighty God of his great mercy to take unto himself the soul of our dear brother here departed, we therefore commit his body to the ground; earth to earth, ashes to ashes, dust to dust; in sure and certain hope of the Resurrection to eternal life.
The Book of Common Prayer 1662: *The Burial of the Dead* Interment; see 18 above

39 Death never takes the wise man by surprise; he is always ready to go.
Jean de la Fontaine 1621–95: *Fables* (1678–9) 'La Mort et le Mourant'

40 They that die by famine die by inches.
Matthew Henry 1662–1714: *An Exposition on the Old and New Testament* (1710)

41 Can storied urn or animated bust
   Back to its mansion call the fleeting
      breath?
Thomas Gray 1716–71: *Elegy Written in a Country Churchyard* (1751)

42 The bodies of those that made such a noise and tumult when alive, when dead, lie as

quietly among the graves of their neighbours as any others.
Jonathan Edwards 1703–58: *Miscellaneous Discourses* sermon on procrastination

43 It matters not how a man dies, but how he lives. The act of dying is not of importance, it lasts so short a time.
Samuel Johnson 1709–84: James Boswell *Life of Samuel Johnson* (1791) 26 October 1769

44 Depend upon it, Sir, when a man knows he is to be hanged in a fortnight, it concentrates his mind wonderfully.
on the execution of Dr Dodd
Samuel Johnson 1709–84: James Boswell *Life of Samuel Johnson* (1791) 19 September 1777

45 My name is Death: the last best friend am
   I.
Robert Southey 1774–1843: 'The Lay of the Laureate' (1816)

46 Now more than ever seems it rich to die,
   To cease upon the midnight with no pain.
John Keats 1795–1821: 'Ode to a Nightingale' (1820)

47 The cemetery is an open space among the ruins, covered in winter with violets and daisies. It might make one in love with death, to think that one should be buried in so sweet a place.
Percy Bysshe Shelley 1792–1822: *Adonais* (1821)

48 He'd make a lovely corpse.
Charles Dickens 1812–70: *Martin Chuzzlewit* (1844)

49 Death must be distinguished from dying, with which it is often confused.
Sydney Smith 1771–1845: H. Pearson *The Smith of Smiths* (1934)

50 Just try and set death aside. It sets you aside, and that's the end of it!
Ivan Turgenev 1818–83: *Fathers and Sons* (1862)

51 This quiet Dust was Gentlemen and Ladies
   And Lads and Girls—
   Was laughter and ability and Sighing
   And Frocks and Curls.
Emily Dickinson 1830–86: 'This quiet Dust was Gentlemen and Ladies' (c.1864)

52 And all our calm is in that balm—
   Not lost but gone before.
Caroline Norton 1808–77: 'Not Lost but Gone Before'

53 For though from out our bourne of time
      and place
   The flood may bear me far,

I hope to see my pilot face to face
When I have crossed the bar.
Alfred, Lord Tennyson 1809–92: 'Crossing the Bar' (1889)

54 In the arts of life man invents nothing; but in the arts of death he outdoes Nature herself, and produces by chemistry and machinery all the slaughter of plague, pestilence and famine.
George Bernard Shaw 1856–1950: *Man and Superman* (1903)

55 There are no dead.
Maurice Maeterlinck 1862–1949: *L'Oiseau bleu* (1909)

56 Death is nothing at all; it does not count. I have only slipped away into the next room.
Henry Scott Holland 1847–1918: sermon preached on Whitsunday 1910

57 Blow out, you bugles, over the rich Dead!
There's none of these so lonely and poor of old,
But, dying, has made us rarer gifts than gold.
Rupert Brooke 1887–1915: 'The Dead' (1914)

58 Webster was much possessed by death
And saw the skull beneath the skin;
And breastless creatures underground
Leaned backward with a lipless grin.
T. S. Eliot 1888–1965: 'Whispers of Immortality' (1919)

59 A man's dying is more the survivors' affair than his own.
Thomas Mann 1875–1955: *The Magic Mountain* (1924)

60 To die will be an awfully big adventure.
J. M. Barrie 1860–1937: *Peter Pan* (1928); see **Last Words** 24

61 Ain't it grand to be blooming well dead?
Leslie Sarony 1897–1985: title of song (1932)

62 Nor dread nor hope attend
A dying animal;
A man awaits his end
Dreading and hoping all.
W. B. Yeats 1865–1939: 'Death' (1933)

63 He knows death to the bone—
Man has created death.
W. B. Yeats 1865–1939: 'Death' (1933)

64 Though lovers be lost love shall not;

And death shall have no dominion.
Dylan Thomas 1914–53: 'And death shall have no dominion' (1936)

65 For here the lover and killer are mingled
who had one body and one heart.
And death, who had the soldier singled
has done the lover mortal hurt.
Keith Douglas 1920–44: 'Vergissmeinnicht, 1943'

66 He shouts play death more sweetly this
Death is a master from Deutschland.
Paul Celan 1920–70: 'Deathfugue' (written 1944)

67   This is death.
To die and know it. This is the Black
Widow, death.
Robert Lowell 1917–77: 'Mr Edwards and the Spider' (1950)

68 One death is a tragedy, a million deaths a statistic.
Joseph Stalin 1879–1953: attributed

69 Let me die a youngman's death
Not a clean & in-between-
The-sheets, holy-water death,
Not a famous-last-words
Peaceful out-of-breath death.
Roger McGough 1937- : 'Let Me Die a Youngman's Death' (1967)

70 If there wasn't death, I think you couldn't go on.
Stevie Smith 1902–71: in *Observer* 9 November 1969

71 This parrot is no more! It has ceased to be! It's expired and gone to meet its maker! This is a late parrot! It's a stiff! Bereft of life it rests in peace — if you hadn't nailed it to the perch it would be pushing up the daisies! It's rung down the curtain and joined the choir invisible! THIS IS AN EX-PARROT!
Graham Chapman 1941–89, **John Cleese** 1939- , et al.: *Monty Python's Flying Circus* (BBC TV programme, 1969)

72 Death is nothing if one can approach it as such. I was just a tiny night-light, suffocated in its own wax, and on the point of expiring.
E. M. Forster 1879–1970: Philip Gardner (ed.) *E. M. Forster: Commonplace Book* (1985)

73 It's not that I'm afraid to die. I just don't want to be there when it happens.
Woody Allen 1935- : *Death* (1975)

74 Deception is not as creative as truth. We do best in life if we look at it with clear

eyes, and I think that applies to coming up to death as well.

of the Hospice movement

Cicely Saunders 1916– : in *Time* 5 September 1988

75 Even death is unreliable: instead of zero it may be some ghastly hallucination, such as the square root of minus one.

Samuel Beckett 1906–89: attributed

76 My breath is folded up
Like sheets in lavender.
The end for me
Arrives like nursery tea.

Graham Greene 1904–91: *A World of My Own* (1992)

77 We die containing a richness of lovers and tribes, tastes we have swallowed, bodies we have plunged into and swum up as if rivers of wisdom, characters we have climbed into as if trees, fears we have hidden as if in caves.

Michael Ondaatje 1943– : *The English Patient* (1992)

78 The key to dying well is for you to decide where, when, how and whom to invite to the last party.

during the last days of his final illness, to a visitor

Timothy Leary 1920–96: in *Daily Telegraph* 3 May 1996; see **Last Words** 31

Debt and Borrowing see also Thrift and Extravagance

see also **Thrift and Extravagance**

PROVERBS AND SAYINGS

1 Access—your flexible friend.

advertising slogan for Access credit card, 1981 onwards

2 American Express? . . . That'll do nicely, sir.

advertising slogan for American Express credit card, 1970s

3 He that goes a-borrowing, goes a sorrowing.

late 15th century, meaning that involving oneself in debt is likely to lead to unhappiness

4 Lend your money and lose your friend.

late 15th century, meaning that debt puts a strain on friendship

5 A man in debt is caught in a net.

American proverb, mid 20th century

6 A national debt, if it is not excessive, will be to us a national blessing.

American proverb; often attributed to Alexander Hamilton (c.1757–1804)

7 Out of debt, out of danger.

mid 17th century, meaning that someone in debt is vulnerable and at risk from others

8 Short reckonings make long friends.

mid 16th century; meaning that the prompt settlement of any debt between friends ensures that their friendship will not be damaged

PHRASES

9 a pound of flesh a payment or penalty which is strictly due but which it is ruthless or inhuman to demand.

with allusion to Shakespeare The Merchant of Venice, *and Shylock's insistence that he had the right to take*

the pound of Antonio's flesh promised in the bargain between them

10 rob Peter to pay Paul take away from one person to pay another; discharge one debt by incurring another.

probably the Apostles St Peter and St Paul as founders of the Church; see **Government** 36

QUOTATIONS

11 Be not made a beggar by banqueting upon borrowing.

Bible: Ecclesiasticus

12 Neither a borrower, nor a lender be;
For loan oft loses both itself and friend,
And borrowing dulls the edge of
      husbandry.

William Shakespeare 1564–1616: *Hamlet* (1601)

13 The human species, according to the best theory I can form of it, is composed of two distinct races, *the men who borrow*, and *the men who lend*.

Charles Lamb 1775–1834: *Essays of Elia* (1823) 'The Two Races of Men'

14 Dreading that climax of all human ills,
The inflammation of his weekly bills.

Lord Byron 1788–1824: *Don Juan* (1819–24)

15 Three things I never lends—my 'oss, my wife, and my name.

R. S. Surtees 1805–64: *Hillingdon Hall* (1845)

16 Annual income twenty pounds, annual expenditure nineteen nineteen six, result happiness. Annual income twenty pounds,

annual expenditure twenty pounds ought and six, result misery.
Charles Dickens 1812–70: *David Copperfield* (1850)

17 Worm or beetle—drought or tempest—on a farmer's land may fall,
Each is loaded full o' ruin, but a mortgage beats 'em all.
William McKendree Carleton 1845–1912: 'The Tramp's Story' (1881)

18 One must have some sort of occupation nowadays. If I hadn't my debts I shouldn't have anything to think about.
Oscar Wilde 1854–1900: *A Woman of No Importance* (1893)

19 In the midst of life we are in debt.
Ethel Watts Mumford 1878–1940 et al.: *Altogether New Cynic's Calendar* (1907); see **Death** 37

20 To take usury is contrary to Scripture; it is contrary to Aristotle; it is contrary to nature, for it is to live without labour; it is to sell time, which belongs to God, for the advantage of wicked men; it is to rob those who use the money lent, and to whom, since they make it profitable, the profits should belong.
R. H. Tawney 1880–1962: *Religion and the Rise of Capitalism* (1926)

21 The National Debt is a very Good Thing and it would be dangerous to pay it off, for fear of Political Economy.
W. C. Sellar 1898–1951 and **R. J. Yeatman** 1898–1968: *1066 and All That* (1930)

22 They hired the money, didn't they?
on the subject of war debts incurred by England and others
Calvin Coolidge 1872–1933: John H. McKee *Coolidge: Wit and Wisdom* (1933)

23 Sixteen tons, what do you get?
Another day older and deeper in debt.
Say brother, don't you call me 'cause I can't go
I owe my soul to the company store.
Merle Travis 1917–83: 'Sixteen Tons' (1947 song)

24 Should we really let our people starve so we can pay our debts?
Julius Nyerere 1922–99: in *Guardian* 21 March 1985

25 You can't put your VISA bill on your American Express card.
P. J. O'Rourke 1947– : *The Bachelor Home Companion* (1987)

26 That will make some sense out of the nonsense of the millennium.
urging cancellation of Third World debt as a way of marking the millennium
Bono 1960– : in *Independent* 14 June 1999

Deception see also **Hypocrisy**, **Lies**

1 **Cheats never prosper.**
early 19th century

2 **Deceit is a lie that wears a smile.**
American proverb, mid 20th century

3 **Fool me once, shame on you; fool me twice, shame on me.**
late 20th century saying, meaning that if someone is deceived twice their own stupidity is to blame

4 **be caught with chaff** be easily deceived or trapped.
*chaff the husks of corn separated from the grain by threshing; from the proverb: see **Experience** 11*

5 **borrowed plumes** a pretentious display not of one's own making.
with reference to the fable of the jay which decked itself in the peacock's feathers

6 **hand a person a lemon** pass off a substandard article as good; swindle a person, do a person down.
*lemon the type of a bad, unsatisfactory, or disappointing thing; see **Satisfaction** 2*

7 **a Potemkin village** a sham or unreal thing.
any of a number of sham villages reputedly built on the orders of Potemkin, favourite of Empress Catherine II of Russia, for her tour of the Crimea in 1787

8 **a wolf in sheep's clothing** a person whose hostile or malicious intentions are concealed by a pretence of gentleness or friendliness.
*with reference to the Bible (Matthew): see **Hypocrisy** 9*

9 **wooden nutmeg** in US usage, a false or fraudulent thing.
*a piece of wood shaped to resemble a nutmeg and fraudulently sold; see **American Cities** 30*

10 Deceive boys with toys, but men with oaths.
Lysander d. 395 BC: Plutarch *Parallel Lives* 'Lysander'

11 And if, to be sure, sometimes you need to conceal a fact with words, do it in such a way that it does not become known, or, if it does become known, that you have a ready and quick defence.
Niccolò Machiavelli 1469–1527: 'Advice to Raffaello Girolami when he went as Ambassador to the Emperor' (October 1522)

12 A false report, if believed during three days, may be of great service to a government.
Catherine de' Medici 1518–89: Isaac D'Israeli *Curiosities of Literature* Second Series vol. 2 (1849)

13 Like strawberry wives, that laid two or three great strawberries at the mouth of their pot, and all the rest were little ones.
describing the tactics of the Commission of Sales, in their dealings with her
Elizabeth I 1533–1603: Francis Bacon *Apophthegms New and Old* (1625)

14 Doubtless the pleasure is as great
Of being cheated, as to cheat.
As lookers-on feel most delight,
That least perceive a juggler's sleight.
Samuel Butler 1612–80: *Hudibras* pt. 2 (1664)

15 An open foe may prove a curse,
But a pretended friend is worse.
John Gay 1685–1732: *Fables* (1727) 'The Shepherd's Dog and the Wolf'

16   Wise fear, you know,
Forbids the robbing of a foe;
But what, to serve our private ends,
Forbids the cheating of our friends?
Charles Churchill 1731–64: *The Ghost* (1763)

17 O what a tangled web we weave,
When first we practise to deceive!
Sir Walter Scott 1771–1832: *Marmion* (1808); see **Child Care** 10

18 You may fool all the people some of the time; you can even fool some of the people all the time; but you can't fool all of the people all the time.
Abraham Lincoln 1809–65: Alexander K. McClure *Lincoln's Yarns and Stories* (1904); also attributed to Phineas Barnum; see **Politics** 24

19 It was beautiful and simple as all truly great swindles are.
O. Henry 1862–1910: *Gentle Grafter* (1908)

20 That branch of the art of lying which consists in very nearly deceiving your friends without quite deceiving your enemies.
on propaganda
Francis M. Cornford 1874–1943: *Microcosmographia Academica* (1922 ed.)

21 A deception that elevates us is dearer than a host of low truths.
Marina Tsvetaeva 1892–1941: *Pushkin and Pugachev* (1937)

22 Macavity, Macavity, there's no one like Macavity,
There never was a Cat of such deceitfulness and suavity.
He always has an alibi, and one or two to spare:
At whatever time the deed took place
MACAVITY WASN'T THERE!
T. S. Eliot 1888–1965: *Old Possum's Book of Practical Cats* (1939) 'Macavity: the Mystery Cat'

23 In wartime . . . truth is so precious that she should always be attended by a bodyguard of lies.
Winston Churchill 1874–1965: *The Second World War* vol. 5 (1951)

24 Propaganda is a soft weapon: hold it in your hands too long, and it will move about like a snake, and strike the other way.
Jean Anouilh 1910–87: *The Lark* (adapted by Lillian Hellman, 1955)

25 It is now a very good day to get out anything we want to bury.
email sent in the aftermath of the terrorist action in America, 11 September 2001; often quoted as 'a good day to bury bad news'
Jo Moore: in *Daily Telegraph* 10 October 2001

Deeds see **Words and Deeds**

Defiance see also Determination and Perseverance

1 Nemo me impune lacessit.
Latin, No one provokes me with impunity, *motto of the Crown of Scotland and of all Scottish regiments*

2 No surrender!
Protestant Northern Irish slogan originating with the defenders of Derry against the Catholic forces of James II in 1689; see **Certainty** 25

3 They haif said: Quhat say they? Lat thame say.
motto of the Earls Marischal of Scotland, inscribed at Marischal College, Aberdeen, 1593; a similarly defiant motto in Greek has been found engraved in remains from classical antiquity

4 You can take a horse to the water, but you can't make him drink.
late 12th century, meaning that even if you create the right circumstances, you cannot persuade someone to do something against their will

PHRASES

5 die in the last ditch die desperately defending something, die fighting to the last extremity.
see 14 below

6 eyeball to eyeball confronting closely; with neither party yielding.
see **Crises** 21

7 kick against the pricks rebel, be recalcitrant, especially to one's own hurt.
with reference to the Bible (Acts) 'It is hard for thee to kick against the pricks'

8 nail one's colours to the mast persist, refuse to give in; be undeterred in one's support for a party or plan of action.
colours the flag or ensign of a ship; see **Indecision** 16

QUOTATIONS

9 They are as venomous as the poison of a serpent: even like the deaf adder that stoppeth her ears;
Which refuseth to hear the voice of the charmer: charm he never so wisely.
Bible: Psalm 58; see **Senses** 1

10 He will give him seven feet of English ground, or as much more as he may be taller than other men.
his offer to the invader Harald Hardrada, before the battle of Stamford Bridge
Harold II c.1019–66: Snorri Sturluson *Heimskringla* (c.1260) 'King Harald's Saga'

11 If I had heard that as many devils would set on me in Worms as there are tiles on the roofs, I should none the less have ridden there.
Martin Luther 1483–1546: to the Princes of Saxony, 21 August 1524; *Sämmtliche Schriften* vol. 16 (1745)

12 I grow, I prosper;
Now, gods, stand up for bastards!
William Shakespeare 1564–1616: *King Lear* (1605-6)

13 . . . What though the field be lost?
All is not lost; the unconquerable will,
And study of revenge, immortal hate,
And courage never to submit or yield:
And what is else not to be overcome?
John Milton 1608–74: *Paradise Lost* (1667)

14 'Do you not see your country is lost?' asked the Duke of Buckingham. 'There is one way never to see it lost' replied William, 'and that is to die in the last ditch.'
William III 1650–1702: Bishop Gilbert Burnet *History of My Own Time* (1838 ed.); see 5 above

15 Should the whole frame of nature round him break,
In ruin and confusion hurled,
He, unconcerned, would hear the mighty crack,
And stand secure amidst a falling world.
Joseph Addison 1672–1719: translation of Horace *Odes*

16 I was ever a fighter, so—one fight more, The best and the last!
Robert Browning 1812–89: 'Prospice' (1864)

17 *No pasarán.*
They shall not pass.
Dolores Ibarruri 1895–1989: radio broadcast, Madrid, 19 July 1936; see **World War I** 1

18 Get up, stand up
Stand up for your rights

Get up, stand up
Never give up the fight.
Bob Marley 1945–81: 'Get up, Stand up' (1973 song)

19 She won't go quietly, that's the problem.
I'll fight to the end.
Diana, Princess of Wales 1961–97: interview on *Panorama*, BBC1 TV, 20 November 1995

Delay see Haste and Delay

Democracy see also Elections, Politics

PROVERBS AND SAYINGS

1 Democracy is better than tyranny.
American proverb, meaning that an imperfect system is better than a bad one

2 The voice of the people is the voice of God.
early 15th century, English version of the Latin vox populi, vox dei; *see 3 below*

QUOTATIONS

3 And those people should not be listened to who keep saying the voice of the people is the voice of God, since the riotousness of the crowd is always very close to madness.
Alcuin c.735–804: letter 164; *Works* (1863); see 2 above

4 Let no one oppose this belief of mine with that well-worn proverb: 'He who builds on the people builds on mud.'
Niccolò Machiavelli 1469–1527: *The Prince* (written 1513)

5 Nor is the people's judgement always true:
The most may err as grossly as the few.
John Dryden 1631–1700: *Absalom and Achitophel* (1681)

6 I never could believe that Providence had sent a few men into the world, ready booted and spurred to ride, and millions ready saddled and bridled to be ridden.
Richard Rumbold c.1622–85: on the scaffold; T. B. Macaulay *History of England* vol. 1 (1849)

7 If one must serve, I hold it better to serve a well-bred lion, who is naturally stronger than I am, than two hundred rats of my own breed.
Voltaire 1694–1778: letter to a friend; Alexis de Tocqueville *The Ancien Régime* (1856)

8 One man shall have one vote.
John Cartwright 1740–1824: *The People's Barrier Against Undue Influence* (1780)

9 All, too, will bear in mind this sacred principle, that though the will of the majority is in all cases to prevail, that will to be rightful must be reasonable; that the minority possess their equal rights, which equal law must protect, and to violate would be oppression.
Thomas Jefferson 1743–1826: inaugural address, 4 March, 1801

10 It is impossible that the whisper of a faction should prevail against the voice of a nation.
Lord John Russell 1792–1878: reply to an Address from a meeting of 150,000 persons at Birmingham on the defeat of the second Reform Bill, October 1831

11 Minorities . . . are almost always in the right.
Sydney Smith 1771–1845: H. Pearson *The Smith of Smiths* (1934)

12 A majority is always the best repartee.
Benjamin Disraeli 1804–81: *Tancred* (1847)

13 Fourscore and seven years ago our fathers brought forth upon this continent a new nation, conceived in liberty, and dedicated to the proposition that all men are created equal . . . we here highly resolve that the dead shall not have died in vain, that this nation, under God, shall have a new birth of freedom; and that government of the people, by the people, and for the people, shall not perish from the earth.
the Lincoln Memorial inscription reads 'by the people, for the people'
Abraham Lincoln 1809–65: address at the Dedication of the National Cemetery at Gettysburg, 19 November 1863, as reported the following day

14 The majority never has right on its side. Never I say! That is one of the social lies that a free, thinking man is bound to rebel against. Who makes up the majority in any given country? Is it the wise men or the fools? I think we must agree that the fools are in a terrible overwhelming majority, all the wide world over. But,

damn it, it can surely never be right that the stupid should rule over the clever!
Henrik Ibsen 1828–1906: *An Enemy of the People* (1882)

15 Democracy substitutes election by the incompetent many for appointment by the corrupt few.
George Bernard Shaw 1856–1950: *Man and Superman* (1903) 'Maxims: Democracy'

16 The world must be made safe for democracy.
Woodrow Wilson 1856–1924: speech to Congress, 2 April 1917

17 No, Democracy is *not* identical with majority rule. Democracy is a *State* which recognizes the subjection of the minority to the majority, that is, an organization for the systematic use of *force* by one class against the other, by one part of the population against another.
Lenin 1870–1924: *State and Revolution* (1919)

18 Democracy is the recurrent suspicion that more than half of the people are right more than half of the time.
E. B. White 1899–1985: in *New Yorker* 3 July 1944

19 Man's capacity for justice makes democracy possible, but man's inclination to injustice makes democracy necessary.
Reinhold Niebuhr 1892–1971: *Children of Light and Children of Darkness* (1944)

20 No one pretends that democracy is perfect or all-wise. Indeed, it has been said that democracy is the worst form of Government except all those other forms that have been tried from time to time.
Winston Churchill 1874–1965: speech, House of Commons, 11 November 1947

21 After each war there is a little less democracy to save.
Brooks Atkinson 1894–1984: *Once Around the Sun* (1951)

22 So Two cheers for Democracy: one because it admits variety and two because it permits criticism. Two cheers are quite enough: there is no occasion to give three. Only Love the Beloved Republic deserves that.
E. M. Forster 1879–1970: *Two Cheers for Democracy* (1951)

23 Democracy means government by discussion, but it is only effective if you can stop people talking.
Clement Attlee 1883–1967: speech at Oxford, 14 June 1957

24 It's not the voting that's democracy, it's the counting.
Tom Stoppard 1937– : *Jumpers* (1972); see **Elections** 16

25 Every government is a parliament of whores. The trouble is, in a democracy the whores are us.
P. J. O'Rourke 1947– : *Parliament of Whores* (1991)

Despair see also Hope, Optimism and Pessimism, Sorrow

PHRASES

1 black dog a metaphorical representation of melancholy or depression.
used particularly by Samuel Johnson (see 6 below) and later by Winston Churchill when alluding to his own periodic bouts of depression

2 dark night of the soul a period of anguish or despair.
a period of spiritual aridity suffered by a mystic, 'Dark night of the soul' being a translation of the Spanish title of a work by St John of the Cross, known in English as The Ascent of Mount Carmel (1578–80); see 15 below

3 legion of the lost ones people who are destitute or abandoned, regarded as beyond hope or help.
after Kipling 'Gentleman-Rankers' (1892) 'To the legion of the lost ones, to the cohort of the damned, to my brethren in their sorrow overseas'

QUOTATIONS

4 My God, my God, look upon me; why hast thou forsaken me?
Bible: Psalm 22

5 Magnanimous Despair alone
Could show me so divine a thing,
Where feeble Hope could ne'er have flown
But vainly flapped its tinsel wing.
Andrew Marvell 1621–78: 'The Definition of Love' (1681)

6 The black dog I hope always to resist, and in time to drive, though I am deprived of almost all those that used to help me.

on his attacks of melancholia

Samuel Johnson 1709–84: letter to Mrs Thrale, 28 June 1783; see 1 above

7 The very knowledge that he lived in vain, That all was over on this side the tomb, Had made Despair a smilingness assume.

Lord Byron 1788–1824: *Childe Harold's Pilgrimage* (1812–18)

8 Everywhere I see bliss, from which I alone am irrevocably excluded.

Mary Shelley 1797–1851: *Frankenstein* (1818)

9 I am in that temper that if I were under water I would scarcely kick to come to the top.

John Keats 1795–1821: letter to Benjamin Bailey, 25 May 1818

10 I give the fight up: let there be an end, A privacy, an obscure nook for me. I want to be forgotten even by God.

Robert Browning 1812–89: *Paracelsus* (1835)

11 Take thy beak from out my heart, and take thy form from off my door! Quoth the Raven, 'Nevermore'.

Edgar Allan Poe 1809–49: 'The Raven' (1845)

12 There is no despair so absolute as that which comes with the first moments of our first great sorrow, when we have not yet known what it is to have suffered and be

healed, to have despaired and have recovered hope.

George Eliot 1819–80: *Adam Bede* (1859)

13 In despair there are the most intense enjoyments, especially when one is very acutely conscious of the hopelessness of one's position.

Fedor Dostoevsky 1821–81: *Notes from Underground* (1864)

14 Not, I'll not, carrion comfort, Despair, not feast on thee;
Not untwist—slack they may be—these last strands of man
In me or, most weary, cry *I can no more*. I can;
Can something, hope, wish day come, not choose not to be.

Gerard Manley Hopkins 1844–89: 'Carrion Comfort' (written 1885)

15 In a real dark night of the soul it is always three o'clock in the morning.

F. Scott Fitzgerald 1896–1940: 'Handle with Care' in *Esquire* March 1936; see 2 above

16 Human life begins on the far side of despair.

Jean-Paul Sartre 1905–80: *Les Mouches* (1943)

17 Despair is the price one pays for setting oneself an impossible aim.

Graham Greene 1904–91: *Heart of the Matter* (1948)

18 Despair, in short, seeks its own environment as surely as water finds its own level.

Alfred Alvarez 1929– : *The Savage God* (1971)

Determination and Perseverance see also Defiance

see also Defiance

PROVERBS AND SAYINGS

1 Constant dropping wears away a stone.

mid 13th century, primarily used to mean that persistence will achieve a difficult or unlikely objective; see 28 below

2 A determined fellow can do more with a rusty monkey wrench than a lot of people can with a machine shop.

American proverb, mid 20th century

3 He that will to Cupar maun to Cupar.

Scottish traditional saying, early 18th century, meaning that if someone is determined on an end they will not be dissuaded; Cupar is a town in Fife, Scotland

4 He who wills the end, wills the means.

late 17th century, meaning that someone sufficiently determined upon an outcome will also be ready to accept whatever is necessary to achieve it

5 If at first you don't succeed, try, try, try again.

mid 19th century; see 46 below

6 It is idle to swallow the cow and choke on the tail.

mid 17th century; meaning that when a serious matter has been accepted, there is no point in quibbling over a trifle, or that it is senseless to give up when a great task is almost completed

7 It's dogged as does it.

mid 19th century, meaning that steady perseverance will bring success

8 Little strokes fell great oaks.

early 15th century, meaning that a person or thing of size and stature can be brought down by a series of small blows

9 Nil carborundum illegitimi.

cod Latin for 'Don't let the bastards grind you down', in circulation during the Second World War, though possibly of earlier origin; often quoted as, 'nil carborundum' or 'illegitimi non carborundum'.

10 Put a stout heart to a stey brae.

Scottish proverbial saying, late 16th century; meaning that determination is needed to climb a steep ('stey') hillside

11 Revenons à ces moutons.

French, literally 'Let us return to these sheep', with allusion to the confused court scene in the Old French Farce de Maistre Pierre Pathelin (c.1470); an exhortation to stop digressing and get back to the subject in hand

12 The show must go on.

American proverb, mid 19th century

13 Slow and steady wins the race.

mid 18th century saying, from the story of the race between the hare and the tortoise, in Aesop's Fables, in which the winner was the slow but persistent tortoise and not the swift but easily distracted hare; see 21 below

14 A stern chase is a long chase.

early 19th century; a stern chase is a chase in which the pursuing ship follows directly in the wake of the pursued

15 The third time pays for all.

late 16th century, meaning that success after initial failure makes up for earlier disappointment

16 We shall not be moved.

title of labour and civil rights song (1931), adapted from an earlier gospel hymn

17 We shall overcome.

title of song, originating from before the American Civil War, adapted as a Baptist hymn ('I'll Overcome Some Day', 1901) by C. Albert Tindley; revived in 1946 as a protest song by black tobacco workers, and in 1963 during the black Civil Rights Campaign

18 Where there's a will there's a way.

mid 17th century, meaning that anything can be done if one has sufficient determination

19 A wilful man must have his way.

early 19th century, meaning that a person set on their own ends will disregard advice in pursuing their chosen course

PHRASES

20 gird up one's loins prepare oneself for mental and physical effort, summon one's courage and determination.

of biblical origin, as in II Kings 'Then said he to Gehazi, Gird up thy loins, and take my staff in thine hand, and go thy way'

21 hare and tortoise the defeat of ability by persistence.

in allusion to Aesop's fable: see 13 above

22 put one's hand to the plough undertake a task; enter on a course of life or conduct.

from the Bible (Luke): see 24 below

QUOTATIONS

23 Faint, yet pursuing.
Bible: Judges

24 No man, having put his hand to the plough, and looking back, is fit for the kingdom of God.
Bible: St Luke; see 22 above

25 Hoc volo, sic iubeo, sit pro ratione voluntas.
I will have this done, so I order it done; let my will replace reasoned judgement.
Juvenal AD c.60–c.130: Satires

26 Thought shall be the harder, heart the keener, courage the greater, as our might lessens.
Anonymous: The Battle of Maldon (c.1000)

27 Here stand I. I can do no other. God help me. Amen.
Martin Luther 1483–1546: speech at the Diet of Worms, 18 April 1521; attributed

28 The drop of rain maketh a hole in the stone, not by violence, but by oft falling.
Hugh Latimer c.1485–1555: The Second Sermon preached before the King's Majesty, 19 April 1549; see 1 above

29   Perseverance, dear my lord,
Keeps honour bright.
William Shakespeare 1564–1616: Troilus and Cressida (1602)

30 Obstinacy in a bad cause, is but constancy in a good.
Thomas Browne 1605–82: Religio Medici (1643)

31 Who would true valour see,
Let him come hither;
One here will constant be,

Come wind, come weather.
There's no discouragement
Shall make him once relent
His first avowed intent
To be a pilgrim.
John Bunyan 1628–88: *The Pilgrim's Progress* (1684)

32 She's as headstrong as an allegory on the banks of the Nile.
Richard Brinsley Sheridan 1751–1816: *The Rivals* (1775)

33 Obstinacy, Sir, is certainly a great vice . . . It happens, however, very unfortunately, that almost the whole line of the great and masculine virtues, constancy, gravity, magnanimity, fortitude, fidelity, and firmness are closely allied to this disagreeable quality.
Edmund Burke 1729–97: *On American Taxation* (1775)

34 I have not yet begun to fight.
as his ship was sinking, 23 September 1779, having been asked whether he had lowered his flag
John Paul Jones 1747–92: Mrs Reginald De Koven *Life and Letters of John Paul Jones* (1914)

35 I have only one eye,—I have a right to be blind sometimes . . . I really do not see the signal!
at the battle of Copenhagen
Horatio, Lord Nelson 1758–1805: Robert Southey *Life of Nelson* (1813); see **Ignorance** 10

36 I am in earnest—I will not equivocate—I will not excuse—I will not retreat a single inch—and I will be heard!
William Lloyd Garrison 1805–79: in *The Liberator* 1 January 1831

37 Let us, then, be up and doing,
With a heart for any fate;
Still achieving, still pursuing,
Learn to labour and to wait.
Henry Wadsworth Longfellow 1807–82: 'A Psalm of Life' (1838); see **Achievement** 7

38   That which we are, we are;
One equal temper of heroic hearts,
Made weak by time and fate, but strong in will
To strive, to seek, to find, and not to yield.
Alfred, Lord Tennyson 1809–92: 'Ulysses' (1842)

39 I purpose to fight it out on this line, if it takes all summer.
Ulysses S. Grant 1822–85: dispatch to Washington, from head-quarters in the field, 11 May 1864

40 The best way out is always through.
Robert Frost 1874–1963: 'A Servant to Servants' (1914)

41 Keep right on to the end of the road,
Keep right on to the end.
Tho' the way be long, let your heart be strong,
Keep right on round the bend.
Harry Lauder 1870–1950: 'The End of the Road' (1924 song)

42 One man that has a mind and knows it can always beat ten men who haven't and don't.
George Bernard Shaw 1856–1950: *The Apple Cart* (1930)

43 Nothing in the world can take the place of persistence. Talent will not; nothing is more common than unsuccessful men with talent. Genius will not; unrewarded genius is almost a proverb. Education will not; the world is full of educated derelicts. Persistence and determination are omnipotent. The slogan 'press on' has solved and always will solve the problems of the human race.
Calvin Coolidge 1872–1933: attributed in the programme of a memorial service for Coolidge in 1933

44 Pick yourself up,
Dust yourself off,
Start all over again.
Dorothy Fields 1905–74: 'Pick Yourself Up' (1936 song)

45 The capacity women have for just hanging on is depressing to contemplate.
Stevie Smith 1902–71: in *Tribune* c.1945

46 If at first you don't succeed, try, try again. Then quit. No use being a damn fool about it.
W. C. Fields 1880–1946: attributed; see 5 above

47 But above all
we have
the ability
to sort peas,
to cup water in our hands,
to seek
the right screw
under the sofa
for hours.
Miroslav Holub 1923– : 'Wings' (1967)

48 We shall not be diverted from our course. To those waiting with bated breath for that favourite media catchphrase, the U-turn, I

have only this to say. 'You turn if you want; the lady's not for turning.'

final line from alteration of the title of Christopher Fry's 1949 play The Lady's Not For Burning

Margaret Thatcher 1925– : speech at Conservative Party Conference in Brighton, 10 October 1980

49 The comeback kid!

Bill Clinton 1946– : description of himself after coming second in the New Hampshire primary, 1992

50 The important thing is not to persist; I think the reason most people fail is that

they are too determined to make something work only because they are attached to it. Talking to Feynman, whatever came up he would say, 'Well, here's another way to look at it.' The least stuck person I have ever known.

Marvin Minsky 1927– : Christopher Sykes (ed.) *No Ordinary Genius* (1994)

51 I will fight for what I believe in until I drop dead. And that's what keeps you alive.

Barbara Castle 1910– : in *Guardian* 14 January 1998

Difference see **Similarity and Difference**

Diplomacy see also **International Relations**

PROVERBS AND SAYINGS

1 A soft answer turneth away wrath.

late 14th century, meaning that refraining from defending oneself against verbal attack may defuse a situation; from the Bible: see **Anger** *4*

PHRASES

2 honest broker an impartial mediator in international, industrial, or other disputes.

from Bismarck: see 7 below

QUOTATIONS

3 An ambassador is an honest man sent to lie abroad for the good of his country.

Henry Wotton 1568–1639: written in the album of Christopher Fleckmore in 1604; Izaak Walton *Reliquiae Wottonianae* (1651)

4 We are prepared to go to the gates of Hell—but no further.

attempting to reach an agreement with Napoleon, c.1800–1

Pope Pius VII 1742–1823: J. M. Robinson *Cardinal Consalvi* (1987)

5 The Congress makes no progress; it dances.

on the Congress of Vienna

Charles-Joseph, Prince de Ligne 1735–1814: Auguste de la Garde-Chambonas *Souvenirs du Congrès de Vienne* (1820)

6 The compact which exists between the North and the South is 'a covenant with death and an agreement with hell'.

William Lloyd Garrison 1805–79: resolution adopted by the Massachusetts Anti-Slavery Society,

27 January 1843; in allusion to the Bible (Isaiah) 'We have made a covenant with death, and with hell are we at agreement'

7 I do not regard the procuring of peace as a matter in which we should play the role of arbiter between different opinions . . . more that of an honest broker who really wants to press the business forward.

Otto von Bismarck 1815–98: speech to the Reichstag, 19 February 1878; see 2 above

8 The agonies of a man who has to finish a difficult negotiation, and at the same time to entertain four royalties at a country house can be better imagined than described.

Lord Salisbury 1830–1903: letter to Lord Lyons, 5 June 1878

9 There is a homely old adage which runs: 'Speak softly and carry a big stick; you will go far.' If the American nation will speak softly, and yet build and keep at a pitch of the highest training a thoroughly efficient navy, the Monroe Doctrine will go far.

Theodore Roosevelt 1858–1919: speech in Chicago, 3 April 1903; see **International Relations** 5, **Woman's Role** 35

10 I gather it has now been decided not to embrace the Russian bear, but to hold out a hand and accept its paw gingerly. No more. The worst of both worlds.

Henry 'Chips' Channon 1897–1958: diary 16 May 1939

11 An appeaser is one who feeds a crocodile hoping it will eat him last.
Winston Churchill 1874–1965: in the House of Commons, January 1940

12 Personally I feel happier now that we have no allies to be polite to and to pamper.
George VI 1895–1952: to Queen Mary, 27 June 1940; John Wheeler-Bennett *King George VI* (1958)

13 Negotiating with de Valera . . . is like trying to pick up mercury with a fork.
to which de Valera replied, 'Why doesn't he use a spoon?'
David Lloyd George 1863–1945: M. J. MacManus *Eamon de Valera* (1944)

14 To jaw-jaw is always better than to war-war.
Winston Churchill 1874–1965: speech at White House, 26 June 1954

15 Mr Khrushchev holds out an olive branch and at the same time tries to hit us over the head with it.
Lyndon Baines Johnson 1908–73: in *Observer* 1 January 1961 'Sayings of the Year 1960'; see **Peace** 5

16 Let us never negotiate out of fear. But let us never fear to negotiate.
John F. Kennedy 1917–63: inaugural address, 20 January 1961

17 Balkan graveyards are full of the broken promises of Slobodan Milosevic.
Bill Clinton 1946– : statement in Washington, 13 October 1998

18 One of the things I learnt when I was negotiating was that until I changed myself I could not change others.
Nelson Mandela 1918– : in *Sunday Times* 16 April 2000

Discontent see Satisfaction and Discontent

Discoveries see Inventions and Discoveries

Disillusion and Cynicism

PROVERBS AND SAYINGS

1 **Blessed is he who expects nothing, for he shall never be disappointed.**
early 18th century; see 11 below

PHRASES

2 **Dead Sea fruit** any outwardly desirable object which on attainment turns out to be worthless; any hollow disappointing thing.
a legendary fruit, of attractive appearance, which dissolved into smoke and ashes when held; see 4 below; Power 33

3 **take the gilt off the gingerbread** strip something of its attractions.
gingerbread was traditionally made in decorative forms which were then gilded

4 **turn to ashes in a person's mouth** turn out to be utterly disappointing or worthless.
probably originally with allusion to the legend of Dead Sea fruit: see 2 above

5 **vanitas vanitatum** vanity of vanities, futility (frequently as an exclamation of disillusionment or pessimism).
late Latin, from the Vulgate translation of the Bible; see Futility 14, Satisfaction and Discontent 25

QUOTATIONS

6 To get practice in being refused.
on being asked why he was begging for alms from a statue
Diogenes 404–323 BC: Diogenes Laertius *Lives of the Philosophers*

7 Kill them all; God will recognize his own.
when asked how the true Catholics could be distinguished from the heretics at the massacre of Béziers, 1209
Arnald-Amaury, abbot of Citeaux d. 1225: Jonathan Sumption *The Albigensian Crusade* (1978)

8 Paris is well worth a mass.
Henri of Navarre, a Huguenot, on becoming King of France
Henri IV 1553–1610: attributed to Henri IV; alternatively to his minister Sully, in conversation with Henri

9 What makes all doctrines plain and clear?
About two hundred pounds a year.
And that which was proved true before,
Prove false again? Two hundred more.
Samuel Butler 1612–80: *Hudibras* pt. 3 (1680)

10 Everything has been said, and we are more than seven thousand years of human thought too late.
Jean de la Bruyère 1645-96: *Les Caractères ou les moeurs de ce siècle* (1688)

11 'Blessed is the man who expects nothing, for he shall never be disappointed' was the ninth beatitude.
Alexander Pope 1688-1744: letter to Fortescue, 23 September 1725; see 1 above

12 And finds, with keen discriminating sight, Black's not so black;—nor white so very white.
George Canning 1770-1827: 'New Morality' (1821)

13 Never glad confident morning again!
Robert Browning 1812-89: 'The Lost Leader' (1845)

14 Take the life-lie away from the average man and straight away you take away his happiness.
Henrik Ibsen 1828-1906: *The Wild Duck* (1884)

15 A man who knows the price of everything and the value of nothing.
definition of a cynic
Oscar Wilde 1854-1900: *Lady Windermere's Fan* (1892)

16 No man in his heart is quite so cynical as a well-bred woman.
W. Somerset Maugham 1874-1965: *A Writer's Notebook* (1949) written in 1896

17 And nothing to look backward to with pride,
And nothing to look forward to with hope.
Robert Frost 1874-1963: 'The Death of the Hired Man' (1914)

18 Disillusionment in living is the finding out nobody agrees with you not those that are and were fighting with you.
Disillusionment in living is the finding out nobody agrees with you not those that are fighting for you. Complete disillusionment is when you realise that no one can for they can't change.
Gertrude Stein 1874-1946: *Making of Americans* (1934)

19 Cynicism is an unpleasant way of saying the truth.
Lillian Hellman 1905-84: *The Little Foxes* (1939)

20 Reason and Progress, the old firm, is selling out! Everyone get out while the going's good. Those forgotten shares you had in the old traditions, the old beliefs are going up—up and up and up.
John Osborne 1929-94: *Look Back in Anger* (1956)

21 If someone tells you he is going to make a 'realistic decision', you immediately understand that he has resolved to do something bad.
Mary McCarthy 1912-89: *On the Contrary* (1961) 'American Realist Playwrights'

22 Like all dreamers, I mistook disenchantment for truth.
Jean-Paul Sartre 1905-80: *Les Mots* (1964) 'Écrire'

23 Man hands on misery to man.
It deepens like a coastal shelf.
Get out as early as you can,
And don't have any kids yourself.
Philip Larkin 1922-85: 'This Be The Verse' (1974)

24 Cynicism is our shared common language, the Esperanto that actually caught on.
Nick Hornby 1957- : *How to be Good* (2001)

Dislikes see **Likes and Dislikes**

Dogs see also **Animals**

PROVERBS AND SAYINGS

1 **Cave canem.**
Latin, beware of the dog; deriving originally from Petronius (d. AD 65)

2 **A dog is for life, not just for Christmas.**
slogan of the National Canine Defence League, from 1978

QUOTATIONS

3 I am his Highness' dog at Kew;
Pray, tell me sir, whose dog are you?
Alexander Pope 1688-1744: 'Epigram Engraved on the Collar of a Dog which I gave to his Royal Highness' (1738)

4 My dog! what remedy remains,
Since, teach you all I can,
I see you, after all my pains,
So much resemble man!
William Cowper 1731-1800: 'On a Spaniel called Beau, killing a young bird' (written 1793)

5 Near this spot are deposited the remains of one who possessed beauty without vanity, strength without insolence, courage without ferocity, and all the virtues of Man, without his vices.
Lord Byron 1788–1824: 'Inscription on the Monument of a Newfoundland Dog' (1808)

6 The more one gets to know of men, the more one values dogs.
also attributed to Mme Roland in the form 'The more I see of men, the more I like dogs'
A. Toussenel 1803–85: *L'Esprit des bêtes* (1847)

7 We were regaled by a dogfight . . . How odd that people of sense should find any pleasure in being accompanied by a beast who is always spoiling conversation.
Lord Macaulay 1800–59: G. O. Trevelyan *Life and Letters of Macaulay* (1876)

8 The great pleasure of a dog is that you may make a fool of yourself with him and not only will he not scold you, but he will make a fool of himself too.
Samuel Butler 1835–1902: *Notebooks* (1912)

9 There is sorrow enough in the natural way
From men and women to fill our day;
But when we are certain of sorrow in store,
Why do we always arrange for more?
*Brothers and Sisters, I bid you beware
Of giving your heart to a dog to tear.*
Rudyard Kipling 1865–1936: 'The Power of the Dog' (1909)

10 I'm a lean dog, a keen dog, a wild dog, and lone;
I'm a rough dog, a tough dog, hunting on my own;
I'm a bad dog, a mad dog, teasing silly sheep;
I love to sit and bay at the moon, to keep fat souls from sleep.
Irene Rutherford McLeod 1891–1964: 'Lone Dog' (1915)

11 Any man who hates dogs and babies can't be all bad.
of W. C. Fields, and often attributed to him
Leo Rosten 1908–97: speech at Masquers' Club dinner, 16 February 1939

12 A door is what a dog is perpetually on the wrong side of.
Ogden Nash 1902–71: 'A Dog's Best Friend is his Illiteracy' (1953)

13 A dog in the home is a piece of moving furniture.
Philippe de Rothschild 1902–88: Cecil Beaton *Self-Portrait with Friends* (1979) November 1955

14 Happiness is a warm puppy.
Charles Monroe Schulz 1922– : title of book (1962); see **Happiness** 28

15 That indefatigable and unsavoury engine of pollution, the dog.
John Sparrow 1906–92: letter to *The Times* 30 September 1975

Doubt see **Certainty and Doubt**

Drawing see **Painting and Drawing**

Dreams see also **Sleep**

1 **Dream of a funeral and you hear of a marriage.**
mid 17th century

2 **Dreams go by contraries.**
early 15th century

3 **Dreams retain the infirmities of our character.**
American proverb, late 19th century

4 **Morning dreams come true.**
mid 16th century, recording a traditional superstition

5 **the gate of horn** in Greek legend, the gates through which true dreams pass.

6 **the ivory gate** in Greek legend, the gate through which false dreams pass.
see 8 below

7 O God! I could be bounded in a nut-shell, and count myself a king of infinite space,

were it not that I have bad dreams.
William Shakespeare 1564–1616: *Hamlet* (1601)

8 That children dream not in the first half year, that men dream not in some countries, are to me sick men's dreams, dreams out of the ivory gate, and visions before midnight.
Thomas Browne 1605–82: 'On Dreams'; see 6 above

9 The dream of reason produces monsters.
Goya 1746–1828: *Los Caprichos* (1799)

10 Was it a vision, or a waking dream?
Fled is that music:—do I wake or sleep?
John Keats 1795–1821: 'Ode to a Nightingale' (1820)

11   The quick Dreams,
The passion-wingèd Ministers of thought.
Percy Bysshe Shelley 1792–1822: *Adonais* (1821)

12 I have spread my dreams under your feet;
Tread softly because you tread on my dreams.
W. B. Yeats 1865–1939: 'He Wishes for the Cloths of Heaven' (1899)

13 The interpretation of dreams is the royal road to a knowledge of the unconscious activities of the mind.
often quoted as, 'Dreams are the royal road to the unconscious'
Sigmund Freud 1856–1939: *The Interpretation of Dreams* (2nd ed., 1909)

14 How many of our daydreams would darken into nightmares if there seemed any danger of their coming true!
Logan Pearsall Smith 1865–1946: *Afterthoughts* (1931)

15 The armoured cars of dreams, contrived to let us do
so many a dangerous thing.
Elizabeth Bishop 1911–79: 'Sleeping Standing Up' (1946)

16 Have you noticed . . . there is never any third act in a nightmare? They bring you to a climax of terror and then leave you there. They are the work of poor dramatists.
Max Beerbohm 1872–1956: S. N. Behrman *Conversations with Max* (1960)

17 All the things one has forgotten scream for help in dreams.
Elias Canetti 1905–94: *Die Provinz der Menschen* (1973)

18 When we dream that we are dreaming, the moment of awakening is at hand.
J. M. Coetzee 1940– : *In the Heart of the Country* (1977)

Dress see also Fashion

1 **Clothes make the man.**
early 15th century, meaning that what one wears is taken by others as an essential signal of status; see 22 below

2 **Fine feathers make fine birds.**
late 16th century, meaning that beautiful clothes confer beauty or style on the wearer

3 **If you want to get ahead, get a hat.**
advertising slogan for the British Hat Council, 1965

4 **Ne'er cast a clout till May be out.**
early 18th century; warning against leaving off old or warm clothes until the end of the month of May (the saying is sometimes mistakenly understood to refer to may blossom)

5 **Nine tailors make a man.**
early 17th century; literally, a gentleman must select his attire from a number of sources (later also associated with bell-ringing, with the nine tailors or

tellers *indicating the nine knells traditionally rung for the death of a man)*

6 Costly thy habit as thy purse can buy,
But not expressed in fancy; rich, not gaudy;
For the apparel oft proclaims the man.
William Shakespeare 1564–1616: *Hamlet* (1601)

7 She wears her clothes, as if they were thrown on her with a pitchfork.
Jonathan Swift 1667–1745: *Polite Conversation* (1738)

8 Let it be observed, that slovenliness is no part of religion; that neither this, nor any text of Scripture, condemns neatness of apparel. Certainly this is a duty, not a sin. 'Cleanliness is, indeed, next to godliness.'
John Wesley 1703–91: *Sermons on Several Occasions* (1788); see **Behaviour** 2

9 No perfumes, but very fine linen, plenty of it, and country washing.
Beau Brummell 1778–1840: *Memoirs of Harriette Wilson* (1825)

10 Beware of all enterprises that require new clothes.
Henry David Thoreau 1817–62: *Walden* (1854) 'Economy'

11   She just wore
Enough for modesty—no more.
Robert Buchanan 1841–1901: 'White Rose and Red' (1873)

12 The sense of being well-dressed gives a feeling of inward tranquillity which religion is powerless to bestow.
Miss C. F. Forbes 1817–1911: R. W. Emerson *Letters and Social Aims* (1876)

13 You should never have your best trousers on when you go out to fight for freedom and truth.
Henrik Ibsen 1828–1906: *An Enemy of the People* (1882)

14 His socks compelled one's attention without losing one's respect.
Saki 1870–1916: *Chronicles of Clovis* (1911)

15 When you're all dressed up and have no place to go.
George Whiting: title of song (1912)

16 Satan himself can't save a woman who wears thirty-shilling corsets under a thirty-guinea costume.
Rudyard Kipling 1865–1936: *Debits and Credits* (1926)

17 From the cradle to the grave, underwear first, last and all the time.
Bertolt Brecht 1898–1956: *The Threepenny Opera* (1928)

18 Where's the man could ease a heart like a satin gown?
Dorothy Parker 1893–1967: 'The Satin Dress' (1937)

19 The trick of wearing mink is to look as though you were wearing a cloth coat. The trick of wearing a cloth coat is to look as though you are wearing mink.
Pierre Balmain 1914–82: in *Observer* 25 December 1955

20 When I was young, I found out that the big toe always ends up making a hole in a sock. So I stopped wearing socks.
Albert Einstein 1879–1955: to Philippe Halsman; A. P. French *Einstein: A Centenary Volume* (1979)

on being asked what she wore in bed:
21 Chanel No. 5.
Marilyn Monroe 1926–62: Pete Martin *Marilyn Monroe* (1956)

22 Clothes don't make the man . . . but they go a long way toward making a businessman.
Thomas Watson Snr. 1874–1956: Robert Sobel *IBM: Colossus in Transition* (1981); see 1 above

23 The American tourist abroad . . . wears clothes suitable for a trip to a disaster area, or for a visit to a museum or zoo: comfortable, casual, brightly coloured, relatively cheap: not calculated to arouse envy or pick up dirt.
Alison Lurie 1926– : *The Language of Clothes* (1981)

24 Life is an adventure, so I make clothes to have adventures in.
Vivienne Westwood 1941– : in 1981; Jane Mulvagh *Vivienne Westwood: An Unfashionable Life* (1998)

25 Haute Couture should be fun, foolish and almost unwearable.
Christian Lacroix 1951– : attributed, 1987

26 The origins of clothing are not practical. They are mystical and erotic. The primitive man in the wolf-pelt was not keeping dry; he was saying: 'Look what I killed. Aren't I the best?'
Katherine Hamnett 1948– : in *Independent on Sunday* 10 March 1991

27 It is totally impossible to be well dressed in cheap shoes.
Hardy Amies 1909– : *The Englishman's Suit* (1994)

28 Every time you open your wardrobe, you look at your clothes and you wonder what you are going to wear. What you are really saying is 'Who am I going to be today?'
Fay Weldon 1931– : in *New Yorker* 26 June 1995

Drink see Food and Drink

Drugs

1 Just say no.
motto of the Nancy Reagan Drug Abuse Fund, founded 1985

2 Almighty God hath not bestowed on mankind a remedy of so universal an extent and so efficacious in curing divers maladies as opiates.
Thomas Sydenham 1624-89: *Observationes Medicae* (1676); MS version given in 1991 ed.

3 Thou hast the keys of Paradise, oh just, subtle, and mighty opium!
Thomas De Quincey 1785-1859: *Confessions of an English Opium Eater* (1822)

4 Cocaine habit-forming? Of course not. I ought to know. I've been using it for years.
Tallulah Bankhead 1903-68: *Tallulah* (1952)

5 In this country, don't forget, a habit is no damn private hell. There's no solitary confinement outside of jail. A habit is hell for those you love.
Billie Holiday 1915-59: *Lady Sings the Blues* (1956, with William F. Duffy)

6 Junk is the ideal product . . . the ultimate merchandise. No sales talk necessary. The client will crawl through a sewer and beg to buy.
William S. Burroughs 1914-97: *The Naked Lunch* (1959)

7 Every form of addiction is bad, no matter whether the narcotic be alcohol or morphine or idealism.
Carl Gustav Jung 1875-1961: *Erinnerungen, Träume, Gedanken* (1962)

8 I'll die young, but it's like kissing God.
on his drug addiction
Lenny Bruce 1925-66: attributed

9 LSD? Nothing much happened, but I did get the distinct impression that some birds were trying to communicate with me.
W. H. Auden 1907-73: George Plimpton (ed.), *The Writer's Chapbook* (1989)

10 We can no more hope to end drug abuse by eliminating heroin and cocaine than we could alter the suicide rate by outlawing high buildings or the sale of rope.
Ben Whittaker 1934- : *The Global Fix* (1987)

11 Alcohol didn't cause the high crime rates of the '20s and '30s, Prohibition did. Drugs don't cause today's alarming crime rates, but drug prohibition does.
quoted by Judge James C. Paine, addressing the Federal Bar Association in Miami, 1991
David Boaz 1953- : 'The Legalization of Drugs' 27 April 1988

12 A drug is neither moral or immoral—it's a chemical compound. The compound itself is not a menace to society until a human being treats it as if consumption bestowed a temporary licence to act like an asshole.
Frank Zappa 1940-93: *The Real Frank Zappa Book* (1989)

13 I experimented with marijuana a time or two. And I didn't like it, and I didn't inhale.
Bill Clinton 1946- : in *Washington Post* 30 March 1992

14 Sure thing, man. I used to be a laboratory myself once.
on being asked to autograph a fan's school chemistry book
Keith Richards 1943- : in *Independent on Sunday* 7 August 1994

Drunkenness see also Alcohol

1 The drunkard's cure is drink again.
American proverb, mid 20th century

2 He that drinks beer, thinks beer.
early 19th century, warning against the effects of intoxication

3 There is truth in wine.
mid 16th century; meaning that a person who is drunk is more likely to speak the truth; the saying is found earlier in Latin as in vino veritas

4 When the wine is in, the wit is out.
late 14th century, meaning that when one is drunk one is likely to be indiscreet or to speak or act foolishly

5 Drink, sir, is a great provoker of three things . . . nose-painting, sleep, and urine. Lechery, sir, it provokes, and unprovokes; it provokes the desire, but it takes away the performance.
William Shakespeare 1564–1616: *Macbeth* (1606)

6 Lo! the poor toper whose untutored sense,
Sees bliss in ale, and can with wine dispense;
Whose head proud fancy never taught to steer,
Beyond the muddy ecstasies of beer.
George Crabbe 1754–1832: 'Inebriety' (1775); see **Ignorance** 14

7 A man who exposes himself when he is intoxicated, has not the art of getting drunk.
Samuel Johnson 1709–84: James Boswell *Life of Samuel Johnson* (1791) 24 April 1779

8 Man, being reasonable, must get drunk;
The best of life is but intoxication.
Lord Byron 1788–1824: *Don Juan* (1819–24)

9 It would be better that England should be free than that England should be compulsorily sober.
William Connor Magee 1821–91: speech on the Intoxicating Liquor Bill, House of Lords, 2 May 1872

10 Licker talks mighty loud w'en it git loose fum de jug.
Joel Chandler Harris 1848–1908: *Uncle Remus: His Songs and His Sayings* (1880)

11 But I'm not so think as you drunk I am.
J. C. Squire 1884–1958: 'Ballade of Soporific Absorption' (1931)

12 Till a lady passing by was heard to say:
'You can tell a man who "boozes" by the company he chooses'
And the pig got up and slowly walked away.
of a pig and a drunk lying side by side in the gutter
Benjamin Hapgood Burt 1880–1950: 'The Pig Got Up and Slowly Walked Away' (1933 song)

13 After a man has had his coffee it's tomorrow: it has to be! . . . And tomorrow it's just a hangover; you ain't still drunk tomorrow.
William Faulkner 1897–1962: *Pylon* (1935)

14 Love makes the world go round? Not at all. Whisky makes it go round twice as fast.
Compton Mackenzie 1883–1972: *Whisky Galore* (1947); see **Love** 8

15 A man you don't like who drinks as much as you do.
definition of an alcoholic
Dylan Thomas 1914–53: Constantine Fitzgibbon *Life of Dylan Thomas* (1965)

16 One more drink and I'd have been under the host.
Dorothy Parker 1893–1967: Howard Teichmann *George S. Kaufman* (1972)

17 Grape is my mulatto mother
In this frozen whited country. Her veined interior
Hangs hot open for me to re-enter
The blood-coloured glasshouse against which the stone world
Thins to a dew and steams off.
Ted Hughes 1930–98: 'Wino' (1967)

18 You're not drunk if you can lie on the floor without holding on.
Dean Martin 1917– : Paul Dickson *Official Rules* (1978)

Duty and Responsibility

1 Everybody's business is nobody's business.
early 17th century, meaning that when something is of some interest to everyone, no single person takes full responsibility for it

2 Every herring must hang by its own gill.
early 17th century, meaning that everyone is accountable for their own actions

3 cat's paw a person who is used by another, typically to carry out an unpleasant or dangerous task.
*originally with allusion to the fable of a monkey which asked a cat to extract its roasted chestnuts from the fire; see **Danger** 16*

4 pass the buck shift the responsibility for something to another person.

buck *an article placed as a reminder before a player whose turn it is to deal at poker; see* 24 *below*

5 wash one's hands of renounce responsibility for; refuse to have any further dealings with.

originally with allusion to the Bible; see **Guilt** *6,* **Indifference** *14*

QUOTATIONS

6 And do thy duty, even if it be humble, rather than another's, even if it be great. To die in one's duty is life: to live in another's is death.

Bhagavadgita 250 BC–AD 250: ch. 3

7 It is much safer to be in a subordinate position than in authority.

Thomas à Kempis c.1380–1471: *The Imitation of Christ*

8 Had I but served God as diligently as I have served the King, he would not have given me over in my grey hairs.

Thomas Wolsey c.1475–1530: George Cavendish *Negotiations of Thomas Wolsey* (1641)

9 Do your duty, and leave the outcome to the Gods.

Pierre Corneille 1606–84: *Horace* (1640)

10 I could not love thee, Dear, so much, Loved I not honour more.

Richard Lovelace 1618–58: 'To Lucasta, Going to the Wars' (1649)

11 England expects that every man will do his duty.

Horatio, Lord Nelson 1758–1805: at the battle of Trafalgar, 21 October 1805; Robert Southey *Life of Nelson* (1813)

12 Stern daughter of the voice of God! O Duty!

William Wordsworth 1770–1850: 'Ode to Duty' (1807)

13 The brave man inattentive to his duty, is worth little more to his country, than the coward who deserts her in the hour of danger.

to troops who had abandoned their lines during the battle of New Orleans, 8 January 1815

Andrew Jackson 1767–1845: attributed

14 Do the work that's nearest, Though it's dull at whiles,

Helping, when we meet them, Lame dogs over stiles.

Charles Kingsley 1819–75: 'The Invitation. To Tom Hughes' (1856)

15 The words *God, Immortality, Duty*—pronounced, with terrible earnestness, how inconceivable was the *first*, how unbelievable the *second*, and yet how peremptory and absolute the third.

George Eliot 1819–80: F. W. H. Myers 'George Eliot', in *Century Magazine* November 1881

16 On an occasion of this kind it becomes more than a moral duty to speak one's mind. It becomes a pleasure.

Oscar Wilde 1854–1900: *The Importance of Being Earnest* (1895)

17 Take up the White Man's burden—
Send forth the best ye breed—
Go, bind your sons to exile
To serve your captives' need.

Rudyard Kipling 1865–1936: 'The White Man's Burden' (1899); see **Race** 5

18 When a stupid man is doing something he is ashamed of, he always declares that it is his duty.

George Bernard Shaw 1856–1950: *Caesar and Cleopatra* (1901)

19 If we believe a thing to be bad, and if we have a right to prevent it, it is our duty to try to prevent it and to damn the consequences.

Lord Milner 1854–1925: speech in Glasgow, 26 November 1909

20 People will do things from a sense of duty which they would never attempt as a pleasure.

Saki 1870–1916: *The Chronicles of Clovis* (1911)

21 A sense of duty is useful in work, but offensive in personal relations. People wish to be liked, not to be endured with patient resignation.

Bertrand Russell 1872–1970: *The Conquest of Happiness* (1930)

22 Power without responsibility: the prerogative of the harlot throughout the ages.

summing up Lord Beaverbrook's political standpoint as a newspaper editor; Stanley Baldwin, Kipling's cousin, subsequently obtained permission to use the phrase in a speech in London on 18 March 1931

Rudyard Kipling 1865–1936: in *Kipling Journal* December 1971

23 I know this—a man got to do what he got to do.
John Steinbeck 1902-68: *Grapes of Wrath* (1939)

24 The buck stops here.
Harry S. Truman 1884-1972: unattributed motto on Truman's desk; see 4 above

25 'Once the rockets are up, who cares where they come down?

That's not my department,' says Wernher von Braun.
Tom Lehrer 1928- : 'Wernher von Braun'

26 Duty is what no-one else will do at the moment.
Penelope Fitzgerald 1916-2000: *Offshore* (1979)

The Earth see also Nature, Pollution and the Environment, The Universe

PHRASES

1 **flood and field** sea and land.
after Shakespeare Othello *'Of moving accidents by flood and field'*

2 **Gaia hypothesis** the theory, put forward by the English scientist James Lovelock (1919-) in 1969, that living matter on the earth collectively defines and regulates the material conditions necessary for the continuance of life.
Gaia, *in Greek mythology, the Earth personified as a goddess, daughter of Chaos; see 17 below*

3 **the glimpses of the moon** the earth by night; sublunary scenes.
after Shakespeare Hamlet *'That thou, dead corse again in complete steel, Revisit'st thus the glimpses of the moon'*

4 **global village** the world considered as a single community linked by telecommunications.
from McLuhan: see **Technology** *18; see also* **The Country** *27*

QUOTATIONS

5 The earth is the Lord's, and all that therein is: the compass of the world, and they that dwell therein.
Bible: Psalm 24

6 Above the smoke and stir of this dim spot, Which men call earth.
John Milton 1608-74: *Comus* (1637)

7 As low as where this earth
Spins like a fretful midge.
Dante Gabriel Rossetti 1828-82: 'The Blessed Damozel' (1870)

8 The earth does not argue,
Is not pathetic, has no arrangements,
Does not scream, haste, persuade,
threaten, promise,

Makes no discriminations, has no conceivable failures,
Closes nothing, refuses nothing, shuts none out.
Walt Whitman 1819-92: 'A Song of the Rolling Earth' (1881)

9 Praise the green earth. Chance has appointed her
home, workshop, larder, middenpit.
Her lousy skin scabbed here and there by
cities provides us with name and nation.
Basil Bunting 1900-85: 'Attis: or, Something Missing' (1931)

10 Topography displays no favourites; North's as near as West.
More delicate than the historians' are the map-makers' colours.
Elizabeth Bishop 1911-79: 'The Map' (1946)

11 Now there is one outstandingly important fact regarding Spaceship Earth, and that is that no instruction book came with it.
R. Buckminster Fuller 1895-1983: *Operating Manual for Spaceship Earth* (1969)

12 God owns heaven
but He craves the earth.
Anne Sexton 1928-74: 'The Earth' (1975)

13 The Alps, the Rockies and all other mountains are related to the earth, the Himalayas to the heavens.
J. K. Galbraith 1908- : *A Life in our Times* (1981)

14 How inappropriate to call this planet Earth when it is clearly Ocean.
Arthur C. Clarke 1917- : in *Nature* 1990; attributed

15 We have a beautiful
mother
Her green lap

immense
Her brown embrace
eternal
Her blue body
everything
we know.
Alice Walker 1944– : 'We Have a Beautiful Mother' (1991)

16 To me, it underscores our responsibility to deal more kindly with one another, and to preserve and cherish the pale blue dot, the

only home we've ever known.
of Earth as photographed by Voyager 1
Carl Sagan 1934–96: *Pale Blue Dot* (1995)

17 Gaia is a tough bitch. People think the earth is going to die and they have to save it, that's ridiculous . . . There's no doubt that Gaia can compensate for our output of greenhouse gases, but the environment that's left will not be happy for any people.
Lynn Margulis 1938– : in *New York Times Biographical Service* January 1996; see 2 above

Eating see Cooking and Eating

Economics see also Business, Debt and Borrowing, Money, Thrift and Extravagance

PROVERBS AND SAYINGS

1 Buy in the cheapest market and sell in the dearest.
late 16th century, sometimes with an implication of sharp practice

2 There's no such thing as a free lunch.
colloquial axiom in American economics from the 1960s, much associated with Milton Friedman; first found in printed form in Robert Heinlein The Moon is a Harsh Mistress *(1966); see* **Universe** 22

PHRASES

3 the dismal science economics.
Thomas Carlyle The Nigger Question *(1849), in a play on* gay science: *see* **Poetry** 1

QUOTATIONS

4 Finance is, as it were, the stomach of the country, from which all the other organs take their tone.
W. E. Gladstone 1809–98: article on finance, 1858; H. C. G. Matthew *Gladstone 1809–1874* (1986)

5 There can be no economy where there is no efficiency.
Benjamin Disraeli 1804–81: address to his constituents, 1 October 1868

6 Lenin was right. There is no subtler, no surer means of overturning the existing basis of society than to debauch the currency.
John Maynard Keynes 1883–1946: *The Economic Consequences of the Peace* (1919)

7 We have always known that heedless self-interest was bad morals; we know now that it is bad economics.
Franklin D. Roosevelt 1882–1945: second inaugural address, 20 January 1937

8 The cold metal of economic theory is in Marx's pages immersed in such a wealth of steaming phrases as to acquire a temperature not naturally its own.
Joseph Alois Schumpeter 1883–1950: *Capitalism, Socialism and Democracy* (1942)

9 What a country calls its vital economic interests are not the things which enable its citizens to live, but the things which enable it to make war.
Simone Weil 1909–43: W. H. Auden *A Certain World* (1971)

10 Everyone is always in favour of general economy and particular expenditure.
Anthony Eden 1897–1977: in *Observer* 17 June 1956

11 It's a recession when your neighbour loses his job; it's a depression when you lose yours.
Harry S. Truman 1884–1972: in *Observer* 13 April 1958

12 In a community where public services have failed to keep abreast of private consumption things are very different. Here, in an atmosphere of private opulence and public squalor, the private goods have full sway.
J. K. Galbraith 1908– : *The Affluent Society* (1958)

13 Expenditure rises to meet income.
C. Northcote Parkinson 1909–93: *The Law and the Profits* (1960)

14 When I have to read economic documents I have to have a box of matches and start moving them into position to simplify and illustrate the points to myself.
Alec Douglas-Home, Lord Home 1903–95: in *Observer* 16 September 1962

15 Small is beautiful. A study of economics as if people mattered.
E. F. Schumacher 1911–77: title of book (1973); see **Quantities** 7

16 Inflation is the one form of taxation that can be imposed without legislation.
Milton Friedman 1912– : in *Observer* 22 September 1974

17 First of all the Georgian silver goes, and then all that nice furniture that used to be in the saloon. Then the Canalettos go.
on privatization; often quoted as 'selling the family silver'
Harold Macmillan 1894–1986: speech to the Tory Reform Group, 8 November 1985

18 If the policy isn't hurting, it isn't working.
on controlling inflation
John Major 1943– : speech in Northampton, 27 October 1989

19 Balancing the budget is like going to heaven. Everybody wants to do it, but nobody wants to do what you have to do to get there.
Phil Gramm 1942– : in a television interview, 16 September 1990

20 The green shoots of economic spring are appearing once again.
often quoted as 'the green shoots of recovery'
Norman Lamont 1942– : speech at Conservative Party Conference, 9 October 1991

21 Trickle-down theory—the less than elegant metaphor that if one feeds the horse enough oats, some will pass through to the road for the sparrows.
J. K. Galbraith 1908– : *The Culture of Contentment* (1992)

22 Every year the international finance system kills more people than the second world war. But at least Hitler was mad, you know.
Ken Livingstone 1945– : in *Sunday Times* 16 April 2000

Education see also **Schools, Teaching, Universities**

PROVERBS AND SAYINGS

1 As the twig is bent, so is the tree inclined.
early 18th century; meaning that early influences have a permanent effect

2 Education doesn't come by bumping your head against the school house.
American proverb, mid 20th century

3 Give me a child for the first seven years, and you may do what you like with him afterwards.
traditionally regarded as a Jesuit maxim; recorded in Lean's Collectanea vol. 3 (1903)

4 It is never too late to learn.
late 17th century

5 Never let your education interfere with your intelligence.
American proverb, mid 20th century

6 Never too old to learn.
late 16th century

7 There is no royal road to learning.
early 19th century, deriving from Euclid; see **Mathematics** 8

PHRASES

8 the groves of Academe the academic community.
from the Roman poet Horace (65–8 BC) Epistles 'And seek for truth in the groves of Academe'

QUOTATIONS

9 Get learning with a great sum of money, and get much gold by her.
Bible: Ecclesiasticus

10 In education there should be no class distinction.
Confucius 551–479 BC: *Analects*

11 Whereas then a rattle is a suitable occupation for infant children, education serves as a rattle for young people when older.
Aristotle 384–322 BC: *Politics*

12 Say not, When I have leisure I will study; perchance thou wilt never have leisure.
Hillel 'The Elder' c.60 BC–AD c.9: in *Talmud* Mishnah 'Pirqei Avot' 2:5

13 And gladly wolde he lerne and gladly
teche.
Geoffrey Chaucer c.1343–1400: *The Canterbury Tales*
'The General Prologue'

14 That lyf so short, the craft so long to lerne.
Geoffrey Chaucer c.1343–1400: *The Parliament of Fowls*; see **Arts** 2, **Medicine** 7

15 I would I had bestowed that time in the
tongues that I have in fencing, dancing,
and bear-baiting. O! had I but followed the
arts!
William Shakespeare 1564–1616: *Twelfth Night*
(1601)

16 Studies serve for delight, for ornament,
and for ability.
Francis Bacon 1561–1626: *Essays* (1625) 'Of Studies'

17 Wear your learning, like your watch in a
private pocket: and do not merely pull it
out and strike it, merely to show that you
have one.
Lord Chesterfield 1694–1773: *Letters to his Son*
(1774) 22 February 1748

18 There mark what ills the scholar's life
assail,
Toil, envy, want, the patron, and the jail.
Samuel Johnson 1709–84: *The Vanity of Human Wishes* (1749)

19 Gie me ae spark o' Nature's fire,
That's a' the learning I desire.
Robert Burns 1759–96: 'Epistle to J. L[aprai]k'
(1786)

20 Example is the school of mankind, and
they will learn at no other.
Edmund Burke 1729–97: *Two Letters on the Proposals for Peace with the Regicide Directory* (9th ed., 1796)

21 What does education often do? It makes a
straight-cut ditch of a free, meandering
brook.
Henry David Thoreau 1817–62: *Journal* c.November 1850

22 Education makes a people easy to lead, but
difficult to drive; easy to govern, but
impossible to enslave.
Lord Brougham 1778–1868: attributed

23 Soap and education are not as sudden as a
massacre, but they are more deadly in the
long run.
Mark Twain 1835–1910: *A Curious Dream* (1872)
'Facts concerning the Recent Resignation'

24 Education is an admirable thing, but it is
well to remember from time to time that
nothing that is worth knowing can be
taught.
Oscar Wilde 1854–1900: *Intentions* (1891)

25 The aim of education is the knowledge not
of facts but of values.
William Ralph Inge 1860–1954: 'The Training of
the Reason' in A. C. Benson (ed.) *Cambridge Essays on Education* (1917)

26 The best thing for being sad . . . is to learn
something.
T. H. White 1906–64: *The Sword in the Stone* (1938)

27 To live for a time close to great minds is
the best kind of education.
John Buchan 1875–1940: *Memory Hold-the-Door*
(1940)

28 It [education] has produced a vast
population able to read but unable to
distinguish what is worth reading, an easy
prey to sensations and cheap appeals.
G. M. Trevelyan 1876–1962: *English Social History*
(1942)

29 The empires of the future are the empires
of the mind.
Winston Churchill 1874–1965: speech at Harvard,
6 September 1943

30 If you educate a man you educate one
person, but if you educate a woman you
educate a family.
Ruby Manikan: in *Observer* 30 March 1947

31 Education ent only books and music—it's
asking questions, all the time. There are
millions of us, all over the country, and no
one, not one of us, is asking questions,
we're all taking the easiest way out.
Arnold Wesker 1932– : *Roots* (1959)

32 Education is the ability to listen to almost
anything without losing your temper or
your self-confidence.
Robert Frost 1874–1963: in *Reader's Digest* April
1960

33 Education is what survives when what has
been learned has been forgotten.
B. F. Skinner 1904–90: in *New Scientist* 21 May 1964

34 The liberally educated person is one who is
able to resist the easy and preferred
answers, not because he is obstinate but
because he knows others worthy of
consideration.
Allan Bloom 1930–92: *The Closing of the American Mind* (1987)

35 Ask me my three main priorities for Government, and I tell you: education, education and education.

Tony Blair 1953– : speech at the Labour Party Conference, 1 October 1996; see **Politics** 15

Effort see also Achievement

1 And all because the lady loves Milk Tray.

advertising slogan for Cadbury's Milk Tray chocolates, 1968 onwards, showing the obstacles overcome to deliver the chocolates

2 Easy come, easy go.

mid 17th century, meaning that something which is acquired without effort will be lost without regret

3 He that would eat the fruit must climb the tree.

early 18th century, meaning that someone who wishes to attain success must first make the necessary effort

4 I didn't get where I am today without—.

managerial catchphrase in BBC television series The Fall and Rise of Reginald Perrin (1976–80), written by David Nobbs

5 If a thing's worth doing, it's worth doing well.

mid 18th century; meaning that if something is worth any effort at all, it should be taken seriously; see Women 39

6 If the sky falls we shall catch larks.

mid 15th century; used dismissively to indicate that something will be attainable only in the most unlikely circumstances

7 Much cry and little wool.

late 15th century, referring to a disturbance without tangible result; in early usage, the image was that of shearing a pig, which cried loudly but produced no wool

8 No pain, no gain.

late 16th century, meaning that nothing worth having can be achieved without effort

9 We're number two. We try harder.

advertising slogan for Avis car rentals

PHRASES

10 improve the shining hour make good use of time; make the most of one's time.

after Isaac Watts (1674–1748): see Work 25

QUOTATIONS

11 *Parturient montes, nascetur ridiculus mus.*

Mountains will go into labour, and a silly little mouse will be born.

Horace 65–8 BC: *Ars Poetica*

12 Also say to them, that they suffre hym this day to wynne his spurres, for if god be pleased, I woll this journey be his, and the honoure therof.

speaking of the Black Prince at the battle of Crécy, 1346; commonly quoted as 'Let the boy win his spurs'

Edward III 1312–77: *The Chronicle of Froissart* (translated by John Bourchier 1523–5); see **Success** 19

13 Things won are done; joy's soul lies in the doing.

William Shakespeare 1564–1616: *Troilus and Cressida* (1602)

14 I had done all that I could; and no man is well pleased to have his all neglected, be it ever so little.

Samuel Johnson 1709–84: letter to Lord Chesterfield, 7 February 1755

15 But the fruit that can fall without shaking, Indeed is too mellow for me.

Lady Mary Wortley Montagu 1689–1762: 'Answered, for Lord William Hamilton' (1758)

16 It is a folly to expect men to do all that they may reasonably be expected to do.

Richard Whately 1787–1863: *Apophthegms* (1854)

17 Say not the struggle naught availeth, The labour and the wounds are vain, The enemy faints not, nor faileth, And as things have been, things remain.

Arthur Hugh Clough 1819–61: 'Say not the struggle naught availeth' (1855)

18 Now, *here*, you see, it takes all the running *you* can do, to keep in the same place. If you want to get somewhere else, you must run at least twice as fast as that!

Lewis Carroll 1832–98: *Through the Looking-Glass* (1872); said by the Red Queen: see **Life Sciences** 4

19 The world is divided into people who do things and people who get the credit. Try, if you can, to belong to the first class. There's far less competition.
Dwight Morrow 1873–1931: letter to his son; Harold Nicolson *Dwight Morrow* (1935)

20 The world is an oyster, but you don't crack it open on a mattress.
Arthur Miller 1915– : *Death of a Salesman* (1949)

21 Our salvation is in striving to achieve what we know we'll never achieve.
Ryszard Kapuscinski 1932– : in *Granta* no. 15, 1985

Elections see also **Democracy**

1 As Maine goes, so goes the nation.
American political saying, c.1840; see 10 below

2 A straw vote only shows which way the hot air blows.
American proverb, early 20th century

3 Vote early and vote often.
American election slogan, already current when quoted by William Porcher Miles in the House of Representatives, 31 March 1858

4 The English people believes itself to be free; it is gravely mistaken; it is free only during the election of Members of Parliament; as soon as the Members are elected, the people is enslaved; it is nothing.
Jean-Jacques Rousseau 1712–78: *Du Contrat social* (1762)

5 The right of election is the very essence of the constitution.
'Junius': *Public Advertiser* 24 April 1769

6 To give victory to the right, not bloody bullets, but peaceful ballots only, are necessary.
usually quoted 'The ballot is stronger than the bullet'
Abraham Lincoln 1809–65: speech, 18 May 1858

7 An election is coming. Universal peace is declared, and the foxes have a sincere interest in prolonging the lives of the poultry.
George Eliot 1819–80: *Felix Holt* (1866)

8 As for our majority . . . one is enough.
now often associated with Churchill
Benjamin Disraeli 1804–81: *Endymion* (1880)

9 The accursed power which stands on Privilege
(And goes with Women, and Champagne, and Bridge)
Broke—and Democracy resumed her reign:
(Which goes with Bridge, and Women and Champagne).
Hilaire Belloc 1870–1953: 'On a Great Election' (1923)

10 As Maine goes, so goes Vermont.
after predicting correctly that Franklin D. Roosevelt would carry all but two states in the election of 1936
James A. Farley 1888–1976: statement to the press, 4 November 1936; see 1 above

11 He has joined what even he would admit to be the majority.
on the death of a supporter of proportional representation
John Sparrow 1906–92: in c.1947; J. A. Gere and John Sparrow (eds.) *Geoffrey Madan's Notebooks* (1981); see **Death** 14

12 If there had been any formidable body of cannibals in the country he would have promised to provide them with free missionaries fattened at the taxpayer's expense.
of Harry Truman's success in the 1948 presidential campaign
H. L. Mencken 1880–1956: in *Baltimore Sun* 7 November 1948

13 Hell, I never vote *for* anybody. I always vote *against*.
W. C. Fields 1880–1946: Robert Lewis Taylor *W. C. Fields* (1950)

14 Don't buy a single vote more than necessary. I'll be damned if I'm going to pay for a landslide.
telegraphed message from his father, read at a Gridiron dinner in Washington, 15 March 1958, and almost certainly JFK's invention
John F. Kennedy 1917–63: J. F. Cutler *Honey Fitz* (1962)

15 Vote for the man who promises least; he'll be the least disappointing.
Bernard Baruch 1870–1965: Meyer Berger *New York* (1960)

16 You won the elections, but I won the count.
replying to an accusation of ballot-rigging
Anastasio Somoza 1925–80: in *Guardian* 17 June 1977; see **Democracy** 24

17 You campaign in poetry. You govern in prose.
Mario Cuomo 1932– : in *New Republic*, Washington, DC, 8 April 1985

18 If voting changed anything, they'd abolish it.
Ken Livingstone 1945– : title of book, 1987

19 Instead of rocking the cradle, they rocked the system.
in her victory speech as President, paying tribute to the women of Ireland
Mary Robinson 1944– : in *The Times* 10 November 1990; see **Women** 3

Emotions

1 Out of the fullness of the heart the mouth speaks.
late 14th century, meaning that overwhelming feeling will express itself in speech; originally with allusion to the Bible (Matthew), 'Out of the abundance of the heart the mouth speaketh'

2 Sing before breakfast, cry before night.
early 17th century, warning against overconfidence in early happiness presaging a reversal of good fortune

PHRASES

3 hard as the nether millstone callous and unyielding, without sympathy or pity.
nether millstone, the lower of the two millstones by which corn is ground; with allusion to Job in the Geneva Bible (1560) 'His heart is as strong as a stone, and as hard as the nether millstone'

4 the pathetic fallacy the attribution of human emotion or responses to inanimate things or animals, especially in art and literature.
from John Ruskin Modern Painters (1856) 'All violent feelings . . . produce . . . a falseness in . . . impressions of external things, which I would generally characterize as the "Pathetic fallacy" '

5 wear one's heart on one's sleeve allow one's feelings to be obvious.
from Shakespeare: see 8 below

6 wring the withers stir the emotions or sensibilities.
after Shakespeare Hamlet 'let the galled jade wince, our withers are unwrung'

QUOTATIONS

7 Even as rain breaks not through a well-thatched house, passions break not through a well-guarded mind.
Pali Tripitaka *c.* 2nd century BC: *Dhammapada* v. 14

8 But I will wear my heart upon my sleeve

For daws to peck at: I am not what I am.
William Shakespeare 1564–1616: *Othello* (1602–4); see 5 above

9   A man whose blood
Is very snow-broth; one who never feels
The wanton stings and motions of the sense.
William Shakespeare 1564–1616: *Measure for Measure* (1604)

10 Our passions are most like to floods and streams;
The shallow murmur, but the deep are dumb.
Walter Ralegh *c.*1552–1618: 'Sir Walter Ralegh to the Queen' (1655)

11 The heart has its reasons which reason knows nothing of.
Blaise Pascal 1623–62: *Pensées* (1670)

12 Calm of mind, all passion spent.
John Milton 1608–74: *Samson Agonistes* (1671)

13 The ruling passion, be it what it will,
The ruling passion conquers reason still.
Alexander Pope 1688–1744: *Epistles to Several Persons* 'To Lord Bathurst' (1733)

14 We shall never learn to feel and respect our real calling and destiny, unless we have taught ourselves to consider every thing as moonshine, compared with the education of the heart.
Sir Walter Scott 1771–1832: to J. G. Lockhart, August 1825

15 There are strings . . . in the human heart that had better not be wibrated.
Charles Dickens 1812–70: *Barnaby Rudge* (1841)

16 As you pass from the tender years of youth into harsh and embittered manhood, make sure you take with you on your journey all the human emotions! Don't leave them on the road, for you will not pick them up afterwards!

Nikolai Gogol 1809–52: *Dead Souls* (1842)

on being told there was no English word equivalent to sensibilité:

17 Yes we have. Humbug.

Lord Palmerston 1784–1865: attributed

18 The world of the emotions that are so lightly called physical.

Colette 1873–1954: *Le Blé en herbe* (1923)

19 The trumpets came out brazenly with the last post. We all swallowed our spittle, chokingly, while our eyes smarted against our wills. A man hates to be moved to folly by a noise.

T. E. Lawrence 1888–1935: *The Mint* (1955)

20 The desires of the heart are as crooked as corkscrews.

W. H. Auden 1907–73: 'Death's Echo' (1937)

21 Now that my ladder's gone
I must lie down where all ladders start
In the foul rag and bone shop of the heart.

W. B. Yeats 1865–1939: 'The Circus Animals' Desertion' (1939)

22 They had been corrupted by money, and he had been corrupted by sentiment. Sentiment was the more dangerous, because you couldn't name its price. A man open to bribes was to be relied upon below a certain figure, but sentiment

might uncoil in the heart at a name, a photograph, even a smell remembered.

Graham Greene 1904–91: *The Heart of the Matter* (1948)

23 Oh heavens, how I long for a little ordinary human enthusiasm. Just enthusiasm—that's all. I want to hear a warm, thrilling voice cry out Hallelujah! Hallelujah! I'm alive!

John Osborne 1929–94: *Look Back in Anger* (1956)

24 A man who has not passed through the inferno of his passions has never overcome them.

Carl Gustav Jung 1875–1961: *Erinnerungen, Träume, Gedanken* (1962)

25 Sentimentality is the emotional promiscuity of those who have no sentiment.

Norman Mailer 1923– : *Cannibals and Christians* (1966)

26 One mad magenta moment and I have paid for it all my life.

Alan Bennett 1934– : *Habeas Corpus* (1973)

27 The heart is an organ of fire.

Michael Ondaatje 1943– : *The English Patient* (1992)

28 The human heart likes a little disorder in its geometry.

Louis de Bernières 1954– : *Captain Corelli's Mandolin* (1994)

29 I was never one who could put my hand on my heart with tears dripping out of either eye, feeling the pain of others.

John Major 1943– : in *Independent* 11 April 2001

Employment see also Work

PROVERBS AND SAYINGS

1 **The labourer is worthy of his hire.**

late 14th century, meaning that someone should be properly recompensed for effort; deriving from the Bible (Luke)

2 **Like master, like man.**

mid 16th century; man here means 'servant'

PHRASES

3 **the butcher, the baker, the candlestick-maker** people of all trades.

from the nursery rhyme 'Rub-a-dub-dub, Three men in a tub'

4 **the oldest profession** prostitution.

see also Politics 33

5 **winter of discontent** a period of difficulty, especially political or industrial unrest; particularly applied to the winter of 1978–79 in Britain, when widespread strikes forced the government out of power.

after Shakespeare Richard III 'Now is the winter of our discontent'; see 29 below

6 For promotion cometh neither from the east, nor from the west: nor yet from the south.
Bible: Psalm 75

7 He who does not teach his son a craft, teaches him brigandage.
The Talmud: *Babylonian Talmud* Qiddushin 29a

8 I hold every man a debtor to his profession.
Francis Bacon 1561–1626: *The Elements of the Common Law* (1596)

9 Thou art not for the fashion of these times, Where none will sweat but for promotion.
William Shakespeare 1564–1616: *As You Like It* (1599)

10   'Tis the curse of service,
Preferment goes by letter and affection,
Not by the old gradation, where each second
Stood heir to the first.
William Shakespeare 1564–1616: *Othello* (1602–4)

11 It is wonderful, when a calculation is made, how little the mind is actually employed in the discharge of any profession.
Samuel Johnson 1709–84: James Boswell *Life of Samuel Johnson* (1791) 6 April 1775

12 To do nothing and get something, formed a boy's ideal of a manly career.
Benjamin Disraeli 1804–81: *Sybil* (1845)

13 For more than five years I maintained myself thus solely by the labour of my hands, and I found, that by working about six weeks in a year, I could meet all the expenses of living.
Henry David Thoreau 1817–62: *Walden* (1854) 'Economy'

14 Which of us . . . is to do the hard and dirty work for the rest—and for what pay? Who is to do the pleasant and clean work, and for what pay?
John Ruskin 1819–1900: *Sesame and Lilies* (1865)

15 Naturally, the workers are perfectly free; the manufacturer does not force them to take his materials and his cards, but he says to them . . . 'If you don't like to be frizzled in my frying pan, you can take a walk into the fire'.
Friedrich Engels 1820–95: *The Condition of the Working Class in England in 1844* (1892); see **Misfortunes** 11

16 The labour of women in the house, certainly, enables men to produce more wealth than they otherwise could; and in this way women are economic factors in society. But so are horses.
Charlotte Perkins Gilman 1860–1935: *Women and Economics* (1898)

17 When domestic servants are treated as human beings it is not worth while to keep them.
George Bernard Shaw 1856–1950: *Man and Superman* (1903)

18 A man who has no office to go to—I don't care who he is—is a trial of which you can have no conception.
George Bernard Shaw 1856–1950: *The Irrational Knot* (1905)

19 Lord Finchley tried to mend the Electric Light
Himself. It struck him dead: And serve him right!
It is the business of the wealthy man
To give employment to the artisan.
Hilaire Belloc 1870–1953: 'Lord Finchley' (1911)

20 All professions are conspiracies against the laity.
George Bernard Shaw 1856–1950: *The Doctor's Dilemma* (1911)

21 Not a penny off the pay, not a second on the day.
often quoted with 'minute' substituted for 'second'
A. J. Cook 1885–1931: speech at York, 3 April 1926

22 The most conservative man in this world is the British Trade Unionist when you want to change him.
Ernest Bevin 1881–1951: speech, Trades Union Congress, 8 September 1927

23 Had the employers of past generations all of them dealt fairly with their men there would have been no unions.
Stanley Baldwin 1867–1947: speech in Birmingham, 14 January 1931

24 Work is of two kinds: first, altering the position of matter at or near the earth's surface relatively to other such matter; second, telling other people to do so. The first kind is unpleasant and ill paid; the second is pleasant and highly paid.
Bertrand Russell 1872–1970: *In Praise of Idleness and Other Essays* (1986) title essay (1932)

25 A professional is a man who can do his job when he doesn't feel like it. An amateur is

a man who can't do his job when he does feel like it.
James Agate 1877–1947: diary 19 July 1945

26 By working faithfully eight hours a day, you may eventually get to be a boss and work twelve hours a day.
Robert Frost 1874–1963: attributed

27 You don't get me I'm part of the union.
John Ford 1948– and **Richard Hudson** 1948– : 'Part of the Union' (1974 song)

28 Industrial relations are like sexual relations. It's better between two consenting parties.
Vic Feather 1908–76: in *Guardian Weekly* 8 August 1976

29 I had known it was going to be a 'winter of discontent'.
James Callaghan 1912– : television interview, 8 February 1979; see 5 above

30 Always suspect any job men willingly vacate for women.
Jill Tweedie 1936–93: *It's Only Me* (1980)

31 Your work parallels your life, but in the sense of a glass full of water where people look at it and say, 'Oh, the water's the same shape as the glass!'
Francis Ford Coppola 1939– : in *Guardian* 15 October 1988

32 McJob: A low-pay, low-prestige, low-dignity, low benefit, no-future job in the service sector.
Douglas Coupland 1961– : *Generation X* (1991)

33 We spend most of our lives working. So why do so few people have a good time doing it? Virgin is the possibility of good times.
Richard Branson 1950– : interview in *New York Times* 28 February 1993

34 I have that normal male thing of valuing myself according to the job I do. When I can't tell someone in one word what I am, then something is missing. I don't represent anything any more.
Michael Portillo 1953– : in *Independent on Sunday* 20 June 1999

Ending see also **Beginning, Change**

PROVERBS AND SAYINGS

1 All good things must come to an end.
mid 15th century, meaning that nothing lasts; although the addition of 'good' is a later development

2 All's well that ends well.
late 14th century, often used with the implication that difficulties have been successfully negotiated

3 And they all lived happily ever after.
traditional ending for a fairy story; see **Optimism** *38*

4 The end crowns the work.
early 16th century, meaning that the fulfilment of a process is its finest and most notable part

5 Everything has an end.
late 14th century, meaning that no condition lasts for ever

6 In my end is my beginning.
motto of Mary, Queen of Scots (1542–87); see **Beginning** *21*

7 The opera isn't over till the fat lady sings.
late 20th century, using an informal description of the culmination of a traditional opera to indicate that a process is not yet complete

PHRASES

8 crack of doom in archaic usage, the thunder-peal supposed to proclaim the Day of Judgement.
originally often as a quotation from Shakespeare's Macbeth

9 the four last things the four things (death, judgement, heaven, and hell) studied in eschatology.

10 the last of the Mohicans the sole survivors of a particular race or kind.
in Fenimore Cooper's novel of that name (1826), the American Indian Uncas, the last survivor of the Mohicans (= Mohegans), an Algonquian people formerly inhabiting Connecticut and Massachusetts

11 when the kissing has to stop when the honeymoon period finishes; when one is forced to recognize harsh realities.
from Browning: see **Kissing** *8*

QUOTATIONS

12 Better is the end of a thing than the beginning thereof.
Bible: Ecclesiastes

13 The rest is silence.
William Shakespeare 1564–1616: *Hamlet* (1601)

14 Finish, good lady; the bright day is done,
And we are for the dark.
William Shakespeare 1564–1616: *Antony and Cleopatra* (1606–7)

15 What if this present were the world's last night?
John Donne 1572–1631: *Holy Sonnets* (after 1609)

16 This is the beginning of the end.
on the announcement of Napoleon's Pyrrhic victory at Borodino, 1812
Charles-Maurice de Talleyrand 1754–1838: attributed; Sainte-Beuve *M. de Talleyrand* (1870); see 20 below

17 All tragedies are finished by a death,
All comedies are ended by a marriage;
The future states of both are left to faith.
Lord Byron 1788–1824: *Don Juan* (1819–24)

18 Some say the world will end in fire,
Some say in ice.
From what I've tasted of desire
I hold with those who favour fire.
Robert Frost 1874–1963: 'Fire and Ice' (1923)

19 This is the way the world ends
Not with a bang but a whimper.
T. S. Eliot 1888–1965: 'The Hollow Men' (1925)

20 Now this is not the end. It is not even the beginning of the end. But it is, perhaps, the end of the beginning.
on the Battle of Egypt
Winston Churchill 1874–1965: speech at the Mansion House, London, 10 November 1942; see 16 above

21 The party's over, it's time to call it a day.
Betty Comden 1919– and **Adolph Green** 1915– : 'The Party's Over' (1956 song)

22 They think it's all over—it is now.
Kenneth Wolstenholme: television commentary in closing moments of the World Cup Final, 30 July 1966

23 Eternity's a terrible thought. I mean, where's it all going to end?
Tom Stoppard 1937– : *Rosencrantz and Guildenstern are Dead* (1967)

24 It ain't over till it's over.
Yogi Berra 1925– : comment on National League pennant race, 1973, quoted in many versions

Enemies see also **Hatred**

PROVERBS AND SAYINGS

1 Dead men don't bite.
*mid 16th century, meaning that killing an enemy puts an end to danger; see **Practicality** 4*

2 The enemies of my enemies are my friends.
American proverb, mid 20th century, meaning that shared enmity provides common ground

3 Love your enemy—but don't put a gun in his hand.
American proverb, mid 20th century, indicating the practical limitations of charity; see 8 below

4 There is no little enemy.
mid 17th century, meaning that any enemy can be dangerous

QUOTATIONS

5 If thine enemy be hungry, give him bread to eat; and if he be thirsty, give him water to drink.
For thou shalt heap coals of fire upon his head, and the Lord shall reward thee.
Bible: Proverbs; see **Forgiveness** 7

6 *Delenda est Carthago.*
Carthage must be destroyed.
*warning included in every speech made by Cato, whatever the subject; see **Peace** 4*
Cato the Elder 234–149 BC: Pliny the Elder *Naturalis Historia*

7 He that is not with me is against me.
Bible: St Matthew

8 Love your enemies, do good to them which hate you.
Bible: St Luke; see 3 above, **Forgiveness** 13

9 There is nothing in the whole world so painful as feeling that one is not liked. It always seems to me that people who hate me must be suffering from some strange form of lunacy.
Sei Shōnagon c.966–c.1013: *The Pillow Book*

10 Heat not a furnace for your foe so hot
That it do singe yourself.
William Shakespeare 1564–1616: *Henry VIII* (1613)

11 People wish their enemies dead—but I do

not; I say give them the gout, give them
the stone!

Lady Mary Wortley Montagu 1689–1762: letter
from Horace Walpole to George Harcourt, 17
September 1778

12 He that wrestles with us strengthens our
nerves, and sharpens our skill. Our
antagonist is our helper.

Edmund Burke 1729–97: *Reflections on the
Revolution in France* (1790)

13 Respect was mingled with surprise,
And the stern joy which warriors feel
In foemen worthy of their steel.

Sir Walter Scott 1771–1832: *The Lady of the Lake*
(1810)

14 He makes no friend who never made a foe.

Alfred, Lord Tennyson 1809–92: *Idylls of the King*
'Lancelot and Elaine' (1859)

15 A man cannot be too careful in the choice
of his enemies.

Oscar Wilde 1854–1900: *The Picture of Dorian Gray*
(1891)

16 You shall judge of a man by his foes as
well as by his friends.

Joseph Conrad 1857–1924: *Lord Jim* (1900)

17 I am the enemy you killed, my friend.
I knew you in this dark: for you so
frowned

Yesterday through me as you jabbed and
killed . . .
Let us sleep now.

Wilfred Owen 1893–1918: 'Strange Meeting'
(written 1918)

18 Scratch a lover, and find a foe.

Dorothy Parker 1893–1967: 'Ballade of a Great
Weariness' (1937)

19 Not while I'm alive 'e ain't!

*reply to the observation that Nye Bevan was
sometimes his own worst enemy*

Ernest Bevin 1881–1951: Roderick Barclay *Ernest
Bevin and the Foreign Office* (1975)

20 I ain't got no quarrel with the Viet Cong.

refusing to be drafted to fight in Vietnam

Muhammad Ali 1942– : at a press conference in
Miami, Florida, February 1966

21 Better to have him inside the tent pissing
out, than outside pissing in.

of J. Edgar Hoover

Lyndon Baines Johnson 1908–73: David
Halberstam *The Best and the Brightest* (1972)

22 Fidel Castro is right. You do not quieten
your enemy by talking with him like a
priest, but by burning him.

at a Communist Party meeting 17 December 1989

Nicolae Ceauşescu 1918–89: in *Guardian* 11 January
1990

England see also Britain, British Towns and Regions

PROVERBS AND SAYINGS

1 **England is the paradise of women, the hell
of horses, and the purgatory of servants.**

late 16th century

2 **An Englishman's word is his bond.**

*early 16th century, meaning that a promise given is
regarded as having the force of a legal agreement*

PHRASES

3 **perfidious Albion** England.

translation of French la perfide Albion, *of late 18th
century origin, with reference to England's alleged
habitual treachery to other nations; Albion is probably
of Celtic origin and related to Latin* albus *'white', in
allusion to the white cliffs of Dover*

QUOTATIONS

4 *Non Angli sed Angeli.*

Not Angles but Angels.

summarizing Bede Historia Ecclesiastica *'They
answered that they were called Angles. "It is well," he*

said, "for they have the faces of angels, and such
should be the co-heirs of the angels of heaven"'

Gregory the Great AD c.540–604: oral tradition

5 This royal throne of kings, this sceptered
isle,
This earth of majesty, this seat of Mars,
This other Eden, demi-paradise,
This fortress built by Nature for herself
Against infection and the hand of war,
This happy breed of men, this little world,
This precious stone set in the silver sea . . .
This blessèd plot, this earth, this realm,
this England.

William Shakespeare 1564–1616: *Richard II* (1595)

6 The English take their pleasures sadly after
the fashion of their country.

Maximilien de Béthune, Duc de Sully 1559–1641:
attributed

7 Let not England forget her precedence of teaching nations how to live.
John Milton 1608–74: *The Doctrine and Discipline of Divorce* (1643)

8 The English are busy; they don't have time to be polite.
Montesquieu 1689–1755: *Pensées et fragments inédits* . . . vol. 2 (1901)

9 The English plays are like their English puddings: nobody has any taste for them but themselves.
Voltaire 1694–1778: Joseph Spence *Anecdotes* (ed. J. M. Osborn, 1966)

10 In England there are sixty different religions, and only one sauce.
Francesco Caracciolo 1752–99: attributed

11 England has saved herself by her exertions, and will, as I trust, save Europe by her example.
replying to a toast in which he had been described as the saviour of his country in the wars with France
William Pitt 1759–1806: R. Coupland *War Speeches of William Pitt* (1915)

12 We must be free or die, who speak the tongue
That Shakespeare spake; the faith and morals hold
Which Milton held.
William Wordsworth 1770–1850: 'It is not to be thought of that the Flood' (1807)

13 I will not cease from mental fight,
Nor shall my sword sleep in my hand,
Till we have built Jerusalem,
In England's green and pleasant land.
William Blake 1757–1827: *Milton* (1804–10) 'And did those feet in ancient time'

14 England is a nation of shopkeepers.
the phrase 'nation of shopkeepers' had been used earlier by Samuel Adams and Adam Smith
Napoleon I 1769–1821: Barry E. O'Meara *Napoleon in Exile* (1822); see **Business** 29

15 For he might have been a Roosian,
A French, or Turk, or Proosian,
Or perhaps Ital-ian!
But in spite of all temptations
To belong to other nations,
He remains an Englishman!
W. S. Gilbert 1836–1911: *HMS Pinafore* (1878)

16 Winds of the World, give answer! They are whimpering to and fro—
And what should they know of England who only England know?
Rudyard Kipling 1865–1936: 'The English Flag' (1892)

17 Ask any man what nationality he would prefer to be, and ninety-nine out of a hundred will tell you that they would prefer to be Englishmen.
Cecil Rhodes 1853–1902: Gordon Le Sueur *Cecil Rhodes* (1913)

18 Englishmen never will be slaves: they are free to do whatever the Government and public opinion allow them to do.
George Bernard Shaw 1856–1950: *Man and Superman* (1903)

19 God! I will pack, and take a train,
And get me to England once again!
For England's the one land, I know,
Where men with Splendid Hearts may go.
Rupert Brooke 1887–1915: 'The Old Vicarage, Grantchester' (1915)

20 Mad dogs and Englishmen
Go out in the midday sun.
Noël Coward 1899–1973: 'Mad Dogs and Englishmen' (1931 song)

21 It is not that the Englishman can't feel—it is that he is afraid to feel. He has been taught at his public school that feeling is bad form. He must not express great joy or sorrow, or even open his mouth too wide when he talks—his pipe might fall out if he did.
E. M. Forster 1879–1970: *Abinger Harvest* (1936) 'Notes on English Character'

22 Down here it was still the England I had known in my childhood: the railway cuttings smothered in wild flowers . . . the red buses, the blue policemen—all sleeping the deep, deep sleep of England, from which I sometimes fear that we shall never wake till we are jerked out of it by the roar of bombs.
George Orwell 1903–50: *Homage to Catalonia* (1938)

23 Let us pause to consider the English,
Who when they pause to consider themselves they get all reticently thrilled and tinglish,
Because every Englishman is convinced of one thing, viz.:
That to be an Englishman is to belong to the most exclusive club there is.
Ogden Nash 1902–71: 'England Expects' (1938)

24 There'll always be an England
While there's a country lane,
Wherever there's a cottage small
Beside a field of grain.
Ross Parker 1914–74 and **Hugh Charles** 1907– : 'There'll always be an England' (1939 song)

25 I am American bred,
  I have seen much to hate here—much to
    forgive,
  But in a world where England is finished
    and dead,
  I do not wish to live.
  Alice Duer Miller 1874-1942: *The White Cliffs* (1940)

26 Think of what our Nation stands for,
  Books from Boots' and country lanes,
  Free speech, free passes, class distinction,
  Democracy and proper drains.
  John Betjeman 1906-84: 'In Westminster Abbey'
  (1940)

27 It [England] is a family in which the young
  are generally thwarted and most of the
  power is in the hands of irresponsible
  uncles and bed-ridden aunts. Still, it is a
  family. It has its private language and its
  common memories, and at the approach of
  an enemy it closes its ranks. A family with
  the wrong members in control.
  George Orwell 1903-50: *The Lion and the Unicorn*
  (1941) 'England Your England'

28 Old maids biking to Holy Communion
  through the mists of the autumn mornings
  . . . these are not only fragments, but
  characteristic fragments, of the English
  scene.
  George Orwell 1903-50: *The Lion and the Unicorn*
  (1941) 'England Your England'; see **Britain** 16

29 An Englishman, even if he is alone, forms
  an orderly queue of one.
  George Mikes 1912- : *How to be an Alien* (1946)

30 This is a letter of hate. It is for you my
  countrymen, I mean those men of my
  country who have defiled it. The men with
  manic fingers leading the sightless, feeble,
  betrayed body of my country to its death
  . . . damn you England.
  John Osborne 1929-94: in *Tribune* 18 August 1961

31 England's not a bad country . . . It's just a
  mean, cold, ugly, divided, tired, clapped-
  out, post-imperial, post-industrial slag-
  heap covered in polystyrene hamburger
  cartons.
  Margaret Drabble 1939- : *A Natural Curiosity*
  (1989)

Entertaining and Hospitality

PROVERBS AND SAYINGS

1 **Always leave the party when you are still
  having a good time.**
  *American proverb, mid 20th century, implying that
  pleasure of this kind is transient*

2 **The company makes the feast.**
  *mid 17th century, meaning that the success of a social
  occasion depends on those present rather than on the
  food and drink provided*

3 **Fish and guests stink after three days.**
  *late 16th century, meaning that one should not
  outstay one's welcome*

4 **Food without hospitality is medicine.**
  American proverb, mid 20th century

5 **It is merry in hall when beards wag all.**
  *early 14th century, meaning when conversation is in
  full flow*

6 **There isn't much to talk about at some
  parties until after one or two couples
  leave.**
  American proverb, mid 20th century

QUOTATIONS

7 Bring hither the fatted calf, and kill it.
  Bible: St Luke; see **Festivals** 29, **Forgiveness** 8

8 Be not forgetful to entertain strangers: for
  thereby some have entertained angels
  unawares.
  Bible: Hebrews

9   Unbidden guests
  Are often welcomest when they are gone.
  William Shakespeare 1564-1616: *Henry VI, Part 1*
  (1592)

10 This day my wife made it appear to me
  that my late entertainment this week cost
  me above £12, an expense which I am
  almost ashamed of, though it is but once
  in a great while, and is the end for which,
  in the most part, we live, to have such a
  merry day once or twice in a man's life.
  Samuel Pepys 1633-1703: diary 6 March 1669

11 He showed me his bill of fare to tempt me
  to dine with him; poh, said I, I value not
  your bill of fare, give me your bill of
  company.
  Jonathan Swift 1667-1745: *Journal to Stella* 2
  September 1711

12 For I, who hold sage Homer's rule the best,
Welcome the coming, speed the going
  guest.
Alexander Pope 1688–1744: *Imitations of Horace*
(1734); 'speed the parting guest' in Pope's
translation of *The Odyssey* (1725-6)

13 Like other parties of the kind, it was first
silent, then talky, then argumentative,
then disputatious, then unintelligible, then
altogethery, then inarticulate, and then
drunk.
Lord Byron 1788–1824: letter to Thomas Moore, 31
October 1815

14 The sooner every party breaks up the
better.
Jane Austen 1775–1817: *Emma* (1816)

15 Everyone knows that the real business of a
ball is either to look out for a wife, to look
after a wife, or to look after somebody
else's wife.
R. S. Surtees 1805-64: *Mr Facey Romford's Hounds*
(1865)

16 If one plays good music, people don't listen
and if one plays bad music people don't
talk.
Oscar Wilde 1854–1900: *The Importance of Being
Earnest* (1895)

17 At a dinner party one should eat wisely
but not too well, and talk well but not too
wisely.
W. Somerset Maugham 1874–1965: *Writer's
Notebook* (1949); written in 1896

18 Some people can stay longer in an hour
than others can in a week.
William Dean Howells 1837–1920: attributed

19 Guests can be, and often are, delightful,
but they should never be allowed to get the
upper hand.
Elizabeth, Countess von Arnim 1866–1941: *All the
Dogs in My Life* (1936)

20 The tumult and the shouting dies,
The captains and the kings depart,
And we are left with large supplies
Of cold blancmange and rhubarb tart.
Ronald Knox 1888–1957: 'After the Party' (1959);
see **Pride** 9

21 I'm a man more dined against than dining.
Maurice Bowra 1898–1971: John Betjeman
Summoned by Bells (1960); in allusion to
Shakespeare *King Lear* 'I am a man More sinned
against than sinning.'

22 The best number for a dinner party is
two—myself and a dam' good head waiter.
Nubar Gulbenkian 1896–1972: in *Daily Telegraph* 14
January 1965

23 Bachelors know all about parties. In fact, a
good bachelor is a living, breathing party
all by himself.
P. J. O'Rourke 1947- : *The Bachelor Home
Companion* (1987)

24 Unless your life is going well you don't
dream of giving a party. Unless you can
look in the mirror and see a benign and
generous and healthy human being, you
shrink from acts of hospitality.
Carol Shields 1935- : *Larry's Party* (1997)

The Environment   see **Pollution and the Environment**

Envy and Jealousy

PROVERBS AND SAYINGS

1 Better be envied than pitied.
*mid 16th century, meaning that even if one is unhappy
it is preferable to be rich and powerful than poor and
vulnerable*

**2 Envy feeds on the living; it ceases when
they are dead.**
American proverb, mid 20th century

**3 The grass is always greener on the other
side of the fence.**
*mid 20th century, meaning that something just out of
reach always appears more desirable than what one
already has*

PHRASES

4 the green-eyed monster jealousy.
from Shakespeare: see 11 below

5 keep up with the Joneses strive not to be
outdone socially by one's neighbours.
*from a comic-strip title, 'Keeping up with the
Joneses—by Pop' in the New York* Globe *1913*

6 nice work if you can get it expressing envy
of what is perceived to be another's more
favourable situation.
title of Gershwin song (1937); see **Courtship** *10*

7 Thou shalt not covet thy neighbour's house, thou shalt not covet thy neighbour's wife, nor his manservant, nor his maidservant, nor his ox, nor his ass, nor any thing that is thy neighbour's.
Bible: Exodus; see 15 below, **Lifestyles** 8

8 Love is strong as death; jealousy is cruel as the grave.
Bible: Song of Solomon

9 Though jealousy be produced by love, as ashes are by fire, yet jealousy extinguishes love as ashes smother the flame.
Marguerite d'Angoulême 1492–1549: *The Heptameron* (1558)

10 Oh! how bitter a thing it is to look into happiness through another man's eyes.
William Shakespeare 1564–1616: *As You Like It* (1599)

11   O! beware, my lord, of jealousy;
It is the green-eyed monster which doth mock
The meat it feeds on.
William Shakespeare 1564–1616: *Othello* (1602–4); see 4 above

12 Malice is of a low stature, but it hath very long arms.
Lord Halifax 1633–95: *Political, Moral, and Miscellaneous Thoughts and Reflections* (1750) 'Of Malice and Envy'

13 Fools out of favour grudge at knaves in place.
Daniel Defoe 1660–1731: *The True-Born Englishman* (1701)

14 If something pleasant happens to you, don't forget to tell it to your friends, to make them feel bad.
Casimir, Comte de Montrond 1768–1843: attributed; Comte J. d'Estourmel *Derniers Souvenirs* (1860)

15 Thou shalt not covet; but tradition Approves all forms of competition.
Arthur Hugh Clough 1819–61: 'The Latest Decalogue' (1862); see 7 above

16 Do we want laurels for ourselves most, Or most that no one else shall have any?
Amy Lowell 1874–1925: 'La Ronde du Diable' (1925); see **Success** 18

17 Jealousy is no more than feeling alone against smiling enemies.
Elizabeth Bowen 1899–1973: *The House in Paris* (1935)

18 To jealousy, nothing is more frightful than laughter.
Françoise Sagan 1935– : *La Chamade* (1965)

19 As we all know from witnessing the consuming jealousy of husbands who are never faithful, people do not confine themselves to the emotions to which they are entitled.
Quentin Crisp 1908–99: *The Naked Civil Servant* (1968)

20 Jealousy is all the fun you *think* they had.
Erica Jong 1942– : *How to Save Your Own Life* (1977)

21 May good confront the man on top and the man below. But let him who is jealous of another's position choke with his envy.
Chinua Achebe 1930– : *Arrow of God* (1988)

Epitaphs see also Death

1 Et in Arcadia ego.
Latin tomb inscription 'And I too in Arcadia', of disputed meaning, often depicted in classical paintings, notably by Poussin in 1655

2 A soldier of the Great War known unto God.
adopted by the War Graves Commission as the standard epitaph for the unidentified dead of World War One

3 hic jacet an epitaph.
*Latin, literally 'here lies', the traditional first two words of a Latin epitaph; see **Death** 31*

4 Go, tell the Spartans, thou who passest by, That here obedient to their laws we lie.
epitaph for the Spartans who died at Thermopylae
Simonides c.556–468 BC: attributed; Herodotus *Histories*

5 And some there be, which have no memorial . . . and are become as though they had never been born . . .
But these were merciful men, whose righteousness hath not been forgotten . . .
Their seed shall remain for ever, and their glory shall not be blotted out.

Their bodies are buried in peace; but their
name liveth for evermore.
Bible: Ecclesiasticus; see 25 below

6 Here lies he who neither feared nor
flattered any flesh.
said of John Knox, as he was buried, 26 November
1572
James Douglas, Earl of Morton c.1516–81: George
R. Preedy *The Life of John Knox* (1940)

7 My friend, judge not me,
Thou seest I judge not thee.
Betwixt the stirrup and the ground
Mercy I asked, mercy I found.
epitaph for a gentleman falling off his horse
William Camden 1551–1623: *Remains Concerning*
Britain (1605)

8 Good friend, for Jesu's sake forbear
To dig the dust enclosed here.
Blest be the man that spares these stones,
And curst be he that moves my bones.
William Shakespeare 1564–1616: epitaph on his
tomb, probably composed by himself

9 Here lies my wife; here let her lie!
Now she's at peace and so am I.
John Dryden 1631–1700: epitaph; attributed but
not traced in his works

10 Life is a jest; and all things show it.
I thought so once; but now I know it.
John Gay 1685–1732: 'My Own Epitaph' (1720)

11 *Si monumentum requiris, circumspice.*
If you seek a monument, gaze around.
Anonymous: inscription in St Paul's Cathedral,
London, attributed to the son of Sir Christopher
Wren, its architect

12   The body of
             Benjamin Franklin, printer,
          (Like the cover of an old book,
             Its contents worn out,
And stripped of its lettering and gilding)
          Lies here, food for worms!
   Yet the work itself shall not be lost,
For it will, as he believed, appear once
                more
             In a new
       And more beautiful edition,
          Corrected and amended
                By its Author!
Benjamin Franklin 1706–90: epitaph for himself
(1728)

13 Under this stone, Reader, survey
Dead Sir John Vanbrugh's house of clay.

Lie heavy on him, Earth! for he
Laid many heavy loads on thee!
Abel Evans 1679–1737: 'Epitaph on Sir John
Vanbrugh, Architect of Blenheim Palace'

14 Where fierce indignation can no longer
tear his heart.
Jonathan Swift 1667–1745: Swift's epitaph; S. Leslie
The Skull of Swift (1928)

15 Here lies one whose name was writ in
water.
John Keats 1795–1821: epitaph for himself; Richard
Monckton Milnes *Life, Letters and Literary Remains of*
John Keats (1848)

16 Were there but a few hearts and intellects
like hers this earth would already become
the hoped-for heaven.
epitaph (1859) inscribed on the tomb of his wife,
Harriet
John Stuart Mill 1806–73: M. St J. Packe *Life of John*
Stuart Mill (1954)

17 Here lie I, Martin Elginbrodde:
Hae mercy o' my soul, Lord God;
As I wad do, were I Lord God,
And ye were Martin Elginbrodde.
George MacDonald 1824–1905: *David Elginbrod*
(1863)

18 Now he belongs to the ages.
of Abraham Lincoln, following his assassination, 15
April 1865
Edwin McMasters Stanton 1814–69: I. M. Tarbell
Life of Abraham Lincoln (1900)

19 This be the verse you grave for me:
'Here he lies where he longed to be;
Home is the sailor, home from sea,
And the hunter home from the hill.'
Robert Louis Stevenson 1850–94: 'Requiem'
(1887)

20 Hereabouts died a very gallant gentleman,
Captain L. E. G. Oates of the Inniskilling
Dragoons. In March 1912, returning from
the Pole, he walked willingly to his death
in a blizzard to try and save his comrades,
beset by hardships.
E. L. Atkinson 1882–1929 and **Apsley Cherry-**
Garrard 1882–1959: epitaph on cairn erected in the
Antarctic, 15 November 1912; see **Last Words** 21

21 They shall grow not old, as we that are left
grow old.
Age shall not weary them, nor the years
condemn.
At the going down of the sun and in the
morning

We will remember them.

particularly associated with Remembrance Day services

Laurence Binyon 1869–1943: 'For the Fallen' (1914)

22 When you go home, tell them of us and say,
'For your tomorrows these gave their today.'

particularly associated with the dead of the Burma campaign of the Second World War, in the form 'For your tomorrow we gave our today'

John Maxwell Edmonds 1875–1958: *Inscriptions Suggested for War Memorials* (1919)

23 Here lies W. C. Fields. I would rather be living in Philadelphia.

W. C. Fields 1880–1946: suggested epitaph for himself; in *Vanity Fair* June 1925

24 Here was the world's worst wound. And here with pride
'Their name liveth for ever' the Gateway claims.
Was ever an immolation so belied

As these intolerably nameless names?

Siegfried Sassoon 1886–1967: 'On Passing the New Menin Gate' (1928); see 5 above

25 We must know,
We will know.

David Hilbert 1862–1943: epitaph on his tombstone

26 Free at last, free at last
Thank God almighty
We are free at last.

epitaph of Martin Luther King (1929–68), quoting a spiritual, with which he ended his 'I have a dream' speech; see Equality 17

Anonymous: Atlanta, Georgia

27 I always thought I'd like my tombstone to be blank. No epitaph, and no name. Well, actually I'd like it to say 'figment'.

Andy Warhol 1927–87: *America* (1985)

28 If I had an epitaph I'd like it to be that 'He encouraged us.'

Tony Benn 1925– : Anthony Clare *In the Psychiatrist's Chair III* (1998)

Equality see also **Human Rights**

1 **A cat may look at a king.**

mid 16th century, meaning that even someone in a lowly position has a right to observe a person of power and influence

2 **Diamond cuts diamond.**

meaning that only a diamond is hard enough to cut another diamond; used of persons who are evenly matched in wit or cunning

3 **Jack is as good as his master.**

early 18th century; Jack is used variously as a familiar name for a sailor, a member of the common people, a serving man, and one who does odd jobs

4 He maketh his sun to rise on the evil and on the good, and sendeth rain on the just and on the unjust.

Bible: St Matthew; see **Weather** 45

5 Hath not a Jew eyes? hath not a Jew hands, organs, dimensions, senses, affections, passions? fed with the same food, hurt with the same weapons, subject to the same diseases, healed by the same means, warmed and cooled by the same winter and summer, as a Christian is? If you prick us, do we not bleed? if you tickle us, do we not laugh? if you poison us, do we not die? and if you wrong us, shall we not revenge?

William Shakespeare 1564–1616: *The Merchant of Venice* (1596–8)

6 Night makes no difference 'twixt the Priest and Clerk;
Joan as my Lady is as good i' th' dark.

Robert Herrick 1591–1674: 'No Difference i' th' Dark' (1648)

7 Sir, there is no settling the point of precedency between a louse and a flea.

on the relative merits of two minor poets

Samuel Johnson 1709–84: James Boswell *Life of Samuel Johnson* (1791) 1783

8 A man's a man for a' that.

Robert Burns 1759–96: 'For a' that and a' that' (1790)

9 There is no method by which men can be both free and equal.

Walter Bagehot 1826–77: in *The Economist* 5 September 1863 'France or England'

10 Make all men equal today, and God has so created them that they shall be all unequal tomorrow.

Anthony Trollope 1815–82: *Autobiography* (1883)

11 When every one is somebodee,
Then no one's anybody.
W. S. Gilbert 1836–1911: *The Gondoliers* (1889)

12 Oh, East is East, and West is West, and
never the twain shall meet,
Till Earth and Sky stand presently at God's
great Judgement Seat;
But there is neither East nor West, Border,
nor Breed, nor Birth,
When two strong men stand face to face,
tho' they come from the ends of earth!
Rudyard Kipling 1865–1936: 'The Ballad of East
and West' (1892)

13 While there is a lower class, I am in it;
while there is a criminal element, I am of
it; while there is a soul in prison, I am not
free.
Eugene Victor Debs 1855–1926: speech at his trial
for sedition in Cleveland, Ohio, 14 September 1918

14 Those who dread a dead-level of income or
wealth . . . do not dread, it seems, a dead-
level of law and order, and of security for
life and property.
R. H. Tawney 1880–1962: *Equality* (4th ed., 1931)

15 The constitution does not provide for first
and second class citizens.
Wendell Willkie 1892–1944: *An American
Programme* (1944)

16 All animals are equal but some animals
are more equal than others.
George Orwell 1903–50: *Animal Farm* (1945)

17 I have a dream that one day on the red
hills of Georgia the sons of former slaves
and the sons of former slave owners will be
able to sit down together at the table of
brotherhood.
Martin Luther King 1929–68: speech at Civil
Rights March in Washington, 28 August 1963; see
Epitaphs 27

18 You can have equality or equality of
opportunity; you cannot have both.
Equality will mean the holding back (or
the new deprivation) of the brighter
children.
Brian Cox 1928– and **Rhodes Boyson** 1925– :
Black Paper 1975 (1975)

Europe see also **Countries and Peoples**, **International Relations**

PHRASES

1 the cockpit of Europe Belgium.
see **Countries and Peoples** 12

2 the Common Market a name for the
European Economic Community or
European Union.
used especially in the 1960s and 1970s; see **Countries
and Peoples** 32

3 the Garden of Europe a traditional name
for Italy.

QUOTATIONS

4 Pray enter
You are learned Europeans and we worse
Than ignorant Americans.
Philip Massinger 1583–1640: *The City Madam*
(1658)

5 The age of chivalry is gone.— That of
sophisters, economists, and calculators,
has succeeded; and the glory of Europe is
extinguished for ever.
Edmund Burke 1729–97: *Reflections on the
Revolution in France* (1790)

6 Roll up that map; it will not be wanted
these ten years.
*of a map of Europe, on hearing of Napoleon's victory
at Austerlitz, December 1805*
William Pitt 1759–1806: Earl Stanhope *Life of the
Rt. Hon. William Pitt* vol. 4 (1862)

7 Better fifty years of Europe than a cycle of
Cathay.
Alfred, Lord Tennyson 1809–92: 'Locksley Hall'
(1842)

8 Whoever speaks of Europe is wrong, [it is]
a geographical concept.
Otto von Bismarck 1815–98: marginal note on a
letter from the Russian Chancellor Gorchakov,
November 1876

9 We are part of the community of Europe
and we must do our duty as such.
Lord Salisbury 1830–1903: speech at Caernarvon,
10 April 1888

10 The European view of a poet is not of
much importance unless the poet writes in
Esperanto.
A. E. Housman 1859–1936: in *Cambridge Review*
1915

11 Purity of race does not exist. Europe is a continent of energetic mongrels.

H. A. L. Fisher 1856–1940: *A History of Europe* (1935)

12 Fog in Channel—Continent isolated.

Russell Brockbank 1913– : newspaper placard in cartoon, *Round the Bend with Brockbank* (1948)

13 If you open that Pandora's Box, you never know what Trojan 'orses will jump out.

on the Council of Europe
Ernest Bevin 1881–1951: Roderick Barclay *Ernest Bevin and the Foreign Office* (1975); see **Problems** 8

14 Yes, it is Europe, from the Atlantic to the Urals, it is Europe, it is the whole of Europe, that will decide the fate of the world.

Charles de Gaulle 1890–1970: speech to the people of Strasbourg, 23 November 1959

15 Leave this Europe where they are never done talking of Man, yet murder men everywhere they find them.

Frantz Fanon 1925–61: *The Wretched of the Earth* (1961)

16 It means the end of a thousand years of history.

on a European federation
Hugh Gaitskell 1906–63: speech at Labour Party Conference, 3 October 1962

17 Without Britain Europe would remain only a torso.

Ludwig Erhard 1897–1977: remark on West German television, 27 May 1962

18 This 'going into Europe' will not turn out to be the thrilling mutual exchange supposed. It is more like nine middle-aged couples with failing marriages meeting in a darkened bedroom in a Brussels hotel for a Group Grope.

E. P. Thompson 1924– : in *Sunday Times* 27 April 1975

19 'We went in,' he said, 'to screw the French by splitting them off from the Germans. The French went in to protect their inefficient farmers from commercial competition. The Germans went in to cleanse themselves of genocide and apply for readmission to the human race.'

on the European Community
Jonathan Lynn 1943– and **Antony Jay** 1930– : *Yes, Minister* (1982) vol. 2

20 We have not successfully rolled back the frontiers of the State in Britain only to see them reimposed at European level, with a European super-State exercising a new dominance from Brussels.

Margaret Thatcher 1925– : speech in Bruges, 20 September 1988

21 In the eighteenth and nineteenth centuries you weren't considered cultured unless you made the European tour, and so it should be.

Edward Heath 1916– : in *Observer* 18 November 1990

22 The policy of European integration is in reality a question of war and peace in the 21st century.

Helmut Kohl 1930– : speech at Louvain University, 2 February 1996

23 I grew up in Europe, where the history comes from.

Eddie Izzard 1962– : *Dress to Kill* (stageshow, San Francisco, 1998)

Evil see **Good and Evil**

Excellence and Mediocrity see also **Perfection**

PROVERBS AND SAYINGS

1 Corruptio optimi pessima.

Latin saying, Corruption of the best becomes the worst; found in English from the early 17th century

2 If something sounds too good to be true, it probably is.

late 20th century saying

3 Jack of all trades and master of none.

early 17th century, meaning that a person who tries to master too many skills will learn none of them properly; see 18 below

PHRASES

4 an admirable Crichton a person who excels in all kinds of studies and pursuits, or who is noted for supreme competence.

originally from James Crichton of Clunie (1560–85?), a Scottish prodigy of intellectual and knightly accomplishments; later in allusion to J. M. Barrie's play The Admirable Crichton (1902) of which the eponymous hero is a butler who takes charge when his master's family is shipwrecked on a desert island

5 the blue ribbon the greatest distinction, the first place or prize.

a ribbon of blue silk, especially that of the Order of the Garter, worn as a badge of honour; see also **Sports** *2*

6 eighth wonder of the world a particularly impressive object.

something worthy to rank with the Seven Wonders of the ancient world; see **Architecture** *4*

7 ne plus ultra the furthest limit reached or attainable; the point of highest attainment, the acme or highest point of a quality.

Latin = not further beyond, the supposed inscription on the Pillars of Hercules (Strait of Gibraltar) prohibiting passage by ships

8 Nature made him, and then broke the mould.
Ludovico Ariosto 1474–1533: *Orlando Furioso* (1532); see **Originality** 2

9 The danger chiefly lies in acting well; No crime's so great as daring to excel.
Charles Churchill 1731–64: *An Epistle to William Hogarth* (1763)

10 The best is the enemy of the good.
Voltaire 1694–1778: *Contes* (1772) 'La Begueule'; derived from an Italian proverb

11 The pretension is nothing; the performance every thing. A good apple is better than an insipid peach.
Leigh Hunt 1784–1859: *The Story of Rimini* (1832 ed.)

12 The best is the best, though a hundred judges have declared it so.
Arthur Quiller-Couch 1863–1944: *Oxford Book of English Verse* (1900) preface

13 The dullard's envy of brilliant men is always assuaged by the suspicion that they will come to a bad end.
Max Beerbohm 1872–1956: *Zuleika Dobson* (1911)

14 The best lack all conviction, while the worst
Are full of passionate intensity.
W. B. Yeats 1865–1939: 'The Second Coming' (1921)

15 She has a Rolls body and a Balham mind.
J. B. Morton ('Beachcomber') 1893–1975: *Morton's Folly* (1933)

16 There's only one real sin, and that is to persuade oneself that the second-best is anything but the second-best.
Doris Lessing 1919– : *Golden Notebook* (1962)

17 If Richard Nixon was second-rate, what in the world *is* third-rate?
Joseph Heller 1923–99: *Good as Gold* (1979)

18 I'm usually called a jack of all trades by people who are scarcely jacks of one.
Jonathan Miller 1934– : in *Daily Telegraph* 24 December 1988; see 3 above

19 To those of you who received honours, awards and distinctions, I say well done. And to the C students, I say you, too, can be president of the United States.
George W. Bush 1946– : in *Sunday Times* 27 May 2001

Excess and Moderation

1 Enough is as good as a feast.
late 14th century, used as a warning against overindulgence, or overdoing something

2 The half is better than the whole.
mid 16th century, advising economy or restraint; from Hesiod Works and Days 'The half is greater than the whole'

3 It is the last straw that breaks the camel's back.
mid 17th century, meaning that the addition of one quite minor problem may prove crushing to someone who is already overburdened; see **Crises** *6*

4 Keep no more cats than will catch mice.
late 17th century, recommending efficiency and the ethic of steady work to justify one's place

5 The last drop makes the cup run over.
mid 17th century, in which the addition of something in itself quite minor causes an excess

6 Less is more.
mid 19th century, meaning that something simple often has more effect; see **Architecture** *16*

7 Moderation in all things.
mid 19th century, from Hesiod Works and Days 'Observe due measure; moderation is best in all things'; see 9 below

8 The pitcher will go to the well once too often.
mid 14th century, meaning that one should not repeat a risky action too often, or push one's luck too far

9 There is measure in all things.
late 14th century; see 7 above

10 You can have too much of a good thing.
late 15th century, meaning that excess even of something which is good in itself can be damaging

PHRASES

11 break a butterfly on a wheel use unnecessary force in destroying something fragile.
*break on the wheel fracture the bones of or dislocate on a wheel as a form of punishment or torture; from Pope: see **Futility** 18*

12 corn in Egypt a plentiful supply.
from the Bible (Genesis) 'Behold, I have heard that there is corn in Egypt: get you down thither and buy for us from thence'

13 embarras de richesse(s) a superfluity of something, more than one needs or wants.
French = embarrassment of riches, from L'embarras des richesses (1726), title of comedy by Abbé d'Allainval

14 gild the lily embellish excessively, add ornament where none is needed.
from alteration of Shakespeare: see 22 below

15 the golden mean the avoidance of extremes, moderation
from the Roman poet Horace (65–8 BC) Odes 'Someone who loves the golden mean'

16 the Matthew principle the principle that more will be given to those who already have.
after the Bible (Matthew) 'Unto every one that hath shall be given, and he shall have abundance'

17 pile Ossa upon Pelion add further problems to an existing difficulty.
from Virgil 'three times they endeavoured to pile Ossa on Pelion, no less, and to roll leafy Olympus on top of Ossa', referring to the Greek legend of how the giants used the Thessalian mountains of Ossa and Pelion in an attempt to scale the heavens and overthrow the gods

QUOTATIONS

18 Nothing in excess.
Anonymous: inscribed on the temple of Apollo at Delphi, and variously ascribed to the Seven Wise Men

19 You will go most safely by the middle way.
Ovid 43 BC–AD C.17: *Metamorphoses*

20 Because thou art lukewarm, and neither cold nor hot, I will spew thee out of my mouth.
Bible: Revelation

21 To many, total abstinence is easier than perfect moderation.
St Augustine of Hippo AD 354–430: *On the Good of Marriage* (AD 401)

22 To gild refinèd gold, to paint the lily . . . Is wasteful and ridiculous excess.
William Shakespeare 1564–1616: *King John* (1591–8); see 14 above

23 By God, Mr Chairman, at this moment I stand astonished at my own moderation!
Lord Clive 1725–74: reply during Parliamentary cross-examination, 1773; G. R. Gleig *The Life of Robert, First Lord Clive* (1848)

24 I know many have been taught to think that moderation, in a case like this, is a sort of treason.
Edmund Burke 1729–97: *Letter to the Sheriffs of Bristol* (1777)

25 The road of excess leads to the palace of wisdom.
William Blake 1757–1827: *The Marriage of Heaven and Hell* (1790–3) 'Proverbs of Hell'

26 Above all, gentlemen, not the slightest zeal.
Charles-Maurice de Talleyrand 1754–1838: P. Chasles *Voyages d'un critique à travers la vie et les livres* (1868)

27 Moderation is a fatal thing, Lady Hunstanton. Nothing succeeds like excess.
Oscar Wilde 1854–1900: *A Woman of No Importance* (1893)

28 Fanaticism consists in redoubling your effort when you have forgotten your aim.
George Santayana 1863–1952: *The Life of Reason* (1905)

29 Up to a point, Lord Copper.
meaning no
Evelyn Waugh 1903–66: *Scoop* (1938)

30 We know what happens to people who stay in the middle of the road. They get run down.
Aneurin Bevan 1897–1960: in *Observer* 6 December 1953

31 I would remind you that extremism in the defence of liberty is no vice! And let me remind you also that moderation in the pursuit of justice is no virtue!
Barry Goldwater 1909–98: accepting the presidential nomination, 16 July 1964

32 There's nothing in the middle of the road but yellow stripes and dead armadillos.
Jim Hightower: attributed, 1984

Excuses see **Apology and Excuses**

Experience see also **Maturity**

---

1 Appetite comes with eating.

mid 17th century, meaning that desire or facility increases as an activity proceeds

2 A burnt child dreads the fire.

mid 13th century, meaning that the memory of past hurt may act as a safeguard in the future

3 Experience is a comb which fate gives a man when his hair is all gone.

*American proverb, mid 20th century; see **Wars** 29*

4 Experience is the best teacher.

mid 16th century, sometimes used with the implication that learning by experience may be painful; see 17 below

5 Experience is the father of wisdom.

mid 16th century, meaning that real understanding of something comes only from direct experience of it

6 Experience keeps a dear school.

mid 18th century, meaning that lessons learned from experience can be painful

7 Live and learn.

early 17th century; often as a resigned or rueful comment on a disagreeable experience

8 Once bitten, twice shy.

mid 19th century, meaning that someone who has suffered an injury will in the future be very cautious of the cause

9 Some folks speak from experience; others, from experience, don't speak.

American proverb, mid 20th century

10 They that live longest, see most.

early 17th century, often used to comment on the experience of old age

11 You cannot catch old birds with chaff.

*late 15th century, meaning that the wise and experienced are not easily fooled; see **Deception** 4*

12 You cannot put an old head on young shoulders.

late 16th century, meaning that you cannot expect someone who is young and inexperienced to show the wisdom and maturity of an older person

13 You should make a point of trying every experience once, excepting incest and folk-dancing.

20th century saying, repeated by Arnold Bax in Farewell My Youth (1943), quoting 'a sympathetic Scot'

14 babes in the wood inexperienced people in a situation calling for experience.

with reference to an old ballad The Children in the Wood, in which a wicked uncle who wishes to steal the children's inheritance causes them to be abandoned in a forest where they die

15 walk before one can run understand elementary points before proceeding to anything more difficult.

*from the proverb: see **Patience** 17*

16 *Experto credite.*

Trust one who has gone through it.

Virgil 70–19 BC: *Aeneid*

17 *Experientia docuit.*

Experience has taught.

commonly quoted as 'Experientia docet [experience teaches]'

Tacitus AD c.56–after 117: *The Histories* bk. 5, ch. 6; see 4 above, 26 below

18 No man's knowledge here can go beyond his experience.

John Locke 1632–1704: *An Essay concerning Human Understanding* (1690)

19 Courts and camps are the only places to learn the world in.

Lord Chesterfield 1694–1773: *Letters to his Son* (1774) 2 October 1747

20 The courtiers who surround him have forgotten nothing and learnt nothing.

of Louis XVIII, at the time of the Declaration of Verona, September 1795

Charles François du Périer Dumouriez 1739–1823: *Examen impartial d'un Écrit intitulé Déclaration de Louis XVIII* (1795); quoted by Napoleon in his Declaration to the French on his return from Elba; a similar saying is attributed to Talleyrand

21 He went like one that hath been stunned,
And is of sense forlorn:
A sadder and a wiser man,
He rose the morrow morn.

Samuel Taylor Coleridge 1772–1834: 'The Rime of the Ancient Mariner' (1798)

22 Axioms in philosophy are not axioms until they are proved upon our pulses: We read

fine things, but never feel them to the full until we have gone the same steps as the author.
John Keats 1795–1821: letter to J. H. Reynolds, 3 May 1818

23 If men could learn from history, what lessons it might teach us! But passion and party blind our eyes, and the light which experience gives is a lantern on the stern, which shines only on the waves behind us!
Samuel Taylor Coleridge 1772–1834: *Table Talk* (1835) 18 December 1831

24 The years teach much which the days never know.
Ralph Waldo Emerson 1803–82: *Essays. Second Series* (1844) 'Experience'

25 Grace is given of God, but knowledge is bought in the market.
Arthur Hugh Clough 1819–61: *The Bothie of Tober-na-Vuolich* (1848)

26 Experientia does it—as papa used to say.
said by Mrs Micawber
Charles Dickens 1812–70: *David Copperfield* (1850) ch. 11; see 17 above

in his case against Ruskin, replying to the question, 'For two days' labour, you ask two hundred guineas?':
27 No, I ask it for the knowledge of a lifetime.
James McNeill Whistler 1834–1903: D. C. Seitz *Whistler Stories* (1913)

28 Experience is the name every one gives to their mistakes.
Oscar Wilde 1854–1900: *Lady Windermere's Fan* (1892)

29 All experience is an arch to build upon.
Henry Brooks Adams 1838–1918: *The Education of Henry Adams* (1907)

30 Experience is not what happens to a man; it is what a man does with what happens to him.
Aldous Huxley 1894–1963: *Texts and Pretexts* (1932)

31 I've been things and seen places.
Mae West 1892–1980: *I'm No Angel* (1933 film)

32 It's a funny old world—a man's lucky if he gets out of it alive.
Walter de Leon and **Paul M. Jones**: *You're Telling Me* (1934 film); spoken by W. C. Fields

33 Experience isn't interesting till it begins to repeat itself—in fact, till it does that, it hardly *is* experience.
Elizabeth Bowen 1899–1973: *Death of the Heart* (1938)

34 We had the experience but missed the meaning.
T. S. Eliot 1888–1965: *Four Quartets* 'The Dry Salvages' (1941)

35 I learned . . . that one can never go back, that one should not ever try to go back—that the essence of life is going forward. Life is really a One Way Street.
Agatha Christie 1890–1976: *At Bertram's Hotel* (1965)

36 I've looked at life from both sides now, From win and lose and still somehow It's life's illusions I recall; I really don't know life at all.
Joni Mitchell 1945– : 'Both Sides Now' (1967 song)

37 Education is when you read the fine print; experience is what you get when you don't.
Pete Seeger 1919– : L. Botts *Loose Talk* (1980)

38 Damaged people are dangerous. They know they can survive.
Josephine Hart: *Damage* (1991)

Exploration see also Travel

1 **Here be dragons.**
alluding to a traditional indication of early mapmakers that a region was unexplored and potentially dangerous

2 **to boldly go** explore freely, unhindered by fear of the unknown.
from the brief given to the Enterprise *in the television series* Star Trek, *written by Gene Roddenberry (from 1966), 'These are the voyages of the starship* Enterprise. Its five-year mission . . . to boldly go where no man has gone before'

3 Now the boundary of Britain is revealed, and everything unknown is held to be glorious.
reporting the speech of a British leader, Calgacus
Tacitus AD c.56–after 117: *Agricola*

4 There is no land unhabitable nor sea innavigable.
Robert Thorne d. 1527: Richard Hakluyt *The Principal Navigations, Voyages, and Discoveries of the English Nation* (1589)

5 They are ill discoverers that think there is no land, when they can see nothing but sea.
Francis Bacon 1561–1626: *The Advancement of Learning* (1605)

6 So geographers, in Afric-maps,
With savage-pictures fill their gaps;
And o'er unhabitable downs
Place elephants for want of towns.
Jonathan Swift 1667–1745: 'On Poetry' (1733)

7 Go West, young man, go West!
John L. B. Soule 1815–91: in *Terre Haute* [Indiana] *Express* (1851); see **America** 18

8 It was a melancholy day for human nature when that stupid Lord Anson, after beating about for three years, found himself again at Greenwich. The circumnavigation of our globe was accomplished, but the illimitable was annihilated and a fatal blow [dealt] to all imagination.
Benjamin Disraeli 1804–81: written 1860, in *Reminiscences* (ed. H. and M. Swartz, 1975)

9 [Faust] never reached a place where he wanted to 'remain'. I cannot even glimpse anywhere worth the attempt.
Fridtjof Nansen 1861–1930: diary, 1909; Alistair Horne (ed.) *Telling Lives* (2000)

10 Why do people so love to wander? I think the civilized parts of the world will suffice for me in the future.
Mary Cassatt 1844–1926: letter to Louisine Havemeyer, 11 February 1911

11 What on earth good accrues from going to the North and South Poles? I never could understand—no one is going there when they can go to Monte Carlo!
John Arbuthnot Fisher 1841–1920: Roland Huntford *The Last Place on Earth* (2000)

12 Polar exploration is at once the cleanest and most isolated way of having a bad time which has been devised.
Apsley Cherry-Garrard 1882–1959: *The Worst Journey in the World* (1922)

13 We shall not cease from exploration
And the end of all our exploring
Will be to arrive where we started
And know the place for the first time.
T. S. Eliot 1888–1965: *Four Quartets* 'Little Gidding' (1942)

14 For a joint scientific and geographical piece of organization, give me Scott; for a Winter Journey, Wilson; for a dash to the pole and nothing else, Amundsen: and if I am in the devil of a hole and want to get out of it, give me Shackleton every time.
Apsley Cherry-Garrard 1882–1959: F. A. Worsley *Shackleton's Boat Journey* (1999)

15 Slim [Lindbergh] flew through miserable weather and stretched science and the art of navigation to find Le Bourget. We could see our destination throughout our entire voyage.
Neil Armstrong 1930– : accepting Lindbergh Award, 10 May 1997

16 I go on expeditions for the same reason an estate agent sells houses—in order to go on paying the bills.
Ranulph Fiennes 1944– : in *Sunday Times* 19 November 2000

Extravagance see **Thrift and Extravagance**

Fact see **Hypothesis and Fact**

Failure see **Success and Failure**

Faith see also Belief

1 Faith will move mountains.

late 19th century, meaning that with the help of faith something naturally impossible can be achieved; in allusion to the Bible: see 2 below

2 If ye have faith as a grain of mustard seed, ye shall say unto this mountain, Remove hence to yonder place; and it shall remove.
Bible: St Matthew; see 1 above

3 Faith without works is dead.
Bible: James

4 The confidence and faith of the heart alone make both God and an idol.
Martin Luther 1483–1546: *Large Catechism* (1529) 'The First Commandment'

5 A man with God is always in the majority.
John Knox c.1505–72: inscription on the Reformation Monument, Geneva

6 At last, by singing and repeating enthusiastic amorous hymns, and ignorantly applying particular texts of scripture, I got my imagination to the proper pitch, and thus was I born again in an instant.
James Lackington 1746–1815: *Memoirs* (1792 ed.)

7 It is necessary to the happiness of man that he be mentally faithful to himself. Infidelity does not consist in believing, or in disbelieving, it consists in professing to believe what one does not believe.
Thomas Paine 1737–1809: *The Age of Reason* pt. 1 (1794)

8 The faith that stands on authority is not faith.
Ralph Waldo Emerson 1803–82: *Essays* (1841) 'The Over-Soul'

9 The Sea of Faith
Was once, too, at the full, and round earth's shore
Lay like the folds of a bright girdle furled.
But now I only hear

Its melancholy, long, withdrawing roar.
Matthew Arnold 1822–88: 'Dover Beach' (1867)

10 The great act of faith is when a man decides he is not God.
Oliver Wendell Holmes Jr. 1841–1935: letter to William James, 24 March 1907

11 And I said to the man who stood at the gate of the year: 'Give me a light that I may tread safely into the unknown.'
    And he replied:
'Go out into the darkness and put your hand into the Hand of God. That shall be to you better than light and safer than a known way.'
quoted by King George VI in his Christmas broadcast, 25 December 1939
Minnie Louise Haskins 1875–1957: *Desert* (1908) 'God Knows'

12 Booth died blind and still by faith he trod,
Eyes still dazzled by the ways of God.
Vachel Lindsay 1879–1931: 'General William Booth Enters into Heaven' (1913)

13 A miracle, my friend, is an event which creates faith. That is the purpose and nature of miracles....Frauds deceive. An event which creates faith does not deceive: therefore it is not a fraud, but a miracle.
George Bernard Shaw 1856–1950: *Saint Joan* (1924)

14 In the darkness . . . the sound of a man Breathing, testing his faith
On emptiness, nailing his questions
One by one to an untenanted cross.
R. S. Thomas 1913–2000: 'Pietà' (1966)

15 A faith is something you die for; a doctrine is something you kill for: there is all the difference in the world.
Tony Benn 1925– : in *Observer* 16 April 1989

16 We're now paying the price for the Eighties and Lord Runcie's kind of effete, liberal elitism amongst bishops which also spread into the theological colleges. There is now a big gap between the faith of those in the pulpit and those in the pews.
George Austin 1931– : in *Guardian* 7 February 1997

Fame see also **Reputation**

1 More people know Tom Fool than Tom Fool knows.

mid 17th century; Tom Fool was a name given to the part of the fool in a play or morris dance

2 Who he?

an editorial interjection after the name of a (supposedly) little-known person, associated particularly with Harold Ross (1892–1951), editor of the New Yorker; repopularized in Britain by the satirical magazine Private Eye

3 a tall poppy a privileged or distinguished person.

perhaps originally in allusion to the legendary Roman king Tarquin striking the heads off poppies in his garden to demonstrate how to treat the leaders of a conquered city

4 Let us now praise famous men, and our fathers that begat us.
Bible: Ecclesiasticus

5 So long as men can breathe, or eyes can see,
So long lives this, and this gives life to thee.
William Shakespeare 1564–1616: sonnet 18

6 Fame is like a river, that beareth up things light and swollen, and drowns things weighty and solid.
Francis Bacon 1561–1626: *Essays* (1625) 'Of Praise'

7 Fame is the spur that the clear spirit doth raise
(That last infirmity of noble mind)
To scorn delights, and live laborious days;
John Milton 1608–74: 'Lycidas' (1638)

8 To be nameless in worthy deeds exceeds an infamous history.
Thomas Browne 1605–82: *Hydriotaphia* (Urn Burial, 1658)

9 Seven wealthy towns contend for HOMER dead
Through which the living HOMER begged his bread.
Anonymous: epilogue to *Aesop at Tunbridge; or, a Few Selected Fables in Verse* By No Person of Quality (1698)

10 Full many a flower is born to blush unseen,
And waste its sweetness on the desert air.
Thomas Gray 1716–71: *Elegy Written in a Country Churchyard* (1751)

11 Every man has a lurking wish to appear considerable in his native place.
Samuel Johnson 1709–84: letter to Joshua Reynolds, 17 July 1771; see **Familiarity** 13

12 I awoke one morning and found myself famous.
on the instantaneous success of Childe Harold
Lord Byron 1788–1824: Thomas Moore *Letters and Journals of Lord Byron* (1830)

13 The deed is all, the glory nothing.
Johann Wolfgang von Goethe 1749–1832: *Faust* pt. 2 (1832) 'Hochgebirg'

14 Martyrdom . . . the only way in which a man can become famous without ability.
George Bernard Shaw 1856–1950: *The Devil's Disciple* (1901)

15 I don't care what you say about me, as long as you say *something* about me, and as long as you spell my name right.
said to a newspaperman in 1912
George M. Cohan 1878–1942: John McCabe *George M. Cohan* (1973)

16 Now who is responsible for this work of development on which so much depends? To whom must the praise be given? To the boys in the back rooms. They do not sit in the limelight. But they are the men who do the work.
Lord Beaverbrook 1879–1964: in *Listener* 27 March 1941; see **Science** 3

17 The celebrity is a person who is known for his well-knownness.
Daniel J. Boorstin 1914– : *The Image* (1961)

18 There's no such thing as bad publicity except your own obituary.
Brendan Behan 1923–64: Dominic Behan *My Brother Brendan* (1965); see **Advertising** 1

19 We're more popular than Jesus now; I don't know which will go first—rock 'n' roll or Christianity.
of The Beatles
John Lennon 1940–80: interview in *Evening Standard* 4 March 1966

20 In the future everybody will be world famous for fifteen minutes.
Andy Warhol 1927–87: *Andy Warhol* (1968)

21 Celebrity is a mask that eats into the face.
John Updike 1932– : *Self-Consciousness: Memoirs* (1989)

22 Oh, the self-importance of fading stars. Never mind, they will be black holes one day.
Jeffrey Bernard 1932–97: in *The Spectator* 18 July 1992

23 The best fame is a writer's fame: it's enough to get a table at a good restaurant, but not enough that you get interrupted when you eat.
Fran Lebowitz 1946– : in *Observer* 30 May 1993 'Sayings of the Week'

24 Define superstar. It has nothing to do with the person. I still walk around the supermarket and buy toilet paper.
Julia Roberts 1967– : in *Sunday Times* 4 March 2001

Familiarity

PROVERBS AND SAYINGS

1 Better the devil you know than the devil you don't know.
mid 19th century, meaning that understanding of the nature of a danger may give one an advantage, and is preferable to something which is completely unknown, and which may well be worse

2 Better wed over the mixen than over the moor.
early 17th century; meaning that it is better to marry a neighbour than a stranger (a mixen is a midden)

3 Blue are the hills that are far away.
late 19th century, meaning that a distant view lends enchantment

4 Come live with me and you'll know me.
early 20th century; the implication is that only by living with a person will you learn their real nature

5 Familiarity breeds contempt.
late 14th century, meaning that we value least the things which are most familiar; see 21 below

6 Good fences make good neighbours.
mid 17th century, meaning that this reduces the possibility of disputes over adjoining land

7 If you lie down with dogs, you will get up with fleas.
late 16th century (earlier in Latin), asserting that human failings, such as dishonesty and foolishness, are contagious

8 A man is known by the company he keeps.
mid 16th century, originally used as a moral maxim or exhortation in the context of preparation for marriage

9 No man is a hero to his valet.
mid 18th century; see Heroes 5

10 There is nothing new under the sun.
late 16th century, from the Bible; see Progress 5

11 What a neighbour gets is not lost.
mid 16th century, meaning that one is likely to benefit from the gain of a neighbour or friend

12 You should know a man seven years before you stir his fire.
early 19th century, used as a caution against over-familiarity on slight acquaintance

QUOTATIONS

13 A prophet is not without honour, save in his own country, and in his own house.
Bible: St Matthew; see **Fame** 11

14 There is nothing that God hath established in a constant course of nature, and which therefore is done every day, but would seem a Miracle, and exercise our admiration, if it were done but once.
John Donne 1572–1631: *LXXX Sermons* (1640) Easter Day, 25 March 1627

15 Old friends are best. King James used to call for his old shoes; they were easiest for his feet.
John Selden 1584–1654: *Table Talk* (1689) 'Friends'

16 We can scarcely hate any one that we know.
William Hazlitt 1778–1830: *Table Talk* (1822) 'On Criticism'

17 Think you, if Laura had been Petrarch's wife,
He would have written sonnets all his life?
Lord Byron 1788–1824: *Don Juan* (1819–24)

18 A maggot must be born i' the rotten cheese to like it.
George Eliot 1819–80: *Adam Bede* (1859)

19 We do not expect people to be deeply moved by what is not unusual. That element of tragedy which lies in the very fact of frequency, has not yet wrought itself into the coarse emotion of mankind.
George Eliot 1819–80: *Middlemarch* (1871–2)

20 There are no conditions of life to which a man cannot get accustomed, especially if he sees them accepted by everyone about him.
Leo Tolstoy 1828–1910: *Anna Karenina* (1875–7)

21 Familiarity breeds contempt—and children.
Mark Twain 1835–1910: *Notebooks* (1935); see 5 above

22 Only the unknown frightens men. But once a man has faced the unknown, that terror becomes known.
Antoine de Saint-Exupéry 1900–44: *Wind, Sand and Stars* (1939)

23 I've grown accustomed to the trace
Of something in the air;
Accustomed to her face.
Alan Jay Lerner 1918–86: 'I've Grown Accustomed to her Face' (1956 song)

24 The mind loves the unknown. It loves images whose meaning is unknown, since the meaning of the mind itself is unknown.
René Magritte 1898–1967: Suzy Gablik *Magritte* (1970)

The Family see also Child Care, Children, Parents

PROVERBS AND SAYINGS

1 The apple never falls far from the tree.
mid 19th century, meaning that family characteristics will assert themselves

2 Blood is thicker than water.
early 19th century, meaning that in the end family ties will always count

3 Blood will tell.
mid 19th century; meaning that family characteristics or heredity will in the end be dominant

4 Children are certain cares, but uncertain comforts.
mid 17th century, emphasizing the continuing responsibility and anxiety of parenthood

5 Like father, like son.
mid 14th century, often used to call attention to similarities in behaviour

6 Like mother, like daughter.
early 14th century; the ultimate allusion is to the Bible (Ezekiel), 'As is the mother, so is her daughter'

7 The shoemaker's son always goes barefoot.
mid 16th century, meaning that the family of a skilled or knowledgeable person are often the last to benefit from their expertise

PHRASES

8 a chip off the old block a child resembling a parent or ancestor, especially in character.
chip something forming a portion of, or derived from, a larger or more important thing, of which it retains the characteristic qualities; see Speeches 10

QUOTATIONS

9 Thy wife shall be as the fruitful vine: upon the walls of thine house.
Thy children like the olive-branches: round about thy table.
Bible: Psalm 128

10 A little more than kin, and less than kind.
William Shakespeare 1564–1616: *Hamlet* (1601)

11 He that hath wife and children hath given hostages to fortune; for they are impediments to great enterprises, either of virtue or mischief.
Francis Bacon 1561–1626: *Essays* (1625) 'Of Marriage and the Single Life'

12 We begin our public affections in our families. No cold relation is a zealous citizen.
Edmund Burke 1729–97: *Reflections on the Revolution in France* (1790)

13 If a man's character is to be abused, say what you will, there's nobody like a relation to do the business.
William Makepeace Thackeray 1811–63: *Vanity Fair* (1847–8)

14 The worst families are those in which the members never really speak their minds to one another; they maintain an atmosphere of unreality, and everyone always lives in an atmosphere of suppressed ill-feeling.
Walter Bagehot 1826–77: *The English Constitution* (ed. 2, 1872) introduction

15 All happy families resemble one another, but each unhappy family is unhappy in its own way.
Leo Tolstoy 1828–1910: *Anna Karenina* (1875–7)

16 Family! . . . the home of all social evil, a charitable institution for comfortable women, an anchorage for house-fathers, and a hell for children.
August Strindberg 1849–1912: *The Son of a Servant* (1886)

17 I detest collaterals. Blood may be thicker than water, but it is also a great deal nastier.
Edith Œ Somerville 1858–1949 and **Martin Ross** 1862–1915: *Some Experiences of an Irish R.M.* (1899)

18 Relations are simply a tedious pack of people, who haven't got the remotest knowledge of how to live, nor the smallest instinct about when to die.
Oscar Wilde 1854–1900: *The Importance of Being Earnest* (1899)

19 The awe and dread with which the untutored savage contemplates his mother-in-law are amongst the most familiar facts of anthropology.
James George Frazer 1854–1941: *The Golden Bough* (2nd ed., 1900)

20 I am the family face;
Flesh perishes, I live on,
Projecting trait and trace
Through time to times anon,
And leaping from place to place
Over oblivion.
Thomas Hardy 1840–1928: 'Heredity' (1917)

21 One would be in less danger
From the wiles of the stranger
If one's own kin and kith
Were more fun to be with.
Ogden Nash 1902–71: 'Family Court' (1931)

22 Believe me, family solidarity is after all the only good thing. I have been deprived of it, so I know.
Marie Curie 1867–1934: to her sister Bronia in 1932; Eve Curie *Madame Curie* (1937)

23 The family—that dear octopus from whose tentacles we never quite escape.
Dodie Smith 1896–1990: *Dear Octopus* (1938)

24 It is no use telling me that there are bad aunts and good aunts. At the core, they are all alike. Sooner or later, out pops the cloven hoof.
P. G. Wodehouse 1881–1975: *The Code of the Woosters* (1938); see **Good and Evil** 10

25 Far from being the basis of the good society, the family, with its narrow privacy and tawdry secrets, is the source of all our discontents.
Edmund Leach 1910–89: BBC Reith Lectures, 1967

26 I have never understood this liking for war. It panders to instincts already catered for within the scope of any respectable domestic establishment.
Alan Bennett 1934– : *Forty Years On* (1969)

27 Family history, of course, has its proper dietary laws. One is supposed to swallow and digest only the permitted parts of it, the halal portions of the past, drained of their redness, their blood.
Salman Rushdie 1947– : *Midnight's Children* (1981)

28 The truth is that it is not the sins of the fathers that descend unto the third generation, but the sorrows of the mothers.
Marilyn French 1929– : *Her Mother's Daughter* (1987); see **Crime** 17

29 Having one child makes you a parent; having two you are a referee.
David Frost 1939– : in *Independent* 16 September 1989

30 [It is] time to turn our attention to pressing challenges like . . . how to make American families more like the Waltons and a little bit less like the Simpsons.
George Bush 1924– : speech, Neenah, Wisconsin, 27 July 1992

Farming

1 **Candlemas day, put beans in the clay; put candles and candlesticks away.**

late 17th century, recording the tradition that the feast of Candlemas, on 2 February, was the time for planting beans

2 **One for the mouse, one for the crow, one to rot, one to grow.**

mid 19th century, traditionally used when sowing seed, and enumerating the ways in which some of the crop will be lost leaving a proportion to germinate

3 **On Saint Thomas the Divine kill all turkeys, geese and swine.**

mid 18th century; 21 December, the traditional feast-day in the Western Church of St Thomas the Apostle, taken as marking the season at which domestic animals not kept through the winter were to be slaughtered

4 **Three acres and a cow.**

regarded as the requirement for self-sufficiency; late 19th century political slogan

5 **first fruits** the first agricultural produce of a season, especially when given as an offering to God

originally alluding to the Bible (Numbers), 'the first fruits of them which they shall offer unto the Lord'

6 A farm is like a man—however great the income, if there is extravagance but little is left.

Cato the Elder 234–149 BC: *On Agriculture*

7 For of all gainful professions, nothing is better, nothing more pleasing, nothing more delightful, nothing better becomes a well-bred man than agriculture.

Cicero 106–43 BC: *De Officiis*

8 O farmers excessively fortunate if only they recognized their blessings!

Virgil 70–19 BC: *Georgics*

9 Cultivators of the earth are the most valuable citizens. they are the most vigorous, the most independent, the most virtuous, and they are tied to their country and wedded to its liberty and interests by the most lasting bands.

Thomas Jefferson 1743–1826: letter to John Jay, 23 August 1785

10 Agriculture is the foundation of manufactures; since the productions of nature are the materials of art.

Edward Gibbon 1737–94: *The Decline and Fall of the Roman Empire* (1776–88)

11 We plough the fields, and scatter
The good seed on the land,
But it is fed and watered
By God's almighty hand.

Jane Montgomery Campbell 1817–78: 'We plough the fields, and scatter' (1861 hymn)

12 Our salvation can only come through the farmer. Neither the lawyers, nor the doctors, nor the rich landlords are going to secure it.

Mahatma Gandhi 1869–1948: speech, Benares, 4 February 1916

13 The Farmer will never be happy again;
He carries his heart in his boots;
For either the rain is destroying his grain
Or the drought is destroying his roots.

A. P. Herbert 1890–1971: 'The Farmer' (1922)

14 Farming looks mighty easy when your plough is a pencil, and you're a thousand miles from the corn field.

Dwight D. Eisenhower 1890–1969: speech, Peoria, 25 September 1956

15 A farm is an irregular patch of nettles bounded by short-term notes, containing a fool and his wife who didn't know enough to stay in the city.

S. J. Perelman 1904–79: *The Most of S. J. Perelman* (1959) 'Acres and Pains'

16 Death may be inevitable but cruelty is not. If we must eat meat, then we must ensure that the animals we kill for our food live the best possible lives before they die.

Desmond Morris 1928– : *The Animal Contract* (1990)

17 Our farms should be starting to jump to life with new-born lambs and calves. Instead, many will feel that spring has been cancelled.

the President of the National Farmers' Union on the foot and mouth epidemic

Ben Gill 1950– : in *Independent* 16 March 2001

Fashion see also **Dress**

PHRASES

1 all the world and his wife everyone with pretensions to fashion.
from Swift Polite Conversation *(1738) 'Pray, Madam, who were the Company? . . . Why, there was all the world, and his wife'*

2 flavour of the month the current fashion; a person who or thing which is especially popular at a given time.
a marketing phrase used in US ice-cream parlours in the 1940s, when a particular flavour of ice-cream would be singled out for the month for special promotion

3 radical chic the fashionable affectation of radical left-wing views or an associated style of dress or life.
coined by Tom Wolfe: see 10 below

QUOTATIONS

4 The women come to see the show, they come to make a show themselves.
Ovid 43 BC–AD c.17: *Ars Amatoria*

5 It is charming to totter into vogue.
Horace Walpole 1717–97: letter to George Selwyn, 2 December 1765

6 Fashion, though Folly's child, and guide of fools,
Rules e'en the wisest, and in learning rules.
George Crabbe 1754–1832: 'The Library' (1808)

7 Fashion is something barbarous, for it produces innovation without reason and imitation without benefit.
George Santayana 1863–1952: *The Life of Reason* (1905)

8 You cannot be both fashionable and first-rate.
Logan Pearsall Smith 1865–1946: *Afterthoughts* (1931) 'In the World'

9 Hip is the sophistication of the wise primitive in a giant jungle.
Norman Mailer 1923– : *Voices of Dissent* (1959) 'The White Negro'

10 Radical Chic . . . is only radical in Style; in its heart it is part of Society and its tradition—Politics, like Rock, Pop, and Camp, has its uses.
Tom Wolfe 1931– : in *New York* 8 June 1970; see 3 above

11 Fashion isn't made to be canned. Fashion in cans becomes quickly obsolete.
Coco Chanel 1883–1971: A. Madsen *Coco Chanel* (1990)

12 We're not curing cancer. We're not putting people into space. It's only clothes. Let's not take ourselves too seriously.
Karl Lagerfeld 1939– : Nicholas Coleridge *The Fashion Conspiracy* (1988)

13 Fashion is more usually a gentle progression of revisited ideas.
Bruce Oldfield 1950– : in *Independent* 9 September 1989

14 I never cared for fashion much. Amusing little seams and witty little pleats. It was the girls I liked.
David Bailey 1938– : in *Independent* 5 November 1990

15 You dress elegant and sophisticated women, I dress sluts.
Gianni Versace 1946–97: to Giorgio Armani, attributed; in *Independent* 15 September 2000

16 Uncool people never hurt anybody—all they do is collect stamps, read science-fiction books and stand on the end of railway platforms staring at trains.
Ben Elton 1959– : in *Radio Times* 18/24 April 1998

17 I'm not interested in fashion. In fact I am bored by it. When someone says that lime green is the new black for this season you just want to tell them to get a life.
Bruce Oldfield 1950– : in *Independent* 19 August 2000

Fate

1 **Fate can be taken by the horns, like a goat, and pushed in the right direction.**

American proverb, mid 20th century, meaning that with sufficient determination one need not be a helpless victim of fate

2 **Hanging and wiving go by destiny.**

mid 16th century; an expression of fatalism about the course of one's life

3 **If you're born to be hanged then you'll never be drowned.**

late 16th century, used to qualify apparent good luck which may have an unhappy outcome

4 **Man proposes, God disposes.**

mid 15th century, often now said in consolation or resignation when plans have been disrupted

5 **The mills of God grind slowly, yet they grind exceeding small.**

*mid 17th century; the current form is from Longfellow: see **God** 18*

6 **We're here
Because
We're here
Because
We're here
Because we're here.**

soldiers' song of the First World War, sung to the tune of 'Auld Lang Syne'

7 **What goes up must come down.**

early 20th century; commonly associated with wartime bombing and anti-aircraft shrapnel, and often used with the implication that an exhilarating rise must be followed by a fall

8 **What must be, must be.**

late 14th century, used to acknowledge the force of circumstances

9 **have a person's name and number on it** (of a bullet) be destined to kill a particular person.

see 17 below

10 **in the lap of the gods** beyond human control.

*from Homer The Iliad 'It lies in the lap of the gods'; see **Chance** 17*

11 **the three sisters** the three goddesses of destiny, the Fates.

12 Canst thou bind the sweet influences of Pleiades, or loose the bands of Orion?
Bible: Job

13 Each man is the smith of his own fortune.
Appius Claudius Caecus fl. 312–279 BC: Sallust *Ad Caesarem Senem de Re Publica Oratio*; see **Self** 2

14   *Dis aliter visum.*
The gods thought otherwise.
Virgil 70–19 BC: *Aeneid*

15 There's a divinity that shapes our ends,
Rough-hew them how we will.
William Shakespeare 1564–1616: *Hamlet* (1601)

16 We are merely the stars' tennis-balls,
struck and bandied
Which way please them.
John Webster c.1580–c.1625: *The Duchess of Malfi* (1623)

17 Every bullet has its billet.
William III 1650–1702: John Wesley's diary, 6 June 1765; see **9** above

18 Must it be? It must be.
Ludwig van Beethoven 1770–1827: String Quartet in F Major, Opus 135, epigraph

19 There once was an old man who said,
'Damn!
It is borne in upon me I am
An engine that moves
In determinate grooves,
I'm not even a bus, I'm a tram.'
Maurice Evan Hare 1886–1967: 'Limerick' (1905)

20 I [Death] was astonished to see him in Baghdad, for I had an appointment with him tonight in Samarra.
W. Somerset Maugham 1874–1965: *Sheppey* (1933)

21 Fate is not an eagle, it creeps like a rat.
Elizabeth Bowen 1899–1973: *The House in Paris* (1935)

22 I go the way that Providence dictates with the assurance of a sleepwalker.
Adolf Hitler 1889–1945: speech in Munich, 15 March 1936

23 The spring is wound up tight. It will uncoil of itself. That is what is so convenient in

tragedy. The least little turn of the wrist will do the job. Anything will set it going.
Jean Anouilh 1910-87: *Antigone* (1944)

24 We may become the makers of our fate when we have ceased to pose as its prophets.
Karl Popper 1902-94: *The Open Society and its Enemies* (1945)

25 Suppose . . . that Lenin had died of typhus in Siberia in 1895 and Hitler had been killed on the western front in 1916. What would the twentieth century have looked like now?
Arthur M. Schlesinger Jr. 1917- : *The Cycles of American History* (1986)

Fear

1 Cowards may die many times before their death.
*late 16th century; see **Courage** 13*

2 Thou shalt not be afraid for any terror by night: nor for the arrow that flieth by day; For the pestilence that walketh in darkness: nor for the sickness that destroyeth in the noon-day.
Bible: Psalm 91

3 Letting 'I dare not' wait upon 'I would,' Like the poor cat i' the adage?
William Shakespeare 1564-1616: *Macbeth* (1606)

4 Present fears
Are less than horrible imaginings.
William Shakespeare 1564-1616: *Macbeth* (1606)

5 Every drop of ink in my pen ran cold.
Horace Walpole 1717-97: letter to George Montagu, 30 July 1752

6 No passion so effectually robs the mind of all its powers of acting and reasoning as fear.
Edmund Burke 1729-97: *On the Sublime and Beautiful* (1757)

7 Wee, sleekit, cow'rin', tim'rous beastie, O what a panic's in thy breastie!
Robert Burns 1759-96: 'To a Mouse' (1786)

8 Better be killed than frightened to death.
R. S. Surtees 1805-64: *Mr Facey Romford's Hounds* (1865)

9 It is my belief that six out of every dozen people who go out hunting are disagreeably conscious of a nervous system, and two out of six are in what is brutally called 'a blue funk'.
Edith Œ Somerville 1858-1949 and **Martin Ross** 1862-1915: *Some Experiences of an Irish R.M.* (1899)

10 The horror! The horror!
Joseph Conrad 1857-1924: *Heart of Darkness* (1902)

11 I will show you fear in a handful of dust.
T. S. Eliot 1888-1965: *The Waste Land* (1922)

12 To fear love is to fear life, and those who fear life are already three parts dead.
Bertrand Russell 1872-1970: *Marriage and Morals* (1929)

13 The only thing we have to fear is fear itself.
Franklin D. Roosevelt 1882-1945: inaugural address, 4 March 1933

14 They cannot scare me with their empty spaces
Between stars—on stars where no human race is.
I have it in me so much nearer home
To scare myself with my own desert places.
Robert Frost 1874-1963: 'Desert Places' (1936)

15 Now a man talks frankly only with his wife, at night, with the blanket over his head.
Isaac Babel 1894-1940: remark *c.*1937, of the Stalinist purges; Solomon Volkov *St Petersburg* (1996)

16 We must travel in the direction of our fear.
John Berryman 1914-72: 'A Point of Age' (1942)

17 There is no terror in a bang, only in the anticipation of it.
Alfred Hitchcock 1899-1980: attributed

18 Terror . . . often arises from a pervasive sense of disestablishment; that things are in the unmaking.
Stephen King 1947- : *Danse Macabre* (1981)

Festivals and Celebrations see also Christmas

1 Barnaby bright, Barnaby bright, the longest day and the shortest night.
mid 17th century; in the Old Style calendar St Barnabas' Day, 11 June, was reckoned the longest day of the year

2 The better the day, the better the deed.
early 17th century, frequently used to justify working on a Sunday or Holy Day

3 A penny for the guy.
traditional saying, used by children displaying a guy to ask for money toward celebrations of Guy Fawkes Night; guy an effigy representing Guy Fawkes: see 24 below

4 If Saint Paul's day be fair and clear, it will betide a happy year.
late 16th century; the feast of the conversion of St Paul is 25 January

5 All Saints' Day 1 November, on which there is a general commemoration of the blessed dead.
sometimes known as All Hallows Day; see 56 below

6 All Souls' Day 2 November, on which the Roman Catholic Church makes supplications on behalf of the dead.

7 April Fool's Day the first of April.
the custom of playing tricks on this day has been observed in many countries for hundreds of years, but its origin is unknown

8 Ash Wednesday the first day of Lent.
from the custom of marking the foreheads of penitents with ashes on that day

9 Bastille Day 14 July, celebrated as a national holiday in France.
the date of the storming of the Bastille in 1789

10 Bonfire Night 5 November, Guy Fawkes Night.
see 24 below

11 Burns Night 25 January.
the annual celebration in honour of the Scottish poet Robert Burns (1759–96), held worldwide on his birthday

12 Canada Day 1 July, observed as a public holiday in Canada.
marking the day in 1867 when four of the former colonial provinces were united under one government as the Dominion of Canada

13 counting of the omer in the Jewish religion, the formal enumeration of the 49 days from the offering at Passover to Pentecost.
omer a sheaf of corn presented as an offering on the second day of Passover

14 Day of Atonement Yom Kippur
see 60 below

15 Ember days a group of three days in each season, observed as days of fasting and prayer in some Christian Churches, and now associated almost entirely with the ordination of ministers.
Ember perhaps alteration of Old English ymbryne period, revolution of time; at first, there were apparently only three groups, perhaps taken over from pagan religious observances connected with seed-time, harvest, and autumn vintage

16 Father's Day a day, usually the third Sunday in June, established for a special tribute to fathers.

17 festival of lights Hanukkah, an eight-day Jewish festival with lights beginning in December; Diwali, a Hindu festival with lights, held over three nights in the period October to November.
Hanukkah (Hebrew 'consecration'), commemorating the rededication of the Temple in 165 BC after its desecration by the Syrians; Diwali (from Hindustani 'row of lights') held to celebrate the new season at the end of the monsoon, and particularly associated with Lakshmi, the goddess of prosperity

18 first-foot the first person to cross a threshold in the New Year, in accordance with a Scottish custom.

19 Forefathers' Day in US usage, 21 December.
the anniversary of the landing of the first settlers at Plymouth, Massachusetts

20 Fourth of July 4 July, a national holiday in the United States.
the anniversary of the adoption of the Declaration of Independence in 1776; see 21, 27 below

21 the Glorious Fourth the Fourth of July.
see 20 above

22 the glorious Twelfth 12 August.
on which the grouse-shooting season opens

23 Good Friday the Friday before Easter Day.
observed as the anniversary of Jesus' Crucifixion

24 Guy Fawkes Night 5 November, Bonfire Night.

Guy Fawkes, *conspirator in the Gunpowder Plot to blow up James I and his Parliament on 5 November 1605, who was arrested in the cellars of the Houses of Parliament the day before the scheduled attack and betrayed his colleagues under torture; he was subsequently executed, and the plot is commemorated by bonfires and fireworks, with the burning of an effigy of Guy Fawkes, annually on 5 November; see 3, 10 above,* **Trust and Treachery** *2*

25 harvest home the festival (now rarely held) celebrating bringing in the harvest.

26 Holy Week the week before Easter Sunday.

after Italian la settimana santa, *French* la semaine sainte

27 Independence Day the Fourth of July.

see 20 above

28 Innocents' Day 28 December.

commemorating the massacre of the innocents, *the young children killed by Herod the Great after the birth of Jesus; see* **Children** *17,* **Cruelty** *2*

29 kill the fatted calf celebrate, especially at a prodigal's return.

from the Bible (Luke): see **Entertaining** *7,* **Forgiveness** *8*

30 Labour Day 1 May in many places; the first Monday of September in North America.

a day celebrated in honour of workers, often as a public holiday

31 Lady Day 25 March.

the feast of the Annunciation to the Virgin Mary

32 Lammas Day 1 August.

Lammas from Old English 'loaf mass', later interpreted as from lamb; *formerly observed as an English harvest festival at which loaves made from the first ripe corn were consecrated*

33 Low Sunday the Sunday after Easter.

perhaps so named in contrast to the high days of Holy Week and Easter

34 many happy returns of the day a greeting to a person on his or her birthday.

35 Mardi Gras Shrove Tuesday in some Catholic countries.

French, = fat Tuesday, in reference to celebrations before the beginning of Lent; see 53 below

36 mark with a white stone regard as specially fortunate or happy.

with allusion to the ancient practice of using a white stone as a memorial of a happy event

37 Maundy Thursday the Thursday before Good Friday.

Maundy *ultimately from Latin* mandatum commandment, *mandate in* mandatum novum *a new commandment (with reference to the Bible (John) 'A new commandment give I unto you'), the opening of the first antiphon sung at the Maundy ceremony of washing the feet of a number of poor people, performed by royal or other eminent people or by ecclesiastics, on the Thursday before Easter, and commonly followed by the distribution of clothing, food, or money*

38 May Day 1 May.

a day of traditional springtime celebrations, probably associated with pre-Christian fertility rites; May Day was designated an international labour day by the International Socialist congress of 1889

39 Memorial Day in the United States, 30 May, or the last Monday in May.

a day on which those who died on active service are remembered

40 Midsummer Day 24 June.

traditionally taken as marking the summer solstice

41 Mothers' Day in North America, the second Sunday in May; in Britain, Mothering Sunday.

a day on which mothers are particularly honoured; see 42 below

42 Mothering Sunday the fourth Sunday in Lent.

mothering *the custom of visiting, communicating with, or giving presents to one's mother (formerly, one's parents) on this day; see 41 above*

43 New Year's Day 1 January.

the first day of the year

44 Oak-Apple Day 29 May.

the anniversary of Charles II's restoration in 1660, when oak-apples or oak-leaves were worn in memory of his hiding in an oak after the battle of Worcester, 1651

45 Palm Sunday the Sunday before Easter.

on which Jesus's entry into Jerusalem is commemorated by processions in which branches of palms are carried

46 Pancake Day Shrove Tuesday.

on which pancakes are traditionally eaten; see 53 below

47 Poppy Day Remembrance Day.

from the artificial red poppies made for wearing on Remembrance Day and sold in aid of needy ex-servicemen and ex-servicewomen (see **World War I** *3); see 49 below*

48 red letter day a pleasantly memorable, fortunate, or happy day.
a saint's day or church festival traditionally indicated in the calendar by red letters

49 Remembrance Day the Sunday nearest to 11 November.
anniversary of the signing of the armistice that ended the First World War on 11 November 1918, when those killed in the wars of 1914–18 and 1939–45 are commemorated; see 47 above

50 Rogation Sunday the Sunday before Ascension Day.
rogation(s) solemn prayers consisting of the litany of the saints chanted on the three days before Ascension Day

51 Rosh Hashana the Jewish New Year, celebrated on the first (and sometimes second) day of the month Tishri (September–October).
Hebrew, = beginning (literally 'head') of the year

52 St Valentine's day 14 February.
traditionally associated with the choosing of sweethearts and the mating of birds

53 Shrove Tuesday the Tuesday before Ash Wednesday.
shrove past tense of shrive hear the confession of, assign penance to, and absolve; the day preceding the start of Lent, when it was formerly customary to be shriven and to take part in festivities; see 35, 46 above; see also Food 8

54 Stir-up Sunday the Sunday before the Sunday on which Advent begins.
so called from the opening words of the collect for the day: 'Stir up, we beseech thee, O Lord, the hearts of thy faithful people'

55 Trafalgar Day 21 October.
the anniversary of the battle of Trafalgar, 1805

56 trick or treat a children's custom of calling at houses at Hallowe'en with the threat of pranks if they are not given a small gift.
on the evening of 31 October, the eve of All Saints' Day; Hallowe'en is of pre-Christian origin, being associated with Samhain, the Celtic festival marking the end of the year and the beginning of winter, when ghosts and spirits were thought to be abroad; it was adopted as a Christian festival but gradually became a secular rather than a Christian observance, involving the dressing up and wearing of masks, and was particularly strong in Scotland; these secular customs were popularized in the US in the late 19th century and later developed into the custom of children playing trick or treat; see 5 above

57 Trinity Sunday the next Sunday after Whit Sunday.
celebrated in honour of the Holy Trinity

58 Twelfth Night the evening of 5 January
the eve of the Epiphany, formerly the last day of the Christmas festivities.

59 Whit Sunday the seventh Sunday after Easter.
literally 'white Sunday', probably from the white robes of the newly baptized at Pentecost; commemorating the descent of the Holy Spirit on the disciples

60 Yom Kippur the most solemn religious fast of the Jewish Year, the last of the ten days of penitence that begin with Rosh Hashana, the Jewish New Year.
Hebrew; see 14 above

QUOTATIONS

61 Tomorrow 'ill be the happiest time of all
the glad New-year;
Of all the glad New-year, mother, the
maddest merriest day;
For I'm to be Queen o' the May, mother,
I'm to be Queen o' the May.
Alfred, Lord Tennyson 1809–92: 'The May Queen' (1832)

62 Gay are the Martian Calends:
December's Nones are gay:
But the proud Ides, when the squadron rides,
Shall be Rome's whitest day!
Lord Macaulay 1800–59: *Lays of Ancient Rome* (1842) 'The Battle of the Lake Regillus'

63 Ring out the old, ring in the new,
Ring, happy bells, across the snow:
The year is going, let him go;
Ring out the false, ring in the true.
Alfred, Lord Tennyson 1809–92: *In Memoriam A. H. H.* (1850)

64 Seasons pursuing each other the indescribable
crowd is gathered, it is the fourth of Seventh-
month, (what salutes of cannon and small-arms!)
Walt Whitman 1819–92: 'Song of Myself' (written 1855)

65 The holiest of all holidays are those
Kept by ourselves in silence and apart;
The secret anniversaries of the heart.
Henry Wadsworth Longfellow 1807–82: 'Holidays' (1877)

66 Time has no divisions to mark its passage, there is never a thunderstorm or blare of trumpets to announce the beginning of a new month or year. Even when a new

century begins it is only we mortals who ring bells and fire off pistols.
Thomas Mann 1875–1955: *The Magic Mountain* (1924)

67 For every year of life we light
A candle on your cake
To mark the simple sort of progress
Anyone can make,
And then, to test your nerve or give
A proper view of death,
You're asked to blow each light, each year,
Out with your own breath.
James Simmons 1933–2001: 'A Birthday Poem' (1969)

68 Never ask the children to tell the class what they did for Easter or Christmas or Confirmation or St Patrick's Day . . .

Nothing points up the inequality of people's lives more starkly than asking innocent children to tell you how they spent what was meant to be a festival.
Maeve Binchy 1940– : in *Irish Times* 14 March 1998

69 The millennium is going to present us with a very sharp portrait of ourselves: drinking is to continue all night and religious observance, as far as possible, is to be kept at bay.
W. F. Deedes 1913– : in *Sunday Times* 15 August 1999

70 The intelligent minority of this world will mark 1 January 2001 as the real beginning of the 21st century and the Third Millennium.
Arthur C. Clarke 1917– : in *Newsweek* 8 January 2001

Fiction and Story-telling see also **Writers**, **Writing**

see also **Writers**, **Writing**

PROVERBS AND SAYINGS

1 Fact is stranger than fiction.
mid 19th century; see **Truth** 5, 28

PHRASES

2 a Canterbury tale a long tedious story.
one of those told on the pilgrimage to the shrine of St Thomas at Canterbury *in Chaucer's* Canterbury Tales

3 a cock and bull story a rambling inconsequential tale, an incredible story.
probably originally with reference to a particular fable

4 a tale of a tub in archaic usage, an apocryphal or incredible tale.
used as the title for a comedy by Jonson (1633) and a satire by Swift (1704), but of earlier origin

5 a whole Megillah a long, tedious, or complicated story.
Megillah each of five books of the Hebrew Scriptures (the Song of Solomon, Ruth, Lamentations, Ecclesiastes, and Esther) appointed to be read on certain Jewish notable days

QUOTATIONS

6 Storys to rede ar delitabill,
Suppos that thai be nocht bot fabill.
John Barbour c.1320–95: *The Bruce* (1375)

7 With a tale forsooth he [the poet] cometh unto you, with a tale which holdeth

children from play, and old men from the chimney corner.
Philip Sidney 1554–86: *The Defence of Poetry* (1595)

8 If this were played upon a stage now, I could condemn it as an improbable fiction.
William Shakespeare 1564–1616: *Twelfth Night* (1601)

9 'Oh! it is only a novel! . . . only Cecilia, or Camilla, or Belinda:' or, in short, only some work in which the most thorough knowledge of human nature, the happiest delineation of its varieties, the liveliest effusions of wit and humour are conveyed to the world in the best chosen language.
Jane Austen 1775–1817: *Northanger Abbey* (1818)

10 I hate things all *fiction* . . . there should always be some foundation of fact for the most airy fabric and pure invention is but the talent of a liar.
Lord Byron 1788–1824: letter to John Murray, 2 April 1817

11 A novel is a mirror which passes over a highway. Sometimes it reflects to your eyes the blue of the skies, at others the churned-up mud of the road.
Stendhal 1783–1842: *Le Rouge et le noir* (1830)

12 Merely corroborative detail, intended to give artistic verisimilitude to an otherwise bald and unconvincing narrative.
W. S. Gilbert 1836–1911: *The Mikado* (1885)

13 The good ended happily, and the bad unhappily. That is what fiction means.
Oscar Wilde 1854–1900: *The Importance of Being Earnest* (1895)

14 Literature is a luxury; fiction is a necessity.
G. K. Chesterton 1874–1936: *The Defendant* (1901) 'A Defence of Penny Dreadfuls'

15 The Story is just the spoiled child of art.
Henry James 1843–1916: *The Ambassadors* (1909 ed.) preface

16 Yes—oh dear yes—the novel tells a story.
E. M. Forster 1879–1970: *Aspects of the Novel* (1927)

17 When in doubt have a man come through the door with a gun in his hand.
Raymond Chandler 1888–1959: attributed

18 A beginning, a muddle, and an end.
on the 'classic formula' for a novel
Philip Larkin 1922–85: in *New Fiction* January 1978

19 The central function of imaginative literature is to make you realize that other people act on moral convictions different from your own.
William Empson 1906–84: *Milton's God* (1981)

20 No stories! No stories! Imagine a world without stories!
But that's exactly what you would have, if all the women were wise.
Margaret Atwood 1939– : *Good Bones* (1992) 'Let Us Now Praise Stupid Women'

21 Most modern fantasy just rearranges the furniture in Tolkien's attic.
Terry Pratchett 1948– : Stan Nicholls (ed.) *Wordsmiths of Wonder* (1993)

Fitness see Health and Fitness

Flattery see Praise and Flattery

Flowers

PROVERBS AND SAYINGS

1 Say it with flowers.
slogan for the Society of American Florists, from 1917

QUOTATIONS

2 That wel by reson men it calle may
The 'dayesye,' or elles the 'ye of day,'
The emperice and flour of floures alle.
Geoffrey Chaucer c.1343–1400: *The Legend of Good Women* 'The Prologue'

3 Bring hither the pink and purple columbine,
With gillyflowers:
Bring coronation, and sops in wine,
Worn of paramours.
Edmund Spenser c.1552–99: *The Shepherd's Calendar* (1579) 'April'

4 I know a bank whereon the wild thyme blows,
Where oxlips and the nodding violet grows
Quite over-canopied with luscious woodbine,
With sweet musk-roses, and with eglantine.
William Shakespeare 1564–1616: *A Midsummer Night's Dream* (1595–6)

5   Daffodils,
That come before the swallow dares, and take
The winds of March with beauty.
William Shakespeare 1564–1616: *The Winter's Tale* (1610–11)

6 I wandered lonely as a cloud
That floats on high o'er vales and hills,
When all at once I saw a crowd,
A host, of golden daffodils;
Beside the lake, beneath the trees,
Fluttering and dancing in the breeze.
William Wordsworth 1770–1850: 'I wandered lonely as a cloud' (1815 ed.)

7 Here are sweet peas, on tiptoe for a flight.
John Keats 1795–1821: 'I stood tip-toe upon a little hill' (1817)

8 Summer set lip to earth's bosom bare,
And left the flushed print in a poppy there.
Francis Thompson 1859–1907: 'The Poppy' (1913)

9 Oh, no man knows
Through what wild centuries
Roves back the rose.
Walter de la Mare 1873–1956: 'All That's Past' (1912)

10 Unkempt about those hedges blows
An English unofficial rose.
Rupert Brooke 1887–1915: 'The Old Vicarage,
Grantchester' (1915)

11 As well as any bloom upon a flower
I like the dust on the nettles, never lost
Except to prove the sweetness of a shower.
Edward Thomas 1878–1917: 'Tall Nettles' (1917)

12 The rose of all the world is not for me.
I want for my part
Only the little white rose of Scotland
That smells sharp and sweet—and breaks
the heart.
Hugh MacDiarmid 1892–1978: 'The Little White
Rose' (1934)

13 Hey, buds below, up is where to grow,
Up with which below can't compare with.
Hurry! It's lovely up here! *Hurry*!
Alan Jay Lerner 1918–86: 'It's Lovely Up Here'
(1965)

14 People from a planet without flowers
would think we must be mad with joy the
whole time to have such things about us.
Iris Murdoch 1919–99: *A Fairly Honourable Defeat*
(1970)

15 From my experience of life I believe my
personal motto should be 'Beware of men
bearing flowers.'
Muriel Spark 1918– : *Curriculum Vitae* (1992)

Food and Drink see also **Alcohol, Cooking and Eating**

PROVERBS AND SAYINGS

1 **An apple-pie without some cheese is like a
kiss without a squeeze.**
traditional saying, early 20th century

2 **Don't eat oysters unless there is an R in the
month.**
*from the tradition that oysters were likely to be unsafe
to eat in the warmer months between May and
August*

3 **God never sends mouths but He sends
meat.**
late 14th century, used in resignation or consolation

4 **A hungry man is an angry man.**
*mid 17th century, meaning that someone deprived of a
basic necessity will not be easily placated*

5 **It's ill speaking between a full man and a
fasting.**
*mid 17th century, meaning that someone in need is
never on good terms with someone who has all they
want*

6 **Oxo gives a meal man-appeal.**
advertising slogan for Oxo beef extract, c. 1960

PHRASES

7 **fish, flesh, and fowl** meat of all kinds,
comprising fish, animals excluding birds,
and poultry.
*originally relating to distinctions made by religious
dietary laws; see **Character** 24*

8 **Lenten fare** food without meat.
*food appropriate to Lent, the period from Ash
Wednesday to Holy Saturday, of which the 40
weekdays are devoted to fasting and penitence in
commemoration of Jesus's fasting in the wilderness;
see **Festivals** 53*

9 **staff of life** bread; a similar staple food of
an area or people.
*from the Biblical phrase break the staff of bread
diminish or cut off the supply of food (Leviticus)*

QUOTATIONS

10 Methinks sometimes I have no more wit
than a Christian or an ordinary man has;
but I am a great eater of beef, and I believe
that does harm to my wit.
William Shakespeare 1564–1616: *Twelfth Night*
(1601)

11 Doubtless God could have made a better
berry, but doubtless God never did.
on the strawberry
William Butler 1535–1618: Izaak Walton *The
Compleat Angler* (3rd ed., 1661)

12 Coffee, (which makes the politician wise,
And see thro' all things with his half-shut
eyes).
Alexander Pope 1688–1744: *The Rape of the Lock*
(1714)

13 A cucumber should be well sliced, and
dressed with pepper and vinegar, and then
thrown out, as good for nothing.
Samuel Johnson 1709–84: James Boswell *Journal of
a Tour to the Hebrides* (1785) 5 October 1773

14 Fair fa' your honest, sonsie face,
Great chieftain o' the puddin'-race!
Robert Burns 1759–96: 'To a Haggis' (1787)

15 An egg boiled very soft is not unwholesome.
Jane Austen 1775–1817: *Emma* (1816)

16 If there is a pure and elevated pleasure in this world it is a roast pheasant with bread sauce. Barn door fowls for dissenters but for the real Churchman, the thirty-nine times articled clerk—the pheasant, the pheasant.
Sydney Smith 1771–1845: letter to R. H. Barham, 15 November 1841

17 Many's the long night I've dreamed of cheese—toasted, mostly.
Robert Louis Stevenson 1850–94: *Treasure Island* (1883)

18 Cauliflower is nothing but cabbage with a college education.
Mark Twain 1835–1910: *Pudd'nhead Wilson* (1894)

19 Look here, Steward, if this is coffee, I want tea; but if this is tea, then I wish for coffee.
Punch: 1902

20 Tea, although an Oriental,
Is a gentleman at least;
Cocoa is a cad and coward,
Cocoa is a vulgar beast.
G. K. Chesterton 1874–1936: 'Song of Right and Wrong' (1914)

21 *What* is the matter with Mary Jane?
She's perfectly well and she hasn't a pain,
And it's lovely rice pudding for dinner again!
What *is* the matter with Mary Jane?
A. A. Milne 1882–1956: 'Rice Pudding' (1924)

22 MOTHER: It's broccoli, dear.
CHILD: I say it's spinach, and I say the hell with it.
E. B. White 1899–1985: *New Yorker* 8 December 1928 (cartoon caption)

23 The ethical value of uncooked food is incomparable. Economically this food has possibilities which no cooked food can have.
Mahatma Gandhi 1869–1948: in *Young India* 13 June 1929

24 The ordinary human being would sooner starve than live on brown bread and raw carrots. And the peculiar evil is this, that the less money you have, the less inclined you feel to spend it on wholesome food . . . When you are underfed, harassed, bored and miserable, you don't *want* to eat dull wholesome food. You want something a little bit 'tasty.'
George Orwell 1903–50: *The Road to Wigan Pier* (1937)

25 Shake and shake
The catsup bottle.
None will come,
And then a lot'll.
Richard Armour 1906–89: 'Going to Extremes' (1949)

26 Milk's leap toward immortality.
of cheese
Clifton Fadiman 1904– : *Any Number Can Play* (1957)

27 Take away that pudding—it has no theme.
Winston Churchill 1874–1965: Lord Home *The Way the Wind Blows* (1976)

28 I'm President of the United States, and I'm not going to eat any more broccoli!
George Bush 1924– : in *New York Times* 23 March 1990

29 A hen's egg is, quite simply, a work of art, a masterpiece of design and construction with, it has to be said, brilliant packaging.
Delia Smith: *How To Cook* (1998)

30 What makes food such a tyranny for women? A man, after all, may in times of crisis, hit the bottle (or another person), but he rarely hits the fridge.
Joanna Trollope 1943– : in *Independent* 28 November 1998

Fools see also **Intelligence**

1 Ask a silly question and you get a silly answer.
early 14th century, often used to indicate that the answer is so obvious that the question should not have been asked

2 Empty vessels make the most sound.
mid 15th century, meaning that foolish and empty-headed people make the most noise

3 A fool and his money are soon parted.
late 16th century

4 Fools build houses and wise men live in them.

late 17th century, meaning that a shrewd person chooses to save themselves trouble, and benefit from the effort expended by another

5 Fortune favours fools.

mid 16th century, meaning that a foolish person is traditionally fortunate

PHRASES

6 wear motley play the fool.

motley *the multicoloured costume of a jester; see 12 below*

7 a wise man of Gotham a fool.

Gotham *a village proverbial for the folly of its inhabitants*

QUOTATIONS

8 Answer not a fool according to his folly, lest thou also be like unto him.
Answer a fool according to his folly, lest he be wise in his own conceit.
Bible: Proverbs

9 As the crackling of thorns under a pot, so is the laughter of a fool.
Bible: Ecclesiastes

10 *Misce stultitiam consiliis brevem:*
Dulce est desipere in loco.
Mix a little foolishness with your prudence: it's good to be silly at the right moment.
Horace 65–8 BC: *Odes*

11 For ye suffer fools gladly, seeing ye yourselves are wise.
Bible: II Corinthians

12 A worthy fool! Motley's the only wear.
William Shakespeare 1564–1616: *As You Like It* (1599); see 6 above

13 The world is full of fools, and he who would not see it should live alone and smash his mirror.
Anonymous: adaptation from an original form attributed to Claude Le Petit (1640–65); *Discours satiriques* (1686)

14 A knowledgeable fool is a greater fool than an ignorant fool.
Molière 1622–73: *Les Femmes savantes* (1672)

15 The rest to some faint meaning make pretence,
But Shadwell never deviates into sense.
John Dryden 1631–1700: *MacFlecknoe* (1682)

16 For fools rush in where angels fear to tread.
Alexander Pope 1688–1744: *An Essay on Criticism* (1711)

17   Be wise with speed;
A fool at forty is a fool indeed.
Edward Young 1683–1765: *The Love of Fame* (1725–8)

18 The picture, placed the busts between,
Adds to the thought much strength:
Wisdom and Wit are little seen,
But Folly's at full length.
Jane Brereton 1685–1740: 'On Mr Nash's Picture at Full Length, between the Busts of Sir Isaac Newton and Mr Pope' (1744)

19 'Tis hard if all is false that I advance
A fool must now and then be right, by chance.
William Cowper 1731–1800: 'Conversation' (1782)

20 A fool sees not the same tree that a wise man sees.
William Blake 1757–1827: *The Marriage of Heaven and Hell* (1790–3) 'Proverbs of Hell'

21 With stupidity the gods themselves struggle in vain.
Friedrich von Schiller 1759–1805: *Die Jungfrau von Orleans* (1801)

22 The ae half of the warld thinks the tither daft.
Sir Walter Scott 1771–1832: *Redgauntlet* (1824)

23 The ultimate result of shielding men from the effects of folly, is to fill the world with fools.
Herbert Spencer 1820–1903: *Essays* (1891) vol. 3 'State Tamperings with Money and Banks'

24 There's a sucker born every minute.
Phineas T. Barnum 1810–91: attributed

25 Better to keep your mouth shut and appear stupid than to open it and remove all doubt.
Mark Twain 1835–1910: James Munson (ed.) *The Sayings of Mark Twain* (1992); attributed, perhaps apocryphal

26 Never give a sucker an even break.
W. C. Fields 1880–1946: title of a W. C. Fields film (1941); the catchphrase (Fields's own) is said to have originated in the musical comedy *Poppy* (1923)

27 So dumb he can't fart and chew gum at the same time.
of Gerald Ford
Lyndon Baines Johnson 1908–73: Richard Reeves *A Ford, not a Lincoln* (1975)

Football see also Sports and Games

PHRASES

1 the beautiful game football.
associated with Pelé: see 8 below

2 golden goal the first goal scored during extra time which ends the match and gives victory to the scoring side.

QUOTATIONS

3 Football, wherein is nothing but beastly fury, and extreme violence, whereof proceedeth hurt, and consequently rancour and malice do remain with them that be wounded.
Thomas Elyot 1499-1546: *Book of the Governor* (1531)

4 Then ye returned to your trinkets; then ye contented your souls
With the flannelled fools at the wicket or the muddied oafs at the goals.
Rudyard Kipling 1865-1936: 'The Islanders' (1903)

5 To say that these men paid their shillings to watch twenty-two hirelings kick a ball is merely to say that a violin is wood and catgut, that *Hamlet* is so much paper and ink. For a shilling the Bruddersford United AFC offered you Conflict and Art.
J. B. Priestley 1894-1984: *Good Companions* (1929)

6 Oh, he's football crazy, he's football mad
And the football it has robbed him o' the wee bit sense he had.
And it would take a dozen skivvies, his clothes to wash and scrub,
Since our Jock became a member of that terrible football club.
Jimmie McGregor 1932- : 'Football Crazy' (1960 song)

7 The great fallacy is that the game is first and last about winning. It is nothing of the kind. The game is about glory, it is about doing things in style and with a flourish, about going out and beating the lot, not waiting for them to die of boredom.
Danny Blanchflower 1926-93: attributed, 1972

8 My life and the beautiful game.
Pelé 1940- : title of autobiography (1977); see 1 above

9 Some people think football is a matter of life and death . . . I can assure them it is much more serious than that.
Bill Shankly 1914-81: in *Sunday Times* 4 October 1981

10 The goal was scored a little bit by the hand of God, another bit by head of Maradona.
on his controversial goal against England in the 1986 World Cup
Diego Maradona 1960- : in *Guardian* 1 July 1986

11 The nice aspect about football is that, if things go wrong, it's the manager who gets the blame.
before his first match as captain of England
Gary Lineker 1960- : in *Independent* 12 September 1990

12 The natural state of the football fan is bitter disappointment, no matter what the score.
Nick Hornby 1957- : *Fever Pitch* (1992)

13 Football is an art more central to our culture than anything the Arts Council deigns to recognize.
Germaine Greer 1939- : in *Independent* 28 June 1996

Foresight see also The Future

PROVERBS AND SAYINGS

1 If a man's foresight were as good as his hindsight, we would all get somewhere.
American proverb, mid 20th century

2 It is easy to be wise after the event.
early 17th century, meaning that the difficult thing is to make a correct judgement without the benefit of hindsight

3 It's too late to shut the stable-door after the horse has bolted.
mid 14th century, meaning that preventive measures taken after things have gone wrong are of little effect; see Mistakes 9

4 Nothing is certain but the unforeseen.
late 19th century, warning against an overconfident belief in a future occurrence

5 Prevention is better than cure.
early 17th century

6 cross a person's palm with silver give a person a coin as payment for fortune-telling.
originally, make the sign of the cross with a coin in the fortune-teller's palm

7 a pricking in one's thumbs a premonition, a foreboding.
*with allusion to Shakespeare Macbeth: see **Good** 26*

8 For which of you, intending to build a tower, sitteth not down first, and counteth the cost, whether he have sufficient to finish it?
Bible: St Luke

9 The best way to suppose what may come, is to remember what is past.
Lord Halifax 1633–95: *Political, Moral, and Miscellaneous Thoughts and Reflections* (1750) 'Miscellaneous: Experience'

10 Prognostics do not always prove prophecies,—at least the wisest prophets make sure of the event first.
Horace Walpole 1717–97: letter to Thomas Walpole, 19 February 1785

11 The best laid schemes o' mice an' men Gang aft a-gley.
Robert Burns 1759–96: 'To a Mouse' (1786); see **Life** 12

12 You can never plan the future by the past.
Edmund Burke 1729–97: *Letter to a Member of the National Assembly* (1791)

13 She felt that those who prepared for all the emergencies of life beforehand may equip themselves at the expense of joy.
E. M. Forster 1879–1970: *Howards End* (1910)

14 The man who has fed the chicken every day throughout its life at last wrings its neck instead, showing that a more refined view as to the uniformity of nature would have been useful to the chicken.
Bertrand Russell 1872–1970: *The Problems of Philosophy* (1912)

15 God damn you all: I told you so.
suggestion for his own epitaph, in conversation with Sir Ernest Barker, 1939
H. G. Wells 1866–1946: Ernest Barker *Age and Youth* (1953)

16 Some of the jam we thought was for tomorrow, we've already eaten.
Tony Benn 1925– : attributed, 1969; see **The Present** 9

17 Science fiction writers foresee the inevitable, and although problems and catastrophes may be inevitable, solutions are not.
Isaac Asimov 1920–92: in *Natural History* April 1975

18 It was déjà vu all over again.
Yogi Berra 1925– : attributed

Forgiveness and Repentance

1 Charity covers a multitude of sins.
early 17th century, meaning that charity as a virtue outweighs many faults; see 12 below

2 A fault confessed is half redressed.
mid 16th century, meaning that by confessing what you have done wrong you have begun to make amends

3 Good to forgive, best to forget.
North American proverb, mid 20th century, meaning that it is even better to forget that you have been injured than to forget the injury

4 Never let the sun go down on your anger.
*mid 17th century, recommending a swift reconciliation after a quarrel; from the Bible: see **Anger** 6*

5 Offenders never pardon.
mid 17th century, meaning that the experience of having wronged someone often fosters a continuing resentment of the victim

6 To know all is to forgive all.
*mid 20th century; see **Insight** 9*

7 heap coals of fire on a person's head cause remorse by returning good for evil.
*with allusion to the Bible (Proverbs): see **Enemies** 5*

8 a prodigal son a spendthrift who subsequently regrets such behaviour; a returned and repentant wanderer.
from the parable in the Bible (Luke) telling the story of the wastrel younger son who repented and was

received back and forgiven by his father, who killed the fatted calf to celebrate his return; see **Entertaining** 7, **Festivals** 29

9 **turn the other cheek** refuse to retaliate, permit or invite another blow or attack.
alluding to the Bible (Matthew): see **Violence** 4

QUOTATIONS

10 Though your sins be as scarlet, they shall be as white as snow.
Bible: Isaiah

11 Lord, how oft shall my brother sin against me, and I forgive him? till seven times?
Jesus saith unto him I say not unto thee, Until seven times: but Until seventy times seven.
Bible: St Matthew

12 Charity shall cover the multitude of sins.
Bible: I Peter; see 1 above

13 We read that we ought to forgive our enemies; but we do not read that we ought to forgive our friends.
speaking of what Bacon refers to as 'perfidious friends'
Cosimo de' Medici 1389–1464: Francis Bacon Apophthegms (1625); see **Enemies** 8

14 And forgive us our trespasses, As we forgive them that trespass against us.
The Book of Common Prayer 1662: Morning Prayer The Lord's Prayer

15 Repentance is but want of power to sin.
John Dryden 1631–1700: Palamon and Arcite (1700)

16 To err is human; to forgive, divine.
Alexander Pope 1688–1744: An Essay on Criticism (1711); see **Computers** 5, **Mistakes** 5

17 Remorse, the fatal egg by pleasure laid.
William Cowper 1731–1800: 'The Progress of Error' (1782)

18   The spirit burning but unbent, May writhe, rebel—the weak alone repent!
Lord Byron 1788–1824: The Corsair (1814)

19 But with the morning cool repentance came.
Sir Walter Scott 1771–1832: Rob Roy (1817)

20 And blessings on the falling out That all the more endears, When we fall out with those we love And kiss again with tears!
Alfred, Lord Tennyson 1809–92: The Princess (1847), song (added 1850)

21 God will pardon me, it is His trade.
on his deathbed
Heinrich Heine 1797–1856: Alfred Meissner Heinrich Heine. Erinnerungen (1856); see **Power** 19

22 After such knowledge, what forgiveness?
T. S. Eliot 1888–1965: 'Gerontion' (1920)

23 I never forgive but I always forget.
Arthur James Balfour 1848–1930: R. Blake Conservative Party (1970)

24 Every one says forgiveness is a lovely idea, until they have something to forgive.
C. S. Lewis 1898–1963: Mere Christianity (1952)

25 I ain't sayin' you treated me unkind You could have done better but I don't mind You just kinda wasted my precious time But don't think twice, it's all right.
Bob Dylan 1941– : 'Don't Think Twice, It's All Right' (1963 song)

26 The stupid neither forgive nor forget; the naïve forgive and forget; the wise forgive but do not forget.
Thomas Szasz 1920– : The Second Sin (1973)

27 God of forgiveness, do not forgive those murderers of Jewish children here.
at an unofficial ceremony at Auschwitz on 26 January 1995, commemorating the 50th anniversary of its liberation
Elie Wiesel 1928– : in The Times 27 January 1995

28 True reconciliation does not consist in merely forgetting the past.
Nelson Mandela 1918– : speech, 7 January 1996

29 I believe any person who asks for forgiveness has to be prepared to give it.
Bill Clinton 1946– : statement after being acquitted by the Senate, 12 February 1999

France see also **Countries and Peoples**, **International Relations**, **Towns and Cities**

1 One Englishman can beat three Frenchmen.
late 16th century; a boastful statement now used of other nationalities and in different proportions

PHRASES

2 la Belle France the country of France, especially viewed in a nostalgic or patriotic manner.

QUOTATIONS

3 France, mother of arts, of warfare, and of laws.
Joachim Du Bellay 1522–60: *Les Regrets* (1558)

4 That sweet enemy, France.
Philip Sidney 1554–86: *Astrophil and Stella* (1591)

5 Tilling and grazing are the two breasts by which France is fed.
Maximilien de Béthune, Duc de Sully 1559–1641: *Mémoires* (1638)

6 They order, said I, this matter better in France.
Laurence Sterne 1713–68: *A Sentimental Journey* (1768)

7 What is not clear is not French.
Antoine de Rivarol 1753–1801: *Discours sur l'Universalité de la Langue Française* (1784)

8 You must hate a Frenchman as you hate the devil.
Horatio, Lord Nelson 1758–1805: Robert Southey *Life of Nelson* (1813)

9 France has more need of me than I have need of France.
Napoleon I 1769–1821: speech, Paris, 31 December 1813

10 Yet, who can help loving the land that has taught us

Six hundred and eighty-five ways to dress eggs?
Thomas Moore 1779–1852: *The Fudge Family in Paris* (1818)

11 France was long a despotism tempered by epigrams.
Thomas Carlyle 1795–1881: *History of the French Revolution* (1837)

12 France, famed in all great arts, in none supreme.
Matthew Arnold 1822–88: 'To a Republican Friend—Continued' (1849)

13 The French soul is stronger than the French mind, and Voltaire shatters against Joan of Arc.
Victor Hugo 1802–85: *Tas de pierres* (1942)

14 If the French noblesse had been capable of playing cricket with their peasants, their chateaux would never have been burnt.
G. M. Trevelyan 1876–1962: *English Social History* (1942)

on speaking French fluently rather than correctly:
15 It's nerve and brass, *audace* and disrespect, and leaping-before-you-look and what-the-hellism, that must be developed.
Diana Cooper 1892–1986: in 1944; Philip Ziegler *Diana Cooper* (1981)

16 Everything ends this way in France. Weddings, christenings, duels, burials, swindlings, affairs of state—everything is a pretext for a good dinner.
Jean Anouilh 1910–87: *Cécile* (1951)

17 How can you govern a country which has 246 varieties of cheese?
Charles de Gaulle 1890–1970: Ernest Mignon *Les Mots du Général* (1962)

18 France is the only place where you can make love in the afternoon without people hammering on your door.
Barbara Cartland 1901–2000: in *Guardian* 24 December 1984

Friendship see also **Relationships**

PROVERBS AND SAYINGS

1 Be kind to your friends: if it weren't for them, you would be a total stranger.
American proverb, mid 20th century

2 A friend in need is a friend indeed.
mid 11th century; a friend in need is one who helps when one is in need or difficulty

3 Love me, love my dog.
early 16th century

4 Oh, the comfort—the inexpressible comfort of feeling safe with a person, having neither to weigh thoughts, nor measure words, but pouring them all out, just as they are, chaff and grain together; knowing that a faithful hand will take and sift them—keep what is worth keeping—and with the breath of kindness blow the rest away.
19th century saying, often attributed to George Eliot or Dinah Mulock Craik (1826–87)

5 Save us from our friends.
late 15th century, meaning that the earnest help of friends can sometimes be unintentionally damaging; see 17 below

6 Two is company, but three is none.
early 18th century; often used with the alternative ending 'three's a crowd'

PHRASES

7 three musketeers three close associates, three inseparable friends.
*translation of French Les Trois Mousquetaires by Alexandre Dumas père; see **Cooperation** 25*

QUOTATIONS

8 Intreat me not to leave thee, or to return from following after thee: for whither thou goest, I will go; and where thou lodgest, I will lodge: thy people shall be my people, and thy God my God.
Bible: Ruth

9 There is a friend that sticketh closer than a brother.
Bible: Proverbs

10 One soul inhabiting two bodies.
reply when asked 'What is a friend?'
Aristotle 384–322 BC: Diogenes Laertius *Lives of Philosophers*

11 I count myself in nothing else so happy
As in a soul remembering my good friends.
William Shakespeare 1564–1616: *Richard II* (1595)

12 It redoubleth joys, and cutteth griefs in halves.
Francis Bacon 1561–1626: *Essays* (1625) 'Of Friendship'

13 It is more shameful to doubt one's friends than to be duped by them.
Duc de la Rochefoucauld 1613–80: *Maximes* (1678)

14 If a man does not make new acquaintance as he advances through life, he will soon find himself left alone. A man, Sir, should keep his friendship in constant repair.
Samuel Johnson 1709–84: James Boswell *Life of Samuel Johnson* (1791) 1755

15 The man that hails you Tom or Jack,
And proves by thumps upon your back
How he esteems your merit,
Is such a friend, that one had need
Be very much his friend indeed
To pardon or to bear it.
William Cowper 1731–1800: 'Friendship' (1782)

16 Should auld acquaintance be forgot
And never brought to mind?
Robert Burns 1759–96: 'Auld Lang Syne' (1796)

17 Give me the avowed, erect and manly foe;
Firm I can meet, perhaps return the blow;
But of all plagues, good Heaven, thy wrath can send,
Save me, oh, save me, from the candid friend.
George Canning 1770–1827: 'New Morality' (1821); see 5 above

18 The only reward of virtue is virtue; the only way to have a friend is to be one.
Ralph Waldo Emerson 1803–82: *Essays* (1841) 'Friendship'

19 [Grant] stood by me when I was crazy, and I stood by him when he was drunk; and now we stand by each other always.
William Sherman 1820–91: in 1864; Geoffrey C. Ward *The Civil War* (1991)

20 Friendships begin with liking or gratitude—roots that can be pulled up.
George Eliot 1819–80: *Daniel Deronda* (1876)

21 A woman can become a man's friend only in the following stages—first an

acquaintance, next a mistress, and only then a friend.
Anton Chekhov 1860–1904: *Uncle Vanya* (1897)

22 I have lost friends, some by death . . . others through sheer inability to cross the street.
Virginia Woolf 1882–1941: *The Waves* (1931)

23 Think where man's glory most begins and ends
And say my glory was I had such friends.
W. B. Yeats 1865–1939: 'The Municipal Gallery Re-visited' (1939)

24 To find a friend one must close one eye. To keep him—two.
Norman Douglas 1868–1952: *Almanac* (1941)

25 My life is spent in a perpetual alternation between two rhythms, the rhythm of attracting people for fear I may be lonely, and the rhythm of trying to get rid of them because I know that I am bored.
C. E. M. Joad 1891–1953: in *Observer* 12 December 1948

26 God's apology for relations.
on friends
Hugh Kingsmill 1889–1949: Michael Holroyd *The Best of Hugh Kingsmill* (1970)

27 Levin wanted friendship and got friendliness; he wanted steak and they offered spam.
Bernard Malamud 1914–86: *A New Life* (1961)

28 Oh I get by with a little help from my friends,
Mm, I get high with a little help from my friends.
John Lennon 1940–80 and **Paul McCartney** 1942– : 'With a Little Help From My Friends' (1967 song)

29 I do not believe that friends are necessarily the people you like best, they are merely the people who got there first.
Peter Ustinov 1921– : *Dear Me* (1977)

30 Who can I tear to pieces, if not my friends?
. . . If they were not my friends, I could not do such violence to them.
Francis Bacon 1909–92: John Russell *Francis Bacon* (1979)

Futility

1 **Dogs bark, but the caravan goes on.**
late 19th century, meaning that trivial criticism will not deflect the progress of something important

2 **In vain the net is spread in the sight of the bird.**
late 14th century, meaning that a person who has seen the process by which someone intends to harm them is unlikely to be in danger

3 **Sue a beggar and catch a louse.**
mid 17th century; meaning that it is pointless to try to obtain restitution from someone without resources

4 **You cannot get a quart into a pint pot.**
late 19th century, used of any situation In which the prospective contents are too large for the container

5 **You cannot get blood from a stone.**
mid 17th century, often used, as a resigned admission, to mean that it is hopeless to try to extort money or sympathy from those who have none; see **Charity** 6

6 **You cannot make bricks without straw.**
mid 17th century, meaning that nothing can be made or achieved if one does not have the correct materials; from the Bible (Exodus): see **Problems** 6

7 **You can't make a silk purse out of a sow's ear.**
early 16th century; meaning that inherent nature cannot be overcome by nurture

PHRASES

8 **cast pearls before swine** offer a good or valuable thing to a person incapable of appreciating it.
with allusion to the Bible (Matthew): see **Value** 18

9 **caviar to the general** a good thing unappreciated by the ignorant.
from Shakespeare Hamlet: *see* **Taste** 3

10 **plough the sand** labour uselessly.
a proverbial type of fruitless activity; see **Revolution** 15

11 **tilt at windmills** attack an imaginary enemy or wrong.
from a story in Cervantes Don Quixote *(1605–15) in which Don Quixote attacked a group of windmills believing them to be giants*

12 **a voice in the wilderness** an unheeded advocate of reform.
with allusion to the Bible (Matthew) 'The voice of one crying in the wilderness'; see also **Preparation** 11

13 **a wild-goose chase** a foolish, fruitless, or hopeless quest, a pursuit of something unattainable.

a horse-race in which the second or any succeeding horse had to follow accurately the course of the leader, like a flight of wild geese; later, an erratic course taken by one person (or thing) and followed (or that may be followed) by another

14 Vanity of vanities, saith the Preacher, vanity of vanities; all is vanity.
Bible: Ecclesiastes; see **Disillusion** 5

15 How weary, stale, flat, and unprofitable Seem to me all the uses of this world.
William Shakespeare 1564–1616: *Hamlet* (1601)

16 To enlarge or illustrate this power and effect of love is to set a candle in the sun.
Robert Burton 1577–1640: *The Anatomy of Melancholy* (1621–51)

17 To endeavour to work upon the vulgar with fine sense, is like attempting to hew blocks with a razor.
Alexander Pope 1688–1744: *Miscellanies* (1727) 'Thoughts on Various Subjects'

18 Who breaks a butterfly upon a wheel?
Alexander Pope 1688–1744: 'An Epistle to Dr Arbuthnot' (1735); see **Excess** 11

19 'My name is Ozymandias, king of kings:
Look on my works, ye Mighty, and despair!'
Nothing beside remains. Round the decay
Of that colossal wreck, boundless and bare
The lone and level sands stretch far away.
Percy Bysshe Shelley 1792–1822: 'Ozymandias' (1819)

20 'Strange friend,' I said, 'here is no cause to mourn.'
'None,' said that other, 'save the undone years,
The hopelessness. Whatever hope is yours,

Was my life also.'
Wilfred Owen 1893–1918: 'Strange Meeting' (written 1918)

21 Pathos, piety, courage—they exist, but are identical, and so is filth. Everything exists, nothing has value.
E. M. Forster 1879–1970: *A Passage to India* (1924)

22 We are the hollow men
We are the stuffed men
Leaning together
Headpiece filled with straw. Alas!
T. S. Eliot 1888–1965: 'The Hollow Men' (1925)

23 Nothing to be done.
Samuel Beckett 1906–89: *Waiting for Godot* (1955)

24 Nothingness haunts being.
Jean-Paul Sartre 1905–80: *Being and Nothingness* (1956)

25 There aren't any good, brave causes left. If the big bang does come, and we all get killed off, it won't be in aid of the old-fashioned, grand design. It'll just be for the Brave New-nothing-very-much-thank-you. About as pointless and inglorious as stepping in front of a bus.
John Osborne 1929–94: *Look Back in Anger* (1956)

26 He's a real nowhere man
Sitting in his nowhere land
Making all his nowhere plans for nobody.
John Lennon 1940–80 and **Paul McCartney** 1942– : 'Nowhere Man' (1966 song)

27 I'm not going to rearrange the furniture on the deck of the Titanic.
having lost five of the last six primaries as President Ford's campaign manager
Rogers Morton 1914–79: *Washington Post* 16 May 1976

28 It seems that I have spent my entire time trying to make life more rational and that it was all wasted effort.
A. J. Ayer 1910–89: in *Observer* 17 August 1986

The Future see also **Foresight**

1 **Coming events cast their shadow before.**
early 19th century, meaning that some initial effects indicating the nature of an event may be felt before it takes place

2 **He that follows freits, freits will follow him.**
Scottish proverbial saying, early 18th century, meaning that someone who looks for portents of the future will find himself dogged by them (freits are omens)

3 **There is no future like the present.**
American proverb, mid 20th century

4 Today you; tomorrow me.
mid 13th century, often used in the context of the inevitability of death to each person

5 Tomorrow is another day.
early 16th century; see **Hope** 21

6 Tomorrow never comes.
early 16th century; used in the context of something which is constantly predicted to be imminent, but which never occurs

PHRASES

7 cast one's bread upon the waters give generously in the expectation of future repayment for one's present kindness.
from the Bible (Ecclesiastes): see **Chance** 19

8 the shape of things to come the way in which future events will develop; the form the future will take.
title of book by H. G. Wells, 1933

9 a straw in the wind a small but significant indicator of the future course of events.
proverbial: see **Meaning** 2

10 the writing on the wall evidence or a sign of approaching disaster; an ominously significant event or situation.
with allusion to the biblical story in Daniel of the writing that appeared on the palace wall at a feast given by Belshazzar, last king of Babylon, foretelling that he would be killed and the city sacked; see also **Success** 17

QUOTATIONS

11 Boast not thyself of to morrow; for thou knowest not what a day may bring forth.
Bible: Proverbs

12 Lord! we know what we are, but know not what we may be.
William Shakespeare 1564-1616: *Hamlet* (1601)

13 For present joys are more to flesh and blood
Than a dull prospect of a distant good.
John Dryden 1631-1700: *The Hind and the Panther* (1687)

14 'We are always doing', says he, 'something for Posterity, but I would fain see Posterity do something for us.'
Joseph Addison 1672-1719: in *The Spectator* 20 August 1714

15 The next Augustan age will dawn on the other side of the Atlantic. There will, perhaps, be a Thucydides at Boston, a Xenophon at New York, and, in time, a Virgil at Mexico, and a Newton at Peru. At

last, some curious traveller from Lima will visit England and give a description of the ruins of St Paul's, like the editions of Balbec and Palmyra.
Horace Walpole 1717-97: letter to Horace Mann, 24 November 1774

16 People will not look forward to posterity, who never look backward to their ancestors.
Edmund Burke 1729-97: *Reflections on the Revolution in France* (1790)

17 So many worlds, so much to do,
So little done, such things to be.
Alfred, Lord Tennyson 1809-92: *In Memoriam A. H. H.* (1850)

18 He seems to think that posterity is a pack-horse, always ready to be loaded.
Benjamin Disraeli 1804-81: speech, 3 June 1862; attributed

19 You cannot fight against the future. Time is on our side.
W. E. Gladstone 1809-98: speech on the Reform Bill, House of Commons, 27 April 1866

20 You will eat, bye and bye,
In that glorious land above the sky;
Work and pray, live on hay,
You'll get pie in the sky when you die.
Joe Hill 1879-1915: 'Preacher and the Slave' (1911 song)

21 Make me a beautiful word for doing things tomorrow; for that surely is a great and blessed invention.
George Bernard Shaw 1856-1950: *Back to Methuselah* (1921)

22 *In the long run* we are all dead.
John Maynard Keynes 1883-1946: *A Tract on Monetary Reform* (1923)

23 I never think of the future. It comes soon enough.
Albert Einstein 1879-1955: in an interview given on the *Belgenland*, December 1930

24 We have trained them [men] to think of the Future as a promised land which favoured heroes attain—not as something which everyone reaches at the rate of sixty minutes an hour, whatever he does, whoever he is.
C. S. Lewis 1898-1963: *The Screwtape Letters* (1942)

25 If you want a picture of the future, imagine a boot stamping on a human face—for ever.
George Orwell 1903-50: *Nineteen Eighty-Four* (1949)

26 They spend their time mostly looking forward to the past.
John Osborne 1929–94: *Look Back in Anger* (1956)

27 The future ain't what it used to be.
Yogi Berra 1925– : attributed

28 And now, we can see a new world coming into view. A world in which there is the very real prospect of a new world order.
George Bush 1924– : speech, in *New York Times* 7 March 1991; see **International Relations** 6

Games see Sports and Games

Gardens see also Flowers

1 The answer lies in the soil.
traditional gardening advice

2 If you would be happy for a week take a wife; if you would be happy for a month kill a pig; but if you would be happy all your life plant a garden.
mid 17th century; the saying exists in a variety of forms, but marriage is nearly always given as one of the ephemeral forms of happiness

3 It is not enough for a gardener to love flowers; he must also hate weeds.
American proverb, mid 20th century

4 One year's seeding makes seven years weeding.
late 19th century; the allusion is to the danger of allowing weeds to grow and seed themselves

5 Parsley seed goes nine times to the Devil.
mid 17th century, meaning that it is often slow to germinate; there was a superstition that parsley, which belonged to the Devil, had to be sown nine times before it would come up

6 Sow dry and set wet.
mid 17th century, meaning that seeds should be sown in dry ground and then given water

7 Walnuts and pears you plant for your heirs.
mid 17th century; meaning that both trees are traditionally slow growing, so that the benefit will be felt by future generations

QUOTATIONS

8 And the Lord God planted a garden eastward in Eden.
Bible: Genesis

9 Sowe Carrets in your Gardens, and humbly praise God for them, as for a singular and great blessing.
Richard Gardiner b. c.1533: *Profitable Instructions for the Manuring, Sowing and Planting of Kitchen Gardens* (1599)

10 Nothing is more pleasant to the eye than green grass kept finely shorn.
Francis Bacon 1561–1626: *Essays* (1625) 'Of Gardens'

11 Annihilating all that's made
To a green thought in a green shade.
Andrew Marvell 1621–78: 'The Garden' (1681)

12 All gardening is landscape-painting.
Alexander Pope 1688–1744: Joseph Spence *Anecdotes* (1966)

13 But though an old man, I am but a young gardener.
Thomas Jefferson 1743–1826: letter to Charles Willson Peale, 20 August 1811

14 A garden was the primitive prison till man with Promethean felicity and boldness luckily sinned himself out of it.
Charles Lamb 1775–1834: letter to William Wordsworth, 22 January 1830

15 What is a weed? A plant whose virtues have not been discovered.
Ralph Waldo Emerson 1803–82: *Fortune of the Republic* (1878)

16 The Glory of the Garden lies in more than meets the eye.
Rudyard Kipling 1865–1936: 'The Glory of the Garden' (1911)

17 The kiss of the sun for pardon,
The song of the birds for mirth,
One is nearer God's Heart in a garden
Than anywhere else on earth.
Dorothy Frances Gurney 1858–1932: 'God's Garden' (1913)

18 Let 'Dig for Victory' be the motto of every
one with a garden and of every able-bodied
man and woman capable of digging an
allotment in their spare time.
Reginald Dorman-Smith 1899–1977: radio
broadcast, 3 October 1939

19 Weeds are not supposed to grow,
But by degrees
Some achieve a flower, although
No one sees.
Philip Larkin 1922–85: 'Modesties' (1951)

20 Perennials are the ones that grow like
weeds, biennials are the ones that die this
year instead of next and hardy annuals are
the ones that never come up at all.
Katharine Whitehorn 1928– : *Observations* (1970)

21 I will keep returning to the virtues of sharp
and swift drainage, whether a plant prefers
to be wet or dry . . . I would have called

this book Better Drains, but you would
never have bought it or borrowed it for
bedtime.
Robin Lane Fox 1946– : *Better Gardening* (1982)

22 I just come and talk to the plants, really—
very important to talk to them, they
respond I find.
Prince Charles 1948– : television interview, 21
September 1986

23 There can be no other occupation like
gardening in which, if you were to creep
behind someone at their work, you would
find them smiling.
Mirabel Osler: *A Gentle Plea for Chaos* (1989)

24 Gardening is the new rock'n'roll. When I
was little, it was all fuddy-duddy Percy
Thrower. Now it's very social and very,
very fashionable.
Ali Ward: in *Independent* 13 June 1998

The Generation Gap see also **Old Age**, **Youth**

PROVERBS AND SAYINGS

1 **Young folks think old folks to be fools, but
old folks know young folks to be fools.**
*late 16th century, asserting the value of the experience
of life which comes with age over youth and
inexperience*

PHRASES

2 **an angry young man** a young man who
feels and expresses anger at the
conventional values of the society around
him.
*originally, a member of a group of socially conscious
writers in the 1950s, including particularly the
playwright John Osborne; the phrase, the title of a
book (1951) by Leslie Paul, was used of Osborne in the
publicity material for his play* Look Back in Anger
*(1956), in which the characteristic views were
articulated by the anti-hero Jimmy Porter; see* **Writers
2**

3 **baby boomer** a person born during the
temporary marked increase in the birth
rate following the Second World War.

4 **Generation X** the generation born after
that of the baby boomers (roughly from
the early 1960s to mid 1970s), typically
perceived to be disaffected and
directionless.
popularized by Douglas Coupland's book Generation
X: tales for an accelerated culture *(1991)*

QUOTATIONS

5 Tiresome, complaining, a praiser of past
times, when he was a boy, a castigator
and censor of the young generation.
Horace 65–8 BC: *Ars Poetica*

6 Age is deformed, youth unkind,
We scorn their bodies, they our mind.
Thomas Bastard 1566–1618: *Chrestoleros* (1598)

7 Crabbed age and youth cannot live
together:
Youth is full of pleasance, age is full of
care.
William Shakespeare 1564–1616: *The Passionate
Pilgrim* (1599)

8 O Man! that from thy fair and shining
youth
Age might but take the things Youth
needed not!
William Wordsworth 1770–1850: 'The Small
Celandine' (1807)

9 Youth, which is forgiven everything,
forgives itself nothing: age, which forgives
itself everything, is forgiven nothing.
George Bernard Shaw 1856–1950: *Man and
Superman* (1903)

10 Where, where but here have Pride and
Truth,

That long to give themselves for wage,
To shake their wicked sides at youth
Restraining reckless middle age?
W. B. Yeats 1865–1939: 'On hearing that the Students of our New University have joined the Agitation against Immoral Literature' (1910)

11 When I was a boy of 14, my father was so ignorant I could hardly stand to have the old man around. But when I got to be 21, I was astonished at how much the old man had learned in seven years.
Mark Twain 1835–1910: attributed in *Reader's Digest* September 1939, but not traced in his works

12 The young man who has not wept is a savage, and the old man who will not laugh is a fool.
George Santayana 1863–1952: *Dialogues in Limbo* (1925)

13 Every generation revolts against its fathers and makes friends with its grandfathers.
Lewis Mumford 1895–90: *The Brown Decades* (1931)

14 Grown-ups never understand anything for themselves, and it is tiresome for children to be always and forever explaining things to them.
Antoine de Saint-Exupéry 1900–44: *Le Petit Prince* (1943)

15 It is the one war in which everyone changes sides.
Cyril Connolly 1903–74: Tom Driberg speech in House of Commons, 30 October 1959

16 Come mothers and fathers,
Throughout the land
And don't criticize
What you can't understand.
Your sons and your daughters
Are beyond your command
Your old road is
Rapidly agin'
Please get out of the new one
If you can't lend your hand
For the times they are a-changin'!
Bob Dylan 1941– : 'The Times They Are A-Changing' (1964 song)

17 Each year brings new problems of Form and Content,
new foes to tug with: at Twenty I tried to vex my elders, past Sixty it's the young whom
I hope to bother.
W. H. Auden 1907–73: 'Shorts I' (1969)

18 When I was young, the old regarded me as an outrageous young fellow, and now that I'm old the young regard me as an outrageous old fellow.
Fred Hoyle 1915–2001: in *Scientific American* March 1995

Genius

PROVERBS AND SAYINGS

1 **Genius is an infinite capacity for taking pains.**
late 19th century

2 **Genius without education is like silver in the mine.**
American proverb, mid 18th century

QUOTATIONS

3 Great wits are sure to madness near allied, And thin partitions do their bounds divide.
John Dryden 1631–1700: *Absalom and Achitophel* (1681)

4 When a true genius appears in the world, you may know him by this sign, that the dunces are all in confederacy against him.
Jonathan Swift 1667–1745: *Thoughts on Various Subjects* (1711)

5 There is more beauty in the works of a great genius who is ignorant of all the rules of art, than in the works of a little genius, who not only knows but scrupulously observes them.
Joseph Addison 1672–1719: in *The Spectator* 10 September 1714

6 The true genius is a mind of large general powers, accidentally determined to some particular direction.
Samuel Johnson 1709–84: *Lives of the English Poets* (1779–81) 'Cowley'

7 Many a genius has been slow of growth. Oaks that flourish for a thousand years do not spring up into beauty like a reed.
G. H. Lewes 1817–78: *The Spanish Drama* (1846)

8 Since when was genius found respectable?
Elizabeth Barrett Browning 1806–61: *Aurora Leigh* (1857)

9 Genius does what it must, and Talent does what it can.
Owen Meredith 1831–91: 'Last Words of a Sensitive Second-Rate Poet' (1868)

10 I have nothing to declare except my genius.
Oscar Wilde 1854–1900: at the New York Custom House; Frank Harris *Oscar Wilde* (1918)

11 Genius is one per cent inspiration, ninety-nine per cent perspiration.
Thomas Alva Edison 1847–1931: said c.1903, in *Harper's Monthly Magazine* September 1932

12 Little minds are interested in the extraordinary; great minds in the commonplace.
Elbert Hubbard 1859–1915: *Thousand and One Epigrams* (1911)

13 Everybody has talent at twenty-five. The difficult thing is to have it at fifty.
Edgar Degas 1834–1917: R. H. Ives Gammell *The Shop-Talk of Edgar Degas* (1961)

14 A man of genius makes no mistakes. His errors are volitional and are the portals of discovery.
James Joyce 1882–1941: *Ulysses* (1922)

15 Geniuses are the luckiest of mortals because what they must do is the same as what they most want to do.
W. H. Auden 1907–73: Dag Hammarskjöld *Markings* (1964)

16 Airing one's dirty linen never makes for a masterpiece.
François Truffaut 1932–84: *Bed and Board* (1972)

Gifts see also Charity

1 **A bird never flew on one wing.**
early 18th century; the saying, which is mainly Scottish and Irish, is frequently used to justify a further gift, especially another drink

2 **Friday's child is loving and giving.**
mid 19th century; see Beauty 5, Sorrow 2, Travel 5, Work 6

3 **Give a thing, and take a thing, to wear the devil's gold ring.**
late 16th century; a schoolchildren's rhyme, chanted when a person gives something and then asks for it back

4 **He gives twice who gives quickly.**
mid 16th century, associating readiness to give with generosity

5 **It is better to give than to receive.**
late 14th century; see 11 below

6 **A small gift usually gets small thanks.**
American proverb, mid 20th century

7 **Greek gift** a gift given with intent to harm.
in allusion to Virgil: see Trust and Treachery 1, 18

8 **manna from heaven** an unexpected or gratuitous benefit.
manna in the Bible (Exodus), the substance miraculously supplied each day as food to the Israelites in the wilderness; see Satisfaction 19

9 Enemies' gifts are no gifts and do no good.
Sophocles c.496–406 BC: *Ajax*

10 Give, and it shall be given unto you; good measure, pressed down, and shaken together, and running over.
Bible: St Luke

11 It is more blessed to give than to receive.
Bible: Acts of the Apostles; see 5 above

12 God loveth a cheerful giver.
Bible: II Corinthians

13 Teach us, good Lord, to serve Thee as
    Thou deservest:
To give and not to count the cost;
To fight and not to heed the wounds;
To toil and not to seek for rest;
To labour and not to ask for any reward
Save that of knowing that we do Thy will.
St Ignatius Loyola 1491–1556: 'Prayer for Generosity' (1548)

14 I am not in the giving vein to-day.
William Shakespeare 1564–1616: *Richard III* (1591)

15 Presents, I often say, endear Absents.
Charles Lamb 1775–1834: *Essays of Elia* (1823) 'A Dissertation upon Roast Pig'

16 Behold, I do not give lectures or a little charity,
When I give I give myself.
Walt Whitman 1819–92: 'Song of Myself' (written 1855)

17 They gave it me,—for an un-birthday
present.
Lewis Carroll 1832–98: *Through the Looking-Glass*
(1872)

18 CHAIRMAN: What is service?
CANDIDATE: The rent we pay for our room
on earth.
*admission ceremony of Toc H (a society, originally of
ex-servicemen and women, founded after the First
World War to promote Christian fellowship and social
service)*
Tubby Clayton 1885–1972: Tresham Lever *Clayton of
Toc H* (1971)

19 Why is it no one ever sent me yet
One perfect limousine, do you suppose?
Ah no, it's always just my luck to get
One perfect rose.
Dorothy Parker 1893–1967: 'One Perfect Rose'
(1937)

20 'The more we ask, the more we have. And,
it is fair enough: asking is not always
easy.'

'And it is said to be hard to accept . . . So
no wonder we have so little.'
Ivy Compton-Burnett 1884–1969: *The Mighty and
their Fall* (1961)

21 I know it's not much, but it's the best I can
do,
My gift is my song and this one's for you.
Elton John 1947– and **Bernie Taupin** 1950– :
'Your Song' (1970 song)

22 Giving presents is one of the most
possessive of things we do . . . It's the way
we keep a hold on other people. Plant
ourselves in their lives.
Penelope Lively 1933– : *Moon Tiger* (1987)

23 When a woman keeps score, no matter
how big or small a gift of love is, it scores
one point; each gift has equal value . . . A
man, however, thinks he scores one point
for a small gift and thirty points for a big
gift.
John Gray 1951– : *Men are from Mars, Women are
from Venus* (1992)

God see also **Belief, The Bible, The Christian Church, Religion**

PROVERBS AND SAYINGS

1 **All things are possible with God.**
late 17th century; see 8 below

2 **God helps them that helps themselves.**
*mid 16th century, often used in urging someone to
action*

3 **The nature of God is a circle of which the
centre is everywhere and the
circumference is nowhere.**
*medieval saying, said to have been traced to a lost
treatise of Empedocles; quoted in the* Roman de la
Rose, *and by St Bonaventura in* Itinerarius Mentis in
Deum

PHRASES

4 **the Ancient of Days** God.
*a scriptural title in the Bible (Daniel) 'the Ancient of
Days did sit, whose garments were white as snow'*

5 **the Lord of Sabaoth** the Lord of Hosts, God.
Hebrew Sabaoth the heavenly hosts

QUOTATIONS

6 The Lord is my shepherd: therefore can I
lack nothing.

He shall feed me in a green pasture: and
lead me forth beside the waters of comfort.
Bible: Psalm 23

7 God is always doing geometry.
Plato 429–347 BC: Plutarch *Moralia; see* **The
Universe** 19

8 With men this is impossible; but with God
all things are possible.
Bible: St Matthew; see 1 above

9 He that loveth not knoweth not God; for
God is love.
Bible: I John

10 A living man is the glory of God.
St Irenaeus c.130–c.200 AD: *Against the Heresies*

11 Praise belongs to God, the Lord of all
Being,
the All-merciful, the All-compassionate,
the Master of the Day of Doom.
The Koran: sura 1

12 Therefore it is necessary to arrive at a
prime mover, put in motion by no other;
and this everyone understands to be God.
St Thomas Aquinas c.1225–74: *Summa Theologicae*
(c.1265); see **Beginning** 13

13 *E'n la sua volontade è nostra pace.*
In His will is our peace.
Dante Alighieri 1265–1321: *Divina Commedia*
'Paradiso'

14 Whatever your heart clings to and confides
in, that is really your God.
Martin Luther 1483–1546: *Large Catechism* (1529)
'The First Commandment'

15 'Twas only fear first in the world made
gods.
Ben Jonson c.1573–1637: *Sejanus* (1603)

16 Batter my heart, three-personed God; for,
you
As yet but knock, breathe, shine, and seek
to mend.
John Donne 1572–1631: *Holy Sonnets* (after 1609)

17 I had rather believe all the fables in the
legend, and the Talmud, and the Alcoran,
than that this universal frame is without a
mind.
Francis Bacon 1561–1626: *Essays* (1625) 'Of Atheism'

18 Though the mills of God grind slowly, yet
they grind exceeding small;
Though with patience He stands waiting,
with exactness grinds He all.
Friedrich von Logau 1604–55: *Sinnegedichte* (1654)
translated by Longfellow; Von Logau's first line is
itself a translation of an anonymous verse in Sextus
Empiricus *Adversus Mathematicos*; see **Fate** 5

19 'God is or he is not.' But to which side
shall we incline? . . . Let us weigh the gain
and the loss in wagering that God is. Let us
estimate the two chances. If you gain, you
gain all; if you lose, you lose nothing.
Wager then without hesitation that he is.
known as Pascal's wager
Blaise Pascal 1623–62: *Pensées* (1670)

20 As you know, God is usually on the side of
the big squadrons against the small.
Comte de Bussy-Rabutin 1618–93: letter to the
Comte de Limoges, 18 October 1677; see **Armed
Forces** 7, **Warfare** 20

21 If the triangles were to make a God they
would give him three sides.
Montesquieu 1689–1755: *Lettres Persanes* (1721)

22 If God did not exist, it would be necessary
to invent him.
Voltaire 1694–1778: *Épîtres* no. 96 'A l'Auteur du
livre des trois imposteurs'

23 God moves in a mysterious way
His wonders to perform.
William Cowper 1731–1800: 'Light Shining out of
Darkness' (1779 hymn)

24 Suppose I had found a *watch* upon the
ground, and it should be enquired how the
watch happened to be in that place . . . the
inference, we think, is inevitable; that the
watch must have had a maker, that there
must have existed, at some time and at
some place or other, an artificer or
artificers, who formed it for the purpose
which we find it actually to answer; who
comprehended its construction, and
designed its use.
William Paley 1743–1805: *Natural Theology* (1802);
see **Life Sciences** 25

25 All service ranks the same with God—
With God, whose puppets, best and worst,
Are we: there is no last nor first.
Robert Browning 1812–89: *Pippa Passes* (1841)

26 Mine eyes have seen the glory of the
coming of the Lord:
He is trampling out the vintage where the
grapes of wrath are stored;
He hath loosed the fateful lightning of his
terrible swift sword:
His truth is marching on.
Julia Ward Howe 1819–1910: 'Battle Hymn of the
Republic' (1862)

27 I will call no being good, who is not what I
mean when I apply that epithet to my
fellow-creatures; and if such a being can
sentence me to hell for not so calling him,
to hell I will go.
John Stuart Mill 1806–73: *Examination of Sir
William Hamilton's Philosophy* (1865)

28 An honest God is the noblest work of man.
after Pope Essay on Man (1734) 'An honest man's the
noblest work of God'
Robert G. Ingersoll 1833–99: *The Gods* (1876)

29 God is dead: but considering the state the
species Man is in, there will perhaps be
caves, for ages yet, in which his shadow
will be shown.
Friedrich Nietzsche 1844–1900: *Die fröhliche
Wissenschaft* (1882)

30 God is subtle but he is not malicious.
Albert Einstein 1879–1955: remark made at
Princeton University, May 1921; R. W. Clark *Einstein*
(1973)

31 It is a mistake to suppose that God is only,
or even chiefly, concerned with religion.
William Temple 1881–1944: R. V. C. Bodley *In
Search of Serenity* (1955)

32 Operationally, God is beginning to resemble not a ruler but the last fading smile of a cosmic Cheshire cat.

Julian Huxley 1887–1975: *Religion without Revelation* (1957 ed.); see **Cats** 3

33 God has been replaced, as he has all over the West, with respectability and air-conditioning.

Imamu Amiri Baraka 1934– : *Midstream* (1963)

34 God, to me, it seems,
is a verb
not a noun,
proper or improper.

R. Buckminster Fuller 1895–1983: *No More Secondhand God* (1963)

35 God is really only another artist. He invented the giraffe, the elephant, and the cat. He has no real style. He just goes on trying other things.

Pablo Picasso 1881–1973: F. Gilot and C. Lake *Life With Picasso* (1964)

36 God seems to have left the receiver off the hook, and time is running out.

Arthur Koestler 1905–83: *The Ghost in the Machine* (1967)

37 The Buddha, the Godhead, resides quite as comfortably in the circuits of a digital computer or the gears of a cycle transmission as he does at the top of a mountain or in the petals of a flower.

Robert M. Pirsig 1928– : *Zen and the Art of Motorcycle Maintenance* (1974)

38 Any God I ever felt in church I brought in with me. And I think all the other folks did too. They come to church to *share* God not find God.

Alice Walker 1944– : *The Colour Purple* (1982)

39 I am not clear that God manoeuvres physical things . . . After all, a conjuring trick with bones only proves that it is as clever as a conjuring trick with bones.

of the Resurrection

David Jenkins 1925– : 'Poles Apart' (BBC radio, 4 October 1984)

40 I think you have to be very careful when you say, 'God is on my side.' I much prefer to say, 'I am on God's side'.

Ann Widdecombe 1947– : Anthony Clare *In the Psychiatrist's Chair III* (1998)

41 Even God has become female. God is no longer the bearded patriarch in the sky. He has had a sex change and turned into Mother Nature.

Fay Weldon 1931– : in *The Times* 29 August 1998

Good and Evil see also **Sin, Virtue**

1 The greater the sinner, the greater the saint.

late 18th century, meaning that a sinner who has reformed is likely to be more virtuous that someone who is morally neutral

2 He that touches pitch shall be defiled.

early 14th century, meaning that a person who chooses to put themselves in contact with wrongdoing will be marked by it; see 14 below

3 Honi soit qui mal y pense.

French, Evil be to him who evil thinks, the motto of the Order of the Garter, originated by Edward III, probably on 23 April of 1348 or 1349

4 Ill weeds grow apace.

late 15th century, used to comment on the apparent success enjoyed by an ill-doer

5 Never do evil that good may come of it.

late 16th century, meaning that the prospect of a good outcome cannot justify wrongdoing

6 The sun loses nothing by shining into a puddle.

early 14th century, of classical origin, meaning that something which is naturally clear and radiant cannot be tainted or diminished by association

7 Two blacks don't make a white.

early 18th century, meaning that one injury or instance of wrongdoing does not justify another

8 Two wrongs don't make a right.

late 18th century, meaning that a first injury does not justify a second in retaliation; see 42 below

9 Where God builds a church, the Devil will build a chapel.

mid 16th century, meaning that the establishment of something which in itself good may also create the opening for something evil; see 23 below

PHRASES

10 cloven hoof the mark of an inherently evil nature.

*a divided hoof, as that of a goat, ascribed to a satyr, the god Pan, or to the Devil; see **The Family** 24*

11 Lord of the Flies Satan, the Devil.

meaning of the Hebrew word which is the origin of Beelzebub, *in the Bible* (II Kings) *the god of the Philistine city Ekron, and in the Gospels, the prince of the devils, often identified with the Devil*

12 the Prince of this world Satan, the Devil.

from the Bible (John) *'the prince of this world is judged'*

13 separate the sheep from the goats sort the good persons or things from the bad or inferior.

from the Bible (Matthew) *'He shall separate the one from another, as a shepherd divideth his sheep from his goats. And he shall set the sheep on his right hand, but the goats on his left'*

QUOTATIONS

14 He that toucheth pitch shall be defiled therewith.

Bible: Ecclesiasticus; see 2 above

15 It is never right to do wrong or to requite wrong with wrong, or when we suffer evil to defend ourselves by doing evil in return.

Socrates 469-399 BC: Plato *Crito*

16 Every art and every investigation, and likewise every practical pursuit or undertaking, seems to aim at some good: hence it has been well said that the Good is That at which all things aim.

Aristotle 384-322 BC: *Nicomachean Ethics*

17 How can Satan cast out Satan?

Bible: St Mark; see also **Warfare** 34

18 For the good that I would I do not: but the evil which I would not, that I do.

Bible: Romans

19 Unto the pure all things are pure.

Bible: Titus; see 37 below

20 With love for mankind and hatred of sins.

often quoted 'Love the sinner but hate the sin'

St Augustine of Hippo AD 354-430: letter 211; J.-P. Migne (ed.) *Patrologiae Latinae* (1845)

21 Good and evil shall not be held equal. Turn away evil with that which is better; and behold the man between whom and thyself there was enmity, shall become, as it were, thy warmest friend.

The Koran: sura 41

22 If all evil were prevented, much good would be absent from the universe. A lion would cease to live, if there were no slaying of animals; and there would be no

patience of martyrs if there were no tyrannical persecution.

St Thomas Aquinas c.1225-74: *Summa Theologicae* (c.1265)

23 For, where God built a church, there the devil would also build a chapel . . . In such sort is the devil always God's ape.

Martin Luther 1483-1546: *Colloquia Mensalia* (1566); see 9 above

24 I come to bury Caesar, not to praise him. The evil that men do lives after them, The good is oft interrèd with their bones.

William Shakespeare 1564-1616: *Julius Caesar* (1599)

25 There is nothing either good or bad, but thinking makes it so.

William Shakespeare 1564-1616: *Hamlet* (1601)

26   By the pricking of my thumbs, Something wicked this way comes.

William Shakespeare 1564-1616: *Macbeth* (1606); see **Foresight** 7

27 Farewell remorse! All good to me is lost; Evil, be thou my good.

John Milton 1608-74: *Paradise Lost* (1667)

28 But if he does really think that there is no distinction between virtue and vice, why, Sir, when he leaves our houses, let us count our spoons.

Samuel Johnson 1709-84: James Boswell *Life of Samuel Johnson* (1791) 14 July 1763

29 It is necessary only for the good man to do nothing for evil to triumph.

Edmund Burke 1729-97: attributed (in a number of forms) to Burke, but not found in his writings

30 One impulse from a vernal wood May teach you more of man, Of moral evil and of good, Than all the sages can.

William Wordsworth 1770-1850: 'The Tables Turned' (1798)

31 He who would do good to another, must do it in minute particulars General good is the plea of the scoundrel, hypocrite and flatterer.

William Blake 1757-1827: *Jerusalem* (1815)

32 It is better to fight for the good, than to rail at the ill.

Alfred, Lord Tennyson 1809-92: *Maud* (1855)

33 Imagine that you are creating a fabric of human destiny with the object of making men happy in the end, giving them peace and rest at last, but that it was essential and inevitable to torture to death only one tiny creature . . . and to found that edifice on its unavenged tears, would you consent to be the architect on those conditions?

Fedor Dostoevsky 1821–81: *The Brothers Karamazov* (1879–80)

34 A belief in a supernatural source of evil is not necessary; men alone are quite capable of every wickedness.

Joseph Conrad 1857–1924: *Under Western Eyes* (1911)

35 In my humble opinion, non-cooperation with evil is as much a duty as is cooperation with good.

Mahatma Gandhi 1869–1948: speech in Ahmadabad, 23 March 1922

36 What we call evil is simply ignorance bumping its head in the dark.

Henry Ford 1863–1947: in *Observer* 16 March 1930

37 To the Puritan all things are impure, as somebody says.

D. H. Lawrence 1885–1930: *Etruscan Places* (1932) 'Cerveteri'; see 19 above

38 I and the public know
What all schoolchildren learn,
Those to whom evil is done
Do evil in return.

W. H. Auden 1907–73: 'September 1, 1939' (1940)

39 As soon as men decide that all means are permitted to fight an evil, then their good becomes indistinguishable from the evil that they set out to destroy.

Christopher Dawson 1889–1970: *The Judgement of the Nations* (1942)

40 The face of 'evil' is always the face of total need.

William S. Burroughs 1914–97: *The Naked Lunch* (1959)

41 It was as though in those last minutes he [Eichmann] was summing up the lessons that this long course in human wickedness had taught us—the lesson of the fearsome, word-and-thought-defying *banality of evil*.

Hannah Arendt 1906–75: *Eichmann in Jerusalem* (1963)

42 Two wrongs don't make a right, but they make a good excuse.

Thomas Szasz 1920– : *The Second Sin* (1973); see 8 above

43 To respond to evil by committing another evil does not eliminate evil but allows it to go on forever.

Václav Havel 1936– : letter, 5 November 1989

44 Mostly, we are good when it makes sense. A good society is one that makes sense of being good.

Ian McEwan 1948– : *Enduring Love* (1998)

Gossip see also **Reputation, Secrecy**

PROVERBS AND SAYINGS

1 Careless talk costs lives.
Second World War security slogan

2 A dog that will fetch a bone will carry a bone.
early 19th century, meaning that someone given to gossip carries talk both ways

3 Give a dog a bad name and hang him.
early 18th century, meaning that once a person's reputation has been blackened his plight is hopeless

4 Gossip is the lifeblood of society.
American proverb, mid 20th century

5 Gossip is vice enjoyed vicariously.
American proverb, early 20th century

6 The greater the truth, the greater the libel.
late 18th century

7 Loose lips sink ships.
American Second World war security slogan

8 A tale never loses in the telling.
mid 16th century, implying that a story is often exaggerated when it is repeated

9 Those who live in glass houses shouldn't throw stones.
mid 17th century, meaning that it is unwise to criticize or slander another if you are vulnerable to retaliation

10 What the soldier said isn't evidence.
mid 19th century, meaning that hearsay evidence alone cannot be relied on; originally from Dickens Pickwick Papers (1837) 'You must not tell us what the soldier, or any other man, said . . . it's not evidence'

PHRASES

11 bush telegraph a rapid informal spreading of information or a rumour; the network through which this takes place.
see 13 below

12 Chinese whispers a game in which a message is distorted by being passed around in a whisper; Russian scandal.
see 14 below

13 hear on the grapevine acquire information by rumour or unofficial communication.
originally from an American Civil War usage, when news was said to be passed 'by grapevine telegraph'; see 11 above

14 Russian scandal Chinese whispers.
see 12 above

QUOTATIONS

15 Many have fallen by the edge of the sword: but not so many as have fallen by the tongue.
Bible: Ecclesiasticus

16 *Che ti fa ciò che quivi pispiglia?*
Vien dietro a me, e lascia dir le genti.
What is it to thee what they whisper there? Come after me and let the people talk.
Dante Alighieri 1265–1321: *Divina Commedia* 'Purgatorio'

17 Enter Rumour, painted full of tongues.
William Shakespeare 1564–1616: *Henry IV, Part 2* (1597); stage direction

18 Be thou as chaste as ice, as pure as snow, thou shalt not escape calumny.
William Shakespeare 1564–1616: *Hamlet* (1601)

19 How these curiosities would be quite forgot, did not such idle fellows as I am put them down.
John Aubrey 1626–97: *Brief Lives* 'Venetia Digby'

20 Love and scandal are the best sweeteners of tea.
Henry Fielding 1707-54: *Love in Several Masques* (1728)

21 It is a matter of great interest what sovereigns are doing; but as to what Grand Duchesses are doing—Who cares?
Napoleon I 1769–1821: letter, 17 December 1811

22 Every man is surrounded by a neighbourhood of voluntary spies.
Jane Austen 1775–1817: *Northanger Abbey* (1818)

23 Gossip is a sort of smoke that comes from the dirty tobacco-pipes of those who diffuse it: it proves nothing but the bad taste of the smoker.
George Eliot 1819-80: *Daniel Deronda* (1876)

24 There is only one thing in the world worse than being talked about, and that is not being talked about.
Oscar Wilde 1854-1900: *The Picture of Dorian Gray* (1891)

25 It takes your enemy and your friend, working together, to hurt you to the heart: the one to slander you and the other to get the news to you.
Mark Twain 1835-1910: *Following the Equator* (1897)

26 Like all gossip—it's merely one of those half-alive things that try to crowd out real life.
E. M. Forster 1879–1970: *A Passage to India* (1924)

27 Blood sport is brought to its ultimate refinement in the gossip columns.
Bernard Ingham 1932- : speech, 5 February 1986

Government see also **International Relations, Parliament, Politics, The Presidency, Society**

PROVERBS AND SAYINGS

1 Divide and rule.
early 17th century, meaning that government control is more easily exercised if possible opponents are separated into factions

PHRASES

2 appeal to Caesar appeal to the highest possible authority.
particularly with allusion to the Bible (Acts), in which Paul the Apostle exercised his right as a Roman citizen to have his case heard in Rome, with the words 'I appeal unto Caesar'

3 bread and circuses the public provision of subsistence and entertainment, especially to assuage the populace.
from Juvenal: see 9 below

4 checks and balances counterbalancing influences by which an organization or system is regulated, typically those ensuring that power in political institutions is not concentrated in the hands of particular individuals or groups.

5 the corridors of power the senior levels of government or administration, where

covert influence is regarded as being exerted and significant decisions are made.
from the title of C. P. Snow's novel The Corridors of Power (1964)

6 the ship of state the state and its affairs, especially when regarded as being subject to adverse or changing circumstances.
a ship as the type of something subject to adverse or changing weather

QUOTATIONS

7 A ruler who governs his state by virtue is like the north polar star, which remains in its place while all the other stars revolve around it.
Confucius 551–479 BC: *Analects*

8 Let them hate, so long as they fear.
Accius 170–c.86 BC: from *Atreus*; Seneca *Dialogues*

9 . . . *Duas tantum res anxius optat,*
Panem et circenses.
Only two things does he [the modern citizen] anxiously wish for—bread and circuses.
Juvenal AD c.60–c.130: *Satires*; see 3 above

10 Because it is difficult to join them together, it is much safer for a prince to be feared than loved, if he is to fail in one of the two.
Niccolò Machiavelli 1469–1527: *The Prince* (written 1513)

11 Though God hath raised me high, yet this I count the glory of my crown: that I have reigned with your loves.
Elizabeth I 1533–1603: The Golden Speech, 1601

12 I will govern according to the common weal, but not according to the common will.
James I 1566–1625: in December, 1621; J. R. Green *History of the English People* vol. 3 (1879)

13 *L'État c'est moi.*
I am the State.
Louis XIV 1638–1715: before the Parlement de Paris, 13 April 1655; probably apocryphal

14 It is a 'beautiful maxim' that it is necessary to save five *sous* on unessential things, and to pour out millions when it is a question of your glory.
Jean-Baptiste Colbert 1619–83: letter to Louis XIV, 1666

15 Governments need both shepherds and butchers.
Voltaire 1694–1778: 'The Piccini Notebooks' (c.1735–50)

16 Little else is requisite to carry a state to the highest degree of opulence from the lowest barbarism but peace, easy taxes, and a tolerable administration of justice: all the rest being brought about by the natural course of things.
Adam Smith 1723–90: in 1755; *Essays on Philosophical Subjects* (1795)

17 I would not give half a guinea to live under one form of government rather than another. It is of no moment to the happiness of an individual.
Samuel Johnson 1709–84: James Boswell *Life of Samuel Johnson* (1791) 31 March 1772

18 A government of laws, and not of men.
John Adams 1735–1826: *Boston Gazette* (1774) 'Novanglus' papers; later incorporated in the Massachusetts Constitution (1780)

19 The happiness of society is the end of government.
John Adams 1735–1826: *Thoughts on Government* (1776)

20 Government, even in its best state, is but a necessary evil . . . Government, like dress, is the badge of lost innocence; the palaces of kings are built upon the ruins of the bowers of paradise.
Thomas Paine 1737–1809: *Common Sense* (1776)

21 My people and I have come to an agreement which satisfies us both. They are to say what they please, and I am to do what I please.
his interpretation of benevolent despotism
Frederick the Great 1712–86: attributed

22 When, in countries that are called civilized, we see age going to the workhouse and youth to the gallows, something must be wrong in the system of government.
Thomas Paine 1737–1809: *The Rights of Man* pt. 2 (1792)

23 A monarchy is a merchantman which sails well, but will sometimes strike on a rock, and go to the bottom; whilst a republic is a raft which would never sink, but then your feet are always in the water.
Fisher Ames 1758–1808: attributed to Ames, speaking in the House of Representatives, 1795; quoted by R. W. Emerson in *Essays* (1844), but not traced in Ames's speeches

24 Away with the cant of 'Measures not men'!—the idle supposition that it is the harness and not the horses that draw the chariot along. If the comparison must be

made, if the distinction must be taken, men are everything, measures comparatively nothing.
George Canning 1770–1827: speech on the Army estimates, 8 December 1802; the phrase 'measures not men' may be found as early as 1742 (in a letter from Chesterfield to Dr Chevenix, 6 March)

25 To govern is to choose.
Duc de Lévis 1764–1830: *Maximes et Réflexions* (1812 ed.)

26 The best government is that which governs least.
John L. O'Sullivan 1813–95: *United States Magazine and Democratic Review* (1837)

27 No Government can be long secure without a formidable Opposition.
Benjamin Disraeli 1804–81: *Coningsby* (1844)

28 This country, with its institutions, belongs to the people who inhabit it. Whenever they shall grow weary of the existing government, they can exercise their constitutional right of amending it, or their revolutionary right to dismember or overthrow it.
Abraham Lincoln 1809–65: first inaugural address, 4 March 1861

29 The Crown is, according to the saying, the 'fountain of honour'; but the Treasury is the spring of business.
Walter Bagehot 1826–77: *The English Constitution* (1867) 'The Cabinet'; see **Royalty** 14

30 A fainéant government is not the worst government that England can have. It has been the great fault of our politicians that they have all wanted to do something.
Anthony Trollope 1815–82: *Phineas Finn* (1869)

31 My faith in the people governing is, on the whole, infinitesimal; my faith in The People governed is, on the whole, illimitable.
Charles Dickens 1812–70: speech at Birmingham and Midland Institute, 27 September 1869

32 The State is not 'abolished', *it withers away.*
Friedrich Engels 1820–95: *Anti-Dühring* (1878)

33 The state is like the human body. Not all of its functions are dignified.
Anatole France 1844–1924: *Les Opinions de M. Jerome Coignard* (1893)

34 I work for a Government I despise for ends I think criminal.
John Maynard Keynes 1883–1946: letter to Duncan Grant, 15 December 1917

35 While the State exists, there can be no freedom. When there is freedom there will be no State.
Lenin 1870–1924: *State and Revolution* (1919)

36 A government which robs Peter to pay Paul can always depend on the support of Paul.
George Bernard Shaw 1856–1950: *Everybody's Political What's What?* (1944); see **Debt** 10

37 BIG BROTHER IS WATCHING YOU.
George Orwell 1903–50: *Nineteen Eighty-Four* (1949)

38 If the Government is big enough to give you everything you want, it is big enough to take away everything you have.
Gerald Ford 1909– : John F. Parker *If Elected* (1960)

39 Many journalists have fallen for the conspiracy theory of government. I do assure you that they would produce more accurate work if they adhered to the cock-up theory.
Bernard Ingham 1932– : in *Observer* 17 March 1985

40 We give the impression of being in office but not in power.
Norman Lamont 1942– : speech, House of Commons, 9 June 1993

41 Thank heavens we do not get all of the government that we are made to pay for.
Milton Friedman 1912– : quoted in the House of Lords, 24 November 1994

Gratitude and Ingratitude

PROVERBS AND SAYINGS

1 **The Devil was sick, the Devil a saint would be; the Devil was well, the devil a saint was he.**
early 17th century, meaning that promises made in adversity may not be kept in prosperity

2 **Don't overload gratitude, if you do, she'll kick.**
American proverb, mid 18th century

3 **Never look a gift horse in the mouth.**
early 16th century, warning against questioning the quality or use of a lucky chance or gift; referring to the fact that it is by a horse's teeth that its age is judged

4 You never miss the water till the well runs dry.

early 17th century, applied to situations in which it is only when a source of support or sustenance has been withdrawn that its importance is understood

5 bite the hand that feeds one injure a benefactor, act ungratefully.

see 14 below

6 A joyful and pleasant thing it is to be thankful.
Bible: Psalm 147

7 Blow, blow, thou winter wind,
Thou art not so unkind
As man's ingratitude.
William Shakespeare 1564–1616: *As You Like It* (1599)

8 How sharper than a serpent's tooth it is
To have a thankless child!
William Shakespeare 1564–1616: *King Lear* (1605–6)

9 I once knew a man out of courtesy help a lame dog over a stile, and he for requital bit his fingers.
William Chillingworth 1602–44: *The Religion of Protestants* (1637)

10   A grateful mind
By owing owes not, but still pays, at once
Indebted and discharged.
John Milton 1608–74: *Paradise Lost* (1667)

11 In most of mankind gratitude is merely a secret hope for greater favours.
Duc de la Rochefoucauld 1613–80: *Maximes* (1678)

12 There are minds so impatient of inferiority, that their gratitude is a species of revenge, and they return benefits, not because recompense is a pleasure, but because obligation is a pain.
Samuel Johnson 1709–84: in *The Rambler* 15 January 1751

13 There's plenty of boys that will come hankering and grovelling around you when you've got an apple, and beg the core off of you; but when they've got one, and you beg for the core and remind them how you give them a core one time, they say thank you 'most to death, but there ain't-a-going to be no core.
Mark Twain 1835–1910: *Tom Sawyer Abroad* (1894)

14 That's the way with these directors, they're always biting the hand that lays the golden egg.
Sam Goldwyn 1882–1974: Alva Johnston *The Great Goldwyn* (1937); see 5 above, **Greed** 5

15 Never in the field of human conflict was so much owed by so many to so few.
on the skill and courage of British airmen
Winston Churchill 1874–1965: speech, House of Commons, 20 August 1940

16 Maybe the only thing worse than having to give gratitude constantly all the time, is having to accept it.
William Faulkner 1897–1962: *Requiem for a Nun* (1951)

17 [Gratitude] is a sickness suffered by dogs.
Joseph Stalin 1879–1953: Nikolai Tolstoy *Stalin's Secret War* (1981)

18 My children are ungrateful: they don't care. That is my great reward. They are free.
Fay Weldon 1931– : *Praxis* (1978)

19 What have the Romans ever done for us?
Graham Chapman 1941–89 et al.: *Monty Python's Life of Brian* (1979 film)

20 He's coming to hate the gratitude of women. It is like being fawned on by rabbits, or like being covered with syrup: you can't get it off. It slows you down, and puts you at a disadvantage.
Margaret Atwood 1939– : *Alias Grace* (1996)

Greatness

1 If any man seek for greatness, let him forget greatness and seek truth.
American proverb, mid 20th century

2 The beauty of Israel is slain upon thy high places: how are the mighty fallen!
Bible: II Samuel

3 Why, man, he doth bestride the narrow
world
Like a Colossus; and we petty men
Walk under his huge legs, and peep about
To find ourselves dishonourable graves.
William Shakespeare 1564–1616: *Julius Caesar*
(1599)

4 But be not afraid of greatness: some men
are born great, some achieve greatness,
and some have greatness thrust upon
them.
William Shakespeare 1564–1616: *Twelfth Night*
(1601)

5 What millions died—that Caesar might be
great!
Thomas Campbell 1777–1844: *Pleasures of Hope*
(1799)

6 Fleas know not whether they are upon the
body of a giant or upon one of ordinary
size.
Walter Savage Landor 1775–1864: *Imaginary
Conversations* (1824)

7 Is it so bad, then, to be misunderstood?
Pythagoras was misunderstood, and
Socrates, and Jesus, and Luther, and
Copernicus, and Galileo, and Newton, and
every pure and wise spirit that ever took
flesh. To be great is to be misunderstood.
Ralph Waldo Emerson 1803–82: *Essays* (1841) 'Self-
Reliance'

8   In me there dwells
No greatness, save it be some far-off touch
Of greatness to know well I am not great.
Alfred, Lord Tennyson 1809–92: *Idylls of the King*
'Lancelot and Elaine' (1859)

9 In historical events great men—
so-called—are but labels serving to give a
name to the event, and like labels they
have the least possible connection with the
event itself.
Leo Tolstoy 1828–1910: *War and Peace* (1868–9)

10 A man is seldom ashamed of feeling that
he cannot love a woman so well when he
sees a certain greatness in her: nature
having intended greatness for men.
George Eliot 1819–80: *Middlemarch* (1871–2)

11 Everything we think of as great has come
to us from neurotics. It is they and they
alone who found religions and create great
works of art. The world will never realise
how much it owes to them and what they
have suffered in order to bestow their gifts
on it.
Marcel Proust 1871–1922: *Guermantes Way* (1921)

12 If I am a great man, then all great men are
frauds.
Andrew Bonar Law 1858–1923: Lord Beaverbrook
Politicians and the War (1932)

13 A man does not attain the status of Galileo
merely because he is persecuted; he must
also be right.
Stephen Jay Gould 1941– : *Ever since Darwin* (1977)

Greed see also Money

1 The more you get the more you want.
mid 14th century

2 Much would have more.
*mid 14th century, meaning that the ownership of
substantial possessions creates in the owner the desire
for still more*

3 The sea refuses no river.
*early 17th century, meaning that the sea's capacity is
so great that anyone who chooses may find a place
there*

**4 Where the carcase is, there shall the
eagles be gathered together.**
*mid 16th century, from the Bible (Matthew)
'Wheresoever the carcase is, there will the eagles be
gathered together'; eagles here as the type of carrion
bird*

PHRASES

5 kill the goose that lays the golden eggs
sacrifice long-term advantage to short-
term gain.
*referring to a traditional story, in which the owner of
the goose killed it in the hope of possessing himself of
a store of golden eggs instead of being contented with
a daily ration; see* **Gratitude** 14

QUOTATIONS

6 Greedy for the property of others,
extravagant with his own.
Sallust 86–35 BC: *Catiline*

7   *Quid non mortalia pectora cogis,*
Auri sacra fames!

To what do you not drive human hearts,
cursed craving for gold!
Virgil 70–19 BC: *Aeneid*

8 Whose God is their belly, and whose glory
is in their shame.
Bible: Philippians

9 Bell, book, and candle shall not drive me
back,
When gold and silver becks me to come
on.
William Shakespeare 1564–1616: *King John*
(1591–8); see **The Supernatural** 2

10   What a rare punishment
Is avarice to itself!
Ben Jonson c.1573–1637: *Volpone* (1606)

11 What, if a dear year come or dearth, or
some loss? And were it not that they are
loath to lay out money on a rope, they
would be hanged forthwith, and
sometimes die to save charges.
Robert Burton 1577–1640: *The Anatomy of
Melancholy* (1621–51)

12 £40,000 a year a moderate income—such
a one as a man *might jog on with.*
Lord Durham 1792–1840: letter from Mr Creevey to
Miss Elizabeth Ord, 13 September 1821

13 Please, sir, I want some more.
Charles Dickens 1812–70: *Oliver Twist* (1838)

14 I'll be sick tonight.
*in reply to his mother's warning 'You'll be sick
tomorrow', when stuffing himself with cakes at tea*
Jack Llewelyn-Davies 1894–1959: Andrew Birkin *J.
M. Barrie and the Lost Boys* (1979); Barrie used the
line in *Little Mary* (1903)

15 If all the rich people in the world divided
up their money among themselves there
wouldn't be enough to go round.
Christina Stead 1902–83: *House of All Nations*
(1938)

16 There is enough in the world for
everyone's need, but not enough for
everyone's greed.
Frank Buchman 1878–1961: *Remaking the World*
(1947)

17 But the music that excels is the sound of
oil wells
As they slurp, slurp, slurp into the barrels
. . .
I want an old-fashioned house
With an old-fashioned fence
And an old-fashioned millionaire.
Marve Fisher: 'An Old-Fashioned Girl' (1954 song)

18 Greed is all right . . . Greed is healthy. You
can be greedy and still feel good about
yourself.
Ivan F. Boesky 1937– : commencement address,
Berkeley, California, 18 May 1986

19 Greed—for lack of a better word—is good.
Greed is right. Greed works.
Stanley Weiser and **Oliver Stone** 1946– : *Wall
Street* (1987 film)

Guilt and Innocence

PROVERBS AND SAYINGS

1 **Confess and be hanged.**
*late 16th century, meaning that guilt must be
confessed and the due punishment accepted for true
repentance*

2 **The guilty one always runs.**
American proverb, mid 20th century

3 **We are all guilty.**
*supposedly typical of the liberal view that all members
of society bear responsibility for its wrongs; used
particularly as a catchphrase by the psychiatrist 'Dr
Heinz Kiosk' in the satirical column of 'Peter Simple'
(pseudonym of Michael Wharton)*

4 **We name the guilty men.**
*supposedly now a cliché of investigative journalism;
Guilty Men (1940) was the title of a tract by Michael
Foot, Frank Owen, and Peter Howard, published under*
*the pseudonym of 'Cato', which attacked the
supporters of Munich and the appeasement policy of
Neville Chamberlain*

QUOTATIONS

5 Everyone's quick to blame the alien.
Aeschylus c.525–456 BC: *The Suppliant Maidens*

6 When Pilate saw that he could prevail
nothing . . . he took water, and washed his
hands before the multitude, saying, I am
innocent of the blood of this just person:
see ye to it.
Bible: St Matthew; see **Duty** 5

7 He that is without sin among you, let him
first cast a stone at her.
Bible: St John; see **Criticism** 3

8 Suspicion always haunts the guilty mind;
The thief doth fear each bush an officer.
William Shakespeare 1564–1616: *Henry VI, Part 3*
(1592)

9 Here's the smell of the blood still: all the
perfumes of Arabia will not sweeten this
little hand.
William Shakespeare 1564–1616: *Macbeth* (1606)

10 He that first cries out stop thief, is often he
that has stolen the treasure.
William Congreve 1670–1729: *Love for Love* (1695)

11 It is better that ten guilty persons escape
than one innocent suffer.
William Blackstone 1723–80: *Commentaries on the
Laws of England* (1765)

12 What hangs people . . . is the unfortunate
circumstance of guilt.
Robert Louis Stevenson 1850–94: *The Wrong Box*
(with Lloyd Osbourne, 1889)

13 Of all means to regeneration Remorse is
surely the most wasteful. It cuts away
healthy tissue with the poisoned. It is a
knife that probes far deeper than the evil.
E. M. Forster 1879–1970: *Howards End* (1910)

14 The innocent and the beautiful
Have no enemy but time.
W. B. Yeats 1865–1939: 'In Memory of Eva Gore
Booth and Con Markiewicz' (1933)

15 It is not only our fate but our business to
lose innocence, and once we have lost
that, it is futile to attempt a picnic in Eden.
Elizabeth Bowen 1899–1973: 'Out of a Book' in
Orion III (1946)

16 Innocence always calls mutely for
protection, when we would be so much
wiser to guard ourselves against it:
innocence is like a dumb leper who has
lost his bell, wandering the world meaning
no harm.
Graham Greene 1904–91: *The Quiet American* (1955)

17 True guilt is guilt at the obligation one
owes to oneself to be oneself. False guilt is

guilt felt at not being what other people
feel one ought to be or assume that one is.
R. D. Laing 1927–89: *Self and Others* (1961)

18 To be absolutely honest, what I feel really
bad about is that I don't feel worse. That's
the ineffectual liberal's problem in a
nutshell.
Michael Frayn 1933– : in *Observer* 8 August 1965

19 I love my work and my children. God
Is distant, difficult. Things happen.
Too near the ancient troughs of blood
Innocence is no earthly weapon.
Geoffrey Hill 1932– : 'Ovid in the Third Reich'
(1968)

20 I brought myself down. I gave them a
sword. And they stuck it in.
Richard Nixon 1913–94: television interview, 19
May 1977

21 Guilt feelings so often arise from
accusations rather than from crimes.
Iris Murdoch 1919–99: *The Sea, The Sea* (1978)

22 Good women always think it is their fault
when someone else is being offensive. Bad
women never take the blame for anything.
Anita Brookner 1938– : *Hotel du Lac* (1984)

*to Albert Speer, who having always denied knowledge
of the Holocaust had said that he was at fault in
having 'looked away':*

23 You cannot look away from something
you don't know. If you looked away, then
you knew.
Gitta Sereny 1923– : recalled on BBC2 *Reputations*,
2 May 1996

24 Innocence is a slippery substance. It seems
you can't possess it and at the same time
know you possess it.
Carol Shields 1935– : *Larry's Party* (1997)

25 I note with considerable satisfaction that I
am whiter than white.
of the inquiry into fraud at the European Commission
Jacques Santer 1937– : at a news conference, 16
March 1999

Habit see **Custom and Habit**

Happiness

1 Blessings brighten as they take their flight.

mid 18th century, meaning that it is only when something is lost that one realizes its value

2 Call no man happy till he dies.

mid 16th century; traditionally attributed to the Athenian statesman and poet Solon (c.640–after 556 BC) in the form 'Call no man happy before he dies, he is at best but fortunate'

3 Happiness is what you make of it.

American proverb, mid 19th century

4 It is a poor heart that never rejoices.

mid 19th century, often used to explain a celebratory action, and implying that circumstances are not in general unrelievedly bad

PHRASES

5 the gaiety of nations general gaiety or amusement.

from Samuel Johnson on the death of David Garrick (1779), 'that stroke of death, which has eclipsed the gaiety of nations'

QUOTATIONS

6 The person who is searching for his own happiness should pull out the dart that he has stuck in himself, the arrow-head of grieving, of desiring, of despair.

Pali Tripitaka *c.* 2nd century BC: *Sutta-Nipāta* [*Woven Cadences*] v. 592

7 *Nil admirari prope res est una, Numici,*
Solaque quae possit facere et servare beatum.
To marvel at nothing is just about the one and only thing, Numicius, that can make a man happy and keep him that way.

Horace 65–8 BC: *Epistles*; see 14 below

8 Happiness lies in conquering one's enemies, in driving them in front of oneself, in taking their property, in savouring their despair, in outraging their wives and daughters.

Genghis Khan 1162–1227: Witold Rodzinski *The Walled Kingdom: A History of China* (1979)

9 Certainly there is no happiness within this circle of flesh, nor is it in the optics of these eyes to behold felicity; the first day of our Jubilee is death.

Thomas Browne 1605–82: *Religio Medici* (1643)

10 But headlong joy is ever on the wing.

John Milton 1608–74: 'The Passion' (1645)

11 One is never as unhappy as one thinks, nor as happy as one hopes.

Duc de la Rochefoucauld 1613–80: *Sentences et Maximes de Morale* (1664)

12 For all the happiness mankind can gain
Is not in pleasure, but in rest from pain.

John Dryden 1631–1700: *The Indian Emperor* (1665)

13 Mirth is like a flash of lightning that breaks through a gloom of clouds, and glitters for a moment: cheerfulness keeps up a kind of daylight in the mind, and fills it with a steady and perpetual serenity.

Joseph Addison 1672–1719: in *The Spectator* 17 May 1712

14 Not to admire, is all the art I know,
To make men happy, and to keep them so.

Alexander Pope 1688–1744: *Imitations of Horace*; see 7 above

15 It cannot reasonably be doubted, but a little miss, dressed in a new gown for a dancing-school ball, receives as complete enjoyment as the greatest orator, who triumphs in the splendour of his eloquence, while he governs the passions and resolutions of a numerous assembly.

David Hume 1711–76: *Essays: Moral and Political* (1741-2) 'The Sceptic'

16 That all who are happy, are equally happy, is not true. A peasant and a philosopher may be equally *satisfied*, but not equally *happy*. Happiness consists in the multiplicity of agreeable consciousness.

Samuel Johnson 1709–84: James Boswell *Life of Samuel Johnson* (1791) February 1766

17 If you will allow me, at my age, a reflection that is scarcely ever made at yours, I must say that if one only knew where one's true happiness lay one would never look for it outside the limits prescribed by the law and by religion.

Pierre Choderlos de Laclos 1741–1803: *Les Liaisons dangereuses* (1782)

18 *Freude, schöner Götterfunken,*
Tochter aus Elysium.

Joy, beautiful radiance of the gods, daughter of Elysium.
Friedrich von Schiller 1759–1805: 'An die Freude' (1785)

19 Happiness is not an ideal of reason but of imagination.
Immanuel Kant 1724–1804: *Fundamental Principles of the Metaphysics of Ethics* (1785)

20 A large income is the best recipe for happiness I ever heard of. It certainly may secure all the myrtle and turkey part of it.
Jane Austen 1775–1817: *Mansfield Park* (1814)

21 Happiness is no laughing matter.
Richard Whately 1787–1863: *Apophthegms* (1854)

22 Cheerfulness gives elasticity to the spirit. Spectres fly before it.
Samuel Smiles 1812–1904: *Self-Help* (1859)

23 Ask yourself whether you are happy, and you cease to be so.
John Stuart Mill 1806–73: *Autobiography* (1873)

24 But a lifetime of happiness! No man alive could bear it: it would be hell on earth.
George Bernard Shaw 1856–1950: *Man and Superman* (1903)

25 For if unhappiness develops the forces of the mind, happiness alone is salutary to the body.
Marcel Proust 1871–1922: *Time Regained* (1926)

26 Happiness makes up in height for what it lacks in length.
Robert Frost 1874–1963: title of poem (1942)

27 Point me out the happy man and I will point you out either egotism, selfishness, evil—or else an absolute ignorance.
Graham Greene 1904–91: *The Heart of the Matter* (1948)

28 Happiness is a warm gun.
John Lennon 1940–80: title of song (1968); see **Dogs** 14

29 Happiness is an imaginary condition, formerly often attributed by the living to the dead, now usually attributed by adults to children, and by children to adults.
Thomas Szasz 1920– : *The Second Sin* (1973)

30 Happiness writes white.
Philip Larkin 1922–85: in conversation with Andrew Motion; in *Independent* 11 October 1999

31 I always say I don't think everyone has the right to happiness or to be loved. Even the Americans have written into their constitution that you have the right to the 'pursuit of happiness'. You have the right to try but that is all.
Claire Rayner 1931– : G. Kinnock and F. Miller (eds.) *By Faith and Daring* (1993); see **Human Rights** 6

Haste and Delay

PROVERBS AND SAYINGS

1 Always in a hurry, always behind.
North American proverb, mid 20th century

2 Delays are dangerous.
late 16th century, used as a warning against procrastination

3 Don't hurry—start early.
American proverb, mid 20th century

4 Haste is from the Devil.
mid 17th century, often used to mean that undue haste results in work being done badly or carelessly

5 Haste makes waste.
late 14th century, meaning that hurried work is likely to be wasteful

6 Make haste slowly.
late 16th century, advising a course of careful preparation; see 13 below

7 More haste, less speed.
mid 14th century, speed here meant originally success rather than swiftness, and the meaning is that hurried work is likely to be less successful

8 Never put off till tomorrow what you can do today.
late 14th century

9 Procrastination is the thief of time.
mid 18th century, meaning that someone who continually puts things off ultimately achieves little; from Edward Young Night Thoughts (1742–5)

PHRASES

10 at the eleventh hour at the latest possible moment.
with reference to the story in the Bible (Matthew) of the labourers who were hired 'about the eleventh hour' to work in the vineyard, and who were given the same payment as those who had worked all day

11 Why tarry the wheels of his chariots?
Bible: Judges

12 He always hurries to the main event and whisks his audience into the middle of things as though they knew already.
Horace 65–8 BC: *Ars Poetica*

13 *Festina lente.*
Make haste slowly.
Augustus 63 BC–AD 14: Suetonius *Lives of the Caesars* 'Divus Augustus'; see 6 above

14 I'll put a girdle round about the earth
In forty minutes.
William Shakespeare 1564–1616: *A Midsummer Night's Dream* (1595–6)

15 I knew a wise man that had it for a by-word, when he saw men hasten to a conclusion. 'Stay a little, that we may make an end the sooner.'
Francis Bacon 1561–1626: *Essays* (1625) 'Of Dispatch'

16 I have protracted my work till most of those whom I wished to please have sunk into the grave; and success and miscarriage are empty sounds.
Samuel Johnson 1709–84: James Boswell *Life of Samuel Johnson* (1791) 1755

17 Though I am always in haste, I am never in a hurry.
John Wesley 1703–91: letter to Miss March, 10 December 1777

18 No admittance till the week after next!
Lewis Carroll 1832–98: *Through the Looking-Glass* (1872)

19 Hesitating doesn't matter if only you win out.
Bertolt Brecht 1898–1956: *The Good Woman of Setzuan* (1938)

20 He gave her a bright fake smile; so much of life was a putting-off of unhappiness for another time. Nothing was ever lost by delay.
Graham Greene 1904–91: *The Heart of the Matter* (1948)

21 ESTRAGON: Charming spot. Inspiring prospects. Let's go.
VLADIMIR: We can't.
ESTRAGON: Why not?
VLADIMIR: We're waiting for Godot.
Samuel Beckett 1906–89: *Waiting for Godot* (1955)

22 If anyone believes that our smiles involve abandonment of the teaching of Marx, Engels and Lenin he deceives himself. Those who wait for that must wait until a shrimp learns to whistle.
Nikita Khrushchev 1894–1971: speech in Moscow, 17 September 1955

23 I think we ought to let him hang there. Let him twist slowly, slowly in the wind.
of Patrick Gray, regarding his nomination as director of the FBI, in a telephone conversation with John Dean
John Ehrlichman 1925–99: in *Washington Post* 27 July 1973

24 I never run for the bus.
Linford Christie 1960– : in *Independent* 19 May 1999

Hatred see also Enemies

1 **Better a dinner of herbs than a stalled ox where hate is.**
mid 16th century, meaning that simple food accompanied by goodwill and affection is preferable to luxury in an atmosphere of ill-will; see 3 below

2 **Curses, like chickens, come home to roost.**
late 14th century, meaning that ill will directed at another is likely to rebound on the originator

3 Better is a dinner of herbs where love is, than a stalled ox and hatred therewith.
Bible: Proverbs; see 1 above

4 For hate is not conquered by hate: hate is conquered by love. This is a law eternal.
Pali Tripitaka *c.* 2nd century BC: *Dhammapada* v. 5

5 I have loved him too much not to feel any hatred for him.
Jean Racine 1639–99: *Andromaque* (1667)

6 Now hatred is by far the longest pleasure;
Men love in haste, but they detest at leisure.
Lord Byron 1788–1824: *Don Juan* (1819–24)

7 The dupe of friendship, and the fool of love; have I not reason to hate and to despise myself? Indeed I do; and chiefly for

not having hated and despised the world enough.
William Hazlitt 1778–1830: *The Plain Speaker* (1826) 'On the Pleasure of Hating'

8 Gr-r-r—there go, my heart's abhorrence!
Water your damned flower-pots, do!
If hate killed men, Brother Lawrence,
God's blood, would not mine kill you!
Robert Browning 1812–89: 'Soliloquy of the Spanish Cloister' (1842)

9 Dante, who loved well because he hated,
Hated wickedness that hinders loving.
Robert Browning 1812–89: 'One Word More' (1855)

10 I tell you there is such a thing as creative hate!
Willa Cather 1873–1947: *The Song of the Lark* (1915)

11 If you hate a person, you hate something in him that is part of yourself. What isn't part of ourselves doesn't disturb us.
Hermann Hesse 1877–1962: *Demian* (1919)

12 Any kiddie in school can love like a fool,
But hating, my boy, is an art.
Ogden Nash 1902–71: 'Plea for Less Malice Toward None' (1933)

13 One cannot overestimate the power of a good rancorous hatred on the part of the *stupid*. The stupid have so much more industry and energy to expend on hating. They build it up like coral insects.
Sylvia Townsend Warner 1893–1978: diary 26 September 1954

14 I never hated a man enough to give him diamonds back.
Zsa Zsa Gabor 1919– : in *Observer* 25 August 1957

15 Always give your best, never get discouraged, never be petty; always remember, others may hate you. Those who hate you don't win unless you hate them. And then you destroy yourself.
address to members of his staff on leaving office after his resignation
Richard Nixon 1913–94: on 9 August 1974

16 Hating gets going, it goes round, it gets older and tighter and older and tighter, until it holds a person inside it like a fist holds a stick.
Ursula K. Le Guin 1929– : *Always Coming Home* (1985)

17 Lets face it:
it knows how to make beauty.
The splendid fire-glow in midnight skies.
Magnificent bursting bombs in rosy dawns.
Wislawa Szymborska 1923– : 'Hatred' (1993)

18 No one is born hating another person because of the colour of his skin, or his background, or his religion. People must learn to hate, and if they can learn to hate, they can be taught to love, for love comes more naturally to the human heart than its opposite.
Nelson Mandela 1918– : *Long Walk to Freedom* (1994)

Health and Fitness

PROVERBS AND SAYINGS

1 **An apple a day keeps the doctor away.**
mid 19th century, meaning that eating an apple each day keeps one healthy

2 **Don't die of ignorance.**
Aids publicity campaign, 1987

3 **Drinka Pinta Milka Day.**
advertising slogan for National Dairy Council, 1958; coined by Bertrand Whitehead

4 **Early to bed and early to rise, makes a man healthy, wealthy, and wise.**
*late 15th century, linking a healthy and sober lifestyle with material success; see **Sleep** 17*

5 **Even your closest friends won't tell you.**
advertising slogan for Listerine mouthwash, US, 1923

6 **I was a seven-stone weakling.**
advertising slogan for Charles Atlas body-building, originally in US

7 **More die of food than famine.**
American proverb, mid 20th century

8 **Slip, slop, slap.**
sun protection slogan, meaning slip on a T-shirt, slop on some suncream, slap on a hat; Australian health education programme, 1980s

9 **There is nothing so good for the inside of a man as the outside of a horse.**
early 20th century, recommending the healthful effects of horse-riding

10 **Those who do not find time for exercise will have to find time for illness.**
traditional saying

11 Life's not just being alive, but being well.
Martial AD c.40–c.104: *Epigrammata*

12 *Orandum est ut sit mens sana in corpore sano.*
You should pray to have a sound mind in a sound body.
Juvenal AD c.60–c.130: *Satires*

13 Look to your health; and if you have it, praise God, and value it next to a good conscience; for health is the second blessing that we mortals are capable of; a blessing that money cannot buy.
Izaak Walton 1593–1683: *The Compleat Angler* (1653)

14 The wise, for cure, on exercise depend; God never made his work for man to mend.
John Dryden 1631–1700: Epistle 'To my honoured kinsman John Driden' (1700)

15 The sovereign invigorator of the body is exercise, and of all the exercises, walking is best.
Thomas Jefferson 1743–1826: letter to Thomas Mann Randolph Jr., 27 August 1786

16 To get back my youth I would do anything in the world, except take exercise, get up early, or be respectable.
Oscar Wilde 1854–1900: *The Picture of Dorian Grey* (1891)

17 Exercise is bunk. If you are healthy, you don't need it: if you are sick you shouldn't take it.
Henry Ford 1863–1947: attributed

18 I sometimes think that running has given me a glimpse of the greatest freedom a man can ever know, because it results in the simultaneous liberation of both body and mind.
Roger Bannister 1929– : *First Four Minutes* (1955)

19 Therapy has become what I think of as the tenth American muse.
Jacob Bronowski 1908–74: attributed

20 Exercise is the yuppie version of bulimia.
Barbara Ehrenreich 1941– : *The Worst Years of Our Lives* (1991) 'Food Worship'

21 The first law of dietetics seems to be: if it tastes good, it's bad for you.
Isaac Asimov 1920–92: attributed

22 In the face of such overwhelming statistical possibilities, hypochondria has always seemed to me to be the only rational position to take on life.
John Diamond: *C: Because Cowards Get Cancer Too* (1998)

23 The only exercise I take is walking behind the coffins of friends who took exercise.
Peter O'Toole 1932– : in *Mail on Sunday* 27 December 1998

Heaven and Hell

1 Hell is wherever heaven is not.
late 16th century

2 Abraham's bosom heaven, the place of rest for the souls of the blessed.
Abraham *the Hebrew patriarch from whom all Jews trace their descent; from the Bible (Luke) 'And it came to pass, that the beggar died, and was carried by the angels into Abraham's bosom'*

3 fire and brimstone torment in hell.
deriving from biblical allusion, as in Revelation 'These both were cast alive into a lake of fire burning with brimstone'

4 the happy hunting-grounds among Native Americans, a fabled country full of game to which warriors go after death.

5 Land of Beulah heaven.
from John Bunyan's Pilgrim's Progress, *where the Land of Beulah is a pleasant and fertile country beyond the Valley of the Shadow of Death, and within sight of the Heavenly City*

6 New Jerusalem the abode of the blessed in heaven.
from the Bible (Revelation) 'And I, John, saw the holy city, new Jerusalem, coming down from God out of heaven'

7 But the children of the kingdom shall be cast out into outer darkness: there shall be weeping and gnashing of teeth.
Bible: St Matthew

8 And I saw a new heaven and a new earth: for the first heaven and the first earth were

passed away; and there was no more sea.
Bible: Revelation

9 PER ME SI VA NELLA CITTÀ DOLENTE,
PER ME SI VA NELL' ETERNO DOLORE,
PER ME SI VA TRA LA PERDUTA GENTE . . .
LASCIATE OGNI SPERANZA VOI CH'ENTRATE!

Through me is the way to the sorrowful
city. Through me is the way to eternal
suffering. Through me is the way to join
the lost people . . . Abandon all hope, you
who enter!
*inscription at the entrance to Hell; the final sentence
now often quoted as 'Abandon hope, all ye who enter
here'*
Dante Alighieri 1265–1321: *Divina Commedia*
'Inferno'

10 Why, this is hell, nor am I out of it:
Thinkst thou that I who saw the face of
God,
And tasted the eternal joys of heaven,
Am not tormented with ten thousand hells
In being deprived of everlasting bliss!
Christopher Marlowe 1564–93: *Doctor Faustus*
(1604)

11 So all we know
Of what they do above,
Is that they happy are, and that they love.
Edmund Waller 1606–87: 'Upon the Death of My
Lady Rich' (1645)

12 Were the happiness of the next world as
closely apprehended as the felicities of this,
it were a martyrdom to live.
Thomas Browne 1605–82: *Hydriotaphia* (Urn Burial,
1658)

13 He ascended into heaven, And sitteth on
the right hand of God the Father
Almighty; From thence he shall come to
judge the quick and the dead.
quick = an archaic term for those who are living
The Book of Common Prayer 1662: *Morning Prayer*
The Apostles' Creed; see **Transport** 16

14 Me miserable! which way shall I fly
Infinite wrath, and infinite despair?
Which way I fly is hell; myself am hell.
John Milton 1608–74: *Paradise Lost* (1667)

15 My idea of heaven is, eating *pâté de foie
gras* to the sound of trumpets.
the view of Smith's friend Henry Luttrell
Sydney Smith 1771–1845: H. Pearson *The Smith of
Smiths* (1934)

16 I will spend my heaven doing good on
earth.
St Teresa of Lisieux 1873–97: T. N. Taylor (ed.) *Soeur
Thérèse of Lisieux* (1912)

17 He has the look of a man who has been in
hell and seen there, not a hopeless
suffering, but meanness and frippery.
on Dostoevsky
W. Somerset Maugham 1874–1965: *A Writer's
Notebook* (1949) written in 1917

18 The true paradises are the paradises that
we have lost.
Marcel Proust 1871–1922: *Time Regained* (1926)

19 Hell, madam, is to love no more.
Georges Bernanos 1888–1948: *Journal d'un curé de
campagne* (1936)

20 Whose love is given over-well
Shall look on Helen's face in hell
Whilst they whose love is thin and wise
Shall see John Knox in Paradise.
Dorothy Parker 1893–1967: 'Partial Comfort' (1937)

21 Hell is other people.
Jean-Paul Sartre 1905–80: *Huis Clos* (1944)

22 What is hell?
Hell is oneself,
Hell is alone, the other figures in it
Merely projections.
T. S. Eliot 1888–1965: *The Cocktail Party* (1950)

23 We are not bound for ever to the circles of
the world, and beyond them is more than
memory.
J. R. R. Tolkien 1892–1973: *The Lord of the Rings* pt.
3 *The Return of the King* (1955)

24 We may be surprised at the people we find
in heaven. God has a soft spot for sinners.
His standards are quite low.
Desmond Tutu 1931– : in *Sunday Times* 15 April
2001

Heroes

1 Better to have lived one day as a tiger than a thousand years as a sheep.
modern saying; see 7 below

PHRASES

2 the Age of Chivalry the time when men behave with courage, honour, and courtesy.
the period during which the knightly social and ethical system prevailed

3 knight in shining armour a chivalrous rescuer or helper, especially of a woman.

QUOTATIONS

4 Cattle die, kinsmen die,
the self must also die;
but glory never dies,
for the man who is able to achieve it.
Anonymous: *Hávamál* ('Sayings of the High One'), c.10th century

5 No man is a hero to his valet.
Mme Cornuel 1605–94: *Lettres de Mlle Aïssé à Madame C* (1787) Letter 13 'De Paris, 1728'; see 9 below; **Familiarity** 9

6 See, the conquering hero comes!
Sound the trumpets, beat the drums!
Thomas Morell 1703–84: *Judas Maccabeus* (1747)

7 In this world I would rather live two days like a tiger, than two hundred years like a sheep.
Tipu Sultan c.1750–99: Alexander Beatson *A View of the Origin and Conduct of the War with Tippoo Sultaun* (1800); see 1 above

8 So faithful in love, and so dauntless in war,
There never was knight like the young Lochinvar.
Sir Walter Scott 1771–1832: *Marmion* (1808) 'Lochinvar'

9 In short, he was a perfect cavaliero,
And to his very valet seemed a hero.
Lord Byron 1788–1824: *Beppo* (1818); see 5 above

10 Every hero becomes a bore at last.
Ralph Waldo Emerson 1803–82: *Representative Men* (1850)

11 Hero-worship is strongest where there is least regard for human freedom.
Herbert Spencer 1820–1903: *Social Statics* (1850)

12 Men reject their prophets and slay them, but they love their martyrs and honour those whom they have slain.
Fedor Dostoevsky 1821–81: *The Brothers Karamazov* (1879–80)

13 Heroing is one of the shortest-lived professions there is.
Will Rogers 1879–1935: newspaper article, 15 February 1925

14 Go to Spain and get killed. The movement needs a Byron.
on being asked by Stephen Spender in the 1930s how best a poet could serve the Communist cause
Harry Pollitt 1890–1960: Frank Johnson *Out of Order* (1982); attributed, perhaps apocryphal

15 ANDREA: Unhappy the land that has no heroes! . . .
GALILEO: No. Unhappy the land that needs heroes.
Bertolt Brecht 1898–1956: *The Life of Galileo* (1939)

16 Show me a hero and I will write you a tragedy.
F. Scott Fitzgerald 1896–1940: Edmund Wilson (ed.) *The Crack-Up* (1945) 'Note-Books E'

17 Faster than a speeding bullet! . . . Look! Up in the sky! It's a bird! It's a plane! It's Superman! Yes, it's Superman! Strange visitor from another planet . . . Who can change the course of mighty rivers, bend steel with his bare hands, and who—disguised as Clark Kent, mild-mannered reporter for a great metropolitan newspaper—fights a never ending battle for truth, justice and the American way!
Anonymous: *Superman* (US radio show, 1940 onwards)

18 If the myth gets bigger than the man, print the myth.
Dorothy Johnson 1905–84: *Indian Country* (1953) 'The Man Who Shot Liberty Valance'; see also **Journalism** 23

19 It was involuntary. They sank my boat.
on being asked how he became a war hero
John F. Kennedy 1917–63: Arthur M. Schlesinger Jr. *A Thousand Days* (1965)

20 In such a regime, I say, you died a good death if your life had inspired someone to come forward and shoot your murderer in the chest—without asking to be paid.
Chinua Achebe 1930- : *A Man of the People* (1966)

21 If I'm such a legend, then why am I so lonely? If I'm a legend, then why do I sit at home for hours staring at the damned phone?
Judy Garland 1922–69: John Gruen *Close-Up* (1968)

22 Ultimately a hero is a man who would argue with the Gods, and so awakens devils to contest his vision.
Norman Mailer 1923- : *The Presidential Papers* (1976)

History

PROVERBS AND SAYINGS

1 Happy is the country which has no history.
early 19th century, meaning that memorable events are likely to be unhappy and disruptive; see 10 below

2 History is a fable agreed upon.
American proverb, mid 20th century

3 History is fiction with the truth left out.
American proverb, mid 20th century

4 History repeats itself.
mid 19th century; see 15, 27, 19 below

PHRASES

5 the Father of History Herodotus (5th century BC), Greek historian.
the first historian to collect materials systematically, test their accuracy to a certain extent, and arrange them in a well-constructed and vivid narrative

6 Whig historian a historian who interprets history as the continuing and inevitable victory of progress over reaction.

QUOTATIONS

7 History is philosophy from examples.
Dionysius of Halicarnassus fl. 30–7 BC: *Ars Rhetorica*

8 If history records good things of good men, the thoughtful hearer is encouraged to imitate what is good.
The Venerable Bede AD 673–735: *Ecclesiastical History of the English People*

9 Whosoever, in writing a modern history, shall follow truth too near the heels, it may happily strike out his teeth.
Walter Ralegh c.1552–1618: *The History of the World* (1614)

10 Happy the people whose annals are blank in history-books!
Montesquieu 1689–1755: attributed to Montesquieu by Thomas Carlyle *History of Frederick the Great*; see 1 above

11 History . . . is, indeed, little more than the register of the crimes, follies, and misfortunes of mankind.
Edward Gibbon 1737–94: *The Decline and Fall of the Roman Empire* (1776–88)

12 What experience and history teach is this—that nations and governments have never learned anything from history, or acted upon any lessons they might have drawn from it.
G. W. F. Hegel 1770–1831: *Lectures on the Philosophy of World History: Introduction* (1830); see 15 below

13 History [is] a distillation of rumour.
Thomas Carlyle 1795–1881: *History of the French Revolution* (1837)

14 History is the essence of innumerable biographies.
Thomas Carlyle 1795–1881: *Critical and Miscellaneous Essays* (1838) 'On History'

15 Hegel says somewhere that all great events and personalities in world history reappear in one fashion or another. He forgot to add: the first time as tragedy, the second as farce.
Karl Marx 1818–83: *The Eighteenth Brumaire of Louis Bonaparte* (1852); see 4, 12 above, 27 below

16 History is a gallery of pictures in which there are few originals and many copies.
Alexis de Tocqueville 1805–59: *L'Ancien régime* (1856)

17 History is past politics, and politics is present history.
E. A. Freeman 1823–92: *Methods of Historical Study* (1886)

18 It has been said that though God cannot alter the past, historians can; it is perhaps because they can be useful to Him in this respect that He tolerates their existence.
Samuel Butler 1835–1902: *Erewhon Revisited* (1901); see **The Past** 16

19 History repeats itself; historians repeat one another.

Rupert Brooke 1887–1915: letter to Geoffrey Keynes, 4 June 1906; see 4 above

20 History is more or less bunk.

Henry Ford 1863–1947: interview with Charles N. Wheeler in *Chicago Tribune* 25 May 1916

21 Human history becomes more and more a race between education and catastrophe.

H. G. Wells 1866–1946: *The Outline of History* (1920)

22 History is not what you thought. *It is what you can remember.*

W. C. Sellar 1898–1951 and **R. J. Yeatman** 1898–1968: *1066 and All That* (1930)

23 And even I can remember
A day when the historians left blanks in their writings,
I mean for things they didn't know.

Ezra Pound 1885–1972: *Draft of XXX Cantos* (1930)

24 A people without history
Is not redeemed from time, for history is a pattern
Of timeless moments. So, while the light fails
On a winter's afternoon, in a secluded chapel

History is now and England.

T. S. Eliot 1888–1965: *Four Quartets* 'Little Gidding' (1942)

25 History gets thicker as it approaches recent times.

A. J. P. Taylor 1906–90: *English History 1914–45* (1965) bibliography

26 History, like wood, has a grain in it which determines how it splits; and those in authority, besides trying to shape and direct events, sometimes find it more convenient just to let them happen.

Malcolm Muggeridge 1903–90: *The Infernal Grove* (1975)

27 Does history repeat itself, the first time as tragedy, the second time as farce? No, that's too grand, too considered a process. History just burps, and we taste again that raw-onion sandwich it swallowed centuries ago.

Julian Barnes 1946– : *A History of the World in 10½ Chapters* (1989); see 4, 15 above

28 What we may be witnessing is not just the end of the Cold War but the end of history as such: that is, the end point of man's ideological evolution and the universalism of Western liberal democracy.

Francis Fukuyama 1952– : in *Independent* 20 September 1989

The Home see also Housework

PROVERBS AND SAYINGS

1 East, west, home's best.

mid 19th century

2 An Englishman's home is his castle.

late 16th century, meaning that a person has the right to refuse entry to his home; reflecting a legal principle, as formulated by the English jurist Edward Coke (1552–1634) 'For a man's house is his castle, et domus sua cuique est tutissimum refugium [and each man's home is his safest refuge]'

3 Every cock will crow upon his own dunghill.

mid 13th century, meaning that everyone is confident and at ease on their home ground

4 Home is home though it's never so homely.

mid 16th century, meaning that no place can compare with one's own home

5 Home is where the heart is.

late 19th century, meaning that one's true home is wherever the person one loves most is

6 Home is where the mortgage is.

American proverb, mid 20th century

7 There's no place like home.

late 16th century; the saying is found earlier in Greek, in the work of the Greek poet Hesiod (c.700 BC); see 14 below

PHRASES

8 fire and flet fire and houseroom.

*flet a dwelling, a house; see **Death** 9*

9 lares and penates the home.

Latin lares the protective gods of the household worshipped in ancient Rome; penates the protective gods of the household, especially the storeroom

10 The foxes have holes, and the birds of the air have nests; but the Son of man hath not where to lay his head.
Bible: St Matthew

11 The accent of one's birthplace lingers in the mind and in the heart as it does in one's speech.
Duc de la Rochefoucauld 1613–80: *Maximes* (1678)

12 I am returned to my own Lares and Penates—to my dogs and cats.
Horace Walpole 1717–97: letter to Rev. William Mason, 25 October 1775; see 9 above

13 Show me a man who cares no more for one place than another, and I will show you in that same person one who loves nothing but himself. Beware of those who are homeless by choice.
Robert Southey 1774–1843: *The Doctor* (1812)

14 Mid pleasures and palaces though we may roam,
Be it ever so humble, there's no place like home.
J. H. Payne 1791–1852: *Clari, or, The Maid of Milan* (1823 opera) 'Home, Sweet Home'; see 7 above

15 What's the good of a home if you are never in it?
George and Weedon Grossmith 1847–1912, 1854–1919: *The Diary of a Nobody* (1894)

16 Any old place I can hang my hat is home sweet home to me.
William Jerome 1865–1932: title of song (1901)

17 Home is the girl's prison and the woman's workhouse.
George Bernard Shaw 1856–1950: *Man and Superman* (1903) 'Maxims: Women in the Home'

18 We make our friends, we make our enemies; but God makes our next-door neighbour.
G. K. Chesterton 1874–1936: *Heretics* (1905)

19 'Home is the place where, when you have to go there,
They have to take you in.'
'I should have called it
Something you somehow haven't to deserve.'
Robert Frost 1874–1963: 'The Death of the Hired Man' (1914)

20   The best
Thing we can do is to make wherever we're lost in
Look as much like home as we can.
Christopher Fry 1907– : *The Lady's not for Burning* (1949)

21 Home is where you come to when you have nothing better to do.
Margaret Thatcher 1925– : in *Vanity Fair* May 1991

Honesty see also **Deception, Lies, Truth**

1 **Children and fools tell the truth.**
mid 16th century, implying that they lack the cunning to see possible danger; tradition sometimes adds drunkards

2 **Confession is good for the soul.**
mid 17th century, meaning that confession is essential to repentance and forgiveness

3 **Honesty is more praised than practised.**
American proverb, mid 20th century, meaning that it is easier to advise another person to be honest than to be honest oneself

4 **Honesty is the best policy.**
early 17th century, meaning that as well as being right, to be honest may also achieve a more successful outcome; see 10 below

5 **It's a sin to steal a pin.**
late 19th century; meaning that even if what is stolen is of little value, the action is still wrong

6 **Sell honestly, but not honesty.**
American proverb, mid 20th century; a play on words meaning that honesty is the essential virtue in commerce

7 Honesty is praised and left to shiver.
Juvenal AD c.60–c.130: *Satires*

8 And those who paint 'em truest praise 'em most.
Joseph Addison 1672–1719: *The Campaign* (1705)

9 'But the Emperor has nothing on at all!' cried a little child.
Hans Christian Andersen 1805–75: *Danish Fairy Legends and Tales* (1846) 'The Emperor's New Clothes'

10 Honesty is the best policy; but he who is governed by that maxim is not an honest man.
Richard Whately 1787–1863: *Apophthegms* (1854); see 4 above

11 The louder he talked of his honour, the faster we counted our spoons.
Ralph Waldo Emerson 1803–82: *The Conduct of Life* (1860)

12 A little sincerity is a dangerous thing, and a great deal of it is absolutely fatal.
Oscar Wilde 1854–1900: *Intentions* (1891)

13 honesty is a good
thing but
it is not profitable to
its possessor
unless it is
kept under control.
Don Marquis 1878–1937: *archys life of mehitabel* (1933)

14 This is hard to answer, so I'll tell the truth.
David Ben-Gurion 1886–1973: at the Zionist Actions Committee session, London, 14 August 1945

15 Always be sincere, even if you don't mean it.
Harry S. Truman 1884–1972: attributed

16 I write the truth and it kills me.
Sarah Kane 1971–99: *Crave* (1998)

17 We need to separate fact from fiction, substance from soundbite, information from innuendo; the public, the electorate, the people who sent us here deserve more than to be spoonfed a cocktail of headline grabbing feelgood stories. They deserve the truth; every member of this house, whether backbencher or minister, has the obligation, the duty, to provide it.
John Major 1943– : in *Guardian* 13 March 2001

Hope see also **Despair, Optimism and Pessimism**

PROVERBS AND SAYINGS

1 A drowning man will clutch at a straw.
mid 16th century, meaning that when hope is slipping away one grasps at the slightest chance

2 He that lives in hope dances to an ill tune.
late 16th century, meaning that hoping for something better may constrain one's freedom of action

3 Hope deferred makes the heart sick.
late 14th century, implying that it is worse to have had one's hopes raised and then dashed, than to have been resigned to not having something; from the Bible: see 9 below

4 Hope is a good breakfast but a bad supper.
mid 17th century, meaning that while it is pleasant to begin something in a hopeful mood, the hopes need to have been fulfilled by the time it ends

5 Hope springs eternal.
mid 18th century, from Pope: see 13 below

6 If it were not for hope, the heart would break.
mid 13th century, referring to the role of hope in warding off complete despair

7 It is better to travel hopefully than to arrive.
*late 19th century, often with the implication that something long sought may be disappointing when achieved; from Stevenson: see **Travel** 28*

8 While there's life there's hope.
mid 16th century, often used as encouragement not to despair in an unpromising situation

QUOTATIONS

9 Hope deferred maketh the heart sick: but when the desire cometh, it is a tree of life.
Bible: Proverbs; see 3 above

10 *Nil desperandum.*
Never despair.
Horace 65–8 BC: *Odes*

11 Who would have thought my shrivelled heart
Could have recovered greenness?
George Herbert 1593–1633: 'The Flower' (1633)

12 I can endure my own despair,
But not another's hope.
William Walsh 1663–1708: 'Song: Of All the Torments'

13 Hope springs eternal in the human breast: Man never Is, but always To be blest.
Alexander Pope 1688–1744: *An Essay on Man* Epistle 1 (1733); see 5 above

14 He that lives upon hope will die fasting.
Benjamin Franklin 1706–90: *Poor Richard's Almanac* (1758)

15 What is hope? nothing but the paint on
the face of Existence; the least touch of
truth rubs it off, and then we see what a
hollow-cheeked harlot we have got hold of.
Lord Byron 1788–1824: letter to Thomas Moore, 28
October 1815

16   O, Wind,
If Winter comes, can Spring be far behind?
Percy Bysshe Shelley 1792–1822: 'Ode to the West
Wind' (1819)

17 Providence has given human wisdom the
choice between two fates: either hope and
agitation, or hopelessness and calm.
Yevgeny Baratynsky 1800–44: 'Two Fates' (1823)

18 Work without hope draws nectar in a
sieve,
And hope without an object cannot live.
Samuel Taylor Coleridge 1772–1834: 'Work
without Hope' (1828)

19 If hopes were dupes, fears may be liars.
Arthur Hugh Clough 1819–61: 'Say not the
struggle naught availeth' (1855)

20 He who has never hoped can never
despair.
George Bernard Shaw 1856–1950: *Caesar and
Cleopatra* (1901)

21 After all, tomorrow is another day.
Margaret Mitchell 1900–49: *Gone with the Wind*
(1936); see **The Future** 5

22 Walk on, walk on, with hope in your
heart,
And you'll never walk alone.
Oscar Hammerstein II 1895–1960: 'You'll Never
Walk Alone' (1945 song)

23 Hope sleeps in our bones like a bear
waiting for spring to rise and walk.
Marge Piercy 1936– : 'Stone, Paper, Knife' (1983)

24 Hope is definitely not the same thing as
optimism. It is not the conviction that
something will turn out well, but the
certainty that something makes sense,
regardless of how it turns out.
Václav Havel 1936– : *Disturbing the Peace* (1986)

Hospitality see **Entertaining and Hospitality**

Housework see also **The Home**

1 **He that will thrive must first ask his wife.**
*late 15th century, meaning that the husband's
material welfare depends on the way in which his wife
manages the household*

2 **It beats as it sweeps as it cleans.**
advertising slogan for Hoover vacuum cleaners, 1919

3 **Persil washes whiter—and it shows.**
advertising slogan for Persil washing powder, 1970s

4 **They that wash on Monday
Have all the week to dry;
They that wash on Tuesday
Are not so much awry;
They that wash on Wednesday
Are not so much to blame;
They that wash on Thursday
Wash for very shame;
They that wash on Friday
Wash in sorry need;
And they that wash on Saturday,
Are lazy folk indeed.**
traditional rhyme

5 **A woman's work is never done.**
*late 16th century, reflecting the traditional
responsibilities of the housewife*

QUOTATIONS

6 There is scarcely any less bother in the
running of a family than in that of an
entire state. And domestic business is no
less importunate for being less important.
Montaigne 1533–92: *Essais* (1580)

7 God walks among the pots and pans.
St Teresa of Ávila 1512–82: *Book of the Foundations*
(1610)

8 Here lies a poor woman who always was
tired,
For she lived in a place where help wasn't
hired.
Her last words on earth were, Dear friends
I am going
Where washing ain't done nor sweeping
nor sewing,
And everything there is exact to my
wishes,

For there they don't eat and there's no
  washing of dishes . . .
Don't mourn for me now, don't mourn for
  me never,
For I'm going to do nothing for ever and
  ever.
Anonymous: epitaph in Bushey churchyard, before
1860; destroyed by 1916

9 Hatred of domestic work is a natural and
admirable result of civilization.
Rebecca West 1892–1983: in *The Freewoman* 6 June
1912

10 The dust comes secretly day after day,
Lies on my ledge and dulls my shining
  things.
But O this dust that I shall drive away
Is flowers and Kings,
Is Solomon's temple, poets, Nineveh.
Viola Meynell 1886–1956: 'Dusting' (1919)

11 Few tasks are more like the torture of
Sisyphus than housework, with its endless
repetition . . . The housewife wears herself
out marking time: she makes nothing,
simply perpetuates the present.
Simone de Beauvoir 1908–86: *The Second Sex*
(1949)

12 MR PRITCHARD: I must dust the blinds and
  then I must raise them.
MRS OGMORE-PRITCHARD: And before you let
  the sun in, mind it wipes its shoes.
Dylan Thomas 1914–53: *Under Milk Wood* (1954)

13 There was no need to do any housework at
all. After the first four years the dirt
doesn't get any worse.
Quentin Crisp 1908–99: *The Naked Civil Servant*
(1968)

14 Conran's Law of Housework—it expands
to fill the time available plus half an hour.
Shirley Conran 1932– : *Superwoman 2* (1977)

15 'I hate discussions of feminism that end up
with who does the dishes,' she said. So do
I. But at the end, there are always the
damned dishes.
Marilyn French 1929– : *The Women's Room* (1977)

16 How often does a house need to be
cleaned, anyway? As a general rule, once
every girlfriend.
P. J. O'Rourke 1947– : *The Bachelor Home
Companion* (1987)

Human Nature see also Behaviour, Character

PROVERBS AND SAYINGS

1 The best of men are but men at best.
*late 17th century, meaning that even someone of great
moral worth is still human and fallible*

2 Man is a wolf to man.
mid 16th century, from Plautus: see 7 below

3 There's nowt so queer as folk.
early 20th century

4 Young saint, old devil.
*early 15th century; meaning that unnaturally good
and moral behaviour at an early age is likely to
change in later life*

PHRASES

5 the old Adam unregenerate human nature
*fallen man as contrasted with the second Adam, Jesus
Christ; see 11 below; Christian Church 11*

QUOTATIONS

6 By nature men are alike. Through practice
they have become far apart.
Confucius 551–479 BC: *Analects*

7 A man is a wolf rather than a man to
another man, when he hasn't yet found
out what he's like.
Plautus c.250–184 BC: *Asinaria*; see 2 above

8 It is part of human nature to hate the man
you have hurt.
Tacitus AD c.56–after 117: *Agricola*

9 One touch of nature makes the whole
  world kin.
William Shakespeare 1564–1616: *Troilus and
Cressida* (1602)

10 God and the doctor we alike adore
But only when in danger, not before;
The danger o'er, both are alike requited,
God is forgotten, and the Doctor slighted.
John Owen c.1563–1622: *Epigrams*; see **Danger** 24

11 O merciful God, grant that the old Adam in
this Child may be so buried, that the new
man may be raised up in him.
The Book of Common Prayer 1662: *Public Baptism
of Infants*; see 5 above

12 On ev'ry hand it will allow'd be,

He's just—nae better than he shou'd be.
Robert Burns 1759-96: 'A Dedication to G[avin]
H[amilton]' (1786)

13 Subdue your appetites my dears, and
you've conquered human natur.
Charles Dickens 1812-70: *Nicholas Nickleby* (1839)

14 But good God, people don't do such things!
Henrik Ibsen 1828-1906: *Hedda Gabler* (1890)

15 Adam was but human—this explains it all.
He did not want the apple for the apple's
sake; he wanted it only because it was
forbidden.
Mark Twain 1835-1910: *Pudd'nhead Wilson* (1894)

16 The natural man has only two primal
passions, to get and beget.
William Osler 1849-1919: *Science and Immortality*
(1904)

17 The terrorist and the policeman both come
from the same basket.
Joseph Conrad 1857-1924: *The Secret Agent* (1907)

18 That is ever the way. 'Tis all jealousy to
the bride and good wishes to the corpse.
J. M. Barrie 1860-1937: *Quality Street* (1913)

19 Goodness has only once found a perfect
incarnation in a human body and never
will again, but evil can always find a home
there. Human nature is not black and
white but black and grey.
Graham Greene 1904-91: 'The Lost Childhood'
(1951)

20 There's a man all over for you, blaming on
his boots the faults of his feet.
Samuel Beckett 1906-89: *Waiting for Godot* (1955)

21 We know that a man can read Goethe or
Rilke in the evening, that he can play Bach
and Schubert, and go to his day's work at
Auschwitz in the morning.
George Steiner 1926- : *Language and Silence*
(1967)

The Human Race

PROVERBS AND SAYINGS

1 Man is the measure of all things.
*mid 16th century, meaning that everything could be
understood in terms of humankind; see 7 below*

PHRASES

2 a man and a brother a fellow human
being.
from the anti-slavery motto Am I not a man and a
brother?*: see* **Race** 1

3 the man on the Clapham omnibus the
average man.
attributed, in the Law Reports *of 1903, to the English
judge Lord Bowen (1853–94)*

4 the naked ape present-day humans
regarded as a species.
title of a book (1967) by Desmond Morris

5 ship of fools the world, humankind.
after The shyp of folys of the worlde *(1509)
translation of German work* Das Narrenschiff *(1494),
literally a ship whose passengers represent various
types of vice, folly, or human failings*

QUOTATIONS

6 And God said, Let us make man in our
image, after our likeness: and let them
have dominion over the fish of the sea, and
over the fowl of the air, and over the
cattle, and over all the earth and over
every creeping thing that creepeth upon
the earth.
Bible: Genesis

7 Man is the measure of all things.
Protagoras b. *c.*485 BC: Plato *Theaetetus*; see 1
above

8 There are many wonderful things, and
nothing is more wonderful than man.
Sophocles *c.*496-406 BC: *Antigone*

9 I am a man, I count nothing human
foreign to me.
Terence *c.*190-159 BC: *Heauton Timorumenos*

10 *Considerate la vostra semenza:
Fatti non foste a viver come bruti,
Ma per seguir virtute e conoscenza.*
Consider your origins: you were not made
to live as brutes, but to follow virtue and
knowledge.
Dante Alighieri 1265-1321: *Divina Commedia*
'Inferno'

11 What a piece of work is a man! How noble
in reason! how infinite in faculty! in form,
in moving, how express and admirable! in

action how like an angel! in apprehension how like a god! the beauty of the world! the paragon of animals! And yet, to me, what is this quintessence of dust?
William Shakespeare 1564–1616: *Hamlet* (1601)

12 How beauteous mankind is! O brave new world,
That has such people in't.
William Shakespeare 1564–1616: *The Tempest* (1611); see **Progress** 1

13 We carry within us the wonders we seek without us: there is all Africa and her prodigies in us.
Thomas Browne 1605–82: *Religio Medici* (1643)

14 Man is only a reed, the weakest thing in nature; but he is a thinking reed.
Blaise Pascal 1623–62: *Pensées* (1670)

15 What is man in nature? A nothing in respect of that which is infinite, an all in respect of nothing, a middle betwixt nothing and all.
Blaise Pascal 1623–62: *Pensées* (1670)

16 Principally I hate and detest that animal called man; although I heartily love John, Peter, Thomas, and so forth.
Jonathan Swift 1667–1745: letter to Pope, 29 September 1725

17 Know then thyself, presume not God to scan;
The proper study of mankind is man.
Alexander Pope 1688–1744: *An Essay on Man* Epistle 2 (1733)

18 Man is a tool-making animal.
Benjamin Franklin 1706–90: James Boswell *Life of Samuel Johnson* (1791) 7 April 1778

19 Out of the crooked timber of humanity no straight thing can ever be made.
Immanuel Kant 1724–1804: *Idee zu einer allgemeinen Geschichte in weltbürgerlicher Absicht* (1784)

20 Drinking when we are not thirsty and making love all year round, madam; that is all there is to distinguish us from other animals.
Pierre-Augustin Caron de Beaumarchais 1732–99: *Le Mariage de Figaro* (1785)

21 Providence has not created mankind entirely independent or entirely free. It is true that around every man a fatal circle is traced, beyond which he cannot pass; but within the wide verge of that circle he is powerful and free.
Alexis de Tocqueville 1805–59: *Democracy in America* (1835–40)

22 Is man an ape or an angel? Now I am on the side of the angels.
Benjamin Disraeli 1804–81: speech at Oxford, 25 November 1864; see **Life Sciences** 12

23 I teach you the superman. Man is something to be surpassed.
Friedrich Nietzsche 1844–1900: *Also Sprach Zarathustra* (1883)

24 Man is the Only Animal that Blushes. Or needs to.
Mark Twain 1835–1910: *Following the Equator* (1897)

25 Will the last generation of the twentieth century differ very much from the first? Will they be healthier and longer-lived, wiser, better, and more intelligent, or will they remain substantially the same as the people we have known and the people whom history has portrayed to us?
Anonymous: in *The Times* 1 January 1901

26 Man, biologically considered, and whatever else he may be into the bargain, is simply the most formidable of all the beasts of prey, and, indeed, the only one that preys systematically on its own species.
William James 1842–1910: in *Atlantic Monthly* December 1904

27 Taking a very gloomy view of the future of the human race, let us suppose that it can only expect to survive for two thousand million years longer, a period about equal to the past age of the earth. Then, regarded as a being destined to live for three-score years and ten, humanity, although it has been born in a house seventy years old, is itself only three days old.
James Jeans 1877–1946: *Eos* (1928)

28 Human kind
Cannot bear very much reality.
T. S. Eliot 1888–1965: *Four Quartets* 'Burnt Norton' (1936)

29 What is man, when you come to think upon him, but a minutely set, ingenious machine for turning, with infinite artfulness, the red wine of Shiraz into urine?
Isak Dinesen 1885–1962: *Seven Gothic Tales* (1934) 'The Dreamers'

30 To say, for example, that a man is made up of certain chemical elements is a satisfactory description only for those who intend to use him as a fertilizer.
H. J. Muller 1890–1967: *Science and Criticism* (1943)

31 Here you could love human beings nearly as God loved them, knowing the worst; you didn't love a pose, a pretty dress, a sentiment artfully assumed.
Graham Greene 1904–91: *The Heart of the Matter* (1948)

32 Man must be invented each day.
Jean-Paul Sartre 1905–80: *Qu'est-ce que la littérature?* (1948)

33 I hate 'Humanity' and all such abstracts: but I love *people*. Lovers of 'Humanity' generally hate *people and children*, and keep parrots or puppy dogs.
Roy Campbell 1901–57: *Light on a Dark Horse* (1951)

34 We're all of us guinea pigs in the laboratory of God. Humanity is just a work in progress.
Tennessee Williams 1911–83: *Camino Real* (1953)

35 In all my work what I try to say is that as human beings we are more alike than we are unalike.
Maya Angelou 1928– : interview in *New York Times* 20 January 1993

Human Rights see also Equality, Justice

1 Liberté! Égalité! Fraternité!
French, Freedom! Equality! Brotherhood!: *motto of the French Revolution, 1789, but of earlier origin*

2 the four freedoms four essential human freedoms as proclaimed in a speech to Congress by Franklin D. Roosevelt in 1941.
see 13 below

3 rights of man rights held to be justifiably belonging to any person; human rights.
associated with the Declaration of the Rights of Man and of the Citizen, adopted by the French National Assembly in 1789 and used as a preface to the French Constitution of 1791

4 No free man shall be taken or imprisoned or dispossessed, or outlawed or exiled, or in any way destroyed, nor will we go upon him, nor will we send against him except by the lawful judgement of his peers or by the law of the land.
Magna Carta 1215: clause 39

5 Magna Charta is such a fellow, that he will have no sovereign.
on the Lords' Amendment to the Petition of Right, 17 May 1628
Edward Coke 1552–1634: J. Rushworth *Historical Collections* (1659)

6 We hold these truths to be self-evident, that all men are created equal, that they are endowed by their Creator with certain unalienable rights, that among these are life, liberty and the pursuit of happiness.
American Declaration of Independence: 4 July 1776; from a draft by Thomas Jefferson (1743–1826); see **Happiness** 31

7 Whatever each man can separately do, without trespassing upon others, he has a right to do for himself; and he has a right to a fair portion of all which society, with all its combinations of skill and force, can do in his favour.
Edmund Burke 1729–97: *Reflections on the Revolution in France* (1790)

8 Any law which violates the inalienable rights of man is essentially unjust and tyrannical; it is not a law at all.
Maximilien Robespierre 1758–94: *Déclaration des droits de l'homme* 24 April 1793

9 Natural rights is simple nonsense: natural and imprescriptible rights, rhetorical nonsense—nonsense upon stilts.
Jeremy Bentham 1748–1832: *Anarchical Fallacies* (1843)

10 Its constitution the glittering and sounding generalities of natural right which make up the Declaration of Independence.
Rufus Choate 1799–1859: letter to the Maine Whig State Central Committee, 9 August 1856; see **Conversation** 4

11 The first duty of a State is to see that every

child born therein shall be well housed, clothed, fed and educated, till it attain years of discretion.
John Ruskin 1819–1900: *Time and Tide* (1867)

12 No man can put a chain about the ankle of his fellow man without at last finding the other end fastened about his own neck.
Frederick Douglass c.1818–1895: speech at Civil Rights Mass Meeting, Washington, DC, 22 October 1883

13 We look forward to a world founded upon four essential human freedoms. The first is freedom of speech and expression—everywhere in the world. The second is freedom of every person to worship God in his own way—everywhere in the world. The third is freedom from want . . . everywhere in the world. The fourth is freedom from fear . . . anywhere in the world.
Franklin D. Roosevelt 1882–1945: message to Congress, 6 January 1941; see 2 above

14 All human beings are born free and equal in dignity and rights.
Anonymous: *Universal Declaration of Human Rights* (1948) article 1

15 A right is not effectual by itself, but only in relation to the obligation to which it corresponds . . . An obligation which goes unrecognized by anybody loses none of the full force of its existence. A right which goes unrecognized by anybody is not worth very much.
Simone Weil 1909–43: *L'Enracinement* (1949)

16 We have talked long enough in this country about equal rights. We have talked for a hundred years or more. It is time now to write the next chapter, and to write it in the books of law.
Lyndon Baines Johnson 1908–73: speech to Congress, 27 November 1963

17 The price of championing human rights is a little inconsistency at times.
David Owen 1938– : speech, House of Commons, 30 March 1977

Humility see **Pride and Humility**

Humour see also **Wit**

1 **collapse of Stout Party** standard dénouement in Victorian humour.
stout party *a fat person; the phrase is supposed to come from Punch, as the characteristic finishing line of a joke, but no actual example has been traced*

2 **Homeric laughter** irrepressible laughter.
proverbially like that of Homer's gods in the Iliad *as they watched lame Hephaestus hobbling*

3 **a merry Andrew** a comic entertainer; a buffoon, a clown.
the suggestion of the antiquary Thomas Hearne (1678–1735) that the original 'merry Andrew' was the traveller and physician Dr Andrew Boorde (1490?–1549) is thought improbable

QUOTATIONS

4 A merry heart doeth good like a medicine.
Bible: Proverbs

5 Delight hath a joy in it either permanent or present. Laughter hath only a scornful tickling.
Philip Sidney 1554–86: *The Defence of Poetry* (1595)

6 A jest's prosperity lies in the ear

Of him that hears it, never in the tongue Of him that makes it.
William Shakespeare 1564–1616: *Love's Labour's Lost* (1595)

7 I love such mirth as does not make friends ashamed to look upon one another next morning.
Izaak Walton 1593–1683: *The Compleat Angler* (1653)

8 We must laugh before we are happy, for fear of dying without having laughed at all.
Jean de la Bruyère 1645–96: *Les Caractères ou les moeurs de ce siècle* (1688)

9 Among all kinds of writing, there is none in which authors are more apt to miscarry than in works of humour, as there is none in which they are more ambitious to excel.
Joseph Addison 1672–1719: in *The Spectator* 10 April 1711

10 I make myself laugh at everything, for fear of having to weep at it.
Pierre-Augustin Caron de Beaumarchais 1732–99: *Le Barbier de Séville* (1775)

11 For what do we live, but to make sport for our neighbours, and laugh at them in our turn?
Jane Austen 1775–1817: *Pride and Prejudice* (1813)

12 Laughter is pleasant, but the exertion is too much for me.
Thomas Love Peacock 1785–1866: *Nightmare Abbey* (1818)

13 We are not amused.
Queen Victoria 1819–1901: attributed; Caroline Holland *Notebooks of a Spinster Lady* (1919) 2 January 1900

14 Everything is funny as long as it is happening to Somebody Else.
Will Rogers 1879–1935: *The Illiterate Digest* (1924)

15 Fun is fun but no girl wants to laugh all of the time.
Anita Loos 1893–1981: *Gentlemen Prefer Blondes* (1925)

16 What do you mean, funny? Funny-peculiar or funny ha-ha?
Ian Hay 1876–1952: *The Housemaster* (1938)

17 Whatever is funny is subversive, every joke is ultimately a custard pie . . . A dirty joke is a sort of mental rebellion.
George Orwell 1903–50: in *Horizon* September 1941 'The Art of Donald McGill'

18 The funniest thing about comedy is that you never know why people laugh. I know *what* makes them laugh but trying to get your hands on the *why* of it is like trying to pick an eel out of a tub of water.
W. C. Fields 1880–1946: R. J. Anobile *A Flask of Fields* (1972)

19 Good taste and humour . . . are a contradiction in terms, like a chaste whore.
Malcolm Muggeridge 1903–90: in *Time* 14 September 1953

20 Laughter would be bereaved if snobbery died.
Peter Ustinov 1921– : in *Observer* 13 March 1955

21 Freud's theory was that when a joke opens a window and all those bats and bogeymen fly out, you get a marvellous feeling of relief and elation. The trouble with Freud is that he never had to play the old Glasgow Empire on a Saturday night after Rangers and Celtic had both lost.
Ken Dodd 1931– : in *Guardian* 30 April 1991; quoted in many, usually much contracted, forms since the mid-1960s

22 Mark my words, when a society has to resort to the lavatory for its humour, the writing is on the wall.
Alan Bennett 1934– : *Forty Years On* (1969)

23 People sometimes divide others into those you laugh at and those you laugh with. The young Auden was someone you could laugh-at-with.
Stephen Spender 1909–95: *W. H. Auden* (1973)

24 The marvellous thing about a joke with a double meaning is that it can only mean one thing.
Ronnie Barker 1929– : *Sauce* (1977)

25 Comedy is tragedy that happens to *other* people.
Angela Carter 1940–92: *Wise Children* (1991)

26 Surely nothing could be that funny.
on being told by Mick Jagger that his wrinkles were laughter lines
George Melly 1926– : in *Independent on Sunday* 1 January 1995 'Quotes of the Year'

Hunting, Shooting, and Fishing

PHRASES

1 big five
a name given by hunters to the five largest and most dangerous of the African mammals: rhinoceros, elephant, buffalo, lion, and leopard.

2 the one that got away traditional angler's description of a large fish that just eluded capture.
from the comment 'you should have seen the one that got away'

QUOTATIONS

3 As no man is born an artist, so no man is born an angler.
Izaak Walton 1593–1683: *The Compleat Angler* (1653)

4 Most of their discourse was about hunting, in a dialect I understand very little.
Samuel Pepys 1633–1703: diary 22 November 1663

5 The dusky night rides down the sky,

And ushers in the morn;
The hounds all join in glorious cry,
The huntsman winds his horn:
And a-hunting we will go.

Henry Fielding 1707–54: *Don Quixote in England* (1733)

6   My hoarse-sounding horn
Invites thee to the chase, the sport of
    kings;
Image of war, without its guilt.

William Somerville 1675–1742: *The Chase* (1735); see 11 below, **Sports** 4

7 Fly fishing may be a very pleasant amusement; but angling or float fishing I can only compare to a stick and a string, with a worm at one end and a fool at the other.

Samuel Johnson 1709–84: attributed; Hawker *Instructions to Young Sportsmen* (1859); also attributed to Jonathan Swift, in *The Indicator* 27 October 1819

8 It is very strange, and very melancholy, that the paucity of human pleasures should persuade us ever to call hunting one of them.

Samuel Johnson 1709–84: Hester Lynch Piozzi *Anecdotes of . . . Johnson* (1786)

9 D'ye ken John Peel with his coat so grey?
D'ye ken John Peel at the break of the day?
D'ye ken John Peel when he's far far away
With his hounds and his horn in the
    morning?

John Woodcock Graves 1795–1886: 'John Peel' (1820)

10 It ar'n't that I loves the fox less, but that I loves the 'ound more.

R. S. Surtees 1805–64: *Handley Cross* (1843)

11 'Unting is all that's worth living for—all time is lost wot is not spent in 'unting—it is like the hair we breathe—if we have it not we die—it's the sport of kings, the image of war without its guilt, and only five-and-twenty per cent of its danger.

R. S. Surtees 1805–64: *Handley Cross* (1843); see 6 above

12 The English country gentleman galloping after a fox—the unspeakable in full pursuit of the uneatable.

Oscar Wilde 1854–1900: *A Woman of No Importance* (1893)

13 When a man wants to murder a tiger he calls it sport; when a tiger wants to murder him, he calls it ferocity.

George Bernard Shaw 1856–1950: *Man and Superman* (1903)

14 The fascination of shooting as a sport depends almost wholly on whether you are at the right or wrong end of a gun.

P. G. Wodehouse 1881–1975: attributed

15 I do not see why I should break my neck because a dog chooses to run after a nasty smell.

on being asked why he did not hunt

Arthur James Balfour 1848–1930: Ian Malcolm *Lord Balfour: A Memory* (1930)

16 A sportsman is a man who, every now and then, simply has to get out and kill something. Not that he's cruel. He wouldn't hurt a fly. It's not big enough.

Stephen Leacock 1869–1944: *My Remarkable Uncle* (1942)

17 Fishing is unquestionably a form of madness but, happily, for the once-bitten there is no cure.

Lord Home 1903–95: *The Way the Wind Blows* (1976)

18 I love fishing. It's like transcendental meditation with a punch-line.

Billy Connolly 1942– : *Gullible's Travels* (1982)

19 They do you a decent death on the hunting-field.

John Mortimer 1923– : *Paradise Postponed* (1985)

20 If killing foxes is necessary for the safety and survival of other species, I—and several million others—will vote for it to continue. But the slaughter ought not to be fun.

Roy Hattersley 1932– : in *Guardian* 21 April 1990

Hypocrisy see also Deception

1 **Do as I say, not as I do.**
mid 16th century, often used to imply hypocrisy

2 **curry favour with** ingratiate oneself with someone through obsequious behaviour.
from an alteration of Middle English curry favel, from the name (Favel or Fauvel) of a chestnut horse in a 14th-century French romance who became a symbol of cunning and duplicity; hence 'to rub down Favel' meant to use the cunning which he personified

3 **holier than thou** characterized by an attitude of self-conscious virtue and piety.
from the Bible (Isaiah) 'Stand by thyself, come not near to me; for I am holier than thou'

4 **holy Willie** a pious hypocrite.
from Robert Burns's poem 'Holy Willie's Prayer' (1785)

5 **shed crocodile tears** put on a display of insincere grief.
from the belief that crocodiles wept while devouring or alluring their prey

6 **a whited sepulchre** a hypocrite, an ostensibly virtuous or pleasant person who is inwardly corrupt.
from the Bible (Matthew): see 10 below

7 Woe unto them that call evil good, and good evil.
Bible: Isaiah

8 My tongue swore, but my mind's unsworn.
on his breaking of an oath
Euripides c.485–c.406 BC: *Hippolytus*

9 Beware of false prophets, which come to you in sheep's clothing, but inwardly they are ravening wolves.
Bible: St Matthew; see **Deception** 8

10 Ye are like unto whited sepulchres, which indeed appear beautiful outward, but are within full of dead men's bones, and of all uncleanness.
Bible: St Matthew; see 6 above

11 I want that glib and oily art

To speak and purpose not.
William Shakespeare 1564–1616: *King Lear* (1605–6)

12 For neither man nor angel can discern Hypocrisy, the only evil that walks Invisible, except to God alone.
John Milton 1608–74: *Paradise Lost* (1667)

13 Hypocrisy is a tribute which vice pays to virtue.
Duc de la Rochefoucauld 1613–80: *Maximes* (1678)

14 Keep up appearances; there lies the test; The world will give thee credit for the rest. Outward be fair, however foul within; Sin if thou wilt, but then in secret sin.
Charles Churchill 1731–64: *Night* (1761)

15 Conventionality is not morality. Self-righteousness is not religion. To attack the first is not to assail the last. To pluck the mask from the face of the Pharisee, is not to lift an impious hand to the Crown of Thorns.
Charlotte Brontë 1816–55: *Jane Eyre* (2nd ed., 1848)

16 In the mouths of many men soft words are like roses that soldiers put into the muzzles of their muskets on holidays.
Henry Wadsworth Longfellow 1807–82: *Table-Talk* (1857) 'Driftwood'

17 I sit on a man's back, choking him and making him carry me, and yet assure myself and others that I am very sorry for him and wish to ease his lot by all possible means—except by getting off his back.
Leo Tolstoy 1828–1910: *What Then Must We Do?* (1886)

18 I hope you have not been leading a double life, pretending to be wicked and being really good all the time. That would be hypocrisy.
Oscar Wilde 1854–1900: *The Importance of Being Earnest* (1895)

19 Hypocrisy is the most difficult and nerve-racking vice that any man can pursue; it needs an unceasing vigilance and a rare detachment of spirit. It cannot, like adultery or gluttony, be practised at spare moments; it is a whole-time job.
W. Somerset Maugham 1874–1965: *Cakes and Ale* (1930)

20 All Reformers, however strict their social conscience, live in houses just as big as they can pay for.
Logan Pearsall Smith 1865-1946: *Afterthoughts* (1931) 'Other People'

21 What makes it so plausible to assume that hypocrisy is the vice of vices is that integrity can indeed exist under the cover of all other vices except this one. Only crime and the criminal, it is true, confront us with the perplexity of radical evil; but only the hypocrite is really rotten to the core.
Hannah Arendt 1906-75: *On Revolution* (1963)

Hypothesis and Fact see also Science

PROVERBS AND SAYINGS

1 The exception proves the rule.
mid 17th century; originally this meant that the recognition of something as an exception proved the existence of a rule, but it is now more often used or understood as justifying divergence from a rule; see 6 below

2 Facts are stubborn things.
early 18th century, used to indicate a core of reality that cannot be adjusted to people's wishes

3 Nullius in verba.
Latin, In the word of none, motto of the Royal Society, emphasizing reliance on experiment rather than authority; from Horace Epistles

4 One story is good till another is told.
late 16th century; meaning that doubt may be cast on an apparently convincing account by a second told from a different angle

5 The proof of the pudding is in the eating.
early 14th century, meaning that the truth of an assertion will be demonstrated by how things actually turn out; proof here means 'test'

6 There is an exception to every rule.
late 16th century; see 1 above

PHRASES

7 chapter and verse exact reference or authority.
the precise reference for a passage of Scripture

8 dot the i's and cross the t's particularize minutely, complete in every detail.

QUOTATIONS

9 Whoever has fixed on his Cause, before he has experimented, can hardly avoid fitting his Experiment to his own Cause . . . rather than the Cause to the truth of the Experiment itself.
Thomas Sprat 1635-1713: *History of the Royal Society* (1667)

10 *Hypotheses non fingo.*
I do not feign hypotheses.
Isaac Newton 1642-1727: *Principia Mathematica* (1713 ed.)

11 It may be so, there is no arguing against facts and experiments.
when told of an experiment which appeared to destroy his theory
Isaac Newton 1642-1727: reported by John Conduit, 1726; D. Brewster *Memoirs of Sir Isaac Newton* (1855)

12 It is the nature of an hypothesis, when once a man has conceived it, that it assimilates every thing to itself, as proper nourishment; and, from the first moment of your begetting it, it generally grows the stronger by every thing you see, hear, read, or understand.
Laurence Sterne 1713-68: *Tristram Shandy* (1759-67)

13 Nothing is too wonderful to be true, if it be consistent with the laws of nature, and in such things as these, experiment is the best test of such consistency.
Michael Faraday 1791-1867: diary, 19 March 1849

14 Now, what I want is, Facts . . . Facts alone are wanted in life.
Charles Dickens 1812-70: *Hard Times* (1854)

15 False views, if supported by some evidence, do little harm, for everyone takes a salutary pleasure in proving their falseness.
Charles Darwin 1809-82: *The Descent of Man* (1871)

16 How seldom is it that theories stand the wear and tear of practice!
Anthony Trollope 1815-82: *Thackeray* (1879)

17 It is a capital mistake to theorize before you have all the evidence. It biases the judgement.
Arthur Conan Doyle 1859-1930: *A Study in Scarlet* (1888)

18 The great tragedy of Science—the slaying of a beautiful hypothesis by an ugly fact.
T. H. Huxley 1825-95: *Collected Essays* (1893-4) 'Biogenesis and Abiogenesis'

19 Roundabout the accredited and orderly fact of every science there ever floats a sort of dust cloud of exceptional observations, of occurrences minute and irregular and seldom met with, which it always proves more easy to ignore than to attend to.
William James 1842-1910: attributed

20 The best scale for an experiment is 12 inches to a foot.
John Arbuthnot Fisher 1841-1920: *Memories* (1919)

21 Facts do not cease to exist because they are ignored.
Aldous Huxley 1894-1963: *Proper Studies* (1927)

22 The grand aim of all science [is] to cover the greatest number of empirical facts by logical deduction from the smallest possible number of hypotheses or axioms.
Albert Einstein 1879-1955: Lincoln Barnett *The Universe and Dr Einstein* (1950 ed.)

23 Aristotle maintained that women have fewer teeth than men; although he was twice married, it never occurred to him to verify this statement by examining his wives' mouths.
Bertrand Russell 1872-1970: *The Impact of Science on Society* (1952)

24 If it looks like a duck, walks like a duck and quacks like a duck, then it just may be a duck.
as a test, during the McCarthy era, of Communist affiliations
Walter Reuther 1907-70: attributed

25 It is a good morning exercise for a research scientist to discard a pet hypothesis every day before breakfast. It keeps him young.
Konrad Lorenz 1903-89: *Das Sogenannte Böse* (1963; translated by Marjorie Latzke as *On Aggression*, 1966)

26 An experiment is a device to make Nature speak intelligibly. After that one has only to listen.
George Wald 1904-97: in *Science* vol. 162 (1968)

27 With five free parameters, a theorist could fit the profile of an elephant.
George Gamow 1904-68: attributed; in *Nature* 21 June 1990

28 If an elderly but distinguished scientist says that something is possible he is almost certainly right, but if he says that it is impossible he is very probably wrong.
Arthur C. Clarke 1917- : in *New Yorker* 9 August 1969; see 29 below

29 When, however, the lay public rallies around an idea that is denounced by distinguished but elderly scientists and supports that idea with great fervour and emotion—the distinguished but elderly scientists are then, after all, probably right.
corollary to Arthur C. Clarke's law; see 28 above
Isaac Asimov 1920-92: Arthur C. Clarke 'Asimov's Corollary' in K. Frazier (ed.) *Paranormal Borderlands of Science* (1981)

30 No *good* model ever accounted for *all* the facts since some data was bound to be misleading if not plain wrong.
James Watson 1928- : Francis Crick *Some Mad Pursuit* (1988)

Idealism see also Hope

PHRASES

1 flower power the ideas of the flower people, hippies who wore flowers as symbols of peace and love; especially the promotion of these as a means of changing the world.

2 starry-eyed idealistic, uplifted, romantic.

3 the vision thing a political view encompassing the longer term.
from the comment by George Bush: see 14 below

QUOTATIONS

4 Where there is no vision, the people perish.
Bible: Proverbs

5 Love and a cottage! Eh, Fanny! Ah, give me indifference and a coach and six!
George Colman, the Elder 1732-94 and **David Garrick** 1717-79: *The Clandestine Marriage* (1766); see **Love** 44, **Marriage** 12

6 Hitch your wagon to a star.
Ralph Waldo Emerson 1803-82: *Society and Solitude* (1870)

7 We are all in the gutter, but some of us are looking at the stars.
Oscar Wilde 1854–1900: *Lady Windermere's Fan* (1892)

8 I am an idealist. I don't know where I'm going but I'm on the way.
Carl Sandburg 1878–1967: *Incidentals* (1907)

9 A cause may be inconvenient, but it's magnificent. It's like champagne or high heels, and one must be prepared to suffer for it.
Arnold Bennett 1867–1931: *The Title* (1918)

10 When they come downstairs from their Ivory Towers, Idealists are very apt to walk straight into the gutter.
Logan Pearsall Smith 1865–1946: *Afterthoughts* (1931) 'Other People'

11 We were the last romantics — chose for theme
Traditional sanctity and loveliness.
W. B. Yeats 1865–1939: 'Coole and Ballylee, 1931' (1933)

12 I submit to you that if a man hasn't discovered something he will die for, he isn't fit to live.
Martin Luther King 1929–68: speech in Detroit, 23 June 1963

13 To dream the impossible dream,
To reach the unreachable star!
Joe Darion 1917–2001: 'The Quest' (1965 song)

14 Oh, the vision thing.
responding to the suggestion that he turn his attention from short-term campaign objectives and look to the longer term
George Bush 1924– : in *Time* 26 January 1987; see 3 above

Ideas see also **Hypothesis and Fact, The Mind, Problems and Solutions, Thinking**

1 I have a cunning plan.
Baldrick's habitual overoptimistic promise in Blackadder (originally in the 1987 television series, written by Richard Curtis and Ben Elton)

2 There is one thing stronger than all the armies in the world; and that is an idea whose time has come.
mid 20th century saying; see 7 below

3 invita Minerva lacking inspiration.
Latin = Minerva (the goddess of wisdom) unwilling

4 King Charles's head an obsession, an *idée fixe*.
with reference to 'Mr Dick', in Dickens's David Copperfield (1850), who could not write or speak on any subject without King Charles's head intruding

5 New opinions are always suspected, and usually opposed, without any other reason but because they are not already common.
John Locke 1632–1704: *An Essay concerning Human Understanding* (1690)

6 General notions are generally wrong.
Lady Mary Wortley Montagu 1689–1762: letter to Edward Wortley Montagu, 28 March 1710

7 A stand can be made against invasion by an army; no stand can be made against invasion by an idea.
Victor Hugo 1802–85: *Histoire d'un Crime* (written 1851–2, published 1877); see 2 above

8 I share no one's ideas. I have my own.
Ivan Turgenev 1818–83: *Fathers and Sons* (1862)

9 Our ideas are only intellectual instruments which we use to break into phenomena; we must change them when they have served their purpose, as we change a blunt lancet that we have used long enough.
Claude Bernard 1813–78: *An Introduction to the Study of Experimental Medicine* (1865)

10 For an idea ever to be fashionable is ominous, since it must afterwards be always old-fashioned.
George Santayana 1863–1952: *Winds of Doctrine* (1913)

11 You see things; and you say 'Why?' But I dream things that never were; and I say 'Why not?'
George Bernard Shaw 1856–1950: *Back to Methuselah* (1921)

12 Marvellous, what ideas the young people

have these days. But I don't believe a word of it.

of the uncertainty principle
Albert Einstein 1879–1955: in 1927; see **Physical Sciences** 8

13 Nothing is more dangerous than an idea, when you have only one idea.
Alain 1868–1951: *Propos sur la religion* (1938)

14 No grand idea was ever born in a conference, but a lot of foolish ideas have died there.
F. Scott Fitzgerald 1896–1940: Edmund Wilson (ed.) *The Crack-Up* (1945) 'Note-Books E'

15 Madmen in authority, who hear voices in the air, are distilling their frenzy from some academic scribbler of a few years back.
John Maynard Keynes 1883–1946: *General Theory* (1947 ed.)

16 *Ideas won't keep*. Something must be done about them.
Alfred North Whitehead 1861–1947: *Dialogues* (1954) 28 April 1938

17 It is better to entertain an idea than to take it home to live with you for the rest of your life.
Randall Jarrell 1914–65: *Pictures from an Institution* (1954)

18 The English approach to ideas is not to kill them, but to let them die of neglect.
Jeremy Paxman 1950– : *The English: a portrait of a people* (1998)

Idleness see also Action and Inaction, Words and Deeds

PROVERBS AND SAYINGS

1 **As good be an addled egg as an idle bird.**
late 16th century, meaning that an idle person will produce nothing

2 **Better to wear out than to rust out.**
mid 16th century, meaning that it is better to remain active than to succumb to idleness; in this form frequently attributed to Richard Cumberland, Bishop of Peterborough (1631–1718)

3 **The devil finds work for idle hands to do.**
early 18th century, meaning that someone who has no work to do will get into mischief

4 **An idle brain is the devil's workshop.**
early 17th century, meaning that those who do not apply themselves to their work are most likely to get into trouble

5 **Idle people have the least leisure.**
late 17th century, meaning that lazy people are the least able to manage their time efficiently

6 **Idleness is never enjoyable unless there is plenty to do.**
American proverb, mid 20th century: see 21 below

7 **Idleness is the root of all evil.**
*early 15th century; the idea has been attributed to the French theologian, monastic reformer, and abbot St Bernard of Clairvaux (1090–1153); see **Money** 24*

8 **If you won't work you shan't eat.**
*mid 16th century, in which essential sustenance is seen as a reward for industry; from the Bible: see **Work** 21*

PHRASES

9 **the bread of idleness** food or sustenance for which one has not worked.
after the Bible (Proverbs) 'She . . . eateth not the bread of idleness'

10 **lotus-eater** a person who spends their time indulging in pleasure and luxury rather than dealing with practical concerns.
the lotus-eaters in Greek mythology were a people who lived on the fruit of the lotus, said to cause a dreamy forgetfulness and an unwillingness to depart; see 17 below

QUOTATIONS

11 Go to the ant thou sluggard; consider her ways, and be wise.
Bible: Proverbs

12 Out ye whores, to work, to work, ye whores, go spin.
commonly quoted as 'Go spin, you jades, go spin'
William Herbert, Lord Pembroke c.1501–70: John Aubrey *Brief Lives* (1898 ed.)

13 He that would thrive
Must rise at five;
He that hath thriven
May lie till seven.
John Clarke d. 1658: 'Diligentia' (1639)

14 Idleness is only the refuge of weak minds.
Lord Chesterfield 1694–1773: *Letters to his Son* (1774) 20 July 1749

15 If you are idle, be not solitary; if you are solitary, be not idle.
Samuel Johnson 1709–84: letter to Boswell, 27 October 1779

16 A man who has nothing to do with his own time has no conscience in his intrusion on that of others.
Jane Austen 1775–1817: *Sense and Sensibility* (1811)

17 Surely, surely, slumber is more sweet than toil, the shore
Than labour in the deep mid-ocean, wind and wave and oar;
Oh rest ye, brother mariners, we will not wander more.
Alfred, Lord Tennyson 1809–92: 'The Lotos-Eaters' (1832); see 10 above

18 The foul sluggard's comfort: 'It will last my time.'
Thomas Carlyle 1795–1881: *Critical and Miscellaneous Essays* (1838) 'Count Cagliostro. Flight Last'

19 How dull it is to pause, to make an end,

To rust unburnished, not to shine in use!
As though to breathe were life.
Alfred, Lord Tennyson 1809–92: 'Ulysses' (1842)

20 Never do to-day what you can put off till to-morrow.
Punch: in 1849

21 It is impossible to enjoy idling thoroughly unless one has plenty of work to do.
Jerome K. Jerome 1859–1927: *Idle Thoughts of an Idle Fellow* (1886); see 6 above

22 Oh! how I hate to get up in the morning, Oh! how I'd love to remain in bed.
Irving Berlin 1888–1989: *Oh! How I Hate to Get Up in the Morning* (1918 song)

23 procrastination is the
art of keeping
up with yesterday.
Don Marquis 1878–1937: *archy and mehitabel* (1927)

24 I was raised to feel that doing nothing was a sin. I had to learn to do nothing.
Jenny Joseph 1932– : in *Observer* 19 April 1998

Ignorance

PROVERBS AND SAYINGS

1 The husband is always the last to know.
early 17th century, relating to marital infidelity

2 Ignorance is bliss.
mid 18th century, from Gray: see 15 below

3 Ignorance is a voluntary misfortune.
American proverb, mid 20th century, meaning that one has chosen not to remedy the condition

4 Nothing so bold as a blind mare.
early 17th century, meaning that those who know least about a situation are least likely to be deterred by it

5 A slice off a cut loaf isn't missed.
late 16th century (first recorded in Shakespeare's Titus Andronicus, *1592), meaning that if something has already been diminished or damaged, further damage may go unnoticed*

6 What the eye doesn't see, the heart doesn't grieve over.
mid 16th century, now sometimes used with the implication that information is being withheld to prevent difficulties

7 What you don't know can't hurt you.
late 16th century

8 When the blind lead the blind, both shall fall into the ditch.
late 9th century, meaning that when a person is guided by someone equally inexperienced, both are likely to come to grief; from the Bible: see **Leadership** 6

PHRASES

9 invincible ignorance in theological terms, ignorance which the person concerned does not have the means to overcome.
translation of scholastic Latin ignorantia invincibilis, *in the* Summa Theologiae *of Thomas Aquinas*

10 turn a Nelson eye to turn a blind eye to, overlook, pretend ignorance of.
Horatio Nelson (1758–1805), British admiral, killed in the battle of Trafalgar, having suffered the loss of an eye and an arm in earlier conflicts: see **Determination** 35

QUOTATIONS

11 I see no other single hindrance such as this hindrance of ignorance, obstructed by which mankind for a long long time runs on and circles on.
Pali Tripitaka *c.* 2nd century BC: *Itivuttaka* [*Thus Was Said*] p. 8

12 If one does not know to which port one is sailing, no wind is favourable.
Seneca ('the Younger') c.4 BC–AD 65: *Epistulae Morales*

13 But those that understood him smiled at one another and shook their heads; but, for mine own part, it was Greek to me.
William Shakespeare 1564–1616: *Julius Caesar* (1599)

14 Lo! the poor Indian, whose untutored mind
Sees God in clouds, or hears him in the wind.
Alexander Pope 1688–1744: *An Essay on Man* Epistle 1 (1733); see **Drunkenness** 6

15   Where ignorance is bliss,
'Tis folly to be wise.
Thomas Gray 1716–71: *Ode on a Distant Prospect of Eton College* (1747); see 2 above

16 Ignorance, madam, pure ignorance.
on being asked why he had defined pastern *as the 'knee' of a horse*
Samuel Johnson 1709–84: James Boswell *Life of Samuel Johnson* (1791) 1755

17 Where people wish to attach, they should always be ignorant. To come with a well-informed mind, is to come with an inability of administering to the vanity of others, which a sensible person would always wish to avoid. A woman especially, if she have the misfortune of knowing any thing, should conceal it as well as she can.
Jane Austen 1775–1817: *Northanger Abbey* (1818)

18 For most men, an ignorant enjoyment is better than an informed one; it is better to conceive the sky as a blue dome than a dark cavity; and the cloud as a golden throne than a sleety mist.
John Ruskin 1819–1900: *Modern Painters* (1856)

19 Ignorance is not innocence but sin.
Robert Browning 1812–89: *The Inn Album* (1875)

20 Ignorance is like a delicate exotic fruit; touch it and the bloom is gone.
Oscar Wilde 1854–1900: *The Importance of Being Earnest* (1895)

21 I know nothing—nobody tells me anything.
John Galsworthy 1867–1933: *Man of Property* (1906)

22 You know everybody is ignorant, only on different subjects.
Will Rogers 1879–1935: in *New York Times* 31 August 1924

23 Happy the hare at morning, for she cannot read
The Hunter's waking thoughts.
W. H. Auden 1907–73: *Dog beneath the Skin* (with Christopher Isherwood, 1935)

24 Ignorance is an evil weed, which dictators may cultivate among their dupes, but which no democracy can afford among its citizens.
William Henry Beveridge 1879–1963: *Full Employment in a Free Society* (1944)

25 As any fule kno.
Geoffrey Willans 1911–58 and **Ronald Searle** 1920– : *Down with Skool!* (1953)

26 Nothing in all the world is more dangerous than sincere ignorance and conscientious stupidity.
Martin Luther King 1929–68: *Strength to Love* (1963)

27 A bishop wrote gravely to the *Times* inviting all nations to destroy 'the formula' of the atomic bomb. There is no simple remedy for ignorance so abysmal.
Peter Medawar 1915–87: *The Hope of Progress* (1972)

28 It was absolutely marvellous working for Pauli. You could ask him anything. There was no worry that he would think a particular question was stupid, since he thought *all* questions were stupid.
Victor Weisskopf 1908–2002: in *American Journal of Physics* 1977

29 Too many people in Britain say with almost a badge of pride that they never did understand maths properly.
David Blunkett 1947– : comment, 16 March 1999

30 Learn to say, 'I don't know'. If used when appropriate, it will be often.
Donald Rumsfeld 1932– : 'Rumsfeld's Rules' (2001)

Imagination

PHRASES

1 **build castles in the air** form unsubstantial or visionary projects.

2 **a castle in Spain** a visionary project, a daydream unlikely to be realized.
the expression is recorded from late Middle English, and it is possible that Spain, as the nearest Moorish country to Christendom, was taken as the type of a region in which the prospective castle-builder had no standing

3 **the vision splendid** the dream of some glorious imagined time.
from Wordsworth 'And by the vision splendid is on his way attended'

QUOTATIONS

4 For the imagination of man's heart is evil from his youth.
Bible: Genesis

5 The lunatic, the lover, and the poet,
Are of imagination all compact.
William Shakespeare 1564–1616: *A Midsummer Night's Dream* (1595–6)

6 I am giddy, expectation whirls me round.
The imaginary relish is so sweet
That it enchants my sense.
William Shakespeare 1564–1616: *Troilus and Cressida* (1602)

7 Though our brother is on the rack, as long as we ourselves are at our ease, our senses will never inform us of what he suffers . . . It is by imagination that we can form any conception of what are his sensations.
Adam Smith 1723–90: *Theory of Moral Sentiments* (2nd ed., 1762)

8 Were it not for imagination, Sir, a man would be as happy in the arms of a chambermaid as of a Duchess.
Samuel Johnson 1709–84: James Boswell *Life of Samuel Johnson* (1791) 9 May 1778

9 [Edmund Burke] is not affected by the reality of distress touching his heart, but by the showy resemblance of it striking his imagination. He pities the plumage, but forgets the dying bird.
on Burke's Reflections on the Revolution in France
Thomas Paine 1737–1809: *The Rights of Man* (1791)

10 Whither is fled the visionary gleam?

Where is it now, the glory and the dream?
William Wordsworth 1770–1850: 'Ode. Intimations of Immortality' (1807)

11 Heard melodies are sweet, but those unheard
Are sweeter; therefore, ye soft pipes, play on;
Not to the sensual ear, but, more endeared,
Pipe to the spirit ditties of no tone.
John Keats 1795–1821: 'Ode on a Grecian Urn' (1820)

12 The same that oft-times hath
Charmed magic casements, opening on the foam
Of perilous seas, in faery lands forlorn.
John Keats 1795–1821: 'Ode to a Nightingale' (1820)

13 His imagination resembled the wings of an ostrich. It enabled him to run, though not to soar.
Lord Macaulay 1800–59: T. F. Ellis (ed.) *Miscellaneous Writings of Lord Macaulay* (1860) 'John Dryden' (1828)

14 He said he should prefer not to know the sources of the Nile, and that there should be some unknown regions preserved as hunting-grounds for the poetic imagination.
George Eliot 1819–80: *Middlemarch* (1871–2)

15 Where there is no imagination there is no horror.
Arthur Conan Doyle 1859–1930: *A Study in Scarlet* (1888)

16 Must then a Christ perish in torment in every age to save those that have no imagination?
George Bernard Shaw 1856–1950: *Saint Joan* (1924)

17 All fantasy should have a solid base in reality.
Max Beerbohm 1872–1956: *Zuleika Dobson* (1946 ed.) note

18 When the imagination sleeps, words are emptied of their meaning.
Albert Camus 1913–60: *Resistance, Rebellion and Death* (1961)

19 Imagination isn't merely a surplus mental department meant for entertainment, but the most essential piece of machinery we

have if we are going to live the lives of
human beings.
Ted Hughes 1930–98: in *Children's Literature in
Education* March 1970

Inaction   see **Action and Inaction**

Inconstancy   see **Constancy and Inconstancy**

Indecision   see also **Certainty and Doubt**

PROVERBS AND SAYINGS

1 **Between two stools one falls to the
ground.**
*late 14th century, meaning that inability to choose
between, or accommodate oneself to, alternative
viewpoints or courses of action may end in disaster*

2 **The cat would eat fish, but would not wet
her feet.**
*early 13th century, commenting on a situation in
which desire for something is checked by
unwillingness to risk discomfort in acquiring it*

3 **Councils of war never fight.**
*mid 19th century, meaning that people discussing
matters in a group never reach the decision to fight,
which an individual would make*

4 **He who hesitates is lost.**
*early 18th century, often used to urge decisive action
on someone; early usages refer specifically to women,
as in Addison Cato (1713) 'The woman that deliberates
is lost'*

5 **If you run after two hares you will catch
neither.**
*early 16th century, meaning that one must decide on
one's goal*

6 **Indecision is fatal, so make up your mind.**
American proverb, mid 20th century

PHRASES

7 **fudge and mudge** evade comment or avoid
making a decision on an issue by waffling;
apply facile solutions to decisions while
trying to appear resolved.
*coined as a political catchphrase by the Labour
politician David Owen in an attack on the leadership
of James Callaghan, 'We are fed up with fudging and
mudging, with mush and slush. We need courage,
conviction, and hard work'*

QUOTATIONS

8 Now, the melancholy god protect thee,
and the tailor make thy doublet of
changeable taffeta, for thy mind is a very
opal.
William Shakespeare 1564–1616: *Twelfth Night*
(1601)

9 I must have a prodigious quantity of mind;
it takes me as much as a week, sometimes,
to make it up.
Mark Twain 1835–1910: *The Innocents Abroad* (1869)

10 There is no more miserable human being
than one in whom nothing is habitual but
indecision.
William James 1842–1910: *The Principles of
Psychology* (1890)

11 The Flying Scotsman is no less splendid a
sight when it travels north to Edinburgh
than when it travels south to London. Mr
Baldwin denouncing sanctions was as
dignified as Mr Baldwin imposing them.
Lord Beaverbrook 1879–1964: in *Daily Express* 29
May 1937

12 The tragedy of a man who could not make
up his mind.
Laurence Olivier 1907–89: introduction to his 1948
screen adaptation of *Hamlet*

13 Often undecided whether to desert a
sinking ship for one that might not float,
he would make up his mind to sit on the
wharf for a day.
of Lord Curzon
Lord Beaverbrook 1879–1964: *Men and Power*
(1956)

14 I'll give you a definite maybe.
Sam Goldwyn 1882–1974: attributed

15 A wrong decision isn't forever; it can always be reversed. The losses from a delayed decision *are* forever; they can never be retrieved.
J. K. Galbraith 1908– : *A Life in our Times* (1981)

16 The archbishop is usually to be found nailing his colours to the fence.
of Archbishop Runcie
Frank Field 1942– : attributed in *Crockfords 1987/88* (1987); Geoffrey Madan records in his *Notebooks* a similar comment was made about A. J. Balfour, c.1904; see **Defiance** 8

Indifference

PHRASES

1 compassion fatigue indifference to charitable appeals on behalf of those who are suffering, experienced as a result of the frequency or number of such appeals.

2 leather or prunella something to which one is completely indifferent.
a misinterpretation of lines from Alexander Pope's Essay on Man (1734): 'Worth makes the Man, and want of it the Fellow;/The rest, is all but Leather or Prunella.' In Pope's poem, a distinction is being drawn between the trade of a cobbler (leather) and the profession of a clergyman (prunella as the material from which a clerical gown is made). The phrase was however taken to denote something of no value

QUOTATIONS

3 They have mouths, and speak not: eyes have they, and see not.
They have ears, and hear not: noses have they, and smell not.
They have hands, and handle not: feet have they, and walk not: neither speak they through their throat.
Bible: Psalm 115

4 It is the disease of not listening, the malady of not marking, that I am troubled withal.
William Shakespeare 1564–1616: *Henry IV, Part 2* (1597)

5 All colours will agree in the dark.
Francis Bacon 1561–1626: *Essays* (1625) 'Of Unity in Religion'

6 And this the burthen of his song,
For ever used to be,
I care for nobody, not I,
If no one cares for me.
Isaac Bickerstaffe 1733–c.1808: *Love in a Village* (1762) 'The Miller of Dee'

7 There is nothing upon the face of the earth so insipid as a medium. Give me love or hate! a friend that will go to jail for me, or an enemy that will run me through the body!
Fanny Burney 1752–1840: *Camilla* (1796)

8 Vacant heart and hand, and eye,—
Easy live and quiet die.
Sir Walter Scott 1771–1832: *The Bride of Lammermoor* (1819)

9 If Jesus Christ were to come to-day, people would not even crucify him. They would ask him to dinner, and hear what he had to say, and make fun of it.
Thomas Carlyle 1795–1881: D. A. Wilson *Carlyle at his Zenith* (1927)

10 The worst sin towards our fellow creatures is not to hate them, but to be indifferent to them: that's the essence of inhumanity.
George Bernard Shaw 1856–1950: *The Devil's Disciple* (1901)

11 Science may have found a cure for most evils; but it has found no remedy for the worst of them all—the apathy of human beings.
Helen Keller 1880–1968: *My Religion* (1927)

12 I wish I could care what you do or where you go but I can't . . . My dear, I don't give a damn.
'Frankly, my dear, I don't give a damn!' in the 1939 screen version by Sidney Howard
Margaret Mitchell 1900–49: *Gone with the Wind* (1936)

13 Cast a cold eye
On life, on death.
Horseman pass by!
W. B. Yeats 1865–1939: 'Under Ben Bulben' (1939)

14 Catholics and Communists have committed great crimes, but at least they have not stood aside, like an established society, and been indifferent. I would rather have blood on my hands than water like Pilate.
Graham Greene 1904–91: *The Comedians* (1966); see **Duty** 5

15 In Germany they came first for the Communists, and I didn't speak up because I wasn't a Communist; and then they came for the trade unionists, and I didn't speak up because I wasn't a trade unionist; and then they came for the Jews, and I didn't speak up because I wasn't a Jew; and then . . . they came for me . . . and by that time there was no-one left to speak up.

Martin Niemöller 1892–1984: quoted in many versions since the Second World War; this version, in *'Quote Unquote' Newsletter* April 2001, was approved by Niemöller as the original in 1971

16 The opposite of love is not hate, it's indifference. The opposite of art is not ugliness, it's indifference. The opposite of faith is not heresy, it's indifference. And the opposite of life is not death, it's indifference.

Elie Wiesel 1928– : in *U.S. News and World Report* 27 October 1986

17 I come from a people who gave the ten commandments to the world. Time has come to strengthen them by three additional ones, which we ought to adopt and commit ourselves to: thou shalt not be a perpetrator; thou shalt not be a victim; and thou shalt never, but never, be a bystander.

Yehuda Bauer 1926– : speech to the German Bundestag, 1998, quoted in his own speech to the Stockholm International Forum on the Holocaust, 26 July 2000; see **Lifestyles** 8

Ingratitude see **Gratitude and Ingratitude**

Innocence see **Guilt and Innocence**

Insight see also **Self-Knowledge**

PHRASES

1 the penny drops understanding dawns.
referring to the mechanism of a penny-in-the-slot machine

2 scales fall from a person's eyes a person receives sudden enlightenment or revelation.
from the Bible (Acts) 'And immediately there fell from his eyes as it had been scales: and he received sight forthwith'

3 third eye in Hinduism and Buddhism, the 'eye of insight' in the forehead of an image of a deity, especially the god Shiva.

QUOTATIONS

4 For the Lord seeth not as man seeth: for man looketh on the outward appearance, but the Lord looketh on the heart.
Bible: I Samuel

5 Each of us touches one place
and understands the whole in that way.
The palm and the fingers feeling in the dark are
how the senses explore the reality of the elephant.
If each of us held a candle there, and if we went in together, we could see it.
on the inferences drawn by men touching different parts of an elephant in the dark
Jalal ad-Din ar-Rumi 1207–73: *Mathnawi*; see **Knowledge** 23

6 Everything I have written seems like straw by comparison with what I have seen and what has been revealed to me.
following a mystical experience, after which he did no more teaching or writing
St Thomas Aquinas c.1225–74: on 6 December 1273

7 I have striven not to laugh at human actions, not to weep at them, nor to hate them, but to understand them.
Baruch Spinoza 1632–77: *Tractatus Politicus* (1677)

8 If the doors of perception were cleansed everything would appear to man as it is, infinite.
William Blake 1757–1827: *The Marriage of Heaven and Hell* (1790–3)

9 *Tout comprendre rend très indulgent.*
To be totally understanding makes one very indulgent.
Mme de Staël 1766–1817: *Corinne* (1807); see **Forgiveness** 6

10 Aye on the shores of darkness there is
   light,
And precipices show untrodden green,
There is a budding morrow in midnight,
There is a triple sight in blindness keen.
John Keats 1795–1821: 'To Homer' (written 1818)

11 The veil of eternity was lifted. The one
great truth which underlies all human
experience, and is the key to all the
mysteries that philosophy has sought in
vain to solve, flashed upon me in a sudden
revelation . . . staggering to my desk, I
wrote . . . '*A strong smell of turpentine
prevails throughout.*'
of his experiences under the influence of ether
Oliver Wendell Holmes 1809–94: *Mechanism in
Thought and Morals* (1871)

12 If we had a keen vision and feeling of all
ordinary human life, it would be like
hearing the grass grow and the squirrel's
heart beat, and we should die of that roar
which lies on the other side of silence.
George Eliot 1819–80: *Middlemarch* (1871–2)

13 One sees great things from the valley; only
small things from the peak.
G. K. Chesterton 1874–1936: *The Innocence of Father
Brown* (1911)

14 It is only with the heart that one can see
rightly; what is essential is invisible to the
eye.
Antoine de Saint-Exupéry 1900–44: *Le Petit Prince*
(1943)

15 Come to the edge.
We might fall.
Come to the edge.
It's too high!
COME TO THE EDGE!
And they came
and he pushed
and they flew . . .
Christopher Logue 1926– : 'Come to the edge'
(1969)

16 Deprivation is for me what daffodils were
for Wordsworth.
Philip Larkin 1922–85: *Required Writing* (1983)

17 The world is like a Mask dancing. If you
want to see it well you do not stand in one
place.
Chinua Achebe 1930– : *Arrow of God* (1988)

18 If we find the answer to that [why it is that
we and the universe exist], it would be the
ultimate triumph of human reason—for
then we would know the mind of God.
Stephen Hawking 1942– : *A Brief History of Time*
(1988)

19 Know what I mean, Harry?
Frank Bruno 1961– : supposed to have been said in
interview with sports commentator Harry
Carpenter, possibly apocryphal

Insults

1 Don't add insult to injury.
*American proverb, mid 18th century, recommending
not to treat someone one has hurt with contempt as
well*

PHRASES

2 bite one's thumb at insult by making the
gesture of biting one's thumb.
in Shakespeare's Romeo and Juliet *(1595), in a scene
between two quarrelling servants, one when
challenged says to the other, 'I do not bite my thumb
at you, sir; but I bite my thumb, sir'*

QUOTATIONS

3 The devil damn thee black, thou cream-
faced loon!

Where gott'st thou that goose look?
William Shakespeare 1564–1616: *Macbeth* (1606)

4 How easy it is to call rogue and villain,
and that wittily! But how hard to make a
man appear a fool, a blockhead, or a
knave, without using any of those
opprobrious terms! To spare the grossness
of the names, and to do the thing yet more
severely, is to draw a full face, and to make
the nose and cheeks stand out, and yet not
to employ any depth of shadowing.
John Dryden 1631–1700: *Of Satire* (1693)

5 An injury is much sooner forgotten than
an insult.
Lord Chesterfield 1694–1773: *Letters to his Son*
(1774) 9 October 1746

6 To-day I pronounced a word which should never come out of a lady's lips it was that I called John a Impudent Bitch.
Marjory Fleming 1803–11: *Journals, Letters and Verses* (1934)

7 The words she spoke of Mrs Harris, lambs could not forgive . . . nor worms forget.
Charles Dickens 1812–70: *Martin Chuzzlewit* (1844)

8 He has to learn that petulance is not sarcasm, and that insolence is not invective.
of Sir Charles Wood
Benjamin Disraeli 1804–81: speech, House of Commons, 16 December 1852

9 Silence is the most perfect expression of scorn.
George Bernard Shaw 1856–1950: *Back to Methuselah* (1921)

10 JUDGE: You are extremely offensive, young man.
SMITH: As a matter of fact, we both are, and the only difference between us is that I am trying to be, and you can't help it.
F. E. Smith 1872–1930: 2nd Earl of Birkenhead *Earl of Birkenhead* (1933)

11 Okie use' ta mean you was from Oklahoma. Now it means you're a dirty son-of-a-bitch. Okie means you're scum. Don't mean nothing itself, it's the way they say it.
John Steinbeck 1902–68: *The Grapes of Wrath* (1939)

12 BESSIE BRADDOCK: Winston, you're drunk.
CHURCHILL: Bessie, you're ugly. But tomorrow I shall be sober.
Winston Churchill 1874–1965: J. L. Lane (ed.) *Sayings of Churchill* (1992)

13 Like being savaged by a dead sheep.
on being criticized by Geoffrey Howe
Denis Healey 1917– : speech in the House of Commons, 14 June 1978

14 I think I detect sarcasm. I can't be doing with sarcasm. You know what they say? Sarcasm is the greatest weapon of the smallest mind.
Alan Ayckbourn 1939– : *Woman in Mind* (1986)

15 I decided the worst thing you can call Paul Keating, quite frankly, is Paul Keating.
John Hewson 1946– : Michael Gordon *A Question of Leadership* (1993)

Intelligence and Intellectuals

PROVERBS AND SAYINGS

1 Elementary, my dear Watson.
remark attributed to Sherlock Holmes, but not found in this form in any book by Arthur Conan Doyle; first found in P.G. Wodehouse Psmith Journalist (1915)

PHRASES

2 the chattering classes the articulate professional people given to free expression of (especially liberal) opinions on society and culture.

3 know a hawk from a handsaw have ordinary discernment.
now chiefly in allusion to Shakespeare Hamlet: *see* **Madness** 4

4 little grey cells intelligence.
the expression used by Agatha Christie's detective Hercule Poirot; see 12 below

5 too clever by half far more clever than is satisfactory or desirable.
see **People** 54

6 trahison des clercs a betrayal of intellectual, artistic, or moral standards by writers, academics, or artists.
French, 'treason of the scholars', title of a book by Julien Benda (1927)

QUOTATIONS

7 Whoever in discussion adduces authority uses not intellect but rather memory.
Leonardo da Vinci 1452–1519: Edward McCurdy (ed.) *Leonardo da Vinci's Notebooks* (1906)

8 The height of cleverness is to be able to conceal it.
Duc de la Rochefoucauld 1613–80: *Maximes* (1678)

9 You beat your pate, and fancy wit will come:
Knock as you please, there's nobody at home.
Alexander Pope 1688–1744: 'Epigram: You beat your pate' (1732)

10 Sir, I have found you an argument; but I am not obliged to find you an understanding.
Samuel Johnson 1709–84: James Boswell *Life of Samuel Johnson* (1791) June 1784

11 Our meddling intellect
Mis-shapes the beauteous forms of
    things:—
We murder to dissect.
William Wordsworth 1770–1850: 'The Tables Turned' (1798)

12 He [Hercule Poirot] tapped his forehead. 'These little grey cells. It is "up to them".'
Agatha Christie 1890–1976: *The Mysterious Affair at Styles* (1920); see 4 above

13 No one in this world, so far as I know— and I have searched the records for years, and employed agents to help me—has ever lost money by underestimating the intelligence of the great masses of the plain people.
H. L. Mencken 1880–1956: in *Chicago Tribune* 19 September 1926

14 'Hullo! friend,' I call out, 'Won't you lend us a hand?' 'I am an intellectual and don't drag wood about,' came the answer. 'You're lucky,' I reply. 'I too wanted to become an intellectual, but I didn't succeed.'
Albert Schweitzer 1875–1965: *Mitteilungen aus Lambarene* (1928)

15 What is a highbrow? He is a man who has found something more interesting than women.
Edgar Wallace 1875–1932: in *New York Times* 24 January 1932

16 As a human being, one has been endowed with just enough intelligence to be able to see clearly how utterly inadequate that intelligence is when confronted with what exists.
Albert Einstein 1879–1955: letter to Queen Elisabeth of Belgium, 19 September 1932

17 Intelligence is quickness to apprehend as distinct from ability, which is capacity to act wisely on the thing apprehended.
Alfred North Whitehead 1861–1947: *Dialogues* (1954) 15 December 1939

18 To the man-in-the-street, who, I'm sorry to say,
Is a keen observer of life,
The word 'Intellectual' suggests straight away
A man who's untrue to his wife.
W. H. Auden 1907–73: *New Year Letter* (1941)

19 An intellectual is someone whose mind watches itself.
Albert Camus 1913–60: *Carnets, 1935–42* (1962)

20 It takes little talent to see clearly what lies under one's nose, a good deal of it to know in which direction to point that organ.
W. H. Auden 1907–73: *Dyer's Hand* (1963) 'Writing'

21 American anti-intellectualism will never again be the same because of Bill Gates. Gates embodies what was supposed to be impossible—the practical intellectual.
Randall E. Stross: *The Microsoft Way* (1996)

International Relations see also **Countries and Peoples, Diplomacy, Government, Politics**

PHRASES

1 **the Auld Alliance** the political relationship of France and Scotland between the 14th and 16th centuries.
auld *is a Scottish form of old*

2 **the balance of power** a state of international equilibrium with no nation predominant.
originally the balance of power in Europe, *as in* London Gazette 1701 *'Your glorious design of re-establishing a just balance of power in Europe', and associated with the political aspirations of Robert Walpole (1676–1745)*

3 **the cold war** the hostility between the Soviet bloc countries and the Western powers which began after the Second World War with the Soviet takeover of the countries of eastern Europe, and which was formally ended in November 1990.
Bernard Baruch (1870–1965), speech to South Carolina Legislature 16 April 1947, 'Let us not be deceived—we are today in the midst of a cold war'; the expression cold war *was suggested to him by H. B. Swope, former editor of the New York World*

4 ethical foreign policy the conduct of foreign policy according to ethical as well as national considerations.

after the British general election of 1997, the aspiration was particularly associated with the incumbency of Robin Cook as Foreign Secretary, but its precise application in individual cases has been controversial

5 the Monroe doctrine a principle of US policy, that any intervention by external powers in the politics of the Americas is a potentially hostile act against the US.

originated by President James Monroe in his annual message to Congress, 2 December 1823; see **Diplomacy** *9*

6 a New World Order a vision of a world ordered differently from the way it is at present; in particular, an optimistic view of the world order or balance of power following the end of the Cold War.

see **The Future** *28*

7 the special relationship the relationship between Britain and the US, regarded as particularly close in terms of common origin and language.

associated with Winston Churchill, as in the House of Commons 7 November 1945, 'We should not abandon our special relationship with the United States and Canada'

8 the Third World the developing countries of Asia, Africa, and Latin America.

the phrase was first applied in the 1950s by French commentators who used tiers monde *to distinguish the developing countries from the capitalist and Communist blocs; see* **Countries** *36,* **Journalism** *27*

9 watchful waiting American policy towards Mexico during Mexico's revolutionary period, 1913–20.

from Woodrow Wilson's State of the Union address, 2 December 1913, 'Our policy of watchful waiting'

QUOTATIONS

10 *Il n'y a plus de Pyrénées.*
The Pyrenees are no more.
on the accession of his grandson to the throne of Spain, 1700
Louis XIV 1638–1715: attributed to Louis by Voltaire in *Siècle de Louis XIV* (1753); but to the Spanish Ambassador to France in the *Mercure Galant* (Paris) November 1700

11 Peace, commerce, and honest friendship with all nations—entangling alliances with none.
Thomas Jefferson 1743–1826: inaugural address, 4th of March 1801

12 If you wish to avoid foreign collision, you had better abandon the ocean.
Henry Clay 1777–1852: speech in the House of Representatives, 22 January 1812

13 In matters of commerce the fault of the Dutch
Is offering too little and asking too much.
The French are with equal advantage content,
So we clap on Dutch bottoms just twenty per cent.
George Canning 1770–1827: dispatch, in cipher, to the English ambassador at the Hague, 31 January 1826

14 The Continent will [not] suffer England to be the workshop of the world.
Benjamin Disraeli 1804–81: speech, House of Commons, 15 March 1838

15 Italy is a geographical expression.
discussing the Italian question with Palmerston in 1847
Prince Metternich 1773–1859: *Mémoires, Documents, etc. de Metternich publiés par son fils* (1883)

16 We have no eternal allies and we have no perpetual enemies. Our interests are eternal and perpetual, and those interests it is our duty to follow.
Lord Palmerston 1784–1865: speech, House of Commons, 1 March 1848

17 In order that he might rob a neighbour whom he had promised to defend, black men fought on the coast of Coromandel, and red men scalped each other by the Great Lakes of North America.
Lord Macaulay 1800–59: *Biographical Essays* (1857) 'Frederic the Great'

18 Lord Palmerston, with characteristic levity had once said that only three men in Europe had ever understood [the Schleswig-Holstein question], and of these the Prince Consort was dead, a Danish statesman (unnamed) was in an asylum, and he himself had forgotten it.
Lord Palmerston 1784–1865: R. W. Seton-Watson *Britain in Europe 1789–1914* (1937)

19 Nations touch at their summits.
Walter Bagehot 1826–77: *The English Constitution* (1867)

20 The very phrase 'foreign affairs' makes an Englishman convinced that I am about to treat of subjects with which he has no concern.
Benjamin Disraeli 1804–81: speech at Manchester, 3 April 1872

21 This policy cannot succeed through speeches, and shooting-matches, and songs; it can only be carried out through blood and iron.
Otto von Bismarck 1815–98: speech in the Prussian House of Deputies, 28 January 1886; see **Warfare** 5

22 Your map of Africa is all very fine, but my map of Africa lies in Europe. Here is Russia and here is France, and we are in the middle; that is my map of Africa.
on colonial policy
Otto von Bismarck 1815–98: to Eugen Wolf, 5 December 1888

23 In a word, we desire to throw no one into the shade [in East Asia], but we also demand our own place in the sun.
Prince Bernhard von Bülow 1849–1929: speech, Reichstag, 6 December 1897; see **Success** 16

24 Just for a word 'neutrality'—a word which in wartime has so often been disregarded—just for a scrap of paper, Great Britain is going to make war on a kindred nation who desires nothing better than to be friends with her.
Theobald von Bethmann Hollweg 1856–1921: summary of a report by Sir E. Goschen to Sir Edward Grey; *The Diary of Edward Goschen 1900–1914* (1980) discusses the contentious origins of this statement; see **Trust** 12

25 Armed neutrality is ineffectual enough at best.
Woodrow Wilson 1856–1924: speech to Congress, 2 April 1917

26 In the field of world policy I would dedicate this Nation to the policy of the good neighbour.
Franklin D. Roosevelt 1882–1945: inaugural address, 4 March 1933

27 Since the day of the air, the old frontiers are gone. When you think of the defence of England you no longer think of the chalk cliffs of Dover; you think of the Rhine. That is where our frontier lies.
Stanley Baldwin 1867–1947: speech, House of Commons, 30 July 1934

28 That four great nations, flushed with victory and stung with injury, stay the hands of vengeance and voluntarily submit their captive enemies to the judgement of the law, is one of the most significant tributes that Power has ever paid to Reason.
Robert H. Jackson 1892–1954: opening statement for the prosecution, International Military Tribunal in Nuremberg, 21 November 1945

29 If Hitler invaded hell I would make at least a favourable reference to the devil in the House of Commons.
Winston Churchill 1874–1965: *The Second World War* (1950) vol. 3

30 If you carry this resolution you will send Britain's Foreign Secretary naked into the conference chamber.
on a motion proposing unilateral nuclear disarmament by the UK
Aneurin Bevan 1897–1960: speech at Labour Party Conference in Brighton, 3 October 1957

31 We face neither East nor West: we face forward.
Kwame Nkrumah 1900–72: conference speech, Accra, 7 April 1960

32 *Ich bin ein Berliner.*
I am a Berliner.
expressing US commitment to the support and defence of West Berlin
John F. Kennedy 1917–63: speech in West Berlin, 26 June 1963

33 We hope that the world will not narrow into a neighbourhood before it has broadened into a brotherhood.
Lyndon Baines Johnson 1908–73: speech at the lighting of the Nation's Christmas Tree, 22 December 1963

34 The great nations have always acted like gangsters, and the small nations like prostitutes.
Stanley Kubrick 1928–99: in *Guardian* 5 June 1963

35 They're Germans. Don't mention the war.
John Cleese 1939– and **Connie Booth**: *Fawlty Towers* 'The Germans' (BBC TV programme, 1975)

36 If Kuwait grew carrots we wouldn't give a damn.
Lawrence Korb 1939– : in *International Herald Tribune* 21 August 1990

37 More than ever before in human history, we share a common destiny. We can master it only if we face it together. And that, my friends, is why we have the United Nations.
Kofi Annan 1938– : in *Sunday Times* 2 January 2000

38 One illusion has been shattered on 11 September: that we can have the good life of the West irrespective of the state of the rest of the world.
Tony Blair 1953– : speech at Lord Mayor's Banquet, London, 12 November 2001

The Internet see Computers and the Internet

Inventions and Discoveries see also Science, Technology

1 **Turkey, heresy, hops, and beer came into England all in one year.**
late 16th century; perhaps referring to 1521. The turkey, found domesticated in Mexico in 1518, was soon afterwards introduced into Europe, in 1521, the Pope conferred on Henry VIII the title Defender of the Faith, in recognition of his opposition to the Lutheran heresy, the hop-plant is believed to have been introduced into the south of England from Flanders between 1520 and 1524, and beer as the name of hopped malt liquor became common only in the 16th century

PHRASES

2 **the best thing since sliced bread** a particularly notable invention or discovery.

3 **reinvent the wheel** be forced by necessity to construct a basic requirement again from the beginning.
the wheel as an essential requirement of modern civilization

QUOTATIONS

4 God hath made man upright; but they have sought out many inventions.
Bible: Ecclesiastes

5 *Eureka!*
I've got it!
Archimedes c.287-212 BC: Vitruvius Pollio *De Architectura*

6 It is well to observe the force and virtue and consequence of discoveries, and these are to be seen nowhere more conspicuously than in those three which were unknown to the ancients, and of which the origins, though recent, are obscure and inglorious; namely, printing, gunpowder, and the mariner's needle [the compass]. For these three have changed the whole face and state of things throughout the world.
Francis Bacon 1561-1626: *Novum Organum* (1620); see **Culture** 11

7 I don't know what I may seem to the world, but as to myself, I seem to have been only like a boy playing on the sea-shore and diverting myself in now and then finding a smoother pebble or a prettier shell than ordinary, whilst the great ocean of truth lay all undiscovered before me.
Isaac Newton 1642-1727: Joseph Spence *Anecdotes* (ed. J. Osborn, 1966)

8 Thus first necessity invented stools,
Convenience next suggested elbow-chairs,
And luxury the accomplished sofa last.
William Cowper 1731-1800: *The Task* (1785) 'The Sofa'

9 What is the use of a new-born child?
when asked what was the use of a new invention
Benjamin Franklin 1706-90: J. Parton *Life and Times of Benjamin Franklin* (1864)

10 Then felt I like some watcher of the skies
When a new planet swims into his ken;
Or like stout Cortez when with eagle eyes
He stared at the Pacific—and all his men
Looked at each other with a wild
    surmise—
Silent, upon a peak in Darien.
John Keats 1795-1821: 'On First Looking into Chapman's Homer' (1817)

11 The discovery of a new dish does more for human happiness than the discovery of a star.
Anthelme Brillat-Savarin 1755-1826: *Physiologie du Goût* (1826)

12 Why sir, there is every possibility that you will soon be able to tax it!
to Gladstone, when asked about the usefulness of electricity
Michael Faraday 1791-1867: W. E. H. Lecky *Democracy and Liberty* (1899 ed.)

13 The example of the discoveries of Nobel is a case in point: powerful explosives have allowed men to do admirable work. They are also a terrible means of destruction in the hands of great criminals who lead people into war. I am among those who think with Nobel that humanity will derive more good than bad from new discoveries.
Pierre Curie 1859-1906: lecture to the Swedish Academy, 1905

14 Name the greatest of all the inventors. Accident.

Mark Twain 1835–1910: *Notebook* (1935)

15 When man wanted to make a machine that would walk he created the wheel, which does not resemble a leg.

Guillaume Apollinaire 1880–1918: *Les Mamelles de Tirésias* (1918)

16 Yes, wonderful things.

when asked what he could see on first looking into the tomb of Tutankhamun, 26 November 1922; his notebook records the words as 'Yes, it is wonderful'
Howard Carter 1874–1939: H. V. F. Winstone *Howard Carter and the discovery of the tomb of Tutankhamun* (1993)

17 That Greek one then is my hero, who watched the bath water rise above his navel and rushed out naked, 'I found it, I found it' into the street in all his shining, and forgot that others would only stare at his genitals.

Dannie Abse 1923– : *Walking under Water* (1952)

18 Whatever Nature has in store for mankind, unpleasant as it may be, men must accept, for ignorance is never better than knowledge.

Enrico Fermi 1901–54: Laura Fermi *Atoms in the Family* (1955)

19 Discovery consists of seeing what everybody has seen and thinking what nobody has thought.

Albert von Szent-Györgyi 1893–1986: Irving Good (ed.) *The Scientist Speculates* (1962)

20 Fleming was like a man who stumbles on a nugget of gold, shows it to a few friends, and then goes off to look for something else. Florey was like a man who goes back to the same spot and creates a gold mine.

Gwyn Macfarlane 1907–87: *Howard Florey* (1979)

21 praise without end the go-ahead zeal of whoever it was invented the wheel; but never a word for the poor soul's sake that thought ahead, and invented the brake.

Howard Nemerov 1920–91: 'To the Congress of the United States, Entering Its Third Century' 26 February 1989

22 The Patent Office is the gatekeeper to the new age.

Tom Stoppard 1937– : *The Invention of Love* (1997)

23 One of the strictures of the scientific ethos is that a discovery does not exist until it is safely reviewed and in print.

Edward O. Wilson 1929– : *Consilience: The Unity of Knowledge* (1998)

Ireland

1 England's difficulty is Ireland's opportunity.

mid 19th century, associated with the aspirations of Irish nationalism

2 Celtic twilight the romantic fairy tale atmosphere of Irish folklore; literature conveying this.

the title of an anthology collected by W. B. Yeats

3 the Emerald Isle Ireland.

William Drennan Erin (1795) 'Nor one feeling of vengeance presume to defile The cause, or the men, of the Emerald Isle'

4 the Flight of the Earls the flight into exile from Ireland of the two Catholic leaders, Hugh O'Neill, Earl of Tyrone, and Rory O'Donnell, Earl of Tyrconnell, 1607.

see 24 below

5 Land of Saints and Scholars Ireland.

saint meaning 'monk' or 'anchorite', alluding to the traditional view of medieval Ireland as a monastic and scholarly land

6 the Wild Geese the Irish Jacobites who fled from Ireland to the Continent after the defeat of James II at the Battle of the Boyne (1690), many of whom later took service with the French forces.

recorded in a poem by M. J. Barry in Spirit of the Nation (1845) 'The wild geese—the wild geese,—'Tis long since they flew, O'er the billowy ocean's bright bosom of blue'

7 Icham of Irlaunde
Ant of the holy londe of irlonde
Gode sir pray ich ye
for of saynte charite,
come ant daunce wyt me,
in irlaunde.

Anonymous: fourteenth century

8 I met wid Napper Tandy, and he took me
   by the hand,
And he said, 'How's poor ould Ireland, and
   how does she stand?'
She's the most disthressful country that
   iver yet was seen,
For they're hangin' men an' women for
   the wearin' o' the Green.
Anonymous: 'The Wearin' o' the Green' (c.1795
ballad)

9 The moment the very name of Ireland is
mentioned, the English seem to bid adieu
to common feeling, common prudence,
and common sense, and to act with the
barbarity of tyrants, and the fatuity of
idiots.
Sydney Smith 1771–1845: *Letters of Peter Plymley*
(1807)

10 The harp that once through Tara's halls
The soul of music shed,
Now hangs as mute on Tara's walls
As if that soul were fled.
Thomas Moore 1779–1852: 'The harp that once
through Tara's halls'(1807)

11 Ulster is Scotland in Ireland.
Gustave de Beaumont 1802–66: *L'Irlande sociale,
politique et religieuse* (1839)

12 Thus you have a starving population, an
absentee aristocracy, and an alien Church,
and in addition the weakest executive in
the world. That is the Irish Question.
Benjamin Disraeli 1804–81: speech in the House of
Commons, 16 February 1844

13 I decided some time ago that if the G.O.M.
[Gladstone] went for Home Rule, the
Orange card would be the one to play.
Please God it may turn out the ace of
trumps and not the two.
Lord Randolph Churchill 1849–94: letter to Lord
Justice FitzGibbon, 16 February 1886; see **Ways and
Means** 18

14 Ulster will fight; Ulster will be right.
Lord Randolph Churchill 1849–94: public letter, 7
May 1886

15 For the great Gaels of Ireland
Are the men that God made mad,
For all their wars are merry,
And all their songs are sad.
G. K. Chesterton 1874–1936: *The Ballad of the White
Horse* (1911)

16 Ireland is the old sow that eats her farrow.
James Joyce 1882–1941: *A Portrait of the Artist as a
Young Man* (1916)

17 In Ireland the inevitable never happens
and the unexpected constantly occurs.
John Pentland Mahaffy 1839–1919: W. B. Stanford
and R. B. McDowell *Mahaffy* (1971)

18 Out of Ireland have we come.
Great hatred, little room,
Maimed us at the start.
W. B. Yeats 1865–1939: 'Remorse for Intemperate
Speech' (1933)

19 Spenser's Ireland
has not altered;—
a place as kind as it is green,
the greenest place I've never seen.
Marianne Moore 1887–1972: 'Spenser's Ireland'
(1941)

20 Clay is the word and clay is the flesh
Where the potato-gatherers like
   mechanized scarecrows move
Along the side-fall of the hill—Maguire
   and his men.
Patrick Kavanagh 1904–67: 'The Great Hunger'
(1947)

21 God made the grass, the air and the rain;
and the grass, the air and the rain made
the Irish; and the Irish turned the grass,
the air and the rain back into God.
Sean O'Faolain 1900–91: in *Holiday* June 1958

22   The famous
Northern reticence, the tight gag of place
And times: yes, yes. Of the 'wee six' I sing.
Seamus Heaney 1939– : 'Whatever You Say Say
Nothing' (1975)

23 Do you not feel that this island is moored
only lightly to the sea-bed, and might be
off for the Americas at any moment?
Sebastian Barry 1955– : *Prayers of Sherkin* (1991)

24 I've said and written a lot about
emigration. But maybe soon I'll be writing
The Flight of Earls in reverse—about
everyone coming back home again.
Liam Reilly: in *Irish Post* 23 August 1997; see **4**
above

25 I'm Irish. We think sideways.
Spike Milligan 1918–2002: in *Independent on
Sunday* 20 June 1999

26 We've never been cool, we're hot. Irish
people are Italians who can't dress,
Jamaicans who can't dance.
Bono 1960– : interview, 25 February 2001; in
Independent 26 February 2001

Jazz see also **Music**

PHRASES

1 beat generation a movement of young people in the 1950s and early 1960s who rejected conventional society, valuing free self-expression and favouring modern jazz.
the phrase was supposedly coined by Jack Kerouac (1922–69) in the course of a conversation

QUOTATIONS

2 Jazz will endure, just as long as people hear it through their feet instead of their brains.
John Philip Sousa 1854–1932: Nat Shapiro (ed.) *An Encyclopedia of Quotations about Music* (1978)

3 It don't mean a thing
If it ain't got that swing.
Irving Mills 1894–1985: 'It Don't Mean a Thing' (1932 song; music by Duke Ellington)

4 Jazz music is to be played sweet, soft, plenty rhythm.
Jelly Roll Morton 1885–1941: *Mister Jelly Roll* (1950)

5 What a terrible revenge by the culture of the Negroes on that of the whites!
Ignacy Jan Paderewski 1860–1941: Nat Shapiro

(ed.) *An Encyclopedia of Quotations about Music* (1978)

6 Playing 'Bop' is like scrabble with all the vowels missing.
Duke Ellington 1899–1974: in *Look* 10 August 1954

7 A jazz musician is a juggler who uses harmonies instead of oranges.
Benny Green 1927– : *The Reluctant Art* (1962)

8 Jazz is the only music in which the same note can be played night after night but differently each time.
Ornette Coleman 1930– : W. H. Mellers *Music in a New Found Land* (1964)

9 If you still have to ask . . . shame on you.
when asked what jazz is; sometimes quoted as, 'Man, if you gotta ask you'll never know'
Louis Armstrong 1901–71: Max Jones et al. *Salute to Satchmo* (1970)

10 [Charlie] Parker was a modern jazz player just as Picasso was a modern player and Pound a modern poet. I hadn't realized that jazz had gone from Lascaux to Jackson Pollock in fifty years.
Philip Larkin 1922–85: *Required Writing* (1983)

Jealousy see **Envy and Jealousy**

Journalism see also **News**

PROVERBS AND SAYINGS

1 All the news that's fit to print.
motto of the New York Times, *from 1896; coined by Adolph S. Ochs (1858–1935)*

2 Top people take *The Times*.
advertising slogan for The Times *newspaper, from January 1959*

PHRASES

3 the fourth estate the press.
a group regarded as having power in the land equivalent to that of one of the three Estates of the Realm, the Crown, the House of Lords, and the House of Commons; from Lord Macaulay in 1843, 'The gallery in which the reporters sit has become a fourth estate of the realm'

4 Page Three a British trademark term for a feature which formerly appeared daily on

page three of the Sun newspaper and included a picture of a topless young woman.
see 32 below, **Women** 13

5 the silly season the months of August and September, when newspapers make up for the lack of serious news with articles on trivial topics.
the time when Parliament and the law courts are in recess; recorded in 1861, when the Saturday Review of 13 July spoke of 'the Silly Season of 1861 setting in a month or two before its time'

6 watch this space! be alert for further news of a particular topic.
space a portion of a newspaper etc. available for a specific purpose, especially for advertising; room which may be acquired for this

7 The journalists have constructed for themselves a little wooden chapel, which they also call the Temple of Fame, in which they put up and take down portraits all day long and make such a hammering you can't hear yourself speak.

Georg Christoph Lichtenberg 1742–99: A. Leitzmann *Georg Christoph Lichtenberg Aphorismen* (1904)

8 *The Times* has made many ministries.

Walter Bagehot 1826–77: *The English Constitution* (1867) 'The Cabinet'

9 All newspaper and journalistic activity is an intellectual brothel from which there is no retreat.

Leo Tolstoy 1828–1910: letter to Prince V. P. Meshchersky, 22 August 1871

10 There are laws to protect the freedom of the press's speech, but none that are worth anything to protect the people from the press.

Mark Twain 1835–1910: 'License of the Press' (1873)

11 When well wetted and beaten into a pulp and mixed with gum and then boiled gently in a pipkin, there is simply nothing equal to *The Times* for stopping cracks or holes in one's canoe, which is, as Mr Pepys would say, an excellent thing in a newspaper.

Mary Kingsley 1862–1900: in *Fortnightly Review* April 1898

12 You furnish the pictures and I'll furnish the war.

message to the artist Frederic Remington in Havana, Cuba, during the Spanish-American War of 1898
William Randolph Hearst 1863–1951: attributed

13 By office boys for office boys.

of the Daily Mail
Lord Salisbury 1830–1903: H. Hamilton Fyfe *Northcliffe, an Intimate Biography* (1930)

14 The men with the muck-rakes are often indispensable to the well-being of society; but only if they know when to stop raking the muck.

Theodore Roosevelt 1858–1919: speech in Washington, 14 April 1906

15 A cynical, mercenary, demagogic, corrupt press will produce in time a people as base as itself.

Joseph Pulitzer 1847–1911: inscribed on the gateway to the Columbia School of Journalism in New York

16 The power of the press is very great, but not so great as the power of suppress.

Lord Northcliffe 1865–1922: office message, *Daily Mail* 1918; Reginald Rose and Geoffrey Harmsworth *Northcliffe* (1959)

17 Comment is free, but facts are sacred.

C. P. Scott 1846–1932: in *Manchester Guardian* 5 May 1921; see 28 below

18 You cannot hope
to bribe or twist,
thank God! the
British journalist.
But, seeing what
the man will do
unbribed, there's
no occasion to.

Humbert Wolfe 1886–1940: 'Over the Fire' (1930)

19 Journalism—an ability to meet the challenge of filling the space.

Rebecca West 1892–1983: in *New York Herald Tribune* 22 April 1956

20 Anyone here been raped and speaks English?

shouted by a British TV reporter in a crowd of Belgian civilians waiting to be airlifted out of the Belgian Congo, c.1960
Anonymous: Edward Behr *Anyone Here been Raped and Speaks English?* (1981)

21 A good newspaper, I suppose, is a nation talking to itself.

Arthur Miller 1915– : in *Observer* 26 November 1961

22 Freedom of the press in Britain means freedom to print such of the proprietor's prejudices as the advertisers don't object to.

Hannen Swaffer 1879–1962: Tom Driberg *Swaff* (1974)

23 When the legend becomes fact, print the legend.

Willis Goldbeck and **James Warner Bellah**: *The Man who Shot Liberty Valance* (1962 film); see also **Heroes** 18

24 Let us today drudge on about our inescapably impossible task of providing every week a first rough draft of a history that will never be completed about a world we can never really understand.

Philip Graham 1915–63: remarks to *Newsweek* correspondents, London, 29 April 1963

25 Success in journalism can be a form of failure. Freedom comes from lack of possessions. The truth-divulging paper must imitate the tramp and sleep under a hedge.

Graham Greene 1904–91: in *New Statesman* 31 May 1968

26 My motto is publish and be sued.

Richard Ingrams 1937– : on BBC Radio 4, 4 May 1977

27 The Third World never sold a newspaper.

Rupert Murdoch 1931– : in *Observer* 1 January 1978; see **International Relations** 8

28 Comment is free but facts are on expenses.

Tom Stoppard 1937– : *Night and Day* (1978); see 17 above

29 Rock journalism is people who can't write interviewing people who can't talk for people who can't read.

Frank Zappa 1940–93: Linda Botts *Loose Talk* (1980)

30 Whenever I see a newspaper I think of the poor trees. As trees they provide beauty, shade and shelter. But as paper all they provide is rubbish.

Yehudi Menuhin 1916–99: attributed, 1982

31 Go to where the silence is and say something.

accepting an award from Columbia University for her

coverage of the 1991 massacre in East Timor by Indonesian troops

Amy Goodman 1957– : in *Columbia Journalism Review* March/April 1994

32 I don't know. The editor did it when I was away.

when asked why he had allowed Page 3 to develop

Rupert Murdoch 1931– : in *Guardian* 25 February 1994; see 4 above

33 When seagulls follow a trawler, it is because they think sardines will be thrown into the sea.

to the media at the end of a press conference, 31 March 1995

Eric Cantona 1966– : in *The Times* 1 April 1995

34 The press is ferocious. It forgives nothing, it only hunts for mistakes.

Diana, Princess of Wales 1961–97: in *Le Monde* 27 August 1997

35 No government in history has been as obsessed with public relations as this one . . . Speaking for myself, if there is a message I want to be off it.

Jeremy Paxman 1950– : in *Daily Telegraph* 3 July 1998

Justice see also **The Law**

1 All's fair in love and war.

early 17th century, meaning that in certain conditions rules do not apply, and any measures are acceptable

2 Be just before you're generous.

mid 18th century, often used in the context of advising that one should settle any obligations before indulging in generosity

3 A fair exchange is no robbery.

mid 16th century, sometimes used of an action regarded as cancelling out an obligation which has been incurred

4 Fair play's a jewel.

early 19th century, applauding the value of honest dealing

5 Give and take is fair play.

late 18th century

6 Give the Devil his due.

late 16th century, meaning that one should acknowledge the strengths and capabilities of even the most unpleasant person

7 One law for the rich and another for the poor.

mid 19th century

8 There are two sides to every question.

early 19th century, meaning that a problem can be seen from more than one angle

9 Turn about is fair play.

mid 18th century, recommending equality of opportunity

10 We all love justice—at our neighbour's expense.

American proverb, mid 20th century

11 What goes around comes around.

modern proverbial saying of US origin, late 20th century, often used as a comment on someone becoming subject to what they have visited on others

12 What's sauce for the goose is sauce for the gander.

late 17th century; meaning that what is suitable for a woman is also suitable for a man, but now sometimes used in wider contexts

13 Jedem das Seine German = 'To each his own'.
inscription on the gate of Buchenwald concentration camp, c. 1937; often quoted as 'Everyone gets what he deserves'; see **World War II** 25

14 Jedburgh justice summary justice.
such as that meted out to Border reivers at Jedburgh in southern Scotland in the 16th century

15 a Roland for an Oliver an appropriate retaliation for a verbal or physical attack, a quid pro quo.
Roland *the legendary nephew of Charlemagne, celebrated with his comrade* Oliver *in the medieval romance* Chanson de Roland

QUOTATIONS

16 Life for life,
Eye for eye, tooth for tooth.
Bible: Exodus; see **Revenge** 3, 8

17 What I say is that 'just' or 'right' means nothing but what is in the interest of the stronger party.
spoken by Thrasymachus
Plato 429–347 BC: *The Republic*

18 Judge not, that ye be not judged.
Bible: St Matthew; see **Prejudice** 1

19 *Nulla iniuria est, quae in volentem fiat.*
No injustice is done to someone who wants that thing done.
usually quoted as 'Volenti non fit iniuria'
Ulpian d. 228: *Corpus Iuris Civilis* Digests

20 Justice is the constant and perpetual wish to render to every one his due.
Justinian AD 483–565: *Institutes*

21 To no man will we sell, or deny, or delay, right or justice.
Magna Carta 1215: clause 40

22 If the parties will at my hands call for justice, then, all were it my father stood on the one side, and the Devil on the other, his cause being good, the Devil should have right.
Thomas More 1478–1535: William Roper *Life of Sir Thomas More*

23 *Fiat justitia et pereat mundus.*
Let justice be done, though the world perish.
Ferdinand I 1503–64: motto; Johannes Manlius *Locorum Communium Collectanea* (1563)

24 The quality of mercy is not strained,

It droppeth as the gentle rain from heaven
Upon the place beneath: it is twice blessed;
It blesseth him that gives and him that takes.
William Shakespeare 1564–1616: *The Merchant of Venice* (1596–8)

25 You manifestly wrong even the poorest ploughman, if you demand not his free consent.
Charles I 1600–49: The King's Reasons for declining the jurisdiction of the High Court of Justice, 21 January 1649

26 I'm armed with more than complete steel—The justice of my quarrel.
Anonymous: *Lust's Dominion* (1657); attributed to Marlowe, though of doubtful authorship

27 A lawyer has no business with the justice or injustice of the cause which he undertakes, unless his client asks his opinion, and then he is bound to give it honestly. The justice or injustice of the cause is to be decided by the judge.
Samuel Johnson 1709–84: James Boswell *Journal of a Tour to the Hebrides* (1785) 15 August 1773

28 Consider what you think justice requires, and decide accordingly. But never give your reasons; for your judgement will probably be right, but your reasons will certainly be wrong.
advice to a newly appointed colonial governor ignorant in the law
William Murray, Lord Mansfield 1705–93: Lord Campbell *The Lives of the Chief Justices of England* (1849)

29 Justice is truth in action.
Benjamin Disraeli 1804–81: speech, House of Commons, 11 February 1851

30 When I hear of an 'equity' in a case like this, I am reminded of a blind man in a dark room—looking for a black hat—which isn't there.
Lord Bowen 1835–94: John Alderson Foote *Pie-Powder* (1911)

31 *J'accuse.*
I accuse.
on the Dreyfus affair
Émile Zola 1840–1902: title of an open letter to the President of the French Republic in *L'Aurore* 13 January 1898

32 A man who is good enough to shed his blood for the country is good enough to be given a square deal afterwards. More than that no man is entitled to, and less than that no man shall have.

Theodore Roosevelt 1858–1919: speech at the Lincoln Monument, Springfield, Illinois, 4 June 1903

33 In England, justice is open to all—like the Ritz Hotel.

James Mathew 1830–1908: R. E. Megarry *Miscellany-at-Law* (1955)

34 Injustice is relatively easy to bear; what stings is justice.

H. L. Mencken 1880–1956: *Prejudices, Third Series* (1922)

35 A long line of cases shows that it is not merely of some importance, but is of fundamental importance that justice should not only be done, but should manifestly and undoubtedly be seen to be done.

Gordon Hewart 1870–1943: Rex v Sussex Justices, 9 November 1923

36 Injustice anywhere is a threat to justice everywhere.

Martin Luther King 1929–68: letter from Birmingham Jail, Alabama, 16 April 1963

37 What good is an ounce of justice in an ocean of shit?

Sony Labou Tansi 1947–95: *The Antipeople* (1983)

38 If this is justice, I am a banana.

on the libel damages awarded against Private Eye *to Sonia Sutcliffe*

Ian Hislop 1960– : comment, 24 May 1989

39 We shouldn't have all these campaigns to get the Birmingham Six released if they'd been hanged. They'd have been forgotten and the whole community would be satisfied.

Lord Denning 1899–1999: in *Spectator* 18 August 1990

40 If it falls to me to start a fight to cut out the cancer of bent and twisted journalism in our country with the simple sword of truth and the trusty shield of British fair play, so be it.

Jonathan Aitken 1942– : statement, London, 10 April 1995

Kissing

1 Kissing goes by favour.

early 17th century, meaning that a kiss is often given as a reward for something done

2 When the gorse is out of bloom, kissing's out of fashion.

mid 19th century; the idea behind the saying is that gorse is always in flower somewhere: see **Love** 14

QUOTATIONS

3 *Da mi basia mille, deinde centum,*
Dein mille altera, dein secunda centum,
Deinde usque altera mille, deinde centum.
Give me a thousand kisses, then a hundred, then another thousand, then a second hundred, then yet another thousand, then a hundred.

Catullus c.84–c.54 BC: *Carmina*

4 I kissed thee ere I killed thee, no way but this,
Killing myself to die upon a kiss.

William Shakespeare 1564–1616: *Othello* (1602–4)

5 Those lips please me which are placed
Close but not too strictly laced:

Yielding I would have them; yet
Not a wimbling tongue admit.

Robert Herrick 1591–1674: 'Kisses Loathsome' (1648)

6 But indeed, dear, these kisses on paper are scarce worth keeping. You gave me one on my neck that night you were in such good-humour, and one on my lips on some forgotten occasion, that I would not part with for a hundred thousand paper ones.

Jane Carlyle 1801–66: letter to Thomas Carlyle, 3 October 1826

7 O Love, O fire! once he drew
With one long kiss my whole soul through
My lips, as sunlight drinketh dew.

Alfred, Lord Tennyson 1809–92: 'Fatima' (1832)

8 What of soul was left, I wonder, when the kissing had to stop?

Robert Browning 1812–89: 'A Toccata of Galuppi's' (1855); see **Ending** 11

9 I wonder who's kissing her now.

Frank Adams and **Will M. Hough**: title of song (1909)

10 You must remember this, a kiss is still a
   kiss,
   A sigh is just a sigh;
   The fundamental things apply,
   As time goes by.
   Herman Hupfeld 1894–1951: 'As Time Goes By'
   (1931 song)

11 A fine romance with no kisses.
   A fine romance, my friend, this is.
   Dorothy Fields 1905–74: 'A Fine Romance' (1936
   song)

12 Where do the noses go? I always wondered
   where the noses would go.
   Ernest Hemingway 1899–1961: *For Whom the Bell
   Tolls* (1940)

13 A kiss can be a comma, a question mark or
   an exclamation point. That's basic spelling

that every woman ought to know.
Mistinguette 1875–1956: in *Theatre Arts* December
1955

14 I wasn't kissing her, I was just whispering
   in her mouth.
   on being discovered by his wife with a chorus girl
   Chico Marx 1891–1961: Groucho Marx and Richard
   J. Anobile *Marx Brothers Scrapbook* (1973)

15 Oh, innocent victims of Cupid,
   Remember this terse little verse;
   To let a fool kiss you is stupid,
   To let a kiss fool you is worse.
   E. Y. Harburg 1898–1981: 'Inscriptions on a Lipstick'
   (1965)

16 Kissing girls is not like science, nor is it like
   sport. It is the third thing when you
   thought there were only two.
   Tom Stoppard 1937– : *The Invention of Love* (1997)

Knowledge

1 **. . . But I know a man who can.**
   advertising slogan for the Automobile Association

2 **The cobbler to his last and the gunner to
   his linstock.**
   *mid 18th century; a fanciful extension of 'Let the
   cobbler stick to his last' (see 8 below). The gunner's
   linstock was a long pole used to hold a match for
   firing a cannon*

3 **Fools ask questions that wise men cannot
   answer.**
   *mid 17th century, meaning that a foolish person may
   put a question to which there is no simple or easily
   given answer*

4 **Knowledge and timber shouldn't be much
   used until they are seasoned.**
   American proverb, mid 19th century

5 **Knowledge is power.**
   *late 16th century; see 26 below, **Arts** 3*

6 **The larger the shoreline of knowledge, the
   longer the shoreline of wonder.**
   North American proverb, mid 20th century

7 **Learning is better than house and land.**
   *late 18th century, reflecting on the difference between
   knowledge and material, and therefore ephemeral,
   possessions*

8 **Let the cobbler stick to his last.**
   *mid 16th century, meaning that people should only
   concern themselves with things they know something*

about (*the cobbler's* last *is a shoemaker's model for
shaping or repairing a shoe or boot*); *see also 2 above*

9 **A little knowledge is a dangerous thing.**
   early 18th century; alteration of Pope: see 29, 41 below

10 **Out of the mouths of babes—.**
   *late 19th century, meaning that young children may
   sometimes speak with disconcerting wisdom; with
   allusion to the Bible (Psalms), 'Out of the mouth of
   very babes and sucklings hast thou ordained strength,
   because of thine enemies'*

11 **When house and land are gone and spent,
   then learning is most excellent.**
   *mid 18th century, contrasting the value of learning
   with the ephemeral nature of material possessions*

12 **have the right sow by the ear** have the
   correct understanding of a situation.
   *see **Practicality** 3*

13 **milk for babes** something easy and
   pleasant to learn.
   *especially in allusion to the Bible (I Corinthians) 'I . . .
   speak unto you . . . even as unto babes in Christ. I
   have fed you with milk, and not with meat'*

14 **'satiable curiosity** a thirst for knowledge
   that cannot be satisfied.
   as exemplified by the Elephant's Child in Kipling's Just
   So Stories, *who was 'full of 'satiable curtiosity': see
   also 43 below*

15 the tree of knowledge knowledge in general, comprising all its branches.
the tree in the Garden of Eden bearing the apple eaten by Eve

QUOTATIONS

16 The fox knows many things—the hedgehog one *big* one.
Archilochus 7th century BC: E. Diehl (ed.) *Anthologia Lyrica Graeca* (3rd ed., 1949–52); see **Character** 42

17 He who knows does not speak.
He who speaks does not know.
Lao Tzu c.604–c.531 BC: *Tao-te Ching* ch. 56

18 He that increaseth knowledge increaseth sorrow.
Bible: Ecclesiastes

19 The price of wisdom is above rubies.
Bible: Job

20 I know nothing except the fact of my ignorance.
Socrates 469–399 BC: Diogenes Laertius *Lives of the Philosophers*

21 Paul, thou art beside thyself; much learning doth make thee mad.
Bible: Acts of the Apostles

22 For now we see through a glass, darkly; but then face to face: now I know in part; but then shall I know even as also I am known.
Bible: I Corinthians

23 Each had but known one part, and no man all;
Hence into deadly error each did fall.
No way to know the All man's heart can find:
Can knowledge e'er accompany the blind?
on blind men's conclusions on touching different parts of an elephant
Sana'i d. c.1131: 'The Blind Men and the Elephant'; see **Insight** 5

24 Everyman, I will go with thee, and be thy guide,
In thy most need to go by thy side.
spoken by 'Knowledge'
Anonymous: *Everyman* (c.1509–19)

25 *Que sais-je?*
What do I know?
on the position of the sceptic
Montaigne 1533–92: *Essais* (1580)

26 Knowledge itself is power.
Francis Bacon 1561–1626: *Meditationes Sacrae* (1597) 'Of Heresies'; see 5 above

27 What song the Syrens sang, or what name Achilles assumed when he hid himself among women, though puzzling questions, are not beyond all conjecture.
Thomas Browne 1605–82: *Hydriotaphia* (Urn Burial, 1658)

28 We have first raised a dust and then complain we cannot see.
George Berkeley 1685–1753: *A Treatise Concerning the Principles of Human Knowledge* (1710)

29 A little learning is a dangerous thing;
Drink deep, or taste not the Pierian spring.
Alexander Pope 1688–1744: *An Essay on Criticism* (1711); see 9 above, **Poetry** 3

30 Knowledge may give weight, but accomplishments give lustre, and many more people see than weigh.
Lord Chesterfield 1694–1773: *Maxims* (1774)

31 Knowledge is of two kinds. We know a subject ourselves, or we know where we can find information upon it.
Samuel Johnson 1709–84: James Boswell *Life of Samuel Johnson* (1791) 18 April 1775

32   Knowledge dwells
In heads replete with thoughts of other men;
Wisdom in minds attentive to their own.
William Cowper 1731–1800: *The Task* (1785) 'The Winter Walk at Noon'

33 Does the eagle know what is in the pit?
Or wilt thou go ask the mole:
Can wisdom be put in a silver rod?
Or love in a golden bowl?
William Blake 1757–1827: *The Book of Thel* (1789) 'Thel's Motto'

34   Do not all charms fly
At the mere touch of cold philosophy?
There was an awful rainbow once in heaven:
We know her woof, her texture; she is given
In the dull catalogue of common things.
Philosophy will clip an Angel's wings.
John Keats 1795–1821: 'Lamia' (1820)

35 Knowledge advances by steps, and not by leaps.
Lord Macaulay 1800–59: T. F. Ellis (ed.) *Miscellaneous Writings of Lord Macaulay* (1860) 'History' (1828)

36 Knowledge comes, but wisdom lingers.
Alfred, Lord Tennyson 1809–92: 'Locksley Hall' (1842)

37 You will find it a very good practice always to verify your references, sir!
Martin Joseph Routh 1755–1854: John William Burgon *Lives of Twelve Good Men* (1888 ed.)

38 It is better to know nothing than to know what ain't so.
Josh Billings 1818–85: *Proverb* (1874)

39 No lesson seems to be so deeply inculcated by the experience of life as that you never should trust experts. If you believe the doctors, nothing is wholesome: if you believe the theologians, nothing is innocent: if you believe the soldiers, nothing is safe. They all require to have their strong wine diluted by a very large admixture of insipid common sense.
Lord Salisbury 1830–1903: letter to Lord Lytton, 15 June 1877

40 Now that I do know it, I shall do my best to forget it.
Arthur Conan Doyle 1859–1930: *A Study in Scarlet* (1887)

41 If a little knowledge is dangerous, where is the man who has so much as to be out of danger?
T. H. Huxley 1825–95: *Collected Essays* vol. 3 (1895) 'On Elementary Instruction in Physiology' (written 1877); see 9 above

42 The motto of all the mongoose family is, 'Run and find out.'
Rudyard Kipling 1865–1936: *The Jungle Book* (1894)

43 I keep six honest serving-men
(They taught me all I knew);
Their names are What and Why and When
And How and Where and Who.
Rudyard Kipling 1865–1936: *Just So Stories* (1902) 'The Elephant's Child'; see 14 above

44 There is no such thing on earth as an uninteresting subject; the only thing that can exist is an uninterested person.
G. K. Chesterton 1874–1936: *Heretics* (1905)

45 For lust of knowing what should not be known,
We take the Golden Road to Samarkand.
James Elroy Flecker 1884–1915: *The Golden Journey to Samarkand* (1913)

46 Owl hasn't exactly got Brain, but he Knows Things.
A. A. Milne 1882–1956: *Winnie-the-Pooh* (1926)

47 Pedantry is the dotage of knowledge.
Holbrook Jackson 1874–1948: *Anatomy of Bibliomania* (1930)

48 Where is the wisdom we have lost in knowledge?
Where is the knowledge we have lost in information?
T. S. Eliot 1888–1965: *The Rock* (1934)

49 An expert is one who knows more and more about less and less.
Nicholas Murray Butler 1862–1947: commencement address at Columbia University; attributed

50 Experts have
their expert fun
ex-cathedra
telling one
just how nothing
can be done.
Piet Hein 1905– : 'Experts' (1966)

51 An expert is someone who knows some of the worst mistakes that can be made in his subject and who manages to avoid them.
Werner Heisenberg 1901–76: *Der Teil und das Ganze* (1969)

52 Not many people know that.
Michael Caine 1933– : title of book (1984)

53 The Admiralty sent the *Beagle* to South America with Darwin on board not because they were interested in evolution but because they knew that the first step to understanding (and, with luck, controlling) the world was to make a map of it. The same is true of the genes.
Steve Jones 1944– : *The Language of the Genes* (1993)

54 That was a little bit more information than I needed to know.
Quentin Tarantino 1963– : *Pulp Fiction* (1994 film); spoken by Uma Thurman

55 Knowledge is good. It does not have to look good or sound good or even do good. It is good just by being knowledge. And the only thing that makes it knowledge is that it is true. You can't have too much of it and there is no little too little to be worth having.
Tom Stoppard 1937– : *The Invention of Love* (1997)

Language see also Meaning, Speech, Swearing, Words

PROVERBS AND SAYINGS

1 The quick brown fox jumps over the lazy dog.

traditional sentence used by keyboarders to ensure that all letters of the alphabet are functioning

PHRASES

2 political correctness the avoidance of forms of expression or action that are perceived to exclude, marginalize, or insult groups of people who are socially disadvantaged or discriminated against.
see 30 below

3 weasel words words or statements that are intentionally ambiguous or misleading.
the expression was popularized by Theodore Roosevelt: see 19 below

4 winged words highly significant or apposite words.
travelling as directly as arrows to the mark; from Homer The Iliad

QUOTATIONS

5 A word fitly spoken is like apples of gold in pictures of silver.
Bible: Proverbs

6 Grammer, the ground of al.
William Langland c.1330–c.1400: *The Vision of Piers Plowman*

7 Syllables govern the world.
John Selden 1584–1654: *Table Talk* (1689)

8 Good heavens! For more than forty years I have been speaking prose without knowing it.
Molière 1622–73: *Le Bourgeois Gentilhomme* (1671)

9 I have laboured to refine our language to grammatical purity, and to clear it from colloquial barbarisms, licentious idioms, and irregular combinations.
Samuel Johnson 1709–84: in *The Rambler* 14 March 1752

10 The true use of speech is not so much to express our wants as to conceal them.
Oliver Goldsmith 1728–74: in *The Bee* 20 October 1759 'On the Use of Language'

11 Language is the dress of thought.
Samuel Johnson 1709–84: *Lives of the English Poets* (1779–81)

12 In language, the ignorant have prescribed laws to the learned.
Richard Duppa 1770–1831: *Maxims* (1830)

13 He who understands baboon would do more towards metaphysics than Locke.
Charles Darwin 1809–82: Notebook M (16 August 1838)

14 Language is fossil poetry.
Ralph Waldo Emerson 1803–82: *Essays. Second Series* (1844) 'The Poet'

15 It is hard for a woman to define her feelings in language which is chiefly made by men to express theirs.
Thomas Hardy 1840–1928: *Far from the Madding Crowd* (1874)

16 I will not go down to posterity talking bad grammar.
while correcting proofs of his last Parliamentary speech, 31 March 1881
Benjamin Disraeli 1804–81: Robert Blake *Disraeli* (1966)

17 The mystery of language was revealed to me. I knew then that 'w-a-t-e-r' meant the wonderful cool something that was flowing over my hand. That living word awakened my soul, gave it light, joy, set it free!
Helen Keller 1880–1968: *The Story of My Life* (1902)

18 A definition is the enclosing a wilderness of idea within a wall of words.
Samuel Butler 1835–1902: *Notebooks* (1912)

19 One of our defects as a nation is a tendency to use what have been called 'weasel words'. When a weasel sucks eggs the meat is sucked out of the egg. If you use a 'weasel word' after another, there is nothing left of the other.
Theodore Roosevelt 1858–1919: speech in St Louis, 31 May 1916; see 3 above

20 The limits of my language mean the limits of my world.
Ludwig Wittgenstein 1889–1951: *Tractatus Logico-Philosophicus* (1922)

21 One picture is worth ten thousand words.
Frederick R. Barnard: in *Printers' Ink* 10 March 1927; see **Words and Deeds** 5

22 The subjunctive mood is in its death throes, and the best thing to do is to put it out of its misery as soon as possible.
W. Somerset Maugham 1874–1965: *A Writer's Notebook* (1949) written in 1941

23 Would you convey my compliments to the purist who reads your proofs and tell him or her that I write in a sort of broken-down patois which is something like the way a Swiss waiter talks, and that when I split an infinitive, God damn it, I split it so it will stay split.
Raymond Chandler 1888–1959: letter to Edward Weeks, 18 January 1947

24 This is the sort of English up with which I will not put.
Winston Churchill 1874–1965: Ernest Gowers *Plain Words* (1948)

25 Colourless green ideas sleep furiously.
illustrating that grammatical structure is independent of meaning
Noam Chomsky 1928– : *Syntactic Structures* (1957)

26 Slang is a language that rolls up its sleeves, spits on its hands and goes to work.
Carl Sandburg 1878–1967: in *New York Times* 13 February 1959

27 Different persons growing up in the same language are like different bushes trimmed and trained to take the shape of identical elephants. The anatomical details of twigs and branches will fulfill the elephantine shape differently from bush to bush, but the overall outward results are alike.
W. V. O. Quine 1908– : *Word and Object* (1960)

28 Save the gerund and screw the whale.
Tom Stoppard 1937– : *The Real Thing* (1988 rev. ed.); see **Pollution** 2

29 Every sentence he [George Bush] manages to utter scatters its component parts like pond water from a verb chasing its own tail.
Clive James 1939– : *The Dreaming Swimmer* (1992)

30 I believe that political correctness can be a form of linguistic fascism, and it sends shivers down the spine of my generation who went to war against fascism.
P. D. James 1920– : in *Paris Review* 1995; see 2 above

31 Soundbite and slogan, strapline and headline, at every turn we meet hyperbole. The soaring inflation of the English language is more urgently in need of control than the economic variety.
Trevor Nunn 1940– : in *Evening Standard* 3 June 1999

Languages see also **Translation**

PHRASES

1 the gift of tongues the power of speaking in unknown languages, regarded as one of the gifts of the Holy Spirit.
from the account in the Bible (Acts) of the coming of the Holy Spirit to the disciples at Pentecost, after which those to whom the disciples preached 'heard them speak with tongues, and magnify God'

2 the Tower of Babel a tower built in an attempt to reach heaven, which God frustrated by confusing the languages of its builders so that they could not understand one another.
from the biblical story (Genesis), which was probably inspired by the Babylonian ziggurat, and may be an attempt to explain the existence of different languages; see 8 below

QUOTATIONS

3 And Frenssh she spak ful faire and fetisly,
After the scole of Stratford atte Bowe,
For Frenssh of Parys was to hire unknowe.
Geoffrey Chaucer c.1343–1400: *The Canterbury Tales* 'The General Prologue'

4 To God I speak Spanish, to women Italian, to men French, and to my horse—German.
Charles V 1500–58: attributed; Lord Chesterfield *Letters to his Son* (1774)

5 It is a thing plainly repugnant to the Word of God, and the custom of the Primitive Church, to have publick Prayer in the Church, or to minister the Sacraments in a tongue not understood of the people.
The Book of Common Prayer 1662: *Articles of Religion* (1562)

6 So now they have made our English tongue a gallimaufry or hodgepodge of all other speeches.
Edmund Spenser c.1552–99: *The Shepherd's Calendar* (1579)

7 Poets that lasting marble seek
Must carve in Latin or in Greek.
Edmund Waller 1606–87: 'Of English Verse' (1645)

8 I am not like a lady at the court of
Versailles, who said: 'What a dreadful pity
that the bother at the tower of Babel
should have got language all mixed up;
but for that, everyone would always have
spoken French.'
Voltaire 1694–1778: letter to Catherine the Great,
26 May 1767; see 2 above

9 I am always sorry when any language is
lost, because languages are the pedigree of
nations.
Samuel Johnson 1709–84: James Boswell *Journal of
a Tour to the Hebrides* (1785) 18 September 1773

10 My English text is chaste, and all licentious
passages are left in the obscurity of a
learned language.
parodied as 'decent obscurity' in the Anti-Jacobin,
1797–8
Edward Gibbon 1737–94: *Memoirs of My Life* (1796)

11 The great breeding people had gone out
and multiplied; colonies in every clime
attest our success; French is the *patois* of
Europe; English is the language of the
world.
Walter Bagehot 1826–77: in *National Review*
January 1856 'Edward Gibbon'

12 Written English is now inert and
inorganic: not stem and leaf and flower,
not even trim and well-joined masonry,
but a daub of untempered mortar.
A. E. Housman 1859–1936: in *Cambridge Review*
1917

13 England and America are two countries
divided by a common language.
George Bernard Shaw 1856–1950: attributed in
this and other forms, but not found in Shaw's
published writings

14 There even are places where English
completely disappears.
In America, they haven't used it for years!
Why can't the English teach their children
how to speak?
Alan Jay Lerner 1918–86: 'Why Can't the English?'
(1956 song)

15 It is very much better to go out in a bowler
and speaking Spanish than in a sombrero
and speaking English.
Prince Philip, Duke of Edinburgh 1921– : in
Observer 15 April 1962

16 Waiting for the German verb is surely the
ultimate thrill.
Flann O'Brien 1911–66: *The Hair of the Dogma*
(1977)

17 To grow
a second tongue, as
harsh a humiliation
as twice to be born.
John Montague 1929– : 'A Grafted Tongue' (1972)

18 We are walking lexicons. In a single
sentence of idle chatter we preserve Latin,
Anglo-Saxon, Norse; we carry a museum
inside our heads, each day we
commemorate peoples of whom we have
never heard.
Penelope Lively 1933– : *Moon Tiger* (1987)

Last Words

PHRASES

1 famous last words said as an ironic
comment on or reply to an overconfident
assertion that may well be proved wrong
by events.

2 Seven Last Words the last seven utterances
of Christ on the Cross.

QUOTATIONS

3 Crito, we owe a cock to Aesculapius;
please pay it and don't forget it.
Socrates 469–399 BC: Plato *Phaedo*

4 I lived uncertain, I die doubtful: O thou
Being of beings, have mercy upon me!
Aristotle 384–322 BC: attributed, probably
apocryphal; a Latin version was current in the early
17th century

5 *Ave Caesar, morituri te salutant.*
Hail Caesar, those who are about to die
salute you.
gladiators saluting the Roman Emperor
Anonymous: Suetonius *Lives of the Caesars*
'Claudius'

6 *O sancta simplicitas!*
O holy simplicity!
at the stake, seeing an aged peasant bringing a bundle of twigs to throw on the pile
John Huss c.1372–1415: J. W. Zincgreff and J. L. Weidner *Apophthegmata* (1653)

7 After his head was upon the block, [he] lift it up again, and gently drew his beard aside, and said, *This hath not offended the king.*
Thomas More 1478–1535: Francis Bacon *Apophthegms New and Old* (1625)

8 I am going to seek a great perhaps . . . Bring down the curtain, the farce is played out.
François Rabelais c.1494–c.1553: attributed, though none of his contemporaries authenticated the remarks, which have become part of the 'Rabelaisian legend'; Jean Fleury *Rabelais et ses oeuvres* (1877)

9 Be of good comfort Master Ridley, and play the man. We shall this day light such a candle by God's grace in England, as (I trust) shall never be put out.
prior to being burned for heresy, 16 October 1555
Hugh Latimer c.1485–1555: John Foxe *Actes and Monuments* (1570 ed.)

10 All my possessions for a moment of time.
Elizabeth I 1533–1603: attributed, but almost certainly apocryphal

11 My design is to make what haste I can to be gone.
Oliver Cromwell 1599–1658: John Morley *Oliver Cromwell* (1900)

12 I am about to take my last voyage, a great leap in the dark.
Thomas Hobbes 1588–1679: John Watkins *Anecdotes of Men of Learning* (1808)

13 Let not poor Nelly starve.
of Nell Gwyn
Charles II 1630–85: Bishop Gilbert Burnet *History of My Own Time* (1724)

14 This is no time for making new enemies.
on being asked to renounce the Devil on his deathbed
Voltaire 1694–1778: attributed

15 Kiss me, Hardy.
Horatio, Lord Nelson 1758–1805: Robert Southey *Life of Nelson* (1813)

16 More light!
Johann Wolfgang von Goethe 1749–1832: attributed; actually 'Open the second shutter, so that more light can come in'

17 They couldn't hit an elephant at this distance.
immediately prior to being killed by enemy fire at the battle of Spotsylvania in the American Civil War
John Sedgwick d. 1864: Robert E. Denney *The Civil War Years* (1992)

18 Die, my dear Doctor, that's the last thing I shall do!
Lord Palmerston 1784–1865: E. Latham *Famous Sayings and their Authors* (1904)

19 Such is life.
Ned Kelly 1855–80: before being hanged, 11 November 1880

20 So little done, so much to do.
Cecil Rhodes 1853–1902: said on the day of his death; Lewis Michell *Life of Rhodes* (1910)

21 I am just going outside and may be some time.
Captain Lawrence Oates 1880–1912: Scott's diary entry, 16–17 March 1912; see **Epitaphs** 20

22 For God's sake look after our people.
Robert Falcon Scott 1868–1912: last diary entry, 29 March 1912

23 We are putting passengers off in small boats . . . Engine room getting flooded . . . CQ.
CQD was the original SOS call for shipping
Anonymous: last signals sent from the *Titanic*, 15 April 1912

24 Why fear death? It is the most beautiful adventure in life.
Charles Frohman 1860–1915: before drowning in the *Lusitania*, 7 May 1915; see **Death** 60

25 Farewell, my friends. I go to glory.
last words before her scarf caught in a car wheel, breaking her neck
Isadora Duncan 1878–1927: Mary Desti *Isadora Duncan's End* (1929)

26 If this is dying, then I don't think much of it.
Lytton Strachey 1880–1932: Michael Holroyd *Lytton Strachey* vol. 2 (1968)

27 How's the Empire?
to his private secretary on the morning of his death, probably prompted by an article in The Times
George V 1865–1936: letter from Lord Wigram, 31 January 1936; see also **British Towns** 38

28 Just before she [Stein] died she asked, 'What *is* the answer?' No answer came. She laughed and said, 'In that case what is the question?' Then she died.
Gertrude Stein 1874–1946: Donald Sutherland *Gertrude Stein, A Biography of her Work* (1951)

29 Tell them I've had a wonderful life.
Ludwig Wittgenstein 1889–1951: Ray Monk
Ludwig Wittgenstein (1990)

30 Now I'll have eine kleine Pause.
Kathleen Ferrier 1912–53: Gerald Moore *Am I Too Loud?* (1962)

31 Why not, why not, why not. Yeah.
Timothy Leary 1920–96: in *Independent* 1 June 1996; see **Death** 78

32 Love? What is it? Most natural painkiller.

What there is . . . LOVE.
William S. Burroughs 1914–97: final entry in journal, 1 August 1997, the day before he died

33 I love you, honey. I know we're all going to die—but there's three of us who are going to do something about it.
final phone call to his wife from the hijacked Flight 93, which crashed south of Pittsburgh, 11 September 2001
Thomas E. Burnett Jnr 1963–2001: in *Independent* 13 September 2001; see **Murder** 26

The Law see also **Crime and Punishment**, **Justice**

PROVERBS AND SAYINGS

1 The devil makes his Christmas pies of lawyers' tongues and clerks' fingers.
late 16th century, in which the lawyers' tongues and clerks' fingers stand for the words and actions of the legal profession as welcomed by the Devil

2 Gray's Inn for walks,
Lincoln's Inn for a wall,
The Inner Temple for a garden,
And the Middle Temple for a hall.
traditional rhyme, mid 17th century; on the four Inns of Court

3 Hard cases make bad law.
mid 19th century, meaning that difficult cases cause the clarity of the law to be obscured by exceptions and strained interpretations; the saying may now also be used to imply that a law framed in response to a particularly distressing case may not be well-thought-out or well-based

4 Home is home, as the Devil said when he found himself in the Court of Session.
Scottish proverbial saying, mid 19th century; the Court of Session is the supreme civil tribunal of Scotland, established in 1532

5 Ignorance of the law is no excuse for breaking it.
early 15th century; see 18 below

6 A man who is his own lawyer has a fool for his client.
early 19th century

7 No one should be judge in his own cause.
mid 15th century, meaning that it is impossible to be impartial where your own interest is involved

8 Possession is nine points of the law.
early 17th century. Although it does not reflect any specific legal ruling, in early use the satisfaction of ten (sometimes twelve) points was commonly asserted to attest to full entitlement or ownership; possession,

represented by nine (or eleven) points is therefore the closest substitute for this

9 Rules are made to be broken.
mid 20th century; see 23 below

PHRASES

10 habeas corpus a writ requiring a person under arrest to be brought before a judge or into court, especially to secure the person's release unless lawful grounds are shown for their detention.
Latin, literally 'thou shalt have the body (in court)'; see 24 below

11 myrmidon of the law a police officer, a minor administrative officer of the law.
Myrmidon a member of a warlike people of ancient Thessaly, whom, according to a Homeric story, Achilles led to the siege of Troy

12 the thin blue line the police as a defensive barrier of the law.
alteration of thin red line: see The Armed Forces 13

13 twelve good men and true a jury.
traditionally composed of twelve men

QUOTATIONS

14 Written laws are like spider's webs; they will catch, it is true, the weak and poor, but would be torn in pieces by the rich and powerful.
Anacharsis 6th century BC: Plutarch *Parallel Lives* 'Solon'

15 *Salus populi suprema est lex.*
The good of the people is the chief law.
Cicero 106–43 BC: *De Legibus*

16 The rusty curb of old father antick, the law.
William Shakespeare 1564–1616: *Henry IV, Part 1* (1597)

17 How long soever it hath continued, if it be against reason, it is of no force in law.
Edward Coke 1552–1634: *The First Part of the Institutes of the Laws of England* (1628)

18 Ignorance of the law excuses no man; not that all men know the law, but because 'tis an excuse every man will plead, and no man can tell how to confute him.
John Selden 1584–1654: *Table Talk* (1689) 'Law'; see 5 above

19 Law is a bottomless pit.
John Arbuthnot 1667–1735: *The History of John Bull* (1712)

20 The hungry judges soon the sentence sign,
And wretches hang that jury-men may dine.
Alexander Pope 1688–1744: *The Rape of the Lock* (1714)

21 Laws, like houses, lean on one another.
Edmund Burke 1729–97: *A Tract on the Popery Laws* (planned c.1765)

22 Bad laws are the worst sort of tyranny.
Edmund Burke 1729–97: *Speech at Bristol, previous to the Late Election* (1780)

23 Laws were made to be broken.
Christopher North 1785–1854: in *Blackwood's Magazine* (May 1830); see 9 above

24 The have-his-carcase, next to the perpetual motion, is vun of the blessedest things as wos ever made.
Charles Dickens 1812–70: *Pickwick Papers* (1837); see 10 above

25 'If the law supposes that,' said Mr Bumble . . . 'the law is a ass—a idiot.'
Charles Dickens 1812–70: *Oliver Twist* (1838)

26 The one great principle of the English law is, to make business for itself.
Charles Dickens 1812–70: *Bleak House* (1853)

27 A jury too frequently have at least one member, more ready to hang the panel than to hang the traitor.
Abraham Lincoln 1809–65: letter 12 June 1863

28 I know no method to secure the repeal of bad or obnoxious laws so effective as their stringent execution.
Ulysses S. Grant 1822–85: inaugural address, 4 March 1869

29 When constabulary duty's to be done,
A policeman's lot is not a happy one.
W. S. Gilbert 1836–1911: *The Pirates of Penzance* (1879)

30 The Law is the true embodiment
Of everything that's excellent.
It has no kind of fault or flaw,
And I, my Lords, embody the Law.
the Lord Chancellor
W. S. Gilbert 1836–1911: *Iolanthe* (1882)

31 However harmless a thing is, if the law forbids it most people will think it wrong.
W. Somerset Maugham 1874–1965: *A Writer's Notebook* (1949) written in 1896

32 I don't know as I want a lawyer to tell me what I cannot do. I hire him to tell me how to do what I want to do.
J. P. Morgan 1837–1913: Ida M. Tarbell *The Life of Elbert H. Gary* (1925)

33 It is obvious that 'obscenity' is not a term capable of exact legal definition; in the practice of the Courts, it means 'anything that shocks the magistrate'.
Bertrand Russell 1872–1970: *Sceptical Essays* (1928) 'The Recrudescence of Puritanism'

34 You know my views about some regulations—they're written for the obedience of fools and the guidance of wise men.
Harry Day: to Douglas Bader, 1931; Paul Brickhill *Reach for the Sky* (1954)

35 No poet ever interpreted nature as freely as a lawyer interprets the truth.
Jean Giraudoux 1882–1944: *La Guerre de Troie n'aura pas lieu* (1935)

36 A verbal contract isn't worth the paper it is written on.
Sam Goldwyn 1882–1974: Alva Johnston *The Great Goldwyn* (1937)

37 Everything not forbidden is compulsory.
T. H. White 1906–64: *The Sword in the Stone* (1938)

38 The art of cross-examination is not the art of examining crossly. It's the art of leading the witness through a line of propositions he agrees to until he's forced to agree to the *one fatal question*.
Clifford Mortimer d. 1960: John Mortimer *Clinging to the Wreckage* (1982)

39 Today, 15 years after 8 May 1945, I know . . . that a life of obedience, led by orders, instructions, decrees and directives, is a very comfortable one in which one's creative thinking is diminished.
Adolf Eichmann 1906–62: memoirs, in *Independent* 13 August 1999

40 Every society gets the kind of criminal it deserves. What is equally true is that every

community gets the kind of law enforcement it insists on.
Robert Kennedy 1925-68: *The Pursuit of Justice* (1964)

41 Loopholes are not always of a fixed dimension. They tend to enlarge as the numbers that pass through wear them away.
Harold Lever 1914-95: speech to Finance Bill Committee, 22 May 1968

42 A lawyer with his briefcase can steal more than a hundred men with guns.
Mario Puzo 1920-99: *The Godfather* (1969)

43 The South African police would leave no stone unturned to see that nothing disturbed the even terror of their lives.
Tom Sharpe 1928- : *Indecent Exposure* (1973)

44 The Court's opinion will accomplish the seemingly impossible feat of leaving this

area of the law more confused than it found it.
William H. Rehnquist 1924- : dissenting opinion in *Roe v. Wade* 1973

45 I have come to regard the Law Courts not as a cathedral, but as a casino.
Richard Ingrams 1937- : in *Guardian* 30 July 1977

46 Asking the ignorant to use the incomprehensible to decide the unknowable.
on the jury system
Hiller B. Zobel 1932- : 'The Jury on Trial' in *American Heritage* July-August 1995

47 Not only did we play the race card, we played it from the bottom of the deck.
on the defence's conduct of the O. J. Simpson trial
Robert Shapiro 1942- : interview, 3 October 1995, in *The Times* 5 October 1995; see **Ways and Means** 18

Leadership

PROVERBS AND SAYINGS

1 **The fish always stinks from the head downwards.**
late 16th century, meaning that as the freshness of a dead fish can be judged from the condition of its head, any corruption in a country or organization will be manifested first in its leaders

2 **A good leader is also a good follower.**
American proverb, mid 20th century

3 **He that cannot obey cannot command.**
late 15th century, meaning that the experience of being under orders teaches one how they should be given

4 **Take me to your leader.**
catchphrase from science-fiction stories

PHRASES

5 **the Nelson touch** a masterly or sympathetic approach to a problem by the person in charge.
supposedly characteristic of Nelson's style of leadership: see 8 below

QUOTATIONS

6 They be blind leaders of the blind. And if the blind lead the blind, both shall fall into the ditch.
Bible: St Matthew; see **Conformity** 12, **Ignorance** 8

7 Since, then, a prince is necessitated to play the animal well, he chooses among the beasts the fox and the lion, because the lion does not protect himself from traps; the fox does not protect himself from wolves. The prince must be a fox, therefore, to recognize the traps and a lion to frighten the wolves.
Niccolò Machiavelli 1469-1527: *The Prince* (written 1513)

8 I believe my arrival was most welcome, not only to the Commander of the Fleet but almost to every individual in it; and when I came to explain to them the '*Nelson touch*', it was like an electric shock. Some shed tears, all approved—'It was new—it was singular—it was simple!'
Horatio, Lord Nelson 1758-1805: letter to Lady Hamilton, 1 October 1805; see 5 above

9 I used to say of him [Napoleon] that his presence on the field made the difference of forty thousand men.
Duke of Wellington 1769-1852: Philip Henry Stanhope *Notes of Conversations with the Duke of Wellington* (1888) 2 November 1831

10 By the structure of the world we often want, at the sudden occurrence of a grave tempest, to change the helmsman—to

replace the pilot of the calm by the pilot of the storm.
Walter Bagehot 1826–77: *The English Constitution* (1867) 'The Cabinet'

11 The art of leadership . . . consists in consolidating the attention of the people against a single adversary and taking care that nothing will split up that attention.
Adolf Hitler 1889–1945: *Mein Kampf* (1925)

12 So long as men worship the Caesars and Napoleons, Caesars and Napoleons will duly arise and make them miserable.
Aldous Huxley 1894–1963: *Ends and Means* (1937)

13 The final test of a leader is that he leaves behind him in other men the conviction and the will to carry on.
Walter Lippmann 1889–1974: in *New York Herald Tribune* 14 April 1945

14 The loyalties which centre upon number one are enormous. If he trips he must be sustained. If he makes mistakes they must be covered. If he sleeps he must not be wantonly disturbed. If he is no good he must be pole-axed. But this last extreme process cannot be carried out every day; and certainly not in the days just after he has been chosen.
Winston Churchill 1874–1965: *The Second World War* vol. 2 (1949)

15 I know that the right kind of leader for the Labour Party is a desiccated calculating

machine who must not in any way permit himself to be swayed by indignation.
Aneurin Bevan 1897–1960: Michael Foot *Aneurin Bevan* (1973)

16 He never said a word of importance in the Senate and he never did a thing. But somehow he managed to create the image of himself as a shining intellectual, a youthful leader who would change the face of the country.
of John F. Kennedy
Lyndon Baines Johnson 1908–73: Robert Dallek *Flawed Giant* (1998)

17 I don't mind how much my Ministers talk, so long as they do what I say.
Margaret Thatcher 1925– : in *Observer* 27 January 1980

18 To grasp and hold a vision, that is the very essence of successful leadership—not only on the movie set where I learned it, but everywhere.
Ronald Reagan 1911– : in *The Wilson Quarterly* Winter 1994; attributed

19 The art of leadership is saying no, not yes. It is very easy to say yes.
Tony Blair 1953– : in *Mail on Sunday* 2 October 1994

20 Leadership is not about being nice. It's about being right and being strong.
Paul Keating 1944– : in *Time* 9 January 1995

21 Leaders should never, ever try to look cool—that's for dictators.
Ben Elton 1959– : in *Radio Times* 18/24 April 1998

Leisure see also Work

1 All work and no play makes Jack a dull boy.
mid 17th century, warning against a lifestyle without any form of relaxation

2 The busiest men have the most leisure.
late 19th century, meaning that someone who is habitually busy is likely to make best use of their time

3 Have a break, have a Kit-Kat.
advertising slogan for Rowntree's Kit-Kat, from c.1955

4 The wisdom of a learned man cometh by opportunity of leisure: and he that hath little business shall become wise.
Bible: Ecclesiasticus

5 The thing which is the most outstanding and chiefly to be desired by all healthy and good and well-off persons, is leisure with honour.
Cicero 106–43 BC: *Pro Sestio*

6 If all the year were playing holidays,
To sport would be as tedious as to work;
But when they seldom come, they wished for come.
William Shakespeare 1564–1616: *Henry IV, Part 1* (1597)

7 Whether we consider the manual industry of the poor, or the intellectual exertions of the superior classes, we shall find that diligent occupation, if not criminally perverted from its purposes, is at once the instrument of virtue and the secret of happiness. Man cannot be safely trusted with a life of leisure.

Hannah More 1745–1833: *Christian Morals* (1813)

8 What is this life if, full of care,
We have no time to stand and stare.

W. H. Davies 1871–1940: 'Leisure' (1911)

9 A perpetual holiday is a good working definition of hell.

George Bernard Shaw 1856–1950: *Parents and Children* (1914)

10 There's sand in the porridge and sand in the bed,
And if this is pleasure we'd rather be dead.

Noël Coward 1899–1973: 'The English Lido' (1928)

11 To be able to fill leisure intelligently is the last product of civilization.

Bertrand Russell 1872–1970: *The Conquest of Happiness* (1930)

12 Cannot avoid contrasting deliriously rapid flight of time when on a holiday with very much slower passage of days, and even hours, in other and more familiar surroundings.

E. M. Delafield 1890–1943: *The Diary of a Provincial Lady* (1930)

13 Man's heart expands to tinker with his car
For this is Sunday morning, Fate's great bazaar.

Louis MacNeice 1907–63: 'Sunday Morning' (1935)

14 It was Einstein who made the real trouble. He announced in 1905 that there was no such thing as absolute rest. After that there never was.

Stephen Leacock 1869–1944: *The Boy I Left Behind Me* (1947)

15 We are closer to the ants than to the butterflies. Very few people can endure much leisure.

Gerald Brenan 1894–1987: *Thoughts in a Dry Season* (1978)

16 To many people holidays are no voyage of discovery, but a ritual of reassurance.

Phillip Adams 1939– : in *Age* 10 September 1983

17 If I am doing nothing, I like to be doing nothing to some purpose. That is what leisure means.

Alan Bennett 1934– : *A Question of Attribution* (1989)

Letters

PROVERBS AND SAYINGS

1 **Do not close a letter without reading it.**
American proverb, mid 20th century

2 **A love letter sometimes costs more than a three-cent stamp.**
American proverb, mid 20th century

3 **Someone, somewhere, wants a letter from you.**
advertising slogan for the British Post Office in the 1960s

QUOTATIONS

4 Ye see how large a letter I have written unto you with mine own hand.

Bible: Galatians

5 There is nothing to write about, you say. Well then, write and let me know just this—that there is nothing to write about; or tell me in the good old style if you are well.

Pliny the Younger AD c.61–c.112: *Letters*

6 Sir, more than kisses, letters mingle souls.

John Donne 1572–1631: 'To Sir Henry Wotton' (1597–8)

7 I knew one that when he wrote a letter he would put that which was most material in the postscript, as if it had been a bymatter.

Francis Bacon 1561–1626: *Essays* (1625) 'Of Cunning'

8 All letters, methinks, should be free and easy as one's discourse, not studied as an oration, nor made up of hard words like a charm.

Dorothy Osborne 1627–95: letter to William Temple, September 1653

9 I have made this [letter] longer than usual, only because I have not had the time to make it shorter.

Blaise Pascal 1623–62: *Lettres Provinciales* (1657)

10 A woman seldom writes her mind but in her postscript.

Richard Steele 1672–1729: in *The Spectator* 31 May 1711

11 You bid me burn your letters. But I must forget you first.
John Adams 1735–1826: letter to Abigail Adams, 28 April 1776

12 It is not in my power to tell thee how I have been affected by this dearest of all letters—it was so unexpected—so new a thing to see the breathing of thy inmost heart upon paper.
Mary Wordsworth 1782–1859: letter to William Wordsworth, 1 August 1810

13 She'll vish there wos more, and that's the great art o' letter writin'.
Charles Dickens 1812–70: *Pickwick Papers* (1837–8)

14 Correspondences are like small-clothes before the invention of suspenders; it is impossible to keep them up.
Sydney Smith 1771–1845: letter to Catherine Crowe, 31 January 1841

15 I would any day as soon kill a pig as write a letter.
on his dislike of personal correspondence
Alfred, Lord Tennyson 1809–92: remark made in the 1850s; Ann Thwaite *Emily Tennyson* (1996)

16 It is wonderful how much news there is when people write every other day; if they wait for a month, there is nothing that seems worth telling.
O. Douglas 1877–1948: *Penny Plain* (1920)

17 Why it should be such an effort to write to the people one loves I can't imagine. It's none at all to write to those who don't really count.
Katherine Mansfield 1888–1923: *Journal of Katherine Mansfield* (1930)

18 Letters of thanks, letters from banks,
Letters of joy from girl and boy,
Receipted bills and invitations
To inspect new stock or to visit relations,
And applications for situations,
And timid lovers' declarations,
And gossip, gossip from all the nations.
W. H. Auden 1907–73: 'Night Mail' (1936)

19 A man seldom puts his authentic self into a letter. He writes it to amuse a friend or to get rid of a social or business obligation, which is to say, a nuisance.
H. L. Mencken 1880–1956: *Minority Report* (1956)

20 Beware of writing to me. I always answer . . . My father spent the last 20 years of his life writing letters. If someone thanked him for a present, he thanked them for thanking him and there was no end to the exchange but death.
Evelyn Waugh 1903–66: letter to Lady Mosley, 30 March 1966

21 Don't think that this is a letter. It is only a small eruption of a disease called friendship.
Jean Renoir 1894–1979: letter to Janine Bazin, 12 June 1974

Liberty

PROVERBS AND SAYINGS

1 **Lean liberty is better than fat slavery.**
early 17th century, asserting that freedom matters more than any material comfort

PHRASES

2 **the bird has flown** the prisoner or fugitive has escaped.
see **Parliament** 13

3 **Liberty Hall** a place where one may do as one likes.
from Goldsmith's She Stoops to Conquer *(1773): 'This is Liberty-hall, gentlemen. You may do just as you please'*

4 **Underground Railroad** in the US, a secret network for helping slaves escape from the South to the North and Canada in the years before the American Civil War.

QUOTATIONS

5 Let my people go.
Bible: Exodus

6 Not bound to swear allegiance to any master, wherever the wind takes me I travel as a visitor.
Horace 65–8 BC: *Epistles*

7 One Cartwright brought a Slave from Russia, and would scourge him, for which he was questioned: and it was resolved, That England was too pure an Air for Slaves to breathe in.
Anonymous: 'In the 11th of Elizabeth' (1568–1569); John Rushworth *Historical Collections* (1680–1722)

8 Why should a man be in love with his fetters, though of gold?
Francis Bacon 1561–1626: *Essay of Death* (1648)

9 Stone walls do not a prison make,
Nor iron bars a cage.
Richard Lovelace 1618–58: 'To Althea, From Prison' (1649)

10 None can love freedom heartily, but good men; the rest love not freedom, but licence.
John Milton 1608–74: *The Tenure of Kings and Magistrates* (1649)

11 Liberty is, to the lowest rank of every nation, little more than the choice of working or starving.
Samuel Johnson 1709–84: 'The Bravery of the English Common Soldier'; in *The British Magazine* January 1760

12 Man was born free, and everywhere he is in chains.
Jean-Jacques Rousseau 1712–78: *Du Contrat social* (1762)

13 How is it that we hear the loudest yelps for liberty among the drivers of negroes?
Samuel Johnson 1709–84: *Taxation No Tyranny* (1775)

14 I know not what course others may take; but as for me, give me liberty, or give me death!
Patrick Henry 1736–99: speech in Virginia Convention, 23 March 1775

15 The tree of liberty must be refreshed from time to time with the blood of patriots and tyrants. It is its natural manure.
Thomas Jefferson 1743–1826: letter to W. S. Smith, 13 November 1787

16 The condition upon which God hath given liberty to man is eternal vigilance; which condition if he break, servitude is at once the consequence of his crime, and the punishment of his guilt.
John Philpot Curran 1750–1817: speech on the right of election of the Lord Mayor of Dublin, 10 July 1790

17 O liberty! O liberty! what crimes are committed in thy name!
Mme Roland 1754–93: A. de Lamartine *Histoire des Girondins* (1847)

18 If men are to wait for liberty till they become wise and good in slavery, they may indeed wait for ever.
Lord Macaulay 1800–59: *Essays Contributed to the Edinburgh Review* (1843) 'Milton'

19 The liberty of the individual must be thus far limited; he must not make himself a nuisance to other people.
John Stuart Mill 1806–73: *On Liberty* (1859)

20 The word 'freedom' means for me not a point of departure but a genuine point of arrival. The point of departure is defined by the word 'order'. Freedom cannot exist without the concept of order.
Prince Metternich 1773–1859: *Mein Politisches Testament* (1880)

21 In giving freedom to the slave, we assure freedom to the free—honourable alike in what we give and what we preserve. We shall nobly save, or meanly lose, the last, best hope of earth.
Abraham Lincoln 1809–65: annual message to Congress, 1 December 1862

22 Liberty means responsibility. That is why most men dread it.
George Bernard Shaw 1856–1950: *Man and Superman* (1903) 'Maxims: Liberty and Equality'

23 Tyranny is always better organized than freedom.
Charles Péguy 1873–1914: *Basic Verities* (1943) 'War and Peace'

24 Freedom is always and exclusively freedom for the one who thinks differently.
Rosa Luxemburg 1871–1919: *Die Russische Revolution* (1918)

25 The most stringent protection of free speech would not protect a man falsely shouting fire in a theatre and causing a panic.
sometimes quoted as, 'shouting fire in a crowded theatre'
Oliver Wendell Holmes Jr. 1841–1935: in *Schenck v. United States* (1919)

26 Liberty is precious—so precious that it must be rationed.
Lenin 1870–1924: Sidney and Beatrice Webb *Soviet Communism* (1936)

27 It's often better to be in chains than to be free.
Franz Kafka 1883–1924: *The Trial* (1925)

28 It is better to die on your feet than to live on your knees.
Dolores Ibarruri 1895–1989: speech in Paris, 3 September 1936; also attributed to Emiliano Zapata

29 I am condemned to be free.
Jean-Paul Sartre 1905–80: *L'Être et le néant* (1943)

30 The enemies of Freedom do not argue; they shout and they shoot.
William Ralph Inge 1860–1954: *End of an Age* (1948)

31 Freedom is the freedom to say that two plus two make four. If that is granted, all else follows.
George Orwell 1903–50: *Nineteen Eighty-Four* (1949)

32 The moment the slave resolves that he will no longer be a slave, his fetters fall. He frees himself and shows the way to others. Freedom and slavery are mental states.
Mahatma Gandhi 1869–1948: *Non-Violence in Peace and War* (1949)

33 Freedom is not something that one people can bestow on another as a gift. They claim it as their own and none can keep it from them.
Kwame Nkrumah 1900–72: speech in Accra, 10 July 1953

34 Liberty is always unfinished business.
American Civil Liberties Union: title of 36th Annual Report, 1 July 1955–30 June 1956

35 Ask the first man you meet what he means by defending freedom, and he'll tell you privately he means defending the standard of living.
Martin Niemöller 1892–1984: address at Augsburg, January 1958; James Bentley *Martin Niemöller* (1984)

36 Liberty is liberty, not equality or fairness or justice or human happiness or a quiet conscience.
Isaiah Berlin 1909–97: *Two Concepts of Liberty* (1958)

37 Let every nation know, whether it wishes us well or ill, that we shall pay any price, bear any burden, meet any hardship, support any friend, oppose any foe to assure the survival and the success of liberty.
John F. Kennedy 1917–63: inaugural address, 20 January 1961

38 Freedom's just another word for nothin' left to lose,
Nothin' ain't worth nothin', but it's free.
Kris Kristofferson 1936– : 'Me and Bobby McGee' (1969 song, with Fred Foster)

39 Of course liberty is not licence. Liberty in my view is conforming to majority opinion.
Hugh Scanlon 1913– : television interview, 9 August 1977

40 Freedom is about the willingness of every single human being to cede to lawful authority a great deal of discretion about what you do, and how you do it.
Rudy Giuliani 1944– : attributed, in *Independent* 10 July 1999

Libraries see also Books, Reading

see also **Books**, **Reading**

PROVERBS AND SAYINGS

1 A library is a repository of medicine for the mind.
American proverb, mid 20th century

QUOTATIONS

2 Let your bookcases and your shelves be your gardens and your pleasure-grounds. Pluck the fruit that grows therein, gather the roses, the spices and the myrrh.
Judah Ibn Tibbon 1120–90: Israel Abrahams *Jewish Life in the Middle Ages* (1932)

3 Come, and take choice of all my library, And so beguile thy sorrow.
William Shakespeare 1564–1616: *Titus Andronicus* (1590)

4 If it were so that I must be a prisoner, if I might have my wish, I would have no other prison than this library, and be chained together with these good authors.
referring to the Bodleian Library, Oxford
James I 1566–1625: attributed

5 No place affords a more striking conviction of the vanity of human hopes, than a public library.
Samuel Johnson 1709–84: in *The Rambler* 23 March 1751

6 With awe, around these silent walks I tread;
These are the lasting mansions of the dead.
George Crabbe 1754–1832: 'The Library' (1808)

7 In his library he had been always sure of leisure and tranquillity; and though

prepared . . . to meet with folly and conceit in every other room in the house, he was used to be free of them there.
Jane Austen 1775–1817: *Pride and Prejudice* (1813)

8 What a sad want I am in of libraries, of books to gather facts from! Why is there not a Majesty's library in every county town? There is a Majesty's jail and gallows in every one.
Thomas Carlyle 1795–1881: diary 18 May 1832

9 We call ourselves a rich nation, and we are filthy and foolish enough to thumb each other's books out of circulating libraries!
John Ruskin 1819–1900: *Sesame and Lilies* (1865)

10 A man should keep his little brain attic stocked with all the furniture that he is likely to use, and the rest he can put away in the lumber room of his library, where he can get it if he wants it.
Arthur Conan Doyle 1859–1930: *The Adventures of Sherlock Holmes* (1892)

11 There is in the British Museum an enormous mind. Consider that Plato is there cheek by jowl with Aristotle; and Shakespeare with Marlowe. This great mind is hoarded beyond the power of any single mind to possess it.
Virginia Woolf 1882–1941: *Jacob's Room* (1922)

12 I've been drunk for about a week now, and I thought it might sober me up to sit in a library.
F. Scott Fitzgerald 1896–1940: *The Great Gatsby* (1925)

13 Cultures of East and West, the entire atlas, Encyclopedias, centuries, dynasties, Symbols, the cosmos, and cosmogonies Are offered from the walls.
Jorge Luis Borges 1899–1986: 'Poem of the Gifts' (1972)

14 What is more important in a library than anything else—than everything else—is the fact that it exists.
Archibald MacLeish 1892–1982: 'The Premise of Meaning' in *American Scholar* 5 June 1972

15 More of my waking life has been spent in libraries than anywhere else. Libraries are reservoirs of strength, grace and wit, reminders of order, calm, continuity, lakes of mental energy, neither warm nor cold, light nor dark. The pleasure they give is steady, unorgiastic, reliable, deep and long-lasting.
Germaine Greer 1939– : *Daddy, We Hardly Knew You* (1989)

16 If you file your waste-paper basket for 50 years, you have a public library.
Tony Benn 1925– : in *Daily Telegraph* 5 March 1994

Lies see also **Deception**, **Truth**

PROVERBS AND SAYINGS

1 **An abomination unto the Lord, but a very present help in time of trouble.**
definition of a lie, an amalgamation of lines from the Bible (Proverbs and Psalms), often attributed to the American politician Adlai Stevenson (1900–65)

2 **Half the truth is often a whole lie.**
mid 18th century, meaning that something which is partially true can still convey a completely false impression

3 **A liar ought to have a good memory.**
mid 16th century, 1st century AD in Latin; implying that one lie is likely to lead to the need for another

4 **A lie can go around the world and back again while the truth is lacing up its boots.**
American proverb, late 19th century; see 16 below

5 **One seldom meets a lonely lie.**
American proverb, mid 20th century; implying that one lie is likely to lead to the need for another

PHRASES

6 **economical with the truth** a person or statement that lies or deliberately withholds information.
*used euphemistically, and deriving from a statement given in evidence by Sir Robert Armstrong: see **Truth** 42*

7 **the liar paradox** the paradox involved in a speaker's statement that he or she is lying or is a (habitual) liar.
said to have been created by the semi-legendary Cretan poet Epimenides, asserting that all Cretans are liars; by this definition, if he is a Cretan, then what he says cannot be true, and Cretans are honest

QUOTATIONS

8 It is the penalty of a liar, that should he even tell the truth, he is not listened to.
The Talmud: *Babylonian Talmud* Sanhedrin 89b

9 The retort courteous . . . the quip modest . . . the reply churlish . . . the reproof valiant . . . the countercheck quarrelsome . . . the lie circumstantial . . . the lie direct.
of the degrees of a lie
William Shakespeare 1564–1616: *As You Like It* (1599)

10 A mixture of a lie doth ever add pleasure.
Francis Bacon 1561–1626: *Essays* (1625) 'Of Truth'

11 No mask like open truth to cover lies,
As to go naked is the best disguise.
William Congreve 1670–1729: *The Double Dealer* (1694)

12 He replied that I must needs be mistaken, or that I *said the thing which was not.* (For they have no word in their language to express lying or falsehood.)
Jonathan Swift 1667–1745: *Gulliver's Travels* (1726)

13 Whoever would lie usefully should lie seldom.
Lord Hervey 1696–1743: *Memoirs of the Reign of George II* (ed. J. W. Croker, 1848)

14 Falsehood has a perennial spring.
Edmund Burke 1729–97: *On American Taxation* (1775)

as a child, when asked whether he had cut down a cherry tree:

15 I can't tell a lie, Pa; you know I can't tell a lie. I did cut it with my hatchet.
George Washington 1732–99: M. L. Weems *Life of George Washington* (10th ed., 1810); see 17 below

16 If you want truth to go round the world you must hire an express train to pull it; but if you want a lie to go round the world, it will fly: it is as light as a feather, and a breath will carry it. It is well said in the old proverb, 'a lie will go round the world while truth is pulling its boots on'.
C. H. Spurgeon 1834–92: *Gems from Spurgeon* (1859); see 4 above

17 I am different from Washington. I have a higher and grander stand of principle. Washington could not lie. I *can* lie but I won't.
Mark Twain 1835–1910: in *Chicago Tribune* 20 December 1871; see 15 above

18 The cruellest lies are often told in silence.
Robert Louis Stevenson 1850–94: *Virginibus Puerisque* (1881)

19 Matilda told such Dreadful Lies,
It made one Gasp and Stretch one's Eyes.
Hilaire Belloc 1870–1953: *Cautionary Tales* (1907) 'Matilda'

20 A little inaccuracy sometimes saves tons of explanation.
Saki 1870–1916: *The Square Egg* (1924)

21 Without lies humanity would perish of despair and boredom.
Anatole France 1844–1924: *La Vie en fleur* (1922)

22 The broad mass of a nation . . . will more easily fall victim to a big lie than to a small one.
Adolf Hitler 1889–1945: *Mein Kampf* (1925)

23 She tells enough white lies to ice a wedding cake.
of Lady Desborough
Margot Asquith 1864–1945: in *Listener* 11 June 1953

24 One sometimes sees more clearly in the man who lies than in the man who tells the truth. Truth, like the light, blinds. Lying, on the other hand, is a beautiful twilight, which gives to each object its value.
Albert Camus 1913–60: attributed; Lord Trevelyan *Diplomatic Channels* (1973)

25 In our country the lie has become not just a moral category but a pillar of the State.
Alexander Solzhenitsyn 1918– : 1974 interview, in *The Oak and the Calf* (1975)

Life see also Life Sciences, Lifestyles

PROVERBS AND SAYINGS

1 Be happy while y'er leevin,
For y'er a lang time deid.
Scottish motto for a house

2 Life is a sexually transmitted disease.
graffito found on the London Underground

3 Life isn't all beer and skittles.
mid 19th century, meaning that life is not unalloyed pleasure or relaxation

4 Life's a bitch, and then you die.
modern saying, late 20th century

5 A live dog is better than a dead lion.
late 14th century, often used in the context of a lesser person taking the place of a greater one who has died; from the Bible: see **Value** 17

6 Man cannot live by bread alone.
*late 19th century, meaning that one needs spiritual as
well as physical sustenance; after the Bible (Matthew)
'Man shall not live by bread alone, but by every word
that proceedeth out of the mouth of God'*

7 Tout passe, tout casse, tout lasse.
*French = everything passes, everything perishes,
everything palls*

PHRASES

8 all flesh whatever has bodily life.
*from the Bible: see **Transience** 7*

9 all human life is there every variety of
human experience.
*used as an advertising slogan for the News of the
World in the late 1950s: see 35 below*

10 the elixir of life a supposed drug or essence
capable of prolonging life indefinitely.
translation of medieval Latin elixir vitae

11 life's rich pageant all the variety of human
experience.
*the first recorded use is by Arthur Marshall (1910–89)
in the monologue The Games Mistress (1937)*

12 mouse and man every living thing.
*alliterative association of the types of animal and
human kind; see **Foresight** 11*

QUOTATIONS

13 All that a man hath will he give for his life.
Bible: Job

14 Not to be born is, past all prizing, best.
Sophocles c.496–406 BC: *Oedipus Coloneus*; see 41
below

15 And life is given to none freehold, but it is
leasehold for all.
Lucretius c.94–55 BC: *De Rerum Natura*

16 'Such,' he said, 'O King, seems to me the
present life of men on earth, in comparison
with that time which to us is uncertain, as
if when on a winter's night you sit feasting
with your ealdormen and thegns,—a
single sparrow should fly swiftly into the
hall, and coming in at one door, instantly
fly out through another.'
The Venerable Bede AD 673–735: *Ecclesiastical
History of the English People*

17 Life well spent is long.
Leonardo da Vinci 1452–1519: Edward McCurdy
(ed.) *Leonardo da Vinci's Notebooks* (1906)

18 All the world's a stage,

And all the men and women merely
players:
They have their exits and their entrances;
And one man in his time plays many
parts,
His acts being seven ages.
William Shakespeare 1564–1616: *As You Like It*
(1599)

19 Life's but a walking shadow, a poor player,
That struts and frets his hour upon the
stage,
And then is heard no more; it is a tale
Told by an idiot, full of sound and fury,
Signifying nothing.
William Shakespeare 1564–1616: *Macbeth* (1606)

20 No arts; no letters; no society; and which
is worst of all, continual fear and danger of
violent death; and the life of man, solitary,
poor, nasty, brutish, and short.
Thomas Hobbes 1588–1679: *Leviathan* (1651)

21 Life is an incurable disease.
Abraham Cowley 1618–67: 'To Dr Scarborough'
(1656)

22 Man that is born of a woman hath but a
short time to live, and is full of misery.
The Book of Common Prayer 1662: *The Burial of
the Dead*

23 Enlarge my life with multitude of days,
In health, in sickness, thus the suppliant
prays;
Hides from himself his state, and shuns to
know,
That life protracted is protracted woe.
Samuel Johnson 1709-84: *The Vanity of Human
Wishes* (1749)

24 Man wants but little here below,
Nor wants that little long.
Oliver Goldsmith 1728–74: 'Edwin and Angelina, or
the Hermit' (1766); see **Alcohol** 16

25 This world is a comedy to those that think,
a tragedy to those that feel.
Horace Walpole 1717–97: letter to Anne, Countess
of Upper Ossory, 16 August 1776

26 Life, like a dome of many-coloured glass,
Stains the white radiance of Eternity,
Until Death tramples it to fragments.
Percy Bysshe Shelley 1792–1822: *Adonais* (1821)

27 Life is real! Life is earnest!
And the grave is not its goal;
Dust thou art, to dust returnest,

Was not spoken of the soul.
Henry Wadsworth Longfellow 1807–82: 'A Psalm of Life' (1838); see **Death** 18

28 I slept, and dreamed that life was beauty;
I woke, and found that life was duty.
Ellen Sturgis Hooper 1816–41: 'Beauty and Duty' (1840)

29 Life must be understood backwards; but
. . . it must be lived forwards.
Sören Kierkegaard 1813–55: *Journals and Papers* (1843)

30 Youth is a blunder; Manhood a struggle;
Old Age a regret.
Benjamin Disraeli 1804–81: *Coningsby* (1844)

31 Our life is frittered away by detail . . .
Simplify, simplify.
Henry David Thoreau 1817–62: *Walden* (1854)

32 The mass of men lead lives of quiet
desperation.
Henry David Thoreau 1817–62: *Walden* (1854)

33 Life would be tolerable but for its
amusements.
George Cornewall Lewis 1806–63: in *The Times* 18 September 1872

34 Life is mostly froth and bubble,
Two things stand like stone,
Kindness in another's trouble,
Courage in your own.
Adam Lindsay Gordon 1833–70: *Ye Wearie Wayfarer* (1866)

35 Cats and monkeys—monkeys and cats—
all human life is there!
Henry James 1843–1916: *The Madonna of the Future* (1879); see 9 above

36 Life is like playing a violin solo in public
and learning the instrument as one goes
on.
Samuel Butler 1835–1902: speech at the Somerville Club, 27 February 1895

37 Life is just one damned thing after another.
Elbert Hubbard 1859–1915: in *Philistine* December 1909; often attributed to Frank Ward O'Malley

38 And Life is Colour and Warmth and Light
And a striving evermore for these;
And he is dead, who will not fight;
And who dies fighting has increase.
Julian Grenfell 1888–1915: 'Into Battle' (1915)

39 I have measured out my life with coffee
spoons.
T. S. Eliot 1888–1965: 'The Love Song of J. Alfred Prufrock' (1917)

40 Life is not a series of gig lamps
symmetrically arranged; life is a luminous
halo, a semi-transparent envelope
surrounding us from the beginning of
consciousness to the end.
Virginia Woolf 1882–1941: *The Common Reader* (1925)

41 Never to have lived is best, ancient writers
say;
Never to have drawn the breath of life,
never to have looked into the eye of day;
The second best's a gay goodnight and
quickly turn away.
W. B. Yeats 1865–1939: 'From *Oedipus at Colonus*' (1928); see 14 above

42 Life is a horizontal fall.
Jean Cocteau 1889–1963: *Opium* (1930)

43 Life is just a bowl of cherries.
Lew Brown 1893–1958: title of song (1931)

44 Birth, and copulation, and death.
That's all the facts when you come to
brass tacks:
Birth, and copulation, and death.
I've been born, and once is enough.
T. S. Eliot 1888–1965: *Sweeney Agonistes* (1932)

45 All that matters is love and work.
Sigmund Freud 1856–1939: attributed

46 To live at all is miracle enough.
Mervyn Peake 1911–68: *The Glassblower* (1950)

47 Life is like a sewer. What you get out of it
depends on what you put into it.
Tom Lehrer 1928– : 'We Will All Go Together When We Go' (1953 song)

48 Oh, isn't life a terrible thing, thank God?
Dylan Thomas 1914–53: *Under Milk Wood* (1954)

49 As far as we can discern, the sole purpose
of human existence is to kindle a light in
the darkness of mere being.
Carl Gustav Jung 1875–1961: *Erinnerungen, Träume, Gedanken* (1962)

50 Life, you know, is rather like opening a tin
of sardines. We are all of us looking for the
key. And, I wonder, how many of you here
tonight have wasted years of your lives
looking behind the kitchen dressers of this
life for that key.
Alan Bennett 1934– : *Beyond the Fringe* (1961 revue) 'Take a Pew'

51 Life is first boredom, then fear.
Philip Larkin 1922–85: 'Dockery & Son' (1964)

52 There's a rule, I think. You get what you want in life, but not your second choice too.
Alison Lurie 1926– : *Real People* (1969)

53 The Answer to the Great Question Of . . . Life, the Universe and Everything . . . [is] Forty-two.
Douglas Adams 1952–2001: *The Hitch Hiker's Guide to the Galaxy* (1979)

54 Life is a rainbow which also includes black.
Yevgeny Yevtushenko 1933– : in *Guardian* 11 August 1987

55 My momma always said life was like a box of chocolates . . . you never know what you're gonna get.
Eric Ross: *Forrest Gump* (1994 film), based on the novel (1986) by Winston Groom; spoken by Tom Hanks

---

Life Sciences see also Life, Nature, Science, Science and Religion

PHRASES

1 animal, vegetable, and mineral the three traditional divisions into which natural objects have been classified.

2 the missing link a hypothetical intermediate type between humans and apes.
a Victorian concept, arising from a simplistic picture of human evolution, representing either a common evolutionary ancestor for both humans and apes, or, in popular thought, some kind of ape-man through which humans had evolved from the other higher primates; it is now clear that human evolution has been much more complex

3 natural selection the process whereby organisms better adapted to their environment tend to survive and produce more offspring.
the theory of its action was first fully expounded by Charles Darwin and it is now believed to be the main process that brings about evolution; see 11, 13 below

4 Red Queen hypothesis the hypothesis that organisms are constantly struggling to keep up with one another in an evolutionary race between predator and prey species.
named from Lewis Carroll's Red Queen; see **Effort** *18*

5 the selfish gene hypothesized as the unit of heredity whose preservation is the ultimate explanation of and rationale for human existence.
title of book (1976) by Richard Dawkins, which did much to popularize the theory of sociobiology

6 survival of the fittest the process or result of natural selection.
from Spencer: see 13 below; see also 3 above, **Business** *33*

QUOTATIONS

7 That which *is* grows, while that which *is not* becomes.
Galen AD 129–199: *On the Natural Faculties*

8 But what if one should tell such people in future that there are more animals living in the scum on the teeth in a man's mouth than there are men in a whole kingdom?
on his observations of micro-organisms
Antoni van Leeuwenhoek 1632–1723: letter to Francis Aston, 17 September 1683

9 Like following life thro' creatures you dissect,
You lose it in the moment you detect.
Alexander Pope 1688–1744: *Epistles to Several Persons* 'To Lord Cobham' (1734)

10 Population, when unchecked, increases in a geometrical ratio. Subsistence only increases in an arithmetical ratio.
Thomas Robert Malthus 1766–1834: *Essay on the Principle of Population* (1798)

11 I have called this principle, by which each slight variation, if useful, is preserved, by the term of Natural Selection.
Charles Darwin 1809–82: *On the Origin of Species* (1859); see 3 above

12 Was it through his grandfather or his grandmother that he claimed his descent from a monkey?
addressed to T. H. Huxley in the debate on Darwin's theory of evolution
Samuel Wilberforce 1805–73: at a meeting of British Association in Oxford, 30 June 1860; see **Human Race** 22, **Science and Religion** 9

13 This survival of the fittest which I have here sought to express in mechanical terms, is that which Mr Darwin has called 'natural selection, or the preservation of favoured races in the struggle for life'.
Herbert Spencer 1820–1903: *Principles of Biology* (1865); see 3, 11 above

14 It has, I believe, been often remarked that a hen is only an egg's way of making another egg.
Samuel Butler 1835–1902: *Life and Habit* (1877)

15 The Microbe is so very small
You cannot make him out at all.
But many sanguine people hope
To see him through a microscope.
Hilaire Belloc 1870–1953: 'The Microbe' (1897)

16 The theory, coarsely enough, and to my Father's great indignation, was defined by a hasty press as being this—that God hid the fossils in the rocks in order to tempt geologists into infidelity.
on Philip Gosse's fundamentalist interpretation of geology (in Omphalos, 1857), subsequently applied to evolution
Edmund Gosse 1849–1928: *Father and Son* (1907)

17 Men will not be content to manufacture life: they will want to improve on it.
J. D. Bernal 1901–71: *The World, the Flesh and the Devil* (1929)

18 Life exists in the universe only because the carbon atom possesses certain exceptional properties.
James Jeans 1877–1946: *The Mysterious Universe* (1930)

19 It has not escaped our notice that the specific pairing we have postulated immediately suggests a possible copying mechanism for the genetic material.
proposing the double helix as the structure of DNA, and hence the chemical mechanism of heredity
Francis Crick 1916– and **James D. Watson** 1928– : in *Nature* 25 April 1953

20 Evolution advances, not by a priori design, but by the selection of what works best out of whatever choices offer. We are the products of editing, rather than of authorship.
George Wald 1904–97: in *Annals of the New York Academy of Sciences* vol. 69 1957

21 The history of the living world can be summarised as the elaboration of ever more perfect eyes within a cosmos in which there is always something more to be seen.
Pierre Teilhard de Chardin 1881–1955: *The Phenomenon of Man* (1959)

22 I'd lay down my life for two brothers or eight cousins.
J. B. S. Haldane 1892–1964: attributed; in *New Scientist* 8 August 1974

23 The biologist passes, the frog remains.
sometimes quoted as 'Theories pass. The frog remains'
Jean Rostand 1894–1977: *Inquiétudes d'un Biologiste* (1967)

24 Water is life's *mater* and *matrix*, mother and medium. There is no life without water.
Albert von Szent-Györgyi 1893–1986: in *Perspectives in Biology and Medicine* Winter 1971

25 [Natural selection] has no vision, no foresight, no sight at all. If it can be said to play the role of watchmaker in nature, it is the *blind* watchmaker.
Richard Dawkins: *The Blind Watchmaker* (1986); see **God** 24

26 The essence of life is statistical improbability on a colossal scale.
Richard Dawkins: *The Blind Watchmaker* (1986)

27 Almost all aspects of life are engineered at the molecular level, and without understanding molecules we can only have a very sketchy understanding of life itself.
Francis Crick 1916– : *What Mad Pursuit* (1988)

28 Life is a copiously branching bush, continually pruned by the grim reaper of extinction, not a ladder of predictable progress.
Stephen Jay Gould 1941– : *Wonderful Life* (1989)

29 Biology is the search for the chemistry that works.
R. J. P. Williams 1926– : lecture in Oxford, June 1996

30 Genes are not like engineering blueprints; they are more like recipes in a cookbook. They tell us what ingredients to use, in what quantities, and in what order—but they do not provide a complete, accurate plan of the final result.
Ian Stewart 1945– : *Life's Other Secret* (1998) preface

31 Students accept astonishing things happening in human genetics without turning a hair but worry about GM soya beans.
Steve Jones 1944– : in *Times Higher Education Supplement* 27 August 1999

32 Today we are learning the language in which God created life.
announcing the deciphering of 90% of the human genome
Bill Clinton 1946– : in *Independent* 27 June 2000

Lifestyles see also **Life**

PROVERBS AND SAYINGS

1 Do as you would be done by.
late 16th century; in Charles Kingsley's The Water-Babies *(1863), Mrs Doasyouwouldbedoneby is the motherly and benevolent figure who is contrasted with her stern sister, Mrs Bedonebyasyoudid*

2 Do unto others as you would they should do unto you.
early 10th century, from the Bible (Matthew): see 15 below; see also **Likes and Dislikes** *13*

3 Make love not war.
student slogan, 1960s

PHRASES

4 the eleventh commandment a rule of conduct regarded as coming next in importance to the Ten Commandments.
often defined as 'Thou shalt not be found out'; see 8 below

5 plain living and high thinking a frugal and philosophic lifestyle.
from Wordsworth: see **Satisfaction** *22*

6 rake's progress a progressive degeneration or decline, especially through self-indulgence.
the title of a series of engravings (1735) by William Hogarth, tracing the rake's life from indulged childhood to the gallows

7 sow one's wild oats commit youthful follies or excesses before settling down.
wild oat a cornfield weed resembling the cultivated oat, supposedly deliberately in its place

8 the Ten Commandments the divine rules of conduct given by God to Moses on Mount Sinai.
as recounted in the Bible (Exodus); the commandments are generally enumerated as: have no other gods; do not make or worship idols; do not take the name of the Lord in vain; keep the sabbath holy; honour one's father and mother; do not kill; do not commit adultery; do not steal; do not give false evidence; do not covet another's property or wife; see **Envy** *7,* **Murder** *8,* **Parents** *4; see also 4 above, 20 below,* **Indifference** *17*

9 this mortal coil the turmoil of life.
from Shakespeare Hamlet: *see* **Death** *27*

QUOTATIONS

10 Thou shalt love thy neighbour as thyself.
Bible: Leviticus; see also St Matthew

11 Fear God, and keep his commandments: for this is the whole duty of man.
Bible: Ecclesiastes

12 A man hath no better thing under the sun, than to eat, and to drink, and to be merry.
Bible: Ecclesiastes

13 We live, not as we wish to, but as we can.
Menander 342–c.292 BC: *The Lady of Andros*

14 1) Refraining from taking life. 2) Refraining from taking what is not given. 3) Refraining from incontinence. 4) Refraining from falsehood. 5) Refraining from strong drink, intoxicants, and liquor, which are occasions of carelessness.
The Five Precepts
Pali Tripitaka *c.* 2nd century BC: *Vinaya, Mahāv.* [*Book of Discipline*]

15 Therefore all things whatsoever ye would that men should do to you, do ye even so to them: for this is the law and the prophets.
Bible: Matthew; see 2 above, **Success** 14

16 Love and do what you will.
St Augustine of Hippo AD 354–430: *In Epistolam Joannis ad Parthos* (AD 413)

17 *Fay ce que vouldras.*
Do what you like.
François Rabelais c.1494–c.1553: *Gargantua* (1534); see 27 below

18 Living is my job and my art.
Montaigne 1533–92: *Essais* (1580)

19 Six hours in sleep, in law's grave study six, Four spend in prayer, the rest on Nature fix.
Edward Coke 1552–1634: translation of a quotation from Justinian *The Pandects*

20 For my part I keep the Commandments, I love my neighbour as my self, and to avoid coveting my neighbour's wife I desire to be coveted by her; which you know is quite another thing.
William Congreve 1670–1729: letter to Mrs Edward Porter, 27 September 1700; see 8 above, **Envy** 7

21 Life is all a VARIORUM,
We regard not how it goes;
Let them cant about DECORUM,
Who have characters to lose.
Robert Burns 1759–96: 'The Jolly Beggars' (1799)

22 A man should have the fine point of his soul taken off to become fit for this world.
John Keats 1795–1821: letter to J. H. Reynolds, 22 November 1817

23 Take short views, hope for the best, and trust in God.
Sydney Smith 1771–1845: Lady Holland *Memoir* (1855)

24 Believe me! The secret of reaping the greatest fruitfulness and the greatest enjoyment from life is *to live dangerously*!
Friedrich Nietzsche 1844–1900: *Die fröhliche Wissenschaft* (1882)

25 Do you want to know the great drama of my life? It's that I have put my genius into my life; all I've put into my works is my talent.
Oscar Wilde 1854–1900: André Gide *Oscar Wilde* (1910)

26 Live all you can; it's a mistake not to. It doesn't so much matter what you do in particular, so long as you have your life. If you haven't had that, what *have* you had?
Henry James 1843–1916: *The Ambassadors* (1903)

27 Do what thou wilt shall be the whole of the Law.
Aleister Crowley 1875–1947: *Book of the Law* (1909); see 17 above

28 Where is the Life we have lost in living?
T. S. Eliot 1888–1965: *The Rock* (1934)

29 Never play cards with a man called Doc. Never eat at a place called Mom's. Never sleep with a woman whose troubles are worse than your own.
Nelson Algren 1909– : in *Newsweek* 2 July 1956

30 Man is born to live, not to prepare for life.
Boris Pasternak 1890–1960: *Doctor Zhivago* (1958)

31 Turn on, tune in and drop out.
Timothy Leary 1920– : lecture, June 1966; *The Politics of Ecstasy* (1968)

32 I've lived a life that's full, I've travelled each and ev'ry highway
And more, much more than this. I did it my way.
Paul Anka 1941– : 'My Way' (1969 song)

33 Expect nothing. Live frugally on surprise.
Alice Walker 1944– : 'Expect nothing' (1973)

34 Another person's life, observed from outside, always has a shape and definition that one's own life lacks.
Pat Barker 1943– : *The Ghost Road* (1995)

35 You only live once, and the way I live, once is enough.
Frank Sinatra 1915–98: attributed, in *The Times* 16 May 1998

Likes and Dislikes see also Criticism, Taste

PROVERBS AND SAYINGS

1 Every man to his taste.
late 16th century, often used to comment on someone else's choice

2 One man's meat is another man's poison.
late 16th century, pointing out that what may be necessary to one person is injurious to another

3 Tastes differ.
early 19th century, meaning that different people will like or approve of different things

4 There is no accounting for tastes.
late 18th century, often used in recognition of a difference in choice between two people

5 You can't please everyone.
late 15th century

6 You're going to like this . . . not a lot . . . but you'll like it!
catchphrase used by Paul Daniels in his conjuring act, especially on television from 1981 onwards

QUOTATIONS

7 To business that we love we rise betime,
And go to 't with delight.
William Shakespeare 1564–1616: *Antony and Cleopatra* (1606–7)

8 I do not love thee, Dr Fell.
The reason why I cannot tell;
But this I know, and know full well,
I do not love thee, Dr Fell.
written while an undergraduate at Christ Church, Oxford, of which Dr Fell was Dean
Thomas Brown 1663–1704: translation of an epigram by Martial AD c.40–c.104

9 People who like this sort of thing will find this the sort of thing they like.
judgement of a book
Abraham Lincoln 1809–65: G. W. E. Russell *Collections and Recollections* (1898)

10 For I've read in many a novel that, unless they've souls that grovel,

Folks *prefer* in fact a hovel to your dreary marble halls.
C. S. Calverley 1831–84: 'In the Gloaming' (1872)

11 I don't care anything about reasons, but I know what I like.
Henry James 1843–1916: *Portrait of a Lady* (1881)

12 Take care to get what you like or you will be forced to like what you get.
George Bernard Shaw 1856–1950: *Man and Superman* (1903) 'Maxims: Stray Sayings'

13 Do not do unto others as you would that they should do unto you. Their tastes may not be the same.
George Bernard Shaw 1856–1950: *Man and Superman* (1903) 'Maxims for Revolutionists: The Golden Rule'; see **Lifestyles** 2, **Success** 14

14 A little of what you fancy does you good.
Fred W. Leigh d. 1924 and **George Arthurs**: title of song (1915)

15 Tiggers don't like honey.
A. A. Milne 1882–1956: *House at Pooh Corner* (1928)

16 In fact, now that you've got me right down to it, the only thing I didn't like about *The Barretts of Wimpole Street* was the play.
Dorothy Parker 1893–1967: review in *New Yorker* 21 February 1931

17 One-fifth of the people are against everything all the time.
Robert Kennedy 1925–68: speech, University of Pennsylvania, 6 May 1964

18 The hippies wanted peace and love. We wanted Ferraris, blondes and switchblades.
Alice Cooper 1948– : in *Independent* 5 May 2001

Logic and Reason

PROVERBS AND SAYINGS

1 There is reason in the roasting of eggs.
mid 17th century, meaning that however odd an action may seem, there is a reason for it

PHRASES

2 chop logic engage in pedantically logical arguments.
chop *exchange or bandy words, later wrongly understood as 'cut into small pieces, mince'*

3 ex pede Herculem inferring the whole of something from an insignificant part.
Latin, from the foot of Hercules, alluding to the story that Pythagoras calculated Hercules's height from the size of Hercules's foot

4 lucus a non lucendo a paradoxical or otherwise absurd derivation; something of which the qualities are the opposite of what its name suggests.
Latin, literally 'a grove from its not shining', i.e. lucus (a grove) is derived from lucere (shine) because there is no light there

5 method in one's madness sense or reason in what appears to be foolish or abnormal behaviour.
from Shakespeare: see **Madness** 5

6 a red herring a distraction introduced to a discussion or argument to divert attention from a more serious question or matter.
from the practice of using the scent of a smoked herring to train hounds to follow a trail

QUOTATIONS

7 I have no other but a woman's reason: I think him so, because I think him so.
William Shakespeare 1564–1616: *The Two Gentlemen of Verona* (1592–3)

8 Reasons are not like garments, the worse for wearing.
Robert Devereux, Earl of Essex 1566–1601: letter to Lord Willoughby, 4 January 1599

9 What ever sceptic could inquire for; For every why he had a wherefore.
Samuel Butler 1612–80: *Hudibras* pt. 1 (1663)

10 I have never yet been able to perceive how anything can be known for truth by consecutive reasoning—and yet it must be.
John Keats 1795–1821: letter to Benjamin Bailey, 22 November 1817

11 I'll not listen to reason . . . Reason always means what someone else has got to say.
Elizabeth Gaskell 1810–65: *Cranford* (1853)

12 'Contrariwise,' continued Tweedledee, 'if it was so, it might be; and if it were so, it would be: but as it isn't, it ain't. That's logic.'
Lewis Carroll 1832–98: *Through the Looking-Glass* (1872)

13 Logical consequences are the scarecrows of fools and the beacons of wise men.
T. H. Huxley 1825–95: *Science and Culture and Other Essays* (1881) 'On the Hypothesis that Animals are Automata'

14 [Logic] is neither a science nor an art, but a dodge.

Benjamin Jowett 1817–93: Lionel A. Tollemache *Benjamin Jowett* (1895)

15 'Is there any other point to which you would wish to draw my attention?'
'To the curious incident of the dog in the night-time.'
'The dog did nothing in the night-time.'
'That was the curious incident,' remarked Sherlock Holmes.

Arthur Conan Doyle 1859–1930: *The Memoirs of Sherlock Holmes* (1894)

16 After all, what was a paradox but a statement of the obvious so as to make it sound untrue?

Ronald Knox 1888–1957: *A Spiritual Aeneid* (1918)

17 Logic must take care of itself.

Ludwig Wittgenstein 1889–1951: *Tractatus Logico-Philosophicus* (1922)

18 Only reason can convince us of those three fundamental truths without a recognition of which there can be no effective liberty: that what we believe is not necessarily true; that what we like is not necessarily good; and that all questions are open.

Clive Bell 1881–1964: *Civilization* (1928)

19 when man determined to destroy himself he picked the was of shall and finding only why smashed it into because.

e. e. cummings 1894–1962: *1 x 1* (1944) no. 26

20 You can't think rationally on an empty stomach, and a whole lot of people can't do it on a full stomach either.

Lord Reith 1889–1971: D. Parker *Radio: The Great Years* (1977)

21 Even logical positivists are capable of love.

A. J. Ayer 1910–89: Kenneth Tynan *Profiles* (1989)

Losing   see **Winning and Losing**

Loss   see **Mourning and Loss**

Love   see also **Courtship, Kissing, Marriage, Relationships, Sex**

PROVERBS AND SAYINGS

1 The course of true love never did run smooth.

late 16th century, originally from Shakespeare: see 29 below

2 It is best to be off with the old love before you are on with the new.

early 19th century

3 Jove but laughs at lover's perjury.

mid 16th century; from the Roman poet Tibullus (c.50–19 BC) and ultimately from the Greek poet Hesiod (c.700 BC)

4 Love and a cough cannot be hid.

early 14th century, meaning that love can no more be concealed than a cough can be suppressed

5 Love begets love.

early 16th century

6 Love is blind.

*late 14th century; Cupid, the god of love, was traditionally portrayed as blind, shooting his arrows at random, but the saying is generally used to mean that a person is often unable to see faults in the one they love; see **Relationships** 1*

7 Love laughs at locksmiths.

early 19th century, meaning that love is too strong a force to be denied by ordinary barriers; from the title of a play (1808) by George Colman, the Younger (1762–1836)

8 Love makes the world go round.

*mid 19th century, from a traditional French song; see **Drunkenness** 15*

9 Love will find a way.

early 17th century, meaning that love is a force which cannot be stemmed or denied

10 One cannot love and be wise.

*early 16th century; the statement 'to love and be wise is scarcely allowed to God' is found in Latin in the writings of the 1st-century Roman writer Publilius Syrus; see **Taxes** 10*

11 The quarrel of lovers is the renewal of love.

early 16th century, meaning that love can be renewed through reconciliation

12 There are as good fish in the sea as ever came out of it.

late 16th century, now often used as a consolation to rejected lovers in the form, 'there are plenty more fish in the sea'

13 'Tis better to have loved and lost, than never to have loved at all.
early 18th century; see 51 below

14 When the furze is in bloom, my love's in tune.
mid 18th century, with the implication that some furze can always be found in bloom; see also **Kissing** *2*

PHRASES

15 Cupid's dart the conquering power of love.
Cupid the Roman god of love, son of Mercury and Venus, represented as a beautiful naked winged boy with a bow and arrows

16 love's young dream the relationship of young lovers; the object of someone's love; a man regarded as a perfect lover.
see 43 below

17 moonlight and roses romance.
title of song by Black and Moret, 1925

18 star-crossed lovers ill-fated lovers.
from Shakespeare Romeo and Juliet *'A pair of star-crossed lovers'*

QUOTATIONS

19 Many waters cannot quench love, neither can the floods drown it.
Bible: Song of Solomon

20 *Omnia vincit Amor: et nos cedamus Amori.*
Love conquers all things: let us too give in to Love.
Virgil 70–19 BC: *Eclogues*

21 And now abideth faith, hope, charity, these three; but the greatest of these is charity.
Bible: I Corinthians

22 There is no fear in love; but perfect love casteth out fear.
Bible: I John

23 You who seek an end of love, love will yield to business: be busy, and you will be safe.
Ovid 43 BC–AD c.17: *Remedia Amoris*

24 Lord, make me an instrument of Your peace!
Where there is hatred let me sow love.
St Francis of Assisi 1181–1226: 'Prayer of St Francis'; attributed

25 The love that moves the sun and the other stars.
Dante Alighieri 1265–1321: *Divina Commedia* 'Paradiso'

26 God defend me, said Dinadan, for the joy of love is too short, and the sorrow thereof, and what cometh thereof, dureth over long.
Thomas Malory d. 1471: *Le Morte D'Arthur* (1485)

27 What thing is love for (well I wot) love is a thing.
It is a prick, it is a sting,
It is a pretty, pretty thing.
George Peele c.1556–96: *The Hunting of Cupid* (c.1591)

28 Where both deliberate, the love is slight;
Who ever loved that loved not at first sight?
Christopher Marlowe 1564–93: *Hero and Leander* (1598)

29 The course of true love never did run smooth.
William Shakespeare 1564–1616: *A Midsummer Night's Dream* (1595–6); see 1 above

30 Whoever loves, if he do not propose
The right true end of love, he's one that goes
To sea for nothing but to make him sick.
John Donne 1572–1631: 'Love's Progress' (c.1600)

31   Then, must you speak
Of one that loved not wisely but too well.
William Shakespeare 1564–1616: *Othello* (1602–4)

32 Love is like linen often changed, the sweeter.
Phineas Fletcher 1582–1650: *Sicelides* (performed 1614)

33 Let me not to the marriage of true minds
Admit impediments. Love is not love
Which alters when it alteration finds.
William Shakespeare 1564–1616: sonnet 116

34 But true love is a durable fire,
In the mind ever burning,
Never sick, never old, never dead,
From itself never turning.
Walter Ralegh c.1552–1618: 'Walsinghame'

35 No cord nor cable can so forcibly draw, or hold so fast, as love can do with a twined thread.
Robert Burton 1577–1640: *The Anatomy of Melancholy* (1621–51)

36 Love is the fart
Of every heart:
It pains a man when 'tis kept close,

And others doth offend, when 'tis let loose.
John Suckling 1609–42: 'Love's Offence' (1646)

37 It's no longer a burning within my veins:
it's Venus entire latched onto her prey.
Jean Racine 1639–99: *Phèdre* (1677)

38 Say what you will, 'tis better to be left
than never to have been loved.
William Congreve 1670–1729: *The Way of the World* (1700); see 51 below

39 If I were young and handsome as I was,
instead of old and faded as I am, and you
could lay the empire of the world at my
feet, you should never share the heart and
hand that once belonged to John, Duke of
Marlborough.
refusing an offer of marriage from the Duke of Somerset
Sarah, Duchess of Marlborough 1660–1744: W. S. Churchill *Marlborough: His Life and Times* vol. 4 (1938)

40 To say a man is fallen in love,—or that he
is deeply in love,—or up to the ears in
love,—and sometimes even over head and
ears in it,—carries an idiomatical kind of
implication, that love is a thing below a
man.
Laurence Sterne 1713–68: *Tristram Shandy* (1759–67)

41 O, my Luve's like a red, red rose
That's newly sprung in June;
O my Luve's like the melodie
That's sweetly play'd in tune.
Robert Burns 1759–96: 'A Red Red Rose' (1796); derived from various folk-songs

42 If I love you, what does that matter to you!
Johann Wolfgang von Goethe 1749–1832: *Wilhelm Meister's Apprenticeship* (1795-6)

43 No, there's nothing half so sweet in life
As love's young dream.
Thomas Moore 1779–1852: 'Love's Young Dream' (1807); see 16 above

44 Love in a hut, with water and a crust,
Is—Love, forgive us!—cinders, ashes,
dust;
Love in a palace is perhaps at last
More grievous torment than a hermit's
fast.
John Keats 1795–1821: 'Lamia' (1820); see **Idealism** 5

45 The magic of first love is our ignorance
that it can ever end.
Benjamin Disraeli 1804–81: *Henrietta Temple* (1837)

46 In the spring a young man's fancy lightly
turns to thoughts of love.
Alfred, Lord Tennyson 1809–92: 'Locksley Hall' (1842)

47 What love is, if thou wouldst be taught,
Thy heart must teach alone—
Two souls with but a single thought,
Two hearts that beat as one.
Friedrich Halm 1806–71: *Der Sohn der Wildnis* (1842)

48 If you could see my legs when I take my
boots off, you'd form some idea of what
unrequited affection is.
Charles Dickens 1812–70: *Dombey and Son* (1848)

49 If thou must love me, let it be for nought
Except for love's sake only.
Elizabeth Barrett Browning 1806–61: *Sonnets from the Portuguese* (1850) no. 14

50 How do I love thee? Let me count the
ways.
I love thee to the depth and breadth and
height
My soul can reach.
Elizabeth Barrett Browning 1806–61: *Sonnets from the Portuguese* (1850) no. 43

51 'Tis better to have loved and lost
Than never to have loved at all.
Alfred, Lord Tennyson 1809–92: *In Memoriam A. H. H.* (1850); see 13, 38 above

52 Love's like the measles—all the worse
when it comes late in life.
Douglas Jerrold 1803–57: *The Wit and Opinions of Douglas Jerrold* (1859)

53 Love is anterior to life,
Posterior to death,
Initial of creation, and
The exponent of breath.
Emily Dickinson 1830–86: 'Love is anterior to life'

54 The love that lasts longest is the love that
is never returned.
W. Somerset Maugham 1874–1965: *A Writer's Notebook* (1949) written in 1894

55 I am the Love that dare not speak its
name.
Lord Alfred Douglas 1870–1945: 'Two Loves' (1896)

56 Yet each man kills the thing he loves,
By each let this be heard,
Some do it with a bitter look,
Some with a flattering word.
The coward does it with a kiss,

The brave man with a sword!
Oscar Wilde 1854–1900: *The Ballad of Reading Gaol* (1898)

57 The fate of love is that it always seems too little or too much.
Amelia E. Barr 1831–1919: *The Belle of Bolling Green* (1904)

58 To us love says humming that the heart's stalled motor has begun working again.
Vladimir Mayakovsky 1893–1930: 'Letter from Paris to Comrade Kostorov on the Nature of Love' (1928)

59 A woman can be proud and stiff
When on love intent;
But Love has pitched his mansion in
The place of excrement;
For nothing can be sole or whole
That has not been rent.
W. B. Yeats 1865–1939: 'Crazy Jane Talks with the Bishop' (1932)

60 Experience shows us that love does not consist in gazing at each other but in looking together in the same direction.
Antoine de Saint-Exupéry 1900–44: *Wind, Sand and Stars* (1939)

61 If I can't love Hitler, I can't love at all.
Rev. A. J. Muste 1885–1967: at a Quaker meeting 1940; in *New York Times* 12 February 1967

62 The life that I have
Is all that I have
And the life that I have
Is yours.
The love that I have
Of the life that I have
Is yours and yours and yours.
given to the British secret agent Violette Szabo (1921–45), for use with the Special Operations Executive
Leo Marks 1920–2001: 'The Life that I Have' (written 1943)

63 How alike are the groans of love to those of the dying.
Malcolm Lowry 1909–57: *Under the Volcano* (1947)

64 Birds do it, bees do it,
Even educated fleas do it.
Let's do it, let's fall in love.
Cole Porter 1891–1964: 'Let's Do It' (1954 song; words added to the 1928 original)

65 Love. Of course, love. Flames for a year, ashes for thirty.
Guiseppe di Lampedusa 1896–1957: *The Leopard* (1957)

66 What will survive of us is love.
Philip Larkin 1922–85: 'An Arundel Tomb' (1964)

67 All you need is love.
John Lennon 1940–80 and **Paul McCartney** 1942– : title of song (1967)

68 Love means not ever having to say you're sorry.
Erich Segal 1937– : *Love Story* (1970)

69 Love doesn't just sit there, like a stone, it has to be made, like bread; remade all the time, made new.
Ursula K. Le Guin 1929– : *The Lathe of Heaven* (1971)

70 Love is mutually feeding each other, not one living on another like a ghoul.
Bessie Head 1937–86: *A Question of Power* (1973)

71 To love someone is to isolate him from the world, wipe out every trace of him, dispossess him of his shadow, drag him into a murderous future. It is to circle around the other like a dead star and absorb him into a black light.
Jean Baudrillard 1929– : *Fatal Strategies* (1983)

72 Love is just a system for getting someone to call you darling after sex.
Julian Barnes 1946– : *Talking It Over* (1991)

73 If grass can grow through cement, love can find you at every time in your life.
Cher 1946– : in *The Times* 30 May 1998

Luck see Chance and Luck

Luxury see Wealth and Luxury

Madness see also Fools, The Mind

1 Whom the gods would destroy, they first make mad.

early 17th century, often used to comment on a foolish action seen as self-destructive in its effect; see 2 below, **Criticism** *22*

2 Whenever God prepares evil for a man, He first damages his mind, with which he deliberates.

Anonymous: scholiastic annotation to Sophocles's *Antigone*; see 1 above

3 I am never better than when I am mad, then methinks I am a brave fellow, then I do wonders. But reason abuseth me, and there's the torment, there's the hell.

Thomas Kyd 1558–94: *The Spanish Tragedy* (1602 ed.)

4 I am but mad north-north-west; when the wind is southerly, I know a hawk from a handsaw.

William Shakespeare 1564–1616: *Hamlet* (1601); see **Intelligence** 3

5 Though this be madness, yet there is method in't.

William Shakespeare 1564–1616: *Hamlet* (1601); see **Logic** 5

6   There is a pleasure sure,
In being mad, which none but madmen know!

John Dryden 1631–1700: *The Spanish Friar* (1681)

7 They called me mad, and I called them mad, and damn them, they outvoted me.

Nathaniel Lee c.1653–92: R. Porter *A Social History of Madness* (1987)

8 Mad, is he? Then I hope he will *bite* some of my other generals.

replying to the Duke of Newcastle, who had complained that General Wolfe was a madman

George II 1683–1760: Henry Beckles Willson *Life and Letters of James Wolfe* (1909)

9 Babylon in all its desolation is a sight not so awful as that of the human mind in ruins.

Scrope Davies c.1783–1852: letter to Thomas Raikes, May 1835

10 Dear Sir,—I am in a madhouse and quite forget your name or who you are.

John Clare 1793–1864: letter, 1860

11 Every one is more or less mad on one point.

Rudyard Kipling 1865–1936: *Plain Tales from the Hills* (1888)

12 As an experience, madness is terrific . . . and in its lava I still find most of the things I write about.

Virginia Woolf 1882–1941: letter to Ethel Smyth, 22 June 1930

13 There was only one catch and that was Catch-22, which specified that a concern for one's own safety in the face of dangers that were real and immediate was the process of a rational mind . . . Orr would be crazy to fly more missions and sane if he didn't, but if he was sane he had to fly them. If he flew them he was crazy and didn't have to; but if he didn't want to he was sane and had to.

Joseph Heller 1923–99: *Catch-22* (1961); see **Circumstance** 7

14 Madness need not be all breakdown. It may also be break-through.

R. D. Laing 1927–89: *The Politics of Experience* (1967)

15 The usefulness of madmen is famous: they demonstrate society's logic flagrantly carried out down to its last scrimshaw scrap.

Cynthia Ozick 1928– : 'The Hole/Birth Catalog' in Francine Klagsbrun (ed.) *The First Ms Reader* (1972)

16 If you talk to God, you are praying; if God talks to you, you have schizophrenia. If the dead talk to you, you are a spiritualist; if God talks to you, you are a schizophrenic.

Thomas Szasz 1920– : *The Second Sin* (1973)

17 The psychopath is the furnace that gives no heat.

Derek Raymond 1931–94: *The Hidden Files* (1992)

Management see also Administration

see also Administration

PROVERBS AND SAYINGS

1 The eye of a master does more work than both his hands.

mid 18th century, meaning that employees work harder when the person who is in charge is present

2 We trained hard . . . but it seemed that every time we were beginning to form up into teams we would be reorganized. I was to learn later in life that we tend to meet any new situation by reorganizing; and a wonderful method it can be for creating the illusion of progress while producing confusion, inefficiency, and demoralization.

late 20th century saying, frequently (and wrongly) attributed to Petronius Arbiter (d. AD 65)

3 Why keep a dog and bark yourself?

late 16th century, often used to advise against carrying out work which can be done for you by somebody else

PHRASES

4 the Peter Principle the principle that members of a hierarchy are promoted until they reach a level at which they are no longer competent.

*from title of book by US educationalist and author Laurence J. Peter (see **Administration** 22)*

5 pour encourager les autres as an example to others, to encourage others.

*French, from Voltaire: see **Ways and Means** 20*

QUOTATIONS

6 Every time I make an appointment, I create a hundred malcontents and one ingrate.

Louis XIV 1638–1715: Voltaire *Siècle de Louis XIV* (1768 ed.)

7 Some great men owe most of their greatness to the ability of detecting in those they destine for their tools the exact quality of strength that matters for their work.

Joseph Conrad 1857–1924: *Lord Jim* (1900)

8 Safe and sane business management . . . reduces itself in the main to a sagacious use of sabotage.

Thorstein Veblen 1857–1929: *The Nature of Peace* (1917)

9 I tell you, sir, the only safeguard of order and discipline in the modern world is a standardized worker with interchangeable parts. That would solve the entire problem of management.

Jean Giraudoux 1882–1944: *The Madwoman of Chaillot* (1945)

10 A good plan violently executed *Now* is better than a perfect plan next week.

George S. Patton 1885–1945: *War As I Knew It* (1947)

11 Perfection of planned layout is achieved only by institutions on the point of collapse.

C. Northcote Parkinson 1909–93: *Parkinson's Law* (1958)

12 An industrial worker would sooner have a £5 note but a countryman must have praise.

Ronald Blythe 1922– : *Akenfield* (1969)

13 Surround yourself with the best people you can find, delegate authority, and don't interfere.

Ronald Reagan 1911– : in *Fortune* September 1986

14 Every organization of today has to build into its very structure the *management of change*.

Peter F. Drucker 1909– : *Post-Capitalist Society* (1993)

15 Management that wants to change an institution must first show it loves that institution.

John Tusa 1936– : in *Observer* 27 February 1994

16 If management are using a word you don't understand, nine times out of ten they are making you redundant.

John Edwards: on BBC Radio Four *Today*, 10 June 1996

17 Try to analyze situations intelligently, anticipate problems and move swiftly to solve them. However, when you're up to your ears in alligators, it is difficult to remember that the reason you're there is to drain the swamp.

Donald Rumsfeld 1932– : *Rumsfeld's Rules* (2001)

Manners see also Behaviour

PROVERBS AND SAYINGS

1 **Civility costs nothing.**
early 18th century, meaning that one should behave with at least minimal courtesy

2 **A civil question deserves a civil answer.**
mid 19th century

3 **Everyone speaks well of the bridge which carries him over.**
late 17th century, meaning that someone is naturally well-disposed towards a source of help, whether or not it has been beneficial to others

4 **Manners maketh man.**
mid fourteenth century; motto of William of Wykeham (1324–1404), bishop of Winchester and founder of Winchester College

5 **Striking manners are bad manners.**
American proverb, mid 20th century

6 **The test of good manners is being able to put up pleasantly with bad ones.**
American proverb, mid 20th century

7 **There is nothing lost by civility.**
late 19th century

QUOTATIONS

8 Leave off first for manners' sake.
Bible: Ecclesiasticus

9 Evil communications corrupt good manners.
Bible: I Corinthians; see **Behaviour** 3

10 Immodest words admit of no defence,
For want of decency is want of sense.
Wentworth Dillon, Lord Roscommon
*c.*1633–1685: *Essay on Translated Verse* (1684)

11 In my mind, there is nothing so illiberal and so ill-bred, as audible laughter.
Lord Chesterfield 1694–1773: *Letters to his Son* (1774) 9 March 1748

12 He is the very pineapple of politeness!
Richard Brinsley Sheridan 1751–1816: *The Rivals* (1775)

13 A man, indeed, is not genteel when he gets drunk; but most vices may be committed very genteelly: a man may debauch his friend's wife genteelly: he may cheat at cards genteelly.
James Boswell 1740–95: *Life of Samuel Johnson* (1791) 6 April 1775

14 The art of pleasing consists in being pleased.
William Hazlitt 1778–1830: *The Round Table* (1817) 'On Manner'

15 Ceremony is an invention to take off the uneasy feeling which we derive from knowing ourselves to be less the object of love and esteem with a fellow-creature than some other person is.
Charles Lamb 1775–1834: *Essays of Elia* (1823) 'A Bachelor's Complaint of the Behaviour of Married People'

16 Curtsey while you're thinking what to say. It saves time.
Lewis Carroll 1832–98: *Through the Looking-Glass* (1872)

17 Very notable was his distinction between coarseness and vulgarity (coarseness, revealing something; vulgarity, concealing something).
E. M. Forster 1879–1970: *The Longest Journey* (1907)

18 Of Courtesy, it is much less
Than Courage of Heart or Holiness,
Yet in my Walks it seems to me
That the Grace of God is in Courtesy.
Hilaire Belloc 1870–1953: 'Courtesy' (1910)

19 Good breeding consists in concealing how much we think of ourselves and how little we think of the other person.
Mark Twain 1835–1910: *Notebooks* (1935)

20 When suave politeness, tempering bigot zeal,
Corrected *I believe* to *One does feel.*
Ronald Knox 1888–1957: 'Absolute and Abitofhell' (1913)

21 'Always be civil to the girls, you never know who they may marry' is an aphorism which has saved many an English spinster from being treated like an Indian widow.
Nancy Mitford 1904–73: *Love in a Cold Climate* (1949)

22 Phone for the fish-knives, Norman
As Cook is a little unnerved;
You kiddies have crumpled the serviettes
And I must have things daintily served.
John Betjeman 1906–84: 'How to get on in Society' (1954)

23 To Americans, English manners are far more frightening than none at all.
Randall Jarrell 1914-65: *Pictures from an Institution* (1954)

24 Manners are especially the need of the plain. The pretty can get away with anything.
Evelyn Waugh 1903-66: in *Observer* 15 April 1962

25 The Japanese have perfected good manners and made them indistinguishable from rudeness.
Paul Theroux 1941- : *The Great Railway Bazaar* (1975)

26 Good manners are a combination of intelligence, education, taste, and style mixed together so that you don't need any of those things.
P. J. O'Rourke 1947- : *Modern Manners* (1984)

Marriage see also Courtship, Love, Sex, The Single Life, Weddings

PROVERBS AND SAYINGS

1 Better be an old man's darling than a young man's slave.
mid 16th century

2 Better one house spoiled than two.
late 16th century, said of two wicked or foolish people joined in marriage

3 A deaf husband and a blind wife are always a happy couple.
late 16th century, meaning that each will remain unaware of drawbacks in the other. The saying is sometimes reversed to a blind husband and a deaf wife

4 The grey mare is the better horse.
mid 16th century, meaning that the wife rules, or is more competent than, the husband

5 Marriage is a lottery.
mid 17th century, referring either to one's choice of partner, or more generally to the element of chance involved in how a marriage will turn out

6 Marriages are made in heaven.
mid 16th century, often used ironically

7 Marry in haste and repent at leisure.
mid 16th century; the formula is also applied to rash steps taken in other circumstances; see 22 below

8 Never marry for money, but marry where money is.
late 19th century, distinguishing between monetary gain as a primary objective and a side benefit

9 There goes more to marriage than four bare legs in a bed.
mid 16th century, meaning that physical compatibility is not enough for a successful marriage

10 Wedlock is a padlock.
late 17th century

11 A young man married is a young man marred.
late 16th century, often used as an argument against marrying too young; see 17 below

PHRASES

12 love in a cottage marriage with insufficient means.
*after Colman: see **Idealism** 5*

13 the weaker vessel a wife, a female partner.
originally in allusion to the Bible (I Peter) 'Giving honour unto the wife, as unto the weaker vessel'

QUOTATIONS

14 Therefore shall a man leave his father and his mother, and shall cleave unto his wife: and they shall be one flesh.
Bible: Genesis

15 What therefore God hath joined together, let not man put asunder.
Bible: St Matthew

16 It is better to marry than to burn.
Bible: I Corinthians

17 A young man married is a man that's marred.
William Shakespeare 1564-1616: *All's Well that Ends Well* (1603-4); see 11 above

18 Wives are young men's mistresses, companions for middle age, and old men's nurses.
Francis Bacon 1561-1626: *Essays* (1625) 'Of Marriage and the Single Life'

19 Then be not coy, but use your time;
And while ye may, go marry:
For having lost but once your prime,
You may for ever tarry.
Robert Herrick 1591-1674: 'To the Virgins, to Make Much of Time' (1648)

20 Marriage is nothing but a civil contract.
John Selden 1584-1654: *Table Talk* (1689) 'Marriage'

21 To have and to hold from this day forward, for better for worse, for richer for poorer,

in sickness and in health, to love, cherish, and to obey, till death us do part.
The Book of Common Prayer 1662: *Solemnization of Matrimony* Betrothal; see 54 below

22 SHARPER: Thus grief still treads upon the heels of pleasure:
Married in haste, we may repent at leisure.
SETTER: Some by experience find those words mis-placed:
At leisure married, they repent in haste.
William Congreve 1670–1729: *The Old Bachelor* (1693); see 7 above

23 I . . . chose my wife, as she did her wedding gown, not for a fine glossy surface, but such qualities as would wear well.
Oliver Goldsmith 1728–74: *The Vicar of Wakefield* (1766)

24 The triumph of hope over experience.
of a man who remarried immediately after the death of a wife with whom he had been unhappy
Samuel Johnson 1709–84: James Boswell *Life of Samuel Johnson* (1791) 1770

25 My definition of marriage . . . it resembles a pair of shears, so joined that they cannot be separated; often moving in opposite directions, yet always punishing anyone who comes between them.
Sydney Smith 1771–1845: Lady Holland *Memoir* (1855)

26 It doesn't much signify whom one marries, for one is sure to find next morning that it was someone else.
Samuel Rogers 1763–1855: Alexander Dyce (ed.) *Table Talk of Samuel Rogers* (1860)

27 Having once embarked upon your marital voyage, it is impossible not to be aware that you make no way and that the sea is not within sight—that in fact, you are exploring a closed basin.
George Eliot 1819–80: *Middlemarch* (1871–2)

28 What man thinks of changing himself so as to suit his wife? And yet men expect that women shall put on altogether new characters when they are married, and girls think that they can do so.
Anthony Trollope 1815–82: *Phineas Redux* (1874)

29 Marriage is like life in this—that it is a field of battle, and not a bed of roses.
Robert Louis Stevenson 1850–94: *Virginibus Puerisque* (1881)

30 It was very good of God to let Carlyle and Mrs Carlyle marry one another and so make only two people miserable instead of four.
Samuel Butler 1835–1902: letter to Miss E. M. A. Savage, 21 November 1884

31 The chains of marriage are so heavy that it takes two to bear them, and sometimes three.
Alexandre Dumas 1824–95: Léon Treich *L'Esprit d'Alexandre Dumas*

32 In married life three is company and two none.
Oscar Wilde 1854–1900: *The Importance of Being Earnest* (1895)

33 Love the quest; marriage the conquest; divorce the inquest.
Helen Rowland 1875–1950: *Reflections of a Bachelor Girl* (1903)

34 Marriage is popular because it combines the maximum of temptation with the maximum of opportunity.
George Bernard Shaw 1856–1950: *Man and Superman* (1903) 'Maxims: Marriage'

35 Being a husband is a whole-time job. That is why so many husbands fail. They cannot give their entire attention to it.
Arnold Bennett 1867–1931: *The Title* (1918)

36 You shall be together when the white wings of death scatter your days.
Ay, you shall be together even in the silent memory of God.
But let there be spaces in your togetherness,
And let the winds of the heavens dance between you.
Kahlil Gibran 1883–1931: *The Prophet* (1923) 'On Marriage'

37 Marriage isn't a word . . . it's a *sentence*!
King Vidor 1895–1982: *The Crowd* (1928 film)

38 By god, D. H. Lawrence was right when he had said there must be a dumb, dark, dull, bitter belly-tension between a man and a woman, and how else could this be achieved save in the long monotony of marriage?
Stella Gibbons 1902–89: *Cold Comfort Farm* (1932)

39 The deep, deep peace of the double-bed after the hurly-burly of the chaise-longue.
on her recent marriage
Mrs Patrick Campbell 1865–1940: Alexander Woollcott *While Rome Burns* (1934)

40 If you cannot have your dear husband for a comfort and a delight, for a breadwinner and a crosspatch, for a sofa, chair or a hot-water bottle, one can use him as a Cross to be Borne.
Stevie Smith 1902-71: *Novel on Yellow Paper* (1936)

41 Marriage is a bribe to make a housekeeper think she's a householder.
Thornton Wilder 1897-1975: *The Merchant of Yonkers* (1939)

42 So they were married—to be the more together—
And found they were never again so much together,
Divided by the morning tea,
By the evening paper,
By children and tradesmen's bills.
Louis MacNeice 1907-63: 'Les Sylphides' (1941)

43 The value of marriage is not that adults produce children but that children produce adults.
Peter De Vries 1910-93: *The Tunnel of Love* (1954)

44 Love and marriage, love and marriage,
Go together like a horse and carriage,
This I tell ya, brother,
Ya can't have one without the other.
Sammy Cahn 1913-93: *Love and Marriage* (1955 song)

45 One doesn't have to get anywhere in a marriage. It's not a public conveyance.
Iris Murdoch 1919-99: *A Severed Head* (1961)

46 Marriage I think
For women
Is the best of opiates.
It kills the thoughts
That think about the thoughts,
It is the best of opiates.
Stevie Smith 1902-71: 'Marriage I Think'

47 I think everybody really will concede that on this, of all days, I should begin my speech with the words 'My husband and I'.
Elizabeth II 1926- : speech at Guildhall, London, on her 25th wedding anniversary, 20 November 1972

48 A divorce is like an amputation; you survive, but there's less of you.
Margaret Atwood 1939- : in *Time*, 1973

49 Marriage is a wonderful invention; but, then again, so is a bicycle repair kit.
Billy Connolly 1942- : Duncan Campbell *Billy Connolly* (1976)

50 Chains do not hold a marriage together. It is threads, hundreds of tiny threads which sew people together through the years. That is what makes a marriage last—more than passion or even sex!
Simone Signoret 1921-85: in *Daily Mail* 4 July 1978

51 There were three of us in this marriage, so it was a bit crowded.
Diana, Princess of Wales 1961-97: interview on *Panorama*, BBC1 TV, 20 November 1995

52 Maybe the Smug Marrieds only mix with other Smug Marrieds and don't know how to relate to individuals any more.
Helen Fielding 1958- : *Bridget Jones's Diary* (1996)

53 I learnt a long time ago that the only people who count in any marriage are the two that are in it.
Hillary Rodham Clinton 1947- : television interview with NBC, 27 January 1998

54 I think we explored the further reaches of 'for better or for worse'.
on her marriage during the 1980s
Mary Archer 1944- : at Jeffrey Archer's trial for perjury, London, 29 June 2001; see 21 above

---

Mathematics see also Quantities and Qualities, Statistics

1 **The good Christian should beware of mathematicians, and all those who make empty prophecies. The danger already exists that mathematicians have made a covenant with the Devil to darken the spirit and to confine man in the bonds of Hell.**
mistranslation of St Augustine's De Genesi ad Litteram; the Latin word mathematicus *means both*

'mathematician' *and* 'astrologer': *see **The Supernatural** 10*

PHRASES

2 **Delian problem** the problem of finding geometrically the side of a cube having twice the volume of a given cube.
from the Delian oracle's pronouncement that a plague In Athens would cease if the cubical altar to Apollo were doubled in size

3 Fermat's last theorem the conjecture that
if *n* is greater than 2 then there is no
integer whose *n*th power can be expressed
as the sum of two smaller *n*th powers.
Pierre de Fermat (1601–65), *French lawyer and
mathematician; the conjecture (of which Fermat noted
that he had 'a truly wonderful proof') has been
demonstrated by calculation to be true for very many
possible values of* n, *and in 1993 a general proof was
announced by the Princeton-based British
mathematician Andrew Wiles*

4 the golden section the division of a line so
that the whole is to the greater part as that
part is to the smaller part.

5 pons asinorum the fifth proposition of the
first book of Euclid.
*Latin, = bridge of asses; so called from the difficulty
which beginners find in 'getting over' it*

6 square the circle construct a square equal
in area to a given circle (a problem
incapable of a purely geometrical solution).

QUOTATIONS

7 Let no one enter who does not know
geometry [mathematics].
*inscription on Plato's door, probably at the Academy
at Athens*
Anonymous: Elias Philosophus *In Aristotelis
Categorias Commentaria*

8 There is no 'royal road' to geometry.
Euclid fl. c.300 BC: addressed to Ptolemy I; Proclus
Commentary on the First Book of Euclid's Elementa;
see **Education** 7

9 If in other sciences we should arrive at
certainty without doubt and truth without
error, it behoves us to place the
foundations of knowledge in mathematics.
Roger Bacon c.1220–c.1292: *Opus Majus*

10 Philosophy is written in that great book
which ever lies before our eyes—I mean
the universe . . . This book is written in
mathematical language and its characters
are triangles, circles and other geometrical
figures, without whose help . . . one
wanders in vain through a dark labyrinth.
often quoted as 'The book of nature is written . . . '
Galileo 1564–1642: *The Assayer* (1623)

11 They are neither finite quantities, or
quantities infinitely small, nor yet nothing.
May we not call them the ghosts of
departed quantities?
on Newton's infinitesimals
George Berkeley 1685–1753: *The Analyst* (1734)

12 Sir Isaac Newton, though so deep in
algebra and fluxions, could not readily
make up a common account: and, when
he was Master of the Mint, used to get
somebody to make up his accounts for
him.
Alexander Pope 1688–1744: Joseph Spence
Anecdotes (ed. J. Osborn, 1966)

13 The most devilish thing is 8 times 8 and 7
times 7 it is what nature itselfe cant
endure.
Marjory Fleming 1803–11: *Journals, Letters and
Verses* (ed. A. Esdaile, 1934)

14 Mathematics are a species of Frenchman; if
you say something to them, they translate
it into their own language and presto! it is
something entirely different.
Johann Wolfgang von Goethe 1749–1832:
attributed; R. L. Weber *A Random Walk in Science*
(1973)

15 What would life be like without arithmetic,
but a scene of horrors?
Sydney Smith 1771–1845: letter to Miss [Lucie
Austen], 22 July 1835

16 I used to love mathematics for its own
sake, and I still do, because it allows for no
hypocrisy and no vagueness, my two *bêtes
noires*.
Stendhal 1783–1842: *La Vie d'Henri Brulard* (1890)

17 'What's the good of *Mercator's* North Poles
and Equators,
Tropics, Zones and Meridian lines?'
So the Bellman would cry: and the crew
would reply,
'They are merely conventional signs!'
Lewis Carroll 1832–98: *The Hunting of the Snark*
(1876)

18 God made the integers, all the rest is the
work of man.
Leopold Kronecker 1823–91: *Jahrsberichte der
Deutschen Mathematiker Vereinigung*

19 I never could make out what those
damned dots meant.
on decimal points
Lord Randolph Churchill 1849–94: W. S. Churchill
Lord Randolph Churchill (1906)

20 Mathematics, rightly viewed, possesses not
only truth, but supreme beauty—a beauty
cold and austere, like that of sculpture.
Bertrand Russell 1872–1970: *Philosophical Essays*
(1910)

21 Mathematics may be defined as the subject
in which we never know what we are

talking about, nor whether what we are saying is true.

Bertrand Russell 1872–1970: *Mysticism and Logic* (1918)

22 Beauty is the first test: there is no permanent place in the world for ugly mathematics.

Godfrey Harold Hardy 1877–1947: *A Mathematician's Apology* (1940)

23 One must divide one's time between politics and equations. But our equations are much more important to me.

Albert Einstein 1879–1955: C. P. Snow 'Einstein' in M. Goldsmith et al. (eds.) *Einstein* (1980)

24 In mathematics you don't understand things. You just get used to them.

John von Neumann 1903–57: Gary Zukav *The Dancing Wu Li Masters* (1979)

25 It is more important to have beauty in one's equations than to have them fit experiment.

he went on to say 'The discrepancy may well be due to minor features . . . that will get cleared up with further developments'

Paul Dirac 1902–84: in *Scientific American* May 1963

26 Points
Have no parts or joints
How then can they combine
To form a line?

J. A. Lindon: M. Gardner *Wheels, Life and Other Mathematical Amusements* (1983)

27 Someone told me that each equation I included in the book would halve the sales.

Stephen Hawking 1942– : *A Brief History of Time* (1988)

Maturity see also Experience

PROVERBS AND SAYINGS

1 **Never send a boy to do a man's job.**
mid 20th century, meaning that someone who is young and inexperienced should not be given too much responsibility

2 **Soon ripe, soon rotten.**
late 14th century (earlier in Latin); a warning against precocity, meaning that notably early achievement is unlikely to be long-lasting

QUOTATIONS

3 More childish valorous than manly wise.

Christopher Marlowe 1564–93: *Tamburlaine the Great* (1590)

4 And so, from hour to hour, we ripe and ripe,
And then from hour to hour, we rot and rot:
And thereby hangs a tale.

William Shakespeare 1564–1616: *As You Like It* (1599)

5 Is not old wine wholesomest, old pippins toothsomest, old wood burn brightest, old linen wash whitest? Old soldiers, sweethearts, are surest, and old lovers are soundest.

John Webster c.1580–c.1625: *Westward Hoe* (1607)

6 Men are but children of a larger growth;
Our appetites as apt to change as theirs,
And full as craving too, and full as vain.

John Dryden 1631–1700: *All for Love* (1678)

7 At twenty years of age, the will reigns; at thirty, the wit; and at forty, the judgement.

Benjamin Franklin 1706–90: *Poor Richard's Almanac* (1741)

8 The imagination of a boy is healthy, and the mature imagination of a man is healthy; but there is a space of life between, in which the soul is in a ferment, the character undecided, the way of life uncertain, the ambition thick-sighted: thence proceeds mawkishness.

John Keats 1795–1821: *Endymion* (1818) preface

9 If you can talk with crowds and keep your virtue,
Or walk with Kings—nor lose the common touch,
If neither foes nor loving friends can hurt you,
If all men count with you, but none too much;
If you can fill the unforgiving minute
With sixty seconds' worth of distance run,
Yours is the Earth and everything that's in it,
And—which is more—you'll be a Man, my son!

Rudyard Kipling 1865–1936: 'If—' (1910)

10 To be adult is to be alone.

Jean Rostand 1894–1977: *Pensées d'un biologiste* (1954)

11 When I was young I hoped that one day I should be able to go into a post office to buy a stamp without feeling nervous and shy: now I realize that I never shall.
Edmund Blunden 1896–1974: Rupert Hart-Davis letter to George Lyttelton, 5 August 1956

12 Immature love says: 'I love you because I need you.' Mature love says: 'I need you because I love you.'
Erich Fromm 1900–80: *The Art of Loving* (1956)

13 One's prime is elusive. You little girls, when you grow up, must be on the alert to recognise your prime at whatever time of your life it may occur.
Muriel Spark 1918– : *The Prime of Miss Jean Brodie* (1961)

14 How many roads must a man walk down Before you can call him a man? . . .

The answer, my friend, is blowin' in the wind,
The answer is blowin' in the wind.
Bob Dylan 1941– : 'Blowin' in the Wind' (1962 song)

15 One of the most obvious facts about grown-ups, to a child, is that they have forgotten what it is like to be a child.
Randall Jarrell 1914–65: Christina Stead *The Man Who Loved Children* (1965)

16 I gave my beauty and my youth to men. I am going to give my wisdom and experience to animals.
Brigitte Bardot 1934– : attributed, June 1987

17 I had always thought that once you grew up you could do anything you wanted—stay up all night or eat ice-cream straight out of the container.
Bill Bryson 1951– : *The Lost Continent* (1989)

Meaning see also Words

PROVERBS AND SAYINGS

1 **Every picture tells a story.**
advertisement for Doan's Backache Kidney Pills (early 1900s)

2 **Straws tell which way the wind blows.**
mid 17th century; see **The Future** 9

PHRASES

3 **gammon and spinach** nonsense, humbug.
with a pun on gammon *bacon, ham. The words* gammon and spinach *are part of the refrain to the song 'A frog he would a-wooing go', and the term is used by Dickens in* David Copperfield *and* Bleak House

QUOTATIONS

4 I pray thee, understand a plain man in his plain meaning.
William Shakespeare 1564–1616: *The Merchant of Venice* (1596–8)

5 Where more is meant than meets the ear.
John Milton 1608–74: 'Il Penseroso' (1645)

6 Egad I think the interpreter is the hardest to be understood of the two!
Richard Brinsley Sheridan 1751–1816: *The Critic* (1779)

7 God and I both knew what it meant once; now God alone knows.
also attributed to Browning, apropos Sordello, *in the form 'When it was written, God and Robert Browning knew what it meant; now only God knows'*
Friedrich Klopstock 1724–1803: C. Lombroso *The Man of Genius* (1891)

8 'Then you should say what you mean,' the March Hare went on. 'I do,' Alice hastily replied; 'at least—at least I mean what I say—that's the same thing, you know.' 'Not the same thing a bit!' said the Hatter. 'Why, you might just as well say that "I see what I eat" is the same thing as "I eat what I see!" '
Lewis Carroll 1832–98: *Alice's Adventures in Wonderland* (1865)

9 You see it's like a portmanteau—there are two meanings packed up into one word.
Lewis Carroll 1832–98: *Through the Looking-Glass* (1872)

10 The meaning doesn't matter if it's only idle chatter of a transcendental kind.
W. S. Gilbert 1836–1911: *Patience* (1881)

11 No one means all he says, and yet very few say all they mean, for words are slippery and thought is viscous.
Henry Brooks Adams 1838–1918: *The Education of Henry Adams* (1907)

12 The little girl had the making of a poet in her who, being told to be sure of her meaning before she spoke, said, 'How can I know what I think till I see what I say?'
Graham Wallas 1858–1932: *The Art of Thought* (1926)

13 Any general statement is like a cheque drawn on a bank. Its value depends on what is there to meet it.
Ezra Pound 1885–1972: *The ABC of Reading* (1934)

14 That was a way of putting it—not very satisfactory:
A periphrastic study in a worn-out poetical fashion,
Leaving one still with the intolerable wrestle
With words and meanings.
T. S. Eliot 1888–1965: *Four Quartets* 'East Coker' (1940)

15 It all depends what you mean by . . .
C. E. M. Joad 1891–1953: answering questions on 'The Brains Trust' (formerly 'Any Questions'), BBC radio (1941–8)

16 If a lady says No, she means Perhaps; if she says Perhaps, she means Yes; if she says Yes, she is no Lady.
If a diplomat says Yes, he means Perhaps; if he says Perhaps, he means No; if he says No, he is no Diplomat.
Lord Dawson of Penn 1864–1945: Francis Watson *Dawson of Penn* (1950)

17 It depends on what the meaning of 'is' is.
Bill Clinton 1946– : videotaped evidence to the grand jury; tapes broadcast 21 September 1998

Means see **Ways and Means**

Medicine see also **Sickness**

PROVERBS AND SAYINGS

1 **The best doctors are Dr Diet, Dr Quiet, and Dr Merryman.**
mid 16th century, outline to an appropriate regime for someone who is ill

2 **Dr Williams' pink pills for pale people.**
patent medicine advertisement, from 1890 on

3 **Keep taking the tablets.**
*supposedly traditional advice from a doctor, especially when little change in the patient's condition is envisaged; see **Pregnancy** 20*

4 **Medicine can prolong life, but death will seize the doctor, too.**
American proverb, mid 20th century

5 **Similia similibus curantur.**
Latin, 'Like cures like'; motto of homeopathic medicine attributed to S. Hahnemann (1755–1843), although not found in this form in Hahnemann's writings

QUOTATIONS

6 Honour a physician with the honour due unto him for the uses which ye may have of him: for the Lord hath created him.
Bible: Ecclesiasticus

7 Life is short, the art long.
Hippocrates c.460–357 BC: *Aphorisms*; see **The Arts** 2

8 Healing is a matter of time, but it is sometimes also a matter of opportunity.
Hippocrates c.460–357 BC: *Precepts*

9 Physician, heal thyself.
Bible: St Luke

10 Confront disease at its onset.
Persius AD 34–62: *Satires*

11 There can be no surgeon who is not also a physician . . . Where the physician is not also a surgeon he is an idol that is nothing but a painted monkey.
Paracelsus c.1493–1541: Walter Pagel *Paracelsus: An introduction to Philosophical Medicine in the Era of the Renaissance* (1958)

12 Diseases desperate grown,
By desperate appliances are relieved,
Or not at all.
William Shakespeare 1564–1616: *Hamlet* (1601); see **Necessity** 3

13 Throw physic to the dogs; I'll none of it.
William Shakespeare 1564–1616: *Macbeth* (1606)

14 The remedy is worse than the disease.
Francis Bacon 1561–1626: *Essays* (1625) 'Of Seditions and Troubles'

15 Physicians of all men are most happy; what good success soever they have, the

world proclaimeth, and what faults they commit, the earth covereth.
Francis Quarles 1592–1644: *Hieroglyphics of the Life of Man* (1638)

16 Cured yesterday of my disease,
I died last night of my physician.
Matthew Prior 1664–1721: 'The Remedy Worse than the Disease' (1727)

17 In disease Medical Men guess: if they cannot ascertain a disease, they call it nervous.
John Keats 1795–1821: J. A. Gere and John Sparrow (eds.) *Geoffrey Madan's Notebooks* (1981); attributed

18 It may seem a strange principle to enunciate as the very first requirement in a Hospital that it should do the sick no harm.
Florence Nightingale 1820–1910: *Notes on Hospitals* (1863 ed.) preface

19 Ah, well, then, I suppose that I shall have to die beyond my means.
at the mention of a huge fee for a surgical operation
Oscar Wilde 1854–1900: R. H. Sherard *Life of Oscar Wilde* (1906)

20 If a lot of cures are suggested for a disease, it means that the disease is incurable.
Anton Chekhov 1860–1904: *The Cherry Orchard* (1904)

21 There is at bottom only one genuinely scientific treatment for all diseases, and that is to stimulate the phagocytes.
George Bernard Shaw 1856–1950: *The Doctor's Dilemma* (1911)

22 Every day, in every way, I am getting better and better.
to be said 15 to 20 times, morning and evening
Émile Coué 1857–1926: *De la suggestion et de ses applications* (1915); see **Achievement** 25

23 One finger in the throat and one in the rectum makes a good diagnostician.
William Osler 1849–1919: *Aphorisms from his Bedside Teachings* (1961)

24 The wounded surgeon plies the steel

That questions the distempered part;
Beneath the bleeding hands we feel
The sharp compassion of the healer's art
Resolving the enigma of the fever chart.
T. S. Eliot 1888–1965: *Four Quartets* 'East Coker' (1940)

25 We shall have to learn to refrain from doing things merely because we know how to do them.
Theodore Fox 1899–1989: speech to Royal College of Physicians, 18 October 1965

26 When our organs have been transplanted
And the new ones made happy to lodge in us,
Let us pray one wish be granted—
We retain our zones erogenous.
E. Y. Harburg 1898–1981: 'Seated One Day at the Organ' (1965)

27 Formerly, when religion was strong and science weak, men mistook magic for medicine; now, when science is strong and religion weak, men mistake medicine for magic.
Thomas Szasz 1920– : *The Second Sin* (1973)

28 Medicinal discovery,
It moves in mighty leaps,
It leapt straight past the common cold
And gave it us for keeps.
Pam Ayres 1947– : 'Oh no, I got a cold' (1976)

29 A cousin of mine who was a casualty surgeon in Manhattan tells me that he and his colleagues had a one-word nickname for bikers: Donors.
Stephen Fry 1957– : *Paperweight* (1992)

30 If you have a stomach ache, in France you get a suppository, in Germany a health spa, in the United States they cut your stomach open and in Britain they put you on a waiting list.
Phil Hammond 1955– and **Michael Mosley**: *Trust Me (I'm a Doctor)* (1999)

Mediocrity see Excellence and Mediocrity

Meeting and Parting

PROVERBS AND SAYINGS

1 The best of friends must part.

early 17th century, meaning that no friendship is so close that separation is impossible

2 Nice to see you—to see you, nice.

catchphrase used by Bruce Forsyth in 'The Generation Game' on BBC Television, 1973 onwards

3 Talk of the Devil, and he is bound to appear.

mid 17th century, meaning that to speak of the Devil may be to invite his presence; often abbreviated to talk of the Devil, *and used when a person just spoken of is seen*

PHRASES

4 nunc dimittis permission to depart, dismissal.

Latin = now you let (your servant) depart, a canticle forming part of the Christian liturgy at evensong and compline, comprising the song of Simeon in the Bible (Luke) (in the Vulgate beginning Nunc dimittis, Domine)

5 ships that pass in the night people whose contact or acquaintance is necessarily fleeting or transitory.

from Longfellow: see **Relationships** 7

QUOTATIONS

6 *Atque in perpetuum, frater, ave atque vale.*
And so, my brother, hail, and farewell evermore!
Catullus *c.84–c.54* BC: *Carmina*

7 Fare well my dear child and pray for me, and I shall for you and all your friends that we may merrily meet in heaven.
Thomas More 1478–1535: last letter to his daughter Margaret Roper, 5 July 1535

8 Good-night, good-night! parting is such sweet sorrow
That I shall say good-night till it be morrow.
William Shakespeare 1564–1616: *Romeo and Juliet* (1595)

9 Ill met by moonlight, proud Titania.
William Shakespeare 1564–1616: *A Midsummer Night's Dream* (1595–6)

10 When shall we three meet again
In thunder, lightning, or in rain?
William Shakespeare 1564–1616: *Macbeth* (1606)

11 Since there's no help, come let us kiss and part,
Nay, I have done: you get no more of me.
Michael Drayton 1563–1631: *Idea* (1619) sonnet 61

12 Gin a body meet a body
Comin thro' the rye,
Gin a body kiss a body
Need a body cry?
Robert Burns 1759–96: 'Comin thro' the rye' (1796)

13 Not many sounds in life, and I include all urban and all rural sounds, exceed in interest a knock at the door.
Charles Lamb 1775–1834: *Essays of Elia* (1823) 'Valentine's Day'

14 The red rose cries, 'She is near, she is near;'
And the white rose weeps, 'She is late;'
The larkspur listens, 'I hear, I hear;'
And the lily whispers, 'I wait.'
Alfred, Lord Tennyson 1809–92: *Maud* (1855)

15 In every parting there is an image of death.
George Eliot 1819–80: *Scenes of Clerical Life* (1858)

16 Dr Livingstone, I presume?
Henry Morton Stanley 1841–1904: *How I found Livingstone* (1872)

17 Parting is all we know of heaven,
And all we need of hell.
Emily Dickinson 1830–86: 'My life closed twice before its close'

18 'Is there anybody there?' said the Traveller,
Knocking on the moonlit door.
Walter de la Mare 1873–1956: 'The Listeners' (1912)

19 We live our lives, for ever taking leave.
Rainer Maria Rilke 1875–1926: *Duineser Elegien* (1948)

20 Goodnight, children . . . everywhere.
Derek McCulloch 1897–1967: *Children's Hour* (BBC Radio programme; closing words normally spoken by 'Uncle Mac' in the 1930s and 1940s)

21 Why don't you come up sometime, and see me?
usually quoted as 'Why don't you come up and see me sometime?'
Mae West 1892–1980: *She Done Him Wrong* (1933 film)

22 Once I leave, I leave. I am not going to speak to the man on the bridge, and I am not going to spit on the deck.
Stanley Baldwin 1867–1947: resignation statement to the Cabinet, 28 May 1937

23 We'll meet again, don't know where,
Don't know when,
But I know we'll meet again some sunny day.
Ross Parker 1914–74 and **Hugh Charles** 1907– : 'We'll Meet Again' (1939 song)

24 Some enchanted evening,
You may see a stranger,
You may see a stranger,
Across a crowded room.
Oscar Hammerstein II 1895–1960: 'Some Enchanted Evening' (1949 song)

25 I'll be back.
James Cameron 1954– : *The Terminator* (1984 film, with Gale Anne Hurd); spoken by Arnold Schwarzenegger

Memory

PROVERBS AND SAYINGS

1 Our memory is always at fault, never our judgement.
American proverb, mid 20th century

PHRASES

2 down memory lane recalling a pleasant past.
Down Memory Lane (1949) *title of a compilation of Mack Sennett comedy shorts*

3 Kim's game a memory-testing game in which players try to remember as many as possible of a set of objects briefly shown to them.
Kim (*the eponymous hero of*) a book by Rudyard Kipling (1865–1936), in which a similar game is played.

4 recherche du temps perdu an evocation of one's early life
French, literally 'in search of the lost time', title of Proust's novel sequence of 1913–27 (in English translation of 1922–31, 'Remembrance of things past'): see 8, 18 below, The Past 15

QUOTATIONS

5 Maybe one day it will be cheering to remember even these things.
Virgil 70–19 BC: *Aeneid*

6 The memories of long love gather like drifting snow, poignant as the mandarin ducks who float side by side in sleep.
Murasaki Shikibu c.978–c.1031: *The Tale of Genji*

7 Old men forget: yet all shall be forgot, But he'll remember with advantages What feats he did that day.
William Shakespeare 1564–1616: *Henry V* (1599)

8 When to the sessions of sweet silent thought

I summon up remembrance of things past.
William Shakespeare 1564–1616: sonnet 30; see 4 above

9 Nobody can remember more than seven of anything.
reason for omitting the eight beatitudes from his catechism
Cardinal Robert Bellarmine 1542–1621: John Bossy *Christianity in the West 1400-1700* (1985)

10 We'll tak a cup o' kindness yet,
For auld lang syne.
Robert Burns 1759–96: 'Auld Lang Syne' (1796); see **The Past** 8

11 You may break, you may shatter the vase, if you will,
But the scent of the roses will hang round it still.
Thomas Moore 1779–1852: 'Farewell!—but whenever' (1807)

12 I remember, I remember,
The house where I was born,
The little window where the sun
Came peeping in at morn.
Thomas Hood 1799–1845: 'I Remember' (1826)

13 In looking on the happy autumn-fields,
And thinking of the days that are no more.
Alfred, Lord Tennyson 1809–92: *The Princess* (1847) song (added 1850)

14 And we forget because we must
And not because we will.
Matthew Arnold 1822–88: 'Absence' (1852)

15 Better by far you should forget and smile
Than that you should remember and be sad.
Christina Rossetti 1830–94: 'Remember' (1862)

16 I've a grand memory for forgetting, David.
Robert Louis Stevenson 1850–94: *Kidnapped*
(1886)

17 I have forgot much, Cynara! gone with the
    wind,
Flung roses, roses, riotously, with the
    throng,
Dancing, to put thy pale, lost lilies out of
    mind.
Ernest Dowson 1867–1900: 'Non Sum Qualis Eram'
(1896); also known as 'Cynara'; see **Absence** 6,
Constancy 16

18 And suddenly the memory revealed itself.
The taste was that of the little piece of
madeleine which on Sunday mornings at
Combray . . . my aunt Léonie used to give
me, dipping it first in her own cup of tea or
tisane.
Marcel Proust 1871–1922: *Swann's Way* (1913, vol. 1
of *Remembrance of Things Past*); see 4 above

19 Midnight shakes the memory
As a madman shakes a dead geranium.
T. S. Eliot 1888–1965: 'Rhapsody on a Windy Night'
(1917)

✓ **20** Someone said that God gave us memory so
that we might have roses in December.
J. M. Barrie 1860–1937: Rectorial Address at St
Andrew's, 3 May 1922

21 In plucking the fruit of memory one runs
the risk of spoiling its bloom.
Joseph Conrad 1857–1924: *The Arrow of Gold* (1924
ed.)

22 What beastly incidents our memories insist
on cherishing! . . . the ugly and disgusting
. . . the beautiful things we have to keep
diaries to remember!
Eugene O'Neill 1888–1953: *Strange Interlude* (1928)

23 A cigarette that bears a lipstick's traces,
An airline ticket to romantic places;
And still my heart has wings
These foolish things
Remind me of you.
Holt Marvell: 'These Foolish Things Remind Me of
You' (1935 song)

24 There should be an invention that bottles
up a memory like a perfume, and it never
faded, never got stale, and whenever I

wanted to I could uncork the bottle, and
live the memory all over again.
Daphne Du Maurier 1907–89: *Rebecca* (1938)

25 Our memories are card-indexes consulted,
and then put back in disorder by
authorities whom we do not control.
Cyril Connolly 1903–74: *The Unquiet Grave* (1944)

26 We met at nine.
We met at eight.
I was on time.
No, you were late.
Ah yes! I remember it well.
Alan Jay Lerner 1918–86: 'I Remember it Well'
(1958 song)

27 Poor people's memory is less nourished
than that of the rich; it has fewer
landmarks in space because they seldom
leave the place where they live, and fewer
reference points in time . . . Of course,
there is the memory of the heart that they
say is the surest kind, but the heart wears
out with sorrow and labour, it forgets
sooner under the weight of fatigue.
Albert Camus 1913–60: *The First Man* (1994)

28 Memories are not shackles, Franklin, they
are garlands.
Alan Bennett 1934– : *Forty Years On* (1969)

29 Everyone seems to remember with great
clarity what they were doing on November
22nd, 1963, at the precise moment they
heard President Kennedy was dead.
Frederick Forsyth 1938– : *The Odessa File* (1972)

30 My memory is certainly in my hands. I can
remember things only if I have a pencil
and I can write with it and play with it. I
think your hand concentrates for you.
Rebecca West 1892–1983: George Plimpton (ed.)
The Writer's Chapbook (1989)

31 Your memory is a monster; *you* forget—*it*
doesn't. It simply files things away. It keeps
things for you, or hides things from you—
and summons them to your recall with a
will of its own. You think you have a
memory; but it has you!
John Irving 1942– : *A Prayer for Owen Meany* (1989)

Men

1 Boys will be boys.
early 17th century, often used ironically

2 I married my husband for life, not for lunch.
20th century saying, origin unknown

3 The way to a man's heart is through his stomach.
early 19th century

4 dead white European male regarded as the stereotypical figure on which literary, cultural, and philosophical studies have traditionally centred.
the acronym DWEM *derives from this*

5 good ol' boy in US usage, a (usually white) male from the Southern States of America, regarded as one of a group conforming to a social and cultural masculine stereotype.

6 Sigh no more, ladies, sigh no more,
Men were deceivers ever.
William Shakespeare 1564–1616: *Much Ado About Nothing* (1598–9)

7 In matters of love men's eyes are always bigger than their bellies. They have violent appetites, 'tis true; but they have soon dined.
John Vanbrugh 1664–1726: *The Relapse* (1696)

8 Man is to be held only by the *slightest* chains, with the idea that he can break them at pleasure, he submits to them in sport.
Maria Edgeworth 1767–1849: *Letters for Literary Ladies* (1795)

9 Men have had every advantage of us in telling their own story. Education has been theirs in so much higher a degree; the pen has been in their hands.
Jane Austen 1775–1817: *Persuasion* (1818)

10 A man . . . is *so* in the way in the house!
Elizabeth Gaskell 1810–65: *Cranford* (1853)

11 The three most important things a man has are, briefly, his private parts, his money, and his religious opinions.
Samuel Butler 1835–1902: *Further Extracts from Notebooks* (1934)

12 Every man over forty is a scoundrel.
George Bernard Shaw 1856–1950: *Man and Superman* (1903) 'Maxims: Stray Sayings'

13 If you wish—
. . . I'll be irreproachably tender;
not a man, but—a cloud in trousers!
Vladimir Mayakovsky 1893–1930: 'The Cloud in Trousers' (1915)

14 Men build bridges and throw railroads across deserts, and yet they contend successfully that the job of sewing on a button is beyond them. Accordingly, they don't have to sew buttons.
Heywood Broun 1888–1939: *Seeing Things at Night* (1921)

15 Somehow a bachelor never quite gets over the idea that he is a thing of beauty and a boy forever.
Helen Rowland 1875–1950: *A Guide to Men* (1922); see **Beauty** 18

16 It's not the men in my life that counts— it's the life in my men.
Mae West 1892–1980: *I'm No Angel* (1933 film)

17 Women want mediocre men, and men are working hard to be as mediocre as possible.
Margaret Mead 1901–78: in *Quote Magazine* 15 June 1958

18 There is, of course, no reason for the existence of the male sex except that sometimes one needs help with moving the piano.
Rebecca West 1892–1983: in *Sunday Telegraph* 28 June 1970

19 Whatever they may be in public life, whatever their relations with men, in their relations with women, all men are rapists, and that's all they are. They rape us with their eyes, their laws, and their codes.
Marilyn French 1929– : *The Women's Room* (1977)

20 Men—athletes especially—have to be like King Kong. When we lose, we can't cry and we can't pout.
Carl Lewis 1961– : in *Observer* 29 July 1984

21 Are all men in disguise except those crying?
Dannie Abse 1923– : 'Encounter at a greyhound bus station' (1986)

22 Every modern male has, lying at the bottom of his psyche, a large, primitive

being covered with hair down to his feet. Making contact with this Wild Man is the step the Eighties male or the Nineties male has yet to take.

Robert Bly 1926– : *Iron John* (1990)

23 Years ago, manhood was an opportunity for achievement, and now it is a problem to be overcome.

Garrison Keillor 1942– : *The Book of Guys* (1994)

24 We are lads. We have burgled houses and nicked car stereos, and we like girls and swear and go to the football and take the piss.

Noel Gallagher 1967– : interview in *Melody Maker* 30 March 1996

25 Men would rather take their trousers off in public when they're drunk than open the shield of their hearts when they are sober.

Stephen Fry 1957– : comment on the work of the Samaritans, 17 May 1996

26 Give me macho, or give me death.

Madonna 1958– : in *Sunday Times* 29 July 2001

Men and Women see also Men, Woman's Role, Women

PROVERBS AND SAYINGS

1 Every Jack has his Jill.

early 17th century, meaning that all lovers have found a mate

2 A good Jack makes a good Jill.

early 17th century, used of the effect of a husband on his wife

3 A man is as old as he feels, and a woman as old as she looks.

late 19th century; both parts of the proverb are sometimes used on their own

QUOTATIONS

4   Just such disparity
As is 'twixt air and angels' purity,
'Twixt women's love, and men's will ever be.

John Donne 1572–1631: 'Air and Angels'

5 He for God only, she for God in him.

John Milton 1608–74: *Paradise Lost* (1667)

6 In every age and country, the wiser, or at least the stronger, of the two sexes, has usurped the powers of the state, and confined the other to the cares and pleasures of domestic life.

Edward Gibbon 1737–94: *The Decline and Fall of the Roman Empire* (1776–88)

7 Man's love is of man's life a thing apart, 'Tis woman's whole existence.

Lord Byron 1788–1824: *Don Juan* (1819–24)

8 The man's desire is for the woman; but the woman's desire is rarely other than for the desire of the man.

Samuel Taylor Coleridge 1772–1834: *Table Talk* (1835) 23 July 1827

9 Man is the hunter; woman is his game.

Alfred, Lord Tennyson 1809–92: *The Princess* (1847)

10 'Tis strange what a man may do, and a woman yet think him an angel.

William Makepeace Thackeray 1811–63: *The History of Henry Esmond* (1852)

11 Man dreams of fame while woman wakes to love.

Alfred, Lord Tennyson 1809–92: *Idylls of the King* 'Merlin and Vivien' (1859)

12 I expect that Woman will be the last thing civilized by Man.

George Meredith 1828–1909: *The Ordeal of Richard Feverel* (1859)

13 Take my word for it, the silliest woman can manage a clever man; but it takes a very clever woman to manage a fool.

Rudyard Kipling 1865–1936: *Plain Tales from the Hills* (1888)

14 All women become like their mothers. That is their tragedy. No man does. That's his.

Oscar Wilde 1854–1900: *The Importance of Being Earnest* (1895)

15 Where young boys plan for what they will achieve and attain, young girls plan for whom they will achieve and attain.

Charlotte Perkins Gilman 1860–1935: *Women and Economics* (1898)

16 Of all human struggles there is none so treacherous and remorseless as the struggle between the artist man and the mother woman.

George Bernard Shaw 1856–1950: *Man and Superman* (1903)

17 Women deprived of the company of men pine, men deprived of the company of women become stupid.

Anton Chekhov 1860–1904: *Notebooks* (1921)

18 A woman can forgive a man for the harm he does her, but she can never forgive him for the sacrifices he makes on her account.

W. Somerset Maugham 1874–1965: *The Moon and Sixpence* (1919)

19 Women have served all these centuries as looking-glasses possessing the magic and delicious power of reflecting the figure of a man at twice its natural size.

Virginia Woolf 1882–1941: *A Room of One's Own* (1929)

20 Me Tarzan, you Jane.

summing up his role in Tarzan, the Ape Man (*1932 film*)

Johnny Weissmuller 1904–84: in *Photoplay Magazine* June 1932; the words occur neither in the film nor the original novel, by Edgar Rice Burroughs

21 In the sex-war thoughtlessness is the weapon of the male, vindictiveness of the female.

Cyril Connolly 1903–74: *The Unquiet Grave* (1944)

22 It is not in giving life but in risking life that man is raised above the animal; that is why superiority has been accorded in humanity not to the sex that brings forth but to that which kills.

Simone de Beauvoir 1908–86: *The Second Sex* (1949)

23 There is more difference within the sexes than between them.

Ivy Compton-Burnett 1884–1969: *Mother and Son* (1955)

24 Why can't a woman be more like a man? Men are so honest, so thoroughly square; Eternally noble, historically fair.

Alan Jay Lerner 1918–86: 'A Hymn to Him' (1956 song)

25 Every woman adores a Fascist,

The boot in the face, the brute
Brute heart of a brute like you.

Sylvia Plath 1932–63: 'Daddy' (1963)

26 Whatever women do they must do twice as well as men to be thought half as good.

Charlotte Whitton 1896–1975: in *Canada Month* June 1963

27 Stand by your man.

Tammy Wynette 1942–98 and **Billy Sherrill**: title of song (1968)

28 Women have very little idea of how much men hate them.

Germaine Greer 1939– : *The Female Eunuch* (1971)

29 Whereas nature turns girls into women, society has to make boys into men.

Anthony Stevens: *Archetype* (1982)

30 My mother said it was simple to keep a man, you must be a maid in the living room, a cook in the kitchen and a whore in the bedroom. I said I'd hire the other two and take care of the bedroom bit.

Jerry Hall: in *Observer* 6 October 1985

31 More and more it appears that, biologically, men are designed for short, brutal lives and women for long miserable ones.

Estelle Ramey: in *Observer* 7 April 1985

32 A man has every season, while a woman has only the right to spring.

Jane Fonda 1937– : in *Daily Mail* 13 September 1989

33 A woman without a man is like a fish without a bicycle.

Gloria Steinem 1934– : attributed

34 Men are from Mars, women are from Venus.

John Gray 1951– : title of book (1992)

35 In societies where men are truly confident of their own worth, women are not merely tolerated but valued.

Aung San Suu Kyi 1945– : videotape speech at NGO Forum on Women, China, early September 1995

Middle Age

PROVERBS AND SAYINGS

1 A fool at forty is a fool indeed.

early 16th century, meaning that someone who has not learned wisdom by the age of forty will never learn it; in this form from Edward Young Universal Passion (1725) 'Be wise with speed; A fool at forty is a fool indeed'

2 Life begins at forty.

mid 20th century, from title of book (1932) by Walter B. Pitkin

3 *Nel mezzo del cammin di nostra vita.*
Midway along the path of our life.
Dante Alighieri 1265–1321: *Divina Commedia*
'Inferno'

4 I am resolved to grow fat and look young
till forty, and then slip out of the world
with the first wrinkle and the reputation of
five-and-twenty.
John Dryden 1631–1700: *The Maiden Queen* (1668)

5 He who thinks to realize when he is older
the hopes and desires of youth is always
deceiving himself, for every decade of a
man's life possesses its own kind of
happiness, its own hopes and prospects.
Johann Wolfgang von Goethe 1749–1832: *Elective
Affinities* (1809)

6 My days are in the yellow leaf;
The flowers and fruits of love are gone;
The worm, the canker, and the grief
Are mine alone!
Lord Byron 1788–1824: 'On This Day I Complete my
Thirty-Sixth Year' (1824)

7 I am past thirty, and three parts iced over.
Matthew Arnold 1822–88: letter to Arthur Hugh
Clough, 12 February 1853

8 Few women, I fear, have had such reason
as I have to think the long sad years of
youth were worth living for the sake of
middle age.
George Eliot 1819–80: letter, 1857

9 Thirty-five is a very attractive age. London
society is full of women of the very highest
birth who have, of their own free choice,
remained thirty-five for years.
Oscar Wilde 1854–1900: *The Importance of Being
Earnest* (1895)

10 At eighteen our convictions are hills from
which we look; at forty-five they are caves
in which we hide.
F. Scott Fitzgerald 1896–1940: 'Bernice Bobs her
Hair' (1920)

11 The afternoon of human life must also
have a significance of its own and cannot
be merely a pitiful appendage to life's
morning.
Carl Gustav Jung 1875–1961: *The Stages of Life*
(1930)

12 One of the pleasures of middle age is to *find
out* that one WAS right, and that one was
much righter than one knew at say 17 or
23.
Ezra Pound 1885–1972: *ABC of Reading* (1934)

13 I have a bone to pick with Fate.
Come here and tell me, girlie,
Do you think my mind is maturing late,
Or simply rotted early?
Ogden Nash 1902–71: 'Lines on Facing Forty' (1942)

14 Years ago we discovered the exact point,
the dead centre of middle age. It occurs
when you are too young to take up golf
and too old to rush up to the net.
Franklin P. Adams 1881–1960: *Nods and Becks*
(1944)

15 At forty-five,
What next, what next?
At every corner,
I meet my Father,
my age, still alive.
Robert Lowell 1917–77: 'Middle Age' (1964)

16 Men at forty
Learn to close softly
The doors to rooms they will not be
Coming back to.
Donald Justice 1925– : 'Men at Forty' (1967)

17 After forty a woman has to choose
between losing her figure or her face. My
advice is to keep your face, and stay sitting
down.
Barbara Cartland 1901–2000: Libby Purves
'Luncheon à la Cartland'; in *The Times* 6 October
1993

18 Women over thirty are at their best, but
men over thirty are too old to recognize it.
Jean-Paul Belmondo 1933– : attributed

19 Fiftieth birthdays should be times of huge
goodwill . . . Only people who put on fake
tan and pretend to be younger than they
are don't get to join the party.
Maeve Binchy 1940– : in *Irish Times* 25 April 1998

The Mind see also Ideas, Logic and Reason, Madness, Thinking

1 A mind is a terrible thing to waste.
motto of the United Negro College Fund; see 23 below

2 the five wits the five (bodily) senses of hearing, sight, smell, taste, and touch.

3 the ghost in the machine the mind viewed as distinct from the body.
a term coined by the philosopher Gilbert Ryle in The Concept of Mind *(1949), for a viewpoint which he regarded as completely misleading*

4 The mind of the perfect man is like a mirror. It does not lean forward or backward in its response to things. It responds to things but conceals nothing of its own.
Zhuangzi *c.*369–286 BC: *Chuang Tzu* ch. 7

5 My mind to me a kingdom is.
Such perfect joy therein I find.
Edward Dyer d. 1607: 'In praise of a contented mind' (1588); attributed

6 The mind is its own place, and in itself
Can make a heaven of hell, a hell of
   heaven.
John Milton 1608–74: *Paradise Lost* (1667)

7 The mind is but a barren soil; a soil which is soon exhausted, and will produce no crop, or only one, unless it be continually fertilized and enriched with foreign matter.
Joshua Reynolds 1723–92: *Discourses on Art* 10 December 1774

8 When people will not weed their own minds, they are apt to be overrun with nettles.
Horace Walpole 1717–97: letter to Caroline, Countess of Ailesbury, 10 July 1779

9 To give a sex to mind was not very consistent with the principles of a man [Rousseau] who argued so warmly, and so well, for the immortality of the soul.
often quoted as, 'Mind has no sex'
Mary Wollstonecraft 1759–97: *A Vindication of the Rights of Woman* (1792)

10 The only means of strengthening one's intellect is to make up one's mind about nothing—to let the mind be a thoroughfare for all thoughts. Not a select party.
John Keats 1795–1821: letter to George and Georgiana Keats, 24 September 1819

11 What is Matter?—Never mind.
What is Mind?—No matter.
Punch: 1855

12 On earth there is nothing great but man; in man there is nothing great but mind.
William Hamilton 1788–1856: *Lectures on Metaphysics and Logic* (1859); attributed in a Latin form to Favorinus in Pico di Mirandola (1463–94) *Disputationes Adversus Astrologiam Divinatricem*

13 The great regions of the mind correspond to the great regions of the brain.
Paul Broca 1824–80: at the Société Anatomique, August 1861

14 To be conscious is an illness—a real thorough-going illness.
Fedor Dostoevsky 1821–81: *Notes from Underground* (1864)

15 With me the horrid doubt always arises whether the convictions of man's mind which has been developed from the mind of the lower animals, are of any value or at all trustworthy.
Charles Darwin 1809–82: Francis Darwin (ed.) *The Life and Letters of Charles Darwin* (1887)

16 O the mind, mind has mountains; cliffs of
   fall
Frightful, sheer, no-man-fathomed. Hold
   them cheap
May who ne'er hung there.
Gerard Manley Hopkins 1844–89: 'No worst, there is none' (written 1885)

17 Minds are like parachutes. They only function when they are open.
James Dewar 1842–1923: attributed

18 If my mental processes are determined wholly by the motions of atoms in my brain, I have no reason for supposing that my beliefs are true. They may be sound chemically, but that does not make them sound logically. And hence I have no reason for supposing my brain to be composed of atoms.
J. B. S. Haldane 1892–1964: *Possible Worlds* (1927)

19 Mind in its purest play is like some bat

That beats about in caverns all alone,
Contriving by a kind of senseless wit
Not to conclude against a wall of stone.
Richard Wilbur 1921– : 'Mind' (1956)

20 Purple haze is in my brain
Lately things don't seem the same.
Jimi Hendrix 1942–70: 'Purple Haze' (1967 song)

21 That's the classical mind at work, runs fine
inside but looks dingy on the surface.
Robert M. Pirsig 1928– : *Zen and the Art of
Motorcycle Maintenance* (1974)

22 Those who are caught in mental cages can
often picture freedom, it just has no
attractive power.
Iris Murdoch 1919–99: *The Sea, The Sea* (1978)

23 What a waste it is to lose one's mind, or
not to have a mind. How true that is.
Dan Quayle 1947– : speech to the United Negro
College Fund, in *The Times* 26 May 1989; see 1
above

24 Consciousness *isn't* intolerable. It is
beautiful: the eternal creation and
dissolution of mental forms.
Martin Amis 1949– : *Time's Arrow* (1991)

25 Every human brain is born not as a blank
tablet (a *tabula rasa*) waiting to be filled in
by experience but as 'an exposed negative
waiting to be slipped into developer fluid'.
on the nature v. nurture debate
Edward O. Wilson 1929– : attributed

Misfortunes see also Adversity

PROVERBS AND SAYINGS

**1 The bread never falls but on its buttered
side.**
*mid 19th century, meaning that if something goes
wrong, the outcome is likely to be as bad as possible*

2 Help you to salt, help you to sorrow.
*mid 17th century, in which salt is regarded as a sign of
bad luck (especially if spilt at table)*

**3 I cried because I had no shoes, until I met a
man who had no feet.**
*modern saying, deriving from a Persian original; see 16
below*

4 If anything can go wrong, it will.
*modern saying reflecting a supposed law of nature,
said to have been coined in 1949 by George Nichols.
Nichols is said to have developed the maxim from a
remark made by a colleague, Captain E. Murphy, and
the rule is otherwise known as Murphy's Law. See 10
below*

5 It is no use crying over spilt milk.
*mid 17th century, meaning that it is pointless to repine
when it is too late to prevent the misfortune*

6 It never rains but it pours.
*early 18th century, meaning that if one thing has gone
wrong, worse will follow*

7 Misfortunes never come singly.
early 14th century

PHRASES

8 a chapter of accidents a series of
misfortunes.
see Chance 23

9 **damnosa hereditas** an inheritance or
tradition bringing more burden than profit.
Latin = inheritance that causes loss, from The
Institutes *of the Roman jurist Gaius (AD c.110–c.180)*

10 **Murphy's law** any of various aphoristic
expressions of the apparent perverseness
and unreasonableness of things.
see 4 above

11 **out of the frying-pan into the fire** from one
unfortunate situation into an even worse
one.
see Employment 15

12 **a poisoned chalice** an assignment, award,
or honour which is likely to prove a
disadvantage or source of problems to the
recipient.
originally from Shakespeare's Macbeth *(1606): 'This
even-handed justice Commends th'ingredience of our
poison'd chalice To our own lips'*

13 **shirt of Nessus** a destructive or
expurgatory force or influence.
*from the classical story of the centaur Nessus slain by
Heracles, whose blood later poisoned Heracles after he
was given a garment smeared with it to wear*

14 **skeleton at the feast** something that spoils
one's pleasure; an intrusive worry or
cause of grief.
*originally in allusion to an ancient Egyptian custom
recorded in Herodotus's* Histories, *which tells of a
wooden corpse in a coffin being carried round at
parties, and shown to guests with the words, 'Look on
this, for this will be your lot when you are dead'*

QUOTATIONS

15 Man is born unto trouble, as the sparks fly upward.
Bible: Job

16 I never complained at the vicissitudes of fortune, nor murmured at the ordinances of Heaven, excepting once, when my feet were bare, and I had not the means of procuring myself shoes. I entered the great mosque at Cufah with a heavy heart when I beheld a man who had no feet. I offered up praise and thanksgiving to God for his bounty, and bore with patience the want of shoes.
Sadi c.1213–91: *The Rose Garden* (1258); see 3 above

17 Misery acquaints a man with strange bedfellows.
William Shakespeare 1564–1616: *The Tempest* (1611); see **Adversity** 1

18 All the misfortunes of men derive from one single thing, which is their inability to be at ease in a room.
Blaise Pascal 1623–62: *Pensées* (1670)

19 In the misfortune of our best friends, we always find something which is not displeasing to us.
Duc de la Rochefoucauld 1613–80: *Réflexions ou Maximes Morales* (1665)

20 If Gladstone fell into the Thames, that would be misfortune; and if anybody pulled him out, that, I suppose, would be a calamity.
Benjamin Disraeli 1804–81: Leon Harris *The Fine Art of Political Wit* (1965)

21 I had never had a piece of toast
Particularly long and wide,
But fell upon the sanded floor,
And always on the buttered side.
James Payn 1830–98: in *Chambers's Journal* 2 February 1884; see 1 above

22 I left the room with silent dignity, but caught my foot in the mat.
George and Weedon Grossmith 1847–1912, 1854–1919: *The Diary of a Nobody* (1894)

23 And always keep a-hold of Nurse
For fear of finding something worse.
Hilaire Belloc 1870–1953: *Cautionary Tales* (1907) 'Jim'

24 One likes people much better when they're battered down by a prodigious siege of misfortune than when they triumph.
Virginia Woolf 1882–1941: diary 13 August 1921

25 boss there is always
a comforting thought
in time of trouble when
it is not our trouble.
Don Marquis 1878–1937: *archy does his part* (1935)

26 My only solution for the problem of habitual accidents . . . is to stay in bed all day. Even then, there is always the chance that you will fall out.
Robert Benchley 1889–1945: *Chips off the old Benchley* (1949)

27   People will take balls,
Balls will be lost always, little boy,
And no one buys a ball back.
John Berryman 1914–72: 'The Ball Poem' (1948)

28 Well, don't you think it's at least possible, just possible that things can happen to us so bad that we don't ever get over them?
Doris Lessing 1919– : *The Golden Notebook* (1962)

29 The fatal law of gravity: when you are down everything falls on you.
Sylvia Townsend Warner 1893–1978: attributed

30 In the words of one of my more sympathetic correspondents, it has turned out to be an 'annus horribilis'.
Elizabeth II 1926– : speech at Guildhall, London, 24 November 1992; see **Time** 8

31 I've no sympathy with people to whom things happen. It may be that their luck was bad, but is that to count in their favour?
Cormac McCarthy 1933– : *All the Pretty Horses* (1993)

Mistakes

1 Homer sometimes nods.

late fourteenth century, meaning that even the greatest expert may make a mistake (nods here means 'becomes drowsy', implying a momentary lack of attention); see 11 below

2 A miss is as good as a mile.

early 17th century, meaning that if you miss the target, it hardly matters by how much; the syntax has been distorted by abridgement: the original form was ' an inch in a miss is as good as an ell' (an ell being a former measure of length equal to about 1.1 metres)

3 Shome mishtake, shurely?

catchphrase in Private Eye *magazine, from the 1980s*

4 There's many a slip 'twixt cup and lip.

mid 16th century, meaning that much can go wrong between the initiation of a process and its completion, often used as a warning

5 To err is human (to forgive divine).

late 16th century (in its quoted form, from Pope, see **Forgiveness** *16); see also* **Computers** *5*

6 a beam in one's eye a fault great compared to another's.

from the Bible (Matthew): see **Self-Knowledge** *3; see also 8 below*

7 an error in the first concoction a fault in the initial stage.

the first of three stages of digestion formerly recognized

8 a mote in a person's eye a fault observed in another person by a person who ignores a greater fault of his or her own.

mote *an irritating particle in the eye; from the Bible (Matthew): see 6 above*

9 shut the stable door when the horse has bolted take preventive measures too late.

from the proverb: see **Foresight** *3*

10 I would rather be wrong, by God, with Plato . . . than be correct with those men.

on Pythagoreans

Cicero 106–43 BC: *Tusculanae Disputationes*

11 I'm aggrieved when sometimes even excellent Homer nods.

Horace 65–8 BC: *Ars Poetica*; see 1 above, **Poets** 17

12 Leave no rubs nor botches in the work.

William Shakespeare 1564–1616: *Macbeth* (1606)

13 Errors, like straws, upon the surface flow; He who would search for pearls must dive below.

John Dryden 1631–1700: *All for Love* (1678)

14 Crooked things may be as stiff and unflexible as straight: and men may be as positive in error as in truth.

John Locke 1632–1704: *An Essay concerning Human Understanding* (1690)

15 Truth lies within a little and certain compass, but error is immense.

Henry St John, Lord Bolingbroke 1678–1751: *Reflections upon Exile* (1716)

16 It is worse than a crime, it is a blunder.

on hearing of the execution of the Duc d'Enghien, 1804

Antoine Boulay de la Meurthe 1761–1840: C.-A. Sainte-Beuve *Nouveaux Lundis* (1870)

17 As she frequently remarked when she made any such mistake, it would be all the same a hundred years hence.

Charles Dickens 1812–70: *Nicholas Nickleby* (1839)

18 'Forward, the Light Brigade!' Was there a man dismayed? Not though the soldier knew Some one had blundered.

Alfred, Lord Tennyson 1809–92: 'The Charge of the Light Brigade' (1854)

19 The man who makes no mistakes does not usually make anything.

Edward John Phelps 1822–1900: speech at the Mansion House, London, 24 January 1889; see **Creativity** 1

20 To lose one parent, Mr Worthing, may be regarded as a misfortune; to lose both looks like carelessness.

Oscar Wilde 1854–1900: *The Importance of Being Earnest* (1895)

21 The report of my death was an exaggeration.

usually quoted as 'Reports of my death have been greatly exaggerated'

Mark Twain 1835–1910: in *New York Journal* 2 June 1897

22 Well, if I called the wrong number, why did you answer the phone?

James Thurber 1894–1961: cartoon caption in *New Yorker* 5 June 1937

23 One Galileo in two thousand years is enough.

on being asked to proscribe the works of Teilhard de Chardin

Pope Pius XII 1876–1958: attributed; Stafford Beer *Platform for Change* (1975)

24 The weak have one weapon: the errors of those who think they are strong.

Georges Bidault 1899–1983: in *Observer* 15 July 1962

25 The road to wisdom?—Well, it's plain and simple to express:
Err
and err
and err again

but less
and less
and less.

Piet Hein 1905– : 'The Road to Wisdom' (1966)

26 Mistakes are a fact of life
It is the response to error that counts.

Nikki Giovanni 1943– : 'Of Liberation' (1970)

27 When people thought the Earth was flat, they were wrong. When people thought the Earth was spherical, they were wrong. But if *you* think that thinking the Earth is spherical is *just as wrong* as thinking the Earth is flat, then your view is wronger than both of them put together.

Isaac Asimov 1920–92: *The Relativity of Wrong* (1989)

28 If all else fails, immortality can always be assured by a spectacular error.

J. K. Galbraith 1908– : attributed

Moderation see **Excess and Moderation**

Money see also **Greed, Poverty, Thrift and Extravagance, Wealth**

PROVERBS AND SAYINGS

1 Bad money drives out good.

early 20th century, meaning that money of lower intrinsic value tends to circulate more freely than money of higher intrinsic and equal nominal value, through what is recognized as money of higher value being hoarded, known as Gresham's law; see 18 below

2 The best things in life are free.

*early 20th century; see **Possessions** 22*

3 Get the money honestly if you can.

American proverb, early 19th century; see 22 below

4 He that cannot pay, let him pray.

early 17th century, meaning that if you have no material resources, prayer is your only resort

5 Money has no smell.

*early 20th century in this form, but originally deriving from a comment made by the Emperor Vespasian (AD 9–79); see **Taxes** 5*

6 Money isn't everything.

early 20th century, often said in consolation or resignation

7 Money is power.

mid 18th century

8 Money is the root of all evil.

mid 15th century, of biblical origin; see 24 below

9 Money makes the mare to go.

late 15th century, referring to money as a source of power

10 Money talks.

mid 17th century, meaning that money has influence; see 40 below

11 Shrouds have no pockets.

mid 19th century; meaning that worldly wealth cannot be kept and used after death

12 Time is money.

*late 16th century, often used to mean that time spent fruitlessly on something represents a real loss of money which could have been earned in that time; see **Time** 32*

13 Where there's muck there's brass.

late 17th century; brass here means 'money'; see 25 below

14 You cannot serve God and Mammon.

mid 16th century, now generally used of wealth regarded as an evil influence; see 23 below

PHRASES

15 the almighty dollar the power of money.

originally with allusion to the American writer Washington Irving (1783–1859): 'The almighty dollar, that great object of universal veneration throughout our land'

16 filthy lucre money, especially when regarded as sordid or distasteful or gained in a dishonourable way.

of biblical origin: see **The Clergy** 6

17 the gnomes of Zurich Swiss financiers or bankers, regarded as having sinister influence.

18 Gresham's Law the tendency for debased money to circulate more freely than money of higher intrinsic and equal nominal value.

Thomas Gresham (d. 1579), English financier and founder of the Royal Exchange'; see 1 above

19 the Old Lady of Threadneedle Street the Bank of England.

Threadneedle Street in the City of London containing the premises of the Bank of England; the name is derived from three-needle, possibly from a tavern with the arms of the City of London Guild of Needlemakers

20 a penny more and up goes the donkey inviting contributions to complete a sum of money.

from the cry of a travelling showman

QUOTATIONS

21 Wine maketh merry: but money answereth all things.
Bible: Ecclesiastes

22 If possible honestly, if not, somehow, make money.
Horace 65-8 BC: *Epistles*; see 3 above, **Wealth** 22

23 No man can serve two masters . . . Ye cannot serve God and mammon.
Bible: St Matthew; see 14 above, **Choice** 5, **Wealth** 9

24 The love of money is the root of all evil.
Bible: I Timothy; see 8 above, **Idleness** 7

25 Money is like muck, not good except it be spread.
Francis Bacon 1561-1626: *Essays* (1625) 'Of Seditions and Troubles'; see 13 above

26 Money speaks sense in a language all nations understand.
Aphra Behn 1640-89: *The Rover* pt. 2 (1681)

27 Money is the sinews of love, as of war.
George Farquhar 1678-1707: *Love and a Bottle* (1698); see **Warfare** 13

28 Take care of the pence, and the pounds will take care of themselves.
William Lowndes 1652-1724. Lord Chesterfield *Letters to his Son* (1774) 5 February 1750; see **Thrift** 7

29 Money, wife, is the true fuller's earth for reputations, there is not a spot or a stain but what it can take out.
John Gay 1685-1732: *The Beggar's Opera* (1728)

30 Money . . . is none of the wheels of trade: it is the oil which renders the motion of the wheels more smooth and easy.
David Hume 1711-76: *Essays: Moral and Political* (1741-2) 'Of Money'

31 I want the whole of Europe to have one currency; it will make trading much easier.
Napoleon I 1769-1821: letter to his brother Louis, 6 May 1807

32 The force of the guinea you have in your pocket depends wholly on the default of a guinea in your neighbour's pocket. If he did not want it, it would be of no use to you.
John Ruskin 1819-1900: *Unto this Last* (1862)

33 Money is like a sixth sense without which you cannot make a complete use of the other five.
W. Somerset Maugham 1874-1965: *Of Human Bondage* (1915)

34 I'm tired of Love: I'm still more tired of Rhyme.
But Money gives me pleasure all the time.
Hilaire Belloc 1870-1953: 'Fatigued' (1923)

35 What is robbing a bank compared with founding a bank?
Bertolt Brecht 1898-1956: *Die Dreigroschenoper* (1928)

36 'My boy,' he says, 'always try to rub up against money, for if you rub up against money long enough, some of it may rub off on you.'
Damon Runyon 1884-1946: in *Cosmopolitan* August 1929, 'A Very Honourable Guy'

37 A bank is a place that will lend you money if you can prove that you don't need it.
Bob Hope 1903- : Alan Harrington *Life in the Crystal Palace* (1959)

38 Money, it turned out, was exactly like sex, you thought of nothing else if you didn't have it and thought of other things if you did.
James Baldwin 1924-87: in *Esquire* May 1961 'Black Boy looks at the White Boy'

39 For I don't care too much for money,

For money can't buy me love.
John Lennon 1940-80 and **Paul McCartney** 1942- : 'Can't Buy Me Love' (1964 song)

40 Money doesn't talk, it swears.
Bob Dylan 1941- : 'It's Alright, Ma (I'm Only Bleeding)' (1965 song); see 10 above

41 From now the pound abroad is worth 14 per cent or so less in terms of other currencies. It does not mean, of course, that the pound here in Britain, in your pocket or purse or in your bank, has been devalued.
Harold Wilson 1916-95: ministerial broadcast, 19 November 1967

42 I listen to money singing. It's like looking down

From long french windows at a provincial town,
The slums, the canal, the churches ornate and mad
In the evening sun. It is intensely sad.
Philip Larkin 1922-85: 'Money' (1974)

43 Those who have some means think that the most important thing in the world is love. The poor know that it is money.
Gerald Brenan 1894-1987: *Thoughts in a Dry Season* (1978)

44 Pennies don't fall from heaven. They have to be earned on earth.
Margaret Thatcher 1925- : in *Observer* 18 November 1979; see **Optimism** 29

Morality

PROVERBS AND SAYINGS

1 **It is one thing to keep your morals on high plane; it's another to keep up with them.**
American proverb, mid 20th century

QUOTATIONS

2 Moral principles please our minds as beef and mutton and pork please our mouths.
Meng-tzu 371-289 BC: *The Book of Mencius*

3 *Cum finis est licitus, etiam media sunt licita.*
The end justifies the means.
Hermann Busenbaum 1600-68: *Medulla Theologiae Moralis* (1650); literally 'When the end is allowed, the means also are allowed'; see 17 below; **Ways and Means** 2

4 That action is best, which procures the greatest happiness for the greatest numbers.
Francis Hutcheson 1694-1746: *An Inquiry into the Original of our Ideas of Beauty and Virtue* (1725); see **Society** 10

5 State a moral case to a ploughman and a professor. The former will decide it as well, and often better than the latter, because he has not been led astray by artificial rules.
Thomas Jefferson 1743-1826: letter to Peter Carr, 10 August 1787

6 We know no spectacle so ridiculous as the British public in one of its periodical fits of morality.
Lord Macaulay 1800-59: *Essays Contributed to the Edinburgh Review* (1843) 'Moore's *Life of Lord Byron*'

7 And many are afraid of God—
And more of Mrs Grundy.
Frederick Locker-Lampson 1821-95: 'The Jester's Plea' (1868); see **Behaviour** 19

8 The highest possible stage in moral culture is when we recognize that we ought to control our thoughts.
Charles Darwin 1809-82: *The Descent of Man* (1871)

9 Morality is the herd-instinct in the individual.
Friedrich Nietzsche 1844-1900: *Die fröhliche Wissenschaft* (1882)

10 Morality is a private and costly luxury.
Henry Brooks Adams 1838-1918: *The Education of Henry Adams* (1907)

11 The nation's morals are like its teeth: the more decayed they are the more it hurts to touch them.
George Bernard Shaw 1856-1950: *The Shewing-up of Blanco Posnet* (1911)

12 Moral indignation is jealousy with a halo.
H. G. Wells 1866-1946: *The Wife of Sir Isaac Harman* (1914)

13 You can't learn too soon that the most useful thing about a principle is that it can always be sacrificed to expediency.
W. Somerset Maugham 1874-1965: *The Circle* (1921)

14 Food comes first, then morals.
Bertolt Brecht 1898-1956: *Die Dreigroschenoper* (1928)

15 In olden days a glimpse of stocking

Was looked on as something shocking
Now, heaven knows,
Anything goes.
Cole Porter 1891–1964: 'Anything Goes' (1934 song)

16 The last temptation is the greatest treason:
To do the right deed for the wrong reason.
T. S. Eliot 1888–1965: *Murder in the Cathedral* (1935)

17 The end cannot justify the means, for the simple and obvious reason that the means employed determine the nature of the ends produced.
Aldous Huxley 1894–1963: *Ends and Means* (1937); see 3 above

18 It is always easier to fight for one's principles than to live up to them.
Alfred Adler 1870–1937: Phyllis Bottome *Alfred Adler* (1939)

19 Morality's *not* practical. Morality's a gesture. A complicated gesture learned from books.
Robert Bolt 1924–95: *A Man for All Seasons* (1960)

20 If people want a sense of purpose, they should get it from their archbishops. They should not hope to receive it from their politicians.
to Henry Fairlie, 1963
Harold Macmillan 1894–1986: H. Fairlie *The Life of Politics* (1968)

21 Even a purely moral act that has no hope of any immediate and visible political effect can gradually and indirectly, over time, gain in political significance.
Václav Havel 1936– : letter to Alexander Dubček, August 1969

22 Finding in 'primitive' languages a dearth of words for moral ideas, many people assumed these ideas did not exist. But the concepts of 'good' or 'beautiful', so essential to Western thought, are meaningless unless they are rooted to things.
Bruce Chatwin 1940–89: *In Patagonia* (1977)

23 Values are tapes we play on the Walkman of the mind: any tune we choose so long as it does not disturb others.
Jonathan Sacks 1948– : *The Persistence of Faith* (1991)

Mourning and Loss see also Sorrow

PROVERBS AND SAYINGS

1 **A bellowing cow soon forgets her calf.**
late 19th century; meaning that the person who laments most loudly is the one who is soonest comforted

2 **Grief is the price we pay for love.**
late 20th century saying; see 26 below

3 **Let the dead bury the dead.**
early 19th century, often used to mean that the past should be left undisturbed; from the Bible (Matthew) 'Let the dead bury their dead'

4 **No flowers by request.**
an intimation that no flowers are desired at a funeral; see **Style** *17*

PHRASES

5 **sackcloth and ashes** a sign of penitence or mourning.
used with biblical allusion to the wearing of sackcloth and having ashes sprinkled on the head, as in Matthew, 'if the mighty works, which were done in you, had been done in Tyre and Sidon, they would have repented long ago in sackcloth and ashes'

6 **wear the green willow** grieve for the loss of a loved one, be in mourning.
a branch or the leaves of the willow as a symbol of grief for unrequited love or the loss of a loved one

QUOTATIONS

7 Blessed are they that mourn: for they shall be comforted.
Bible: St Matthew

8 Grief fills the room up of my absent child,
Lies in his bed, walks up and down with me,
Puts on his pretty looks, repeats his words,
Remembers me of all his gracious parts,
Stuffs out his vacant garments with his form:
Then have I reason to be fond of grief.
William Shakespeare 1564–1616: *King John* (1591–8)

9   All my pretty ones?
Did you say all? O hell-kite! All?
What! all my pretty chickens and their dam,

At one fell swoop?
William Shakespeare 1564–1616: *Macbeth* (1606);
see **Thoroughness** 6

10   O more than moon,
Draw not up seas to drown me in thy
   sphere,
Weep me not dead, in thine arms, but
   forbear
To teach the sea what it may do too soon.
John Donne 1572–1631: 'A Valediction: of Weeping'

11 He first deceased; she for a little tried
To live without him: liked it not, and died.
Henry Wotton 1568–1639: 'Upon the Death of Sir
Albertus Moreton's Wife' (1651)

12 How often are we to die before we go quite
off this stage? In every friend we lose a part
of ourselves, and the best part.
Alexander Pope 1688–1744: letter to Jonathan
Swift, 5 December 1732

13 She lived unknown, and few could know
When Lucy ceased to be;
But she is in her grave, and, oh,
The difference to me!
William Wordsworth 1770–1850: 'She dwelt
among the untrodden ways' (1800)

14 I have had playmates, I have had
   companions,
In my days of childhood, in my joyful
   school-days,—
All, all are gone, the old familiar faces.
Charles Lamb 1775–1834: 'The Old Familiar Faces'

15 Bombazine would have shown a deeper
sense of her loss.
Elizabeth Gaskell 1810–65: *Cranford* (1853)

16 They told me, Heraclitus, they told me you
   were dead,
They brought me bitter news to hear and
   bitter tears to shed.
I wept as I remembered how often you
   and I
Had tired the sun with talking and sent
   him down the sky.
William Cory 1823–92: 'Heraclitus' (1858);
translation of Callimachus 'Epigram'

17 Dead! and . . . never called me mother.
Mrs Henry Wood 1814–87: *East Lynne* (dramatized
by T. A. Palmer, 1874, the words do not occur in the
novel of 1861)

18 He was my North, my South, my East and
   West,
My working week and my Sunday rest,
My noon, my midnight, my talk, my song;

I thought that love would last for ever: I
   was wrong.
W. H. Auden 1907–73: 'Funeral Blues' (1936)

19 Bereavement is a universal and integral
part of our experience of love. It follows
marriage as normally as marriage follows
courtship or as autumn follows summer.
C. S. Lewis 1898–1963: *A Grief Observed* (1961)

20 All I have I would have given gladly not to
be standing here today.
following the assassination of J. F. Kennedy
Lyndon Baines Johnson 1908–73: first speech to
Congress as President, 27 November 1963

21 Widow. The word consumes itself.
Sylvia Plath 1932–63: 'Widow' (1971)

22 I can't think of a more wonderful
thanksgiving for the life I have had than
that everyone should be jolly at my
funeral.
Lord Mountbatten 1900–79: Richard Hough
Mountbatten (1980)

23 People are mourning on both sides of this
conflict. In our prayers we shall quite
rightly remember those who are bereaved
in our own country and the relations of
the young Argentinian soldiers who were
killed. Common sorrow could do
something to reunite those who were
engaged in this struggle. A shared anguish
can be a bridge of reconciliation. Our
neighbours are indeed like us.
Robert Runcie 1921–99: sermon in St. Paul's
Cathedral, service of thanksgiving at the end of the
Falklands war, 26 July 1982

24 Do not stand at my grave and weep:
I am not there. I do not sleep.
I am a thousand winds that blow.
I am the diamond glints on snow . . .
Do not stand at my grave and cry;
I am not there, I did not die.
Anonymous: quoted in letter left by British soldier
Stephen Cummins when killed by the IRA, March
1989; origin uncertain, attributed to various
authors

25 The number of casualties will be more
than any of us can bear.
*following the destruction of the World Trade Center in
New York, 11 September 2001*
Rudy Giuliani 1944– : in *The Times* 12 September
2001

26 Nothing that can be said can begin to take away the anguish and pain of these moments. Grief is the price we pay for love.

Elizabeth II 1926– : message to prayer service for the families of British victims of the terrorist attacks in New York, 21 September 2001; see 2 above

Murder see also Death

1 **Blood will have blood.**

late Middle English, meaning that killing will provoke further killing; in this form from Shakespeare Macbeth 'It will have blood, they say blood will have blood'

2 **Guns don't kill people; people kill people.**

National Rifle Association slogan; see 25 below

3 **Killing no murder.**

mid 17th century; see 13 below

4 **Lizzie Borden took an axe**
And gave her mother forty whacks;
When she saw what she had done
She gave her father forty-one!

popular rhyme in circulation after the acquittal of Lizzie Borden, in June 1893, from the charge of murdering her father and stepmother at Fall River, Massachusetts on 4 August 1892

5 **Murder will out.**

early 14th century, meaning that the crime of murder can never be successfully concealed; see 11 below

PHRASES

6 **licensed to kill** supposedly indicating that an agent is authorized by the Security Service to kill when engaged in counter-espionage.

associated particularly with Ian Fleming's thriller-hero James Bond

7 **mark of Cain** the stigma of a murderer, a sign of infamy.

the sign placed on Cain after the murder of Abel, originally as a sign of divine protection in exile; see also **Canada** 2, **Order** 7, **Travel** 8

QUOTATIONS

8 Thou shalt not kill.

Bible: Exodus; see 18 below; **Lifestyles** 8

9 Whoso slays a soul not to retaliate for a soul slain, nor for corruption done in the land, shall be as if he had slain mankind altogether.

The Koran: sura 5

10 Will no one rid me of this turbulent priest?

of Thomas Becket, Archbishop of Canterbury, murdered in Canterbury Cathedral, December 1170

Henry II 1133–89: oral tradition

11 Mordre wol out; that se we day by day.

Geoffrey Chaucer c.1343–1400: The Canterbury Tales 'The Nun's Priest's Tale'; see 5 above

12 Murder most foul, as in the best it is;
But this most foul, strange, and unnatural.

William Shakespeare 1564–1616: Hamlet (1601)

13 Killing no murder briefly discourst in three questions.

an apology for tyrannicide

Edward Sexby d. 1658: title of pamphlet (1657); see 3 above

14 Assassination is the quickest way.

Molière 1622–73: Le Sicilien (1668)

15 Murder considered as one of the fine arts.

Thomas De Quincey 1785–1859: in Blackwood's Magazine February 1827; essay title

16 In that case, if we are to abolish the death penalty, let the murderers take the first step.

Alphonse Karr 1808–90: in Les Guêpes January 1849

17 She had very thick ankles.

his justification for poisoning his wife's half-sister, Helen Abercromby

Thomas Griffiths Wainewright 1794–1852: in Dictionary of National Biography (1917–)

18 Thou shalt not kill; but need'st not strive Officiously to keep alive.

Arthur Hugh Clough 1819–61: 'The Latest Decalogue' (1862); see 8 above

19 It was not until several weeks after he had decided to murder his wife that Dr Bickleigh took any active steps in the matter. Murder is a serious business.

Francis Iles 1893–1970: Malice Aforethought (1931)

20 Any man has to, needs to, wants to
Once in a lifetime, do a girl in.

T. S. Eliot 1888–1965: Sweeney Agonistes (1932)

21 Kill a man, and you are an assassin. Kill millions of men, and you are a conqueror. Kill everyone, and you are a god.
Jean Rostand 1894–1977: *Pensées d'un biologiste* (1939)

22 Roast beef and Yorkshire, or roast pork and apple sauce, followed up by suet pudding and driven home, as it were, by a cup of mahogany-brown tea, have put you in just the right mood. Your pipe is drawing sweetly, the sofa cushions are soft underneath you, the fire is well alight, the air is warm and stagnant. In these blissful circumstances, what is it that you want to read about?
    Naturally, about a murder.
George Orwell 1903–50: *Decline of the English Murder and other essays* (1965) title essay, written 1946

23 Television has brought back murder into the home—where it belongs.
Alfred Hitchcock 1899–1980: in *Observer* 19 December 1965

24 It might or might not be right to kill, but sometimes it is necessary.
Gerry Adams 1948– : view of the protagonist in a short story; *Before the Dawn* (1996)

25 The National Rifle Association says guns don't kill people, people do. But I think the gun helps. Just standing there, going 'Bang!'—that's not going to kill too many people.
Eddie Izzard 1962– : *Dress to Kill* (stageshow, San Francisco, 1998); see 2 above

26 I love you . . . That is what they were all saying down their phones, from the hijacked planes and the burning towers. There is only love, and then oblivion. Love was all they had to set against the hatred of their murderers.
of the last messages received from those trapped by terrorist attacks, 11 September 2001
Ian McEwan 1948– : in *Guardian* 15 September 2001; see **Last Words** 33

Music see also Jazz, Musicians, Singing

PROVERBS AND SAYINGS

1 Every good boy deserves favour.
traditional mnemonic for the notes (E, G. B, D, F) on the lines of the treble clef stave

2 Music helps not the toothache.
mid 17th century

PHRASES

3 music of the spheres the harmonious sound supposed to be produced by the motion of the celestial globes imagined by the older astronomers as revolving round the earth and respectively carrying with them the moon, sun, planets, and fixed stars.
*see **The Universe** 3*

4 promenade concert a concert of classical music at which a part of the audience stands in an area without seating, for which tickets are sold at a reduced price.
the most famous series of such concerts is the annual BBC Promenade Concerts (known as the Proms), instituted by Sir Henry Wood in 1895

5 Tin Pan Alley the world of composers and publishers of popular music.
from the name given to a district in New York (28th Street, between 5th Avenue and Broadway) where many songwriters, arrangers, and music publishers were formerly based

6 the tune the old cow died of a tedious badly played piece of music.

QUOTATIONS

7 If music be the food of love, play on;
Give me excess of it, that, surfeiting,
The appetite may sicken, and so die.
William Shakespeare 1564–1616: *Twelfth Night* (1601)

8 Music has charms to soothe a savage breast.
William Congreve 1670–1729: *The Mourning Bride* (1697)

9 Too beautiful for our ears, and much too many notes, dear Mozart.
of The Abduction from the Seraglio (1782)
Joseph II 1741–90: F. X. Niemetschek *Life of Mozart* (1798)

10 Melody is the essence of music. I compare a good melodist to a fine racer, and counterpoints to hack post-horses.
Wolfgang Amadeus Mozart 1756–91: remark to Michael Kelly, 1786; Michael Kelly *Reminiscences* (1826)

11 A carpenter's hammer, in a warm summer noon, will fret me into more than midsummer madness. But those unconnected, unset sounds are nothing to the measured malice of music.
Charles Lamb 1775–1834: *Elia* (1823)

12 Hark, the dominant's persistence till it must be answered to!
Robert Browning 1812–89: 'A Toccata of Galuppi's' (1855)

13 But I struck one chord of music,
Like the sound of a great Amen.
Adelaide Ann Procter 1825–64: 'A Lost Chord' (1858)

14 Hell is full of musical amateurs: music is the brandy of the damned.
George Bernard Shaw 1856–1950: *Man and Superman* (1903)

15 There is music in the air.
Edward Elgar 1857–1934: R. J. Buckley *Sir Edward Elgar* (1905)

16 The symphony must be like the world. It must embrace everything.
Gustav Mahler 1860–1911: remark to Sibelius, Helsinki, 1907

17 It is only that which cannot be expressed otherwise that is worth expressing in music.
Frederick Delius 1862–1934: in *Sackbut* September 1920 'At the Crossroads'

18 Extraordinary how potent cheap music is.
Noël Coward 1899–1973: *Private Lives* (1930)

19 Music begins to atrophy when it departs too far from the dance . . . poetry begins to atrophy when it gets too far from music.
Ezra Pound 1885–1972: *The ABC of Reading* (1934)

20 The whole trouble with a folk song is that once you have played it through there is nothing much you can do except play it over again and play it rather louder.
Constant Lambert 1905–51: *Music Ho!* (1934)

21 Down the road someone is practising scales,
The notes like little fishes vanish with a wink of tails.
Louis MacNeice 1907–63: 'Sunday Morning' (1935)

22 The whole problem can be stated quite simply by asking, 'Is there a meaning to music?' My answer to that would be, 'Yes.' And 'Can you state in so many words what the meaning is?' My answer to that would be, 'No.'
Aaron Copland 1900–90: *What to Listen for in Music* (1939)

23 If I don't practise for one day, I know it; if I don't practise for two days, the critics know it; if I don't practise for three days, the audience knows it.
Ignacy Jan Paderewski 1860–1941: attributed; Nat Shapiro *An Encyclopedia of Quotations about Music* (1978)

24 Good music is that which penetrates the ear with facility and quits the memory with difficulty.
Thomas Beecham 1879–1961: speech, c.1950; in *New York Times* 9 March 1961

25 The notes I handle no better than many pianists. But the pauses between the notes—ah, that is where the art resides!
Artur Schnabel 1882–1951: in *Chicago Daily News* 11 June 1958

26 Music is your own experience, your thoughts, your wisdom. If you don't live it, it won't come out of your horn.
Charlie Parker 1920–55: Nat Shapiro and Nat Hentoff *Hear Me Talkin' to Ya* (1955)

27 I don't know whether I like it, but it's what I meant.
on his 4th symphony
Ralph Vaughan Williams 1872–1958: Christopher Headington *Bodley Head History of Western Music* (1974)

28 The hills are alive with the sound of music,
With songs they have sung for a thousand years.
The hills fill my heart with the sound of music,
My heart wants to sing ev'ry song it hears.
Oscar Hammerstein II 1895–1960: 'The Sound of Music' (1959 song)

29 You just pick a chord, go twang, and you've got music.
Sid Vicious 1957–79: attributed

30 Music is spiritual. The music business is not.
Van Morrison: in *The Times* 6 July 1990

31 Why waste money on psychotherapy when you can listen to the B Minor Mass?
Michael Torke 1961– : in *Observer* 23 September 1990 'Sayings of the Week'

32 Improvisation is too good to leave to chance.
Paul Simon 1942- : in *Observer* 30 December 1990

33 Icelandic peoples were the ones who memorized sagas . . . We were the first rappers of Europe.
Björk 1965- : attributed, January 1996

34 The rhythm hammers us, hits us and possesses us, making us prisoners of noise. It's like a drug.
of popular music
Jeanne Moreau 1928- : in *Guardian* 13 August 1997

Musicians see also Jazz, Music

PHRASES

1 The Fab Four George Harrison, John Lennon, Paul McCartney, and Ringo Starr.
the four members of the pop and rock group the Beatles

2 the waltz king Johann Strauss (1825-99).
he composed many famous waltzes, such as The Blue Danube *(1867)*

QUOTATIONS

3 Tallis is dead and Music dies.
William Byrd 1543-1623: 'Ye Sacred Muses'

4 Difficult do you call it, Sir? I wish it were impossible.
on the performance of a celebrated violinist
Samuel Johnson 1709-84: William Seward *Supplement to the Anecdotes of Distinguished Persons* (1797)

5 Some cry up Haydn, some Mozart, Just as the whim bites; for my part I care not a farthing candle For either of them, or for Handel.
Charles Lamb 1775-1834: 'Free Thoughts on Several Eminent Composers' (1830)

6 Hats off, gentlemen—a genius!
on Chopin
Robert Schumann 1810-56: 'An Opus 2' (1831); H. Pleasants (ed.) *Schumann on Music* (1965)

7 We are the music makers, We are the dreamers of dreams . . . We are the movers and shakers Of the world for ever, it seems.
Arthur O'Shaughnessy 1844-81: 'Ode' (1874); see **Change** 22

8 Please do not shoot the pianist. He is doing his best.
printed notice in a dancing saloon
Anonymous: Oscar Wilde *Impressions of America* 'Leadville' (c.1882-3)

9 I have been told that Wagner's music is better than it sounds.
Bill Nye 1850-96: Mark Twain *Autobiography* (1924)

10 It will be generally admitted that Beethoven's Fifth Symphony is the most sublime noise that has ever penetrated into the ear of man.
E. M. Forster 1879-1970: *Howards End* (1910)

11 Ravel refuses the Legion of Honour, but all his music accepts it.
Erik Satie 1866-1925: Jean Cocteau *Le Discours d'Oxford* (1956)

12 Bach almost persuades me to be a Christian.
Roger Fry 1866-1934: Virginia Woolf *Roger Fry* (1940)

13 Children are given Mozart because of the small *quantity* of the notes; grown-ups avoid Mozart because of the great *quality* of the notes.
Artur Schnabel 1882-1951: *My Life and Music* (1961)

14 Many musicians do not consider George Gershwin a serious composer. But they should understand that, serious or not, he is a composer—that is, a man who lives in music and expresses everything, serious or not, sound or superficial, by means of music, because it is his native language.
Arnold Schoenberg 1874-1951: Robert Kimball and Alfred Simon *The Gershwins* (1973)

15 There are two golden rules for an orchestra: start together and finish together. The public doesn't give a damn what goes on in between.
Thomas Beecham 1879-1961: Harold Atkins and Archie Newman *Beecham Stories* (1978)

16 If I play Tchaikovsky I play his melodies and skip his spiritual struggles . . . If there's any time left over I fill in with a lot of runs up and down the keyboard.
Liberace 1919-87: Stuart Hall and Paddy Whannel (eds.) *The Popular Arts* (1964)

17 Whether the angels play only Bach in praising God I am not quite sure; I am sure, however, that en famille they play Mozart.
Karl Barth 1886–1968: in *New York Times* 11 December 1968

18 A musician, if he's a messenger, is like a child who hasn't been handled too many times by man, hasn't had too many fingerprints across his brain.
Jimi Hendrix 1942–70: in *Life Magazine* (1969)

19 Most people get into bands for three very simple rock and roll reasons: to get laid, to get fame, and to get rich.
Bob Geldof 1954– : in *Melody Maker* 27 August 1977

20 If anyone has conducted a Beethoven performance, and then doesn't have to go to an osteopath, then there's something wrong.
Simon Rattle 1955– : in *Guardian* 31 May 1990

21 Ballads and babies. That's what happened to me.
on reaching the age of fifty
Paul McCartney 1942– : in *Time* 8 June 1992

22 Beethoven tells you what it's like to be Beethoven and Mozart tells you what it's like to be human. Bach tells you what it's like be the universe.
Douglas Adams 1952–2001: attributed, in *Independent* 17 May 2001

Names

1 By Tre, Pol, and Pen, you shall know the Cornish men.
traditional saying, mid 16th century, referring to the frequency of these elements in Cornish names

2 If the cap fits, wear it.
mid 18th century, used with reference to the assumed suitability of a name or description to a person's behaviour

3 If the shoe fits, wear it.
late 18th century, meaning that one has to accept it when a particular comment is shown to apply to oneself; found mainly in the US

QUOTATIONS

4 God hath also highly exalted him, and given him a name which is above every name:
That at the name of Jesus every knee should bow.
Bible: Philippians

5 What's in a name? that which we call a rose
By any other name would smell as sweet.
William Shakespeare 1564–1616: *Romeo and Juliet* (1595)

6 JAQUES: I do not like her name.
ORLANDO: There was no thought of pleasing you when she was christened.
William Shakespeare 1564–1616: *As You Like It* (1599)

7 If you should have a boy do not christen him John . . . 'Tis a bad name and goes against a man. If my name had been Edmund I should have been more fortunate.
John Keats 1795–1821: letter to his sister-in-law, 13 January 1820

8 A nickname is the heaviest stone that the devil can throw at a man.
William Hazlitt 1778–1830: *Sketches and Essays* (1839) 'Nicknames'

9 With a name like yours, you might be any shape, almost.
Lewis Carroll 1832–98: *Through the Looking-Glass* (1872)

10 I have fallen in love with American names,
The sharp, gaunt names that never get fat,
The snakeskin-titles of mining-claims,
The plumed war-bonnet of Medicine Hat,
Tucson and Deadwood and Lost Mule Flat.
Stephen Vincent Benét 1898–1943: 'American Names' (1927)

11 Dear 338171 (May I call you 338?).
Noël Coward 1899–1973: letter to T. E. Lawrence, 25 August 1930

12 A self-made man may prefer a self-made name.
on Samuel Goldfish changing his name to Samuel Goldwyn
Learned Hand 1872–1961: Bosley Crowther *Lion's Share* (1957)

13 The name of a man is a numbing blow from which he never recovers.
Marshall McLuhan 1911–80: *Understanding Media* (1964)

14 Every Tom, Dick and Harry is called Arthur.
to Arthur Hornblow, who was planning to name his son Arthur
Sam Goldwyn 1882–1974: Michael Freedland *The Goldwyn Touch* (1986)

15 No, I'm breaking it in for a friend.
when asked if Groucho were his real name
Groucho Marx 1895–1977: attributed

16 Just as crystallization of surnames was one of the steps in human civilization, their relinquishment gradually increases as we revert to savagery.
Anthony Powell 1905–2000: *Fisher King* (1986)

17 We do have these extraordinary names . . . When you see the sign 'African Primates Meeting' you expect someone to produce bananas.
at his retirement service as Archbishop of Cape Town, 23 June 1996
Desmond Tutu 1931—: in *Daily Telegraph* 24 June 1996

Nature see also **The Earth**, **Life Sciences**

PROVERBS AND SAYINGS

1 Nature abhors a vacuum.
mid 16th century; see 19 below

2 You can drive out nature with a pitchfork but she keeps on coming back.
mid 16th century, from the Roman poet Horace (65–8 BC) Epistles 'You may drive out nature with a pitchfork, but she will always return'

PHRASES

3 balance of nature a state of equilibrium produced by the interaction of living organisms, ecological balance.

4 Nature red in tooth and claw a ruthless personification of the creative and regulative physical power conceived of as operating in the material world.
from Tennyson: see 12 below

QUOTATIONS

5 Nature does nothing without purpose or uselessly.
Aristotle 384–322 BC: *Politics*

6 Be not blind, but open-eyed, to the great wonders of Nature, familiar, everyday objects though they be to thee. But men are more wont to be astonished at the sun's eclipse than at his unfailing rise.
Orchoth Zadikkim c.15th century: *Orchoth Zaddikim*

7 In her inventions nothing is lacking, and nothing is superfluous.
Leonardo da Vinci 1452–1519: Edward McCurdy (ed.) *Leonardo da Vinci's Notebooks* (1906)

8 And this our life, exempt from public haunt,
Finds tongues in trees, books in the running brooks,
Sermons in stones, and good in everything.
William Shakespeare 1564–1616: *As You Like It* (1599)

9 All things are artificial, for nature is the art of God.
Thomas Browne 1605–82: *Religio Medici* (1643)

10   I have learned
To look on nature, not as in the hour
Of thoughtless youth; but hearing oftentimes
The still, sad music of humanity.
William Wordsworth 1770–1850: 'Lines composed . . . above Tintern Abbey' (1798)

11 There is a pleasure in the pathless woods,
There is a rapture on the lonely shore,
There is society, where none intrudes,
By the deep sea, and music in its roar:
I love not man the less, but nature more.
Lord Byron 1788–1824: *Childe Harold's Pilgrimage* (1812–18)

12 Who trusted God was love indeed
And love Creation's final law—
Though Nature, red in tooth and claw
With ravine, shrieked against his creed.
Alfred, Lord Tennyson 1809–92: *In Memoriam A. H. H.* (1850); see 4 above

13 I believe a leaf of grass is no less than the journey-work of the stars,
And the pismire is equally perfect, and a grain of sand, and the egg of the wren,
And the tree toad is a chef-d'oeuvre for the highest,

And the running blackberry would adorn
the parlours of heaven.
Walt Whitman 1819–92: 'Song of Myself' (written
1855)

14 What a book a devil's chaplain might write
on the clumsy, wasteful, blundering, low,
and horridly cruel works of nature!
Charles Darwin 1809–82: letter to J. D. Hooker, 13
July 1856

15 Nature is not a temple, but a workshop,
and man's the workman in it.
Ivan Turgenev 1818–83: *Fathers and Sons* (1862)

16 In nature there are neither rewards nor
punishments—there are consequences.
Robert G. Ingersoll 1833–99: *Some Reasons Why*
(1881)

17 For nature, heartless, witless nature,
Will neither care nor know
What stranger's feet may find the meadow
And trespass there and go.
A. E. Housman 1859–1936: *Last Poems* (1922) no.
40

18 Nature, Mr Allnutt, is what we are put
into this world to rise above.
James Agee 1909–55: *The African Queen* (1951 film);
not in the novel by C. S. Forester

19 BRICK: Well, they say nature hates a
vacuum, Big Daddy.
BIG DADDY: That's what they say, but
sometimes I think that a vacuum is a
hell of a lot better than some of the stuff
that nature replaces it with.
Tennessee Williams 1911–83: *Cat on a Hot Tin Roof*
(1955); see 1 above

20 Christianity deposes Mother Nature and
begets, on her prostrate body, Science,
which proceeds to destroy Nature.
Ted Hughes 1930–98: in *Your Environment* Summer
1970

21 People thought they could explain and
conquer nature—yet the outcome is that
they destroyed it and disinherited
themselves from it.
Václav Havel 1936– : Lewis Wolpert *The Unnatural
Nature of Science* (1993)

Necessity

1 Any port in a storm.
*mid 18th century, meaning that when one is in trouble
or difficulty, support or shelter from any source is
welcome*

2 Beggars can't be choosers.
*mid 16th century, meaning that someone who is
destitute is in no position to criticize what may be
offered; see **Sex** 34*

**3 Desperate diseases must have desperate
remedies.**
*mid 16th century, meaning that in a difficult or
dangerous situation it may be necessary to take
extreme and risky measures; see **Medicine** 12,
Revolution 5*

4 Even a worm will turn.
*mid 16th century, meaning that even a meek person
will resist or retaliate if pushed too far*

5 Hunger drives the wolf out of the wood.
*late 15th century, meaning that even the fiercest
animal will be driven from shelter by necessity*

**6 If the mountain will not come to
Mahomet, Mahomet must go to the
mountain.**
*early 17th century, used in the context of an
apparently insoluble situation. The saying refers to a*

story of Muhammad recounted by Bacon in his Essays,
*in which the Prophet called a hill to him, and when it
did not move, made this remark*

7 Make a virtue of necessity.
*proverbial saying, late 14th century, meaning that one
should do with a good grace what is unavoidable; see
17 below*

8 Necessity is the mother of invention.
*mid 16th century, meaning that need is often a spur to
the creative process*

9 Necessity knows no law.
*late 14th century, meaning that someone in extreme
need will disregard rules or prohibitions; see 20 below*

10 Necessity sharpens industry.
American proverb, mid 20th century

11 Needs must when the devil drives.
*mid 15th century, used in recognition of overwhelming
force of circumstance*

12 When all fruit fails, welcome haws.
*early 18th century, often used of someone taking of
necessity an older or otherwise unsuitable lover*

13 Who says A must say B.
*mid 19th century; only recorded in English from North
American sources, and meaning that if a first step is
taken, the second will inevitably follow*

14 the breath of life a necessity.

from the Bible (Genesis) 'all in whose nostrils was the breath of life'

15 a wing and a prayer reliance on hope or the slightest chance in a desperate situation.

a song (1943) by H. Adamson, recounting an emergency landing by an aircraft: see **Crises** *18*

QUOTATIONS

16 Nothing have I found stronger than Necessity.

Euripides c.485–c.406 BC: *Alcestis*

17 All places that the eye of heaven visits
Are to a wise man ports and happy
  havens.
Teach thy necessity to reason thus;
There is no virtue like necessity.

William Shakespeare 1564–1616: *Richard II* (1595); see 7 above

18 Must! Is *must* a word to be addressed to princes? Little man, little man! thy father, if he had been alive, durst not have used that word.

to Robert Cecil, on his saying she must go to bed

Elizabeth I 1533–1603: J. R. Green *A Short History of the English People* (1874)

19 Cruel necessity.

on the execution of Charles I, 1649

Oliver Cromwell 1599–1658: Joseph Spence *Anecdotes* (1820)

20 Necessity hath no law. Feigned necessities, imaginary necessities . . . are the greatest cozenage that men can put upon the Providence of God, and make pretences to break known rules by.

Oliver Cromwell 1599–1658: speech to Parliament, 12 September 1654; see 9 above

21 Necessity never made a good bargain.

Benjamin Franklin 1706–90: *Poor Richard's Almanac* (1735)

22 The superfluous, a very necessary thing.

Voltaire 1694–1778: *Le Mondain* (1736)

23 Necessity is the plea for every infringement of human freedom: it is the argument of tyrants; it is the creed of slaves.

William Pitt 1759–1806: speech, House of Commons, 18 November 1783

24 What throws a monkey wrench in
A fella's good intention?
That nasty old invention—
Necessity!

E. Y. Harburg 1898–1981: 'Necessity' (1947)

25 Necessity has the face of a dog.

Gabriel García Márquez 1928– : *In Evil Hour* (1968)

News see also Journalism

1 Bad news travels fast.

late 16th century, meaning that bad news is more likely to be talked about

2 No news is good news.

early 17th century, often used in consolation or resignation

QUOTATIONS

3 Tell it not in Gath, publish it not in the streets of Askelon.

Bible: II Samuel

4 How beautiful upon the mountains are the feet of him that bringeth good tidings.

Bible: Isaiah

5 What news on the Rialto?

William Shakespeare 1564–1616: *The Merchant of Venice* (1596–8)

6 Ill news hath wings, and with the wind doth go,

Comfort's a cripple and comes ever slow.

Michael Drayton 1563–1631: *The Barons' Wars* (1603)

7 The nature of bad news infects the teller.

William Shakespeare 1564–1616: *Antony and Cleopatra* (1606–7)

8 A master passion is the love of news.

George Crabbe 1754–1832: 'The Newspaper' (1785)

9 When a dog bites a man, that is not news, because it happens so often. But if a man bites a dog, that is news.

John B. Bogart 1848–1921: F. M. O'Brien *The Story of the [New York] Sun* (1918); often attributed to Charles A. Dana

10 News is what a chap who doesn't care much about anything wants to read. And it's only news until he's read it. After that it's dead.

Evelyn Waugh 1903–66: *Scoop* (1938)

11 You might get bigger audiences for 'Noble Rover, the labrador, who saved beautiful

baby in fire', but that ain't news—just an insidious form of patronising propaganda.
on the desirability of promoting 'good news' stories
John Simpson 1944- : interview in *Radio Times* 9 August 1997

Night see Day and Night

Old Age see also Middle Age

1 **The gods send nuts to those who have no teeth.**
early 20th century, meaning that opportunities or pleasures often come too late to be enjoyed

2 **There's many a good tune played on an old fiddle.**
early 20th century, meaning that age is not necessarily an indicator of incapacity

3 **There's no fool like an old fool.**
mid 16th century, often used to suggest that the folly of an older person is often particularly worthy of castigation

4 **Indian summer** a tranquil late period of life.
a period of fine weather in late autumn: see **Weather** 25

5 **threescore and ten** the age of seventy.
in reference to the biblical span of a person's life: see 7 below

6 Then shall ye bring down my grey hairs with sorrow to the grave.
Bible: Genesis

7 The days of our age are threescore years and ten; and though men be so strong that they come to fourscore years: yet is their strength then but labour and sorrow; so soon passeth it away, and we are gone.
Bible: Psalm 90; see 5 above

8   Last scene of all,
That ends this strange eventful history,
Is second childishness, and mere oblivion,
Sans teeth, sans eyes, sans taste, sans everything.
William Shakespeare 1564-1616: *As You Like It* (1599)

9 No spring, nor summer beauty hath such grace,

As I have seen in one autumnal face.
John Donne 1572-1631: 'The Autumnal' (c.1600)

10 Age will not be defied.
Francis Bacon 1561-1626: *Essays* (1625) 'Of Regimen of Health'

11 Every man desires to live long; but no man would be old.
Jonathan Swift 1667-1745: *Thoughts on Various Subjects* (1727 ed.)

12 How happy he who crowns in shades like these,
A youth of labour with an age of ease.
Oliver Goldsmith 1728-74: *The Deserted Village* (1770)

13 Those that desire to write or say anything to me have no time to lose; for time has shaken me by the hand and death is not far behind.
John Wesley 1703-91: letter to Ezekiel Cooper, 1 February 1791

14 The abbreviation of time, and the failure of hope, will always tinge with a browner shade the evening of life.
Edward Gibbon 1737-94: *Memoirs of My Life* (1796)

15 Age does not make us childish, as men tell,
It merely finds us children still at heart.
Johann Wolfgang von Goethe 1749-1832: *Faust* pt. 1 (1808)

16 Grow old along with me!
The best is yet to be.
Robert Browning 1812-89: 'Rabbi Ben Ezra' (1864)

17 It is better to be seventy years young than forty years old!
Oliver Wendell Holmes 1809-94: reply to invitation from Julia Ward Howe to her seventieth birthday party, 27 May 1889

18 The tragedy of old age is not that one is old, but that one is young.
Oscar Wilde 1854-1900: *The Picture of Dorian Grey* (1891)

19 When you are old and grey and full of
   sleep,
And nodding by the fire, take down this
   book
And slowly read and dream of the soft look
Your eyes had once, and of their shadows
   deep.
W. B. Yeats 1865–1939: 'When You Are Old' (1893)

20 I grow old . . . I grow old . . .
I shall wear the bottoms of my trousers
   rolled.
T. S. Eliot 1888–1965: 'The Love Song of J. Alfred
Prufrock' (1917)

21 Oh, to be seventy again!
on seeing a pretty girl on his eightieth birthday
Georges Clemenceau 1841–1929: James Agate
diary, 19 April 1938; also attributed to Oliver
Wendell Holmes Jnr.

22 An aged man is but a paltry thing,
A tattered coat upon a stick, unless
Soul clap its hands and sing, and louder
   sing
For every tatter in its mortal dress.
W. B. Yeats 1865–1939: 'Sailing to Byzantium'
(1928)

23 From the earliest times the old have
   rubbed it into the young that they are
   wiser than they, and before the young had
   discovered what nonsense this was they
   were old too, and it profited them to carry
   on the imposture.
W. Somerset Maugham 1874–1965: *Cakes and Ale*
(1930)

24 Old age is the most unexpected of all things
   that happen to a man.
Leon Trotsky 1879–1940: diary 8 May 1935

25 You will recognize, my boy, the first sign of
   old age: it is when you go out into the
   streets of London and realize for the first
   time how young the policemen look.
Seymour Hicks 1871–1949: C. R. D. Pulling *They
Were Singing* (1952)

26 Do not go gentle into that good night,
Old age should burn and rave at close of
   day;
Rage, rage against the dying of the light.
Dylan Thomas 1914–53: 'Do Not Go Gentle into
that Good Night' (1952)

27 To me old age is always fifteen years older
   than I am.
Bernard Baruch 1870–1965: in *Newsweek* 29
August 1955

28 Considering the alternative, it's not too
   bad at all.
*when asked what he felt about the advancing years on
his seventy-second birthday*
Maurice Chevalier 1888–1972: Michael Freedland
Maurice Chevalier (1981)

29 Hope I die before I get old.
Pete Townshend 1945– : 'My Generation' (1965
song)

30 Will you still need me, will you still feed
   me,
When I'm sixty four?
John Lennon 1940–80 and **Paul McCartney**
1942– : 'When I'm Sixty Four' (1967 song)

31 What is called the serenity of age is only
   perhaps a euphemism for the fading power
   to feel the sudden shock of joy or sorrow.
Arthur Bliss 1891–1975: *As I Remember* (1970)

32 The man who works and is not bored is
   never old.
Pablo Casals 1876–1973: J. Lloyd Webber (ed.) *Song
of the Birds* (1985)

33 When I am an old woman I shall wear
   purple
With a red hat which doesn't go, and
   doesn't suit me.
Jenny Joseph 1932– : 'Warning' (1974)

34 While there's snow on the roof, it doesn't
   mean the fire has gone out in the furnace.
John G. Diefenbaker 1895–1979: approaching his
80th birthday, Ottawa, 17 September 1975

35 It is pleasanter to help the young than the
   old. The young need crutches for a time,
   and then throw them away . . . Give the
   old crutches, and they use them for ever,
   complaining of their poor quality the
   while.
Fay Weldon 1931– : *Praxis* (1978)

36 With full-span lives having become the
   norm, people may need to learn how to be
   aged as they once had to learn how to be
   adult.
Ronald Blythe 1922– : *The View in Winter* (1979)

37 The unending problem of growing old was
   not how he changed, but how things did.
Toni Morrison 1931– : *Tar Baby* (1981)

38 I saw how hard it is for our own society
   ever to become wise while old people are
   ostracized.
George Monbiot: *No Man's Land* (1994)

39 Old people have one advantage compared
   with young ones. They have been young

themselves, and young people haven't been old.
Lord Longford 1905–2001: in *Independent* 6 March 1999

Opinion

1 He that complies against his will is of his own opinion still.
late 17th century, from Samuel Butler: see 14 below

2 So many men, so many opinions.
late 14th century, meaning that the greater the number of people involved, the greater the number of different opinions there will be; from Terence (c.190–159 BC) Phormio 'There are as many opinions as there are people: each has his own correct way'

3 Those who never retract their opinions, love themselves more than they love truth.
American proverb, mid 20th century

4 Thought is free.
late 14th century; meaning that while speech and action can be limited, one's powers of imagination and speculation cannot be regulated

5 The wish is father to the thought.
late 16th century, meaning that one's opinions are often influenced by one's wishes; from Shakespeare 2 Henry IV 'Thy wish was father, Harry, to that thought'

6 appeal from Philip drunk to Philip sober suggest that an opinion or decision represents a passing mood only.
alluding to a judgement given by Philip of Macedon, father of Alexander the Great

7 hearts and minds emotional and intellectual support; complete approval.

8 no comment I do not intend to express an opinion.
traditional expression of refusal to answer journalists' questions

9 vox populi expressed general opinion.
Latin = voice of the people; see Democracy 2

10 Some recluses and brahmins so called,
Are deeply attached to their own views:
People who only see one side of things
Engage in quarrels and disputes.
Pali Tripitaka *c.* 2nd century BC: *The Udāna* [Solemn Utterances]

11 A plague of opinion! a man may wear it on both sides, like a leather jerkin.
William Shakespeare 1564–1616: *Troilus and Cressida* (1602)

12 Opinion in good men is but knowledge in the making.
John Milton 1608–74: *Areopagitica* (1644)

13 They that approve a private opinion, call it opinion; but they that mislike it, heresy: and yet heresy signifies no more than private opinion.
Thomas Hobbes 1588–1679: *Leviathan* (1651)

14 He that complies against his will,
Is of his own opinion still;
Which he may adhere to, yet disown,
For reasons to himself best known.
Samuel Butler 1612–80: *Hudibras* pt. 3 (1680); see 1 above

15 Some praise at morning what they blame at night;
But always think the last opinion right.
Alexander Pope 1688–1744: *An Essay on Criticism* (1711)

16 Have not the wisest of men in all ages, not excepting Solomon himself,—have they not had their Hobby-Horses . . . and so long as a man rides his Hobby-Horse peaceably and quietly along the King's highway, and neither compels you or me to get up behind him,—pray, Sir, what have either you or I to do with it?
Laurence Sterne 1713–68: *Tristram Shandy* (1759–67)

17 Every man has a right to utter what he thinks truth, and every other man has a right to knock him down for it. Martyrdom is the test.
Samuel Johnson 1709–84: James Boswell *Life of Samuel Johnson* (1791) 1780

18 A man can brave opinion, a woman must submit to it.
Mme de Staël 1766–1817: *Delphine* (1802)

19 If all mankind minus one were of one opinion, and only one person were of the contrary opinion, mankind would be no more justified in silencing that one person, than he, if he had the power, would be justified in silencing mankind.

John Stuart Mill 1806–73: *On Liberty* (1859)

20 There are nine and sixty ways of
   constructing tribal lays,
   And—every—single—one—of—them—
   is—right!

Rudyard Kipling 1865–1936: 'In the Neolithic Age' (1893)

21 It were not best that we should all think alike; it is difference of opinion that makes horse-races.

Mark Twain 1835–1910: *Pudd'nhead Wilson* (1894)

22 Thank God, in these days of enlightenment and establishment, everyone has a right to his own opinions, and chiefly to the

opinion that nobody else has a right to theirs.

Ronald Knox 1888–1957: *Reunion All Round* (1914)

23 An intellectual hatred is the worst,
   So let her think opinions are accursed.

W. B. Yeats 1865–1939: 'A Prayer for My Daughter' (1920)

24 The opinions that are held with passion are always those for which no good ground exists; indeed the passion is the measure of the holder's lack of rational conviction.

Bertrand Russell 1872–1970: *Sceptical Essays* (1928)

25 Why should you mind being wrong if someone can show you that you are?

A. J. Ayer 1910–89: attributed

26 You might very well think that. I couldn't possibly comment.

the Chief Whip's habitual response to questioning
Michael Dobbs 1948– : *House of Cards* (televised 1990)

Opportunity

PROVERBS AND SAYINGS

1 **All is fish that comes to the net.**

early 16th century, meaning that everything can be used to advantage

2 **All is grist that comes to the mill.**

mid 17th century, meaning that all experience or knowledge is useful (grist is corn that is ground to make flour)

3 **A bleating sheep loses a bite.**

late 16th century, meaning that opportunities may be lost through idle chatter

4 **Every dog has his day.**

mid 16th century, meaning that everyone, however insignificant, has a moment of strength and power

5 **He that will not when he may, when he will he shall have nay.**

late 10th century, meaning that if an opportunity is not taken when offered, it may well not occur again

6 **It's not what you know, but whom you know.**

American proverb, mid 20th century

7 **Make hay while the sun shines.**

mid 16th century, meaning that one should take advantage of favourable circumstances which may not last

8 **The mill cannot grind with the water that is past.**

early 17th century, meaning that an opportunity that has been missed cannot then be used

9 **No time like the present.**

mid 16th century; often used to urge swift and immediate action

10 **Opportunities look for you when you are worth finding.**

North American proverb, mid 20th century

11 **Opportunity never knocks twice at any man's door.**

mid 16th century, meaning that a chance once missed will not occur again

12 **Opportunity never knocks for persons not worth a rap.**

American proverb, mid 20th century

13 **A postern door makes a thief.**

mid 15th century, referring to the opportunity offered by a back or side entrance

14 **Strike while the iron is hot.**

late 14th century, meaning that one should take advantage of opportunity; the allusion was originally to the work of a blacksmith; see 29 below

15 Take the goods the gods provide.

late 17th century, meaning that one should accept and be grateful for unearned benefits

16 Time and tide wait for no man.

late 14th century; often used as an exhortation to act, in the knowledge that a favourable moment will not last for ever

17 When one door shuts, another opens.

late 16th century, meaning that as one possible course of action is closed off, another opportunity offers

18 When the cat's away, the mice will play.

early 17th century, meaning that many will take advantage of a situation in which rules are not enforced or authority is lacking

19 The world is one's oyster.

early 17th century, meaning that opportunities are unlimited; an oyster as a delicacy and a source of pearls. Perhaps originally with allusion to Shakespeare's Merry Wives of Windsor (1597), 'the world's mine oyster, which I, with sword will open'

PHRASES

20 room at the top opportunity to join an élite or the top ranks of a profession

*see **Ambition** 5*

21 streets paved with gold proverbial view of a city in which opportunities for advancement are easy.

as in George Colman the Younger's The Heir at Law (1797) 'Oh, London is a fine town, A very famous city, Where all the streets are paved with gold'

22 take time by the forelock not let a chance slip away.

from the personification of Time as bald except for a forelock; see 28 below

23 window of opportunity a free or suitable interval or period of time for a particular event or action.

deriving from launch window, a period outside which the planned launch of a spacecraft cannot take place if the journey is to be completed, owing to the changing positions of the planets; especially used in connection with the US–Soviet arms race

---

QUOTATIONS

24 Time is that wherein there is opportunity, and opportunity is that wherein there is no great time.
Hippocrates c.460–357 BC: *Precepts*

25 How oft the sight of means to do ill deeds

Makes ill deeds done!
William Shakespeare 1564–1616: *King John* (1591–8)

26 There is a tide in the affairs of men,
Which, taken at the flood, leads on to fortune;
Omitted, all the voyage of their life
Is bound in shallows and in miseries.
William Shakespeare 1564–1616: *Julius Caesar* (1599)

27 If any man can shew any just cause, why they may not lawfully be joined together, let him now speak, or else hereafter for ever hold his peace.
The Book of Common Prayer 1662: *Solemnization of Matrimony*

28 But on occasion's forelock watchful wait.
John Milton 1608–74: *Paradise Regained* (1671); see 22 above

29 We must beat the iron while it is hot, but we may polish it at leisure.
John Dryden 1631–1700: *Aeneis* (1697); see 14 above

30 *La carrière ouverte aux talents.*
The career open to the talents.
Napoleon I 1769–1821: Barry E. O'Meara *Napoleon in Exile* (1822); see 31 below

31 To the very last he [Napoleon] had a kind of idea; that, namely, of *La carrière ouverte aux talents*, The tools to him that can handle them.
Thomas Carlyle 1795–1881: *Critical and Miscellaneous Essays* (1838) 'Sir Walter Scott'; see 30 above

32 Never the time and the place
And the loved one all together!
Robert Browning 1812–89: 'Never the Time and the Place' (1883)

33 If only I could get down to Sidcup! I've been waiting for the weather to break. He's got my papers, this man I left them with, it's got it all down there, I could prove everything.
Harold Pinter 1930– : *The Caretaker* (1960)

34 She's got a ticket to ride, but she don't care.
John Lennon 1940–80 and **Paul MacCartney** 1942– : 'Ticket to Ride' (1965 song)

35 I opened the door for a lot of people, and they just ran through and left me holding the knob.
Bo Diddley 1928– : in 1971; M. Wrenn *Bitch, Bitch, Bitch* (1988)

Optimism and Pessimism see also Despair, Hope

PROVERBS AND SAYINGS

1 **All's for the best in the best of all possible worlds.**
early 20th century, from Voltaire; see 17 below

2 **Another day, another dollar.**
American proverb, mid 20th century

3 **The darkest hour is just before dawn.**
mid 17th century, suggesting that the experience of complete despair may mean that matters have reached the lowest point and may shortly improve

4 **Don't count your chickens before they are hatched.**
late 16th century, meaning that one should not make, or act upon, an assumption (usually favourable) which may turn out to be ill-founded; see 13 below

5 **Don't halloo till you are out of the wood.**
late 18th century, meaning that you should not exult until danger and difficulty are past (halloo means shout in order to attract attention)

6 **Every cloud has a silver lining.**
mid 19th century, meaning that even the gloomiest circumstance has some hopeful element in it; see 32 below

7 **God's in his heaven; all's right with the world.**
from early 16th century in the form 'God is where he was'; now largely replaced by this quotation from Browning; see 19 below

8 **If ifs and ands were pots and pans, there'd be no work for tinkers' hands.**
mid 19th century; traditional response to an over-optimistic conditional expression, in which ands is the plural form of and 'if'

9 **If wishes were horses, beggars would ride.**
early 17th century, meaning that what one wishes is often far from reality

10 **It's an ill wind that blows nobody any good.**
mid 16th century, meaning that good luck may arise from the source of another's misfortune

11 **The sharper the storm, the sooner it's over.**
meaning that the more intense something is, the shorter time it is likely to last

12 **When things are at the worst they begin to mend.**
mid 18th century; meaning that when a bad situation has reached its worst possible point, the next change must reflect at least a small improvement

PHRASES

13 **count one's chickens** be overoptimistic, assume too much.
from the proverb: see 4 above

14 **sell the bear's skin before one has caught the bear** act upon an assumption of success which may turn out to be ill-founded.
early versions of the phrase, from the 16th century, have lion or beast; see also **Business** 17

QUOTATIONS

15 Sin is behovely, but all shall be well and all shall be well and all manner of thing shall be well.
Julian of Norwich 1343–after 1416: *Revelations of Divine Love*

16 Yet where an equal poise of hope and fear
Does arbitrate the event, my nature is
That I incline to hope, rather than fear,
And gladly banish squint suspicion.
John Milton 1608–74: *Comus* (1637)

17 In this best of possible worlds . . . all is for the best.
usually quoted as 'All is for the best in the best of all possible worlds'
Voltaire 1694–1778: *Candide* (1759); see 1above, 27 below

18 There's a gude time coming.
Sir Walter Scott 1771–1832: *Rob Roy* (1817)

19 The lark's on the wing;
The snail's on the thorn:
God's in his heaven—
All's right with the world!
Robert Browning 1812–89: *Pippa Passes* (1841); see 7 above

20 I have known him come home to supper with a flood of tears, and a declaration that nothing was now left but a jail; and go to bed making a calculation of the expense of putting bow-windows to the house, 'in case anything turned up,' which was his favourite expression.
of Mr Micawber
Charles Dickens 1812–70: *David Copperfield* (1850)

21 In front the sun climbs slow, how slowly,
But westward, look, the land is bright.
Arthur Hugh Clough 1819–61: 'Say not the struggle naught availeth' (1855)

22 Nothing to do but work,
Nothing to eat but food,
Nothing to wear but clothes
To keep one from going nude.
Benjamin Franklin King 1857–94: 'The Pessimist'

23 If way to the Better there be, it exacts a full
look at the worst.
Thomas Hardy 1840–1928: 'De Profundis' (1902)

24 Are we downhearted?
No! Let 'em all come!
Charles Knight and **Kenneth Lyle**: 'Here we are!
Here we are again!!' (1914 song)

25 'Twixt the optimist and pessimist
The difference is droll:
The optimist sees the doughnut
But the pessimist sees the hole.
McLandburgh Wilson 1892– : *Optimist and
Pessimist* (c.1915)

26 Cheer up! the worst is yet to come!
Philander Chase Johnson 1866–1939: in
Everybody's Magazine May 1920

27 The optimist proclaims that we live in the
best of all possible worlds; and the
pessimist fears this is true.
James Branch Cabell 1879–1958: *The Silver Stallion*
(1926); see **17** above

28 Grab your coat, and get your hat,
Leave your worry on the doorstep,
Just direct your feet
To the sunny side of the street.
Dorothy Fields 1905–74: 'On the Sunny Side of the
Street' (1930 song)

29 Every time it rains, it rains
Pennies from heaven.
Don't you know each cloud contains
Pennies from heaven?
Johnny Burke 1908–64: 'Pennies from Heaven'
(1936 song); see **Money** 44, **Surprise** 6

30 It's no go my honey love, it's no go my
poppet;
Work your hands from day to day, the
winds will blow the profit.
The glass is falling hour by hour, the glass
will fall for ever,

But if you break the bloody glass you
won't hold up the weather.
Louis MacNeice 1907–63: 'Bagpipe Music' (1938)

31 You've got to ac-cent-tchu-ate the positive
Elim-my-nate the negative
Latch on to the affirmative
Don't mess with Mister In-between.
Johnny Mercer 1909–76: 'Ac-cent-tchu-ate the
Positive' (1944 song)

32 There are bad times just around the
corner,
There are dark clouds travelling through
the sky
And it's no good whining
About a silver lining
For we know from experience that they
won't roll by.
Noël Coward 1899–1973: 'There are Bad Times Just
Around the Corner' (1953 song); see **6** above

33 Everything's coming up roses.
Stephen Sondheim 1930– : title of song (1959)

34 When you're depressed, there *are* no
molehills.
Randall Jarrell 1914–65: William H. Pritchard
Randall Jarrell: A Literary Life (1990); see **Value** 12

35 If we see light at the end of the tunnel,
It's the light of the oncoming train.
Robert Lowell 1917–77: 'Since 1939' (1977); see
Adversity 5

36 I don't consider myself a pessimist. I think
of a pessimist as someone who is waiting
for it to rain. And I feel soaked to the skin.
Leonard Cohen 1934– : in *Observer* 2 May 1993

37 Pessimism was dear to him in its
impersonation of profundity and its
implication of arcane knowledge.
Candia McWilliam 1955– : *Debatable Land* (1994)

38 I don't mind grappling with the fact that
there is no Santa Claus, but I still want to
be allowed to believe in living happily ever
after.
Vanessa Feltz 1962– : in *Sunday Times* 2
September 2001; see **Ending** 3

Order and Chaos

1 The Devil is in the details.
late 20th century, meaning that the most difficult part of planning and achieving something is the detailed specification rather than the overall concept; see **Architecture** *19*

2 A place for everything, and everything in its place.
mid 17th century, often associated with Samuel Smiles; see **Administration** *8*

3 alarms and excursions confused noise and bustle.
alarums and excursions an old stage-direction occurring in Shakespeare 3 Henry VI *and* Richard III

4 all hell let loose a state of utter confusion and uproar, utter pandemonium.
from Milton: see 11 below

5 flutter the dovecots startle or perturb a sedate or conventionally-minded community.
from Shakespeare's Coriolanus 'like an eagle in a dove-cote, I Fluttered your Volscians in Corioli'

6 a pretty kettle of fish an awkward state of affairs, a mess.
kettle a long pan for cooking fish in liquid; see also **Royalty** *32*

7 raise Cain make a disturbance, cause trouble.
*Cain the eldest son of Adam, who in the Bible (*Genesis*) is said to have murdered his younger brother Abel; see also* **Canada** *2,* **Murder** *7,* **Travel** *8*

8 shipshape and Bristol fashion with all in good order.
Bristol a city and port in the west of England; originally a nautical expression

9 Sturm und Drang (a period of) emotion, stress, or turbulence.
German, literally 'storm and stress', title of a 1776 play by Friedrich Maximilian Klinger (1752–1831)

10 All things began in order, so shall they end, and so shall they begin again; according to the ordainer of order and mystical mathematics of the city of heaven.
Thomas Browne 1605–82: *The Garden of Cyrus* (1658)

11 But wherefore thou alone? Wherefore with thee
Came not all hell broke loose?
John Milton 1608–74: *Paradise Lost* (1667); see 4 above

12 With ruin upon ruin, rout on rout,
Confusion worse confounded.
John Milton 1608–74: *Paradise Lost* (1667)

13 Lo! thy dread empire, Chaos! is restored;
Light dies before thy uncreating word:
Thy hand, great Anarch! lets the curtain fall;
And universal darkness buries all.
Alexander Pope 1688–1744: *The Dunciad* (1742)

14 Good order is the foundation of all good things.
Edmund Burke 1729–97: *Reflections on the Revolution in France* (1790)

15 Chaos often breeds life, when order breeds habit.
Henry Brooks Adams 1838–1918: *The Education of Henry Adams* (1907)

16 Things fall apart; the centre cannot hold;
Mere anarchy is loosed upon the world,
The blood-dimmed tide is loosed, and everywhere
The ceremony of innocence is drowned.
W. B. Yeats 1865–1939: 'The Second Coming' (1921)

17 I'm interested in anything about revolt, disorder, chaos, especially activity that appears to have no meaning. It seems to me to be the road toward freedom.
Jim Morrison 1943–71: in *Time* 24 January 1968

18 I'm at my best in a messy, middle-of-the-road muddle.
Harold Wilson 1916–95: remark in Cabinet, 21 January 1975; Philip Ziegler *Wilson* (1993)

Originality

PHRASES

1 an Arabian bird a unique specimen.
a phoenix, in allusion to Shakespeare Cymbeline *'She is alone the Arabian bird, and I have lost the wager'*

2 break the mould make impossible the repetition of a certain type of creation; put an end to a pattern of events or behaviour by setting markedly different standards.
originally with reference to Ariosto: see **Excellence** 8

QUOTATIONS

3 The saying of the noble and glorious Aeschylus, who declared that his tragedies were large cuts taken from Homer's mighty dinners.
Aeschylus c.525–456 BC: Athenaeus *Deipnosophistae*

4 Nothing has yet been said that's not been said before.
Terence c.190–159 BC: *Eunuchus*

5 It could be said of me that in this book I have only made up a bunch of other men's flowers, providing of my own only the string that ties them together.
Montaigne 1533–92: *Essais* (1580)

6 They lard their lean books with the fat of others' works.
Robert Burton 1577–1640: *The Anatomy of Melancholy* (1621–51)

7 Not wrung from speculations and subtleties, but from common sense, and observation; not picked from the leaves of any author, but bred among the weeds and tares of mine own brain.
Thomas Browne 1605–82: *Religio Medici* (1643)

8 He invades authors like a monarch; and what would be theft in other poets, is only victory in him.
of Ben Jonson
John Dryden 1631–1700: *An Essay of Dramatic Poesy* (1668)

9 The original writer is not he who refrains from imitating others, but he who can be imitated by none.
François-René Chateaubriand 1768–1848: *Le Génie du Christianisme* (1802)

10 Never forget what I believe was observed to you by Coleridge, that every great and original writer, in proportion as he is great and original, must himself create the taste by which he is to be relished.
William Wordsworth 1770–1850: letter to Lady Beaumont, 21 May 1807

11 Make copies, young man, many copies. You can only become a good artist by copying the masters.
Jean Ingres 1780–1867: to Degas; A. Vollard *Souvenirs d'un marchand de tableaux* (1937)

12 The truth is that the propensity of man to imitate what is before him is one of the strongest parts of his nature.
Walter Bagehot 1826–77: *Physics and Politics* (1872) 'Nation-Making'

13 Immature poets imitate; mature poets steal.
T. S. Eliot 1888–1965: *The Sacred Wood* (1920) 'Philip Massinger'

14 If you steal from one author, it's plagiarism; if you steal from many, it's research.
Wilson Mizner 1876–1933: Alva Johnston *The Legendary Mizners* (1953)

15 No plagiarist can excuse the wrong by showing how much of his work he did not pirate.
Learned Hand 1872–1961: *Sheldon v. Metro-Goldwyn Pictures Corp.* 1936

16 It is sometimes necessary to repeat what we all know. All map-makers should place the Mississippi in the same location, and avoid originality.
Saul Bellow 1915– : *Mr Sammler's Planet* (1969)

17 Let's have some new clichés.
Sam Goldwyn 1882–1974: attributed, perhaps apocryphal

Painting and Drawing see also **The Arts**, **Photography**, Sculpture

1 A good painter can draw a devil as well as an angel.
late 16th century

2 Not a day without a line.
traditional saying, attributed to the Greek artist Apelles (fl. 325 BC) by Pliny the Elder

PHRASES

3 Giotto's O the perfect circle supposedly drawn freehand by Giotto (*c.*1267–1337), Italian painter.

4 warts and all including features or qualities that are not appealing or attractive.
from Cromwell: see 6 below

QUOTATIONS

5 Good painters imitate nature, bad ones spew it up.
Cervantes 1547–1616: *El Licenciado Vidriera* (1613)

6 Remark all these roughnesses, pimples, warts, and everything as you see me; otherwise I will never pay a farthing for it.
to the painter Lely; see 4 above
Oliver Cromwell 1599–1658: Horace Walpole *Anecdotes of Painting in England* vol. 3 (1763)

7 An imitation in lines and colours on any surface of all that is to be found under the sun.
of painting
Nicolas Poussin 1594–1665: letter to M. de Chambray, 1665

8 A mere copier of nature can never produce anything great.
Joshua Reynolds 1723–92: *Discourses on Art* 14 December 1770

9 The sound of water escaping from mill-dams, etc., willows, old rotten planks, slimy posts, and brickwork . . . those scenes made me a painter and I am grateful.
John Constable 1776–1837: letter to John Fisher, 23 October 1821

10 *Le dessin est la probité de l'art.*
Drawing is the true test of art.
J. A. D. Ingres 1780–1867: *Pensées d'Ingres* (1922)

11 I have seen, and heard, much of Cockney impudence before now; but never expected to hear a coxcomb ask two hundred guineas for flinging a pot of paint in the public's face.
on Whistler's Nocturne in Black and Gold
John Ruskin 1819–1900: *Fors Clavigera* (1871–84) letter 79, 18 June 1877

12 I own I like definite form in what my eyes are to rest upon; and if landscapes were sold, like the sheets of characters of my boyhood, one penny plain and twopence coloured, I should go the length of twopence every day of my life.
Robert Louis Stevenson 1850–94: *Travels with a Donkey* (1879)

13 You should not paint the chair, but only what someone has felt about it.
Edvard Munch 1863–1944: written *c.*1891; R. Heller *Munch* (1984)

14 Treat nature in terms of the cylinder, the sphere, the cone, all in perspective.
Paul Cézanne 1839–1906: letter to Emile Bernard, 1904; Emile Bernard *Paul Cézanne* (1925)

15 Monet is only an eye, but what an eye!
Paul Cézanne 1839–1906: attributed

16 What I dream of is an art of balance, of purity and serenity devoid of troubling or depressing subject matter . . . a soothing, calming influence on the mind, rather like a good armchair which provides relaxation from physical fatigue.
Henri Matisse 1869–1954: *Notes d'un peintre* (1908)

17 A man like Picasso studies an object as a surgeon dissects a corpse.
Guillaume Apollinaire 1880–1918: *Les Peintres cubistes* (1913)

18 It's with my brush that I make love.
often quoted as 'I paint with my prick'
Pierre Auguste Renoir 1841–1919: A. André *Renoir* (1919)

19 An active line on a walk, moving freely without a goal. A walk for walk's sake.
Paul Klee 1879–1940: *Pedagogical Sketchbook* (1925)

20 Every time I paint a portrait I lose a friend.
John Singer Sargent 1856–1925: N. Bentley and E. Esar *Treasury of Humorous Quotations* (1951)

21 No, painting is not made to decorate apartments. It's an offensive and defensive weapon against the enemy.
Pablo Picasso 1881–1973: interview with Simone Téry, 24 March 1945, in Alfred H. Barr *Picasso* (1946)

22 I am a painter and I nail my pictures together.
Kurt Schwitters 1887–1948: R. Hausmann *Am Anfang war Dada* (1972)

23 Picasso is Spanish, I am too. Picasso is a genius. I am too. Picasso will be seventy-two and I about forty-eight. Picasso is known in every country of the world; so am I. Picasso is a Communist; I am not.
Salvador Dali 1904–89: lecture in Madrid, 12 October 1951

24 When I was the age of these children I could draw like Raphael: it took me many years to learn how to draw like these children.
to Herbert Read, when visiting an exhibition of childen's drawings
Pablo Picasso 1881–1973: quoted in letter from Read to *The Times* 27 October 1956

25 There was a reviewer a while back who wrote that my pictures didn't have any beginning or any end. He didn't mean it as a compliment, but it was. It was a fine compliment.
Jackson Pollock 1912–56: Francis V. O'Connor *Jackson Pollock* (1967)

26 Painting is saying 'Ta' to God.
Stanley Spencer 1891–1959: letter from Spencer's daughter Shirin to *Observer* 7 February 1988

27 If Botticelli were alive today he'd be working for *Vogue*.
Peter Ustinov 1921– : in *Observer* 21 October 1962

28 A product of the untalented, sold by the unprincipled to the utterly bewildered.
on abstract art
Al Capp 1907–79: in *National Observer* 1 July 1963

29 I rarely draw what I see—I draw what I feel in my body.
Barbara Hepworth 1903–75: Alan Bowness *Barbara Hepworth—Drawings from a Sculptor's Landscape* (1966)

30 All painting, no matter what you're painting, is abstract in that it's got to be organized.
David Hockney 1937– : *David Hockney* (1976)

31 I find a particular delight in taking the caricature as far as I can. It satisfies me to stretch the human frame about and recreate it and yet keep a likeness.
Gerald Scarfe 1936– : *Scarfe by Scarfe* (1986)

32 What I see is a marvellous painting. But how are you going to make it? And, of course, as I don't know how to make it, I rely then on chance and accident making it for me.
Francis Bacon 1909–92: David Sylvester (ed.) *Interviews with Francis Bacon: the brutality of fact* (ed. 3, 1987)

33 Mostly painting is like putting a message in a bottle and flinging it into the sea.
Howard Hodgkin 1932– : in *Observer* 10 June 2001

The Paranormal see also The Supernatural

PROVERBS AND SAYINGS

1 **It's life, Jim, but not as we know it.**
late 20th century saying associated with the television series Star Trek *(1966–); the saying does not occur in the series but derives from the 1987 song 'Star Trekkin'' sung by The Firm*

2 **The truth is out there.**
catchphrase from The X Files *(American television series, 1993–), created by Chris Carter (1957–), in which two special agents repeatedly investigate cases which appear to involve the paranormal; final proof of extra-terrestrial activity, however, is always lacking*

PHRASES

3 **Bermuda triangle** a place where people or objects vanish without explanation.
an area of the West Atlantic Ocean where a disproportionately large number of ships and aeroplanes are said to have been mysteriously lost

4 **Close Encounter** term used for a supposed encounter with a UFO.
divided into categories, from a Close Encounter of the First Kind (sighting but no physical evidence), through Second (physical evidence left) and Third (extra-terrestrials beings observed) to a Close Encounter of the Fourth Kind, which involves abduction by aliens; see 6 below

5 **near-death experience** an unusual experience taking place on the brink of

death and recounted by a person on recovery.
see 15, 18 below

6 Unidentified Flying Object a mysterious object seen in the sky for which it is claimed no orthodox scientific explanation can be found.
often abbreviated to UFO. It is often supposed that UFOs, if real, must be vehicles carrying extraterrestrials, although other theories are put forward; see 4 above

QUOTATIONS

7 When the consciousness-principle getteth outside [the body it sayeth to itself] 'Am I dead or am I not dead?' It cannot determine. It seeth its relatives and connections as it had been used to seeing them before. It even heareth the wailings.
The Tibetan Book of the Dead 8th century: bk. 1, pt. 1

8 GLENDOWER: I can call spirits from the vasty deep.
HOTSPUR: Why, so can I, or so can any man;
But will they come when you do call for them?
William Shakespeare 1564–1616: *Henry IV, Part 1* (1597)

9 No testimony is sufficient to establish a miracle, unless the testimony be of such a kind, that its falsehood would be more miraculous than the fact which it endeavours to establish.
David Hume 1711–76: 'Of Miracles' (1748)

10 Call the death by any name Your Highness will, attribute it to whom you will, or say it might have been prevented how you will, it is the same death eternally—inborn, inbred, engendered in the corrupted humours of the vicious body itself, and that only—Spontaneous Combustion, and none other of all the deaths that can be died.
Charles Dickens 1812–70: *Bleak House* (1853)

11 From the astrologer came the astronomer, from the alchemist the chemist, from the mesmerist the experimental psychologist. The quack of yesterday is the professor of tomorrow.
Arthur Conan Doyle 1859–1930: *Tales of Terror and Mystery* (1922)

12 Indubitably, Magic is one of the subtlest and most difficult of the sciences and arts.
There is more opportunity for errors of comprehension, judgement and practice than in any other branch of physics.
Aleister Crowley 1875–1947: *The Confessions of Aleister Crowley* (1929)

13 About astrology and palmistry: they are good because they make people vivid and full of possibilities. They are communism at its best. Everybody has a birthday and almost everybody has a palm.
Kurt Vonnegut 1922– : *Wampeters, Foma and Granfalloons* (1974)

14 The fancy that extraterrestrial life is by definition of a higher order than our own is one that soothes all children, and many writers.
Joan Didion 1934– : *The White Album* (1979)

15 This was reality and all else an illusion.
on his near-death experience; see 5 above
Michael Bentine 1922–96: *The Door Marked Summer* (1981)

16 My boy, *The War of the Worlds* was just a dress rehearsal.
on the reality of alien invasion
Orson Welles 1915–85: Michael Munn *X-Rated: The Paranormal Experiences of the Movie Star Greats* (1996)

17 Black magic operates most effectively in preconscious, marginal areas. Casual curses are the most effective.
William S. Burroughs 1914–97: *The Western Lands* (1987)

18 Did you know that I was dead? The first time that I tried to cross the river I was frustrated, but my second attempt succeeded. It was most extraordinary. My thoughts became persons.
on his near-death experience; see 5 above
A. J. Ayer 1910–89: in *Sunday Telegraph* 28 August 1988

19 Mr Geller may have psychic powers by means of which he can bend spoons; if so, he appears to be doing it the hard way.
James Randi 1928– : *The Supernatural A-Z: the truth and the lies* (1995)

20 I don't believe in astrology; I'm a Sagittarius and we're sceptical.
Arthur C. Clarke 1917– : attributed; Nigel Rees *Cassell Dictionary of Humorous Quotations* (1999)

21 There is no such thing as magic, only acting.
Paul Daniels 1938– : *Under No Illusion* (2000, with Chris Gidney)

22 I was sued by a woman who claimed that she became pregnant because she watched me on the television and I bent her contraceptive coil.
Uri Geller 1946– : in *Sunday Times* 17 December 2000

Parents see also **Child Care, The Family**

PROVERBS AND SAYINGS

1 **It is a wise child that knows its own father.**
late 16th century, meaning that a child's legal paternity might not reflect an actual blood link; see 6 below

2 **My son is my son till he gets him a wife, but my daughter's my daughter all the days of her life.**
late 17th century; meaning that while a man who establishes his own family relegates former blood ties to second place, a woman's filial role is not affected by her marriage

3 **Praise the child, and you make love to the mother.**
early 19th century

QUOTATIONS

4 Honour thy father and thy mother.
Bible: Exodus; see **Lifestyles** 8

5 A wise son maketh a glad father: but a foolish son is the heaviness of his mother.
Bible: Proverbs

6 It is a wise father that knows his own child.
William Shakespeare 1564–1616: *The Merchant of Venice* (1596–8); see 1 above

7 The joys of parents are secret, and so are their griefs and fears.
Francis Bacon 1561–1626: *Essays* (1625) 'Of Parents and Children'

8 After God comes my Papa—that was ever the motto, the axiom of my childhood and I cling to it still!
Wolfgang Amadeus Mozart 1756–91: letter to his father and sister, 7 March 1778

9 A slavish bondage to parents cramps every faculty of the mind.
Mary Wollstonecraft 1759–97: *A Vindication of the Rights of Woman* (1792)

10 The mother's yearning, that completest type of the life in another life which is the essence of real human love, feels the presence of the cherished child even in the debased, degraded man.
George Eliot 1819–80: *Adam Bede* (1859)

11 For the hand that rocks the cradle
Is the hand that rules the world.
William Ross Wallace d. 1881: 'What rules the world' (1865); see **Women** 3

12 If I were damned of body and soul,
I know whose prayers would make me whole,
Mother o' mine, O mother o' mine.
Rudyard Kipling 1865–1936: *The Light That Failed* (1891)

13 Children begin by loving their parents; after a time they judge them; rarely, if ever, do they forgive them.
Oscar Wilde 1854–1900: *A Woman of No Importance* (1893)

14 Few misfortunes can befall a boy which bring worse consequences than to have a really affectionate mother.
W. Somerset Maugham 1874–1965: *A Writer's Notebook* (1949); written in 1896

15 The natural term of the affection of the human animal for its offspring is six years.
George Bernard Shaw 1856–1950: *Heartbreak House* (1919)

16 Your children are not your children.
They are the sons and daughters of Life's longing for itself.
They came through you but not from you
And though they are with you yet they belong not to you.
Kahlil Gibran 1883–1931: *The Prophet* (1923) 'On Children'

17 The affection you get back from children is sixpence given as change for a sovereign.
Edith Nesbit 1858–1924: J. Briggs *A Woman of Passion* (1987)

18 The fundamental defect of fathers, in our competitive society, is that they want their children to be a credit to them.
Bertrand Russell 1872–1970: *Sceptical Essays* (1928) 'Freedom versus Authority in Education'

19 Children aren't happy with nothing to ignore,
And that's what parents were created for.
Ogden Nash 1902–71: 'The Parent' (1933)

20 Nothing has a stronger influence on their children than the unlived lives of their parents.
Carl Gustav Jung 1875–1961: attributed; in *Boston Magazine* June 1978

21 There is no good father, that's the rule. Don't lay the blame on men but on the bond of paternity, which is rotten. To beget children, nothing better; to *have* them, what iniquity!
Jean-Paul Sartre 1905–80: *Les Mots* (1964) 'Lire'

22 Do they know they're old,
These two who are my father and my mother
Whose fire from which I came, has now grown cold?
Elizabeth Jennings 1926–2001: 'One Flesh' (1967)

23 No matter how old a mother is she watches her middle-aged children for signs of improvement.
Florida Scott-Maxwell: *Measure of my Days* (1968)

24 In our society mothers take the place elsewhere occupied by the Fates, the System, Negroes, Communism or Reactionary Imperialist Plots; mothers go on getting blamed until they're eighty, but shouldn't take it personally.
Katharine Whitehorn 1928– : *Observations* (1970)

25 Children always assume the sexual lives of their parents come to a grinding halt at their conception.
Alan Bennett 1934– : *Getting On* (1972)

26 It doesn't matter who my father was; it matters who I remember he was.
Anne Sexton 1928–74: diary, 1 January 1972

27 There must be many fathers around the country who have experienced the cruellest, most crushing rejection of all: their children have ended up supporting the wrong team.
Nick Hornby 1957– : *Fever Pitch* (1992)

28 I have reached the age when a woman begins to perceive that she is growing into the person she least plans to resemble: her mother.
Anita Brookner 1938– : *Incidents in the Rue Laugier* (1995)

29 I feel like the roots of a great bunch of flowers. The grower gets all the praise, the flowers get the adoration, while the roots that started it all must remain under the ground unnoticed.
view of the father of Noel and Liam
Thomas Gallagher: in *Independent* 23 August 1997

30 Who needs a mother once the milk has gone?
Esther Dyson 1951– : remark aged 5, in *Independent* 11 January 1999

31 My father was a management genius. But what I really wanted was a dad.
Michael Jackson 1958– : speech at the Oxford Union, 6 March 2001

Parliament

PROVERBS AND SAYINGS

1 I spy strangers!
the conventional formula demanding the exclusion from the House of non-members to whose presence attention is thus drawn

2 Who goes home?
formal question asked by the doorkeeper when the House of Commons adjourns

PHRASES

3 Administration of All the Talents a coalition government, ironically regarded.
the Ministry of Lord Grenville, 1806–7, a short-lived coalition ironically regarded as possessing all possible talents in its members

4 apply for the Chiltern Hundreds resign from the House of Commons.
Chiltern Hundreds a crown manor, the administration of which is a nominal office under the Crown and so requires an MP to vacate his or her seat

5 the best club in London the House of Commons.

6 Father of the House of Commons the member with the longest continuous service.

7 His or Her Majesty's Opposition the principal party opposed to the governing party in the British Parliament.

John Cam Hobhouse, in Recollections of a Long Life *(1865), said of a debate in 1826, 'When I invented the phrase 'His Majesty's Opposition' [Canning] paid me a compliment on the fortunate hit'*

8 Leader of the House (in the House of Commons) an MP chosen from the party in office to plan the Government's legislative programme and arrange the business of the House; (in the House of Lords) the peer who acts as spokesman for the Government.

9 Mr Balfour's poodle the House of Lords.

title of a book by Roy Jenkins Mr Balfour's Poodle. An account of the struggle between the House of Lords and the government of Mr Asquith *(1954); ultimately in allusion to Lloyd George: see 23 below*

10 the West Lothian question the constitutional anomaly that MPs for Scottish and Welsh constituencies are unable to vote on Scottish or Welsh matters that have been devolved to those assemblies, but are able to vote on equivalent matters concerning England, whilst MPs for English constituencies have no reciprocal influence on Scottish or Welsh policy.

West Lothian is the name of a former parliamentary constituency in Central Scotland, whose MP, Tam Dalyell, persistently raised this question in Parliament in debates on Scottish and Welsh devolution during 1977-8

QUOTATIONS

11 A parliament can do any thing but make a man a woman, and a woman a man.
Henry Herbert, Lord Pembroke *c.*1534–1601: quoted in 4th Earl of Pembroke's speech, 11 April 1648, proving himself Chancellor of Oxford

12 I have neither eye to see, nor tongue to speak here, but as the House is pleased to direct me.
the Speaker, on being asked if he had seen any of the five MPs whom the King had ordered to be arrested
William Lenthall 1591–1662: to Charles I, 4 January 1642; John Rushworth *Historical Collections. The Third Part* (1692)

13 I see all the birds are flown.
after attempting to arrest the Five Members
Charles I 1600–49: in the House of Commons, 4 January 1642; see **Liberty** 2

14 Take away that fool's bauble, the mace.
often quoted as, 'Take away these baubles'
Oliver Cromwell 1599–1658: at the dismissal of the Rump Parliament, 20 April 1653

15 Your representative owes you, not his industry only, but his judgement; and he betrays, instead of serving you, if he sacrifices it to your opinion.
Edmund Burke 1729–97: speech, Bristol, 3 November 1774

16 Though we cannot out-vote them we will out-argue them.
on the practical value of speeches in the House of Commons
Samuel Johnson 1709–84: James Boswell *Life of Samuel Johnson* (1791) 3 April 1778

17 The duty of an Opposition [is] very simple . . . to oppose everything, and propose nothing.
Edward Stanley, 14th Earl of Derby 1799–1869: quoting 'Mr Tierney, a great Whig authority', in the House of Commons, 4 June 1841

18 Your business is not to govern the country but it is, if you think fit, to call to account those who do govern it.
W. E. Gladstone 1809–98: speech to the House of Commons, 29 January 1855

19 England is the mother of Parliaments.
John Bright 1811–89: speech at Birmingham, 18 January 1865; see **Britain** 3

20 A cabinet is a combining committee—a *hyphen* which joins, a *buckle* which fastens, the legislative part of the state to the executive part of the state.
Walter Bagehot 1826–77: *The English Constitution* (1867) 'The Cabinet'

21 I am dead; dead, but in the Elysian fields.
to a peer, on his elevation to the House of Lords
Benjamin Disraeli 1804–81: W. Monypenny and G. Buckle *Life of Benjamin Disraeli* vol. 5 (1920)

22 When in that House MPs divide,
If they've a brain and cerebellum too,
They have to leave that brain outside,
And vote just as their leaders tell 'em to.
W. S. Gilbert 1836–1911: *Iolanthe* (1882)

23 The leal and trusty mastiff which is to watch over our interests, but which runs away at the first snarl of the trade unions

... A mastiff? It is the right hon. Gentleman's poodle.

on the House of Lords and A. J. Balfour
David Lloyd George 1863–1945: speech, House of Commons, 26 June 1907; see 9 above

24 They [parliament] are a lot of hard-faced men who look as if they had done very well out of the war.
Stanley Baldwin 1867–1947: J. M. Keynes *Economic Consequences of the Peace* (1919)

25 Think of it! A second Chamber selected by the Whips. A seraglio of eunuchs.
Michael Foot 1913– : speech, *Hansard* 3 February 1969

26 It is, I think, good evidence of life after death.
on the quality of debate in the House of Lords
Donald Soper 1903–98: in *Listener* 17 August 1978

27 Parliament itself would not exist in its present form had people not defied the law.
Arthur Scargill 1938– : evidence to House of Commons Select Committee on Employment, 2 April 1980

28 The only safe pleasure for a parliamentarian is a bag of boiled sweets.
Julian Critchley 1930–2000: in *Listener* 10 June 1982

29 Being an MP is a good job, the sort of job all working-class parents want for their children—clean, indoors and no heavy lifting.
Diane Abbott 1953– : in *Independent* 18 January 1994

30 Being an MP feeds your vanity and starves your self-respect.
Matthew Parris 1949– : in *The Times* 9 February 1994

31 There can be no place in a 21st-century parliament for people with 15th-century titles upholding 19th-century prejudices.
Paddy Ashdown 1941– : comment, 24 November 1998

32 In the last Parliament, the House of Commons had more MPs called John than all the women MPs put together.
Tessa Jowell 1947– : in *Independent on Sunday* 14 March 1999 'Quotes'

33 To say that change at Westminster happens at a snail's pace is to insult the pace of snails.
Oona King 1967– : in *The Times* 25 November 2000

Parting see **Meeting and Parting**

The Past see also History, Memory, The Present

PROVERBS AND SAYINGS

1 **Nostalgia isn't what it used to be.**
graffito; taken as title of book by Simone Signoret, 1978

2 **Old sins cast long shadows.**
early 20th century; current usage is likely to refer to the wrong done by one generation affecting its descendants

3 **The past always looks better than it was; it's only pleasant because it isn't here.**
American proverb, late 19th century

4 **The past at least is secure.**
American proverb, early 19th century

5 **Things past cannot be recalled.**
late 15th century, meaning that what has already happened cannot be changed

6 **What's done cannot be undone.**
mid 15th century

PHRASES

7 **ancien régime** the old system or style of things.
French = former regime, the system of government in France before the Revolution of 1789

8 **auld lang syne** times long past.
*literally 'old long since'; especially as the title and refrain of a traditional song (see **Memory** 10)*

9 **a fly in amber** a curious relic of the past, preserved into the present.
alluding to the fossilized bodies of insects often found trapped in amber

10 **the good old days** the past.
*regarded as better than the present; see 33 below, **The Present** 15*

11 **the naughty nineties** the 1890s.
regarded as a time of liberalism and permissiveness, especially in Britain and France

12 once upon a time at some vague time in the past.
usually as a conventional opening of a story

13 the roaring twenties the 1920s.
regarded as a period of postwar buoyancy following the end of the First World War

14 the swinging sixties the 1960s.
regarded as a period of release from accepted social and cultural conventions

15 temps perdu the past, contemplated with nostalgia and a sense of irretrievability.
French, literally 'time lost', originally with allusion to Proust: see **Memory** *4*

QUOTATIONS

16 Even a god cannot change the past.
literally 'The one thing which even God cannot do is to make undone what has been done'
Agathon b. *c.*445: Aristotle *Nicomachaean Ethics*; see **History** 18

17 *Mais où sont les neiges d'antan?*
But where are the snows of yesteryear?
François Villon b. 1431: *Le Grand Testament* (1461) 'Ballade des dames du temps jadis'

18 O! call back yesterday, bid time return.
William Shakespeare 1564–1616: *Richard II* (1595)

19 Antiquities are history defaced, or some remnants of history which have casually escaped the shipwreck of time.
Francis Bacon 1561–1626: *The Advancement of Learning* (1605)

20 There never was a merry world since the fairies left off dancing, and the Parson left conjuring.
John Selden 1584–1654: *Table Talk* (1689)

21 Old mortality, the ruins of forgotten times.
Thomas Browne 1605–82: *Hydriotaphia* (Urn Burial, 1658)

22 Think of it, soldiers; from the summit of these pyramids, forty centuries look down upon you.
Napoleon I 1769–1821: speech, 21 July 1798, before the Battle of the Pyramids

23 Thy Naiad airs have brought me home,
To the glory that was Greece
And the grandeur that was Rome.
Edgar Allan Poe 1809–49: 'To Helen' (1831)

24 The splendour falls on castle walls
And snowy summits old in story.
Alfred, Lord Tennyson 1809–92: *The Princess* (1847), song (added 1850)

25 The moving finger writes; and, having writ,
Moves on: nor all thy piety nor wit
Shall lure it back to cancel half a line,
Nor all thy tears wash out a word of it.
Edward Fitzgerald 1809–83: *The Rubáiyát of Omar Khayyám* (1859)

26 I have gazed upon the face of Agamemnon.
on discovering a gold mask at Mycenae, 1876; traditional version of his telegram to the minister at Athens: 'This one is very like the picture which my imagination formed of Agamemnon long ago'
Heinrich Schliemann 1822–90: W. M. Calder and D. A. Traill *Myth, Scandal, and History* (1986)

27 What are those blue remembered hills,
What spires, what farms are those?
That is the land of lost content,
I see it shining plain,
The happy highways where I went
And cannot come again.
A. E. Housman 1859–1936: *A Shropshire Lad* (1896)

28 Those who cannot remember the past are condemned to repeat it.
George Santayana 1863–1952: *The Life of Reason* (1905)

29 Stands the Church clock at ten to three?
And is there honey still for tea?
Rupert Brooke 1887–1915: 'The Old Vicarage, Grantchester' (1915)

30 The past is the only dead thing that smells sweet.
Edward Thomas 1878–1917: 'Early one morning in May I set out' (1917)

31 I tell you the past is a bucket of ashes.
Carl Sandburg 1878–1967: 'Prairie' (1918)

32 Things ain't what they used to be.
Ted Persons: title of song (1941)

33 In every age 'the good old days' were a myth. No one ever thought they were good at the time. For every age has consisted of crises that seemed intolerable to the people who lived through them.
Brooks Atkinson 1894–1984: *Once Around the Sun* (1951); see 10 above

34 The past is never dead. It's not even past.
William Faulkner 1897–1962: *Requiem for a Nun* (1951)

35 The past is a foreign country: they do things differently there.
L. P. Hartley 1895–1972: *The Go-Between* (1953)

36 An old teapot, used daily, can tell me more of my past than anything I recorded of it.

Continuity . . . continuity . . . it is that which we cannot write down, it is that we cannot compass, record or control.

Sylvia Townsend Warner 1893–1978: letter to Alyse Gregory, 26 May 1953

37 People who are always praising the past
And especially the times of faith as best
Ought to go and live in the Middle Ages
And be burnt at the stake as witches and
   sages.

Stevie Smith 1902–71: 'The Past' (1957)

38 Yesterday, all my troubles seemed so far
   away,
Now it looks as though they're here to
   stay.
Oh I believe in yesterday.

John Lennon 1940–80 and **Paul McCartney** 1942– : 'Yesterday' (1965 song)

39 A man who has once looked with the archaeological eye will never see quite normally. He will be wounded by what other men call trifles. It is possible to refine the sense of time until an old show in the grass or a pile of nineteenth century beer bottles in an abandoned mining town tolls in one's head like a hall clock.

Loren Eiseley 1907–77: *The Night Country* (1971)

40 Hindsight is always twenty-twenty.

Billy Wilder 1906– : J. R. Columbo *Wit and Wisdom of the Moviemakers* (1979)

41 Reading about sex in yesterday's novels is like watching people smoke in old films.

Fay Weldon 1931– : in *Guardian* 1 December 1989

42 Thanks to modern technology . . . history now comes equipped with a fast-forward button.

Gore Vidal 1925– : *Screening History* (1992)

43 So the years hang like old clothes, forgotten in the wardrobe of our minds. Did I wear that? Who was I then?

Brian Moore 1921– : *No Other Life* (1993)

44 I think that today's youth have a tendency to live in the present and work for the future—and to be totally ignorant of the past.

Steven Spielberg 1947– : in *Independent on Sunday* 22 August 1999

Patience see also **Determination, Haste and Delay**

1 **All commend patience, but none can endure to suffer.**
American proverb, mid 20th century

2 **All things come to those who wait.**
early 16th century; often used as an adjuration to patience

3 **Be the day weary or be the day long, at last it ringeth to evensong.**
early 16th century, meaning that even the most difficult time will come to an end

4 **Bear and forbear.**
late 16th century, recommending patience and tolerance

5 **First things first.**
late 19th century

6 **Hurry no man's cattle.**
early 19th century, sometimes used as an injunction to be patient with someone

7 **It is a long lane that has no turning.**
mid 19th century, commonly used as an assertion that an unfavourable situation will eventually change for the better

8 **The longest way round is the shortest way home.**
mid 17th century, meaning that not trying to take a short cut is often the most effective way

9 **Nothing should be done in haste but gripping a flea.**
mid 17th century, used as a warning against rash action

10 **One step at a time.**
mid 19th century; recommending cautious progression along a desired route

11 **Patience is a virtue.**
late 14th century, often used as an exhortation

12 **Rome was not built in a day.**
mid 16th century, used to warn against trying to achieve too much at once

13 **Slow but sure.**
late 17th century; sure here means 'sure-footed, deliberate'

14 **Softly, softly, catchee monkey.**
early 20th century, advocating caution or guile as the best way to achieve an end

15 There is luck in leisure.

late 17th century, meaning that it is often advisable to wait before acting

16 A watched pot never boils.

mid 19th century; meaning that to pay too close an attention to the development of desired event appears to inhibit the result

17 We must learn to walk before we can run.

mid 14th century, meaning that a solid foundation is necessary for faster progress; see **Experience** *15*

18 What can't be cured must be endured.

late 16th century, meaning that there is no point in complaining about what is unavoidable

19 the patience of Job unending patience.

the patriarch Job, whose patience and exemplary piety were tried by dire and undeserved misfortunes, and who, in spite of his bitter lamentations, remained finally confident in the goodness and justice of God (see 20 below); see **Sympathy** *6*

20 The Lord gave, and the Lord hath taken away; blessed be the name of the Lord.
Bible: Job; see 19 above

21 Let patience have her perfect work.
Bible: James

22 Let nothing trouble you, nothing frighten you. All things are passing; God never changes. Patient endurance attains all things. Whoever possesses God lacks nothing: God alone suffices.
St Teresa of Ávila 1512-82: 'St Teresa's Bookmark'; found in her breviary after her death

23 Still have I borne it with a patient shrug, For sufferance is the badge of all our tribe.
William Shakespeare 1564-1616: *The Merchant of Venice* (1596-8)

24 Beware the fury of a patient man.
John Dryden 1631-1700: *Absalom and Achitophel* (1681)

25 Our patience will achieve more than our force.
Edmund Burke 1729-97: *Reflections on the Revolution in France* (1790)

26 Patience, that blending of moral courage with physical timidity.
Thomas Hardy 1840-1928: *Tess of the d'Urbervilles* (1891)

27 We had better wait and see.
referring to the rumour that the House of Lords was to be flooded with new Liberal peers to ensure the passage of the Finance Bill
Herbert Asquith 1852-1928: phrase used repeatedly in speeches in 1910; Roy Jenkins *Asquith* (1964)

28 I am extraordinarily patient, provided I get my own way in the end.
Margaret Thatcher 1925- : in *Observer* 4 April 1989

Patriotism

1 I'm backing Britain.

slogan coined by workers at the Colt factory, Surbiton, Surrey in 1968, and subsequently used in a national campaign

2 It's an ill bird that fouls its own nest.

mid 13th century; a condemnation of a person who brings his own family, home, or country into disrepute by his words or actions

3 Lousy but loyal.

London East End slogan at George V's Jubilee (1935)

4 King and country the objects of allegiance for a patriot whose head of State is a king.

5 Queen and country the objects of allegiance for a patriot whose head of State is a queen.

6 *Dulce et decorum est pro patria mori.*
Lovely and honourable it is to die for one's country.
Horace 65-8 BC: *Odes*; see **Warfare** 38

7 Not that I loved Caesar less, but that I loved Rome more.
William Shakespeare 1564-1616: *Julius Caesar* (1599)

8 Never was patriot yet, but was a fool.
John Dryden 1631-1700: *Absalom and Achitophel* (1681)

9 What pity is it
That we can die but once to serve our
country!
Joseph Addison 1672–1719: *Cato* (1713)

10 Be England what she will,
With all her faults, she is my country still.
Charles Churchill 1731–64: *The Farewell* (1764)

11 Patriotism is the last refuge of a scoundrel.
Samuel Johnson 1709–84: James Boswell *Life of
Samuel Johnson* (1791) 7 April 1775

12 I only regret that I have but one life to lose
for my country.
prior to his execution by the British for spying
Nathan Hale 1755–76: Henry Phelps Johnston
Nathan Hale, 1776 (1914)

13 These are the times that try men's souls.
The summer soldier and the sunshine
patriot will, in this crisis, shrink from the
service of their country; but he that stands
it *now*, deserves the love and thanks of
men and women.
Thomas Paine 1737–1809: *The Crisis* (December
1776)

14 Breathes there the man, with soul so dead,
Who never to himself hath said,
This is my own, my native land!
Sir Walter Scott 1771–1832: *The Lay of the Last
Minstrel* (1805)

15 Our country! In her intercourse with
foreign nations, may she always be in the
right; but our country, right or wrong.
Stephen Decatur 1779–1820: toast at Norfolk,
Virginia, April 1816; A. S. Mackenzie *Life of Stephen
Decatur* (1846); see 16 below

16 My toast would be, may our country be
always successful, but whether successful
or otherwise, always right.
John Quincy Adams 1767–1848: letter to John
Adams, 1 August 1816; see 15 above

17 A steady patriot of the world alone,
The friend of every country but his own.
on the Jacobins, extreme political radicals
George Canning 1770–1827: 'New Morality' (1821)

18 We don't want to fight, yet by jingo! if we
do,
We've got the ships, we've got the men,
and got the money too.
the origin of the term jingoism
G. W. Hunt 1829?–1904: 'We Don't Want to Fight'
(1878 song)

19 If I should die, think only this of me:
That there's some corner of a foreign field

That is for ever England.
Rupert Brooke 1887–1915: 'The Soldier' (1914)

20 Standing, as I do, in view of God and
eternity, I realize that patriotism is not
enough. I must have no hatred or
bitterness towards anyone.
*on the eve of her execution for helping Allied soldiers
to escape from occupied Belgium*
Edith Cavell 1865–1915: in *The Times* 23 October
1915

21 I vow to thee, my country—all earthly
things above—
Entire and whole and perfect, the service of
my love.
Cecil Spring-Rice 1859–1918: 'I Vow to Thee, My
Country' (1918)

22 You'll never have a quiet world till you
knock the patriotism out of the human
race.
George Bernard Shaw 1856–1950: *O'Flaherty V.C.*
(1919)

23 You think you are dying for your country;
you die for the industrialists.
Anatole France 1844–1924: in *L'Humanité* 18 July
1922

24 Patriotism is a lively sense of collective
responsibility. Nationalism is a silly cock
crowing on its own dunghill.
Richard Aldington 1892–1962: *The Colonel's
Daughter* (1931)

25 That this House will in no circumstances
fight for its King and Country.
D. M. Graham 1911–99: motion worded by Graham
for a debate at the Oxford Union, of which he was
Librarian, 9 February 1933 (passed by 275 votes to
153)

*on H. G. Wells's comment on 'an alien and uninspiring
court':*
26 I may be uninspiring, but I'll be damned if
I'm an alien!
George V 1865–1936: Sarah Bradford *George VI*
(1989); attributed, perhaps apocryphal

27 If I had to choose between betraying my
country and betraying my friend, I hope I
should have the guts to betray my
country.
E. M. Forster 1879–1970: *Two Cheers for Democracy*
(1951)

28 And so, my fellow Americans: ask not
what your country can do for you—ask
what you can do for your country.
John F. Kennedy 1917–63: inaugural address, 20
January 1961

29 I would die for my country but I could never let my country die for me.
Neil Kinnock 1942– : speech at Labour Party Conference, 30 September 1986

30 The cricket test—which side do they cheer for? . . . Are you still looking back to where you came from or where you are?
on the loyalties of Britain's immigrant population
Norman Tebbit 1931– : interview in *Los Angeles Times*; in *Daily Telegraph* 20 April 1990

Peace see also Warfare

PROVERBS AND SAYINGS

1 **After a storm comes a calm.**
late 14th century, often used with the implication that a calm situation is only achieved after stress and turmoil

2 **Ban the bomb.**
US anti-nuclear slogan, 1953 onwards, adopted by the Campaign for Nuclear Disarmament

3 **Nothing can bring you peace but yourself.**
American proverb, mid 19th century

PHRASES

4 **a Carthaginian peace** a peace settlement which imposes very severe terms on the defeated side.
*referring to the ultimate destruction of Carthage by Rome in the Punic Wars; see **Enemies** 6*

5 **an olive branch** a branch of an olive tree as an emblem of peace; any token of peace or goodwill.
*alluding to the Bible (Genesis) 'And the dove came in to him in the evening; and lo, in her mouth was an olive leave pluckt off: so Noah knew that the waters were abated from off the earth'; see **Diplomacy** 15*

6 **peace with honour** a phrase recorded from the 17th century.
used most famously by Disraeli: see 14 below

QUOTATIONS

7 They shall beat their swords into plowshares, and their spears into pruninghooks: nation shall not lift up sword against nation, neither shall they learn war any more.
Bible: Isaiah; see **Broadcasting** 2

8 The peace of God, which passeth all understanding, shall keep your hearts and minds through Christ Jesus.
Bible: Philippians

9 They make a wilderness and call it peace.
Tacitus AD c.56–after 117: *Agricola*

10 The naked, poor, and manglèd Peace,

Dear nurse of arts, plenties, and joyful births.
William Shakespeare 1564–1616: *Henry V* (1599)

11 . . . Peace hath her victories
No less renowned than war.
John Milton 1608–74: 'To the Lord General Cromwell' (written 1652)

12 It's a maxim not to be despised, 'Though peace be made, yet it's interest that keeps peace.'
Oliver Cromwell 1599–1658: speech to Parliament, 4 September 1654

13 Give peace in our time, O Lord.
The Book of Common Prayer 1662: *Morning Prayer*; see 21 below

14 Lord Salisbury and myself have brought you back peace—but a peace I hope with honour.
Benjamin Disraeli 1804–81: speech on returning from the Congress of Berlin, 16 July 1878; see 6 above, 21 below

15 In the arts of peace Man is a bungler.
George Bernard Shaw 1856–1950: *Man and Superman* (1903)

16 War makes rattling good history; but Peace is poor reading.
Thomas Hardy 1840–1928: *The Dynasts* (1904)

17 It is easier to make war than to make peace.
Georges Clemenceau 1841–1929: speech at Verdun, 20 July 1919

18 Peace is indivisible.
Maxim Litvinov 1876–1951: note to the Allies, 25 February 1920

19 I have many times asked myself whether there can be more potent advocates of peace upon earth through the years to come than this massed multitude of silent witnesses to the desolation of war.
George V 1865–1936: message read at Terlincthun Cemetery, Boulogne, 13 May 1922

20 I am not only a pacifist but a militant pacifist. I am willing to fight for peace.

Nothing will end war unless the people themselves refuse to go to war.
Albert Einstein 1879–1955: interview with G. S. Viereck, January 1931

21 This is the second time in our history that there has come back from Germany to Downing Street peace with honour. I believe it is peace for our time.
Neville Chamberlain 1869–1940: speech from 10 Downing Street, 30 September 1938; see 13, 14 above

22 One observes, they have gone too long without a war here. Where is morality to come from in such a case, I ask? Peace is nothing but slovenliness, only war creates order.
Bertolt Brecht 1898–1956: *Mother Courage* (1939)

23 Go placidly amid the noise and the haste, and remember what peace there may be in silence.
Max Ehrmann 1872–1945: 'Desiderata' (1948); often wrongly dated to 1692, the date of foundation of a church in Baltimore whose vicar circulated the poem in 1956

24 The work, my friend, is peace. More than an end of this war—an end to the beginnings of all wars.
Franklin D. Roosevelt 1882–1945: undelivered address for Jefferson Day, 13 April 1945 (the day after Roosevelt died)

25 The grim fact is that we prepare for war like precocious giants and for peace like retarded pygmies.
Lester Pearson 1897–1972: speech in Toronto, 14 March 1955

26 I think that people want peace so much that one of these days governments had better get out of the way and let them have it.
Dwight D. Eisenhower 1890–1969: broadcast discussion, 31 August 1959

27 You can't separate peace from freedom because no one can be at peace unless he has his freedom.
Malcolm X 1925–65: speech in New York, 7 January 1965

28 Give peace a chance.
John Lennon 1940–80 and **Paul McCartney** 1942– : title of song (1969)

29 Kissinger brought peace to Vietnam the same way Napoleon brought peace to Europe: by losing.
Joseph Heller 1923–99: *Good as Gold* (1979)

30 Enough of blood and tears. Enough.
Yitzhak Rabin 1922–95: at the signing of the Israel-Palestine Declaration, Washington, 13 September 1993

31 You can't switch on peace like a light.
Mo Mowlam 1949– : in *Independent* 6 September 1999

People see also Musicians, Poets, The Presidency, Writers

PROVERBS AND SAYINGS

1 **The cat, the rat, and Lovell the dog, rule all England under the hog.**
contemporary rhyme referring to William Catesby, Richard Ratcliffe, and Francis Lovell, favourites of Richard III (1452–85), whose personal emblem was a white boar

PHRASES

2 **the Angelic Doctor** St Thomas Aquinas (1225–74), Italian philosopher, theologian, and Dominican friar.

3 **the Black Prince** Edward, Prince of Wales (1330–76), eldest son of Edward III of England.
the name Black Prince apparently derives from the black armour he wore when fighting

4 **Bonnie Prince Charlie** Charles Edward Stuart, the Young Pretender.
Scottish appellation for Charles Edward Stuart, who led the Jacobite uprising of 1745–6; see 24 below

5 **the Corsican ogre** Napoleon I (1769–1821), Emperor of France.
in reference to his Corsican birthplace; see 13 below

6 **the Desert Fox** Erwin Rommel (1891–1944), German Field Marshal.
from his early successes in the North African campaign, 1941–2

7 **the Grand Old Man** William Ewart Gladstone (1809–98).
recorded from 1882, and popularly abbreviated as GOM; Gladstone won his last election in 1892 at the age of eighty-three

8 the Great Deliverer William III of Great Britain (1650-1702).

in reference to William's role in securing the Protestant succession on the overthrow of his Catholic father-in-law, James II, in 1688

9 the Iron Duke the first Duke of Wellington (1769-1852).

10 the Iron Lady Margaret Thatcher (1925-).

name given to Margaret Thatcher in 1976 by the Soviet newspaper Red Star, which accused her of trying to revive the cold war

11 the Jersey Lily the actresss Lillie Langtry, (1853-1929).

born in Jersey, she was noted for her beauty and became known as 'the Jersey Lily' from the title of a portrait of her painted by Millais

12 the Lady of the Lamp Florence Nightingale (1820-1910), English nurse and medical reformer.

from her nightly rounds in army hospital at Scutari in the Crimean War

13 the little Corporal Napoleon I.

referring to his rank in the French Revolutionary army, and his diminutive height; see 5 above

14 the Maid of Orleans Joan of Arc (c.1412-31).

translation of French la Pucelle; Orleans in reference to her relieving of the besieged city in 1429

15 the Merry Monarch Charles II (1630-85).

from Rochester: see 30 below

16 the Nine Days' Queen Lady Jane Grey (1537-54).

named as his successor by her cousin, the dying Edward VI, she was deposed after nine days on the throne, and was executed in the following year

17 Old Blood and Guts George Patton (1885-1945).

name given to General Patton by his men; see **Warfare** *48*

18 the Old Pretender James Stuart (1688-1766), the son of the exiled James II of England, and focus of Jacobite loyalties.

from his assertion of his claim to the British throne against the house of Hanover; see 24 below, **Royalty** *20,* **Writers** *20*

19 the People's William William Ewart Gladstone (1809-98), British Liberal statesman.

coined by the newspaper proprietor Edward Levy-Lawson (1833-1916)

20 the Scourge of God Attila, the leader of the Huns in the 5th century AD.

translation of Latin flagellum Dei

21 Stupor Mundi Frederick II (1194-1250), Holy Roman Emperor.

Latin = wonder of the world

22 the Widow at Windsor Queen Victoria (1819-1901).

the Queen's husband, Prince Albert, predeceased her by forty years

23 the Young Chevalier Charles Edward Stuart, the Young Pretender.

his father, James Stuart, the Old Pretender, was known by the sobriquet of The Chevalier (de St George); see 4 above, 24 below

24 the Young Pretender Charles Edward Stuart (1720-88).

son of James Stuart, the Old Pretender, who asserted the Stuart claim to the British throne against the house of Hanover: see 4, 18, 23 above, **Royalty** *20*

QUOTATIONS

25 The master of those who know.
of Aristotle
Dante Alighieri 1265-1321: *Divina Commedia* 'Inferno'

26 As time requireth, a man of marvellous mirth and pastimes, and sometime of as sad gravity, as who say: a man for all seasons.
of Sir Thomas More
Robert Whittington: *Vulgaria* (1521); see **Character** 23

27 The wisest fool in Christendom.
of James I of England
Henri IV (of Navarre) 1553-1610: attributed both to Henri IV and Sully

28 Had Cleopatra's nose been shorter, the whole face of the world would have changed.
Blaise Pascal 1623-62: *Pensées* (1670)

29 He had a head to contrive, a tongue to persuade, and a hand to execute any mischief.
of the Parliamentarian John Hampden
Edward Hyde, Earl of Clarendon 1609-74: *The History of the Rebellion* (1703)

30 A merry monarch, scandalous and poor.
John Wilmot, Lord Rochester 1647-80: 'A Satire on King Charles II' (1697); see 15 above

31 Our Garrick's a salad; for in him we see

Oil, vinegar, sugar, and saltness agree.
of David Garrick
Oliver Goldsmith 1728–74: *Retaliation* (1774)

32 He snatched the lightning shaft from heaven, and the sceptre from tyrants.
of Benjamin Franklin, inventor of the lightning conductor and American statesman
A. R. J. Turgot 1727–81: inscription for a bust

33 If a man were to go by chance at the same time with Burke under a shed, to shun a shower, he would say—'this is an extraordinary man.'
of Edmund Burke
Samuel Johnson 1709–84: James Boswell *Life of Samuel Johnson* (1791) 15 May 1784

34 That hyena in petticoats, Mrs Wollstonecraft.
of Mary Wollstonecraft
Horace Walpole 1717–97: letter to Hannah More, 26 January 1795

35 Mad, bad, and dangerous to know.
of Byron, after their first meeting
Lady Caroline Lamb 1785–1828: diary, March 1812; Elizabeth Jenkins *Lady Caroline Lamb* (1932)

36 An Archangel a little damaged.
of Coleridge
Charles Lamb 1775–1834: letter to Wordsworth, 26 April 1816

37 The seagreen Incorruptible.
of Robespierre
Thomas Carlyle 1795–1881: *History of the French Revolution* (1837)

38 He has occasional flashes of silence, that make his conversation perfectly delightful.
of Macaulay
Sydney Smith 1771–1845: Lady Holland *Memoir* (1855)

39 A sophistical rhetorician, inebriated with the exuberance of his own verbosity.
of Gladstone
Benjamin Disraeli 1804–81: in *The Times* 29 July 1878

40 He was imperfect, unfinished, inartistic; he was worse than provincial—he was parochial.
of H. D. Thoreau
Henry James 1843–1916: *Hawthorne* (1879)

41 There never was a Churchill from John of Marlborough down that had either morals or principles.
W. E. Gladstone 1809–98: in conversation in 1882, recorded by Captain R. V. Briscoe; R. F. Foster *Lord Randolph Churchill* (1981)

42 A lath of wood painted to look like iron.
of Lord Salisbury
Otto von Bismarck 1815–98: attributed, but vigorously denied by Sidney Whitman in *Personal Reminiscences of Prince Bismarck* (1902)

43 Her conception of God was certainly not orthodox. She felt towards Him as she might have felt towards a glorified sanitary engineer; and in some of her speculations she seems hardly to distinguish between the Deity and the Drains.
Lytton Strachey 1880–1932: *Eminent Victorians* (1918) 'Florence Nightingale'

44 A good man fallen among Fabians.
of George Bernard Shaw
Lenin 1870–1924: Arthur Ransome *Six Weeks in Russia in 1919* (1919) 'Notes of Conversations with Lenin'

45 He seemed at ease and to have the look of the last gentleman in Europe.
of Oscar Wilde
Ada Leverson 1865–1936: *Letters to the Sphinx* (1930)

46 I remember, when I was a child, being taken to the celebrated Barnum's circus, which contained an exhibition of freaks and monstrosities, but the exhibit on the programme which I most desired to see was the one described as 'The Boneless Wonder'. My parents judged that that spectacle would be too revolting and demoralizing for my youthful eyes, and I have waited 50 years to see the boneless wonder sitting on the Treasury Bench.
of Ramsay MacDonald
Winston Churchill 1874–1965: speech in the House of Commons, 28 January 1931; see **The Body** 4

47 This extraordinary figure of our time, this syren, this goat-footed bard, this half-human visitor to our age from the hag-ridden magic and enchanted woods of Celtic antiquity.
John Maynard Keynes 1883–1946: *Essays in Biography* (1933) 'Mr Lloyd George'

48 To us he is no more a person now but a whole climate of opinion.
W. H. Auden 1907–73: 'In Memory of Sigmund Freud' (1940)

49 If only Bapu knew the cost of setting him up in poverty!
of Mahatma Gandhi
Sarojini Naidu 1879–1949: A. Campbell-Johnson *Mission with Mountbatten* (1951)

50 He can't see a belt without hitting below it.
of Lloyd George
Margot Asquith 1864–1945: in *Listener* 11 June 1953

51 A modest man who has a good deal to be modest about.
of Clement Attlee
Winston Churchill 1874–1965: in *Chicago Sunday Tribune Magazine of Books* 27 June 1954

52 In a world of voluble hates, he plotted to make men like, or at least tolerate one another.
of Stanley Baldwin
G. M. Trevelyan 1876–1962: in *Dictionary of National Biography 1941–50* (1959)

53 What, when drunk, one sees in other women, one sees in Garbo sober.
of Greta Garbo
Kenneth Tynan 1927–80: *Curtains* (1961)

54 Too clever by half.
of Iain Macleod; the term had been applied by an earlier Lord Salisbury (1830–1903) to Disraeli's amendment on Disestablishment, 30 March 1868. See **Intelligence** 5
Lord Salisbury 1893–1972: speech, House of Lords, 7 March 1961

55 She would rather light a candle than curse the darkness, and her glow has warmed the world.
on learning of Eleanor Roosevelt's death
Adlai Stevenson 1900–65: in *New York Times* 8 November 1962

56 In defeat unbeatable: in victory unbearable.
of Lord Montgomery
Winston Churchill 1874–1965: Edward Marsh *Ambrosia and Small Beer* (1964)

57 No, *no. Jimmy Stewart* for governor— Reagan for his best friend.
on hearing that Ronald Reagan was seeking nomination as Governor of California, 1966
Jack Warner 1892–1978: Max Wilk *The Wit and Wisdom of Hollywood* (1972)

58 The Stag at Bay with the mentality of a fox at large.
of Harold Macmillan
Bernard Levin 1928– : *The Pendulum Years* (1970)

59 It is not necessary that every time he rises he should give his famous imitation of a semi-house-trained polecat.
of Norman Tebbit
Michael Foot 1913– : speech, House of Commons, 2 March 1978

60 She cannot see an institution without hitting it with her handbag.
of Margaret Thatcher
Julian Critchley 1930–2000: in *The Times* 21 June 1982

61 Comrades, this man has a nice smile, but he's got iron teeth.
of Mikhail Gorbachev
Andrei Gromyko 1909–89: speech to Soviet Communist Party Central Committee, 11 March 1985

62 She has the eyes of Caligula, but the mouth of Marilyn Monroe.
of Margaret Thatcher
François Mitterrand 1916–96: comment to his new European Minister Roland Dumas; in *Observer* 25 November 1990

63 A man who so much resembled a Baked Alaska—sweet, warm and gungy on the outside, hard and cold within.
of C. P. Snow
Francis King 1923– : *Yesterday Came Suddenly* (1993)

64 She's a gay man trapped in a woman's body.
of Madonna
Boy George 1961– : *Take It Like a Man* (1995)

65 She was the People's Princess, and that is how she will stay . . . in our hearts and in our memories forever.
Tony Blair 1953– : on hearing of the death of Diana, Princess of Wales, 31 August 1997

Peoples see Countries and Peoples

Perfection see also Excellence and Mediocrity

1 **Trifles make perfection, but perfection is no trifle.**
American proverb, mid 20th century

2 Nothing is an unmixed blessing.
Horace 65-8 BC: *Odes*

3 How many things by season seasoned are
To their right praise and true perfection!
William Shakespeare 1564-1616: *The Merchant of Venice* (1596-8)

4 Perfection is the child of Time.
Joseph Hall 1574-1656: *Works* (1625)

5 Whoever thinks a faultless piece to see,
Thinks what ne'er was, nor is, nor e'er shall be.
Alexander Pope 1688-1744: *An Essay on Criticism* (1711)

6 Pictures of perfection as you know make me sick and wicked.
Jane Austen 1775-1817: letter to Fanny Knight, 23 March 1817

7 Faultily faultless, icily regular, splendidly null,
Dead perfection, no more.
Alfred, Lord Tennyson 1809-92: *Maud* (1855)

8 Faultless to a fault.
Robert Browning 1812-89: *The Ring and the Book* (1868-9)

9 The pursuit of perfection, then, is the pursuit of sweetness and light . . . He who works for sweetness and light united, works to make reason and the will of God prevail.
Matthew Arnold 1822-88: *Culture and Anarchy* (1869); see **Virtue** 26

10 Finality is death. Perfection is finality. Nothing is perfect. There are lumps in it.
James Stephens 1882-1950: *The Crock of Gold* (1912)

11 The intellect of man is forced to choose Perfection of the life, or of the work.
W. B. Yeats 1865-1939: 'The Choice' (1933)

12 Perfection is finally attained not when there is no longer anything to add but when there is no longer anything to take away, when a body has been stripped down to its nakedness.
Antoine de Saint-Exupéry 1900-44: *Wind, Sand and Stars* (1939)

13 Perfection is terrible, it cannot have children.
Sylvia Plath 1932-63: 'The Munich Mannequins' (1965)

14 Here we are perfect. Metaphysical greenbirds
Perch over sunlit leaves; our feet converse
With the refreshing grass.
Douglas Dunn 1942- : 'The Garden' (1972)

Perseverance see Determination and Perseverance

Pessimism see Optimisim and Pessimism

Philosophy see also Logic and Reason

1 **How many angels can dance on the head of a pin?**
regarded satirically as a characteristic speculation of scholastic philosophy, particularly as exemplified by 'Doctor Scholasticus' (Anselm of Laon, d. 1117) and as used in medieval comedies; see 7 below

2 **Occam's razor** the principle that in explaining a thing no more assumptions should be made than are necessary.
an ancient philosophical principle often attributed to the English scholastic philosopher William of Occam (c.1285-1349), but earlier in origin; see 5 below

3 The unexamined life is not worth living.
Socrates 469–399 BC: Plato *Apology*

4 There is nothing so absurd but some philosopher has said it.
Cicero 106–43 BC: *De Divinatione*

5 No more things should be presumed to exist than are absolutely necessary.
William of Occam c.1285–1349: not found in this form in his writings, although he frequently used similar expressions, e.g. 'Plurality should not be assumed unnecessarily'; *Quodlibeta* (c.1324); see 2 above

6 How charming is divine philosophy!
Not harsh and crabbèd, as dull fools suppose,
But musical as is Apollo's lute.
John Milton 1608–74: *Comus* (1637)

7 Some who are far from atheists, may make themselves merry with that conceit of thousands of spirits dancing at once upon a needle's point.
Ralph Cudworth 1617–88: *The True Intellectual System of the Universe* (1678); see 1 above

8 The same principles which at first lead to scepticism, pursued to a certain point bring men back to common sense.
George Berkeley 1685–1753: *Three Dialogues between Hylas and Philonous* (1734)

9 Superstition sets the whole world in flames; philosophy quenches them.
Voltaire 1694–1778: *Dictionnaire philosophique* (1764) 'Superstition'

10 I have tried too in my time to be a philosopher; but, I don't know how, cheerfulness was always breaking in.
Oliver Edwards 1711–91: James Boswell *Life of Samuel Johnson* (1791) 17 April 1778

11 I am tempted to say of metaphysicians what Scaliger used to say of the Basques: they are said to understand one another, but I don't believe a word of it.
Nicolas-Sébastien Chamfort 1741–94: *Maximes et Pensées* (1796)

12 When philosophy paints its grey on grey, then has a shape of life grown old. By philosophy's grey on grey it cannot be rejuvenated but only understood. The owl of Minerva spreads its wings only with the falling of the dusk.
G. W. F. Hegel 1770–1831: *Philosophy of Right* (1821)

13 The philosophers have only interpreted the world in various ways; the point is to change it.
Karl Marx 1818–83: *Theses on Feuerbach* (written 1845, published 1888)

14 Metaphysics is the finding of bad reasons for what we believe upon instinct; but to find these reasons is no less an instinct.
F. H. Bradley 1846–1924: *Appearance and Reality* (1893)

15 What I understand by 'philosopher': a terrible explosive in the presence of which everything is in danger.
Friedrich Nietzsche 1844–1900: *Ecce Homo* (1908) 'Die Unzeitgemässen'

16 The Socratic manner is not a game at which two can play.
Max Beerbohm 1872–1956: *Zuleika Dobson* (1911)

17 He [Wittgenstein] thinks nothing empirical is Knowable—I asked him to admit that there was not a rhinoceros in the room, but he wouldn't.
Bertrand Russell 1872–1970: letter to Lady Ottoline Morrell, November 1911

18 The safest general characterization of the European philosophical tradition is that it consists of a series of footnotes to Plato.
Alfred North Whitehead 1861–1947: *Process and Reality* (1929)

19 To ask the hard question is simple.
W. H. Auden 1907–73: title of poem (1933)

20 What is your aim in philosophy?—To show the fly the way out of the fly-bottle.
Ludwig Wittgenstein 1889–1951: *Philosophische Untersuchungen* (1953)

21 Students of the heavens are separable into astronomers and astrologers as readily as are the minor domestic ruminants into sheep and goats, but the separation of philosophers into sages and cranks seems to be more sensitive to frames of reference.
W. V. O. Quine 1908– : *Theories and Things* (1981)

22 What we do today, we don't have to do tomorrow. We don't even *think* about tomorrow. I was tellin' somebody that the other day; they say that's *existentialism*. I say, well, they probably copied that off of me.
Miles Davis 1926–91: Charles Shaar Murray *Shots From the Hip* (1991)

Photography

PROVERBS AND SAYINGS

1 The camera never lies.
20th century saying; see 7 below

PHRASES

2 candid camera the technique of photographing or filming people without their knowledge, chiefly in situations set up for the amusement of television viewers.

QUOTATIONS

3 I longed to arrest all beauty that came before me, and at length the longing has been satisfied.
Julia Margaret Cameron 1815–79: *Annals of My Glass House* (1874)

4 The photographer is like the cod which produces a million eggs in order that one may reach maturity.
George Bernard Shaw 1856–1950: introduction to the catalogue for Alvin Langdon Coburn's exhibition at the Royal Photographic Society, 1906; Bill Jay and Margaret Moore *Bernard Shaw and Photography* (1989)

5 To me, photography is the simultaneous recognition, in a fraction of a second, of the significance of an event as well as of a precise organization of forms which give that event its proper expression.
Henri Cartier-Bresson 1908– : *The Decisive Moment* (1952)

6 If your pictures aren't good enough, you aren't close enough.
of photojournalism
Robert Capa 1913–54: Russell Miller *Magnum: Fifty years at the Front Line of History* (1997)

7 The camera's eye
Does not lie,
But it cannot show
The life within.
W. H. Auden 1907–73: 'Runner' (1962); see 1 above

8 Nothing attracts me like a closed door. I cannot let my camera rest until I have pried it open.
Margaret Bourke-White 1906–71: *Portrait of Myself* (1964)

9 A photograph is a secret about a secret. The more it tells you the less you know.
Diane Arbus 1923–71: Patricia Bosworth *Diane Arbus: a Biography* (1985)

10 A photograph is not only an image (as a painting is an image), an interpretation of the real; it is also a trace, something directly stencilled off the real, like a footprint or a death mask.
Susan Sontag 1933– : in *New York Review of Books* 23 June 1977

11 It takes a lot of imagination to be a good photographer. You need less imagination to be a painter, because you can invent things. But in photography everything is so ordinary; it takes a lot of looking before you learn to see the ordinary.
David Bailey 1938– : interview in *The Face* December 1984

12 All you can do with most ordinary photographs is stare at them—they stare back, blankly—and presently your concentration begins to fade. They stare you down. I mean, photography is all right if you don't mind looking at the world from the point of view of a paralysed cyclops—*for a split second*.
David Hockney 1937– : as told to Lawrence Weschler, *Cameraworks* (1984)

13 Most things in life are moments of pleasure and a lifetime of embarrassment; photography is a moment of embarrassment and a lifetime of pleasure.
Tony Benn 1925– : in *Independent* 21 October 1989

14 It's more important to click with people than to click the shutter.
Alfred Eisenstaedt 1898–1995: in *Life* 24 August 1995

Physical Sciences see also Science

1 **cold fusion** nuclear fusion occurring at or close to room temperature.
claims for its discovery in 1989 are generally held to have been mistaken

2 **fourth dimension** a postulated spatial dimension additional to those determining length, area, and volume.
the phrase is recorded from the late 19th century, and is now also used in physics to denote time as analogous to linear dimensions

3 **laws of thermodynamics** three laws describing the general direction of physical change in the universe.
see 10, 16 below; see also Arts and Sciences 14

4 **Maxwell's demon** a hypothetical being imagined as controlling a hole in a partition dividing a gas-filled container into two parts, and allowing only fast-moving molecules to pass in one direction, and slow-moving molecules in the other.
this would result in one side of the container becoming warmer and the other colder, in violation of the second law of thermodynamics. The name derives from the Scottish physicist James Clerk Maxwell (1831–79); see 16 below

5 **perpetual motion** the motion of a hypothetical machine which, once activated, would run forever unless subject to an external force or to wear.
although impossible according to the first and second laws of thermodynamics, the development of such a mechanism has been attempted by many inventors; see 3 above

6 **quark confinement** the hypothesis that free quarks can never be seen in isolation.
quark any of a number of subatomic particles carrying a fractional electric charge, postulated as building blocks of the hadrons. The name (originally quork) was invented in the 1960s by Murray Gell-Mann; it was changed by association with the line 'Three quarks for Muster Mark' in Joyce's Finnegans Wake (1939)

7 **Schrödinger's cat** a paradox concerning a cat in a sealed box containing a lethal device triggered by radioactive decay; an outside observer cannot know whether the device has been set off and the cat killed. According to quantum mechanics the cat is in an indeterminate state, some

combination of alive and dead, until the box is opened, at which point it will be found to be one or the other.
suggested in 1935 by the Austrian theoretical physicist Erwin Schrödinger (1887–1961), to illustrate the conceptual difficulties of quantum mechanics

8 **uncertainty principle** the principle that the momentum and position of a particle cannot both be precisely determined at the same time.
see Ideas 12, Science 26

9 There was a young lady named Bright,
Whose speed was far faster than light;
She set out one day
In a relative way
And returned on the previous night.
Arthur Buller 1874–1944: 'Relativity' in *Punch* 19 December 1923

10 If someone points out to you that your pet theory of the universe is in disagreement with Maxwell's equations—then so much the worse for Maxwell's equations. If it is found to be contradicted by observation—well, these experimentalists do bungle things sometimes. But if your theory is found to be against the second law of thermodynamics I can give you no hope; there is nothing for it but to collapse in deepest humiliation.
Arthur Eddington 1882–1944: *The Nature of the Physical World* (1928); see 3 above

11 If we assume that the last breath of, say, Julius Caesar has by now become thoroughly scattered through the atmosphere, then the chances are that each of us inhales one molecule of it with every breath we take.
now usually quoted as the 'dying breath of Socrates'
James Jeans 1877–1946: *An Introduction to the Kinetic Theory of Gases* (1940)

12 When Rutherford was done with the atom all the solidity was pretty well knocked out of it.
Stephen Leacock 1869–1944: *The Boy I Left Behind Me* (1947)

13 I remembered the line from the Hindu scripture, the *Bhagavad Gita* . . . 'I am become death, the destroyer of worlds.'

on the explosion of the first atomic bomb near Alamogordo, New Mexico, 16 July 1945

J. Robert Oppenheimer 1904–67: Len Giovannitti and Fred Freed *The Decision to Drop the Bomb* (1965)

14 In some sort of crude sense which no vulgarity, no humour, no overstatement can quite extinguish, the physicists have known sin; and this is a knowledge which they cannot lose.

J. Robert Oppenheimer 1904–67: lecture at Massachusetts Institute of Technology, 25 November 1947

15 If I could remember the names of all these particles I'd be a botanist.

Enrico Fermi 1901–54: R. L. Weber *More Random Walks in Science* (1973)

16 Heat won't pass from a cooler to a hotter, You can try it if you like but you'd far better notter.

Michael Flanders 1922–75 and **Donald Swann** 1923–94: 'The First and Second Law' (1956 song); see 3, 4 above

17 It would be a poor thing to be an atom in a world without physicists. And physicists are made of atoms. A physicist is an atom's way of knowing about atoms.

George Wald 1904–97: foreword to L. J. Henderson *The Fitness of the Environment* (1958)

18 We do not know why they have the masses they do; we do not know why they transform into another the way they do; we do not know anything! The one concept that stands like the Rock of Gibraltar in our sea of confusion is the Pauli [exclusion] principle.

of elementary particles

George Gamow 1904–68: in *Scientific American* July 1959

19 Anybody who is not shocked by this subject has failed to understand it.

of quantum mechanics

Niels Bohr 1885–1962: attributed; in *Nature* 23 August 1990

20 Neutrinos, they are very small They have no charge and have no mass And do not interact at all.

John Updike 1932– : 'Cosmic Gall ' (1964)

21 There is no democracy in physics. We can't say that some second-rate guy has as much right to opinion as Fermi.

Luis Walter Alvarez 1911–88: D. S. Greenberg *The Politics of Pure Science* (1969)

22 I am acutely aware of the fact that the marriage between mathematics and physics, which was so enormously fruitful in past centuries, has recently ended in divorce.

Freeman Dyson 1923– : in *Bulletin of the American Mathematical Society* September 1972

23 The trade of chemist (fortified, in my case, by the experience of Auschwitz) teaches you to overcome, indeed to ignore, certain revulsions that are neither necessary or congenital: matter is matter, neither noble nor vile, infinitely transformable, and its proximate origin is of no importance whatsoever. Nitrogen is nitrogen, it passes miraculously from the air into plants, from these into animals, from animals into us; when its function in our body is exhausted, we eliminate it, but it still remains nitrogen, aseptic, innocent.

Primo Levi 1919–87: *The Periodic Table* (1975)

24 Good morning, and a special welcome to those of you who are new to the field of quantum solar energy conversion.

opening a lecture at Strathclyde University, immediately after her husband's trial for perjury; the audience included many journalists

Mary Archer 1944– : in *Sunday Times* 29 July 2001

Pleasure

PROVERBS AND SAYINGS

1 A good time was had by all.

title of a collection of poems published in 1937 by Stevie Smith (1902–71), taken from the characteristic conclusion of accounts of social events in parish magazines

2 Stop me and buy one.

Wall's ice cream, from spring 1922

PHRASES

3 cakes and ale merrymaking, good things.

from Shakespeare Twelfth Night: *see* **Virtue** 22

4 forbidden fruit illicit pleasure.
the fruit forbidden to Adam in the Bible (Genesis) 'But of the tree of the knowledge of good and evil, thou shalt not eat of it'

5 pleased as Punch showing or feeling great pleasure.
Punch the grotesque hook-nosed humpbacked principal character of Punch and Judy, a traditional puppet-show in which Punch is shown nagging, beating, and finally killing a succession of characters, including his wife Judy

6 the primrose path the pursuit of pleasure, especially with disastrous consequences.
in allusion to Shakespeare Hamlet: see Words and Deeds 12

7 a song in one's heart a feeling of joy or pleasure.
originally with allusion to Lorenz Hart 'With a Song in my Heart', 1930 song

8 teddy bears' picnic an occasion of innocent enjoyment.
a song (c.1932) by Jimmy Kennedy and J. W. Bratton

9 wine, women, and song proverbially required by men for carefree entertainment and pleasure.
see 11 below

QUOTATIONS

10 Everyone is dragged on by their favourite pleasure.
Virgil 70–19 BC: *Eclogues*

11 Who loves not woman, wine, and song
Remains a fool his whole life long.
Martin Luther 1483–1546: attributed; later inscribed in the Luther room in the Wartburg, but with no proof of authorship; see 9 above, 18 below

12 Pleasure is nothing else but the intermission of pain.
John Selden 1584–1654: *Table Talk* (1689) 'Pleasure'

13 I shouldn't be surprised if the greatest rule of all weren't to give pleasure.
Molière 1622–73: *La Critique de l'école des femmes* (1663)

14 Music and women I cannot but give way to, whatever my business is.
Samuel Pepys 1633–1703: diary 9 March 1666

15 Great lords have their pleasures, but the people have fun.
Montesquieu 1689–1755: *Pensées et fragments inédits . . .* vol. 2 (1901)

16 A man enjoys the happiness he feels, a woman the happiness she gives.
Pierre Choderlos de Laclos 1741–1803: *Les Liaisons dangereuses* (1782)

17 One half of the world cannot understand the pleasures of the other.
Jane Austen 1775–1817: *Emma* (1816)

18 Let us have wine and women, mirth and laughter,
Sermons and soda-water the day after.
Lord Byron 1788–1824: *Don Juan* (1819–24); see 11 above

19 The greatest pleasure I know, is to do a good action by stealth, and to have it found out by accident.
Charles Lamb 1775–1834: 'Table Talk by the late Elia' in *The Athenaeum* 4 January 1834

20 The Puritan hated bear-baiting, not because it gave pain to the bear, but because it gave pleasure to the spectators.
Lord Macaulay 1800–59: *History of England* vol. 1 (1849)

21 The great pleasure in life is doing what people say you cannot do.
Walter Bagehot 1826–77: in *Prospective Review* 1853 'Shakespeare'

22 A fool bolts pleasure, then complains of moral indigestion.
Minna Antrim 1861–1950: *Naked Truth and Veiled Allusions* (1902)

23 Lying in bed would be an altogether perfect and supreme experience if only one had a coloured pencil long enough to draw on the ceiling.
G. K. Chesterton 1874–1936: *Tremendous Trifles* (1909) 'On Lying in Bed'

24 It's always the good feel rotten. Pleasure's for those who are bad.
Sergei Yesenin 1895–1925: 'Pleasure's for the Bad' (1923)

25 It is a curious thing that people only ask if you are enjoying yourself when you aren't.
Edith Nesbit 1858–1924: *Five of Us, and Madeline* (1925)

26 I admit it is better fun to punt than to be punted, and that a desire to have all the fun is nine-tenths of the law of chivalry.
Dorothy L. Sayers 1893–1957: *Gaudy Night* (1935)

27 People must not do things for fun. We are not here for fun. There is no reference to fun in any Act of Parliament.
A. P. Herbert 1890–1971: *Uncommon Law* (1935)

28 All the things I really like to do are either illegal, immoral, or fattening.
Alexander Woollcott 1887–1943: R. E. Drennan *Wit's End* (1973)

29 In love, as in gluttony, pleasure is a matter of the utmost precision.
Italo Calvino 1923–85: Charles Fourier *Theory of the Four Movements* (1971)

30 There's no greater bliss in life than when the plumber eventually comes to unblock your drains. No writer can give that sort of pleasure.
Victoria Glendinning 1937– : in *Observer* 3 January 1993

31 No pleasure is worth giving up for the sake of two more years in a geriatric home in Weston-super-Mare.
Kingsley Amis 1922–95: in *The Times* 21 June 1994; attributed

---

Poetry see also **Writing**

PHRASES

1 the gay science the art of poetry.
Provencal gai saber; see **Economics** *3*

2 Mount Parnassus poetry.
a mountain in central Greece, just north of Delphi. Held to be sacred by the ancient Greeks, it was associated with Apollo and the Muses

3 the Pierian spring the source of poetic inspiration.
from Pieria, a district in northern Thessaly, that in classical mythology was reputed home of the Muses and the location of a spring sacred to them; see **Knowledge** *29*

4 stuffed owl of poetry which treats trivial or inconsequential subjects in a grandiose manner.
the stuffed owl title of 'an anthology of bad verse' (1930); ultimately from Wordsworth Miscellaneous Sonnets (1827) 'The presence even of a stuffed owl for her Can cheat the time'

QUOTATIONS

5 Skilled or unskilled, we all scribble poems.
Horace 65–8 BC: *Epistles*

6 'By God,' quod he, 'for pleynly, at a word, Thy drasty rymyng is nat worth a toord!'
Geoffrey Chaucer c.1343–1400: *The Canterbury Tales* 'Sir Thopas'

7 I am two fools, I know,
For loving, and for saying so
In whining poetry.
John Donne 1572–1631: 'The Triple Fool'

8 All poets are mad.
Robert Burton 1577–1640: *The Anatomy of Melancholy* (1621–51) 'Democritus to the Reader'

9 For rhyme the rudder is of verses, With which like ships they steer their courses.
Samuel Butler 1612–80: *Hudibras* pt. 1 (1663)

10 Rhyme being no necessary adjunct or true ornament of poem or good verse, in longer works especially, but the invention of a barbarous age, to set off wretched matter and lame metre.
John Milton 1608–74: *Paradise Lost* (1667) 'The Verse' (preface, added 1668)

11 All that is not prose is verse; and all that is not verse is prose.
Molière 1622–73: *Le Bourgeois Gentilhomme* (1671)

12 BOSWELL: Sir, what is poetry?
JOHNSON: Why Sir, it is much easier to say what it is not. We all *know* what light is; but it is not easy to *tell* what it is.
Samuel Johnson 1709–84: James Boswell *Life of Samuel Johnson* (1791) 12 April 1776

13 Some rhyme a neebor's name to lash;
Some rhyme (vain thought!) for needfu' cash;
Some rhyme to court the countra clash,
An' raise a din;
For me, an aim I never fash;
I rhyme for fun.
Robert Burns 1759–96: 'To J. S[mith]' (1786)

14 Poetry is the spontaneous overflow of powerful feelings: it takes its origin from emotion recollected in tranquillity.
William Wordsworth 1770–1850: *Lyrical Ballads* (2nd ed., 1802)

15 That willing suspension of disbelief for the moment, which constitutes poetic faith.
Samuel Taylor Coleridge 1772–1834: *Biographia Literaria* (1817)

16 If poetry comes not as naturally as the leaves to a tree it had better not come at all.

John Keats 1795–1821: letter to John Taylor, 27 February 1818

17 Poetry is the record of the best and happiest moments of the happiest and best minds.

Percy Bysshe Shelley 1792–1822: *A Defence of Poetry* (written 1821)

18 Poets are the unacknowledged legislators of the world.

Percy Bysshe Shelley 1792–1822: *A Defence of Poetry* (written 1821)

19 Prose = words in their best order;—poetry = the *best* words in the best order.

Samuel Taylor Coleridge 1772–1834: *Table Talk* (1835) 12 July 1827

20 Prose is when all the lines except the last go on to the end. Poetry is when some of them fall short of it.

Jeremy Bentham 1748–1832: M. St. J. Packe *The Life of John Stuart Mill* (1954)

21 What is a modern poet's fate?
To write his thoughts upon a slate;
The critic spits on what is done,
Gives it a wipe—and all is gone.

Thomas Hood 1799–1845: 'A Joke'; Hallam Tennyson *Alfred Lord Tennyson* (1897)

22 Everything you invent is true: you can be sure of that. Poetry is a subject as precise as geometry.

Gustave Flaubert 1821–80: letter to Louise Colet, 14 August 1853

23 The difference between genuine poetry and the poetry of Dryden, Pope, and all their school, is briefly this: their poetry is conceived and composed in their wits, genuine poetry is conceived and composed in the soul.

Matthew Arnold 1822–88: *Essays in Criticism Second Series* (1888) 'Thomas Gray'

24 I said 'a line will take us hours maybe,
Yet if it does not seem a moment's thought
Our stitching and unstitching has been naught.'

W. B. Yeats 1865–1939: 'Adam's Curse' (1904)

25 All a poet can do today is warn.

Wilfred Owen 1893–1918: preface (written 1918) in *Poems* (1963)

26 Poetry is not a turning loose of emotion, but an escape from emotion; it is not the expression of personality but an escape from personality.

T. S. Eliot 1888–1965: *The Sacred Wood* (1920) 'Tradition and Individual Talent'

27 A poem should not mean
But be.

Archibald MacLeish 1892–1982: 'Ars Poetica' (1926)

28 In our language rhyme is a barrel. A barrel of dynamite. The line is a fuse. The line smoulders to the end and explodes; and the town is blown sky-high in a stanza.

Vladimir Mayakovsky 1893–1930: 'Conversation with an Inspector of Taxes about Poetry' (1926)

29 Experience has taught me, when I am shaving of a morning, to keep watch over my thoughts, because, if a line of poetry strays into my memory, my skin bristles so that the razor ceases to act . . . The seat of this sensation is the pit of the stomach.

A. E. Housman 1859–1936: lecture at Cambridge, 9 May 1933

30 Poetry is not the most important thing in life . . . I'd much rather lie in a hot bath reading Agatha Christie and sucking sweets.

Dylan Thomas 1914–53: Joan Wyndham *Love is Blue* (1986) 6 July 1943

31 There's nothing in the world for which a poet will give up writing, not even when he is a Jew and the language of his poems is German.

Paul Celan 1920–70: letter to relatives, 2 August 1948

32 For twenty years I've stared my level best
To see if evening—any evening —would suggest
A patient etherized upon a table;
In vain. I simply wasn't able.
on contemporary poetry

C. S. Lewis 1898–1963: 'A Confession' (1964); see **Day** 15

33 I'd as soon write free verse as play tennis with the net down.

Robert Frost 1874–1963: Edward Lathem *Interviews with Robert Frost* (1966)

34 Most people ignore most poetry
because
most poetry ignores most people.

Adrian Mitchell 1932– : *Poems* (1964)

35 It is barbarous to write a poem after Auschwitz.

Theodor Adorno 1903–69: I. Buruma *Wages of Guilt* (1994)

36 A poet's hope: to be,
like some valley cheese,
local, but prized elsewhere.
W. H. Auden 1907–73: 'Shorts II' (1976)

37 The notion of expressing sentiments in
short lines having similar sounds at their
ends seems as remote as mangoes on the
moon.
Philip Larkin 1922–85: letter to Barbara Pym, 22
January 1975

38 My favourite poem is the one that starts
'Thirty days hath September' because it
actually tells you something.
Groucho Marx 1895–1977: Ned Sherrin *Cutting Edge*
(1984); attributed

39 I think poetry should be alive. You should
be able to dance it.
Benjamin Zephaniah 1958– : in *Sunday Times* 23
August 1987

40 As well as between tongue and teeth,
poetry happens between the ears and
behind the left nipple.
Douglas Dunn 1942– : in *Observer* 23 March 1997

41 The beginning of a poem is always a
moment of tiny revelation, a new way of
seeing something, which almost
simultaneously attracts language to it.
Carol Ann Duffy 1965– : in *Independent* 2 October
1999

Poets

1 the Father of English poetry Geoffrey
Chaucer (*c*.1342–1400).
*regarded as traditional starting-point for English
literature and as the first great English poet*

2 the fleshly school of poetry a group of late
19th-century poets associated with Dante
Gabriel Rossetti.
the term was coined in the Contemporary Review *of
October 1871 by the Scottish writer Robert Buchanan*

3 the Good Gray Poet the American poet
Walt Whitman (1819–92).
*the sobriquet was first applied to him in a book of this
title (1866) by his friend, the journalist William
O'Connor*

4 the Lake Poets the poets Samuel Taylor
Coleridge, Robert Southey, and William
Wordsworth.
they lived in and were inspired by the Lake District

5 the Peasant Poet John Clare (1793–1864).
*his popularity became part of a vogue for rural poetry
and 'ploughman' poets*

6 Poet Laureate an eminent poet appointed
as a member of the British royal
household.
*the Poet Laureate was formerly expected to write
poems for state occasions, but since Victorian times
the post has carried no specific duties*

7 the Theban eagle the Greek lyric poet
Pindar (*c*.518–*c*.438 BC)
*the name derives from three passages in poems by
Pindar in which an eagle is mentioned without its
connection to the context being clear; traditionally,
the bird has been taken as an image of the poet*

QUOTATIONS

8 The worshipful father and first founder and
embellisher of ornate eloquence in our
English, I mean Master Geoffrey Chaucer.
William Caxton *c*.1421–91: Caxton's edition
(*c*.1478) of Chaucer's translation of Boethius *De
Consolacione Philosophie*

9 Dr Donne's verses are like the peace of
God; they pass all understanding.
James I 1566–1625: remark recorded by Archdeacon
Plume (1630–1704)

10 'Tis sufficient to say, according to the
proverb, that here is God's plenty.
of Chaucer
John Dryden 1631–1700: *Fables Ancient and Modern*
(1700)

11 Ev'n copious Dryden, wanted, or forgot,
The last and greatest art, the art to blot.
Alexander Pope 1688–1744: *Imitations of Horace*
(1737)

12 The living throne, the sapphire-blaze,
Where angels tremble, while they gaze,
He saw; but blasted with excess of light,
Closed his eyes in endless night.
of Milton
Thomas Gray 1716–71: *The Progress of Poesy* (1757)

13 Milton, Madam, was a genius that could
cut a Colossus from a rock; but could not
carve heads upon cherry-stones.
*to Hannah More, who had expressed a wonder that
the poet who had written* Paradise Lost *should write
such poor sonnets*
Samuel Johnson 1709–84: James Boswell *Life of
Samuel Johnson* (1791) 13 June 1784

14 The reason Milton wrote in fetters when
he wrote of Angels and God, and at liberty
when of Devils and Hell, is because he was
a true Poet, and of the Devil's party
without knowing it.
William Blake 1757–1827: *The Marriage of Heaven
and Hell* (1790–3)

15 With Donne, whose muse on dromedary
trots,
Wreathe iron pokers into true-love knots.
Samuel Taylor Coleridge 1772–1834: 'On Donne's
Poetry' (1818)

16 A cloud-encircled meteor of the air,
A hooded eagle among blinking owls.
of Coleridge
Percy Bysshe Shelley 1792–1822: 'Letter to Maria
Gisborne' (1820)

17 We learn from Horace, Homer sometimes
sleeps;
We feel without him: Wordsworth
sometimes wakes.
Lord Byron 1788–1824: *Don Juan* (1819–24); see
Mistakes 11

18 He spoke, and loosed our heart in tears.
He laid us as we lay at birth
On the cool flowery lap of earth.
of Wordsworth
Matthew Arnold 1822–88: 'Memorial Verses, April
1850' (1852)

19 In poetry, no less than in life, he is 'a
beautiful and ineffectual angel, beating in
the void his luminous wings in vain'.
Matthew Arnold 1822–88: *Essays in Criticism*
Second Series (1888) 'Shelley' (quoting from his
own essay on Byron in the same work)

20 Chaos, illumined by flashes of lightning.
on Robert Browning's 'style'
Oscar Wilde 1854–1900: Ada Leverson *Letters to
the Sphinx* (1930)

21 You who desired so much—in vain to
ask—
Yet fed your hunger like an endless task,
Dared dignify the labor, bless the quest—
Achieved that stillness ultimately best,
Being, of all, least sought for: Emily, hear!
Hart Crane 1899–1932: 'To Emily Dickinson' (1927)

22 How unpleasant to meet Mr Eliot!
With his features of clerical cut,

And his brow so grim
And his mouth so prim
And his conversation, so nicely
Restricted to What Precisely
And If and Perhaps and But.
T. S. Eliot 1888–1965: 'Five-Finger Exercises' (1936)

23 The high-water mark, so to speak, of
Socialist literature is W. H. Auden, a sort
of gutless Kipling.
George Orwell 1903–50: *The Road to Wigan Pier*
(1937)

24 You were silly like us; your gift survived it
all:
The parish of rich women, physical decay,
Yourself. Mad Ireland hurt you into poetry.
W. H. Auden 1907–73: 'In Memory of W. B. Yeats'
(1940)

25 *Hugo—hélas!*
Hugo—alas!
when asked who was the greatest 19th-century poet
André Gide 1869–1951: Claude Martin *La Maturité
d'André Gide* (1977)

26 To see him fumbling with our rich and
delicate language is to experience all the
horror of seeing a Sèvres vase in the hands
of a chimpanzee.
of Stephen Spender
Evelyn Waugh 1903–66: in *The Tablet* 5 May 1951

27 Self-contempt, well-grounded.
on the foundation of T. S. Eliot's work
F. R. Leavis 1895–1978: in *Times Literary Supplement*
21 October 1988; see **Self-Esteem** 11

28 Auden of the last years, when he had
begun to resemble in his own person an
ample, flopping, ambulatory volume of the
OED in carpet slippers.
Seamus Heaney 1939– : in *London Review of Books*
4 June 1987

29 It has to be said that if Heaney belonged to
an unfashionable race—were he a
Welshman for instance—his poetry—
perfectly pleasant, mild stuff—would have
been lucky to make it into the parish
magazine.
A. N. Wilson 1950– : in *Evening Standard* 24
January 1997

Political Parties see also Capitalism and Communism, Politicians, Politics

1 I am a Marxist—of the Groucho tendency.
slogan found at Nanterre in Paris, 1968

2 Labour isn't working.
on a poster showing a long queue outside an unemployment office; British Conservative Party slogan, 1978

3 Meet the challenge—make the change.
Labour Party slogan, 1989

PHRASES

4 Big Blue Machine in Canada, informal name for the Ontario Progressive Conservative party, especially during the premiership of William Davis (1971-85), or for the group of people responsible for the party's campaigns and political organization.

5 big tent the doctrine or belief that a political party (or coalition of parties) should permit and encourage a broad spectrum of views and opinions among its members rather than insist on strict adherence to party policy; a party run on these lines.

6 clear blue water as seen by some Conservatives, the gap between their political aims and aspirations and those of the Labour Party.
from blend of clear water, the distance between two boats, and blue water, the open sea, with a play on blue as the traditional colour of Conservatism

7 the Grand Old Party the American Republican Party.

8 the magic circle an inner group of politicians viewed as choosing the leader of the Conservative Party before this became an electoral matter.
coined by Iain Macleod in a critical article in the Spectator on the 'emergence' of Alec Douglas-Home in succession to Harold Macmillan in 1963

9 Selsdon man an advocate or adherent of the policies outlined at a conference of Conservative Party leaders held at the Selsdon Park Hotel, January 1970, from the view of a political opponent.
from the Selsdon Park Hotel, Croydon, Surrey, after Piltdown man a fraudulent fossil composed of a human cranium and an ape jaw that was presented in 1912 as a genuine hominid of great antiquity

10 somewhere to the right of Genghis Khan holding right-wing views of the most extreme kind.
Genghis Khan (1162–1227), the founder of the Mongol empire, as the type of a repressive and tyrannical ruler

QUOTATIONS

11 Party is little less than an inquisition, where men are under such a discipline in carrying on the common cause, as leaves no liberty of private opinion.
Lord Halifax 1633–95: *Political, Moral, and Miscellaneous Thoughts and Reflections* (1750) 'Of Parties'

12 Party-spirit, which at best is but the madness of many for the gain of a few.
Alexander Pope 1688–1744: letter to Edward Blount, 27 August 1714

13 I have always said, the first Whig was the Devil.
Samuel Johnson 1709–84: James Boswell *Life of Johnson* (1791) 28 April 1778; see 17 below

14 PRINCE OF WALES: True blue and Mrs Crewe.
MRS CREWE: Buff and blue and all of you.
toast proposed by George IV when Prince of Wales to Mrs Crewe, in honour of her support for the Whigs and Charles James Fox in the Westminster election of 1784 (buff and blue were the Whig colours)
George IV 1762–1830: at a dinner at Carlton House, May 1784; Amanda Foreman *Georgiana Duchess of Devonshire* (1998); see **Trust and Treachery** 16

15 If I could not go to Heaven but with a party, I would not go there at all.
Thomas Jefferson 1743–1826: letter to Francis Hopkinson, 13 March 1789

16 Let me . . . warn you in the most solemn manner against the baneful effects of the spirit of party.
George Washington 1732–99: President's address retiring from public life, 17 September 1796

17 God will not always be a Tory.
Lord Byron 1788–1824: letter 2 February 1821; see 13 above

18 I always voted at my party's call,
And I never thought of thinking for myself
at all.
W. S. Gilbert 1836–1911: *HMS Pinafore* (1878)

19 Damn your principles! Stick to your party.
Benjamin Disraeli 1804–81: attributed to Disraeli
and believed to have been said to Edward Bulwer-
Lytton; E. Latham *Famous Sayings and their Authors*
(1904)

20 We are Republicans and don't propose to
leave our party and identify ourselves with
the party whose antecedents are rum,
Romanism, and rebellion.
Samuel Dickinson Burchard 1812–91: speech at
the Fifth Avenue Hotel, New York, 29 October 1884

21 We are all socialists now.
*during the passage of the 1888 budget, noted for the
reduction of the National Debt*
William Harcourt 1827–1904: attributed; Hubert
Bland 'The Outlook' in G. B. Shaw (ed.) *Fabian
Essays in Socialism* (1889)

22 Then raise the scarlet standard high!
Within its shade we'll live or die.
Tho' cowards flinch and traitors sneer,
We'll keep the red flag flying here.
James M. Connell 1852–1929: 'The Red Flag' (1889
song)

23 When in office, the Liberals forget their
principles and the Tories remember their
friends.
Thomas Kettle 1880–1916: Nicholas Mansergh *The
Irish Question* (ed. 3, 1975)

24 To the ordinary working man, the sort you
would meet in any pub on Saturday night,
Socialism does not mean much more than
better wages and shorter hours and
nobody bossing you about.
George Orwell 1903–50: *The Road to Wigan Pier*
(1937)

25 I am reminded of four definitions: A
Radical is a man with both feet firmly
planted—in the air. A Conservative is a
man with two perfectly good legs who,
however, has never learned to walk
forward. A Reactionary is a somnambulist
walking backwards. A Liberal is a man
who uses his legs and his hands at the
behest—at the command—of his head.
Franklin D. Roosevelt 1882–1945: radio address to
New York Herald Tribune Forum, 26 October 1939

26 Conservatives do not believe that the
political struggle is the most important

thing in life . . . The simplest of them prefer
fox-hunting—the wisest religion.
Lord Hailsham 1907–2001: *The Case for
Conservatism* (1947)

27 I fear my Socialism is purely cerebral; I do
not like the masses in the flesh.
Harold Nicolson 1886–1968: letter to Vita
Sackville-West, 7 May 1948

28 The language of priorities is the religion of
Socialism.
Aneurin Bevan 1897–1960: speech at Labour Party
Conference in Blackpool, 8 June 1949

29 If they [the Republicans] will stop telling
lies about the Democrats, we will stop
telling the truth about them.
Adlai Stevenson 1900–65: speech during 1952
Presidential campaign; J. B. Martin *Adlai Stevenson
and Illinois* (1976)

30 Under democracy one party always
devotes its energies to trying to prove that
the other party is unfit to rule—and both
commonly succeed and are right.
H. L. Mencken 1880–1956: *Minority Report* (1956)

31 I am a free man, an American, a United
States Senator, and a Democrat, in that
order.
Lyndon Baines Johnson 1908–73: in *Texas Quarterly*
Winter 1958

32 Fascism is not in itself a new order of
society. It is the future refusing to be born.
Aneurin Bevan 1897–1960: Leon Harris *The Fine Art
of Political Wit* (1965)

33 There are some of us . . . who will fight
and fight and fight again to save the Party
we love.
Hugh Gaitskell 1906–63: speech at Labour Party
Conference, 5 October 1960

34 As usual the Liberals offer a mixture of
sound and original ideas. Unfortunately
none of the sound ideas is original and
none of the original ideas is sound.
Harold Macmillan 1894–1986: speech to London
Conservatives, 7 March 1961

35 Loyalty is the Tory's secret weapon.
Lord Kilmuir 1900–67: Anthony Sampson *Anatomy
of Britain* (1962)

36 This party is a moral crusade or it is
nothing.
Harold Wilson 1916–95: speech at the Labour
Party Conference, 1 October 1962

37 The Labour Party owes more to
Methodism than to Marxism.
Morgan Phillips 1902–63: James Callaghan *Time
and Chance* (1987)

38 An independent is a guy who wants to take the politics out of politics.
Adlai Stevenson 1900–65: Bill Adler *The Stevenson Wit* (1966)

39 The Provisional IRA is no more a left-wing movement than Hitler's National Socialist Party was.
Garret Fitzgerald 1926– : comment, 1973

40 This party is a bit like an old stage-coach. If you drive along at a rapid rate, everyone aboard is either so exhilarated or so seasick that you don't have a lot of difficulty.
of the Labour Party
Harold Wilson 1916–95: Anthony Sampson *The Changing Anatomy of Britain* (1982)

41 Socialism can only arrive by bicycle.
José Antonio Viera Gallo 1943– : Ivan Illich *Energy and Equity* (1974) epigraph

42 The longest suicide note in history.
on the Labour Party's election manifesto New Hope for Britain (1983)
Gerald Kaufman 1930– : Denis Healey *The Time of My Life* (1989)

43 A dead or dying beast lying across a railway line and preventing other trains from getting through.
of the Labour Party
Roy Jenkins 1920– : in *Guardian* 16 May 1987

44 I have only one firm belief about the American political system, and that is this: God is a Republican and Santa Claus is a Democrat.
P. J. O'Rourke 1947– : *Parliament of Whores* (1991)

45 International life is right-wing, like nature. The social contract is left-wing, like humanity.
Régis Debray 1940– : *Charles de Gaulle* (1994)

46 I did not vote Labour because they've heard of Oasis and nobody is going to vote Tory because William Hague has got a baseball cap.
Ben Elton 1959– : in *Radio Times* 18 April 1998

47 No man or woman is indispensable and no individual is more important than the party and thereby the democratic health of our country.
William Hague 1961– : resignation speech as Conservative leader, 8 June 2001

Politicians see also **People, Political Parties, Politics, Speeches**

1 Mummy, what's that man for?
remark by a small child to its mother; commonly cited as originally said of a late 19th/early 20th century politician; the earliest known instance is a cartoon in Punch *in 1906 where it is applied to a man carrying a bag of golf clubs; see also 9 below*

2 A politician is an animal who can sit on a fence and yet keep both ears to the ground.
American proverb, mid 20th century

3 Politicians also have no leisure, because they are always aiming at something beyond political life itself, power and glory, or happiness.
Aristotle 384–322 BC: *Nicomachean Ethics*

4 This judgement I have of you that you will not be corrupted by any manner of gift and that you will be faithful to the state; and that without respect of my private will you will give me that counsel which you think best.
to William Cecil, appointing him her Secretary of State in 1558
Elizabeth I 1533–1603: Conyers Read *Mr Secretary Cecil and queen Elizabeth* (1955)

5 He that goeth about to persuade a multitude, that they are not so well governed as they ought to be, shall never want attentive and favourable hearers.
Richard Hooker c.1554–1600: *Of the Laws of Ecclesiastical Polity* (1593)

6   Get thee glass eyes;
And, like a scurvy politician, seem
To see the things thou dost not.
William Shakespeare 1564–1616: *King Lear* (1605–6)

7 The greatest art of a politician is to render vice serviceable to the cause of virtue.
Henry St John, Lord Bolingbroke 1678–1751: comment (c.1728); Joseph Spence *Observations, Anecdotes, and Characters* (1820)

8 A minister who moves about in society is in a position to read the signs of the times even in a festive gathering, but one who remains shut up in his office learns nothing.
Duc de Choiseul 1719–85: Jack F. Bernard *Talleyrand* (1973)

9 What is that fat gentleman in such a passion about?
as a child, on hearing Charles James Fox speak in Parliament
Charles Shaw-Lefevre, Lord Eversley 1794–1888: G. W. E. Russell *Collections and Recollections* (1898); see also 1 above

10 If a due participation of office is a matter of right, how are vacancies to be obtained? Those by death are few; by resignation none.
usually quoted as, 'Few die and none resign'
Thomas Jefferson 1743–1826: letter to E. Shipman and others, 12 July 1801

11 What I want is men who will support me when I am in the wrong.
replying to a politician who said 'I will support you as long as you are in the right'
Lord Melbourne 1779–1848: Lord David Cecil *Lord M* (1954)

12 The greatest gift of any statesman rests not in knowing what concessions to make, but recognising when to make them.
Prince Metternich 1773–1859: *Concessionen und Nichtconcessionen* (1852)

13 With malice toward none; with charity for all; with firmness in the right, as God gives us to see the right, let us strive on to finish the work we are in.
Abraham Lincoln 1809–65: Second Inaugural Address, 4 March 1865

14 A constitutional statesman is in general a man of common opinion and uncommon abilities.
Walter Bagehot 1826–77: *Biographical Studies* (1881) 'The Character of Sir Robert Peel'

15 An honest politician is one who when he's bought stays bought.
Simon Cameron 1799–1889: attributed

16 He knows nothing; and he thinks he knows everything. That points clearly to a political career.
George Bernard Shaw 1856–1950: *Major Barbara* (1907)

17 'Do you pray for the senators, Dr Hale?' 'No, I look at the senators and I pray for the country.'
Edward Everett Hale 1822–1909: Van Wyck Brooks *New England Indian Summer* (1940)

18 He [Labouchere] did not object to the old man always having a card up his sleeve, but he did object to his insinuating that the Almighty had placed it there.
on Gladstone's 'frequent appeals to a higher power'
Henry Labouchere 1831–1912: Earl Curzon *Modern Parliamentary Eloquence* (1913); see **Secrecy** 15

19 We all know that Prime Ministers are wedded to the truth, but like other married couples they sometimes live apart.
Saki 1870–1916: *The Unbearable Bassington* (1912)

20 If you want to succeed in politics, you must keep your conscience well under control.
David Lloyd George 1863–1945: Lord Riddell, diary, 23 April 1919

21 did you ever
notice that when
a politician
does get an idea
he usually
gets it all wrong.
Don Marquis 1878–1937: *archys life of mehitabel* (1933)

22 a politician is an arse upon which everyone has sat except a man.
e. e. cummings 1894–1962: *1 x 1* (1944) no. 10

23 Forever poised between a cliché and an indiscretion.
on the life of a Foreign Secretary
Harold Macmillan 1894–1986: in *Newsweek* 30 April 1956

24 I am not going to spend any time whatsoever in attacking the Foreign Secretary . . . If we complain about the tune, there is no reason to attack the monkey when the organ grinder is present.
during a debate on the Suez crisis
Aneurin Bevan 1897–1960: speech, House of Commons, 16 May 1957

25 A politician is a man who understands government, and it takes a politician to run a government. A statesman is a politician who's been dead 10 or 15 years.
Harry S. Truman 1884–1972: in *New York World Telegram and Sun* 12 April 1958

26 A political leader must keep looking over his shoulder all the time to see if the boys are still there. If they aren't still there, he's no longer a political leader.

Bernard Baruch 1870–1965: in *New York Times* 21 June 1965

27 The ability to foretell what is going to happen tomorrow, next week, next month, and next year. And to have the ability afterwards to explain why it didn't happen.

describing the qualifications desirable in a prospective politician

Winston Churchill 1874–1965: B. Adler *Churchill Wit* (1965)

28 I think a Prime Minister has to be a butcher and know the joints. That is perhaps where I have not been quite competent, in knowing all the ways that you can cut up a carcass.

R. A. Butler 1902–82: in *Listener* 28 June 1966

29 The best time to listen to a politician is when he's on the stump on a street corner in the rain late at night when he's exhausted. Then he doesn't lie.

Theodore H. White 1915–86: in *New York Times* 5 January 1969

30 In politics, if you want anything said, ask a man. If you want anything done, ask a woman.

Margaret Thatcher 1925– : in 1970; in *People* (New York) 15 September 1975

31 A statesman is a politician who places himself at the service of the nation. A

politician is a statesman who places the nation at his service.

Georges Pompidou 1911–74: in *Observer* 30 December 1973

32 The average footslogger in the New South Wales Right . . . generally speaking carries a dagger in one hand and a Bible in the other and doesn't put either to really elegant use.

Neville Wran 1926– : in 1973; Michael Gordon *A Question of Leadership* (1993)

33 All political lives, unless they are cut off in midstream at a happy juncture, end in failure, because that is the nature of politics and of human affairs.

Enoch Powell 1912–98: *Joseph Chamberlain* (1977)

34 In politics you must always keep running with the pack. The moment that you falter and they sense that you are injured, the rest will turn on you like wolves.

R. A. Butler 1902–82: Dennis Walters *Not Always with the Pack* (1989)

35 There are no true friends in politics. We are all sharks circling, and waiting, for traces of blood to appear in the water.

Alan Clark 1928–99: diary 30 November 1990

36 Politicians are entitled to change their minds. But when they adjust their principles some explanation is necessary.

Roy Hattersley 1932– : in *Observer* 21 March 1999

Politics see also **Democracy, Elections, Government, International Relations, Parliament, Political Parties, Politicians, The Presidency**

PROVERBS AND SAYINGS

1 **In politics a man must learn to rise above principle.**

American proverb, mid 20th century

2 **It'll play in Peoria.**

catchphrase of the Nixon administration (early 1970s) meaning 'it will be acceptable to middle America', but originating in a standard music hall joke of the 1930s

3 **The personal is political.**

1970s feminist slogan, coined by Carol Hanisch (1945–)

4 **Politics makes strange bedfellows.**

mid 19th century, meaning that political alliances in a common cause may bring together those of widely differing views

PHRASES

5 **midnight appointment** in US politics, an appointment made during the last hours of an administration.

originally with particular reference to those made by the 2nd President John Adams (1735–1826)

6 **October surprise** in the US, an unexpected but popular political act or speech made just prior to a November election in an attempt to win votes.

used especially with reference to an alleged conspiracy in which members of the 1980 Republican campaign team are said to have made an arms deal with Iran to delay the release of US hostages in Iran until after the election

7 **a smoke-filled room** regarded as the characteristic venue of those in control of a

party meeting to arrange a political decision.

*from Kirke Simpson news report, filed 12 June 1920,
'[Warren] Harding of Ohio was chosen by a group of
men in a smoke-filled room early today as Republican
candidate for President'; usually attributed to Harry
Daugherty, one of Harding's supporters, who appears
merely to have concurred with this version of events,
when pressed for comment by Simpson.*

8 the third way in politics, a middle way between conventional right- and left-wing ideologies or policies; an ideology founded on political centrism or neutrality.

*in the 1990s the third way became identified with the
political programmes of centre-left parties in Western
Europe and North America, characterized by both
market-driven economic policy and a concern for
social justice*

9 the two nations the rich and poor members of a society seen as effectively divided into separate nations by the presence or absence of wealth.

*from Disraeli: see **Wealth** 25*

QUOTATIONS

10 Man is by nature a political animal.
Aristotle 384–322 BC: *Politics*

11 State business is a cruel trade; good nature is a bungler in it.
Lord Halifax 1633–95: *Political, Moral, and
Miscellaneous Thoughts and Reflections* (1750)
'Wicked Ministers'

12 Most schemes of political improvement are very laughable things.
Samuel Johnson 1709–84: James Boswell *Life of
Samuel Johnson* (1791) 26 October 1769

13 Magnanimity in politics is not seldom the truest wisdom; and a great empire and little minds go ill together.
Edmund Burke 1729–97: *On Conciliation with
America* (1775)

14 I agree with you that in politics the middle way is none at all.
John Adams 1735–1826: letter to Horatio Gates, 23
March 1776

15 What is the first part of politics? Education. The second? Education. And the third? Education.
Jules Michelet 1798–1874: *Le Peuple* (1846); see
Education 35

16 Finality is not the language of politics.
Benjamin Disraeli 1804–81: speech, House of
Commons, 28 February 1859

17 Politics is the art of the possible.
Otto von Bismarck 1815–98: in conversation with
Meyer von Waldeck, 11 August 1867; see 30, 35
below, **Science** 24

18 In politics, there is no use looking beyond the next fortnight.
Joseph Chamberlain 1836–1914: letter from A. J.
Balfour to 3rd Marquess of Salisbury, 24 March 1886

19 A statesman . . . must wait until he hears the steps of God sounding through events; then leap up and grasp the hem of his garment.
Otto von Bismarck 1815–98: A. J. P. Taylor *Bismarck*
(1955)

20 Politics, as a practice, whatever its professions, has always been the systematic organization of hatreds.
Henry Brooks Adams 1838–1918: *The Education of
Henry Adams* (1907)

21 I never dared be radical when young
For fear it would make me conservative when old.
Robert Frost 1874–1963: 'Precaution' (1936)

22 Politics is war without bloodshed while war is politics with bloodshed.
Mao Zedong 1893–1976: lecture, 1938; *Selected
Works* (1965)

23 He may be a son of a bitch, but he's our son of a bitch.
on President Somoza of Nicaragua, 1938
Franklin D. Roosevelt 1882–1945: attributed

24 The trouble with this country is that there are too many politicians who believe, with a conviction based on experience, that you can fool all of the people all of the time.
Franklin P. Adams 1881–1960: *Nods and Becks*
(1944); see **Deception** 18

25 All reactionaries are paper tigers. In appearance, the reactionaries are terrifying, but in reality they are not so powerful. From a long-term point of view, it is not the reactionaries but the people who are really powerful.
Mao Zedong 1893–1976: interview with Anne
Louise Strong, August 1946; *Selected Works* (1961)

26 We have a great objective—the light on the hill—which we aim to reach by working for the betterment of mankind not only here but anywhere we may give a helping hand.
Joseph Benedict 'Ben' Chifley 1885–1951: speech
to the Annual Conference of the New South Wales
branch of the Australian Labor Party, 12 June 1949

27 Political language . . . is designed to make lies sound truthful and murder respectable, and to give an appearance of solidity to pure wind.
George Orwell 1903–50: *Shooting an Elephant* (1950) 'Politics and the English Language'

28 Men enter local politics solely as a result of being unhappily married.
C. Northcote Parkinson 1909–93: *Parkinson's Law* (1958)

29 Politics are too serious a matter to be left to the politicians.
replying to Attlee's remark that 'De Gaulle is a very good soldier and a very bad politician'
Charles de Gaulle 1890–1970: Clement Attlee *A Prime Minister Remembers* (1961)

30 Politics is not the art of the possible. It consists in choosing between the disastrous and the unpalatable.
J. K. Galbraith 1908– : letter to President Kennedy, 2 March 1962; see 17 above

31 A week is a long time in politics.
probably first said at the time of the 1964 sterling crisis
Harold Wilson 1916–95: Nigel Rees *Sayings of the Century* (1984)

32 The liberals can understand everything but people who don't understand them.
Lenny Bruce 1925–66: John Cohen (ed.) *The Essential Lenny Bruce* (1967)

33 Politics is supposed to be the second oldest profession. I have come to realize that it bears a very close resemblance to the first.
Ronald Reagan 1911– : at a conference in Los Angeles, 2 March 1977; see **Employment** 4

when asked what his biggest problem was:
34 Events, dear boy. Events.
Harold Macmillan 1894–1986: attributed

35 Let us teach ourselves and others that politics can be not only the art of the possible, especially if this means the art of speculation, calculation, intrigue, secret deals, and pragmatic manoeuvring, but that it can even be the art of the impossible, namely, the art of improving ourselves and the world.
Václav Havel 1936– : speech, Prague, 1 January 1990; see 17 above

36 If something makes you cry, you have to do something about it. That's the difference between politics and guilt.
Bill Clinton 1946– : *On the Make* (1994)

37 Safe is spelled D-U-L-L. Politics has got to be a fun activity, otherwise people turn their back on it.
Alan Clark 1928–99: on being selected as parliamentary candidate for Kensington and Chelsea, 24 January 1997

38 Politics is a marathon, not a sprint.
Ken Livingstone 1945– : in *New Statesman* 10 October 1997

Pollution and the Environment see also **The Earth**, Nature

see also **The Earth**, Nature

PROVERBS AND SAYINGS

1 **Kills all known germs.**
advertising slogan for Domestos bleach, 1959

2 **Save the whale.**
environmental slogan associated with the alarm over the rapidly declining whale population which led in 1985 to a moratorium on commercial whaling; see also **Language** *28*

3 **Think globally, act locally.**
Friends of the Earth slogan, c.1985

QUOTATIONS

4 Woe to her that is filthy and polluted, to the oppressing city!
Bible: Zephaniah

5 Woe unto them that join house to house, that lay field to field, till there be no place.
Bible: Isaiah

6 It goes so heavily with my disposition that this goodly frame, the earth, seems to me a sterile promontory; this most excellent canopy, the air, look you, this brave o'erhanging firmament, this majestical roof fretted with golden fire, why, it appears no other thing to me but a foul and pestilent congregation of vapours.
William Shakespeare 1564–1616: *Hamlet* (1601)

7 O all ye Green Things upon the Earth, bless ye the Lord: praise him, and magnify him for ever.
The Book of Common Prayer 1662: Benedicite

8 The parks are the lungs of London.
William Pitt, Earl of Chatham 1708–78: speech by William Windham, House of Commons, 30 June 1808

9 And did the Countenance Divine
Shine forth upon our clouded hills?
And was Jerusalem builded here
Among these dark Satanic mills?
William Blake 1757–1827: *Milton* (1804–10) 'And did those feet in ancient time'

10 The river Rhine, it is well known,
Doth wash your city of Cologne;
But tell me, Nymphs, what power divine
Shall henceforth wash the river Rhine?
Samuel Taylor Coleridge 1772–1834: 'Cologne' (1834)

11 What would the world be, once bereft
Of wet and wildness? Let them be left,
O let them be left, wildness and wet;
Long live the weeds and the wilderness yet.
Gerard Manley Hopkins 1844–89: 'Inversnaid' (written 1881)

12 Dirt is only matter out of place.
John Chipman Gray 1839–1915: *Restraints on the Alienation of Property* (2nd ed., 1895)

13 Man has been endowed with reason, with the power to create, so that he can add to what he's been given. But up to now he hasn't been a creator, only a destroyer. Forests keep disappearing, rivers dry up, wild life's become extinct, the climate's ruined and the land grows poorer and uglier every day.
Anton Chekhov 1860–1904: *Uncle Vanya* (1897)

14 The sanitary and mechanical age we are now entering makes up for the mercy it grants to our sense of smell by the ferocity with which it assails our sense of hearing. As usual, what we call 'progress' is the exchange of one nuisance for another nuisance.
Havelock Ellis 1859–1939: *Impressions and Comments* (1914)

15 I think that I shall never see
A billboard lovely as a tree.
Perhaps, unless the billboards fall,
I'll never see a tree at all.
Ogden Nash 1902–71: 'Song of the Open Road' (1933); see **Trees** 14

16 Clear the air! clean the sky! wash the wind!
T. S. Eliot 1888–1965: *Murder in the Cathedral* (1935)

17 Come, friendly bombs, and fall on Slough!

It isn't fit for humans now,
There isn't grass to graze a cow.
Swarm over, Death!
John Betjeman 1906–84: 'Slough' (1937)

18 Over increasingly large areas of the United States, spring now comes unheralded by the return of the birds, and the early mornings are strangely silent where once they were filled with the beauty of bird song.
Rachel Carson 1907–64: *The Silent Spring* (1962)

19 Make it a *green* peace.
Bill Darnell: at a meeting of the Don't Make a Wave Committee, which preceded the formation of Greenpeace, in Vancouver, 1970; Robert Hunter *The Greenpeace Chronicle* (1979)

20 We have met the enemy and he is us.
the cartoon-strip character, Pogo the opossum, looking at litter under a tree; used as an Earth Day poster in 1971
Walt Kelly 1913–73: *Pogo* cartoon, 1970

21 The sea is the universal sewer.
Jacques Cousteau 1910–97: testimony before the House Committee on Science and Astronautics, 28 January 1971

22 There should be supermarkets that sell things and supermarkets that buy things back, and until that equalizes, there'll be more waste than there should be.
Andy Warhol 1927–87: *Philosophy of Andy Warhol (From A to B and Back Again)* (1975)

23 It is not what they built. It is what they knocked down.
It is not the houses. It is the spaces between the houses.
It is not the streets that exist. It is the streets that no longer exist.
James Fenton 1949– : *German Requiem* (1981)

24 If I were a Brazilian without land or money or the means to feed my children, I would be burning the rain forest too.
Sting 1951– : in *International Herald Tribune* 14 April 1989

25 I do not know of any environmental group in any country that does not view its government as an adversary.
Gro Harlem Brundtland 1939– : in *Time* 25 September 1989

26 The poor tread lightest upon the earth. The higher our income, the more resources we control and the more havoc we wreak.
Paul Harrison 1936– : in *Guardian* 1 May 1992

27 We live in a world where emissions from our refrigerators have caused the ozone layer to evaporate and we'll get skin cancer if we sunbathe. If that's not a science fiction scenario, I don't know what is.
William Gibson 1948- : in *Newsweek* 5 June 1995

28 The greenest political party there has ever been was the Nazi party. The Nazis were great believers in purity, that nature should not be interfered with.
Steve Jones 1944- : in *Times Higher Education Supplement* 27 August 1999

Possessions

1 **Finders keepers (losers weepers).**
early 19th century

2 **Findings keepings.**
mid 19th century

3 **Keep a thing seven years and you'll always find a use for it.**
early 17th century, recommending caution and thrift

4 **Light come, light go.**
late 14th century, meaning that something gained without effort can be lost without much regret

5 **What you have, hold.**
mid 15th century, with reference to an uncompromising position based on a refusal to make any concessions

6 **What you spend, you have.**
early 14th century; meaning that the only real possessions one has are those of which one can dispose

7 **You cannot lose what you never had.**
late 16th century, used in consolation or resignation

PHRASES

8 **dead men's shoes** a property or position coveted by a prospective successor but available only on a person's death.
*from the proverb: see **Ambition** 3*

9 **ewe lamb** a person's most cherished possession.
from the Bible: see 11 below

QUOTATIONS

10 The sage does not accumulate for himself.
The more he uses for others, the more he has himself.
The more he gives to others, the more he possesses of his own.
Lao Tzu c.604-c.531 BC: *Tao-te Ching* ch. 81

11 The poor man had nothing, save one little ewe lamb.
Bible: II Samuel; see 9 above

12 How many things I can do without!
on looking at a multitude of wares exposed for sale
Socrates 469-399 BC: Diogenes Laertius *Lives of the Philosophers*

13 For we brought nothing into this world, and it is certain we can carry nothing out.
Bible: I Timothy

14 There are only two families in the world, as a grandmother of mine used to say: the haves and the have-nots.
Cervantes 1547-1616: *Don Quixote* (1605)

15 Well! some people talk of morality, and some of religion, but give me a little snug property.
Maria Edgeworth 1767-1849: *The Absentee* (1812)

16 Property has its duties as well as its rights.
Thomas Drummond 1797-1840: letter to the Earl of Donoughmore, 22 May 1838

17 Property is theft.
Pierre-Joseph Proudhon 1809-65: *Qu'est-ce que la propriété?* (1840)

18 Things are in the saddle,
And ride mankind.
Ralph Waldo Emerson 1803-82: 'Ode' Inscribed to W. H. Channing (1847)

19 Have nothing in your houses that you do not know to be useful, or believe to be beautiful.
William Morris 1834-96: *Hopes and Fears for Art* (1882) 'Making the Best of It'

20 Conspicuous consumption of valuable goods is a means of reputability to the gentleman of leisure.
Thorstein Veblen 1857-1929: *Theory of the Leisure Class* (1899)

21 Never be afraid of throwing away what you have, if you *can* throw it away, it is not really yours.
R. H. Tawney 1880-1962: diary 1912, in *Dictionary of National Biography* 1961-1970 (1981)

22 The moon belongs to everyone,

The best things in life are free.
Buddy De Sylva 1895–1950 and **Lew Brown** 1893–1958: 'The Best Things in Life are Free' (1927 song); see **Money** 2

23 People don't resent having nothing nearly as much as too little.
Ivy Compton-Burnett 1884–1969: *A Family and a Fortune* (1939)

24 The goal of all inanimate objects is to resist man and ultimately to defeat him.
Russell Baker 1925– : in *New York Times* 18 June 1968

25 Man must choose whether to be rich in things or in the freedom to use them.
Ivan Illich 1926– : *Deschooling Society* (1971)

26 The thrill was in the trying on, in the buying. The moment after she had acquired something new it became meaningless to her.
Judith Krantz 1932– : *Scruples* (1978)

27 If men are to respect each other for what they are, they must cease to respect each other for what they own.
A. J. P. Taylor 1906–90: *Politicians, Socialism and Historians* (1980)

28 People who get through life dependent on other people's possessions are always the first to lecture you on how little possessions count.
Ben Elton 1959– : *Stark* (1989)

29 The metamorphosis of consumption from vice to virtue is one of the most important yet least examined phenomena of the twentieth century.
Jeremy Rifkin 1945– : *The End of Work* (1995)

Poverty see also Money, Wealth

PROVERBS AND SAYINGS

1 **Both poverty and prosperity come from spending money—prosperity from spending it wisely.**
American proverb, mid 20th century

2 **Empty sacks will never stand upright.**
mid 17th century; meaning that those in an extremity of need cannot survive

3 **A moneyless man goes fast through the market.**
meaning that someone without resources is unable to pause to buy anything (or, in a modern variant, rushes to wherever what they lack may be found)

4 **Poverty comes from God, but not dirt.**
American proverb, mid 20th century

5 **Poverty is no disgrace, but it's a great inconvenience.**
late 16th century

6 **Poverty is not a crime.**
late 16th century

7 **Stretch your arm no further than your sleeve will reach.**
mid 16th century; meaning that you should not spend more than you can afford

8 **When poverty comes in at the door, love flies out of the window.**
mid 17th century, meaning that the strains of living in poverty often destroy a loving relationship

PHRASES

9 **on the breadline** in the poorest conditions in which it is possible to live.
the breadline in North American usage was a queue of people waiting to receive free food

10 **poor as Job** very poor.
in the Bible (Job), the formerly wealthy figure of Job, deprived of his possessions, becomes a type of abject poverty

11 **the submerged tenth** the supposed fraction of the population permanently living in poverty.
from William Booth (1829–1912) In Darkest England (1890) 'This Submerged Tenth—is it, then, beyond the reach of the nine-tenths in the midst of whom they live?'

QUOTATIONS

12 What mean ye that ye beat my people to pieces, and grind the faces of the poor?
Bible: Isaiah

13 The poor always ye have with you.
Bible: St John

14 The misfortunes of poverty carry with them nothing harder to bear than that it makes men ridiculous.
Juvenal AD c.60–c.130: *Satires*

15 I can get no remedy against this consumption of the purse: borrowing only

lingers and lingers it out, but the disease is incurable.

William Shakespeare 1564–1616: *Henry IV, Part 2* (1597)

16 I want there to be no peasant in my kingdom so poor that he is unable to have a chicken in his pot every Sunday.

Henri IV (of Navarre) 1553–1610: Hardouin de Péréfixe *Histoire de Henry le Grand* (1681); see **Progress** 16

17 Come away; poverty's catching.

Aphra Behn 1640–89: *The Rover* pt. 2 (1681)

18 Give me not poverty lest I steal.

Daniel Defoe 1660–1731: in *Review* 15 September 1711; later incorporated into *Moll Flanders* (1721)

19 Laws grind the poor, and rich men rule the law.

Oliver Goldsmith 1728–74: *The Traveller* (1764)

20 Resolve not to be poor: whatever you have, spend less. Poverty is a great enemy to human happiness; it certainly destroys liberty, and it makes some virtues impracticable, and others extremely difficult.

Samuel Johnson 1709–84: letter to Boswell, 7 December 1782

21 The murmuring poor, who will not fast in peace.

George Crabbe 1754–1832: 'The Newspaper' (1785)

22 The poor are Europe's blacks.

Nicolas-Sébastien Chamfort 1741–94: *Maximes et Pensées* (1796)

23 Oh! God! that bread should be so dear, And flesh and blood so cheap!

Thomas Hood 1799–1845: 'The Song of the Shirt' (1843)

24 Economy was always 'elegant', and money-spending always 'vulgar' and ostentatious— a sort of sour-grapeism, which made us very peaceful and satisfied.

Elizabeth Gaskell 1810–65: *Cranford* (1853)

25 Like dear St Francis of Assisi I am wedded to Poverty: but in my case the marriage is not a success.

Oscar Wilde 1854–1900: letter June 1899

26 The greatest of evils and the worst of crimes is poverty.

George Bernard Shaw 1856–1950: *Major Barbara* (1907)

27 The poor cannot always reach those whom they want to love, and they can hardly ever escape from those whom they no longer love.

E. M. Forster 1879–1970: *Howards End* (1910)

28 She was not so much a person as an implication of dreary poverty, like an open door in a mean house that lets out the smell of cooking cabbage and the screams of children.

Rebecca West 1892–1983: *The Return of the Soldier* (1918)

29 There's nothing surer, The rich get rich and the poor get children.

Gus Kahn 1886–1941 and **Raymond B. Egan** 1890–1952: 'Ain't We Got Fun' (1921 song)

30 Brother can you spare a dime?

E. Y. Harburg 1898–1981: title of song (1932)

31 How can you frighten a man whose hunger is not only in his own cramped stomach but in the wretched bellies of his children? You can't scare him—he has known a fear beyond every other.

John Steinbeck 1902–68: *The Grapes of Wrath* (1939)

32 Anyone who has ever struggled with poverty knows how extremely expensive it is to be poor.

James Baldwin 1924–87: *Nobody Knows My Name* (1961) 'Fifth Avenue, Uptown: a letter from Harlem'

33 Born down in a dead man's town The first kick I took was when I hit the ground.

Bruce Springsteen 1949– : 'Born in the USA' (1984 song)

34 When I give food to the poor they call me a saint. When I ask why the poor have no food they call me a communist.

Helder Camara 1909–99: attributed

35 I never saw a beggar yet who would recognise guilt if it bit him on his unwashed ass.

Tony Parsons 1953– : *Dispatches from the Front Line of Popular Culture* (1994)

Power

1 Big fish eat little fish.

early 13th century, meaning that the rich and powerful are likely to prey on those who are less strong, and often used with the implication that each predator is in turn victim to a stronger one

2 He who pays the piper calls the tune.

late 19th century, meaning that the person financially responsible for something can control what is done; see 12 below

3 In the country of the blind the one eyed man is king.

early 16th century, meaning that someone of moderate ability will dominate those with none

4 Kings have long arms.

mid 16th century, meaning that a king's power reaches a long way

5 Might is right.

early 14th century

6 A mouse may help a lion.

mid 16th century; alluding to Aesop's fable of the lion and the rat, in which a rat saved a lion which had become trapped in a net by gnawing through the cords which bound it

7 Power corrupts.

late 19th century; see 25 below

8 Set a beggar on horseback, and he'll ride to the Devil.

late 16th century, meaning that a person unused to power will make unwise use of it

9 They that dance must pay the fiddler.

mid 17th century, meaning that you must be prepared to make recompense for the provision of an essential service

10 We have ways of making you talk.

supposedly the characteristic threat of an inquisitor in a 1930s film, but not traced in this form; 'We have ways of making men talk' occurs in Lives of a Bengal Lancer *(1935)*

11 éminence grise a person who exercises power or influence in a certain sphere without holding an official position.

the term was originally applied to Cardinal Richelieu's grey-cloaked private secretary, Père Joseph (1577–1638); see **Royalty** *39*

12 pay the piper (and call the tune) pay the cost of (and so have the right to control) an activity or undertaking.

from the proverb: see 2 above

13 the powers that be the authorities concerned, the people exercising political or social control.

from the Bible (Romans), 'For there is no power but of God: the powers that be are ordained of God'

14   Man, proud man,
Drest in a little brief authority.
William Shakespeare 1564–1616: *Measure for Measure* (1604)

15 All rising to great place is by a winding stair.
Francis Bacon 1561–1626: *Essays* (1625) 'Of Great Place'

16 Power is so apt to be insolent and Liberty to be saucy, that they are very seldom upon good terms.
Lord Halifax 1633–95: *Political, Moral, and Miscellaneous Thoughts and Reflections* (1750) 'Of Prerogative, Power and Liberty'

17 Nature has left this tincture in the blood, That all men would be tyrants if they
could.
Daniel Defoe 1660–1731: *The History of the Kentish Petition* (1712–13)

18 Those who have been once intoxicated with power, and have derived any kind of emolument from it, even though for but one year, can never willingly abandon it.
Edmund Burke 1729–97: *Letter to a Member of the National Assembly* (1791)

19 I shall be an autocrat: that's my trade. And the good Lord will forgive me: that's his.
Catherine the Great 1729–96: attributed; see **Forgiveness** 21

20   The good old rule
Sufficeth them, the simple plan,
That they should take who have the
power,
And they should keep who can.
William Wordsworth 1770–1850: 'Rob Roy's Grave' (1807)

21 The fundamental article of my political creed is that despotism, or unlimited sovereignty, or absolute power, is the same in a majority of a popular assembly, an aristocratic council, an oligarchical junto, and a single emperor.
John Adams 1735–1826: letter to Thomas Jefferson, 13 November 1815

22 Power concedes nothing without a demand. It never did, and it never will.
Frederick Douglass c.1818–95: letter to Gerrit Smith, 30 March 1849

23 I claim not to have controlled events, but confess plainly that events have controlled me.
Abraham Lincoln 1809–65: letter to A. G. Hodges, 4 April 1864

24 'The question is,' said Humpty Dumpty, 'which is to be master—that's all.'
Lewis Carroll 1832–98: *Through the Looking-Glass* (1872)

25 Power tends to corrupt and absolute power corrupts absolutely.
Lord Acton 1834–1902: letter to Bishop Mandell Creighton, 3 April 1887; see 7 above

26 Whatever happens we have got
The Maxim Gun, and they have not.
Hilaire Belloc 1870–1953: *The Modern Traveller* (1898)

27 The hand that signed the paper felled a city;
Five sovereign fingers taxed the breath,
Doubled the globe of dead and halved a country;
These five kings did a king to death.
Dylan Thomas 1914–53: 'The hand that signed the paper felled a city' (1936)

28 Every Communist must grasp the truth, 'Political power grows out of the barrel of a gun'.
Mao Zedong 1893–1976: speech, 6 November 1938

29 The finest plans are always ruined by the littleness of those who ought to carry them out, for the Emperors can actually do nothing.
Bertolt Brecht 1898–1956: *Mother Courage* (1939)

30 Who controls the past controls the future: who controls the present controls the past.
George Orwell 1903–50: *Nineteen Eighty-Four* (1949)

31 You only have power over people as long as you don't take *everything* away from them. But when you've robbed a man of *everything* he's no longer in your power — he's free again.
Alexander Solzhenitsyn 1918– : *The First Circle* (1968)

32 Power is the great aphrodisiac.
Henry Kissinger 1923– : in *New York Times* 19 January 1971

33 Power? It's like a Dead Sea fruit. When you achieve it, there is nothing there.
Harold Macmillan 1894–1986: Anthony Sampson *The New Anatomy of Britain* (1971); see **Disillusion** 2

34 When you make your peace with authority, you become an authority.
Jim Morrison 1943–71: Andrew Doe and John Tobler *In Their Own Words: The Doors* (1988)

35 Every dictator uses religion as a prop to keep himself in power.
Benazir Bhutto 1953– : interview on *60 Minutes*, CBS-TV, 8 August 1986

36 Seven months ago I could give a single command and 541,000 people would immediately obey it. Today I can't get a plumber to come to my house.
H. Norman Schwarzkopf III 1934– : in *Newsweek* 11 November 1991

Practicality

PROVERBS AND SAYINGS

1 **Cut your coat according to your cloth.**
mid 16th century, meaning that actions taken should suit one's circumstances or resources

2 **You cannot make an omelette without breaking eggs.**
mid 19th century, often used in the context of a regrettable political necessity which is said to be justified because it will benefit the majority

3 This man hath the right sow by the ear.
of Thomas Cranmer, June 1529
Henry VIII 1491–1547: *Acts and Monuments of John Foxe* ['Fox's Book of Martyrs'], 1570; see **Knowledge** 12

4 A dead woman bites not.
pressing for the execution of Mary Queen of Scots in 1587
Patrick, Lord Gray d. 1612: oral tradition; William Camden *Annals of the Reign of Queen Elizabeth* (1615); see **Enemies** 1

5 My lord, we make use of you, not for your bad legs, but for your good head.
to William Cecil, who suffered from gout
Elizabeth I 1533–1603: F. Chamberlin *Sayings of Queen Elizabeth* (1923)

6 Common sense is the best distributed commodity in the world, for every man is convinced that he is well supplied with it.
René Descartes 1596–1650: *Le Discours de la méthode* (1637)

7 And he gave it for his opinion, that whoever could make two ears of corn or two blades of grass to grow upon a spot of ground where only one grew before, would deserve better of mankind, and do more essential service to his country than the whole race of politicians put together.
Jonathan Swift 1667–1745: *Gulliver's Travels* (1726) 'A Voyage to Brobdingnag'

8 'Tis use alone that sanctifies expense, And splendour borrows all her rays from sense.
Alexander Pope 1688–1744: *Epistles to Several Persons* 'To Lord Burlington' (1731)

9 Common sense is not so common.
Voltaire 1694–1778: *Dictionnaire philosophique* (1765) 'Sens Commun'

10 Whenever our neighbour's house is on fire, it cannot be amiss for the engines to play a little on our own.
Edmund Burke 1729–97: *Reflections on the Revolution in France* (1790)

11 How horrible it is to have so many people killed!—And what a blessing that one cares for none of them!
after the battle of Albuera, 16 May 1811
Jane Austen 1775–1817: letter to Cassandra Austen, 31 May 1811

12 Put your trust in God, my boys, and keep your powder dry.
Valentine Blacker 1728–1823: 'Oliver's Advice'; often attributed to Oliver Cromwell himself

13 It's grand, and you canna expect to be baith grand and comfortable.
J. M. Barrie 1860–1937: *The Little Minister* (1891)

14 Praise the Lord and pass the ammunition.
moving along a line of sailors passing ammunition by hand to the deck
Howell Forgy 1908–83: at Pearl Harbor, 7 December 1941; later the title of a song by Frank Loesser, 1942

15 Common sense is nothing more than a deposit of prejudices laid down in the mind before you reach eighteen.
Albert Einstein 1879–1955: Lincoln Barnett *The Universe and Dr Einstein* (1950 ed.)

16 Life is too short to stuff a mushroom.
Shirley Conran 1932– : *Superwoman* (1975)

17 I'm up to my neck in the real world, every day. Just you try doing your VAT return with a head full of goblins.
Terry Pratchett 1948– : in *Sunday Times* 27 February 2000

Praise and Flattery

1 Flattery is soft soap, and soft soap is ninety percent lye.
American proverb, mid 19th century

2 Flattery, like perfume, should be smelled, not swallowed.
American proverb, mid 19th century; see 15 below

3 Give credit where credit is due.
late 18th century

4 Imitation is the sincerest form of flattery.
early 19th century, from Charles Caleb Colton (1780–1832) Lacon (1820)

5 damn with faint praise commend so feebly as to imply disapproval.
from Pope: see 11 below

6 But when I tell him he hates flatterers,
He says he does, being then most flattered.
William Shakespeare 1564–1616: *Julius Caesar*
(1599)

7 It has been well said that 'the arch-
flatterer with whom all the petty flatterers
have intelligence is a man's self.'
Francis Bacon 1561–1626: *Essays* (1625) 'Of Love'

8 Nothing so soon the drooping spirits can
raise
As praises from the men, whom all men
praise.
Abraham Cowley 1618–67: 'Ode upon a Copy of
Verses of My Lord Broghill's' (1663)

9 Of whom to be dispraised were no small
praise.
John Milton 1608–74: *Paradise Regained* (1671)

10 He who discommendeth others obliquely
commendeth himself.
Thomas Browne 1605–82: *Christian Morals* (1716)

11 Damn with faint praise, assent with civil
leer,
And without sneering, teach the rest to
sneer.
Alexander Pope 1688–1744: 'An Epistle to Dr
Arbuthnot' (1735); see 5 above

12 Madam, before you flatter a man so grossly
to his face, you should consider whether or
not your flattery is worth his having.
Samuel Johnson 1709–84: Fanny Burney's diary,
August 1778

13 And even the ranks of Tuscany

Could scarce forbear to cheer.
Lord Macaulay 1800–59: *Lays of Ancient Rome*
(1842) 'Horatius'

14 The advantage of doing one's praising for
oneself is that one can lay it on so thick
and exactly in the right places.
Samuel Butler 1835–1902: *The Way of All Flesh*
(1903)

15 I suppose flattery hurts no one, that is, if
he doesn't inhale.
Adlai Stevenson 1900–65: television broadcast, 30
March 1952; see 2 above

16 It would be nice if sometimes the kind
things I say were considered worthy of
quotation. It isn't difficult, you know, to be
witty or amusing when one has something
to say that is destructive, but damned hard
to be clever and quotable when you are
singing someone's praises.
Noël Coward 1899–1973: William Marchant *The
Pleasure of His Company* (1981)

17 If you are flattering a woman, it pays to be
a little more subtle. You don't have to
bother with men, they believe any
compliment automatically.
Alan Ayckbourn 1939– : *Round and Round the
Garden* (1975)

18 Please don't be too effusive.
*to the Prime Minister, on the speech he was to make
to celebrate her golden wedding*
Elizabeth II 1926– : in *Daily Telegraph* 21 November
1997

19 I can't think of many toadies that have
prospered, or many toadies who have
become household names.
Betty Boothroyd 1929– : in *Mail on Sunday* 12 April
1998

Prayer

**1 The family that prays together stays
together.**
*motto devised by Al Scalpone for the Roman Catholic
Family Rosary Crusade, 1947*

2 Laborare est orare.
*Latin, To work is to pray, a traditional motto of the
Benedictine order, also found in the form 'Ora, lege,
et labora [Pray, read, and work]'*

3 the Lord's Prayer the prayer taught by
Christ to his disciples, beginning 'Our
Father'.
the term is a translation of Latin oratio Dominica,
*and is first recorded in the Book of Common Prayer of
1549*

4 sacrifice of praise (and thanksgiving) an
offering of praise to God.
*with reference to the Bible (Leviticus) 'He shall offer
with the sacrifice of thanksgiving unleavened cakes
mingled with oil'*

5 tell one's beads say one's prayers.

the beads of a rosary or paternoster, used for keeping count of the prayers said

QUOTATIONS

6 O gods, grant me this in return for my piety.

Catullus c.84–c.54 BC: *Carmina*

7 Ask, and it shall be given you; seek, and ye shall find; knock, and it shall be opened unto you.

Bible: St Matthew; see **Action** 10

8 Christ beside me,
Christ before me,
Christ behind me,
Christ within me,
Christ beneath me,
Christ above me.

St Patrick fl. 5th cent.: 'St Patrick's Breastplate'

9 Perform the prayer
at the sinking of the sun to the darkening
   of the night
and the recital of dawn.

The Koran: sura 17

10 God be in my head,
And in my understanding.

Anonymous: *Sarum Missal* (11th century)

11 Prayer in my opinion is nothing else than an intimate sharing between friends.

St Teresa of Ávila 1512–82: *Life of the Mother Teresa of Jesus* (1611)

12 My words fly up, my thoughts remain
   below:
Words without thoughts never to heaven
   go.

William Shakespeare 1564–1616: *Hamlet* (1601)

13 I throw myself down in my Chamber, and I call in, and invite God, and his Angels thither, and when they are there, I neglect God and his Angels, for the noise of a fly, for the rattling of a coach, for the whining of a door.

John Donne 1572–1631: *LXXX Sermons* (1640) 12 December 1626 'At the Funeral of Sir William Cokayne'

14 O Lord! thou knowest how busy I must be this day: if I forget thee, do not thou forget me.

prayer before the Battle of Edgehill, 1642

Jacob Astley 1579–1652: Sir Philip Warwick *Memoires* (1701)

15 At my devotion I love to use the civility of my knee, my hat, and hand.

Thomas Browne 1605–82: *Religio Medici* (1643)

16 Be still and cool in thy own mind and spirit from thy own thoughts, and then thou wilt feel the principle of God to turn thy mind to the Lord God.

George Fox 1624–91: diary 1658

17 No praying, it spoils business.

Thomas Otway 1652–85: *Venice Preserved* (1682)

18 O God, if there be a God, save my soul, if I have a soul!

prayer of a common soldier before the battle of Blenheim, 1704

Anonymous: in *Notes and Queries* 9 October 1937

19 One single grateful thought raised to heaven is the most perfect prayer.

G. E. Lessing 1729–81: *Minna von Barnhelm* (1767)

20   Did not God
Sometimes withhold in mercy what we
   ask,
We should be ruined at our own request.

Hannah More 1745–1833: *Moses in the Bulrushes* (1782)

21 He prayeth well, who loveth well
Both man and bird and beast.

Samuel Taylor Coleridge 1772–1834: 'The Rime of the Ancient Mariner' (1798)

22 And lips say, 'God be pitiful,'
Who ne'er said, 'God be praised.'

Elizabeth Barrett Browning 1806–61: 'The Cry of the Human' (1844)

23   More things are wrought by prayer
Than this world dreams of.

Alfred, Lord Tennyson 1809–92: *Idylls of the King* 'The Passing of Arthur' (1869)

24 Whatever a man prays for, he prays for a miracle. Every prayer reduces itself to this: Great God, grant that twice two be not four.

Ivan Turgenev 1818–83: *Poems in Prose* (1881) 'Prayer'

25 To lift up the hands in prayer gives God glory, but a man with a dungfork in his hand, a woman with a slop-pail, give him glory too. He is so great that all things give him glory if you mean they should.

Gerard Manley Hopkins 1844–89: 'The Principle or Foundation' (1882)

26 You can't pray a lie.

Mark Twain 1835–1910: *Adventures of Huckleberry Finn* (1885)

27 Frederick Douglass used to tell me that when he was a Maryland slave, and a good Methodist, he would go into the farthest corner of the tobacco fields and pray to God to bring him liberty; but God never answered his prayers until he prayed with his heels.

Susan B. Anthony 1820–1906: R. C. Dorr *Susan B. Anthony* (1928)

28 Often when I pray I wonder if I am not posting letters to a non-existent address.

C. S. Lewis 1898–1963: letter to Arthur Greeves, 24 December 1930; W. Hooper (ed.) *They Stand Together* (1979)

29 The wish for prayer is a prayer in itself.

Georges Bernanos 1888–1948: *Journal d'un curé de campagne* (1936)

30 School prayer . . . bears about as much resemblance to real spiritual experience as that freeze-dried astronaut food bears to a nice standing rib roast.

Anna Quindlen 1953– : in *New York Times* 7 December 1994

31 Surely the form of a prayer does not matter, and the only distinction God makes is between good will and ill; or so I have come to believe.

Margaret Atwood 1939– : *Alias Grace* (1996)

32 The prayers of the dying are especially precious to God, because they will soon be in His presence.

Basil Hume 1923–99: in *Independent* 18 June 1999

Pregnancy and Birth

PROVERBS AND SAYINGS

**1 And the child that is born of the Sabbath day,
Is bonny, and blithe, and good and gay.**

mid 19th century; see **Beauty** 5, **Gifts** 2, **Sorrow** 2, **Travel** 5, **Work** 6

**2 Jeannie Jeannie, full of hopes
Read a book by Marie Stopes
But to judge from her condition
She must have read the wrong edition.**

1920s skipping rhyme; Marie Stopes (1880–1958) was a Scottish birth-control campaigner

3 No moon, no man.

late 19th century, recording the traditional belief that a child born at the time of the new moon or just before its appearance will not live to grow up

QUOTATIONS

4 In sorrow thou shalt bring forth children.

Bible: Genesis

5 The queen of Scots is this day leichter of a fair son, and I am but a barren stock.

Elizabeth I 1533–1603: in 1566; Sir James Melville *Memoirs of His Own Life* (1827 ed.)

6 Our birth is but a sleep and a forgetting . . .
Not in entire forgetfulness,
And not in utter nakedness,
But trailing clouds of glory do we come.

William Wordsworth 1770–1850: 'Ode. Intimations of Immortality' (1807)

7 What you say of the pride of giving life to an immortal soul is very fine, dear, but I own I can not enter into that; I think much more of our being like a cow or a dog at such moments; when our poor nature becomes so very animal and unecstatic.

Queen Victoria 1819–1901: letter to the Princess Royal, 15 June 1858

8 In the dark womb where I began
My mother's life made me a man.
Through all the months of human birth
Her beauty fed my common earth.
I cannot see, nor breathe, nor stir,
But through the death of some of her.

John Masefield 1878–1967: 'C. L. M.' (1910)

9 We want better reasons for having children than not knowing how to prevent them.

Dora Russell 1894–1986: *Hypatia* (1925)

10 Death and taxes and childbirth! There's never any convenient time for any of them.

Margaret Mitchell 1900–49: *Gone with the Wind* (1936); see **Certainty** 3

11 I am not yet born; O fill me
With strength against those who would freeze my
humanity, would dragoon me into a lethal automaton,
would make me a cog in a machine, a thing with

one face, a thing.
Louis MacNeice 1907–63: 'Prayer Before Birth' (1944)

12 Abortions will not let you forget.
You remember the children you got that
   you did not get . . .
Gwendolyn Brooks 1917–2000: 'The Mother' (1945)

13 Love set you going like a fat gold watch.
The midwife slapped your footsoles, and
   your bald cry
Took its place among the elements.
Sylvia Plath 1932–63: 'Morning Song' (1965)

14 A fast word about oral contraception. I
asked a girl to go to bed with me and she
said 'no'.
Woody Allen 1935– : at a nightclub in Washington,
April 1965

15 If men could get pregnant, abortion would
be a sacrament.
Florynce Kennedy 1916–2001: in *Ms.* March 1973

16 With its heart bursting, the infant sinks into
hell . . . the mother is driving it out. At the
same time she is holding it in, preventing its
passage. It is she who is the enemy. She who
stands between the child and life. Only one
of them can prevail. It is mortal combat.
Frederick Leboyer: *Birth Without Violence* (1975)

17 No phallic hero, no matter what he does to
himself or to another to prove his courage,
ever matches the solitary, existential
courage of the woman who gives birth.
Andrea Dworkin 1946– : *Our Blood* (1976)

18 No test tube can breed love and affection. No
frozen packet of semen ever read a story to a
sleepy child.
Shirley Williams 1930– : in *Daily Mirror* 2 March
1978

19 If men had to have babies, they would only
ever have one each.
Diana, Princess of Wales 1961–97: in *Observer* 29
July 1984

20 Protestant women may take the pill. Roman
Catholic women must keep taking The
Tablet.
Irene Thomas 1919–2001: in *Guardian* 28 December
1990; see **Medicine** 3

21 Large numbers of gynaecologists refer to it
as not fertility but futility, which I think is
quite interesting. And when I was brought
up as a young gynaecologist in training,
people thought I was mad wanting to be in
a futility clinic.
Robert Winston 1940– : Anthony Clare *In the
Psychiatrist's Chair II* (1995)

Prejudice and Tolerance see also **Race and Racism**

PROVERBS AND SAYINGS

1 Judge not, that ye be not judged.
*late 15th century, used as a warning against overhasty
criticism of someone; from the Bible (Matthew): see
Justice 18*

2 Live and let live.
*early 17th century, often used in the context of
coexistence between deeply divided groups*

3 No tree takes so deep a root as a prejudice.
*American proverb, mid 20th century, emphasizing how
difficult it is to eradicate prejudice*

**4 There's none so blind as those who will not
see.**
*mid 16th century, used in reference to someone who is
unwilling to recognize unwelcome facts*

**5 There's none so deaf as those who will not
hear.**
*mid 16th century, used to refer to someone who chooses
not to listen to unwelcome information*

QUOTATIONS

6 *Sine ira et studio.*
With neither anger nor partiality.
Tacitus AD c.56–after 117: *Annals*

7 Hear the other side.
St Augustine of Hippo AD 354–430: *De Duabus
Animabus contra Manicheos*

8 Sir Roger told them, with the air of a man
who would not give his judgement rashly,
that much might be said on both sides.
Joseph Addison 1672–1719: in *The Spectator* 20 July
1711

9 There is, however, a limit at which
forbearance ceases to be a virtue.
Edmund Burke 1729–97: *Observations on a late
Publication on the Present State of the Nation* (2nd ed.,
1769)

10 Drive out prejudices through the door, and they will return through the window.
Frederick the Great 1712–86: letter to Voltaire, 19 March 1771

11 When prejudice commands, reason is silent.
Helvétius 1715–71: De l'homme (1773)

12 Prejudice is the child of ignorance.
William Hazlitt 1778–1830: 'On Prejudice' (1830)

13 Who's 'im, Bill?
A stranger!
'Eave 'arf a brick at 'im.
Punch: 1854

14 Tolerance is only another name for indifference.
W. Somerset Maugham 1874–1965: A Writer's Notebook (1949) written in 1896

15 Make hatred hated!
to public school teachers
Anatole France 1844–1924: speech in Tours, August 1919; Carter Jefferson Anatole France: The Politics of Scepticism (1965)

16 I decline utterly to be impartial as between the fire brigade and the fire.
replying to complaints of his bias in editing the British Gazette during the General Strike
Winston Churchill 1874–1965: speech, House of Commons, 7 July 1926

17 Bigotry tries to keep truth safe in its hand With a grip that kills it.
Rabindranath Tagore 1861–1941: Fireflies (1928)

18 Oh who is that young sinner with the handcuffs on his wrists?
And what has he been after that they groan and shake their fists?
And wherefore is he wearing such a conscience-stricken air?

Oh they're taking him to prison for the colour of his hair.
A. E. Housman 1859–1936: Collected Poems (1939) 'Additional Poems' no. 18

19 Intolerance of groups is often, strangely enough, exhibited more strongly against small differences than against fundamental ones.
Sigmund Freud 1856–1939: Moses and Monotheism (1938)

20 You might as well fall flat on your face as lean over too far backward.
James Thurber 1894–1961: 'The Bear Who Let It Alone' in New Yorker 29 April 1939

21 Four legs good, two legs bad.
George Orwell 1903–50: Animal Farm (1945)

22 We should therefore claim, in the name of tolerance, the right not to tolerate the intolerant.
Karl Popper 1902–94: The Open Society and Its Enemies (1945)

23 When people feel deeply, impartiality is bias.
Lord Reith 1889–1971: Into the Wind (1945)

24 PLEASE ACCEPT MY RESIGNATION. I DON'T WANT TO BELONG TO ANY CLUB THAT WILL ACCEPT ME AS A MEMBER.
Groucho Marx 1895–1977: Groucho and Me (1959)

25 What is objectionable, what is dangerous about extremists is not that they are extreme but that they are intolerant.
Robert Kennedy 1925–68: The Pursuit of Justice (1964)

26 Human diversity makes tolerance more than a virtue, it makes it a requirement for survival.
René Dubos 1901–82: Celebrations of Life (1981)

Preparation and Readiness

PROVERBS AND SAYINGS

1 Be prepared.
motto of the Scout and Guide organizations, deriving from the initials of Robert Baden-Powell (1857–1941), the founder

2 Don't cross the bridge till you come to it.
mid 19th century, warning that you should not concern yourself with possible difficulties unless and until they arise

3 The early bird catches the worm.
mid 17th century, meaning that someone who is energetic and efficient is most likely to be successful

4 The early man never borrows from the late man.
mid 17th century, meaning that someone who has made their preparations has no need to turn to someone less efficient

5 Forewarned is forearmed.
early 16th century, meaning that if one has been warned in advance about a problem one can make preparations for dealing with it

6 For want of a nail the shoe was lost; for want of a shoe the horse was lost; and for want of a horse the man was lost.
early 17th century; late 15th century in French. The

saying is often quoted allusively to imply that one apparently small circumstance can result in a large-scale disaster

7 Here's one I made earlier.
catchphrase popularized by children's television programme Blue Peter, from 1963, as a culmination to directions for making a model out of empty yoghurt pots, coat-hangers, and similar domestic items

8 Hope for the best and prepare for the worst.
mid 16th century, recommending a balance between optimism and realism

9 If you want peace, you must prepare for war.
mid 16th century, meaning that a country in a state of military preparedness is unlikely to be attacked; see **Warfare** 11

PHRASES

10 armed at all points prepared in every particular.
recorded from late Middle English, but often referring directly to a First Folio variant reading of Shakespeare Hamlet

QUOTATIONS

11 The voice of him that crieth in the wilderness, Prepare ye the way of the Lord.
Bible: Isaiah; see **Futility** 12

12 Watch therefore: for ye know not what hour your Lord doth come.
Bible: St Matthew

13   Not a mouse

Shall disturb this hallowed house:
I am sent with broom before,
To sweep the dust behind the door.
William Shakespeare 1564–1616: A Midsummer Night's Dream (1595-6)

14 No time like the present.
Mrs Manley 1663–1724: The Lost Lover (1696)

15 Barkis is willin'.
Charles Dickens 1812–70: David Copperfield (1850)

16 I think the necessity of being *ready* increases. Look to it.
Abraham Lincoln 1809–65: the whole of a letter to Governor Andrew Curtin of Pennsylvania, 8 April 1861

17 No plan of operations reaches with any certainty beyond the first encounter with the enemy's main force.
often quoted as 'no plan survives first contact with the enemy'
Helmuth von Moltke 1800–91: Kriegsgechichtiche Einzelschriften (1880)

18 In preparing for battle I have always found that plans are useless, but planning is indispensable.
Dwight D. Eisenhower 1890–1969: Richard Nixon Six Crises (1962); attributed

19 Go ahead, make my day.
Joseph C. Stinson 1947– : Sudden Impact (1983 film); spoken by Clint Eastwood

20 First things first, second things never.
Shirley Conran 1932– : Superwoman (1975)

21 We are ready for any unforeseen event which may or may not happen.
George W. Bush 1946– : in Guardian 30 December 2000

The Present see also **The Past**

PROVERBS AND SAYINGS

1 Enjoy the present moment and don't grieve for the future.
American proverb, mid 20th century

2 Jam tomorrow and jam yesterday, but never jam today.
late 19th century, from Carroll: see 9 below

QUOTATIONS

3 *Carpe diem, quam minimum credula postero.*
Seize the day, put no trust in the future.
Horace 65–8 BC: Odes

4 Take therefore no thought for the morrow: for the morrow shall take thought for the things of itself. Sufficient unto the day is the evil thereof.
Bible: St Matthew; see **Worry** 4

5 Can ye not discern the signs of the times?
Bible: St Matthew

6 Praise they that will times past, I joy to see My self now live: this age best pleaseth me.
Robert Herrick 1591–1674: 'The Present Time Best Pleaseth' (1648)

7 The present is the funeral of the past,

And man the living sepulchre of life.
John Clare 1793–1864: 'The present is the funeral of the past' (written 1845)

8 Unborn TO-MORROW, and dead YESTERDAY,
Why fret about them if TO-DAY be sweet!
Edward Fitzgerald 1809–83: *The Rubáiyát of Omar Khayyám* (1859)

9 The rule is, jam to-morrow and jam yesterday—but never jam today.
Lewis Carroll 1832–98: *Through the Looking-Glass* (1872); see 2 above, **Foresight** 16

10 To-morrow for the young the poets exploding like bombs,
The walks by the lake, the weeks of perfect communion;
To-morrow the bicycle races
Through the suburbs on summer evenings: but to-day the struggle.
W. H. Auden 1907–73: 'Spain 1937' (1937)

11 Exhaust the little moment. Soon it dies.
And be it gash or gold it will not come
Again in this identical disguise.
Gwendolyn Brooks 1917–2000: 'Exhaust the little moment' (1949)

12 Like a monkey scratching for the wrong fleas, every age assiduously seeks out in

itself those vices which it does not in fact have, while ignoring the large, red, beady-eyed crawlers who scuttle around unimpeded.
Katharine Whitehorn 1928– : *Observations* (1970)

13 Life is one tenth Here and Now, nine-tenths a history lesson. For most of the time the Here and Now is neither now nor here.
Graham Swift 1949– : *Waterland* (1984)

14 Things are both more trivial than they ever were, and more important than they ever were, and the difference between the trivial and the important doesn't seem to matter. But the nowness of everything is absolutely wondrous.
on his heightened awareness of things, in the face of his imminent death
Dennis Potter 1935–94: interview with Melvyn Bragg on Channel 4, March 1994, in *Seeing the Blossom* (1994)

15 It's not perfect, but to me on balance Right Now is a lot better than the Good Old Days.
Maeve Binchy 1940– : in *Irish Times* 15 November 1997; see **The Past** 10

The Presidency see also **America, Politicians**

PHRASES

1 **bully pulpit** a public office or position of authority that provides its occupant with an outstanding opportunity to speak out on any issue.
from Roosevelt's personal view of the presidency: see 6 below

2 **just a heart-beat away from the Presidency** the vice-president's position.
from Adlai Stevenson (1900–65), speech at Cleveland, Ohio, 23 October 1952, 'The Republican party did not have to . . . encourage the excesses of its Vice-Presidential nominee [Richard Nixon]—the young man who asks you to set him one heart-beat from the Presidency of the United States'

QUOTATIONS

3 My country has in its wisdom contrived for me the most insignificant office that ever the invention of man contrived or his imagination conceived.
of the vice-presidency
John Adams 1735–1826: letter to Abigail Adams, 19 December 1793

4 A citizen, first in war, first in peace, and first in the hearts of his countrymen.
Henry Lee 1756–1818: *Funeral Oration on the death of General Washington* (1800)

5 As President, I have no eyes but constitutional eyes; I cannot see you.
Abraham Lincoln 1809–65: reply to the South Carolina Commissioners; attributed

6 I have got such a bully pulpit!
Theodore Roosevelt 1858–1919: in *Outlook* (New York) 27 February 1909; see 1 above, 20 below

7 Log-cabin to White House.
William Roscoe Thayer 1859–1923: title of biography (1910) of James Garfield (1831–81)

8 How do they know?
reaction to the death of President Calvin Coolidge in 1933
Dorothy Parker 1893–1967: Malcolm Cowley *Writers at Work* 1st Series (1958)

9 When I was a boy I was told that anybody could become President. I'm beginning to believe it.
Clarence Darrow 1857–1938: Irving Stone *Clarence Darrow for the Defence* (1941)

10 He'll sit right here and he'll say do this, do that! And nothing will happen. Poor Ike— it won't be a bit like the Army.
of Eisenhower
Harry S. Truman 1884–1972: *Harry S. Truman* (1973)

11 No easy problems ever come to the President of the United States. If they are easy to solve, somebody else has solved them.
Dwight D. Eisenhower 1890–1969: in *Parade Magazine* 8 April 1962

12 The lines he loved to hear were: 'Don't let it be forgot, that once there was a spot, for one brief shining moment that was known as Camelot.' . . . There'll be great Presidents again . . . but there'll never be another Camelot again.
on the Kennedy White House, quoting Alan Jay Lerner
Jacqueline Kennedy Onassis 1929–94: in *Life* 6 December 1963

13 The vice-presidency isn't worth a pitcher of warm piss.
John Nance Garner 1868–1967: O. C. Fisher *Cactus Jack* (1978)

14 The answer to the runaway Presidency is not the messenger-boy Presidency. The American democracy must discover a middle way between making the President a tsar and making him a puppet.
Arthur M. Schlesinger Jr. 1917– : *The Imperial Presidency* (1973) preface

15 There can be no whitewash at the White House.
on Watergate
Richard Nixon 1913–94: television speech, 30 April 1973

16 Anybody that wants the presidency so much that he'll spend two years organizing and campaigning for it is not to be trusted with the office.
David Broder 1929– : in *Washington Post* 18 July 1973

17 The US presidency is a Tudor monarchy plus telephones.
Anthony Burgess 1917–93: George Plimpton (ed.) *Writers at Work* 4th Series (1977)

18 When the President does it, that means that it is not illegal.
Richard Nixon 1913–94: David Frost *I Gave Them a Sword* (1978)

19 Ronald Reagan . . . is attempting a great breakthrough in political technology—he has been perfecting the Teflon-coated Presidency. He sees to it that nothing sticks to him.
Patricia Schroeder 1940– : speech in the US House of Representatives, 2 August 1983

20 If the President has a bully pulpit, then the First Lady has a white glove pulpit . . . more refined, restricted, ceremonial, but it's a pulpit all the same.
Nancy Reagan 1923– : in *New York Times* 10 March 1988; see 6 above

21 Poor George [Bush], he can't help it—he was born with a silver foot in his mouth.
Ann Richards 1933– : keynote speech at the Democratic convention, in *Independent* 20 July 1988; see **Wealth** 8

22 Somewhere out in this audience may even be someone who will one day follow in my footsteps, and preside over the White House as the President's spouse. I wish him well!
Barbara Bush 1925– : remarks at Wellesley College Commencement, 1 June 1990

23 To those of you who received honours, awards and distinctions, I say well done. And to the C students, I say you, too, can be president of the United States.
George W. Bush 1946– : in *Sunday Times* 27 May 2001

Pride and Humility see also **Self-Esteem and Self-Assertion**

PROVERBS AND SAYINGS

1 Pride feels no pain.
early 17th century, implying that inordinate self-esteem will not allow the admission that one might be suffering

2 Pride goes before a fall.
late 14th century, often with the implication that proud and haughty behaviour will contribute to its own downfall; see 4 below

3 as proud as Lucifer very proud, arrogant.
Lucifer *the rebel angel whose fall from heaven Jerome and other early Christian writers considered was alluded to in the Bible (Isaiah) (where the word is an epithet of the king of Babylon); Satan, the Devil*

QUOTATIONS

4 Pride goeth before destruction, and an haughty spirit before a fall.
Bible: Proverbs; see 2 above

5 Blessed are the meek: for they shall inherit the earth.
Bible: St Matthew; see 11 below

6 He that is down needs fear no fall,
He that is low no pride.
He that is humble ever shall
Have God to be his guide.
John Bunyan 1628–88: *The Pilgrim's Progress* (1684) 'Shepherd Boy's Song'

7 We are so very 'umble.
Charles Dickens 1812–70: *David Copperfield* (1850)

8 I can trace my ancestry back to a protoplasmal primordial atomic globule. Consequently, my family pride is something in-conceivable. I can't help it. I was born sneering.
W. S. Gilbert 1836–1911: *The Mikado* (1885)

9 The tumult and the shouting dies—
The captains and the kings depart—

Still stands Thine ancient Sacrifice,
An humble and a contrite heart.
Lord God of Hosts, be with us yet,
Lest we forget—lest we forget!
Rudyard Kipling 1865–1936: 'Recessional' (1897); see **Entertaining** 20

10 The clever men at Oxford
Know all that there is to be knowed.
But they none of them know one half as much
As intelligent Mr Toad!
Kenneth Grahame 1859–1932: *Wind in the Willows* (1908)

11 We have the highest authority for believing that the meek shall inherit the earth; though I have never found any particular corroboration of this aphorism in the records of Somerset House.
F. E. Smith 1872–1930: *Contemporary Personalities* (1924); see 5 above

12 I have often wished I had time to cultivate modesty . . . But I am too busy thinking about myself.
Edith Sitwell 1887–1964: in *Observer* 30 April 1950

13 No one can make you feel inferior without your consent.
Eleanor Roosevelt 1884–1962: in *Catholic Digest* August 1960

14 In 1969 I published a small book on Humility. It was a pioneering work which has not, to my knowledge, been superseded.
Lord Longford 1905–2001: in *Tablet* 22 January 1994

Problems and Solutions see also Ways and Means

1 Jim'll fix it.
catchphrase of a BBC television series (1975–94) starring Jimmy Savile in which participants had their wishes fulfilled

2 When all you have is a hammer, everything looks like a nail.
late 20th century (chiefly North American), often used to comment on the wholesale application of one solution or method to the solution of any problem

3 a chicken-and-egg problem an unresolved question as to which of two things caused

the other.
from the riddle, Which came first, the chicken or the egg?

4 cut the Gordian knot solve a problem by force or by evading the conditions.
in allusion to an intricate knot tied by Gordius, king of Gordium, Phrygia, and cut through by Alexander the Great in response to the prophecy that only the future ruler of Asia could loosen it

5 Frankenstein's monster something which has developed beyond the management or control of its originator.
Frankenstein the title of a novel (1818) by Mary Shelley whose eponymous main character constructed and gave life to a human monster

6 make bricks without straw perform a task without provision of the necessary materials or means.

from the Bible (Exodus), in allusion to Pharaoh's decree to the taskmasters set over the Israelites in Egypt 'Ye shall no more give the people straw to make brick, as heretofore: let them go and gather straw for themselves'; see **Futility** *6*

7 Open Sesame a (marvellous or irresistible) means of securing access to what would usually be inaccessible.

the magic words by which, in the tale of Ali Baba and the Forty Thieves in the Arabian Nights, *the door of the robbers' cave was made to open*

8 Pandora's box a thing which once activated will give rise to many unmanageable problems.

in Greek mythology, the gift of Jupiter to Pandōra, 'all-gifted', the first mortal woman, on whom, when made by Vulcan, all the gods and goddesses bestowed gifts; the box enclosed all human ills, which flew out when it was foolishly opened (or in a later version, it contained all the blessings of the gods, which with the exception of hope escaped and were lost when the box was opened); see **Europe** *13*

9 philosophers' stone a universal cure or solution.

the supreme object of alchemy, a substance supposed to change any metal into gold or silver and (according to some) to cure all diseases and prolong life indefinitely

10 the sixty-four thousand dollar question the crucial issue, a difficult question, a dilemma.

the top prize in a broadcast quiz show

11 sorcerer's apprentice a person who having instigated a process is unable to control it.

translating French l'apprenti sorcier, *a symphonic poem by Paul Dukas (1897) after* der Zauberlehrling, *a ballad by Goethe (1797)*

12 there's the rub there is the difficulty.

a rub here is literally an impediment in bowls by which a bowl is hindered in or diverted from its proper course; from Shakespeare: see **Death** *27*

QUOTATIONS

13 Probable impossibilities are to be preferred to improbable possibilities.
Aristotle 384–322 BC: *Poetics*

14 One hears only those questions for which one is able to find answers.
Friedrich Nietzsche 1844–1900: *The Gay Science* (1882)

15 How often have I said to you that when you have eliminated the impossible, whatever remains, *however improbable*, must be the truth?
Arthur Conan Doyle 1859–1930: *The Sign of Four* (1890)

16 The fascination of what's difficult
Has dried the sap out of my veins, and rent
Spontaneous joy and natural content
Out of my heart.
W. B. Yeats 1865–1939: 'The Fascination of What's Difficult' (1910)

17 There is always a well-known solution to every human problem—neat, plausible, and wrong.
Henry Louis Mencken 1880–1956: *Prejudices* 2nd series (1920)

18 Another nice mess you've gotten me into.
Stan Laurel 1890–1965: *Another Fine Mess* (1930 film) and many other Laurel and Hardy films; spoken by Oliver Hardy

19 It isn't that they can't see the solution. It is that they can't see the problem.
G. K. Chesterton 1874–1936: *Scandal of Father Brown* (1935)

20 We haven't got the money, so we've got to think!
Ernest Rutherford 1871–1937: in *Bulletin of the Institute of Physics* (1962); see 26 below

21 Let me have the best solution worked out. Don't argue the matter. The difficulties will argue for themselves.
on the Mulberry floating harbours
Winston Churchill 1874–1965: minute to Lord Mountbatten, 30 May 1942

22 What we're saying today is that you're either part of the solution or you're part of the problem.
Eldridge Cleaver 1935–98: speech in San Francisco, 1968; R. Scheer *Eldridge Cleaver, Post Prison Writings and Speeches* (1969)

23 Problems worthy
of attack
prove their worth
by hitting back.
Piet Hein 1905– : 'Problems' (1969)

24 Houston, we've had a problem.
on Apollo 13 space mission, 14 April 1970
James Lovell 1928– : in *The Times* 15 April 1970

25 Einstein was a man who could ask immensely simple questions. And what his life showed, and his work, is that when the

answers are simple too, then you hear God thinking.
Jacob Bronowski 1908-74: *The Ascent of Man* (1973)

26 Rutherford was a disaster. He started the 'something for nothing' tradition . . . the notion that research can always be done on the cheap . . . The war taught us differently. If you want quick and effective results you must put the money in.
Edward Bullard 1907-80: P. Grosvenor and J.McMillan *The British Genius* (1973); see 20 above

27 If a problem is too difficult to solve, one cannot claim that it is solved by pointing at all the efforts made to solve it.
Hannes Alfven 1908-95: quoted by Lord Flowers in 1976; A. Sampson *The Changing Anatomy of Britain* (1982)

28 What I cannot create, I do not understand. Know how to solve every problem that has been solved.
written on his blackboard at Caltech, as he left it for the last time in January 1988
Richard Feynman 1918-88: Christopher Sykes (ed.) *No Ordinary Genius* (1994)

Progress see also Change

see also **Change**

PHRASES

1 **brave new world** utopia produced by technological and social advance.
title of a satirical novel by Aldous Huxley (1932), after Shakespeare Tempest: *see **Human Race** 12*

2 **future shock** a state of distress or disorientation due to rapid social or technological change.
from Alvin Toffler in Horizon *1965, 'The dizzy disorientation brought on by the premature arrival of the future'; definition of* future shock

3 **Great Leap Forward** an unsuccessful attempt made under Mao Zedong in China 1958-60 to hasten the process of industrialization and improve agricultural production.

4 **quantum leap** a sudden, significant or very evident (usually large) increase or advance.
from the term quantum jump *in Physics, referring to an abrupt transition from one quantum state to another*

QUOTATIONS

5 The thing that hath been, it is that which shall be; and that which is done is that which shall be done: and there is no new thing under the sun.
Bible: Ecclesiastes; see **Familiarity** 10

6 Forgetting those things which are behind, and reaching forth unto those things which are before,
I press toward the mark.
Bible: Philippians

7 We are like dwarfs on the shoulders of giants, so that we can see more than they, and things at a greater distance, not by virtue of any sharpness of sight on our part, or any physical distinction, but because we are carried high and raised up by their giant size.
Bernard of Chartres d. c.1130: John of Salisbury *The Metalogicon* (1159)

8 If I have seen further it is by standing on the shoulders of giants.
Isaac Newton 1642-1727: letter to Robert Hooke, 5 February 1676

9 Not to go back, is somewhat to advance, And men must walk at least before they dance.
Alexander Pope 1688-1744: *Imitations of Horace*

10 Nothing in progression can rest on its original plan. We may as well think of rocking a grown man in the cradle of an infant.
Edmund Burke 1729-97: *Letter to the Sheriffs of Bristol* (1777)

11 The European talks of progress because by an ingenious application of some scientific acquirements he has established a society which has mistaken comfort for civilization.
Benjamin Disraeli 1804-81: *Tancred* (1847)

12 Belief in progress is a doctrine of idlers and Belgians. It is the individual relying upon his neighbours to do his work.
Charles Baudelaire 1821-67: *Journaux intimes* (1887) 'Mon coeur mis à nu'

13 The reasonable man adapts himself to the world: the unreasonable one persists in trying to adapt the world to himself. Therefore all progress depends on the unreasonable man.
George Bernard Shaw 1856–1950: *Man and Superman* (1903)

14 One step forward two steps back.
Lenin 1870–1924: title of book (1904)

15 The new growth in the plant swelling against the sheath, which at the same time imprisons and protects it, must still be the truest type of progress.
Jane Addams 1860–1935: *Democracy and Social Ethics* (1907)

16 The slogan of progress is changing from the full dinner pail to the full garage.
sometimes paraphrased as, 'a car in every garage and a chicken in every pot'
Herbert Hoover 1874–1964: speech in New York, 22 October 1928; see **Poverty** 16

17 In time to come, I tell them, we'll be equal to any living now. If cripples, then no matter; we shall just have been run over
by 'New Man' in the wagon of his 'Plan'.
Boris Pasternak 1890–1960: 'When I Grow Weary' (1932)

18 Want is one only of five giants on the road of reconstruction . . . the others are Disease, Ignorance, Squalor and Idleness.
William Henry Beveridge 1879–1963: *Social Insurance and Allied Services* (1942)

19 pity this busy monster, manunkind, not. Progress is a comfortable disease.
e. e. cummings 1894–1962: *1 x 1* (1944) no. 14

20 'Change' is scientific, 'progress' is ethical; change is indubitable, whereas progress is a matter of controversy.
Bertrand Russell: *Unpopular Essays* (1950) 'Philosophy and Politics'

21 Man aspires to the stars. But if he can get his sewage and refuse distributed and utilised in orderly fashion he will be doing very well.
Roy Bridger: in *The Times* 13 July 1959

22 Is it progress if a cannibal uses knife and fork?
Stanislaw Lec 1909–66: *Unkempt Thoughts* (1962)

23 Things can only get better.
Jamie Petrie and **Peter Cunnah**: title of song (1992), used as a slogan by the Labour party in the 1997 general election campaign

24 For 80 per cent of humanity the Middle Ages ended suddenly in the 1950s; or perhaps better still, they were *felt* to end in the 1960s.
Eric Hobsbawm 1917– : *Age of Extremes* (1994)

Publishing see also Books

see also **Books**

PHRASES

1 **printer's devil** an errand-boy or junior assistant in a printing office.
devil *a person employed in a subordinate position to work under the direction of or for a particular person; see 8 below*

2 **river of white** a white line or streak down a printed page where spaces between words on consecutive lines are close together.

QUOTATIONS

3 I, according to my copy, have done set it in imprint, to the intent that noble men may see and learn the noble acts of chivalry, the gentle and virtuous deeds that some knights used in those days.
William Caxton c.1421–91: Thomas Malory *Le Morte D'Arthur* (1485) prologue

4 You shall see them on a beautiful quarto page where a neat rivulet of text shall meander through a meadow of margin.
Richard Brinsley Sheridan 1751–1816: *The School for Scandal* (1777)

5 Never literary attempt was more unfortunate than my Treatise of Human Nature. It fell *dead-born from the press.*
David Hume 1711–76: *My Own Life* (1777)

6 The poem will please if it is lively—if it is stupid it will fail—but I will have none of your damned cutting and slashing.
Lord Byron 1788–1824: letter to his publisher John Murray, 6 April 1819

7 Publish and be damned.
replying to Harriette Wilson's blackmail threat, c. 1825
Duke of Wellington 1769–1852: attributed

8 For you know, dear—I may, without
vanity, hint—
Though an angel should write, still 'tis
devils must print.
Thomas Moore 1779–1852: *The Fudges in England*
(1835); see 1 above

9 Now Barabbas was a publisher.
alteration in a Bible of the verse 'Now Barabbas was a
robber'
Thomas Campbell 1777–1844: attributed, in
Samuel Smiles *A Publisher and his Friends* (1891); also
attributed, wrongly, to Byron

10 University printing presses exist, and are
subsidised by the Government for the
purpose of producing books which no one
can read; and they are true to their high
calling.
Francis M. Cornford 1874–1943: *Microcosmographia
Academica* (1908)

11 For several days after my first book was
published I carried it about in my pocket,
and took surreptitious peeps at it to make
sure that the ink had not faded.
J. M. Barrie 1860–1937: speech at the Critics' Circle
in London, 26 May 1922

12 Of all the literary scenes
Saddest this sight to me:
The graves of little magazines
Who died to make verse free.
Keith Preston 1884–1927: 'The Liberators'

13 Gutenberg made everybody a reader.
Xerox makes everybody a publisher.
Marshall McLuhan 1911–80: in *Guardian Weekly* 12
June 1977

14 If I had been someone not very clever, I
would have done an easier job like
publishing. That's the easiest job I can
think of.
A. J. Ayer 1910–89: attributed

15 The whole world of publishing has
changed. The accountants have moved in.
It's now the bottom line, not is it a good
book?
Hammond Innes 1913– : interview in *Daily
Telegraph* 3 August 1996

Punctuality

PROVERBS AND SAYINGS

1 Better late than never.
*early 14th century, meaning that even if one has
missed the first chance of doing something, it is better
to attempt it than not to do it at all*

**2 Cathedral time is five minutes later than
standard time.**
*order of service leaflet, Christ Church Cathedral,
Oxford, 1990s*

3 First come, first served.
late 14th century

**4 Punctuality is the art of guessing correctly
how late the other party is going to be.**
American proverb, mid 20th century

5 Punctuality is the politeness of princes.
mid 19th century; see 10 below

6 Punctuality is the soul of business.
mid 19th century

QUOTATIONS

7 You come most carefully upon your hour.
William Shakespeare 1564–1616: *Hamlet* (1601)

8 I was nearly kept waiting.
Louis XIV 1638–1715: attribution queried, among
others, by E. Fournier in *L'Esprit dans l'Histoire* (1857)

9 Recollect that painting and punctuality
mix like oil and vinegar, and that genius
and regularity are utter enemies, and must
be to the end of time.
Thomas Gainsborough 1727–88: letter to the Hon.
Edward Stratford, 1 May 1772

10 Punctuality is the politeness of kings.
Louis XVIII 1755–1824: *Souvenirs de J. Lafitte* (1844);
attributed; see 5 above

11 The only way of catching a train I have
ever discovered is to miss the train before.
G. K. Chesterton 1874–1936: *Tremendous Trifles*
(1909)

12 An artist must organize his life. Here is the
exact timetable of my daily activities. Get
up: 7.18 am; be inspired: 10.23 to 11.47
am. I take lunch at 12.11 pm and leave
the table at 12.14 pm.
Erik Satie 1866–1925: *Memoirs of an Amnesiac*
(1914)

13 But think how early I go.

when criticized for continually arriving late for work in the City in 1919

Lord Castlerosse 1891–1943: Leonard Mosley *Castlerosse* (1956); remark also claimed by Howard Dietz at MGM

14 We've been waiting 700 years, you can have the seven minutes.

on arriving at Dublin Castle for the handover by British forces on 16 January 1922, and being told that he was seven minutes late

Michael Collins 1880–1922: Tim Pat Coogan *Michael Collins* (1990); attributed, perhaps apocryphal

15 I have noticed that the people who are late are often so much jollier than the people who have to wait for them.

E. V. Lucas 1868–1938: *365 Days and One More* (1926)

16 We must leave exactly on time . . . From now on everything must function to perfection.

to a station-master

Benito Mussolini 1883–1945: Giorgio Pini *Mussolini* (1939)

17 My Aunt Minnie would always be punctual and never hold up production, but who would pay to see my Aunt Minnie?

on Marilyn Monroe's unpunctuality

Billy Wilder 1906– : P. F. Boller and R. L. Davis *Hollywood Anecdotes* (1988)

18 Punctuality is the virtue of the bored.

Evelyn Waugh 1903–66: diary 26 March 1962

19 I will surprise God because I'm late. I was always very punctual with the Devil.

on his imminent death

Jeffrey Bernard 1932–97: in *Guardian* 6 September 1997

Punishment see Crime and Punishment

Quantities and Qualities

PROVERBS AND SAYINGS

1 How long is a piece of string?

traditional saying

2 Little fish are sweet.

early 19th century; meaning that small gifts are always acceptable

3 Many a little makes a mickle.

*mid 13th century, the proper form of the next proverb (*mickle *in Scottish usage means 'a great quantity or amount')*

4 Many a mickle makes a muckle.

late 18th century; an alteration of the previous proverb which is actually nonsensical, since muckle *is a variant of* mickle *and both mean 'a large quantity or amount'*

5 The more the merrier.

late 14th century

6 The nearer the bone, the sweeter the meat.

late 14th century, meaning that the juiciest meat lies next to the bone, or that the meat closest to the bone is particularly precious because it may represent one's last scrap of food

7 Never mind the quality, feel the width.

used as the title of a television comedy series (1967–9) about a tailoring business in the East End of London, ultimately probably an inversion of a cloth trade saying

8 Small is beautiful.

title of a book by E. F. Schumacher, 1973; see **Economics** 15

9 There is safety in numbers.

late 17th century; now with the implication that a number of people will be unscathed where an individual might be in danger

10 The whole is more than the sum of the parts.

traditional saying, probably deriving from Aristotle; see **Causes and Consequences** 16

PHRASES

11 Benjamin's portion the largest share.

the youngest son of the patriarch Jacob, who according to the Bible (Genesis) was given a larger share than his other brothers by his brother Joseph, 'He took and sent messes [portions of food] unto them before him: but Benjamin's mess was five times so much as any of theirs'

12 the eye of a needle a minute opening or space through which it is difficult to pass.

chiefly in echoes of the Bible (Matthew): see **Wealth** 16

13 **horn of plenty** a cornucopia, an overflowing stock; an abundant source.
translation of Latin cornu copiae a mythical horn able to provide whatever is desired

14 **the number of the beast** six hundred and sixty-six.
after the Bible (Revelation) 'Let him that hath understanding count the number of the beast: for it is the number of a man: and his number is six hundred threescore and six' (the beast was traditionally identified with Antichrist)

15 **their name is legion** they are innumerable.
from the story in the Bible (Mark) of the reply of the 'man with an unclean spirit' who was to be healed by Jesus, 'My name is Legion, for we are many'

16 **tip of the iceberg** a known or recognizable part of something (especially a difficulty) evidently much larger.
the part of an iceberg visible above the water

17 **Uncle Tom Cobley and all** a whole lot of people.
the last of a long list of people in the song 'Widecombe Fair'

18 **a widow's cruse** a seemingly slight resource which is in fact not readily exhausted.
in allusion to the story in the Bible (I Kings) of the cruse of oil belonging to the widow to whom Elijah was sent for sustenance

QUOTATIONS

19 The works of Creation are described as being completed in six days, the same formula for a day being repeated six times. The reason for this is that six is the number of perfection.
St. Augustine of Hippo AD 354–430: *The City of God*

20 Thick as autumnal leaves that strew the brooks
In Vallombrosa.
John Milton 1608–74: *Paradise Lost* (1667)

21 So, naturalists observe, a flea
Hath smaller fleas that on him prey;
And these have smaller fleas to bite 'em,

And so proceed *ad infinitum*.
Jonathan Swift 1667–1745: 'On Poetry' (1733)

22 Nothing is more contrary to the organization of the mind, of the memory, and of the imagination . . . It's just tormenting the people with trivia!!!
on the introduction of the metric system
Napoleon I 1769–1821: *Mémoires . . . écrits à Ste-Hélène* (1823–5)

23 I think no virtue goes with size.
Ralph Waldo Emerson 1803–82: 'The Titmouse' (1867)

24 I'll sing you twelve O.
Green grow the rushes O.
What is your twelve O?
Twelve for the twelve apostles,
Eleven for the eleven who went to heaven,
Ten for the ten commandments,
Nine for the nine bright shiners,
Eight for the eight bold rangers,
Seven for the seven stars in the sky,
Six for the six proud walkers,
Five for the symbol at your door,
Four for the Gospel makers,
Three for the rivals,
Two, two, the lily-white boys,
Clothed all in green O,
One is one and all alone
And ever more shall be so.
Anonymous: 'The Dilly Song'; existing in various versions from the nineteenth century, possibly of earlier origin; see **The Skies** 7

25 It is our national joy to mistake for the first-rate, the fecund rate.
Dorothy Parker 1893–1967: review of Sinclair Lewis *Dodsworth*; in *New Yorker* 16 March 1929

26 Less is a bore.
Robert Venturi 1925– : *Complexity and Contradiction in Architecture* (1966); see **Architecture** 16, **Excess** 6

27 I'm only a four-dimensional creature. Haven't got a clue how to visualise infinity. Even Einstein hadn't. I know because I asked him.
Patrick Moore 1923– : in *Sunday Times* 15 April 2001

Quotations

PROVERBS AND SAYINGS

1 The devil can quote Scripture for his own ends.

*late 16th century, meaning that it is possible for someone engaged in wrongdoing to quote selectively from the Bible in apparent support of their position, and alluding to the temptation of Christ by the Devil in the Bible (Matthew); see **The Bible** 11*

PHRASES

2 cap verses reply to one previously quoted with another, that begins with the final or initial letter of the first, or that rimes or otherwise corresponds with it.

QUOTATIONS

3 Confound those who have said our remarks before us.
Aelius Donatus 4th century: St Jerome *Commentary on Ecclesiastes*

4 Classical quotation is the *parole* of literary men all over the world.
Samuel Johnson 1709–84: James Boswell *Life of Samuel Johnson* (1791) 8 May 1781

5 A proverb is one man's wit and all men's wisdom.
Lord John Russell 1792–1878: R. J. Mackintosh *Sir James Mackintosh* (1835)

6 I hate quotation. Tell me what you know.
Ralph Waldo Emerson 1803–82: diary May 1849

7 He wrapped himself in quotations—as a beggar would enfold himself in the purple of emperors.
Rudyard Kipling 1865–1936: *Many Inventions* (1893)

8 OSCAR WILDE: How I wish I had said that.
WHISTLER: You will, Oscar, you will.
James McNeill Whistler 1834–1903: R. Ellman *Oscar Wilde* (1987)

9 But I have long thought that if you knew a column of advertisements by heart, you could achieve unexpected felicities with them. You can get a happy quotation anywhere if you have the eye.
Oliver Wendell Holmes Jr. 1841–1935: letter to Harold Laski, 31 May 1923

10 It is a good thing for an uneducated man to read books of quotations.
Winston Churchill 1874–1965: *My Early Life* (1930)

11 I always have a quotation for everything—it saves original thinking.
Dorothy L. Sayers 1893–1957: *Have His Carcase* (1932)

12 Misquotation is, in fact, the pride and privilege of the learned. A widely-read man never quotes accurately, for the rather obvious reason that he has read too widely.
Hesketh Pearson 1887–1964: *Common Misquotations* (1934)

13 Windbags can be right. Aphorists can be wrong. It is a tough world.
James Fenton 1949– : in *Times* 21 February 1985

14 A quotation is what a speaker wants to say—unlike a soundbite which is all that an interviewer allows you to say.
Tony Benn 1925– : letter to Antony Jay, August 1996

Race and Racism see also Equality, Prejudice and Tolerance

PROVERBS AND SAYINGS

1 Am I not a man and a brother.

*motto on the seal of the British and Foreign Anti-Slavery Society, 1787, depicting a kneeling slave in chains uttering these words (subsequently a popular Wedgwood cameo); see **Human Race** 2*

2 Black is beautiful.

slogan of American civil rights campaigners, mid-1960s

3 Power to the people.

slogan of the Black Panther movement, from c.1968 onwards

PHRASES

4 rainbow coalition a political alliance of minority peoples and other disadvantaged groups.

from Jesse Jackson: see 32, 34 below

5 the white man's burden the supposed task of whites to civilize blacks.

*from Kipling, originally in specific allusion to the United States' role in the Philippines: see **Duty** 17*

QUOTATIONS

6 You call me misbeliever, cut-throat dog,
And spit upon my Jewish gabardine,
And all for use of that which is mine own.
William Shakespeare 1564–1616: *The Merchant of Venice* (1596–8)

7 When I recovered a little I found some black people about me . . . I asked them if we were not to be eaten by those white men with horrible looks, red faces, and loose hair.
Olaudah Equiano c.1745–c.1797: *Narrative of the Life of Olaudah Equiano* (1789)

8 You have seen how a man was made a slave; you shall see how a slave was made a man.
Frederick Douglass c.1818–1895: *Narrative of the Life of Frederick Douglass* (1845)

9 The only good Indian is a dead Indian.
at Fort Cobb, January 1869
Philip Henry Sheridan 1831–88: attributed

10 Because a man has a black face and a different religion from our own, there is no reason why he should be treated as a brute.
Edward VII 1841–1910: letter to Lord Granville, 30 November 1875

11 The gentleman will please remember that when his half-civilized ancestors were hunting the wild boar in Silesia, mine were princes of the earth.
in reply to a taunt by a Senator of German descent
Judah Benjamin 1811–84: B. Perley Poore *Perley's Reminiscences* (1886)

12 The so-called white races are really pinko-grey.
E. M. Forster 1879–1970: *A Passage to India* (1924)

13 How odd
Of God
To choose
The Jews.
to which Cecil Browne replied: 'But not so odd/As those who choose/A Jewish God/But spurn the Jews.'
William Norman Ewer 1885–1976: *Week-End Book* (1924)

14 I, too, sing America.
I am the darker brother.
They send me to eat in the kitchen

When company comes.
Langston Hughes 1902–67: 'I, Too' (1925)

15 If my theory of relativity is proven correct, Germany will claim me as a German and France will declare that I am a citizen of the world. Should my theory prove untrue, France will say that I am a German and Germany will declare that I am a Jew.
Albert Einstein 1879–1955: address at the Sorbonne, Paris, possibly early December 1929; in *New York Times* 16 February 1930

16 After all, who remembers today the extermination of the Armenians?
Adolf Hitler 1889–1945: comment, 22 August 1939

17 I herewith commission you to carry out all preparations with regard to . . . a *total solution* of the Jewish question in those territories of Europe which are under German influence.
Hermann Goering 1893–1946: instructions to Heydrich, 31 July 1941; W. L. Shirer *The Rise and Fall of the Third Reich* (1962)

18 You've got to be taught to be afraid
Of people whose eyes are oddly made,
Of people whose skin is a different shade.
You've got to be carefully taught.
Oscar Hammerstein II 1895–1960: 'You've Got to be Carefully Taught' (1949)

19 Some of my best friends are white boys.
when I meet 'em
I treat 'em
just the same as if they was people.
Ray Durem 1915–63: 'Broadminded' (written 1951)

20 You can be up to your boobies in white satin, with gardenias in your hair and no sugar cane for miles, but you can still be working on a plantation.
Billie Holiday 1915–59: *Lady Sings the Blues* (1956, with William Duffy)

21 You gotta say this for the white race—its self-confidence knows no bounds. Who else could go to a small island in the South Pacific where there's no poverty, no crime, no unemployment, no war and no worry—and call it a 'primitive society'?
Dick Gregory 1932– : *From the Back of the Bus* (1962)

22 I want to be the white man's brother, not his brother-in-law.
Martin Luther King 1929–68: in *New York Journal-American* 10 September 1962

23 Segregation now, segregation tomorrow and segregation forever!
George Wallace 1919– : inaugural speech as Governor of Alabama, 14 January 1963

24 There are no 'white' or 'coloured' signs on the foxholes or graveyards of battle.
John F. Kennedy 1917–63: message to Congress on proposed Civil Rights Bill, 19 June 1963

25 Being a star has made it possible for me to get insulted in places where the average Negro could never *hope* to go and get insulted.
Sammy Davis Jnr. 1925–90: *Yes I Can* (1965)

26 It comes as a great shock around the age of 5, 6 or 7 to discover that the flag to which you have pledged allegiance, along with everybody else, has not pledged allegiance to you. It comes as a great shock to see Gary Cooper killing off the Indians and, although you are rooting for Gary Cooper, that the Indians are you.
speaking for the proposition that 'The American Dream is at the expense of the American Negro'
James Baldwin 1924–87: Cambridge Union, England, 17 February 1965

27 Though it be a thrilling and marvellous thing to be merely young and gifted in such times, it is doubly so, doubly dynamic—to be young, gifted and *black*.
Lorraine Hansberry 1930–65: *To be young, gifted and black: Lorraine Hansberry in her own words* (1969) adapted by Robert Nemiroff

28 As I look ahead, I am filled with foreboding. Like the Roman, I seem to see 'the River Tiber foaming with much blood'.
on the probable consequences of immigration
Enoch Powell 1912–98: speech at the Annual Meeting of the West Midlands Area Conservative Political Centre, Birmingham, 20 April 1968; see **Warfare** 14

29 And if the white man thought that Asians were a low, filthy nation, Asians could still smile with relief—at least, they were not Africans. And if the white man thought that Africans were a low, filthy nation, Africans in southern Africa could still smile—at least, they were not bushmen. They all have their monsters.
Bessie Head 1937–86: *Maru* (1971)

30 The basic tenet of Black consciousness is that the Black man must reject all value systems that seek to make him a foreigner in the country of his birth and reduce his basic human dignity.
Steve Biko 1946–77: statement as witness, 3 May 1976

31 There are no 'mixed' marriages. It just looks that way. People don't mix races; they abandon them or pick them.
Toni Morrison 1931– : *Tar Baby* (1981)

32 When I look out at this convention, I see the face of America, red, yellow, brown, black, and white. We are all precious in God's sight—the real rainbow coalition.
Jesse Jackson 1941– : speech at Democratic National Convention, Atlanta, 19 July 1988; see 4 above

33 Growing up, I came up with this name: I'm a Cablinasian.
explaining his rejection of 'African-American' as the term to describe his Caucasian, Afro-American, Native American, Thai, and Chinese ancestry
Tiger Woods 1975– : interview, 21 April 1997

34 Maybe there is no rainbow nation after all because it does not have the colour black.
at the funeral of a black child reportedly shot dead by a white farmer
Winnie Madikizela-Mandela 1934– : in *Irish Times* 25 April 1998 'Quotes of the Week'; see 4 above

Rank and Title see also **Class**

1 **Everybody loves a lord.**
mid 19th century

2 **If two ride on a horse, one must ride behind.**
late 16th century; meaning that of two people engaged on the same task, one must take a subordinate role

3 **Where Macgregor sits is the head of the table.**
mid 19th century, sometimes attributed to 'Rob Roy' MacGregor. Other names are used as well as Macgregor

4 I made the carles lords, but who made the carlines ladies?

of the wives of Scots Lords of Session

James I 1566–1625: E. Grenville Murray *Embassies and Foreign Courts* (1855)

5 'Tis from high life high characters are drawn;
A saint in crape is twice a saint in lawn.

Alexander Pope 1688–1744: 'To Lord Cobham' (1734)

6 Nobility is a graceful ornament to the civil order. It is the Corinthian capital of polished society.

Edmund Burke 1729–97: *Reflections on the Revolution in France* (1790)

7 The rank is but the guinea's stamp,
The man's the gowd for a' that!

Robert Burns 1759–96: 'For a' that and a' that' (1790)

8 I am an ancestor.

taunted on his lack of ancestry when made Duke of Abrantes, 1807

Marshal Junot 1771–1813: attributed

9 Kind hearts are more than coronets,
And simple faith than Norman blood.

Alfred, Lord Tennyson 1809–92: 'Lady Clara Vere de Vere' (1842)

10 The stately homes of England,
How beautiful they stand!
Amidst their tall ancestral trees,
O'er all the pleasant land.

Felicia Hemans 1793–1835: 'The Homes of England' (1849); see 15 below

11 The order of nobility is of great use, too, not only in what it creates, but in what it prevents. It prevents the rule of wealth—the religion of gold. This is the obvious and natural idol of the Anglo-Saxon.

Walter Bagehot 1826–77: *The English Constitution* (1867)

12 Titles distinguish the mediocre, embarrass the superior, and are disgraced by the inferior.

George Bernard Shaw 1856–1950: *Man and Superman* (1903)

13 A fully-equipped duke costs as much to keep up as two Dreadnoughts; and dukes are just as great a terror and they last longer.

David Lloyd George 1863–1945: speech at Newcastle, 9 October 1909

14 When I want a peerage, I shall buy it like an honest man.

Lord Northcliffe 1865–1922: Tom Driberg *Swaff* (1974)

15 The Stately Homes of England,
How beautiful they stand,
To prove the upper classes
Have still the upper hand.

Noël Coward 1899–1973: 'The Stately Homes of England' (1938 song); see 10 above

16 A medal glitters, but it also casts a shadow.

a reference to the envy caused by the award of honours

Winston Churchill 1874–1965: in 1941; Kenneth Rose *King George V* (1983)

17 Not a reluctant peer but a persistent commoner.

of his ultimately successful fight to disclaim his inherited title of Viscount Stansgate

Tony Benn 1925– : at a press conference, 23 November 1960

18 There is no stronger craving in the world than that of the rich for titles, except perhaps that of the titled for riches.

Hesketh Pearson 1887–1964: *The Pilgrim Daughters* (1961)

19 What harm have I ever done to the Labour Party?

declining the offer of a peerage

R. H. Tawney 1880–1962: in *Evening Standard* 18 January 1962

20 As far as the fourteenth earl is concerned, I suppose Mr Wilson, when you come to think of it, is the fourteenth Mr Wilson.

replying to Harold Wilson's remark (on Home's becoming leader of the Conservative party) that 'the whole [democratic] process has ground to a halt with a fourteenth Earl'

Lord Home 1903–95: in *Daily Telegraph* 22 October 1963

21 People fail you, children disappoint you, thieves break in, moths corrupt, but an OBE goes on for ever.

Fay Weldon 1931– : *Praxis* (1978)

22 She needed no royal title to continue to generate her particular brand of magic.

of his sister, Diana, Princess of Wales

Lord Spencer 1964– : tribute at her funeral, 7 September 1997

23 This is the stuff that all of our childhood fantasies come from. You know, courtliness, civility and honour.
on his knighthood
Steven Spielberg 1947– : in *Sunday Times* 4 February 2001

Readiness see **Preparation and Readiness**

Reading see also **Books**

1 Have you read any good books lately?
catchphrase used by Richard Murdoch in radio comedy series Much-Binding-in-the-Marsh, *written by Richard Murdoch and Kenneth Horne, started 2 January 1947*

2 He that runs may read.
proverbial saying, late 16th century, meaning very clear and readable; originally with allusion to the Bible (Habakkuk), reinforced by John Keble's 'Septuagesima' (1827), 'There is a book, who runs may read'

3 The man who reads is the man who leads.
American proverb, mid 20th century

QUOTATIONS

4 When he was reading, he drew his eyes along over the leaves, and his heart searched into the sense, but his voice and tongue were silent.
of St Ambrose
St Augustine of Hippo AD 354–430: *Confessions* (AD 397–8)

5 POLONIUS: What do you read, my lord?
HAMLET: Words, words, words.
William Shakespeare 1564–1616: *Hamlet* (1601)

6 Choose an author as you choose a friend.
Wentworth Dillon, Lord Roscommon c.1633–85: *Essay on Translated Verse* (1684)

7 He had read much, if one considers his long life; but his contemplation was much more than his reading. He was wont to say that if he had read as much as other men, he should have known no more than other men.
John Aubrey 1626–97: *Brief Lives* 'Thomas Hobbes'

8 Reading is to the mind what exercise is to the body.
Richard Steele 1672–1729: in *The Tatler* 18 March 1710

9 The bookful blockhead, ignorantly read, With loads of learned lumber in his head.
Alexander Pope 1688–1744: *An Essay on Criticism* (1711)

10 A man ought to read just as inclination leads him; for what he reads as a task will do him little good.
Samuel Johnson 1709–84: James Boswell *Life of Samuel Johnson* (1791) 14 July 1763

11 Digressions, incontestably, are the sunshine;—they are the life, the soul of reading;—take them out of this book for instance,—you might as well take the book along with them.
Laurence Sterne 1713–68: *Tristram Shandy* (1759–67)

12 Much have I travelled in the realms of gold,
And many goodly states and kingdoms seen.
John Keats 1795–1821: 'On First Looking into Chapman's Homer' (1817)

13 People say that life is the thing, but I prefer reading.
Logan Pearsall Smith 1865–1946: *Afterthoughts* (1931) 'Myself'

14 What do we ever get nowadays from reading to equal the excitement and the revelation in those first fourteen years?
Graham Greene 1904–91: *The Lost Childhood and Other Essays* (1951) title essay

15 What really knocks me out is a book that, when you're all done reading it, you wish the author that wrote it was a terrific friend of yours and you could call him up on the phone whenever you felt like it.
J. D. Salinger 1919– : *Catcher in the Rye* (1951)

16 Don't read too much now: the dude
Who lets the girl down before
The hero arrives, the chap
Who's yellow and keeps the store,
Seem far too familiar. Get stewed:
Books are a load of crap.
Philip Larkin 1922–85: 'Study of Reading Habits' (1964)

17 Curiously enough, one cannot *read* a book: one can only reread it. A good reader, a major reader, an active and creative reader is a rereader.
Vladimir Nabokov 1899–1977: *Lectures on Literature* (1980) 'Good Readers and Good Writers'

18 Reading one book is like eating one crisp.
Diane Duane 1952– : *So You Want to Be a Wizard* (1983)

19 Any writer worth his salt knows that only a small proportion of literature does more than partly compensate people for the damage they have suffered in learning to read.
Rebecca West 1892–1983: Peter Vansittart *Path from a White Horse* (1985)

20 The world may be full of fourth-rate writers but it's also full of fourth-rate readers.
Stan Barstow 1928– : in *Daily Mail* 15 August 1989

21 You know, I would like to like reading. I've been trying to get myself to read for such a long time. I've got piles of books that I wanna read, but I just get distracted.
Melanie Chisholm 1974– : in *Independent* 20 March 2000

Reality see also **Appearance, Hypothesis and Fact**

1 **Where's the beef?**
advertising slogan for Wendy's Hamburgers in campaign launched 9 January 1984, and subsequently taken up by Walter Mondale in a televised debate with Gary Hart from Atlanta, 11 March 1984: 'When I hear your new ideas I'm reminded of that ad, "Where's the beef?"' '

PHRASES

2 **cloud cuckoo land** a state of unrealistic or absurdly over-optimistic fantasy.
a translation of Greek Nephelokokkugia, the name of the city built by the birds in the Greek poet Aristophanes' comedy Birds (414 BC)

3 **opium of the people** something regarded as inducing a false and unrealistic sense of contentment among people.
from Marx: see **Religion** *21; see also* **Sport** *25*

4 **the real Simon Pure** the real or genuine person or thing.
a character in Centlivre's A Bold Stroke for a Wife (1717), who is impersonated by another character during part of the play

QUOTATIONS

5 Every thing, saith Epictetus, hath two handles, the one to be held by, the other not.
Robert Burton 1577–1640: *The Anatomy of Melancholy* (1621–51)

6 I refute it *thus.*
kicking a large stone by way of refuting Bishop Berkeley's theory of the non-existence of matter
Samuel Johnson 1709–84: James Boswell *Life of Samuel Johnson* (1791) 6 August 1763

7 All theory, dear friend, is grey, but the golden tree of actual life springs ever green.
Johann Wolfgang von Goethe 1749–1832: *Faust* pt. 1 (1808) 'Studierzimmer'

8 What is rational is actual and what is actual is rational.
G. W. F. Hegel 1770–1831: *Grundlinien der Philosophie des Rechts* (1821)

9 All that we see or seem
Is but a dream within a dream.
Edgar Allan Poe 1809–49: 'A Dream within a Dream' (1849)

10 Do you think that the things people make fools of themselves about are any less real and true than the things they behave sensibly about? They are more true: they are the only things that are true.
George Bernard Shaw 1856–1950: *Candida* (1898)

11 Between the idea
And the reality
Between the motion
And the act
Falls the Shadow.
T. S. Eliot 1888–1965: 'The Hollow Men' (1925)

12 They said, 'You have a blue guitar,
You do not play things as they are.'
The man replied, 'Things as they are
Are changed upon the blue guitar.'
Wallace Stevens 1879–1955: 'The Man with the
Blue Guitar' (1937)

13 BLANCHE: I don't want realism.
MITCH: Naw, I guess not.
BLANCHE: I'll tell you what I want. Magic!
Tennessee Williams: *A Streetcar Named Desire*
(1947)

14 Reality goes bounding past the satirist like
a cheetah laughing as it lopes ahead of the
greyhound.
Claud Cockburn 1904–81: *Crossing the Line* (1958)

15 Perhaps the rare and simple pleasure of
being seen for what one is compensates for
the misery of being it.
Margaret Drabble 1939– : *A Summer Bird-Cage*
(1963)

16 The camera makes everyone a tourist in
other people's reality, and eventually in
one's own.
Susan Sontag 1933– : in *New York Review of Books*
18 April 1974

17 Each person experiences his own reality,
and no one else can be the judge of what
that reality really is.
Shirley Maclaine 1934– : *Out on a Limb* (1983)

18 Reality's not strange, not unexpected.
Reality doesn't reside in the sudden
hallucination of events. Reality is
uneventfulness, vacancy, flatness. Reality
is that nothing happens. How many of the
events of history have occurred . . . for no
other reason, fundamentally, than the
desire to make things happen?
Graham Swift 1949– : *Waterland* (1984)

Reason see **Logic and Reason**

Rebellion see **Revolution and Rebellion**

Relationships see also **Friendship, Hatred, Love**

PROVERBS AND SAYINGS

1 **L'amour est aveugle; l'amitié ferme les
yeux.**
French proverb: Love is blind; friendship closes its eyes;
see **Love** 6

QUOTATIONS

2 Am I my brother's keeper?
Bible: Genesis

3 Difficult or easy, pleasant or bitter, you are
the same you: I cannot live with you—or
without you.
Martial AD c.40–c.104: *Epigrammata*

4 He who has a thousand friends has not a
friend to spare,
And he who has one enemy will meet him
everywhere.
Ali ibn-Abi-Talib c.602–661: *A Hundred Sayings*

5 In necessary things, unity; in doubtful
things, liberty; in all things, charity.
Richard Baxter 1615–91: motto

6 Friendship is a disinterested commerce
between equals; love, an abject intercourse
between tyrants and slaves.
Oliver Goldsmith 1728–74: *The Good-Natured Man*
(1768)

7 Ships that pass in the night, and speak
each other in passing;
Only a signal shown and a distant voice in
the darkness;
So on the ocean of life we pass and speak
one another,
Only a look and a voice; then darkness
again and a silence.
Henry Wadsworth Longfellow 1807–82: *Tales of a
Wayside Inn* pt. 3 (1874); see **Meeting** 5

8 Love, friendship, respect do not unite
people as much as common hatred for
something.
Anton Chekhov 1860–1904: *Notebooks* (1921)

9 Personal relations are the important thing
for ever and ever, and not this outer life of
telegrams and anger.
E. M. Forster 1879–1970: *Howards End* (1910)

10 I may be wrong, but I have never found deserting friends conciliates enemies.
Margot Asquith 1864–1945: *Lay Sermons* (1927)

11 No human relation gives one possession in another—every two souls are absolutely different. In friendship or in love, the two side by side raise hands together to find what one cannot reach alone.
Kahlil Gibran 1883–1931: *Beloved Prophet: the love letters of Kahlil Gibran and Mary Haskell and her private journal* (1972)

12 The meeting of two personalities is like the contact of two chemical substances: if there is any reaction, both are transformed.
Carl Gustav Jung 1875–1961: *Modern Man in Search of a Soul* (1933)

13 She experienced all the cosiness and irritation which can come from living with thoroughly nice people with whom one has nothing in common.
Barbara Pym 1913–80: *Less than Angels* (1955)

14 Almost all of our relationships begin and most of them continue as forms of mutual exploitation, a mental or physical barter, to be terminated when one or both parties run out of goods.
W. H. Auden 1907–73: *The Dyer's Hand* (1963)

15 It is easier to live through someone else than to become complete yourself.
Betty Friedan 1921– : *The Feminine Mystique* (1963)

16 And it seems to me you lived your life
Like a candle in the wind.
Never knowing who to cling to

When the rain set in . . .
Elton John 1947– and **Bernie Taupin** 1950– : 'Candle in the Wind' (song, 1973)

17 Never marry a man who hates his mother, because he'll end up hating you.
Jill Bennett 1931–90: in *Observer* 12 September 1982

18 The ones we choose to love become our anchor
when the hawser of the blood-tie's hacked, or frays.
Tony Harrison 1953– : *v* (1985)

19 Men love women, women love children; children love hamsters—it's quite hopeless.
Alice Thomas Ellis 1932– : attributed, 1987

20 There are those who never stretch out the hand for fear it will be bitten. But those who never stretch out the hand will never feel it clasped in friendship.
Michael Heseltine 1933– : *Where There's a Will* (1987)

21 Here's how men think. Sex, work—and those are reversible, depending on age—sex, work, food, sports and lastly, begrudgingly, relationships. And here's how women think. Relationships, relationships, relationships, work, sex, shopping, weight, food.
Carrie Fisher 1956– : *Surrender the Pink* (1990)

22 Their relationship consisted
In discussing if it existed.
Thom Gunn 1929– : 'Jamesian' (1992)

23 If we were actually to comprehend other people we would not be able to use them for our own ends.
Candia McWilliam 1955– : *Debatable Land* (1994)

Religion see also **The Bible, The Christian Church, Clergy, God, Prayer, Science and Religion**

PROVERBS AND SAYINGS

1 Man's extremity is God's opportunity.
early 17th century, meaning that great distress or danger may prompt a person to turn to God for help

PHRASES

2 graven image an idol.
*in allusion to the second commandment in the Bible (Exodus) 'Thou shalt not make unto thee any graven image'; see **Lifestyles** 8*

3 people of the Book the Jews and Christians as regarded by Muslims.
those whose religion entails adherence to a book of divine revelation

QUOTATIONS

4 Is that which is holy loved by the gods because it is holy, or is it holy because it is loved by the gods?
Plato 429–347 BC: *Euthyphro*

5 *Tantum religio potuit suadere malorum.*

So much wrong could religion induce.
Lucretius c.94–55 BC: *De Rerum Natura*

6 Render therefore unto Caesar the things
which are Caesar's; and unto God the
things that are God's.
Bible: St Matthew

7 I go into the Muslim mosque and the
Jewish synagogue and the Christian
church and I see one altar.
Jalal ad-Din ar-Rumi 1207–73: Coleman Barks and
John Moyne (eds.) *The Essential Rumi* (1999)

8 I count religion but a childish toy,
And hold there is no sin but ignorance.
Christopher Marlowe 1564–93: *The Jew of Malta*
(c.1592)

9 One religion is as true as another.
Robert Burton 1577–1640: *The Anatomy of
Melancholy* (1621–51)

10 A good honest and painful sermon.
Samuel Pepys 1633–1703: diary 17 March 1661

11 They are for religion when in rags and
contempt; but I am for him when he walks
in his golden slippers, in the sunshine and
with applause.
John Bunyan 1628–88: *The Pilgrim's Progress* (1678)

12 'People differ in their discourse and
profession about these matters, but men of
sense are really but of one religion.' . . .
'Pray, my lord, what religion is that which
men of sense agree in?' 'Madam,' says the
earl immediately, 'men of sense never tell
it.'
1st Earl of Shaftesbury 1621–83: Bishop Gilbert
Burnet *History of My Own Time* vol. 1 (1724)

13 We have just enough religion to make us
hate, but not enough to make us love one
another.
Jonathan Swift 1667–1745: *Thoughts on Various
Subjects* (1711)

14 I went to America to convert the Indians;
but oh, who shall convert me?
John Wesley 1703–91: diary 24 January 1738

15 Putting moral virtues at the highest, and
religion at the lowest, religion must still be
allowed to be a collateral security, at least,
to virtue; and every prudent man will
sooner trust to two securities than to one.
Lord Chesterfield 1694–1773: *Letters to his Son*
(1774) 8 January 1750

16 It is our first duty to serve society, and,
after we have done that, we may attend
wholly to the salvation of our own souls. A

youthful passion for abstracted devotion
should not be encouraged.
Samuel Johnson 1709–84: James Boswell *Life of
Samuel Johnson* (1791) February 1766

17 Orthodoxy is my doxy; heterodoxy is
another man's doxy.
William Warburton 1698–1779: to Lord Sandwich;
Joseph Priestley *Memoirs* (1807)

18 My country is the world, and my religion
is to do good.
Thomas Paine 1737–1809: *The Rights of Man* pt. 2
(1792)

19 Any system of religion that has any thing
in it that shocks the mind of a child cannot
be a true system.
Thomas Paine 1737–1809: *The Age of Reason* pt. 1
(1794)

20 In vain with lavish kindness
The gifts of God are strown;
The heathen in his blindness
Bows down to wood and stone.
Reginald Heber 1783–1826: 'From Greenland's icy
mountains' (1821 hymn); see **Armed Forces** 32

21 Religion . . . is the opium of the people.
Karl Marx 1818–83: *A Contribution to the Critique of
Hegel's Philosophy of Right* (1843–4); see **Reality** 3

22 Things have come to a pretty pass when
religion is allowed to invade the sphere of
private life.
on hearing an evangelical sermon
Lord Melbourne 1779–1848: G. W. E. Russell
Collections and Recollections (1898)

23 So long as man remains free he strives for
nothing so incessantly and so painfully as
to find someone to worship.
Fedor Dostoevsky 1821–81: *The Brothers Karamazov*
(1879–80)

24 So many gods, so many creeds,
So many paths that wind and wind,
While just the art of being kind
Is all the sad world needs.
Ella Wheeler Wilcox 1855–1919: 'The World's
Need'

25 To become a popular religion, it is only
necessary for a superstition to enslave a
philosophy.
William Ralph Inge 1860–1954: *Idea of Progress*
(1920)

26 There's no reason to bring religion into it. I
think we ought to have as great a regard

for religion as we can, so as to keep it out of as many things as possible.

Sean O'Casey 1880–1964: *The Plough and the Stars* (1926)

27 Religion is the frozen thought of men out of which they build temples.

Jiddu Krishnamurti 1895–1986: in *Observer* 22 April 1928

28 Zen . . . does not confuse spirituality with thinking about God while one is peeling potatoes. Zen spirituality is just to peel the potatoes.

Alan Watts 1915–73: *The Way of Zen* (1957)

29 Religions are kept alive by heresies, which are really sudden explosions of faith. Dead religions do not produce them.

Gerald Brenan 1894–1987: *Thoughts in a Dry Season* (1978)

30 If even a dog's tooth is truly worshipped it glows with light. The venerated object is

endowed with power, that is the simple sense of the ontological proof.

Iris Murdoch 1919–99: *The Sea, The Sea* (1978)

31 Religion to me has always been the wound, not the bandage.

Dennis Potter 1935–94: interview with Melvyn Bragg on Channel 4, March 1994, in *Seeing the Blossom* (1994)

32 It [religion] can trap us in language *about* mysteries rather than open us to the mysteries themselves.

Richard Holloway 1933– : introduction to *The Gospel According to Luke* (1998)

33 A sense of the sacred without a sense of humour becomes leaden.

Robert Runcie 1921–2000: on *Loose Ends*, BBC Radio 4, 15 April 2000

34 It is time the West confronted its ignorance of Islam. Jews, Muslims and Christians are all children of Abraham.

Tony Blair 1953– : Labour Party conference, Brighton, 2 October 2001

Repentance see **Forgiveness and Repentance**

Reputation see also **Fame**

PROVERBS AND SAYINGS

1 **Brave men lived before Agamemnon.**

early 19th century, meaning that to be remembered the exploits of a hero must be recorded; from Horace: see **Biography** 2

2 **Common fame is seldom to blame.**

mid 17th century, meaning that reputation is generally founded on fact rather than rumour

3 **De mortuis nil nisi bonum.**

Latin, literally 'Of the dead, speak kindly or not at all'; see 8 below

4 **The devil is not so black as he is painted.**

mid 16th century, meaning that someone may not be as bad as their reputation

5 **A good reputation stands still; a bad one runs.**

American proverb, mid 20th century

6 **He that has an ill name is half hanged.**

late 14th century, meaning that someone with a bad reputation is already half way to being condemned on any charge brought against him

7 **A man's best reputation for his future is his record of the past.**

American proverb, mid 20th century

8 **Never speak ill of the dead.**

mid 16th century; see 3 above

9 **No smoke without fire.**

late Middle English, meaning that rumour is generally founded on fact

10 **One man may steal a horse, while another may not look over a hedge.**

mid 16th century; meaning that while one person is endlessly indulged, another is treated with suspicion on the slightest evidence

11 **Throw dirt enough, and some will stick.**

mid 17th century, meaning that persistent slander will in the end be believed

PHRASES

12 **a blot on one's escutcheon** a mark on one's reputation.

escutcheon *an heraldic shield or emblem bearing one's coat of arms*

13 **Caesar's wife** a person required to be above suspicion.

Julius Caesar, according to oral tradition, had divorced his wife after unfounded allegations were made against her: see 16 below

14 rest on one's laurels cease to strive for further glory.

*laurels leaves of the bay-tree as an emblem of victory or distinction; see **Success** 18*

15 A good name is rather to be chosen than great riches.

Bible: Proverbs

16 Caesar's wife must be above suspicion.

Julius Caesar 100–44 BC: oral tradition, based on Plutarch *Parallel Lives* 'Julius Caesar'; see 13 above

17 Woe unto you, when all men shall speak well of you!

Bible: St Luke

18 *Non è il mondan romore altro che un fiato di vento, ch'or vien quinci ed or qien quindi, e muta nome perchè muta lato.*

The reputation which the world bestows
is like the wind, that shifts now here now there,
its name changed with the quarter whence it blows.

Dante Alighieri 1265–1321: *Divina Commedia* 'Purgatorio'

19 Who steals my purse steals trash; 'tis something, nothing;
'Twas mine, 'tis his, and has been slave to thousands;
But he that filches from me my good name
Robs me of that which not enriches him,
And makes me poor indeed.

William Shakespeare 1564–1616: *Othello* (1602–4)

20 They come together like the Coroner's Inquest, to sit upon the murdered reputations of the week.

William Congreve 1670–1729: *The Way of the World* (1700)

21 At ev'ry word a reputation dies.

Alexander Pope 1688–1744: *The Rape of the Lock* (1714)

22 We owe respect to the living; to the dead we owe only truth.

Voltaire 1694–1778: 'Première Lettre sur Oedipe' in *Oeuvres* (1785)

23 The devil's most devilish when respectable.

Elizabeth Barrett Browning 1806–61: *Aurora Leigh* (1857)

24 What is merit? The opinion one man entertains of another.

Lord Palmerston 1784–1865: Thomas Carlyle *Shooting Niagara: and After?* (1867)

25 Always providing you have enough courage—or money—you can do without a reputation.

Margaret Mitchell 1900–49: *Gone with the Wind* (1936)

26 Honour is like a match, you can only use it once.

Marcel Pagnol 1895–1974: *Marius* (1946)

27 I'm the girl who lost her reputation and never missed it.

Mae West 1892–1980: P. F. Boller and R. L. Davis *Hollywood Anecdotes* (1988)

28 How do I want to be remembered when I die? As a fighter pilot? Look, I want to be remembered so that other people, when they talk about me, smile. That's how I want to be remembered. I don't give a damn about being a fighter pilot. The thing is this: I want to leave warmth behind.

Douglas Bader 1910–82: speech, 4 September 1982

29 You can't shame or humiliate modern celebrities. What used to be called shame and humiliation is now called publicity.

P. J. O'Rourke 1947– : *Give War a Chance* (1992)

30 I think that's just another word for a washed-up has-been.

on being an 'icon'

Bob Dylan 1941– : in *Mail on Sunday* 18 January 1998

Revenge

1 Don't cut off your nose to spite your face.

mid 16th century, warning against spiteful revenge which is likely to result in your own hurt or loss

2 Don't get mad, get even.

late 20th century

3 An eye for an eye makes the whole world blind.

*modern saying, often attributed to Mahatma Gandhi (1869–1948); see 8 below, **Justice** 16*

4 He laughs best who laughs last.

early 17th century, meaning that the most successful person is the one who is finally triumphant

5 He who laughs last, laughs longest.

early 20th century development of 4 above

6 Revenge is a dish that can be eaten cold.

late 19th century, meaning that vengeance need not be exacted immediately

7 Revenge is sweet.

mid 16th century; see 19 below

PHRASES

8 an eye for an eye revenge, retaliation in kind.

from the Bible (Exodus): see 3 above, **Justice** *16*

9 squeeze until the pips squeak exact the maximum payment from.

originally with reference to Eric Geddes: see 21 below

QUOTATIONS

10 Vengeance is mine; I will repay, saith the Lord.

Bible: Romans

11 Indeed, revenge is always the pleasure of a paltry, feeble, tiny mind.

Juvenal AD c.60–c.130: *Satires*

12 Men should be either treated generously or destroyed, because they take revenge for slight injuries—for heavy ones they cannot.

Niccolò Machiavelli 1469–1527: *The Prince* (written 1513)

13   Caesar's spirit, ranging for revenge, With Ate by his side, come hot from hell, Shall in these confines, with a monarch's voice Cry, 'Havoc!' and let slip the dogs of war.

William Shakespeare 1564–1616: *Julius Caesar* (1599); see **Warfare** 6

14 Revenge is a kind of wild justice, which the more man's nature runs to, the more ought law to weed it out.

Francis Bacon 1561–1626: *Essays* (1625) 'Of Revenge'

15 A man that studieth revenge keeps his own wounds green.

Francis Bacon 1561–1626: *Essays* (1625) 'Of Revenge'

16 Heaven has no rage, like love to hatred turned,
Nor Hell a fury, like a woman scorned.

William Congreve 1670–1729: *The Mourning Bride* (1697); see **Women** 4

17 We hand folks over to God's mercy, and show none ourselves.

George Eliot 1819–80: *Adam Bede* (1859)

18 *Sic semper tyrannis!* The South is avenged.

having shot President Lincoln, 14 April 1865

John Wilkes Booth 1838–65: '*Sic semper tyrannis* [Thus always to tyrants]'—motto of the State of Virginia; in *New York Times* 15 April 1865 (the second part of the statement possibly apocryphal)

19 It may be that vengeance is sweet, and that the gods forbade vengeance to men because they reserved for themselves so delicious and intoxicating a drink. But no one should drain the cup to the bottom. The dregs are often filthy-tasting.

Winston Churchill 1874–1965: *The River War* (1899); see 7 above

20 Beware of the man who does not return your blow: he neither forgives you nor allows you to forgive yourself.

George Bernard Shaw 1856–1950: *Man and Superman* (1903)

21 The Germans, if this Government is returned, are going to pay every penny; they are going to be squeezed as a lemon is squeezed—until the pips squeak.

Eric Geddes 1875–1937: speech at Cambridge, 10 December 1918; see 9 above

22 If you start throwing hedgehogs under me, I shall throw a couple of porcupines under you.

Nikita Khrushchev 1894–1971: in *New York Times* 7 November 1963

23 Get your retaliation in first.

Carwyn James 1929–83: attributed, 1971

24 You can't be fuelled by bitterness. It can eat you up, but it cannot drive you.

Benazir Bhutto 1953– : *Daughter of Destiny* (1989)

Revolution and Rebellion

1 Every revolution was first a thought in one man's mind.
American proverb, mid 19th century

2 Revolutions are not made by men in spectacles.
American proverb, late 19th century

3 Revolutions are not made with rosewater.
early 19th century

4 Whosoever draws his sword against the prince must throw the scabbard away.
early 17th century, meaning that anyone who tries to assassinate or depose a monarch must remain constantly on the defence; see **Warfare** *7, 9*

QUOTATIONS

5 A desperate disease requires a dangerous remedy.
Guy Fawkes 1570–1606: remark, 6 November 1605; see **Necessity** 3

6 The surest way to prevent seditions (if the times do bear it) is to take away the matter of them.
Francis Bacon 1561–1626: *Essays* (1625) 'Of Seditions and Troubles'

7 Rebellion to tyrants is obedience to God.
John Bradshaw 1602–59: supposititious epitaph; Henry S. Randall *Life of Thomas Jefferson* (1865)

8 When the people contend for their liberty, they seldom get anything by their victory but new masters.
Lord Halifax 1633–95: *Political, Moral, and Miscellaneous Thoughts and Reflections* (1750) 'Of Prerogative, Power and Liberty'

9 He wished . . . that all the great men in the world and all the nobility could be hanged, and strangled with the guts of priests.
quoting 'an ignorant, uneducated man'; often quoted as 'I should like . . . the last of the kings to be strangled with the guts of the last priest'
Jean Meslier c.1664–1733: *Testament* (1864)

10 *Après nous le déluge.*
After us the deluge.
Madame de Pompadour 1721–64: Madame du Hausset *Mémoires* (1824)

11 A little rebellion now and then is a good thing.
Thomas Jefferson 1743–1826: letter to James Madison, 30 January 1787

12 LOUIS XVI: It is a big revolt.
LA ROCHEFOUCAULD-LIANCOURT: No, Sir, a big revolution.
on a report reaching Versailles of the Fall of the Bastille, 1789
Duc de la Rochefoucauld-Liancourt 1747–1827: F. Dreyfus *La Rochefoucauld-Liancourt* (1903)

13 Bliss was it in that dawn to be alive,
But to be young was very heaven!
William Wordsworth 1770–1850: 'The French Revolution, as it Appeared to Enthusiasts' (1809)

14 A share in two revolutions is living to some purpose.
Thomas Paine 1737–1809: Eric Foner *Tom Paine and Revolutionary America* (1976)

15 Those who have served the cause of the revolution have ploughed the sea.
Simón Bolívar 1783–1830: attributed; see **Futility** 10

16 Maximilien Robespierre was nothing but the hand of Jean Jacques Rousseau, the bloody hand that drew from the womb of time the body whose soul Rousseau had created.
Heinrich Heine 1797–1856: *Zur Geschichte der Religion und Philosophie in Deutschland* (1834)

17 Revolutions are not made; they come. A revolution is as natural a growth as an oak. It comes out of the past. Its foundations are laid far back.
Wendell Phillips 1811–84: speech, 8 January 1852

18 The social order destroyed by a revolution is almost always better than that which immediately preceded it, and experience shows that the most dangerous moment for a bad government is generally that in which it sets about reform.
Alexis de Tocqueville 1805–59: *L'Ancien régime* (1856)

19 Better to abolish serfdom from above than to wait till it begins to abolish itself from below.
Tsar Alexander II 1818–81: speech in Moscow, 30 March 1856

20 I will die like a true-blue rebel. Don't waste any time in mourning—organize.
prior to his death by firing squad
Joe Hill 1879–1915: farewell telegram to Bill Haywood, 18 November 1915

21 The Germans turned upon Russia the most grisly of all weapons. They transported

Lenin in a sealed truck, like a plague bacillus, from Switzerland into Russia.
Winston Churchill 1874–1965: *The World Crisis* (1929)

22 Not believing in force is the same thing as not believing in gravitation.
Leon Trotsky 1879–1940: G. Maximov *The Guillotine at Work* (1940)

23 What is a rebel? A man who says no.
Albert Camus 1913–60: *L'Homme révolté* (1951)

24 History will absolve me.
Fidel Castro 1927– : title of pamphlet (1953)

25 Would it not be easier
In that case for the government
To dissolve the people
And elect another?
on the 1953 uprising in East Germany
Bertolt Brecht 1898–1956: 'The Solution' (1953)

26 Those who make peaceful revolution impossible will make violent revolution inevitable.
John F. Kennedy 1917–63: speech at the White House, 13 March 1962

27 The Revolution is made by man, but man must forge his revolutionary spirit from day to day.
Ernesto ('Che') Guevara 1928–67: *Socialism and Man in Cuba* (1968)

28 Ev'rywhere I hear the sound of marching, charging feet, boy,
'Cause summer's here and the time is right for fighting in the street, boy.
Mick Jagger 1943– and **Keith Richards** 1943– : 'Street Fighting Man' (1968 song)

29 The most radical revolutionary will become a conservative on the day after the revolution.
Hannah Arendt 1906–75: in *New Yorker* 12 September 1970

30 We must try to find ways to starve the terrorist and the hijacker of the oxygen of publicity on which they depend.
Margaret Thatcher 1925– : speech, 15 July 1985

31 We will make no distinction between the terrorists who committed these acts and those who harbour them.
after the terrorist attacks of 11 September
George W. Bush 1946– : televised address, 11 September 2001

Rivers

PROVERBS AND SAYINGS

1 All rivers run into the sea.
early 16th century; originally with biblical allusion to the Bible (Ecclesiastes), 'All the rivers run into the sea; yet the sea is not full; unto the place from whence the rivers come, thither they return again'

2 Says Tweed to Till—
'What gars ye rin sae still?'
Says Till to Tweed—
'Though ye rin with speed
And I rin slaw,
For ae man that ye droon
I droon twa.'
traditional rhyme

PHRASES

3 the Father of Waters the Mississippi.
see 4 below

4 Old Man River the Mississippi.
see 3 above, 13 below

QUOTATIONS

5 Because of you your land never pleads for showers, nor does its parched grass pray to Jupiter the Rain-giver.
of the River Nile
Tibullus c.50–19 BC: *Elegies*

6 Sweet Thames, run softly, till I end my song.
Edmund Spenser c.1552–99: *Prothalamion* (1596)

7 And he spoke to the river Tiber,
As it rolls by the towers of Rome.
Oh, Tiber! father Tiber
To whom the Romans pray,
A Roman's life, a Roman's arms,
Take thou in charge this day!
Lord Macaulay 1800–59: *Lays of Ancient Rome* (1842) 'Horatius'

8 Way down upon the Swanee River,
Far, far, away,
There's where my heart is turning ever;
There's where the old folks stay.
Stephen Collins Foster 1826–64: 'The Old Folks at Home' (1851 song)

9 I come from haunts of coot and hern,
I make a sudden sally
And sparkle out among the fern,
To bicker down a valley.
Alfred, Lord Tennyson 1809–92: 'The Brook' (1855)

10   Even the weariest river
Winds somewhere safe to sea.
Algernon Charles Swinburne 1837–1909: 'The Garden of Proserpine' (1866)

11 Then I saw the Congo, creeping through the black,
Cutting through the forest with a golden track.
Vachel Lindsay 1879–1931: 'The Congo' (1914)

12 I've known rivers:
I've known rivers ancient as the world and older than the flow of human blood in human veins.
Langston Hughes 1902–67: 'The Negro Speaks of Rivers' (1921)

13 Ol' man river, dat ol' man river,

He must know sumpin', but don't say nothin',
He jus' keeps rollin',
He jus' keeps rollin' along.
Oscar Hammerstein II 1895–1960: 'Ol' Man River' (1927 song); see 4 above, **Singing** 13

14 I do not know much about gods; but I think that the river
Is a strong brown god—sullen, untamed and intractable.
T. S. Eliot 1888–1965: *Four Quartets* 'The Dry Salvages' (1941)

15 The Thames is liquid history.
to an American who had compared the Thames disparagingly with the Mississippi
John Burns 1858–1943: in *Daily Mail* 25 January 1943

16 I may be smelly, and I may be old,
Rough in my pebbles, reedy in my pools,
But where my fish float by I bless their swimming
And I like people to bathe in me, especially women.
Stevie Smith 1902–71: 'The River God' (1950)

Royalty

PROVERBS AND SAYINGS

1 The king can do no wrong.
mid 17th century, meaning that something cannot be wrong if it is done by someone of sovereign power, who alone is not subject to the laws of the land; translation of the Latin legal maxim rex non potest peccare

2 A king's chaff is worth more than other men's corn.
early 17th century, meaning that even minor benefits available to those attending on a sovereign are more substantial than the best that can be offered by those of lesser status

PHRASES

3 born in the purple born into an imperial or royal reigning family.
purple the dye traditionally used for fabric worn by persons of imperial or royal rank; see 8 below

4 the Chrysanthemum Throne the throne of Japan.
the chrysanthemum is the crest of the imperial family

5 the divine right of kings the doctrine that monarchs have authority from God alone, independently of their subjects' will.
see 18 below

6 the King over the Water an exiled sovereign as seen by those loyal to his cause.
*18th-century Jacobite toast to James Francis Edward Stuart (1688–1766) and his son Charles Edward Stuart (1720–88), who from exile in France and Italy asserted their right to the British throne against the House of Hanover; see 20 below, **People** 18, 24*

7 the Peacock Throne the former throne of the Kings of Delhi, later that of the Shahs of Iran.
adorned with precious stones forming an expanded peacock's tail, the throne was taken to Persia by Nadir Shah (1688–1747), king of Persia, who in 1739 captured Delhi

8 wear the purple hold the office of a sovereign or emperor.
purple the dye traditionally used for fabric worn by persons of imperial or royal rank; see 3 above

QUOTATIONS

9 Whoso pulleth out this sword of this stone and anvil is rightwise King born of all England.
Thomas Malory d. 1471: *Le Morte D'Arthur* (1470)

10 The anger of the sovereign is death.
Duke of Norfolk 1473?–1554: William Roper *Life of Sir Thomas More*

11 I know I have the body of a weak and feeble woman, but I have the heart and stomach of a king, and of a king of England too.
Elizabeth I 1533–1603: speech to the troops at Tilbury on the approach of the Armada, 1588

12 Not all the water in the rough rude sea Can wash the balm from an anointed king.
William Shakespeare 1564–1616: *Richard II* (1595)

13 Uneasy lies the head that wears a crown.
William Shakespeare 1564–1616: *Henry IV, Part 2* (1597)

14 He is the fountain of honour.
Francis Bacon 1561–1626: *An Essay of a King* (1642); attribution doubtful; see **Government** 29

15 A subject and a sovereign are clean different things.
Charles I 1600–49: speech on the scaffold, 30 January 1649

16 But methought it lessened my esteem of a king, that he should not be able to command the rain.
Samuel Pepys 1633–1703: diary 19 July 1662

17 Titles are shadows, crowns are empty things,
The good of subjects is the end of kings.
Daniel Defoe 1660–1731: *The True-Born Englishman* (1701)

18 The Right Divine of Kings to govern wrong.
Alexander Pope 1688–1744: *The Dunciad* (1742); see 5 above

19 God save our gracious king!
Long live our noble king!
God save the king!
Anonymous: 'God save the King', attributed to various authors of the mid eighteenth century, including Henry Carey c.1687–1743

20 God bless the King, I mean the Faith's Defender;
God bless—no harm in blessing—the Pretender;
But who Pretender is, or who is King,
God bless us all—that's quite another thing.
John Byrom 1692–1763: 'To an Officer in the Army, Extempore, Intended to allay the Violence of Party-Spirit' (1773); see 6 above, **People** 18, 24

21 The influence of the Crown has increased, is increasing, and ought to be diminished.
John Dunning 1731–83: resolution passed in the House of Commons, 6 April 1780

22 A confused, but somehow a sort of solemn, recollection of a lady in diamonds, and a long black hood.
memory of being touched by Queen Anne for scrofula at the age of two; see **Sickness** 6
Samuel Johnson 1709–84: Hester Lynch Piozzi *Anecdotes of . . . Johnson* (1786)

23 Monarchy is only the string that ties the robber's bundle.
Percy Bysshe Shelley 1792–1822: *A Philosophical View of Reform* (written 1819–20)

24 The king neither administers nor governs, he reigns.
Louis Adolphe Thiers 1797–1877: in *Le National*, 4 February 1830

25 I will be good.
on being shown a chart of the line of succession, 11 March 1830
Queen Victoria 1819–1901: Theodore Martin *The Prince Consort* (1875)

26 The Emperor is everything, Vienna is nothing.
Prince Metternich 1773–1859: letter to Count Bombelles, 5 June 1848

27 George the First was always reckoned Vile, but viler George the Second;
And what mortal ever heard
Any good of George the Third?
When from earth the Fourth descended
God be praised the Georges ended!
Walter Savage Landor 1775–1864: epigram in *The Atlas*, 28 April 1855

28 Above all things our royalty is to be reverenced, and if you begin to poke about it you cannot reverence it . . . Its mystery is its life. We must not let in daylight upon magic.
Walter Bagehot 1826–77: *The English Constitution* (1867)

29 The Sovereign has, under a constitutional monarchy such as ours, three rights—the right to be consulted, the right to encourage, the right to warn.
Walter Bagehot 1826–77: *The English Constitution* (1867)

30 Everyone likes flattery; and when you come to Royalty you should lay it on with a trowel.

Benjamin Disraeli 1804–81: to Matthew Arnold; G. W. E. Russell *Collections and Recollections* (1898)

31 We could not go anywhere without sending word ahead so that life might be put on parade for us.

Infanta Eulalia of Spain 1864–1958: *Court Life from Within* (1915)

32 Well, Mr Baldwin! *this* is a pretty kettle of fish!

after Edward VIII had told her he was prepared to give up the throne to marry Mrs Simpson

Queen Mary 1867–1953: said on 17 November 1936; James Pope-Hennessy *Life of Queen Mary* (1959); see **Order** 6

33 At long last I am able to say a few words of my own . . . you must believe me when I tell you that I have found it impossible to carry the heavy burden of responsibility and to discharge my duties as King as I would wish to do without the help and support of the woman I love.

Edward VIII 1894–1972: radio broadcast following his abdication, 11 December 1936

34 The whole world is in revolt. Soon there will be only five Kings left—the King of England, the King of Spades, the King of Clubs, the King of Hearts and the King of Diamonds.

King Farouk 1920–65: addressed to the author at a conference in Cairo, 1948; Lord Boyd-Orr *As I Recall* (1966)

35 The family firm.

description of the British monarchy

George VI 1895–1952: attributed

36 Royalty is the gold filling in a mouthful of decay.

John Osborne 1929–94: 'They call it cricket' in T. Maschler (ed.) *Declaration* (1957)

37 To be Prince of Wales is not a position. It is a predicament.

Alan Bennett 1934– : *The Madness of King George* (1995 film)

38 I'd like to be a queen in people's hearts but I don't see myself being Queen of this country.

Diana, Princess of Wales 1961–97: interview on *Panorama*, BBC1 TV, 20 November 1995

39 The *éminence cerise*, the bolster behind the throne.

of Queen Elizabeth, the Queen Mother

Will Self 1961– : in *Independent on Sunday* 8 August 1999; see **Power** 11

Russia

PROVERBS AND SAYINGS

1 Scratch a Russian and you find a Tartar.

early 19th century, meaning that if a person is harmed their real national character will be revealed

QUOTATIONS

2 God of frostbite, God of famine,
beggars, cripples by the yard,
farms with no crops to examine—
that's him, that's your Russian God.

Prince Peter Vyazemsky 1792–1878: 'The Russian God' (1828)

3 Russia has two generals in whom she can confide—Generals Janvier [January] and Février [February].

Nicholas I 1796–1855: attributed; *Punch* 10 March 1855

4 Through reason Russia can't be known,
No common yardstick can avail you:
She has a nature all her own —
Have faith in her, all else will fail you.

F. I. Tyutchev 1803–73: 'Through reason Russia can't be known' (1866)

5 Every country has its own constitution; ours is absolutism moderated by assassination.

Anonymous: Ernst Friedrich Herbert, Count Münster, quoting 'an intelligent Russian', in *Political Sketches of the State of Europe, 1814–1867* (1868)

6 The Lord God has given us vast forests, immense fields, wide horizons; surely we ought to be giants, living in such a country as this.

Anton Chekhov 1860–1904: *The Cherry Orchard* (1904)

7 I cannot forecast to you the action of Russia. It is a riddle wrapped in a mystery inside an enigma.

Winston Churchill 1874–1965: radio broadcast, 1 October 1939

8 [Russian Communism is] the illegitimate child of Karl Marx and Catherine the Great.
Clement Attlee 1883–1967: speech at Aarhus University, 11 April 1956

9 The Soviet Union has indeed been our greatest menace, not so much because of what it has done, but because of the excuses it has provided us for our failures.
J. William Fulbright 1905–95: in *Observer* 21 December 1958

10 The idea of restructuring [perestroika] . . . combines continuity and innovation, the historical experience of Bolshevism and the contemporaneity of socialism.
Mikhail Sergeevich Gorbachev 1931– : speech on the seventieth anniversary of the Russian Revolution, 2 November 1987

11 Russia can be an empire or a democracy, but it cannot be both.
Zbigniew Brzezinski 1928– : in *Foreign Affairs* March/April 1994

12 Today is the last day of an era past.
at a Berlin ceremony to end the Soviet military presence in Germany
Boris Yeltsin 1931– : in *Guardian* 1 September 1994

Satisfaction and Discontent

PROVERBS AND SAYINGS

1 Acorns were good till bread was found.
proverbial saying, late 16th century; meaning that until something better is found, what one has will be judged satisfactory

2 The answer is a lemon.
early 20th century; a lemon as the type of something unsatisfactory, perhaps referring to the least valuable symbol in a fruit machine; see **Deception** *6*

3 Go further and fare worse.
mid 16th century, meaning that it is often wise to take what is on offer

4 Half a loaf is better than no bread.
mid 16th century, meaning that to have part of something is better than having nothing at all

5 Something is better than nothing.
mid 16th century, meaning that even a possession of intrinsically little value is preferable to being empty-handed

6 What you've never had you never miss.
early 20th century

PHRASES

7 all gas and gaiters a satisfactory state of affairs.
originally recorded in Dickens Nicholas Nickleby (1839) 'all is gas and gaiters'

8 all Sir Garnet highly satisfactory, all right.
Sir Garnet Wolseley (1833–1913), leader of several successful military expeditions; see **Armed Forces** *31*

9 a dusty answer an unsatisfactory answer, a disappointing response.
from Meredith: see **Certainty** *14*

10 a fly in the ointment a trifling circumstance that spoils the enjoyment or agreeableness of a thing.
after the Bible (Ecclesiastes) 'Dead flies cause the ointment of the apothecary to send forth a stinking savour'

11 sour grapes an expression or attitude of deliberate disparagement of a desired but unattainable object.
alluding to Aesop's fable of 'The Fox and the Grapes', in which a fox unable to reach the grapes contented himself with the reflection that they must be sour

QUOTATIONS

12 My soul, do not seek immortal life, but exhaust the realm of the possible.
Pindar 518–438 BC: *Pythian Odes*

13 Those who are contented and at ease when the occasion comes and live in accord with the course of Nature cannot be affected by sorrow or joy. This is what the ancients called release from bondage. Those who cannot release themselves are so because they are bound by material things.
Zhuangzi c.369–286 BC: *Chuang Tzu* ch. 6

14 It is called Nirvana because of the getting rid of craving.
Pali Tripitaka c. 2nd century BC: *Samyutta-nikāya* [*Kindred Sayings*] pt. 1, p. 39

15 So long as the great majority of men are not deprived of either property or honour, they are satisfied.
Niccolò Machiavelli 1469–1527: *The Prince* (written 1513)

16 Some have too much, yet still do crave;
I little have, and seek no more.
They are but poor, though much they
have,
And I am rich with little store.
Edward Dyer d. 1607: 'In praise of a contented mind' (1588)

17 'Tis just like a summer birdcage in a garden; the birds that are without despair to get in, and the birds that are within despair, and are in a consumption, for fear they shall never get out.
John Webster c.1580–c.1625: *The White Devil* (1612)

18 About six or seven o'clock, I walk out into a common that lies hard by the house, where a great many young wenches keep sheep and cows and sit in the shade singing of ballads . . . I talk to them, and find they want nothing to make them the happiest people in the world, but the knowledge that they are so.
Dorothy Osborne 1627–95: letter to William Temple, 2 June 1653

19 We loathe our manna, and we long for quails.
John Dryden 1631–1700: *The Medal* (1682); see **Gifts** 8

20 The stoical scheme of supplying our wants, by lopping off our desires, is like cutting off our feet when we want shoes.
Jonathan Swift 1667–1745: *Thoughts on Various Subjects* (1711)

21 Contented wi' little and cantie wi' mair,
Whene'er I forgather wi' Sorrow and Care,
I gie them a skelp, as they're creeping along,
Wi' a cog o' gude swats and an auld Scotish sang.
Robert Burns 1759–96: 'Contented wi' little' (1796)

22 Plain living and high thinking are no more:
The homely beauty of the good old cause
Is gone.
William Wordsworth 1770–1850: 'O friend! I know not which way I must look' (1807); see **Lifestyles** 5

23 That all was wrong because not all was right.
George Crabbe 1754–1832: 'The Convert' (1812)

24 In pale contented sort of discontent.
John Keats 1795–1821: 'Lamia' (1820)

25 Ah! *Vanitas Vanitatum!* Which of us is happy in this world? Which of us has his desire? or, having it, is satisfied?—Come,

children, let us shut up the box and the puppets, for our play is played out.
William Makepeace Thackeray 1811–63: *Vanity Fair* (1847–8); see **Disillusion** 5, **Futility** 14

26 Oh, the little more, and how much it is!
And the little less, and what worlds away!
Robert Browning 1812–89: 'By the Fireside' (1855)

27 It is better to be a human being dissatisfied than a pig satisfied; better to be Socrates dissatisfied than a fool satisfied.
John Stuart Mill 1806–73: *Utilitarianism* (1863)

28 It is an uneasy lot at best, to be what we call highly taught and yet not to enjoy: to be present at this great spectacle of life and never to be liberated from a small hungry shivering self.
George Eliot 1819–80: *Middlemarch* (1871–2)

29 A book of verses underneath the bough,
A jug of wine, a loaf of bread—and Thou
Beside me singing in the wilderness—
Oh, wilderness were paradise enow!
Edward Fitzgerald 1809–83: *The Rubáiyát of Omar Khayyám* (1879 ed.)

30 I'm afraid you've got a bad egg, Mr Jones.
Oh no, my Lord, I assure you! Parts of it are excellent!
Punch: cartoon caption, 1895, showing a curate breakfasting with his bishop; see **Character** 19

31 As long as I have a want, I have a reason for living. Satisfaction is death.
George Bernard Shaw 1856–1950: *Overruled* (1916)

32 Content is disillusioning to behold: what is there to be content about?
Virginia Woolf 1882–1941: diary 5 May 1920

33 He spoke with a certain what-is-it in his voice, and I could see that, if not actually disgruntled, he was far from being gruntled.
P. G. Wodehouse 1881–1975: *The Code of the Woosters* (1938)

34 When you don't have any money, the problem is food. When you have money, it's sex. When you have both it's health.
J. P. Donleavy 1926– : *The Ginger Man* (1955)

35 Let us be frank about it: most of our people have never had it so good.
Harold Macmillan 1894–1986: speech at Bedford, 20 July 1957; 'You Never Had It So Good' was the Democratic Party slogan during the 1952 US election campaign

36 There are some things in every country

that you must be born to endure; and another 100 years of general satisfaction with Americans and America could not reconcile this expatriate to cranberry sauce, peanut butter and drum majorettes.
Alistair Cooke 1908– : *Talk About America* (1968)

37 I've had this business that anything is better than nothing. There are times when

nothing has to be better than anything.
Penelope Gilliatt 1933–93: *Sunday, Bloody Sunday* (1971)

38 You ask if they were happy. This is not a characteristic of a European. To be contented—that's for the cows.
Coco Chanel 1883–1971: A. Madsen *Coco Chanel* (1990)

Schools see also Children, Education, Teaching

see also **Children, Education, Teaching**

PROVERBS AND SAYINGS

**1 No more Latin, no more French,
No more sitting on a hard board bench.**
traditional children's rhyme for the end of school term

PHRASES

2 the happiest days of your life school days.
from the title of a film (1950) based on a play by John Dighton

QUOTATIONS

3 Alexander at the head of the world never tasted the true pleasure that boys of his own age have enjoyed at the head of school.
Horace Walpole 1717–97: letter, 6 May 1736

4 Public schools are the nurseries of all vice and immorality.
Henry Fielding 1707–54: *Joseph Andrews* (1742)

5 There is now less flogging in our great schools than formerly, but then less is learned there; so that what the boys get at one end they lose at the other.
Samuel Johnson 1709–84: James Boswell *Life of Samuel Johnson* (1791) 1775

6 My object will be, if possible, to form Christian men, for Christian boys I can scarcely hope to make.
on appointment to the Headmastership of Rugby School
Thomas Arnold 1795–1842: letter to Revd John Tucker, 2 March 1828

7 EDUCATION.—At Mr Wackford Squeers's Academy, Dotheboys Hall, at the delightful village of Dotheboys, near Greta Bridge in Yorkshire, Youth are boarded, clothed, booked, furnished with pocket-money, provided with all necessaries, instructed in all languages living and dead,

mathematics, orthography, geometry, astronomy, trigonometry, the use of the globes, algebra, single stick (if required), writing, arithmetic, fortification, and every other branch of classical literature. Terms, twenty guineas per annum. No extras, no vacations, and diet unparalleled.
Charles Dickens 1812–70: *Nicholas Nickleby* (1839)

8 'I don't care a straw for Greek particles, or the digamma, no more does his mother. What is he sent to school for? . . . If he'll only turn out a brave, helpful, truth-telling Englishman, and a gentleman, and a Christian, that's all I want,' thought the Squire.
Thomas Hughes 1822–96: *Tom Brown's Schooldays* (1857)

9 You send your child to the schoolmaster, but 'tis the schoolboys who educate him.
Ralph Waldo Emerson 1803–82: *Conduct of Life* (1860) 'Culture'

10 Forty years on, when afar and asunder Parted are those who are singing to-day.
E. E. Bowen 1836–1901: 'Forty Years On' (Harrow School Song, published 1886)

11 Make the boy interested in natural history if you can; it is better than games.
Robert Falcon Scott 1868–1912: last letter to his wife, in *Scott's Last Expedition* (1913)

12 Headmasters have powers at their disposal with which Prime Ministers have never yet been invested.
Winston Churchill 1874–1965: *My Early Life* (1930)

13 The only good things about skool are the BOYS wizz who are noble brave fearless etc. although you hav various swots, bulies,

cissies, milksops, greedy guts and oiks with whom i am forced to mingle hem-hem.
Geoffrey Willans 1911–58 and **Ronald Searle** 1920– : *Down With Skool!* (1953)

14 The dread of beatings! Dread of being late! And, greatest dread of all, the dread of games!
John Betjeman 1906–84: *Summoned by Bells* (1960)

15 I am putting old heads on your young shoulders . . . all my pupils are the crème de la crème.
Muriel Spark 1918– : *The Prime of Miss Jean Brodie* (1961)

16 When I lost my leather tawse for ever I lost my fear of my pupils and they lost their fear of me.
A. S. Neill 1883–1973: Jonathan Croall *Neill of Summerhill: the Permanent Rebel* (1983)

17 Schools are for schooling, not social engineering.
Brian Cox 1928– and **Rhodes Boyson** 1925– : *Black Paper 1975* (1975)

18 Dear Parents
    If you don't believe everything your child tells you about school, I will not believe everything your child tells me about home.
John Rae 1931– : *Letters from School* (1987)

19 Let me say this very slowly indeed. Watch my lips: no selection by examination or interview under a Labour government.
David Blunkett 1947– : in *Daily Telegraph* (electronic edition) 5 October 1995; see **Taxes** 19

20 The day of the bog-standard comprehensive is over.
Alastair Campbell 1957– : press briefing, 12 February 2001

Science see also **Arts and Sciences, Hypothesis and Fact, Inventions and Discoveries, Life Sciences, Physical Sciences, Science and Religion, Technology**

PROVERBS AND SAYINGS

1 Much science, much sorrow.
early 17th century, suggesting that learning may increase one's awareness of difficult questions

2 Science has no enemy but the ignorant.
mid 16th century, from Latin Scientia non habet inimicum nisi ignorantem

PHRASES

3 backroom boys people who provide vital scientific and technical support for those in the field who become public figures.
the expression derives from Lord Beaverbrook: see **Fame** 16

QUOTATIONS

4 Lucky is he who has been able to understand the causes of things.
of Lucretius
Virgil 70–19 BC: *Georgics*

5 That all things are changed, and that nothing really perishes, and that the sum of matter remains exactly the same, is sufficiently certain.
Francis Bacon 1561–1626: *Cogitationes de Natura Rerum*

6 Books must follow sciences, and not sciences books.
Francis Bacon 1561–1626: *Resuscitatio* (1657)

7 The changing of bodies into light, and light into bodies, is very conformable to the course of Nature, which seems delighted with transmutations.
Isaac Newton 1642–1727: *Opticks* (1730 ed.)

8 Nature, and Nature's laws lay hid in night. God said, *Let Newton be!* and all was light.
Alexander Pope 1688–1744: 'Epitaph: Intended for Sir Isaac Newton' (1730); see 17 below

9 Where observation is concerned, chance favours only the prepared mind.
Louis Pasteur 1822–95: address given on the inauguration of the Faculty of Science, University of Lille, 7 December 1854

10 Scientific truth should be presented in different forms, and should be regarded as equally scientific, whether it appears in the robust form and the vivid colouring of a physical illustration, or in the tenuity and paleness of a symbolic expression.
James Clerk Maxwell 1831–79: address to the British Association, 15 September 1870

11 When you can measure what you are speaking about, and express it in numbers, you know something about it; but when you cannot measure it, when you cannot express it in numbers, your knowledge is of a meagre and unsatisfactory kind: it may be the beginning of knowledge, but you have scarcely, in your thoughts, advanced to the stage of *science*, whatever the matter may be.

often quoted as 'If you cannot measure it, then it is not science'

Lord Kelvin 1824–1907: *Popular Lectures and Addresses* vol. 1 (1889) 'Electrical Units of Measurement', delivered 3 May 1883

12 Science is nothing but trained and organized common sense, differing from the latter only as a veteran may differ from a raw recruit: and its methods differ from those of common sense only as far as the guardsman's cut and thrust differ from the manner in which a savage wields his club.

T. H. Huxley 1825–95: *Collected Essays* (1893–4) 'The Method of Zadig'

13 In science, we must be interested in things, not in persons.

Marie Curie 1867–1934: in c.1904; Eve Curie *Madame Curie* (1937)

14 Science is built up of facts, as a house is built of stones; but an accumulation of facts is no more a science than a heap of stones is a house.

Henri Poincaré 1854–1912: *Science and Hypothesis* (1905)

15 The outcome of any serious research can only be to make two questions grow where one question grew before.

Thorstein Veblen 1857–1929: *University of California Chronicle* (1908) 'Evolution of the Scientific Point of View'

16 In science the credit goes to the man who convinces the world, not to the man to whom the idea first occurs.

Francis Darwin 1848–1925: in *Eugenics Review* April 1914 'Francis Galton'

17 It did not last: the Devil howling 'Ho! Let Einstein be!' restored the status quo.

J. C. Squire 1884–1958: 'In continuation of Pope on Newton' (1926); see 8 above

18 I ask you to look both ways. For the road to a knowledge of the stars leads through the atom; and important knowledge of the atom has been reached through the stars.

Arthur Eddington 1882–1944: *Stars and Atoms* (1928)

19 It is much easier to make measurements than to know exactly what you are measuring.

J. W. N. Sullivan 1886–1937: comment, 1928; R. L. Weber *More Random Walks in Science* (1982)

20 All science is either physics or stamp collecting.

Ernest Rutherford 1871–1937: J. B. Birks *Rutherford at Manchester* (1962)

21 The aim of science is not to open the door to infinite wisdom, but to set a limit to infinite error.

Bertolt Brecht 1898–1956: *Life of Galileo* (1939)

22 The importance of a scientific work can be measured by the number of previous publications it makes it superfluous to read.

David Hilbert 1862–1943: attributed; Lewis Wolpert *The Unnatural Nature of Science* (1993)

23 A new scientific truth does not triumph by convincing its opponents and making them see the light, but rather because its opponents eventually die, and a new generation grows up that is familiar with it.

Max Planck 1858–1947: *A Scientific Autobiography* (1949)

24 If politics is the art of the possible, research is surely the art of the soluble. Both are immensely practical-minded affairs.

Peter Medawar 1915–87: in *New Statesman* 19 June 1964; see **Politics** 17

25 Basic research is what I am doing when I don't know what I am doing.

Wernher von Braun 1912–77: R. L. Weber *A Random Walk in Science* (1973)

26 In effect, we have redefined the task of science to be the discovery of laws that will enable us to predict events up to the limits set by the uncertainty principle.

Stephen Hawking 1942– : *A Brief History of Time* (1988); see **Physical Sciences** 8

27 The priest persuades humble people to endure their hard lot; the politician urges them to rebel against it; and the scientist thinks of a method that does away with the hard lot altogether.

Max Perutz 1914– : *Is Science Necessary* (1989)

28 Science is an integral part of culture. It's not this foreign thing, done by an arcane priesthood. It's one of the glories of human intellectual tradition.

Stephen Jay Gould 1941– : in *Independent* 24 January 1990

Science and Religion

1 creation science the reinterpretation of scientific knowledge in accord with belief in the literal truth of the Bible.
especially regarding the origin of matter, life, and humankind described in Genesis

2 God of the gaps God as an explanation for phenomena not yet explained by science; God thought of as acting only in those spheres not otherwise accounted for.
see 11 below

QUOTATIONS

3 Science is for the cultivation of religion, not for worldly enjoyment.
Sadi c.1213–91: *The Rose Garden* (1258)

4 In disputes about natural phenomena one must begin not with the authority of Scriptural passage but with sensory experience and necessary demonstrations. For the Holy Scripture and nature derive equally from the Godhead, the former as the dictation of the Holy Spirit and the latter as the most obedient executrix of God's orders.
Galileo 1564–1642: letter to Christina Lotharinga, Arch-Duchess of Tuscany

5 It is God who is the ultimate reason of things, and the knowledge of God is no less the beginning of science than his essence and will are the beginning of beings.
Gottfried Wilhelm Leibniz 1646–1716: *Letter on a General Principle Useful in Explaining the Laws of Nature* (1687)

6 An Aristotle was but the rubbish of an Adam, and Athens but the rudiments of Paradise.
Robert South 1634–1716: *Twelve Sermons . . .* (1692)

7 If ignorance of nature gave birth to the Gods, knowledge of nature is destined to destroy them.
Paul Henri, Baron d'Holbach 1723–89: *Système de la Nature* (1770)

8 The atoms of Democritus
And Newton's particles of light

Are sands upon the Red Sea shore
Where Israel's tents do shine so bright.
William Blake 1757–1827: *MS Note-Book*

9 I asserted—and I repeat—that a man has no reason to be ashamed of having an ape for his grandfather. If there were an ancestor whom I should feel shame in recalling it would rather be a *man*—a man of restless and versatile intellect—who, not content with an equivocal success in his own sphere of activity, plunges into scientific questions with which he has no real acquaintance, only to obscure them by an aimless rhetoric, and distract the attention of his hearers from the real point at issue by eloquent digressions and skilled appeals to religious prejudice.
replying to Bishop Samuel Wilberforce in the debate on Darwin's theory of evolution
T. H. Huxley 1825–95: at a meeting of the British Association in Oxford, 30 June 1860; see **Life Sciences** 12

10 Terms like grace, new birth, justification . . . terms, in short, which with St Paul are literary terms, theologians have employed as if they were scientific terms.
Matthew Arnold 1822–88: *Literature and Dogma* (1873)

11 There are reverent minds who ceaselessly scan the fields of Nature and the books of Science in search of gaps—gaps which they will fill up with God. As if God lived in gaps?
Henry Drummond 1851–97: *The Ascent of Man* (1894); see 2 above

12 Science without religion is lame, religion without science is blind.
Albert Einstein 1879–1955: *Science, Philosophy and Religion: a Symposium* (1941)

13 We have grasped the mystery of the atom and rejected the Sermon on the Mount.
Omar Bradley 1893–1981: speech on Armistice Day, 1948; see **The Christian Church** 12

14 There is no evil in the atom; only in men's souls.
Adlai Stevenson 1900–65: speech at Hartford, Connecticut, 18 September 1952

15 The means by which we live have outdistanced the ends for which we live. Our scientific power has outrun our spiritual power. We have guided missiles and misguided men.

Martin Luther King 1929-68: *Strength to Love* (1963)

16 How is it that hardly any major religion has looked at science and concluded, 'This is better than we thought! The Universe is much bigger than our prophets said, grander, more subtle, more elegant'?

Carl Sagan 1934-96: *Pale Blue Dot* (1995)

17 Science offers the best answers to the meaning of life. Science offers you the privilege before you die of understanding why you were ever born in the first place.

Richard Dawkins 1941- : in *Break the Science Barrier with Richard Dawkins* (Channel 4) 1 September 1996

Scotland

PHRASES

1 the curse of Scotland the nine of diamonds in a pack of cards.

perhaps from its resemblance to the armorial bearings, nine lozenges on a saltire, of Lord Stair, from his part in sanctioning the Massacre of Glencoe in 1692; see 6 below

2 the land of cakes Scotland.

cake a piece of thin oaten bread

QUOTATIONS

3 So long as there shall but one hundred of us remain alive, we will never subject ourselves to the dominion of the English. For it is not glory, it is not riches, neither is it honour, but it is freedom alone that we fight and contend for, which no honest man will lose but with his life.

to the Pope, asserting the independence of Scotland

Declaration of Arbroath: letter sent by the Scottish Parliament, 6 April 1320

4 It came with a lass, and it will pass with a lass.

of the crown of Scotland, which had come to the Stuarts through the female line, on learning of the birth of Mary Queen of Scots, December 1542

James V 1512-42: Robert Lindsay of Pitscottie (c.1500-65) *History of Scotland* (1728)

5 Stands Scotland where it did?

William Shakespeare 1564-1616: *Macbeth* (1606)

6 It's a great work of charity be be exact in rooting out that damnable sept, the worst in all the Highlands.

on hearing that Alasdair Maclan, chief of the Glencoe MacDonalds, had been too late in taking the required oath of loyalty to William III; see 1 above

Lord Stair 1648-1707: letter to Thomas Livingston, 11 January 1692

7 Now there's ane end of ane old song.

as he signed the engrossed exemplification of the Act of Union, 1706; see 22 below

James Ogilvy, Lord Seafield 1664-1730: *The Lockhart Papers* (1817)

8 The noblest prospect which a Scotchman ever sees, is the high road that leads him to England!

Samuel Johnson 1709-84: James Boswell *Life of Samuel Johnson* (1791) 6 July 1763

9 My heart's in the Highlands, my heart is not here;
My heart's in the Highlands a-chasing the deer.

Robert Burns 1759-96: 'My Heart's in the Highlands' (1790)

10 Scots, wha hae wi' Wallace bled,
Scots, wham Bruce has aften led,
Welcome to your gory bed,—
Or to victorie.

Robert Burns 1759-96: 'Robert Bruce's March to Bannockburn' (1799) (also known as 'Scots, Wha Hae')

11 O Caledonia! stern and wild,
Meet nurse for a poetic child!

Sir Walter Scott 1771-1832: *The Lay of the Last Minstrel* (1805)

12 From the lone shieling of the misty island
Mountains divide us, and the waste of seas—
Yet still the blood is strong, the heart is Highland,
And we in dreams behold the Hebrides!

John Galt 1779-1839: 'Canadian Boat Song' (1829); translated from the Gaelic; attributed

13 There are few more impressive sights in the world than a Scotsman on the make.

J. M. Barrie 1860-1937: *What Every Woman Knows* (1918)

14 It is never difficult to distinguish between a Scotsman with a grievance and a ray of sunshine.
P. G. Wodehouse 1881–1975: *Blandings Castle and Elsewhere* (1935)

15 O flower of Scotland, when will we see your like again,
that fought and died for your bit hill and glen
and stood against him, proud Edward's army,
and sent him homeward tae think again.
Roy Williamson 1936–90: 'O Flower of Scotland' (1968)

16 Scotland, land of the omnipotent No.
Alan Bold 1943– : 'A Memory of Death' (1969)

17 Who owns this landscape?
The millionaire who bought it or
the poacher staggering downhill in the early morning
with a deer on his back?
Norman McCaig 1910–96: 'A Man in Assynt' (1969)

18 Scotland small? Our multiform, our infinite Scotland *small?*
Only as a patch of hillside may be a cliché corner

To a fool who cries 'Nothing but heather!'
Hugh MacDiarmid 1892–1978: *Direadh* 1 (1974)

19 It's nae good blamin' it oan the English fir colonising us. Ah don't hate the English. They're just wankers. We can't even pick a decent vibrant, healthy culture to be colonised by.
Irvine Welsh 1957– : *Trainspotting* (1994)

20 I don't want a Stormont. I don't want a wee pretendy government in Edinburgh.
on the prospective Scottish Parliament; often quoted as 'a wee pretendy Parliament'
Billy Connolly 1942– : interview on *Breakfast with Frost* (BBC TV), 9 February 1997

21 It is Scotland's rightful heritage that its people should create a modern Parliament . . . This entire issue is above and beyond any political party.
of Scottish devolution, in the Referendum campaign
Sean Connery 1930– : speech in Edinburgh, 7 September 1997

22 The Scottish Parliament which adjourned on 25 March in the year 1707 is hereby reconvened.
Winifred Ewing 1929– : in the Scottish Parliament, 12 May 1999; see 7 above

Sculpture

PHRASES

1 **fig leaf** representation of the leaf of a fig tree, often used for concealing the genitals in paintings and sculpture.
with particular reference to the story of Adam and Eve in the Bible (Genesis), when having eaten of the tree of the knowledge of good and evil and become ashamed of their nakedness, 'they sewed fig leaves together, and made themselves aprons'

2 **Elgin Marbles** a collection of classical Greek marble sculptures and architectural fragments, chiefly from the frieze and pediment of the Parthenon in Athens.
they were brought to England in 1802–12 by the diplomat and art connoisseur Thomas Bruce (1766–1841), the 7th Earl of Elgin; see 4 below

QUOTATIONS

3 The marble not yet carved can hold the form

Of every thought the greatest artist has.
Michelangelo 1475–1564: Sonnet 15

4 Dull is the eye that will not weep to see
Thy walls defaced, thy mouldering shrines removed
By British hands, which it had best behoved
To guard those relics ne'er to be restored.
of the Parthenon
Lord Byron 1788–1824: *Childe Harold's Pilgrimage* (1812–18); see 2 above

5 All his statues are so constrained by agony that they seem to wish to break themselves. They all seem ready to succumb to the pressure of despair that fills them.
of Michelangelo
Auguste Rodin 1840–1917: *On Art and Artists* (1911)

6 Carving is interrelated masses conveying an emotion: a perfect relationship between

the mind and the colour, light and weight which is the stone, made by the hand which feels.

Barbara Hepworth 1903–75: Herbert Read (ed.) *Unit One* (1934)

7 The first hole made through a piece of stone is a revelation.

Henry Moore 1898–1986: in *Listener* 18 August 1937

8 The old ideas of nobility and sacrifice have become a howitzer squatting at Hyde Park like a petrified toad, and the hero has become a cabinet minister on a pedestal in bronze boots.

on modern sculpture

Geoffrey Grigson 1905–85: *Henry Moore* (1944)

9 Why don't they stick to murder and leave art to us?

on hearing that his statue of Lazarus in New College chapel, Oxford, kept Khrushchev awake at night

Jacob Epstein 1880–1959: attributed

10 Most statues seem sad and introspective, they hold their breath between coming and going,
They lament their devoured, once shuddering stone.

Dannie Abse 1923– : 'At the Tate'

11 It's amazing what you can do with an E in A-level art, twisted imagination and a chainsaw.

after winning the 1995 Turner Prize

Damien Hirst 1965– : in *Observer* 3 December 1995

The Sea

PROVERBS AND SAYINGS

1 The good seaman is known in bad weather.

American proverb, mid 18th century

2 He that would go to sea for pleasure would go to hell for a pastime.

late 19th century, with reference to the dangers involved in going to sea

3 One hand for oneself and one for the ship.

late 18th century, meaning literally, hold on with one hand, and work the ship with the other

PHRASES

4 Davy Jones's locker the deep, especially as the grave of those who are drowned at sea.

Davy Jones the evil spirit of the sea

5 the long forties the sea area between the NE coast of Scotland and the SW coast of Norway.

from its depth of over 40 fathoms

6 the roaring forties stormy ocean tracts between latitude 40 and 50 degrees south.

7 the seven seas the Arctic, Antarctic, North and South Pacific, North and South Atlantic, and Indian Oceans.

QUOTATIONS

8 They that go down to the sea in ships: and occupy their business in great waters;
These men see the works of the Lord: and his wonders in the deep.

Bible: Psalm 107

9 Full fathom five thy father lies;
Of his bones are coral made:
Those are pearls that were his eyes:
Nothing of him that doth fade,
But doth suffer a sea-change
Into something rich and strange.

William Shakespeare 1564–1616: *The Tempest* (1611); see **Change** 24

10 Now would I give a thousand furlongs of sea for an acre of barren ground.

William Shakespeare 1564–1616: *The Tempest* (1611)

11 The dominion of the sea, as it is an ancient and undoubted right of the crown of England, so it is the best security of the land . . . The wooden walls are the best walls of this kingdom.

Thomas Coventry 1578–1640: speech to the Judges, 17 June 1635; see **Armed Forces** 14

12 What is a ship but a prison?

Robert Burton 1577–1640: *The Anatomy of Melancholy* (1621–51)

13 Water, water, everywhere,
And all the boards did shrink;
Water, water, everywhere,
Nor any drop to drink.

Samuel Taylor Coleridge 1772–1834: 'The Rime of the Ancient Mariner' (1798)

14 It [the Channel] is a mere ditch, and will be crossed as soon as someone has the courage to attempt it.

Napoleon I 1769–1821: letter to Consul Cambacérès, 16 November 1803

15 A wet sheet and a flowing sea,
A wind that follows fast
And fills the white and rustling sail
And bends the gallant mast.
Allan Cunningham 1784–1842: 'A Wet Sheet and a Flowing Sea' (1825)

16 Rocked in the cradle of the deep.
Emma Hart Willard 1787–1870: title of song (1840), inspired by a prospect of the Bristol Channel

17 Break, break, break,
On thy cold grey stones, O Sea!
And I would that my tongue could utter
The thoughts that arise in me.
Alfred, Lord Tennyson 1809–92: 'Break, Break, Break' (1842)

18 I must go down to the sea again, to the lonely sea and the sky,
And all I ask is a tall ship and a star to steer her by,
And the wheel's kick and the wind's song and the white sail's shaking,
And a grey mist on the sea's face and a grey dawn breaking.
John Masefield 1878–1967: 'Sea Fever'; 'I must down to the seas' in the original of 1902, possibly a misprint

19 'A man who is not afraid of the sea will soon be drownded,' he said 'for he will be going out on a day he shouldn't. But we do be afraid of the sea, and we do only be drownded now and again.'
John Millington Synge 1871–1909: The Aran Islands (1907)

20 The dragon-green, the luminous, the dark, the serpent-haunted sea.
James Elroy Flecker 1884–1915: 'The Gates of Damascus' (1913)

21 The snotgreen sea. The scrotumtightening sea.
James Joyce 1882–1941: Ulysses (1922)

22 The sea hates a coward!
Eugene O'Neill 1888–1953: Mourning becomes Electra (1931)

23 They didn't think much to the Ocean:
The waves, they were fiddlin' and small,
There was no wrecks and nobody drownded,
Fact, nothing to laugh at at all.
Marriott Edgar 1880–1951: 'The Lion and Albert' (1932)

24 It is an interesting biological fact that all of us have in our veins the exact same percentage of salt in our blood that exists in the ocean, and therefore, we have salt in our blood, in our sweat, in our tears. We are tied to the ocean. And when we go back to the sea—whether it is to sail or to watch it—we are going back from whence we came.
John F. Kennedy 1917–63: speech, Newport, Rhode Island, 14 September 1962

25 The sea has such extraordinary moods that sometimes you feel this is the only sort of life—and 10 minutes later you're praying for death.
Prince Philip, Duke of Edinburgh 1921– : in Independent 31 December 1998

26 When you are up there, it's like trying to hang on to a telegraph pole in an earthquake.
90 feet up the mast of her boat Kingfisher
Ellen MacArthur 1977– : in Daily Telegraph 16 February 2001

The Seasons see also Weather

1 A cherry year, a merry year; a plum year, a dumb year.
late 17th century, recording the tradition that a good crop of cherries is a promising sign for the year

2 It is not spring until you can plant your foot upon twelve daisies.
mid 19th century; meaning that mild spring weather is only assured when daisies are flowering thickly on the grass

3 May chickens come cheeping.
late 19th century, meaning that the weakness of chickens born in May is apparent from their continuous feeble cries. The proverb has also been linked to the idea that marriage in May is unlucky, and that children of such marriages are less likely to survive; see **Weddings** 3

4 One swallow does not make a summer.
mid 16th century, meaning that a single sign such as the arrival of one migratory swallow does not mean that the summer's settled weather has fully arrived

5 On the first of March, the crows begin to search.

mid 19th century; meaning that crows traditionally pair off on this day

6 A swarm in May is worth a load of hay; a swarm in June is worth a silver spoon; but a swarm in July is not worth a fly.

traditional beekeepers' saying, mid 17th century; meaning that the later in the year it is, the less time there will be for bees to collect pollen from flowers in blossom

7 Winter never rots in the sky.

early 17th century; meaning that the arrival of winter is not delayed

PHRASES

8 a blackthorn winter a period of cold weather in early spring.

at the time when the blackthorn is in flower

9 fall of the leaf autumn.

10 February fill-dyke the month of February.

referring to the month's rain and snows; see **Weather** *4*

QUOTATIONS

11 Sumer is icumen in,
Lhude sing cuccu!
Groweth sed, and bloweth med,
And springth the wude nu.

Anonymous: 'Cuckoo Song' (*c*.1250), sung annually at Reading Abbey gateway and first recorded by John Fornset, a monk of Reading Abbey; see 23 below

12 In a somer seson, whan softe was the sonne.

William Langland *c*.1330–*c*.1400: *The Vision of Piers Plowman*

13 Whan that Aprill with his shoures soote
The droghte of March hath perced to the roote.

Geoffrey Chaucer *c*.1343–1400: *The Canterbury Tales* 'The General Prologue'

14 I sing of brooks, of blossoms, birds, and bowers:
Of April, May, of June, and July-flowers.
I sing of May-poles, Hock-carts, wassails, wakes,
Of bride-grooms, brides, and of their bridal-cakes.

Robert Herrick 1591–1674: 'The Argument of his Book' from *Hesperides* (1648)

15 Early autumn—

rice field, ocean,
one green.

Matsuo Basho 1644–94: translated by Lucien Stryk

16 The way to ensure summer in England is to have it framed and glazed in a comfortable room.

Horace Walpole 1717–97: letter to Revd William Cole, 28 May 1774

17 Snowy, Flowy, Blowy,
Showery, Flowery, Bowery,
Hoppy, Croppy, Droppy,
Breezy, Sneezy, Freezy.

George Ellis 1753–1815: 'The Twelve Months'

18 Season of mists and mellow fruitfulness,
Close bosom-friend of the maturing sun;
Conspiring with him how to load and bless
With fruit the vines that round the thatch-eaves run.

John Keats 1795–1821: 'To Autumn' (1820)

19 A tedious season they await
Who hear November at the gate.

Alexander Pushkin 1799–1837: *Eugene Onegin* (1833)

20 No warmth, no cheerfulness, no healthful ease,
No comfortable feel in any member—
No shade, no shine, no butterflies, no bees,
No fruits, no flowers, no leaves, no birds,—
November!

Thomas Hood 1799–1845: 'No!' (1844)

21 Oh, to be in England
Now that April's there,
And whoever wakes in England
Sees, some morning, unaware,
That the lowest boughs and the brushwood sheaf
Round the elm-tree bole are in tiny leaf,
While the chaffinch sings on the orchard bough
In England—now!

Robert Browning 1812–89: 'Home-Thoughts, from Abroad' (1845)

22 In winter I get up at night
And dress by yellow candle-light.
In summer, quite the other way,—
I have to go to bed by day.

Robert Louis Stevenson 1850–94: 'Bed in Summer' (1885)

23 Winter is icummen in,

Lhude sing Goddamm,
Raineth drop and staineth slop,
And how the wind doth ramm!
Sing: Goddamm.
Ezra Pound 1885–1972: 'Ancient Music' (1917); see 11 above

24 April is the cruellest month, breeding
Lilacs out of the dead land, mixing
Memory and desire, stirring
Dull roots with spring rain.
T. S. Eliot 1888–1965: *The Waste Land* (1922)

25 I want to go south, where there is no
autumn, where the cold doesn't crouch
over one like a snow-leopard waiting to
pounce. The heart of the North is dead,
and the fingers of cold are corpse fingers.
D. H. Lawrence 1885–1930: letter to J. Middleton Murry, 3 October 1924

26 Summer time an' the livin' is easy,
Fish are jumpin' an' the cotton is high.
Du Bose Heyward 1885–1940 and **Ira Gershwin** 1896–1983: 'Summertime' (1935 song)

27 It is about five o'clock in an evening that
the first hour of spring strikes—autumn
arrives in the early morning, but spring at
the close of a winter day.
Elizabeth Bowen 1899–1973: *The Death of the Heart* (1938)

28 June is bustin' out all over.
Oscar Hammerstein II 1895–1960: title of song (1945)

29 August creates as she slumbers, replete
and satisfied.
Joseph Wood Krutch 1893–1970: *Twelve Seasons* (1949)

30 What of October, that ambiguous month,
the month of tension, the unendurable
month?
Doris Lessing 1919– : *Martha Quest* (1952)

31 For man, autumn is a time of harvest, of
gathering together. For nature, it is a time
of sowing, of scattering abroad.
Edwin Way Teale 1899–1980: *Autumn Across America* (1956)

32 Work seethes in the hands of spring,
That strapping dairymaid.
Boris Pasternak 1890–1960: *Doctor Zhivago* (1958) 'Zhivago's Poems: March'

33 There is something about winter
which pares things down to their essentials
a bare tree
a black hedge
hold their own stark throne in our hearts.
Moya Cannon 1956– : 'Winter Paths' (1997)

Secrecy

1 **Dead men tell no tales.**
mid 17th century, often used to imply that a person's knowledge of a secret will die with them

2 **Don't ask, don't tell.**
summary of the Clinton administration's compromise policy on homosexuals serving in the armed forces, as described by Sam Nunn (1938–) in May 1993

3 **Fields have eyes and woods have ears.**
early 13th century, meaning that one may always be spied on by unseen watchers or listeners

4 **Listeners never hear any good of themselves.**
mid 17th century

5 **Little pitchers have large ears.**
mid 16th century, meaning that children overhear what is not meant for them (a pitcher's ears are its handles)

6 **Never tell tales out of school.**
mid 16th century; a warning against indiscretion

7 **No names, no pack-drill.**
early 20th century, meaning that if nobody is named as being responsible, nobody can be blamed or punished (pack-drill a military punishment of walking up and down carrying full equipment); the expression is now used generally to express an unwillingness to provide detailed information

8 **One does not wash one's dirty linen in public.**
early 19th century; meaning that discreditable matters should be dealt with privately

9 **Sch . . . you know who.**
advertising slogan for Schweppes mineral drinks, 1960s

10 **A secret is either too good to keep or too bad not to tell.**
American proverb, mid 20th century

11 Those who hide can find.

early 15th century, meaning that those who have concealed something know where it is to be found

12 Three may keep a secret, if two of them are dead.

mid 16th century; meaning that the only way to keep a secret is to tell no-one else

13 Walls have ears.

late 16th century; meaning that care should be taken for possible eavesdroppers

14 Will the real — please stand up?

catchphrase from an American TV game show (1955–66) in which a panel was asked to identify the 'real' one of three candidates all claiming to be a particular person; after the guesses were made, the compère would request the 'real' candidate to stand up

PHRASES

15 an ace up one's sleeve something effective held in reserve, a hidden advantage.

*an ace as the card of highest value in a card-game; see **Politicians** 18*

16 quiet American a person suspected of being an undercover agent or spy.

with allusion to Graham Greene's The Quiet American (1955)

17 a skeleton in the cupboard a secret source of discredit, pain, or shame.

brought into literary use by Thackeray in 1845, 'there is a skeleton in every house'; see 32 below

18 a smoking pistol a piece of incontrovertible incriminating evidence.

on the assumption that a person found with a smoking pistol or gun must be the guilty party; particularly associated with Barber B. Conable's comment on a Watergate tape revealing President Nixon's wish to limit FBI involvement in the investigation: 'I guess we have found the smoking pistol, haven't we?'

19 something nasty in the woodshed a traumatic experience or a concealed unpleasantness in a person's background.

from Stella Gibbons Cold Comfort Farm (1932), the repeated assertion 'I saw something nasty in the woodshed' being Aunt Ada Doom's method of ensuring her family's continued attendance on her

QUOTATIONS

20 DUKE: And what's her history?
VIOLA: A blank, my lord. She never told her love,

But let concealment, like a worm i' the bud,
Feed on her damask cheek.
William Shakespeare 1564–1616: *Twelfth Night* (1601)

21 I would not open windows into men's souls.
Elizabeth I 1533–1603: oral tradition, the words very possibly originating in a letter drafted by Bacon; J. B. Black *Reign of Elizabeth 1558–1603* (1936)

22 For secrets are edged tools,
And must be kept from children and from fools.
John Dryden 1631–1700: *Sir Martin Mar-All* (1667)

23 Secrets with girls, like loaded guns with boys,
Are never valued till they make a noise.
George Crabbe 1754–1832: *Tales of the Hall* (1819) 'The Maid's Story'

24 We never knows wot's hidden in each other's hearts; and if we had glass winders there, we'd need keep the shutters up, some on us, I do assure you!
Charles Dickens 1812–70: *Martin Chuzzlewit* (1844)

25 After the first silence the small man said to the other: 'Where does a wise man hide a pebble?' And the tall man answered in a low voice: 'On the beach.' The small man nodded, and after a short silence said: 'Where does a wise man hide a leaf?' And the other answered: 'In the forest.'
G. K. Chesterton 1874–1936: *The Innocence of Father Brown* (1911)

26 I shall be but a short time tonight. I have seldom spoken with greater regret, for my lips are not yet unsealed. Were these troubles over I would make a case, and I guarantee that not a man would go into the lobby against us.
on the Abyssinian crisis; usually quoted 'My lips are sealed'
Stanley Baldwin 1867–1947: speech, House of Commons, 10 December 1935

27 We dance round in a ring and suppose,
But the Secret sits in the middle and knows.
Robert Frost 1874–1963: 'The Secret Sits' (1942)

28 Once the toothpaste is out of the tube, it is awfully hard to get it back in.
on the Watergate affair
H. R. Haldeman 1929– : to John Dean, 8 April 1973

29 That's another of those irregular verbs, isn't it? I give confidential briefings; you leak; he has been charged under Section 2a of the Official Secrets Act.

Jonathan Lynn 1943- and **Antony Jay** 1930- : *Yes Prime Minister* (1987) vol. 2 'Man Overboard'

30 Truth is suppressed, not to protect the country from enemy agents but to protect the Government of the day against the people.

Roy Hattersley 1932- : in *Independent* 18 February 1995

31 If a man cannot keep a measly affair secret, what is he doing in charge of the Intelligence Service?

on the break-up of the marriage of Foreign Secretary Robin Cook

Frederick Forsyth 1938- : in *Guardian* 14 January 1998

32 Everyone has a skeleton in their closet. The difference between Bill Clinton and myself is that he has a walk-in closet.

Pat Buchanan 1938- : in *Sunday Times* 21 November 1999; see 17 above

The Self

1 Deny self for self's sake.

American proverb, mid 18th century, meaning that the result of self-denial is likely to be self-improvement

2 Every man is the architect of his own fortune.

mid 16th century, meaning that each person is ultimately responsible for what happens to them; see **Fate** *13*

QUOTATIONS

3 The commander of three armies may be taken away but the will of even a common man may not be taken away from him.

Confucius 551-479 BC: *Analects* ch. 9, v. 25

4 If a man should conquer in battle a thousand and a thousand more, and another man should conquer himself, his would be the greater victory, because the greatest of victories is the victory over oneself.

Pali Tripitaka c. 2nd century BC: *Dhammapada* v. 103

5 If I am not for myself who is for me; and being for my own self what am I? If not now when?

Hillel 'The Elder' c.60 BC–AD c.9: *Pirqe Aboth*

6 I am made all things to all men.

Bible: I Corinthians

7 Every man's ordure well to his own sense doth smell.

Montaigne 1533-92: *Essais* (1580, Florio's translation of 1603), quoting the Latin of Erasmus (c.1469-1536)

8 This above all: to thine own self be true, And it must follow, as the night the day,

Thou canst not then be false to any man.

William Shakespeare 1564-1616: *Hamlet* (1601)

9 Who is it that can tell me who I am?

William Shakespeare 1564-1616: *King Lear* (1605-6)

10 But I do nothing upon my self, and yet I am mine own *Executioner*.

John Donne 1572-1631: *Devotions upon Emergent Occasions* (1624)

11 It is the nature of extreme self-lovers, as they will set a house on fire, and it were but to roast their eggs.

Francis Bacon 1561-1626: *Essays* (1625) 'Of Wisdom for a Man's Self'

12 The self is hateful.

Blaise Pascal 1623-62: *Pensées* (1670)

13 It is not contrary to reason to prefer the destruction of the whole world to the scratching of my finger.

David Hume 1711-76: *A Treatise upon Human Nature* (1739)

14 I am—yet what I am, none cares or knows;
My friends forsake me like a memory lost:
I am the self-consumer of my woes.

John Clare 1793-1864: 'I Am' (1848)

15 Do I contradict myself?
Very well then I contradict myself,
(I am large, I contain multitudes.)

Walt Whitman 1819-92: 'Song of Myself' (written 1855)

16 It matters not how strait the gate,
How charged with punishments the scroll,
I am the master of my fate:

I am the captain of my soul.
W. E. Henley 1849–1903: 'Invictus. In Memoriam R.T.H.B.' (1888)

17 Rose is a rose is a rose is a rose, is a rose.
Gertrude Stein 1874–1946: *Sacred Emily* (1913)

18 I am I plus my surroundings, and if I do not preserve the latter I do not preserve myself.
José Ortega y Gasset 1883–1955: *Meditaciones del Quijote* (1914)

19 Through the Thou a person becomes I.
Martin Buber 1878–1965: *Ich und Du* (1923)

20 We are all serving a life-sentence in the dungeon of self.
Cyril Connolly 1903–74: *The Unquiet Grave* (1944)

21 The whole human way of life has been destroyed and ruined. All that's left is the bare, shivering human soul, stripped to the last shred, the naked force of the human psyche for which nothing has changed because it was always cold and shivering and reaching out to its nearest neighbour, as cold and lonely as itself.
Boris Pasternak 1890–1960: *Doctor Zhivago* (1958)

22 The image of myself which I try to create in my own mind in order that I may love myself is very different from the image which I try to create in the minds of others in order that they may love me.
W. H. Auden 1907–73: *Dyer's Hand* (1963) 'Hic et Ille'

23 Some thirty inches from my nose
The frontier of my Person goes,
And all the untilled air between

Is private *pagus* or demesne.
W. H. Auden 1907–73: 'Prologue: the Birth of Architecture' (1966)

24 I am not a number, I am a free man!
Patrick McGoohan 1928– et al.: Number Six, in *The Prisoner* (TV series 1967–68)

25 Gandhi says create and preserve the image of your choice. The image of my choice is not Beatle George.
George Harrison 1943–2001: in *Rolling Stone* 19 December 1974

26 My one regret in life is that I am not someone else.
Woody Allen 1935– : Eric Lax *Woody Allen and his Comedy* (1975)

27 Human beings have an inalienable right to invent themselves; when that right is pre-empted it is called brain-washing.
Germaine Greer 1939– : in *The Times* 1 February 1986

28 Personal isn't the same as important.
Terry Pratchett 1948– : *Men at Arms* (1993)

29 'You' your joys and your sorrows, your memories and ambitions, your sense of personal identity and free will, are in fact no more than the behaviour of a vast assembly of nerve cells and their associated molecules.
Francis Crick 1916– : *The Astonishing Hypothesis: The Scientific Search for the Soul* (1994)

30 Each child hunts for a solution to the boredom of being no one but itself.
Candia McWilliam 1955– : *Debatable Land* (1994)

31 I think of who I am as what I've done.
Esther Dyson 1951– : in *Independent* 11 January 1999

Self-Esteem and Self-Assertion see also Pride and Humility

1 Because I'm worth it.
advertising slogan for L'Oreal, from mid 1980s

2 Here's tae us; wha's like us?
Gey few, and they're a' deid.
Scottish toast, probably of 19th-century origin

3 Self-praise is no recommendation.
early 19th century, meaning that a person's own favourable account of themselves is of dubious worth

4 a fly on the wheel a person who overestimates his or her own influence.
see 10 below

5 hide one's light under a bushel conceal one's merits.
with allusion to the Bible (Matthew) 'Neither do men light a candle, and put it under a bushel, but on a candlestick; and it giveth light unto all that are in the house'

6 little tin god a self-important person.

tin *implicitly contrasted with precious metals; an object of unjustified veneration*

7 pooh-bah a person having much influence or holding many offices at the same time, especially one perceived as pompously self-important.

from the name of a character in W. S. Gilbert's The Mikado *(1885)*

QUOTATIONS

8 Seest thou a man wise in his own conceit? There is more hope of a fool than of him.
Bible: Proverbs

9 Lord I am not worthy that thou shouldest come under my roof.
Bible: St Matthew

10 It was prettily devised of Aesop, 'The fly sat upon the axletree of the chariot-wheel and said, what a dust do I raise.'
Francis Bacon 1561–1626: *Essays* (1625) 'Of Vain-Glory'; see 4 above

11   Oft-times nothing profits more
Than self esteem, grounded on just and
   right
Well managed.
John Milton 1608–74: *Paradise Lost* (1667); see
Poets 27

12 Where he falls short, 'tis Nature's fault
   alone;
Where he succeeds, the merit's all his
   own.
of the actor, Thomas Sheridan
Charles Churchill 1731–64: *The Rosciad* (1761)

13 The axis of the earth sticks out visibly through the centre of each and every town or city.
Oliver Wendell Holmes 1809–94: *The Autocrat of the Breakfast-Table* (1858)

14 He was like a cock who thought the sun had risen to hear him crow.
George Eliot 1819–80: *Adam Bede* (1859)

15 To be commonly above others, still more to think yourself above others, is to be below them every now and then, and sometimes much below.
Walter Bagehot 1826–77: in *National Review* July 1859 'John Milton'

16 As for conceit, what man will do any good who is not conceited? Nobody holds a good opinion of a man who has a low opinion of himself.
Anthony Trollope 1815–82: *Orley Farm* (1862)

on the suggestion that his attacks on John Bright were too harsh as Bright was a self-made man:

17 I know he is and he adores his maker.
Benjamin Disraeli 1804–81: Leon Harris *The Fine Art of Political Wit* (1965)

18 You must stir it and stump it,
And blow your own trumpet,
Or trust me, you haven't a chance.
W. S. Gilbert 1836–1911: *Ruddigore* (1887)

19 It is easy—terribly easy— to shake a man's faith in himself. To take advantage of that to break a man's spirit is devil's work.
George Bernard Shaw 1856–1950: *Candida* (1898)

20 The affair between Margot Asquith and Margot Asquith will live as one of the prettiest love stories in all literature.
Dorothy Parker 1893–1967: review of Margot Asquith's *Lay Sermons* in *New Yorker* 22 October 1927

21 Anything you can do, I can do better,
I can do anything better than you.
Irving Berlin 1888–1989: 'Anything You Can Do' (1946 song)

22 Early in life I had to choose between honest arrogance and hypocritical humility. I chose honest arrogance and have seen no occasion to change.
Frank Lloyd Wright 1867–1959: Herbert Jacobs *Frank Lloyd Wright* (1965)

23 I'm the greatest.
Muhammad Ali (Cassius Clay) 1942– : catchphrase used from 1962, in *Louisville Times* 16 November 1962

24 It's easy to be independent when you've got money. But to be independent when you haven't got a thing—that's the Lord's test.
Mahalia Jackson 1911–72: *Movin' On Up* (with Evan McLoud Wylie 1966)

25 That's it baby, when you got it, flaunt it.
Mel Brooks 1926– : *The Producers* (1968 film)

26 Pretentious? *Moi?*
John Cleese 1939– and **Connie Booth**: *Fawlty Towers* 'The Psychiatrist' (BBC TV programme, 1979)

27 Well, I don't want to be any more egotistical than possible. I have total confidence in my ability.
Robert Hawke 1929– : on entering Parliament, 1980; T. Thompson and E. Butel (eds.) *The World According to Hawke* (1983)

28 Shyness is egotism out of its depth.
Penelope Keith 1940– : in *Daily Mail* 27 June 1988

29 In the company of those she found unimportant, her spirits sank: she felt insignificant, plain and ordinary as though ordinariness was contagious.

Alice Thomas Ellis 1932– : *The Inn at the Edge of the World* (1990)

30 Our deepest fear is not that we are inadequate. Our deepest fear is that we are powerful beyond measure. It is our light, not our darkness, that most frightens us.

Marianne Williamson 1953– : *A Return to Love* (1992)

31 Our mistreatment was just not right, and I was tired of it.

of her refusal, on 1 December 1955, to surrender her

seat on a segregated bus in Alabama to a white man

Rosa Parks 1913– : *Quiet Strength* (1994)

32 I need people's good opinion. This is something in myself I dislike because I even need the good opinion of people who I don't admire. I am afraid of them. I am afraid of what they will say to me. I am afraid of their tongues and their indifference.

Ruth Rendell 1930– : Anthony Clare *In the Psychiatrist's Chair II* (1995)

33 Arrogance is a highly under-appreciated character trait.

Sting 1951– : in *Independent* 23 June 2001

Self-Interest see also Self-Sacrifice

PROVERBS AND SAYINGS

1 Every man for himself and God for us all.

mid 16th century, meaning that ultimately God is concerned for humankind while individuals are concerned only for themselves

2 Every man for himself, and the Devil take the hindmost.

early 16th century, meaning that each person must look out for their own interests, and that the weakest is likely to come to disaster

3 Hear all, see all, say nowt, tak'all, keep all, gie nowt, and if tha ever does owt for nowt do it for thysen.

early 15th century, now associated with Yorkshire, and caricaturing supposedly traditional Yorkshire attributes, in the picture of someone who is shrewd, taciturn, grasping, and selfish

4 If you want a thing done well, do it yourself.

mid 17th century, meaning that no-one else has so much interest in your own welfare

5 If you would be well served, serve yourself.

mid 17th century, meaning that no-one else has so much interest in your own welfare

6 Near is my kirtle, but nearer is my smock.

mid 15th century, used as a justification for putting one's own interests first (a kirtle is a woman's skirt or gown, and a smock is an undergarment)

7 Near is my shirt, but nearer is my skin.

late 16th century, a justification of self-interest

8 Self-interest is the rule, self-sacrifice the exception.

American proverb, mid 20th century

9 Self-preservation is the first law of nature.

mid 17th century, meaning that the instinct for self-preservation is inbuilt and instinctive

PHRASES

10 bow down in the house of Rimmon pay lip-service to a principle; sacrifice one's principles for the sake of conformity.

Rimmon a deity worshipped in ancient Damascus; after the Bible (2 Kings) 'I bow myself in the house of Rimmon'

11 cultivate one's garden attend to one's own affairs.

after Voltaire: see 23 below

12 dog in the manger a person who selfishly refuses to let others enjoy benefits for which he or she personally has no use.

from Aesop's fable of a dog which jumped into a manger and would not let the ox or horse eat the hay

13 an eye to the main chance consideration for one's own interests.

the main chance literally, in the game of hazard, a number (5, 6, 7, or 8) called by a player before throwing the dice

14 I'm all right, Jack expressing selfish complacency and unconcern for others.

originally in nautical use

15 law of the jungle a system in which brute force and self-interest are paramount.

the supposed code of survival in jungle life

16 not in my back yard expressing an objection to the siting of something regarded as unpleasant in one's own locality, while by implication finding it acceptable elsewhere.

originating in the United States in derogatory references to the anti-nuclear movement, and in Britain particularly associated with reports of the then Environment Secretary Nicholas Ridley's opposition in 1988 to housing developments near his home; the acronym NIMBY derives from this

17 **take the Fifth (Amendment)** in America, decline to incriminate oneself.

appeal to Article V of the ten original amendments (1791) to the Constitution of the United States, which states that 'no person . . . shall be compelled in any criminal case to be a witness against himself'

QUOTATIONS

18 *Cui bono?*
To whose profit?
Cicero 106–43 BC: *Pro Roscio Amerino*; quoting L. Cassius Longinus Ravilla

19 Men are nearly always willing to believe what they wish.
Julius Caesar 100–44 BC: *De Bello Gallico*

20 To rise by other's fall
I deem a losing gain;
All states with others' ruins built
To ruin run amain.
Robert Southwell c.1561–95: 'Content and Rich' (1595)

21 Thus God and nature linked the gen'ral frame,
And bade self-love and social be the same.
Alexander Pope 1688–1744: *An Essay on Man* Epistle 3 (1733)

22 And this is law, I will maintain,
Unto my dying day, Sir,
That whatsoever King shall reign,
I will be the Vicar of Bray, sir!
Anonymous: 'The Vicar of Bray' (1734 song)

23 *Il faut cultiver notre jardin.*
We must cultivate our garden.
Voltaire 1694–1778: *Candide* (1759); see 11 above

24 It is not from the benevolence of the butcher, the brewer, or the baker, that we expect our dinner, but from their regard to their own interest. We address ourselves not to their humanity but their self love.
Adam Smith 1723–90: *Wealth of Nations* (1776)

25 All sensible people are selfish, and nature is tugging at every contract to make the terms of it fair.
Ralph Waldo Emerson 1803–82: *The Conduct of Life* (1860)

26 We are all special cases. We all want to appeal against something! Everyone insists on his innocence, at all costs, even if it means accusing the rest of the human race and heaven.
Albert Camus 1913–60: *La Chute* (1956)

27 He would, wouldn't he?
on being told that Lord Astor claimed that her allegations, concerning himself and his house parties at Cliveden, were untrue
Mandy Rice-Davies 1944– : *at the trial of Stephen Ward, 29 June 1963*

28 Selflessness . . . is always the greatest insult to the ghetto, for selflessness is a luxury to the poor, it beckons to the spineless, the undifferentiated, the inept, the derelict, the drowning—a poor man is nothing without the fierce thorns of his ego.
Norman Mailer 1923– : *Miami and the Siege of Chicago* (1968)

29 Fourteen heart attacks and he had to die in my week. In MY week.
when ex-President Eisenhower's death prevented her photograph appearing on the cover of Newsweek
Janis Joplin 1943–70: *in* New Musical Express *12 April 1969*

30 We are now in the Me Decade—seeing the upward roll of . . . the third great religious wave in American history . . . and this one has the mightiest, holiest roll of all, the beat that goes . . . *Me . . . Me . . . Me . . . Me.*
Tom Wolfe 1931– : *Mauve Gloves and Madmen* (1976)

31 It's the first time in recorded history that turkeys have been known to vote for an early Christmas.
on the collapse of the pact between Labour and the Liberals
James Callaghan 1912– : *in the House of Commons, 28 March 1979*

Self-Knowledge

1 Know thyself.

late fourteenth century, inscribed in Greek on the temple of Apollo at Delphi; Plato, in Protagoras, *ascribes the saying to the Seven Wise Men of the 6th century* BC

QUOTATIONS

2 I do not know whether I was then a man dreaming I was a butterfly, or whether I am now a butterfly dreaming I am a man.

Zhuangzi c.369–286 BC: *Chuang Tzu* (1889)

3 Why beholdest thou the mote that is in thy brother's eye, but considerest not the beam that is in thine own eye?

Bible: St Matthew; see **Mistakes** 6, 8

4 The path of self knowledge must never be abandoned, nor is there on this journey a soul so much a giant that it has no need to return often to the stage of an infant and suckling.

St Teresa of Ávila 1512–82: *Life of the Mother Teresa of Jesus* (1611)

5 He knows the universe and does not know himself.

Jean de la Fontaine 1621–95: *Fables* (1678–9) 'Démocrite et les Abdéritains'

6 Satire is a sort of glass, wherein beholders do generally discover everybody's face but their own.

Jonathan Swift 1667–1745: *The Battle of the Books* (1704)

7 All our knowledge is, ourselves to know.

Alexander Pope 1688–1744: *An Essay on Man* Epistle 4 (1734)

8 O wad some Pow'r the giftie gie us
To see oursels as others see us!
It wad frae mony a blunder free us,
And foolish notion.

Robert Burns 1759–96: 'To a Louse' (1786)

9 How little do we know that which we are!
How less what we may be!

Lord Byron 1788–1824: *Don Juan* (1819–24)

10 I do not know myself, and God forbid that I should.

Johann Wolfgang von Goethe 1749–1832: J. P. Eckermann *Gespräche mit Goethe* (1836–48) 10 April 1829

11 Resolve to be thyself: and know, that he Who finds himself, loses his misery.

Matthew Arnold 1822–88: 'Self-Dependence' (1852)

12 No, when the fight begins within himself, A man's worth something.

Robert Browning 1812–89: 'Bishop Blougram's Apology' (1855)

13 The tragedy of a man who has found himself out.

J. M. Barrie 1860–1937: *What Every Woman Knows* (performed 1908, published 1918)

14 The chief requirement of the good life, is to live without any image of oneself.

Iris Murdoch 1919–99: *The Bell* (1958)

15 Between the ages of twenty and forty we are engaged in the process of discovering who we are, which involves learning the difference between accidental limitations which it is our duty to outgrow and the necessary limitations of our nature beyond which we cannot trespass with impunity.

W. H. Auden 1907–73: *Dyer's Hand* (1963) 'Reading'

16 There are few things more painful than to recognize one's own faults in others.

John Wells 1936– : in *Observer* 23 May 1982

17 [Alfred Hitchcock] thought of himself as looking like Cary Grant. That's tough, to think of yourself one way and look another.

Tippi Hedren 1935– : interview in California, 1982; P. F. Boller and R. L. Davis *Hollywood Anecdotes* (1988)

Self-Sacrifice see also Self-Interest

1 labour of love a task undertaken for the love of a person or for the work itself.
from the Bible (I Thessalonians) 'Your work of faith and labour of love'

2 the supreme sacrifice the laying down of one's life for another or for one's country.
see 10 below

3 Greater love hath no man than this, that a man lay down his life for his friends.
Bible: St John; see **Trust and Treachery** 35

4 I am no longer my own, but yours. Put me to what you will, rank me with whom you will; put me to doing, put me to suffering; let me be employed for you or laid aside for you, exalted for you or brought low for you; let me be full, let me be empty; let me have all things, let me have nothing.
Methodist Service Book: The Covenant Prayer (based on the words of Richard Alleine in the First Covenant Service, 1782)

5 Deny yourself! You must deny yourself! That is the song that never ends.
Johann Wolfgang von Goethe 1749–1832: *Faust* pt. 1 (1808) 'Studierzimmer'

6 It is a far, far better thing that I do, than I have ever done; it is a far, far better rest that I go to, than I have ever known.
Sydney Carton's thoughts on the steps of the guillotine, taking the place of Charles Darnay whom he has smuggled out of prison
Charles Dickens 1812–70: *A Tale of Two Cities* (1859)

7 From the standpoint of pure reason, there are no good grounds to support the claim that one should sacrifice one's own happiness to that of others.
W. Somerset Maugham 1874–1965: *A Writer's Notebook* (1949) written in 1896

8 Self-sacrifice enables us to sacrifice other people without blushing.
George Bernard Shaw 1856–1950: *Man and Superman* (1903) 'Maxims: Self-Sacrifice'

9 I gave my life for freedom — This I know:
For those who bade me fight had told me so.
William Norman Ewer 1885–1976: 'Five Souls' (1917)

10 The love that never falters, the love that pays the price,
The love that makes undaunted the final sacrifice.
Cecil Spring-Rice 1859–1918: 'I Vow to Thee, My Country' (1918); see 2 above

11 A woman will always sacrifice herself if you give her the opportunity. It is her favourite form of self-indulgence.
W. Somerset Maugham 1874–1965: *The Circle* (1921)

12 I do not think you have ever realised the shock, which the attitude you took up caused your family and the whole nation. It seemed inconceivable to those who had made such sacrifices during the war that you, as their King, refused a lesser sacrifice.
Queen Mary 1867–1953: letter to the Duke of Windsor, July 1938

13 I have nothing to offer but blood, toil, tears and sweat.
Winston Churchill 1874–1965: speech, House of Commons, 13 May 1940

14 She's the sort of woman who lives for others—you can always tell the others by their hunted expression.
C. S. Lewis 1898–1963: *The Screwtape Letters* (1942)

15 To gain that which is worth having, it may be necessary to lose everything else.
Bernadette Devlin McAliskey 1947– : preface to *The Price of My Soul* (1969)

16 Perhaps only those who sacrifice themselves completely are truly memorable.
Paul Scott 1920–78: letter to F. Weinbaum, 26 October 1975

Selling see Buying and Selling

The Senses see also The Body

1 deaf as an adder completely deaf.
after the Bible: see Defiance 9

2 the five senses the special bodily faculties of sight, hearing, smell, taste, and touch.

3 I have heard of thee by the hearing of the ear: but now mine eye seeth thee.
The Bible: Job

4 By convention there is colour, by convention sweetness, by convention bitterness, but in reality there are atoms and space.
Democritus c.460–c.370 BC: fragment 125

5 When in recollection he withdraws all his senses from the attractions of the pleasures of sense, even as a tortoise withdraws all its limbs, then his is a serene wisdom.
Bhagavadgita: ch. 2, v. 58

6 Nor will the sweetest delight of gardens afford much comfort in sleep; wherein the dullness of that sense shakes hands with delectable odours; and though in the bed of Cleopatra, can hardly with any delight raise up the ghost of a rose.
Thomas Browne 1605–82: *The Garden of Cyrus* (1658)

7 When I consider how my light is spent,
E're half my days, in this dark world and
   wide,
And that one talent which is death to hide
Lodged with me useless.
on his blindness
John Milton 1608–74: 'When I consider how my light is spent' (1673)

8 Whatever withdraws us from the power of our senses; whatever makes the past, the distant, or the future predominate over the present, advances us in the dignity of thinking beings.
Samuel Johnson 1709–84: *A Journey to the Western Islands of Scotland* (1775)

9 O for a life of sensations rather than of thoughts!
John Keats 1795–1821: letter to Benjamin Bailey, 22 November 1817

10   Any nose
May ravage with impunity a rose.
Robert Browning 1812–89: *Sordello* (1840)

11 You see, but you do not observe.
Arthur Conan Doyle 1859–1930: *The Adventures of Sherlock Holmes* (1892)

12 Friday I tasted life. It was a vast morsel. A Circus passed the house—still I feel the red in my mind though the drums are out. The Lawn is full of south and the odours tangle, and I hear to-day for the first time the river in the tree.
Emily Dickinson 1830–86: letter to Mrs J. G. Holland, May 1866

13 Fortissimo at last!
on seeing Niagara Falls
Gustav Mahler 1860–1911: K. Blaukopf *Gustav Mahler* (1973)

14 Does it matter?—losing your sight? . . .
There's such splendid work for the blind;
And people will always be kind,
As you sit on the terrace remembering
And turning your face to the light.
Siegfried Sassoon 1886–1967: 'Does it Matter?' (1918)

15 I test my bath before I sit,
And I'm always moved to wonderment
That what chills the finger not a bit
Is so frigid upon the fundament.
Ogden Nash 1902–71: 'Samson Agonistes' (1942)

16 Each day I live in a glass room
Unless I break it with the thrusting
Of my senses and pass through
The splintered walls to the great landscape.
Mervyn Peake 1911–68: 'Each day I live in a glass room' (1967)

17 My left hand is my thinking hand. The right is only a motor hand.
Barbara Hepworth 1903–75: *A Pictorial Autobiography* (1970)

18 I can hear people smile.
David Blunkett 1947– : in *Independent* 14 July 2001

Sex see also **Love, Marriage, The Single Life**

PROVERBS AND SAYINGS

1 Did the earth move for you?
supposedly said to one's partner after sexual intercourse, after Hemingway: see 27 below

2 Dirty water will quench fire.
mid 16th century, mainly used to mean that a man's sexual needs can be satisfied by any woman, however ugly or immoral

3 Post coitum omne animal triste..
Latin = After coition every animal is sad

PHRASES

4 the beast with two backs a man and woman having sexual intercourse.
from Shakespeare Othello: see 12 below

5 a gay Lothario a libertine, a rake.
from Nicholas Rowe (1674–1718) The Fair Penitent (1703) 'Is this that haughty, gallant, gay Lothario?'

QUOTATIONS

6 Someone asked Sophocles, 'How is your sex-life now? Are you still able to have a woman?' He replied, 'Hush, man; most gladly indeed am I rid of it all, as though I had escaped from a mad and savage master.'
Sophocles c.496–406 BC: Plato *Republic*

7 I have never yet seen anyone whose desire to build up his moral power was as strong as sexual desire.
Confucius 551–479 BC: *Analects*

8 Give me chastity and continency—but not yet!
St Augustine of Hippo AD 354–430: *Confessions* (AD 397–8)

9 And after wyn on Venus moste I thynke,
For al so siker as cold engendreth hayl,
A likerous mouth moste han a likerous
tayl.
Geoffrey Chaucer c.1343–1400: *The Canterbury Tales* 'The Wife of Bath's Prologue'

10 Licence my roving hands, and let them go,
Behind, before, above, between, below.
O my America, my new found land,
My kingdom, safeliest when with one man
manned.
John Donne 1572–1631: 'To His Mistress Going to Bed' (c.1595)

11 Is it not strange that desire should so many years outlive performance?
William Shakespeare 1564–1616: *Henry IV, Part 2* (1597)

12 Your daughter and the Moor are now making the beast with two backs.
William Shakespeare 1564–1616: *Othello* (1602–4); see 4 above

13 Die: die for adultery! No:
The wren goes to't, and the small gilded fly
Does lecher in my sight.
Let copulation thrive.
William Shakespeare 1564–1616: *King Lear* (1605–6)

14 This trivial and vulgar way of coition; it is the foolishest act a wise man commits in all his life, nor is there any thing that will more deject his cooled imagination, when he shall consider what an odd and unworthy piece of folly he hath committed.
Thomas Browne 1605–82: *Religio Medici* (1643)

15 The Duke returned from the wars today and did pleasure me in his top-boots.
Sarah, Duchess of Marlborough 1660–1744: oral tradition, attributed in various forms; see I. Butler *Rule of Three* (1967)

16 I'll come no more behind your scenes, David; for the silk stockings and white bosoms of your actresses excite my amorous propensities.
Samuel Johnson 1709–84: James Boswell *Life of Samuel Johnson* (1791) 1750

17 The pleasure is momentary, the position ridiculous, and the expense damnable.
Lord Chesterfield 1694–1773: attributed

18 Not tonight, Josephine.
Napoleon I 1769–1821: attributed, but probably apocryphal; R. H. Horne *The History of Napoleon* (1841) describes the circumstances in which the affront may have occurred

19 'Tisn't beauty, so to speak, nor good talk necessarily. It's just It. Some women'll stay in a man's memory if they once walked down a street.
Rudyard Kipling 1865–1936: *Traffics and Discoveries* (1904); see **Women** 12

20 When I hear his steps outside my door I lie down on my bed, close my eyes, open my legs, and think of England.
Lady Hillingdon 1857–1940: diary 1912 (original untraced, perhaps apocryphal); J. Gathorne-Hardy *The Rise and Fall of the British Nanny* (1972)

21 i like my body when it is with your body. It is so quite new a thing. Muscles better and nerves more.
e. e. cummings 1894–1962: 'Sonnets–Actualities' no. 8 (1925)

22 You're neither unnatural, nor abominable, nor mad; you're as much a part of what people call nature as anyone else; only you're unexplained as yet—you've not got your niche in creation.
on lesbianism
Radclyffe Hall 1883–1943: *The Well of Loneliness* (1928)

23   While we think of it, and talk of it Let us leave it alone, physically, keep apart.
For while we have sex in the mind, we truly have none in the body.
D. H. Lawrence 1885–1930: 'Leave Sex Alone' (1929)

24 Chastity—the most unnatural of all the sexual perversions.
Aldous Huxley 1894–1963: *Eyeless in Gaza* (1936)

25 Pornography is the attempt to insult sex, to do dirt on it.
D. H. Lawrence 1885–1930: *Phoenix* (1936) 'Pornography and Obscenity'

26 Give a man a free hand and he'll try to put it all over you.
Mae West 1892–1980: *Klondike Annie* (1936 film)

27 But did thee feel the earth move?
Ernest Hemingway 1899–1961: *For Whom the Bell Tolls* (1940); see 1 above

28 It doesn't matter what you do in the bedroom as long as you don't do it in the street and frighten the horses.
Mrs Patrick Campbell 1865–1940: Daphne Fielding *The Duchess of Jermyn Street* (1964)

29 The only unnatural sex act is that which you cannot perform.
Alfred Kinsey 1894–1956: attributed; in *Time* 21 January 1966

30 I think Lawrence tried to portray this [sex] relation as in a real sense an act of holy communion. For him flesh was sacramental of the spirit.
as defence witness in the case against Penguin Books for publishing Lady Chatterley's Lover
Bishop John Robinson 1919–83: in *The Times* 28 October 1960

31 I can't get no satisfaction I can't get no girl reaction.
Mick Jagger 1943– and **Keith Richards** 1943– : '(I Can't Get No) Satisfaction' (1965 song)

32 I have heard some say . . . [homosexual] practices are allowed in France and in other NATO countries. We are not French, and we are not other nationals. We are British, thank God!
on the 2nd reading of the Sexual Offences Bill
Field Marshal Montgomery 1887–1976: speech, House of Lords, 24 May 1965

33 The orgasm has replaced the Cross as the focus of longing and the image of fulfilment.
Malcolm Muggeridge 1903–90: *Tread Softly* (1966)

34 My dear fellow, buggers can't be choosers.
on being told he should not marry anyone as plain as his fiancée
Maurice Bowra 1898–1971: Hugh Lloyd-Jones *Maurice Bowra: a Celebration* (1974); possibly apocryphal; see **Necessity** 2

35 Is sex dirty? Only if it's done right.
Woody Allen 1935– : *Everything You Always Wanted to Know about Sex* (1972 film)

36 Traditionally, sex has been a very private, secretive activity. Herein perhaps lies its powerful force for uniting people in a strong bond. As we make sex less secretive, we may rob it of its power to hold men and women together.
Thomas Szasz 1920– : *The Second Sin* (1973)

37 Sexual intercourse began In nineteen sixty-three (Which was rather late for me) — Between the end of the *Chatterley* ban And the Beatles' first LP.
Philip Larkin 1922–85: 'Annus Mirabilis' (1974)

38 Is that a gun in your pocket, or are you just glad to see me?
usually quoted as 'Is that a pistol in your pocket . . . '
Mae West 1892–1980: Joseph Weintraub *Peel Me a Grape* (1975)

39 On bisexuality: It immediately doubles your chances for a date on Saturday night.
Woody Allen 1935– : in *New York Times* 1 December 1975

40 Seduction is often difficult to distinguish from rape. In seduction, the rapist bothers to buy a bottle of wine.
Andrea Dworkin 1946- : speech to women at *Harper & Row*, 1976; in *Letters from a War Zone* (1988)

41 Don't knock masturbation. It's sex with someone I love.
Woody Allen 1935- : *Annie Hall* (1977 film, with Marshall Brickman)

42 That [sex] was the most fun I ever had without laughing.
Woody Allen 1935- : *Annie Hall* (1977 film, with Marshall Brickman)

43 Sex has never been an obsession with me. It's just like eating a bag of crisps. Quite nice, but nothing marvellous. Sex is not simply black and white. There's a lot of grey.
Boy George 1961- : in *Sun* 21 October 1982

44 Love is two minutes fifty-two seconds of squishing noises.
Johnny Rotten 1957- : in *Daily Mirror*, 1983

45 I'll have what she's having.
woman to waiter, seeing Sally acting an orgasm
Nora Ephron 1941- : *When Harry Met Sally* (1989 film)

46 Gay men may seek sex without emotion; lesbians often end up in emotion without sex.
Camille Paglia 1947- : in *Esquire* October 1991

47 Sex and taxes are in many ways the same. Tax does to cash what males do to genes. It dispenses assets among the population as a whole. Sex, not death, is the great leveller.
Steve Jones 1944- : speech to the Royal Society; in *Independent* 25 January 1997

Shakespeare see also Acting, The Theatre

PHRASES

1 the Scottish play Shakespeare's *Macbeth*.
in theatrical tradition it is regarded as unlucky to speak of this play by its title

2 the Swan of Avon Shakespeare.
after Ben Jonson's line 'Sweet Swan of Avon' (1623)

QUOTATIONS

3 He was not of an age, but for all time!
Ben Jonson c.1573-1637: 'To the Memory of My Beloved, the Author, Mr William Shakespeare' (1623)

4 Thou hadst small Latin, and less Greek.
Ben Jonson c.1573-1637: 'To the Memory of My Beloved, the Author, Mr William Shakespeare' (1623)

5 His mind and hand went together: And what he thought, he uttered with that easiness, that we have scarce received from him a blot.
John Heming 1556-1630 and **Henry Condell** d. 1627: First Folio Shakespeare (1623) preface

6 [Shakespeare] is the very Janus of poets; he wears almost everywhere two faces; and you have scarce begun to admire the one, ere you despise the other.
John Dryden 1631-1700: *Essay on the Dramatic Poetry of the Last Age* (1672)

7 His comedies will remain wit as long as the English tongue is understood, for that he handles the ways of men.
John Aubrey 1626-97: *Brief Lives* 'William Shakespeare'

8 Shakespeare has united the powers of exciting laughter and sorrow not only in one mind but in one composition . . . That this is a practice contrary to the rules of criticism will be readily allowed; but there is always an appeal open from criticism to nature.
Samuel Johnson 1709-84: *Plays of William Shakespeare . . .* (1765) preface

9 Was there ever such stuff as great part of Shakespeare? Only one must not say so! But what think you?—what?—Is there not sad stuff? what?—what?
George III 1738-1820: to Fanny Burney; Fanny Burney, diary, 19 December 1785

10 Scorn not the Sonnet; Critic, you have frowned,
Mindless of its just honours; with this key Shakespeare unlocked his heart.
William Wordsworth 1770-1850: 'Scorn not the Sonnet' (1827)

11 Others abide our question. Thou art free. We ask and ask: Thou smilest and art still,

Out-topping knowledge.
Matthew Arnold 1822–88: 'Shakespeare' (1849)

12 With the single exception of Homer, there is no eminent writer, not even Sir Walter Scott, whom I can despise so entirely as I despise Shakespeare when I measure my mind against his.
George Bernard Shaw 1856–1950: in *Saturday Review* 26 September 1896

13 When I read Shakespeare I am struck with wonder
That such trivial people should muse and thunder
In such lovely language.
D. H. Lawrence 1885–1930: 'When I Read Shakespeare' (1929)

14 Brush up your Shakespeare,
Start quoting him now.

Brush up your Shakespeare
And the women you will wow.
Cole Porter 1891–1964: 'Brush Up your Shakespeare' (1948 song)

15 Shakespeare is so tiring. You never get a chance to sit down unless you're a king.
Josephine Hull ?1886–1957: in *Time* 16 November 1953

16 Shakespeare—the nearest thing in incarnation to the eye of God.
Laurence Olivier 1907–89: in *Kenneth Harris Talking To* (1971) 'Sir Laurence Olivier'

17 There is a sense in which every writer in English owes a debt to Shakespeare. He is our theatrical DNA.
Richard Eyre 1943– : 'Changing Stages' (BBC2 TV programme) 5 November 2000

Sickness see also Health and Fitness, Medicine

1 Coughs and sneezes spread diseases. Trap the germs in your handkerchief.
Second World War health slogan (1942)

2 A creaking door hangs longest.
late 17th century, usually meaning that someone who is apparently in poor health may well outlive the ostensibly stronger

3 Feed a cold and starve a fever.
mid 19th century (probably intended as two separate admonitions, but sometimes interpreted to mean that if you feed a cold you will have to starve a fever later)

4 the Black Death the great epidemic of plague in Europe in the 14th century.
the name 'black death' is modern, and was apparently introduced by Mrs. Penrose (Mrs. Markham) in 1823; earlier writers call it the (great) pestilence, the plague, or the great death; see 8 below

5 the falling sickness an archaic term for epilepsy.

6 the king's evil scrofula.
from the belief that a cure could be obtained by the sovereign's touching the sores; see Royalty 22

7 white death tuberculosis.
after Black Death

8 And times without number it happened that two priests would be on their way to bury someone, holding a cross before them, only to find that bearers carrying three or four additional biers would fall in behind them; so that whereas the priests had thought they only had one burial to attend to, they in fact had six or eight, and sometimes more.
during the Black Death; see 4 above
Boccaccio 1313–75: *Decameron* (1348–58)

9 I saw a dead corpse in a coffin lie in the close unburied—and a watch is constantly kept there, night and day, to keep the people in—the plague making us cruel as dogs one to another.
Samuel Pepys 1633–1703: diary, 4 September 1665

10 Here am I, dying of a hundred good symptoms.
Alexander Pope 1688–1744: to George, Lord Lyttelton, 15 May 1744; Joseph Spence *Anecdotes* (ed. J. Osborn, 1966)

11 To know ourselves diseased, is half our cure.
Edward Young 1683–1765: *Night Thoughts* (1742–5) 'Night 9'

12 How few of his friends' houses would a man choose to be at when he is sick.
Samuel Johnson 1709–84: James Boswell *Life of Samuel Johnson* (1791) 1783

13 It is a most extraordinary thing, but I never read a patent medicine advertisement without being impelled to the conclusion that I am suffering from the particular disease therein dealt with in its most virulent form.

Jerome K. Jerome 1859–1927: *Three Men in a Boat* (1889)

14 'Ye can call it influenza if ye like,' said Mrs Machin. 'There was no influenza in my young days. We called a cold a cold.'

Arnold Bennett 1867–1931: *The Card* (1911)

15 I enjoy convalescence. It is the part that makes illness worth while.

George Bernard Shaw 1856–1950: *Back to Methuselah* (1921)

16 Human nature seldom walks up to the word 'cancer'.

Rudyard Kipling 1865–1936: *Debits and Credits* (1926)

17 Venerable Mother Toothache
Climb down from the white battlements,
Stop twisting in your yellow fingers
The fourfold rope of nerves.

John Heath-Stubbs 1918– : 'A Charm Against the Toothache' (1954)

18 My final word, before I'm done,
Is 'Cancer can be rather fun'.
Thanks to the nurses and Nye Bevan
The NHS is quite like heaven
Provided one confronts the tumour
With a sufficient sense of humour.

J. B. S. Haldane 1892–1964: 'Cancer's a Funny Thing' (1968)

19 Did God who gave us flowers and trees,
Also provide the allergies?

E. Y. Harburg 1898–1981: 'A Nose is a Nose is a Nose' (1965)

20 I know the colour rose, and it is lovely,
But not when it ripens in a tumour;
And healing greens, leaves and grass, so springlike,
In limbs that fester are not springlike.

Dannie Abse 1923– : 'Pathology of Colours' (1968)

21 Everyone I've met so far has a cold. The entire population of the British Isles seems to do absolutely nothing from one year's end to another except shuffle round in small circles sneezing voluptuously into each other's faces . . . a sort of merry-go-round of reinfection. What chance of survival has one got?

Lawrence Durrell 1912–90: Gerald Durrell *Birds, Beasts and Relatives* (1969)

22 A man's illness is his private territory and, no matter how much he loves you and how close you are, you stay an outsider. You are healthy.

Lauren Bacall 1924– : *By Myself* (1978)

23 Illness is not something a person *has*; it's another way of *being*.

Jonathan Miller 1934– : *The Body in Question* (1978)

24 Societies need to have one illness which becomes identified with evil, and attaches blame to its 'victims'.

Susan Sontag 1933– : *AIDS and its Metaphors* (1989)

25 Meningitis. It was a word you had to bite on to say it. It had a fright and a hiss in it.

Seamus Deane 1940– : *Reading in the Dark* (1996)

26 and I swear sometimes
when I put my head to his chest
I can hear the virus humming
like a refrigerator.

of Aids

Mark Doty 1953– : 'Atlantis' (1996)

27 People mean well and do not see how distancing insistent cheeriness is, how it denies another's reality, denies a sick person the space or right to be sick and in pain.

Marilyn French 1929– : *A Season in Hell* (1998)

28 It's all about losing your brain without losing your mind.

on his fight against Parkinson's disease

Michael J. Fox 1961– : in *The Times* 16 September 2000

Silence see also **Speech**

1 A shut mouth catches no flies.

late 16th century; a warning against the dangers of idle talk

2 Silence is a still noise.

American proverb, late 19th century

3 Silence means consent.

late 14th century; translation of a Latin tag, 'qui tacet consentire videtur [he who is silent seems to consent]', said to have been spoken by Thomas More (1478–1535) when asked at his trial why he was silent on being asked to acknowledge the king's supremacy over the Church. The principle is not accepted in modern English law

4 Speech is silver, but silence is golden.

mid 19th century, meaning that discretion can be more valuable than the most eloquent words; see **Speech** *5*

5 A still tongue makes a wise head.

mid 16th century; meaning that a person who is not given to idle talk, and who listens to others, is likely to be wise

6 Silence is a woman's finest ornament.
Auctoritates Aristotelis: a compilation of medieval propositions

7 Shallow brooks murmur most, deep silent slide away.
Philip Sidney 1554–86: *Arcadia* (1581)

8 Silence is the virtue of fools.
Francis Bacon 1561–1626: *De Dignitate et Augmentis Scientiarum* (1623)

9 No voice; but oh! the silence sank
Like music on my heart.
Samuel Taylor Coleridge 1772–1834: 'The Rime of the Ancient Mariner' (1798)

10 Thou still unravished bride of quietness,
Thou foster-child of silence and slow time.
John Keats 1795–1821: 'Ode on a Grecian Urn' (1820)

11 Under all speech that is good for anything there lies a silence that is better. Silence is deep as Eternity; speech is shallow as Time.
Thomas Carlyle 1795–1881: *Critical and Miscellaneous Essays* (1838) 'Sir Walter Scott'

12 Speech is often barren; but silence also does not necessarily brood over a full nest. Your still fowl, blinking at you without remark, may all the while be sitting on one addled egg; and when it takes to cackling will have nothing to announce but that addled delusion.
George Eliot 1819–80: *Felix Holt* (1866)

13 Elected Silence, sing to me
And beat upon my whorlèd ear.
Gerard Manley Hopkins 1844–89: 'The Habit of Perfection' (written 1866)

14 People talking without speaking
People hearing without listening
People writing songs that voices never share
And no one dare disturb the sound of silence.
Paul Simon 1942– : 'Sound of Silence' (1964 song)

15 Silence is often a good policy on some subjects in politics, but silence is regarded as a sort of sin now, and it has to be filled with a lot of gossip and sound bites.
Douglas Hurd 1930– : in *Independent* 23 April 2001

Similarity and Difference

1 All cats are grey in the dark.

mid 16th century; meaning that darkness obscures inessential differences

2 Birds of a feather flock together.

mid 16th century; meaning that people of the same (usually, unscrupulous) character associated together; see 11 below

3 Comparisons are odious.

mid 15th century, often used to suggest that to compare two different things or persons is unhelpful or misleading; see 15 below

4 Extremes meet.

mid 18th century, meaning that opposite extremes have much in common

5 From the sweetest wine, the tartest vinegar.

late 16th century; used to mean that the strongest hate comes from former love

6 Like breeds like.

mid 16th century, meaning that a particular kind of event may well be the genesis of a similar occurrence

7 Like will to like.

late 14th century, meaning that those of similar nature and inclination are drawn together

8 One nail drives out another.

mid 13th century, meaning like will counter like

9 Two of a trade never agree.

early 17th century; meaning that close association with someone makes disagreement over policy and principles more likely

10 When Greek meets Greek, then comes the tug of war.

late 17th century, meaning that when two people of a similar kind are opposed, there is a struggle for supremacy; see 18 below

PHRASES

11 birds of a feather those of like character.

from the proverb: see 2 above

12 of the same leaven of the same sort or character.

leaven an agency which exercises a transforming influence from within, of biblical origin as in Matthew, 'Take heed and beware of the leaven of the Pharisees'; see Sin 3

13 rara avis a person or thing of a kind rarely encountered; a unique or exceptional person.

Latin, from the Roman satirist Juvenal (c.60–c.140) Rara avis in terris nigroque simillima cycno. 'A rare bird on this earth, like nothing so much as a black swan'

QUOTATIONS

14 The road up and the road down are one and the same.

Heraclitus c.540–c.480 BC: H. Diels and W. Kranz *Die Fragmente der Vorsokratiker* (7th ed., 1954) fragment 60

15 Comparisons are odorous.

William Shakespeare 1564–1616: *Much Ado About Nothing* (1598–9); see 3 above

16   Feel by turns the bitter change
Of fierce extremes, extremes by change
    more fierce.

John Milton 1608–74: *Paradise Lost* (1667)

17 Dark with excessive bright.

John Milton 1608–74: *Paradise Lost* (1667)

18 When Greeks joined Greeks, then was the tug of war!

Nathaniel Lee c.1653–92: *The Rival Queens* (1677); see 10 above

19 No caparisons, Miss, if you please!—
Caparisons don't become a young woman.

Richard Brinsley Sheridan 1751–1816: *The Rivals* (1775)

20   Near all the birds
Will sing at dawn,—and yet we do not
    take
The chaffering swallow for the holy lark.

Elizabeth Barrett Browning 1806–61: *Aurora Leigh* (1857)

21 One of the most common defects of half-instructed minds is to think much of that in which they differ from others, and little of that in which they agree with others.

on the evils of sectarianism

Walter Bagehot 1826–77: in *Economist* 11 June 1870

22 Out of intense complexities intense simplicities emerge.

Winston Churchill 1874–1965: *The World Crisis* (1923–9)

23 World is crazier and more of it than we
    think,
Incorrigibly plural. I peel and portion
A tangerine and spit the pips and feel
The drunkenness of things being various.

Louis MacNeice 1907–63: 'Snow' (1935)

24 If we cannot end now our differences, at least we can help make the world safe for diversity.

John F. Kennedy 1917–63: address at American University, Washington, DC, 10 June 1963

25 Without deviation from the norm, progress is not possible.

Frank Zappa 1940–93: attributed, in *New York* 20 June 1994

Sin see also **Good and Evil**

1 Satan rebuking sin.

proverbial expression recorded from the early 17th century, originally meaning that the worst possible stage has been reached; in later use, an ironic comment on the nature of the person delivering the rebuke

2 What is got over the Devil's back is spent under his belly.

late 16th century; meaning that what is gained improperly will be spent on folly and debauchery

3 the old leaven traces of an unregenerate condition.

*leaven an agency which exercises a transforming influence from within, as in the Bible (1 Corinthians) 'Purge out therefore the old leaven'; see **Similarity** 12*

4 original sin the tendency to evil supposedly innate in all humans

held to be inherited from Adam in consequence of the Fall of Man

5 the seven deadly sins those entailing damnation.

traditionally pride, covetousness, lust, envy, gluttony, anger, and sloth

6 the sin against the Holy Ghost the only sin regarded as putting its perpetrator beyond redemption; an ultimate and irredeemable wrong.

in Christian theology, based on the interpretation of several Gospel passages: see 10 below

7 Be sure your sin will find you out.
Bible: Numbers

8 There is no peace, saith the Lord, unto the wicked.
Bible: Isaiah; see **Action** 12

9 If thine eye offend thee, pluck it out, and cast it from thee: it is better for thee to enter into life with one eye, rather than having two eyes to be cast into hell fire.
Bible: St Matthew

10 The blasphemy against the Holy Ghost shall not be forgiven unto men.
Bible: St Matthew; see **6** above

11 The wages of sin is death.
Bible: Romans

12 No one ever suddenly became depraved.
Juvenal AD c.60–c.130: *Satires*

13 We make ourselves a ladder out of our vices if we trample the vices themselves underfoot.
St Augustine of Hippo AD 354–430: Sermon no. 176 ('On the Ascension of the Lord')

14 I have sinned exceedingly in thought, word, and deed, through my fault, through my fault, through my most grievous fault.
The Missal: *The Ordinary of the Mass*

15   Commit
The oldest sins the newest kind of ways.
William Shakespeare 1564–1616: *Henry IV, Part 2* (1597)

16 Nothing emboldens sin so much as mercy.
William Shakespeare 1564–1616: *Timon of Athens* (c.1607)

17 I should renounce the devil and all his works, the pomps and vanity of this wicked world, and all the sinful lusts of the flesh.
The Book of Common Prayer 1662: *Catechism*; see **Temptation** 4

18 We have erred, and strayed from thy ways like lost sheep. We have followed too much the devices and desires of our own hearts.
The Book of Common Prayer 1662: *Morning Prayer General Confession*

19 Had laws not been, we never had been blamed;
For not to know we sin is innocence.
William D'Avenant 1606–68: 'The Philosopher's Disquisition directed to the Dying Christian' (1672)

20 It is public scandal that constitutes offence, and to sin in secret is not to sin at all.
Molière 1622–73: *Le Tartuffe* (1669)

21 Vice came in always at the door of necessity, not at the door of inclination.
Daniel Defoe 1660–1731: *Moll Flanders* (1721)

22 I waive the quantum o' the sin;
The hazard of concealing;
But och! it hardens a' within,

And petrifies the feeling!
Robert Burns 1759-96: 'Epistle to a Young Friend' (1786)

23 Vice is detestable; I banish all its appearances from my coteries; and I would banish its reality, too, were I sure I should then have any thing but empty chairs in my drawing-room.
Fanny Burney 1752-1840: *Camilla* (1796)

24 That Calvinistic sense of innate depravity and original sin from whose visitations, in some shape or other, no deeply thinking mind is always and wholly free.
Herman Melville 1819-91: *Hawthorne and His Mosses* (1850)

25 She [the Catholic Church] holds that it were better for sun and moon to drop from heaven, for the earth to fail, and for all the many millions who are upon it to die of starvation in extremest agony, as far as temporal affliction goes, than that one soul, I will not say, should be lost, but should commit one single venial sin, should tell one wilful untruth . . . or steal one poor farthing without excuse.
John Henry Newman 1801-90: *Lectures on Anglican Difficulties* (1852)

26 For the sin ye do by two and two ye must pay for one by one!
Rudyard Kipling 1865-1936: 'Tomlinson' (1892)

27 The only difference between the saint and the sinner is that every saint has a past, and every sinner has a future.
Oscar Wilde 1854-1900: *A Woman of No Importance* (1893)

28 When I'm good, I'm very, very good, but when I'm bad, I'm better.
Mae West 1892-1980: *I'm No Angel* (1933 film)

when asked by Mrs Coolidge what a sermon had been about:

29 'Sins,' he said. 'Well, what did he say about sin?' 'He was against it.'
Calvin Coolidge 1872-1933: John H. McKee *Coolidge: Wit and Wisdom* (1933); perhaps apocryphal

30 All sins are attempts to fill voids.
Simone Weil 1909-43: *La Pesanteur et la grâce* (1948)

31 There are different kinds of wrong. The people sinned against are not always the best.
Ivy Compton-Burnett 1884-1969: *The Mighty and their Fall* (1961)

32 All sin tends to be addictive, and the terminal point of addiction is what is called damnation.
W. H. Auden 1907-73: *A Certain World* (1970) 'Hell'

33 Sins become more subtle as you grow older. You commit sins of despair rather than lust.
Piers Paul Read 1941- : in *Daily Telegraph* 3 October 1990

Singing see also Music

PROVERBS AND SAYINGS

1 Why should the devil have all the best tunes?
commonly attributed to the English evangelist Rowland Hill (1744–1833); many hymns are sung to popular secular melodies, and this practice was especially favoured by the Methodists

QUOTATIONS

2 The exercise of singing is delightful to Nature, and good to preserve the health of man. It doth strengthen all parts of the breast, and doth open the pipes.
William Byrd 1543-1623: *Psalms, Sonnets and Songs* (1588)

3 I can suck melancholy out of a song as a weasel sucks eggs.
William Shakespeare 1564-1616: *As You Like It* (1599)

4 If a man were permitted to make all the ballads, he need not care who should make the laws of a nation.
Andrew Fletcher of Saltoun 1655-1716: 'An Account of a Conversation concerning a Right Regulation of Government for the Good of Mankind. In a Letter to the Marquis of Montrose' (1704)

5 An exotic and irrational entertainment,
which has been always combated, and
always has prevailed.

of Italian opera

Samuel Johnson 1709–84: *Lives of the English Poets*
(1779–81) 'Hughes'

6 Sentimentally I am disposed to harmony.
But organically I am incapable of a tune.

Charles Lamb 1775–1834: *Essays of Elia* (1823) 'A
Chapter on Ears'

7 Nothing can be more disgusting than an
oratorio. How absurd to see 500 people
fiddling like madmen about Israelites in the
Red Sea!

Sydney Smith 1771–1845: Hesketh Pearson *The
Smith of Smiths* (1934)

8 Every tone [of the songs of the slaves] was
a testimony against slavery, and a prayer
to God for deliverance from chains.

Frederick Douglass c.1818–1895: *Narrative of the
Life of Frederick Douglass* (1845)

9 A wandering minstrel I—
A thing of shreds and patches.
Of ballads, songs and snatches,
And dreamy lullaby!

W. S. Gilbert 1836–1911: *The Mikado* (1885); see
Character 25

10 You think that's noise—you ain't heard
nuttin' yet!

*first said in a café, competing with the din from a
neighbouring building site, in 1906; subsequently an
aside in the 1927 film* The Jazz Singer

Al Jolson 1886–1950: Martin Abramson *The Real
Story of Al Jolson* (1950); also the title of a Jolson
song, 1919, in the form 'You Ain't Heard Nothing
Yet'

11 Everyone suddenly burst out singing;

And I was filled with such delight
As prisoned birds must find in freedom.

Siegfried Sassoon 1886–1967: 'Everyone Sang'
(1919)

12 Tenors get women by the score.

James Joyce 1882–1941: *Ulysses* (1922)

13 Jerry Kern didn't write 'Ol' Man River', *my*
husband did! What Kern wrote was dum-
dum-*dee*-dum.

Dorothy Hammerstein: attributed, probably
apocryphal; Stephen Citron *The Wordsmiths: Oscar
Hammerstein 2nd and Alan Jay Lerner* (1995); see
Rivers 13

14 A good lyric should be rhymed
conversation.

Ira Gershwin 1896–1983: Philip Furia *Ira Gershwin*
(1966)

15 No opera plot can be sensible, for in
sensible situations people do not sing. An
opera plot must be, in both senses of the
word, a melodrama.

W. H. Auden 1907–73: in *Times Literary Supplement*
2 November 1967

16 Words make you think a thought. Music
makes you feel a feeling. A song makes
you feel a thought.

E. Y. Harburg 1898–1981: lecture given at the New
York YMCA in 1970

17 In writing songs I've learned as much from
Cézanne as I have from Woody Guthrie.

Bob Dylan 1941– : Clinton Heylin *Dylan: Behind the
Shades* (1991)

18 It's the only song I've ever written where I
get goose bumps every time I play it.

of 'Candle in the Wind'

Elton John 1947– : in *Daily Telegraph* 9 September
1997

The Single Life see also **Marriage**

PROVERBS AND SAYINGS

1 Why buy a cow when milk is so cheap?

*mid 17th century, putting forward an argument for
choosing the least troublesome alternative; frequently
used as an argument against marriage*

PHRASES

2 old maid a single woman regarded as too
old for marriage.

figuratively, a prim and fussy person; see 10 below

QUOTATIONS

3 I would be married, but I'd have no wife,
I would be married to a single life.

Richard Crashaw c.1612–49: 'On Marriage' (1646)

4 Marriage has many pains, but celibacy has
no pleasures.

Samuel Johnson 1709–84: *Rasselas* (1759)

5 It is amusing that a virtue is made of the
vice of chastity; and it's a pretty odd sort of
chastity at that, which leads men straight

into the sin of Onan, and girls to the waning of their colour.
Voltaire 1694–1778: letter to M. Mariott, 28 March 1766

6 It is a truth universally acknowledged, that a single man in possession of a good fortune, must be in want of a wife.
Jane Austen 1775–1817: *Pride and Prejudice* (1813)

7 Marriage may often be a stormy lake, but celibacy is almost always a muddy horsepond.
Thomas Love Peacock 1785–1866: *Melincourt* (1817)

8 Single women have a dreadful propensity for being poor—which is one very strong argument in favour of matrimony.
Jane Austen 1775–1817: letter to Fanny Knight, 13 March 1817

9 Even quarrels with one's husband are preferable to the ennui of a solitary existence.
Elizabeth Patterson Bonaparte 1785–1879: Eugene L. Didier *The Life and Letters of Madame Bonaparte* (1879)

10 Being an old maid is like death by drowning, a really delightful sensation after you cease to struggle.
Edna Ferber 1887–1968: R. E. Drennan *Wit's End* (1973); see 2 above

11 I am that twentieth-century failure, a happy undersexed celibate.
Denise Coffey: Ned Sherrin *Cutting Edge* (1984)

12 Nobody dies from lack of sex. It's lack of love we die from.
Margaret Atwood 1939– : *The Handmaid's Tale* (1986)

13 We are a select group, without personal obligation, social encumbrance, or any socks that match.
P. J. O'Rourke 1947– : *The Bachelor Home Companion* (1987)

14 Deep down, we remain human, very human and have all the desires to love and be loved by one person . . . Every time I did a marriage, every time I see people married, I say: 'That could have been me.'
Basil Hume 1923–99: attributed; in 1992

Situation see Circumstance and Situation

The Skies see also The Universe

PHRASES

1 the evening star the planet Venus, seen shining in the western sky after sunset.
see 15 below

2 the Great Bear in astronomy, the constellation Ursa Major.
named from the story in Greek mythology that the nymph Callisto was turned into a bear and placed as a constellation in the heavens by Zeus. The seven brightest stars form a familiar formation variously called the Plough, Big Dipper, or Charles's Wain, and include the Pointers; see 7, 30 below

3 the merry dancers in Scotland, the aurora borealis.
see 5 below

4 the mother of the months the moon.

5 the northern lights the aurora borealis.
alluding to the streamers of light appearing in the sky; see 3 above

6 the queen of tides the moon.

7 the seven stars a former name for the Pleiades and the Great Bear.
*there are six stars in the Pleiades visible to the naked eye: the eldest Pleiad, Merope, was 'the lost Pleiad'; see also 2 above, **Quantities** 24*

QUOTATIONS

8 And God made two great lights; the greater light to rule the day, and the lesser light to rule the night: he made the stars also.
Bible: Genesis

9 And ther he saugh, with ful avysement The erratik sterres, herkenyng armonye With sownes ful of hevenyssh melodie.
Geoffrey Chaucer c.1343–1400: *Troilus and Criseyde*

10 The fool will turn the whole art of astronomy inside out! But, as the Holy Scripture reports, Joshua ordered the sun to stand still and not the earth.
on Copernicus' suggestion that the earth moved round the sun
Martin Luther 1483–1546: *Table Talk*, 4 June 1539

11 Queen and huntress, chaste and fair,
   Now the sun is laid to sleep,
   Seated in thy silver chair,
   State in wonted manner keep:
   Hesperus entreats thy light,
   Goddess, excellently bright.
   Ben Jonson c.1573–1637: *Cynthia's Revels* (1600)

12   The moon's an arrant thief,
   And her pale fire she snatches from the
       sun.
   William Shakespeare 1564–1616: *Timon of Athens*
   (c.1607)

13 Busy old fool, unruly sun,
   Why dost thou thus,
   Through windows, and through curtains
       call on us?
   John Donne 1572–1631: 'The Sun Rising'

14 But it does move.
   after his recantation, that the earth moves around the
   sun, in 1632
   Galileo Galilei 1564–1642: attributed; Baretti *Italian*
   Library (1757) possibly has the earliest appearance
   of the phrase

15   The evening star,
   Love's harbinger.
   John Milton 1608–74: *Paradise Lost* (1667); see 1
   above

16 The hornèd Moon, with one bright star
   Within the nether tip.
   Samuel Taylor Coleridge 1772–1834: 'The Rime of
   the Ancient Mariner' (1798)

17 Twinkle, twinkle, little star,
   How I wonder what you are!
   Up above the world so high,
   Like a diamond in the sky!
   Ann Taylor 1782–1866 and **Jane Taylor** 1783–1824:
   'The Star' (1806)

18 I am the daughter of Earth and Water,
   And the nursling of the Sky;
   I pass through the pores of the ocean and
       shores;
   I change, but I cannot die.
   Percy Bysshe Shelley 1792–1822: 'The Cloud' (1819)

19 Look at the stars! look, look up at the
       skies!
   O look at all the fire-folk sitting in the air!
   The bright boroughs, the circle-citadels
       there!
   Gerard Manley Hopkins 1844–89: 'The Starlight
   Night' (written 1877)

20 The night has a thousand eyes,
   And the day but one;
   Yet the light of the bright world dies,

With the dying sun.
F. W. Bourdillon 1852–1921: 'Light' (1878)

21 Slowly, silently, now the moon
   Walks the night in her silver shoon.
   Walter de la Mare 1873–1956: 'Silver' (1913)

22 I have loved the stars too fondly to be
   fearful of the night.
   Sarah Williams: 'The Old Astronomer to His Pupil'
   (1920)

23 The heaventree of stars hung with humid
   nightblue fruit.
   James Joyce 1882–1941: *Ulysses* (1922)

24 We have seen
   The moon in lonely alleys make
   A grail of laughter of an empty ash can.
   Hart Crane 1899–1932: 'Chaplinesque' (1926)

25 Had I been a man I might have explored
   the Poles, or climbed Mount Everest, but as
   it was, my spirit found outlet in the air.
   Amy Johnson 1903–41: Margot Asquith (ed.) *Myself*
   When Young (1938)

26 The moon is nothing
   But a circumambulating aphrodisiac
   Divinely subsidized to provoke the world
   Into a rising birth-rate.
   Christopher Fry 1907– : *The Lady's not for Burning*
   (1949)

27 Don't tell me that man doesn't belong out
   there. Man belongs wherever he wants to
   go—and he'll do plenty well when he gets
   there.
   Wernher von Braun 1912–77: in *Time* 17 February
   1958

28 Houston, Tranquillity Base here. The Eagle
   has landed.
   Neil Armstrong 1930– : on landing on the moon,
   on 20 July 1969

29 Nothing is more symptomatic of the
   enervation, of the decompression of the
   Western imagination, than our incapacity
   to respond to the landings on the Moon.
   Not a single great poem, picture, metaphor
   has come of this breathtaking act, of
   Prometheus' rescue of Icarus or of Phaeton
   in flight towards the stars.
   George Steiner 1926– : 'Modernity, Mythology
   and Magic', lecture at the 1994 Salzburg Festival

30 Our windy, untidy loft
   where old people had flung up old junk
   they'd thought might come in handy

ploughs, ladles, bears, lions, a clatter of heroes.
Moya Cannon 1956– : 'The Stars' (1997); see 2 above

Sleep see also **Dreams**

1 One hour's sleep before midnight is worth two after.
mid 17th century

2 Six hours sleep for a man, seven for a woman, and eight for a fool.
early 17th century, implying that the more sleep a person needs, the less vigorous and effective they are likely to be

3 Some sleep five hours; nature requires seven, laziness nine, and wickedness eleven.
American proverb, mid 20th century

4 We never sleep.
motto of the American detective agency founded by Allan Pinkerton (c.1855)

PHRASES

5 the land of Nod sleep.
a pun on the biblical place-name in the Bible (Genesis) of the land to which Cain was exiled after the killing of Abel, after Swift Polite Conversation *(1731–8) 'I'm going to the Land of Nod'; see also* **Canada** *2*

QUOTATIONS

6 The sleep of a labouring man is sweet.
Bible: Ecclesiastes

7 Care-charmer Sleep, son of the sable Night, Brother to Death, in silent darkness born.
Samuel Daniel 1563–1619: *Delia* (1592) sonnet 54

8 Not to be a-bed after midnight is to be up betimes.
William Shakespeare 1564–1616: *Twelfth Night* (1601)

9 Golden slumbers kiss your eyes, Smiles awake you when you rise: Sleep, pretty wantons, do not cry, And I will sing a lullaby.
Thomas Dekker 1570–1641: *Patient Grissil* (1603)

10 Methought I heard a voice cry, 'Sleep no more!
Macbeth does murder sleep,' the innocent sleep,
Sleep that knits up the ravelled sleave of care,
The death of each day's life, sore labour's bath,
Balm of hurt minds, great nature's second course.
William Shakespeare 1564–1616: *Macbeth* (1606)

11 What hath night to do with sleep?
John Milton 1608–74: *Comus* (1637)

12 And so to bed.
Samuel Pepys 1633–1703: diary 20 April 1660

13 Tired Nature's sweet restorer, balmy sleep!
Edward Young 1683–1765: *Night Thoughts* (1742–5)

14 Turn the key deftly in the oilèd wards, And seal the hushèd casket of my soul.
John Keats 1795–1821: 'Sonnet to Sleep' (written 1819)

15 Must we to bed indeed? Well then, Let us arise and go like men, And face with an undaunted tread The long black passage up to bed.
Robert Louis Stevenson 1850–94: 'North-West Passage. Good-Night' (1885)

16 The cool kindliness of sheets, that soon
Smooth away trouble; and the rough male kiss
Of blankets.
Rupert Brooke 1887–1915: 'The Great Lover' (1914)

17 Early to rise and early to bed makes a male healthy and wealthy and dead.
James Thurber 1894–1961: 'The Shrike and the Chipmunks' in *New Yorker* 18 February 1939; see **Health** 4

18 Sleep is when all the unsorted stuff comes flying out as from a dustbin upset in a high wind.
William Golding 1911–93: *Pincher Martin* (1956)

19 I love sleep because it is both pleasant and safe to use.
Fran Lebowitz 1946– : *Metropolitan Life* (1978)

Smoking

1 Happiness is a cigar called Hamlet.

advertising slogan for Hamlet cigars, UK

2 Smoking can seriously damage your health.

government health warning now required by British law to be printed on cigarette packets; in form 'Smoking can damage your health' from early 1970s

3 You're never alone with a Strand.

advertising slogan for Strand cigarettes, 1960; the image of loneliness was so strongly conveyed by the solitary smoker that sales were in fact adversely affected

4 I do hold it, and will affirm it (before any prince in Europe) to be the most sovereign and precious weed that ever the earth tendered to the use of man.

of tobacco

Ben Jonson c.1573–1637: *Every Man in His Humour* (1598)

5 A custom loathsome to the eye, hateful to the nose, harmful to the brain, dangerous to the lungs, and in the black, stinking fume thereof, nearest resembling the horrible Stygian smoke of the pit that is bottomless.

James I 1566–1625: *A Counterblast to Tobacco* (1604)

6 The lungs of the tobacconist are rotted, the liver spotted, the brain smoked like the backside of the pig-woman's booth here, and the whole body within, black as her pan you saw e'en now without.

Ben Jonson c.1573–1637: *Bartholomew Fair* (1614)

7 He who lives without tobacco is not worthy to live.

Molière 1622–73: *Don Juan* (performed 1665)

8 The pipe with solemn interposing puff, Makes half a sentence at a time enough;

The dozing sages drop the drowsy strain, Then pause, and puff—and speak, and pause again.

William Cowper 1731–1800: 'Conversation' (1782)

9 This very night I am going to leave off tobacco! Surely there must be some other world in which this unconquerable purpose shall be realized.

Charles Lamb 1775–1834: letter to Thomas Manning, 26 December 1815

10 The roots of tobacco plants must go clear through to hell.

Thomas Alva Edison 1847–1931: in *American Heritage* 12 July 1885

11 A cigarette is the perfect type of a perfect pleasure. It is exquisite, and it leaves one unsatisfied. What more can one want?

Oscar Wilde 1854–1900: *The Picture of Dorian Gray* (1891)

12 The wretcheder one is, the more one smokes; and the more one smokes, the wretcheder one gets—a vicious circle!

George du Maurier 1834–96: *Peter Ibbetson* (1892)

13 What this country needs is a really good 5-cent cigar.

Thomas R. Marshall 1854–1925: in *New York Tribune* 4 January 1920

14 I smoked my first cigarette and kissed my first woman on the same day. I have never had time for tobacco since.

Arturo Toscanini 1867–1957: in *Observer* 30 June 1946

15 But the cigarette, well, I love stroking this lovely tube of delight.

Dennis Potter 1935–94: interview with Melvyn Bragg on Channel 4, March 1994; *Seeing the Blossom* (1994)

16 It has been said that cigarettes are the only product that, if used according to the manufacturer's instructions, have a very high chance of killing you.

Michael Buerk 1946– : in *Sunday Times* 11 July 1999

Society see also Government, Human Race

1 If every man would sweep his own doorstep the city would soon be clean.
early 17th century; meaning that if everyone fulfils their own responsibilities, what is necessary will be done

2 One half of the world does not know how the other half lives.
early 17th century, often used to comment on a lack of communication between neighbouring groups

PHRASES

3 body politic the state viewed as an aggregate of its invidual members; organized society.

4 pillar of society a person regarded as a particularly responsible citizen, a mainstay of the social fabric.
pillar in the sense of a person regarded as a mainstay or support for something is recorded from Middle English; Pillars of Society was the English title (1888) of a play by Ibsen

QUOTATIONS

5 No man is an Island, entire of it self; every man is a piece of the Continent, a part of the main; if a clod be washed away by the sea, Europe is the less, as well as if a promontory were.
John Donne 1572–1631: *Devotions upon Emergent Occasions* (1624)

6 The only way by which any one divests himself of his natural liberty and puts on the bonds of civil society is by agreeing with other men to join and unite into a community.
John Locke 1632–1704: *Second Treatise of Civil Government* (1690)

7 Society is indeed a contract . . . it becomes a partnership not only between those who are living, but between those who are living, those who are dead, and those who are to be born.
Edmund Burke 1729–97: *Reflections on the Revolution in France* (1790)

8 The general will rules in society as the private will governs each separate individual.
Maximilien Robespierre 1758–94: *Lettres à ses commettans* (2nd series) 5 January 1793

9 Only in the state does man have a rational existence . . . Man owes his entire existence to the state, and has his being within it alone. Whatever worth and spiritual reality he possesses are his solely by virtue of the state.
G. W. F. Hegel 1770–1831: *Lectures on the Philosophy of World History: Introduction* (1830)

10 The greatest happiness of the greatest number is the foundation of morals and legislation.
Jeremy Bentham 1748–1832: *The Commonplace Book*; Bentham claimed that either Joseph Priestley (1733–1804) or Cesare Beccaria (1738–94) passed on the 'sacred truth'; see **Morality** 4

11 Wherever a man goes, men will pursue him and paw him with their dirty institutions, and, if they can, constrain him to belong to their desperate oddfellow society.
Henry David Thoreau 1817–62: *Walden* (1854) 'The Village'

12 When society requires to be rebuilt, there is no use in attempting to rebuild it on the old plan.
John Stuart Mill 1806–73: *Dissertations and Discussions* vol. 1 (1859) 'Essay on Coleridge'

13 From each according to his abilities, to each according to his needs.
Karl Marx 1818–83: *Critique of the Gotha Programme* (written 1875, but of earlier origin)

14 The Social Contract is nothing more or less than a vast conspiracy of human beings to lie to and humbug themselves and one another for the general Good. Lies are the mortar that bind the savage individual man into the social masonry.
H. G. Wells 1866–1946: *Love and Mr Lewisham* (1900)

15 There is no such thing as the State
And no one exists alone;
Hunger allows no choice
To the citizen or the police;
We must love one another or die.
W. H. Auden 1907–73: 'September 1, 1939' (1940)

16 Society is based on the assumption that everyone is alike and no one is alive.
Hugh Kingsmill 1889–1949: Michael Holroyd *Hugh Kingsmill* (1964)

17 If a free society cannot help the many who are poor, it cannot save the few who are rich.
John F. Kennedy 1917–63: inaugural address, 20 January 1961

18 In your time we have the opportunity to move not only toward the rich society and the powerful society, but upward to the Great Society.
Lyndon Baines Johnson 1908–73: speech at University of Michigan, 22 May 1964

19 We started off trying to set up a small anarchist community, but people wouldn't obey the rules.
Alan Bennett 1934– : *Getting On* (1972)

20 There is no such thing as Society. There are individual men and women, and there are families.
Margaret Thatcher 1925– : in *Woman's Own* 31 October 1987

21 Polluted rivers, filthy streets, bodies bedded down in doorways are no advertisement for a prosperous or caring society.
Michael Heseltine 1933– : speech at Conservative Party Conference 10 October 1989

Solitude

PROVERBS AND SAYINGS

1 **Better alone than in bad company.**
American proverb, late 17th century

2 **He travels fastest who travels alone.**
late 19th century, implying that single-minded pursuit of an objective is more easily achieved by someone without family commitments; see 13 below

3 **The lone sheep is in danger of the wolf.**
late 16th century, stressing the importance of mutual support

PHRASES

4 **send to Coventry** refuse to speak to; ostracize.
perhaps after circumstances recorded in Clarendon The History of the Rebellion (1703) 'At Bromicham, a town so generally wicked, that it had risen upon small parties of the King's, and killed, or taken them prisoners, and sent them to Coventry' (Coventry being then strongly held for Parliament)

QUOTATIONS

5 It is not good that the man should be alone; I will make him an help meet for him.
Bible: Genesis; see 18, 19 below

6 He who is unable to live in society, or who has no need because he is sufficient for himself, must be either a beast or a god.
Aristotle 384–322 BC: *Politics*

7 Never less idle than when wholly idle, nor less alone than when wholly alone.
Scipio Africanus 236–c.184 BC: Cicero *De Officiis*

8 In solitude
What happiness? who can enjoy alone,
Or all enjoying, what contentment find?
John Milton 1608–74: *Paradise Lost* (1667)

9 I am monarch of all I survey,
My right there is none to dispute;
From the centre all round to the sea
I am lord of the foul and the brute.
William Cowper 1731–1800: 'Verses Supposed to be Written by Alexander Selkirk' (1782); Selkirk (1621–1721) was the prototype of 'Robinson Crusoe'

10 Anythin' for a quiet life, as the man said wen he took the sitivation at the lighthouse.
Charles Dickens 1812–70: *Pickwick Papers* (1837)

11 I long for scenes where man hath never trod
A place where woman never smiled or wept
There to abide with my Creator God.
John Clare 1793–1864: 'I Am' (1848)

12 It is a fine thing to be out on the hills alone. A man can hardly be a beast or a fool alone on a great mountain.
Francis Kilvert 1840–79: diary 29 May 1871

13 Down to Gehenna or up to the Throne,
He travels the fastest who travels alone.
Rudyard Kipling 1865–1936: 'The Winners' (*The Story of the Gadsbys*, 1890); see 2 above

14 My heart is a lonely hunter that hunts on a lonely hill.
Fiona McLeod 1855–1905: 'The Lonely Hunter' (1896); reworked by Carson McCullers as 'The heart is a lonely hunter' for the title of a novel, 1940

15 Man goes into the noisy crowd to drown his own clamour of silence.
Rabindranath Tagore 1861–1941: 'Stray Birds' (1916)

16 I want to be alone.
Greta Garbo 1905–90: *Grand Hotel* (1932 film), the phrase already being associated with Garbo

17 You come into the world alone and you go out of the world alone yet it seems to me you are more alone while living than even going and coming.
Emily Carr 1871–1945: *Hundreds and Thousands: The Journals of Emily Carr* (1966) 16 July 1933

18 God created man and, finding him not sufficiently alone, gave him a companion to make him feel his solitude more keenly.
Paul Valéry 1871–1945: *Tel Quel 1* (1941); see 5 above

19 [Barrymore] would quote from Genesis the text which says, 'It is not good for man to be alone,' and then add, 'But O my God, what a relief.'
John Barrymore 1882–1942: Alma Power-Waters *John Barrymore* (1941); see 5 above

20 Please fence me in baby the world's too big out here and I don't like it without you.
Humphrey Bogart 1899–1957: telegram to Lauren Bacall; Lauren Bacall *By Myself* (1978); see **The Country and the Town** 22

21 Oh, no no no, it was too cold always
(Still the dead one lay moaning)
I was much too far out all my life
And not waving but drowning.
Stevie Smith 1902–71: 'Not Waving but Drowning' (1957)

22 We're all of us sentenced to solitary confinement inside our own skins, for life!
Tennessee Williams 1911–83: *Orpheus Descending* (1958)

23 How does it feel
To be on your own
With no direction home
Like a complete unknown
Like a rolling stone?
Bob Dylan 1941– : *Like a Rolling Stone* (1965 song)

24 All the lonely people, where do they all come from?
John Lennon 1940–80 and **Paul McCartney** 1942– : 'Eleanor Rigby' (1966 song)

25 Many a housewife staring at the back of her husband's newspaper, or listening to his breathing in bed is lonelier than any spinster in a rented room.
Germaine Greer 1939– : *The Female Eunuch* (1970)

26 What Chekhov saw in our failure to communicate was something positive and precious: the private silence in which we live, and which enables us to endure our own solitude.
V. S. Pritchett 1900– : *Myth Makers* (1979)

27 Thirty years is a very long time to live alone and life doesn't get any nicer.
on widowhood, at the age of 92
Frances Partridge 1900– : G. Kinnock and F. Miller *By Faith and Daring* (1993)

Solutions see Problems and Solutions

Sorrow see also Mourning and Loss, Suffering

PROVERBS AND SAYINGS

1 **Misery loves company.**
late 16th century, now predominantly current in the United States

2 **Wednesday's child is full of woe.**
traditional rhyme, mid 19th century; see **Beauty** 5, **Gifts** 2, **Travel** 5, **Work** 6

PHRASES

3 **de profundis** a cry of appeal from the depths (of sorrow).
Latin = from the depths, the initial words of Psalm 130: see **Suffering** 5

4 **Man of Sorrows** a name for Jesus Christ.
deriving from a prophecy in the Bible (Isaiah), 'He is despised and rejected of men; a man of sorrows, and acquainted with grief'

QUOTATIONS

5 By the waters of Babylon we sat down and wept: when we remembered thee, O Sion.
Bible: Psalm 137

6 *Sunt lacrimae rerum et mentem mortalia tangunt.*
There are tears shed for things even here and mortality touches the heart.
Virgil 70–19 BC: *Aeneid*

7 Small sorrows speak; great ones are silent.
Seneca ('the Younger') c.4 BC–AD 65: *Hippolytus*

8 . . . *Nessun maggior dolore,*
Che ricordarsi del tempo felice
Nella miseria.

There is no greater pain than to remember
a happy time when one is in misery.
Dante Alighieri 1265–1321: *Divina Commedia*
'Inferno'

9 If you have tears, prepare to shed them
now.
William Shakespeare 1564–1616: *Julius Caesar*
(1599)

10 When sorrows come, they come not single
spies,
But in battalions.
William Shakespeare 1564–1616: *Hamlet* (1601)

11 We think caged birds sing, when indeed
they cry.
John Webster c.1580–c.1625: *The White Devil* (1612)

12 All my joys to this are folly,
Naught so sweet as Melancholy.
Robert Burton 1577–1640: *The Anatomy of
Melancholy* (1621–51)

13 Nothing is here for tears.
John Milton 1608–74: *Samson Agonistes* (1671)

14 Grief is a species of idleness.
Samuel Johnson 1709–84: letter to Mrs Thrale, 17
March 1773

15 For a tear is an intellectual thing;
And a sigh is the sword of an Angel King.
William Blake 1757–1827: *Jerusalem* (1815)

16 I tell you, hopeless grief is passionless.
Elizabeth Barrett Browning 1806–61: 'Grief'
(1844)

17 Tears, idle tears, I know not what they
mean,
Tears from the depth of some divine
despair.
Alfred, Lord Tennyson 1809–92: *The Princess*
(1847), song (added 1850)

18 Áh! ás the heart grows older
It will come to such sights colder
By and by, nor spare a sigh
Though worlds of wanwood leafmeal lie;
And yet you *will* weep and know why.
Gerard Manley Hopkins 1844–89: 'Spring and Fall:
to a young child' (written 1880)

19 MEDVEDENKO: Why do you wear black all
the time?
MASHA: I'm in mourning for my life, I'm
unhappy.
Anton Chekhov 1860–1904: *The Seagull* (1896)

20 Laugh and the world laughs with you;
Weep, and you weep alone;
For the sad old earth must borrow its
mirth,
But has trouble enough of its own.
Ella Wheeler Wilcox 1855–1919: 'Solitude'; see
Sympathy 3

21 All the old statues of Victory have wings:
but Grief has no wings. She is the
unwelcome lodger that squats on the
hearth-stone between us and the fire and
will not move or be dislodged.
Arthur Quiller-Couch 1863–1944: Armistice Day
anniversary sermon, Cambridge, November 1923

22 Now laughing friends deride tears I cannot
hide,
So I smile and say 'When a lovely flame
dies,
Smoke gets in your eyes.'
Otto Harbach 1873–1963: 'Smoke Gets in your
Eyes' (1933 song)

23 Sob, heavy world,
Sob as you spin
Mantled in mist, remote from the happy.
W. H. Auden 1907–73: *The Age of Anxiety* (1947)

24 He felt the loyalty we all feel to
unhappiness—the sense that that is where
we really belong.
Graham Greene 1904–91: *The Heart of the Matter*
(1948)

25 How small and selfish is sorrow. But it
bangs one about until one is senseless.
shortly after the death of George VI
Queen Elizabeth, the Queen Mother 1900–2002:
letter to Edith Sitwell, 1952; Victoria Glendinning
Edith Sitwell (1983)

26 No one ever told me that grief felt so like
fear.
C. S. Lewis 1898–1963: *A Grief Observed* (1961)

27 Total grief is like a minefield. No knowing
when one will touch the tripwire.
Sylvia Townsend Warner 1893–1978: diary 11
December 1969

Speech see also Conversation

1 How now, brown cow?
a traditional elocution exercise

2 Length begets loathing.
mid 18th century, in reference to verbosity

3 Who knows most, speaks least.
mid 17th century

PHRASES

4 have kissed the Blarney stone be eloquent and persuasive.
a stone, at Blarney castle near Cork in Ireland, said to give the gift of persuasive speech to anyone who kisses it; the verb to blarney 'talk flatteringly' derives from this

5 a silver tongue a gift of eloquence or persuasiveness.
see Silence 4

QUOTATIONS

6 The words of his mouth were softer than butter, having war in his heart: his words were smoother than oil, and yet they be very swords.
Bible: Psalm 55

7 Then said they unto him, Say now Shibboleth: and he said Sibboleth: for he could not frame to pronounce it right. Then they took him, and slew him.
Bible: Judges

8 The reason why we have two ears and only one mouth is that we may listen the more and talk the less.
to a youth who was talking nonsense
Zeno 333–261 BC: Diogenes Laertius *Lives of the Philosophers*

9 The tongue can no man tame; it is an unruly evil.
Bible: James; see **The Body** 8

10 Somwhat he lipsed, for his wantownesse, To make his Englissh sweete upon his tonge.
Geoffrey Chaucer c.1343–1400: *The Canterbury Tales* 'The General Prologue'

11 It has been well said, that heart speaks to heart, whereas language only speaks to the ears.
St Francis de Sales 1567–1622: letter to the Archbishop of Bourges, 5 October 1604, which John

Henry Newman paraphrased for his motto as '*cor ad cor loquitur* [heart speaks to heart]'

12   Her voice was ever soft, Gentle and low, an excellent thing in woman.
William Shakespeare 1564–1616: *King Lear* (1605–6)

13 I do not much dislike the matter, but The manner of his speech.
William Shakespeare 1564–1616: *Antony and Cleopatra* (1606–7)

14 Continual eloquence is tedious.
Blaise Pascal 1623–62: *Pensées* (1670)

15 Most men make little other use of their speech than to give evidence against their own understanding.
Lord Halifax 1633–95: *Political, Moral, and Miscellaneous Thoughts and Reflections* (1750) 'Of Folly and Fools'

16 Faith, that's as well said, as if I had said it myself.
Jonathan Swift 1667–1745: *Polite Conversation* (1738)

when asked if he found his stammering very inconvenient:

17 No, Sir, because I have time to think before I speak, and don't ask impertinent questions.
Erasmus Darwin 1731–1802: 'Reminiscences of My Father's Everyday Life', an appendix by Francis Darwin to his edition of Charles Darwin *Autobiography* (1877)

18 When you have nothing to say, say nothing.
Charles Caleb Colton c.1780–1832: *Lacon* (1820)

19 And, when you stick on conversation's burrs, Don't strew your pathway with those dreadful *urs.*
Oliver Wendell Holmes 1809–94: 'A Rhymed Lesson' (1848)

20 Human speech is like a cracked kettle on which we tap crude rhythms for bears to dance to, while we long to make music that will melt the stars.
Gustave Flaubert 1821–80: *Madame Bovary* (1857)

21 Take care of the sense, and the sounds will take care of themselves.
Lewis Carroll 1832–98: *Alice's Adventures in Wonderland* (1865); see **Thrift** 7

22 Half the sorrows of women would be averted if they could repress the speech they know to be useless; nay, the speech they have resolved not to make.
George Eliot 1819–80: *Felix Holt* (1866)

23 I don't want to talk grammar, I want to talk like a lady.
George Bernard Shaw 1856–1950: *Pygmalion* (1916)

24 What can be said at all can be said clearly; and whereof one cannot speak thereof one must be silent.
Ludwig Wittgenstein 1889–1951: *Tractatus Logico-Philosophicus* (1922)

25 Speech is civilization itself. The word, even the most contradictory word, preserves contact — it is silence which isolates.
Thomas Mann 1875–1955: *The Magic Mountain* (1924)

26 You like potato and I like po-tah-to,
You like tomato and I like to-mah-to;
Potato, po-tah-to, tomato, to-mah-to—
Let's call the whole thing off!
Ira Gershwin 1896–1983: 'Let's Call the Whole Thing Off' (1937 song)

27　　　Speech impelled us

To purify the dialect of the tribe
And urge the mind to aftersight and foresight.
T. S. Eliot 1888–1965: *Four Quartets* 'Little Gidding' (1942)

28 Nagging is the repetition of unpalatable truths.
Edith Summerskill 1901–80: speech to the Married Women's Association, House of Commons, 14 July 1960

29 Never express yourself more clearly than you think.
Niels Bohr 1885–1962: Abraham Pais *Einstein Lived Here* (1994)

30 Sentence structure is innate but whining is acquired.
Woody Allen 1935– : 'Remembering Needleman' (1976)

31　　　Here is the News,
Said the absolute speaker. Between him and us
A great gulf was fixed where pronunciation
Reigned tyrannically
Seamus Heaney 1939– : 'A Sofa in the Forties' (1996)

Speeches

PROVERBS AND SAYINGS

1 Unaccustomed as I am . . .
clichéistic opening words by a public speaker

PHRASES

2 the rubber chicken circuit the circuit followed by professional speakers.
referring to what is regarded as the customary menu for the lunch or dinner preceding the speech

3 the Rupert of Debate Edward Stanley (1799–1869), later 14th Earl of Derby.
a description by the British novelist and politician Edward Bulwer-Lytton (1803–73), likening his parliamentary style to the dashing cavalry charges of Prince Rupert

4 talking to Buncombe ostentatious and irrelevant speechmaking.
from Felix Walker, excusing a long, dull, irrelevant speech in the House of Representatives, c.1820, 'I'm talking to Buncombe', Buncombe being his constituency; the word bunkum *derives from this*

QUOTATIONS

5 When asked what was first in oratory, [he] replied to his questioner, 'action,' what second, 'action,' and again third, 'action'.
Demosthenes c.384—c.322 BC: Cicero *Brutus*

6 Grasp the subject, the words will follow.
Cato the Elder 234–149 BC: Caius Julius Victor *Ars Rhetorica*

7 Friends, Romans, countrymen, lend me your ears.
William Shakespeare 1564–1616: *Julius Caesar* (1599)

8 But all was false and hollow; though his tongue
Dropped manna, and could make the worse appear
The better reason.
John Milton 1608–74: *Paradise Lost* (1667)

9 And adepts in the speaking trade
Keep a cough by them ready made.
Charles Churchill 1731–64: *The Ghost* (1763)

10 Not merely a chip of the old 'block', but the old block itself.

on the younger Pitt's maiden speech, February 1781
Edmund Burke 1729–97: N. W. Wraxall *Historical Memoirs of My Own Time* (1904 ed.); see **The Family** 8

11 The Right Honourable gentleman is indebted to his memory for his jests, and to his imagination for his facts.

Richard Brinsley Sheridan 1751–1816: speech in reply to Mr Dundas; T. Moore *Life of Sheridan* (1825)

12 He [Lord Charles Beresford] is one of those orators of whom it was well said, 'Before they get up, they do not know what they are going to say; when they are speaking, they do not know what they are saying; and when they have sat down, they do not know what they have said.'

Winston Churchill 1874–1965: speech, House of Commons, 20 December 1912

13 M. Clemenceau . . . is one of the greatest living orators, but he knows that the finest eloquence is that which gets things done and the worst is that which delays them.

David Lloyd George 1863–1945: speech at Paris Peace Conference, 18 January 1919

14 If I am to speak for ten minutes, I need a week for preparation; if fifteen minutes, three days; if half an hour, two days; if an hour, I am ready now.

Woodrow Wilson 1856–1924: Josephus Daniels *The Wilson Era* (1946)

15 If you don't say anything, you won't be called on to repeat it.

Calvin Coolidge 1872–1933: attributed

16 He [Winston Churchill] mobilized the English language and sent it into battle to steady his fellow countrymen and hearten those Europeans upon whom the long dark night of tyranny had descended.

Ed Murrow 1908–65: broadcast, 30 November 1954

17 It was the nation and the race dwelling all round the globe that had the lion's heart. I had the luck to be called upon to give the roar. I also hope that I sometimes suggested to the lion the right place to use his claws.

Winston Churchill 1874–1965: speech at Westminster Hall, 30 November 1954

18 I take the view, and always have, that if you cannot say what you are going to say in twenty minutes you ought to go away and write a book about it.

Lord Brabazon 1884–1964: speech, House of Lords, 21 June 1955

19 I do not object to people looking at their watches when I am speaking. But I strongly object when they start shaking them to make certain they are still going.

Lord Birkett 1883–1962: in *Observer* 30 October 1960

20 Do you remember that in classical times when Cicero had finished speaking, the people said, 'How well he spoke', but when Demosthenes had finished speaking, they said, 'Let us march.'

introducing John F. Kennedy in 1960
Adlai Stevenson 1900–65: Bert Cochran *Adlai Stevenson*

21 Humming, Hawing and Hesitation are the three Graces of contemporary Parliamentary oratory.

Julian Critchley 1930–2000: *Westminster Blues* (1985)

Sports and Games see also **Cricket, Football, Hunting, Shooting, and Fishing, Winning and Losing**

PROVERBS AND SAYINGS

1 **Nice guys finish last.**
after Leo Durocher: see 18 below

PHRASES

2 **the blue ribbon of the turf** the Derby.
from Disraeli Lord George Bentinck (1852); a horse bred and sold by Lord George subsequently won the Derby, and Lord George coined this phrase in explaining to Disraeli his bitter disappointment at not still owning the horse, with the words 'you do not know what the Derby is'; see **Excellence** 5

3 **rumble in the jungle** the boxing match between Muhammad Ali and George Foreman in Zaire in 1974.

4 **the sport of kings** horse-racing.
*the term was originally applied to war and later hunting; see **Hunting** 6*

5 There is plenty of time to win this game, and to thrash the Spaniards too.
receiving news of the Armada while playing bowls on Plymouth Hoe
Francis Drake c.1540–96: attributed, in *Dictionary of National Biography* (1917–)

6 When we have matched our rackets to these balls,
We will in France, by God's grace, play a set
Shall strike his father's crown into the hazard.
William Shakespeare 1564–1616: *Henry V* (1599)

7 Chaos umpire sits,
And by decision more embroils the fray.
John Milton 1608–74: *Paradise Lost* (1667)

8 I am sorry I have not learned to play at cards. It is very useful in life: it generates kindness and consolidates society.
Samuel Johnson 1709–84: James Boswell *Journal of a Tour to the Hebrides* (1785) 21 November 1773

9 What a sad old age you are preparing for yourself.
to a young diplomat who boasted of his ignorance of whist
Charles-Maurice de Talleyrand 1754–1838: J. Amédée Pichot *Souvenirs Intimes sur M. de Talleyrand* (1870)

10 The harmless art of knucklebones has seen the fall of the Roman empire and the rise of the United States.
Robert Louis Stevenson 1850–94: *Across the Plains* (1892) 'The Lantern-Bearers'

11 And it's not for the sake of a ribboned coat, Or the selfish hope of a season's fame,
But his Captain's hand on his shoulder smote—
'Play up! play up! and play the game!'
Henry Newbolt 1862–1938: 'Vitaï Lampada' (1897)

12 To play billiards well is a sign of an ill-spent youth.
Charles Roupell: attributed; D. Duncan *Life of Herbert Spencer* (1908)

13 Take me out to the ball game, Take me out with the crowd.
Buy me some peanuts and cracker-jack— I don't care if I never get back.
Jack Norworth 1879–1959: 'Take Me Out to the Ball Game' (1908 song)

14 Golf is a good walk spoiled.
Mark Twain 1835–1910: Alex Ayres *Greatly Exaggerated: the Wit and Wisdom of Mark Twain* (1988); attributed

15 We was robbed!
after Jack Sharkey beat Max Schmeling (of whom Jacobs was manager) in the heavyweight title fight, 21 June 1932
Joe Jacobs 1896–1940: Peter Heller *In This Corner* (1975)

16 For when the One Great Scorer comes to mark against your name,
He writes—not that you won or lost—but how you played the Game.
Grantland Rice 1880–1954: 'Alumnus Football' (1941)

17 Love-thirty, love-forty, oh! weakness of joy,
The speed of a swallow, the grace of a boy,
With carefullest carelessness, gaily you won,
I am weak from your loveliness, Joan Hunter Dunn.
John Betjeman 1906–84: 'A Subaltern's Love-Song' (1945)

18 I called off his players' names as they came marching up the steps behind him . . . All nice guys. They'll finish last. Nice guys. Finish last.
casual remark at a practice ground in the presence of a number of journalists, July 1946
Leo Durocher 1906–91: *Nice Guys Finish Last* (1975); see 1 above

when asked by the coroner if he had intended to 'get Doyle in trouble':
19 Mister, it's my *business* to get him in trouble.
following the death of Jimmy Doyle from his injuries after fighting Robinson, 24 June 1947
Sugar Ray Robinson 1920–89: Sugar Ray Robinson with Dave Anderson *Sugar Ray* (1970)

20 Serious sport has nothing to do with fair play. It is bound up with hatred, jealousy, boastfulness, and disregard of all the rules.
George Orwell 1903–50: *Shooting an Elephant* (1950) 'I Write as I Please'

21 Don't look back. Something may be gaining on you.
a baseball pitcher's advice
Satchel Paige 1906–82: in *Collier's* 13 June 1953

22 If you watch a game, it's fun. If you play it, it's recreation. If you work at it, it's golf.
Bob Hope 1903– : in *Reader's Digest* October 1958

23 What I know most surely about morality and the duty of man I owe to sport.
often quoted as, ' . . . I owe to football'
Albert Camus 1913–60: Herbert R. Lottman *Albert Camus* (1979)

24 Float like a butterfly, sting like a bee.
summary of his boxing strategy
Muhammad Ali 1942- : G. Sullivan *Cassius Clay Story* (1964); probably originated by Drew 'Bundini' Brown

25 In America, it is sport that is the opiate of the masses.
Russell Baker 1925- : in *New York Times* 3 October 1967; see **Reality** 3

26 It's gonna be a thrilla, a chilla, and a killa, When I get the gorilla in Manila.
of his fight with Joe Frazier
Muhammad Ali 1942- : in 1975

27 All you have to do is keep the five players who hate your guts away from the five who are undecided.
on baseball
Casey Stengel 1891-1975: John Samuel (ed.) *The Guardian Book of Sports Quotes* (1985)

28 You cannot be serious!
John McEnroe 1959- : said to tennis umpire at Wimbledon, early 1980s

29 If people don't want to come out to the ball park, nobody's going to stop 'em.
Yogi Berra 1925- : attributed

30 New Yorkers love it when you spill your guts out there. Spill your guts at Wimbledon and they make you stop and clean it up.
Jimmy Connors 1952- : at Flushing Meadow; in *Guardian* 24 December 1984 'Sports Quotes of the Year'

31 The thing about sport, any sport, is that swearing is very much part of it.
Jimmy Greaves 1940- : in *Observer* 1 January 1989

32 Everything about sport is derived from the hunt: there is no sport in existence that does not base itself either on the chase or on aiming, the two key elements of primeval hunting.
Desmond Morris 1928- : *The Animal Contract* (1990)

33 Boxing's just show business with blood.
Frank Bruno 1961- : in *Guardian* 20 November 1991; also attributed to David Belasco in 1915

34 Baseball is very big with my people. It figures. It's the only way we can get to shake a bat at a white man without starting a riot.
Dick Gregory 1932- : D. H. Nathan (ed.) *Baseball Quotations* (1991)

35 Running's like breathing. It's something that comes really naturally.
Cathy Freeman 1973- : interview in *Daily Telegraph* 16 July 2000

Statistics see also Mathematics, Quantities and Qualities

PHRASES

1 the law of averages the supposed principle that future events are likely to turn out so that they balance any past deviation from a presumed average.
the term derives initially from Henry Thomas Buckle's The History of Civilization in England (1857): 'The great advance made by the statisticians consists in applying to these inquiries [into crime] the doctrine of averages, which no one thought of doing before the eighteenth century'. The first (sceptical) reference to 'Mr Buckle's "Law of Averages" ' is found in 1875

2 vital statistics quantitative data concerning the population, such as the number of births, marriages, and deaths; informally, the measurements of a woman's bust, waist, and hips.

QUOTATIONS

3 We are just statistics, born to consume resources.
Horace 65-8 BC: *Epistles*

4 A witty statesman said, you might prove anything by figures.
Thomas Carlyle 1795-1881: *Chartism* (1839)

5 Every moment dies a man,
Every moment one is born.
Alfred, Lord Tennyson 1809-92: 'The Vision of Sin' (1842); see 6 below

6 Every moment dies a man,
Every moment 1$\frac{1}{16}$ is born.
Charles Babbage 1792-1871: parody of Tennyson's 'Vision of Sin' in an unpublished letter to the poet; in *New Scientist* 4 December 1958; see 5 above

7 There are three kinds of lies: lies, damned lies and statistics.
Benjamin Disraeli 1804-81: attributed; Mark Twain *Autobiography* (1924)

8 Long and painful experience has taught me one great principle in managing business for other people, viz., if you want to inspire confidence, *give plenty of statistics.*
Lewis Carroll 1832–98: C. L. Dodgson *Three Years in a Curatorship by One Whom It Has Tried* (1886)

9 He uses statistics as a drunken man uses lampposts—for support rather than for illumination.
Andrew Lang 1844–1912: attributed

10 [The War Office kept three sets of figures:] one to mislead the public, another to mislead the Cabinet, and the third to mislead itself.
Herbert Asquith 1852–1928: Alistair Horne *Price of Glory* (1962)

11 If your experiment needs statistics, you ought to have done a better experiment.
Ernest Rutherford 1871–1937: Norman T. J. Bailey *The Mathematical Approach to Biology and Medicine* (1967)

12 Statistics are the triumph of the quantitative method, and the quantitative method is the victory of sterility and death.
Hilaire Belloc 1870–1953: *The Silence of the Sea* (1941)

13 The so-called science of poll-taking is not a science at all but a mere necromancy. People are unpredictable by nature, and although you can take a nation's pulse, you can't be sure that the nation hasn't just run up a flight of stairs.
E. B. White 1899–1985: in *New Yorker* 13 November 1948

14 From the fact that there are 400,000 species of beetles on this planet, but only 8,000 species of mammals, he [Haldane] concluded that the Creator, if He exists, has a special preference for beetles.
J. B. S. Haldane 1892–1964: report of lecture, 7 April 1951

15 One of the thieves was saved. (*Pause*) It's a reasonable percentage.
Samuel Beckett 1906–89: *Waiting for Godot* (1955)

16 Counting counts only when we have learnt how to count what counts.
Alan Ryan 1940– : in *Independent* 26 April 2001

Story-telling see **Fiction and Story-telling**

Strength and Weakness

PROVERBS AND SAYINGS

1 Every tub must stand on its own bottom.
mid 16th century; meaning that it is necessary to support oneself by one's own efforts

2 If you don't like the heat, get out of the kitchen.
mid 20th century, meaning that if you choose to work in a particular sphere you must also deal with its pressures; see 25 below

3 It is the pace that kills.
mid 19th century, used as a warning against working under extreme pressure

4 A reed before the wind lives on, while mighty oaks do fall.
late 14th century, meaning that a something which bends to the force of the wind is less likely to be broken than something which tries to withstand it

5 Strength through joy.
German Labour Front slogan from 1933, coined by Robert Ley (1890–1945)

6 The weakest go to the wall.
early 16th century; usually said to derive from the installation of seating (around the walls) in the churches of the late Middle Ages

7 You are the weakest link . . . goodbye.
catchphrase used by Anne Robinson on the television game-show The Weakest Link *(2000–); see* **Cooperation** *2*

PHRASES

8 Achilles heel a person's only vulnerable spot, a weak point.
from the legend of the only point at which Achilles could be wounded after he was dipped into the River Styx, his mother having held him so that his heel was protected from the river water by her grasp

9 broken reed a person who fails to give support, a weak or ineffectual person.
from the Bible (Isaiah) 'thou trustest in the staff of this broken reed, on Egypt'

10 built on sand lacking a firm foundation; unstable; ephemeral.

from the parable in the Bible (Matthew) of the two houses founded respectively on rock and on sand

11 steal someone's thunder use another person's idea, and spoil the effect the originator hoped to achieve by acting on it first.

originally thunder as a stage effect, after John Dennis: see **The Theatre** *9*

12 a tiger in one's tank energy, spirit, animation.

from an Esso petrol advertising slogan: see **Transport** *3*

13 a tower of strength a source of strong and reliable support.

perhaps originally alluding to the Book of Common Prayer *'O Lord . . . be unto them a tower of strength'*

QUOTATIONS

14 A threefold cord is not quickly broken.
Bible: Ecclesiastes

15 All the world knows that the weak overcomes the strong and the soft overcomes the hard.
But none can practice it.
Lao Tzu *c.604–c.531 BC: Tao-te Ching*

16 If God be for us, who can be against us?
Bible: Romans

17 The gods are on the side of the stronger.
Tacitus *AD c.56–after 117: Histories; see* **Armed Forces** 7

18 One hair of a woman can draw more than a hundred pair of oxen.
James Howell *c.1593–1666: Familiar Letters (1645–55); see* **Beauty** 1

19 The concessions of the weak are the concessions of fear.
Edmund Burke *1729–97: On Conciliation with America (1775)*

20 The thing is, you see, that the strongest man in the world is the man who stands most alone.
Henrik Ibsen *1828–1906: An Enemy of the People (1882)*

21 The weak are strong because they are reckless. The strong are weak because they have scruples.
Otto von Bismarck *1815–98: quoted by Henry Kissinger to James Callaghan, 1975; James Callaghan* Time and Chance *(1987)*

22 I am as strong as a bull moose and you can use me to the limit.
'Bull Moose' subsequently became the popular name of the Progressive Party
Theodore Roosevelt *1858–1919: letter to Mark Hanna, 27 June 1900*

23 This is the law of the Yukon, that only the Strong shall thrive;
That surely the Weak shall perish, and only the Fit survive.
Robert W. Service *1874–1958: 'The Law of the Yukon' (1907)*

24 Nothing is wasted, nothing is in vain:
The seas roll over but the rocks remain.
A. P. Herbert *1890–1971: Tough at the Top (operetta c.1949)*

25 If you can't stand the heat, get out of the kitchen.
Harry Vaughan: *in* Time *28 April 1952; associated with Harry S. Truman, but attributed by him to Vaughan, his 'military jester'; see 2 above*

26 The most potent weapon in the hands of the oppressor is the mind of the oppressed.
Steve Biko *1946–77: statement as witness, 3 May 1976*

27 Toughness doesn't have to come in a pinstripe suit.
Dianne Feinstein *1933– : in* Time *4 June 1984*

28 People assumed I was a lot stronger than I was because I had a big mouth and a shaved head. I acted tough to cover the vulnerability.
Sinéad O'Connor *1966– : in* Irish Times *22 November 1997*

Style *see also* **Language**

PROVERBS AND SAYINGS

1 The style is the man.
early 20th century, meaning that one's chosen style reflects one's essential characteristics; see 11 *below*

PHRASES

2 purple patch an ornate or elaborate passage in a literary composition.
from Horace: see 4 below

QUOTATIONS

3 I strive to be brief, and I become obscure.
Horace 65-8 BC: *Ars Poetica*

4 Works of serious purpose and grand
promises often have a purple patch or two
stitched on, to shine far and wide.
Horace 65-8 BC: *Ars Poetica*; see 2 above

5 I have revered always not crude verbosity,
but holy simplicity.
St Jerome c. AD 342-420: letter 'Ad Pammachium'

6 More matter with less art.
William Shakespeare 1564-1616: *Hamlet* (1601)

7 He does it with a better grace, but I do it
more natural.
William Shakespeare 1564-1616: *Twelfth Night*
(1601)

8 When we see a natural style, we are quite
surprised and delighted, for we expected to
see an author and we find a man.
Blaise Pascal 1623-62: *Pensées* (1670)

9 Style is the dress of thought; a modest
dress,
Neat, but not gaudy, will true critics
please.
Samuel Wesley 1662-1735: 'An Epistle to a Friend
concerning Poetry' (1700)

10 True wit is Nature to advantage dressed,
What oft was thought, but ne'er so well
expressed.
Alexander Pope 1688-1744: *An Essay on Criticism*
(1711)

11 These things [subject matter] are external
to the man; style is the man.
Comte de Buffon 1707-88: *Discours sur le style*;
address given to the Académie Française, 25 August
1753; see 1 above

12 The moving accident is not my trade;
To freeze the blood I have no ready arts:
'Tis my delight, alone in summer shade,
To pipe a simple song for thinking hearts.
William Wordsworth 1770-1850: 'Hart-Leap Well'
(1800)

13 Style is life! It is the very life-blood of
thought!
Gustave Flaubert 1821-80: letter to Louise Colet, 7
September 1853

14 People think that I can teach them style.
What stuff it all is! Have something to say,
and say it as clearly as you can. That is the
only secret of style.
Matthew Arnold 1822-88: G. W. E. Russell
Collections and Recollections (1898)

15 I don't wish to sign my name, though I am
afraid everybody will know who the writer
is: one's style is one's signature always.
sending a letter for publication
Oscar Wilde 1854-1900: letter to the *Daily
Telegraph*, 2 February 1891

16 As to the Adjective: when in doubt, strike
it out.
Mark Twain 1835-1910: *Pudd'nhead Wilson* (1894)

17 No flowers, by request.
*summarizing the principle of conciseness for
contributors to the* Dictionary of National Biography
Alfred Ainger 1837-1904: speech to contributors, 8
July 1897; see **Mourning** 4

18 No iron can stab the heart with such force
as a full stop put just at the right place.
Isaac Babel 1894-c.1939: *Guy de Maupassant* (1932)

19 'Feather-footed through the plashy fen
passes the questing vole' . . . 'Yes,' said the
Managing Editor. 'That must be good
style.'
Evelyn Waugh 1903-66: *Scoop* (1938)

20 The Mandarin style . . . is beloved by
literary pundits, by those who would make
the written word as unlike as possible to
the spoken one.
Cyril Connolly 1903-74: *Enemies of Promise* (1938)

21 I am well aware that an addiction to silk
underwear does not necessarily imply that
one's feet are dirty. Nonetheless, style, like
sheer silk, too often hides eczema.
Albert Camus 1913-60: *The Fall* (1956)

22 It's not what I do, but the way I do it. It's
not what I say, but the way I say it.
Mae West 1892-1980: G. Eells and S. Musgrove
Mae West (1989)

23 My style flows from the fingers. The eye
and ear approve or amend.
Bernard Malamud 1914-86: George Plimpton (ed.)
The Writer's Chapbook (1989)

Success and Failure see also Winning and Losing

PROVERBS AND SAYINGS

1 The bigger they are, the harder they fall.

early 20th century, commonly attributed in its current form to the fighter Robert Fitzsimmons, prior to a fight c.1900

2 From clogs to clogs is only three generations.

late 19th century, said to be a Lancashire proverb; the clog, a shoe with a thick wooden sole, was worn by manual workers in the north of England. The implication is that the energy and ability required to raise a person's material status from poverty is often not continued to the third generation, and that the success is therefore not sustained

3 From shirtsleeves to shirtsleeves in three generations.

early 20th century; meaning that wealth gained in one generation will be lost by the third. The saying is often attributed to the Scottish-born American industrialist and philanthropist Andrew Carnegie (1835–1919) but is not found in his writings

4 From the sublime to the ridiculous is only one step.

late 19th century; see 28, 29 below

5 Let them laugh that win.

mid 16th century, meaning that triumphant laughter should be witheld until success is assured

6 Nothing succeeds like success.

mid 19th century, meaning that someone already regarded as successful is likely to attract more support

7 The only place where success comes before work is in a dictionary.

modern saying

8 The race is not to the swift, nor the battle to the strong.

mid 17th century, meaning that the person with the most apparent advantages will not necessarily be successful; see 20 below

9 A rising tide lifts all boats.

mid 20th century, usually taken to mean that a prosperous society benefits everybody; in America the expression was particularly associated with John Fitzgerald Kennedy (1917–63)

10 Success has many fathers, while failure is an orphan.

mid 20th century, meaning that once something is seen to succeed many people will claim to have initiated it, while responsibility for failure is likely to be disclaimed; see 41 below

11 Up like a rocket, down like a stick.

late 19th century, meaning that sudden marked success is likely to be followed by equally sudden failure; see 27 below

12 You win a few, you lose a few.

mid 20th century, meaning that one has to accept failure as well as success, and used as an expression of consolation or resignation

PHRASES

13 the bitch goddess material or worldly success as an object of attainment.
from William James: see 34 below

14 the golden rule a basic principle which should always be followed to ensure success in general or in a particular activity.
*the term is sometimes specifically used of the injunction given by Jesus in the Bible: see **Lifestyles** 15, **Likes** 13*

15 one's finest hour the time of one's greatest success.
*now particularly associated with Churchill: see **World War II** 11*

16 place in the sun one's share of good fortune or prosperity; a favourable situation or position, prominence.
*associated with German nationalism (see **International Relations** 23) but earlier recorded in the writings of Pascal (translation 1688)*

17 weighed in the balance and found wanting having failed to meet the test of a particular situation
*in the Bible (Daniel), part of the judgement made on King Belshazzar by the writing on the wall: see **The Future** 10*

18 win one's laurels succeed publicly, achieve one's due reward of acknowledgement and praise.
*laurels the foliage of the bay-tree (real or imaginary) as an emblem of victory or of distinction; see **Envy** 16, **Reputation** 14, **Youth** 14*

19 win one's spurs attain distinction, achieve one's first honours.
*spurs as an emblem of knighthood, especially gained by an act of valour; see **Effort** 12*

20 The race is not to the swift, nor the battle to the strong.
Bible: Ecclesiastes; see 8 above

21 *Veni, vidi, vici.*
I came, I saw, I conquered.
Julius Caesar 100–44 BC: inscription displayed in Caesar's Pontic triumph, according to Suetonius *Lives of the Caesars* 'Divus Julius'; or, according to Plutarch *Parallel Lives* 'Julius Caesar', written in a letter by Caesar, announcing the victory of Zela which concluded the Pontic campaign

22 For what shall it profit a man, if he shall gain the whole world, and lose his own soul?
Bible: St Mark; see **Wales** 10

23 Of all I had, only honour and life have been spared.
usually quoted 'All is lost save honour'
Francis I of France 1494–1547: letter to his mother following his defeat at Pavia, 1525

24 MACBETH: If we should fail,—
LADY MACBETH: We fail!
But screw your courage to the sticking-place,
And we'll not fail.
William Shakespeare 1564–1616: *Macbeth* (1606)

25 'Tis not in mortals to command success,
But we'll do more, Sempronius; we'll deserve it.
Joseph Addison 1672–1719: *Cato* (1713)

26 The conduct of a losing party never appears right: at least it never can possess the only infallible criterion of wisdom to vulgar judgements—success.
Edmund Burke 1729–97: *Letter to a Member of the National Assembly* (1791)

27 As he rose like a rocket, he fell like the stick.
on Edmund Burke losing the parliamentary debate on the French Revolution to Charles James Fox
Thomas Paine 1737–1809: *Letter to the Addressers on the late Proclamation* (1792); see 11 above

28 The sublime and the ridiculous are often so nearly related, that it is difficult to class them separately. One step above the sublime, makes the ridiculous; and one step above the ridiculous, makes the sublime again.
Thomas Paine 1737–1809: *The Age of Reason* pt. 2 (1795); see 4 above, 29 below

29 There is only one step from the sublime to the ridiculous.
to De Pradt, Polish ambassador, after the retreat from Moscow in 1812
Napoléon I 1769–1821: D. G. De Pradt *Histoire de l'Ambassade dans le grand-duché de Varsovie en 1812* (1815); see 4, 28 above

30 It was roses, roses, all the way.
Robert Browning 1812–89: 'The Patriot' (1855)

31 I have climbed to the top of the greasy pole.
on becoming Prime Minister
Benjamin Disraeli 1804–81: W. Monypenny and G. Buckle *Life of Benjamin Disraeli* vol. 4 (1916)

32 Success is a science; if you have the conditions, you get the result.
Oscar Wilde 1854–1900: letter ?March–April 1883

33 All you need in this life is ignorance and confidence; then success is sure.
Mark Twain 1835–1910: letter to Mrs Foote, 2 December 1887

34 The moral flabbiness born of the exclusive worship of the bitch-goddess *success*.
William James 1842–1910: letter to H. G. Wells, 11 September 1906; see 13 above

35 The world continues to offer glittering prizes to those who have stout hearts and sharp swords.
F. E. Smith 1872–1930: Rectorial Address, Glasgow University, 7 November 1923

36 Anybody seen in a bus over the age of 30 has been a failure in life.
Loelia, Duchess of Westminster 1902–93: in *The Times* 4 November 1993 (obituary); habitual remark

37 You [the Mensheviks] are pitiful isolated individuals; you are bankrupts; your role is played out. Go where you belong from now on — into the dustbin of history!
Leon Trotsky 1879–1940: *History of the Russian Revolution* (1933)

38 How to win friends and influence people.
Dale Carnegie 1888–1955: title of book (1936)

39 History to the defeated
May say Alas but cannot help or pardon.
W. H. Auden 1907–73: 'Spain 1937' (1937)

40 Success is relative:
It is what we can make of the mess we have made of things.
T. S. Eliot 1888–1965: *The Family Reunion* (1939)

41 Victory has a hundred fathers, but no-one wants to recognise defeat as his own.
Count Galeazzo Ciano 1903–44: diary, 9 September 1942; see 10 above

42 And all my endeavours are unlucky
   explorers
come back, abandoning the expedition.
Keith Douglas 1920-44: 'On Return from Egypt,
1943-4' (1946)

43 If *A* is a success in life, then *A* equals *x* plus
y plus *z*. Work is *x*; *y* is play; and *z* is
keeping your mouth shut.
Albert Einstein 1879-1955: in *Observer* 15 January
1950

44 For a writer, success is always temporary,
success is only a delayed failure. And it is
incomplete.
Graham Greene 1904-91: *A Sort of Life* (1971)

45 Whenever a friend succeeds, a little
something in me dies.
Gore Vidal 1925- : in *Sunday Times Magazine* 16
September 1973

46 Is it possible to succeed without any act of
betrayal?
Jean Renoir 1894-1979: *My Life and My Films* (1974)

47 Ever tried. Ever failed. No matter. Try
again. Fail again. Fail better.
Samuel Beckett 1906-89: *Worstward Ho* (1983)

48 In the United States there's a Puritan ethic
and a mythology of success. He who is
successful is good. In Latin countries, in
Catholic countries, a successful person is a
sinner.
Umberto Eco 1932- : in *International Herald Tribune*
14 December 1988

49 Fame has a bloody long sell-by date. You
reach a certain level and it is pumped with
preservatives, like long-life milk. But
success is like fresh fruit: it perishes every
day.
Luke Goss 1968- : in *Observer* 11 March 2001

Suffering see also **Mourning and Loss**, **Sorrow**, **Sympathy and Consolation**

PROVERBS AND SAYINGS

1 Beauty without cruelty.
slogan for Animal Rights

2 Crosses are ladders that lead to heaven.
*early 17th century, meaning that the way to heaven is
through suffering; crosses refers either to the crucifix,
or more generally to troubles or misfortunes*

3 Ee, it was agony, Ivy.
catchphrase from Ray's a Laugh (*BBC radio
programme, 1949-61), written by Ted Ray*

QUOTATIONS

4 They that sow in tears: shall reap in joy.
Bible: Psalm 126

5 Out of the deep have I called unto thee, O
Lord: Lord, hear my voice.
Bible: Psalm 130; see **Sorrow** 3

6 Nothing happens to anybody which he is
not fitted by nature to bear.
Marcus Aurelius AD 121-80: *Meditations*

7 All those who suffer in the world do so
because of their desire for their own
happiness.
Shantideva c.685-763: *Bodhicaryāvatāra* ch. 8, v.
129

8 If you bear the cross gladly, it will bear
you.
Thomas à Kempis c.1380-1471: *The Imitation of
Christ*

9 Be grateful for, not blind to the many,
many sufferings which thou art spared;
thou art no better than those who have
been searched out and racked by them.
Orchoth Zadikkim c.15th century: *Orchoth
Zaddikim*

10 He jests at scars, that never felt a wound.
William Shakespeare 1564-1616: *Romeo and Juliet*
(1595)

11   The worst is not,
So long as we can say, 'This is the worst.'
William Shakespeare 1564-1616: *King Lear*
(1605-6)

12 Our torments also may in length of time
Become our elements.
John Milton 1608-74: *Paradise Lost* (1667)

13 No pain, no palm; no thorns, no throne;
no gall, no glory; no cross, no crown.
William Penn 1644-1718: *No Cross, No Crown* (1669
pamphlet)

14 To each his suff'rings, all are men,
Condemned alike to groan;
The tender for another's pain,

Th' unfeeling for his own.
Thomas Gray 1716–71: *Ode on a Distant Prospect of Eton College* (1747)

15 Thank you, madam, the agony is abated.
aged four, having had hot coffee spilt over his legs
Lord Macaulay 1800–59: G. O. Trevelyan *Life and Letters of Lord Macaulay* (1876)

16 Misery such as mine has no pride. I care not who knows that I am wretched.
Jane Austen 1775–1817: *Sense and Sensibility* (1811)

17 Suffering is permanent, obscure and dark, And shares the nature of infinity.
William Wordsworth 1770–1850: *The Borderers* (1842)

18 Sorrow and silence are strong, and patient endurance is godlike.
Henry Wadsworth Longfellow 1807–82: *Evangeline* (1847)

19   For frequent tears have run The colours from my life.
Elizabeth Barrett Browning 1806–61: *Sonnets from the Portuguese* (1850)

20 After great pain, a formal feeling comes— The Nerves sit ceremonious, like Tombs— The stiff Heart questions was it He, that bore, And Yesterday, or Centuries before?
Emily Dickinson 1830–86: 'After great pain, a formal feeling comes' (1862)

21 The toad beneath the harrow knows Exactly where each tooth-point goes; The butterfly upon the road Preaches contentment to that toad.
Rudyard Kipling 1865–1936: 'Pagett, MP' (1886); see **Adversity** 8

22 What does not kill me makes me stronger.
Friedrich Nietzsche 1844–1900: *Twilight of the Idols* (1889)

23 Nothing begins, and nothing ends, That is not paid with moan; For we are born in other's pain, And perish in our own.
Francis Thompson 1859–1907: 'Daisy' (1913)

24 Tragedy ought really to be a great kick at misery.
D. H. Lawrence 1885–1930: letter to A. W. McLeod, 6 October 1912

25 It is not true that suffering ennobles the character; happiness does that sometimes, but suffering, for the most part, makes men petty and vindictive.
W. Somerset Maugham 1874–1965: *The Moon and Sixpence* (1919)

26 Too long a sacrifice Can make a stone of the heart. O when may it suffice?
W. B. Yeats 1865–1939: 'Easter, 1916' (1921)

27 The point is that nobody likes having salt rubbed into their wounds, even if it is the salt of the earth.
Rebecca West 1892–1983: *The Salt of the Earth* (1935); see **Virtue** 11

28 About suffering they were never wrong, The Old Masters: how well they understood Its human position; how it takes place While someone else is eating or opening a window or just walking dully along.
W. H. Auden 1907–73: 'Musée des Beaux Arts' (1940)

29 That was how his life happened. No mad hooves galloping in the sky, But the weak, washy way of true tragedy— A sick horse nosing around the meadow for a clean place to die.
Patrick Kavanagh 1904–67: 'The Great Hunger' (1947)

30 Willy Loman never made a lot of money. His name was never in the paper. He's not the finest character that ever lived. But he's a human being, and a terrible thing is happening to him. So attention must be paid.
Arthur Miller 1915– : *Death of a Salesman* (1949)

31 How can you expect a man who's warm to understand one who's cold?
Alexander Solzhenitsyn 1918– : *One Day in the Life of Ivan Denisovich* (1962)

32 Children's talent to endure stems from their ignorance of alternatives.
Maya Angelou 1928– : *I Know Why The Caged Bird Sings* (1969)

33 The most extreme agony is to feel that one has been utterly forsaken.
Bruno Bettelheim 1903–90: *Surviving and other essays* (1979)

34 Scars have the strange power to remind us that our past is real.
Cormac McCarthy 1933– : *All the Pretty Horses* (1993)

Suicide

PHRASES

1 assisted suicide the suicide of a patient suffering from an incurable disease, effected by the taking of lethal drugs provided by a doctor for this purpose.

2 kamikaze pilot in the Second World War, the pilot of a Japanese aircraft loaded with explosives and making a deliberate suicidal crash on an enemy target.

kamikaze = Japanese, from kami *'divinity'* + kaze *'wind'*, originally referring to the gale that, in Japanese tradition, destroyed the fleet of invading Mongols in 1281

QUOTATIONS

3 For who would bear the whips and scorns of time,
The oppressor's wrong, the proud man's contumely,
The pangs of disprized love, the law's delay,
The insolence of office, and the spurns
That patient merit of the unworthy takes,
When he himself might his quietus make
With a bare bodkin?
William Shakespeare 1564–1616: *Hamlet* (1601)

4 In chains and darkness, wherefore should I stay,
And mourn in prison, while I keep the key?
Lady Mary Wortley Montagu 1689–1762: 'Verses on Self-Murder' (1749)

5 All this buttoning and unbuttoning.
Anonymous: 18th-century suicide note

6   Nor at all can tell
Whether I mean this day to end myself,
Or lend an ear to Plato where he says,
That men like soldiers may not quit the post

Allotted by the Gods.
Alfred, Lord Tennyson 1809–92: 'Lucretius' (1868)

7 The thought of suicide is a great source of comfort: with it a calm passage is to be made across many a bad night.
Friedrich Nietzsche 1844–1900: *Jenseits von Gut und Böse* (1886)

8 In this life there's nothing new in dying,
But nor, of course, is living any newer.
his final poem, written in his own blood the day before he hanged himself in his Leningrad hotel room
Sergei Yesenin 1895–1925: 'Goodbye, my Friend, Goodbye' (1925)

9 Guns aren't lawful;
Nooses give;
Gas smells awful;
You might as well live.
Dorothy Parker 1893–1967: 'Résumé' (1937)

10 A suicide kills two people, Maggie, that's what it's for!
Arthur Miller 1915– : *After the Fall* (1964)

11 But suicides have a special language.
Like carpenters they want to know *which tools*.
They never ask *why build*.
Anne Sexton 1928–74: 'Wanting to Die' (1966)

12 It's better to burn out
Than to fade away.
Neil Young 1945– : 'My My, Hey Hey (Out of the Blue)' (1978 song, with Jeff Blackburn); quoted by Kurt Cobain in his suicide note, 8 April 1994

13 Suicide is no more than a trick played on the calendar.
Tom Stoppard 1937– : *The Dog It Was That Died* (1983)

14 Without the possibility of suicide, I would have killed myself long ago.
E. M. Cioran 1911–95: in *Independent* 2 December 1989

The Supernatural see also The Paranormal

PROVERBS AND SAYINGS

1 From ghoulies and ghosties and long-leggety beasties

And things that go bump in the night,
Good Lord, deliver us!
'The Cornish or West Country Litany'; see 4 below

PHRASES

2 bell, book, and candle the formulaic requirements for laying a curse on someone.

with allusion to the rite of excommunication, 'Do to the book, quench the candle, ring the bell'; see **Crime** *30,* **Greed** *9*

3 the good neighbours fairies; witches.

4 things that go bump in the night supernatural manifestations as a source of night-time terror.

from 'The Cornish or West Country Litany': see 1 above

5 the wee folk fairies.

6 a witch of Endor a medium.

from the story in the Bible (I Samuel) of 'a woman that hath a familiar spirit at Endor', who with its help conjured up the spirit of the dead prophet Samuel for Saul; see 21 below

QUOTATIONS

7 Then a spirit passed before my face; the hair of my flesh stood up.
Bible: Job

8 May the gods avert this omen.
Cicero 106–43 BC: *Third Philippic*

9 For we wrestle not against flesh and blood, but against principalities, against powers, against the rulers of the darkness of this world, against spiritual wickedness in high places.
Bible: Ephesians

10 Hence, a devout Christian must avoid astrologers and all impious soothsayers, especially when they tell the truth, for fear of leading his soul into error by consorting with demons and entangling himself with the bonds of such association.
St Augustine of Hippo AD 354–430: *De Genesi ad Litteram*; see **Mathematics** 1

11 There are more things in heaven and earth, Horatio,
Than are dreamt of in your philosophy.
William Shakespeare 1564–1616: *Hamlet* (1601); see **Universe** 11

12 Double, double toil and trouble;
Fire burn and cauldron bubble.
William Shakespeare 1564–1616: *Macbeth* (1606)

13 There is a superstition in avoiding superstition.
Francis Bacon 1561–1626: *Essays* (1625) 'Of Superstition'

14 Anno 1670, not far from Cirencester, was an apparition; being demanded whether a good spirit or a bad? returned no answer, but disappeared with a curious perfume and most melodious twang. Mr W. Lilly believes it was a fairy.
John Aubrey 1626–97: *Miscellanies* (1696) 'Apparitions'

15 All argument is against it; but all belief is for it.
of the existence of ghosts
Samuel Johnson 1709–84: James Boswell *Life of Samuel Johnson* (1791) 31 March 1778

16 He dug up a fairy-mount against my advice, and had no luck afterwards.
Maria Edgeworth 1767–1849: *Castle Rackrent* (1800)

17 Superstition is the poetry of life.
Johann Wolfgang von Goethe 1749–1832: *Maximen und Reflexionen* (1819) 'Literatur und Sprache'

18 Up the airy mountain,
Down the rushy glen,
We daren't go a-hunting,
For fear of little men.
William Allingham 1824–89: 'The Fairies' (1850)

19 The Universe of Magic is in the mind of a man: the setting is but Illusion even to the thinker.
Aleister Crowley 1875–1947: in *Equinox* 1909

20 There are fairies at the bottom of our garden!
Rose Fyleman 1877–1957: 'The Fairies' (1918)

21 Oh, the road to En-dor is the oldest road
And the craziest road of all!
Straight it runs to the Witch's abode
As it did in the days of Saul,
And nothing has changed of the sorrow in store
For such as go down on the road to En-dor!
Rudyard Kipling 1865–1936: 'En-dor' (1914–19); see 6 above

22 Every time a child says 'I don't believe in fairies' there is a little fairy somewhere that falls down dead.
J. M. Barrie 1860–1937: *Peter Pan* (1928)

23 There are many strange things in the world beyond our knowledge, and maybe there are ghosts too, though I do not understand why they should come back to this world when they have gone from it.
Peig Sayers 1873–1958: *The Western Island* (1944)

24 Do not meddle in the affairs of Wizards, for they are subtle and quick to anger.
J. R. R. Tolkien 1892–1973: *The Lord of the Rings* pt. 1 *The Fellowship of the Ring* (1954)

25 The twilight is the crack between the worlds. It is the door to the unknown.
Carlos Castaneda c.1925–98: *Tales of Power* (1974)

26 In every generation there is a Chosen One. She alone will stand against the vampires, the demons, and the forces of darkness. She is the Slayer.
Joss Whedon 1964– : *Buffy the Vampire Slayer* (TV series, 1997–), episode 1, opening words

27 I would love to meet a ghost, even though I don't believe in them. The reason is that if I met one, I would ask it some sensible questions about the afterlife and nobody seems to do that, do they?
Paul Daniels 1938– : *Under No Illusion* (2000, with Chris Gidney)

28 I have yet to meet a single child who has told me that they want to be a Satanist or are interested in the occult because of the book.
on the influence of her Harry Potter books
J. K. Rowling 1965– : in 2000

Surprise

PROVERBS AND SAYINGS

1 The age of miracles is past.
late sixteenth century, often used ironically, or as a comment on failure

2 Nobody expects the Spanish Inquisition.
from a Monty Python *script: see 14 below*

3 The unexpected always happens.
late 19th century, warning against an overconfident belief that something cannot occur

4 Wonders will never cease.
late 18th century, often used ironically to comment on an unusual circumstance

5 You could have knocked me down with a feather.
mid 19th century saying, expressing great surprise

PHRASES

6 pennies from heaven unexpected benefits, especially financial ones.
song-title, 1936: see **Optimism** 29

7 a Scarborough warning very short notice, no notice at all.
proverbial; explained by Thomas Fuller as relating to the surprise capture of Scarborough Castle by Thomas Stafford in 1557, but the first recorded use predates this by eleven years

QUOTATIONS

8 O wonderful, wonderful, and most wonderful wonderful! and yet again wonderful, and after that, out of all whooping!
William Shakespeare 1564–1616: *As You Like It* (1599)

9 Surprises are foolish things. The pleasure is not enhanced, and the inconvenience is often considerable.
Jane Austen 1775–1817: *Emma* (1816)

10 I'm Gormed—and I can't say no fairer than that!
Charles Dickens 1812–70: *David Copperfield* (1850)

11 'Curiouser and curiouser!' cried Alice.
Lewis Carroll 1832–98: *Alice's Adventures in Wonderland* (1865)

12 I turned to Aunt Agatha, whose demeanour was now rather like that of one who, picking daisies on the railway, has just caught the down express in the small of the back.
P. G. Wodehouse 1881–1975: *The Inimitable Jeeves* (1923)

13 It was quite the most incredible event that has ever happened to me in my life. It was almost as incredible as if you fired a 15-inch shell at a piece of tissue paper and it came back and hit you.
on the back-scattering effect of metal foil on alpha-particles
Ernest Rutherford 1871–1937: E. N. da C. Andrade *Rutherford and the Nature of the Atom* (1964)

14 Nobody expects the Spanish Inquisition! Our chief weapon is surprise—surprise and fear . . . fear and surprise . . . our two weapons are fear and surprise—and ruthless efficiency . . .
Graham Chapman 1941–89 et al.: *Monty Python's Flying Circus* (BBC TV programme, 1970); see 2 above

Swearing

1 Excuse (or pardon) my French.
an informal apology for swearing

PHRASES

2 four-letter word any of several short words referring to sexual or excretory functions, regarded as coarse or offensive.

3 not Pygmalion likely not bloody likely.
a humorous euphemism deriving from Shaw's Pygmalion (1916), which caused a public sensation at the time of the first London production; see **Transport** *13*

QUOTATIONS

4 Swear not at all; neither by heaven; for it is God's throne:
Nor by the earth; for it is his footstool.
Bible: St Matthew

5 You taught me language; and my profit on't
Is, I know how to curse: the red plague rid you,
For learning me your language!
William Shakespeare 1564–1616: *The Tempest* (1611)

6 'Our armies swore terribly in Flanders,' cried my uncle Toby,—'but nothing to this.'
Laurence Sterne 1713–68: *Tristram Shandy* (1759–67)

7 Though 'Bother it' I may
Occasionally say,
I never use a big, big D—
W. S. Gilbert 1836–1911: *HMS Pinafore* (1878)

8 A swear word in a rustic slum
A simple swear word is to some,

To Masefield something more.
Max Beerbohm 1872–1956: *Fifty Caricatures* (1912)

9 If ever I utter an oath again may my soul be blasted to eternal damnation!
George Bernard Shaw 1856–1950: *Saint Joan* (1924)

10 Orchestras only need to be sworn at, and a German is consequently at an advantage with them, as English profanity, except in America, has not gone beyond the limited terminology of perdition.
George Bernard Shaw 1856–1950: Harold Schonberg *The Great Conductors* (1967)

11 I doubt if there are very many rational people in this world to whom the word 'fuck' is particularly diabolical or revolting or totally forbidden.
Kenneth Tynan 1927–80: *BBC-3* (television programme) 13 November 1965

12 The man who first abused his fellows with swear words instead of bashing their brains out with a club should be counted among those who laid the foundations of civilization.
John Cohen 1911– : in *Observer* 21 November 1965

13 Don't swear, boy. It shows a lack of vocabulary.
Alan Bennett 1934– : *Forty Years On* (1969)

14 Expletive deleted.
Anonymous: *Submission of Recorded Presidential Conversations to the Committee on the Judiciary of the House of Representatives by President Richard M. Nixon* 30 April 1974

15 Swear words are neutral; they only become objectionable when someone is offended by them. The art of good manners (as well as bad manners) is knowing who will be offended by what.
John Rae 1931– : *Letters from School* (1987)

Sympathy and Consolation

1 God makes the back to the burden.
early 19th century, an assertion that nothing is truly insupportable used in resignation or consolation

2 God tempers the wind to the shorn lamb.
mid 17th century, meaning that God so arranges it that bad luck does not unduly plague the weak or unfortunate

3 Laugh and the world laughs with you, weep and you weep alone.

late 19th century; see **Sorrow** *20*

4 Nothing so bad but it might have been worse.

late 19th century, used in resignation or consolation

5 Pity is akin to love.

early 17th century

PHRASES

6 a Job's comforter a person who aggravates distress while seeking to give comfort.

Job the biblical patriarch, who responded to the exhortations of his friends, 'miserable comforters are ye all'; see **Patience** *19*

7 milk of human kindness compassion, sympathy.

originally from Shakespeare's Lady Macbeth: see 14 below; see also **Writers** *19*

8 tea and sympathy hospitality and consolation offered to a distressed person.

the phrase was used as a film title in 1956

QUOTATIONS

9 Heaven and Earth are not ruthful;
To them the Ten Thousand Things are but
    as straw dogs.

Ten Thousand Things *all life forms;* straw dogs *sacrificial tokens*

Lao-tsu c.604–c.531 BC: *Tao-Tê-Ching*

10 If you want me to weep, you must first feel grief yourself.

Horace 65–8 BC: *Ars Poetica*

11 O divine Master, grant that I may not so
    much seek
To be consoled as to console;
To be understood as to understand.

St Francis of Assisi 1181–1226: 'Prayer of St Francis'; attributed

12 For pitee renneth soone in gentil herte.

Geoffrey Chaucer c.1343–1400: *The Canterbury Tales* 'The Knight's Tale'

13 But yet the pity of it, Iago! O! Iago, the pity of it, Iago!

William Shakespeare 1564–1616: *Othello* (1602–4)

14 Yet I do fear thy nature;
It is too full o' the milk of human kindness

To catch the nearest way.

William Shakespeare 1564–1616: *Macbeth* (1606); see 7 above

15 We are all strong enough to bear the misfortunes of others.

Duc de la Rochefoucauld 1613–80: *Maximes* (1678)

16 If a madman were to come into this room with a stick in his hand, no doubt we should pity the state of his mind; but our primary consideration would be to take care of ourselves. We should knock him down first, and pity him afterwards.

Samuel Johnson 1709–84: House of Commons, 3 April 1776

17 Our sympathy is cold to the relation of distant misery.

Edward Gibbon 1737–94: *The Decline and Fall of the Roman Empire* (1776–88)

18 Then cherish pity, lest you drive an angel
    from your door.

William Blake 1757–1827: 'Holy Thursday' (1789)

19 Nobody can tell what I suffer! But it is always so. Those who do not complain are never pitied.

Jane Austen 1775–1817: *Pride and Prejudice* (1813)

20 They charge me with fanaticism. If to be feelingly alive to the sufferings of my fellow-creatures is to be a fanatic, I am one of the most incurable fanatics ever permitted to be at large.

William Wilberforce 1759–1833: in House of Commons, 19 June 1816

21 Hatred is a tonic, it makes one live, it inspires vengeance; but pity kills, it makes our weakness weaker.

Honoré de Balzac 1799–1850: *La Peau de Chagrin* (1831)

22 Only the hopeless are starkly sincere and . . . only the unhappy can either give or take sympathy.

Jean Rhys c.1890–1979: *The Left Bank* (1927)

23 If you see anybody fallen by the wayside and lying in the ditch, it isn't much good climbing into the ditch and lying by his side.

Dick Sheppard 1880–1937: Carolyn Scott *Dick Sheppard* (1977)

24 Intellectual disgrace
Stares from every human face,
And the seas of pity lie

Locked and frozen in each eye.
W. H. Auden 1907–73: 'In Memory of W. B. Yeats'
(1940)

25 Any victim demands allegiance.
Graham Greene 1904–91: *The Heart of the Matter*
(1948)

26 The fact that I have no remedy for the
sorrows of the world is no reason for my
accepting yours. It simply supports the
strong probability that yours is a fake.
H. L. Mencken 1880–1956: *Minority Report* (1956)

27 When times get rough,
And friends just can't be found
Like a bridge over troubled water

I will lay me down.
Paul Simon 1942– : 'Bridge over Troubled Water'
(1970 song)

28 You can't cry on a shoulder that's wearing
a shoulder pad.
Steven Spielberg 1947– : in *Rolling Stone* 22 July
1982

29 We didn't have counsellors rushing
around every time somebody let off a gun,
you know, asking 'Are you all right—are
you sure you don't have a ghastly
problem?' You just got on with it.
on his shipmates in the Second World War
Prince Philip, Duke of Edinburgh 1921– : BBC TV
interview, August 1999

Taste

PHRASES

1 arbiter elegantiarum an authority on
matters of taste or etiquette.
Latin: see 2 below

QUOTATIONS

2 *Elegantiae arbiter.*
The arbiter of taste.
of Petronius
Tacitus AD c.56–after 117: *Annals*; see 1 above

3 The play, I remember, pleased not the
million; 'twas caviar to the general.
William Shakespeare 1564–1616: *Hamlet* (1601);
see **Futility** 9

4 Between good sense and good taste there is
the same difference as between cause and
effect.
Jean de la Bruyère 1645–96: *Les Caractères ou les
moeurs de ce siècle* (1688) 'Des Jugements'

5 Our tastes greatly alter. The lad does not
care for the child's rattle, and the old man
does not care for the young man's whore.
Samuel Johnson 1709–84: James Boswell *Life of
Samuel Johnson* (1791) Spring 1766

6 Could we teach taste or genius by rules,
they would be no longer taste and genius.
Joshua Reynolds 1723–92: *Discourses on Art* 14
December 1770

7 Rules and models destroy genius and art.
William Hazlitt 1778–1830: *Sketches and Essays*
(1839) 'On Taste'

8 She had
A heart—how shall I say?—too soon made
glad,
Too easily impressed; she liked whate'er
She looked on, and her looks went
everywhere.
Robert Browning 1812–89: 'My Last Duchess'
(1842)

9 A difference of taste in jokes is a great
strain on the affections.
George Eliot 1819–80: *Daniel Deronda* (1876)

10 It's worse than wicked, my dear, it's
vulgar.
Punch: Almanac (1876)

11 Taste is the feminine of genius.
Edward Fitzgerald 1809–83: letter to J. R. Lowell,
October 1877

12 Nowhere probably is there more true
feeling, and nowhere worse taste, than in
a churchyard.
Benjamin Jowett 1817–93: Evelyn Abbott and Lewis
Campbell (eds.) *Letters of Benjamin Jowett* (1899)

of the wallpaper in the room where he was dying:
13 One of us must go.
Oscar Wilde 1854–1900: attributed, probably
apocryphal

14 Good taste is better than bad taste, but bad
taste is better than no taste, and men
without individuality have no taste — at
any rate no taste that they can impose on
their publics.
Arnold Bennett 1867–1931: in *Evening Standard* 21
August 1930

15 The kind of people who always go on about whether a thing is in good taste invariably have very bad taste.
Joe Orton 1933–67: in *Transatlantic Review* Spring 1967

16 So they is some people who suddenly get loads of money who become very tasteless. How has you two managed to avoid that?
interviewing David and Victoria Beckham
Ali G 1970– : in *Sunday Times* 11 February 2001

Taxes

1 Can't pay, won't pay.
anti-Poll Tax slogan, c.1990; see 3 below

2 Peter's pence an annual tax of one penny from every householder having land of a certain value, paid to the papal see at Rome from Anglo-Saxon times until discontinued in 1534 after Henry VIII's break with Rome.
St Peter regarded by Roman Catholics as the first bishop of the Church at Rome

3 poll tax a tax levied on every adult, without reference to their income or resources.
such taxes were levied in England in 1377, 1379, and 1380; the last of these is generally regarded as having contributed to the 1381 Peasants' Revolt. From the mid 1980s, the term was used informally for the community charge, a usage which reflected the tax's deep unpopularity; see 1 above

4 scot and lot a tax levied by a municipal corporation on its members for the defraying of expenses.

5 Money has no smell.
quashing an objection to a tax on public lavatories
Vespasian AD 9–79: traditional summary; Suetonius *Lives of the Caesars* 'Vespasian'; see **Money** 5

6 Neither will it be, that a people overlaid with taxes should ever become valiant and martial.
Francis Bacon 1561–1626: *Essays* (1625) 'Of the True Greatness of Kingdoms'

7 The art of taxation consists in so plucking the goose as to obtain the largest possible amount of feathers with the smallest possible amount of hissing.
Jean-Baptiste Colbert 1619–83: attributed

8 *Excise.* A hateful tax levied upon commodities.
Samuel Johnson 1709–84: *A Dictionary of the English Language* (1755)

9 Taxation without representation is tyranny.
James Otis 1725–83: watchword (c.1761) of the American Revolution; in *Dictionary of American Biography*

10 To tax and to please, no more than to love and to be wise, is not given to men.
Edmund Burke 1729–97: *On American Taxation* (1775); see **Love** 10

11 There is no art which one government sooner learns of another than that of draining money from the pockets of the people.
Adam Smith 1723–90: *Wealth of Nations* (1776)

12 The art of government is to make two-thirds of a nation pay all it possibly can pay for the benefit of the other third.
Voltaire 1694–1778: attributed; Walter Bagehot *The English Constitution* (1867)

13 All taxes must, at last, fall upon agriculture.
Edward Gibbon 1737–1794: quoting Artaxerxes, in *The Decline and Fall of the Roman Empire* (1776–88)

14 In this world nothing can be said to be certain, except death and taxes.
Benjamin Franklin 1706–90: letter to Jean Baptiste Le Roy, 13 November 1789; see **Certainty** 3

15 The Chancellor of the Exchequer is a man whose duties make him more or less of a taxing machine. He is intrusted with a certain amount of misery which it is his duty to distribute as fairly as he can.
Robert Lowe 1811–92: speech, House of Commons, 11 April 1870

16 Death is the most convenient time to tax rich people.
David Lloyd George 1863–1945: in *Lord Riddell's Intimate Diary of the Peace Conference and After*, 1918–23 (1933)

17 Income Tax has made more Liars out of the American people than Golf.
Will Rogers 1879–1935: *The Illiterate Digest* (1924) 'Helping the Girls with their Income Taxes'

18 Only the little people pay taxes.
Leona Helmsley c.1920– : addressed to her housekeeper in 1983, and reported at her trial for tax evasion; in *New York Times* 12 July 1989

19 Read my lips: no new taxes.
campaign pledge on taxation
George Bush 1924– : in *New York Times* 19 August 1988; see **Schools** 19

Teaching see also Education, Schools, Universities

PROVERBS AND SAYINGS

1 He teaches ill who teaches all.
early 17th century

2 He that teaches himself has a fool for his master.
early 17th century

3 Nobody forgets a good teacher.
Teacher Training Agency slogan, late 20th century

QUOTATIONS

4 A man who reviews the old so as to find out the new is qualified to teach others.
Confucius 551–479 BC: *Analects*

5 Even while they teach, men learn.
Seneca ('the Younger') c.4 BC–AD 65: *Epistulae Morales*

6 There is no such whetstone, to sharpen a good wit and encourage a will to learning, as is praise.
Roger Ascham 1515–68: *The Schoolmaster* (1570)

7 Men must be taught as if you taught them not,
And things unknown proposed as things forgot.
Alexander Pope 1688–1744: *An Essay on Criticism* (1711)

8 Delightful task! to rear the tender thought,
To teach the young idea how to shoot.
James Thomson 1700–48: *The Seasons* (1746) 'Spring'; see **Children** 3

9 It is no matter what you teach them [children] first, any more than what leg you shall put into your breeches first.
Samuel Johnson 1709–84: James Boswell *Life of Samuel Johnson* (1791) 26 July 1763

10 Few have been taught to any purpose who have not been their own teachers.
Joshua Reynolds 1723–92: *Discourses on Art* 11 December 1769

11 C-l-e-a-n, clean, verb active, to make bright, to scour. W-i-n, win, d-e-r, der, winder, a casement. When the boy knows this out of the book, he goes and does it.
Charles Dickens 1812–70: *Nicholas Nickleby* (1839)

12 Be a governess! Better be a slave at once!
Charlotte Brontë 1816–55: *Shirley* (1849)

13 He who can, does. He who cannot, teaches.
George Bernard Shaw 1856–1950: *Man and Superman* (1903)

14 A teacher affects eternity; he can never tell where his influence stops.
Henry Brooks Adams 1838–1918: *The Education of Henry Adams* (1907)

15 For every person who wants to teach there are approximately thirty who don't want to learn—much.
W. C. Sellar 1898–1951 and **R. J. Yeatman** 1898–1968: *And Now All This* (1932)

16 We teachers can only help the work going on, as servants wait upon a master.
Maria Montessori 1870–1952: *The Absorbent Mind* (1949)

17 That is the difference between good teachers and great teachers: good teachers make the best of a pupil's means: great teachers foresee a pupil's ends.
Maria Callas 1923–77: *Kenneth Harris Talking To* (1971) 'Maria Callas'

18 A teacher should have maximal authority and minimal power.
Thomas Szasz 1920– : *The Second Sin* (1973) 'Education'

19 Knowledge has to be sucked into the brain, not pushed into it.
Victor Weisskopf 1908–2002: *The Privilege of Being a Physicist* (1989)

20 I wouldn't wish teaching on my worst enemy's dog.
Louis de Bernières 1954– : in *Sunday Times* 18 March 2001

Technology see also **Inventions and Discoveries, Science**

PROVERBS AND SAYINGS

1 Let your fingers do the walking.
1960s advertisement for Bell system Telephone Directory Yellow Pages

2 Science finds, industry applies, man conforms.
subtitle of guidebook to 1933 Chicago World's Fair

3 Vorsprung durch Technik.
German = Progress through technology; advertising slogan for Audi motors, from 1986

PHRASES

4 the white heat of technology the most advanced form of technology.
from a misquotation of Harold Wilson: see 19 below

QUOTATIONS

5 Give me but one firm spot on which to stand, and I will move the earth.
on the action of a lever
Archimedes c.287–212 BC: Pappus *Synagoge*; see **Arts and Sciences** 8

6 I sell here, Sir, what all the world desires to have—POWER.
of his engineering works
Matthew Boulton 1728–1809: James Boswell *Life of Samuel Johnson* (1791) 22 March 1776

7 Man is a tool-using animal . . . Without tools he is nothing, with tools he is all.
Thomas Carlyle 1795–1881: *Sartor Resartus* (1834)

8 This extraordinary metal [iron], the soul of every manufacture, and the mainspring perhaps of civilized society.
Samuel Smiles 1812–1904: *Men of Invention and Industry* (1884)

9 One machine can do the work of fifty ordinary men. No machine can do the work of one extraordinary man.
Elbert Hubbard 1859–1915: *Thousand and One Epigrams* (1911)

10 Your worship is your furnaces,
Which, like old idols, lost obscenes,
Have molten bowels; your vision is
Machines for making more machines.
Gordon Bottomley 1874–1948: 'To Ironfounders and Others' (1912)

11 Machines are worshipped because they are beautiful, and valued because they confer power; they are hated because they are hideous, and loathed because they impose slavery.
Bertrand Russell 1872–1970: *Sceptical Essays* (1928) 'Machines and Emotions'

12 But far above and far as sight endures
Like whips of anger
With lightning's danger
There runs the quick perspective of the future.
Stephen Spender 1909–95: 'The Pylons' (1933)

13 This is not the age of pamphleteers. It is the age of the engineers. The spark-gap is mightier than the pen.
Lancelot Hogben 1895–1975: *Science for the Citizen* (1938); see **Ways and Means** 11

14 One servant is worth a thousand gadgets.
Joseph Alois Schumpeter 1883–1950: J. K. Galbraith *A Life in our Times* (1981)

15 When you see something that is technically sweet, you go ahead and do it and you argue about what to do about it only after you have had your technical success. That is the way it was with the atomic bomb.
J. Robert Oppenheimer 1904–67: in *In the Matter of J. Robert Oppenheimer, USAEC Transcript of Hearing Before Personnel Security Board* (1954)

16 It has been said that an engineer is a man who can do for ten shillings what any fool can do for a pound.
Nevil Shute 1899–1960: *Slide Rule* (1954)

17 Technology . . . the knack of so arranging the world that we need not experience it.
Max Frisch 1911–91: *Homo Faber* (1957)

18 The new electronic interdependence recreates the world in the image of a global village.
Marshall McLuhan 1911–80: *The Gutenberg Galaxy* (1962); see **The Country** 27, **The Earth** 4

19 The Britain that is going to be forged in the white heat of this revolution will be no place for restrictive practices or for outdated methods on either side of industry.
referring to the 'technological revolution'
Harold Wilson 1916–95: speech at the Labour Party Conference, 1 October 1963; see 4 above

20 The medium is the message.
Marshall McLuhan 1911–80: *Understanding Media* (1964)

21 When this circuit learns your job, what are you going to do?
Marshall McLuhan 1911–80: *The Medium is the Massage* (1967)

22 Inanimate objects are classified scientifically into three major categories— those that don't work, those that break down, and those that get lost.
Russell Baker 1925– : in *New York Times* 18 June 1968

23 The first rule of intelligent tinkering is to save all the parts.
Paul Ralph Ehrlich 1932– : in *Saturday Review* 5 June 1971

24 Any sufficiently advanced technology is indistinguishable from magic.
Arthur C. Clarke 1917– : *The Lost Worlds of 2001* (1972)

25 For a successful technology, reality must take precedence over public relations, for nature cannot be fooled.
Richard Phillips Feynman 1918–88: Appendix to the *Rogers Commission Report on the Space Shuttle Challenger Accident* 6 June 1986

26 Machines are the new proletariat. The working class is being given its walking papers.
Jacques Attali 1943– : *Millenium: Winners and Losers in the Coming World Order* (1991)

27 The thing with high-tech is that you always end up using scissors.
David Hockney 1937– : in *Observer* 10 July 1994

28 Technology happens. It's not good, it's not bad. Is steel good or bad?
Andrew Grove 1936– : in *Time* 29 December 1997

Temptation

PROVERBS AND SAYINGS

1 Naughty but nice.
advertising slogan for cream-cakes in the first half of the 1980s; earlier, the title of a 1939 film

2 Stolen fruit is sweet.
early 17th century, meaning that the knowledge that something is forbidden makes it more attractive

3 Stolen waters are sweet.
late 14th century; meaning that something which has been obtained secretly or illicitly seems particularly attractive

PHRASES

4 the pomps and vanities of this wicked world ostentatious display as a type of worldly temptation.
after the answer in the Catechism: *see **Sin** 17*

5 the world, the flesh, and the devil the temptations of earthly life.
from Book of Common Prayer: *see 10 below*

QUOTATIONS

6 Get thee behind me, Satan.
Bible: St Matthew

7 And lead us not into temptation, but deliver us from evil.
Bible: St Matthew

8 Watch and pray, that ye enter not into temptation: the spirit indeed is willing but the flesh is weak.
Bible: St Matthew

9   Is this her fault or mine?
The tempter or the tempted, who sins most?
William Shakespeare 1564–1616: *Measure for Measure* (1604)

10 From all the deceits of the world, the flesh, and the devil,
Good Lord, deliver us.
The Book of Common Prayer 1662: *The Litany*; see 5 above

11 What's done we partly may compute,
But know not what's resisted.
Robert Burns 1759–96: 'Address to the Unco Guid' (1787); see **Virtue** 13

12 It may almost be a question whether such wisdom as many of us have in our mature years has not come from the dying out of the power of temptation, rather than as the results of thought and resolution.
Anthony Trollope 1815–82: *The Small House at Allington* (1864)

13 I can resist everything except temptation.
Oscar Wilde 1854–1900: *Lady Windermere's Fan* (1892)

14 There are several good protections against temptations, but the surest is cowardice.
Mark Twain 1835–1910: *Following the Equator* (1897)

15 Temptations came to him, in middle age, tentatively and without insistence, like a neglected butcher-boy who asks for a Christmas box in February for no more hopeful reason than that he didn't get one in December.
Saki 1870–1916: *The Chronicles of Clovis* (1911)

16 If we are to be punished for the sins we have committed, at least we should be praised for our yearning for the sins we have not committed.
paraphrasing the poet Mirza Ghalib (1797–1849)
Jawaharlal Nehru 1889–1964: letter to Indira Gandhi, 7 May 1943

17 The Lord above made liquor for temptation
To see if man could turn away from sin.
The Lord above made liquor for temptation—but

With a little bit of luck,
With a little bit of luck,
When temptation comes you'll give right in!
Alan Jay Lerner 1918–86: 'With a Little Bit of Luck' (1956 song)

18 This extraordinary pride in being exempt from temptation that you have not yet risen to the level of! Eunuchs boasting of their chastity!
C. S. Lewis 1898–1963: 'Unreal Estates' in Kingsley Amis and Robert Conquest (eds.) *Spectrum IV* (1965)

19 I've looked on a lot of women with lust. I've committed adultery in my heart many times. This is something that God recognizes I will do — and I have done it — and God forgives me for it.
Jimmy Carter 1924– : in *Playboy* November 1976

20 Who was it said a temptation resisted is a true measure of character? Certainly no one in Beverly Hills.
Joan Collins 1933– : in *Independent* 18 July 1998

The Theatre see also Acting, Shakespeare

PHRASES

1 the ghost walks money is available and salaries will paid.
has been explained by the story that an actor playing the ghost of Hamlet's father refused to 'walk again' until the cast's overdue salaries had been paid

2 a mess of plottage a theatrical production with a poorly constructed plot.
by analogy with mess of pottage: *see* **Value** 13

QUOTATIONS

3 Tragedy is thus a representation of an action that is worth serious attention, complete in itself and of some amplitude . . . by means of pity and fear bringing about the purgation of such emotions.
Aristotle 384–322 BC: *Poetics*

4 For what's a play without a woman in it?
Thomas Kyd 1558–94: *The Spanish Tragedy* (1592)

5   Can this cockpit hold
The vasty fields of France? or may we cram
Within this wooden O the very casques

That did affright the air at Agincourt?
William Shakespeare 1564–1616: *Henry V* (1599)

6   The play's the thing
Wherein I'll catch the conscience of the king.
William Shakespeare 1564–1616: *Hamlet* (1601)

7 Then to the well-trod stage anon,
If Jonson's learnèd sock be on,
Or sweetest Shakespeare fancy's child,
Warble his native wood-notes wild.
John Milton 1608–74: 'L'Allegro' (1645); see **Acting** 2

8 Ay, now the plot thickens very much upon us.
George Villiers, Duke of Buckingham 1628–87: *The Rehearsal* (1672); see **Circumstance** 9

9 Damn them! They will not let my play run, but they steal my thunder!
on hearing his new thunder effects used at a performance of Macbeth, *following the withdrawal of one of his own plays after only a short run*
John Dennis 1657–1734: William S. Walsh *A Handy-Book of Literary Curiosities* (1893); see **Strength** 11

10 There still remains, to mortify a wit,
The many-headed monster of the pit.
Alexander Pope 1688–1744: *Imitations of Horace*;
see **Class** 6

11 'Do you come to the play without knowing
what it is?' 'O yes, Sir, yes, very
frequently; I have no time to read play-
bills; one merely comes to meet one's
friends, and show that one's alive.'
Fanny Burney 1752–1840: *Evelina* (1778)

12 The composition of a tragedy requires
testicles.
*on being asked why no woman had ever written 'a
tolerable tragedy'*
Voltaire 1694–1778: letter from Byron to John
Murray, 2 April 1817

13 NINA: Your play's hard to act, there are no
living people in it.
TREPLEV: Living people! We should show
life neither as it is nor as it ought to be,
but as we see it in our dreams.
Anton Chekhov 1860–1904: *The Seagull* (1896)

14 Things on stage should be as complicated
and as simple as in life. People dine, just
dine, while their happiness is made and
their lives are smashed. If in Act I you
have a pistol hanging on the wall, then it
must fire in the last act.
Anton Chekhov 1860–1904: attributed; Donald
Rayfield *Anton Chekhov* (1997)

15 *Étonne-moi.*
Astonish me.
Sergei Diaghilev 1872–1929: to Jean Cocteau;
Wallace Fowlie (ed.) *Journals of Jean Cocteau* (1956)

16 There's no business like show business.
Irving Berlin 1888–1989: title of song (1946)

17 We never closed.
*of the Windmill Theatre, London, during the Second
World War*
Vivian van Damm c.1889–1960: *Tonight and Every
Night* (1952)

18 It's a sound you can't get in the movies or
television . . . the sound of a wonderful,
deep silence that means you've hit them
where they live.
Shelley Winters 1922– : in *Theatre Arts* June 1956

19 Don't clap too hard—it's a very old
building.
John Osborne 1929–94: *The Entertainer* (1957)

20 The theatre is the only institution in the
world which has been dying for four
thousand years and has never succumbed.
John Steinbeck 1902–68: *Once There Was a War*
(1958)

21 Satire is what closes Saturday night.
George S. Kaufman 1889–1961: Scott Meredith
George S. Kaufman and his Friends (1974)

22 The weasel under the cocktail cabinet.
on being asked what his plays were about
Harold Pinter 1930– : J. Russell Taylor *Anger and
After* (1962)

23 I go to the theatre to be entertained, I
want to be taken out of myself, I don't
want to see lust and rape and incest and
sodomy and so on, I can get all that at
home.
Alan Bennett 1934– : Alan Bennett et al. *Beyond
the Fringe* (1963) 'Man of Principles'

24 I can do you blood and love without the
rhetoric, and I can do you blood and
rhetoric without the love, and I can do you
all three concurrent or consecutive, but I
can't do you love and rhetoric without the
blood. Blood is compulsory—they're all
blood, you see.
Tom Stoppard 1937– : *Rosencrantz and Guildenstern
are Dead* (1967)

25 Welcome to the Theatre,
To the magic, to the fun!
Where painted trees and flowers grow,
And laughter rings fortissimo,
And treachery's sweetly done.
Lee Adams: 'Welcome to the Theatre' (1970 song)

26 I've never much enjoyed going to plays . . .
The unreality of painted people standing
on a platform saying things they've said to
each other for months is more than I can
overlook.
John Updike 1932– : George Plimpton (ed.) *Writers
at Work* 4th Series (1977)

27 The theatre exists in movement.
Peter Brook 1925– : *Threads of Time* (1998)

28 Theatre is often regarded in Britain as the
cricket of the arts, meaning archaic,
quaint, thinly attended, and not done as
well as it used to be.
Richard Eyre 1943– : in *Independent* 25 March 2000

Thinking see also **Ideas, The Mind**

PROVERBS AND SAYINGS

1 Great minds think alike.
early 17th century, now often used ironically

2 Perish the thought!
saying used, often ironically, to show that one finds a suggestion or idea completely ridiculous; the phrase probably derives from 'perish that thought!' in Colley Cibber's Richard III *(1700)*

3 Two heads are better than one.
late 14th century, meaning that it is advisable to discuss a problem with another person

PHRASES

4 an agonizing reappraisal a reassessment of a policy or position painfully forced on one by a radical change of circumstance, or by a realization of what the existing circumstances really are.
from John Foster Dulles (1888–1959) in 1953, 'If . . . the European Defence Community should not be effective; if France and Germany remain apart . . . That would compel an agonizing reappraisal of basic United States policy'

5 lateral thinking a way of thinking which seeks the solution to intractable problems through unorthodox methods, or elements which would normally be ignored by logical thinking.
from Edward de Bono (1933–) The Use of Lateral Thinking (1967) 'Some people are aware of another sort of thinking which . . . leads to those simple ideas that are obvious only after they have been thought of . . . the term "lateral thinking" has been coined to describe this other sort of thinking; "vertical thinking" is used to denote the conventional logical process'

6 positive thinking the practice or result of concentrating one's mind on the good and constructive aspects of a matter so as to eliminate destructive attitudes and emotions.
The Power of Positive Thinking title of a book (1952) by Norman Vincent Peale (1898–1993)

QUOTATIONS

7 His thinking does not produce smoke after the flame, but light after smoke.
Horace 65–8 BC: *Ars Poetica*

8 Whatsoever things are true, whatsoever things are honest, whatsoever things are just, whatsoever things are pure, whatsoever things are lovely, whatsoever things are of good report; if there be any virtue and if there be any praise, think on these things.
Bible: Philippians

9 To change your mind and to follow him who sets you right is to be nonetheless the free agent that you were before.
Marcus Aurelius AD 121–80: *Meditations*

10 The important thing is not to think much but to love much.
St Teresa of Ávila 1512–82: *The Interior Castle* (1588)

11 Yond' Cassius has a lean and hungry look;
He thinks too much: such men are
   dangerous.
William Shakespeare 1564–1616: *Julius Caesar* (1599)

12 *Je pense, donc je suis.*
I think, therefore I am.
usually quoted as, 'Cogito, ergo sum', from the 1641 Latin edition
René Descartes 1596–1650: *Le Discours de la méthode* (1637); see 29 below

13 A man, doubtful of his dinner, or trembling at a creditor, is not much disposed to abstracted meditation, or remote enquiries.
Samuel Johnson 1709–84: *Lives of the English Poets* (1779–81) 'Collins'

14 Two things fill the mind with ever new and increasing wonder and awe, the more often and the more seriously reflection concentrates upon them: the starry heaven above me and the moral law within me.
Immanuel Kant 1724–1804: *Critique of Practical Reason* (1788)

15 I never could find any man who could think for two minutes together.
Sydney Smith 1771–1845: *Sketches of Moral Philosophy* (1849)

16 Stung by the splendour of a sudden
   thought.
Robert Browning 1812–89: 'A Death in the Desert' (1864)

17 How often misused words generate misleading thoughts.
Herbert Spencer 1820–1903: *Principles of Ethics* (1879)

18 It is quite a three-pipe problem, and I beg that you won't speak to me for fifty minutes.
Arthur Conan Doyle 1859–1930: *The Adventures of Sherlock Holmes* (1892)

19 Sometimes I sits and thinks, and then again I just sits.
Punch: 1906

20 How can I tell what I think till I see what I say?
E. M. Forster 1879–1970: *Aspects of the Novel* (1927)

21 Pooh began to feel a little more comfortable, because when you are a Bear of Very Little Brain, and you Think of Things, you find sometimes that a Thing which seemed very Thingish inside you is quite different when it gets out into the open and has other people looking at it.
A. A. Milne 1882–1956: *The House at Pooh Corner* (1928)

22 A man of action forced into a state of thought is unhappy until he can get out of it.
John Galsworthy 1867–1933: *Maid in Waiting* (1931)

23 *Doublethink* means the power of holding two contradictory beliefs in one's mind simultaneously, and accepting both of them.
George Orwell 1903–50: *Nineteen Eighty-Four* (1949)

24 He can't think without his hat.
Samuel Beckett 1906–89: *Waiting for Godot* (1955)

25 It is a far, far better thing to have a firm anchor in nonsense than to put out on the troubled seas of thought.
J. K. Galbraith 1908– : *The Affluent Society* (1958)

26 What was once thought can never be unthought.
Friedrich Dürrenmatt 1921– : *The Physicists* (1962)

27 The real question is not whether machines think but whether men do.
B. F. Skinner 1904–90: *Contingencies of Reinforcement* (1969)

28 The question of whether a mechanical device could ever be said to think— perhaps even to experience feelings, or to have a mind—is not really a new one. But it has been given a new impetus, even an urgency, by the advent of modern computer technology.
Roger Penrose 1931– : *The Emperor's New Mind* (1989)

29 *I think, therefore I am* is the statement of an intellectual who underrates toothaches.
Milan Kundera 1929– : *Immortality* (1991); see 12 above

Thoroughness see also **Determination and Perseverance**

PROVERBS AND SAYINGS

1 Do not spoil the ship for a ha'porth of tar.
early 17th century, used generally to warn against risking loss or failure through unwillingness to allow relatively trivial expenditure; ship is a dialectal pronunciation of sheep, and the original literal sense was 'do not allow sheep to die for the lack of a trifling amount of tar', tar being used to protect sores and wounds on sheep from flies

2 In for a penny, in for a pound.
late 17th century, meaning that if one is to be involved at all, it may as well be fully

3 Nothing venture, nothing gain.
early 17th century, a later variant of nothing venture, nothing have

4 Nothing venture, nothing have.
late 14th century, meaning that one must be prepared to take some risks to achieve a desired end

5 One might as well be hanged for a sheep as a lamb.
late 17th century, meaning that if one is going to incur a severe penalty it may as well be for something substantial

PHRASES

6 at one fell swoop at a single blow, in one go.
swoop the sudden pouncing of a bird of prey from a height on its quarry, especially with allusion to Shakespeare Macbeth: *see* **Mourning** *9*

7 flesh and fell entirely.
the whole substance of the body (fell the skin)

8 go the extra mile make an extra effort, do more than is strictly asked or required.
in a revue song (1957) by Joyce Grenfell, 'Ready . . . To go the extra mile', but perhaps ultimately in allusion

to the Bible (Matthew) 'And whosoever shall compel thee to go a mile, go with him twain'

9 to destroy root and branch to destroy thoroughly, radically.

perhaps originally with reference to the Bible (Malachi), 'The day that cometh shall burn them up . . . that it shall leave them neither root nor branch'

10 Whatsoever thy hand findeth to do, do it with thy might.
Bible: Ecclesiastes

11 There must be a beginning of any great matter, but the continuing unto the end until it be thoroughly finished yields the true glory.
Francis Drake c.1540–96: dispatch to Sir Francis Walsingham, 17 May 1587

12 The shortest way to do many things is to do only one thing at once.
Samuel Smiles 1812–1904: *Self-Help* (1859)

13 Climb ev'ry mountain, ford ev'ry stream
Follow ev'ry rainbow, till you find your
dream!
Oscar Hammerstein II 1895–1960: *Climb Ev'ry Mountain* (1959 song)

Thrift and Extravagance see also **Debt and Borrowing, Poverty, Wealth**

1 Make do and mend.
wartime slogan, 1940s

2 Most people consider thrift a fine virtue in ancestors.
American proverb, mid 20th century

3 A penny saved is a penny earned.
mid 17th century, used as an exhortation to thrift

4 Penny wise and pound foolish.
early 17th century, meaning that too much concern with saving small sums may result in larger loss if necessary expenditure on maintenance and safety has been withheld

5 Spare at the spigot, and let out the bung-hole.
mid 17th century; referring to the practice of being overcareful on the one hand, and carelessly generous on the other. (A spigot is a peg or pin used to regulate the flow of liquid through a tap on a cask, and a bung-hole is a hole through which a cask is filled or emptied, and which is closed by a bung)

6 Spare well and have to spend.
mid 16th century; meaning that the person who is thrifty and careful with their resources can use them lavishly when the occasion offers

7 Take care of the pence and the pounds will take care of themselves.
*mid 18th century, meaning that thrift and small savings will grow to substantial wealth; see **Money** 28, **Speech** 21*

8 Thrift is a great revenue.
mid 17th century, meaning that care with expenditure is one of the best ways of providing an income for oneself

9 Wilful waste makes woeful want.
early 18th century, meaning that deliberate misuse of resources is likely to lead to severe shortage

10 Plenty has made me poor.
Ovid 43 BC–AD c.17: *Metamorphoses*

11 Thrift, thrift, Horatio! the funeral baked meats
Did coldly furnish forth the marriage tables.
William Shakespeare 1564–1616: *Hamlet* (1601)

12 In squandering wealth was his peculiar art:
Nothing went unrewarded, but desert.
Beggared by fools, whom still he found too late:
He had his jest, and they had his estate.
John Dryden 1631–1700: *Absalom and Achitophel* (1681)

13 Mun, a had na' been the-erre abune two hours when—*bang*—went saxpence!!!
Punch: 1868

14 Economy is going without something you do want in case you should, some day, want something you probably won't want.
Anthony Hope 1863–1933: *The Dolly Dialogues* (1894)

15 From the foregoing survey of conspicuous leisure and consumption, it appears that the utility of both alike for the purposes of reputability lies in the element of waste that is common to both. In the one case it

is a waste of time and effort, in the other it is a waste of goods.
Thorstein Veblen 1857–1929: *Theory of the Leisure Class* (1899)

16 All decent people live beyond their incomes nowadays, and those who aren't respectable live beyond other peoples'.
Saki 1870–1916: *Chronicles of Clovis* (1911)

17 We could have saved sixpence. We have saved fivepence. (*Pause*) But at what cost?
Samuel Beckett 1906–89: *All That Fall* (1957)

18 If a champion spends his money foolishly, they ridicule him for that, and if he doesn't spend it, they call him cheap. Well, I'd rather have them criticize me for not spending it and wind up keeping my money.
Rocky Marciano 1923–69: Everett M. Skehan *Rocky Marciano* (1983)

19 Prudence is the other woman in Gordon's life.
of Gordon Brown, Chancellor of the Exchequer
Anonymous: an unidentified aide, in March 1998

Time see also Transience

PROVERBS AND SAYINGS

1 Give us back our eleven days.
slogan protesting against the adoption of the Gregorian Calendar in 1752, which meant that 14 September followed immediately after 2 September; see 12 below

2 Never is a long time.
*late 14th century, often used to indicate that circumstances may ultimately change; see **Change** 6*

3 Spring forward, fall back.
a reminder that clocks are moved forward in spring and back in the fall (autumn)

4 There is a time for everything.
late 14th century, meaning that there is always a suitable time to do something; from the Bible: see 18 below

5 Time is a great healer.
late 14th century, meaning that initial pain is felt less keenly with the passage of time; see 43 below

6 Time will tell.
mid 16th century, meaning that the true nature of something is likely to emerge over a period of time, and that conversely it is only after time has passed that something can be regarded as settled

7 Time works wonders.
late 16th century; often used to suggest that with the passage of time something initially unknown and unwelcome will become familiar and acceptable

PHRASES

8 annus mirabilis a remarkable or auspicious year.
modern Latin = wonderful year in Annus Mirabilis: the year of wonders, *title of poem (1667) by Dryden; see **Misfortunes** 30*

9 at the Greek Calends never.
calends the first day of the month in the ancient Roman calendar; the Greek Calends will never come as the Greeks did not use calends in reckoning time

10 for the duration until the end of something, especially a war; hence, informally, for a very long time.
used first of the 1914–18 war from the term of enlistment 'for four years or the duration of the war'

11 a movable feast an event which takes place at no regular time.
*a religious feast day (especially Easter Day and the other Christian holy days whose dates are related to it) which does not occur on the same calendar date each year; see **Towns and Cities** 25*

12 Old Style the method of calculating dates using the Julian calendar.
in England and Wales it was superseded by the use of the Gregorian calendar in 1752; see 1 above

13 once in a blue moon very rarely, practically never.
to say that the moon is blue is recorded in the sixteenth century as a proverbial assertion of something that could not be true

14 till kingdom come for an indefinitely long period.
kingdom come the next world, eternity; from thy kingdom come in the Lord's Prayer

15 time immemorial legally, a time up to the beginning of the reign of Richard I in 1189; generally, a longer time than anyone can remember or trace.

16 time's arrow the direction of travel from past to future in time considered as a physical dimension.
from Arthur Eddington (1882–1944) The Nature of the Physical World (1928) 'Let us draw an arrow

arbitrarily. If as we follow the arrow we find more and more of the random element in the world, then the arrow is pointing towards the future; if the random element decreases the arrow points towards the past . . . I shall use the phrase "time's arrow" to express this one-way property of time which has no analogue in space.'

17 world without end for ever, eternally.

translation of Late Latin in saecula saeculorum to the ages of ages, as used in Morning Prayer and other services, 'As it was in the beginning, is now, and ever shall be: world without end.'

QUOTATIONS

18 To every thing there is a season, and a time to every purpose under the heaven: A time to be born, and a time to die . . . A time to weep, and a time to laugh; a time to mourn, and a time to dance.
Bible: Ecclesiastes; see 4 above

19 *Sed fugit interea, fugit inreparabile tempus.*
But meanwhile it is flying, irretrievable time is flying.
usually quoted as 'tempus fugit [time flies]'
Virgil 70–19 BC: Georgics; see **Transience** 3

20 *Tempus edax rerum.*
Time the devourer of everything.
Ovid 43 BC–AD c.17: Metamorphoses

21 Every instant of time is a pinprick of eternity.
Marcus Aurelius AD 121–80: Meditations

22 I am Time grown old to destroy the world, Embarked on the course of world annihilation.
Bhagavad Gita 250 BC–AD 250: ch. 11

23 Time is . . . Time was . . . Time is past.
Robert Greene c.1560–92: Friar Bacon and Friar Bungay (1594)

24 I wasted time, and now doth time waste me.
William Shakespeare 1564–1616: Richard II (1595)

25 Time hath, my lord, a wallet at his back, Wherein he puts alms for oblivion.
William Shakespeare 1564–1616: Troilus and Cressida (1602)

26 To-morrow, and to-morrow, and to-morrow,
Creeps in this petty pace from day to day,
To the last syllable of recorded time;
And all our yesterdays have lighted fools
The way to dusty death.
William Shakespeare 1564–1616: Macbeth (1606)

27 Even such is Time, which takes in trust Our youth, our joys, and all we have, And pays us but with age and dust.
Walter Ralegh c.1552–1618: written the night before his death, and found in his Bible in the Gatehouse at Westminster

28 There was never any thing by the wit of man so well devised, or so sure established, which in continuance of time hath not been corrupted.
The Book of Common Prayer 1662: The Preface Concerning the Service of the Church

29 But at my back I always hear Time's wingèd chariot hurrying near: And yonder all before us lie Deserts of vast eternity.
Andrew Marvell 1621–78: 'To His Coy Mistress' (1681)

30 Time, like an ever-rolling stream, Bears all its sons away.
Isaac Watts 1674–1748: 'O God, our help in ages past' (1719 hymn)

31 I recommend to you to take care of minutes: for hours will take care of themselves.
Lord Chesterfield 1694–1773: Letters to his Son (1774) 6 November 1747

32 Remember that time is money.
Benjamin Franklin 1706–90: Advice to a Young Tradesman (1748); see **Money** 12

33 O aching time! O moments big as years!
John Keats 1795–1821: 'Hyperion: A Fragment' (1820)

34 Men talk of killing time, while time quietly kills them.
Dion Boucicault 1820–90: London Assurance (1841)

35 He said, 'What's time? Leave Now for dogs and apes!
Man has Forever.'
Robert Browning 1812–89: 'A Grammarian's Funeral' (1855)

36 Lost, yesterday, somewhere between Sunrise and Sunset, two golden hours, each set with sixty diamond minutes. No reward is offered, for they are gone forever.
Horace Mann 1796–1859: 'Lost, Two Golden Hours'

37 Time is
Too slow for those who wait,
Too swift for those who fear,
Too long for those who grieve,

Too short for those who rejoice;
But for those who love,
Time is eternity.
Henry Van Dyke 1852–1933: 'Time is too slow for those who wait' (1905), read at the funeral of Diana, Princess of Wales; the original form of the last line is 'Time is not'

38 Time, you old gypsy man,
Will you not stay,
Put up your caravan
Just for one day?
Ralph Hodgson 1871–1962: 'Time, You Old Gipsy Man' (1917)

39 Ah! the clock is always slow;
It is later than you think.
Robert W. Service 1874–1958: 'It Is Later Than You Think' (1921)

40 Half our life is spent trying to find something to do with the time we have rushed through life trying to save.
Will Rogers 1879–1935: letter in *New York Times* 29 April 1930

41 Time present and time past
Are both perhaps present in time future,
And time future contained in time past.
T. S. Eliot 1888–1965: *Four Quartets* 'Burnt Norton' (1936)

42 Three o'clock is always too late or too early for anything you want to do.
Jean-Paul Sartre 1905–80: *La Nausée* (1938)

43 Time has too much credit . . . It is not a great healer. It is an indifferent and perfunctory one. Sometimes it does not heal at all. And sometimes when it seems to, no healing has been necessary.
Ivy Compton-Burnett 1884–1969: *Darkness and Day* (1951); see 5 above

44 VLADIMIR: That passed the time.
ESTRAGON: It would have passed in any case.
VLADIMIR: Yes, but not so rapidly.
Samuel Beckett 1906–89: *Waiting for Godot* (1955)

45 The distinction between past, present and future is only an illusion, however persistent.
Albert Einstein 1879–1955: letter to Michelangelo Besso, 21 March 1955

46 And meanwhile time goes about its immemorial work of making everyone look and feel like shit.
Martin Amis 1949– : *London Fields* (1989)

Title see **Rank and Title**

Tolerance see **Prejudice and Tolerance**

The Town see **The Country and the Town**

Towns and Cities see also **American Cities and States**, **British Towns and Regions**

PROVERBS AND SAYINGS

1 **All roads lead to Rome.**
late 14th century, earlier in Latin

2 **Next year in Jerusalem!**
traditionally the concluding words of the Jewish Passover service, expressing the hope of the Diaspora that Jews dispersed throughout the world would once more be reunited

3 **See Naples and die.**
implying that after seeing Naples, one could have nothing left on earth to wish for; Goethe noted it as an Italian proverb in his diary in 1787

PHRASES

4 **the cities of the plain** Sodom and Gomorrah, on the plain of Jordan in ancient Palestine.
from the Bible (Genesis), the ancient cities destroyed by fire from heaven, because of the wickedness of their inhabitants

5 **the City of the Seven Hills** Rome.

6 **City of the Tribes** Galway.
the term tribes of Galway was used for Irish families or communities having the same surname

7 **City of the Violated Treaty** Limerick.
referring to the Treaty of Limerick of 1691

8 **City of the Violet Crown** Athens.

translating an epithet used by Pindar (c.518–c.438 BC) and Aristophanes (c.450–c.385 BC)

9 **the Eternal City** Rome.

translating the Latin urbs aeterna, *occurring in Ovid and Tibullus, and frequently found in the official documents of the Empire*

10 **the Forbidden City** Lhasa.

the centre of Tibetan Buddhism, closed to foreign visitors until the 20th century. The name Forbidden City *is also given to an area of Beijing (Peking) containing the former imperial palaces*

11 **the Holy City** Jerusalem.

12 **the Venice of the North** St Petersburg.

QUOTATIONS

13 He could boast that he inherited it brick and left it marble.

referring to the city of Rome
Augustus 63 BC–AD 14: Suetonius *Lives of the Caesars* 'Divus Augustus'

14 Once did she hold the gorgeous East in fee, And was the safeguard of the West.

William Wordsworth 1770–1850: 'On the Extinction of the Venetian Republic' (1807)

15 Sun-girt city, thou hast been
Ocean's child, and then his queen;
Now is come a darker day,
And thou soon must be his prey.

of Venice
Percy Bysshe Shelley 1792–1822: 'Lines written amongst the Euganean Hills' (1818)

16 While stands the Coliseum, Rome shall stand;
When falls the Coliseum, Rome shall fall;
And when Rome falls—the World.

Lord Byron 1788–1824: *Childe Harold's Pilgrimage* (1812–18)

17 Let there be light! said Liberty,
And like sunrise from the sea,
Athens arose!

Percy Bysshe Shelley 1792–1822: *Hellas* (1822)

18 Moscow: those syllables can start
A tumult in the Russian heart.

Alexander Pushkin 1799–1837: *Eugene Onegin* (1833)

19 Match me such marvel, save in Eastern clime,—
A rose-red city—half as old as Time!

John William Burgon 1813–88: *Petra* (1845)

20 Petersburg, the most abstract and premeditated city on earth.

Fedor Dostoevsky 1821–81: *Notes from Underground* (1864)

21 God made the harbour, and that's all right, but Satan made Sydney.

Anonymous: unnamed Sydney citizen; Mark Twain *More Tramps Abroad* (1897)

22 The last time I saw Paris
Her heart was warm and gay,
I heard the laughter of her heart in ev'ry street café.

Oscar Hammerstein II 1895–1960: 'The Last Time I saw Paris' (1941 song)

23 STREETS FLOODED. PLEASE ADVISE.

telegraph message on arriving in Venice
Robert Benchley 1889–1945: R. E. Drennan (ed.) *Wits End* (1973)

24 No history much? Perhaps. Only this ominous
Dark beauty flowering under veils,
Trapped in the spectrum of a dying style:
A village like an instinct left to rust,
Composed around the echo of a pistol-shot.

Lawrence Durrell 1912–90: 'Sarajevo' (1951)

25 Paris is a movable feast.

Ernest Hemingway 1899–1961: *A Movable Feast* (1964) epigraph; see **Time** 11

26 Venice is like eating an entire box of chocolate liqueurs in one go.

Truman Capote 1924–84: in *Observer* 26 November 1961

27 Rome's just a city like anywhere else. A vastly overrated city, I'd say. It trades on belief just as Stratford trades on Shakespeare.

Anthony Burgess 1917–93: *Inside Mr Enderby* (1963)

28 By God what a site! By man what a mess!

of Sydney
Clough Williams-Ellis 1883–1978: *Architect Errant* (1971)

29 Toronto is a kind of New York operated by the Swiss.

Peter Ustinov 1921– : in *Globe & Mail* 1 August 1987; attributed

30 Saigon is like all the other great modern cities of the world. It's the mess left over from people getting rich.

P. J. O'Rourke 1947– : *Give War a Chance* (1992)

Transience see also Opportunity, Time

1 **And this, too, shall pass away.**

traditional saying said to be true for all times and situations; the story is told by Edward Fitzgerald in Polonius (1852) 'The Sultan asked for a signet motto, that should hold good for Adversity or Prosperity. Solomon gave him—"This also shall pass away"'

2 **Sic transit gloria mundi**.

Latin = Thus passes the glory of the world; said during the coronation of a new Pope, while flax is burned (used at the coronation of Alexander V in Pisa, 7 July 1409, but earlier in origin)

3 **Time flies.**

late 14th century, from Virgil: see **Time** *19*

4 Like that of leaves is a generation of men.
Homer: *The Iliad*

5 For a thousand years in thy sight are but as yesterday: seeing that is past as a watch in the night.
Bible: Psalm 90

6 *Eheu fugaces, Postume, Postume, Labuntur anni.*
Ah me, Postumus, Postumus, the fleeting years are slipping by.
Horace 65-8 BC: *Odes*

7 All flesh is as grass, and all the glory of man as the flower of grass. The grass withereth, and the flower thereof falleth away.
Bible: I Peter; see **Life** 8

8 Gather ye rosebuds while ye may,
Old Time is still a-flying:
And this same flower that smiles to-day,
To-morrow will be dying.
Robert Herrick 1591-1674: 'To the Virgins, to Make Much of Time' (1648)

9 But transient is the smile of fate:
A little rule, a little sway,
A sunbeam in a winter's day,
Is all the proud and mighty have
Between the cradle and the grave.
John Dyer 1700-58: *Grongar Hill* (1726)

10 Though nothing can bring back the hour
Of splendour in the grass, of glory in the flower;
We will grieve not, rather find

Strength in what remains behind.
William Wordsworth 1770-1850: 'Ode. Intimations of Immortality' (1807)

11 I never nursed a dear gazelle,
To glad me with its soft black eye,
But when it came to know me well,
And love me, it was sure to die!
Thomas Moore 1779-1852: *Lalla Rookh* (1817) 'The Fire-Worshippers'; see **Value** 28

12 He who binds to himself a joy
Doth the winged life destroy
But he who kisses the joy as it flies
Lives in Eternity's sunrise.
William Blake 1757-1827: *MS Note-Book*

13 They are not long, the days of wine and roses.
Ernest Dowson 1867-1900: 'Vitae Summa Brevis' (1896)

14 Look thy last on all things lovely,
Every hour.
Walter de la Mare 1873-1956: 'Fare Well' (1918)

15 He will be just like the scent on a pocket handkerchief.
on being asked what place Arthur Balfour would have in history
David Lloyd George 1863-1945: Thomas Jones diary 9 June 1922

16 The sunlight on the garden
Hardens and grows cold,
We cannot cage the minute
Within its net of gold.
Louis MacNeice 1907-63: 'Sunlight on the Garden' (1938)

17 Treaties, you see, are like girls and roses: they last while they last.
Charles de Gaulle 1890-1970: speech at Elysée Palace, 2 July 1963

18 And it seems to me you lived your life
Like a candle in the wind.
of Marilyn Monroe, later revised for Diana Princess of Wales
Elton John 1947- and **Bernie Taupin** 1950- : 'Candle in the Wind' (song, 1973); see **Singing** 18

19 We are all of us balloons dancing in a world of pins.
Anthony Montague Browne 1923- : *Long Sunset* (1995)

Translation

1 Traduttore traditore.
Italian, meaning 'translators, traitors'

2 Translator General Philemon Holland (1552–1637).
he translated the work of Livy, Pliny, Plutarch, Suetonius, and others; Thomas Fuller named him the 'translator general in his age' and said that 'these books alone of his turning into English will make a country gentleman a competent library'

3 Such is our pride, our folly, or our fate,
That few, but such as cannot write,
   translate.
John Denham 1615–69: 'To Richard Fanshaw' (1648)

4 He is translation's thief that addeth more,
As much as he that taketh from the store
Of the first author.
Andrew Marvell 1621–78: 'To His Worthy Friend Dr Witty' (1651)

5 Some hold translations not unlike to be
The wrong side of a Turkey tapestry.
James Howell c.1593–1666: *Familiar Letters* (1645–55)

6 It is a pretty poem, Mr Pope, but you must not call it Homer.
when pressed by Pope to comment on 'My Homer', i.e. his translation of Homer's Iliad
Richard Bentley 1662–1742: John Hawkins (ed.) *The Works of Samuel Johnson* (1787)

7 It appears to me that men are hired to run down men of genius under the mask of translators.
William Blake 1757–1827: *Annotations to Boyd's Dante* (written c.1800)

8 The vanity of translation; it were as wise to cast a violet into a crucible that you might discover the formal principle of its colour and odour, as seek to transfuse from one language to another the creations of a poet. The plant must spring again from its seed, or it will bear no flower.
Percy Bysshe Shelley 1792–1822: *A Defence of Poetry* (written 1821)

9 A translation is no translation unless it will give you the music of a poem along with the words of it.
John Millington Synge 1871–1909: *The Aran Islands* (1907)

10 The original Greek is of great use in elucidating Browning's translation of the *Agamemnon*.
Robert Yelverton Tyrrell 1844–1914: Ulick O'Connor *Oliver St John Gogarty* (1964)

11 Translations (like wives) are seldom strictly faithful if they are in the least attractive.
Roy Campbell 1901–57: in *Poetry Review* June–July 1949

12 It has never occurred to Anderson that one foreign language can be translated into another. He assumes that every strange tongue exists only by virtue of its not being English.
Tom Stoppard 1937– : *Where Are They Now?* (1973)

13 The original is unfaithful to the translation.
on Henley's translation of Beckford's Vathek
Jorge Luis Borges 1899–1986: *Sobre el 'Vathek' de William Beckford*; in *Obras Completas* (1974)

Transport

1 Clunk, click, every trip.
road safety campaign promoting the use of seat-belts, 1971

2 Let the train take the strain.
British Rail slogan, 1970 onwards

3 Put a tiger in your tank.
advertising slogan for Esso petrol, 1964; see **Strength** 12

PHRASES

4 a magic carpet a means of sudden and effortless travel.

a mythical carpet able to transport a person on it to any desired place

5 seven-league boots the ability to travel very fast on foot.

boots enabling the wearer to go seven leagues at each stride, from the fairy story of Hop o' my Thumb.

QUOTATIONS

6 The driving is like the driving of Jehu, the son of Nimshi; for he driveth furiously.
Bible: II Kings

7 There was a rocky valley between Buxton and Bakewell . . . You enterprised a railroad . . . you blasted its rocks away . . . And now, every fool in Buxton can be at Bakewell in half-an-hour, and every fool in Bakewell at Buxton.
John Ruskin 1819–1900: *Praeterita* vol. 3 (1889)

8 There is *nothing*—absolutely nothing—half so much worth doing as simply messing about in boats.
Kenneth Grahame 1859–1932: *The Wind in the Willows* (1908)

9 The poetry of motion! The *real* way to travel! The *only* way to travel! Here today—in next week tomorrow! Villages skipped, towns and cities jumped—always somebody else's horizon! O bliss! O poop-poop! O my! O my!
on the car
Kenneth Grahame 1859–1932: *The Wind in the Willows* (1908)

10 What good is speed if the brain has oozed out on the way?
Karl Kraus 1874–1936: in *Die Fackel* September 1909 'The Discovery of the North Pole'

11 Railway termini. They are our gates to the glorious and the unknown. Through them we pass out into adventure and sunshine, to them, alas! we return.
E. M. Forster 1879–1970: *Howards End* (1910)

12 Sir, Saturday morning, although recurring at regular and well-foreseen intervals, always seems to take this railway by surprise.
W. S. Gilbert 1836–1911: letter to the station-master at Baker Street, on the Metropolitan line; John Julius Norwich *Christmas Crackers* (1980)

13 Walk! Not bloody likely. I am going in a taxi.
George Bernard Shaw 1856–1950: *Pygmalion* (1916); see **Swearing** 3

14 To George F. Babbitt, as to most prosperous citizens of Zenith, his motor car was poetry and tragedy, love and heroism. The office was his pirate ship but the car his perilous excursion ashore.
Sinclair Lewis 1885–1951: *Babbitt* (1922)

15 Men travel faster now, but I do not know if they go to better things.
Willa Cather 1873–1947: *Death Comes for the Archbishop* (1927)

16 [There are] only two classes of pedestrians in these days of reckless motor traffic—the quick, and the dead.
Lord Dewar 1864–1930: George Robey *Looking Back on Life* (1933); see **Heaven** 13

17 After the first powerful plain manifesto The black statement of pistons, without more fuss
But gliding like a queen, she leaves the station.
Stephen Spender 1909–95: 'The Express' (1933)

18 Home James, and don't spare the horses.
Fred Hillebrand 1893– : title of song (1934)

19 This is the Night Mail crossing the Border, Bringing the cheque and the postal order, Letters for the rich, letters for the poor, The shop at the corner, the girl next door.
W. H. Auden 1907–73: 'Night Mail' (1936)

20 Oh! I have slipped the surly bonds of earth And danced the skies on laughter-silvered wings; . . .
And, while with silent lifting mind I've trod
The high, untrespassed sanctity of space, Put out my hand and touched the face of God.
quoted by Ronald Reagan following the explosion of the space shuttle Challenger, *January 1986*
John Gillespie Magee 1922–41: 'High Flight' (1943)

21 It looks like a poached egg—we can't make that.
on seeing the Morris Minor prototype in 1945
Lord Nuffield 1877–1963: attributed

22 That life-quickening atmosphere of a big railway station where everything is something trembling on the brink of something else.
Vladimir Nabokov 1899–1977: *Spring in Fialta and other stories* (1956) 'Spring in Fialta'

23 I think that cars today are almost the exact equivalent of the great Gothic cathedrals: I mean the supreme creation of an era, conceived with passion by unknown artists, and consumed in image if not in usage by a whole population which appropriates them as a purely magical object.

Roland Barthes 1915–80: *Mythologies* (1957) 'La nouvelle Citroën'

24 The automobile changed our dress, manners, social customs, vacation habits, the shape of our cities, consumer purchasing patterns, common tastes and positions in intercourse.

John Keats 1920– : *The Insolent Chariots* (1958)

25 There is no class of person more moved by hatred than the motorist and the policeman is a convenient receptacle for his feeling.

C. W. Hewitt: speech to the Lawyers' Club of the London School of Economics, 22 October 1959

26 The car has become an article of dress without which we feel uncertain, unclad and incomplete in the urban compound.

Marshall McLuhan 1911–80: *Understanding Media* (1964)

27 I myself see the car crash as a tremendous sexual event really: a liberation of human and machine libido (if there is such a thing).

J. G. Ballard 1930– : in *Penthouse* September 1970

28 I was astonished at the effect my successful landing in France had on the nations of the world. To me, it was like a match lighting a bonfire.

of the first solo transatlantic flight

Charles Lindbergh 1902–74: *Autobiography of Values* (1978)

29 I have seldom heard a train go by and not wished I was on it. Those whistles sing bewitchment: railways are irresistible bazaars, snaking along perfectly level no matter what the landscape, improving your mood with speed, and never upsetting your drink.

Paul Theroux 1941– : *The Great Railway Bazaar* (1975)

30 We have now to plan no longer for soft little animals pottering about on their own two legs, but for hard steel canisters hurtling about with these same little animals inside them.

Hugh Casson 1910– : Clough Williams-Ellis *Around the World in 90 Years* (1978)

31 Commuter—one who spends his life
In riding to and from his wife;
A man who shaves and takes a train,
And then rides back to shave again.

E. B. White 1899–1985: 'The Commuter' (1982)

32 There are only two emotions in a plane: boredom and terror.

Orson Welles 1915–85: interview to celebrate his 70th birthday, in *The Times* 6 May 1985

33 You have your own company, your own temperature control, your own music— and don't have to put up with dreadful human beings sitting alongside you.

on cars compared to public transport

Steven Norris 1945– : comment to Commons Environment Select Committee, in *Daily Telegraph* 9 February 1995

34 Railways and the Church have their critics, but both are the best ways of getting a man to his ultimate destination.

Revd W. Awdry 1911–97: in *Daily Telegraph* 22 March 1997; obituary

---

Travel see also **Countries and Peoples, Exploration**

PROVERBS AND SAYINGS

1 **Been there, done that, got the T-shirt.**

evoking a jaded tourist as the image of someone who is bored by too much sight-seeing; see **Boredom** 1

2 **Go abroad and you'll hear news of home.**

late 17th century, meaning that information about one's immediate vicinity may have become more widely publicized

3 **If it's Tuesday, this must be Belgium.**

late 20th century saying, from the title of a 1969 film written by David Shaw

4 **Is your journey *really* necessary?**

1939 slogan, coined to discourage Civil Servants from going home for Christmas

5 **Thursday's child has far to go.**

traditional rhyme, mid 19th century; see **Beauty** 5, **Gifts** 2, **Pregnancy and Birth** 1, **Sorrow** 2, **Work** 6

6 Travel broadens the mind.
early 20th century

7 Travelling is one way of lengthening life, at least in appearance.
American proverb, mid 20th century

PHRASES

8 curse of Cain the fate of someone compelled to lead a wandering life.
after the Bible (Genesis) 'a fugitive . . . shalt thou [Cain] be in the earth'; see also **Canada** *2,* **Murder** *7,* **Order** *7*

9 genius loci the presiding god or spirit of a particular place.
originally with reference to Virgil Aeneid 'He prays to the spirit of the place and to Earth'; later with genius *taken as referring to the body of associations connected with or inspirations derived from a place, rather than to a tutelary deity*

10 round Robin Hood's barn by a circuitous route.
Robin Hood a popular English outlaw traditionally famous from medieval times, Robin Hood's barn an out-of-the-way place

11 Sabbath day's journey an easy journey.
the distance a Jew might travel on the Sabbath (approximately two-thirds of a mile); in the Bible (Acts) the distance from Mount Olivet to Jerusalem is described as being 'a Sabbath day's journey'

12 wild blue yonder the far distance; a remote place.
from R. Crawford Army Air Corps (song, 1939) 'Off we go into the wild blue yonder, Climbing high into the sun'

QUOTATIONS

13 And the Lord said unto Satan, Whence comest thou? Then Satan answered the Lord, and said, From going to and fro in the earth, and from walking up and down in it.
Bible: Job

14 They change their clime, not their frame of mind, who rush across the sea.
Horace 65–8 BC: *Epistles*

15 Ay, now am I in Arden; the more fool I. When I was at home I was in a better place; but travellers must be content.
William Shakespeare 1564–1616: *As You Like It* (1599)

16 He disdains all things above his reach, and preferreth all countries before his own.
Thomas Overbury 1581–1613: *Miscellaneous Works* (1632) 'An Affected Traveller'

17 Travel, in the younger sort, is a part of education; in the elder, a part of experience. He that travelleth into a country before he hath some entrance into the language, goeth to school, and not to travel.
Francis Bacon 1561–1626: *Essays* (1625) 'Of Travel'

18 See one promontory (said Socrates of old), one mountain, one sea, one river, and see all.
Robert Burton 1577–1640: *The Anatomy of Melancholy* (1621–51)

19 I always love to begin a journey on Sundays, because I shall have the prayers of the church, to preserve all that travel by land, or by water.
Jonathan Swift 1667–1745: *Polite Conversation* (1738)

20 So it is in travelling; a man must carry knowledge with him, if he would bring home knowledge.
Samuel Johnson 1709–84: James Boswell *Life of Samuel Johnson* (1791) 17 April 1778

21 Worth seeing, yes; but not worth going to see.
on the Giant's Causeway
Samuel Johnson 1709–84: James Boswell *Life of Samuel Johnson* (1791) 12 October 1779

22 Travelling is the ruin of all happiness! There's no looking at a building here after seeing Italy.
Fanny Burney 1752–1840: *Cecilia* (1782)

23   I am become a name;
For always roaming with a hungry heart.
Alfred, Lord Tennyson 1809–92: 'Ulysses' (1842)

24 It is not worthwhile to go around the world to count the cats in Zanzibar.
Henry David Thoreau 1817–62: *Walden* (1854) 'Conclusion'

25 'Abroad', that large home of ruined reputations.
George Eliot 1819–80: *Felix Holt* (1866)

26 Of all noxious animals, too, the most noxious is a tourist. And of all tourists the most vulgar, ill-bred, offensive and loathsome is the British tourist.
Francis Kilvert 1840–79: diary 5 April 1870

27 For my part, I travel not to go anywhere, but to go. I travel for travel's sake. The great affair is to move.
Robert Louis Stevenson 1850–94: *Travels with a Donkey* (1879)

28 To travel hopefully is a better thing than to arrive, and the true success is to labour.
Robert Louis Stevenson 1850–94: *Virginibus Puerisque* (1881); see **Hope** 7

29 A man travels the world in search of what he needs and returns home to find it.
George Moore 1852–1933: *The Brook Kerith* (1916)

30 How 'ya gonna keep 'em down on the farm (after they've seen Paree)?
Sam M. Lewis 1885–1959 and **Joe Young** 1889–1939: title of song (1919)

31 I like my 'abroad' to be Catholic and sensual.
Henry ('Chips') Channon 1897–1958: diary 18 January 1924

32 In America there are two classes of travel—first class, and with children.
Robert Benchley 1889–1945: *Pluck and Luck* (1925)

33 São Paulo is like Reading, only much farther away.
Peter Fleming 1907–71: *Brazilian Adventure* (1933)

34 A good traveller is one who does not know where he is going to, and a perfect traveller does not know where he came from.
Lin Yutang 1895–1976: *The Importance of Living* (1938)

35 Frogs . . . are slightly better than Huns or Wops, but abroad is unutterably bloody and foreigners are fiends.
Nancy Mitford 1904–73: *The Pursuit of Love* (1945)

36 Why do the wrong people travel, travel,
When the right people stay back home?
Noël Coward 1899–1973: 'Why do the Wrong People Travel?' (1961 song)

37 I did not fully understand the dread term 'terminal illness' until I saw Heathrow for myself.
Dennis Potter 1935–94: in *Sunday Times* 4 June 1978

38 In the middle ages people were tourists because of their religion, whereas now they are tourists because tourism is their religion.
Robert Runcie 1921–99: speech in London, 6 December 1988

39 The Devil himself had probably re-designed Hell in the light of information he had gained from observing airport layouts.
Anthony Price 1928– : *The Memory Trap* (1989)

40 Tourists look at themselves as the be all and end all, but they are not. They are just another crop, like cotton was in the past.
Lord Glenconner 1926– : in *Sunday Times* 7 January 2001

Treachery see **Trust and Treachery**

Trees

PROVERBS AND SAYINGS

1 **Beware of an oak, it draws the stroke; avoid an ash, it counts the flash; creep under the thorn, it can save you from harm.**
late 19th century, recording traditional beliefs on where to shelter from lightning during a thunderstorm

2 **Every elm has its man.**
early 20th century; perhaps referring to the readiness of the tree to drop its branches on the unwary. Elm wood was also traditionally used for coffins

PHRASES

3 **upas tree** in folklore, a Javanese tree alleged to poison its surroundings and said to be fatal to approach.
an account of the tree given in the London Magazine *of 1783 was said to be translated from one written in Dutch by Mr Foersch, a surgeon at Samarang in 1773, but was in fact invented by the writer and critic George Steevens (1736–1800)*

QUOTATIONS

4 Something sweet is the whisper of the pine, O goatherd, that makes her music by yonder springs.
Theocritus c.300–260 BC: *Idylls*

5 Generations pass while some trees stand, and old families last not three oaks.
Thomas Browne 1605–82: *Hydriotaphia* (Urn Burial, 1658)

6 Under the cherry—
blossom soup,

blossom salad.
Matsuo Basho 1644–94: translated by Lucien Stryk

7 He that plants trees loves others beside
himself.
Thomas Fuller 1654–1734: *Gnomologia* (1732)

8 The poplars are felled, farewell to the shade
And the whispering sound of the cool
colonnade.
William Cowper 1731–1800: 'The Poplar-Field'
(written 1784)

9 O leave this barren spot to me!
Spare, woodman, spare the beechen tree.
Thomas Campbell 1777–1844: 'The Beech-Tree's
Petition' (1800)

10 And since to look at things in bloom
Fifty springs are little room,
About the woodlands I will go
To see the cherry hung with snow.
A. E. Housman 1859–1936: *A Shropshire Lad* (1896)

11 Of all the trees that grow so fair,
Old England to adorn,
Greater are none beneath the Sun,
Than Oak, and Ash, and Thorn.
Rudyard Kipling 1865–1936: *Puck of Pook's Hill*
(1906) 'A Tree Song'

12 For pines are gossip pines the wide world
through
And full of runic tales to sigh or sing.
James Elroy Flecker 1884–1915: *Golden Journey to
Samarkand* (1913) 'Brumana'

13 I like trees because they seem more
resigned to the way they have to live than
other things do.
Willa Cather 1873–1947: *O Pioneers!* (1913)

14 I think that I shall never see
A poem lovely as a tree.
Joyce Kilmer 1886–1918: 'Trees' (1914); see
Pollution 15

15 O chestnut-tree, great-rooted blossomer,
Are you the leaf, the blossom or the bole?
W. B. Yeats 1865–1939: 'Among School Children'
(1928)

16 I am for the woods against the world,
But are the woods for me?
Edmund Blunden 1896–1974: 'The Kiss' (1931)

17 In every wood, in every spring,
there is a different green.
J. R. R. Tolkien 1892–1973: *The Fellowship of the
Ring* (1954)

18 Now dream
of that sweet
equal republic
where the juniper
talks to the oak,
the thistle,
the bandaged elm,
and the jolly jolly chestnut.
Tom Paulin 1949– : 'The Book of Juniper' (1983)

19 Hugging trees has a calming effect on me.
I'm talking about enormous trees that will
be there when we are all dead and gone.
I've hugged trees in every part of this little
island.
Gerry Adams 1948– : in *Independent* 7 July 2001

Trust and Treachery

PROVERBS AND SAYINGS

1 Fear the Greeks bearing gifts.
*late 19th century; originally from Virgil: see 18 below;
see also 15 below, **Gifts** 7*

**2 Please to remember the Fifth of November,
Gunpowder Treason and Plot.
We know no reason why gunpowder
treason
Should ever be forgot.**
*traditional rhyme on the Gunpowder Plot (1605); see
Festivals 24*

**3 Promises, like pie-crust, are made to be
broken.**
late 17th century

4 Would you buy a used car from this man?
campaign slogan directed against Richard Nixon, 1968

**5 You cannot run with the hare and hunt
with the hounds.**
*mid 15th century, meaning that you must take one of
two opposing sides; see 11 below*

PHRASES

6 drop the pilot abandon a trustworthy
adviser.
*from dropping the pilot, caption to Tenniel's cartoon,
and title of poem, on Bismarck's dismissal as German
Chancellor by the young Kaiser; in* Punch *29 March
1890*

7 fifth column an organized body sympathizing with and working for the enemy within a country at war or otherwise under attack.

translating Spanish quinta columna, *an extra body of supporters claimed by General Mola as being within Madrid when he besieged the city with four columns of Nationalist forces in 1936*

8 Judas kiss an act of betrayal.

Judas *Iscariot, the disciple who betrayed Jesus, after the Bible (Matthew), 'And he that betrayed him gave them a sign, saying, Whomsoever I shall kiss, that same is he: hold him fast'; see 37 below*

9 night of the long knives a ruthless or decisive action held to resemble a treacherous massacre.

after the massacre (according to legend) of the Britons by Hengist in 472, or of Ernst Roehm and his associates by Hitler on 29–30 June 1934

10 Punic faith treachery.

from Latin Punica fide *'with Carthaginian trustworthiness' (Sallust* Jugurtha*), reflecting the traditional hostility of Rome to Carthage*

11 run with the hare and hunt with the hounds try to remain on good terms with both sides in a quarrel; play a double role.

see 5 above

12 a scrap of paper a treaty or pledge which one does not intend to honour.

said to have been used by the German Chancellor, Bethmann-Hollweg (1856–1921) in connection with German violation of Belgian neutrality in August 1914; see **International Relations** *24*

13 sell down the river let down, betray.

originally of selling a troublesome slave to the owner of a sugar cane plantation on the lower Mississippi, where conditions were harsher than in the northern slave states

14 thirty pieces of silver a material gain for which a principle has been betrayed.

from the price for which Judas betrayed Jesus to the Jewish authorities, as told in the Bible (Matthew): 'and they covenanted with him for thirty pieces of silver'; see **Death** *15*

15 Trojan horse a person or device deliberately set to bring about an enemy's downfall or to undermine from within.

a hollow wooden statue of a horse in which the Greeks are said to have concealed themselves to enter Troy: see 18 below; see also **Computers** *7*

16 true blue faithful, staunch, and unwavering.

perhaps with regard to the blue of the sky, or to some specially fast dye; from the mid 17th century applied specifically to the Scottish Presbyterian or Whig party,

and later (in the current sense), to the Tory, or Conservative, Party; see **Political Parties** *14*

QUOTATIONS

17 O put not your trust in princes, nor in any child of man: for there is no help in them.
Bible: Psalm 146

18   *Equo ne credite, Teucri.*
Quidquid id est, timeo Danaos et dona
*   ferentes.*
Do not trust the horse, Trojans. Whatever it is, I fear the Greeks even when they bring gifts.
Virgil 70–19 BC: *Aeneid*; see 1, 15 above, see also **Gifts** 7

19 *Et tu, Brute?*
You too, Brutus?
said to his friend Brutus as he was assassinated by him
Julius Caesar 100–44 BC: traditional rendering of Suetonius *Lives of the Caesars* 'Divus Julius'

20 This night, before the cock crow, thou shalt deny me thrice.
Bible: St Matthew

21 *Quis custodiet ipsos custodes?*
Who is to guard the guards themselves?
Juvenal AD c.60–c.130: *Satires*

22 The smylere with the knyf under the cloke.
Geoffrey Chaucer c.1343–1400: *The Canterbury Tales* 'The Knight's Tale'

23 I know what it is to be a subject, what to be a Sovereign, what to have good neighbours, and sometimes meet evil-willers.
the traditional version concludes: 'and in trust I have found treason'
Elizabeth I 1533–1603: speech to a Parliamentary deputation at Richmond, 12 November 1586; John Neale *Elizabeth I and her Parliaments 1584–1601* (1957), from a report 'which the Queen herself heavily amended in her own hand'

24 Treason doth never prosper, what's the reason?
For if it prosper, none dare call it treason.
John Harington 1561–1612: *Epigrams* (1618)

25 There is nothing makes a man suspect much, more than to know little.
Francis Bacon 1561–1626: *Essays* (1625) 'Of Suspicion'

26 It is better to suffer wrong than to do it, and happier to be sometimes cheated than not to trust.
Samuel Johnson 1709–84: in *Rambler* 18 December 1750

27 Caesar had his Brutus—Charles the First, his Cromwell—and George the Third— ('Treason,' cried the Speaker) . . . *may profit by their example. If this* be treason, make the most of it.
Patrick Henry 1736–99: speech in the Virginia assembly, May 1765

to the Emperor of Russia, who had spoken bitterly of those who had betrayed the cause of Europe:
28 That, Sire, is a question of dates.
often quoted as, 'treason is a matter of dates'
Charles-Maurice de Talleyrand 1754–1838: Duff Cooper *Talleyrand* (1932)

29 Just for a handful of silver he left us,
Just for a riband to stick in his coat.
of Wordsworth's apparent betrayal of his radical principles by accepting the position of poet laureate
Robert Browning 1812–89: 'The Lost Leader' (1845)

30 And trust me not at all or all in all.
Alfred, Lord Tennyson 1809–92: *Idylls of the King* 'Merlin and Vivien' (1859)

31 A promise made is a debt unpaid, and the trail has its own stern code.
Robert W. Service 1874–1958: 'The Cremation of Sam McGee' (1907)

32 To trust people is a luxury in which only the wealthy can indulge; the poor cannot afford it.
E. M. Forster 1879–1970: *Howards End* (1910)

33 Anyone can rat, but it takes a certain amount of ingenuity to re-rat.
on rejoining the Conservatives twenty years after leaving them for the Liberals, c.1924
Winston Churchill 1874–1965: Kay Halle *Irrepressible Churchill* (1966)

34 He trusted neither of them as far as he could spit, and he was a poor spitter, lacking both distance and control.
P. G. Wodehouse 1881–1975: *Money in the Bank* (1946)

35 Greater love hath no man than this, that he lay down his friends for his life.
on Harold Macmillan sacking seven of his Cabinet on 13 July 1962
Jeremy Thorpe 1929– : D. E. Butler and Anthony King *The General Election of 1964* (1965); see **Self-Sacrifice** 3

36 To betray, you must first belong.
Kim Philby 1912–88: in *Sunday Times* 17 December 1967

37 Judas was paid! I am sacrificing my whole political life.
response to a heckler's call of 'Judas', having advised Conservatives to vote Labour at the coming general election
Enoch Powell 1912–98: speech at Bull Ring, Birmingham, 23 February 1974; see **8** above

38 I think the greatest of all human virtues is loyalty. It embraces all the best of the human character: courage, faith, love and charity.
Douglas Bader 1910–82: speech, 4 September 1982

39 He who wields the knife never wears the crown.
Michael Heseltine 1933– : in *New Society* 14 February 1986

40 It is rather like sending your opening batsmen to the crease only for them to find the moment that the first balls are bowled that their bats have been broken before the game by the team captain.
Geoffrey Howe 1926– : resignation speech as Deputy Prime Minister, House of Commons 13 November 1990

41 After first confidences between people moving towards friendship, a rest between exchanges of information somehow hastens, not impedes, the growing trust.
Candia McWilliam 1955– : *Debatable Land* (1994)

Truth see also **Honesty**, **Lies**

1 Believe it or not.
title of syndicated newspaper feature (from 1918), written by Robert L. Ripley

2 Many a true word is spoken in jest.
late 14th century, meaning that an apparent joke may often include a shrewd comment, or that what is spoken of as unlikely or improbable may in the future turn out to be true

3 Se non è vero, è molto ben trovato.
*Italian = If it is not true, it is a happy invention; common saying from the 16th century; see **9** below*

4 Tell the truth and shame the devil.
mid 16th century, meaning that by telling the truth one is taking the right course however embarrassing or difficult it may be

5 Truth is stranger than fiction.

early 19th century, implying that no invention can be as remarkable as what may actually happen; from Byron: see 28 below; see also **Fiction** 1

6 Truth lies at the bottom of a well.

mid 16th century, sometimes used to imply that the truth of a situation can be hard to find

7 Truth will out.

mid 15th century; meaning that in the end what has really happened will become apparent

8 What everybody says must be true.

late 14th century, sometimes used ironically to assert that popular gossip is often inaccurate

PHRASES

9 ben trovato happily invented; appropriate though untrue.

Italian, literally 'well found': see 3 above

10 the truth, the whole truth, and nothing but the truth the absolute truth, without concealment or addition.

part of the formula of the oath taken by witnesses in court

QUOTATIONS

11 Great is Truth, and mighty above all things.

Bible: I Esdras

12 But, my dearest Agathon, it is truth which you cannot contradict; you can without any difficulty contradict Socrates.

Socrates 469-399 BC: Plato *Symposium*

13 Plato is dear to me, but dearer still is truth.

Aristotle 384-322 BC: attributed

14 And ye shall know the truth, and the truth shall make you free.

Bible: St John; see 37 below

15 Truth will come to light; murder cannot be hid long.

William Shakespeare 1564-1616: *The Merchant of Venice* (1596-8)

16 What is truth? said jesting Pilate; and would not stay for an answer.

Francis Bacon 1561-1626: *Essays* (1625) 'Of Truth'

17 Many from . . . an inconsiderate zeal unto truth, have too rashly charged the troops of error, and remain as trophies unto the enemies of truth.

Thomas Browne 1605-82: *Religio Medici* (1643)

18 Though all the winds of doctrine were let loose to play upon the earth, so Truth be

in the field, we do injuriously by licensing and prohibiting to misdoubt her strength. Let her and Falsehood grapple; who ever knew Truth put to the worse, in a free and open encounter?

John Milton 1608-74: *Areopagitica* (1644)

19 True and False are attributes of speech, not of things. And where speech is not, there is neither Truth nor Falsehood.

Thomas Hobbes 1588-1679: *Leviathan* (1651)

20 It is one thing to show a man that he is in error, and another to put him in possession of truth.

John Locke 1632-1704: *An Essay concerning Human Understanding* (1690)

21 I design plain truth for plain people.

John Wesley 1703-91: *Sermons on Several Occasions* (1746)

22 They make truth serve as a stalking-horse to error.

Henry St John, Lord Bolingbroke 1678-1751: *Letters on the Study and Use of History* (1752)

23 It is commonly said, and more particularly by Lord Shaftesbury, that ridicule is the best test of truth.

Lord Chesterfield 1694-1773: *Letters to his Son* (1774) 6 February 1752

24 In lapidary inscriptions a man is not upon oath.

Samuel Johnson 1709-84: James Boswell *Life of Samuel Johnson* (1791) 1775

25 If God were to hold out enclosed in His right hand all Truth, and in His left hand just the active search for Truth, though with the condition that I should always err therein, and He should say to me: Choose! I should humbly take His left hand and say: Father! Give me this one; absolute Truth belongs to Thee alone.

G. E. Lessing 1729-81: *Eine Duplik* (1778)

26 A truth that's told with bad intent
Beats all the lies you can invent.

William Blake 1757-1827: 'Auguries of Innocence' (c.1803)

27 I am certain of nothing but the holiness of the heart's affections and the truth of imagination—what the imagination seizes as beauty must be truth—whether it existed before or not.

John Keats 1795-1821: letter to Benjamin Bailey, 22 November 1817; see **Beauty** 19

28 'Tis strange—but true; for truth is always strange;

Stranger than fiction.
Lord Byron 1788-1824: *Don Juan* (1819-24); see 5 above

29 What I tell you three times is true.
Lewis Carroll 1832-98: *The Hunting of the Snark* (1876)

30 It is the customary fate of new truths to begin as heresies and to end as superstitions.
T. H. Huxley 1825-95: *Science and Culture and Other Essays* (1881) 'The Coming of Age of the Origin of Species'

31 The truth is rarely pure, and never simple.
Oscar Wilde 1854-1900: *The Importance of Being Earnest* (1895)

32 Truth is the most valuable thing we have. Let us economize it.
Mark Twain 1835-1910: *Following the Equator* (1897); see 42 below

33 A platitude is simply a truth repeated until people get tired of hearing it.
Stanley Baldwin 1867-1947: speech, House of Commons, 29 May 1924

34 An exaggeration is a truth that has lost its temper.
Kahlil Gibran 1883-1931: *Sand and Foam* (1926)

35 Truth is a pathless land, and you cannot approach it by any path whatsoever, by any religion, by any sect.
Jiddu Krishnamurti 1895-1986: speech in Holland, 3 August 1929

36 The truth is often a terrible weapon of aggression. It is possible to lie, and even to murder, for the truth.
Alfred Adler 1870-1937: *The Problems of Neurosis* (1929)

37 The truth which makes men free is for the most part the truth which men prefer not to hear.
Herbert Agar 1897-1980: *A Time for Greatness* (1942); see 14 above

38 There are no whole truths; all truths are half-truths. It is trying to treat them as whole truths that plays the devil.
Alfred North Whitehead 1861-1947: *Dialogues* (1954)

39 Truth exists; only lies are invented.
Georges Braque 1882-1963: *Le Jour et la nuit: Cahiers 1917-52*

40 One of the favourite maxims of my father was the distinction between the two sorts of truths, profound truths recognized by the fact that the opposite is also a profound truth, in contrast to trivialities where opposites are obviously absurd.
Niels Bohr 1885-1962: S. Rozental *Niels Bohr* (1967)

41 Truth is not merely what we are thinking, but also why, to whom and under what circumstances we say it.
Václav Havel 1936- : *Temptation* (1985)

42 It contains a misleading impression, not a lie. It was being economical with the truth.
the phrase 'economy of truth' was earlier used by Edmund Burke (1729-97)
Robert Armstrong 1927- : referring to a letter during the 'Spycatcher' trial, Supreme Court, New South Wales, in *Daily Telegraph* 19 November 1986; see 32 above, **Lies** 6

43 In exceptional circumstances it is necessary to say something that is untrue in the House of Commons.
William Waldegrave 1946- : in *Guardian* 9 March 1994

The Universe see also The Earth, The Skies

PHRASES

1 **big bang** the explosion of dense matter which according to current cosmological theories marked the origin of the universe.
see 16 below

2 **the four elements** earth, air, fire, and water.
collectively regarded as constituents of the material world by ancient and medieval philosophers

3 **Ptolemaic system** the theory that the earth is the stationary centre of the universe, with the planets moving in epicyclic orbits within surrounding concentric spheres.
after Ptolemy (2nd century), Greek astronomer and geographer; see 6 below, see also **Music** *3*

QUOTATIONS

4 Is it not worthy of tears that, when the number of worlds is infinite, we have not yet become lords of a single one?
when asked why he wept on hearing from Anaxarchus that there was an infinite number of worlds
Alexander the Great 356-323 BC: Plutarch *Moralia*

5 The universe and I exist together, and all things and I are one.
Zhuangzi c.369–286 BC: *Chuang Tzu* ch. 2

6 Had I been present at the Creation, I would have given some useful hints for the better ordering of the universe.
on studying the Ptolemaic system
Alfonso 'the Wise' of Castile 1221–84: attributed; see 3 above

7 The eternal silence of these infinite spaces [the heavens] terrifies me.
Blaise Pascal 1623–62: *Pensées* (1670)

on hearing that Margaret Fuller 'accepted the universe':
8 'Gad! she'd better!'
Thomas Carlyle 1795–1881: William James *Varieties of Religious Experience* (1902)

9 Not a sound. The universe sleeps, resting a huge ear on its paw with mites of stars.
Vladimir Mayakovsky 1893–1930: 'The Cloud in Trousers' (1915)

10 The world is everything that is the case.
Ludwig Wittgenstein 1889–1951: *Tractatus Logico-Philosophicus* (1922)

11 Now, my own suspicion is that the universe is not only queerer than we suppose, but queerer than we *can* suppose . . . I suspect that there are more things in heaven and earth than are dreamed of, or can be dreamed of, in any philosophy.
J. B. S. Haldane 1892–1964: *Possible Worlds and Other Essays* (1927) 'Possible Worlds'; see **The Supernatural** 11

12 From the intrinsic evidence of his creation, the Great Architect of the Universe now begins to appear as a pure mathematician.
James Jeans 1877–1946: *The Mysterious Universe* (1930)

13 This, now, is the judgement of our scientific age—the third reaction of man upon the universe! This universe is not hostile, nor yet is it friendly. It is simply indifferent.
John H. Holmes 1879–1964: *The Sensible Man's View of Religion* (1932)

14 The eternal mystery of the world is its comprehensibility . . . The fact that it is comprehensible is a miracle.
usually quoted as 'The most incomprehensible fact about the universe is that it is comprehensible'
Albert Einstein 1879–1955: in *Franklin Institute Journal* March 1936 'Physics and Reality'

15 Ptolemy made a universe, which lasted 1400 years. Newton, also, made a universe, which lasted 300 years. Einstein has made a universe, and I can't tell you how long that will last.
George Bernard Shaw 1856–1950: David Cassidy *Einstein and Our World* (1995)

16 One [idea] was that the Universe started its life a finite time ago in a single huge explosion. . . . This big bang idea seemed to me to be unsatisfactory.
Fred Hoyle 1915–2001: *The Nature of the Universe* (1950); see 1 above

17 Space isn't remote at all. It's only an hour's drive away if your car could go straight upwards.
Fred Hoyle 1915–2001: in *Observer* 9 September 1979

18 We are the children of chaos, and the deep structure of change is decay. At root, there is only corruption, and the unstemmable tide of chaos. Gone is purpose; all that is left is direction. This is the bleakness we have to accept as we peer deeply and dispassionately into the heart of the Universe.
Peter Atkins 1940– : *The Second Law* (1984)

19 The Greeks said God was always doing geometry, modern physicists say he's playing roulette, everything depends on the observer, the universe is a totality of observations, it's a work of art created by us.
Iris Murdoch 1919–99: *The Good Apprentice* (1985); see **God** 7

20 What is it that breathes fire into the equations and makes a universe for them to describe . . . Why does the universe go to all the bother of existing?
Stephen Hawking 1942– : *A Brief History of Time* (1988)

21 Space is almost infinite. As a matter of fact, we think it is infinite.
Dan Quayle 1947– : in *Daily Telegraph* 8 March 1989

22 It is often said that there is no such thing as a free lunch. The Universe, however, is a free lunch.
Alan Guth 1947– : in *Harpers* November 1994; see **Economics** 2

23 I think it is likely that there is life out there. I fear we shall never know about it.
Richard Dawkins 1941– : *Seven Wonders of the World* (BBC TV) 9 April 1997

Universities see also Education, Teaching

1 **Lady Margaret Hall for ladies,
St Hugh's for girls,
St Hilda's for wenches,
Somerville for women.**
Oxford saying, c. 1930s

2 **the Ivy League** a group of long-established
eastern US universities of high academic
and social prestige, including Harvard,
Yale, Princeton, and Columbia.

3 **redbrick university** a British university
founded in the late 19th or early 20th
century, usually in a large industrial city,
and especially as contrasted with Oxford
and Cambridge.
see 24 below

4 **town and gown** non-members and
members of a university in a particular
place.
gown as worn by members of a university

5 A Clerk there was of Oxenford also,
That unto logyk hadde longe ygo.
As leene was his hors as is a rake,
And he was nat right fat, I undertake,
But looked holwe, and therto sobrely.
Geoffrey Chaucer c.1343–1400: *The Canterbury Tales*
'The General Prologue'

6 Universities incline wits to sophistry and
affectation.
Francis Bacon 1561–1626: *Valerius Terminus of the
Interpretation of Nature*

7 Aye, 'tis well enough for a servant to be
bred at an University. But the education is
a little too pedantic for a gentleman.
William Congreve 1670–1729: *Love for Love* (1695)

8 The discipline of colleges and universities is
in general contrived, not for the benefit of
the students, but for the interest, or more
properly speaking, for the ease of the
masters.
Adam Smith 1723–90: *Wealth of Nations* (1776)

9 To the University of Oxford I acknowledge
no obligation; and she will as cheerfully
renounce me for a son, as I am willing to
disclaim her for a mother. I spent fourteen

months at Magdalen College: they proved
the fourteen months the most idle and
unprofitable of my whole life.
Edward Gibbon 1737–94: *Memoirs of My Life* (1796)

10 The most prominent requisite to a lecturer,
though perhaps not really the most
important, is a good delivery; for though
to all true philosophers science and nature
will have charms innumerable in every
dress, yet I am sorry to say that the
generality of mankind cannot accompany
us one short hour unless the path is
strewed with flowers.
Michael Faraday 1791–1867: *Advice to a Lecturer*
(1960); from his letters and notebook written at
age 21

11 The true University of these days is a
collection of books.
Thomas Carlyle 1795–1881: *On Heroes, Hero-
Worship, and the Heroic* (1841)

12 A classic lecture, rich in sentiment,
With scraps of thundrous epic lilted out
By violet-hooded Doctors, elegies
And quoted odes, and jewels five-words-
    long,
That on the stretched forefinger of all Time
Sparkle for ever.
Alfred, Lord Tennyson 1809–92: *The Princess*
(1847)

13 A whaleship was my Yale College and my
Harvard.
Herman Melville 1819–91: *Moby Dick* (1851)

14 Nor can I do better, in conclusion, than
impress upon you the study of Greek
literature, which not only elevates above
the vulgar herd, but leads not infrequently
to positions of considerable emolument.
Thomas Gaisford 1779–1855: Christmas Day
Sermon in the Cathedral, Oxford; W. Tuckwell
Reminiscences of Oxford (2nd ed., 1907)

15 Home of lost causes, and forsaken beliefs,
and unpopular names, and impossible
loyalties!
of Oxford
Matthew Arnold 1822–88: *Essays in Criticism* First
Series (1865)

16 A University should be a place of light, of
liberty, and of learning.
Benjamin Disraeli 1804–81: speech, House of
Commons, 11 March 1873

17 Undergraduates owe their happiness chiefly to the consciousness that they are no longer at school. The nonsense which was knocked out of them at school is all put gently back at Oxford or Cambridge.
Max Beerbohm 1872–1956: *More* (1899)

18 Very nice sort of place, Oxford, I should think, for people that like that sort of place. They teach you to be a gentleman there. In the Polytechnic they teach you to be an engineer or such like.
George Bernard Shaw 1856–1950: *Man and Superman* (1903)

19 Gentlemen: I have not had your advantages. What poor education I have received has been gained in the University of Life.
Horatio Bottomley 1860–1933: speech at the Oxford Union, 2 December 1920

20 Our American professors like their literature clear and cold and pure and very dead.
Sinclair Lewis 1885–1951: Nobel Prize Address, 12 December 1930

21 Princeton is a wonderful little spot. A quaint and ceremonious village of puny demigods on stilts.
Albert Einstein 1879–1955: letter to Queen Elisabeth of Belgium, 20 November 1933

22 We always eat Oxford marmalade at Camblidge. Better scholars, better plofessors at Camblidge, but better marmalade at Oxford.
Arthur Ransome 1884–1967: *Missee Lee* (1941)

23 I am told that today rather more than 60 per cent of the men who go to the universities go on a Government grant. This is a new class that has entered upon the scene . . . They are scum.
W. Somerset Maugham 1874–1965: in *Sunday Times* 25 December 1955

24 I don't think one 'comes down' from Jimmy's university. According to him, it's not even red brick, but white tile.
John Osborne 1929–94: *Look Back in Anger* (1956); see 3 above

25 The delusion that there are thousands of young people about who are capable of benefiting from university training, but have somehow failed to find their way there, is . . . a necessary component of the expansionist case . . . More will mean worse.
Kingsley Amis 1922–95: in *Encounter* July 1960

26 Four times, under our educational rules, the human pack is shuffled and cut—at eleven-plus, sixteen-plus, eighteen-plus and twenty-plus—and happy is he who comes top of the deck on each occasion, but especially the last. This is called Finals, the very name of which implies that nothing of importance can happen after it.
David Lodge 1935– : *Changing Places* (1975)

27 City of perspiring dreams.
of Cambridge
Frederic Raphael 1931– : *The Glittering Prizes* (1976); see **British Towns** 17

28 There is one thing that a professor can be absolutely certain of: almost every student entering the university believes, or says he believes, that truth is relative.
Allan Bloom 1930–92: *The Closing of the American Mind* (1987)

29 Why am I the first Kinnock in a thousand generations to be able to get to a university?
later plagiarized by the American politician Joe Biden
Neil Kinnock 1942– : speech in party political broadcast, 21 May 1987

30 As to our universities, I've come to the conclusion that they are élitist where they should be egalitarian and egalitarian where they should be élitist.
David Lodge 1935– : *Nice Work* (1989)

Value

1 Gold may be bought too dear.
mid 16th century, meaning that wealth may be acquired at too great a price

2 If you pay peanuts, you get monkeys.
mid 20th century, meaning that a poor rate of pay will attract only poorly qualified and incompetent staff (peanuts here means 'a small sum of money')

3 It is a poor dog that's not worth whistling for.

mid 16th century, meaning that a dog is of no value if the owner will not even go to the trouble of whistling for it

4 Little things please little minds.

late 16th century

5 Nothing comes of nothing.

late 14th century

6 Nothing for nothing.

early 18th century, summarizing the attitude that if nothing will be offered unless a return is assured

7 Worth a guinea a box.

advertising slogan for Beecham's pills, from c.1859, from the chance remark of a lady purchaser

8 The worth of a thing is what it will bring.

mid 16th century, meaning that the real value of something can only be measured by what another person is willing to pay for it

PHRASES

9 the end of the rainbow the place where something precious is found at last.

with allusion to the proverbial belief in the existence of a crock of gold (or something else of great value) at the end of a rainbow; see 14 below

10 golden calf something, especially wealth, as an object of excessive or unworthy worship.

from the story in the Bible (Exodus) of the idol made and worshipped by the Israelites in disobedience to Moses

11 holy of holies a thing regarded as sacrosanct.

the inner chamber of the sanctuary in the Jewish Temple, separated by a veil from the outer chamber

12 make a mountain out of a molehill laying unnecessary stress on a small matter.

see Optimism 34

13 mess of pottage a material or trivial comfort gained at the expense of something more important.

the price, according to the Bible (Genesis), for which Esau sold his birthright to his brother Jacob; see Theatre 2

14 pot of gold an imaginary reward; a jackpot; an ideal.

supposedly to be found at the end of the rainbow: see 9 above

15 pride of place the most prominent or important position among a group of things.

in falconry, the high position from which a falcon or similar bird swoops down on its prey; first recorded in Shakespeare's Macbeth

QUOTATIONS

16 Thirty spokes share the wheel's hub;
It is the centre hole that makes it useful.
Shape clay into a vessel;
It is the space within that makes it useful.
Cut doors and windows for a room;
It is the holes which make it useful.
Therefore profit comes from what is there;
Usefulness from what is not there.
Lao-tsu c.604–c.531 BC: *Tao-Tê-Ching*

17 A living dog is better than a dead lion.
Bible: Ecclesiastes; see **Life** 5

18 Neither cast ye your pearls before swine.
Bible: St Matthew; see **Futility** 8

19 Men do not weigh the stalk for that it was,
When once they find her flower, her glory, pass.
Samuel Daniel 1563–1619: *Delia* (1592) sonnet 32

20 O monstrous! but one half-pennyworth of bread to this intolerable deal of sack!
William Shakespeare 1564–1616: *Henry IV, Part 1* (1597)

21   Of one whose hand,
Like the base Indian, threw a pearl away
Richer than all his tribe.
William Shakespeare 1564–1616: *Othello* (1602–4)

22   Then on the shore
Of the wide world I stand alone and think
Till love and fame to nothingness do sink.
John Keats 1795–1821: 'When I have fears that I may cease to be' (written 1818)

23 It is not that pearls fetch a high price *because* men have dived for them; but on the contrary, men dive for them because they fetch a high price.
Richard Whately 1787–1863: *Introductory Lectures on Political Economy* (1832)

24 An acre in Middlesex is better than a principality in Utopia.
Lord Macaulay 1800–59: *Essays Contributed to the Edinburgh Review* (1843) 'Lord Bacon'

25 Every man is wanted, and no man is wanted much.
Ralph Waldo Emerson 1803–82: *Essays. Second Series* (1844) 'Nominalist and Realist'

26 You can calculate the worth of a man by the number of his enemies, and the importance of a work of art by the harm that is spoken of it.
Gustave Flaubert 1821–80: letter to Louise Colet, 14 June 1853

27 Nothink for nothink 'ere, and precious
little for sixpence.
Punch: in 1869

28 I never loved a dear Gazelle—
Nor anything that cost me much:
High prices profit those who sell,
But why should I be fond of such?
Lewis Carroll 1832–98: *Phantasmagoria* (1869)
'Theme with Variations'; see **Transience** 11

29 It is the peculiar beauty of this method,
gentlemen, and the one that endears it to
the really scientific mind that under no
circumstances can it possibly be of the
smallest possible utility to anyone.
H. J. A. Smith 1826–83: C. H. Pearson *Biographical
Sketches and Recollections of Henry John Skipton Scott*
(1894)

30 I cannot help it that my pictures do not
sell. Nevertheless the time will come when
people will see that they are worth more
than the price of the paint.
Vincent Van Gogh 1853–90: letter to his brother
Theo, 20 October 1888

31 It has long been an axiom of mine that the
little things are infinitely the most
important.
Arthur Conan Doyle 1859–1930: *Adventures of
Sherlock Holmes* (1892)

32 No more impressive warning can be given
to those who would confine knowledge
and research to what is apparently useful,
than the reflection that conic sections were
studied for eighteen hundred years merely
as an abstract science, without regard to
any utility other than to satisfy the craving
for knowledge on the part of
mathematicians, and that then at the end
of this long period of abstract study, they
were found to be the necessary key with
which to attain the knowledge of the most
important laws of nature.
Alfred North Whitehead 1861–1947: *Introduction
to Mathematics* (1911)

33 Nothing that costs only a dollar is worth
having.
Elizabeth Arden 1876–1966: attributed; in *Fortune*
October 1973

34 One of me is worth forty thousand of you.
John McEnroe 1959– : to the crowd at the Queen's
Club tournament, in *Sunday Times* 24 June 1984

35 How do you put an estimate on a 6ft
hamster? We don't sell too many of those.
valuing items from the Millennium Dome for auction
Derek Sadler: in *Mail on Sunday* 25 February 2001

Violence

1 Burn, baby, burn.
*black extremist slogan in use during the Los Angeles
riots, August 1965*

PHRASES

2 blood and thunder violence and bloodshed,
especially in fiction.

QUOTATIONS

3 Force, unaided by judgement, collapses
through its own weight.
Horace 65–8 BC: *Odes*

4 Resist not evil: but whosoever shall smite
thee on thy right cheek, turn to him the
other also.
Bible: St Matthew; see 7 below, **Forgiveness** 9

5 All they that take the sword shall perish
with the sword.
Bible: St Matthew

6   Who overcomes
By force, hath overcome but half his foe.
John Milton 1608–74: *Paradise Lost* (1667)

7 Wisdom has taught us to be calm and
    meek,
To take one blow, and turn the other
    cheek;
It is not written what a man shall do
If the rude caitiff smite the other too!
Oliver Wendell Holmes 1809–94: 'Non-
Resistance' (1861); see 4 above

8 If you strike a child take care that you
strike it in anger, even at the risk of
maiming it for life. A blow in cold blood
neither can nor should be forgiven.
George Bernard Shaw 1856–1950: *Man and
Superman* (1903) 'Maxims: How to Beat Children'

9 Non-violence is the first article of my faith.
It is also the last article of my creed.
Mahatma Gandhi 1869–1948: speech at Shahi Bag,
18 March 1922, on a charge of sedition

10 A man may build himself a throne of bayonets, but he cannot sit on it.
quoted by Boris Yeltsin at the time of the failed military coup in Russia, August 1991
William Ralph Inge 1860–1954: *Philosophy of Plotinus* (1923)

11 Where force is necessary, there it must be applied boldly, decisively and completely. But one must know the limitations of force; one must know when to blend force with a manoeuvre, a blow with an agreement.
Leon Trotsky 1879–1940: *What Next?* (1932)

12 Pale Ebenezer thought it wrong to fight, But Roaring Bill (who killed him) thought it right.
Hilaire Belloc 1870–1953: 'The Pacifist' (1938)

13 In violence, we forget who we are.
Mary McCarthy 1912–89: *On the Contrary* (1961) 'Characters in Fiction'

14 I don't think there is anything particularly wrong about hitting a woman—although I don't recommend doing it in the same way that you'd hit a man.
Sean Connery 1930– : in *Playboy* November 1965

15 A riot is at bottom the language of the unheard.
Martin Luther King 1929–68: *Where Do We Go From Here?* (1967)

16 I say violence is necessary. It is as American as cherry pie.
H. Rap Brown 1943– : speech at Washington, 27 July 1967

17 Keep violence in the mind Where it belongs.
Brian Aldiss 1925– : *Barefoot in the Head* (1969) 'Charteris'

18 The only thing that's been a worse flop than the organization of non-violence has been the organization of violence.
Joan Baez 1941– : *Daybreak* (1970)

19 The quietly pacifist peaceful always die to make room for men who shout.
Alice Walker 1944– : 'The QPP' (1973)

20 Not hard enough.
when asked how hard she had slapped a policeman
Zsa Zsa Gabor 1919– : in *Independent* 21 September 1989

21 The terrible thing about terrorism is that ultimately it destroys those who practise it. Slowly but surely, as they try to extinguish life in others, the light within them dies.
Terry Waite 1939– : in *Guardian* 20 February 1992

22 It's very unfashionable to say this, but rape actually isn't the worst thing that can happen to a woman if you're safe, alive and unmarked after the event.
Fay Weldon 1931– : in *Radio Times* 4 July 1998

Virtue see also Good and Evil, Sin

PROVERBS AND SAYINGS

1 **The good die young.**
late 17th century, often used ironically; see **Youth** 2

2 **Good men are scarce.**
early 17th century

3 **He lives long who lives well.**
mid 16th century, meaning that the reputation derived from living a good and moral life will mean that one's name will last

4 **No good deed goes unpunished.**
modern humorous saying, sometimes attributed to Oscar Wilde but not traced in his writings

5 **See no evil, hear no evil, speak no evil.**
early 20th century; conventionally represented by 'the three wise monkeys' covering their eyes, ears, and mouth respectively with their hands, and used

particularly to imply a deliberate refusal to notice something that is wrong

6 **Virtue is its own reward.**
early 16th century; meaning that the satisfaction of knowing that one has observed appropriate moral standards should be all that is sought

PHRASES

7 **the book of life** the record of those achieving salvation.
after the Bible (Revelation) 'I will not blot out his name out of the book of life'

8 **a cardinal virtue** a particular strength or attribute.
each of the chief moral attributes (originally of scholastic philosophy), justice, prudence, temperance, and fortitude, which with the three theological virtues

*of faith, hope, and charity, comprise the seven virtues;
cardinal meaning 'a hinge'*

9 **odour of sanctity** a state of holiness or
saintliness.

*translation of French odeur de sainteté a sweet or
balsamic odour reputedly emitted by the bodies of
saints at or after death*

10 **pure as the driven snow** completely pure.

*driven of snow that has been piled into drifts or made
smooth by the wind; see 48 below*

11 **salt of the earth** of complete kindness,
honesty, and reliability.

after the Bible (Matthew) 'Ye are the salt of the earth'

12 **sans peur et sans reproche** without fear
and without blame, fearless and blameless.

*French; Chevalier sans peur et sans reproche
'Fearless, blameless knight' was the description in
contemporary chronicles of Pierre Bayard (1476–1524)*

13 **the unco guid** those who are professedly
strict in matters of morals and religion.

*originally alluding to Robert Burns 'Address to the
Unco Guid, or the Rigidly Righteous': see* **Temptation**
11

14 **Victorian values** values based on high
standards of self-reliance and personal
morality supposedly typical of the reign of
Queen Victoria (1819–1901), but
alternatively regarded as representing a
restrictive moral earnestness.

*associated particularly with Margaret Thatcher as
Conservative Prime Minister: see 51 below*

15 **without any spot or wrinkle** without any
moral stain or blemish.

*originally in Tyndale's translation of the Bible
(Ephesians)*

QUOTATIONS

16 Strait is the gate, and narrow is the way,
which leadeth unto life, and few there be
that find it.
Bible: St Matthew

17 *Puro e disposto a salire alle stelle.*
Pure and ready to mount to the stars.
Dante Alighieri 1265–1321: *Divina Commedia*
'Purgatorio'

18 Would that we had spent one whole day
well in this world!
Thomas à Kempis c.1380–1471: *The Imitation of
Christ*

19 We may not look at our pleasure to go to
heaven in feather-beds; it is not the way.
Thomas More 1478–1535: William Roper *Life of Sir
Thomas More*

20 Our goodness derives not from our
capacity to think but to love.
St Teresa of Ávila 1512–82: *Book of the Foundations*
(1610)

21 How far that little candle throws his
beams!
So shines a good deed in a naughty world.
William Shakespeare 1564–1616: *The Merchant of
Venice* (1596–8)

22 Dost thou think, because thou art
virtuous, there shall be no more cakes and
ale?
William Shakespeare 1564–1616: *Twelfth Night*
(1601); see **Pleasure** 3

23 Virtue is like a rich stone, best plain set.
Francis Bacon 1561–1626: *Essays* (1625) 'Of Beauty'

24 I cannot praise a fugitive and cloistered
virtue, unexercised and unbreathed, that
never sallies out and sees her adversary,
but slinks out of the race, where that
immortal garland is to be run for, not
without dust and heat.
John Milton 1608–74: *Areopagitica* (1644)

25 I am not the less human for being devout.
Molière 1622–73: *Le Tartuffe* (1669)

26 Instead of dirt and poison we have rather
chosen to fill our hives with honey and
wax; thus furnishing mankind with the
two noblest of things, which are sweetness
and light.
Jonathan Swift 1667–1745: *The Battle of the Books*
(1704); see **Behaviour** 11

27 When men grow virtuous in their old age,
they only make a sacrifice to God of the
devil's leavings.
Alexander Pope 1688–1744: *Miscellanies* (1727)
'Thoughts on Various Subjects'

28 Virtue she finds too painful an endeavour,
Content to dwell in decencies for ever.
Alexander Pope 1688–1744: *Epistles to Several
Persons* 'To a Lady' (1735)

29 Let humble Allen, with an awkward
shame,
Do good by stealth, and blush to find it
fame.
Alexander Pope 1688–1744: *Imitations of Horace*
(1738)

30 The virtue which requires to be ever
guarded is scarce worth the sentinel.
Oliver Goldsmith 1728–74: *The Vicar of Wakefield*
(1766)

31 Tell me, ye divines, which is the most virtuous man, he who begets twenty bastards, or he who sacrifices an hundred thousand lives?
Horace Walpole 1717–97: letter to Sir Horace Mann, 7 July 1778

32 Minute attention to propriety stops the growth of virtue.
Mary Wollstonecraft 1759–97: letter to Everina Wollstonecraft, 4 March 1787

33 Virtue knows to a farthing what it has lost by not having been vice.
Horace Walpole 1717–97: L. Kronenberger *The Extraordinary Mr Wilkes* (1974)

34   That best portion of a good man's life,
His little, nameless, unremembered, acts
Of kindness and of love.
William Wordsworth 1770–1850: 'Lines composed a few miles above Tintern Abbey' (1798)

35 The greatest offence against virtue is to speak ill of it.
William Hazlitt 1778–1830: *Sketches and Essays* (1839) 'On Cant and Hypocrisy'

36 My strength is as the strength of ten, Because my heart is pure.
Alfred, Lord Tennyson 1809–92: 'Sir Galahad' (1842)

37 More people are flattered into virtue than bullied out of vice.
R. S. Surtees 1805–64: *The Analysis of the Hunting Field* (1846)

38 I expect to pass through this world but once; any good thing therefore that I can do, or any kindness that I can show to any fellow-creature, let me do it now; let me not defer or neglect it, for I shall not pass this way again.
Stephen Grellet 1773–1855: attributed; see John o' London *Treasure Trove* (1925) for some of the many other claimants to authorship

39 Be good, sweet maid, and let who will be clever.
Charles Kingsley 1819–75: 'A Farewell' (1858)

40 If some great Power would agree to make me always think what is true and do what is right, on condition of being turned into a sort of clock and wound up every morning before I got out of bed, I should instantly close with the offer.
T. H. Huxley 1825–95: 'On Descartes' *Discourse on Method*' (written 1870)

41 Few things are harder to put up with than the annoyance of a good example.
Mark Twain 1835–1910: *Pudd'nhead Wilson* (1894)

42 No people do so much harm as those who go about doing good.
Mandell Creighton 1843–1901: *The Life and Letters of Mandell Creighton* by his wife (1904)

43 What is virtue but the Trade Unionism of the married?
George Bernard Shaw 1856–1950: *Man and Superman* (1903)

44 She was poor but she was honest
Victim of a rich man's game.
First he loved her, then he left her,
And she lost her maiden name . . .
Anonymous: 'She was Poor but she was Honest'; sung by British soldiers in the First World War

45 'Goodness, what beautiful diamonds!'
'Goodness had nothing to do with it.'
Mae West 1892–1980: *Night After Night* (1932 film)

46 If all the good people were clever,
And all clever people were good,
The world would be nicer than ever
We thought that it possibly could.
But somehow, 'tis seldom or never
The two hit it off as they should;
The good are so harsh to the clever,
The clever so rude to the good!
Elizabeth Wordsworth 1840–1932: 'Good and Clever'

47 Courage is not simply *one* of the virtues but the form of every virtue at the testing point.
C. S. Lewis 1898–1963: Cyril Connolly *The Unquiet Grave* (1944)

48 I'm as pure as the driven slush.
Tallulah Bankhead 1903–68: in *Saturday Evening Post* 12 April 1947; see 10 above

49 Terrible is the temptation to be good.
Bertolt Brecht 1898–1956: *The Caucasian Chalk Circle* (1948)

50   What after all
Is a halo? It's only one more thing to keep clean.
Christopher Fry 1907– : *The Lady's not for Burning* (1949)

51 I was asked whether I was trying to restore Victorian values. I said straight out I was. And I am.
Margaret Thatcher 1925– : speech to the British Jewish Community, 21 July 1983, referring to an interview with Brian Walden on 17 January 1983; see 14 above

Wales

1 Land of my Fathers Wales.

from the opening words of the first verse of the Welsh national anthem by Evan James; see 5, 8 below

2 Little England beyond Wales the English-speaking area of Pembrokeshire (Dyfed).

a name first recorded in Camden's Britannia *(1586)*

QUOTATIONS

3 Who dare compare the English, the most degraded of all the races under heaven, with the Welsh?

Giraldus Cambrensis 1146?–1220?: attributed

4 Though it appear a little out of fashion,
There is much care and valour in this
    Welshman.

William Shakespeare 1564–1616: *Henry V* (1599)

5 Wales, Wales, sweet are thy hills and
    vales,
Thy speech, thy song,
To thee belong,
O may they live ever in Wales.

Evan James: 'Land of My Fathers' (1856); see 1 above

6 Among our ancient mountains,
And from our lovely vales,
Oh, let the prayer re-echo:
'God bless the Prince of Wales!'

George Linley 1798–1865: 'God Bless the Prince of Wales' (1862 song); translated from the Welsh original by J. C. Hughes (1837–87)

7 'I often think,' he continued, 'that we can trace almost all the disasters of English history to the influence of Wales!'

Evelyn Waugh 1903–66: *Decline and Fall* (1928)

8 The land of my fathers. My fathers can have it.

Dylan Thomas 1914–53: in *Adam* December 1953; see 1 above

9 There is no present in Wales,
And no future;
There is only the past,
Brittle with relics . . .
And an impotent people,
Sick with inbreeding,
Worrying the carcase of an old song.

R. S. Thomas 1913–2000: 'Welsh Landscape' (1955)

10 It profits a man nothing to give his soul for the whole world . . . But for Wales—!

Robert Bolt 1924–95: *A Man for All Seasons* (1960); see **Success** 22

11 I wanted a play that would paint the full face of sensuality, rebellion and revivalism. In South Wales these three phenomena have played second fiddle only to Rugby Union which is a distillation of all three.

Gwyn Thomas 1913–81: introduction to *Jackie the Jumper* (1962)

12 Everyday when I wake up, I thank the Lord I'm Welsh.

Cerys Matthews 1969– : 'International Velvet' (1998 song)

13 The Welsh remain the only race whom you can vilify without being called a racist.

A. N. Wilson 1950– : in *Sunday Times* 23 April 2000

14 What are they for? They are always so pleased with themselves.

of the Welsh; comment made on BBC2's Room 101 *programme*

Anne Robinson 1944– : in *Daily Telegraph* 7 March 2001

Warfare see also **The Armed Forces, Peace, Wars**

PROVERBS AND SAYINGS

1 A bayonet is a weapon with a worker at each end.

British pacifist slogan (1940)

2 A bigger bang for a buck.

Charles E. Wilson's defence policy, in Newsweek *22 March 1954*

3 War will cease when men refuse to fight.

pacifist slogan, from c.1936; often quoted as 'Wars will cease . . . '

4 When war is declared, Truth is the first casualty.

epigraph to Arthur Ponsonby's Falsehood in Wartime *(1928), perhaps deriving from Johnson: see 21 below; attributed also to Hiram Johnson, speaking in the US Senate, 1918, but not recorded in his speech*

PHRASES

5 **blood and iron** military force as distinguished from diplomacy.
translation of German Blut und Eisen: *see* **International Relations** 21

6 **dogs of war** the havoc accompanying war.
from Shakespeare Julius Caesar: *see* **Revenge** 13

7 **draw one's sword against** take up arms against, attack.
see **Revolution** 4

8 **just war** a war which is deemed to be morally or theologically justifiable.
in the Middle Ages, St Thomas Aquinas laid down three conditions which a just war *must meet: it had to be authorized by the sovereign, the cause must be just, and those engaging in it must have the intention of advancing good or avoiding evil; see 34 below*

9 **throw away the scabbard** abandon all thought of making peace.
from the proverb: see **Revolution** 4

QUOTATIONS

10 He saith among the trumpets, Ha, ha; and he smelleth the battle afar off, the thunder of the captains, and the shouting.
Bible: Job

11 We make war that we may live in peace.
Aristotle 384–322 BC: *Nicomachean Ethics*; see **Preparation** 9

12 Laws are silent in time of war.
Cicero 106–43 BC: *Pro Milone*

13 The sinews of war, unlimited money.
Cicero 106–43 BC: *Fifth Philippic*; see **Money** 27

14 I see wars, horrible wars, and the Tiber foaming with much blood.
Virgil 70–19 BC: *Aeneid*; see **Race** 28

15 Wars begin when you will, but they do not end when you please.
Niccolò Machiavelli 1469–1527: *History of Florence* (1521–4)

16 Once more unto the breach, dear friends, once more;
Or close the wall up with our English dead!
In peace there's nothing so becomes a man
As modest stillness and humility:
But when the blast of war blows in our ears,
Then imitate the action of the tiger;
Stiffen the sinews, summon up the blood,

Disguise fair nature with hard-favoured rage.
William Shakespeare 1564–1616: *Henry V* (1599)

17 For what can war, but endless war still breed?
John Milton 1608–74: 'On the Lord General Fairfax at the Siege of Colchester' (written 1648)

18 Force, and fraud, are in war the two cardinal virtues.
Thomas Hobbes 1588–1679: *Leviathan* (1651)

19 One to destroy, is murder by the law;
And gibbets keep the lifted hand in awe;
To murder thousands, takes a specious name,
'War's glorious art', and gives immortal fame.
Edward Young 1683–1765: *The Love of Fame* (1725–8)

20 God is on the side not of the heavy battalions, but of the best shots.
Voltaire 1694–1778: 'The Piccini Notebooks' (c.1735–50); see **The Armed Forces** 7, **God** 20

21 Among the calamities of war may be jointly numbered the diminution of the love of truth, by the falsehoods which interest dictates and credulity encourages.
Samuel Johnson 1709–84: in *The Idler* 11 November 1758; see **4** above

22 There never was a good war, or a bad peace.
Benjamin Franklin 1706–90: letter to Josiah Quincy, 11 September 1783

23 War is the national industry of Prussia.
Comte de Mirabeau 1749–91: attributed to Mirabeau by Albert Sorel (1842–1906), based on Mirabeau's introduction to *De la monarchie prussienne sous Frédéric le Grand* (1788)

24 In war, three-quarters turns on personal character and relations; the balance of manpower and materials counts only for the remaining quarter.
Napoléon I 1769–1821: 'Observations sur les affaires d'Espagne, Saint-Cloud, 27 août 1808'

25 Next to a battle lost, the greatest misery is a battle gained.
Duke of Wellington 1769–1852: in *Diary of Frances, Lady Shelley 1787–1817* (ed. R. Edgcumbe)

26 Everything is very simple in war, but the simplest thing is difficult. These difficulties accumulate and produce a friction which

no man can imagine exactly who has not seen war.
Karl von Clausewitz 1780–1831: *On War* (1832–4)

27 War is nothing but a continuation of politics with the admixture of other means.
commonly rendered as 'War is the continuation of politics by other means'
Karl von Clausewitz 1780–1831: *On War* (1832–4)

28 He knew that the essence of war is violence, and that moderation in war is imbecility.
Lord Macaulay 1800–59: *Essays Contributed to the Edinburgh Review* (1843) 'John Hampden'

29 All the business of war, and indeed all the business of life, is to endeavour to find out what you don't know by what you do; that's what I called 'guessing what was at the other side of the hill'.
Duke of Wellington 1769–1852: in *The Croker Papers* (1885)

30 It is well that war is so terrible. We should grow too fond of it.
Robert E. Lee 1807–70: after the battle of Fredericksburg, December 1862; attributed

31 There is many a boy here to-day who looks on war as all glory, but, boys, it is all hell.
William Sherman 1820–91: speech at Columbus, Ohio, 11 August 1880

32 Everlasting peace is a dream, and not even a pleasant one; and war is a necessary part of God's arrangement of the world . . . Without war the world would deteriorate into materialism.
Helmuth von Moltke 1800–91: letter to Dr J. K. Bluntschli, 11 December 1880

of possible German involvement in the Balkans:
33 Not worth the healthy bones of a single Pomeranian grenadier.
Otto von Bismarck 1815–98: George O. Kent *Bismarck and his Times* (1978); see **World War II** 21

34 I do wish people would not deceive themselves by talk of a just war. There is no such thing as a just war. What we are doing is casting out Satan by Satan.
Charles Hamilton Sorley 1895–1915: letter to his mother from Aldershot, March 1915; see 8 above, **Good and Evil** 17

35 War is hell, and all that, but it has a good deal to recommend it. It wipes out all the small nuisances of peace-time.
Ian Hay 1876–1952: *The First Hundred Thousand* (1915)

36 Once lead this people into war and they will forget there ever was such a thing as tolerance.
Woodrow Wilson 1856–1924: John Dos Passos *Mr Wilson's War* (1917)

37 My subject is War, and the pity of War. The Poetry is in the pity.
Wilfred Owen 1893–1918: preface (written 1918) in *Poems* (1963)

38 If you could hear, at every jolt, the blood
Come gargling from the froth-corrupted lungs,
Obscene as cancer, bitter as the cud
Of vile, incurable sores on innocent tongues,—
My friend, you would not tell with such high zest
To children ardent for some desperate glory,
The old Lie: Dulce et decorum est
Pro patria mori.
Wilfred Owen 1893–1918: 'Dulce et Decorum Est'; see **Patriotism** 6

39 Waste of Blood, and waste of Tears,
Waste of youth's most precious years,
Waste of ways the saints have trod,
Waste of Glory, waste of God,
War!
G. A. Studdert Kennedy 1883–1929: 'Waste' (1919)

40 War is too serious a matter to entrust to military men.
Georges Clemenceau 1841–1929: attributed to Clemenceau, e.g. in Hampden Jackson *Clemenceau and the Third Republic* (1946); but also to Briand and Talleyrand

41 The bomber will always get through. The only defence is in offence, which means that you have to kill more women and children more quickly than the enemy if you want to save yourselves.
Stanley Baldwin 1867–1947: speech, House of Commons, 10 November 1932

42 Wars may be fought with weapons, but they are won by men.
George S. Patton 1885–1945: in *Cavalry Journal* September 1933

43 We can manage without butter but not, for example, without guns. If we are attacked we can only defend ourselves with guns not with butter.
Joseph Goebbels 1897–1945: speech in Berlin, 17 January 1936; see 44 below

44 We have no butter . . . but I ask you—would you rather have butter or guns? . . .

preparedness makes us powerful. Butter merely makes us fat.

Hermann Goering 1893–1946: speech at Hamburg, 1936; W. Frischauer *Goering* (1951); see 43 above

45 Little girl . . . Sometime they'll give a war and nobody will come.

Carl Sandburg 1878–1967: *The People, Yes* (1936); 'Suppose They Gave a War and Nobody Came?' was the title of a 1970 film

46 In war, whichever side may call itself the victor, there are no winners, but all are losers.

Neville Chamberlain 1869–1940: speech at Kettering, 3 July 1938

47 War always finds a way.

Bertolt Brecht 1898–1956: *Mother Courage* (1939)

48 War will be won by Blood and Guts alone.

George Patton 1885–1945: address to fellow officers, Fort Benning, Georgia, 1940; see **People** 17

49 Probably the battle of Waterloo *was* won on the playing-fields of Eton, but the opening battles of all subsequent wars have been lost there.

George Orwell 1903–50: *The Lion and the Unicorn* (1941) 'England Your England'; see **Wars** 14

50 What difference does it make to the dead, the orphans and the homeless, whether the mad destruction is wrought under the name of totalitarianism or the holy name of liberty or democracy?

Mahatma Gandhi 1869–1948: *Non-Violence in Peace and War* (1942)

51 Older men declare war. But it is youth who must fight and die.

Herbert Hoover 1874–1964: speech at the Republican National Convention, Chicago, 27 June 1944

52 I have never met anyone who wasn't against war. Even Hitler and Mussolini were, according to themselves.

David Low 1891–1963: in *New York Times Magazine* 10 February 1946

53 The quickest way of ending a war is to lose it.

George Orwell 1903–50: in *Polemic* May 1946

54 In war: resolution. In defeat: defiance. In victory: magnanimity. In peace: goodwill.

Winston Churchill 1874–1965: *The Second World War* vol. 1 (1948)

55 Every gun that is made, every warship launched, every rocket fired signifies, in the final sense, a theft from those who hunger and are not fed, those who are cold and are not clothed. This world in arms is not spending money alone. It is spending the sweat of its labourers, the genius of its scientists, the hopes of its children.

Dwight D. Eisenhower 1890–1969: speech in Washington, 16 April 1953

56 Mankind must put an end to war or war will put an end to mankind.

John F. Kennedy 1917–63: speech to United Nations General Assembly, 25 September 1961

57 Dead battles, like dead generals, hold the military mind in their dead grip and Germans, no less than other peoples, prepare for the last war.

Barbara W. Tuchman 1912–89: *August 1914* (1962)

58 Rule 1, on page 1 of the book of war, is: 'Do not march on Moscow' . . . [Rule 2] is: 'Do not go fighting with your land armies in China.'

Lord Montgomery 1887–1976: speech, House of Lords, 30 May 1962

59 History is littered with the wars which everybody knew would never happen.

Enoch Powell 1912–98: speech to the Conservative Party Conference, 19 October 1967

60 The conventional army loses if it does not win. The guerrilla wins if he does not lose.

Henry Kissinger 1923– : in *Foreign Affairs* January 1969

61 War is the most exciting and dramatic thing in life. In fighting to the death you feel terribly relaxed when you manage to come through.

Moshe Dayan 1915–81: in *Observer* 13 February 1972

62 If the Third World War is fought with nuclear weapons, the fourth will be fought with bows and arrows.

Lord Mountbatten 1900–79: in *Maclean's* 17 November 1975

63 I love the smell of napalm in the morning. It smells like victory.

John Milius and **Francis Ford Coppola** 1939– : *Apocalypse Now* (1979 film)

64 One began to hear it said that World War I was the chemists' war, World War II was the physicists' war, World War III (may it never come) will be the mathematicians' war.

Philip J. Davis 1923– and **Reuben Hersh** 1927– : *The Mathematical Experience* (1981)

65 Once you're committed to war, then be

ferocious enough to do whatever is necessary to get it over with as quickly as possible in victory.

H. Norman Schwarzkopf III 1934– : in *New York Times* 28 January 1991

66 When you're in the battlefield, survival is all there is. Death is the only great

emotion.

Sam Fuller 1912– : in *Guardian* 26 February 1991

67 It now does look as if air power has prevailed in the Balkans and that the time to redefine how victory in war may be won has come.

John Keegan 1934– : in *Daily Telegraph* 4 June 1999

Wars see also World War I, World War II

PROVERBS AND SAYINGS

1 Hey, hey, LBJ, how many kids have you killed today?
anti-Vietnam marching slogan

2 Remember the Alamo!
Texan battle-cry at the battle of San Jacinto, 1836, referring to the defence of a Franciscan mission in the Texan War of Independence, in which all the defenders were killed

PHRASES

3 the late unpleasantness the war that took place recently.
originally the American Civil War

QUOTATIONS

4 Men said openly that Christ and His saints slept.
of twelfth-century England during the civil war between Stephen and Matilda
Anonymous: *Anglo-Saxon Chronicle* for 1137

5 The singeing of the King of Spain's Beard.
on the expedition to Cadiz, 1587
Francis Drake c.1540–96: Francis Bacon *Considerations touching a War with Spain* (1629)

6 The dimensions of this mercy are above my thoughts. It is, for aught I know, a crowning mercy.
on the battle of Worcester, 1651
Oliver Cromwell 1599–1658: letter to William Lenthall, Speaker of the Parliament of England, 4 September 1651

7 They now *ring* the bells, but they will soon *wring* their hands.
on the declaration of war with Spain, 1739
Robert Walpole 1676–1745: W. Coxe *Memoirs of Sir Robert Walpole* (1798)

8 What a glorious morning is this.
on hearing gunfire at Lexington, 19 April 1775; traditionally quoted 'What a glorious morning for America'
Samuel Adams 1722–1803: J. K. Hosmer *Samuel Adams* (1886)

9 Men, you are all marksmen—don't one of you fire until you see the white of their eyes.
at Bunker Hill, 1775
Israel Putnam 1718–90: R. Frothingham *History of the Siege of Boston* (1873) ; also attributed to William Prescott, 1726–95

10 We beat them to-day or Molly Stark's a widow.
John Stark 1728–1822: before the battle of Bennington, 16 August 1777; in *Cyclopaedia of American Biography*

11 *Guerra a cuchillo.*
War to the knife.
at the siege of Saragossa, 4 August 1808, replying to the suggestion that he should surrender
José de Palafox 1780–1847: as reported; he actually said: '*Guerra y cuchillo* [War and the knife]'; José Gòmez de Arteche y Moro *Guerra de la Independencia* (1875)

12 Up Guards and at them!
Duke of Wellington 1769–1852: in *The Battle of Waterloo* by a Near Observer [J. Booth] (1815); later denied by Wellington

13 Hard pounding this, gentlemen; let's see who will pound longest.
at the battle of Waterloo
Duke of Wellington 1769–1852: Sir Walter Scott *Paul's Letters* (1816)

14 The battle of Waterloo was won on the playing fields of Eton.
Duke of Wellington 1769–1852: oral tradition, but not found in this form of words; C. F. R. Montalembert *De l'avenir politique de l'Angleterre* (1856); see **Warfare** 49

15 Half a league, half a league,
Half a league onward,

All in the valley of Death
Rode the six hundred . . .
Cannon to right of them,
Cannon to left of them,
Cannon in front of them
Volleyed and thundered.

Alfred, Lord Tennyson 1809–92: 'The Charge of the Light Brigade' (1854)

16 *J'y suis, j'y reste.*
Here I am, and here I stay.

at the taking of the Malakoff fortress during the Crimean War, 8 September 1855

Comte de Macmahon 1808–93: G. Hanotaux *Histoire de la France Contemporaine* (1903–8)

17 There is Jackson with his Virginians, standing like a stone wall. Let us determine to die here, and we will conquer.

referring to General T. J. ('Stonewall') Jackson at the battle of Bull Run, 21 July, 1861 (in which Bee himself was killed)

Barnard Elliott Bee 1823–61: B. Perley Poore *Perley's Reminiscences* (1886)

18 All quiet along the Potomac to-night,
No sound save the rush of the river,
While soft falls the dew on the face of the
      dead—
The picket's off duty forever.

Ethel Lynn Beers 1827–79: 'The Picket Guard' (1861); the first line is also attributed to George B. McClellan (1826–85)

19 Give them the cold steel, boys!

Lewis Addison Armistead 1817–63: attributed during the American Civil War, 1863

20 Hold out. Relief is coming.

usually quoted as 'Hold the fort! I am coming!'

William Tecumsah Sherman 1820–91: flag signal from Kennesaw Mountain to General John Murray Corse at Allatoona Pass, 5 October 1864

21 Don't cheer, men; those poor devils are dying.

John Woodward ('Jack') Philip 1840–1900: at the battle of Santiago, 4 July 1898; in *Dictionary of American Biography* vol. 14 (1934)

22 The Cavaliers (Wrong but Wromantic) and the Roundheads (Right but Repulsive).

of the two sides in the English Civil War

W. C. Sellar 1898–1951 and **R. J. Yeatman** 1898–1968: *1066 and All That* (1930)

23 We are not about to send American boys 9 or 10,000 miles away from home to do what Asian boys ought to be doing for themselves.

Lyndon Baines Johnson 1908–73: speech at Akron University, 21 October 1964

24 They've got to draw in their horns and stop their aggression, or we're going to bomb them back into the Stone Age.

on the North Vietnamese

Curtis E. LeMay 1906–90: *Mission with LeMay* (1965)

25 It became necessary to destroy the town to save it.

statement by unidentified US Army Major, referring to Ben Tre in Vietnam

Anonymous: Associated Press Report, *New York Times* 8 February 1968

26 Just rejoice at that news and congratulate our forces and the Marines . . . Rejoice!

on the recapture of South Georgia; usually quoted as 'Rejoice, rejoice'

Margaret Thatcher 1925– : to newsmen outside Downing Street, 25 April 1982

27 I counted them all out and I counted them all back.

on the number of British aeroplanes (which he was not permitted to disclose) joining the raid on Port Stanley in the Falkland Islands

Brian Hanrahan 1949– : BBC broadcast report, 1 May 1982

28 Gotcha!

Anonymous: headline on the sinking of the *General Belgrano*, in *Sun* 4 May 1982

29 The Falklands thing was a fight between two bald men over a comb.

Jorge Luis Borges 1899–1986: in *Time* 14 February 1983; see **Experience** 3

30 The mother of battles.

popular interpretation of his description of the approaching Gulf War

Saddam Hussein 1937– : speech in Baghdad, 6 January 1991; *The Times*, 7 January 1991, reported that Saddam had no intention of relinquishing Kuwait and was ready for the 'mother of all wars'

31 That killed head straining through the windscreen
with its frill of bubbles in the eye-sockets
is not trying to tell you something—
it is telling you something.

Helen Dunmore 1952– : 'Poem on the Obliteration of 100,000 Iraqi Soldiers' (1994)

32 Serbs out, Nato in, refugees back.

George Robertson 1946– : summing up the Nato objective in Kosovo, 7 June 1999

33 It is time for us to win the first war of the 21st century.

of the 'war on terrorism'

George W. Bush 1946– : at a White House press conference, 16 September 2001

Ways and Means

1 Catching's before hanging.

early 19th century, meaning that an essential step must be taken before the consequence can ensue

2 The end justifies the means.

*late 16th century; see **Morality** 3*

3 Fight fire with fire.

mid 19th century, meaning that one should counter like with like

4 Fire is a good servant but a bad master.

early 17th century, acknowledging that fire is both essential for living and potentially destructive

5 First catch your hare.

early 19th century, referring to the first essential step that must be taken before a process can begin; often attributed to the English cook Hannah Glasse (fl. 1747), but her directions for making hare soup are, 'Take your hare when it is cased' (cased here meaning 'skinned')

6 Give a man enough rope and he will hang himself.

mid 17th century, often used to mean that someone given enough licence or freedom will defeat themselves through their own mistakes

7 Honey catches more flies than vinegar.

mid 17th century, meaning that soft or ingratiating words achieve more than sharpness

8 If you can't beat them, join them.

mid 20th century; often used in consolation or resignation

9 It is good to make a bridge of gold to a flying enemy.

late 16th century, meaning that it is wiser to give passage to an enemy in flight, who may be desperate

10 An old poacher makes the best gamekeeper.

late 14th century, meaning that someone who has formerly taken part in wrongdoing knows best how to counter it in others

11 The pen is mightier than the sword.

*late 16th century, meaning that written words may often have more lasting force than military strength; see **Technology** 13, **Writing** 28*

12 Set a thief to catch a thief.

mid 17th century; used to imply that the person best placed to catch someone out in dishonest practices is one whose own nature tends that way

13 There are more ways of killing a cat than choking it with cream.

mid 19th century; meaning that there are more ways of achieving an end than giving an opponent a glut of what they most want

14 There are more ways of killing a dog than choking it with butter.

mid 19th century; meaning that there are more ways of achieving an end than giving an opponent a glut of what they most want

15 There are more ways of killing a dog than hanging it.

late 17th century; meaning that there are more ways than one of achieving an end

16 There is nothing like leather.

late 17th century, referring to the toughness and durability of leather. The saying comes from one of Aesop's fables, in which a leatherworker contributed this opinion to a discussion on how to fortify a city

17 drive a coach and six through make useless by the disregard of law or custom.

from Stephen Rice (1637–1715) 'I will drive a coach and six horses through the Act of Settlement'

18 play the — card introduce a specified (advantageous) factor.

*from Lord Randolph Churchill: see **Ireland** 13; see also **The Law** 47*

19 It is in life as it is in ways, the shortest way is commonly the foulest, and surely the fairer way is not much about.

Francis Bacon 1561–1626: *The Advancement of Learning* (1605)

20 *Dans ce pays-ci il est bon de tuer de temps en temps un amiral pour encourager les autres.*

In this country [England] it is thought well to kill an admiral from time to time to encourage the others.

referring to the execution of Admiral John Byng, 1757

Voltaire 1694–1778: *Candide* (1759); see **Management** 5

21 A servant's too often a negligent elf;
—If it's business of consequence, DO IT YOURSELF!

R. H. Barham 1788–1845: 'The Ingoldsby Penance!—Moral' (1842)

22 They sought it with thimbles, they sought
it with care;
They pursued it with forks and hope;
They threatened its life with a railway-
share;

They charmed it with smiles and soap.
Lewis Carroll 1832–98: *The Hunting of the Snark*
(1876)

23 The colour of the cat doesn't matter as
long as it catches the mice.
quoting a Chinese proverb
Deng Xiaoping 1904–97: in *Financial Times* 18
December 1986

Weakness see Strength and Weakness

Wealth and Luxury see also Money, Thrift and Extravagance

1 A diamond is forever.
advertising slogan for De Beers Consolidated Mines,
1940s onwards

2 If you really want to make a million . . . the
quickest way is to start your own religion.
previously attributed to L. Ron Hubbard 1911–86 in B.
Corydon and L. Ron Hubbard Jr. L. Ron Hubbard
(1987), but attribution subsequently rejected by L. Ron
Hubbard Jr., who also dissociated himself from the
book

3 Money makes a man.
early 16th century, meaning that possession of wealth
confers status

4 Money makes money.
late 16th century, implying that those who are already
wealthy are likely to become more so

5 The rich man has his ice in the summer and
the poor man gets his in the winter.
early 20th century, contrasting luxury with hardship
through apparent equality

6 the affluent society a society in which
material wealth is widely distributed, a
rich society.
usually in allusion to the book The Affluent Society
(1958) by the Canadian-born economist John Kenneth
Galbraith

7 Aladdin's cave a place of great riches.
in the Arabian Nights, the cave in which Aladdin
found an old lamp which, when rubbed, brought a
genie to obey his will; see Chance 15

8 born with a silver spoon in one's mouth
born in affluence.
see Class 33, Presidency 21

9 the Mammon of unrighteousness wealth
ill-used or ill-gained.
Mammon (ultimately from Hebrew māmōn money,
wealth), in early use, (the proper name of) the devil of
covetousness, later with personification, wealth
regarded as an idol or an evil influence; see Money 23

10 the Midas touch the ability to turn one's
actions to financial advantage.
Midas, in classical legend a king of Phrygia whose
touch was said to turn all things to gold

11 milk and honey abundance, comfort,
prosperity.
with allusion to the biblical description of the
promised land: see 14 below

12 poor little rich girl a wealthy girl or
woman whose money brings her no
happiness.
title of a 1925 song by Noël Coward

13 Tom Tiddler's ground a place where money
or profit is readily made.
a children's game in which one player tries to catch
the others who run on to his or her territory crying
'We're on Tom Tiddler's ground, picking up gold and
silver'

14 A land flowing with milk and honey.
Bible: Exodus; see 11 above

15 Lay not up for yourselves treasures upon
earth, where moth and rust doth corrupt,
and where thieves break through and
steal:
But lay up for yourselves treasures in
heaven.
Bible: St Matthew

16 It is easier for a camel to go through the
eye of a needle, than for a rich man to
enter into the kingdom of God.
Bible: St Matthew; see **Quantities** 12

17   I glory
More in the cunning purchase of my
  wealth
Than in the glad possession.
Ben Jonson c.1573–1637: *Volpone* (1606)

18 Riches are for spending.
Francis Bacon 1561–1626: *Essays* (1625) 'Of Expense'

19   Let none admire
That riches grow in hell; that soil may best
Deserve the precious bane.
John Milton 1608–74: *Paradise Lost* (1667)

20 It was very prettily said, that we may learn
the little value of fortune by the persons on
whom heaven is pleased to bestow it.
Richard Steele 1672–1729: in *The Tatler* 27 July 1710

21 We are all Adam's children but silk makes
the difference.
Thomas Fuller 1654–1734: *Gnomologia* (1732)

22 Get place and wealth, if possible, with
  grace;
If not, by any means get wealth and place.
Alexander Pope 1688–1744: *Imitations of Horace*
(1738); see **Money** 22

23 The chief enjoyment of riches consists in
the parade of riches.
Adam Smith 1723–90: *Wealth of Nations* (1776)

24 We are not here to sell a parcel of boilers
and vats, but the potentiality of growing
rich, beyond the dreams of avarice.
at the sale of Thrale's brewery
Samuel Johnson 1709–84: James Boswell *Life of
Samuel Johnson* (1791) 6 April 1781

25 'Two nations; between whom there is no
intercourse and no sympathy; who are as
ignorant of each other's habits, thoughts,
and feelings, as if they were dwellers in
different zones, or inhabitants of different
planets . . . ' 'You speak of—' said
Egremont, hesitatingly, 'THE RICH AND THE
POOR.'
Benjamin Disraeli 1804–81: *Sybil* (1845); see
Politics 9

26 I spend my life ministering to the swinish
luxury of the rich.
William Morris 1834–96: attributed, c.1877; W. R.
Lethaby *Philip Webb* (1935)

27 The man who dies . . . rich dies disgraced.
Andrew Carnegie 1835–1919: In *North American
Review* June 1889 'Wealth'

28 In every well-governed state, wealth is a
sacred thing; in democracies it is the only
sacred thing.
Anatole France 1844–1924: *L'Île des pingouins*
(1908)

29 To be clever enough to get all that money,
one must be stupid enough to want it.
G. K. Chesterton 1874–1936: *Wisdom of Father
Brown* (1914)

30 Her voice is full of money.
F. Scott Fitzgerald 1896–1940: *The Great Gatsby*
(1925)

31 Let me tell you about the very rich. They
are different from you and me.
F. Scott Fitzgerald 1896–1940: *All the Sad Young
Men* (1926) 'Rich Boy'; to which Ernest Hemingway
replied, 'Yes, they have more money', in *Esquire*
August 1936 'The Snows of Kilimanjaro'

32 I am absolutely convinced that no wealth
in the world can help humanity forward,
even in the hands of the most devoted
worker in this cause . . . Can anyone
imagine Moses, Jesus, or Gandhi with the
moneybags of Carnegie?
Albert Einstein 1879–1955: *Mein Weltbild* (1934)

33 The necessities were going by default to
save the luxuries until I hardly knew
which were necessities and which luxuries.
Frank Lloyd Wright 1867–1959: *Autobiography*
(1945)

34 A kiss on the hand may be quite
  continental,
But diamonds are a girl's best friend.
Leo Robin 1900–84: 'Diamonds are a Girl's Best
Friend' (1949 song)

35 If you can actually count your money,
then you are not really a rich man.
J. Paul Getty 1892–1976: in *Observer* 3 November
1957

36 The greater the wealth, the thicker will be
the dirt.
J. K. Galbraith 1908– : *The Affluent Society* (1958)

37 I want to spend, and spend, and spend.
*said to reporters on arriving to collect her husband's
football pools winnings of £152,000*
Vivian Nicholson 1936– : in *Daily Herald* 28
September 1961

38 The saddest thing I can imagine is to get
used to luxury.
Charlie Chaplin 1889–1977: *My Autobiography*
(1964)

39 I've been rich and I've been poor: rich is better.

Sophie Tucker c.1884–1966: attributed

40 The minute you walked in the joint,
I could see you were a man of distinction,
A real big spender . . .

Hey! big spender, spend a little time with me.

Dorothy Fields 1905–74: 'Big Spender' (1966 song)

41 Having money is rather like being a blonde. It is more fun but not vital.

Mary Quant 1934– : in *Observer* 2 November 1986

Weather

PROVERBS AND SAYINGS

1 April showers bring forth May flowers.

mid 16th century, referring to the value of rain during April to early growth

2 As the day lengthens, so the cold strengthens.

early 17th century, recording the tradition that the coldest weather arrives when days begin to grow lighter

3 A dripping June sets all in tune.

mid 18th century; meaning that rain in June is beneficial to all crops and plants

4 February fill dyke, be it black or be it white.

mid 16th century; meaning that February is a month likely to bring heavy rain (black) or snow (white); see **Seasons** 10

5 A green Yule makes a fat churchyard.

mid 17th century, meaning that a mild winter is traditionally unhealthy

6 If Candlemas day be sunny and bright, winter will have another flight; if Candlemas day be cloudy with rain, winter is gone and won't come again.

late 17th century; in the Church calendar 2 February is the date of the feast of the Purification of the Virgin Mary and the Presentation of Christ in the Temple. This is known as Candlemas Day because candles are blessed at services on that day

7 If in February there be no rain, 'tis neither good for hay nor grain.

early 18th century; meaning that a drought in February will be damaging to crops later in the year

8 Long foretold, long last; short notice, soon past.

mid 19th century; meaning that if there is a long gap between the signs that the weather will change and the change itself, then the predicted weather will last a long time. If the intervening period is a short one, then the predicted weather will be of correspondingly short duration

9 March borrowed from April three days, and they were ill.

traditional saying, mid 17th century; implying that bad weather in early April reflects the influence of March; see 22 below

10 March comes in like a lion, and goes out like a lamb.

early 17th century; meaning that weather is traditionally stormy at the beginning of March, but calm at the end

11 A peck of March dust is worth a king's ransom.

early 16th century, meaning that March is traditionally a wet month, and dust is rare (a peck was a dry measure of two gallons)

12 Rain before seven, fine before eleven.

mid 19th century

13 Rain, rain, go away, Come again another day.

traditional rhyme, mid 17th century

14 Red sky at night, shepherd's delight; red sky in the morning, shepherd's warning.

late 14th century, meaning that good and bad weather respectively is presaged by a red sky at sunset and dawn

15 Robin Hood could brave all weathers but a thaw wind.

mid 19th century; a thaw wind is a cold wind which accompanies the breaking up of frost

16 Saint Swithin's day, if thou be fair, for forty days it will remain; Saint Swithin's day, if thou bring rain, for forty days it will remain.

early 17th century; St Swithin's day is 15 July, and the tradition may have its origin in the heavy rain said to have occurred when his relics were to be transferred to a shrine in Winchester cathedral

17 September blow soft till the fruit's in the loft.

late 16th century, expressing the hope that fine weather often traditional in September will hold until *a crop of apples or other fruit has been picked and stored*

18 So many mists in March, so many frosts in May.

early 17th century; meaning that mist or fog in March presages frost in May

19 There is no such thing as bad weather, only the wrong clothes.

late 20th century saying

20 When the oak is before the ash, then you will only get a splash; when the ash is before the oak, then you may expect a soak.

mid 19th century; a traditional way of predicting whether the summer will be wet or dry on the basis of whether the oak or the ash is first to come into leaf in the spring

21 When the wind is in the east, 'tis neither good for man nor beast.

early 17th century, referring to the traditional bitterness of the east wind

22 borrowed days in Scottish tradition, the last three days of March (Old Style).

said to have been borrowed from April and to be particularly stormy; see 9 above

23 the bow of promise a rainbow.

after the Bible (Genesis) 'I do set my bow in the cloud, and it shall be for a token of a covenant between me and the earth'

24 Groundhog Day in North American usage, a day (in most areas 2 February) which, if sunny, is believed to indicate wintry weather to come.

from the story that, if there is enough sun for the groundhog (a woodchuck) to see its shadow, it retires underground for further hibernation

25 Indian summer a period of calm dry warm weather in late autumn in the northern US or elsewhere

see Old Age 4

26 London particular a dense fog affecting London.

see 41 below

27 queen's weather fine weather.

of the kind supposedly associated with public appearances by Queen Victoria

28 St Luke's summer a period of fine weather occurring about the feast of St Luke (18 October).

29 St Martin's summer a period of fine weather occurring about Martinmas (11 November).

QUOTATIONS

30 'After sharpest shoures,' quath Pees 'most shene is the sonne;
Is no weder warmer than after watry cloudes.'
Pees *Peace*
William Langland c.1330–c.1400: *The Vision of Piers Plowman*

31 For I have seyn of a ful misty morwe
Folowen ful ofte a myrie someris day.
Geoffrey Chaucer c.1343–1400: *Troilus and Criseyde*

32 There is no such thing as bad weather. All weather is good because it is God's.
St Teresa of Ávila 1512–82: attributed; H. Ward and J. Wild (eds.) *The Lion Christian Quotation Collection* (1997)

33 The uncertain glory of an April day.
William Shakespeare 1564–1616: *The Two Gentlemen of Verona* (1592–3)

34 So foul and fair a day I have not seen.
William Shakespeare 1564–1616: *Macbeth* (1606)

35 Rainy days—
silkworms droop
on mulberries.
Matsuo Basho 1644–94: translated by Lucien Stryk

36 When two Englishmen meet, their first talk is of the weather.
Samuel Johnson 1709–84: in *The Idler* 24 June 1758

37 The best sun we have is made of Newcastle coal.
Horace Walpole 1717–97: letter to George Montagu, 15 June 1768

38 The frost performs its secret ministry, Unhelped by any wind.
Samuel Taylor Coleridge 1772–1834: 'Frost at Midnight' (1798)

39 It is impossible to live in a country which is continually under hatches . . . Rain! Rain! Rain!
John Keats 1795–1821: letter to J. H. Reynolds from Devon, 10 April 1818

40 O wild West Wind, thou breath of Autumn's being,
Thou, from whose unseen presence the leaves dead
Are driven, like ghosts from an enchanter fleeing,

Yellow, and black, and pale, and hectic
red,
Pestilence-stricken multitudes.
Percy Bysshe Shelley 1792–1822: 'Ode to the West Wind' (1819)

41 This is a London particular . . . A fog, miss.
Charles Dickens 1812–70: *Bleak House* (1853); see 26 above

42 Welcome, wild North-easter!
Shame it is to see
Odes to every zephyr;
Ne'er a verse to thee.
Charles Kingsley 1819–75: 'Ode to the North-East Wind' (1858)

43 There is a sumptuous variety about the New England weather that compels the stranger's admiration—and regret. The weather is always doing something there; always attending strictly to business; always getting up new designs and trying them on the people to see how they will go.
Mark Twain 1835–1910: speech to New England Society, 22 December 1876

44 When men were all asleep the snow came flying,
In large white flakes falling on the city brown,
Stealthily and perpetually settling and loosely lying,
Hushing the latest traffic of the drowsy town.
Robert Bridges 1844–1930: 'London Snow' (1890)

45 The rain, it raineth on the just
And also on the unjust fella:
But chiefly on the just, because
The unjust steals the just's umbrella.
Lord Bowen 1835–94: Walter Sichel *Sands of Time* (1923); see **Equality** 4

46 The fog comes
on little cat feet.
It sits looking
over harbour and city
on silent haunches
and then moves on.
Carl Sandburg 1878–1967: 'Fog' (1916)

47 The yellow fog that rubs its back upon the window-panes.
T. S. Eliot 1888–1965: 'The Love Song of J. Alfred Prufrock' (1917)

48 This is the weather the cuckoo likes,
And so do I;

When showers betumble the chestnut spikes,
And nestlings fly.
Thomas Hardy 1840–1928: 'Weathers' (1922)

49 No one can tell me,
Nobody knows,
Where the wind comes from,
Where the wind goes.
A. A. Milne 1882–1956: 'Wind on the Hill' (1927)

50 The first fall of snow is not only an event, but it is a magical event. You go to bed in one kind of world and wake up to find yourself in another quite different, and if this is not enchantment, then where is it to be found?
J. B. Priestley 1894–1984: *Apes and Angels* (1928) 'First Snow'

51 Thank heavens, the sun has gone in, and I don't have to go out and enjoy it.
Logan Pearsall Smith 1865–1946: *Afterthoughts* (1931)

52 It ain't a fit night out for man or beast.
W. C. Fields 1880–1946: adopted by Fields but claimed by him not to be original; letter, 8 February 1944

53 I believe we should all behave quite differently if we lived in a warm, sunny climate all the time.
Noël Coward 1899–1973: *Brief Encounter* (1945)

54 You can call this rain bad weather, but it is not. It is simply weather, and weather means rough weather. It reminds us forcibly that its element is water, falling water. And water is hard.
Heinrich Böll 1917–85: *Irish Journal* (1957, translated Leila Vennewitz)

55   We just sit tight while wind dives
And strafes invisibly. Space is a salvo,
We are bombarded by the empty air.
Strange, it is a huge nothing that we fear.
Seamus Heaney 1939– : 'Storm on the Island' (1966)

56 A woman rang to say she heard there was a hurricane on the way. Well don't worry, there isn't.
weather forecast on the night before serious gales in southern England
Michael Fish 1944– : BBC TV, 15 October 1987

57 Wet spring had merged imperceptibly into bleak autumn. For months the sky had remained a depthless grey. Sometimes it

rained, but mostly it was just dull . . . It was like living inside Tupperware.
Bill Bryson 1951– : *The Lost Continent* (1989)

58 It was the wrong kind of snow.
explaining disruption on British Rail
Terry Worrall: in *The Independent* 16 February 1991

Weddings see also **Marriage**

1 Always a bridesmaid, never a bride.
late 19th century, recording the belief that to be a bridesmaid too often is unlucky for one's own chances of marriage

2 Happy is the bride that the sun shines on.
mid 17th century

3 Marry in May, rue for aye.
*late 17th century; see **Seasons** 3*

4 Now you will feel no rain, for each of you will be shelter for the other. Now you will feel no cold, for each of you will be warmth for the other.
from the saying known as the 'Apache Blessing'

5 One wedding brings another.
mid 17th century

QUOTATIONS

6 As the bridegroom rejoiceth over the bride.
Bible: Isaiah

7 With this Ring I thee wed, with my body I thee worship, and with all my worldly goods I thee endow.
The Book of Common Prayer 1662: *Solemnization of Matrimony* Wedding

8 O! how short a time does it take to put an end to a woman's liberty!
Fanny Burney 1752–1840: diary 20 July 1768

9 What woman, however old, has not the bridal-favours and raiment stowed away, and packed in lavender, in the inmost cupboards of her heart?
William Makepeace Thackeray 1811–63: *The Virginians* (1857–9)

10 The flowers in the bride's hand are sadly like the garland which decked the heifers of sacrifice in old times.
Thomas Hardy 1840–1928: *Jude the Obscure* (1896)

11 If it were not for the presents, an elopement would be preferable.
George Ade 1866–1944: *Forty Modern Fables* (1901)

12 Why am I always the bridesmaid,
Never the blushing bride?
Fred W. Leigh d. 1924: 'Why Am I Always the Bridesmaid?' (1917 song, with Charles Collins and Lily Morris)

13 I'm getting married in the morning,
Ding dong! The bells are gonna chime.
Pull out the stopper;
Let's have a whopper;
But get me to the church on time!
Alan Jay Lerner 1918–86: 'Get Me to the Church on Time' (1956 song)

14 O God, and the wedding! All her family and her friends
and only a handful of mine all scroungy and bearded
just wait to get at the drinks and food.
Gregory Corso 1930– : 'Marriage' (1960)

15 I think weddings is sadder than funerals, because they remind you of your own wedding. You can't be reminded of your own funeral because it hasn't happened. But weddings always make me cry.
Brendan Behan 1923–64: *Richard's Cork Leg*

16 I love to cry at weddings, anybody's weddings anytime!
. . . anybody's weddings just so long as it's not mine!
Dorothy Fields 1905–74: 'I Love to Cry at Weddings' (1966)

17 All weddings are similar but every marriage is different. Death comes to everyone but one mourns alone.
John Berger 1926– : *The White Bird* (1985)

18 The trouble
with being best man is, you don't get a chance to prove it.
Les A. Murray 1938– : *The Boys Who Stole the Funeral* (1989)

19 It's pretty easy. Just say 'I do' whenever anyone asks you a question.
Richard Curtis 1956– : *Four Weddings and a Funeral* (1994 film)

Winning and Losing   see also **Success and Failure**

1 All your base are belong to us.

late 20th century saying, deriving from the poor English translation of the Japanese video game Zero Wing, released 1989

2 Heads I win, tails you lose.

late 17th century, meaning I win in any event; heads and tails the obverse and reverse images on a coin

3 What you lose on the swings you gain on the roundabouts.

early 20th century, meaning that ones losses and gains tend to cancel one another out; see 18 below, **Circumstance** 11

4 You can't win them all.

mid 20th century, used as an expression of consolation or resignation

5 Pyrrhic victory a victory gained at too great a cost.

like that of Pyrrhus over the Romans at Asculum in 279 BC: see 6 below

6 One more such victory and we are lost.

on defeating the Romans at Asculum, 279 BC

Pyrrhus 319-272 BC: Plutarch *Parallel Lives* 'Pyrrhus'; see 5 above

7 The only safe course for the defeated is to expect no safety.

Virgil 70-19 BC: *Aeneid*

8 The happy state of winning the palm without the dust of racing.

Horace 65-8 BC: *Epistles*

9 Know ye not that they which run in a race run all, but one receiveth the prize.

Bible: I Corinthians

10 *Vae victis.*

Down with the defeated!

cry (already proverbial) of the Gallic King, Brennus, on capturing Rome (390 BC)

Livy 59 BC–AD 17: *Ab Urbe Condita*

11 Eclipse first, the rest nowhere.

comment on a horse-race at Epsom, 3 May 1769; Eclipse was the most famous racehorse of the 18th century, one of the ancestors in the direct male line of all thoroughbred racehorses throughout the world

Dennis O'Kelly c.1720-87: in *Annals of Sporting* (1822); *Dictionary of National Biography* gives the occasion as the Queen's Plate at Winchester, 1769

12 When in doubt, win the trick.

Edmond Hoyle 1672-1769: *Hoyle's Games Improved* (ed. Charles Jones, 1790) 'Twenty-four Short Rules for Learners' (though attributed to Hoyle, this may well have been an editorial addition by Jones, since it is not found in earlier editions)

13 'The game,' said he, 'is never lost till won.'

George Crabbe 1754-1832: *Tales of the Hall* (1819) 'Gretna Green'

14 The politicians of New York . . . see nothing wrong in the rule, that to the victor belong the spoils of the enemy.

William Learned Marcy 1786-1857: speech to the Senate, 25 January 1832

15 EVERYBODY has won, and all must have prizes.

Lewis Carroll 1832-98: *Alice's Adventures in Wonderland* (1865)

16 We are not interested in the possibilities of defeat; they do not exist.

on the Boer War during 'Black Week', December 1899

Queen Victoria 1819-1901: Lady Gwendolen Cecil *Life of Robert, Marquis of Salisbury* (1931)

17 The important thing in life is not the victory but the contest; the essential thing is not to have won but to have fought well.

Baron Pierre de Coubertin 1863-1937: speech on the Olympic Games, London, 24 July 1908

18 What's lost upon the roundabouts we pulls up on the swings!

Patrick Reginald Chalmers 1872-1942: 'Roundabouts and Swings' (1912); see 3 above

19 Honey, I just forgot to duck.

to his wife, on losing the World Heavyweight title, 23 September 1926

Jack Dempsey 1895-1983: J. and B. P. Dempsey *Dempsey* (1977); after a failed attempt on his life in 1981, Ronald Reagan quipped to his wife 'Honey, I forgot to duck'

20 What is our aim? . . . Victory, victory at all costs, victory in spite of all terror; victory, however long and hard the road may be; for without victory, there is no survival.

Winston Churchill 1874-1965: speech, House of Commons, 13 May 1940

21 The war situation has developed not necessarily to Japan's advantage.
announcing Japan's surrender, in a broadcast to his people after atom bombs had destroyed Hiroshima and Nagasaki
Emperor Hirohito 1901–89: on 15 August 1945

22 Man is not made for defeat. A man can be destroyed but not defeated.
Ernest Hemingway 1899–1961: *The Old Man and the Sea* (1952)

23 Sure, winning isn't everything. It's the only thing.
Henry 'Red' Sanders: in *Sports Illustrated* 26 December 1955; often attributed to Vince Lombardi

24 Defeat doesn't finish a man—quit does. A man is not finished when he's defeated.

He's finished when he quits.
Richard Nixon 1913–94: William Safire *Before the Fall* (1975)

25 A man able to think isn't defeated—even when he is defeated.
Milan Kundera 1929– : in *Sunday Times* 20 May 1984

26 The moment of victory is much too short to live for that and nothing else.
Martina Navratilova 1956– : in *Independent* 21 June 1989

27 Winning is everything. The only ones who remember you when you come second are your wife and your dog.
Damon Hill 1960– : in *Sunday Times* 18 December 1994

Wit and Wordplay see also Humour

PROVERBS AND SAYINGS

1 Brevity is the soul of wit.
early 17th century, from Shakespeare: see 5 below

PHRASES

2 Attic salt refined, delicate, poignant wit.
Attic of Attica, district of ancient Greece, or Athens, its chief city

3 esprit de l'escalier a clever remark that occurs to one after the opportunity to make it is lost.
French = staircase wit, from Denis Diderot (1713–84) Paradoxe sur le Comédien (written 1773–8) 'The witty riposte one thinks of only when one has left the drawing-room and is already on the way downstairs'

QUOTATIONS

4 I am not only witty in myself, but the cause that wit is in other men.
William Shakespeare 1564–1616: *Henry IV, Part 2* (1597)

5 Brevity is the soul of wit.
William Shakespeare 1564–1616: *Hamlet* (1601); see 1 above, 17 below

6 A thing well said will be wit in all languages.
John Dryden 1631–1700: *An Essay of Dramatic Poesy* (1668)

7   Wit will shine
Through the harsh cadence of a rugged line.
John Dryden 1631–1700: 'To the Memory of Mr Oldham' (1684)

8 A man who could make so vile a pun would not scruple to pick a pocket.
John Dennis 1657–1734: editorial note in *The Gentleman's Magazine* (1781)

9 Apt Alliteration's artful aid.
Charles Churchill 1731–64: *The Prophecy of Famine* (1763)

10 If I reprehend any thing in this world, it is the use of my oracular tongue, and a nice derangement of epitaphs!
Richard Brinsley Sheridan 1751–1816: *The Rivals* (1775)

11 There's no possibility of being witty without a little ill-nature; the malice of a good thing is the barb that makes it stick.
Richard Brinsley Sheridan 1751–1816: *The School for Scandal* (1777)

12 His wit invites you by his looks to come, But when you knock it never is at home.
William Cowper 1731–1800: 'Conversation' (1782)

13 What is an Epigram? a dwarfish whole, Its body brevity, and wit its soul.
Samuel Taylor Coleridge 1772–1834: 'Epigram' (1809)

14 Those who cannot miss an opportunity of saying a good thing . . . are not to be trusted with the management of any great question.
William Hazlitt 1778–1830: *Characteristics* (1823)

15 [A pun] is a pistol let off at the ear; not a feather to tickle the intellect.
Charles Lamb 1775–1834: *Last Essays of Elia* (1833) 'Popular Fallacies'

16 Wit is the epitaph of an emotion.
Friedrich Nietzsche 1844–1900: *Menschliches, Allzumenschliches* (1867–80)

17 Impropriety is the soul of wit.
W. Somerset Maugham 1874–1965: *The Moon and Sixpence* (1919); see 5 above

18 If, with the literate, I am
Impelled to try an epigram,
I never seek to take the credit;
We all assume that Oscar said it.
Dorothy Parker 1893–1967: 'A Pig's-Eye View of Literature' (1937)

19 There's a hell of a distance between wise-cracking and wit. Wit has truth in it; wise-cracking is simply callisthenics with words.
Dorothy Parker 1893–1967: in *Paris Review* Summer 1956

20 Satire is a lesson, parody is a game.
Vladimir Nabokov 1899–1977: *Strong Opinions* (1974)

21 I shouldn't call myself a satirist. To be a satirist, you have to know better than everyone else, and I've never done that.
Philip Larkin 1922–85: A. N. Wilson *Penfriends from Porlock* (1988)

22 Satire is dependent on strong beliefs, and on strong beliefs wounded.
Anita Brookner 1938– : in *Spectator* 23 March 1989

Woman's Role see also Men and Women

PROVERBS AND SAYINGS

1 Burn your bra.
feminist slogan, 1970s

2 Silence is a woman's best garment.
mid 16th century; often used as recommending a traditionally submissive and discreet role for women

3 Votes for women.
slogan of the women's suffrage movement, adopted when it proved impossible to use a banner with the longer slogan 'Will the Liberal Party Give Votes for Women?' made by Emmeline Pankhurst, Christabel Pankhurst, and Annie Kenney

4 A woman's place is in the home.
mid 19th century, reflecting the traditional view of a woman's role

PHRASES

5 the angel in the house a woman who is completely devoted to her husband and family.
from the title of a poem (1854–62) by Coventry Patmore; often used pejoratively

QUOTATIONS

6 Men are the managers of the affairs of women.
The Koran: sura 4

7 The First Blast of the Trumpet Against the Monstrous Regiment of Women.
regiment 'rule or government over a country', directed against the rule of Mary Tudor in England

and Mary of Lorraine in Scotland (as regent for her daughter Mary Queen of Scots)
John Knox c.1505–72: title of pamphlet (1558)

8 I am obnoxious to each carping tongue,
Who says my hand a needle better fits,
A poet's pen, all scorn, I should thus wrong.
Anne Bradstreet c.1612–72: 'The Prologue' (1650)

9 Why then should women be denied the benefits of instruction? If knowledge and understanding had been useless additions to the sex, God almighty would never have given them capacities.
Daniel Defoe 1660–1731: *An Essay Upon Projects* (1697) 'Of Academies: An Academy for Women'

10 If all men are born free, how is it that all women are born slaves?
Mary Astell 1668–1731: *Some Reflections upon Marriage* (1706 ed.)

11 A woman's preaching is like a dog's walking on his hinder legs. It is not done well; but you are surprised to find it done at all.
Samuel Johnson 1709–84: James Boswell *Life of Samuel Johnson* (1791) 31 July 1763

12 In the new code of laws which I suppose it will be necessary for you to make I desire you would remember the ladies, and be more generous and favourable to them than your ancestors. Do not put such unlimited power into the hands of the husbands. Remember all men would be tyrants if they could.

Abigail Adams 1744–1818: letter to John Adams, 31 March 1776

13 A man is in general better pleased when he has a good dinner upon his table, than when his wife talks Greek.

Samuel Johnson 1709–84: John Hawkins (ed.) *The Works of Samuel Johnson* (1787) 'Apophthegms, Sentiments, Opinions, etc.'

14 Can anything be more absurd than keeping women in a state of ignorance, and yet so vehemently to insist on their resisting temptation?

Vicesimus Knox 1752–1821: Mary Wollstonecraft *A Vindication of the Rights of Woman* (1792)

15 I do not wish them [women] to have power over men; but over themselves.

Mary Wollstonecraft 1759–97: *A Vindication of the Rights of Woman* (1792)

16 Religion is an all-important matter in a public school for girls. Whatever people say, it is the mother's safeguard, and the husband's. What we ask of education is not that girls should think, but that they should believe.

Napoleon I 1769–1821: 'Note sur L'Établissement D'Écouen' 15 May 1807

17 That little man . . . he says women can't have as much rights as men, cause Christ wasn't a woman. Where did your Christ come from? From God and a woman. Man had nothing to do with Him.

Sojourner Truth c.1797–1883: speech at Women's Rights Convention, Akron, Ohio, 1851

18 Woman stock is rising in the market. I shall not live to see women vote, but I'll come and rap at the ballot box.

Lydia Maria Child 1802–80: letter to Sarah Shaw, 3 August 1856

19 I should like to know what is the proper function of women, if it is not to make reasons for husbands to stay at home, and still stronger reasons for bachelors to go out.

George Eliot 1819–80: *The Mill on the Floss* (1860)

20 I want to be something so much worthier than the doll in the doll's house.

Charles Dickens 1812–70: *Our Mutual Friend* (1865)

21 The Queen is most anxious to enlist every one who can speak or write to join in checking this mad, wicked folly of 'Woman's Rights', with all its attendant horrors, on which her poor feeble sex is bent, forgetting every sense of womanly feeling and propriety.

Queen Victoria 1819–1901: letter to Theodore Martin, 29 May 1870

22 Inferior to us God made you, and inferior to the end of time you will remain.

on the admission of women to university

John William Burgon 1813–88: University Sermon, New College, Oxford, 8 June 1884

23 The one point on which all women are in furious secret rebellion against the existing law is the saddling of the right to a child with the obligation to become the servant of a man.

George Bernard Shaw 1856–1950: *Getting Married* (1911)

24 We are here to claim our right as women, not only to be free, but to fight for freedom. That it is our right as well as our duty.

Christabel Pankhurst 1880–1958: in *Votes for Women* 31 March 1911

25 I myself have never been able to find out precisely what feminism is: I only know that people call me a feminist whenever I express sentiments that differentiate me from a doormat or a prostitute.

Rebecca West 1892–1983: in *The Clarion* 14 November 1913

26 Woman is the nigger of the world.

Yoko Ono 1933– : remark made in a 1968 interview for *Nova* magazine and adopted by John Lennon as the title of a song (1972)

27 But if God had wanted us to think just with our wombs, why did He give us a brain?

Clare Booth Luce 1903–87: in *Life* 16 October 1970

28 Women's Liberation is just a lot of foolishness. It's the men who are discriminated against. They can't bear children. And no-one's likely to do anything about that.

Golda Meir 1898–1978: in *Newsweek* 23 October 1972

29 The sadness of the women's movement is that they don't allow the necessity of love. See, I don't personally trust any revolution where love is not allowed.

Maya Angelou 1928– : in *California Living* 14 May 1975

30 We are becoming the men we wanted to marry.

Gloria Steinem 1934– : in *Ms* July/August 1982

31 I didn't fight to get women out from behind the vacuum cleaner to get them onto the board of Hoover.
Germaine Greer 1939– : in *Guardian* 27 October 1986

32 Today the problem that has no name is how to juggle work, love, home and children.
Betty Friedan 1921– : *The Second Stage* (1987)

33 Feminism is the most revolutionary idea there has ever been. Equality for women demands a change in the human psyche more profound then anything Marx dreamed of. It means valuing parenthood as much as we value banking.
Polly Toynbee 1946– : in *Guardian* 19 January 1987

34 I could have stayed home and baked cookies and had teas. But what I decided was to fulfil my profession, which I entered before my husband was in public life.
Hillary Rodham Clinton 1947– : comment on questions raised by rival Democratic contender Edmund G. Brown Jr.; in *Albany Times-Union* 17 March 1992

35 Women have been trained to speak softly and carry lipstick. Those days are over.
Bella Abzug 1920–98: attributed; in *Times* 2 April 1998; see **Diplomacy** 9

Women see also **Men and Women**

PROVERBS AND SAYINGS

1 Far-fetched and dear-bought is good for ladies.
mid 14th century, meaning that expensive or exotic articles are suitable for women

2 The female of the species is more deadly than the male.
early 20th century; from Kipling: see 40 below

3 The hand that rocks the cradle rules the world.
mid 19th century, referring to the strength of a woman's indirect influence on the male world; see **Elections** 19, **Parents** 11

4 Hell hath no fury like a woman scorned.
late 17th century, meaning that a woman whose love has turned to hate is the most savage of creatures; a fury *here may be either one of the avenging deities of classical mythology, or more generally someone in a state of frenzied rage; see* **Revenge** 16

5 Long and lazy, little and loud; fat and fulsome, pretty and proud.
late 16th century; categorizing supposed physical and temperamental characteristics in women

6 A whistling woman and a crowing hen are neither fit for God nor men.
early 18th century; both the woman and the hen are considered unnatural, and therefore unlucky

7 A woman, a dog, and a walnut tree, the more you beat them the better they be.
late 16th century; the walnut tree was beaten firstly to bring down the fruit, and then to break down long shoots and encourage short fruit-bearing ones

8 A woman and a ship ever want mending.
late 16th century, meaning that both women and ships require constant attention and expenditure

PHRASES

9 daughter of Eve a woman, especially one regarded as showing a typically feminine trait.

10 Essex girl a derogatory term applied to a type of young woman, supposedly to be found in and around Essex, and variously characterized as unintelligent, promiscuous, and materialistic.
she is typically the butt of politically incorrect jokes; see also **Class** 3

11 the fair sex the female sex, women collectively.
see 34 below

12 It girl an actress or model, usually vivacious and outgoing, considered to have particular sex appeal. In later use, also a young woman who has achieved celebrity because of her socialite lifestyle.
coined by the screenwriter Elinor Glyn (1864-1943) and personified by the actress Clara Bow (1905-65). The use of it *meaning sex appeal is first recorded in Kipling: see* **Sex** 19

13 page three girl a model whose nude or semi-nude photograph appears as part of a regular series in a tabloid newspaper.
after the standard page position in the Sun, *a British newspaper*

QUOTATIONS

14 This is now bone of my bones, and flesh of my flesh: she shall be called Woman, because she was taken out of Man.
Bible: Genesis

15 Who can find a virtuous woman? for her price is far above rubies.
Bible: Proverbs

16 The greatest glory of a woman is to be least talked about by men.
Pericles c.495–429 BC: Thucydides *History of the Peloponnesian War*

17   *Varium et mutabile semper Femina.*
Fickle and changeable always is woman.
Virgil 70–19 BC: *Aeneid*

18 Whoever has a daughter and does not bury her alive, nor insult her nor favour his son over her, Allah will enter him into Paradise.
Ahmad ibn Hanbal 780–855: *Musnad* no. 1957

19 And what is bettre than wisedoom? Womman. And
what is bettre than a good womman? Nothyng.
Geoffrey Chaucer c.1343–1400: *The Canterbury Tales* 'The Tale of Melibee'

20 Frailty, thy name is woman!
William Shakespeare 1564–1616: *Hamlet* (1601)

21 The weaker sex, to piety more prone.
William Alexander, Earl of Stirling c.1567–1640: 'Doomsday' 5th Hour (1637)

22 She floats, she hesitates; in a word, she's a woman.
Jean Racine 1639–99: *Athalie* (1691)

23 She knows her man, and when you rant and swear,
Can draw you to her *with a single hair.*
John Dryden 1631–1700: translation of Persius *Satires*

24 I have never had any great esteem for the generality of the fair sex, and my only consolation for being of that gender has been the assurance it gave me of never being married to anyone amongst them.
Lady Mary Wortley Montagu 1689–1762: letter to Mrs Calthorpe, 7 December 1723

25 Woman's at best a contradiction still.
Alexander Pope 1688–1744: *Epistles to Several Persons* 'To a Lady' (1735)

26 Women, then, are only children of a larger growth.
Lord Chesterfield 1694–1773: *Letters to his Son* (1774) 5 September 1748

27 Here's to the maiden of bashful fifteen
Here's to the widow of fifty

Here's to the flaunting, extravagant quean;
And here's to the housewife that's thrifty.
Richard Brinsley Sheridan 1751–1816: *The School for Scandal* (1777)

28 Auld nature swears, the lovely dears
Her noblest work she classes, O;
Her prentice han' she tried on man,
An' then she made the lasses, O.
Robert Burns 1759–96: 'Green Grow the Rashes' (1787)

29 O Woman! in our hours of ease,
Uncertain, coy, and hard to please,
And variable as the shade
By the light quivering aspen made;
When pain and anguish wring the brow,
A ministering angel thou!
Sir Walter Scott 1771–1832: *Marmion* (1808); see **Charity** 9

30 All the privilege I claim for my own sex . . . is that of loving longest, when existence or when hope is gone.
Jane Austen 1775–1817: *Persuasion* (1818)

31 In her first passion woman loves her lover,
In all the others all she loves is love.
Lord Byron 1788–1824: *Don Juan* (1819–24)

32 Eternal Woman draws us upward.
Johann Wolfgang von Goethe 1749–1832: *Faust* pt. 2 (1832) 'Hochgebirg'

33   The woman is so hard
Upon the woman.
Alfred, Lord Tennyson 1809–92: *The Princess* (1847)

34 Only the male intellect, clouded by sexual impulse, could call the undersized, narrow-shouldered, broad-hipped, and short-legged sex the fair sex.
Arthur Schopenhauer 1788–1860: 'On Women' (1851); see **11** above

35 The happiest women, like the happiest nations, have no history.
George Eliot 1819–80: *The Mill on the Floss* (1860)

36 Women—one half the human race at least—care fifty times more for a marriage than a ministry.
Walter Bagehot 1826–77: *The English Constitution* (1867) 'The Monarchy'

37 Woman was God's second blunder.
Friedrich Nietzsche 1844–1900: *Der Antichrist* (1888)

38 When you get to a man in the case,
They're like as a row of pins—

For the Colonel's Lady an' Judy O'Grady
Are sisters under their skins!
Rudyard Kipling 1865–1936: 'The Ladies' (1896)

39 The prime truth of woman, the universal
mother . . . that if a thing is worth doing, it
is worth doing badly.
G. K. Chesterton 1874–1936: *What's Wrong with the World* (1910) 'Folly and Female Education'; see
Effort 5

40 The female of the species is more deadly
than the male.
Rudyard Kipling 1865–1936: 'The Female of the Species' (1919); see 2 above

41 Women have no wilderness in them,
They are provident instead,
Content in the tight hot cell of their hearts
To eat dusty bread.
Louise Bogan 1897–1970: 'Women' (1923)

42 The perpetual hunger to be beautiful and
that thirst to be loved which is the real
curse of Eve.
Jean Rhys c.1890–1979: *The Left Bank* (1927) 'Illusion'

43 Certain women should be struck regularly,
like gongs.
Noël Coward 1899–1973: *Private Lives* (1930)

44 The great and almost only comfort about
being a woman is that one can always
pretend to be more stupid than one is and
no one is surprised.
Freya Stark 1893–1993: *The Valleys of the Assassins* (1934)

45 Woman may born you, love you, an'
mourn you,
But a woman is a sometime thing.
Du Bose Heyward 1885–1940 and **Ira Gershwin** 1896–1983: 'A Woman is a Sometime Thing' (1935 song)

46 The great question that has never been
answered and which I have not yet been
able to answer, despite my thirty years of
research into the feminine soul, is 'What
does a woman want?'
Sigmund Freud 1856–1939: to Marie Bonaparte; Ernest Jones *Sigmund Freud: Life and Work* (1955)

47 Women would rather be right than be
reasonable.
Ogden Nash 1902–71: 'Frailty, Thy Name is a Misnomer' (1942)

48 One is not born a woman: one becomes
one.
Simone de Beauvoir 1908–86: *Le deuxième sexe* (1949)

49 There is nothin' like a dame.
Oscar Hammerstein II 1895–1960: title of song (1949)

50 Thank heaven for little girls!
For little girls get bigger every day.
Alan Jay Lerner 1918–86: 'Thank Heaven for Little Girls' (1958 song)

51 Women never have young minds. They
are born three thousand years old.
Shelagh Delaney 1939– : *A Taste of Honey* (1959)

52 I got a twenty dollar piece says
There ain't nothin' I can't do.
I can make a dress out of a feed bag an' I
can make a man out of you.
'Cause I'm a woman
W-O-M-A-N
I'll say it again.
Jerry Leiber 1933– : 'I'm a Woman' (1962 song)

53 From birth to 18 a girl needs good parents.
From 18 to 35, she needs good looks. From
35 to 55, good personality. From 55 on,
she needs good cash.
Sophie Tucker 1884–1966: Michael Freedland *Sophie* (1978)

54 She takes just like a woman, yes, she does
She makes love just like a woman, yes, she
does
And she aches just like a woman
But she breaks like a little girl.
Bob Dylan 1941– : 'Just Like a Woman' (1966 song)

55 Sisterhood is powerful.
Robin Morgan 1941– : title of book (1970)

56 Being a woman is of special interest only to
aspiring male transsexuals. To actual
women, it is merely a good excuse not to
play football.
Fran Lebowitz 1946– : *Metropolitan Life* (1978)

57 The freedom women were supposed to
have found in the Sixties largely boiled
down to easy contraception and abortion:
things to make life easier for men, in fact.
Julie Burchill 1960– : *Damaged Goods* (1986)

58 a woman is not
a potted plant
her leaves trimmed
to the contours
of her sex.
Alice Walker 1944– : 'A woman is not a potted plant'

59 You can now see the Female Eunuch the
world over . . . spreading herself wherever
blue jeans and Coca-Cola may go.

Wherever you see nail varnish, lipstick, brassieres, and high heels, the Eunuch has set up her camp.
Germaine Greer 1939– : *The Female Eunuch* (20th anniversary ed., 1991)

60 There is no female Mozart because there is no female Jack the Ripper.
Camille Paglia 1947– : in *International Herald Tribune* 26 April 1991

61 You can have it all, but you can't do it all.
Michelle Pfeiffer 1959– : attributed; in *Guardian* 4 January 1996

Wordplay see Wit and Wordplay

Words see also Language, Meaning, Names, Words and Deeds

1 All words are pegs to hang ideas on.
American proverb, late 19th century

2 Hard words break no bones.
late 17th century, meaning that the damage done by verbal attack is limited

3 I before e, except after c.
traditional spelling rule, 19th century

4 If you take hyphens seriously you will surely go mad.
said to be from a style book in use with Oxford University Press, New York; perhaps apocryphal

5 Sticks and stones may break my bones, but words will never hurt me.
late 19th century; meaning that verbal attack does no real injury

QUOTATIONS

6 And once sent out a word takes wing beyond recall.
Horace 65–8 BC: *Epistles*

7 Throughout the world, if it were sought,
Fair words enough a man shall find.
They be good cheap; they cost right naught;
Their substance is but only wind.
Thomas Wyatt c.1503–42: 'Throughout the world, if it were sought' (1557)

8 But words are words; I never yet did hear
That the bruisèd heart was piercèd through the ear.
William Shakespeare 1564–1616: *Othello* (1602–4)

9 Words are the tokens current and accepted for conceits, as moneys are for values.
Francis Bacon 1561–1626: *The Advancement of Learning* (1605)

10 Words are wise men's counters, they do but reckon by them: but they are the money of fools, that value them by the authority of an Aristotle, a Cicero, or a Thomas, or any other doctor whatsoever, if but a man.
Thomas Hobbes 1588–1679: *Leviathan* (1651)

11 Words are like leaves; and where they most abound,
Much fruit of sense beneath is rarely found.
Alexander Pope 1688–1744: *An Essay on Criticism* (1711)

12 I am not yet so lost in lexicography as to forget that words are the daughters of earth, and that things are the sons of heaven. Language is only the instrument of science, and words are but the signs of ideas: I wish, however, that the instrument might be less apt to decay, and that signs might be permanent, like the things which they denote.
Samuel Johnson 1709–84: *A Dictionary of the English Language* (1755)

13 It's exactly where a thought is lacking
That, just in time, a word shows up instead.
Goethe 1749–1832: *Faust* (1808)

14 'Do you spell it with a "V" or a "W"?' inquired the judge. 'That depends upon the taste and fancy of the speller, my Lord,' replied Sam [Weller].
Charles Dickens 1812–70: *Pickwick Papers* (1837)

15 'When *I* use a word,' Humpty Dumpty said in a rather scornful tone, 'it means just what I choose it to mean—neither more nor less.'
Lewis Carroll 1832–98: *Through the Looking-Glass* (1872)

16 Some word that teems with hidden meaning—like Basingstoke.
W. S. Gilbert 1836–1911: *Ruddigore* (1887)

17 I fear those big words, Stephen said, which make us so unhappy.
James Joyce 1882–1941: *Ulysses* (1922)

18 Words are, of course, the most powerful drug used by mankind.
Rudyard Kipling 1865–1936: speech, 14 February 1923

19 I could not write the words Mr Joyce uses: my prudish hands would refuse to form the letters.
George Bernard Shaw 1856–1950: *Table Talk of G. B. S.* (1925)

20 My spelling is Wobbly. It's good spelling but it Wobbles, and the letters get in the wrong places.
A. A. Milne 1882–1956: *Winnie-the-Pooh* (1926)

21 The Greeks had a word for it.
Zoë Akins 1886–1958: title of play (1930)

22 I gotta use words when I talk to you.
T. S. Eliot 1888–1965: *Sweeney Agonistes* (1932)

23   Words strain,
Crack and sometimes break, under the burden,
Under the tension, slip, slide, perish,
Decay with imprecision, will not stay in place,
Will not stay still.
T. S. Eliot 1888–1965: *Four Quartets* 'Burnt Norton' (1936)

24 Today words have become battles. The right words, battles won; the wrong words, battles lost.
Erich von Ludendorff 1865–1937: George C. Bruntz *Allied Propaganda and the Collapse of the German Empire in 1918* (1938)

25 Words are chameleons, which reflect the colour of their environment.
Learned Hand 1872–1961: in *Commissioner v. National Carbide Corp.* (1948)

26 There is no use indicting words, they are no shoddier than what they peddle.
Samuel Beckett 1906–89: *Malone Dies* (1958)

27 Man does not live by words alone, despite the fact that he sometimes has to eat them.
Adlai Stevenson 1900–65: *The Wit and Wisdom of Adlai Stevenson* (1965)

28 The day of the jewelled epigram is passed and, whether one likes it or not, one is moving into the stern puritanical era of the four-letter word.
Noel Annan 1916–2000: in the House of Lords, 1966; George Greenfield *Scribblers for Bread* (1989)

29 MIKE: There's no word in the Irish language for what you were doing.
WILSON: In Lapland they have no word for snow.
Joe Orton 1933–67: *The Ruffian on the Stair* (rev. ed. 1967)

30 If *Miss* means respectably unmarried, and *Mrs* respectably married, then *Ms* means nudge, nudge, wink, wink.
Angela Carter 1940–92: 'The Language of Sisterhood' in Christopher Ricks (ed.) *The State of the Language* (1980)

31 In my youth there were words you couldn't say in front of a girl; now you can't say 'girl'.
Tom Lehrer 1928– : interview in *The Oldie* 1996; in *Sunday Telegraph* 10 March 1996

Words and Deeds

PROVERBS AND SAYINGS

1 Actions speak louder than words.
early 17th century, meaning that real feeling is expressed not by what someone says but by what they do

2 Brag is a good dog, but Holdfast is better.
early 18th century, meaning that perseverance is a better quality than ostentation

3 Example is better than precept.
early 15th century

4 Fine words butter no parsnips.
mid 17th century, meaning that nothing is ever achieved by fine words alone (butter was the traditional garnish for parsips)

5 One picture is worth ten thousand words.
*early 20th century; see **Language** 21*

6 An ounce of practice is worth a pound of precept.
late 16th century, meaning that a small amount of practical assistance is worth more than a great deal of advice

7 Practise what you preach.

late 14th century, meaning that you should follow the advice you give to others

8 Talk is cheap.

mid 19th century meaning that it is easier to say than to do something

9 Threatened men live long.

mid 16th century; meaning that threats are often not put into effect, and those who express resentment are actually much less dangerous than those who conceal animosity

QUOTATIONS

10 But be ye doers of the word, and not hearers only.

Bible: James

11 Woord is but wynd; leff woord and tak the dede.

John Lydgate c.1370–c.1451: *Secrets of Old Philosophers*

12 Do not, as some ungracious pastors do,
Show me the steep and thorny way to
   heaven,
Whiles, like a puffed and reckless libertine,
Himself the primrose path of dalliance
   treads,
And recks not his own rede.

William Shakespeare 1564–1616: *Hamlet* (1601); see **Pleasure** 6

13 Oh that thou hadst like others been all
   words,
And no performance.

Philip Massinger 1583–1640: *The Parliament of Love* (1624)

14 Here lies a great and mighty king
Whose promise none relies on;
He never said a foolish thing,
Nor ever did a wise one.

on Charles II

John Wilmot, Lord Rochester 1647–80: 'The King's Epitaph' (alternatively 'Here lies our sovereign lord the King'); in C. E. Doble et al. *Thomas Hearne: Remarks and Collections* (1885–1921) 17 November 1706; see 15 below

15 This is very true: for my words are my own, and my actions are my ministers'.

reply to Lord Rochester's epitaph

Charles II 1630–85: in *Thomas Hearne: Remarks and Collections* (1885–1921) 17 November 1706; see 14 above

16 Because half a dozen grasshoppers under a fern make the field ring with their importunate chink, whilst thousands of great cattle, reposed beneath the shadow of the British oak, chew the cud and are silent, pray do not imagine that those who make the noise are the only inhabitants of the field.

Edmund Burke 1729–97: *Reflections on the Revolution in France* (1790)

17 I prefer the talents of action—of war—of the senate—or even of science—to all the speculations of those mere dreamers of another existence.

Lord Byron 1788–1824: letter to Annabella Milbanke, 29 November 1813

18 The end of man is an action and not a thought, though it were the noblest.

Thomas Carlyle 1795–1881: *Sartor Resartus* (1834)

19 Considering how foolishly people act and how pleasantly they prattle, perhaps it would be better for the world if they talked more and did less.

W. Somerset Maugham 1874–1965: *A Writer's Notebook* (1949) written in 1892

20 People who could not tell a lathe from a lawn mower and have never carried the responsibilities of management never tire of telling British management off for its alleged inefficiency.

Keith Joseph 1918–94: in *The Times* 9 August 1974

21 Enough of talking—it is time now to do.

Tony Blair 1953– : on taking office as Prime Minister; Downing Street, 2 May 1997

22 What do you mean by this word '*we*'? *you*'re not going to war, are you? It's like watching the football and saying, 'We beat Germany 5–1!' No, *you* didn't! *you* watched it on the telly!

Jeremy Hardy: 'Jeremy Hardy Speaks to the Nation' BBC Radio 4, 6 September 2001

Work see also Employment, Idleness, Leisure

1 Arbeit macht frei.

German, Work liberates, words inscribed on the gates of Dachau concentration camp, 1933, and subsequently on those of Auschwitz

2 Every man to his trade.

late 16th century, meaning that one should operate within one's own area of expertise

3 Fools and bairns should never see half-done work.

early 18th century, meaning that the unwise and the inexperienced may judge the quality of a finished article from its rough unfinished state

4 One volunteer is worth two pressed men.

early 18th century; a pressed man was someone forcibly enlisted by the press gang, a body of men which in the 18th and 19th centuries was employed to enlist men forcibly into service in the army or navy

5 Practice makes perfect.

mid 16th century, often used as an encouragement

6 Saturday's child works hard for its living.

*mid 19th century; see **Beauty** 5, **Gifts** 2, **Pregnancy** 1, **Sorrow** 2, **Travel** 5*

7 A short horse is soon curried.

mid 14th century; meaning that a slight task is soon completed (literally, that it does not take long to rub down a short horse with a curry-comb)

8 Too many cooks spoil the broth.

late 16th century, meaning that the involvement of too many people is likely to mean that something is done badly

9 Two boys are half a boy, and three boys are no boy at all.

mid 20th century; meaning that the more boys there are present, the less work will be done

10 Where bees are, there is honey.

early 17th century, meaning that industrious work is necessary to create riches

11 Work expands so as to fill the time available.

mid 20th century, from Parkinson: see 38 below

12 the bread of idleness food or sustenance for which one has not worked.

after the Bible (Proverbs) 'She . . . eateth not the bread of idleness'

13 burn the midnight oil study late into the night.

see 24 below

14 by the sweat of one's brow by one's own hard work.

from the Bible: see 18 below

15 daily bread a livelihood.

after the Bible (Matthew) 'Give us this day our daily bread' (part of the Lord's Prayer)

16 ply the labouring oar do much of the work.

labouring oar the hardest to pull, originally with allusion to Dryden Aeneid 'three Trojans tug at ev'ry lab'ring oar'

17 sing for one's supper provide a service in order to earn a benefit.

after the nursery rhyme Little Tommy Tucker

18 In the sweat of thy face shalt thou eat bread.

Bible: Genesis; see 14 above

19 For it is commonly said: completed labours are pleasant.

Cicero 106–43 BC: *De Finibus*

20 Come unto me, all ye that labour and are heavy laden, and I will give you rest . . .
For my yoke is easy, and my burden is light.

Bible: St Matthew

21 If any would not work, neither should he eat.

Bible: II Thessalonians; see **Idleness** 8

22 Set thy heart upon thy work but never upon its reward. Work not for a reward: but never cease to do thy work.

Bhagavadgita: ch. 2, v. 47

23 The labour we delight in physics pain.

William Shakespeare 1564–1616: *Macbeth* (1606)

24 We spend our midday sweat, our midnight oil;
We tire the night in thought, the day in toil.

Francis Quarles 1592–1644: *Emblems* (1635); see 13 above

25 How doth the little busy bee
Improve each shining hour,
And gather honey all the day

From every opening flower!
Isaac Watts 1674–1748: 'Against Idleness and Mischief' (1715); see **Effort** 10

26 If you have great talents, industry will improve them: if you have but moderate abilities, industry will supply their deficiency.
Joshua Reynolds 1723–92: *Discourses on Art* 11 December 1769

27 The world is too much with us; late and soon,
Getting and spending, we lay waste our powers.
William Wordsworth 1770–1850: 'The world is too much with us' (1807)

28 Who first invented work—and tied the free And holy-day rejoicing spirit down
To the ever-haunting importunity
Of business?
Charles Lamb 1775–1834: letter to Bernard Barton, 11 September 1822

29 My life is one demd horrid grind!
Charles Dickens 1812–70: *Nicholas Nickleby* (1839)

30 Blessèd are the horny hands of toil!
James Russell Lowell 1819–91: 'A Glance Behind the Curtain' (1844)

31 For men must work, and women must weep,
And there's little to earn, and many to keep,
Though the harbour bar be moaning.
Charles Kingsley 1819–75: 'The Three Fishers' (1858)

32 Labour without joy is base. Labour without sorrow is base. Sorrow without labour is base. Joy without labour is base.
John Ruskin 1819–1900: *Time and Tide* (1867)

33 Generations have trod, have trod, have trod;
And all is seared with trade; bleared, smeared with toil.
Gerard Manley Hopkins 1844–89: 'God's Grandeur' (written 1877)

34 I like work: it fascinates me. I can sit and look at it for hours. I love to keep it by me: the idea of getting rid of it nearly breaks my heart.
Jerome K. Jerome 1859–1927: *Three Men in a Boat* (1889)

35 Work is love made visible.
Kahlil Gibran 1883–1931: *The Prophet* (1923)

36 Who built Thebes of the seven gates?

In the books you will find the names of kings.
Did the kings haul up the lumps of rock?
. . .
Where, the evening that the wall of China was finished
Did the masons go?
Bertolt Brecht 1898–1956: 'Questions From A Worker Who Reads' (1935)

37 Why should I let the toad *work*
Squat on my life?
Can't I use my wit as a pitchfork
And drive the brute off?
Philip Larkin 1922–85: 'Toads' (1955)

38 Work expands so as to fill the time available for its completion.
C. Northcote Parkinson 1909–93: *Parkinson's Law* (1958); see 11 above

39 Without work, all life goes rotten, but when work is soulless, life stifles and dies.
Albert Camus 1913–60: attributed; E. F. Schumacher *Good Work* (1979)

40 It has been my experience that one cannot, in any shape or form, depend on human relations for lasting reward. It is only work that truly satisfies.
Bette Davis 1908–89: *The Lonely Life* (1962)

41 Work was like a stick. It had two ends. When you worked for the knowing you gave them quality; when you worked for a fool you simply gave him eye-wash.
Alexander Solzhenitsyn 1918– : *One Day in the Life of Ivan Denisovich* (1962)

42 I had known it was going to be a 'winter of discontent'.
following extensive strikes; echoing Shakespeare's Richard III
James Callaghan 1912– : television interview, 8 February 1979

43 It's true hard work never killed anybody, but I figure why take the chance?
Ronald Reagan 1911– : interview, *Guardian* 31 March 1987

44 I have long been of the opinion that if work were such a splendid thing the rich would have kept more of it for themselves.
Bruce Grocott 1940– : in *Observer* 22 May 1988

45 Where I come from in Wales, we white men dig for black coal and in America your black men pick white cotton. To me it's the same thing.
Tom Jones 1940– ; L. Ellis and B. Sutherland *Tom Jones: Close Up* (2000)

World War I see also The Armed Forces, Warfare

PROVERBS AND SAYINGS

1 Ils ne passeront pas.
French, They shall not pass, slogan used by the French army at the defence of Verdun in 1916; variously attributed to Marshal Pétain and to General Robert Nivelle, and taken up by the Republicans in the Spanish Civil War in the form 'No pasarán!'; *see* **Defiance** 17

PHRASES

2 the Angels of Mons protective spirits supposedly seen over the First World War battlefield.
the origin was in fact a short story, 'The Angel of Mons' (1915) by Arthur Machen (1843–1947), which circulated widely by word of mouth as a factual account

3 Flanders poppy a red poppy used as an emblem of the soldiers of the Allies who fell in the First World War.
chosen as a flower which grew on the battlefields: see 15 below

4 lions led by donkeys associated with British soldiers during the First World War.
attributed to Max Hoffman (1869–1927) in Alan Clark The Donkeys (1961); this attribution has not been traced elsewhere, and the phrase is of much earlier origin

5 the Old Contemptibles the British army in France in 1914.
referring to the German Emperor's alleged mention of a 'contemptible little army'

6 the war to end wars the war of 1914–18, as a war intended to make further wars impossible.
after the title of book by H. G. Wells in 1914, The War That Will End War

QUOTATIONS

7 If there is ever another war in Europe, it will come out of some damned silly thing in the Balkans.
Otto von Bismarck 1815–98: quoted in speech, House of Commons, 16 August 1945

8 The lamps are going out all over Europe; we shall not see them lit again in our lifetime.
on the eve of the First World War
Edward Grey 1862–1933: *25 Years* (1925)

9 Do your duty bravely. Fear God. Honour the King.
Lord Kitchener 1850–1916: message to soldiers of the British Expeditionary Force, August 1914

10 *Gott strafe England!*
God punish England!
Alfred Funke b. 1869: *Schwert und Myrte* (1914)

11 Belgium put the kibosh on the Kaiser.
Alf Ellerton: title of song (1914)

12 Now, God be thanked Who has matched us with His hour,
And caught our youth, and wakened us from sleeping,
With hand made sure, clear eye, and sharpened power,
To turn, as swimmers into cleanness leaping.
Rupert Brooke 1887–1915: 'Peace' (1914)

13 Oh! we don't want to lose you but we think you ought to go
For your King and your Country both need you so.
Paul Alfred Rubens 1875–1917: 'Your King and Country Want You' (1914 song)

14 My centre is giving way, my right is retreating, situation excellent, I am attacking.
Ferdinand Foch 1851–1929: message sent during the first Battle of the Marne, September 1914; R. Recouly *Foch* (1919)

15 In Flanders fields the poppies blow
Between the crosses, row on row.
John McCrae 1872–1918: 'In Flanders Fields' (1915); see 3 above

16 What passing-bells for these who die as cattle?
Only the monstrous anger of the guns.
Only the stuttering rifles' rapid rattle
Can patter out their hasty orisons.
Wilfred Owen 1893–1918: 'Anthem for Doomed Youth' (written 1917)

17 *Lafayette, nous voilà!*
Lafayette, we are here.
Charles E. Stanton 1859–1933: at the tomb of Lafayette in Paris, 4 July 1917

18 Over there, over there,
Send the word, send the word over there
That the Yanks are coming, the Yanks are coming . . .

We'll be over, we're coming over
And we won't come back till it's over, over
  there.
George M. Cohan 1878–1942: 'Over There' (1917
song); see **World War II** 1

19 If I were fierce, and bald, and short of
    breath,
I'd live with scarlet Majors at the Base,
And speed glum heroes up the line to
    death.
Siegfried Sassoon 1886–1967: 'Base Details' (1918)

20 O Death, where is thy sting-a-ling-a-ling,
O grave, thy victory?
The bells of Hell go ting-a-ling-a-ling
For you but not for me.
Anonymous: 'For You But Not For Me' (First World
War song); see **Death** 22

21 My home policy: I wage war; my foreign
policy: I wage war. All the time I wage
war.
Georges Clemenceau 1841–1929: speech to French
Chamber of Deputies, 8 March 1918

22 At eleven o'clock this morning came to an
end the cruellest and most terrible war
that has ever scourged mankind. I hope we
may say that thus, this fateful morning,
came to an end all wars.
David Lloyd George 1863–1945: speech, House of
Commons, 11 November 1918

23 This is not a peace treaty, it is an armistice
for twenty years.
Ferdinand Foch 1851–1929: at the signing of the
Treaty of Versailles, 1919; Paul Reynaud *Mémoires*
(1963)

24 You are all a lost generation.
*of the young who served in the First World War;
phrase borrowed (in translation) from a French garage*

mechanic, *whom Stein heard address it disparagingly
to an incompetent apprentice*
Gertrude Stein 1874–1946: Ernest Hemingway
subsequently took it as his epigraph to *The Sun Also
Rises* (1926)

25 Who will remember, passing through this
    Gate,
The unheroic Dead who fed the guns?
Who shall absolve the foulness of their
    fate,—
Those doomed, conscripted, unvictorious
    ones?
Siegfried Sassoon 1886–1967: 'On Passing the New
Menin Gate' (1928)

26 All quiet on the western front.
Erich Maria Remarque 1898–1970: English title of
Im Westen nichts Neues (1929 novel)

27 See that little stream—we could walk to it
in two minutes. It took the British a month
to walk it—a whole empire walking very
slowly, dying in front and pushing forward
behind. And another empire walked very
slowly backward a few inches a day,
leaving the dead like a million bloody rugs.
F. Scott Fitzgerald 1896–1940: *Tender is the Night*
(1934)

28 Oh what a lovely war.
Joan Littlewood 1914– and **Charles Chilton**
1914– : title of stage show (1963)

29 The First World War had begun—imposed
on the statesmen of Europe by railway
timetables.
A. J. P. Taylor 1906–90: *The First World War* (1963)

30 The Somme is like the Holocaust. It
revealed things about mankind that we
cannot come to terms with and cannot
forget. It can never become the past.
Pat Barker 1943– : on winning the Booker Prize,
November 1995

World War II see also Warfare

1 **Overpaid, overfed, oversexed, and over
here.**
*of American troops in Britain during the Second World
War; associated with Tommy Trinder, but probably not
his invention; see* **World War I** *18*

2 **the Baedeker raids** a series of German
reprisal air raids in 1942 on places in

Britain of cultural and historical
importance.
*after the series of guidebooks published by Karl
Baedeker (1801–59), German publisher*

3 **the Battle of Britain** a series of air battles
fought over Britain (August–October
1940), in which the RAF successfully
resisted raids by the numerically superior
German air force.
*from Winston Churchill, 18 June 1940, 'What General
Weygand called the Battle of France is over. I expect*

*that the Battle of Britain is about to begin'; the words
'The Battle of Britain is about to begin' appeared in
the order of the day for pilots on 10 July*

4 the desert rats soldiers of the 7th British
armoured division in the North African
desert campaign of 1941–2.
the badge of the division was a jerboa

5 the forgotten army the British army in
Burma after the fall of Rangoon in 1942
and the evacuation west, and the
subsequent cutting by the Japanese of the
supply link from India to Nationalist
China.
*said to derive from Lord Louis Mountbatten's
encouragement to his troops after taking over as
supreme Allied commander in South-East Asia, 'You
are not the Forgotten Army—no one's even heard of
you'*

QUOTATIONS

6 How horrible, fantastic, incredible it is that
we should be digging trenches and trying
on gas-masks here because of a quarrel in
a far away country between people of
whom we know nothing.
on Germany's annexation of the Sudetenland
Neville Chamberlain 1869–1940: radio broadcast,
27 September 1938

7 We're gonna hang out the washing on the
Siegfried Line.
Jimmy Kennedy and **Michael Carr**: title of song
(1939)

8 We shall not flag or fail. We shall go on to
the end. We shall fight in France, we shall
fight on the seas and oceans, we shall fight
with growing confidence and growing
strength in the air, we shall defend our
island, whatever the cost may be. We shall
fight on the beaches, we shall fight on the
landing grounds, we shall fight in the fields
and in the streets, we shall fight in the
hills; we shall never surrender.
Winston Churchill 1874–1965: speech, House of
Commons, 4 June 1940

9 This little steamer, like all her brave and
battered sisters, is immortal. She'll go
sailing proudly down the years in the epic
of Dunkirk. And our great-grand-children,
when they learn how we began this war
by snatching glory out of defeat, and then
swept on to victory, may also learn how
the little holiday steamers made an
excursion to hell and came back glorious.
J. B. Priestley 1894–1984: radio broadcast, 5 June
1940; see **Crises** 5

10 France has lost a battle. But France has
not lost the war!
Charles de Gaulle 1890–1970: proclamation, 18
June 1940

11 Let us therefore brace ourselves to our
duty, and so bear ourselves that, if the
British Empire and its Commonwealth lasts
for a thousand years, men will still say,
'This was their finest hour.'
Winston Churchill 1874–1965: speech, House of
Commons, 18 June 1940; see **Success** 15

12 I'm glad we've been bombed. It makes me
feel I can look the East End in the face.
Queen Elizabeth, the Queen Mother 1900–2002:
to a London policeman, 13 September 1940

13 We have the men—the skill—the
wealth—and above all, the will . . . We
must be the great arsenal of democracy.
Franklin D. Roosevelt 1882–1945: 'Fireside Chat'
radio broadcast, 29 December 1940

14 Yesterday, December 7, 1941—a date
which will live in infamy—the United
States of America was suddenly and
deliberately attacked by naval and air
forces of the Empire of Japan.
Franklin D. Roosevelt 1882–1945: address to
Congress, 8 December 1941

15 Sighted sub, sank same.
*on sinking a Japanese submarine in the Atlantic region
(the first US naval success in the war)*
Donald Mason 1913– : radio message, 28 January
1942

16 I came through and I shall return.
*on reaching Australia, having broken through
Japanese lines en route from Corregidor*
Douglas MacArthur 1880–1964: statement in
Adelaide, 20 March 1942

17 Don't let's be beastly to the Germans
When our Victory is ultimately won.
Noël Coward 1899–1973: 'Don't Let's Be Beastly to
the Germans' (1943 song)

18 I think we might be going a bridge too far.
*expressing reservations about the Arnhem 'Market
Garden' operation*
Frederick ('Boy') Browning 1896–1965: to Field
Marshal Montgomery on 10 September 1944

19 The Third Fleet's sunken and damaged
ships have been salvaged and are retiring
at high speed toward the enemy.
*on hearing claims that the Japanese had virtually
annihilated the US fleet*
W. F. ('Bull') Halsey 1882–1959: report, 14 October
1944

20 Nuts!

Anthony McAuliffe 1898–1975: replying to the German demand for surrender at Bastogne, Belgium, 22 December 1944

21 I would not regard the whole of the remaining cities of Germany as worth the bones of one British Grenadier.

supporting the continued strategic bombing of German cities

Arthur Harris 1892–1984: letter to Norman Bottomley, deputy Chief of Air Staff, 29 March 1945; Max Hastings *Bomber Command* (1979); see **Warfare** 33

22 It may almost be said, 'Before Alamein we never had a victory. After Alamein we never had a defeat.'

Winston Churchill 1874–1965: *Second World War* (1951)

23 So on and on
we walked without thinking of rest
passing craters, passing fire,
under the rocking sky of '41

tottering crazy on its smoking columns.

Yevgeny Yevtushenko 1933– : 'The Companion' (1954)

24 Who do you think you are kidding, Mister Hitler?
If you think we're on the run?
We are the boys who will stop your little game
We are the boys who will make you think again.

Jimmy Perry: 'Who do you think you are kidding, Mister Hitler' (theme song of *Dad's Army*, BBC television, 1968–77)

25 This happened near the core
Of a world's culture. This
Occurred among higher things.
This was a philosophical conclusion.
Everybody gets what he deserves.
The bare drab rubble of the place.
The dull damp stone. The rain.
The emptiness. The human lack.

Alan Bold 1943– : 'June 1967 at Buchenwald' (1969); see **Justice** 13

Worry

1 Care killed the cat.

late 16th century;the meaning of care has shifted somewhat from 'worry, grief' to 'care, caution'; see 8 below

2 Do not meet troubles half-way.

late 19th century, warning against anxiety about something that has not yet happened

3 It is not work that kills, but worry.

late 19th century, meaning that direct effort is less stressful than constant concern

4 Sufficient unto the day is the evil thereof.

mid 18th century, used to mean that dealing with unpleasant matters should be left until it becomes necessary; from the Bible: see **The Present** *4*

5 Worry is interest paid on trouble before it falls due.

American proverb, early 20th century

6 Worry is like a rocking chair: both give you something to do, but neither gets you anywhere.

American proverb, mid 20th century

QUOTATIONS

7 O polished perturbation! golden care!

That keep'st the ports of slumber open wide
To many a watchful night!

William Shakespeare 1564–1616: *Henry IV, Part 2* (1597)

8 What though care killed a cat, thou hast mettle enough in thee to kill care.

William Shakespeare 1564–1616: *Much Ado About Nothing* (1598–9); see 1 above

9 In trouble to be troubled
Is to have your trouble doubled.

Daniel Defoe 1660–1731: *The Farther Adventures of Robinson Crusoe* (1719)

10 Nothing puzzles me more than time and space; and yet nothing troubles me less, as I never think about them.

Charles Lamb 1775–1834: letter to Thomas Manning, 2 January 1810

11 What's the use of worrying?
It never was worth while,
So, pack up your troubles in your old kit-bag,
And smile, smile, smile.

George Asaf 1880–1951: 'Pack up your Troubles' (1915 song)

12 Neurosis is the way of avoiding non-being by avoiding being.

Paul Tillich 1886–1965: *The Courage To Be* (1952)

13 I'm not [biting my fingernails]. I'm biting my knuckles. I finished the fingernails months ago.

while directing Cleopatra *(1963)*

Joseph L. Mankiewicz 1909– : Dick Sheppard *Elizabeth* (1975)

14 Paul Getty . . . had always been vastly, immeasurably wealthy, and yet went about looking like a man who cannot quite remember whether he remembered to turn the gas off before leaving home.

Bernard Levin 1928– : *The Pendulum Years* (1970)

15 A neurosis is a secret you don't know you're keeping.

Kenneth Tynan 1927–80: Kathleen Tynan *Life of Kenneth Tynan* (1987)

16 Men show their love by not worrying. A man questions 'How can you worry about someone whom you admire and trust?'

John Gray 1951– : *Men are from Mars, Women are from Venus* (1992)

Writers see also Poets, Shakespeare

1 Aesthetic Movement a literary and artistic movement which flourished in England in the 1880s.

devoted to 'art for art's sake' and rejecting the notion that art should have a social or moral purpose, its chief exponents included Oscar Wilde, Max Beerbohm, and others associated with the journal the Yellow Book; *see* **The Arts** *5, 16*

2 angry young men a group of socially conscious writers in the 1950s, including particularly the playwright John Osborne.

see **The Generation Gap** *2*

3 Bloomsbury Group a group of writers, artists, and philosophers living in or associated with Bloomsbury in the early 20th century.

the group included Virginia Woolf, Lytton Strachey, Vanessa Bell, Duncan Grant, and Roger Fry

4 Kaleyard School a group of late 19th-century fiction writers, including J. M. Barrie.

they described local town life in Scotland in a romantic vein and with much use of the vernacular; kaleyard *in Scots means literally 'kitchen garden'*

5 Will you have all in all for prose and verse? Take the miracle of our age, Sir Philip Sidney.

Richard Carew 1555–1620: William Camden *Remains concerning Britain* (1614) 'The Excellency of the English Tongue'

6 That great Cham of literature, Samuel Johnson.

Tobias Smollett 1721–71: letter to John Wilkes, 16 March 1759

7 Why, Sir, if you were to read Richardson for the story, your impatience would be so much fretted that you would hang yourself.

Samuel Johnson 1709–84: James Boswell *Life of Samuel Johnson* (1791) 6 April 1772

8 What should I do with your strong, manly, spirited sketches, full of variety and glow?—How could I possibly join them on to the little bit (two inches wide) of ivory on which I work with so fine a brush, as produces little effect after much labour?

Jane Austen 1775–1817: letter to J. Edward Austen, 16 December 1816

9 The Big Bow-Wow strain I can do myself like any now going; but the exquisite touch, which renders ordinary commonplace things and characters interesting, from the truth of the description and the sentiment, is denied to me.

of Jane Austen

Sir Walter Scott 1771–1832: diary 14 March 1826

10 Swift was *anima Rabelaisii habitans in sicco*—the soul of Rabelais dwelling in a dry place.

Samuel Taylor Coleridge 1772–1834: *Table Talk* (1835) 15 June 1830

11 Johnson hewed passages through the Alps, while Gibbon levelled walks through parks and gardens.

George Colman, the Younger 1762–1836: *Random Records* (1830)

12 Voltaire speaks to a party, Molière speaks to society, Shakespeare speaks to mankind.

Victor Hugo 1802–85: *Littérature et philosophie mêlées* (1834)

13 Thou large-brained woman and large-hearted man.

Elizabeth Barrett Browning 1806–61: 'To George Sand—A Desire' (1844)

14 A rake among scholars, and a scholar among rakes.

of Richard Steele

Lord Macaulay 1800–59: *Essays Contributed to the Edinburgh Review* (1850) 'The Life and Writings of Addison'

15 He describes London like a special correspondent for posterity.

Walter Bagehot 1826–77: *National Review* 7 October 1858 'Charles Dickens'

16 It is leviathan retrieving pebbles. It is a magnificent but painful hippopotamus resolved at any cost, even at the cost of its dignity, upon picking up a pea which has got into a corner of its den.

of Henry James

H. G. Wells 1866–1946: *Boon* (1915)

17 E. M. Forster never gets any further than warming the teapot. He's a rare fine hand at that. Feel this teapot. Is it not beautifully warm? Yes, but there ain't going to be no tea.

Katherine Mansfield 1888–1923: diary, May 1917

18 The humour of Dostoievsky is the humour of a bar-loafer who ties a kettle to a dog's tail.

W. Somerset Maugham 1874–1965: *A Writer's Notebook* (1949) written in 1917

19 The cheerful clatter of Sir James Barrie's cans as he went round with the milk of human kindness.

Philip Guedalla 1889–1944: *Supers and Supermen* (1920) 'Some Critics'; see **Sympathy** 7

20 The work of Henry James has always seemed divisible by a simple dynastic arrangement into three reigns: James I, James II, and the Old Pretender.

Philip Guedalla 1889–1944: *Supers and Supermen* (1920); see **People** 18

21 A dogged attempt to cover the universe with mud, an inverted Victorianism, an attempt to make crossness and dirt succeed where sweetness and light failed.

of James Joyce's Ulysses

E. M. Forster 1879–1970: *Aspects of the Novel* (1927); see **Behaviour** 11

22 It was like watching someone organize her own immortality. Every phrase and gesture was studied. Now and again, when she said something a little out of the ordinary, she wrote it down herself in a notebook.

of Virginia Woolf

Harold Laski 1893–1950: letter to Oliver Wendell Holmes, 30 November 1930

23 Shaw's plays are the price we pay for Shaw's prefaces.

James Agate 1877–1947: diary 10 March 1933

24 She is so odd a blend of Little Nell and Lady Macbeth. It is not so much the familiar phenomenon of a hand of steel in a velvet glove as a lacy sleeve with a bottle of vitriol concealed in its folds.

of Dorothy Parker

Alexander Woollcott 1887–1943: *While Rome Burns* (1934)

25 Coleridge was a drug addict. Poe was an alcoholic. Marlowe was stabbed by a man whom he was treacherously trying to stab. Pope took money to keep a woman's name out of a satire; then wrote a piece so that she could still be recognized anyhow. Chatterton killed himself. Byron was accused of incest. *Do you still want to be a writer—and if so, why?*

Bennett Cerf 1898–1971: *Shake Well Before Using* (1948)

26 English literature's performing flea.

of P. G. Wodehouse

Sean O'Casey 1880–1964: P. G. Wodehouse *Performing Flea* (1953)

27 The mama of dada.

of Gertrude Stein

Clifton Fadiman 1904– : *Party of One* (1955)

28 The magic of Shaw's words may still bewitch posterity . . . but it will find that he has nothing to say.

A. J. P. Taylor 1906–90: in *Observer* 22 July 1956

29 For years a secret shame destroyed my peace—
I'd not read Eliot, Auden or MacNeice.
But then I had a thought that brought me hope—
Neither had Chaucer, Shakespeare, Milton, Pope.

Justin Richardson: 'Take Heart, Illiterates' (1966)

30 He could not blow his nose without moralising on the state of the handkerchief industry.

of George Orwell

Cyril Connolly 1903–74: in *Sunday Times* 29 September 1968

31 We were put to Dickens as children but it never quite took. That unremitting humanity soon had me cheesed off.
Alan Bennett 1934– : *The Old Country* (1978)

32 He's the Shakespeare of science fiction.
of H. G. Wells
Brian Aldiss 1925– : interview, 'Bookmark', BBC2 TV, 24 August 1996

33 My problem is not being great. I'm in the second league, not among the gods like Jane Austen and Henry James and Tolstoy.
Iris Murdoch 1919–99: in *The Times* 9 February 1999

Writing see also **Books, Fiction and Story-telling, Originality, Poetry, Style, Words**

see also **Books, Fiction and Story-telling, Originality, Poetry, Style, Words**

PROVERBS AND SAYINGS

1 **The art of writing is the art of applying the seat of the pants to the seat of the chair.**
American proverb, mid 20th century

2 **He who would write and can't write can surely review.**
American proverb, mid 19th century

PHRASES

3 **cacoethes scribendi** an irresistible desire to write.
from Juvenal (see 7 below); Latin from Greek kakoēthes *use as noun of adjective* kakoēthes *ill-disposed*

4 **disjecta membra** scattered fragments, especially of a written work.
Latin, an alteration of disjecti membra poetae, *as used by the poet Horace, 'in our case you would not recognize, as you would in the case of Ennius, the limbs, even though you had dismembered him, of a poet'*

QUOTATIONS

5 It is a foolish thing to make a long prologue, and to be short in the story itself.
Bible: II Maccabees

6 You will have written exceptionally well if, by skilful arrangement of your words, you have made an ordinary one seem original.
Horace 65–8 BC: *Ars Poetica*

7   *Tenet insanabile multos*
Scribendi cacoethes et aegro in corde senescit.
Many suffer from the incurable disease of writing, and it becomes chronic in their sick minds.
Juvenal AD c.60–c.130: *Satires*; see 3 above

8 If writing did not exist, what terrible depressions we should suffer from.
Sei Shōnagon c.966–c.1013: *The Pillow Book of Sei Shōnagon*

9 Go, litel bok, go, litel myn tragedye,
Ther God thi makere yet, er that he dye,
So sende myght to make in som comedye!
Geoffrey Chaucer c.1343–1400: *Troilus and Criseyde*

10 In the mind, as in the body, there is the necessity of getting rid of waste, and a man of active literary habits will write for the fire as well as for the press.
Jerome Cardan 1501–76: William Osler *Aequanimites* (1904); epigraph

11 And, as imagination bodies forth
The forms of things unknown, the poet's pen
Turns them to shapes, and gives to airy nothing
A local habitation and a name.
William Shakespeare 1564–1616: *A Midsummer Night's Dream* (1595–6)

12 If all the earth were paper white
And all the sea were ink
'Twere not enough for me to write
As my poor heart doth think.
John Lyly c.1554–1606: 'If all the earth were paper white'

13 So all my best is dressing old words new,
Spending again what is already spent.
William Shakespeare 1564–1616: sonnet 76

14 The last thing one knows in constructing a work is what to put first.
Blaise Pascal 1623–62: *Pensées* (1670)

15 Of every four words I write, I strike out three.
Nicolas Boileau 1636–1711: *Satire* (2). A M. Molière (1665)

16   What in me is dark
Illumine, what is low raise and support;
That to the height of this great argument

I may assert eternal providence,
And justify the ways of God to men.
John Milton 1608–74: *Paradise Lost* (1667); see
Alcohol 20

17 Learn to write well, or not to write at all.
**John Sheffield, Duke of Buckingham and
Normanby** 1648–1721: 'An Essay upon Satire' (1689)

18 Writing, when properly managed (as you
may be sure I think mine is) is but a
different name for conversation.
Laurence Sterne 1713–68: *Tristram Shandy*
(1759–67)

19 Any fool may write a most valuable book
by chance, if he will only tell us what he
heard and saw with veracity.
Thomas Gray 1716–71: letter to Horace Walpole, 25
February 1768

20 You write with ease, to show your
    breeding,
But easy writing's vile hard reading.
Richard Brinsley Sheridan 1751–1816: 'Clio's
Protest' (written 1771, published 1819)

21 Read over your compositions, and where
ever you meet with a passage which you
think is particularly fine, strike it out.
Samuel Johnson 1709–84: quoting a college tutor;
James Boswell *Life of Samuel Johnson* (1791) 30 April
1773

22 No man but a blockhead ever wrote,
except for money.
Samuel Johnson 1709–84: James Boswell *Life of
Samuel Johnson* (1791) 5 April 1776

23 Another damned, thick, square book!
Always scribble, scribble, scribble! Eh! Mr
Gibbon?
William Henry, Duke of Gloucester 1743–1805:
Henry Best *Personal and Literary Memorials* (1829);
also attributed to the Duke of Cumberland and
King George III; D. M. Low *Edward Gibbon* (1937)

24 Let other pens dwell on guilt and misery. I
quit such odious subjects as soon as I can.
Jane Austen 1775–1817: *Mansfield Park* (1814)

25 Until you understand a writer's ignorance,
presume yourself ignorant of his
understanding.
Samuel Taylor Coleridge 1772–1834: *Biographia
Literaria* (1817)

26 I am convinced more and more day by day
that fine writing is next to fine doing the
top thing in the world.
John Keats 1795–1821: letter to J. H. Reynolds, 24
August 1819

27 When my sonnet was rejected, I
exclaimed, 'Damn the age; I will write for
Antiquity!'
Charles Lamb 1775–1834: letter to B. W. Proctor 22
January 1829

28 Beneath the rule of men entirely great
The pen is mightier than the sword.
Edward George Bulwer-Lytton 1803–73: *Richelieu*
(1839); see **Ways and Means** 11

29 A losing trade, I assure you, sir: literature
is a drug.
George Borrow 1803–81: *Lavengro* (1851)

30 Writers, like teeth, are divided into incisors
and grinders.
Walter Bagehot 1826–77: *Estimates of some
Englishmen and Scotchmen* (1858) 'The First
Edinburgh Reviewers'

31 They shut me up in prose—
As when a little girl
They put me in the closet—
Because they liked me 'still'.
Emily Dickinson 1830–86: 'They shut me up in
prose' (c.1862)

32 The business of the poet and novelist is to
show the sorriness underlying the grandest
things, and the grandeur underlying the
sorriest things.
Thomas Hardy 1840–1928: notebook entry for 19
April 1885

33 A writer must be as objective as a chemist:
he must abandon the subjective line; he
must know that dung-heaps play a very
reasonable part in a landscape, and that
evil passions are as inherent in life as good
ones.
Anton Chekhov 1860–1904: letter to M. V. Kiselev,
14 January 1887

34 Only connect! . . . Only connect the prose
and the passion, and both will be exalted,
and human love will be seen at its height.
E. M. Forster 1879–1970: *Howards End* (1910)

35 My theory of writing I can sum up in one
sentence. An author ought to write for the
youth of his own generation, the critics of
the next, and the schoolmasters of ever
after.
F. Scott Fitzgerald 1896–1940: letter to the
Booksellers' Convention, April 1920

36 True literature can exist only where it is
created not by diligent and trustworthy
officials, but by madmen, heretics,
dreamers, rebels and sceptics. But when a
writer must be sensible . . . there can be no

bronze literature, there can only be a newspaper literature, which is read today, and used for wrapping soap tomorrow.
Yevgeny Zamyatin 1884–1937: 'I am Afraid' (1921)

37 This writing business. Pencils and what-not. Over-rated, if you ask me. Silly stuff. Nothing in it.
A. A. Milne 1882–1956: *Winnie-the-Pooh* (1926)

38 A woman must have money and a room of her own if she is to write fiction.
Virginia Woolf 1882–1941: *A Room of One's Own* (1929)

39 I am a camera with its shutter open, quite passive, recording, not thinking.
Christopher Isherwood 1904–86: *Goodbye to Berlin* (1939) 'Berlin Diary' Autumn 1930

40 Remarks are not literature.
Gertrude Stein 1874–1946: *Autobiography of Alice B. Toklas* (1933)

41 Literature is news that STAYS news.
Ezra Pound 1885–1972: *The ABC of Reading* (1934)

42 Manuscripts don't burn.
Mikhail Bulgakov 1891–1940: *The Master and Margarita* (1966–67)

43 There is no need for the writer to eat a whole sheep to be able to tell you what mutton tastes like. It is enough if he eats a cutlet. But he should do that.
W. Somerset Maugham 1874–1965: *A Writer's Notebook* (1949) written in 1941

44 A writer's ambition should be . . . to trade a hundred contemporary readers for ten readers in ten years' time and for one reader in a hundred years.
Arthur Koestler 1905–83: in *New York Times Book Review* 1 April 1951

45 Writing is not a profession but a vocation of unhappiness.
Georges Simenon 1903–89: interview in *Paris Review* Summer 1955

46 The writer's only responsibility is to his art. He will be completely ruthless if he is a good one. . . . If a writer has to rob his mother, he will not hesitate; the *Ode on a Grecian Urn* is worth any number of old ladies.
William Faulkner 1897–1962: in *Paris Review* Spring 1956

47 The most essential gift for a good writer is a built-in, shock-proof shit detector. This is the writer's radar and all great writers have had it.
Ernest Hemingway 1899–1961: in *Paris Review* Spring 1958

48 A writer must refuse, therefore, to allow himself to be transformed into an institution.
Jean-Paul Sartre 1905–80: refusing the Nobel Prize at Stockholm, 22 October 1964

49 Good prose is like a window-pane.
George Orwell 1903–50: *Collected Essays* (1968) vol. 1 'Why I Write'

50 Nothing I wrote in the thirties saved one Jew from Auschwitz.
W. H. Auden 1907–73: attributed

51 The shelf life of the modern hardback writer is somewhere between the milk and the yoghurt.
Calvin Trillin: in *Sunday Times* 9 June 1991; attributed

52 One of the things a writer is for is to say the unsayable, speak the unspeakable and ask difficult questions.
Salman Rushdie 1947– : in *Independent on Sunday* 10 September 1995

53 I come from a backward place: your duty is supplied by life around you. One guy plants bananas; another plants cocoa; I'm a writer, I plant lines. There's the same clarity of occupation, and the sense of devotion.
Derek Walcott 1930– : in *Guardian* 12 July 1997

Youth see also **Children, Generation Gap**

1 **Wanton kittens make sober cats.**

early 18th century, meaning that someone who in youth is light-minded and lascivious may be soberly behaved in later life

2 **Whom the gods love die young.**

mid 16th century, meaning that the happiest fate is to die before health and strength are lost; see 6 below, **Virtue** 1

3 **Youth must be served.**

early 19th century, meaning that some indulgence should be given to the wishes and enthusiasms of youth

4 salad days the period when one is young and inexperienced, one's time of youth.

from Shakespeare's Antony and Cleopatra *(1606–7)* 'My salad days, When I was green in judgment'

5 an ugly duckling a young person who shows no promise at all of the beauty and success that will eventually come with maturity.

in allusion to a tale by Hans Andersen of a cygnet in a brood of ducks

QUOTATIONS

6 Whom the gods love dies young.

Menander 342–c.292 BC: *Dis Exapaton*; see 2 above, **Virtue** 1

7 In delay there lies no plenty;
Then come kiss me, sweet and twenty,
Youth's a stuff will not endure.

William Shakespeare 1564–1616: *Twelfth Night* (1601)

8 Young men are fitter to invent than to judge, fitter for execution than for counsel, and fitter for new projects than for settled business.

Francis Bacon 1561–1626: *Essays* (1625) 'Of Youth and Age'

9 To find a young fellow that is neither a wit in his own eye, nor a fool in the eye of the world, is a very hard task.

William Congreve 1670–1729: *Love for Love* (1695)

10 The atrocious crime of being a young man . . . I shall neither attempt to palliate nor deny.

William Pitt, Earl of Chatham 1708–78: speech, House of Commons, 2 March 1741

11 In gallant trim the gilded vessel goes;
Youth on the prow, and Pleasure at the helm.

Thomas Gray 1716–71: 'The Bard' (1757)

12 Heaven lies about us in our infancy!
Shades of the prison-house begin to close
Upon the growing boy,

William Wordsworth 1770–1850: 'Ode. Intimations of Immortality' (1807)

13 Live as long as you may, the first twenty years are the longest half of your life.

Robert Southey 1774–1843: *The Doctor* (1812)

14 Oh, talk not to me of a name great in story;
The days of our youth are the days of our glory;

And the myrtle and ivy of sweet two-and-twenty
Are worth all your laurels, though ever so plenty.

Lord Byron 1788–1824: 'Stanzas Written on the Road between Florence and Pisa, November 1821'; see **Success** 18

15 The Youth of a Nation are the trustees of Posterity.

Benjamin Disraeli 1804–81: *Sybil* (1845)

16 I remember my youth and the feeling that will never come back any more—the feeling that I could last for ever, outlast the sea, the earth, and all men; the deceitful feeling that lures us on to joys, to perils, to love, to vain effort—to death; the triumphant conviction of strength, the heat of life in the handful of dust, the glow in the heart that with every year grows dim, grows cold, grows small, and expires—and expires, too soon, too soon—before life itself.

Joseph Conrad 1857–1924: *Youth* (1902)

17 I'm not young enough to know everything.

J. M. Barrie 1860–1937: *The Admirable Crichton* (performed 1902, published 1914)

18 Youth would be an ideal state if it came a little later in life.

Herbert Henry Asquith 1852–1928: in *Observer* 15 April 1923

19 It is better to waste one's youth than to do nothing with it at all.

Georges Courteline 1858–1929: *La Philosophie de Georges Courteline* (1948)

20 The force that through the green fuse drives the flower
Drives my green age.

Dylan Thomas 1914–53: 'The force that through the green fuse drives the flower' (1934)

21 It's that second time you hear your love song sung,
Makes you think perhaps, that
Love like youth is wasted on the young.

Sammy Cahn 1913–93: 'The Second Time Around' (1960 song)

22 It is thinking about themselves that is really the curse of the younger generation—they appear to have no other subject which interests them at all.

Harold Macmillan 1894–1986: the 'Tuesday memorandum', a draft of a letter to the Queen, advising on his successor but not sent, 1963; D. R. Thorpe *Alec Douglas-Home* (1996)

23 Being young is not having any money;
being young is not minding not having
any money.

Katharine Whitehorn 1928– : *Observations* (1970)

24 Youth is something very new: twenty
years ago no one mentioned it.

Coco Chanel 1883–1971: Marcel Haedrich *Coco
Chanel, Her Life, Her Secrets* (1971)

25 We have created a child who will be so
exposed to the media that he will be lost to
his parents by the time he is 12.

David Bowie 1947– : in *Melody Maker* 22 January
1972

26 Remember that as a teenager you are at
the last stage in your life when you will be
happy to hear that the phone is for you.

Fran Lebowitz 1946– : *Social Studies* (1981)

27 Youth is vivid rather than happy, but
memory always remembers the happy
things.

Bernard Lovell 1913– : in *The Times* 20 August 1993

28 Being young is greatly overestimated . . .
Any failure seems so total. Later on you
realize you can have another go.

Mary Quant 1934—: interview in *Observer* 5 May
1996-

Keyword Index

action (*cont.*)

A. this day	ACTION 2
a. to the word	ACTING 3
A. without thought	ACTION 3
again third, 'a.'	SPEECHES 5
end of man is an a.	WORDS AND DEEDS 18
man of a. forced into	THINKING 22
prefer the talents of a.	WORDS AND DEEDS 17
they must have a.	ACTION 23
truth in a.	JUSTICE 29

actions A. receive their tincture CUSTOM 12

A. speak louder than words	WORDS AND DEEDS 1
laugh at human a.	INSIGHT 7
my a. are my ministers'	WORDS AND DEEDS 15

actor a. is a kind of a guy ACTING 11

actors A. are cattle ACTING 9

a. are not heart surgeons ACTING 16

actress a. to be a success ACTING 10

acts a. the most slowly ARCHITECTURE 13

desires but a. not	ACTION 21
little, nameless, unremembered, a.	VIRTUE 34

actual rational is a. REALITY 8

adage cat i' the a. FEAR 3

Adam A. was born hungry COOKING 20

A. was but human	HUMAN NATURE 15
all A.'s children	WEALTH 21
old A.	HUMAN NATURE 5
old A.	HUMAN NATURE 11
rubbish of an A.	SCIENCE AND RELIG 6
second A.	CHRISTIAN CH 11
When A. and Eve	BRITISH TOWNS 33
When A. dalfe	CLASS 8
When A. delved	CLASS 2

add no longer anything to a. PERFECTION 12

adder a. that stoppeth her ears DEFIANCE 9

brings forth the a.	DANGER 23
deaf as an a.	SENSES 1

addeth translation's thief that a. TRANSLATION 4

addiction a. is bad DRUGS 7

prisoners of a. BUYING 10

addictive sin tends to be a. SIN 32

addled a. egg IDLENESS 1

one a. egg SILENCE 12

address letters to a non-existent a. PRAYER 28

adjective As to the A. STYLE 16

adjourned Scottish Parliament which a. SCOTLAND 22

administered a. is best ADMINISTRATION 4

administers a. nor governs ROYALTY 24

administration A. of All the Talents PARLIAMENT 3

a. of justice GOVERNMENT 16

administrative a. won't ADMINISTRATION 26

admirable a. Crichton EXCELLENCE 4

admiral kill an a. from time to time WAYS 20

admirari Nil a. HAPPINESS 7

admiration exercise our a. FAMILIARITY 14

admire begun to a. the one SHAKESPEARE 6

Not to a. HAPPINESS 14

admittance a. till the week after HASTE 18

adult a. is alone MATURITY 10

child becomes an a.	CHILDREN 24
occupation of an a.	ACTING 13

adultery a. being a most conventional CONFORMITY 14

committed a. in my heart	TEMPTATION 19
die for a.	SEX 13

adults a. produce children MARRIAGE 43

a. to children HAPPINESS 29

advance A. Australia AUSTRALIA 9

A. Australia	AUSTRALIA 15
somewhat to a.	PROGRESS 9

advanced sufficiently a. technology TECHNOLOGY 24

advantage not necessarily to Japan's a. WINNING 21

old have one a.	OLD AGE 39
take a mean a.	APOLOGY 17
undertaking of great A.	BUSINESS 25
with equal a.	INTERNAT REL 13

adventure awfully big a. DEATH 60

most beautiful a. LAST WORDS 24

adventures A. are for the adventurous DANGER 1

a. of his soul	CRITICISM 14
clothes to have a. in	DRESS 24

adversary against a single a. LEADERSHIP 11

adversity A. doth best discover ADVERSITY 11

A., if a man	ADVERSITY 15
A. makes strange bedfellows	ADVERSITY 1
dose of a.	ADVERSITY 2
hundred that will stand a.	ADVERSITY 12
learn to endure a.	ADVERSITY 14
uses of a.	ADVERSITY 10

advertise a. food to hungry people ADVERTISING 13

a. what you can't fulfil	ADVERTISING 4
pays to a.	ADVERTISING 8

advertisement one effective a. ADVERTISING 8

patent medicine a.	SICKNESS 13
soul of an a.	ADVERTISING 7

advertisements column of a. by heart QUOTATIONS 9

advertisers a. don't object to JOURNALISM 22

a. 'sizzling' AMERICA 38

advertising A. is the rattling ADVERTISING 12

A. may be described	ADVERTISING 9
a. we deserve	ADVERTISING 11
calls it a.	ADVERTISING 18
money I spend on a.	ADVERTISING 10

advice a. is good or bad ADVICE 16

A. is seldom welcome	ADVICE 14
a. is worth having	ADVICE 18
Ask a.	ADVICE 1
I never give any a.	ADVICE 15
pass on good a.	ADVICE 19
when you seek a.	ADVICE 23

advise PLEASE A. TOWNS 23

advocates a. of peace PEACE 19

aeroplanes it wasn't the a. BEAUTY 31

Aesculapius owe a cock to A. LAST WORDS 3

aesthetic A. Movement WRITERS 1

affable sign of an a. man BODY 19

affair a. between Margot Asquith SELF-ESTEEM 20

keep a measly a. secret SECRECY 31

affairs a. of men OPPORTUNITY 26

affectation sophistry and a. UNIVERSITIES 6

affection A. beaming in one eye CHARACTER 34

a. of the human	PARENTS 15
a. you get back	PARENTS 17
by letter and a.	EMPLOYMENT 10

affections holiness of the heart's a. TRUTH 27

afflictions a. of Job BIBLE 12

affluent a. society WEALTH 6

afraid a. of God MORALITY 7

a. of their tongues	SELF-ESTEEM 32
a. of the sea	SEA 19
a. to die	DEATH 73
he is a. to feel	ENGLAND 21
taught to be a.	RACE 18

Africa A. always brings AFRICA 6

A. and her prodigies	HUMAN RACE 13
A. and the English tongue	AFRICA 11
A. lies in Europe	INTERNAT REL 22
A. of the millions	AFRICA 8
A. resembles a revolver	AFRICA 9
A. was swaddled in lies	AFRICA 13
something new out of A.	AFRICA 1
woman of A.	AFRICA 14

African A. Primates meeting NAMES 17

Africans A. could still smile RACE 29

A. experience people AFRICA 9

after happily ever a. ENDING 3

afterlife questions about the a. SUPERNATURAL 27

after-life no longer believe in an a. CREATIVITY 15

afternoon a. of human life MIDDLE AGE 11

make love in the a. FRANCE 18

again déja vu all over a. FORESIGHT 18

against a. everything LIKES 17

anyone who wasn't a. war	WARFARE 52
God was a. art	ARTS 20
He was a. it	SIN 29

I always vote a.	ELECTIONS 13
who can be a. us	STRENGTH 16
with me is a. me	ENEMIES 7
Agamemnon face of A.	PAST 26
lived before A.	REPUTATION 1
agapanthus Beware of the A.	DANGER 33
age A. does not make us childish	OLD AGE 15
a. going to the workhouse	GOVERNMENT 22
A. is deformed	GENERATION GAP 6
a. is the most unexpected	OLD AGE 24
A. might but take	GENERATION GAP 8
a. of ease	OLD AGE 12
A. shall not weary them	EPITAPHS 21
a. to write an autobiography	BIOGRAPHY 19
a., which forgives itself	GENERATION GAP 9
A. will not be defied	OLD AGE 10
Crabbed a.	GENERATION GAP 7
days of our a.	OLD AGE 7
every a. assiduously	PRESENT 12
gatekeeper to the new a.	INVENTIONS 22
Of cold a.	CONSTANCY 9
serenity of a.	OLD AGE 31
very attractive a.	MIDDLE AGE 9
was not of an a.	SHAKESPEARE 3
with a. and dust	TIME 27
aged a. man is but a paltry	OLD AGE 22
a. thrush	BIRDS 16
learn how to be a.	OLD AGE 36
agenbite a. of inwit	CONSCIENCE 7
A. of inwit	CONSCIENCE 16
agenda item of the a.	ADMINISTRATION 20
ages belongs to the a.	EPITAPHS 18
seven a.	LIFE 18
agnosticism all that a. means	BELIEF 22
agonizing a. reappraisal	THINKING 4
agony about the a. of creation	CREATIVITY 16
a. is abated	SUFFERING 15
constrained by a.	SCULPTURE 5
it was a., Ivy	SUFFERING 3
most extreme a.	SUFFERING 33
agree a. in the dark	INDIFFERENCE 5
a. with others	SIMILARITY 21
a. with the book of God	CENSORSHIP 2
trade never a.	SIMILARITY 9
agreement a. with hell	DIPLOMACY 6
blow with an a.	VIOLENCE 11
agrees nobody a. with you	DISILLUSION 18
agriculture A. is the foundation	FARMING 10
at last, fall upon a.	TAXES 13
well-bred man than a.	FARMING 7
ahead a., get a hat	DRESS 3
aid Apt Alliteration's artful a.	WIT 9
aim all things a.	GOOD 16
forgotten your a.	EXCESS 28
impossible a.	DESPAIR 17
shooting without a.	ACTION 3
aiming a. at a million	ACHIEVEMENT 20
on the chase or on a.	SPORTS 32
air a. and angels' purity	MEN AND WOMEN 4
a. power has prevailed in the Balkans	WARFARE 67
bombarded by the empty a.	WEATHER 55
castles in the a.	IMAGINATION 1
Clear the a.	POLLUTION 16
excellent canopy, the a.	POLLUTION 6
feet planted in the a.	POLITICAL PART 25
hot a. blows	ELECTIONS 2
music in the a.	MUSIC 15
outlet in the a.	SKIES 25
pattern of subtle a.	CATS 15
too pure an A.	LIBERTY 7
air-conditioning respectability and a.	GOD 33
aircraft a. is missing	ARMED FORCES 6
airline a. ticket	MEMORY 23
airport observing a. layouts	TRAVEL 39
aitches lose but our a.	CLASS 15
Aladdin A.'s cave	WEALTH 7
A.'s lamp	CHANCE 15

Alamein After A. never had a defeat	WORLD W II 22
Alamo Remember the A.	WARS 2
alarms a. and excursions	ORDER 3
alas Hugo—a.	POETS 25
May say A.	SUCCESS 39
Albion perfidious A.	ENGLAND 3
alcohol A. didn't cause	DRUGS 11
a. has taken out of me	ALCOHOL 31
a. or morphine	DRUGS 7
A. will preserve anything	ALCOHOL 1
ale bliss in a.	DRUNKENNESS 6
cakes and a.	PLEASURE 3
no more cakes and a.	VIRTUE 22
alehouse by an Englishman, an a.	ARCHITECTURE 1
Alexander A. at the head	SCHOOLS 3
Some talk of A.	ARMED FORCES 23
algebra a. and fluxions	MATHS 12
algebraic weaves a. patterns	COMPUTERS 8
alibi He always has an a.	DECEPTION 22
alibis a. for its evil deeds	CORRUPTION 1
alien damned if I'm an a.	PATRIOTISM 26
quick to blame the a.	GUILT 5
alike all places were a.	CATS 9
everyone is a.	SOCIETY 16
Great minds think a.	THINKING 1
men are a.	HUMAN NATURE 6
we are more a.	HUMAN RACE 35
alive gets out of it a.	EXPERIENCE 32
half-a. things	GOSSIP 26
Hallelujah! I'm a.	EMOTIONS 23
in that dawn to be a.	REVOLUTION 13
Life's not just being a.	HEALTH 11
no one is a.	SOCIETY 16
Not while I'm a.	ENEMIES 19
Officiously to keep a.	MURDER 18
poetry should be a.	POETRY 39
show that one's a.	THEATRE 11
that's what keeps you a.	DETERMINATION 51
tumult when a.	DEATH 42
all A. for one	COOPERATION 25
a. in respect of nothing	HUMAN RACE 15
A.-merciful	GOD 11
a. must have prizes	WINNING 15
A. my pretty ones	MOURNING 9
a. our yesterdays	TIME 26
a. shall be well	OPTIMISM 15
a. that a man hath	LIFE 13
a. things to all men	CONFORMITY 2
a. things to all men	SELF 6
God for us a.	SELF-INTEREST 1
his a. neglected	EFFORT 14
know a. is to forgive	FORGIVENESS 6
man for a. seasons	PEOPLE 26
not at all or a. in all	TRUST 30
teaches ill who teaches a.	TEACHING 1
Will you have a. in all	WRITERS 5
You can have it a.	WOMEN 61
allegiance a. to any master	LIBERTY 6
Any victim demands a.	SYMPATHY 25
not pledged a. to you	RACE 4
allegory headstrong as an a.	DETERMINATION 32
alleluia A. is our song	CHRISTIAN CH 41
allergies Also provide the a.	SICKNESS 19
alley Tin Pan A.	MUSIC 5
alleys lowest and vilest a.	COUNTRY AND TOWN 17
alliance Auld A.	INTERNAT REL 1
alliances a. with none	INTERNAT REL 11
allies a. to be polite to	DIPLOMACY 12
no eternal a.	INTERNAT REL 16
alligators up to your ears in a.	MANAGEMENT 17
alliteration Apt A.'s artful aid	WIT 9
allowed revolution where love is not a.	
	WOMAN'S ROLE 29
almighty a. dollar	MONEY 15
A. had placed it there	POLITICIANS 18
alms a. for oblivion	TIME 25
aloha A. State	AMERICAN CITIES 1

Australia (*cont.*)
A. has a marvellous sky — AUSTRALIA 18
A. is a huge rest home — AUSTRALIA 26
expectations of A. — AUSTRALIA 13
happened in A. — AUSTRALIA 30
last year in A. — COUNTRIES 35
take A. right back — AUSTRALIA 29
Australian A. republic — AUSTRALIA 24
Australians A. wouldn't give a XXXX — AUSTRALIA 2
authentic puts his a. self — LETTERS 19
author amended By its A. — EPITAPHS 12
Choose an a. — READING 2
expected to see an a. — STYLE 8
same steps as the a. — EXPERIENCE 22
wish the a. that wrote it — READING 15
authority a. uses not intellect — INTELLIGENCE 7
cede to a lawful a. — LIBERTY 40
faith that stands on a. — FAITH 8
little brief a. — POWER 14
make your peace with a. — POWER 34
maximal a. and minimal power — TEACHING 18
than in a. — DUTY 7
authorized A. Version — BIBLE 1
authors with these good a. — LIBRARIES 4
authorship editing rather than a. — LIFE SCI 20
autobiography age to write an a. — BIOGRAPHY 19
a. is an obituary — BIOGRAPHY 20
autocracy a. turned upside down — CAPITALISM 12
autocrat a.: that's my trade — POWER 19
automobile a. changed our dress — TRANSPORT 24
autres encourager les a. — MANAGEMENT 5
pour encourager les a. — WAYS 20
autumn a. arrives in — SEASONS 27
a. follows summer — MOURNING 19
a. is a time of harvest — SEASONS 31
Early a. — SEASONS 15
happy a.-fields — MEMORY 13
thou breath of A.'s being — WEATHER 40
autumnal one a. face — OLD AGE 9
availeth struggle naught a. — EFFORT 17
avarice a. to itself — GREED 10
rich, beyond the dreams of a. — WEALTH 24
ave a. atque vale — MEETING 6
avenged South is a. — REVENGE 18
average A. made lethal — CONFORMITY 15
good for the a. man — CLASS 24
one day become Mr A. — CONFORMITY 17
averages law of a. — STATISTICS 1
avert a. this omen — SUPERNATURAL 8
avis rara a. — SIMILARITY 13
avoid managed to a. that — TASTE 16
manages to a. them — KNOWLEDGE 51
avoiding by a. being — WORRY 12
Avon swan of A. — SHAKESPEARE 2
awaits man a. his end — DEATH 62
awake A.! for Morning — DAY 13
awakened a. a sleeping giant — CAUSES 29
awakening a. is at hand — DREAMS 18
away one that got a. — HUNTING 2
When the cat's a. — OPPORTUNITY 18
awe increasing wonder and a. — THINKING 14
awful it's a. — BOREDOM 8
awkward a. squad — ARMED FORCES 12
awoke a. one morning — FAME 12
axe Lizzie Borden took an a. — MURDER 4
axes a. are being ground — CENSORSHIP 9
axioms A. in philosophy — EXPERIENCE 22
hypotheses or a. — HYPOTHESIS 22
axis a. of the earth — SELF-ESTEEM 13
Aztecs disbelief of the A. — CERTAINTY 23

babel bother at the tower of B. — LANGUAGES 8
Tower of B. — LANGUAGES 2
babes b. in the wood — EXPERIENCE 14
milk for b. — KNOWLEDGE 13

mouths of b. — KNOWLEDGE 10
babies Ballads and b. — MUSICIANS 21
hates dogs and b. — DOGS 11
If men had to have b. — PREGNANCY 19
no longer sing to the b. — CHILD CARE 17
putting milk into b. — CHILD CARE 11
baboon He who understands b. — LANGUAGE 13
baby b. boomer — GENERATION GAP 3
Burn, b., burn — VIOLENCE 1
interval by a b. — CENSORSHIP 8
saved beautiful b. — NEWS 11
when the b. isn't looking — CHILD CARE 1
Babylon B. in all its desolation — MADNESS 9
waters of B. — SORROW 5
Bach angels play only B. — MUSICIANS 17
B. almost persuades me — MUSICIANS 12
B. tells you — MUSICIANS 22
bachelor b. never quite gets over — MEN 15
bachelors B. know all about parties — ENTERTAINING 23
stronger reasons for b. to go out — WOMAN'S ROLE 19
back boys in the b. rooms — FAME 16
come b. to this world — SUPERNATURAL 23
Don't look b. — SPORTS 7
I'll be b. — MEETING 25
in the small of the b. — SURPRISE 12
I sit on a man's b. — HYPOCRISY 17
makes the b. to the burden — SYMPATHY 1
not in my b. yard — SELF-INTEREST 16
Not to go b. — PROGRESS 9
over the Devil's b. — SIN 2
those before cried 'b.!' — COURAGE 24
backbone b. of the Army — ARMED FORCES 32
no more b. than a chocolate éclair — CHARACTER 38
backing I'm b. Britain — PATRIOTISM 1
backroom b. boys — SCIENCE 3
backs beast with two b. — SEX 4
beast with two b. — SEX 12
backward b. to their ancestors — FUTURE 16
b. to with pride — DISILLUSION 1
backwards understood b. — LIFE 29
bad bad b. is better than — TASTE 14
b. book is as much of a labour — BOOKS 18
b. colour — APPEARANCE 7
b. ended unhappily — FICTION 13
b. excuse is better — APOLOGY 2
B. laws are the worst — LAW 22
b. men combine — COOPERATION 22
B. money — MONEY 1
b. news infects — NEWS 7
B. news travels fast — NEWS 1
b. penny always turns up — CHARACTER 2
b. times just around — OPTIMISM 32
B. women never take — GUILT 22
can't be all b. — DOGS 11
come to a b. end — EXCELLENCE 13
dog a b. name — GOSSIP 3
feel really b. about — GUILT 18
from b. to worse — CHANGE 36
good or b. — GOOD 25
Hard cases make b. law — LAW 3
in b. company — SOLITUDE 1
it's bad for you — HEALTH 21
mad, b. and dangerous — PEOPLE 35
make them feel b. — ENVY 14
no such thing as b. weather — WEATHER 19
no such thing as b. weather — WEATHER 32
Nothing so b. — SYMPATHY 4
pay to see b. movies — CINEMA 15
so b. that we don't ever — MISFORTUNES 28
their luck was b. — MISFORTUNES 31
thing as b. publicity — FAME 18
those who are b. — PLEASURE 24
two legs b. — PREJUDICE 21
when I'm b., I'm better — SIN 28
when she was b. — BEHAVIOUR 21
badge b. of all our tribe — PATIENCE 23
badly always turn out b. — CLERGY 1

worth doing b. — WOMEN 39
Baedeker B. raids — WORLD W II 2
bag out of a tattered b. — CHARACTER 14
Baghdad astonished to see him in B. — FATE 20
bags other people's b. — BUSINESS 36
bah 'B.,' said Scrooge — CHRISTMAS 9
bairns Fools and b. should never see — WORK 3
bake b. so shall you brew — CAUSES 1
so shall you b. — CAUSES 2
baked stayed home and b. cookies — WOMAN'S ROLE 34
baked Alaska resembled a B. — PEOPLE 63
baker butcher, the b. — EMPLOYMENT 4
Bakewell B. in half-an-hour — TRANSPORT 7
balance art of b. — PAINTING 16
b. of nature — NATURE 3
b. of power — INTERNAT REL 2
redress the b. — AMERICA 15
weighed in the b. — SUCCESS 17
balances checks and b. — GOVERNMENT 4
balancing B. the budget — ECONOMICS 19
bald b. street breaks — DAY 12
between two b. men over a comb — WARS 29
baldness far side of b. — BODY 22
Baldwin B. denouncing sanctions — INDECISION 11
Balfour B.'s poodle — PARLIAMENT 9
Balham B. mind — EXCELLENCE 15
Balkan B. graveyards are full — DIPLOMACY 17
Balkans air power has prevailed in the B. — WARFARE 67
damned silly thing in the B. — WORLD W I 7
ball b. no question makes — CHANCE 26
business of a b. — ENTERTAINING 15
hirelings kick a b. — FOOTBALL 5
out to the b. game — SPORTS 13
out to the b. park — SPORTS 29
ballads B. and babies — MUSICIANS 21
make all the b. — SINGING 4
balloons b. dancing in a world of pins — TRANSIENCE 19
ballot b. is stronger — ELECTIONS 6
rap at the b. box — WOMAN'S ROLE 18
balls B. will be lost — MISFORTUNES 27
our rackets to these b. — SPORTS 6
balm wash the b. — ROYALTY 12
bamboo b. curtain — CAPITALISM 4
ban B. the bomb — PEACE 2
recommend they b. it — CENSORSHIP 15
banality b. of evil — GOOD 41
manufacture of b. — BROADCASTING 9
banana I am a b. — JUSTICE 38
bananas produce b. — NAMES 17
bandage wound, not the b. — RELIGION 31
bands b. of Orion — FATE 12
people get into b. — MUSICIANS 19
pursue Culture in b. — CULTURE 19
bane Deserve the precious b. — WEALTH 19
baneful b. effects of the spirit — POLITICAL PART 16
bang b.—went saxpence — THRIFT 13
big b. — FUTILITY 25
big b. — UNIVERSE 1
bigger b. for a buck — WARFARE 2
Kiss Kiss B. Bang — CINEMA 19
Not with a b. — ENDING 19
standing there, going 'B.' — MURDER 25
terror in a b. — FEAR 17
This big b. idea — UNIVERSE 16
bank b. is a place — MONEY 37
cry all the way to the b. — CRITICISM 23
robbing a b. — MONEY 35
banker Scotch b. — CANADA 18
banking as much as we value b. — WOMAN'S ROLE 33
place for b. and prostitution — COUNTRY AND TOWN 23
banks letters from b. — LETTERS 18
banned book should be b. — CENSORSHIP 10
banner star-spangled b. — AMERICA 14
banqueting b. upon borrowing — DEBT 11
banter how does fortune b. us — CHANCE 21
bar crossed the b. — DEATH 53
Barabbas always save b. — CHOICE 22

B. was a publisher — PUBLISHING 9
barb b. that makes it stick — WIT 11
barbarian He [the Briton] is a b. — BRITAIN 9
barbarians b. are to arrive — CULTURE 14
barbarisms colloquial b. — LANGUAGE 9
barbarity b. of tyrants — IRELAND 9
barbarous b. to write a poem — POETRY 35
invention of a b. age — POETRY 10
victorious in b. ages — CULTURE 13
bard goat-footed b. — PEOPLE 47
barefoot son always goes b. — FAMILY 7
bargain made a good b. — NECESSITY 20
never was a better b. — CONSTANCY 5
two to make a b. — COOPERATION 9
bargains rule for b. — BUSINESS 31
bark come out as I do, and b. — ARGUMENT 13
dog and b. yourself — MANAGEMENT 3
Dogs b. — FUTILITY 1
barking b. dog — ACTION 4
Barkis B. is willin' — PREPARATION 15
Barmecide B. feast — COOKING 12
barmy b. army — CRICKET 1
barn round Robin Hood's b. — TRAVEL 10
Barnaby B. bright — FESTIVALS 1
barrel b. of a gun — POWER 28
barren but a b. stock — PREGNANCY 5
barrier beyond an impassable b. — ANIMALS 36
bars Stars and B. — AMERICA 8
base All your b. are belong to us — WINNING 1
b. in reality — IMAGINATION 17
people as b. as itself — JOURNALISM 15
baseball B. is very big — SPORTS 34
Hague has got a b. cap — POLITICAL PART 46
bashing b. their brains out — SWEARING 12
basic b. research is what — SCIENCE 25
basin exploring a closed b. — MARRIAGE 27
Basingstoke like B. — WORDS 16
basket come from the same b. — HUMAN NATURE 17
eggs in one b. — CAUTION 6
eggs in one b. — CAUTION 28
bastards b. grind you down — DETERMINATION 9
he who begets twenty b. — VIRTUE 31
stand up for b. — DEFIANCE 12
Bastille B. Day — FESTIVALS 9
Voltaire in the B. — CENSORSHIP 18
bat b. at a white man — SPORTS 34
b. for the length of time — CRICKET 15
like some b. — MIND 19
bath be tired of B. — BRITISH TOWNS 28
lie in a hot b. — POETRY 18
test my b. before — SENSES 15
bathe like people to b. in me — RIVERS 16
baton marshal's b. — AMBITION 7
bats b. have been broken — TRUST 40
battalions But in b. — SORROW 10
side not of the heavy b. — WARFARE 20
side of the big b. — ARMED FORCES 7
batter B. my heart — GOD 16
battered b. his head — CATS 14
battle B. of Britain — WORLD W II 3
b. to the strong — SUCCESS 8
b. to the strong — SUCCESS 20
field of b. — MARRIAGE 29
France has lost a b. — WORLD W II 9
he smelleth the b. afar — WARFARE 10
Next to a b. lost — WARFARE 25
battlefield b. is the heart of man — BEAUTY 24
battles Dead b., like dead generals — WARFARE 57
mother of b. — WARS 30
opening b. of all subsequent wars — WARFARE 49
right words, b. won — WORDS 24
baubles Take away these b. — PARLIAMENT 14
bay b. at the moon — DOGS 10
B. State — AMERICAN CITIES 2
bayonet b. is a weapon with — WARFARE 1
bayonets throne of b. — VIOLENCE 10
bazaar Fate's great b. — LEISURE 13

bazaars railways are irresistible b. — TRANSPORT 29
be B. what you would seem — BEHAVIOUR 1
  How less what we may b. — SELF-KNOWLEDGE 9
  not mean But b. — POETRY 27
  that which shall b. — PROGRESS 5
  To b., or not to be — CHOICE 14
  What must b., must be — FATE 8
beach only pebble on the b. — COURTSHIP 9
beaches fight on the b. — WORLD W II 8
beacons b. of wise men — LOGIC 13
beads tell one's b. — PRAYER 5
beak b. from out my heart — DESPAIR 11
  He takes in his b. — BIRDS 18
beaker b. full of the warm South — ALCOHOL 14
beam b. in one's eye — MISTAKES 6
  considerest not the b. — SELF-KNOWLEDGE 3
beans b. in the clay — FARMING 1
bear any of us can b. — MOURNING 25
  B. and forbear — PATIENCE 4
  b. market — BUSINESS 17
  B. of Very Little Brain — THINKING 21
  B. State — AMERICAN CITIES 3
  b. the cross gladly — SUFFERING 8
  B. up—trust to time — ADVICE 20
  b. very much reality — HUMAN RACE 28
  b. waiting for spring — HOPE 23
  embrace the Russian b. — DIPLOMACY 10
  fitted by nature to b. — SUFFERING 6
  Great B. — SKIES 2
  sell the b.'s skin — OPTIMISM 14
bear-baiting history of b. — ANIMALS 34
  Puritan hated b. — PLEASURE 20
beard b. usually means that — APPEARANCE 25
  drew his b. aside — LAST WORDS 7
  singeing of the King of Spain's B. — WARS 5
bearded all scroungy and b. — WEDDINGS 14
beards when b. wag all — ENTERTAINING 5
bears for b. to dance to — SPEECH 20
  teddy b.' picnic — PLEASURE 8
beast b. lying across a railway — POLITICAL PART 43
  b. or a fool — SOLITUDE 12
  b. or a god — SOLITUDE 6
  b. who is always spoiling — DOGS 7
  b. with two backs — SEX 4
  b. with two backs — SEX 12
  Beauty killed the B. — BEAUTY 31
  call this b. to mind — ANIMALS 22
  for man or b. — WEATHER 52
  number of the b. — QUANTITIES 14
  regardeth the life of his b. — ANIMALS 11
  serpent subtlest b. — ANIMALS 14
  what rough b. — CHRISTMAS 13
beastie tim'rous b. — FEAR 7
beastly b. to the Germans — WORLD W II 17
beasts king of b. — ANIMALS 6
beat b. generation — JAZZ 1
  b. their swords — PEACE 7
  can't b. them, join them — WAYS 8
  more you b. them — WOMEN 7
  We b. them to-day or — WARS 10
beatings dread of b. — SCHOOLS 14
Beatles B.'s first LP — SEX 37
beats b. as it sweeps — HOUSEWORK 2
beauteous How b. mankind is — HUMAN RACE 12
beautiful All things bright and b. — ANIMALS 19
  always make it b. — BEAUTY 20
  b. catastrophe — AMERICAN CITIES 56
  b. face is a mute — BEAUTY 7
  b. game — FOOTBALL 1
  b. game — FOOTBALL 8
  b. people have done nothing — BEAUTY 38
  b. things in the world — BEAUTY 21
  b. upon the mountains — NEWS 4
  believe to be b. — POSSESSIONS 14
  Black is b. — RACE 2
  hunger to be b. — WOMEN 42
  innocent and the b. — GUILT 14

It is b. — MIND 24
  love of what is b. — CULTURE 6
  most b. woman in the room — BEAUTY 28
  Ordinary made b. — CONFORMITY 15
  Small is b. — ECONOMICS 15
  Small is b. — QUANTITIES 8
  Too b. for our ears — MUSIC 9
  When a woman isn't b. — BEAUTY 26
beauty American b. rose — BUSINESS 33
  arrest all b. — PHOTOGRAPHY 3
  b. and my youth — MATURITY 16
  b. and naught else — BEAUTY 22
  b. being only skin-deep — BEAUTY 32
  B. crieth in an attic — CANADA 8
  B. draws with a single — BEAUTY 1
  b. faded — BEAUTY 15
  b. in building — ARCHITECTURE 7
  b. in one's equations — MATHS 25
  b. in the works — GENIUS 5
  B. is a good letter — BEAUTY 2
  b. is a joy — BEAUTY 18
  B. is all very well — BEAUTY 27
  B. is in the eye — BEAUTY 3
  b. is mysterious — BEAUTY 24
  B. is no quality — BEAUTY 16
  B. is only skin deep — BEAUTY 4
  B. is past change — BEAUTY 23
  B. is the first test — MATHS 22
  B. is the lover's gift — BEAUTY 14
  B. is truth — BEAUTY 19
  B. killed the Beast — BEAUTY 31
  b. myth moves for men — BEAUTY 36
  B. too rich for use — BEAUTY 12
  B. without cruelty — SUFFERING 1
  b. without vanity — ANIMALS 30
  b. without vanity — DOGS 5
  how to make b. — HATRED 17
  life was b. — LIFE 28
  Love built on b. — BEAUTY 11
  no excellent b. — BEAUTY 13
  secret b. she holds — AUSTRALIA 27
  struggle for superhuman b. — BEAUTY 34
  terrible b. is born — CHANGE 45
  thing of b. — MEN 15
  truth, but supreme b. — MATHS 20
  walks in b. — BEAUTY 17
  where B. was — BEAUTY 30
  winds of March with b. — FLOWERS 5
  world's b. becomes enough — BEAUTY 35
beaver b. works and plays — ANIMALS 1
because B. it's there — ACHIEVEMENT 24
  B. We're here — FATE 6
  she did this b. — BOOKS 27
  smashed it into b. — LOGIC 19
becomes that which *is not* b. — LIFE SCI 7
bed And so to b. — SLEEP 12
  As you make your b. — CAUSES 3
  b. at the same time — CONSTANCY 19
  b. of roses — MARRIAGE 29
  Early to b. — HEALTH 4
  early to b. — SLEEP 17
  go to b. by day — SEASONS 22
  legs in a b. — MARRIAGE 9
  Lying in b. — PLEASURE 23
  mind is not a b. — CERTAINTY 21
  Not to be a-b. — SLEEP 8
  passage up to b. — SLEEP 15
  reds under the b. — CAPITALISM 7
  remain in b. — IDLENESS 22
  stay in b. — MISFORTUNES 26
bedfellows Politics makes strange b. — POLITICS 4
  strange b. — ADVERSITY 1
  strange b. — MISFORTUNES 17
bedroom what you do in the b. — SEX 28
bedrooms in the nation's b. — CENSORSHIP 16
bee b. works — ANIMALS 1
  How doth the little busy b. — WORK 25

benefit b. of clergy	CLERGY 5
benevolence b. of the butcher	SELF-INTEREST 24
b. of the passive order	CHARITY 19
Benjamin B.'s portion	QUANTITIES 11
bent b. her contraceptive	PARANORMAL 22
twig is b.	EDUCATION 1
bereaved Laughter would be b.	HUMOUR 20
bereavement B. is a universal	MOURNING 19
Berliner *Ich bin ein B.*	INTERNAT REL 32
Bermuda B. triangle	PARANORMAL 3
berry made a better b.	FOOD 11
beside Christ b. me	PRAYER 8
thou art b. thyself	KNOWLEDGE 21
best administered is b.	ADMINISTRATION 4
All is for the b.	OPTIMISM 17
All's for the b.	OPTIMISM 1
aren't always at their b.	BEHAVIOUR 30
b. and happiest moments	POETRY 17
b. is good enough	ARTS 8
b. is the best	EXCELLENCE 12
b. is the enemy	EXCELLENCE 10
b. is yet to be	OLD AGE 16
b. lack all conviction	EXCELLENCE 14
b. of all possible worlds	OPTIMISM 27
b. of friends	MEETING 1
b. of men	HUMAN NATURE 1
b. of times	CIRCUMSTANCE 20
b. of us being unfit	CRIME 33
b. people you can find	MANAGEMENT 13
b. thing since sliced	INVENTIONS 2
b. things in life	MONEY 2
b. things in life	POSSESSIONS 22
b. way out	DETERMINATION 40
b. words	POETRY 19
Corruption of the b.	EXCELLENCE 1
East, west, home's b.	HOME 1
Hope for the b.	PREPARATION 8
past all prizing, b.	LIFE 14
trouble with being b. man	WEDDINGS 18
bestride b. the narrow world	GREATNESS 3
best-seller b. is the gilded tomb	BOOKS 19
best-sellers all the great b.	BOOKS 21
Bethlehem slouches towards B.	CHRISTMAS 13
betray guts to b. my country	PATRIOTISM 27
To b., you must first	TRUST 36
betrayal any act of b.	SUCCESS 46
better b. and better	MEDICINE 22
B. Drains	GARDENS 21
b. hap to worse	CHANGE 27
B. is the end	ENDING 12
b. man than I am	CHARACTER 36
b. mouse-trap	ACHIEVEMENT 21
b. part of biography	BIOGRAPHY 14
b. than he shou'd be	HUMAN NATURE 12
b. than his neighbour	BRITISH TOWNS 40
b. than it sounds	MUSICIANS 9
b. the day	FESTIVALS 2
b. to have loved	LOVE 51
b. your condition	CHANGE 2
could have done b.	FORGIVENESS 25
Fail b.	SUCCESS 47
far, far b. thing	SELF-SACRIFICE 6
for b. for worse	MARRIAGE 21
from worse to b.	CHANGE 33
further reaches of 'for b.'	MARRIAGE 54
Gad! she'd b.	UNIVERSE 8
go to b. things	TRANSPORT 15
nothing b. to do	HOME 21
past always looks b.	PAST 3
rich is b.	WEALTH 39
Things can only get b.	PROGRESS 23
way to the B.	OPTIMISM 23
between B. two stools	INDECISION 1
Beulah Land of B.	HEAVEN 5
beverage b. of hell	ALCOHOL 17
beware B. of desperate steps	CAUTION 23
b. of giving your heart	DOGS 9

B. of men bearing flowers	FLOWERS 15
B. of the Agapanthus	DANGER 33
Let the buyer b.	BUYING 2
bewildered utterly b.	PAINTING 28
beyond b. the veil	DEATH 12
bias impartiality is b.	PREJUDICE 23
Bible B. in the other	POLITICIANS 32
B. of the 17th	CULTURE 35
English B., a book	BIBLE 15
not reading the same B.	BIBLE 23
To read in de B.	BIBLE 20
used the B.	BIBLE 17
bicker b. down a valley	RIVERS 9
bicycle arrive by b.	POLITICAL PART 41
fish without a b.	MEN AND WOMEN 33
king rides a b.	COUNTRIES 34
so is a b. repair kit	MARRIAGE 49
bicycling b. to Holy Communion	BRITAIN 16
biennials b. are the ones that die	GARDENS 20
big b. bang	FUTILITY 25
b. bang	UNIVERSE 1
B. Blue machine	POLITICAL PART 4
B. BROTHER IS WATCHING YOU	GOVERNMENT 37
b. enough to take away	GOVERNMENT 38
B. fish eat little	POWER 1
b. five	HUNTING 1
b. tent	POLITICAL PART 5
b. way of doing things	CHARITY 25
b. words which make us so unhappy	WORDS 17
Hey! b. spender	WEALTH 40
I am b.	CINEMA 12
side of the b. squadrons	GOD 20
This b. bang idea	UNIVERSE 16
victim to a b. lie	LIES 22
bigger b. bang for a buck	WARFARE 2
b. they are	SUCCESS 1
Universe is much b.	SCIENCE AND RELIG 16
biggest b. electric train set	CINEMA 13
bigotry B. tries to keep truth	PREJUDICE 17
bike he got on his b.	ACTION 2
bikers nickname for b.: donors	MEDICINE 29
biking b. to Holy Communion	ENGLAND 28
bill b. of company	ENTERTAINING 11
billabong camped by a b.	AUSTRALIA 17
billboard b. lovely as a tree	POLLUTION 15
billet Every bullet has its b.	FATE 7
billiards like a brilliant player of b.	CONVERSATION 10
To play b. well	SPORTS 12
billion b. dollar country	AMERICA 23
b. minus one	CHANCE 30
bills children and trademen's b.	MARRIAGE 42
inflammation of his weekly b.	DEBT 14
to go on paying the b.	EXPLORATION 16
bind b. the sweet influences	FATE 1
b. your sons to exile	DUTY 17
Safe b.	CAUTION 17
binds b. to himself a joy	TRANSIENCE 12
bingeing [b.] gives you a feeling	COOKING 36
biographers picklocks of b.	BIOGRAPHY 13
biographical noble and b. friend	BIOGRAPHY 8
biographies innumerable b.	HISTORY 14
biography better part of b.	BIOGRAPHY 14
B. is about Chaps	BIOGRAPHY 12
Judas who writes the b.	BIOGRAPHY 10
no history; only b.	BIOGRAPHY 7
biologist b. passes	LIFE SCI 23
biology B. is the search	LIFE SCI 29
bird Arabian b.	ORIGINALITY 1
beauty of b. song	POLLUTION 18
b. has flown	LIBERTY 5
b. in a cage	BELIEF 2
b. in the hand	CAUTION 2
b. in the hand	CERTAINTY 4
b. never flew	GIFTS 1
B. of Freedom	AMERICA 4
B. thou never wert	BIRDS 11
catch the b. of paradise	CHOICE 26

born (*cont.*)

B. on the fourth of July	AMERICA 25
b. sneering	PRIDE 8
b. three thousand years old	WOMEN 51
b. to be hanged	FATE 3
b. to live	LIFESTYLES 30
b. to set it right	CIRCUMSTANCE 14
b. unto trouble	MISFORTUNES 15
fell *dead-b. from the press*	PUBLISHING 5
future refusing to be b.	POLITICAL PART 32
house where I was b.	MEMORY 12
I am not yet b.	PREGNANCY 11
I've been b.	LIFE 44
I was b. again	FAITH 6
Man was b. free	LIBERTY 12
moment one is b.	STATISTICS 5
not b. a woman	WOMEN 48
Not to be b.	LIFE 14
some men are b. great	GREATNESS 4
sucker b. every minute	FOOLS 24
those who are to be b.	SOCIETY 7
to the manner b.	BEHAVIOUR 12
to the manner b.	CUSTOM 9
twice to be b.	LANGUAGES 17
understanding why you were ever b.	
	SCIENCE AND RELIG 17
unto us a child is b.	CHRISTMAS 4
where I was b.	BIOGRAPHY 18
boroughs bright b.	SKIES 19
borrow *men who b.*	DEBT 13
borrowed b. days	WEATHER 22
b. plumes	DECEPTION 5
March b. from April	WEATHER 9
borrower b., nor a lender	DEBT 12
borrowers Your *b. of books*	BOOKS 10
borrowing banqueting upon b.	DEBT 11
b. dulls the edge	DEBT 12
b. only lingers	POVERTY 15
He that goes a-b.	DEBT 3
borrows early man never b.	PREPARATION 4
bosom Abraham's bosom	HEAVEN 2
b. of a single state	CANADA 7
She has no b.	BODY 24
bosoms white b. of your actresses	SEX 16
boss b. there is always	MISFORTUNES 25
get to the b.	EMPLOYMENT 26
bossing nobody b. you about	POLITICAL PART 24
Boston B. man is the east wind	AMERICAN CITIES 49
this is good old B.	AMERICAN CITIES 50
Thucydides at B.	FUTURE 15
Boswelliana lues B.	BIOGRAPHY 1
botanist I'd be a b.	PHYSICAL 15
Botany Bay seek for at B.	AUSTRALIA 11
botches no rubs nor b.	MISTAKES 12
bother b. with people I hate	BEHAVIOUR 29
Though 'B. it' I may	SWEARING 7
Botticelli If B. were alive	PAINTING 29
bottle hit the b.	FOOD 30
message in a b.	PAINTING 33
shake the catsup b.	FOOD 25
bottles wine in old b.	CHANGE 16
wine in old b.	CHANGE 23
bottom at the b. of our garden	SUPERNATURAL 20
now the b. line	PUBLISHING 15
stand on its own b.	STRENGTH 1
bottomless Law is a b. pit	LAW 19
bought Gold may be b. too dear	VALUE 1
I b. the company	BUSINESS 7
one who when he's b.	POLITICIANS 15
boundaries b., usually unnatural	COUNTRIES 29
bounded b. in a nut-shell	DREAMS 7
bouquet b. is better	ALCOHOL 27
bourgeois astonish the b.	CLASS 15
b. are other people	CLASS 18
b. climb up on them	BOOKS 13
B. . . . is an epithet	CLASS 19
b. prefers comfort	CLASS 22

small-town b.	CONFORMITY 14
bourgeoisie b. in the long run	CLASS 23
bourne b. of time and place	DEATH 53
bow b. down in the house	SELF-INTEREST 10
b. of promise	WEATHER 23
Cupid's b.	BODY 6
every knee should b.	NAMES 4
bowels b. of Christ	CERTAINTY 4
bowl B. fast, bowl faster	CRICKET 12
b. of cherries	LIFE 43
b. of night	DAY 13
lurk within the b.	COOKING 23
when I am going to bowl	CRICKET 16
bowler b. and speaking Spanish	LANGUAGES 15
bowls those who play at b.	CAUTION 21
bows B. down to wood	RELIGION 20
will be fought with b. and arrows	WARFARE 62
bow windows b. to the house	OPTIMISM 20
bow-wow Big B. strain	WRITERS 9
box Pandora's b.	PROBLEMS 8
Worth a guinea a b.	VALUE 7
boxing B.'s just show business	SPORTS 33
boy b. forever	MEN 15
b. playing on the sea-shore	INVENTIONS 7
country out of the b.	COUNTRY AND TOWN 3
cruel as a small b.	CRUELTY 16
good ol' b.	MEN 5
misfortunes can befall a b.	PARENTS 14
Never send a b.	MATURITY 9
schoolrooms for 'the boy'	CRIME 34
To be a soaring human b.	CHILDREN 15
When I was a b.	GENERATION GAP 11
boyfriend thing called the B.	COURTSHIP 13
boys backroom b.	SCIENCE 3
b. are still there	POLITICIANS 26
b. get at one end	SCHOOLS 1
b. in the back rooms	FAME 16
B. will be boys	MEN 1
b. with toys	DECEPTION 10
B. wizz who are noble	SCHOOLS 13
Christian b. I can scarcely	SCHOOLS 6
for office b.	JOURNALISM 13
not about to send American b.	WARS 23
society has to make b. into	MEN AND WOMEN 29
Two b. are half a boy	WORK 9
bra Burn your b.	WOMAN'S ROLE 9
Bracknell savage as Lady B.	CLASS 30
brae stout heart to a stey b.	DETERMINATION 10
brag B. is a good dog	WORDS AND DEEDS 2
brain atoms in my b.	MIND 18
Bear of Very Little B.	THINKING 21
b. attic stocked	LIBRARIES 10
b. has oozed out	TRANSPORT 11
fingerprints across his b.	MUSICIANS 18
great regions of the b.	MIND 13
harmful to the b.	SMOKING 5
haze that is my b.	MIND 20
human b. is born	MIND 25
idle b.	IDLENESS 4
leave that b. outside	PARLIAMENT 22
losing your b.	SICKNESS 28
My b.? It's my second	BODY 30
Owl hasn't exactly got B.	KNOWLEDGE 46
puzzle their b.	ALCOHOL 11
sucked into the b.	TEACHING 19
tares of mine own b.	ORIGINALITY 7
why did He give us a b.	WOMAN'S ROLE 27
brained Thou large-b. woman	WRITERS 13
brains b. of a Minerva	ACTING 10
feet instead of their b.	JAZZ 2
brain-washing called b.	SELF 27
brake invented the b.	INVENTIONS 21
branch destroy root and b.	THOROUGHNESS 9
olive b.	PEACE 5
branchy Towery city and b. between towers	
	BRITISH TOWNS 31
brandy b. of the damned	MUSIC 14

must drink b. — ALCOHOL 12
brass muck there's b. — MONEY 13
brassiere Art is not a *brassiere* — ARTS 37
brave b. deserve the fair — COURAGE 8
b. man inattentive — DUTY 13
b. man with a sword — LOVE 56
B. men lived before — REPUTATION 1
B. New-nothing-very-much — FUTILITY 25
b. new world — PROGRESS 1
Fortune favours the b. — COURAGE 7
home of the b. — AMERICA 14
Many b. men lived before — BIOGRAPHY 2
None but the b. — COURAGE 17
O b. new world — HUMAN RACE 12
one half of mankind b. — COURAGE 21
bravest b. of all categories — COURAGE 32
brawling with a b. woman — ARGUMENT 8
bray Vicar of B. — SELF-INTEREST 22
Brazil Charley's aunt from B. — COUNTRIES 21
In B. they throw flowers — COUNTRIES 28
Brazilian B. without land — POLLUTION 24
breach honoured in the b. — CUSTOM 9
Once more unto the b. — WARFARE 16
bread better than no b. — SATISFACTION 4
b. and circuses — GOVERNMENT 3
b. and circuses — GOVERNMENT 9
b. never falls — MISFORTUNES 1
b. of idleness — IDLENESS 9
b. of idleness — WORK 12
b. should be so dear — POVERTY 23
b. upon the waters — CHANCE 19
b. upon the waters — FUTURE 7
daily b. — WORK 15
He took the b. — BELIEF 14
HOMER begged his b. — FAME 9
live by b. alone — LIFE 6
made like b. — LOVE 69
one half-pennyworth of b. — VALUE 20
shalt thou eat b. — WORK 18
since sliced b. — INVENTIONS 2
till b. was found — SATISFACTION 1
breadline on the b. — POVERTY 9
break B., break, break — SEA 1
b. one's duck — CRICKET 2
b. them at pleasure — MEN 8
b. the mould — ORIGINALITY 2
cruel to b. people's legs — CRUELTY 17
designed to b. human beings — CRIME 50
Have a b. — LEISURE 3
heart would b. — HOPE 6
nature round him b. — DEFIANCE 15
sucker an even b. — FOOLS 26
they do not b. — COUNTRIES 31
those that b. down — TECHNOLOGY 22
breakdown need not be all b. — MADNESS 14
breakfast B., Dinner, Lunch — COOKING 29
Hope is a good b. — HOPE 4
sing before b. — EMOTIONS 2
things before b. — BELIEF 21
breaking b. it in — NAMES 15
breaks b. a butterfly — FUTILITY 18
b. like a little girl — WOMEN 54
party b. up the better — ENTERTAINING 14
break-through may also be b. — MADNESS 14
breast all parts of the b. — SINGING 2
soothe a savage b. — MUSIC 8
breastie panic's in thy b. — FEAR 7
breasts b. by which France is fed — FRANCE 5
breath b. bigger than a circustent — BEGINNING 22
b. is folded up — DEATH 76
b. of life — NECESSITY 14
b. of Socrates — PHYSICAL 11
call the fleeting b. — DEATH 41
drawn the b. — LIFE 41
exponent of b. — LOVE 53
Out with your own b. — FESTIVALS 67
they hold their b. — SCULPTURE 10

waste of b. — ARMED FORCES 36
breathe As though to b. were life — IDLENESS 19
like the hair we b. — HUNTING 11
men can b. — FAME 5
summer's morn to b. — COUNTRY AND TOWN 4
breathes B. there the man — PATRIOTISM 14
breathing b. of thy inmost heart — LETTERS 12
Running's like b. — SPORTS 35
breathless b. hush in the Close — CRICKET 6
bred b. in the bone — CHARACTER 16
breeches B. Bible — BIBLE 2
put into your b. — TEACHING 9
breed b. of their horses — CHILDREN 11
endless war still b. — WARFARE 17
this happy b. — ENGLAND 5
breeding Burgundy without any b. — ALCOHOL 25
Good b. consists — MANNERS 19
breeds Familiarity b. contempt — FAMILIARITY 5
Like b. like — SIMILARITY 6
breezy B., Sneezy, Freezy — SEASONS 17
brevity B. is the soul of wit — WIT 1
B. is the soul of wit — WIT 5
Its body b. — WIT 13
brew b., so shall you bake — CAUSES 2
so shall you b. — CAUSES 1
bribe b. or twist — JOURNALISM 18
Marriage is a b. — MARRIAGE 41
without a b. — CORRUPTION 10
bribed b. by their loyalties — CORRUPTION 16
bribes b. he had taken — CORRUPTION 15
man open to b. — EMOTIONS 22
brick carried a piece of b. — BUYING 5
'Eave 'arf a b. at 'im — PREJUDICE 13
inherited it b. — TOWNS 13
not even red b. — UNIVERSITIES 24
bricks b. without straw — FUTILITY 6
make b. without straw — PROBLEMS 6
brickwork posts, and b. — PAINTING 9
bridal-favours b. and raiment — WEDDINGS 9
bride b. of quietness — SILENCE 10
b. that the sun shines on — WEDDINGS 2
flowers in the b.'s hand — WEDDINGS 10
jealousy to the b. — HUMAN NATURE 18
never a b. — WEDDINGS 1
Never the blushing b. — WEDDINGS 12
rejoiceth over the b. — WEDDINGS 6
bridegroom b. rejoiceth over — WEDDINGS 6
brides bride-grooms, b. — SEASONS 14
bridesmaid Always a b. — WEDDINGS 1
always the b. — WEDDINGS 12
bridge b. built from the known — ARTS AND SCI 10
b. of asses — MATHS 5
b. of gold to a flying enemy — WAYS 9
b. of reconciliation — MOURNING 23
b. over troubled water — SYMPATHY 27
b. that carries him — MANNERS 3
b. too far — WORLD W II 18
Champagne, and B. — ELECTIONS 9
Don't cross the b. — PREPARATION 2
keep the b. with me — COOPERATION 24
London B. is broken down — BRITISH TOWNS 6
man on the bridge — MEETING 22
brief little b. authority — POWER 14
strive to be b. — STYLE 3
brigandage teaches him b. — EMPLOYMENT 7
bright All things b. and beautiful — ANIMALS 19
b. day is done — ENDING 4
b. day that brings — DANGER 23
Dark with excessive b. — SIMILARITY 17
land is b. — OPTIMISM 21
brighten Blessings b. — HAPPINESS 1
brilliant envy of b. men — EXCELLENCE 13
brimstone fire and b. — HEAVEN 3
bring what it will b. — VALUE 19
bringing b. me up by hand — CHILD CARE 7
brink something trembling on the b. — TRANSPORT 22
brisking b. about the life — CATS 6

Bristol B. fashion ORDER 8
Britain Battle of B. WORLD W II 3
boundary of B. is revealed EXPLORATION 3
I'm backing B. PATRIOTISM 1
State in B. EUROPE 20
Without B. Europe would EUROPE 17
Britannia Cool B. BRITAIN 1
Rule, B. BRITAIN 6
When I think of Cool B. BRITAIN 17
British bones of one B. Grenadier WORLD W II 21
B. Grenadier ARMED FORCES 23
B. is unique BRITAIN 11
By B. hands SCULPTURE 4
loathsome is the B. tourist TRAVEL 26
officer of B. rule AFRICA 11
ridiculous as the B. MORALITY 6
We are B., thank God SEX 32
British Museum B. is an enormous mind LIBRARIES 11
Briton glory in the name of B. BRITAIN 8
Britons B. alone use 'Might' BRITAIN 10
B. never will be slaves BRITAIN 6
broad land of the b. acres BRITISH TOWNS 21
broadened b. into a brotherhood INTERNAT REL 33
broadens Travel b. the mind TRAVEL 6
broccoli eat any more b. FOOD 28
It's b., dear FOOD 22
broke b. the mould EXCELLENCE 8
If it ain't b. ACTION 5
broken bats have been b. TRUST 40
b. reed STRENGTH 9
Laws were made to be b. LAW 23
made to be b. TRUST 3
not quickly b. STRENGTH 14
Rules are made to be b. LAW 9
broker honest b. DIPLOMACY 2
honest b. DIPLOMACY 7
brook free, meandering b. EDUCATION 21
broom sent with a b. before PREPARATION 13
brooms New b. sweep clean CHANGE 7
broth Too many cooks spoil the b. WORK 8
brothel intellectual b. JOURNALISM 9
brother Am I my b.'s keeper RELATIONSHIPS 2
BIG B. IS WATCHING YOU GOVERNMENT 37
B. can you spare a dime POVERTY 30
b. sin against me FORGIVENESS 11
B. to Death SLEEP 7
closer than a b. FRIENDSHIP 9
man and a b. HUMAN RACE 2
man and a b. RACE 1
white man's b. RACE 22
brotherhood broadened into a b. INTERNAT REL 33
crown thy good with b. AMERICA 24
table of b. EQUALITY 17
brother-in-law not his b. RACE 22
brothers All arts are b. ARTS 1
b. or eight cousins LIFE SCI 22
live together as b. COOPERATION 29
brow sweat of one's b. WORK 14
brown b. embrace eternal EARTH 15
How now, b. cow SPEECH 1
strong b. god RIVERS 14
browner tinge with a b. shade OLD AGE 14
browning safety-catch of my B. CULTURE 21
bruise tread on it and b. it CRUELTY 10
bruised b. in a new place CHANGE 36
brush b. that I make love PAINTING 18
B. up your Shakespeare SHAKESPEARE 14
work with so fine a b. WRITERS 8
brushers b. of noblemen's clothes CRITICISM 4
brutal short, b. lives MEN AND WOMEN 31
brutality b. and sadistic conduct BIBLE 21
brute Brute heart of a b. MEN AND WOMEN 25
treated as a b. RACE 10
brutes made to live as b. HUMAN RACE 10
brutish b. and short LIFE 20
Brutus You too, B. TRUST 19
bubble b. reputation ARMED FORCES 16

froth and b. LIFE 34
bubbles frill of b. in the eye-sockets WARS 31
buck bigger bang for a b. WARFARE 2
b. stops here DUTY 24
pass the b. DUTY 4
bucket b. of ashes PAST 31
stick inside a swill b. ADVERTISING 12
buckeye B. State AMERICAN CITIES 5
buckle b. which fastens PARLIAMENT 20
Buckley B.'s chance CHANCE 16
bud worm i' the b. SECRECY 20
Buddha B., the Godhead GOD 37
budget Balancing the b. ECONOMICS 19
buds Hey, b. below FLOWERS 13
bug not a b., it's a feature COMPUTERS 1
bugger B. Bognor BRITISH TOWNS 38
buggers b. can't be choosers SEX 34
bugles Blow out, you b. DEATH 57
build Birds b. CREATIVITY 8
b. a church CHRISTIAN CH 7
b. a tower FORESIGHT 8
b. shopping malls BUSINESS 50
easier to b. two chimneys ARCHITECTURE 2
Fools b. houses FOOLS 4
never ask *why* b. SUICIDE 11
building be able to read a b. ARCHITECTURE 22
beauty in b. ARCHITECTURE 7
b. hath three conditions ARCHITECTURE 5
first b. erected by ARCHITECTURE 1
it's a very old b. THEATRE 19
Modern body b. is ritual BODY 35
No good b. without ARCHITECTURE 3
buildings architecture applies only to b. ARCHITECTURE 15
our b. shape us ARCHITECTURE 14
builds b. on mud DEMOCRACY 4
built b. in a day PATIENCE 12
b. on sand STRENGTH 10
b. Thebes of the seven gates WORK 36
bulimia yuppie version of b. HEALTH 20
bull b. market BUSINESS 19
milk the b. BELIEF 17
strong as a b. moose STRENGTH 22
bullet Every b. has its billet FATE 17
stronger than the b. ELECTIONS 6
bullied b. out of vice VIRTUE 37
bully b. is always a coward COURAGE 2
b. pulpit PRESIDENCY 1
such a b. pulpit PRESIDENCY 6
bump go b. in the night SUPERNATURAL 1
go b. in the night SUPERNATURAL 4
bumping b. your head EDUCATION 2
Bunbury invalid called B. APOLOGY 14
Buncombe talking to B. SPEECHES 4
bung-hole let out the b. THRIFT 5
bungle b. raising your children CHILD CARE 13
bungler good nature is a b. POLITICS 11
Man is a b. PEACE 15
bunk Exercise is b. HEALTH 17
more or less b. HISTORY 20
bunkers Give up and live in b. ARCHITECTURE 23
burden bear any b. LIBERTY 37
conjure away the b. ARTS 14
heavy b. of responsibility ROYALTY 33
makes the back to the b. SYMPATHY 1
my b. is light WORK 20
White Man's b. DUTY 17
white man's b. RACE 5
bureaucrats b. will care more ADMINISTRATION 9
Guidelines for b. ADMINISTRATION 23
burglars fear of b. is not only CRIME 47
burgundy naïve domestic B. ALCOHOL 25
burial thought they had only one b. SICKNESS 8
burials b., swindlings, affairs of state FRANCE 16
buried b. in so sweet a place DEATH 47
Burke B. under a shed PEOPLE 33
burn better to b. out SUICIDE 12

cathedrals (*cont.*)
great Gothic c. — TRANSPORT 23
Catherine Marx and C. the Great — RUSSIA 8
catholic C. and Communist are alike — ARGUMENT 22
C. and sensual — TRAVEL 31
C. Church has never really — CHRISTIAN CH 42
C. women must keep taking — PREGNANCY 20
if I was not a C. — CHRISTIAN CH 38
miserable Irish C. childhood — CHILDREN 28
you may as well be a C. — CHRISTIAN CH 43
Catholics C. and Communists — INDIFFERENCE 14
cats All c. are grey — SIMILARITY 1
C. and monkeys — LIFE 35
C. look down on us — ANIMALS 31
C., no less liquid — CATS 10
C. seem to go on — CATS 13
count the c. in Zanzibar — TRAVEL 24
fight like Kilkenny c. — CATS 4
Keep no more c. — EXCESS 4
Naming of C. — CATS 11
to my dogs and c. — HOME 12
Wanton kittens make sober c. — YOUTH 1
cattle Actors are c. — ACTING 9
C. die — HEROES 4
Hurry no man's c. — PATIENCE 6
these who die as c. — WORLD W I 16
thousands of great c. — WORDS AND DEEDS 16
caught c. the bear — OPTIMISM 14
c. with chaff — DECEPTION 4
shoots him gets c. — CAUTION 32
cauldron c. bubble — SUPERNATURAL 12
cauliflower C. is nothing but cabbage — FOOD 18
cause already in the c. — CAUSES 22
always has some c. — CAUSES 16
any just c. — OPPORTUNITY 27
between c. and effect — TASTE 4
c. may be inconvenient — IDEALISM 9
c. of dullness — BOREDOM 3
Experiment to his own C. — HYPOTHESIS 9
First C. — BEGINNING 13
good old c. — SATISFACTION 22
his c. being good — JUSTICE 22
judge in his own c. — LAW 7
causes good, brave c. — FUTILITY 25
Home of lost c. — UNIVERSITIES 15
understand the c. of things — SCIENCE 4
caution c. in love — CAUTION 30
C. is the parent — CAUTION 4
cautious c. of his own words — CONVERSATION 4
cavaliero he was a perfect c. — HEROES 9
cavaliers C. (Wrong but Wromantic) — WARS 22
cave Aladdin's c. — WEALTH 7
C. canem — DOGS 1
caves c. for ages yet — GOD 29
c. in which we hide — MIDDLE AGE 10
caviar C. for peasants — CLASS 24
c. to the general — FUTILITY 9
c. to the general — TASTE 3
cease c. upon the midnight — DEATH 46
War will c. when men refuse — WARFARE 3
ceiling draw on the c. — PLEASURE 23
celebrity C. is a mask — FAME 21
c. is a person — FAME 17
celestial C. Empire — COUNTRIES 2
celibacy carrying c. to extremes — COURTSHIP 14
c. has no pleasures — SINGLE 4
c. is almost always — SINGLE 7
celibate happy undersexed c. — SINGLE 11
cell tight hot c. of their hearts — WOMEN 41
cellos c. of the deep farms — BIRDS 21
cells assembly of nerve c. — SELF 29
c. and gibbets — CRIME 34
little grey c. — INTELLIGENCE 4
little grey c. — INTELLIGENCE 12
Celtic C. antiquity — PEOPLE 47
C. twilight — IRELAND 2
cement grass can grow through c. — LOVE 73

cemetery c. is an open space — DEATH 47
censorship beginning of c. — CENSORSHIP 19
extreme form of c. — CENSORSHIP 7
centennial C. State — AMERICAN CITIES 6
centre c. cannot hold — ORDER 16
c. is everywhere — GOD 3
centuries c. look down — PAST 22
Through what wild c. — FLOWERS 9
century c. belongs to Canada — CANADA 9
c. differ very much — HUMAN RACE 25
new c. begins — FESTIVALS 66
real beginning of the 21st c. — FESTIVALS 70
twentieth c. have looked like — FATE 25
Cerberus sop to C. — APOLOGY 9
cerebral Socialism is purely c. — POLITICAL PART 27
ceremony C. is an invention — MANNERS 15
c. of innocence — ORDER 16
cerise *éminence c.* — ROYALTY 39
certain It is c. — BELIEF 12
Nothing is c. — CERTAINTY 3
Nothing is c. — FORESIGHT 4
certainties begin with c. — CERTAINTY 8
hot for c. — CERTAINTY 14
chaff caught with c. — DECEPTION 4
king's c. is worth — ROYALTY 2
old birds with c. — EXPERIENCE 11
tastes like c. — ABSENCE 11
chaffering c. swallow — SIMILARITY 20
chaffinch c. sings — SEASONS 21
chain c. about the ankle — HUMAN RIGHTS 12
c. is no stronger — COOPERATION 2
chained c. together with these — LIBRARIES 4
chains better to be in c. — LIBERTY 27
by the *slightest* c. — MEN 8
C. do not hold — MARRIAGE 50
c. of marriage — MARRIAGE 31
he is in c. — LIBERTY 12
lose but their c. — CLASS 13
chainsaw imagination and a c. — SCULPTURE 11
chair paint the c. — PAINTING 13
to the seat of the c. — WRITING 1
chairs any thing but empty c. — SIN 23
chaise-longue hurly-burly of the c. — MARRIAGE 39
chalice poisoned c. — MISFORTUNES 12
chalices priests and golden c. — CLERGY 7
challenge Meet the c. — POLITICAL PART 3
Cham great C. of literature — WRITERS 6
chamber C. selected by the Whips — PARLIAMENT 25
into the conference c. — INTERNAT REL 30
chambermaid in the arms of a c. — IMAGINATION 8
more worth than his c. — CRISES 11
chameleons Words are c. — WORDS 25
champagne C., and Bridge — ELECTIONS 9
C. certainly gives one — ALCOHOL 15
C. or high heels — IDEALISM 9
c. teetotaller — ALCOHOL 21
championing c. human rights — HUMAN RIGHTS 17
chance Blind c. — CHANCE 2
Buckley's c. — CHANCE 16
c. and accident — PAINTING 32
c. favours only the prepared — SCIENCE 9
eye to the main c. — SELF-INTEREST 13
Give peace a c. — PEACE 28
Last C. Gulch — CHILDREN 25
Moses took a c. — CHANCE 11
never eliminate c. — CHANCE 28
too good to leave to c. — MUSIC 32
why take the c. — WORK 43
chancellor C. of the Exchequer — TAXES 15
chances change by course — CHANGE 2
Chanel C. No. 5 — DRESS 21
change beauty is past c. — BEAUTY 23
before you make a c. — CHANGE 2
bound to c. — CHANCE 25
by c. more fierce — SIMILARITY 16
certain relief in c. — CHANGE 36
C. and decay — CHANGE 39

cheese (*cont.*)
like some valley c.	POETRY 36
varieties of c.	FRANCE 17

chefs C. do it anonymously   COOKING 38

chemical certain c. elements   HUMAN RACE 30
| two c. substances | RELATIONSHIPS 12 |

chemist as objective as a c.   WRITING 33
| trade of c. | PHYSICAL 23 |

chemistry c. and machinery   DEATH 54
| c. that works | LIFE SCI 29 |

chemists c.' war   WARFARE 64

cheque statement is like a c.   MEANING 3

Chernobyl cultural C.   CULTURE 31
| cultural C. | CULTURE 32 |

cherries bowl of c.   LIFE 43
| c., hops, and women | BRITISH TOWNS 30 |

cherry as American as c. pie   VIOLENCE 16
c. hung with snow	TREES 10
c. year	SEASONS 1
Under the c.	TREES 6

cherry-stones carve heads upon c.   POETS 13

Cheshire C. cat   CATS 3
| cosmic C. cat | GOD 32 |
| face of the C. Cat | BRITAIN 15 |

chestnut c.-tree, great-rooted blossomer   TREES 15
| jolly jolly c. | TREES 18 |

chestnuts c. out of the fire   DANGER 16

chevalier Young C.   PEOPLE 23

chew fart and c. gum   FOOLS 27

chewing gum c. for the eyes   BROADCASTING 3

chic radical c.   FASHION 3
| Radical C. | FASHION 10 |

chicken c.-and-egg problem   PROBLEMS 3
c. in his pot	POVERTY 16
C. Tikka Masala	BRITAIN 19
Left wing, c. wing	CAPITALISM 26
man who has fed the c.	FORESIGHT 14
Mother Carey's c.	BIRDS 6
rubber c. circuit	SPEECHES 2

chickens all my pretty c.   MOURNING 9
count one's c.	OPTIMISM 13
Curses, like c.	HATRED 2
Don't count your c.	OPTIMISM 4
May c. come	SEASONS 3
stealin' no chickens	ANIMALS 2

chieftain c. of the puddin'-race   FOOD 14

child change in the c.   CHILD CARE 9
cherished c.	PARENTS 10
c. becomes an adult	CHILDREN 24
c. born therein	HUMAN RIGHTS 11
C. is father of the Man	CHILDREN 14
c. is not a vase	CHILDREN 7
c. is owed the greatest respect	CHILDREN 6
c. is the father	CHARACTER 5
c. makes you a parent	FAMILY 29
c. shall lead them	COOPERATION 19
c.'s strength	BELIEF 19
c. who hasn't been handled	MUSICIANS 18
c. who will be so exposed	YOUTH 25
first c. is made of glass	CHILD CARE 16
Give me a c.	EDUCATION 3
have a thankless c.	GRATITUDE 8
If you strike a c.	VIOLENCE 8
knows his own c.	PARENTS 6
leave a c. alone	CHILDREN 16
like to be a c.	MATURITY 15
Monday's c.	BEAUTY 5
my absent c.	MOURNING 8
never was a c. so lovely	CHILD CARE 6
Praise the c.	PARENTS 3
right to a c. with the obligation	WOMAN'S ROLE 23
Saturday's c. works hard	WORK 6
shocks the mind of a c.	RELIGION 19
spoiled c. of art	FICTION 15
spoil the c.	CHILD CARE 2
Thursday's c. has far to go	TRAVEL 5
Train up a c.	CHILD CARE 3

unto us a c. is born	CHRISTMAS 4
use of a new-born c.	INVENTIONS 9
Wednesday's c.	SORROW 2
wise c. that knows	PARENTS 1

childbirth Death and taxes and c.   PREGNANCY 10

childhood C. is measured out   CHILDREN 22
C. is the kingdom	CHILDREN 18
C. is the Last Chance	CHILDREN 25
c. is timeless	CHILDREN 26
miserable Irish Catholic c.	CHILDREN 28
one moment in c.	CHILDREN 20
what my lousy c. was like	BIOGRAPHY 18

childish Age does not make us c.   OLD AGE 15
| c. valorous | MATURITY 3 |

childishness second c.   OLD AGE 8

children art of dealing with c.   CHILD CARE 14
breeds contempt—and c.	FAMILIARITY 21
bring forth c.	PREGNANCY 4
bungle raising your c.	CHILD CARE 13
C. always assume	PARENTS 25
C. and fools	HONESTY 1
c. and tradesmen's bills	MARRIAGE 42
c. are a bitter disappointment	CHILD CARE 8
C. are certain cares	FAMILY 4
c. are not your children	PARENTS 16
C. aren't happy	PARENTS 19
c. at play	CHILDREN 8
C. begin by loving	PARENTS 13
c. have ended up	PARENTS 27
c. how to speak	LANGUAGES 14
c. is sixpence	PARENTS 17
c. like the olive-branches	FAMILY 9
c. love hamsters	RELATIONSHIPS 19
c. of Abraham	RELIGION 34
c. of a larger growth	MATURITY 6
c. of a larger growth	WOMEN 26
c. of Israel	COUNTRIES 3
c., playing or quarrelling	CHANCE 29
c. produce adults	MARRIAGE 43
c.'s hearts are glad	CHRISTMAS 15
C. should be seen	CHILDREN 1
C.'s talent to endure	SUFFERING 32
c. still at heart	OLD AGE 15
C. sweeten labours	CHILDREN 10
c. to adults	HAPPINESS 29
c. to be a credit	PARENTS 18
devil's c.	CHANCE 4
dogs than of their c.	CHILDREN 11
draw like these c.	PAINTING 24
first class, and with c.	TRAVEL 32
Goodnight, c.	MEETING 20
Heaven protects c.	DANGER 3
hell for c.	FAMILY 16
holdeth c. from play	FICTION 7
influence on their c.	PARENTS 20
it cannot have c.	PERFECTION 13
kept from c.	SECRECY 22
My c. are c.	GRATITUDE 18
Never ask the c.	FESTIVALS 68
not much about having c.	CHILDREN 23
other people's c.	CHILDREN 27
poor get c.	POVERTY 29
reasons for having c.	PREGNANCY 9
Suffer the little c.	CHILDREN 5
their c. are naïve	CHILD CARE 10
They can't bear c.	WOMAN'S ROLE 28
tiresome for c.	GENERATION GAP 3
To beget c.	PARENTS 21
violations committed by c.	CHILDREN 19
wife and c.	FAMILY 11
wretched bellies of his c.	POVERTY 31
You remember the c.	PREGNANCY 12

Chile Small earthquake in C.   BOREDOM 10

Chiltern Hundreds apply for the C.   PARLIAMENT 4

chimney old men from the c.   FICTION 7

chimneys easier to build two c.   ARCHITECTURE 2

chimpanzee hands of a c.   POETS 26

china fighting with your land armies in C.	WARFARE 58	C. have burnt each other	CHRISTIAN CH 23
Chinese C. wall	BUSINESS 20	**Christmas** asks for a C. box	TEMPTATION 15
C. whispers	GOSSIP 12	C. Day in the Workhouse	CHRISTMAS 11
no one can destroy the C.	COUNTRIES 31	C. is the Disneyfication	CHRISTMAS 17
chinks fill hup the c.	COOKING 22	C.-morning bells	CHRISTMAS 15
chip c. off the old block	FAMILY 8	C. should fall out	CHRISTMAS 7
c. of the old 'block'	SPEECHES 10	C. won't be Christmas	CHRISTMAS 10
chips C. with everything	CHOICE 28	did for Easter or C.	FESTIVALS 68
known by his c.	APPEARANCE 4	dreaming of a white C.	CHRISTMAS 14
chivalry age of c.	EUROPE 5	Let them know it's C.	CHARITY 27
Age of C.	HEROES 2	not just for C.	DOGS 2
law of c.	PLEASURE 26	shopping days to C.	CHRISTMAS 1
noble acts of c.	PUBLISHING 3	'Twas the night before C.	CHRISTMAS 8
chlorine about the properties of c.	ARTS AND SCI 12	twelve days of C.	CHRISTMAS 2
chocolate entire box of c.	TOWNS 26	vote for an early C.	SELF-INTEREST 31
no more backbone than a c. éclair	CHARACTER 38	white Christmas	CHRISTMAS 3
chocolates box of c.	LIFE 55	x. is a good time	CHRISTMAS 16
choice c. in rotten apples	CHOICE 8	**chrysanthemum** C. Throne	ROYALTY 4
c. of all my library	LIBRARIES 3	**church** c. for his mother	CHRISTIAN CH 14
c. of working	LIBERTY 11	c. is an anvil	CHRISTIAN CH 4
has a c. has trouble	CHOICE 3	c. is God	CHRISTIAN CH 3
Hobson's c.	CHOICE 10	c. to *share* God	GOD 3
image of your c.	SELF 25	c. with stumbling-blocks	CHRISTIAN CH 7
independent c.	CHOICE 17	dog who goes to c.	BEHAVIOUR 6
not your second c. too	LIFE 52	get me to the c. on time	WEDDINGS 13
obvious c.	CHOICE 6	God builds a c.	GOOD 9
terrible c.	CHOICE 19	I will build my c.	CHRISTIAN CH 13
you takes your c.	CHOICE 9	Railways and the C.	TRANSPORT 34
choices sum of all the c.	CHOICE 29	some to c. repair	CHRISTIAN CH 20
choke c. on the tail	DETERMINATION 6	Spaniard will be a c.	ARCHITECTURE 1
choking c. him and making him	HYPOCRISY 17	Stands the C. clock	PAST 29
choleric captain's but a c. word	CLASS 11	where God built a c.	GOOD 23
choose *believe what we c.*	BELIEF 20	**Churchill** never was a C.	PEOPLE 41
C. an author	READING 6	**churchmen** single life doth well with c.	CLERGY 8
c. not to be	DESPAIR 14	**Church of England** C. begins	CRICKET 10
c. to be Faraday	ARTS AND SCI 9	dangers which beset the C.	CHRISTIAN CH 35
ones we c. to love	RELATIONSHIPS 18	If the C. were to fail	CHRISTIAN CH 26
To c. The Jews	RACE 13	**churchyard** green Yule makes a fat c.	WEATHER 5
To govern is to c.	GOVERNMENT 25	than in a c.	TASTE 12
woman can hardly ever c.	CHOICE 18	**churchyards** c. yawn	DAY 5
choosers Beggars can't be c.	NECESSITY 2	**CIA** C. were suddenly to splash	BIOGRAPHY 23
buggers can't be c.	SEX 34	**cigar** c. called Hamlet	SMOKING 1
choosing c. between the disastrous	POLITICS 30	good 5-cent c.	SMOKING 13
chop c. logic	LOGIC 2	**cigarette** c. is the perfect	SMOKING 11
chopper cheap and chippy c.	CRIME 38	c. that bears	MEMORY 23
chord I struck one c.	MUSIC 13	c., well, I love	SMOKING 15
You just pick a c.	MUSIC 29	smoked my first c.	SMOKING 14
chosen after he has been c.	LEADERSHIP 14	**cigarettes** c. are the only	SMOKING 16
c. people	COUNTRIES 4	**Cinderella** If I made C.	CINEMA 14
few are c.	CHOICE 13	**cinders** c., ashes, dust	LOVE 44
Christ cause C. wasn't a woman	WOMAN'S ROLE 17	**cinema** c. is truth	CINEMA 17
C. and His saints slept	WARS 4	**circle** fatal c. is traced	HUMAN RACE 21
C. beside me	PRAYER 8	God is a c.	GOD 3
C. perish in torment	IMAGINATION 16	magic c.	POLITICAL PART 8
C. receive thy saule	DEATH 9	square the c.	MATHS 6
Christendom cockpit of C.	COUNTRIES 12	wheel has come full c.	CIRCUMSTANCE 9
wisest fool in C.	PEOPLE 27	**circuit** When this c. learns your job	TECHNOLOGY 21
christened when she was c.	NAMES 6	**circumference** c. is nowhere	GOD 3
Christian C. boys I can scarcely	SCHOOLS 6	**circumlocution** C. Office	ADMINISTRATION 7
C. ideal has not been tried	CHRISTIAN CH 29	**circumnavigation** c. of our globe	EXPLORATION 4
C. religion not only	CHRISTIAN CH 22	**circumspice** *Si monumentum requiris*, c.	EPITAPHS 11
If you're going to be a C.	CHRISTIAN CH 43	**circumstance** clutch of c.	COURAGE 26
Jewish synagogue and the C. church	RELIGION 7	grain of c.	ADVERSITY 16
maybe a C. third	CLERGY 21	**circumstances** C. alter cases	CIRCUMSTANCE 1
persuades me to be a C.	MUSICIANS 12	New c.	CIRCUMSTANCE 2
Scratch the C.	CHRISTIAN CH 28	**circus** proceedings into a c.	BROADCASTING 8
Christianity C. better than Truth	CHRISTIAN CH 24	**circuses** bread and c.	GOVERNMENT 8
C. deposes Mother Nature	NATURE 20	bread and c.	GOVERNMENT 9
C. is the most materialistic	CHRISTIAN CH 32	**circustent** breath bigger than a c.	BEGINNING 22
C. was the religion	CLERGY 14	**cities** c. for our best morality	COUNTRY AND TOWN 12
Disneyfication of C.	CHRISTMAS 17	c. of the plain	TOWNS 4
heart of C.	CHRISTIAN CH 30	flower of c.	BRITISH TOWNS 22
His C. was muscular	CHRISTIAN CH 27	shape of our c.	TRANSPORT 24
muscular C.	CHRISTIAN CH 9	**citizen** zealous c.	FAMILY 12
rock 'n' roll or C.	FAME 19	**citizens** most valuable c.	FARMING 9
that definition of C.	CHRISTIAN CH 46	second class c.	EQUALITY 15
Christians blood of C.	CHRISTIAN CH 15	**city** c. consists in men	ARMED FORCES 15

only the wrong c.	WEATHER 19
out of these wet c.	ALCOHOL 6
require new c.	DRESS 10
She wears her c.	DRESS 7
years hang like old c.	PAST 43
clothing origins of c.	DRESS 26
sheep's c.	HYPOCRISY 9
wolf in sheep's c.	DECEPTION 8
cloud c. as a golden throne	IGNORANCE 18
c. cuckoo land	REALITY 2
c. has a silver lining	OPTIMISM 6
c. in trousers	MEN 13
lonely as a c.	FLOWERS 6
Long White C.	COUNTRIES 6
clouds trailing c. of glory	PREGNANCY 6
cloudy if Candlemas day be c.	WEATHER 6
clout Ne'er cast a c.	DRESS 4
cloven c. hoof	GOOD 10
out pops the c. hoof	FAMILY 24
club BELONG TO ANY C.	PREJUDICE 24
best c. in London	PARLIAMENT 5
most exclusive c.	ENGLAND 23
that terrible football c.	FOOTBALL 6
clue invariably a c.	CRIME 40
clunk C., click, every trip	TRANSPORT 1
clutch c. at a straw	HOPE 1
c. of circumstance	COURAGE 26
coach c. and six	IDEALISM 5
drive a c. and six	WAYS 17
looking for a body in the c.	CINEMA 14
rattling of a c.	PRAYER 13
coal dig for black c.	WORK 45
made mainly of c.	ADMINISTRATION 16
made of Newcastle c.	WEATHER 37
coalition rainbow c.	RACE 4
real rainbow c.	RACE 32
coals c. of fire	FORGIVENESS 7
c. of fire upon his head	ENEMIES 5
coarseness c., revealing something	MANNERS 7
coast Gold C.	AFRICA 3
Slave C.	AFRICA 4
coat c. so grey	HUNTING 9
c. upon a stick	OLD AGE 22
Cut your c.	PRACTICALITY 1
riband to stick in his c.	TRUST 29
cobbler c. stick to his last	KNOWLEDGE 1
c. to his last	KNOWLEDGE 2
Cobley Uncle Tom C.	QUANTITIES 17
Coca-Cola blue jeans and C.	WOMEN 59
cocaine C. habit-forming	DRUGS 4
cock before the c. crow	TRUST 20
c. will crow	HOME 3
c. with lively din	BIRDS 8
like a c. who thought	SELF-ESTEEM 14
many a good c.	CHARACTER 14
Nationalism is a silly c.	PATRIOTISM 24
owe a c. to Aesculapius	LAST WORDS 3
cock and bull c. story	FICTION 3
cockney C. impudence	PAINTING 11
cockpit c. of Christendom	COUNTRIES 12
c. of Europe	EUROPE 1
cocksure c. of anything	CERTAINTY 12
stupid are c.	CERTAINTY 24
cocktail weasel under the c. cabinet	THEATRE 22
cock-up c. theory	GOVERNMENT 39
cocoa C. is a cad	FOOD 20
cod photographer is like the c.	PHOTOGRAPHY 4
code trail has its own stern c.	TRUST 31
coffee After a man has had his c.	DRUNKENNESS 13
c., I want tea	FOOD 19
C., which makes the politician	FOOD 12
life with c. spoons	LIFE 39
coffin plate on a c.	APPEARANCE 18
coffins walking behind the c.	HEALTH 23
cogito C., ergo sum	THINKING 12
coil bent her contraceptive c.	PARANORMAL 22
shuffled off this mortal c.	DEATH 27

this mortal c.	LIFESTYLES 9
coincidence Twice is c.	CHANCE 34
coition After c.	SEX 3
vulgar way of c.	SEX 14
cold as c. and lonely	SELF 21
called a c. a cold	SICKNESS 14
can be eaten c.	REVENGE 6
Cast a c. eye	INDIFFERENCE 13
Charity is c.	CHARITY 17
c. fusion	PHYSICAL 1
C. hands	BODY 1
c. metal	ECONOMICS 8
C. on Monday	COOKING 33
c. relation	FAMILY 12
c. war	INTERNAT REL 3
Feed a c.	SICKNESS 3
fingers of c.	SEASONS 25
fuel to c. people	ADVERTISING 13
Give them the c. steel	WARS 19
hard and c. within	PEOPLE 63
ink in my pen ran c.	FEAR 5
in love with a c. climate	COUNTRIES 14
met so far has a c.	SICKNESS 21
one who's c.	SUFFERING 31
past the common c.	MEDICINE 28
so the c. strengthens	WEATHER 6
you will feel no c.	WEDDINGS 4
Coliseum While stands the C.	TOWNS 16
collapse c. of civilization	AMERICAN CITIES 62
c. of Stout Party	HUMOUR 1
on the point of c.	MANAGEMENT 11
collaterals I detest c.	FAMILY 17
college cabbage with a c. education	FOOD 18
colleges discipline of c.	UNIVERSITIES 8
Collins marry Mr C.	CHOICE 16
collision avoid foreign c.	INTERNAT REL 12
Cologne wash your city of C.	POLLUTION 10
colonies c. in your wife's name	CAUTION 31
New c. seek for	AUSTRALIA 11
colonised culture to be c. by	SCOTLAND 19
Colossus C. from a rock	POETS 13
Like a C.	GREATNESS 3
colour any c. that he wants	CHOICE 20
bad c.	APPEARANCE 7
By convention there is c.	SENSES 4
C. and Warmth	LIFE 38
c. of his hair	PREJUDICE 18
c. of the cat doesn't matter	WAYS 23
know the c. rose	SICKNESS 20
coloured no 'white' or 'c.' signs	RACE 24
twopence c.	PAINTING 12
colourless C. green ideas	LANGUAGE 25
colours c. dont quite match	APPEARANCE 23
c. from my life	SUFFERING 19
C. seen by candlelight	CONSTANCY 14
c. to the fence	INDECISION 16
c. will agree	INDIFFERENCE 5
lines and c.	PAINTING 7
nail one's c.	DEFIANCE 8
columbine pink and purple c.	FLOWERS 3
column Fifth c.	TRUST 7
comb between two bald men over a c.	WARS 29
Experience is a c.	EXPERIENCE 2
combinations irregular c.	LANGUAGE 9
combine When bad men c.	COOPERATION 22
combining c. committee	PARLIAMENT 20
combustion Spontaneous C.	PARANORMAL 10
come C. again another day	WEATHER 13
c. into the world alone	SOLITUDE 17
c. out as I do	ARGUMENT 13
C. to the edge	INSIGHT 15
c. to those who wait	PATIENCE 2
c. up and see me	MEETING 21
C. with me to the Casbah	CINEMA 1
death is not c.	DEATH 20
Easy c., easy go	EFFORT 2
First c., first served	PUNCTUALITY 3

conspiracy (*cont.*)
c. theory of government | GOVERNMENT 39
c. to make you happy | AMERICA 39
constable c.'s handbook | BIBLE 17
constancy c. in a good | DETERMINATION 30
Tell me no more of c. | CONSTANCY 9
constant c. as the northern star | CONSTANCY 6
C. dropping wears away | DETERMINATION 1
C., in Nature | CHANGE 32
here will c. be | DETERMINATION 31
constitution C. and the laws of England | CRICKET 8
c. does not provide | EQUALITY 15
c. the glittering | HUMAN RIGHTS 10
essence of the c. | ELECTIONS 5
its own c. | RUSSIA 15
constitutional c. eyes | PRESIDENCY 5
c. right | GOVERNMENT 28
construction mind's c. | APPEARANCE 14
consulted right to be c. | ROYALTY 29
consume born to c. resources | STATISTICS 3
consumer c. isn't a moron | ADVERTISING 15
c. is the king | BUYING 9
In a c. society | BUYING 10
consumption Conspicuous c. | POSSESSIONS 20
c. of the purse | POVERTY 15
metamorphosis of c. | POSSESSIONS 29
contact no plan survives first c. | PREPARATION 17
word preserves c. | SPEECH 25
contemporary hundred c. readers | WRITING 44
contempt Familiarity breeds c. | FAMILIARITY 21
Familiarity breeds c. | FAMILIARITY 5
contemptibles Old C. | WORLD W I 5
contender I could have been a c. | ACHIEVEMENT 28
content C. is disillusioning | SATISFACTION 32
land of lost c. | PAST 27
travellers must be c. | TRAVEL 15
contented C. wi' little | SATISFACTION 21
To be c. | SATISFACTION 38
contention bone of c. | ARGUMENT 7
contentment Preaches c. | SUFFERING 21
contest not the victory but the c. | WINNING 17
continence chastity and c. | SEX 8
continent brought forth upon this c. | DEMOCRACY 13
C. isolated | EUROPE 12
Dark C. | AFRICA 2
drifting c. | AFRICA 8
swallowed by an alien c. | CANADA 14
continuance in c. of time | TIME 28
continuation c. of politics by other means | WARFARE 27
continued soever it hath c. | LAW 17
continuing c. unto the end | THOROUGHNESS 11
continuity C. . . . . continuity | PAST 36
contraception easy c. and abortion | WOMEN 57
word about oral c. | PREGNANCY 14
contraceptive bent her c. coil | PARANORMAL 22
contract c. isn't worth the paper | LAW 36
indeed a c. | SOCIETY 7
nothing but a civil c. | MARRIAGE 20
tugging at every c. | SELF-INTEREST 25
contradict Do I c. myself | SELF 15
truth you cannot c. | TRUTH 12
contradiction at best a c. still | WOMEN 25
contradictory unrelated and even c. | CHARACTER 42
contraries Dreams go by c. | DREAMS 2
contrariwise 'C.,' continued Tweedledee | LOGIC 12
contrast enjoyment from a c. | CIRCUMSTANCE 22
control conscience well under c. | POLITICIANS 20
c. our thoughts | MORALITY 8
kept under c. | HONESTY 13
wrong members in c. | ENGLAND 27
controlled events have c. me | POWER 23
controlling (with luck, c.) the world | KNOWLEDGE 53
controls c. the past | POWER 30
new c. | CIRCUMSTANCE 2
convalescence I enjoy c. | SICKNESS 15
convenience C. next suggested | INVENTIONS 8
c. to liberty | CLASS 22

conveniences c. so much sought after | AUSTRALIA 10
convenient c. that there be gods | BELIEF 9
convention By c. there is colour | SENSES 4
conventional c. signs | MATHS 17
c. way to rise | CONFORMITY 14
conventionality C. is not morality | HYPOCRISY 15
conversation c. among gentlemen | CONVERSATION 9
c. perfectly delightful | PEOPLE 38
c.'s burrs | SPEECH 19
different name for c. | WRITING 18
no such thing as c. | CONVERSATION 18
proper subject of c. | CONVERSATION 8
rhymed c. | SINGING 14
spoiling c. | DOGS 7
subjects for elegant c. | CONVERSATION 17
conversations pictures or c. | BOOKS 12
convert who shall c. me | RELIGION 14
converted c. a man | CENSORSHIP 6
conveyance It's not a public c. | MARRIAGE 45
conviction best lack all c. | EXCELLENCE 14
c. and the will | LEADERSHIP 13
lack of rational c. | OPINION 24
convictions c. are hills | MIDDLE AGE 10
convinced c. beyond doubt | CERTAINTY 22
convinces c. the world | SCIENCE 16
convincing less c. than one | APOLOGY 19
cook between a chef and a c. | COOKING 38
c. in the kitchen | MEN AND WOMEN 30
C. is a little unnerved | MANNERS 22
c. is no better | COOKING 4
cookery Kissing don't last: c. do | COOKING 24
cookies stayed home and baked c. | WOMAN'S ROLE 34
cooking C. is the most ancient | COOKING 20
missionary position of c. | COOKING 37
cooks as c. go, she went | COOKING 28
c. who sport white caps | COOKING 3
count the c. | COOKING 14
Devil sends c. | COOKING 7
Too many c. spoil the broth | WORK 8
cool Be still and c. | PRAYER 16
C. Britannia | BRITAIN 1
try to look c. | LEADERSHIP 21
When I think of C. Britannia | BRITAIN 19
cooler c. to a hotter | PHYSICAL 16
coolness produced is c. | ARGUMENT 4
cooperation c. is unnecessary | COOPERATION 8
c. with good | GOOD 35
don't believe in c. | COOPERATION 7
Government and c. | COOPERATION 26
coot haunts of c. | RIVERS 9
copier c. of nature | PAINTING 8
copies Make c. | ORIGINALITY 11
many c. | HISTORY 16
Copperfield that David C. kind of crap | BIOGRAPHY 18
cops C. are like a doctor | CRIME 46
copulation Birth and c. | LIFE 44
Let c. thrive | SEX 13
copybook Gods of the C. Headings | CAUSES 24
coral build it up like c. insects | HATRED 13
cord threefold c. | STRENGTH 14
core ain't-a-going to be no c. | GRATITUDE 13
cork c. out of my lunch | ALCOHOL 26
corkscrews crooked as c. | EMOTIONS 20
corn c. in Egypt | EXCESS 12
make two ears of c. | PRACTICALITY 7
other men's c. | ROYALTY 2
corner c. of a foreign field | PATRIOTISM 19
just around the c. | OPTIMISM 32
on a street c. | POLITICIANS 29
coronets more than c. | RANK 9
corporal little C. | PEOPLE 23
corporation c. to have a conscience | BUSINESS 30
corporations [c.] cannot commit treason | BUSINESS 24
corpore *mens sana in c. sano* | HEALTH 12
corpse c. in a coffin | SICKNESS 9
good wishes to the c. | HUMAN NATURE 18
He'd make a lovely c. | DEATH 48

reform the c.	CRIME 31
crimson c. thread of kinship	AUSTRALIA 16
cringe Cultural C.	AUSTRALIA 21
cultural c.	AUSTRALIA 29
cripple cannot meet a c.	CONVERSATION 17
Comfort's a c.	NEWS 6
crises c. that seemed intolerable	PAST 33
crisis C.? What Crisis	CRISES 24
drama out of a c.	CRISES 3
nature fit for a great c.	CHARACTER 35
There cannot be a c.	CRISES 23
crisp eating one c.	READING 18
crisps like eating a bag of c.	SEX 43
criterion c. of wisdom	SUCCESS 26
critic c. is a man who knows	CRITICISM 26
c. is he who relates	CRITICISM 14
c. spits on what is done	POETRY 21
in honour of a c.	CRITICISM 21
criticism best place for c.	CRITICISM 1
c. is only applied	CRITICISM 15
C. is something you can avoid	CRITICISM 2
c.'s motto	CREATIVITY 17
from c. to nature	SHAKESPEARE 8
it permits c.	DEMOCRACY 22
People ask you for c.	CRITICISM 18
criticisms most penetrating of c.	CRITICISM 20
criticize c. what you can't understand	GENERATION GAP 16
criticized c. is not always	CRITICISM 24
If you are not c.	CRITICISM 30
critics c. are all ready made	CRITICISM 10
C. are like brushers	CRITICISM 4
c. know it	MUSIC 23
c. of the next	WRITING 35
You know who the c. are	CRITICISM 13
crocodile appeaser is one who feeds a c.	DIPLOMACY 5
c. tears	HYPOCRISY 5
crooked c. as corkscrews	EMOTIONS 20
C. things may be as stiff	MISTAKES 14
c. timber of humanity	HUMAN RACE 19
crop just another c., like cotton	TRAVEL 40
makes a good c.	CAUSES 5
cross bear the c. gladly	SUFFERING 8
c. a person's palm	FORESIGHT 6
c. the Rubicon	CRISES 4
c. the t's	HYPOTHESIS 8
C. to be borne	MARRIAGE 40
Don't c. the bridge	PREPARATION 2
inability to c. the street	FRIENDSHIP 22
no c., no crown	SUFFERING 13
replaced the C.	SEX 33
untenanted c.	FAITH 14
crosses Between the c., row on row	WORLD W I 15
C. are ladders	SUFFERING 2
cross-examination art of c.	LAW 38
crossness make c. and dirt succeed	WRITERS 21
crow before the cock c.	TRUST 20
cock will c.	HOME 3
one for the c.	FARMING 2
risen to hear him c.	SELF-ESTEEM 14
crowd c. of men	CONFORMITY 9
c. will always save Barabbas	CHOICE 22
crowded Across a c. room	MEETING 24
it was a bit c.	MARRIAGE 51
crowds talk with c.	MATURITY 9
crowing whistling woman and a c. hen	WOMEN 6
crown City of the Violet C.	TOWNS 8
C. is, according	GOVERNMENT 29
C. of Thorns	HYPOCRISY 15
c. thy good	AMERICA 24
glory of my c.	GOVERNMENT 11
head that wears a c.	ROYALTY 13
influence of the C.	ROYALTY 21
never wears the c.	TRUST 39
no cross, no c.	SUFFERING 13
strike his father's c.	SPORTS 6
crowning c. glory	BODY 5

c. mercy	WARS 6
crowns end c. the work	ENDING 4
crows c. begin to search	SEASONS 5
crucible America is God's C.	AMERICA 26
cast a violet into a c.	TRANSLATION 8
crucify would not even c. him	INDIFFERENCE 9
cruel c. and unusual punishment	CRIME 11
c. and unusual punishment	CRIME 26
c. as a small boy	CRUELTY 16
c. as the grave	ENVY 8
C., but composed	CATS 8
C. necessity	NECESSITY 19
c. only to be kind	CRUELTY 6
c. to be kind	CRUELTY 12
c. trade	POLITICS 21
c. works of nature	NATURE 14
Not that he's c.	HUNTING 16
wicked are c.	ANIMALS 11
cruellest c. month	SEASONS 24
cruelty Beauty without c.	SUFFERING 1
c. is not	FARMING 16
C., like every other vice	CRUELTY 9
c. with a good conscience	CRUELTY 11
To end c.	CHRISTIAN CH 46
crumbs covetous of their c.	CHARITY 17
crusade party is a moral c.	POLITICAL PART 36
cruse widow's c.	QUANTITIES 18
crust c. over a volcano	CULTURE 17
crutches Give the old crutches	OLD AGE 35
cry beer to c. into	ALCOHOL 24
can't c. on a shoulder	SYMPATHY 28
c. all the way to the bank	CRITICISM 23
c. before night	EMOTIONS 2
c. before you're hurt	COURAGE 5
c. wolf	DANGER 11
If something makes you c.	POLITICS 36
indeed they c.	SORROW 11
love to c. at weddings	WEDDINGS 16
Much c.	EFFORT 7
we can't c.	MEN 20
crying c. over spilt milk	MISFORTUNES 5
except those c.	MEN 21
cuckoo cloud c. land	REALITY 2
C.! Shall I call thee bird	BIRDS 10
Lhude sing c.	SEASONS 11
produce . . . ? The c. clock	CULTURE 23
weather the c. likes	WEATHER 48
cucumber c. should be well sliced	FOOD 13
cuddled c. by a complete stranger	CHILD CARE 19
cui C. bono	SELF-INTEREST 18
culpa mea c.	APOLOGY 8
cultivate c. one's garden	SELF-INTEREST 11
c. our garden	SELF-INTEREST 23
cultivators C. of the earth	FARMING 9
cultural c. Chernobyl	CULTURE 31
c. Chernobyl	CULTURE 32
C. Cringe	AUSTRALIA 21
c. cringe	AUSTRALIA 29
culture American c.	CANADA 13
central to our c.	FOOTBALL 13
core Of a world's c.	WORLD W II 25
C. may even be described	CULTURE 22
c. of the 1990s	CULTURE 34
c. to be colonised by	SCOTLAND 19
hears the word c.	CULTURE 29
hear the word c.	CULTURE 21
hear the word 'c.'	CULTURE 26
integral part of c.	SCIENCE 28
mechanics of c.	ARTS 29
own c. is not to die	CULTURE 28
Popular c. is a contradiction	CULTURE 33
pursue C. in bands	CULTURE 16
cultured C. people are merely	CULTURE 19
weren't considered c.	EUROPE 21
cultures C. of East and West	LIBRARIES 13
two c.	ARTS AND SCI 2
cunning c. purchase of my wealth	WEALTH 17

cunning (cont.)
I have a c. plan — IDEAS 1
cup c. o' kindness — MEMORY 10
c. run over — EXCESS 5
Full c., steady hand — CAUTION 7
'twixt c. and lip — MISTAKES 4
Cupar will to C. — DETERMINATION 3
cupboard skeleton in the c. — SECRECY 17
Cupid C.'s bow — BODY 6
C.'s dart — LOVE 15
victims of C. — KISSING 15
curate c.'s egg — CHARACTER 19
like a shabby c. — ARTS AND SCI 15
very name of a C. — CLERGY 16
cure better than c. — FORESIGHT 5
drunkard's c. is drink — DRUNKENNESS 1
for c., on exercise depend — HEALTH 14
half our c. — SICKNESS 11
No c., no pay — BUSINESS 10
once-bitten there is no c. — HUNTING 17
cured C. yesterday — MEDICINE 16
What can't be c. — PATIENCE 18
cures c. are suggested — MEDICINE 20
Like c. like — MEDICINE 5
curfew c. tolls the knell — DAY 8
curiosities c. would be quite forgot — GOSSIP 19
curiosity c. about the future — BIOGRAPHY 19
'satiable c. — KNOWLEDGE 14
curious c. engine — BODY 12
curiouser C. and curiouser — SURPRISE 11
curl Who had a little c. — BEHAVIOUR 21
currency debauch the c. — ECONOMICS 2
Europe to have one c. — MONEY 31
curried short horse is soon c. — WORK 7
curry c. favour — HYPOCRISY 2
curse c. of Cain — TRAVEL 3
c. of Scotland — SCOTLAND 1
c. the darkness — PEOPLE 55
foe may prove a c. — DECEPTION 15
I know how to c. — SWEARING 5
real c. of Eve — WOMEN 42
cursed c. that rascally thief — CRIME 30
curses Casual c. are the most effective — PARANORMAL 17
C., like chickens — HATRED 2
curst c. be he that moves — EPITAPHS 8
curtain bamboo c. — CAPITALISM 4
Bring down the c. — LAST WORDS 8
iron c. — CAPITALISM 6
iron c. — CAPITALISM 20
lets the c. fall — ORDER 13
curtsey C. while you're thinking — MANNERS 16
custard pie joke is ultimately a c. — HUMOUR 17
custodiet Quis c. — TRUST 21
custom conforms to c. — CONFORMITY 10
C. is mummified — CUSTOM 1
c. must give way to truth — CUSTOM 7
C. reconciles us — CUSTOM 13
C. that is before all law — CUSTOM 10
C., that unwritten law — CUSTOM 11
follow the c. — BEHAVIOUR 14
Lest one good c. — CHANGE 42
customer c. is always right — BUSINESS 5
c. is never wrong — BUSINESS 34
customers people of c. — BUSINESS 29
customs c. of his tribe — BRITAIN 9
cut c. his ear off — ARTS AND SCI 16
c. my conscience — CONSCIENCE 19
c. the Gordian knot — PROBLEMS 4
C. your coat — PRACTICALITY 1
cuts c. taken from Homer — ORIGINALITY 3
Diamond c. diamond — EQUALITY 2
cutting c. edge of the mind — ACTION 26
damned c. and slashing — PUBLISHING 6
cycle c. of Cathay — EUROPE 7
cyclops paralysed c. — PHOTOGRAPHY 12
cylinder in terms of the c. — PAINTING 14
cynical c. as a well-bred woman — DISILLUSION 16

cynicism C. is an unpleasant way — DISILLUSION 19
C. our shared common language — DISILLUSION 24

d never use a big, big D — SWEARING 7
dad girls in slacks remember d. — CHRISTMAS 15
really wanted was a d. — PARENTS 31
dada mama of d. — WRITERS 27
daddy D., what did you do — ARMED FORCES 2
daffodils D., That come before — FLOWERS 9
d. were for Wordsworth — INSIGHT 16
host, of golden d. — FLOWERS 6
daft thinks the tither d. — FOOLS 22
dagger d. in one hand — POLITICIANS 32
daily d. bread — WORK 15
dairymaid That strapping d. — SEASONS 32
daisies upon twelve d. — SEASONS 2
daisy 'd.,' or elles — FLOWERS 2
dam chickens and their d. — MOURNING 9
damage d. they have suffered — READING 19
d. your health — SMOKING 2
damaged Archangel a little d. — PEOPLE 36
D. people are dangerous — EXPERIENCE 38
damages d. his mind — MADNESS 2
dame nothin' like a d. — WOMEN 49
dames struts his d. — BIRDS 8
dammed saved by being d. — COUNTRIES 17
damn D. the age — WRITING 27
d. the consequences — DUTY 19
d. with faint praise — PRAISE 5
D. with faint praise — PRAISE 11
d. you England — ENGLAND 30
I don't give a d. — INDIFFERENCE 12
damnation blasted to eternal d. — SWEARING 9
damnations Twenty-nine distinct d. — BIBLE 16
damned brandy of the d. — MUSIC 14
d. lies and statistics — STATISTICS 7
d. of body and soul — PARENTS 12
one d. thing — LIFE 37
public be d. — BUSINESS 32
Publish and be d. — PUBLISHING 7
damnosa d. hereditas — MISFORTUNES 2
Damocles sword of D. — DANGER 19
Danaos timeo D. — TRUST 18
dance able to d. it — POETRY 39
before they d. — PROGRESS 9
d. is a measured pace — DANCE 7
D. is the hidden language — DANCE 17
d. must pay the fiddler — POWER 9
d. on the head of a pin — PHILOSOPHY 1
dancer form the d. — DANCE 12
d. wyt me, in irlaunde — IRELAND 9
departs too far from d. — MUSIC 19
face the music and d. — DANCE 14
On with the d. — DANCE 9
When you go to d. — DANCE 1
will you join the d. — DANCE 10
dancer d. from the dance — DANCE 12
shoes to be a d. — DANCE 2
dancers merry d. — SKIES 3
nation of d. — AFRICA 7
dances d. and its music — DANCE 16
d. to an ill tune — HOPE 2
no progress; it d. — DIPLOMACY 5
dancing d. cheek-to-cheek — DANCE 13
d. dogs and bears — ANIMALS 25
[D. is] a perpendicular — DANCE 15
d. is love's proper — DANCE 6
fairies left off d. — PAST 20
like a Mask d. — INSIGHT 17
Line d. is as sinful — DANCE 18
manners of a d. master — BEHAVIOUR 18
more than d. shoes — DANCE 2
dandy Candy is d. — ALCOHOL 23
I'm a Yankee Doodle D. — AMERICA 25
Dane-geld paying the D. — CORRUPTION 14

danger as to be out of d.   KNOWLEDGE 41
   Avoiding d. is no safer   DANGER 31
   common d.   DANGER 2
   d. chiefly lies   EXCELLENCE 9
   everything is in d.   PHILOSOPHY 15
   nettle of d.   DANGER 22
   One would be in less d.   FAMILY 21
   only when in d.   HUMAN NATURE 10
   out of d.   DEBT 7
   post of d.   DANGER 8
   twenty per cent of its d.   HUNTING 11
dangerous Damaged people are d.   EXPERIENCE 38
   d. to know   PEOPLE 35
   Delays are d.   HASTE 2
   knowledge is a d. thing   KNOWLEDGE 9
   learning is a d. thing   KNOWLEDGE 29
   most d. moment   REVOLUTION 18
   Nothing is more d.   IDEAS 13
   so many a d. thing   DREAMS 15
dangerously live d.   LIFESTYLES 24
dangers D. by being despised   DANGER 26
   perils and d.   DAY 6
Dante D., who loved well   HATRED 9
dare Letting 'I d. not'   FEAR 3
   none d. call it treason   TRUST 24
dares Who d. wins   DANGER 9
Darien upon a peak in D.   INVENTIONS 10
dark agree in the d.   INDIFFERENCE 5
   as good i' th' d.   EQUALITY 6
   blind man in a d. room   JUSTICE 30
   d. and stormy night   BEGINNING 7
   D. Continent   AFRICA 2
   d. night of the soul   DESPAIR 2
   D. with excessive bright   SIMILARITY 17
   feeling in the d.   INSIGHT 5
   grey in the d.   SIMILARITY 1
   head in the d.   GOOD 36
   leap in the d.   LAST WORDS 12
   one stride comes the d.   DAY 9
   we are for the d.   ENDING 14
   We work in the d.   ARTS 19
darkeneth d. counsel   ADVICE 12
darker I am the d. brother   RACE 14
darkest d. hour   OPTIMISM 3
darkly through a glass, d.   KNOWLEDGE 22
darkness cast out into outer d.   HEAVEN 7
   clutch out of the d.   CRIME 47
   curse the d.   PEOPLE 55
   d. buries all   ORDER 13
   d. there is light   INSIGHT 10
   leaves the world to d.   DAY 8
   Lighten our d.   DAY 6
   light in the d.   LIFE 49
   rear of d.   BIRDS 8
   rulers of the d.   SUPERNATURAL 9
darling old man's d.   MARRIAGE 1
   someone to call you d.   LOVE 72
dart Cupid's d.   LOVE 15
data d. was bound to be misleading   HYPOTHESIS 30
date d. on Saturday night   SEX 39
   d. which will live in infamy   WORLD W II 14
dates treason is a matter of d.   TRUST 28
dating d. in your thirties   COURTSHIP 17
   D. is a social engagement   COURTSHIP 16
daughter d. of Eve   WOMEN 9
   d. of Nigeria   AFRICA 14
   d. of the voice of God   DUTY 12
   d. on the stage   ACTING 8
   d.'s my daughter   PARENTS 2
   Like mother, like d.   FAMILY 6
   Whoever has a d.   WOMEN 18
daughters d. of Life's longing   PARENTS 16
   words are the d. of earth   WORDS 12
dauntless d. in war   HEROES 8
dauphin daylight's d.   BIRDS 15
Davy D. Jones's locker   SEA 4
dawn Bliss was it in that d.   REVOLUTION 13

   by the d.'s early   AMERICA 28
   just before d.   OPTIMISM 3
   sing at d.   SIMILARITY 20
day Action this d.   ACTION 2
   Another d.   OPTIMISM 3
   another d. older   DEBT 23
   arrow that flieth by d.   FEAR 2
   As the d. lengthens   WEATHER 2
   Be the day d.   PATIENCE 3
   better the d.   FESTIVALS 2
   breaks the blank d.   DAY 12
   bright d. is done   ENDING 14
   built in a d.   PATIENCE 12
   call it a d.   ENDING 21
   cares that infest the d.   DAY 11
   dog has his d.   OPPORTUNITY 4
   go to bed by d.   SEASONS 22
   hard d.'s night   DAY 22
   I have lost a d.   CHARITY 13
   jocund d. stands tiptoe   DAY 4
   knell of parting d.   DAY 8
   lived one d. as a tiger   HEROES 1
   make my d.   PREPARATION 19
   Not a d. without a line   PAINTING 2
   second on the d.   EMPLOYMENT 21
   Seize the d.   PRESENT 3
   So foul and fair a d.   WEATHER 34
   spent one whole d. well   VIRTUE 18
   Sufficient unto the d.   PRESENT 4
   Sufficient unto the d.   WORRY 4
   Tomorrow is another d.   FUTURE 5
   tomorrow is another d.   HOPE 21
   to rule the d.   SKIES 8
   what a d. may bring   FUTURE 11
   write every other d.   LETTERS 16
daydreams d. would darken   DREAMS 14
   exotic d.   CONFORMITY 14
daylight d. appears plainer   DAY 1
   d. in the mind   HAPPINESS 14
   d.'s dauphin   BIRDS 15
   let in d. upon magic   ROYALTY 28
days Ancient of D.   GOD 4
   borrowed d.   WEATHER 22
   d. are in the yellow   MIDDLE AGE 6
   D. are where we live   DAY 21
   d. never d.   EXPERIENCE 24
   d. of wine and roses   TRANSIENCE 13
   d. that are no more   MEMORY 13
   d. to Christmas   CHRISTMAS 1
   ends of smoky d.   DAY 16
   first 1,000 d.   BEGINNING 23
   good old d.   PAST 10
   happiest d. of your life   SCHOOLS 2
   multitude of d.   LIFE 23
   Nine Days' Queen   PEOPLE 16
   only three d. old   HUMAN RACE 27
   our eleven d.   TIME 1
   salad d.   YOUTH 4
   stink after three d.   ENTERTAINING 3
   takes less than three d.   CRICKET 14
   twelve d. of Christmas   CHRISTMAS 2
dazzled d. by the ways of God   FAITH 12
dead After that it's d.   NEWS 10
   Am I d. or am I not dead   PARANORMAL 7
   Better red than d.   CAPITALISM 3
   better than a d. lion   LIFE 5
   Blessed are the d.   DEATH 2
   blooming well d.   DEATH 61
   Born down in a d. man's town   POVERTY 33
   charity more than the d.   CHARITY 18
   cold and pure and very d.   UNIVERSITIES 20
   consistent people are the d.   CHANGE 46
   contend for HOMER d.   FAME 9
   d. 10 or 15 years   POLITICIANS 25
   d. and destroyed   DEATH 17
   D.! and . . . never called   MOURNING 17
   D. battles, like dead generals   WARFARE 57

dead (*cont.*)
d. bury the dead	MOURNING 3
d. fish swim	CONFORMITY 13
d. generations	CUSTOM 17
d. Indian	RACE 9
D. men don't bite	ENEMIES 1
d. men's bones	HYPOCRISY 10
d. men's shoes	AMBITION 3
d. men's shoes	POSSESSIONS 8
D. men tell no tales	SECRECY 1
d. shall not have died	DEMOCRACY 13
d. talk to you	MADNESS 16
d. thing that smells sweet	PAST 30
d. we owe only truth	REPUTATION 22
d. white European	MEN 4
d., who will not fight	LIFE 38
d. woman bites not	PRACTICALITY 4
democracy of the d.	CUSTOM 18
fell d.-*born from the press*	PUBLISHING 5
God is d.	GOD 29
I am d.	PARLIAMENT 21
if two of them are d.	SECRECY 12
judge the quick and the d.	HEAVEN 13
Kennedy was d.	MEMORY 29
know that I was d.	PARANORMAL 18
living dog better than a d. lion	VALUE 17
long time d.	LIFE 1
mansions of the d.	LIBRARIES 6
Never old, never d.	LOVE 34
Not many d.	BOREDOM 10
over the rich D.	DEATH 57
past is never d.	PAST 34
quick and the d.	TRANSPORT 16
speak ill of the d.	REPUTATION 8
There are no d.	DEATH 55
they're a' d.	SELF-ESTEEM 2
those who are d.	SOCIETY 7
three parts d.	FEAR 12
told me you were d.	MOURNING 16
unheroic D. who fed the guns	WORLD W I 25
until I drop d.	DETERMINATION 51
wealthy and d.	SLEEP 17
we are all d.	FUTURE 22
we'd rather be d.	LEISURE 10
Weep me not d.	MOURNING 10
with soul so d.	PATRIOTISM 14

dead-end d. kid — CRIME 12
deadener habit is a great d. — CUSTOM 22
dead-level d. of income — EQUALITY 14
deadly d. in the long run — EDUCATION 23
more d. than the male	WOMEN 2
more d. than the male	WOMEN 40
seven d. sins	SIN 5

Dead Sea D. fruit — DISILLUSION 2
like a D. fruit	POWER 33

deaf d. as an adder — SENSES 1
d. husband	MARRIAGE 3
none so d.	PREJUDICE 5

deal new d. — AMERICA 30
square d. afterwards	JUSTICE 32

deals D. are my art form — BUSINESS 47
dean no dogma, no D. — CLERGY 20
dear bread should be so d. — POVERTY 23
D. 338171	NAMES 11
Far-fetched and d.-bought	WOMEN 1
Gold may be bought too d.	VALUE 1
Plato is d. to me	TRUTH 13

death abolish the d. penalty — MURDER 16
All in the valley of D.	WARS 15
arts of d.	DEATH 54
Black D.	SICKNESS 4
Black Widow, d.	DEATH 67
Brother to D.	SLEEP 7
care a whit for d.	CONSCIENCE 9
certain, except d. and taxes	TAXES 14
copulation, and d.	LIFE 44
covenant with d.	DIPLOMACY 6

d. and taxes	CERTAINTY 3
D. and taxes and childbirth	PREGNANCY 10
D. be not proud	DEATH 29
d. hath ten thousand	DEATH 33
D. is a master	DEATH 66
[D. is] nature's way	DEATH 3
d. is not come	DEATH 20
d. is not far behind	OLD AGE 13
D. is nothing	DEATH 56
D. is nothing	DEATH 72
D. is the great leveller	DEATH 4
D. is the most convenient time	TAXES 16
D. is the only great emotion	WARFARE 66
d. is unreliable	DEATH 75
D. may be inevitable	FARMING 16
D. must be distinguished	DEATH 49
D. never takes the wise	DEATH 39
d. of some of her	PREGNANCY 8
d. on the hunting-field	HUNTING 19
D. pays all debts	DEATH 5
d. shall have no dominion	DEATH 64
d., the destroyer	PHYSICAL 5
D. tramples it	LIFE 26
d., where is thy sting	DEATH 22
D., where is thy sting-a-ling	WORLD W I 20
d., who had the soldier	DEATH 65
d. will seize the doctor	MEDICINE 4
Defer not charities till d.	CHARITY 16
die a youngman's d.	DEATH 69
died a good d.	HEROES 20
end to the exchange but d.	LETTERS 20
everything except d.	DEATH 8
Finality is d.	PERFECTION 10
finished by a d.	ENDING 17
frightened to d.	FEAR 8
give me d.	LIBERTY 14
If there wasn't d.	DEATH 70
image of d.	MEETING 15
in its d. throes	LANGUAGE 22
in love with d.	DEATH 47
just, and mighty D.	DEATH 31
laws of d.	COOPERATION 26
live in another's d.	DUTY 6
Love is as strong as d.	ENVY 8
Man has created d.	DEATH 63
matter of life and d.	FOOTBALL 9
My name is D.	DEATH 45
new terror to d.	BIOGRAPHY 8
no one his d.	DEATH 24
nothing but d.	CERTAINTY 19
One d. is a tragedy	DEATH 68
our Jubilee is d.	HAPPINESS 9
owe God a d.	DEATH 26
possessed by d.	DEATH 58
posterior to d.	LOVE 53
praying for d.	SEA 25
put the worst to d.	CRIME 33
Reports of my d.	MISTAKES 21
Satisfaction is d.	SATISFACTION 31
set d. aside	DEATH 50
shadow of d.	DANGER 20
sovereign is d.	ROYALTY 10
till d. us do part	MARRIAGE 21
up the line to d.	WORLD W I 19
wages of sin is d.	SIN 11
we are in d.	DEATH 37
When d. approached	BIRDS 7
white d.	SICKNESS 7
Why fear d.	LAST WORDS 24

death-sentence d. without a whimper — CHOICE 23
debate Rupert of D. — SPEECHES 13
debt d. of nature — DEATH 25
deeper in d.	DEBT 23
man in d.	DEBT 5
national d.	DEBT 6
National D.	DEBT 21
Out of d.	DEBT 7

promise made is a d. unpaid	TRUST 31
we are in d.	DEBT 19
debtor d. to his profession	EMPLOYMENT 8
debts Death pays all d.	DEATH 5
dies pays all d.	DEATH 30
If I hadn't my d.	DEBT 18
pay our d.	DEBT 24
decade d. of a man's life	MIDDLE AGE 5
decay Change and d.	CHANGE 39
mouthful of d.	ROYALTY 36
deceit D. is a lie	DECEPTION 2
deceive D. boys with toys	DECEPTION 10
Frauds d.	FAITH 13
practise to d.	DECEPTION 17
deceived willingness to be d.	BELIEF 27
deceivers Men were d.	MEN 6
deceiving d. your enemies	DECEPTION 20
December roses in D.	MEMORY 20
decencies Content to dwell in d.	VIRTUE 28
decency For want of d.	MANNERS 10
decent aristocracy to what is d.	CLASS 19
d. obscurity	LANGUAGES 10
deception D. is not as creative	DEATH 74
d. that elevates us	DECEPTION 21
deceptive Appearances are d.	APPEARANCE 2
decimal on d. points	MATHS 19
decision losses from a delayed d.	INDECISION 15
realistic d.	DISILLUSION 21
deck bottom of the d.	LAW 47
declare nothing to d.	GENIUS 10
decorate d. apartments	PAINTING 21
decorum cant about D.	LIFESTYLES 21
Dulce et d. est	PATRIOTISM 6
deduction logical d.	HYPOTHESIS 22
deed better the d.	FESTIVALS 2
d. is all	FAME 13
good d. in a naughty world	VIRTUE 21
No good d. goes unpunished	VIRTUE 4
tak the d.	WORDS AND DEEDS 11
thought, word, and d.	SIN 14
deeds means to do ill d.	OPPORTUNITY 25
nameless in worthy d.	FAME 8
deep cradle of the d.	SEA 16
d. are dumb	EMOTIONS 10
d. silent slide away	SILENCE 7
Out of the d.	SUFFERING 5
Still waters run d.	CHARACTER 11
wonders in the d.	SEA 8
defaced thy walls d.	SCULPTURE 4
defeat After Alamein never had a d.	WORLD W II 22
In d.: defiance	WARFARE 54
In d. unbeatable	PEOPLE 56
possibilities of d.	WINNING 16
recognize d. as his own	SUCCESS 41
defeated able to think isn't d.	WINNING 25
destroyed but not d.	WINNING 22
Down with the d.	WINNING 10
History to the d.	SUCCESS 39
not finished when he's d.	WINNING 24
only safe course for the d.	WINNING 7
people can't be d.	ARMED FORCES 8
defence best form of d.	COURAGE 1
d. of England	INTERNAT REL 27
Never make a d.	APOLOGY 10
only d. is in offence	WARFARE 41
defend d. to the death	CENSORSHIP 4
d. us from all perils	DAY 6
defending d. the standard	LIBERTY 35
deferred Hope d.	HOPE 3
Hope d.	HOPE 9
defiance In defeat: d.	WARFARE 54
defied Age will not be d.	OLD AGE 10
defiled pitch shall be d.	GOOD 2
pitch shall be d.	GOOD 14
definite d. maybe	INDECISION 14
definition d. is the enclosing	LANGUAGE 18
d. of hell	LEISURE 9

exact legal d.	LAW 33
shape and d.	LIFESTYLES 34
definitive do nothing d.	ARMED FORCES 22
deformed Age is d.	GENERATION GAP 6
degraded most d. of all the races	WALES 3
degrees boil at different d.	ANGER 11
set down to it by d.	ADVERSITY 15
deity D. and the Drains	PEOPLE 43
déja vu D. all over again	FORESIGHT 18
delay deny, or d.	JUSTICE 21
ever lost by d.	HASTE 20
delayed losses from a d. decision	INDECISION 15
only a d. failure	SUCCESS 44
delays D. are dangerous	HASTE 2
delegate d. authority	MANAGEMENT 13
when in trouble, d.	ADMINISTRATION 23
delenda D. est Carthago	ENEMIES 6
deleted Expletive d.	SWEARING 14
Delian D. problem	MATHS 2
deliberate Where both d.	LOVE 28
delight D. hath a joy in it	HUMOUR 5
firmness, and d.	ARCHITECTURE 5
go to it with d.	LIKES 5
labour we d. in	WORK 23
source of much d.	BODY 32
Studies serve for d.	EDUCATION 16
tube of d.	SMOKING 15
delightful guests can be d.	ENTERTAINING 19
delitabill Storys to rede ar d.	FICTION 6
deliver d. us from evil	TEMPTATION 7
deliverance d., both alike requited	DANGER 24
deliverer Great D.	PEOPLE 8
Delphic D. oracle	ADVICE 8
déluge *Apres nous le d.*	REVOLUTION 10
delusion added d.	SILENCE 12
demand nothing without a d.	POWER 22
demigods puny d. on stilts	UNIVERSITIES 21
demi-tasses villainous d.	CLASS 20
democracies in d. it is the only sacred thing	WEALTH 28
democracy arsenal of d.	WORLD W II 13
D. and proper drains	ENGLAND 26
d. can afford	IGNORANCE 24
D. is a *State*	DEMOCRACY 17
D. is better	DEMOCRACY 1
D. is the recurrent	DEMOCRACY 18
d. is the worst	DEMOCRACY 20
D. means government	DEMOCRACY 23
d. of the dead	CUSTOM 18
D. resumed her reign	ELECTIONS 9
D. substitutes election	DEMOCRACY 15
d. the whores are us	DEMOCRACY 25
d. unbearable	BROADCASTING 17
empire or a d.	RUSSIA 11
holy name of liberty or d.	WARFARE 50
justice makes d.	DEMOCRACY 19
little less d.	DEMOCRACY 21
no d. in physics	PHYSICAL 21
pollution of d.	CORRUPTION 18
safe for d.	DEMOCRACY 16
Two cheers for D.	DEMOCRACY 22
Under d. one party	POLITICAL PART 30
voting that's d.	DEMOCRACY 24
democrat Santa Claus is a D.	POLITICAL PART 44
Senator, and a D.	POLITICAL PART 31
democratic d. health of our country	POLITICAL PART 47
democrats lies about the D.	POLITICAL PART 29
demolition d. of a man	CRUELTY 15
demon Maxwell's d.	PHYSICAL 4
denial d. of life	DANGER 32
deny d., or delay	JUSTICE 21
D. self for self's sake	SELF 1
thou shalt d. me thrice	TRUST 20
You must d. yourself	SELF-SACRIFICE 5
denying they were d.	AUSTRALIA 31
depart he will not d. from it	CHILD CARE 3
department That's not my d.	DUTY 25
departure d. is defined	LIBERTY 20

depends d. on what the meaning	MEANING 17
d. what you mean	MEANING 15
depraved suddenly became d.	SIN 12
depravity sense of innate d.	SIN 24
depressed When you're depressed	OPTIMISM 34
depression d. when you lose yours	ECONOMICS 11
depressions what terrible d.	WRITING 8
deprivation D. is for me	INSIGHT 16
deputy read by d.	BOOKS 5
derangement nice d. of epitaphs	WIT 10
descent d. from a monkey	LIFE SCI 12
desert D. Fox	PEOPLE 6
d. rats	WORLD W II 4
my own d. places	FEAR 14
on the d. air	FAME 10
ship of the d.	ANIMALS 9
deserve advertising we d.	ADVERTISING 11
have done nothing to d.	BEAUTY 38
somehow haven't to d.	HOME 19
we'll d. it	SUCCESS 25
deserves criminal it d.	LAW 40
Everybody gets what he d.	WORLD W II 25
face he d.	APPEARANCE 28
good boy d. favour	MUSIC 1
desiccated d. calculating machine	LEADERSHIP 15
design not by a priori d.	LIFE SCI 20
designs Official d.	ARCHITECTURE 20
desipere d. in loco	FOOLS 10
desirable physically d.	APPEARANCE 31
desire d. accomplished is sweet	ACHIEVEMENT 11
d. for desires	BOREDOM 5
d. for their own happiness	SUFFERING 7
d. is for the woman	MEN AND WOMEN 8
d. should so many years	SEX 11
get your heart's desire	ACHIEVEMENT 23
provokes the d.	DRUNKENNESS 5
strong as sexual d.	SEX 7
Which of us has his d.	SATISFACTION 25
desired d. so much	POETS 21
desires d. but acts not	ACTION 21
d. of the heart	EMOTIONS 20
devices and d.	SIN 18
lopping off our d.	SATISFACTION 20
desiring d., of despair	HAPPINESS 6
desolation d. of war	PEACE 19
despair can never d.	HOPE 20
carrion comfort D.	DESPAIR 14
D. a smilingness assume	DESPAIR 7
D. is the price one pays	DESPAIR 17
D. seeks its own	DESPAIR 18
d. so absolute	DESPAIR 12
endure my own d.	HOPE 12
far side of d.	DESPAIR 16
In d. there are the most	DESPAIR 13
Magnaminious D.	DESPAIR 5
Mighty, and d.	FUTILITY 19
Never d.	HOPE 10
perish of d.	LIES 21
pressure of d.	SCULPTURE 5
sins of d.	SIN 33
some divine d.	SORROW 17
desperandum Nil desperandum	HOPE 10
desperate Beware of d. steps	CAUTION 23
D. diseases	NECESSITY 3
Diseases d. grown	MEDICINE 12
desperation lives of quiet d.	LIFE 32
despise can d. so entirely	SHAKESPEARE 12
Government I d.	GOVERNMENT 34
you d. the other	SHAKESPEARE 6
despised Dangers by being d.	DANGER 26
despotism d. or unlimited sovereignty	POWER 21
France was long a d.	FRANCE 11
destination could see our d.	EXPLORATION 15
destiny Anatomy is d.	BODY 14
fabric of human d.	GOOD 33
share a common d.	INTERNAT REL 37
walking with d.	CRISES 17

wiving go by d.	FATE 2
destroy d. the town to save it	WARS 25
Doth the winged life d.	TRANSIENCE 12
gods wish to d.	CRITICISM 22
man determined to d.	LOGIC 19
Whom the gods would d.	MADNESS 1
destroyed Carthage must be d.	ENEMIES 6
d. but not defeated	WINNING 22
ought to be d.	CENSORSHIP 2
treated generously or d.	REVENGE 12
destroyer d. of worlds	PHYSICAL 13
only a d.	POLLUTION 13
destroys d. those who practise it	VIOLENCE 21
destruction based on d. and despair	CIRCUMSTANCE 24
d. of the whole world	SELF 13
Pride goeth before d.	PRIDE 4
urge for d.	CREATIVITY 6
detail corroborative d.	FICTION 12
frittered away by d.	LIFE 31
details Devil is in the d.	ORDER 1
God is in the d.	ARCHITECTURE 19
suppresses idle d.	DAY 20
detect moment you d.	LIFE SCI 9
detector shock-proof shit d.	WRITING 47
determination Persistence and d.	DETERMINATION 43
determined d. fellow can do more	DETERMINATION 2
detest d. at leisure	HATRED 6
detrimental d. to keep it	ANGER 13
Deutschland master from D.	DEATH 66
de Valera Negotiating with D.	DIPLOMACY 13
deviation Without d. from the norm	SIMILARITY 25
devices d. and desires	SIN 18
devil apology for the D.	BIBLE 19
as you hate the d.	FRANCE 8
Better the d. you know	FAMILIARITY 1
covenant with the D.	MATHS 1
d. can cite Scripture	BIBLE 11
d. can quote Scripture	QUOTATIONS 1
d. damn thee	INSULTS 3
d. finds work	IDLENESS 3
d. have all the best	SINGING 1
D. howling 'Ho'	SCIENCE 17
D. is in the details	ORDER 1
d. is not so black	REPUTATION 4
d. looks after his own	CHANCE 3
d. makes his Christmas pies	LAW 1
d.'s children	CHANCE 4
D. sends cooks	COOKING 7
d.'s gold ring	GIFTS 3
D. should have right	JUSTICE 22
d.'s most devilish	REPUTATION 23
d.'s walking parody	ANIMALS 23
d.'s workshop	IDLENESS 4
D. take the hindmost	SELF-INTEREST 2
D. was sick	GRATITUDE 1
D. whoops	ARTS 18
D. will build a chapel	GOOD 9
d. would also build	GOOD 23
Drink and the d.	ALCOHOL 18
easier to raise the D.	BEGINNING 5
first Whig was the D.	POLITICAL PART 13
Give the D. his due	JUSTICE 6
good painter can draw a d.	PAINTING 1
Haste is from the D.	HASTE 4
home, as the D. said	LAW 4
nine times to the D.	GARDENS 5
of the D.'s party	POETS 14
old d.	HUMAN NATURE 4
over the D.'s back	SIN 2
printer's d.	PUBLISHING 1
reference to the d.	INTERNAT REL 29
renounce the d.	SIN 17
ride to the D.	POWER 8
sacrifice to God of the d.'s leavings	VIRTUE 27
shame the d.	TRUTH 4
sups with the D.	CAUTION 9
Talk of the D.	MEETING 3

d. within a dream	REALITY 9
d. yourself into a character	CHARACTER 18
glory and the d.	IMAGINATION 10
I have a d.	EQUALITY 17
love's young d.	LOVE 16
love's young d.	LOVE 43
salesman is got to d.	BUSINESS 37
sleep: perchance to d.	DEATH 27
vision, or a waking d.	DREAMS 10
dreamed d. of cheese	FOOD 17
d. that life was beauty	LIFE 28
dreamers d. of dreams	MUSICIANS 7
mere d. of another existence	WORDS AND DEEDS 17
dreaming d. I was a butterfly	SELF-KNOWLEDGE 2
d. of a white Christmas	CHRISTMAS 14
d. spires	BRITISH TOWNS 17
dreams armoured cars of d.	DREAMS 15
City of perspiring d.	UNIVERSITIES 27
D. go by contraries	DREAMS 2
d. is the royal road	DREAMS 13
d. or swords	BOOKS 17
D. retain the infirmities	DREAMS 3
I have bad d.	DREAMS 7
Morning d. come true	DREAMS 4
quick D.	DREAMS 11
rich, beyond the d. of avarice	WEALTH 24
scream for help in d.	DREAMS 17
see it in our d.	THEATRE 13
you tread on my d.	DREAMS 12
dreamt d. of in your philosophy	SUPERNATURAL 11
dregs d. are often filthy-tasting	REVENGE 19
dress article of d. without	TRANSPORT 26
changed our d., manners	TRANSPORT 24
d. of thought	LANGUAGE 11
d. of thought	STYLE 9
I d. sluts	FASHION 15
dressed d. up and no place to go	DRESS 15
dressing d. old words new	WRITING 13
drifting d. continent	AFRICA 8
drink d. and drive	ALCOHOL 2
D. and the devil	ALCOHOL 18
d., and to be merry	LIFESTYLES 12
D. deep, or taste not	KNOWLEDGE 29
D. is a great provoker	DRUNKENNESS 5
d. one another's healths	ALCOHOL 19
drunkard's cure is d.	DRUNKENNESS 1
little d. below	ALCOHOL 16
Nor any drop to d.	SEA 13
One more d.	DRUNKENNESS 16
reason why I don't d.	ALCOHOL 29
Refraining from strong d.	LIFESTYLES 14
strong d. is raging	ALCOHOL 8
you can't make him d.	DEFIANCE 4
drinka D. Pinta Milka Day	HEALTH 3
drinking d. is to continue	FESTIVALS 69
D. when we are not thirsty	HUMAN RACE 20
drinks d. as much as you	DRUNKENNESS 15
d. beer, thinks beer	DRUNKENNESS 2
dripping d. June sets all in tune	WEATHER 3
drive cannot d. you	REVENGE 24
can't d. the car	CRITICISM 26
difficult to d.	EDUCATION 22
drink and d.	ALCOHOL 2
d. a coach and six	WAYS 15
drives when the devil d.	NECESSITY 11
driving like the d. of Jehu	TRANSPORT 6
dromedary muse on d. trots	POETS 15
drop because of that missing d.	CHARITY 25
d. makes the cup run	EXCESS 5
d. out	LIFESTYLES 24
d. the pilot	TRUST 6
Nor any d. to drink	SEA 13
dropping Constant d. wears away	DETERMINATION 1
drops penny d.	INSIGHT 5
drought d. is destroying his roots	FARMING 13
d. of March	SEASONS 13
drove Sussex won't be d.	BRITISH TOWNS 10

drown I d. twa	RIVERS 2
drowned BETTER D. THAN DUFFERS	ACHIEVEMENT 26
d. now and again	SEA 19
nobody d.	SEA 23
you'll never be d.	FATE 3
drowning d. man will clutch	HOPE 1
like death by d.	SINGLE 10
not waving but d.	SOLITUDE 11
drudge his mother d.	ARTS 23
drug d. is neither moral or immoral	DRUGS 12
hope to end d. abuse	DRUGS 10
It's like a d.	MUSIC 34
literature is a d.	WRITING 29
most powerful d. used	WORDS 18
drugs D. don't cause today's	DRUGS 11
drum marching to a different d.	CONFORMITY 3
drummer hears a different d.	CONFORMITY 8
drunk appeal from Philip d.	OPINION 6
art of getting d.	DRUNKENNESS 7
d. for about a week	LIBRARIES 12
genteel when he gets d.	MANNERS 13
inarticulate, and then d.	ENTERTAINING 13
must get d.	DRUNKENNESS 8
think as you d. I am	DRUNKENNESS 11
What d., one sees	PEOPLE 53
when he was d.	FRIENDSHIP 19
when they're d.	MEN 25
Winston, you're d.	INSULTS 12
you ain't still d. tomorrow	DRUNKENNESS 13
You're not d.	DRUNKENNESS 18
drunkard d.'s cure is drink	DRUNKENNESS 1
drunken d. man uses lampposts	STATISTICS 9
sailors and d. men	DANGER 3
drunkenness d. of things being	SIMILARITY 23
dry dwelling in a d. place	WRITERS 10
into a d. Martini	ALCOHOL 6
Sow d.	GARDENS 6
till the well runs d.	GRATITUDE 4
Dryden D. wanted, or forgot	POETS 11
poetry of D.	POETRY 23
duchess chambermaid as of a D.	IMAGINATION 8
duchesses D. are doing	GOSSIP 21
duck break one's d.	CRICKET 2
D. and cover	CRISES 1
forgot to d.	WINNING 19
If it looks like a d.	HYPOTHESIS 24
duckling ugly d.	YOUTH 5
ducks d. who float	MEMORY 6
due Give the Devil his d.	JUSTICE 6
render everyone his d.	JUSTICE 20
duffers BETTER DROWNED THAN D.	ACHIEVEMENT 26
duke Iron D.	PEOPLE 9
dukes drawing room full of d.	ARTS AND SCI 15
d. are just as great	RANK 13
dulce D. et decorum est	PATRIOTISM 6
dull d. at whiles	DUTY 14
d. in himself	BOREDOM 3
d. it is to pause	IDLENESS 19
makes d. men witty	ANGER 7
makes Jack a d. boy	LEISURE 1
Safe is spelled D.	POLITICS 37
dullard d.'s envy	EXCELLENCE 13
dullness cardinal sin is d.	CINEMA 23
d. in others	BOREDOM 3
dum wrote d.-dum-*dee*-dum	SINGING 13
dumb deep are d.	EMOTIONS 10
d. son of a bitch	ARMED FORCES 45
d. year	SEASONS 1
So d. he can't fart	FOOLS 27
takes 40 d. animals	CRUELTY 1
dunces d. are all in confederacy	GENIUS 4
dungeon d. of self	SELF 20
dungfork d. in his hand	PRAYER 25
dunghill crowing on its own d.	PATRIOTISM 24
crow upon his own d.	HOME 3
Dunkirk appeals to the D. spirit	CRISES 20
D. spirit	CRISES 5

dupe d. of friendship — HATRED 7
duped than to be d. — FRIENDSHIP 13
dupes If hopes were d. — HOPE 19
duration for the d. — TIME 10
dusk d. with a light behind — APPEARANCE 21
falling of the d. — PHILOSOPHY 12
dust d. comes secretly — HOUSEWORK 10
d. enclosed here — EPITAPHS 8
d. of exploded beliefs — BELIEF 24
d. on the nettles — FLOWERS 11
d. the blinds — HOUSEWORK 12
d. thou art — DEATH 18
D. thou art — LIFE 27
d. to dust — DEATH 38
D. yourself off — DETERMINATION 44
Grind them into the d. — CRICKET 12
handful of d. — FEAR 11
life in the handful of d. — YOUTH 16
peck of March d. — WEATHER 11
raised a d. — KNOWLEDGE 28
This quiet D. — DEATH 51
To sweep the d. — PREPARATION 13
what a d. do I raise — SELF-ESTEEM 10
winning the palm without the d. — WINNING 8
with age and d. — TIME 27
dustbin d. of history — SUCCESS 37
d. upset — SLEEP 18
dusty d. answer — CERTAINTY 14
d. answer — SATISFACTION 9
eat d. bread — WOMEN 41
Dutch fault of the D. — INTERNAT REL 13
duties Property has its d. — POSSESSIONS 16
duty declares that it is his d. — DUTY 18
die in one's d. is life — DUTY 6
Do your d. — DUTY 9
Do your d. bravely — WORLD W I 9
d. bade me fight — ARMED FORCES 36
d. is the king's — CONSCIENCE 11
d. is useful in work — DUTY 21
D. is what no-one else will do — DUTY 26
d. of an Opposition — PARLIAMENT 17
d. of a soldier — ARMED FORCES 3
d. of man — LIFESTYLES 11
d. to serve society — RELIGION 16
d. to speak one's mind — DUTY 16
every man will do his d. — DUTY 11
from a sense of d. — DUTY 20
Immortality, D. — DUTY 15
inattentive to his d. — DUTY 13
life was d. — LIFE 28
voice of God! O D. — DUTY 12
We must do our d. — EUROPE 9
dwarfish What is an Epigram? a d. whole — WIT 13
dwarfs d. on the shoulders — PROGRESS 7
dyer like the d.'s hand — CIRCUMSTANCE 15
dying attend a d. animal — DEATH 62
dead or d. beast — POLITICAL PART 43
distinguished from d. — DEATH 49
d. breath of Socrates — PHYSICAL 11
d. for four thousand years — THEATRE 20
d. is more the survivors' — DEATH 59
d. of a hundred — SICKNESS 10
d. of the light — OLD AGE 26
d. without having laughed — HUMOUR 8
feel that he is d. — CRUELTY 5
If this is d. — LAST WORDS 26
indisposeth us for d. — DEATH 35
key to d. well — DEATH 78
nothing new in d. — SUICIDE 8
prayers of the d. — PRAYER 32
those of the d. — LOVE 63
those poor devils are d. — WARS 21
tree without it d. — CUSTOM 5
dyke February fill-d. — SEASONS 10
February fill d. — WEATHER 4
dynamite barrel of d. — POETRY 28

e I before e, except after c — WORDS 3
each To e. his own — JUSTICE 13
eagle Does the e. know — KNOWLEDGE 33
e. among blinking owls — POETS 16
E. has landed — SKIES 28
Fate is not an e. — FATE 21
Theban e. — POETS 7
eagles e. be gathered — GREED 4
E. don't catch flies — CHARACTER 6
ear cut his e. off — ARTS AND SCI 16
e. of him that hears it — HUMOUR 6
hearing of the e. — SENSES 3
heart was pierced through the e. — WORDS 8
out of a sow's e. — FUTILITY 7
penetrates the e. — MUSIC 24
resting a huge e. — UNIVERSE 9
right sow by the e. — PRACTICALITY 3
sow by the e. — KNOWLEDGE 12
than meets the e. — MEANING 5
earl fourteenth e. — RANK 20
earlier one I made e. — PREPARATION 7
earls Flight of the E. — IRELAND 4
early always too late or too e. — TIME 42
e. bird catches — PREPARATION 3
e. man never borrows — PREPARATION 4
E. to bed — HEALTH 4
E. to rise — SLEEP 17
get up e. — HEALTH 16
start e. — HASTE 3
think how e. I go — PUNCTUALITY 13
Vote e. — ELECTIONS 3
earned penny saved is a penny e. — THRIFT 3
earnest die in e. — DEATH 32
Life is e. — LIFE 27
earrings e. for under £1 — BUSINESS 49
ears adder that stoppeth her e. — DEFIANCE 9
between the e. — POETRY 40
e., and hear not — INDIFFERENCE 3
keep both e. to the ground — POLITICIANS 2
lend me your e. — SPEECHES 7
pitchers have large e. — SECRECY 5
Too beautiful for our e. — MUSIC 9
two e. and only one mouth — SPEECH 8
Walls have e. — SECRECY 13
wolf by the e. — CRISES 13
wolf by the e. — DANGER 12
woods have e. — SECRECY 3
earth all e. to love — BRITISH TOWNS 34
begins with a heap of e. — BEGINNING 18
but He craves the e. — EARTH 12
call this planet E. — EARTH 14
daughter of E. — SKIES 18
Did the e. move — SEX 8
e. does not argue — EARTH 8
e.; for it is his footstool — SWEARING 4
E. has not anything — BRITISH TOWNS 25
e. is the Lord's — EARTH 5
e. to earth — DEATH 38
feel the e. move — SEX 27
flowery lap of e. — POETS 18
girdle round the e. — HASTE 14
going to and fro in the e. — TRAVEL 13
heaven and a new e. — HEAVEN 9
heaven and the e. — BEGINNING 17
If all the e. were paper — WRITING 12
I will move the e. — TECHNOLOGY 5
Lie heavy on him, E. — EPITAPHS 9
low as where this e. — EARTH 7
more things in heaven and e. — SUPERNATURAL 11
On e. there is nothing — MIND 12
salt of the e. — VIRTUE 11
serious e. — CHRISTIAN CH 34
Spaceship E. — EARTH 11
surly bonds of e. — TRANSPORT 20
they shall inherit the e. — PRIDE 5
thought the E. was flat — MISTAKES 27
Which men call e. — EARTH 6

either happy could I be with e. — CHOICE 15
elaboration e. of ever more perfect eyes — LIFE SCI 21
elasticity e. to the spirit — HAPPINESS 22
elbow e. has a fascination — BEAUTY 25
elbow-chairs suggested e. — INVENTIONS 8
elderly I see it as an e. lady — CHRISTIAN CH 44
elders tried to vex my e. — GENERATION GAP 17
elect e. another — REVOLUTION 25
elected E. Silence, sing — SILENCE 13
election e. by the incompetent — DEMOCRACY 15
  e. is coming — ELECTIONS 7
  only during the e. — ELECTIONS 4
  right of e. — ELECTIONS 5
elections You won the e. — ELECTIONS 16
electric biggest e. train set — CINEMA 13
  body e. — BODY 17
  mend the E. Light — EMPLOYMENT 19
electrical e. skin and glaring eyes — CATS 6
electricity usefulness of e. — INVENTIONS 12
electrification e. of the whole — CAPITALISM 16
electronic e. interdependence recreates — TECHNOLOGY 18
elegant e. and sophisticated women — FASHION 15
elegantiarum arbiter e. — TASTE 1
elegy whole of Gray's E. — ACHIEVEMENT 15
elementary E., my dear Watson — INTELLIGENCE 1
elements Become our e. — SUFFERING 12
  four e. — UNIVERSE 2
elephant e., the only harmless — ANIMALS 13
  profile of an e. — HYPOTHESIS 2
  reality of the e. — INSIGHT 5
  They couldn't hit an e. — LAST WORDS 17
elephants take the shape of e. — LANGUAGE 27
elevates deception that e. us — DECEPTION 21
  e. above the vulgar herd — UNIVERSITIES 14
eleven fine before e. — WEATHER 12
  our e. days — TIME 1
eleven-plus e., sixteen-plus — UNIVERSITIES 26
eleventh at the e. hour — HASTE 10
  e. commandment — LIFESTYLES 4
Elgin E. Marbles — SCULPTURE 2
Elginbrodde Here lie I, Martin E. — EPITAPHS 17
eliminate e. evil — GOOD 43
eliminated e. the impossible — PROBLEMS 15
Eliot unpleasant to meet Mr E. — POETS 22
elite Internet is an e. organisation — COMPUTERS 16
élitist é. where they should be — UNIVERSITIES 30
elixir e. of life — LIFE 10
elm Every e. has its man — TREES 2
elms City of E. — AMERICAN CITIES 8
elopement e. would be preferable — WEDDINGS 11
eloquence Continual e. — SPEECH 14
  embellisher of ornate e. — POETS 8
  finest e. — SPEECHES 13
else happening to Somebody E. — HUMOUR 14
Elysian in the E. fields — PARLIAMENT 21
Elysium daughter of E. — HAPPINESS 18
embarras e. de richesse — EXCESS 13
embarrassment e. of riches — EXCESS 13
  keeps us in our place is e. — CLASS 31
  moment of e. — PHOTOGRAPHY 13
ember E. days — FESTIVALS 15
embody e. the Law — LAW 30
embrace brown e. eternal — EARTH 15
  It must e. everything — MUSIC 16
emendation e. wrong — CRITICISM 9
emerald E. Isle — IRELAND 3
emergencies e. of life — FORESIGHT 13
emigration written alot about e. — IRELAND 24
Emily E., hear — POETS 21
éminence é. cerise — ROYALTY 39
  é. grise — POWER 11
emolument positions of considerable e. — UNIVERSITIES 14
emotion conveying an e. — SCULPTURE 6
  Death is the only great e. — WARFARE 66
  e. without sex — SEX 46
  origin from e. — POETRY 14
  turning loose of e. — POETRY 26

  Wit is the epitaph of an e. — WIT 16
emotional e. promiscuity — EMOTIONS 25
  Gluttony is an e. escape — COOKING 34
emotions all the human e. — EMOTIONS 16
  confine themselves to the e. — ENVY 19
  e. in a plane — TRANSPORT 32
  gamut of the e. — ACTING 7
  strikes at the e. — BROADCASTING 16
  world of the e. — EMOTIONS 18
emperice e. and flour of floures — FLOWERS 2
emperor dey makes you E. — CRIME 42
  E. has nothing on — HONESTY 9
  E. is everything — ROYALTY 26
emperors E. can actually do — POWER 29
empire Celestial E. — COUNTRIES 2
  disposed of an e. — BRITAIN 12
  E. City — AMERICAN CITIES 12
  e. or a democracy — RUSSIA 11
  E. State — AMERICAN CITIES 13
  E. State of the South — AMERICAN CITIES 14
  great e. and little minds — POLITICS 13
  How's the E. — LAST WORDS 27
  ideological e. — COUNTRIES 36
  lost an e. — BRITAIN 13
  relic of E. — BRITAIN 15
  Roman, nor an e. — COUNTRIES 13
  To found a great e. — BUSINESS 29
  Westward the course of e. — AMERICA 11
  whole e. walking very slowly — WORLD W I 27
empires e. of the mind — EDUCATION 29
empirical nothing e. is Knowable — PHILOSOPHY 17
employee e. tends to rise — ADMINISTRATION 22
employers e. of past generations — EMPLOYMENT 23
employment e. to the artisan — EMPLOYMENT 19
emptiness e. The human lack — WORLD W II 25
  great Australian E. — AUSTRALIA 23
  testing his faith on e. — FAITH 14
empty Bring on the e. horses — CINEMA 9
  E. sacks will never stand — POVERTY 2
  e. spaces Between stars — FEAR 14
  E. vessels — FOOLS 2
  fear of e. spaces — CANADA 19
  leave a man's hands e. — CREATIVITY 17
enchanted Some e. evening — MEETING 24
enchantment Distance lends e. — APPEARANCE 6
  distance lends e. — COUNTRY AND TOWN 11
  Land of E. — AMERICAN CITIES 24
encounter Close E. — PARANORMAL 4
encourage right to e. — ROYALTY 29
encouraged He e. us — EPITAPHS 28
encouragement in love without e. — COURTSHIP 8
  sympathy and e. — COOPERATION 27
encourager e. les autres — MANAGEMENT 5
  pour e. les autres — WAYS 20
encyclopedias E., centuries — LIBRARIES 3
end beginning is my e. — BEGINNING 21
  beginning of the e. — ENDING 16
  Better is the e. — ENDING 12
  boys get at one e. — SCHOOLS 5
  came to an e. all wars — WORLD W I 22
  come to an e. — ENDING 1
  continuing unto the e. — THOROUGHNESS 11
  do not e. when you please — WARFARE 15
  e. as superstitions — TRUTH 30
  e. cannot justify — MORALITY 17
  e. crowns the work — ENDING 4
  e. for which — ENTERTAINING 10
  e. in doubts — CERTAINTY 8
  e. is my beginning — ENDING 6
  e. justifies the means — MORALITY 3
  e. justifies the means — WAYS 2
  e. of ane old song — SCOTLAND 7
  e. of a thousand years — EUROPE 16
  e. of civilization — CULTURE 3
  e. of history — HISTORY 28
  e. of love — LOVE 23

sells e. to get a toy	CAUSES 18
teacher affects e.	TEACHING 14
Time is e.	TIME 37
etherized e. upon a table	DAY 15
E. upon a table	POETRY 32
ethical e. foreign policy	INTERNAT REL 4
e. value of uncooked food	FOOD 23
Ethiop jewel in an E.'s ear	BEAUTY 12
Eton on the playing-fields of E.	WARFARE 49
on the playing fields of E.	WARS 14
eunuch Female E.	WOMEN 59
Time's e.	CREATIVITY 8
eunuchs E. boasting of their chastity	TEMPTATION 18
seraglio of e.	PARLIAMENT 25
euphemism e. for the fading power	OLD AGE 31
Eureka E.! I've got it	INVENTIONS 5
Europe Africa lies in E.	INTERNAT REL 22
cockpit of E.	EUROPE 1
community of E.	EUROPE 9
E. by her example	ENGLAND 11
E. is a continent	EUROPE 11
E. is the unfinished	AMERICA 37
E. that will decide	EUROPE 14
E. to have one currency	MONEY 31
E., where the history	EUROPE 23
E. would remain a torso	EUROPE 17
fifty years of E.	EUROPE 7
Garden of E.	EUROPE 3
glory of E.	EUROPE 5
keep up with Western E.	BRITAIN 14
lamps are going out all over E.	WORLD W I 8
last gentleman in E.	PEOPLE 45
poor are E.'s blacks	POVERTY 22
sick man of E.	COUNTRIES 11
This 'going into E.'	EUROPE 18
Transformations in Eastern E.	CAPITALISM 31
Whoever speaks of E.	EUROPE 8
European E. integration	EUROPE 22
E. male	MEN 4
E. super-State	EUROPE 20
E. view of a poet	EUROPE 10
unless you made the E. tour	EUROPE 21
Europeans second-hand E.	AUSTRALIA 19
You are learned E.	EUROPE 4
eve Adam dalfe and E. spane	CLASS 8
Adam delved and E. span	CLASS 2
daughter of E.	WOMEN 9
real curse of E.	WOMEN 42
even e. terror of their lives	LAW 43
get e.	REVENGE 2
evening e. full of the linnet's	DAY 14
e. is spread out	DAY 15
e. of life	OLD AGE 14
e. settles down	DAY 16
e. star	SKIES 1
e. star	SKIES 15
five o'clock in an e.	SEASONS 27
It is a beauteous e.	DAY 10
Now came still e.	DAY 7
Rilke in the e.	HUMAN NATURE 21
Some enchanted e.	MEETING 24
To see if e.	POETRY 32
evensong full-hearted e.	BIRDS 16
ringeth to e.	PATIENCE 3
event as the e. decides	ADVICE 16
hurries to the main e.	HASTE 12
name to the e.	GREATNESS 9
significance of an e.	PHOTOGRAPHY 5
wise after the e.	FORESIGHT 2
events e. cast their shadow	FUTURE 1
E., dear boy	POLITICS 34
e. have controlled me	POWER 23
e. overlapping each other	CIRCUMSTANCE 23
shape and direct e.	HISTORY 26
ever E. the same	CHANGE 11
for e. hold his peace	OPPORTUNITY 27
Hardly e.	CERTAINTY 16

Everest climbed Mount E.	SKIES 25
everlasting e. bliss	HEAVEN 10
evermore name liveth for e.	EPITAPHS 5
every E. day, in every way	MEDICINE 22
E. man for himself	SELF-INTEREST 1
E. man for himself	SELF-INTEREST 2
everybody E. has won	WINNING 15
e. is ignorant	IGNORANCE 22
E.'s business	DUTY 1
What e. says	TRUTH 8
everyday e. story	COUNTRY AND TOWN 1
Everyman E., I will go with thee	KNOWLEDGE 24
everyone e. is alike	SOCIETY 16
E. suddenly burst out	SINGING 11
stop e. from doing it	ADMINISTRATION 12
To be like e. else	CONFORMITY 16
You can't please e.	LIKES 5
everything Chips with e.	CHOICE 28
E. exists	FUTILITY 21
E. has an end	ENDING 5
E. has been said	DISILLUSION 10
e. in its place	ADMINISTRATION 8
E. is funny	HUMOUR 14
e. passes	LIFE 7
e. that is the case	UNIVERSE 10
Macaulay is of e.	CERTAINTY 12
Money isn't e.	MONEY 6
place for e.	ORDER 2
robbed a man of *e.*	POWER 31
sans e.	OLD AGE 8
tell e.	BOREDOM 2
time for e.	TIME 4
Universe and Everything	LIFE 53
voices talking about e.	BOOKS 29
We can't all do e.	ACHIEVEMENT 12
everywhere Water, water, e.	SEA 13
evidence before you have all the e.	HYPOTHESIS 17
e. of life	PARLIAMENT 26
give e. against	SPEECH 15
soldier said isn't e.	GOSSIP 10
supported by some e.	HYPOTHESIS 15
evil banality of e.	GOOD 41
book is a great e.	BOOKS 2
call e. good	HYPOCRISY 7
deeper than the evil	GUILT 13
deliver us from e.	TEMPTATION 7
Do e. in return	GOOD 38
eliminate e.	GOOD 43
E., be thou my good	GOOD 27
E. be to him	GOOD 3
e. can always find a home	HUMAN NATURE 19
E. communications	BEHAVIOUR 3
E. communications corrupt	MANNERS 9
e. cradling	BELIEF 13
E. doers	CONSCIENCE 3
e. from his youth	IMAGINATION 4
e. in return	GOOD 15
e. is simply ignorance	GOOD 36
e. that men do	GOOD 24
e. that walks Invisible	HYPOCRISY 5
e. to triumph	GOOD 29
e. were prevented	GOOD 22
e. which I would not	GOOD 18
face of 'e.'	GOOD 40
fight an e.	GOOD 39
God prepares e.	MADNESS 2
Good and e. shall not be held	GOOD 21
identified with e.	SICKNESS 24
is the e. thereof	PRESENT 4
I will fear no e.	DANGER 20
king's e.	SICKNESS 6
necessary e.	GOVERNMENT 20
Never do e.	GOOD 5
no e. in the atom	SCIENCE AND RELIG 14
non-cooperation with e.	GOOD 35
punishment is e.	CRIME 25
root of all e.	IDLENESS 7

faces (*cont.*)
they have everybody's f. — ACTING 4
fact by an ugly f. — HYPOTHESIS 18
F. is stranger — FICTION 1
foundation of f. — FICTION 10
Mistakes are a f. — MISTAKES 26
reaching after f. — CERTAINTY 10
When the legend becomes f. — JOURNALISM 23
faction whisper of a f. — DEMOCRACY 10
factories used to be prayer f. — CHRISTIAN CH 40
factory f. we make cosmetics — BUSINESS 45
facts accounted for *all* the f. — HYPOTHESIS 30
built up of f. — SCIENCE 14
empirical f. — HYPOTHESIS 22
F. alone are wanted — HYPOTHESIS 14
f. and experiments — HYPOTHESIS 11
f. are on expenses — JOURNALISM 28
f. are scared — JOURNALISM 17
F. are stubborn — HYPOTHESIS 2
F. do not cease to exist — HYPOTHESIS 21
imagination for his f. — SPEECHES 11
knowledge not of f. — EDUCATION 25
faculty cramps every f. — PARENTS 9
fade simply f. away — ARMED FORCES 37
Than to f. away — SUICIDE 12
faded beauty f. — BEAUTY 15
faery f. lands forlorn — IMAGINATION 12
fail F. better — SUCCESS 47
People f. you — RANK 21
failed f. in literature — CRITICISM 13
failure Any f. seems so total — YOUTH 28
end in f. — POLITICIANS 33
f. in life — SUCCESS 36
f. is an orphan — SUCCESS 10
F. of planning — COURAGE 34
only a delayed f. — SUCCESS 44
twentieth-century f. — SINGLE 11
failures provided us for our f. — RUSSIA 9
fainéant f. government — GOVERNMENT 30
faint damn with f. praise — PRAISE 5
Damn with f. praise — PRAISE 11
F. heart never won — COURAGE 6
F. yet pursuing — DETERMINATION 23
fair brave deserves the f. — COURAGE 17
brave deserve the f. — COURAGE 8
British f. play — JUSTICE 40
f. as is the rose — BEAUTY 9
f. exchange is no robbery — JUSTICE 3
f. in love and war — JUSTICE 1
f. of face — BEAUTY 5
f. play — JUSTICE 5
F. play's a jewel — JUSTICE 4
f. sex — WOMEN 11
If Saint Paul's day be f. — FESTIVALS 4
My f. lady — BRITISH TOWNS 6
Outward be f. — HYPOCRISY 14
right and f. — ARGUMENT 16
short-legged sex the f. sex — WOMEN 34
So foul and f. a day — WEATHER 34
to do with f. play — SPORTS 20
to show more f. — BRITISH TOWNS 25
Turn about is f. play — JUSTICE 9
fairer f. way is not much about — WAYS 19
fairies f. at the bottom — SUPERNATURAL 20
f. left off dancing — PAST 20
I don't believe in f. — SUPERNATURAL 22
fairness not equality or f. — LIBERTY 36
fairy believes it was a f. — SUPERNATURAL 14
He dug up a f.-mount — SUPERNATURAL 16
faith event which creates f. — FAITH 13
explosions of f. — RELIGION 29
f. and morals hold — ENGLAND 12
f. in honest doubt — CERTAINTY 13
f. in the people — GOVERNMENT 31
f. is something you die — FAITH 15
f. of the heart — FAITH 4
f. of those in the pulpit — FAITH 16

f. shines equal — COURAGE 25
f. that stands on authority — FAITH 8
f. unfaithful — CONSTANCY 15
F. will move mountains — FAITH 1
f. without f. — CERTAINTY 19
F. without works — FAITH 3
first article of my f. — VIOLENCE 9
great act of f. — FAITH 10
If ye have f. — FAITH 2
kept the f. — ACHIEVEMENT 13
now abideth f. — LOVE 21
Punic f. — TRUST 10
Sea of F. — FAITH 9
shake a man's f. — SELF-ESTEEM 19
still by f. he trod — FAITH 12
testing his f. — FAITH 14
thou of little f. — CERTAINTY 7
faithful f. in love — HEROES 8
f. to himself — FAITH 7
f. to thee, Cynara — CONSTANCY 16
f. to the state — POLITICIANS 4
seldom strictly f. — TRANSLATION 11
fake yours is a f. — SYMPATHY 26
falcon dapple-dawn-drawn F. — BIRDS 15
Falklands F. thing was a fight — WARS 29
fall diggeth a pit shall f. — CAUSES 14
divided we f. — COOPERATION 18
dividing we f. — AMERICA 12
f. flat on your face — PREJUDICE 20
f. for anything — CHARACTER 47
f. of the leaf — SEASONS 9
f. out with those we love — FORGIVENESS 20
f. without shaking — EFFORT 15
fear I to f. — AMBITION 10
fear no f. — PRIDE 6
harder they f. — SUCCESS 1
haughty spirit before a f. — PRIDE 4
horizontal f. — LIFE 42
Pride goes before a f. — PRIDE 2
rise by other's f. — SELF-INTEREST 20
Spring forward, f. back — TIME 3
Things f. apart — ORDER 16
When thieves f. out — CRIME 10
fallacy pathetic f. — EMOTIONS 4
fallen anybody f. by the wayside — SYMPATHY 23
f. among Fabians — PEOPLE 44
f. by the edge — GOSSIP 15
f. in love — LOVE 40
how are the mighty f. — GREATNESS 2
falling amidst a f. world — DEFIANCE 15
but by oft f. — DETERMINATION 28
f. domino — CAUSES 26
f. sickness — SICKNESS 5
falls apple never f. — FAMILY 1
As a tree f. — DEATH 1
f. on top of you — MISFORTUNES 29
false Beware of f. prophets — HYPOCRISY 9
f. guilt is guilt — GUILT 17
f. report — DECEPTION 12
f. that I advance — FOOLS 19
Ring out the f. — FESTIVALS 63
True and F. are attributes — TRUTH 19
falsehood F. has a perennial spring — LIES 14
Refraining from f. — LIFESTYLES 14
falsely kept him f. true — CONSTANCY 15
falseness proving their f. — HYPOTHESIS 15
falter moment that you f. — POLITICIANS 34
falters love that never f. — SELF-SACRIFICE 10
fame blush to find it f. — VIRTUE 29
Common f. is seldom — REPUTATION 7
F. has a bloody long — SUCCESS 49
F. is like a river — FAME 6
F. is the spur — FAME 7
F. vaporizes — CHARACTER 46
love and f. to nothingness do sink — VALUE 22
Man dreams of f. — MEN AND WOMEN 11
Temple of F. — JOURNALISM 7

fine (*cont.*)

think is particularly f.	WRITING 21
very f. cat	CATS 7
finer for the f. folk	CLASS 24
finest f. hour	SUCCESS 15
their f. hour	WORLD W II 11
finger chills the f.	SENSES 15
f. in the throat	MEDICINE 23
moving f. writes	PAST 25
scratching of my f.	SELF 13
fingernails finished the f. months ago	WORRY 13
paring his f.	ARTS 25
fingerprints f. across his brain	MUSICIANS 18
fingers f. do the walking	TECHNOLOGY 1
f. of cold	SEASONS 25
F. were made before forks	COOKING 6
in your yellow f.	SICKNESS 17
style flows from the f.	STYLE 23
finish F., good lady	ENDING 14
f. the job	ACHIEVEMENT 27
f. together	MUSICIANS 15
Nice guys f. last	SPORTS 1
started so I'll f.	BEGINNING 8
finished England is f.	ENGLAND 25
f. in half the time	COOPERATION 27
f. my course	ACHIEVEMENT 13
not f. when he's defeated	WINNING 24
this will not be f.	BEGINNING 23
finite f. quantities	MATHS 11
fire bad as a f.	CHANGE 13
before you stir his f.	FAMILIARITY 12
breathes f. into the equations	UNIVERSE 20
chestnuts out of the f.	DANGER 16
coals of f.	FORGIVENESS 7
don't one of you f. until you see	WARS 9
dreads the f.	EXPERIENCE 2
Fight f. with fire	WAYS 3
f. and brimstone	HEAVEN 3
F. and fleet	DEATH 9
f. and flet	HOME 8
f. brigade and the fire	PREJUDICE 16
f. from which I came	PARENTS 22
f.-glow in midnight skies	HATRED 17
f. has gone out	OLD AGE 34
f. in a crowded theatre	LIBERTY 25
f. in the last act	THEATRE 14
F. is a good servant	WAYS 4
f. to be lit	CHILDREN 7
f. upon his head	ENEMIES 5
heart is an organ of f.	EMOTIONS 27
her pale f.	SKIES 12
I didn't f. him	ARMED FORCES 45
into the f.	MISFORTUNES 11
kindles f.	ABSENCE 10
Love is a durable f.	LOVE 34
neighbour's house is on f.	PRACTICALITY 10
No smoke without f.	REPUTATION 9
play with f.	DANGER 5
set a house on f.	SELF 11
spark o' Nature's fire	EDUCATION 19
walk into the f.	EMPLOYMENT 15
wall next door catches f.	CRISES 10
will quench f.	SEX 2
world will end in f.	ENDING 18
write for the f.	WRITING 10
fire-folk look at all the f.	SKIES 19
firm family f.	ROYALTY 35
old f. is selling out	DISILLUSION 20
firmness f., and delight	ARCHITECTURE 5
first always a f. time	BEGINNING 14
cast the f. stone	CRITICISM 3
done for the f. time	CUSTOM 19
Eclipse f., the rest nowhere	WINNING 11
f. and second class	EQUALITY 15
F. Cause	BEGINNING 13
F. come, first served	PUNCTUALITY 3
F. Fleet	AUSTRALIA 5

f. fruits	FARMING 5
f. great sorrow	DESPAIR 12
F. impressions	BEGINNING 2
f. in a village	AMBITION 6
f. in the hearts	PRESIDENCY 4
f. Kinnock in a thousand	UNIVERSITIES 29
f. of human qualities	COURAGE 30
f. step	BEGINNING 6
f. step that is difficult	ACHIEVEMENT 16
F. things first	PATIENCE 5
F. things first	PREPARATION 20
f. war of the 21st century	WARS 33
magic of f. love	LOVE 45
no last nor f.	GOD 25
people who got there f.	FRIENDSHIP 29
retaliation in f.	REVENGE 23
truck with f. impulses	CAUTION 25
what to put f.	WRITING 14
firstborn her f. son	CHRISTMAS 5
first-foot f.	FESTIVALS 18
first-rate fashionable and f.	FASHION 8
mistake for the f.	QUANTITIES 25
fish Big f. eat little	POWER 1
cat would eat f.	INDECISION 2
dominion over the f.	HUMAN RACE 6
f. always stinks	LEADERSHIP 1
F. and guests stink	ENTERTAINING 3
f., flesh, and fowl	FOOD 7
f. in the sea	LOVE 12
f. is the movement	CATS 15
f. swim with the stream	CONFORMITY 13
f. that comes to the net	OPPORTUNITY 1
f. without a bicycle	MEN AND WOMEN 33
Give a man a f.	CHARITY 3
kettle of f.	ORDER 6
Little f. are sweet	QUANTITIES 2
neither f. nor flesh	CHARACTER 24
pretty kettle of f.	ROYALTY 32
surrounded by f.	ADMINISTRATION 16
fishes notes like little f.	MUSIC 21
fish-guts Keep your own f.	CHARITY 4
fishing angling or float f.	HUNTING 7
F. is a form of madness	HUNTING 17
fish-knives Phone for the f.	MANNERS 22
fist f. holds a stick	HATRED 16
fit f. for this world	LIFESTYLES 22
fitness no test of f. for it	CHILD CARE 12
fits If the cap f.	NAMES 2
If the shoe f.	NAMES 3
fittest f. who perished	CHANGE 50
survival of the f.	BUSINESS 33
survival of the f.	LIFE SCI 6
survival of the f.	LIFE SCI 13
five big f.	HUNTING 1
f. senses	SENSES 2
f. wits	MIND 2
happens *before* you count to f.	ANGER 14
only f. Kings left	ROYALTY 34
five-and-twenty reputation of f.	MIDDLE AGE 4
fix don't f. it	ACTION 5
Jim'll f. it	PROBLEMS 1
fizzy f., explosive stuff	CHRISTIAN CH 39
flabby f. exterior	CHARACTER 44
flag f. to which you have pledged	RACE 26
keep the red f. flying	POLITICAL PART 22
Trade follows the f.	BUSINESS 16
flagpole run it up the f.	ADVERTISING 2
flames F. for a year	LOVE 65
world in f.	PHILOSOPHY 9
Flanders F. poppy	WORLD W I 3
In F. fields	WORLD W I 15
swore terribly in F.	SWEARING 6
flashes f. of silence	PEOPLE 38
flat how f. and empty	AMERICAN CITIES 63
thought the Earth was f.	MISTAKES 27
Very f., Norfolk	BRITISH TOWNS 39
flattered f. any flesh	EPITAPHS 6

f. into virtue — VIRTUE 37
flatterers all the petty f. — PRAISE 7
tell him he hates f. — PRAISE 6
flattering f. a woman — PRAISE 17
flattery Everyone likes f. — ROYALTY 30
f. hurts no one — PRAISE 15
F. is soft soap — PRAISE 1
F., like perfume — PRAISE 2
sincerest form of f. — PRAISE 4
your f. is worth — PRAISE 12
flaunt f. it — SELF-ESTEEM 25
flavour f. of the month — FASHION 2
flaw no fault or f. — LAW 30
flea gripping a f. — PATIENCE 9
literature's performing f. — WRITERS 26
louse and a f. — EQUALITY 7
fleas F. know not whether — GREATNESS 6
get up with the f. — FAMILIARITY 7
smaller f. to bite 'em — QUANTITIES 21
flee f. when no man pursueth — COURAGE 11
fleet Fire and f. — DEATH 9
First F. — AUSTRALIA 5
Fleming F. was like a man — INVENTIONS 20
flesh All f. is as grass — TRANSIENCE 7
clay is the f. — IRELAND 20
come out in the f. — CHARACTER 16
flattered any f. — EPITAPHS 6
f. and fell — THOROUGHNESS 7
f., and fowl — FOOD 7
f. has bodily life — LIFE 8
f. is weak — TEMPTATION 8
f. of my flesh — WOMEN 14
F. perishes — FAMILY 20
f. was sacramental — SEX 30
hair of my f. — SUPERNATURAL 7
lusts of the f. — SIN 17
neither f. nor flesh — CHARACTER 24
not against f. and blood — SUPERNATURAL 9
pound of f. — DEBT 9
they shall be one f. — MARRIAGE 14
way of all f. — DEATH 13
world, the f., and the devil — TEMPTATION 5
world, the f., and the devil — TEMPTATION 10
fleshly f. school of poetry — POETS 2
flet fire and f. — HOME 8
flew f. through miserable weather — EXPLORATION 15
pushed and they f. — INSIGHT 15
flexible f. friend — DEBT 1
flies catches no f. — SILENCE 1
Eagles don't catch f. — CHARACTER 6
Honey catches more f. — WAYS 7
Lord of the F. — GOOD 11
time f. — TIME 19
Time f. — TRANSIENCE 3
flight as they take their f. — HAPPINESS 1
first solo transatlantic flight — TRANSPORT 28
F. of the Earls — IRELAND 4
F. of the Earls in reverse — IRELAND 24
flinched f., but he always went on — COURAGE 32
fling f. away ambition — AMBITION 11
f. the ringleaders — CRIME 29
float F. like a butterfly — SPORTS 24
floats f. on high — FLOWERS 6
She f., she hesitates — WOMEN 22
flock f. together — SIMILARITY 2
flog f. the rank and file — CRIME 29
flogging f. in our great schools — SCHOOLS 5
flood f. and field — EARTH 1
taken at the f. — OPPORTUNITY 26
flooded Engine room getting f. — LAST WORDS 23
STREETS F. — TOWNS 23
floods f. drown it — LOVE 19
floor f. without holding on — DRUNKENNESS 18
Florence Silicon Valley is the F. — COMPUTERS 21
Florey F. was like a man — INVENTIONS 20
flow f. of soul — CONVERSATION 3
flower f. of cities — BRITISH TOWNS 22

f. of safety — DANGER 22
f. of Scotland — SCOTLAND 15
f. power — IDEALISM 1
f. that's free — BRITISH TOWNS 41
f. thereof falleth away — TRANSIENCE 7
full many a f. — FAME 10
her f., her glory, pass — VALUE 19
other men's f. — ORIGINALITY 5
petals of a f. — GOD 37
Some achieve a f. — GARDENS 19
through the green fuse drives the f. — YOUTH 20
flower-pots Water your damned f. — HATRED 8
flowers Beware of men bearing f. — FLOWERS 15
bring forth May f. — WEATHER 1
flour of f. — FLOWERS 2
f. and Kings — HOUSEWORK 10
f. get the adoration — PARENTS 29
f. in the bride's hand — WEDDINGS 10
gardener to love f. — GARDENS 3
gave us f. and trees — SICKNESS 19
In Brazil they throw f. — COUNTRIES 28
No f. by request — MOURNING 4
No f., by request — STYLE 17
No fruits, no f. — SEASONS 20
path is strewed with f. — UNIVERSITIES 10
planet without f. — FLOWERS 14
Say it with f. — FLOWERS 1
flowery Showery, F., Bowery — SEASONS 17
flowing land f. with milk and honey — WEALTH 14
flown bird has f. — LIBERTY 2
birds are f. — PARLIAMENT 13
flutter f. the dovecotes — ORDER 5
fly f. in amber — PAST 9
f. in the ointment — SATISFACTION 10
f. on the wheel — SELF-ESTEEM 4
f. sat upon the axle-tree — SELF-ESTEEM 4
f. the way out — PHILOSOPHY 20
He wouldn't hurt a f. — HUNTING 16
His wisdom made the f. — ANIMALS 27
man is not a f. — BODY 15
noise of a f. — PRAYER 13
Pigs may f. — BELIEF 4
pigs might f. — BELIEF 7
which way shall I f. — HEAVEN 14
fly-bottle way out of the f. — PHILOSOPHY 20
flying Unidentified F. Object — PARANORMAL 6
Flying Scotsman F. is no less splendid — INDECISION 11
foe find a f. — ENEMIES 18
f. may prove a curse — DECEPTION 15
furnace for your f. — ENEMIES 10
robbing of a f. — DECEPTION 16
who never made a f. — ENEMIES 14
willing f. — ARMED FORCES 9
foemen f. worthy of their steel — ENEMIES 13
foes judge of a man by his f. — ENEMIES 16
fog f. comes on little cat feet — WEATHER 46
F. in Channel — EUROPE 12
f., miss — WEATHER 41
yellow f. that rubs its back — WEATHER 47
fold Do not f. — COMPUTERS 1
folk queer as f. — HUMAN NATURE 3
story of country f. — COUNTRY AND TOWN 1
trouble with a f. song — MUSIC 20
wee f. — SUPERNATURAL 5
folk-dancing incest and f. — EXPERIENCE 13
folks strokes for different f. — CHOICE 1
folktales f. of the village — CULTURE 35
follies f. and misfortunes — HISTORY 11
follow f. the custom — BEHAVIOUR 14
follower also a good f. — LEADERSHIP 2
follows He that f. freits — FUTURE 2
folly according to his f. — FOOLS 8
effects of f. — FOOLS 23
Fashion, though F.'s child — FASHION 6
f.'s all they've taught — COURTSHIP 7
F.'s at full length — FOOLS 18
f. to be wise — IGNORANCE 15

fox (cont.)

f. from a fax-machine	COUNTRY AND TOWN 28
f. knows many things	KNOWLEDGE 16
galloping after a f.	HUNTING 12
loves the f. less	HUNTING 10
prince must be a f.	LEADERSHIP 7
quick brown f.	LANGUAGE 1

foxes f. have a sincere — ELECTIONS 7

f. have holes	HOME 10
If killing f. is necessary	HUNTING 20
second to the f.	CHARACTER 42

foxholes f. or graveyards — RACE 24

fox-hunting prefer f. — POLITICAL PART 26

fragments characteristic f. — ENGLAND 28

tramples it to f.	LIFE 26

frailty F., thy name is woman — WOMEN 20

frame f. of nature — DEFIANCE 15

framed f. and glazed — SEASONS 16

France breasts by which F. is fed — FRANCE 5

F. all is permitted	COUNTRIES 32
F. has lost a battle	WORLD W II 10
F. has more need of me	FRANCE 9
F. was long a despotism	FRANCE 11
F. will say that I am	RACE 15
La Belle F.	FRANCE 2
matter better in F.	FRANCE 6
sweet enemy, F.	FRANCE 4
vasty fields of F.	THEATRE 5

Francis dear St F. of Assissi — POVERTY 25

Frankenstein F.'s monster — PROBLEMS 5

fraternité Égalité! F. — HUMAN RIGHTS 1

fraud Force, and f., are in war — WARFARE 18

frauds F. deceive — FAITH 13

great men are f.	GREATNESS 12

freak still an A I f. — CONFORMITY 17

freckled whatever is fickle, f. — BEAUTY 23

free believes itself to be f. — ELECTIONS 4

best things in life are f.	POSSESSIONS 22
born f.	HUMAN RIGHTS 14
but it's f.	LIBERTY 38
chains than to be f.	LIBERTY 27
condemned to be f.	LIBERTY 29
England should be f.	DRUNKENNESS 9
Everybody favours f. speech	CENSORSHIP 9
everything f. in America	AMERICA 35
flower that's f.	BRITISH TOWNS 41
f. agent that you were	THINKING 9
f. and equal	EQUALITY 9
F. at last	EPITAPHS 26
f. lunch	ECONOMICS 2
f. man shall be taken	HUMAN RIGHTS 4
f. or die	ENGLAND 12
F. Quebec	CANADA 15
f. society cannot help	SOCIETY 17
f. speech would not	LIBERTY 25
he's f. again	POWER 31
I am a f. man	POLITICAL PART 31
I am a f. man	SELF 24
ignorant and f.	CULTURE 10
Land of the F.	AMERICA 6
land of the f.	AMERICA 14
man a f. hand	SEX 26
Man was born f.	LIBERTY 12
powerful and f.	HUMAN RACE 21
prison, I am not f.	EQUALITY 13
things in life are f.	MONEY 2
Thought is f.	OPINION 4
truth shall make you f.	TRUTH 14
truth which makes men f.	TRUTH 37
Universe is a f. lunch	UNIVERSE 22
workers are perfectly f.	EMPLOYMENT 15
write f. verse	POETRY 33
yearning to breathe f.	AMERICA 22

freedom better organized than f. — LIBERTY 23

Bird of F.	AMERICA 4
can often picture f.	MIND 22
enemies of F.	LIBERTY 30

f. alone that we fight	SCOTLAND 3
F. and slavery	LIBERTY 32
f. and truth	DRESS 13
F. and Whisky	ALCOHOL 13
F. cannot exist	LIBERTY 20
F. comes from lack	JOURNALISM 25
f. depends on being courageous	COURAGE 12
f. for the one	LIBERTY 24
F. is about the willingness	LIBERTY 40
F. is not something	LIBERTY 33
F. is the freedom to say	LIBERTY 31
F. of the press	JOURNALISM 22
F.'s just another word	LIBERTY 38
f. there will be no State	GOVERNMENT 35
f. to offend	CENSORSHIP 21
f. to the slave	LIBERTY 21
f. to use them	POSSESSIONS 25
f. women were supposed to have	WOMEN 57
greatest f. a man can ever know	HEALTH 18
infringement of human f.	NECESSITY 23
means by defending f.	LIBERTY 35
my life for f.	SELF-SACRIFICE 9
not f., but licence	LIBERTY 10
regard for human f.	HEROES 11
road towards f.	ORDER 17
separate peace from f.	PEACE 27
to fight for f.	WOMAN'S ROLE 24

freedoms four essential human f. — HUMAN RIGHTS 13

four f.	HUMAN RIGHTS 2

freehold given to none f. — LIFE 15

freeze f. my humanity — PREGNANCY 11

to f. the blood	STYLE 12

freits He that follows f. — FUTURE 2

French always have spoken F. — LANGUAGES 8

clear is not F.	FRANCE 7
Excuse my F.	SWEARING 1
F. are with equal advantage	INTERNAT REL 13
F. is the patois	LANGUAGES 11
F. noblesse had been	FRANCE 14
F. she spak ful faire	LANGUAGES 3
F. soul is stronger	FRANCE 13
F. went in to protect	EUROPE 19
men, F.	LANGUAGES 4
no more F.	SCHOOLS 1
on speaking F. fluently	FRANCE 15
We are not F.	SEX 32
We F., we English	CANADA 12

Frenchman species of F. — MATHS 14

You must hate a F.	FRANCE 8

Frenchmen beat three F. — FRANCE 1

frequency very fact of f. — FAMILIARITY 19

fresh f. fields — CHANGE 20

f. woods	CHANGE 30

fret f. a passage — APPEARANCE 15

Freud trouble with F. — HUMOUR 21

Freude F., schöner Götterfunken — HAPPINESS 18

friction f. which no man can imagine — WARFARE 26

Friday F.'s child is loving — GIFTS 2

Good F.	FESTIVALS 23

fridge he rarely hits the f. — FOOD 30

friend as you choose a f. — READING 6

become a man's f.	FRIENDSHIP 21
betraying my f.	PATRIOTISM 27
Boldness be my f.	COURAGE 14
breaking it in for a f.	NAMES 15
candid f.	FRIENDSHIP 17
diamonds are a girl's best f.	WEALTH 34
enemy and your f.	GOSSIP 25
four-legged f.	ANIMALS 29
f. in need	FRIENDSHIP 2
f. is to be one	FRIENDSHIP 18
f. of every country	PATRIOTISM 17
f. that sticketh closer	FRIENDSHIP 9
f. that will go to jail	INDIFFERENCE 1
He makes no f.	ENEMIES 14
In every f. we lose	MOURNING 12
Is such a f.	FRIENDSHIP 15

last best f. am I	DEATH 45
lose a f.	PAINTING 20
lose your f.	DEBT 4
much-loved and elegant f.	ARCHITECTURE 21
pretended f. is worse	DECEPTION 15
Reagan for his best f.	PEOPLE 57
'Strange friend,' I said	FUTILITY 20
To find a f.	FRIENDSHIP 24
Whenever a f. succeeds	SUCCESS 45
friendliness friendship and f.	FRIENDSHIP 27
friends as well as by his f.	ENEMIES 16
Be kind to your f.	FRIENDSHIP 1
best f. are white boys	RACE 19
book is the best of f.	BOOKS 11
cheating of our f.	DECEPTION 16
closest f. won't tell you	HEALTH 5
comes to meet one's f.	THEATRE 11
deceiving your f.	DECEPTION 20
deserting f. conciliates	RELATIONSHIPS 10
doubt one's f.	FRIENDSHIP 13
enemies are my f.	ENEMIES 2
few of his f.' houses	SICKNESS 12
forgive our f.	FORGIVENESS 13
f. are necessarily	FRIENDSHIP 29
f. ashamed to look	HUMOUR 7
f. do not need it	APOLOGY 15
f. in politics	POLITICIANS 35
f. must part	MEETING 1
F., Romans, countrymen	SPEECHES 7
f. with its grandfathers	GENERATION GAP 13
has a thousand f.	RELATIONSHIPS 4
help from my f.	FRIENDSHIP 28
his life for his f.	SELF-SACRIFICE 3
How to win f.	SUCCESS 38
If they were not my f.	FRIENDSHIP 30
I had such f.	FRIENDSHIP 23
I have lost f.	FRIENDSHIP 22
intimate sharing between f.	PRAYER 11
lay down his f. for his life	TRUST 35
less f. you will have	ARGUMENT 3
misfortune of our best f.	MISFORTUNES 19
no absent f.	ABSENCE 15
Old f. are best	FAMILIARITY 15
reckonings make long f.	DEBT 8
remembering my good f.	FRIENDSHIP 11
Save us from our f.	FRIENDSHIP 5
tell it to your f.	ENVY 14
Tories remember their f.	POLITICAL PART 23
We make our f.	HOME 18
friendship clasped in f.	RELATIONSHIPS 20
disease called f.	LETTERS 21
dupe of f.	HATRED 7
F. a disinterested commerce	RELATIONSHIPS 6
f. closes its eyes	RELATIONSHIPS 1
f. in constant repair	FRIENDSHIP 14
Levin wanted f.	FRIENDSHIP 27
moving towards f.	TRUST 41
friendships F. begin with liking	FRIENDSHIP 20
fright f. and a hiss	SICKNESS 25
frighten by God, they f. me	ARMED FORCES 25
frightened f. to death	FEAR 8
frightening never more f.	CERTAINTY 22
frightens Only the unknown f.	FAMILIARITY 22
frivolous memoirs of the f.	BIOGRAPHY 15
frog f. remains	LIFE SCI 23
leap-splash—a f.	ANIMALS 15
frogs F. . . . are slightly better than Huns	TRAVEL 35
f. don't die for 'fun'	CRUELTY 4
frontier f. of my Person	SELF 23
frontiers f. are gone	INTERNAT REL 27
rolled back the f.	EUROPE 20
frost f. performs its secret ministry	WEATHER 38
frostbite God of f.	RUSSIA 2
frosts so many f. in May	WEATHER 18
froth Life is mostly f.	LIFE 34
frozen f. music	ARCHITECTURE 8
Locked and f.	SYMPATHY 24

fruit Dead Sea f.	DISILLUSION 2
exotic f.	IGNORANCE 20
forbidden f.	PLEASURE 4
f. of memory	MEMORY 21
f. that can fall	EFFORT 2
He that would eat the f.	EFFORT 3
humid nightblue f.	SKIES 23
known by its f.	CHARACTER 13
like a Dead Sea f.	POWER 33
Stolen f. is sweet	TEMPTATION 2
success is like fresh f.	SUCCESS 49
till the f.'s in the loft	WEATHER 17
When all f. fails	NECESSITY 12
fruitfulness mellow f.	SEASONS 18
fruits first f.	FARMING 5
No f., no flowers	SEASONS 20
frying pan frizzled in my f.	EMPLOYMENT 15
out of the f.	MISFORTUNES 11
fuck They f. you up	CHILD CARE 1
word 'f.' is particularly diabolical	SWEARING 11
fudge f. and mudge	INDECISION 7
fugaces Eheu f. Labuntur anni	TRANSIENCE 6
fugitive f. and cloistered virtue	VIRTUE 24
fulfil what you can't f.	ADVERTISING 2
full F. cup, steady hand	CAUTION 7
f. man and a fasting	FOOD 5
fuller's earth f.'s for reputations	MONEY 29
fun Cancer can be rather f.	SICKNESS 18
expert f.	KNOWLEDGE 50
frogs don't die for 'f.'	CRUELTY 4
F. is fun	HUMOUR 15
f. you *think* they had	ENVY 20
got to be a f. activity	POLITICS 37
Haute Couture should be f.	DRESS 25
have all the f.	PLEASURE 26
I rhyme for f.	POETRY 13
most f. I ever had	SEX 42
no reference to f.	PLEASURE 27
people have f.	PLEASURE 15
slaughter ought not to be f.	HUNTING 20
two is f.	CHILDREN 2
function Form follows f.	ARCHITECTURE 10
functions f. are dignified	GOVERNMENT 33
fundament frigid upon the f.	SENSES 15
fundamental f. things of life	KISSING 10
funeral Dream of a f.	DREAMS 7
for the f. expenses	ADVERSITY 13
f. baked meats	THRIFT 11
jolly at my f.	MOURNING 22
One f. makes many	DEATH 6
present is the f.	PRESENT 7
funerals weddings is sadder than f.	WEDDINGS 15
funk blue f.	FEAR 9
funny Everything is f.	HUMOUR 14
f. ha-ha	HUMOUR 16
f. is subversive	HUMOUR 17
f. old world	EXPERIENCE 32
nothing could be that f.	HUMOUR 26
funny-peculiar F. or funny ha-ha	HUMOUR 16
fur to make a f. coat	CRUELTY 1
furiously he driveth f.	TRANSPORT 6
ideas sleep f.	LANGUAGE 25
furnace f. for your foe	ENEMIES 10
gone out in the f.	OLD AGE 34
psychopath is the f.	MADNESS 17
furnaces Your worship is your f.	TECHNOLOGY 10
furniture don't trip over the f.	ACTING 2
f. so charming	BOOKS 12
piece of moving f.	DOGS 13
rearranges the f.	FICTION 21
rearrange the f.	FUTILITY 27
stocked with all the f.	LIBRARIES 10
further explored the f. reaches	MARRIAGE 54
f. away than anywhere else	COUNTRY AND TOWN 26
Go f. and fare	SATISFACTION 3
Hell—but no f.	DIPLOMACY 4
fury full of sound and f.	LIFE 19

fury (*cont.*)
f. of the patient man	PATIENCE 24
Hell hath no f.	WOMEN 4
nothing but beastly f.	FOOTBALL 3

furze f. is in bloom — LOVE 14

fuse force that through the green f. — YOUTH 20
| line is a f. | POETRY 28 |

fusion cold f. — PHYSICAL 1
futility not fertility but f. — PREGNANCY 21
future controls the f. — POWER 30
curiosity about the f.	BIOGRAPHY 19
empires of the f.	EDUCATION 29
every sinner has a f.	SIN 27
fight against the f.	FUTURE 19
f. ain't what it used to be	FUTURE 27
F. as a promised land	FUTURE 24
f. refusing to be born	POLITICAL PART 32
f. shock	PROGRESS 2
grieve for the f.	PRESENT 1
I have seen the f.	CAPITALISM 15
I never think of the f.	FUTURE 23
lets the f. in	CHILDREN 20
no f. like the present	FUTURE 3
past, present and future	TIME 45
picture of the f.	FUTURE 25
plan the f.	FORESIGHT 12
present in time f.	TIME 41
quick perspective of the f.	TECHNOLOGY 12
reputation for his f.	REPUTATION 7
work for the f.	PAST 44

gabardine spit upon my Jewish g. — RACE 6
gadgets servant is worth a thousand g. — TECHNOLOGY 14
Gaels G. of Ireland — IRELAND 15
gag g. of place — IRELAND 22
Gaia G. hypothesis — EARTH 2
| G. is a tough bitch | EARTH 17 |
gaiety g. of nations — HAPPINESS 5
gain another man's g. — CIRCUMSTANCE 3
g. of a few	POLITICAL PART 12
g. that which is worth	SELF-SACRIFICE 15
g. the whole world	SUCCESS 22
g., you gain all	GOD 19
No pain, no g.	EFFORT 8
Nothing venture, nothing g.	THOROUGHNESS 3
without some g.	CIRCUMSTANCE 5
gaining may be g. on you — SPORTS 21
gaiters all gas and g. — SATISFACTION 7
Galatians great text in G. — BIBLE 16
Galileo One G. is enough — MISTAKES 23
| status of G. | GREATNESS 13 |
gall g. and wormwood — ADVERSITY 3
gallant g. gentleman — EPITAPHS 20
gallimaufry g. or hodgepodge — LANGUAGES 6
gallop G. about doing good — CHARITY 24
gallows youth to the g. — GOVERNMENT 22
game beautiful g. — FOOTBALL 1
beautiful g.	FOOTBALL 8
g. at which two can play	PHILOSOPHY 16
g. is about glory	FOOTBALL 7
g. is never lost till won	WINNING 13
how you played the G.	SPORTS 16
If you watch a g.	SPORTS 22
It's more than a g.	CRICKET 4
most of the g.	ACTION 8
out to the ball g.	SPORTS 13
play the g.	SPORTS 11
take seriously any g.	CRICKET 14
time to win this g.	SPORTS 5
woman is his g.	MEN AND WOMEN 9
gamekeeper old poacher makes the best g. — WAYS 10
games better than g. — SCHOOLS 11
| dread of g. | SCHOOLS 14 |
| g. should be seen | CHILDREN 8 |
gammon g. and spinach — MEANING 3

gamut g. of the emotions — ACTING 7
gangsters acted like g. — INTERNAT REL 34
gaps God lived in g. — SCIENCE AND RELIG 11
| God of the g. | SCIENCE AND RELIG 2 |
garage full g. — PROGRESS 16
garbage G. in, garbage out — COMPUTERS 2
Garbo sees in G. sober — PEOPLE 53
garden at the bottom of our g. — SUPERNATURAL 20
book is like a g.	BOOKS 1
Cabbage G.	AUSTRALIA 4
cultivate one's g.	SELF-INTEREST 11
cultivate our g.	SELF-INTEREST 23
g. of England	BRITISH TOWNS 18
G. of Europe	EUROPE 3
G. State	AMERICAN CITIES 17
g. was the primitive prison	GARDENS 14
Glory of the G.	GARDENS 16
God planted a g.	GARDENS 8
God's Heart in a g.	GARDENS 18
God the first g. made	COUNTRY AND TOWN 9
plant a g.	GARDENS 2
woman in a g.	BIBLE 18
gardener g. to love flowers — GARDENS 3
| I am but a young g. | GARDENS 13 |
gardenias g. in your hair — RACE 20
gardening g. is landscape-painting — GARDENS 12
| G. is the new rock'n'roll | GARDENS 24 |
| occupation like g. | GARDENS 23 |
gardens Sowe Carrets in your G. — GARDENS 9
| your shelves be your g. | LIBRARIES 1 |
garlands they are g. — MEMORY 28
garment grasp the hem of his g. — POLITICS 19
| like a g. wear | BRITISH TOWNS 25 |
| Silence is a woman's best g. | WOMAN'S ROLE 2 |
garments Reasons are not like g. — LOGIC 8
garnet all Sir G. — SATISFACTION 8
Garrick G.'s a salad — PEOPLE 31
gas all g. and gaiters — SATISFACTION 7
fret about death by nerve g.	ARCHITECTURE 23
G. smells awful	SUICIDE 9
remembered to turn the g. off	WORRY 14
gash be it g. or gold — PRESENT 11
gate g. of horn — DREAMS 5
g. of the year	FAITH 11
ivory g.	DREAMS 6
ivory g.	DREAMS 8
November at the g.	SEASONS 19
poor man at his g.	CLASS 14
Strait is the g.	VIRTUE 16
gatekeeper Patent Office is the g. — INVENTIONS 22
gates g. of Hell—but no further — DIPLOMACY 4
| g. to the glorious and the unknown | TRANSPORT 11 |
| logic a g. stretched out | COMPUTERS 11 |
Gath Tell it not in G. — NEWS 3
gather G. ye rosebuds while ye may — TRANSIENCE 8
gay g. goodnight — LIFE 41
g. Lothario	SEX 5
g. man trapped	PEOPLE 64
G. men may seek sex	SEX 46
g. science	POETRY 1
gazelle never loved a dear G. — VALUE 28
| nursed a dear g. | TRANSIENCE 11 |
gazing g. at each other — LOVE 60
geese g. and swine — FARMING 3
| Wild G. | IRELAND 6 |
Gehenna Down to G. — SOLITUDE 13
gene selfish g. — LIFE SCI 5
general caviar to the g. — FUTILITY 9
caviar to the g.	TASTE 3
G. good is the plea	GOOD 31
G. notions	IDEAS 6
generalities g. of natural right — HUMAN RIGHTS 10
| glittering g. | CONVERSATION 4 |
General Motors good for G. — BUSINESS 39
generals *bite* some of my other g. — MADNESS 8
| law for g. | ARMED FORCES 45 |
| Russia has two g. | RUSSIA 3 |

generation beat g.	JAZZ 1
Every g. revolts	GENERATION GAP 13
g. away from extinction	CHRISTIAN CH 45
g. of men	TRANSIENCE 4
g. was stolen	AUSTRALIA 31
G. X	GENERATION GAP 4
lost g.	WORLD W I 24
stolen g.	AUSTRALIA 8
Will the last g.	HUMAN RACE 25
generations G. have trod	WORK 33
in a thousand g.	UNIVERSITIES 29
in three g.	SUCCESS 3
It takes three g.	CLASS 1
only three g.	SUCCESS 2
generous always g. ones	CAUTION 25
just before you're g.	JUSTICE 2
generously treated g. or destroyed	REVENGE 12
genes G. are not like	LIFE SCI 30
true of the g.	KNOWLEDGE 53
what males do to g.	SEX 47
genetic mechanism for g. material	LIFE SCI 19
genetics geography and g.	AMERICA 36
happening in human g.	LIFE SCI 31
Geneva G. Bible	BIBLE 3
Genghis Khan right of G.	POLITICAL PART 10
genitals stare at his g.	INVENTIONS 17
genius declare except my g.	GENIUS 10
destroy g. and art	TASTE 7
feminine of g.	TASTE 11
g. a better discerning	ALCOHOL 11
g. appears in the world	GENIUS 4
G. does what it must	GENIUS 9
g. found respectable	GENIUS 8
g. has been of slow growth	GENIUS 7
g. into my life	LIFESTYLES 25
g. is a mind	GENIUS 6
G. is an infinite capacity	GENIUS 1
G. is one percent	GENIUS 11
g. loci	TRAVEL 9
g. makes no mistakes	GENIUS 14
g. of Einstein	CAUSES 28
g. that could cut a Colossus	POETS 13
g. who is ignorant	GENIUS 5
G. without education	GENIUS 2
gentlemen—a g.	MUSICIANS 6
Picasso is a g.	PAINTING 23
run down men of g.	TRANSLATION 7
teach taste or g.	TASTE 6
geniuses G. are the luckiest	GENIUS 15
genocide cleanse themselves of g.	EUROPE 19
genome 90% of the human g.	LIFE SCI 32
genteel g. when he gets drunk	MANNERS 13
gentle Do not go g.	OLD AGE 26
g. rain from heaven	JUSTICE 24
parfit g. knight	CHARACTER 27
gentleman generations to make a g.	CLASS 1
g. in black velvet	ANIMALS 8
g. in Whitehall	ADMINISTRATION 15
last g. in Europe	PEOPLE 45
mariner with the g.	CLASS 9
no g. could mean to	APOLOGY 12
teach you to be a g.	UNIVERSITIES 18
too pedantic for a g.	UNIVERSITIES 7
who was then the g.	CLASS 2
gentlemanly werry g. ideas	ALCOHOL 15
gentlemen conversation among g.	CONVERSATION 9
Dust was G.	DEATH 51
g. and the players	CLASS 4
nation of g.	CRICKET 13
genuine g. poetry is conceived	POETRY 23
geographers g., in Afric-maps	EXPLORATION 6
geographical g. concept	EUROPE 8
Italy is a g. expression	INTERNAT REL 15
joint scientific and g.	EXPLORATION 4
geography g. and genetics	AMERICA 36
G. is about Maps	BIOGRAPHY 12
too much g.	CANADA 11

geologists g. into infidelity	LIFE SCI 16
geometrical g. ratio	LIFE SCI 10
geometry always doing g.	GOD 7
as precise as g.	POETRY 22
God was always doing g.	UNIVERSE 19
little disorder in its g.	EMOTIONS 28
royal road to g.	MATHS 8
who does not know g.	MATHS 7
George G. the First was always	ROYALTY 27
Georgia red hills of G.	EQUALITY 17
geranium shakes a dead g.	MEMORY 19
geriatric years in a g. home	PLEASURE 31
German poems is G.	POETRY 31
to my horse —G.	LANGUAGES 4
Waiting for the G. verb	LANGUAGES 16
Germans beastly to the G.	WORLD W II 17
G. went in to cleanse	EUROPE 19
They're G.	INTERNAT REL 35
Germany G. all is prohibited	COUNTRIES 32
G. will declare that I am	RACE 15
mystical heart of g.	COUNTRIES 40
remaining cities of G.	WORLD W II 21
germs Kills all known g.	POLLUTION 1
Gershwin G. a serious composer	MUSICIANS 14
gerund Save the g.	LANGUAGE 28
gesture Morality's a g.	MORALITY 19
get g. anywhere in marriage	MARRIAGE 45
g. something	EMPLOYMENT 12
G. up, stand up	DEFIANCE 8
g. what you like	LIKES 12
what you g.	APPEARANCE 11
You don't g. me	EMPLOYMENT 27
gets What a neighbour g.	FAMILIARITY 11
getting G. and spending	WORK 27
ghost g. in the machine	MIND 3
g. of a rose	SENSES 6
g. of the deceased Roman	CHRISTIAN CH 19
g. walks	THEATRE 1
love to meet a g.	SUPERNATURAL 27
ghosties ghoulies and g.	SUPERNATURAL 1
ghosts by our lack of g.	CANADA 12
g. of departed quantities	MATHS 11
maybe there are g. too	SUPERNATURAL 23
ghoul like a g.	LOVE 70
ghoulies g. and ghosties	SUPERNATURAL 1
giant awakened a sleeping g.	CAUSES 29
body of a g.	GREATNESS 6
hand of the g.	CHILDREN 4
one g. leap	ACHIEVEMENT 29
soul so much a g.	SELF-KNOWLEDGE 4
giants like precocious g.	PEACE 25
one of five g.	PROGRESS 18
shoulders of g.	PROGRESS 7
shoulders of g.	PROGRESS 8
we ought to be g.	RUSSIA 6
gibbets g. for 'the man'	CRIME 34
Gibraltar G. in our sea	PHYSICAL 18
giddy I am g.	IMAGINATION 6
gift any manner of g.	POLITICIANS 4
Beauty is the lover's g.	BEAUTY 14
bestow on another as a g.	LIBERTY 33
g. horse in the mouth	GRATITUDE 3
g. of love	GIFTS 23
g. of tongues	LANGUAGES 1
g. survived it all	POETS 24
Greek g.	GIFTS 7
My g. is my song	GIFTS 21
small g.	GIFTS 6
gifted young, g. and *black*	RACE 27
giftie g. gie us	SELF-KNOWLEDGE 8
gifts even when they bring gifts	TRUST 18
g. and do no good	GIFTS 9
Greeks bearing g.	TRUST 1
gigantic but a g. mistake	AMERICA 33
gild g. the lily	EXCESS 14
gill hang by its own g.	DUTY 2
gilt g. off the gingerbread	DISILLUSION 3

gingerbread gilt off the g.   DISILLUSION 3
Giotto G.'s O   PAINTING 3
   tactile values of G.   COUNTRIES 22
giraffes G.!—a People who live   ANIMALS 28
gird g. up one's loins   DETERMINATION 21
girdle g. round the earth   HASTE 14
girl breaks like a little g.   WOMEN 54
   can't get no g. reaction   SEX 31
   diamonds are a g.'s best friend   WEALTH 34
   do a g. in   MURDER 20
   Essex g.   WOMEN 10
   g. is like a melody   BEAUTY 29
   g. wants to laugh   HUMOUR 15
   It g.   WOMEN 12
   man chases a g.   COURTSHIP 12
   page three g.   WOMEN 13
   policeman and a pretty g.   CINEMA 18
   poor little rich g.   WEALTH 12
   say in front of a g.   WORDS 31
   There was a little g.   BEHAVIOUR 21
girlfriend once every g.   HOUSEWORK 16
girls bombers named for g.   ARMED FORCES 43
   g. who wear glasses   APPEARANCE 26
   It was the g. I liked   FASHION 14
   like g. and roses   TRANSIENCE 17
   nature turns g. into women   MEN AND WOMEN 29
   not that g. should think   WOMAN'S ROLE 16
   Secrets with g.   SECRECY 23
   St Hugh's for g.   UNIVERSITIES 1
   Thank heaven for little g.   WOMEN 50
   we like g.   MEN 24
give better to g.   GIFTS 5
   G., and it shall be given   GIFTS 10
   g. and not to count   GIFTS 13
   G. and take   JUSTICE 5
   G. a thing   GIFTS 3
   g. than to receive   GIFTS 11
   prepared to g. it   FORGIVENESS 29
   want them to g. it   ADVICE 23
given I would have g. gladly   MOURNING 20
   taking what is not g.   LIFESTYLES 14
giver cheerful g.   GIFTS 12
gives blesseth him that g.   JUSTICE 24
   happiness she g.   PLEASURE 16
   He g. twice   GIFTS 4
   more he g. to others   POSSESSIONS 10
giving g. vein   GIFTS 14
   loving and giving   GIFTS 2
glad g. confident morning   DISILLUSION 13
   just g. to see me   SEX 38
gladly bear the cross g.   SUFFERING 8
   g. wolde he lerne   EDUCATION 13
   I would have given g.   MOURNING 20
Gladstone If G. fell into the Thames   MISFORTUNES 20
Glasgow G. Empire on a Saturday   HUMOUR 21
   G. man and an Edinburgh man   BRITISH TOWNS 40
   G.'s miles better   BRITISH TOWNS 3
   I belong to G.   BRITISH TOWNS 37
glass break the bloody g.   OPTIMISM 30
   dome of many-coloured g.   LIFE 26
   first child is made of g.   CHILD CARE 16
   Get thee g. eyes   POLITICIANS 6
   live in a g. room   SENSES 16
   live in g. houses   GOSSIP 9
   same shape as the g.   EMPLOYMENT 31
   Satire is a sort of g.   SELF-KNOWLEDGE 6
   through a g., darkly   KNOWLEDGE 22
glasses girls who wear g.   APPEARANCE 26
   ladder and some g.   COUNTRY AND TOWN 18
glib g. and oily art   HYPOCRISY 11
glimpses g. of the moon   EARTH 3
glittering g. and sounding   HUMAN RIGHTS 10
   g. generalities   CONVERSATION 4
   g. prizes   SUCCESS 35
glitters All that g.   APPEARANCE 1
   medal g.   RANK 16
global g. village   EARTH 4

   image of a g. village   TECHNOLOGY 18
globally Think g.   POLLUTION 3
glorious g. Devon   BRITISH TOWNS 33
   G. Fourth   FESTIVALS 21
   g. morning for America   WARS 8
   g. Twelfth   FESTIVALS 22
glory all the g. of man   TRANSIENCE 7
   all things give him g.   PRAYER 25
   children ardent for some desperate g.   WARFARE 38
   crowning g.   BODY 5
   days of our g.   YOUTH 14
   eyes have seen the g.   GOD 26
   game is about g.   FOOTBALL 7
   g. and the dream   IMAGINATION 10
   g. in the name   BRITAIN 8
   g. in the triumph   DANGER 25
   g. is in their shame   GREED 8
   g. never dies   HEROES 4
   g. nothing   FAME 13
   g. of Europe   EUROPE 5
   g. of Gothic   ARCHITECTURE 11
   g. of my crown   GOVERNMENT 11
   G. of the Garden   GARDENS 16
   g. that was Greece   PAST 23
   g. was I had such friends   FRIENDSHIP 23
   greatest g. of a woman   WOMEN 16
   her flower, her g., pass   VALUE 19
   I go to g.   LAST WORDS 25
   it is a g. to her   BODY 10
   living man is the g.   GOD 10
   looks on war as all g.   WARFARE 31
   Old G.   AMERICA 7
   question of your g.   GOVERNMENT 14
   Solomon in all his g.   BEAUTY 8
   Thus passes the g.   TRANSIENCE 2
   trailing clouds of g.   PREGNANCY 6
   uncertain g. of an April day   WEATHER 33
   yields the true g.   THOROUGHNESS 11
glove steel in a velvet g.   WRITERS 24
   white g. pulpit   PRESIDENCY 20
gloves cat in g.   CAUTION 3
glow g. has warmed the world   PEOPLE 55
glow-worm I am a g.   CHARACTER 45
gluttony G. is an emotional escape   COOKING 34
   love, as in g.   PLEASURE 29
GM G. soya beans   LIFE SCI 31
gnashing g. of teeth   HEAVEN 7
gnat strain at a g.   BELIEF 8
gnomes g. of Zurich   MONEY 17
go better 'ole, g. to it   ADVICE 21
   Easy come, easy g.   EFFORT 2
   G. ahead, make my day   PREPARATION 19
   G. further and fare   SATISFACTION 3
   G., litel bok   WRITING 9
   g. out of the world alone   SOLITUDE 17
   G. West, young man   AMERICA 14
   I g. to glory   LAST WORDS 25
   In the name of God, g.   ACTION 18
   Let my people g.   LIBERTY 5
   Light come, light g.   POSSESSIONS 4
   no place to g.   DRESS 15
   One of us must g.   TASTE 13
   quickly g.   CONSTANCY 2
   Rain, rain, g. away   WEATHER 13
   to boldly g.   EXPLORATION 2
   To g. away is to die   ABSENCE 12
   we think you ought to g.   WORLD W I 13
goal golden g.   FOOTBALL 2
   without a g.   PAINTING 19
goals oafs at the g.   FOOTBALL 4
goat g. feet dance   DANCE 5
   horns, like a g.   FATE 1
goat-footed g. bard   PEOPLE 47
goats sheep from the g.   GOOD 13
goblins head full of g.   PRACTICALITY 17
God afraid of G.   MORALITY 7
   After G. comes my Papa   PARENTS 8

grass (*cont.*)
snake in the g.	DANGER 18
splendour in the g.	TRANSIENCE 10
two blades of g.	PRACTICALITY 7
While the g. grows	ACHIEVEMENT 9
With the refreshing g.	PERFECTION 14

grasshoppers half a dozen g.   WORDS AND DEEDS 16
grassroots tremendous g. revolution   COMPUTERS 20
grateful g. mind   GRATITUDE 10
One single g. thought	PRAYER 19

gratia ars g. artis   ARTS 4
gratitude Don't overload g.   GRATITUDE 9
g. is a secret hope	GRATITUDE 11
g. is a species of revenge	GRATITUDE 12
hate the g. of women	GRATITUDE 20
having to give g.	GRATITUDE 16
liking of g.	FRIENDSHIP 20

grave Between the cradle and the g.   TRANSIENCE 9
cradle to the g.	DRESS 17
cruel as the g.	ENVY 8
Do not stand at my g.	MOURNING 24
g. is not its goal	LIFE 27
g., where is thy victory	DEATH 22
kind of healthy g.	COUNTRY AND TOWN 15
she is in her g.	MOURNING 13
sorrow to the g.	OLD AGE 6
white man's g.	AFRICA 5

graven g. image   RELIGION 2
graves g. of little magazines   PUBLISHING 12
g. of their neighbours	DEATH 42
g. with our teeth	COOKING 25

graveyards Balkan g. are full   DIPLOMACY 1
foxholes or g.	RACE 24

gravitation not believing in g.   REVOLUTION 22
gravity fatal law of g.   MISFORTUNES 29
Gray whole of G.'s Elegy   ACHIEVEMENT 15
grazing Tilling and g.   FRANCE 5
greasy top of the g. pole   SUCCESS 31
great Caesar might be g.   GREATNESS 5
close to g. minds	EDUCATION 27
Everything we think of as g.	GREATNESS 11
G. Bear	SKIES 2
G. Bible	BIBLE 4
g. book is a great evil	BOOKS 2
g. is to be misunderstood	GREATNESS 7
G. is Truth	TRUTH 11
G. Leap Forward	PROGRESS 3
g. men are frauds	GREATNESS 12
g. men—so-called	GREATNESS 9
g. minds in the commonplace	GENIUS 12
G. minds think alike	THINKING 1
g. regions of the mind	MIND 13
G. Society	SOCIETY 18
g. things from the valley	INSIGHT 13
I am not g.	GREATNESS 8
nothing g. but man	MIND 12
problem is not being g.	WRITERS 33
some men are born g.	GREATNESS 4

Great Britain G. has lost an empire   BRITAIN 13
natives of G.	BRITAIN 7

greater G. love hath no man   SELF-SACRIFICE 3
g. the sinner	GOOD 1
g. the truth	GOSSIP 6
Thy necessity is yet g.	CHARITY 14

greatest g. happiness   MORALITY 4
g. number	SOCIETY 10
g. of these is charity	LOVE 21
I'm the g.	SELF-ESTEEM 23

greatness g. not to be exact   BUSINESS 27
g. thrust upon them	GREATNESS 3
If any man seek for g.	GREATNESS 1
intended g. for men	GREATNESS 10
owe most of their g.	MANAGEMENT 7
touch of g.	GREATNESS 2

Greece glory that was G.   PAST 23
If you take G. apart	COUNTRIES 37
isles of G.	COUNTRIES 16

greed enough for everyone's g.   GREED 16
Greed is all right	GREED 18
G. is good	GREED 19

greedy G. for the property   GREED 6
Greek at the G. Calends   TIME 9
G. gift	GIFTS 7
G. in its origin	COUNTRIES 20
G. one then is my hero	INVENTIONS 17
half G., half Latin	BROADCASTING 6
it was all G. to me	IGNORANCE 13
Latin or in G.	LANGUAGES 7
less G.	SHAKESPEARE 4
original G. is of much use	TRANSLATION 10
straw for G. particles	SCHOOLS 8
study of G. literature	UNIVERSITIES 14
When G. meets Greek	SIMILARITY 10
when his wife talks G.	WOMAN'S ROLE 13

Greeks G. bearing gifts   TRUST 1
G. had a word for it	WORDS 21
I fear the G. even	TRUST 18
When G. joined Greeks	SIMILARITY 18

green all ye G. Things   POLLUTION 7
charity are always g.	CHARITY 5
Colourless g. ideas	LANGUAGE 25
Drives my g. age	YOUTH 20
g. and pleasant land	ENGLAND 13
G. belts should be the start	COUNTRY AND TOWN 24
G. grow the rushes O	QUANTITIES 24
g. lap immense	EARTH 15
g. shoots of recovery	ECONOMICS 20
g. Yule makes a fat churchyard	WEATHER 5
keeps his own wounds g.	REVENGE 15
kind as it is g.	IRELAND 19
life springs ever g.	REALITY 7
lime g. is the new black	FASHION 17
Make it a *g.* peace	POLLUTION 19
One g.	SEASONS 15
Praise the g. earth	EARTH 9
there is a different g.	TREES 17
To a g. thought	GARDENS 11
wearin' o' the G.	IRELAND 8
Wherever g. is worn	CHANGE 45

greenbirds Metaphysical g.   PERFECTION 14
greener grass is always g.   ENVY 3
greenest g. political party   POLLUTION 28
green-eyed g. monster   ENVY 4
g. monster	ENVY 11

greenhouse g. gases   EARTH 17
greenness Could have recovered g.   HOPE 11
greens healing g.   SICKNESS 20
grenadier bones of a single Pomeranian g.   WARFARE 33
British G.	ARMED FORCES 23

Gresham G.'s Law   MONEY 18
grew once you g. up   MATURITY 17
grey All cats are g.   SIMILARITY 1
black and g.	HUMAN NATURE 19
bring down my g. hairs	OLD AGE 6
Good G. Poet	POETS 3
in my g. hairs	DUTY 8
little g. cells	INTELLIGENCE 4
little g. cells	INTELLIGENCE 12
philosophy paints its g.	PHILOSOPHY 12
remained a depthless g.	WEATHER 57
There's a lot of g.	SEX 43
When you are old and g.	OLD AGE 19

grief feel g. yourself   SYMPATHY 10
g. felt so like fear	SORROW 26
G. fills the room	MOURNING 8
G. has no wings	SORROW 21
G. is a species	SORROW 14
g. is like minefield	SORROW 27
G. is the price	MOURNING 2
G. is the price we pay	MOURNING 26
hopeless g.	SORROW 9
Thine be the g.	CONSTANCY 8

griefs cutteth g. in halves   FRIENDSHIP 12
g. and fears	PARENTS 7

hair (*cont.*)

not your yellow h.	BODY 23
One h. of a woman	STRENGTH 18
red faces, and loose h.	RACE 7
when his h. is all gone	EXPERIENCE 3
with a single h.	BEAUTY 1
woman have long h.	BODY 10
you have lovely h.	BEAUTY 26
hairs bring down my grey h.	OLD AGE 6
in my grey h.	DUTY 8
halal h. portions of the past	FAMILY 27
half all truths are h.-truths	TRUTH 38
h.-alive things	GOSSIP 26
H. a loaf	SATISFACTION 4
h. is better	EXCESS 2
h. of the people	DEMOCRACY 18
h. of the warld	FOOLS 22
H. the money I spend	ADVERTISING 10
H. the truth	LIES 2
longest h. of your life	YOUTH 13
One h. of the world	PLEASURE 17
other h. lives	SOCIETY 2
overcome but h. his foe	VIOLENCE 6
thought h. as good	MEN AND WOMEN 26
too clever by h.	INTELLIGENCE 5
Too clever by h.	PEOPLE 54
Well begun is h. done	BEGINNING 12
Halifax Hell, Hull, and H.	BRITISH TOWNS 2
hall fly swiftly into the h.	LIFE 16
Liberty H.	LIBERTY 3
merry in h.	ENTERTAINING 5
Middle Temple for a h.	LAW 2
hallelujah H.! I'm alive	EMOTIONS 23
halloo Don't h.	OPTIMISM 5
halo jealousy with a h.	MORALITY 12
life is a luminous h.	LIFE 40
What after all Is a h.	VIRTUE 50
halt How long h. ye	CERTAINTY 6
halved trouble h.	COOPERATION 16
hamburger polystyrene h. cartons	ENGLAND 31
Hamlet cigar called H.	SMOKING 1
had not written *H.*	ARTS AND SCI 19
H. is so much paper	FOOTBALL 5
H. without the Prince	ABSENCE 7
hammer all you have is a h.	PROBLEMS 2
carpenter's h.	MUSIC 11
hammering make such a h.	JOURNALISM 7
hammers worn out many h.	CHRISTIAN CH 4
hamster estimate on a 6ft h.	VALUE 35
hamsters children love h.	RELATIONSHIPS 19
hand bird in the h.	CAUTION 2
bird in the h.	CERTAINTY 4
biting the h.	GRATITUDE 9
bringing me up by h.	CHILD CARE 7
God's almighty h.	FARMING 11
h. is the cutting edge	ACTION 26
h. of God	FOOTBALL 10
h. of Jean Jacques Rousseau	REVOLUTION 16
h. that feeds	GRATITUDE 5
h. that rocks	PARENTS 11
h. that rocks the cradle	WOMEN 3
h. that signed the paper	POWER 27
h. to execute	PEOPLE 29
h. to the plough	DETERMINATION 22
h. to the plough	DETERMINATION 24
made by the h.	SCULPTURE 6
man a free h.	SEX 26
mind and h. went together	SHAKESPEARE 5
never stretch out the h.	RELATIONSHIPS 20
One h. for oneself	SEA 3
One h. washes	COOPERATION 14
sound of the single h.	COOPERATION 21
steady h.	CAUTION 7
sweeten this little h.	GUILT 5
thinking h.	SENSES 17
thy h. findeth to do	THOROUGHNESS 10
what thy right h. doeth	CHARITY 11

whom you take by the h.	DANCE 1
written with mine own h.	LETTERS 4
your white h.	BODY 12
handbag hitting it with her h.	PEOPLE 60
handbook constable's h.	BIBLE 17
Handel or for H.	MUSICIANS 5
handful h. of dust	FEAR 11
life in the h. of dust	YOUTH 16
handicraft sphere of h.	BROADCASTING 9
handkerchief scent on a pocket h.	TRANSIENCE 15
state of the h. industry	WRITERS 30
handle him that can h. them	OPPORTUNITY 31
handles Every thing hath two h.	REALITY 5
hands Beneath the bleeding h.	MEDICINE 24
Cold h.	BODY 1
given two h. and two legs	BODY 36
h., and handle not	INDIFFERENCE 3
h. are a sort of feet	BODY 14
Holding h. at midnight	COURTSHIP 10
horny h. of toil	WORK 30
I think with my h.	BODY 34
labour of my h.	EMPLOYMENT 13
leave a man's h. empty	CREATIVITY 17
Licence my roving h.	SEX 10
Many h. make light work	COOPERATION 12
memory is in my h.	MEMORY 30
more work than both his h.	MANAGEMENT 1
no h. but yours	CHRISTIAN CH 2
raise h. together	RELATIONSHIPS 11
spits on its h.	LANGUAGE 26
washed his h.	GUILT 6
wash one's h.	DUTY 5
work for idle h.	IDLENESS 3
handsaw hawk from a h.	INTELLIGENCE 3
hawk from a h.	MADNESS 4
handsome H. is	BEHAVIOUR 5
hang enough rope and he will h. himself	WAYS 6
H. a thief when he's young	CRIME 4
h. my hat	HOME 16
let him h. there	HASTE 23
ready to h. the panel	LAW 27
We must h. together	COOPERATION 23
wretches h.	LAW 20
hanged born to be h.	FATE 3
Confess and be h.	GUILT 1
h., drawn, and quartered	CRIME 22
h. for a sheep	THOROUGHNESS 5
h. for stealing horses	CRIME 24
h. in a fortnight	DEATH 44
if they'd been hanged	JUSTICE 39
ill name is half h.	REPUTATION 6
Little thieves are h.	CRIME 7
hanging capacity women have for just h. on	DETERMINATION 45
Catching's before h.	WAYS 1
H. and wiving	FATE 2
H. is too good for him	CRIME 23
h. men an' women	IRELAND 8
killing a dog than h. it	WAYS 15
hanging-look h. to me	APPEARANCE 16
hangs thereby h. a tale	MATURITY 4
What h. people	GUILT 12
happen Accidents will h.	CHANCE 1
cannot h. to him	ARMED FORCES 40
everybody knew would never h.	WARFARE 59
h. tomorrow, next week	POLITICIANS 27
h. to somebody else	CHANCE 33
make things h.	REALITY 18
may or may not h.	PREPARATION 21
people to whom things h.	MISFORTUNES 31
things can h.	MISFORTUNES 28
Things h.	GUILT 19
We make things h.	CHANCE 36
happened LSD? Nothing much h.	DRUGS 7
happens dependent on what h. to her	CHOICE 18
h. anywhere	BOREDOM 9
Nothing h.	BOREDOM 8

hate (*cont.*)

h. any one that we know	FAMILIARITY 16
h. is conquered by love	HATRED 4
h. something in him	HATRED 11
h. the man you have hurt	HUMAN NATURE 8
h. the sin	GOOD 20
h. to get up	IDLENESS 22
how much men h. them	MEN AND WOMEN 28
If h. killed men	HATRED 8
I h. quotation	QUOTATIONS 6
I h. television	BROADCASTING 7
I have seen much to h.	ENGLAND 25
immortal h.	DEFIANCE 13
learn to h.	HATRED 18
Let them h.	GOVERNMENT 8
love is not h.	INDIFFERENCE 16
not to h. them	INDIFFERENCE 10
people who h. me	ENEMIES 9
players who h. your guts	SPORTS 27
religion to make us h.	RELIGION 13
roughness breedeth h.	CRIME 21
stalled ox where h. is	HATRED 1
This is a letter of h.	ENGLAND 30
hated I never h. a man enough	HATRED 14
loved well because he h.	HATRED 9
hates h. dogs and babies	DOGS 11
man who h. his mother	RELATIONSHIPS 17
tell him he h. flatterers	PRAISE 6
world of voluble h.	PEOPLE 52
hating don't give way to h.	CHARACTER 39
H. gets going	HATRED 16
h., my boy, is an art	HATRED 12
hatred common h. for something	RELATIONSHIPS 8
H. is a tonic	SYMPATHY 21
h., little room	IRELAND 18
h. on the part	HATRED 13
intellectual h.	OPINION 23
love to h. turned	REVENGE 16
Make h. hated	PREJUDICE 15
more moved by h.	TRANSPORT 25
not to feel any h.	HATRED 5
set against the h.	MURDER 26
stalled ox and h.	HATRED 3
hatreds systematic organization of h.	POLITICS 20
hats H. off, gentlemen	MUSICIANS 6
haunted h. town it is to me	BRITISH TOWNS 32
haunts h. of coot	RIVERS 9
haute couture H. should be fun	DRESS 25
have h.-his-carcase, next to the perpetual	LAW 24
h. to take you in	HOME 19
I'll h. what she's having	SEX 45
more we h.	GIFTS 20
take away everything you h.	GOVERNMENT 38
What you h., hold	POSSESSIONS 5
What you spend, you h.	POSSESSIONS 6
You can h. it all	WOMEN 61
have-nots haves and the h.	POSSESSIONS 14
haves h. and the have-nots	POSSESSIONS 14
havoc Cry, 'H.'	REVENGE 13
hawk h. from a handsaw	INTELLIGENCE 9
h. from a handsaw	MADNESS 4
hawkeye H. State	AMERICAN CITIES 22
hawks H. will not pick out	COOPERATION 6
haws welcome h.	NECESSITY 12
hay antic h.	DANCE 3
antic h.	DANCE 5
h. while the sun shines	OPPORTUNITY 7
live on h.	FUTURE 20
neither good for h. nor grain	WEATHER 7
So *that's* what h. looks like	COUNTRY AND TOWN 20
worth a load of h.	SEASONS 6
Haydn Some cry up H.	MUSICIANS 5
haze Purple h.	MIND 20
he H. would	SELF-INTEREST 27
Who h.	FAME 2
head at the command—of his h.	POLITICAL PART 25
at the h. of school	SCHOOLS 3

bumping its h.	GOOD 36
for you good h.	PRACTICALITY 5
God be in my h.	PRAYER 10
h. full of goblins	PRACTICALITY 17
h. of Maradona	FOOTBALL 10
h. on young shoulders	EXPERIENCE 12
h. to contrive	PEOPLE 29
hit us over the h.	DIPLOMACY 15
If you can keep your h.	CRISES 15
keep your h.	CRISES 19
King Charles's h.	IDEAS 4
makes a wise h.	SILENCE 5
stinks from the h.	LEADERSHIP 1
Uneasy lies the h.	ROYALTY 13
weak in the h.	BRITISH TOWNS 12
where to lay his h.	HOME 10
headline strapline and h.	LANGUAGE 31
headmasters H. have powers	SCHOOLS 12
headpiece H. filled with straw	FUTILITY 22
heads H. I win	WINNING 2
h. replete with thoughts	KNOWLEDGE 32
Two h. are better	THINKING 3
headstrong h. as an allegory	DETERMINATION 32
heal Physician, h. thyself	MEDICINE 9
healer h.'s art	MEDICINE 24
Time is a great h.	TIME 5
healing H. is a matter of time	MEDICINE 8
no h. has been necessary	TIME 43
health damage your h.	SMOKING 2
drink one another's h.	ALCOHOL 19
have both, it's h.	SATISFACTION 34
h. and no wealth	BRITISH TOWNS 9
in sickness and in h.	MARRIAGE 21
Look to your h.	HEALTH 13
no h. in us	ACTION 19
healthy generous and h. human being	ENTERTAINING 24
Greed is h.	GREED 18
h. and wealthy	SLEEP 17
h. man does not torture	CRUELTY 13
h., wealthy, and wise	HEALTH 4
h., you don't need it	HEALTH 17
Heaney H. belonged	POETS 29
hear H. all, see all	SELF-INTEREST 3
h. in my imagination	CREATIVITY 5
h. it through their feet	JAZZ 2
h. no evil	VIRTUE 5
h. on the grapevine	GOSSIP 13
h. people smile	SENSES 18
H. the other side	PREJUDICE 7
men prefer not to h.	TRUTH 37
nothing of what you h.	BELIEF 1
one may h.	CONVERSATION 12
those who will not h.	PREJUDICE 5
heard ain't h. nuttin' yet	SINGING 10
I will be h.	DETERMINATION 36
seen and not h.	CHILDREN 1
hearers favourable h.	POLITICIANS 5
not h. only	WORDS AND DEEDS 10
hearing h. of the ear	SENSES 3
h. without listening	SILENCE 14
our sense of h.	POLLUTION 14
heart anniversaries of the h.	FESTIVALS 65
ás the h. grows older	SORROW 18
Batter my h.	GOD 16
beak from out my h.	DESPAIR 11
Because my h. is pure	VIRTUE 36
bigger the h.	BODY 3
bone shop of the h.	EMOTIONS 21
breaks the h.	FLOWERS 12
committed adultery in my h.	TEMPTATION 19
desires of the h.	EMOTIONS 20
ease a h.	DRESS 18
education of the h.	EMOTIONS 14
Faint h. never won	COURAGE 6
faith of the h.	FAITH 4
Fourteen h. attacks	SELF-INTEREST 29
fullness of the h.	EMOTIONS 1

get your h.'s desire	ACHIEVEMENT 23	don't like the h.	STRENGTH 2
giving your h. to a dog	DOGS 9	furnace that gives no h.	MADNESS 17
had the lion's h.	SPEECHES 17	H. not a furnace	ENEMIES 10
h. and hand that once	LOVE 39	H. won't pass	PHYSICAL 16
h. and stomach	ROYALTY 11	white h. of technology	TECHNOLOGY 4
h. beats so that I can	DANCE 13	white h. of this revolution	TECHNOLOGY 19
h. doesn't grieve over	IGNORANCE 6	**heated** h. argument ever	ARGUMENT 4
h. for any fate	DETERMINATION 37	**heathen** h. in his blindness	RELIGION 20
h. grow fonder	ABSENCE 2	**heather** Nothing but h.	SCOTLAND 18
h. has its reasons	EMOTIONS 11	**Heathrow** saw H. for myself	TRAVEL 37
h. in tears	POETS 18	**heaven** all we know of h.	MEETING 17
h. in the business	BUSINESS 40	eternal joys of h.	HEAVEN 10
h. is a lonely hunter	SOLITUDE 14	God created the h.	BEGINNING 17
h. is an organ of fire	EMOTIONS 27	God owns h.	EARTH 12
h. is Highland	SCOTLAND 12	God's in his h.	OPTIMISM 7
H. of England	BRITISH TOWNS 23	God's in his h.	OPTIMISM 19
h. of man	BEAUTY 24	going to h.	ECONOMICS 19
H. of oak	ARMED FORCES 20	go to h. in feather-beds	VIRTUE 19
h. of oak	CHARACTER 21	H. but with a party	POLITICAL PART 15
h. on one's sleeve	EMOTIONS 5	H. in a rage	BIRDS 9
h. *prefers* to move	ADVERSITY 16	H. lies about us in our infancy	YOUTH 12
h. speaks to heart	SPEECH 11	H. protects children	DANGER 3
h.'s stalled motor	LOVE 58	H. will protect	CLASS 20
h. that has truly loved	CONSTANCY 11	hoped-for h.	EPITAPHS 16
h. that never rejoices	HAPPINESS 4	I'm in H.	DANCE 13
h. that one can see	INSIGHT 14	in h. and earth	UNIVERSE 11
h. the keener	DETERMINATION 26	I saw a new h.	HEAVEN 8
h. to a stey brae	DETERMINATION 10	I will spend my h.	HEAVEN 16
h. upon my sleeve	EMOTIONS 8	ladders that lead to h.	SUFFERING 2
h. upon paper	LETTERS 12	made in h.	MARRIAGE 6
h. was pierced through the ear	WORDS 8	make of h. a hell	MIND 6
h. was warm and gay	TOWNS 22	manna from h.	GIFTS 8
h. wears out with sorrow	MEMORY 27	merrily meet in h.	MEETING 7
h. would break	HOPE 6	more things in h. and earth	SUPERNATURAL 11
holiness of the h.'s affections	TRUTH 27	My idea of h.	HEAVEN 15
hope in your h.	HOPE 22	neither by h.	SWEARING 4
human h. likes a little disorder	EMOTIONS 28	Or what's a h. for	AMBITION 19
If thy h. fails thee	AMBITION 10	Pennies don't fall from h.	MONEY 44
imagination of a man's h.	IMAGINATION 4	Pennies from h.	OPTIMISM 29
inmost cupboards of her h.	WEDDINGS 9	pennies from h.	SURPRISE 6
left my h. in San Francisco	AMERICAN CITIES 59	serve in h.	AMBITION 13
looketh on the h.	INSIGHT 4	starry h. above me	THINKING 14
makes the h. sick	HOPE 3	Thank h. for little girls	WOMEN 50
maketh the h. sick	HOPE 9	things are the sons of h.	WORDS 12
Man's h. expands	LEISURE 13	treasures in h.	WEALTH 15
man's h. is small	BRITISH TOWNS 34	wherever h. is not	HEAVEN 1
merry h.	APPEARANCE 13	**heavens** Himalayas to the h.	EARTH 13
merry h.	HUMOUR 4	**heaventree** h. of stars	SKIES 23
my h. is turning ever	RIVERS 8	**heaviness** h. of his mother	PARENTS 5
My h.'s in the Highlands	SCOTLAND 10	**heavy** h. that it takes two	MARRIAGE 31
my shrivelled h.	HOPE 11	**Hebrides** behold the H.	SCOTLAND 12
mystical h. of Germany	COUNTRIES 40	**hedge** look over a h.	REPUTATION 10
my true love hath my h.	CONSTANCY 5	**hedgehog** h. one *big* one	KNOWLEDGE 16
no longer tear his h.	EPITAPHS 14	**hedgehogs** belongs to the h.	CHARACTER 42
plague your h.	BEAUTY 6	start throwing h.	REVENGE 22
put my hand on my h.	EMOTIONS 29	**heel** Achilles h.	STRENGTH 8
Shakespeare unlocked his h.	SHAKESPEARE 10	**heels** champagne or high h.	IDEALISM 9
song in one's h.	PLEASURE 7	prayed with his h.	PRAYER 27
squirrel's h. beat	INSIGHT 12	**height** carries weight and governs h.	BODY 32
stone out of the h.	SUFFERING 26	Happiness makes up in h.	HAPPINESS 26
strings . . . in the human h.	EMOTIONS 15	**Heineken** H. refreshes	ALCOHOL 4
Vacant h.	INDIFFERENCE 8	**heirs** plant for your h.	GARDENS 7
warm h.	BODY 1	**Helen** H.'s face in hell	HEAVEN 20
way to a man's h.	MEN 3	**hell** agreement with h.	DIPLOMACY 6
Whatever your h. clings to	GOD 14	all h. broke loose	ORDER 11
where the h. is	HOME 5	all h. let loose	ORDER 4
heart-beat Just a h. away	PRESIDENCY 2	all we need of h.	MEETING 17
hearts first in the h.	PRESIDENCY 4	bells of H. go ting-a-ling	WORLD W I 20
h. and minds	OPINION 7	beverage of h.	ALCOHOL 17
h. and minds	PEACE 8	boys, it is all h.	WARFARE 31
h. that beat as one	LOVE 47	cast into h. fire	SIN 9
h. when they are sober	MEN 25	clear through to h.	SMOKING 10
hidden in each other's h.	SECRECY 24	definition of h.	LEISURE 9
Kind h. are more than	RANK 9	gates of H.	DIPLOMACY 4
men with Splendid H.	ENGLAND 19	go to h. like lambs	BRITISH TOWNS 35
queen in people's h.	ROYALTY 38	habit is h.	DRUGS 5
heat can't stand the h.	STRENGTH 25	Helen's face in h.	HEAVEN 20

hell (*cont.*)

H. hath no fury	WOMEN 4
H., Hull, and Halifax	BRITISH TOWNS 2
H. is full	MUSIC 14
H. is oneself	HEAVEN 22
H. is other people	HEAVEN 21
H. is wherever heaven is not	HEAVEN 1
H., madam, is to love	HEAVEN 19
h. of heaven	MIND 6
h. of horses	ENGLAND 1
h. on earth	HAPPINESS 24
If Hitler invaded h.	INTERNAT REL 29
in the bonds of H.	MATHS 1
I say the h. with it	FOOD 22
made an excursion to h.	WORLD W II 20
man who has been in h.	HEAVEN 17
myself am h.	HEAVEN 14
probably re-designed H.	TRAVEL 39
reign in h.	AMBITION 13
riches grow in h.	WEALTH 19
road to h.	ACTION 9
sentence me to h.	GOD 27
to h. for a pastime	SEA 2
War is h., and all that	WARFARE 35
why they invented H.	CRUELTY 11
Why, this is h.	HEAVEN 10
hellhound h. is always a hellhound	CHARACTER 40
hell-kite O h.! All	MOURNING 9
helluva New York,—a h. town	AMERICAN CITIES 53
helm Pleasure at the h.	YOUTH 11
help any belief in h.	COOPERATION 32
cannot h. one poor man	CHARITY 21
do something to *h.*	COOPERATION 28
God h. me	DETERMINATION 27
h. from my friends	FRIENDSHIP 28
h. in time of trouble	LIES 1
h. meet for him	SOLITUDE 5
h. me when I fell	CHILD CARE 5
h. the feeble up	CHARITY 15
h. thou mine unbelief	BELIEF 10
no h. in them	TRUST 17
only h. the work going on	TEACHING 16
without the h. and support	ROYALTY 33
you can't h. it	INSULTS 10
helper antagonist is our h.	ENEMIES 12
helps Every little h.	COOPERATION 4
God h. them	GOD 2
hem grasp the h. of his garment	POLITICS 19
hen better take a wet h.	CHOICE 26
h. is only an egg's way	LIFE SCI 14
Heraclitus They told me, H.	MOURNING 16
herb h. at your feet	CRUELTY 10
herbs dinner of h.	HATRED 1
dinner of h.	HATRED 3
Herculem ex pede H.	LOGIC 3
Hercules some of H.	ARMED FORCES 23
herd instinct Morality is the h.	MORALITY 9
here h. Because We're here	FATE 6
h. for the beer	ALCOHOL 5
H. I am, and here I stay	WARS 16
one tenth H. and Now	PRESENT 13
hereditas damnosa h.	MISFORTUNES 9
heresies begin as h.	TRUTH 30
kept alive by h.	RELIGION 29
heresy h., hops, and beer	INVENTIONS 1
h. signifies no more	OPINION 13
hero Greek one then is my h.	INVENTIONS 17
h. becomes a bore	HEROES 10
h. has become a cabinet	SCULPTURE 8
h. to his valet	FAMILIARITY 9
h. to his valet	HEROES 5
No phallic h.	PREGNANCY 17
See, the conquering h.	HEROES 6
Show me a h.	HEROES 16
valet seemed a h.	HEROES 9
who aspires to be a h.	ALCOHOL 12
Herod Oh, for an hour of H.	CHILDREN 17

out-Herod H.	CRUELTY 2
heroes clatter of h.	SKIES 30
land that needs h.	HEROES 15
speed glum h. up the line	WORLD W I 19
world's brave h.	ARMED FORCES 23
heroic temper of h. hearts	DETERMINATION 38
heroing H. is one of the shortest	HEROES 13
hero-worship H. is strongest	HEROES 11
herring Every h. must hang by	DUTY 2
good red h.	CHARACTER 24
red h.	LOGIC 6
hesitates h. is lost	INDECISION 4
She floats, she h.	WOMEN 22
hesitating H. doesn't matter	HASTE 19
hesitation Hawing and H.	SPEECHES 21
heterodoxy h. is another man's	RELIGION 17
hic H. *jacet*	DEATH 31
h. jacet	EPITAPHS 22
hidden h. in each other's hearts	SECRECY 24
h. persuaders	ADVERTISING 14
Nature is often h.	CHARACTER 28
hide h. one's light	SELF-ESTEEM 5
Those who h. can find	SECRECY 11
wise man h. a leaf	SECRECY 25
high h. man, with a great thing	ACHIEVEMENT 20
h. thinking	LIFESTYLES 5
None climbs so h.	ACHIEVEMENT 14
Pile it h.	BUSINESS 13
wickedness in h. places	SUPERNATURAL 9
highbrow What is a h.	INTELLIGENCE 15
higher h. the monkey climbs	AMBITION 2
highland heart is H.	SCOTLAND 12
highlands My heart's in the H.	SCOTLAND 12
worst in all the H.	SCOTLAND 6
high-tech thing with h.	TECHNOLOGY 27
highway each and every h.	LIFESTYLES 32
passes over a h.	FICTION 11
highways happy h.	PAST 27
hijacker terrorist and h.	REVOLUTION 30
hill at the other side of the h.	WARFARE 29
city upon a h.	AMERICA 10
hunter home from the h.	EPITAPHS 19
light on the h.	POLITICS 26
hills Blue are the h.	FAMILIARITY 3
blue remembered h.	PAST 27
City of the Seven H.	TOWNS 3
convictions are h.	MIDDLE AGE 10
h. are alive	MUSIC 28
out on the h. alone	SOLITUDE 12
sweet are thy h. and vales	WALES 5
Himalayas H. to the heavens	EARTH 13
himself Every man for h.	SELF-INTEREST 1
Every man for h.	SELF-INTEREST 2
hind-legs sheep on its h.	CONFORMITY 9
hindmost Devil take the h.	SELF-INTEREST 2
hindrance h. of h.	IGNORANCE 11
hindsight as good as his h.	FORESIGHT 1
h. is always twenty-twenty	PAST 40
hip H. is the sophistication	FASHION 9
smite h. and thigh	CRIME 16
hippies h. wanted peace and love	LIKES 18
Hippocrene blushful H.	ALCOHOL 14
hippopotamus magnificent but painful h.	WRITERS 16
hire worthy of his h.	EMPLOYMENT 1
hired h. the money	DEBT 22
Hiroshima Einstein leads to H.	CAUSES 28
hissing smallest possible amount of h.	TAXES 7
historian Whig h.	HISTORY 6
historians h. can	HISTORY 18
h. left blanks	HISTORY 23
h. repeat one another	HISTORY 19
history all the disasters of English h.	WALES 7
country which has no h.	HISTORY 1
draft of a h.	JOURNALISM 24
dustbin of h.	SUCCESS 37
end of h.	HISTORY 28
Family h., of course	FAMILY 27

Father of H.	HISTORY 5	**holiday** perpetual h.	LEISURE 9
happiest women have no h.	WOMEN 35	Roman h.	CRUELTY 3
h. defaced	PAST 19	Roman h.	CRUELTY 8
H. gets thicker	HISTORY 25	time when on h.	LEISURE 12
h. has portrayed	HUMAN RACE 25	**holidays** h. are no voyage	LEISURE 16
H. is a fable	HISTORY 2	holiest of all h.	FESTIVALS 65
H. is bunk	HISTORY 20	playing h.	LEISURE 6
H. is littered with the wars	WARFARE 59	**holier** h. than thou	HYPOCRISY 3
H. is not what you thought	HISTORY 22	**holiness** Courage of Heart, or H.	MANNERS 18
H. is now	HISTORY 24	h. of the heart's affections	TRUTH 27
h. is on our side	CAPITALISM 21	social h.	CHRISTIAN CH 21
H. is past politics	HISTORY 17	**Holland** H. lies so low	COUNTRIES 17
H. is the essence	HISTORY 14	**hollow** We are the h. men	FUTILITY 22
H. just burps	HISTORY 27	**Hollywood** H. is a place where	AMERICAN CITIES 58
H., like wood	HISTORY 26	invited to H.	CINEMA 11
h. now comes equipped	PAST 42	**holocaust** Somme is like the H.	WORLD W I 30
h. of art	ARTS 21	**holy** but h. simplicity	STYLE 5
h. records good things	HISTORY 8	H. City	TOWNS 11
H. repeats itself	HISTORY 4	H. Land	COUNTRIES 5
H. repeats itself	HISTORY 19	h. loved by the gods	RELIGION 4
H. to the defeated	SUCCESS 39	h. of holies	VALUE 11
H. will absolve me	REVOLUTION 24	h. simplicity	LAST WORDS 6
h. with lightning	CINEMA 5	h. time is quiet	DAY 10
h. worth bothering about	AUSTRALIA 30	H. Week	FESTIVALS 26
learned anything from h.	HISTORY 12	h. Willie	HYPOCRISY 4
learn from h.	EXPERIENCE 23	neither h., nor Roman	COUNTRIES 13
No h. much	TOWNS 24	**holy-day** h. rejoicing spirit	WORK 28
no h.; only biography	BIOGRAPHY 7	**Holy Ghost** blasphemy against the H.	SIN 10
strange eventful h.	OLD AGE 8	pencil of the H.	BIBLE 12
Thames is liquid h.	RIVERS 15	sin against the H.	SIN 6
thousand years of h.	EUROPE 16	**home** Charity begins at h.	CHARITY 1
too much h.	CANADA 11	East, west h.'s best	HOME 1
War makes good h.	PEACE 16	get all that at h.	THEATRE 23
where the h. comes from	EUROPE 23	harvest h.	FESTIVALS 25
writing a modern h.	HISTORY 9	hear news of h.	TRAVEL 2
history-books blank in h.	HISTORY 10	h. is his castle	HOME 2
hit h. them where they live	THEATRE 18	H. is home	HOME 4
h. us over the head	DIPLOMACY 15	H. is home	LAW 4
They couldn't h. an elephant	LAST WORDS 17	H. is the girl's prison	HOME 17
hitch h. your wagon	IDEALISM 6	H. is the place	HOME 19
Hitler Even H. and Mussolini were	WARFARE 52	H. is the sailor	EPITAPHS 19
H. had been killed	FATE 25	H. is where the heart is	HOME 5
H. invaded hell	INTERNAT REL 29	H. is where the mortgage is	HOME 6
H.'s National Socialist	POLITICAL PART 39	H. is where you come	HOME 21
H. was mad	ECONOMICS 22	H. James	TRANSPORT 18
If I can't love H.	LOVE 61	H. of lost causes	UNIVERSITIES 15
you are kidding, Mister H.	WORLD W II 24	h. of the brave	AMERICA 14
hitting h. below it	PEOPLE 50	h. sweet home to me	HOME 16
worth by h. back	PROBLEMS 23	Look as much like h.	HOME 20
wrong about h. a woman	VIOLENCE 14	murder into the h.	MURDER 23
hoarded h. beyond the power	LIBRARIES 11	My h. policy	WORLD W I 21
hoary h. sort of land	AUSTRALIA 18	nobody at h.	INTELLIGENCE 9
hobby horses had their H.	OPINION 16	no place like h.	HOME 7
hobgoblin h. of little minds	CHANGE 37	no place like h.	HOME 14
Hobson H.'s choice	CHOICE 10	shortest way h.	PATIENCE 8
hodgepodge h. of all other speeches	LANGUAGES 6	What's the good of a h.	HOME 15
hoe tickle her with a h.	AUSTRALIA 14	when you knock it never is at h.	WIT 12
hog England under the h.	PEOPLE 1	Who goes h.	PARLIAMENT 2
hoist h. with one's own petard	CAUSES 12	woman's place is in the h.	WOMAN'S ROLE 4
hold h. on other people	GIFTS 22	your child tells me about h.	SCHOOLS 1
H. the fort	WARS 20	**homeless** h. by choice	HOME 13
keep a-h. of Nurse	MISFORTUNES 23	houses to the h.	ADVERTISING 13
What you have, h.	POSSESSIONS 5	**homely** though it's never so h.	HOME 4
holdfast H. is better	WORDS AND DEEDS 2	**Homer** contend for H. dead	FAME 9
holding h. on to the sides	CHARACTER 49	cuts taken from H.	ORIGINALITY 3
without h. on	DRUNKENNESS 18	H. nods	MISTAKES 11
hole centre h. that makes it useful	VALUE 16	H. sometimes nods	MISTAKES 1
first h. made through	SCULPTURE 7	H. sometimes sleeps	POETS 17
h. in the stone	DETERMINATION 28	must not call it H.	TRANSLATION 6
if I am in the devil of a h.	EXPLORATION 14	single exception of H.	SHAKESPEARE 12
in a round h.	CIRCUMSTANCE 14	**Homeric** H. laughter	HUMOUR 2
into the round h.	CIRCUMSTANCE 18	**homes** stately h. of England	RANK 10
knows of a better h.	ADVICE 21	**homosexual** in a h. relationship	CONSTANCY 17
making a h. in a sock	DRESS 20	**honest** buy it like an h. man	RANK 14
pessimist sees the h.	OPTIMISM 25	h. and intelligent	ARGUMENT 22
When you are in a h.	APOLOGY 7	h. arrogance	SELF-ESTEEM 22
holes foxes have h.	HOME 10	h. broker	DIPLOMACY 2

honest (*cont.*)
h. broker	DIPLOMACY 7
h. God	GOD 28
h. men come by their own	CRIME 10
h. politician	POLITICIANS 15
h., sonsie face	FOOD 14
not an h. man	HONESTY 10
poor but she was h.	VIRTUE 44

honestly Get the money h.
	MONEY 3
h., but not honesty	HONESTY 6
If possible h.	MONEY 22

honesty h. is a good thing
	HONESTY 13
H. is more praised	HONESTY 3
H. is praised	HONESTY 7
H. is the best policy	HONESTY 4
H. is the best policy	HONESTY 10

honey H. catches more flies
	WAYS 7
h. still for tea	PAST 29
milk and h.	WEALTH 11
Tiggers don't like h.	LIKES 15
Where bees are, there is h.	WORK 10

honi H. soit qui mal y pense
	GOOD 3

honour All is lost save h.
	SUCCESS 23
civility and h.	RANK 23
either property or h.	SATISFACTION 15
fountain of h.	GOVERNMENT 29
fountain of h.	ROYALTY 14
h. among thieves	COOPERATION 15
H. a physician	MEDICINE 6
H. is like a match	REPUTATION 26
h. rooted in dishonour	CONSTANCY 15
H. the King	WORLD W I 9
H. thy father	PARENTS 4
hurt that H. feels	CORRUPTION 13
Keeps h. bright	DETERMINATION 29
leisure with h.	LEISURE 5
Loved I not h. more	DUTY 10
peace with h.	PEACE 6
peace with h.	PEACE 14
peace with h.	PEACE 21
post of h.	DANGER 8
prophet is not without h.	FAMILIARITY 13
refuses the Legion of H.	MUSICIANS 11
safety, h., and welfare	ARMED FORCES 18
talked of his h.	HONESTY 11

honoured h. in the breach
	CUSTOM 9

hood long black h.
	ROYALTY 22

hoof cloven h.
	GOOD 10
horse's h.	ANIMALS 5

hook receiver off the h.
	GOD 36

hooter because the h. hoots
	BRITISH TOWNS 35

Hoover get them onto the board of H.
	WOMAN'S ROLE 31

hope Abandon all h.
	HEAVEN 9
any h. for them	CUSTOM 16
best h. of earth	LIBERTY 21
dread nor h. attend	DEATH 62
equal poise of h.	OPTIMISM 16
faith, h., charity	LOVE 21
forward to with h.	DISILLUSION 17
He that lives in h.	HOPE 2
h. and agitation in	HOPE 17
H. could ne'er have flown	DESPAIR 5
H. deferred	HOPE 3
H. deferred	HOPE 9
h. for greater favours	GRATITUDE 11
h. for the best	LIFESTYLES 23
H. for the best	PREPARATION 8
h. in your heart	HOPE 22
H. is a good breakfast	HOPE 4
h. over experience	MARRIAGE 24
H. sleeps in our bones	HOPE 23
H. springs eternal	HOPE 5
H. springs eternal	HOPE 13
h., wish day may come	DESPAIR 14
If it were not for h.	HOPE 6
life there's hope	HOPE 8
lives upon h.	HOPE 14

not another's h.	HOPE 12
recovered h.	DESPAIR 12
we sell h.	BUSINESS 45
Whatever h. is yours	FUTILITY 20
What is h.	HOPE 15
when h. is gone	WOMEN 30
Work without h.	HOPE 18

hoped He who has never h.
	HOPE 20

hoped-for h. heaven
	EPITAPHS 16

hopefully better to travel h.
	HOPE 7
To travel h.	TRAVEL 28

hopeless h. are starkly sincere
	SYMPATHY 22
h. grief	SORROW 16

hopelessness h. and calm
	HOPE 17
h. of one's position	DESPAIR 13
undone years, The h.	FUTILITY 20

hopes happy as one h.
	HAPPINESS 11
h. and prospects	MIDDLE AGE 5
If h. were dupes	HOPE 19
no great h. from Birmingham	BRITISH TOWNS 27
vanity of human h.	LIBRARIES 5

hops cherries, h., and women
	BRITISH TOWNS 30
heresy, h., and beer	INVENTIONS 1

horizons wide h.
	RUSSIA 6

horizontal h. desire
	DANCE 15
h. fall	LIFE 42

horn come out of your h.
	MUSIC 26
cow's h.	ANIMALS 5
gate of h.	DREAMS 5
h. of plenty	QUANTITIES 13
hounds and his h.	HUNTING 9

horned h. Moon
	SKIES 16

horns Fate can be taken by the h.
	FATE 1
h. of a dilemma	CIRCUMSTANCE 8

horny h. hands of toil
	WORK 30

horribilis annus h.
	MISFORTUNES 30

horrible h. imaginings
	FEAR 4

horror h. of sunsets
	DAY 17
h.! The horror	FEAR 10
there is no h.	IMAGINATION 15

horrors scene of h.
	MATHS 15

horse camel is a h.
	ADMINISTRATION 27
Do not trust the horse	TRUST 18
for want of a h.	PREPARATION 6
gift h. in the mouth	GRATITUDE 3
good h.	APPEARANCE 7
h. enough oats	ECONOMICS 21
h. has bolted	FORESIGHT 3
h. has bolted	MISTAKES 9
h., my wife, and my name	DEBT 15
h.'s hoof	ANIMALS 5
h. to the water	DEFIANCE 4
If two ride on a h.	RANK 2
mare is the better h.	MARRIAGE 4
may steal a h.	REPUTATION 10
outside of a h.	HEALTH 9
owe it to h. and hound	ANIMALS 21
short h. is soon curried	WORK 7
sick h. nosing around	SUFFERING 29
stable is not a h.	CHARACTER 9
to my h.—German	LANGUAGES 4
Trojan h.	COMPUTERS 7
Trojan h.	TRUST 15

horseback Set a beggar on h.
	POWER 8

horseman H. pass by
	INDIFFERENCE 13

horsepond always a muddy h.
	SINGLE 7

horse races opinion that makes h.
	OPINION 21

horses breed of their h.
	CHILDREN 11
Bring on the empty h.	CINEMA 9
don't spare the h.	TRANSPORT 18
frighten the h.	SEX 28
hack post-h.	MUSIC 10
harness and not the h.	GOVERNMENT 24
hell of h.	ENGLAND 1
H. for courses	CHOICE 4
h. in midstream	CHANGE 18
h. may not be stolen	CRIME 24

h. of instruction	ANGER 9
If wishes were h.	OPTIMISM 9
hospital requirement in a H.	MEDICINE 18
hospitality h. is medicine	ENTERTAINING 4
host under the h.	DRUNKENNESS 16
hostages h. to fortune	FAMILY 11
hostile universe is not h.	UNIVERSE 13
hot h. for certainties	CERTAINTY 14
H. on Sunday	COOKING 33
iron while it is h.	OPPORTUNITY 29
It's red h., mate	CENSORSHIP 15
never been cool, we're h.	IRELAND 26
pot is soon h.	ANGER 2
while the iron is h.	OPPORTUNITY 14
hotter cooler to a h.	PHYSICAL 16
hound I loves the h. more	HUNTING 10
owe it to horse and h.	ANIMALS 21
hounds h. all join in	HUNTING 5
h. and his horn	HUNTING 9
hunt with the h.	TRUST 5
hunt with the h.	TRUST 11
hour accompany us one short h.	UNIVERSITIES 10
at the eleventh h.	HASTE 10
darkest h.	OPTIMISM 3
finest h.	SUCCESS 15
h. come round at last	CHRISTMAS 3
h. upon the stage	LIFE 19
Improve each shining h.	WORK 25
improve the shining h.	EFFORT 10
longer in an h.	ENTERTAINING 18
matched us with His h.	WORLD W I 12
most carefully upon your h.	PUNCTUALITY 7
Oh, for an h. of Herod	CHILDREN 26
One h.'s sleep before	SLEEP 1
their finest h.	WORLD W II 11
witching h.	DAY 3
ye know not what h.	PREPARATION 12
hours chase the glowing H.	DANCE 9
eight h. a day	EMPLOYMENT 26
h. will take care of themselves	TIME 31
I see the h. pass	ACTION 28
look at it for h.	WORK 34
Six h. in sleep	LIFESTYLES 19
Six h. sleep	SLEEP 2
sleep five h.	SLEEP 3
two golden h.	TIME 36
wages and shorter h.	POLITICAL PART 24
house all through the h.	CHRISTMAS 8
angel in the h.	WOMAN'S ROLE 5
doll in the doll's h.	WOMAN'S ROLE 20
h. and land	KNOWLEDGE 7
h. and land	KNOWLEDGE 11
h. is a machine	ARCHITECTURE 12
h. is built of stones	SCIENCE 13
H. is pleased to direct	PARLIAMENT 12
h. need to be cleaned	HOUSEWORK 16
h. of Rimmon	SELF-INTEREST 10
h. where I was born	MEMORY 12
If a h. be divided	COOPERATION 20
in the way in the h.	MEN 10
join h. to house	POLLUTION 5
labour of women in the h.	EMPLOYMENT 16
Leader of the H.	PARLIAMENT 8
mind to sell his h.	BUYING 5
one h. spoiled	MARRIAGE 2
serious h.	CHRISTIAN CH 34
well-thatched h.	EMOTIONS 7
housed h., clothed, fed	HUMAN RIGHTS 11
houseful three is a h.	CHILDREN 2
householder think she's a h.	MARRIAGE 41
housekeeper make a h. think	MARRIAGE 41
House of Commons devil in the H.	INTERNAT REL 29
Father of the H.	PARLIAMENT 6
untrue in the H.	TRUTH 43
houses few of his friends' h.	SICKNESS 12
Fools build h.	FOOLS 4
have nothing in your h.	POSSESSIONS 19

H. are built to live in	ARCHITECTURE 6
h. just as big	HYPOCRISY 20
Laws, like h.	LAW 21
live in glass h.	GOSSIP 9
spaces between the h.	POLLUTION 23
wasn't for the h. in between	COUNTRY AND TOWN 18
housetop corner of the h.	ARGUMENT 8
housetops proclaim from the h.	ADVERTISING 6
house-trained semi-h. polecat	PEOPLE 59
housewife h. that's thrifty	WOMEN 27
h. wears herself out	HOUSEWORK 11
Many a h. staring	SOLITUDE 25
housework Conran's Law of h.	HOUSEWORK 14
h., with its endless repetition	HOUSEWORK 11
no need to do any h.	HOUSEWORK 13
Houston H., we've had a problem	PROBLEMS 24
hovel prefer in fact a h.	LIKES 10
how H. and Where	KNOWLEDGE 43
H. NOT TO DO IT	ADMINISTRATION 7
H. now, brown cow	SPEECH 1
h. you do it	LIBERTY 40
howitzer h. squatting	SCULPTURE 8
howling h. coyote	ANIMALS 2
huddled Your h. masses	AMERICA 22
hues all her lovely h.	BIRDS 17
hugging H. trees has a calming effect	TREES 19
Hugo H.—alas	POETS 25
Hull Hell, H., and Halifax	BRITISH TOWNS 2
human all h. life	LIFE 9
all h. life is there	LIFE 35
conquered h. natur	HUMAN NATURE 13
depend on h. relations	WORK 40
dreadful h. beings sitting	TRANSPORT 33
he's a h. being	SUFFERING 30
h. being dissatisfied	SATISFACTION 27
h. beings we are more alike	HUMAN RACE 35
H. kind cannot bear	HUMAN RACE 28
H. life begins	DESPAIR 16
H. life is a sad show	ARTS 14
H. nature seldom walks	SICKNESS 16
h. zoo	COUNTRY AND TOWN 25
I count nothing h.	HUMAN RACE 9
it's like to be h.	MUSICIANS 22
knowledge of h. nature	FICTION 9
lives of h. beings	IMAGINATION 19
lose its h. face	CAPITALISM 27
love h. beings	HUMAN RACE 31
not the less h. for being devout	VIRTUE 25
To be a soaring h. boy	CHILDREN 15
To err is h.	COMPUTERS 2
To err is h.	FORGIVENESS 16
To err is h.	MISTAKES 5
treated as h. beings	EMPLOYMENT 17
we remain h.	SINGLE 14
humanity can help h. forward	WEALTH 32
crooked timber of h.	HUMAN RACE 19
freeze my h.	PREGNANCY 11
h., although it has been born	HUMAN RACE 27
I hate H.	HUMAN RACE 33
left-wing, like h.	POLITICAL PART 45
music of h.	NATURE 10
teach governments h.	CRIME 27
That unremitting h.	WRITERS 31
humble He that is h.	PRIDE 6
We are so very h.	PRIDE 7
humbug H.	CHRISTMAS 9
Yes we have. H.	EMOTIONS 17
humiliation as harsh a h.	LANGUAGES 17
born of h.	ARTS 31
shame and h.	REPUTATION 29
humility hypocritical h.	SELF-ESTEEM 22
small book on H.	PRIDE 14
humming H., Hawing	SPEECHES 21
madly h., demented refrigerator	ACTING 14
virus h.	SICKNESS 26
humour Good taste and h.	HUMOUR 19
h. of a bar-loafer	WRITERS 18

importunate business is no less i.   HOUSEWORK 6
importunity ever-haunting i. Of business   WORK 28
impossibilities Probable i.   PROBLEMS 13
impossible art of the i.   POLITICS 35
  because it is i.   BELIEF 12
  eliminated the i.   PROBLEMS 15
  i. aim   DESPAIR 17
  i. dream   IDEALISM 13
  i. takes a little longer   ACHIEVEMENT 2
  i. to enjoy idling   IDLENESS 21
  I wish it were i.   MUSICIANS 4
  says that it is i.   HYPOTHESIS 28
  six i. things   BELIEF 21
  With men this is i.   GOD 8
imposture carry on the i.   OLD AGE 23
impotence i. and sodomy   CLASS 27
imprecision Decay with i.   WORDS 23
impressed Too easily i.   TASTE 8
impressions First i.   BEGINNING 2
imprint set it in I.   PUBLISHING 3
imprisoned I. in every fat man   BODY 25
  i. or dispossessed   HUMAN RIGHTS 4
improbability statistical i.   LIFE SCI 26
improbable *however* i.   PROBLEMS 15
  i. possibilities   PROBLEMS 13
impropriety I. is the soul of wit   WIT 17
improve how to i. what's proposed   ADVICE 24
  I. each shining hour   WORK 25
  i. the shining hour   EFFORT 10
  want to i. on it   LIFE SCI 17
improvement signs of i.   PARENTS 23
improves Anger i. nothing   ANGER 1
improvisation I. is too good   MUSIC 32
impudence Cockney i.   PAINTING 11
impudent called John a I. Bitch   INSULTS 6
impulse first i.   ACTION 17
  i. from a vernal wood   GOOD 30
  i. of the moment   BEHAVIOUR 20
impulses truck with first i.   CAUTION 25
impunity provokes me with i.   DEFIANCE 1
impure all things are i.   GOOD 37
in Garbage i.   COMPUTERS 2
inability i. to cross the street   FRIENDSHIP 5
inaccuracy i. sometimes saves   LIES 20
inaction i. sap the vigour   ACTION 14
inadequate i. that intelligence   INTELLIGENCE 16
inanimate goal of all i. objects   POSSESSIONS 24
in-between mess with Mister I.   OPTIMISM 31
incapacity courted by I.   CAUTION 24
incarnation i. in a human body   HUMAN NATURE 19
incest i. and folk-dancing   EXPERIENCE 13
  see lust and rape and i.   THEATRE 23
Inch says 'Not an i.'   CERTAINTY 25
inches die by i.   DEATH 40
incident i. of the dog   LOGIC 15
incisors divided into i. and grinders   WRITING 30
inclination door of i.   SIN 21
  just as i. leads him   READING 10
inclusion Life being all i.   ARTS 24
income dead-level of i.   EQUALITY 14
  Expenditure rises to meet i.   ECONOMICS 13
  higher our i.   POLLUTION 26
  however great the i.   FARMING 6
  i. is the best recipe   HAPPINESS 20
  I. Tax has made more Liars   TAXES 17
  i. twenty pounds   DEBT 16
  moderate i.   GREED 12
incomes live beyond their i. nowadays   THRIFT 16
incompetence his level of i.   ADMINISTRATION 22
incompetent election by the i.   DEMOCRACY 15
incomplete i. in the urban compound   TRANSPORT 26
incomprehensible i. to decide the unknowable   LAW 46
  most i. fact   UNIVERSE 14
inconsistency i. at times   HUMAN RIGHTS 17
inconstancy in Nature were i.   CHANGE 32
inconstant i. woman   CONSTANCY 10
incontinence Refraining from i.   LIFESTYLES 14

inconvenience great i.   POVERTY 5
  i. is often considerable   SURPRISE 9
  made without i.   CHANGE 33
inconvenient cause may be i.   IDEALISM 9
incorruptible seagreen I.   PEOPLE 37
increase who dies fighting has i.   LIFE 38
increased has i., is increasing   ROYALTY 21
incurable i. disease   LIFE 21
indecision habitual but i.   INDECISION 10
  I. is fatal   INDECISION 6
independence Declaration of I.   HUMAN RIGHTS 10
  I. Day   FESTIVALS 27
independent easy to be i.   SELF-ESTEEM 24
  i. choice   CHOICE 17
  i. is a guy   POLITICAL PART 38
  i. or entirely free   HUMAN RACE 21
India I. is identifiable   COUNTRIES 26
  I. . . . is not a place   COUNTRIES 33
Indian I. summer   OLD AGE 4
  I. summer   WEATHER 25
  like an I. widow   MANNERS 21
  Like the base I.   VALUE 21
  Lo! the poor I.   IGNORANCE 14
  only good I.   RACE 9
Indians America to convert the I.   RELIGION 14
  I. are you   RACE 26
Indies augmentation of the I.   BODY 11
indifference another name for i.   PREJUDICE 14
  i. and a coach and six   IDEALISM 5
  it's i.   INDIFFERENCE 16
indifferent i. to them   INDIFFERENCE 10
  It is simply i.   UNIVERSE 13
  society, and been i.   INDIFFERENCE 14
indigestion moral i.   PLEASURE 22
  reaps i.   COOKING 26
indignation i. can no longer tear   EPITAPHS 14
  i. is jealousy   MORALITY 12
indiscretion cliché and an i.   POLITICIANS 23
individual bind the savage i.   SOCIETY 14
  i. calamity   CRISES 12
  i. men and women   SOCIETY 20
  no i. is more important   POLITICAL PART 47
individualism rugged i.   AMERICA 29
individuals how to relate to i.   MARRIAGE 52
indivisible Peace is i.   PEACE 18
indulgent makes one very i.   INSIGHT 9
industrial I. relations are like sexual   EMPLOYMENT 2
industrialists die for the i.   PATRIOTISM 23
industrious stupid and i.   ARMED FORCES 38
industry i. applies   TECHNOLOGY 2
  i. will supply their deficiency   WORK 26
  Modern i. seems to be inefficient   BUSINESS 44
  national i. of Prussia   WARFARE 23
  Necessity sharpens i.   NECESSITY 10
  not his i.   PARLIAMENT 15
  that of a major i.   BROADCASTING 9
inefficient Modern industry seems to be i.   BUSINESS 44
inequality i. of people's lives   FESTIVALS 68
inertia I. can develop its own momentum   ACTION 29
inessential save five *sous* on i. things   GOVERNMENT 14
inevitable arguing with the i.   ARGUMENT 17
  Death may be i.   FARMING 16
  i. never happens   IRELAND 17
  writers foresee the i.   FORESIGHT 7
infamy date which will live in i.   WORLD W II 14
infancy Heaven lies about us in our i.   YOUTH 12
infant At first the i.   CHILDREN 3
infanticide indefensible as i.   CENSORSHIP 10
infects i. the teller   NEWS 7
inferior disgraced by the i.   RANK 12
  I. to us God made you   WOMAN'S ROLE 22
  make you feel i.   PRIDE 13
inferno i. of his passions   EMOTIONS 24
infidelity geologists into i.   LIFE SCI 16
  I. does not consist   FAITH 7
  smacks of i.   CHANGE 41
  There is no i.   CONSTANCY 13

judgement (*cont.*)
j. will probably be right   JUSTICE 28
never our j.   MEMORY 1
people's j.   DEMOCRACY 5
replace reasoned j.   DETERMINATION 25
judges j. have declared it so   EXCELLENCE 12
j. soon the sentence sign   LAW 20
judging considers j. others   CRITICISM 5
Judy Colonel's Lady an' J. O'Grady   WOMEN 38
jug git loose fum de j.   DRUNKENNESS 10
juggernaut Prudence is a wooden J.   CAUTION 27
juggle how to j. work, love, home   WOMAN'S ROLE 32
juggler j. who uses harmonies   JAZZ 7
perceive a j.'s sleight   DECEPTION 14
July Born on the fourth of J.   AMERICA 25
Fourth of J.   FESTIVALS 20
June dripping J. sets all in tune   WEATHER 3
J. is bustin' out   SEASONS 28
jungle concrete j.   COUNTRY AND TOWN 4
law of the j.   SELF-INTEREST 15
rumble in the j.   SPORTS 3
juniper j. talks to the oak   TREES 18
junk flung up old j.   SKIES 30
J. is the ideal product   DRUGS 6
Juno bird of J.   BIRDS 5
Jupiter J. the Rain-giver   RIVERS 5
jury j. too frequently have   LAW 27
jury-men j. may dine   LAW 20
just any j. cause   OPPORTUNITY 27
j. before you're generous   JUSTICE 2
'j.' or 'right' means nothing   JUSTICE 17
j. war   WARFARE 8
no such thing as a j. war   WARFARE 34
rain, it raineth on the j.   WEATHER 45
sendeth rain on the j.   EQUALITY 4
justice call for j.   JUSTICE 22
Jedburgh j.   JUSTICE 14
j., I am a banana   JUSTICE 38
J. is in one scale   CRISES 13
j. is open to all   JUSTICE 33
J. is the constant   JUSTICE 20
J. is truth   JUSTICE 29
j. makes democracy   DEMOCRACY 19
j. of my own quarrel   JUSTICE 26
j. or human happiness   LIBERTY 36
j. or injustice   JUSTICE 27
j. should not only be done   JUSTICE 35
kind of wild j.   REVENGE 14
Let j. be done   JUSTICE 23
ounce of j.   JUSTICE 37
poetic j.   CAUSES 13
pursuit of j.   EXCESS 31
right or J.   JUSTICE 21
think j. requires   JUSTICE 28
threat to j. everywhere   JUSTICE 36
truth, j. and the American way   HEROES 17
We all love j.   JUSTICE 10
What stings is j.   JUSTICE 34
justifies end j. the means   MORALITY 3
justify j. God's ways to man   ALCOHOL 20
j. the ways of God   WRITING 16
justitia Fiat j.   JUSTICE 23

kaiser put the kibosh on the K.   WORLD W I 11
kaleyard K. School   WRITERS 4
kamikaze k. pilot   SUICIDE 2
Kansas not in K. any more   CHANGE 47
karma k. is working from another   BODY 36
Keating you can call Paul K.   INSULTS 15
keep Ideas won't k.   IDEAS 16
If you can k. your head   CRISES 15
K. a thing seven years   POSSESSIONS 5
K. right on   DETERMINATION 41
k. up with the Joneses   ENVY 5
k. up with them   MORALITY 1

K. your own shop   BUSINESS 8
should k. who can   POWER 20
too good to k.   SECRECY 10
worth while to k. them   EMPLOYMENT 17
keeper Am I my brother's k.   RELATIONSHIPS 2
keepers Finders k.   POSSESSIONS 1
keeping k. up with yesterday   IDLENESS 23
keepings Findings k.   POSSESSIONS 2
Kennedy K. was dead   MEMORY 29
Kent everybody knows K.   BRITISH TOWNS 30
Some places of K.   BRITISH TOWNS 9
Kentish K. miles   BRITISH TOWNS 9
kettle k. of fish   ORDER 6
pretty k. of fish   ROYALTY 32
ties a k. to a dog's tail   WRITERS 18
key k. can open any door   CORRUPTION 3
looking for the k.   LIFE 50
Turn the k. deftly   SLEEP 14
while I keep the k.   SUICIDE 4
keystone K. State   AMERICAN CITIES 23
kibosh put the k. on the Kaiser   WORLD W I 11
kick first k. I took   POVERTY 33
great k. at misery   SUFFERING 24
if you do, she'll k.   GRATITUDE 2
k. against the pricks   DEFIANCE 7
k. to come to the top   DESPAIR 9
kicks how I get my k.   BUSINESS 47
kid dead-end k.   CRIME 12
kiddies k. have crumpled the serviettes   MANNERS 22
kidding you are k., Mister Hitler   WORLD W II 24
kids don't have any k.   DISILLUSION 23
how many k. have you killed today   WARS 1
Kilkenny fight like K. cats   CATS 4
kill as soon k. a pig   LETTERS 15
enough in thee to k. care   WORRY 8
Eternal in man cannot k.   DEATH 19
get out and k. something   HUNTING 16
Guns don't k. people   MURDER 2
k. a good book   CENSORSHIP 3
K. a man   MURDER 21
k. the fatted calf   FESTIVALS 29
K. them all   DISILLUSION 7
licensed to k.   MURDER 6
not going to k. too many   MURDER 25
right to k.   MURDER 24
something you k. for   FAITH 15
Thou shalt not k.   MURDER 8
Thou shalt not k.   MURDER 18
What does not k. me   SUFFERING 22
killed Better be k.   FEAR 8
Care k. the cat   WORRY 1
enemy you k.   ENEMIES 17
Go to Spain and get k.   HEROES 14
hard work never k. anybody   WORK 43
He must try and get k.   ARMED FORCES 31
how many kids have you k. today   WARS 1
If hate k. men   HATRED 8
k. myself long ago   SUICIDE 14
knows he cannot be k.   ARMED FORCES 40
Look what I k.   DRESS 26
so many people k.   PRACTICALITY 11
who k. him   VIOLENCE 12
killer lover and k. are mingled   DEATH 65
killing If k. foxes is necessary   HUNTING 20
K. myself to die   KISSING 4
K. no murder   MURDER 3
K. no murder   MURDER 13
Men talk of k. time   TIME 34
more ways of k. a cat   WAYS 13
more ways of k. a dog   WAYS 14
more ways of k. a dog   WAYS 15
kills it k. me   HONESTY 16
K. all known germs   POLLUTION 1
k. the thing he loves   LOVE 56
not work that k.   WORRY 3
pace that k.   STRENGTH 3
pity k.   SYMPATHY 21

suicide k. two people	SUICIDE 10	coward does it with a k.	LOVE 56
that which k.	MEN AND WOMEN 22	die upon a k.	KISSING 4
Kim K.'s game	MEMORY 3	immortal with a k.	BEAUTY 10
kin little more than k.	FAMILY 10	Judas k.	TRUST 8
makes the whole world k.	HUMAN NATURE 9	k. again with tears	FORGIVENESS 20
one's own k. and kith	FAMILY 21	k. and part	MEETING 11
kind art of being k.	RELIGION 24	k. can be a comma	KISSING 13
cruel only to be k.	CRUELTY 6	k. is still a kiss	KISSING 10
cruel to be k.	CRUELTY 12	K. Kiss Bang Bang	CINEMA 19
k. as it is green	IRELAND 19	K. me, Hardy	LAST WORDS 15
K. hearts are more than	RANK 9	k. of the sun	GARDENS 17
k. things I say	PRAISE 16	k. the place to make it well	CHILD CARE 5
k. to Belfast	BRITISH TOWNS 44	like a k. without a squeeze	FOOD 1
k. to your friends	FRIENDSHIP 1	rough male k.	SLEEP 16
less than k.	FAMILY 10	To let a k. fool you	KISSING 15
people will always be k.	SENSES 14	With one long k.	KISSING 7
kindle k. light in the darkness	LIFE 49	**kissed** k. my first woman	SMOKING 14
kindliness k. of sheets	SLEEP 16	k. the Blarney stone	SPEECH 4
kindness cup o' k.	MEMORY 10	**kisses** Give me a thousand k.	KISSING 3
generates k.	SPORTS 8	k. on paper	KISSING 6
K. in another's trouble	LIFE 34	more than k.	LETTERS 6
k. of strangers	CHARITY 22	romance with no k.	KISSING 11
milk of human k.	SYMPATHY 7	**kissing** I wasn't k. her	KISSING 14
milk of human k.	SYMPATHY 14	K. don't last	COOKING 24
milk of human k.	WRITERS 19	K. girls	KISSING 16
king cat may look at a k.	EQUALITY 1	K. goes by favour	KISSING 1
consumer is the k.	BUYING 9	k. had to stop	KISSING 8
duty is the k.'s	CONSCIENCE 11	k. has to stop	ENDING 11
esteem of a k.	ROYALTY 16	k.'s out of fashion	KISSING 2
fight for its K.	PATRIOTISM 25	like k. God	DRUGS 8
from an anointed k.	ROYALTY 12	who's k. her now	KISSING 9
God save our gracious k.	ROYALTY 19	**Kissinger** K. brought peace	PEACE 29
Here lies a great and mighty k.	WORDS AND DEEDS 14	**kit-bag** pack up your troubles in your old k.	WORRY 11
K. and Country	ARMED FORCES 10	**kitchen** get out of the k.	STRENGTH 2
K. and country	PATRIOTISM 4	get out of the k.	STRENGTH 25
k. can do no wrong	ROYALTY 1	**kith** one's own kin and k.	FAMILY 21
K. Charles's head	IDEAS 4	**Kit-Kat** have a K.	LEISURE 3
K. James Bible	BIBLE 5	**kitten** trouble with a k.	CATS 12
K. of all these	DEATH 17	**kittens** Wanton k. make sober cats	YOUTH 1
k. of beasts	ANIMALS 6	**kleine** eine k. Pause	LAST WORDS 30
K. of Great Britain	CORRUPTION 12	**knaves** grudge at k.	ENVY 13
k. of infinite space	DREAMS 7	**knee** civility of my k.	PRAYER 15
K. over the Water	ROYALTY 6	every k. should bow	NAMES 4
k. rides a bicycle	COUNTRIES 34	**knees** live on your k.	LIBERTY 28
k.'s chaff is worth	ROYALTY 2	**knell** k. of parting day	DAY 8
k.'s evil	SICKNESS 6	**knew** looked away, then you k.	GUILT 23
offended the k.	LAST WORDS 7	**knife** cannibal uses k. and fork	PROGRESS 22
one eyed man is k.	POWER 3	He who wields the k.	TRUST 39
rightwise K. born	ROYALTY 9	k. that probes far deeper	GUILT 13
stomach of a k.	ROYALTY 11	smyler with the k.	TRUST 22
unless you're a k.	SHAKESPEARE 15	War to the k.	WARS 11
waltz k.	MUSICIANS 2	**knight** k. in shining armour	HEROES 3
who is K.	ROYALTY 20	parfit gentil knight	CHARACTER 27
you, as their K.	SELF-SACRIFICE 12	There was never a k.	HEROES 8
your K. and your Country	WORLD W I 13	white k.	BUSINESS 22
kingdom k. where nobody dies	CHILDREN 8	**knives** carry long k.	COOKING 3
till k. come	TIME 14	night of the long k.	TRUST 9
to me a k. is	MIND 5	**knob** holding the k.	OPPORTUNITY 35
kingdom of God fit for the k.	DETERMINATION 24	**knock** k., and it shall be opened	PRAYER 7
King Kong have to be like K.	MEN 20	K. as you please	INTELLIGENCE 7
kings cabbages—and k.	CONVERSATION 14	k. at the door	MEETING 13
divine right of k.	ROYALTY 5	k., breathe, shine	GOD 16
end of k.	ROYALTY 17	k. him down first	SYMPATHY 16
flowers and K.	HOUSEWORK 10	k. him down for it	OPINION 17
K. have long arms	POWER 4	when you k. it never is at home	WIT 12
k. to be strangled	REVOLUTION 9	**knocked** k. me down with a feather	SURPRISE 5
only five K. left	ROYALTY 34	**knocking** K. on the moonlit door	MEETING 18
politeness of k.	PUNCTUALITY 10	**knocks** k. you down	ARGUMENT 12
sport of k.	HUNTING 6	never k. twice	OPPORTUNITY 11
sport of k.	HUNTING 11	Opportunity never k.	OPPORTUNITY 12
sport of k.	SPORTS 4	**knot** cut the Gordian k.	PROBLEMS 4
walk with K.	MATURITY 9	**knots** pokers into true-love k.	POETS 15
kinship thread of k.	AUSTRALIA 16	**know** As any fule k.	IGNORANCE 25
kinsmen k. die	HEROES 4	Better the devil you k.	FAMILIARITY 1
Kipling sort of gutless K.	POETS 23	better to k. nothing	KNOWLEDGE 38
kirtle Near is my k.	SELF-INTEREST 6	does not k. himself	SELF-KNOWLEDGE 5
kiss come k. me, sweet and twenty	YOUTH 7	does not k. where he is going	TRAVEL 34

last (*cont.*)
l. to know	IGNORANCE 1
Long foretold, long l.	WEATHER 8
Look thy l. on all things	TRANSIENCE 14
Nice guys finish l.	SPORTS 1
no l. nor first	GOD 25
prepare for the l. war	WARFARE 57
Seven L. Words	LAST WORDS 2
We were the l. romantics	IDEALISM 11
who laughs l.	REVENGE 4
world's l. night	ENDING 15

lasts Love that l. longest — LOVE 54
late always too l. or too early — TIME 42
Better l. than never	PUNCTUALITY 1
Dread of being l.	SCHOOLS 14
guessing correctly how l.	PUNCTUALITY 4
human thought too l.	DISILLUSION 10
l. to shut the stable-door	FORESIGHT 3
l. unpleasantness	WARS 3
never come l.	BEHAVIOUR 29
never too l. to mend	CHANGE 4
people who are l.	PUNCTUALITY 15
She is l.	MEETING 14
surprise God because I'm l.	PUNCTUALITY 19
too l. to learn	EDUCATION 24
You were l.	MEMORY 26

later if it came a little l. in life — YOUTH 18
l. than you think	TIME 39

lateral l. thinking — THINKING 5
lath l. of wood — PEOPLE 42
lathe tell a l. from a lawn mower — WORDS AND DEEDS 20
Latin carve in L. — LANGUAGES 7
half Greek, half L.	BROADCASTING 6
No more L.	SCHOOLS 1
small L.	SHAKESPEARE 4

Latins L. are tenderly enthusiastic — COUNTRIES 28
laugh l. all the time — HUMOUR 15
L. and the world laughs	SORROW 20
L. and the world laughs	SYMPATHY 3
l. at everything	HUMOUR 10
l. at human actions	INSIGHT 7
l. at them in our turn	HUMOUR 11
Let them l.	SUCCESS 5
must l. before we are happy	HUMOUR 8
nothing to l. at	SEA 23
old man who will not l.	GENERATION GAP 12
those you l. at	HUMOUR 23
why people l.	HUMOUR 18

laughable very l. things — POLITICS 12
laugh-at-with someone you could l. — HUMOUR 23
laughing ever had without l. — SEX 42
no l. matter	HAPPINESS 21

laughs He who l. last — REVENGE 5
l. with a harvest	AUSTRALIA 14
Love l. at locksmiths	LOVE 7
who l. last	REVENGE 4

laughter audible l. — MANNERS 14
exciting l. and sorrow	SHAKESPEARE 8
grail of l.	SKIES 24
Homeric l.	HUMOUR 2
L. hath only a scornful	HUMOUR 5
L. is pleasant	HUMOUR 12
l. of a fool	FOOLS 9
l. of her heart	TOWNS 22
L. would be bereaved	HUMOUR 20
more frightful than l.	ENVY 18

launched l. a thousand ships — BEAUTY 10
laureate Poet L. — POETS 6
laurels rest on one's l. — REPUTATION 14
want l. for ourselves most	ENVY 16
win one's l.	SUCCESS 18
worth all your l.	YOUTH 14

lava l. I still find most — MADNESS 12
lavatory l. for its humour — HUMOUR 22
lavender packed in l. — WEDDINGS 9
sheets in l.	DEATH 76

law before all l. — CUSTOM 10

chief l.	LAW 15
Custom, that unwritten l.	CUSTOM 11
dead-level of l.	EQUALITY 14
defied the l.	PARLIAMENT 27
Every land has its own l.	COUNTRIES 1
father antick, the l.	LAW 16
Gresham's L.	MONEY 18
Hard cases make bad l.	LAW 3
if the l. forbids it	LAW 31
Ignorance of the l.	LAW 5
Ignorance of the l.	LAW 18
it is of no force in l.	LAW 17
kind of l. enforcement	LAW 40
l. is a ass	LAW 25
L. is a bottomless pit	LAW 19
L. is the true embodiment	LAW 30
l. more confused	LAW 44
l. of averages	STATISTICS 1
l. of the jungle	SELF-INTEREST 15
l. of the Medes	CHANGE 21
l.'s delay	SUICIDE 3
l.'s grave study six	LIFESTYLES 19
l. which violates	HUMAN RIGHTS 8
love as well as l.	CORRUPTION 10
Murphy's l.	MISFORTUNES 10
myrmidon of the l.	LAW 11
Necessity hath no l.	NECESSITY 20
Necessity knows no l.	NECESSITY 9
nine points of the l.	LAW 8
Nor l., nor duty	ARMED FORCES 36
One l. for the rich	JUSTICE 7
ought l. to weed it	REVENGE 14
prescribed by the l.	HAPPINESS 17
principle of the English l.	LAW 26
this is the royal L.	BIBLE 14
whole of the L.	LIFESTYLES 27

law courts L. not as a cathedral — LAW 45
lawful All ambitions are l. — AMBITION 20
lawn Get your tanks off my l. — ARGUMENT 23
tell a lathe from a l. mower	WORDS AND DEEDS 20
twice a saint in l.	RANK 5

laws Bad l. are the worst — LAW 22
Constitution and the l. of England	CRICKET 8
government of l.	GOVERNMENT 18
had l. not been	SIN 19
l. are like spider's webs	LAW 14
L. are silent in time of war	WARFARE 12
L. grind the poor	POVERTY 19
L., like houses	LAW 21
l. of God	CAUSES 13
l. of nature	BRITAIN 9
l. to the learned	LANGUAGE 12
L. were made to be broken	LAW 23
New lords, new l.	CHANGE 8
obnoxious l.	LAW 28
warfare, and of l.	FRANCE 3
who would make the l.	SINGING 4

lawyer his own l. — LAW 6
l. has no business	JUSTICE 27
l. interprets the truth	LAW 35
l. to tell me	LAW 32
l. with his briefcase	LAW 42

lawyers pies of l.' tongues — LAW 1
lays constructing tribal l. — OPINION 20
laziness l. nine — SLEEP 3
lazy clever and l. — ARMED FORCES 38
only l. ones	BEAUTY 33

LBJ L., how many kids — WARS 1
lead blind l. the blind — LEADERSHIP 6
easy to l.	EDUCATION 22
l. the blind	IGNORANCE 8
l. us not into temptation	TEMPTATION 7

leader l. for the Labour Party — LEADERSHIP 15
l. is also a good follower	LEADERSHIP 2
l. must keep looking	POLITICIANS 26
L. of the House	PARLIAMENT 8
l. who would change	LEADERSHIP 16

Take me to your l.	LEADERSHIP 4
test of a l.	LEADERSHIP 13
leaders L. should never	LEADERSHIP 21
l. tell 'em to	PARLIAMENT 22
leadership art of l.	LEADERSHIP 11
essence of successful l.	LEADERSHIP 18
L. is not about being nice	LEADERSHIP 20
l. is saying no	LEADERSHIP 19
leads man who l.	READING 3
leaf Are you the l.	TREES 15
fall of the l.	SEASONS 9
fig l.	SCULPTURE 1
in the yellow l.	MIDDLE AGE 6
wise man hide a l.	SECRECY 25
league Half a l. onward	WARS 15
Ivy L.	UNIVERSITIES 2
seven-l. boots	TRANSPORT 5
leak l. will sink a ship	CAUSES 19
you l.	SECRECY 29
leaking not attractive—you are l.	APPEARANCE 30
lean I'm a l. dog	DOGS 10
l. and hungry look	THINKING 4
L. liberty	LIBERTY 1
l. on one another	LAW 21
l. over too far backward	PREJUDICE 20
leap Great L. Forward	PROGRESS 3
l. in the dark	LAST WORDS 12
l.-splash—a frog	ANIMALS 15
Look before you l.	CAUTION 14
one giant l.	ACHIEVEMENT 29
quantum l.	PROGRESS 4
leaping l.-before-you-look	FRANCE 15
leaps moves in mighty l.	MEDICINE 28
learn craft so long to l.	EDUCATION 14
gladly wolde he l.	EDUCATION 13
is to l. something	EDUCATION 26
l. how to be aged	OLD AGE 36
l. the world in	EXPERIENCE 19
l. to do nothing	IDLENESS 24
l. to hate	HATRED 18
L. to write well	WRITING 17
Live and l.	EXPERIENCE 7
thirty who don't want to l.	TEACHING 15
too late to l.	EDUCATION 4
too old to l.	EDUCATION 6
while they teach, men l.	TEACHING 5
learned In writing songs I've l.	SINGING 17
laws to the l.	LANGUAGE 12
l. anything from l.	HISTORY 12
l. has been forgotten	EDUCATION 33
l. in seven years	GENERATION GAP 11
loads of l. lumber	READING 9
Nobody is born l.	CLERGY 3
privilege of the l.	QUOTATIONS 12
learning age of a state, l.	CULTURE 7
A little l.	KNOWLEDGE 29
encourage a will to l.	TEACHING 6
Get l. with a great sum	EDUCATION 9
l. doth make thee mad	KNOWLEDGE 21
l. I desire	EDUCATION 19
L. is better than house	KNOWLEDGE 7
l. is most excellent	KNOWLEDGE 11
l., like your watch	EDUCATION 17
l. the instrument	LIFE 36
of liberty, and of l.	UNIVERSITIES 16
road to l.	EDUCATION 7
learnt l. nothing	EXPERIENCE 20
leasehold l. for all	LIFE 15
least man who promises l.	ELECTIONS 15
that which governs l.	GOVERNMENT 26
leather l. or prunella	INDIFFERENCE 2
There is nothing like l.	WAYS 16
leave for ever taking l.	MEETING 14
l. a child alone	CHILDREN 16
l. his father	MARRIAGE 14
l. it to a torrent of change	CHANGE 43
L. off first	MANNERS 8

l. the party	ENTERTAINING 1
Once I leave, I l.	MEETING 22
two couples l.	ENTERTAINING 6
leaven of the same l.	SIMILARITY 12
old l.	SIN 3
leaves l. to a tree	POETRY 16
l. trimmed to the contours	WOMEN 58
Like that of l.	TRANSIENCE 4
Thick as autumnal l.	QUANTITIES 20
whose unseen presence the l. dead	WEATHER 40
Words are like l.	WORDS 11
leaving Became him like the l.	DEATH 28
lechery L., sir, it provokes	DRUNKENNESS 5
lecture classic l.	UNIVERSITIES 12
lecturer requisite to a l.	UNIVERSITIES 10
lectures l. or a little charity	GIFTS 16
left better to be l.	LOVE 38
l. our country	AUSTRALIA 12
L. wing, chicken wing	CAPITALISM 26
let not thy l. know	CHARITY 11
left-wing l., like humanity	POLITICAL PART 45
no more a l. movement	POLITICAL PART 39
leg does not resemble a l.	INVENTIONS 15
l., a source of much delight	BODY 32
l. you shall put	TEACHING 9
legal exact l. definition	LAW 33
legend fables in the l.	GOD 17
If I'm such a l.	HEROES 21
When the l. becomes fact	JOURNALISM 23
legion l. of the lost	DESPAIR 3
their name is l.	QUANTITIES 15
legislation imposed without l.	ECONOMICS 16
legislators l. of the world	POETRY 18
legs better pair of l.	BODY 16
cruel to break people's l.	CRUELTY 17
dog's walking on his hinder l.	WOMAN'S ROLE 11
Four l. good	PREJUDICE 21
given two hands and two l.	BODY 36
If you could see my l.	LOVE 48
l. in a bed	MARRIAGE 9
long and lofty l.	BIRDS 19
not for your bad l.	PRACTICALITY 5
leisure At l. married	MARRIAGE 22
conspicuous l.	THRIFT 15
detest at l.	HATRED 6
endure so much l.	LEISURE 15
fill l. intelligently	LEISURE 11
have the most l.	LEISURE 2
least l.	IDLENESS 5
l. with honour	LEISURE 5
life of l.	LEISURE 7
luck in l.	PATIENCE 15
opportunity of l.	LEISURE 4
polish it at l.	OPPORTUNITY 29
Politicians have no l.	POLITICIANS 3
repent at l.	MARRIAGE 7
sure of l. and tranquillity	LIBRARIES 7
That is what l. means	LEISURE 17
When I have l.	EDUCATION 12
lemon answer is a l.	SATISFACTION 2
hand a person a l.	DECEPTION 6
squeezed as a l.	REVENGE 21
lend l. me your ears	SPEECHES 7
L. your money	DEBT 4
men who l.	DEBT 13
lender borrower, nor a l.	DEBT 12
lends Three things I never l.	DEBT 15
length L. begets loathing	SPEECH 2
what it lacks in l.	HAPPINESS 26
lengthening one way of l. life	TRAVEL 7
lengthens As the day l.	WEATHER 2
Lenin L. had died of typhus	FATE 25
L. he deceives himself	HASTE 22
L. in a sealed truck	REVOLUTION 21
L. was right	ECONOMICS 6
lente *Festina l.*	HASTE 13
Lenten L. fare	FOOD 8

light (*cont.*)
dying of the l. OLD AGE 26
excess of l. POETS 12
faster than l. PHYSICAL 9
Give me a l. FAITH 11
how my l. is spent SENSES 7
I travel l. BODY 26
Let there be l. BEGINNING 17
Let there be l. TOWNS 17
l. after smoke THINKING 7
l. at the end ADVERSITY 5
l. at the end OPTIMISM 35
L. come, light go POSSESSIONS 4
l. fantastic DANCE 4
l. fantastic toe DANCE 8
L.(God's eldest daughter) ARCHITECTURE 7
l. in the darkness LIFE 49
l., not our darkness SELF-ESTEEM 30
l. on the hill POLITICS 26
l., shade, and perspective BEAUTY 20
L. the blue touch paper DANGER 7
l. under a bushel SELF-ESTEEM 5
l. which experience gives EXPERIENCE 23
mend the Electric L. EMPLOYMENT 19
More l. LAST WORDS 16
noose of l. DAY 13
particles of l. SCIENCE AND RELIG 8
peace like a l. PEACE 31
place of l., of liberty UNIVERSITIES 16
shed l. on the human soul CINEMA 21
sweetness and l. BEHAVIOUR 11
sweetness and l. PERFECTION 9
sweetness and l. VIRTUE 26
truth will come to l. TRUTH 15
Warmth and L. LIFE 38
We all *know* what l. is POETRY 12
with a l. behind her APPEARANCE 21
lighten L. our darkness DAY 6
lighthouse l. with his eyes ANIMALS 28
sitivation at the l. SOLITUDE 10
lightning being struck by l. CHANCE 37
flashes of l. POETS 20
history with l. CINEMA 5
L. never strikes CHANCE 9
l. shaft from heaven PEOPLE 32
like a flash of l. HAPPINESS 13
Shakespeare by flashes of l. ACTING 6
lights festival of l. FESTIVALS 17
northern l. SKIES 9
two great l. SKIES 8
like but you'll l. it LIKES 6
Do what you l. LIFESTYLES 17
I know what I l. CRITICISM 17
I know what I l. LIKES 11
l. about *The Barretts* LIKES 16
L. breeds like SIMILARITY 6
L. cures like MEDICINE 5
l. is not necessarily LOGIC 18
l., or at least tolerate PEOPLE 52
l. this sort of thing LIKES 9
l. to like reading READING 21
l. what you get LIKES 12
L. will to like SIMILARITY 7
man you don't l. DRUNKENNESS 15
people you l. FRIENDSHIP 29
things I really l. PLEASURE 28
To be l. everyone else CONFORMITY 16
wha's l. us SELF-ESTEEM 2
whether I l. it MUSIC 27
liked I l. it so much BUSINESS 7
l. it not MOURNING 11
People wish to be l. DUTY 21
she l. whate'er She looked on TASTE 8
that one is not l. ENEMIES 1
likely Not bloody l. TRANSPORT 13
not Pygmalion l. SWEARING 3
likeness after our l. HUMAN RACE 6

keep a l. PAINTING 31
likerous l. mouth SEX 9
liking l. or gratitude FRIENDSHIP 20
lilacs L. out of the dead land SEASONS 24
lilies Consider the l. BEAUTY 8
l. out of mind MEMORY 17
peacocks and l. BEAUTY 21
Lillabullero dozen bars of L. ARGUMENT 11
lily gild the l. EXCESS 14
Jersey L. PEOPLE 11
l. whispers, 'I wait' MEETING 14
paint the l. EXCESS 22
poppy or a l. ARTS 16
limbs Yours are the l. APPEARANCE 27
limitations accidental l. SELF-KNOWLEDGE 15
limits l. of my language LANGUAGE 20
l. prescribed by the law HAPPINESS 17
limousine One perfect l. GIFTS 19
Lincoln L. was, London is BRITISH TOWNS 5
line cancel half a l. PAST 25
combine To form a l. MATHS 26
L. dancing is as sinful DANCE 18
l. on a walk PAINTING 19
l. will take us hours POETRY 24
Not a day without a l. PAINTING 2
now the bottom l. PUBLISHING 15
there is no Party l. CONFORMITY 11
thin blue l. LAW 12
thin red l. ARMED FORCES 13
linen Airing one's dirty l. GENIUS 16
l., plenty of it DRESS 9
Love is like l. LOVE 32
old l. wash whitest MATURITY 5
wash one's dirty l. SECRECY 8
women or l. APPEARANCE 10
lines I'm a writer, I plant l. WRITING 53
Just say the l. ACTING 12
l. and colours PAINTING 7
l. except the last POETRY 20
sentiments in short l. POETRY 37
linguistic l. fascism LANGUAGE 30
lining About a silver l. OPTIMISM 32
cloud has a silver l. OPTIMISM 6
link missing l. LIFE SCI 2
than its weakest l. COOPERATION 2
You are the weakest l. STRENGTH 5
linnet full of the l.'s wings DAY 14
linstock gunner to his l. KNOWLEDGE 2
lion better than a dead l. LIFE 5
bold as a l. COURAGE 11
had the l.'s heart SPEECHES 17
l. and the calf COOPERATION 30
l. in the way DANGER 13
l.'s mouth DANGER 14
l.'s provider ANIMALS 7
l. to frighten the wolves LEADERSHIP 7
living dog better than a dead l. VALUE 17
March comes in like a l. WEATHER 10
mouse may help a l. POWER 6
serve a well-bred l. DEMOCRACY 7
twist the l.'s tail BRITAIN 5
lions l. led by donkeys WORLD W I 4
lip 'twixt cup and l. MISTAKES 4
lips l. that touch liquor ALCOHOL 17
Loose l. sink ships GOSSIP 7
My l. are sealed SECRECY 26
out of a lady's l. INSULTS 6
Read my l. TAXES 19
soul through My l. KISSING 7
Those l. please me KISSING 5
Watch my l. SCHOOLS 19
lipsed Somwhat he l. SPEECH 10
lipstick l.'s traces MEMORY 23
speak softly and carry l. WOMAN'S ROLE 35
liquid Cats, no less l. CATS 10
Thames is l. history RIVERS 15
liquor Good l. ALCOHOL 11

love (*cont.*)
off with the old l.	LOVE 2
ones we choose to l.	RELATIONSHIPS 18
opposite of l.	INDIFFERENCE 16
Pity is akin to l.	SYMPATHY 5
price we pay for l.	MOURNING 2
revolution where l. is not allowed	WOMAN'S ROLE 29
save the Party we l.	POLITICAL PART 33
service of my l.	PATRIOTISM 21
sex with someone I l.	SEX 41
show their l. by not worrying	WORRY 16
sinews of l.	MONEY 27
support of the woman I l.	ROYALTY 33
survive of us is l.	LOVE 66
taught to l.	HATRED 18
There is only l.	MURDER 26
thing in the world is l.	MONEY 43
those whom they no longer l.	POVERTY 27
thoughts of l.	LOVE 46
to think but to l.	VIRTUE 20
'Twixt women's l.	MEN AND WOMEN 4
unlucky in l.	CHANCE 10
waters cannot quench l.	LOVE 19
What there is . . . L.	LAST WORDS 32
What thing is l.	LOVE 27
Whom the gods l. die young	YOUTH 2
woman wakes to l.	MEN AND WOMEN 11
Work is l. made visible	WORK 35
yet jealousy extinguishes l.	ENVY 9

loved be l. by one person
	SINGLE 14
feared than to be l.	GOVERNMENT 10
heart that has truly l.	CONSTANCY 11
holy l. by the gods	RELIGION 4
I have l. him too much	HATRED 5
I l. thee once	CONSTANCY 8
l. and lost	LOVE 13
l. and lost	LOVE 51
l. Caesar less	PATRIOTISM 7
l. not at first sight	LOVE 28
l. not wisely	LOVE 31
l. one all together	OPPORTUNITY 32
l. well because he hated	HATRED 9
never to have been l.	LOVE 38
thirst to be l.	WOMEN 42

love letter l. sometimes costs
	LETTERS 2

loveliness miracle of l.
	BEAUTY 25
sanctity and l.	IDEALISM 11
weak from your l.	SPORTS 17

Lovell L. the dog
	PEOPLE 1

lovely Hurry! It's l. up here
	FLOWERS 13
on all things l.	TRANSIENCE 14
what a l. war	WORLD W I 28
You have l. eyes	BEAUTY 26

lover Beauty is the l.'s gift
	BEAUTY 14
done the l. mortal hurt	DEATH 65
l., and the poet	IMAGINATION 6
l.'s perjury	LOVE 3
Scratch a l.	ENEMIES 18
true l. of mine	COURTSHIP 1
woman loves her l.	WOMEN 31

lovers old l. are soundest
	MATURITY 5
quarrel of l.	LOVE 11
star-crossed l.	LOVE 18

loves all she l. is love
	WOMEN 31
believe that God l. them	BELIEF 33
Everybody l. a lord	RANK 1
kills the thing he l.	LOVE 56
lady l. Milk Tray	EFFORT 1
l. nothing but himself	HOME 13
l. the fox less	HUNTING 10
people one l.	LETTERS 17
reigned with your l.	GOVERNMENT 11

loveth He that l. not
	GOD 9
prayeth well, who l. well	PRAYER 21

loving discharge for l.
	ARMED FORCES 46
l. and giving	GIFTS 2
l. longest	WOMEN 30

one for l.	POETRY 7

low casualties were l.
	ARMED FORCES 43
l. as where this earth	EARTH 7
l. man seeks	ACHIEVEMENT 20
l. opinion of himself	SELF-ESTEEM 16
L. Sunday	FESTIVALS 33
upper station of l. life	CLASS 11

lowbrow militant l.
	CULTURE 24

Lowells L. talk to the Cabots
	AMERICAN CITIES 50

lower immorality of the l. classes
	CLASS 16
l. classes had such white skins	CLASS 21

loyal Lousy but l.
	PATRIOTISM 3
l. to his own career	AMBITION 21

loyalties bribed by their l.
	CORRUPTION 16
l. which centre	LEADERSHIP 14

loyalty greatest of virtues is l.
	TRUST 38
L. is the Tory's secret	POLITICAL PART 35
l. we all feel	SORROW 24

LSD L.? Nothing much happened
	DRUGS 7
PC is the L. of the '90s	COMPUTERS 14

lucendo lucus a non l.
	LOGIC 4

Lucifer as proud as L.
	PRIDE 3

luck All you know about it [l.]
	CHANCE 25
but it is l.	CHANCE 29
devil's l.	CHANCE 4
diligence bring l.	CHANCE 22
Fools for l.	CHANCE 6
l. in leisure	PATIENCE 15
l. in odd numbers	CHANCE 13
mother of good l.	CHANCE 5
their l. was bad	MISFORTUNES 31
want their l. buttered	CHANCE 27
What we call l.	CHANCE 36
With a little bit of l.	TEMPTATION 17
you'll have good l.	CHANCE 12

luckiest l. of mortals
	GENIUS 15

lucky Australia is a l. country
	AUSTRALIA 22
born l.	CHANCE 8
L. at cards	CHANCE 10
L. Country	AUSTRALIA 6
l. if he gets out	EXPERIENCE 32
Third time l.	CHANCE 14

lucrative l. to cheat
	CRIME 35

lucre filthy l.
	MONEY 16
greedy of filthy l.	CLERGY 6

lucus l. a non lucendo
	LOGIC 4

Lucy When l. ceased to be
	MOURNING 13

lues l. Boswelliana
	BIOGRAPHY 1

Luke St L.'s summer
	WEATHER 28

lukewarm Because thou art l.
	EXCESS 9

lumber loads of learned l.
	READING 9
l. room of his library	LIBRARIES 10

lumps There are l. in
	PERFECTION 10

lunacy strange form of l.
	ENEMIES 9

lunatic l. brandishing a hatchet
	DANGER 30
l., the lover	IMAGINATION 5

lunatics l. have taken charge
	CINEMA 6

lunch cork out of my l.
	ALCOHOL 26
free l.	ECONOMICS 2
ladies who l.	CHARITY 8
life, not for l.	MEN 2
L. is for wimps	COOKING 35
Universe is a free l.	UNIVERSE 22

lungs dangerous to the l.
	SMOKING 5
l. of the tobacconist	SMOKING 6
parks are the l.	POLLUTION 8

lust crazy with l.
	ADVERTISING 18
despair rather than l.	SIN 33
lot of women with l.	TEMPTATION 19

lusts l. of the flesh
	SIN 17

luxuries necessities and which l.
	WEALTH 33

luxury costly l.
	MORALITY 10
Literature is a l.	FICTION 14
l., the accomplished sofa	INVENTIONS 8
selflessness is a l.	SELF-INTEREST 28
swinish l. of the rich	WEALTH 26
to get used to l.	WEALTH 38

man (*cont.*)

animal called m.	HUMAN RACE 16
Any m. has to	MURDER 20
ask a m.	POLITICIANS 30
Clothes make the m.	DRESS 1
degraded m.	PARENTS 10
demolition of a m.	CRUELTY 15
do a m.'s job	MATURITY 1
dreaming I am a m.	SELF-KNOWLEDGE 2
father of the M.	CHILDREN 14
for m. or beast	WEATHER 52
Grand Old M.	PEOPLE 7
I know a m. who can	COOPERATION 1
I know a m. who can	KNOWLEDGE 1
inside of a m.	HEALTH 9
last thing civilized by M.	MEN AND WOMEN 12
Like master, like m.	EMPLOYMENT 2
make a m. a woman	PARLIAMENT 11
m. and a brother	HUMAN RACE 2
m. and a brother	RACE 1
M., biologically considered	HUMAN RACE 26
m. bites a dog	NEWS 9
M. cannot live by bread	LIFE 6
M. dreams of fame	MEN AND WOMEN 11
m. enjoys the happiness	PLEASURE 16
m. for all seasons	CHARACTER 23
m. for all seasons	PEOPLE 26
M. hands on misery	DISILLUSION 23
M. has created death	DEATH 63
M. has Forever	TIME 35
m. in our image	HUMAN RACE 6
M. is a tool-making animal	HUMAN RACE 18
M. is a wolf to man	HUMAN NATURE 2
M. is born unto trouble	MISFORTUNES 15
m. . . . is *so* in the way	MEN 10
M. is something to be surpassed	HUMAN RACE 23
M. is the hunter	MEN AND WOMEN 9
M. is the measure	HUMAN RACE 1
M. is the measure	HUMAN RACE 7
M. is the only Animal	HUMAN RACE 24
M. is to be held	MEN 8
m. must be a nonconformist	CONFORMITY 6
Manners maketh m.	MANNERS 4
M. of Sorrows	SORROW 4
m. on the Clapham omnibus	HUMAN RACE 3
M. proposes	FATE 4
m.'s a man for a' that	EQUALITY 8
m.'s desire	MEN AND WOMEN 8
M.'s inhumanity to man	CRUELTY 7
man's the gowd for a' that	RANK 7
M. that is born of a woman	LIFE 22
m. thinks of changing	MARRIAGE 28
M. wants but little	LIFE 24
Money makes a m.	WEALTH 3
more wonderful than m.	HUMAN RACE 8
mouse and m.	LIFE 12
never done talking of M.	EUROPE 15
never known a m. like this Man	CHRISTIAN CH 33
new m. may be raised	HUMAN NATURE 11
Nine tailor make a m.	DRESS 5
noblest work of m.	GOD 28
No m. is an Island	SOCIETY 5
no m. is wanted much	VALUE 25
No moon, no m.	PREGNANCY 3
nothing great but m.	MIND 12
nowhere m.	FUTILITY 26
oft proclaims the m.	DRESS 6
Old M. River	RIVERS 4
piece of work is a m.	HUMAN RACE 11
rights of m.	HUMAN RIGHTS 3
she was taken out of M.	WOMEN 14
slave was made a m.	RACE 8
So much resemble m.	DOGS 4
Stand by your m.	MEN AND WOMEN 27
what a m. may do	MEN AND WOMEN 10
What is m.	HUMAN RACE 15
what's that m. for	POLITICIANS 1

wolf rather than a m.	HUMAN NATURE 7
woman be more like a m.	MEN AND WOMEN 24
woman without a m.	MEN AND WOMEN 33
you can call him a m.	MATURITY 14
you'll be a M.	MATURITY 9
manage clever woman to m. a fool	MEN AND WOMEN 13
management as a 'm. bishop'	CLERGY 22
blight is m.	BROADCASTING 18
father was a m. genius	PARENTS 31
m. are using a word	MANAGEMENT 16
m. of change	MANAGEMENT 14
M. that wants to change	MANAGEMENT 15
sane business m.	MANAGEMENT 4
telling British m. off	WORDS AND DEEDS 20
manager m. who gets the blame	FOOTBALL 11
No m. ever got fired	COMPUTERS 4
managers m. of affairs of women	WOMAN'S ROLE 6
man-appeal gives a meal m.	FOOD 6
Manchester M. after midnight	BRITISH TOWNS 46
What m. says today	BRITISH TOWNS 11
mandarin M. style	STYLE 20
manger dog in the m.	SELF-INTEREST 12
laid him in a m.	CHRISTMAS 5
mangoes m. on the moon	POETRY 37
mangrove held together by m. roots	AMERICAN CITIES 54
manhood M. a struggle	LIFE 30
m. was an opportunity	MEN 23
manifesto first powerful plain m.	TRANSPORT 17
Manila gorilla in M.	SPORTS 26
man-in-the-street m., who, I'm sorry to say	INTELLIGENCE 18
mankind How beauteous m. is	HUMAN RACE 12
M. must put an end to war	WARFARE 56
proper study of m.	HUMAN RACE 17
silencing m.	OPINION 19
slain m. altogether	MURDER 9
speaks to m.	WRITERS 12
manly m. wise	MATURITY 3
manna loathe our m.	SATISFACTION 19
m. from heaven	GIFTS 8
manner all m. of things	OPTIMISM 15
m. of his speech	SPEECH 13
to the m. born	BEHAVIOUR 12
to the m. born	CUSTOM 9
manners art of good m.	SWEARING 15
changed our dress, m.	TRANSPORT 24
corrupt good m.	BEHAVIOUR 3
corrupt good m.	MANNERS 9
for m.' sake	MANNERS 8
M. are especially	MANNERS 24
m. are more frightening	MANNERS 23
M. maketh man	MANNERS 4
m. of a dancing master	BEHAVIOUR 18
Oh, the m.	BEHAVIOUR 13
other m.	CHANGE 10
perfected good m.	MANNERS 25
Striking m. are bad	MANNERS 5
test of good m.	MANNERS 6
manoeuvre blend force with a m.	VIOLENCE 11
manpower balance of m. and materials	WARFARE 24
mansion Back to its m.	DEATH 41
Love has pitched his m.	LOVE 59
mansions m. of the dead	LIBRARIES 6
manufacture content to m. life	LIFE SCI 17
soul of every m.	TECHNOLOGY 8
manufacturer m.'s instructions	SMOKING 16
manufactures foundation of m.	FARMING 10
manunkind busy monster, m.	PROGRESS 19
manure It is its natural m.	LIBERTY 15
what she lacks: m.	COUNTRIES 25
manuscripts M. don't burn	WRITING 42
many makes so m. of them	APPEARANCE 19
m. are called	CHOICE 13
M. hands make light work	COOPERATION 12
m. things I can do without	POSSESSIONS 12
owed by so m.	GRATITUDE 15
shortest way to do m. things	THOROUGHNESS 12

medicinal M. discovery	MEDICINE 28
medicine good like a m.	HUMOUR 4
hospitality is m.	ENTERTAINING 4
M. can prolong life	MEDICINE 4
m. for magic	MEDICINE 27
m. for the mind	LIBRARIES 1
patent m. advertisement	SICKNESS 13
Medicine Hat war-bonnet of M.	NAMES 10
mediocre distinguish the m.	RANK 12
m. men	MEN 17
middle-aged and m.	BROADCASTING 18
mediocrity last refuge of m.	BEHAVIOUR 4
meditation disposed to abstracted m.	THINKING 13
transcendental m. with a punch-line	HUNTING 18
medium insipid as a m.	INDIFFERENCE 7
m. is the message	TECHNOLOGY 20
mother and m.	LIFE SCI 24
meek Blessed are the M.	PRIDE 5
m. shall inherit	PRIDE 11
meet Extremes m.	SIMILARITY 4
m. in heaven	MEETING 7
m. troubles half-way	WORRY 2
never the twain shall m.	EQUALITY 12
We'll m. again	MEETING 23
we three m. again	MEETING 10
meeting as if I was a public m.	CONVERSATION 16
meets When Greek m. Greek	SIMILARITY 10
Megillah whole M.	FICTION 5
melancholy m. god protect thee	INDECISION 8
m. out of a song	SINGING 3
so sweet as M.	SORROW 12
mellow too m. for me	EFFORT 15
melodies I play his m.	MUSICIANS 16
m. are sweet	IMAGINATION 11
melody ful of hevenyssh m.	SKIES 9
girl is like a m.	BEAUTY 29
M. is the essence	MUSIC 10
m. That's sweetly play'd	LOVE 41
melting-pot great M.	AMERICA 26
member ACCEPT ME AS A M.	PREJUDICE 24
unruly m.	BODY 8
membra disjecta m.	WRITING 4
même c'est la m. chose	CHANGE 40
memoirs m. of the frivolous	BIOGRAPHY 15
write one's m.	BIOGRAPHY 16
memorable completely are truly m.	SELF-SACRIFICE 16
memorandum m. is written not to inform	
	ADMINISTRATION 24
memorial have no m.	EPITAPHS 5
M. Day	FESTIVALS 39
memories m. are card-indexes	MEMORY 25
M. are not shackles	MEMORY 28
m. insist on cherishing	MEMORY 22
m. of long love	MEMORY 6
memory bottles up a m.	MEMORY 24
down m. lane	MEMORY 2
fruit of m.	MEMORY 21
God gave us m.	MEMORY 20
have a good m.	LIES 3
intellect but rather m.	INTELLIGENCE 7
m. for forgetting	MEMORY 16
m. for his jests	SPEECHES 11
m. is always at fault	MEMORY 1
m. is a monster	MEMORY 31
m. is in my hands	MEMORY 30
m. of a Macaulay	ACTING 10
m. revealed itself	MEMORY 18
Midnight shakes the m.	MEMORY 19
no force can abolish m.	BOOKS 20
quits the m.	MUSIC 24
men all m. would be tyrants if they could	
	WOMAN'S ROLE 12
all things to all m.	SELF 6
best of m.	HUMAN NATURE 1
city consists in m.	ARMED FORCES 15
company of m.	MEN AND WOMEN 17
For fear of little m.	SUPERNATURAL 18

have power over m.	WOMAN'S ROLE 15
how much m. hate them	MEN AND WOMEN 28
If m. could get pregnant	PREGNANCY 15
If m. had to have babies	PREGNANCY 19
intended greatness for m.	GREATNESS 10
Measures not m.	GOVERNMENT 24
mediocre m.	MEN 17
m. alone are quite capable	GOOD 34
m. are alike	HUMAN NATURE 6
M. are but children	MATURITY 6
m. are created equal	HUMAN RIGHTS 6
m. are rapists	MEN 19
m. bearing flowers	FLOWERS 15
m., French	LANGUAGES 4
M. have had every advantage	MEN 9
m. in disguise	MEN 21
m. in my life	MEN 16
m. must work	WORK 31
m. over thirty	MIDDLE AGE 18
M. seldom make passes	APPEARANCE 26
M. were deceivers	MEN 6
m. we wanted to marry	WOMAN'S ROLE 30
m. who are discriminated against	WOMAN'S ROLE 28
m., women, and clergyman	CLERGY 18
more I see of m.	DOGS 6
schemes o' mice an' m.	FORESIGHT 11
So many m.	OPINION 2
We are the hollow m.	FUTILITY 22
we've got the m.	PATRIOTISM 18
menace our greatest m.	RUSSIA 9
mend Make do and m.	THRIFT 1
never too late to m.	CHANGE 4
seek to m.	GOD 16
they begin to m.	OPTIMISM 12
mending woman and a ship ever want m.	WOMEN 8
meningitis M.. It was a word	SICKNESS 25
mens m. sana in corpore sano	HEALTH 12
mental m. cages	MIND 22
m. states	LIBERTY 32
Mercator M.'s North Poles	MATHS 17
merchandise mechanical arts and m.	CULTURE 7
ultimate m.	DRUGS 6
merchant m. shall hardly keep	BUSINESS 23
merchantman monarchy is a m.	GOVERNMENT 23
mercies m. of the wicked	ANIMALS 11
mercury m. with a fork	DIPLOMACY 13
mercy crowning m.	WARS 2
Hae m. o' my soul	EPITAPHS 17
Lord in His m. be kind	BRITISH TOWNS 44
M. I asked	EPITAPHS 7
over to God's m.	REVENGE 17
quality of m.	JUSTICE 24
so much as m.	SIN 16
withhold in m.	PRAYER 20
merit he esteems your m.	FRIENDSHIP 15
m.'s all his own	SELF-ESTEEM 12
m. for a bishopric	CLERGY 17
M. in appearance	APPEARANCE 9
What is m.	REPUTATION 24
merrier more the m.	QUANTITIES 5
merrily m. meet in heaven	MEETING 7
merry drink, and to be m.	LIFESTYLES 12
m. Andrew	HUMOUR 3
m. dancers	SKIES 3
m. day once or twice	ENTERTAINING 10
m. heart	APPEARANCE 13
m. heart	HUMOUR 4
m. in hall	ENTERTAINING 5
M. Monarch	PEOPLE 15
m. monarch	PEOPLE 30
m. year	SEASONS 1
wars are m.	IRELAND 15
mess Another nice m.	PROBLEMS 18
By man what a m.	TOWNS 28
m. left over from other people	TOWNS 30
m. of plottage	THEATRE 2
m. of pottage	VALUE 13

suddenly get loads of m.	TASTE 16
taking m. from poor people	CHARITY 28
Time is m.	MONEY 12
to get all that m.	WEALTH 29
using its m.	CAPITALISM 25
voice is full of m.	WEALTH 30
world in arms is not spending m. alone	WARFARE 55
You pays your m.	CHOICE 9
moneybags with the m. of Carnegie	WEALTH 32
moneyless m. man goes fast	POVERTY 3
mongrels continent of energetic m.	EUROPE 11
monk make the m.	APPEARANCE 5
monkey attack the m.	POLITICIANS 24
descent from a m.	LIFE SCI 12
higher the m. climbs	AMBITION 2
nothing but a painted m.	MEDICINE 11
softly, catchee m.	PATIENCE 14
monkeys army of m.	CHANCE 32
Cats and m.	LIFE 35
million m. banging	COMPUTERS 17
pay peanuts, you get m.	VALUE 2
three wise m.	VIRTUE 5
monogamist kind of serial m.	CONSTANCY 20
monologues intersecting m.	CONVERSATION 18
monopoly m. profits	BUSINESS 35
m. stage of capitalism	CAPITALISM 14
monotony m. of marriage	MARRIAGE 38
Monroe M. doctrine	INTERNAT REL 5
mouth of Marilyn M.	PEOPLE 62
monster busy m., manunkind	PROGRESS 19
Frankenstein's m.	PROBLEMS 5
green-eyed m.	ENVY 4
green-eyed m.	ENVY 11
many-headed m.	CLASS 6
many-headed m. of the pit	THEATRE 10
memory is a m.	MEMORY 31
monsters reason produces m.	DREAMS 9
monstrous m. carbuncle	ARCHITECTURE 21
M. Regiment of Women	WOMAN'S ROLE 7
With m. head	ANIMALS 23
Monte Carlo when they can go to M.	EXPLORATION 11
montes *Parturient m.*	EFFORT 11
month cruellest m.	SEASONS 24
flavour of the m.	FASHION 2
if they wait for a m.	LETTERS 16
R in the m.	FOOD 2
months mother of the m.	SKIES 9
Montreal O God! O M.	CANADA 8
monument seek a m.	EPITAPHS 11
monumental M. City	AMERICAN CITIES 27
monumentum *Si m. requiris*	EPITAPHS 11
moods such extraordinary m.	SEA 25
moon glimpses of the m.	EARTH 3
horned m.	SKIES 16
landings on the M.	SKIES 29
m. belongs to everyone	POSSESSIONS 22
m. in lonely alleys	SKIES 24
m. is nothing	SKIES 26
m.'s an arrant thief	SKIES 12
No m., no man	PREGNANCY 3
now the m.	SKIES 21
O more than m.	MOURNING 10
once in a blue m.	TIME 13
moonlight Ill met by m.	MEETING 9
m. and music	DANCE 14
m. and roses	LOVE 17
moonlit Knocking on the m. door	MEETING 18
moonshine every thing as m.	EMOTIONS 14
moor mixen than the m.	FAMILIARITY 2
Moore M.'s law	COMPUTERS 6
moored m. only lightly	IRELAND 23
moose strong as a bull m.	STRENGTH 22
moral act on m. convictions	FICTION 19
blending of m. courage	PATIENCE 26
build up his m. power	SEX 7
drug is neither m. or immoral	DRUGS 12
m. act that has no hope	MORALITY 21

M. courage is a rarer commodity	COURAGE 33
m. evil and of good	GOOD 30
m. indigestion	PLEASURE 22
M. indignation is jealousy	MORALITY 12
m. law within me	THINKING 14
m. or immoral book	BOOKS 15
m. principles please	MORALITY 2
m. virtues at the highest	RELIGION 15
not just a m. category	LIES 25
party is a m. crusade	POLITICAL PART 36
stage in m. culture	MORALITY 8
words for m. ideas	MORALITY 22
moralist problem for the m.	BOREDOM 6
moralists delight to m.	CRUELTY 11
morality cities for our best m.	COUNTRY AND TOWN 12
Conventionality is not m.	HYPOCRISY 15
fits of m.	MORALITY 6
M. is a private	MORALITY 10
M. is the herd-instinct	MORALITY 9
M.'s *not* practical	MORALITY 19
some people talk of m.	POSSESSIONS 15
surely about m.	SPORTS 23
morals Food comes first, then m.	MORALITY 14
m. are like its teeth	MORALITY 11
m. of a whore	BEHAVIOUR 18
m. on a high plane	MORALITY 1
m. or principles	PEOPLE 41
self-interest was bad m.	ECONOMICS 7
more believing m. and more	BELIEF 32
days that are no m.	MEMORY 13
I want some m.	GREED 13
Less is m.	ARCHITECTURE 16
Less is m.	EXCESS 6
little m., and how much	SATISFACTION 26
m. about less	KNOWLEDGE 49
m. equal than others	EQUALITY 16
m. he has himself	POSSESSIONS 10
m. Piglet wasn't there	ABSENCE 14
m. the merrier	QUANTITIES 5
m. things in heaven	UNIVERSE 11
M. will mean worse	UNIVERSITIES 25
m. you get	GREED 1
Much would have m.	GREED 2
She'll vish there wos m.	LETTERS 13
mores O m.	BEHAVIOUR 13
mori *pro patria m.*	PATRIOTISM 6
moriar *Non omnis m.*	DEATH 21
morituri *m. te salutant*	LAST WORDS 5
morning appendage to life's m.	MIDDLE AGE 11
Auschwitz in the m.	HUMAN NATURE 21
beauty of the m.	BRITISH TOWNS 25
getting married in the m.	WEDDINGS 13
glad confident m.	DISILLUSION 13
glorious m. for America	WARS 8
hate to get up in the m.	IDLENESS 22
in the early m.	SEASONS 27
M. dreams come true	DREAMS 4
M. has broken	DAY 19
M. in the bowl of night	DAY 13
m.'s minion	BIRDS 15
some m., unaware	SEASONS 21
moron consumer isn't a m.	ADVERTISING 15
morphine m. or idealism	DRUGS 7
Morris M. Minor prototype	TRANSPORT 21
morrow thought for the m.	PRESENT 4
mortal It is m. combat	PREGNANCY 16
tatter in its m. dress	OLD AGE 21
this m. coil	LIFESTYLES 9
mortality m., the ruins	PAST 21
mortar daub of untempered m.	LANGUAGES 12
Lies are the m.	SOCIETY 14
mortgage m. beats 'em all	DEBT 17
where the m. is	HOME 6
Morton M.'s fork	CHOICE 12
mortuis De m. nil	REPUTATION 3
Moscow Do not march on M.	WARFARE 58
M.: those syllables	TOWNS 18

name at the n. of Jesus — NAMES 4
colonies in your wife's n. — CAUTION 31
committed in thy n. — LIBERTY 17
dare not speak its n. — LOVE 55
dog a bad n. — GOSSIP 3
glory in the n. — BRITAIN 8
good n. is rather — REPUTATION 15
I do not like her n. — NAMES 6
If my n. had been Edmund — NAMES 7
ill n. is half hanged — REPUTATION 6
In the n. of God, go — ACTION 18
its n. changed — REPUTATION 18
local habitation and a n. — WRITING 11
my good n. — REPUTATION 19
n. Achilles assumed — KNOWLEDGE 27
n. and nation — EARTH 9
n. and number — FATE 9
n. great in story — YOUTH 14
n. liveth for evermore — EPITAPHS 5
n. of a man — NAMES 13
n. the guilty men — GUILT 4
n. was writ in water — EPITAPHS 15
problem that has no n. — WOMAN'S ROLE 32
quite forget your n. — MADNESS 10
self-made n. — NAMES 12
spared the n. — CRITICISM 7
spell my n. right — FAME 15
their n. is legion — QUANTITIES 15
Their n. liveth for ever — EPITAPHS 24
What's in a n. — NAMES 5
wife, and my n. — DEBT 15
With a n. like yours — NAMES 9
nameless intolerably n. names — EPITAPHS 24
little, n., unremembered, acts — VIRTUE 34
n. in worthy deeds — FAME 8
names in love with American n. — NAMES 10
n. of all these particles — PHYSICAL 15
No n., no pack-drill — SECRECY 7
things with their n. — BELIEF 29
naming N. of Cats — CATS 11
napalm I love the smell of n. — WARFARE 63
Naples See N. and die — TOWNS 3
Napoleon N. brought peace — PEACE 29
Napoleons Caesars and N. — LEADERSHIP 12
narcotic n. be alcohol — DRUGS 7
narrative unconvincing n. — FICTION 12
narrow n. into a neighbourhood — INTERNAT REL 33
n. is the way — VIRTUE 16
neck is n. — BIRDS 19
two n. words — DEATH 31
nastier great deal n. — FAMILY 17
how much n. I would be — CHRISTIAN CH 38
nasty n., brutish, and short — LIFE 20
something n. in the woodshed — SECRECY 19
when we turn n. — CHARACTER 50
nation in the n.'s bedrooms — CENSORSHIP 16
n. at his service — POLITICIANS 31
n., conceived in liberty — DEMOCRACY 13
n. expects to be ignorant — CULTURE 10
n. of dancers — AFRICA 7
n. of shopkeepers — ENGLAND 14
n. of shopkeepers — BUSINESS 29
n. shall not lift up sword — PEACE 7
N. shall speak peace — BROADCASTING 2
n. talking to itself — JOURNALISM 21
n. . . . will more easily — LIES 22
no rainbow n. — RACE 34
rich and lazy n. — CORRUPTION 14
so goes the n. — ELECTIONS 1
two-thirds of a n. pay — TAXES 12
voice of a n. — DEMOCRACY 10
what our N. stands for — ENGLAND 26
national n. debt — DEBT 6
N. Debt — DEBT 21
nationalism N. is a silly cock — PATRIOTISM 24
nationality n. he would prefer — ENGLAND 17
nations four great n. — INTERNAT REL 28

friendship with all n. — INTERNAT REL 11
gaiety of n. — HAPPINESS 5
gossip from all the n. — LETTERS 18
n. have always acted — INTERNAT REL 34
n. how to live — ENGLAND 7
N. touch — INTERNAT REL 19
n. which have put mankind — CULTURE 18
Other n. use 'force' — BRITAIN 10
pedigree of n. — LANGUAGES 9
to belong to other n. — ENGLAND 15
two n. — POLITICS 9
Two n. — WEALTH 25
two n. warring — CANADA 7
native in his n. place — FAME 11
my n. land — PATRIOTISM 14
no harm to England's n. people — AUSTRALIA 28
Nato Serbs out, N. in — WARS 32
natural do it more n. — STYLE 7
interested in n. history — SCHOOLS 11
n. man has only two — HUMAN NATURE 16
N. rights is nonsense — HUMAN RIGHTS 9
n. selection — LIFE SCI 3
N. Selection — LIFE SCI 11
see a n. style — STYLE 8
twice as n. — APPEARANCE 20
nature balance of n. — NATURE 3
book of n. — MATHS 10
but n. more — NATURE 11
By n. men are alike — HUMAN NATURE 6
conquer n. — NATURE 21
Constant in N. — CHANGE 32
copier of n. — PAINTING 8
cruel works of n. — NATURE 14
debt of n. — DEATH 25
deposes Mother N. — NATURE 20
frame of n. — DEFIANCE 15
from criticism to n. — SHAKESPEARE 8
great n.'s second course — SLEEP 10
Habit is second n. — CUSTOM 8
he outdoes N. — DEATH 54
Holy Scripture and n. — SCIENCE AND RELIG 4
ignorance of n. — SCIENCE AND RELIG 7
inherit the human n. — CULTURE 13
In n. there are neither — NATURE 16
mirror up to n. — ACTING 3
most important laws of n. — VALUE 32
N. abhors a vacuum — NATURE 1
n. cannot be fooled — TECHNOLOGY 25
N. does nothing — NATURE 5
N. has in store — INVENTIONS 13
n. having intended — GREATNESS 10
n., heartless — NATURE 17
n. in terms — PAINTING 14
N. is not a temple — NATURE 15
N. is often hidden — CHARACTER 28
n. is subdued — CIRCUMSTANCE 15
n. is the art — NATURE 9
n. is tugging at — SELF-INTEREST 25
n. itselfe cant endure — MATHS 13
N. made him — EXCELLENCE 8
N., Mr Allnutt — NATURE 18
n. of God — GOD 3
N. red in tooth — NATURE 4
N., red in tooth — NATURE 12
n. replaces it with — NATURE 19
N.'s great masterpiece — ANIMALS 13
N.'s laws lay hid — SCIENCE 8
N. speak intelligibly — HYPOTHESIS 26
N.'s sweet restorer — SLEEP 13
n.'s way of telling you — DEATH 3
N. that is above all art — CUSTOM 10
n. turns girls into women — MEN AND WOMEN 29
n. with a pitchfork — NATURE 2
one touch of n. — HUMAN NATURE 9
painters imitate n. — PAINTING 5
poet ever interpreted n. — LAW 35
productions of n. — FARMING 10

photography P. is truth — CINEMA 17
physic Throw p. to the dogs — MEDICINE 13
physical p. illustration — SCIENCE 10
so lightly called p. — EMOTIONS 18
physician died last night of my p. — MEDICINE 16
Honour a p. — MEDICINE 6
p. can bury his mistakes — ARCHITECTURE 17
P., heal thyself — MEDICINE 9
who is not also a p. — MEDICINE 11
physicians P. of all men — MEDICINE 15
physicists p. are made of atoms — PHYSICAL 17
p. have known sin — PHYSICAL 14
p.' war — WARFARE 64
physics marriage between mathematics and p. — PHYSICAL 22
no democracy in p. — PHYSICAL 21
p. or stamp collecting — SCIENCE 20
p. pain — WORK 23
pianist shoot the p. — MUSICIANS 8
pianists no better than many p. — MUSIC 25
piano help with moving the p. — MEN 18
Picasso P. is Spanish — PAINTING 23
P. studies an object — PAINTING 17
P. was there first — CRITICISM 29
Piccadilly P. with a poppy or a lily — ARTS 1
pick p. it up — CHANCE 12
p. the one I never tried — CHOICE 24
P. yourself up — DETERMINATION 44
picklocks p. of biographers — BIOGRAPHY 13
picnic p. in Eden — GUILT 15
teddy bears' p. — PLEASURE 8
picture One p. is worth ten thousand words — WORDS AND DEEDS 5
p. is worth ten thousand — LANGUAGE 21
p. tells a story — MEANING 1
pictures gallery of p. — HISTORY 16
nail my p. together — PAINTING 22
P. are for entertainment — CINEMA 20
p. aren't good enough — PHOTOGRAPHY 6
p. are so powerful — BROADCASTING 20
p. didn't have any beginning — PAINTING 25
P. of perfection — PERFECTION 6
p. of silver — LANGUAGE 5
p. or conversations — BOOKS 14
p. that got small — CINEMA 12
You furnish the p. — JOURNALISM 2
pie p. in the sky — FUTURE 20
pie-crust Promises, like p. — TRUST 3
Pierian P. spring — POETRY 3
pies devil makes his Christmas p. — LAW 1
piety in return for my p. — PRAYER 6
weaker sex, to p. more prone — WOMEN 21
pig as soon kill a p. — LETTERS 15
expect from a p. — CHARACTER 15
kill a p. — GARDENS 2
p. got up — DRUNKENNESS 14
p. satisfied — SATISFACTION 27
pigs P. may fly — BELIEF 4
p. might fly — BELIEF 7
P. treat us as equals — ANIMALS 31
Pilate said jesting P. — TRUTH 16
water like P. — INDIFFERENCE 14
pile P. it high — BUSINESS 13
p. Ossa upon Pelion — EXCESS 17
pilfering p., unprotected race — COUNTRIES 18
pilgrim To be a p. — DETERMINATION 31
pill Protestant women may take the p. — PREGNANCY 20
pillar p. of society — SOCIETY 4
p. of the State — LIES 25
pillars not one of its p. — CHRISTIAN CH 25
pills pink p. for pale people — MEDICINE 2
pilot drop the p. — TRUST 6
every p. knows that — ARMED FORCES 40
I hope to see my p. — DEATH 53
kamikaze p. — SUICIDE 2
p. of the calm — LEADERSHIP 10
pin on the head of a p. — PHILOSOPHY 1

See a p. — CHANCE 12
steal a p. — HONESTY 5
pine whisper of the p. — TREES 4
pineapple p. of politeness — MANNERS 12
pines p. are gossip pines — TREES 12
pink p. pills for pale people — MEDICINE 2
pinko-grey really p. — RACE 12
pinprick p. of eternity — TIME 21
pins balloons dancing in a world of p. — TRANSIENCE 19
pinstripe come in a p. suit — STRENGTH 27
pint p. . . . why that's very nearly — BODY 27
quart into a p. pot — FUTILITY 4
pinta P. Milka Day — HEALTH 3
pipe his p. might fall out — ENGLAND 21
p. with solemn — SMOKING 8
three-p. problem — THINKING 18
Your p. is drawing sweetly — MURDER 22
piper pays the p. — POWER 2
pay the p. — POWER 12
pipes open the p. — SINGING 2
pippins old p. toothsomest — MATURITY 5
pips until the p. squeak — REVENGE 9
until the p. squeak — REVENGE 21
pirate office was his p. ship — TRANSPORT 14
pismire p. is equally perfect — NATURE 13
piss pitcher of warm p. — PRESIDENCY 13
take the p. — MEN 24
pissing p. out — ENEMIES 21
pistol echo of a p.-shot — TOWNS 24
p. hanging on the wall — THEATRE 14
p. in your pocket — SEX 38
p. let off at the ear — WIT 15
p. misses fire — ARGUMENT 12
reach for my p. — CULTURE 21
smoking p. — SECRECY 18
pistols p. and cartridges — ARMED FORCES 33
ring bells and fire off p. — FESTIVALS 66
pistons black statement of p. — TRANSPORT 17
pit diggeth a p. — CAUSES 14
Law is a bottomless p. — LAW 19
many-headed monster of the p. — THEATRE 10
what is in the p. — KNOWLEDGE 33
pitch p. shall be defiled — GOOD 2
p. shall be defiled — GOOD 14
pitcher p. of warm piss — PRESIDENCY 13
p. will go to the well — EXCESS 8
pitchers Little p. have large — SECRECY 5
pitchfork nature with a p. — NATURE 2
thrown on her with a p. — DRESS 7
pitied complain are never p. — SYMPATHY 19
envied than p. — ENVY 1
pities p. the plumage — IMAGINATION 9
pitiful God be p. — PRAYER 2
pity by means of p. and fear — THEATRE 3
p. him afterwards — SYMPATHY 16
P. is akin to love — SYMPATHY 5
p. kills — SYMPATHY 21
p. of it, Iago — SYMPATHY 13
p. renneth soone — SYMPATHY 12
Poetry is in the p. — WARFARE 37
seas of p. lie — SYMPATHY 24
Then cherish p. — SYMPATHY 18
place bourne of time and p. — DEATH 53
cares no more for one p. — HOME 13
get wealth and p. — WEALTH 22
keep in the same p. — EFFORT 18
no p. like home — HOME 7
no p. to go — DRESS 15
p. for everything — ADMINISTRATION 8
p. for everything — ORDER 2
p. in the sun — INTERNAT REL 23
p. in the sun — SUCCESS 16
pride of p. — VALUE 15
tight gag of p. — IRELAND 22
time and p. — BEGINNING 19
time and p. for everything — CIRCUMSTANCE 4
time and the p. — OPPORTUNITY 32

plough hand to the p. — DETERMINATION 22
hand to the p. — DETERMINATION 24
p. is a pencil — FARMING 14
p. the fields — FARMING 11
p. the sand — FUTILITY 10
ploughed p. the sea — REVOLUTION 15
ploughman even the poorest p. — JUSTICE 25
p. and a professor — MORALITY 5
ploughshares swords into p. — PEACE 7
pluck p. it out — SIN 9
plum p. year — SEASONS 1
plumage If you have bright p. — CHARACTER 51
pities the p. — IMAGINATION 9
plumber can't get a p. — POWER 36
p. eventually comes — PLEASURE 30
plumes borrowed p. — DECEPTION 5
plunder What a place to p. — BRITISH TOWNS 26
plural Incorrigibly p. — SIMILARITY 23
plus ne p. ultra — EXCELLENCE 7
P. ça change — CHANGE 40
p. de Pyrénées. — INTERNAT REL 10
ply p. the labouring oar — WORK 16
poacher old p. makes the best gamekeeper — WAYS 10
p. staggering downhill — SCOTLAND 17
pocket garden carried in the p. — BOOKS 1
gun in your p. — SEX 38
not scruple to pick a p. — WIT 8
pound in your p. — MONEY 41
your neighbour's p. — MONEY 32
pockets Shrouds have no p. — MONEY 11
poem author of that p. — ACHIEVEMENT 15
barbarous to write a p. — POETRY 35
Every good p. — ARTS AND SCI 4
greatest p. — AMERICA 19
It is a pretty p. — TRANSLATION 6
music of a p. — TRANSLATION 9
ornament of a p. — POETRY 10
p. lovely as a tree — TREES 14
p. should not mean — POETRY 27
poems P. are made by fools — CREATIVITY 9
we all scribble p. — POETRY 5
poet All a p. can do — POETRY 25
he was a true P. — POETS 14
lack their sacred p. — BIOGRAPHY 2
lover, and the p. — IMAGINATION 5
modern p.'s fate — POETRY 21
Peasant P. — POETS 5
p. ever interpreted nature — LAW 35
P. Laureate — POETS 6
p. ranks far below — ARTS 7
p.'s hope — POETRY 36
p. will give up writing — POETRY 31
p. writes in Esperanto — EUROPE 10
poetic constitutes p. faith — POETRY 15
nurse for a p. child — SCOTLAND 11
p. justice — CAUSES 13
poetry campaign in p. — ELECTIONS 17
Father of English p. — POETS 1
If p. comes not — POETRY 16
In whining p. — POETRY 7
Ireland hurt you into p. — POETS 24
Language is fossil p. — LANGUAGE 14
p. begins to atrophy — MUSIC 19
p. cannot celebrate them — ARTS AND SCI 15
p. ignores most people — POETRY 34
P. is a subject — POETRY 22
p. is conceived — POETRY 23
P. is eloquent painting — ARTS 6
P. is in the pity — WARFARE 37
P. is not a turning — POETRY 26
P. is the record — POETRY 17
P. is when some of them — POETRY 20
p., no less than in life — POETS 19
p. of motion — TRANSPORT 9
p. should be alive — POETRY 39
p. strays into my memory — POETRY 29
p. = the *best* words — POETRY 19

Superstition is the p. — SUPERNATURAL 17
what is p. — POETRY 12
poets All p. are mad — POETRY 8
Lake P. — POETS 4
mature p. steal — ORIGINALITY 13
P. are the unacknowledged — POETRY 18
P. that lasting marble — LANGUAGES 7
p. witty — ARTS AND SCI 3
point it scores one p. — GIFTS 23
mad on one p. — MADNESS 11
upon a needle's p. — PHILOSOPHY 7
Up to a p. — EXCESS 29
points armed at all p. — PREPARATION 10
P. Have no parts — MATHS 26
poised p. between a cliché — POLITICIANS 23
poison another man's p. — LIKES 2
p. and antidote — BIBLE 22
poisoned p. chalice — MISFORTUNES 12
poisoner famous p. or a successful poisoner — CRIME 54
pokers p. into true-love knots — POETS 15
Pol By Tre, P., and Pen — NAMES 1
polar P. exploration is at once — EXPLORATION 12
pole for a dash to the p. — EXPLORATION 14
P. first, a pope second — CLERGY 21
top of the greasy p. — SUCCESS 31
pole-axed he must be p. — LEADERSHIP 24
polecat semi-house-trained p. — PEOPLE 59
poles explored the P. — SKIES 25
going to the North and South P. — EXPLORATION 11
policeman p. and a pretty girl — CINEMA 18
p. is a convenient receptacle — TRANSPORT 25
p.'s lot is not a happy one — LAW 29
terrorist and the p. — HUMAN NATURE 17
policemen blue p. — ENGLAND 22
how young the p. look — OLD AGE 25
policy ethical foreign p. — INTERNAT REL 4
Honesty is the best p. — HONESTY 4
Honesty is the best p. — HONESTY 10
p. of the good neighbour — INTERNAT REL 26
polish p. it at leisure — OPPORTUNITY 29
polished O p. perturbation — WORRY 7
polite allies to be p. to — DIPLOMACY 12
time to be p. — ENGLAND 8
politeness pineapple of p. — MANNERS 12
p. of kings — PUNCTUALITY 10
p. of princes — PUNCTUALITY 5
suave p. — MANNERS 20
politic body p. — SOCIETY 3
political All p. lives — POLITICIANS 33
by nature a p. animal — POLITICS 10
gain in p. significance — MORALITY 21
greenest p. party — POLLUTION 28
personal is p. — POLITICS 3
points to a p. career — POLITICIANS 16
p. correctness — LANGUAGE 2
p. correctness — LANGUAGE 30
P. Economy — DEBT 21
p. leader must keep — POLITICIANS 26
P. power grows out of — POWER 28
schemes of p. improvement — POLITICS 12
politician art of a p. — POLITICIANS 7
honest p. — POLITICIANS 15
like a scurvy p. — POLITICIANS 6
listen to a p. — POLITICIANS 29
makes the p. wise — FOOD 12
p. does get an idea — POLITICIANS 21
p. is an arse — POLITICIANS 22
p. is a statesman — POLITICIANS 31
p. urges them to rebel — SCIENCE 27
p. who's been dead — POLITICIANS 25
politicians fault of our p. — GOVERNMENT 30
left to the p. — POLITICS 29
p. and civil servants — CULTURE 26
P. are entitled — POLITICIANS 36
p. complain that TV — BROADCASTING 8
P. have no leisure — POLITICIANS 3
whole race of p. — PRACTICALITY 7

prince (*cont.*)
p. must be a fox | LEADERSHIP 7
P. of this world | GOOD 12
p. to be feared | GOVERNMENT 10
sword against the p. | REVOLUTION 4
To be P. of Wales | ROYALTY 37
princes addressed to p. | NECESSITY 18
mine were p. of the earth | RACE 11
politeness of p. | PUNCTUALITY 5
put not your trust in p. | TRUST 17
princess like a Sleeping P. | AUSTRALIA 18
People's P. | PEOPLE 65
Princeton P. is a wonderful spot | UNIVERSITIES 21
principle little of the p. left | ADMINISTRATION 18
Matthew p. | EXCESS 16
Peter P. | MANAGEMENT 4
p. of the English law | LAW 26
rise above p. | POLITICS 1
standing up for a p. | ARGUMENT 24
thing about a p. | MORALITY 13
principles adjust their p. | POLITICIANS 36
Damn your p. | POLITICAL PART 19
fight for one's p. | MORALITY 18
Liberals forget their p. | POLITICAL PART 23
morals or p. | PEOPLE 41
print *devils* must p. | PUBLISHING 8
licence to p. money | BROADCASTING 10
news that's fit to p. | JOURNALISM 1
p. the legend | JOURNALISM 23
p. the myth | HEROES 18
read the fine p. | EXPERIENCE 37
printer p.'s devil | PUBLISHING 1
printers P.' Bible | BIBLE 6
printing P., and the Protestant | CULTURE 11
p., gunpowder | INVENTIONS 6
priorities language of p. | POLITICAL PART 28
p. for Government | EDUCATION 35
prisms prunes and p. | BEHAVIOUR 9
prison at home in p. | CRIME 43
do not a p. make | LIBERTY 9
Home is the girl's p. | HOME 17
I would have no other p. | LIBRARIES 4
mourn in p. | SUICIDE 4
primitive p. | GARDENS 14
p., I am not free | EQUALITY 13
Shades of the p.-house | YOUTH 12
ship but a p. | SEA 12
to p. for the colour | PREJUDICE 18
prisoner thoughts of a p. | CRIME 49
prisoners p. of addiction | BUYING 10
p. of noise | MUSIC 34
prisons Jails and p. are designed | CRIME 50
privacy p. and tawdry secrets | FAMILY 25
private his p. parts | MEN 11
liberty of p. opinion | POLITICAL PART 11
P. faces in public places | BEHAVIOUR 28
p. opulence | ECONOMICS 12
p., secretive activity | SEX 36
p. territory | SICKNESS 22
p. will governs | SOCIETY 8
sphere of p. life | RELIGION 22
privilege power which stands on P. | ELECTIONS 9
prize one receiveth the p. | WINNING 9
prized local but p. | POETRY 36
prizes all must have p. | WINNING 15
glittering p. | SUCCESS 35
probable P. impossibilities | PROBLEMS 13
problem can't see the p. | PROBLEMS 19
have a ghastly p. | SYMPATHY 29
Houston, we've had a p. | PROBLEMS 24
part of the p. | PROBLEMS 22
p. is too difficult | PROBLEMS 27
p. that has no name | WOMAN'S ROLE 32
p. to be overcome | MEN 23
three-pipe p. | THINKING 18
problems anticipate p. and move | MANAGEMENT 17
No easy p. ever come | PRESIDENCY 11

P. worthy of attack | PROBLEMS 23
proclaim p. from the housetops | ADVERTISING 6
proclaims apparel oft p. the man | DRESS 6
procrastination p. is the art | IDLENESS 23
P. is the thief of time | HASTE 9
procreant Always the p. urge | CREATIVITY 7
prodigal p. son | FORGIVENESS 8
prodigies Africa and her p. | HUMAN RACE 13
production river of p. | CULTURE 19
products p. of editing | LIFE SCI 20
profanity p., except in America | SWEARING 10
profession debtor to his p. | EMPLOYMENT 8
decided was to fulfil my p. | WOMAN'S ROLE 34
discharge of any p. | EMPLOYMENT 11
liberal p. | AMBITION 14
oldest p. | EMPLOYMENT 4
second oldest p. | POLITICS 33
professional p. is a man who can | EMPLOYMENT 25
professions of all gainful p. | FARMING 7
p. are conspiracies | EMPLOYMENT 20
shortest-lived p. | HEROES 13
professor ploughman and a p. | MORALITY 5
p. of tomorrow | PARANORMAL 11
professors better p. at Camblidge | UNIVERSITIES 22
professsor p. can be absolutely certain | UNIVERSITIES 28
profit Form follows p. | BEAUTY 37
High prices p. those who sell | VALUE 28
p. comes from what is there | VALUE 16
To whose profit | SELF-INTEREST 18
what shall it p. a man | SUCCESS 22
profitable p. to its possessor | HONESTY 13
profits monopoly p. | BUSINESS 35
profound p. truths recognized | TRUTH 40
profundis de p. | SORROW 3
profundity impersonation of p. | OPTIMISM 37
prognostics p. do not always prove | FORESIGHT 10
progress Congress makes no p. | DIPLOMACY 5
illusion of p. | MANAGEMENT 2
ladder of predictable p. | LIFE SCI 28
p. is a matter of controversy | PROGRESS 20
p. is not possible | SIMILARITY 25
P. through technology | TECHNOLOGY 3
rake's p. | LIFESTYLES 6
Reason and P. | DISILLUSION 20
work in p. | HUMAN RACE 34
progression p. of revisited ideas | FASHION 3
prohibited that is not expressly p. | COUNTRIES 32
prohibition Communism is like p. | CAPITALISM 18
P. did | DRUGS 11
P. makes you want to cry | ALCOHOL 24
projections figures in it Merely p. | HEAVEN 22
proletariat dictatorship of the p. | CAPITALISM 5
Machines are the new p. | TECHNOLOGY 26
prologue make a long p. | WRITING 1
p. to a very dull play | COURTSHIP 6
promenade p. concert | MUSIC 4
promiscuity emotional p. | EMOTIONS 25
promise bow of p. | WEATHER 23
P., large promise | ADVERTISING 7
p. made is a debt unpaid | TRUST 31
Whose p. none relies on | WORDS AND DEEDS 14
promised Future as a p. land | FUTURE 24
promises man who p. least | ELECTIONS 15
P., like pie-crust | TRUST 3
p. of Slobodan Milosevic | DIPLOMACY 17
promising they first call p. | CRITICISM 22
promotion p. cometh neither | EMPLOYMENT 7
sweat but for p. | EMPLOYMENT 9
You'll get no p. | ARMED FORCES 39
pronounce p. it right | SPEECH 7
pronunciation where p. Reigned | SPEECH 31
proof America is the p. | AMERICA 37
p. of the pudding | HYPOTHESIS 5
proofs purist who reads your p. | LANGUAGE 23
Proosian Turk, or P. | ENGLAND 15
propaganda patronising p. | NEWS 11
P. is a soft weapon | DECEPTION 24

pure (*cont.*)
truth is rarely p. — TRUTH 31
purify p. the dialect — SPEECH 27
puritan P. all things are impure — GOOD 37
P. hated bear-baiting — PLEASURE 20
purity P. of race — EUROPE 11
purple born in the p. — ROYALTY 3
in the p. of emperors — QUOTATIONS 7
I shall wear p. — OLD AGE 33
noon a p. glow — DAY 14
P. haze — MIND 20
p. patch — STYLE 2
p. patch or two — STYLE 4
wear the p. — ROYALTY 8
purpose Gone is p. — UNIVERSE 18
happy sense of p. — ARGUMENT 24
nothing to some p. — LEISURE 17
nothing without p. — NATURE 5
out of p. — AMERICA 36
speak and p. not — HYPOCRISY 11
time for every p. — TIME 18
want a sense of p. — MORALITY 20
purse consumption of the p. — POVERTY 15
p. out of a sow's ear — FUTILITY 7
steals my p. steals trash — REPUTATION 19
pursue p. Culture in bands — CULTURE 16
pursuing Faint yet p. — DETERMINATION 23
still p. — ACHIEVEMENT 7
still p. — DETERMINATION 37
pursuit p. of happiness — HAPPINESS 31
p. of happiness — HUMAN RIGHTS 6
p. of perfection — PERFECTION 9
pushed p. and they flew — INSIGHT 15
p. in the right direction — FATE 1
put P. me to what you will — SELF-SACRIFICE 4
p. off till tomorrow — HASTE 8
with which I will not p. — LANGUAGE 24
putting way of p. it — MEANING 14
putting-off p. of unhappiness — HASTE 20
puzzles Nothing p. me more — WORRY 10
Pygmalion not P. likely — SWEARING 3
pygmies like retarded p. — PEACE 25
pyramids children but like p. — BOOKS 13
summit of these p. — PAST 22
Pyrenees P. are no more — INTERNAT REL 10
Pyrrhic P. victory — WINNING 5

quack q. of yesterday — PARANORMAL 11
quails long for Q. — SATISFACTION 19
Quaker Q. City — AMERICAN CITIES 36
Q. State — AMERICAN CITIES 37
qualities q. as would wear well — MARRIAGE 23
q., the imperious will — CHARACTER 35
Q. too elevated — CHARACTER 32
quality Never mind the q. — QUANTITIES 7
q. of mercy — JUSTICE 24
q. of the notes — MUSICIANS 13
Q. time? There's always — CHILD CARE 20
q. which guarantees all — COURAGE 30
quantitative triumph of the q. method — STATISTICS 12
quantities ghosts of departed q. — MATHS 11
quantity *q.* of the notes — MUSICIANS 13
quantum q. leap — PROGRESS 4
q. solar energy — PHYSICAL 24
quark q. confinement — PHYSICAL 6
quarrel justice of my own q. — JUSTICE 26
no q. with the Viet Cong — ENEMIES 20
one to make a q. — ARGUMENT 18
q. in a far away country — WORLD W II 6
q. of lovers — LOVE 11
two to make a q. — ARGUMENT 2
quarrels Engage in q. and disputes — OPINION 10
q. with one's husband — SINGLE 9
quart q. into a pint pot — FUTILITY 4
quarto beautiful q. page — PUBLISHING 4

Quebec Free Q. — CANADA 15
queen I'm to be Q. o' the May — FESTIVALS 61
Nine Days' Queen — PEOPLE 16
Ocean's child, and then his q. — TOWNS 15
Q. and country — PATRIOTISM 5
Q. and huntress — SKIES 11
q. in people's hearts — ROYALTY 38
q. of Scots is this day — PREGNANCY 5
Q. of the West — AMERICAN CITIES 38
q. of tides — SKIES 6
q.'s weather — WEATHER 27
Red Q. hypothesis — LIFE SCI 4
Queensberry Q. Rules — BEHAVIOUR 10
queer q. as folk — HUMAN NATURE 3
queerer q. than we *can* suppose — UNIVERSE 19
quench waters cannot q. — LOVE 19
questing passes the q. vole — STYLE 19
question Ask a silly q. — FOOLS 1
ask him the same q. — COUNTRIES 27
ask the hard q. — PHILOSOPHY 19
civil q. — MANNERS 2
If you put the q. in wrong — COMPUTERS 9
one fatal q. — LAW 38
Others abide our q. — SHAKESPEARE 11
q. causes it to disappear — COUNTRIES 26
q. is which is to be — POWER 24
sixty-four thousand dollar q. — PROBLEMS 10
that is the q. — CHOICE 14
two sides to every q. — JUSTICE 8
what is the q. — LAST WORDS 28
questioning Q. is not the mode — CONVERSATION 9
questions *all* q. were stupid — IGNORANCE 11
ask difficult q. — WRITING 52
ask it some sensible q. — SUPERNATURAL 27
Fools ask q. — KNOWLEDGE 3
haven't thought up the q. — COMPUTERS 10
hears only those q. — PROBLEMS 14
make two q. grow — SCIENCE 15
nailing his q. — FAITH 13
q., all the time — EDUCATION 31
q. are open — LOGIC 18
q. the distempered part — MEDICINE 24
Them that asks no q. — CAUTION 29
though puzzling q. — KNOWLEDGE 27
queue orderly q. of one — ENGLAND 29
quick judge the q. and the dead — HEAVEN 13
q. and the dead — TRANSPORT 16
q. brown fox — LANGUAGE 1
quicker liquor is q. — ALCOHOL 23
quickest q. way of ending a war — WARFARE 53
quickly get it over with as q. as possible — WARFARE 65
It were done q. — ACTION 16
Q. come — CONSTANCY 2
twice who gives q. — GIFTS 4
quiet All q. along the Potomac to-night — WARS 18
All q. on the western front — WORLD W I 26
Anythin' for a q. life — SOLITUDE 10
Dr Q. — MEDICINE 1
lives of q. desperation — LIFE 32
never have a q. world — PATRIOTISM 22
q. American — SECRECY 16
q. as a nun — DAY 10
q. die — INDIFFERENCE 8
q. life — BUSINESS 35
quieten q. your enemy — ENEMIES 22
quietly q. among the graves — DEATH 42
q. pacifist peaceful — VIOLENCE 19
She won't go q. — DEFIANCE 19
quietness bride of q. — SILENCE 10
quietus might his q. make — SUICIDE 2
quip q. modest — LIES 9
quis Q. *custodiet* — TRUST 21
quit Then q. — DETERMINATION 46
quits finished when he q. — WINNING 24
quiver q. full of them — CHILDREN 4
quotation Classical q. is the parole — QUOTATIONS 4
considered worthy of q. — PRAISE 16

read (*cont.*)

people who can't r.	JOURNALISM 29
people who don't r.	BOOKS 30
population able to r.	EDUCATION 28
praise and don't r.	BOOKS 16
Pray, r., and work	PRAYER 2
r. any good books lately	READING 1
r. by deputy	BOOKS 5
r., by preference	ARTS AND SCI 5
r. just as inclination	READING 10
R. my lips	TAXES 19
r. Richardson for the story	WRITERS 7
r. the fine print	EXPERIENCE 37
r. the Riot Act	CRIME 14
r. the same book	BOOKS 3
r. too widely	QUOTATIONS 12
servants to r.	CENSORSHIP 14
she cannot r.	IGNORANCE 23
suffered in learning to r.	READING 19
superfluous to r.	SCIENCE 22
What do you r.	READING 5
what is it you want to r.	MURDER 22
reader made everybody a r.	PUBLISHING 13
one r. in a hundred years	WRITING 44
readers full of fourth-rate r.	READING 20
reading easy writing's vile hard r.	WRITING 20
he was r.	READING 4
I prefer r.	READING 13
like to like r.	READING 21
Peace is poor r.	PEACE 16
r. Agatha Christie	POETRY 30
r. is right	CRITICISM 9
R. is to the mind	READING 8
R. one book	READING 18
r. or non-reading	BOOKS 9
São Paulo is like R.	TRAVEL 33
soul of r.	READING 11
substitute for r.	BOOKS 24
without r. it	LETTERS 1
you're all done r. it	READING 15
reads man who r.	READING 3
ready always r. to go	DEATH 39
critics are all r. made	CRITICISM 10
necessity of being r.	PREPARATION 16
r. for any unforeseen	PREPARATION 21
those for which we are r.	BOOKS 22
Reagan R. for his best friend	PEOPLE 57
real any less r. and true	REALITY 10
Be r., don't get caught	ACTING 15
born in the r. world	CLASS 33
crowd out r. life	GOSSIP 26
Life is r.	LIFE 27
new dimensions of the 'r.'	CINEMA 21
our past is r.	SUFFERING 34
r. — please stand up	SECRECY 14
r. Simon Pure	REALITY 4
r. world be redefined to suit	COMPUTERS 22
realism I don't want r.	REALITY 13
realistic r. decision	DISILLUSION 21
reality bear very much r.	HUMAN RACE 28
experiences his own r.	REALITY 17
idea And the r.	REALITY 11
R. goes bounding past	REALITY 14
r. must take precedence	TECHNOLOGY 25
R.'s not strange	REALITY 18
solid base in r.	IMAGINATION 17
This was r.	PARANORMAL 15
tourist in other people's r.	REALITY 16
realms r. of gold	READING 12
reap r. a character	CAUSES 21
r. in joy	SUFFERING 4
r. the whirlwind	CAUSES 8
r. the whirlwind	CAUSES 15
shall he also r.	CAUSES 17
sow, so you r.	CAUSES 4
reappraisal agonizing r.	THINKING 4
reaps r. indigestion	COOKING 26

reason age of r.	CULTURE 2
appear The better r.	SPEECHES 8
Can they r.	ANIMALS 16
dream of r.	DREAMS 9
erring R.'s spite	CIRCUMSTANCE 16
feast of r.	CONVERSATION 2
How noble in r.	HUMAN RACE 11
ideal of r.	HAPPINESS 19
if it be against r.	LAW 17
kills r. itself	CENSORSHIP 3
passion conquers r.	EMOTIONS 13
Power has paid to R.	INTERNAT REL 28
r. abuseth me	MADNESS 3
R. always means	LOGIC 11
R. and Progress	DISILLUSION 20
r. in the roasting	LOGIC 1
r. is silent	PREJUDICE 11
r. knows nothing of	EMOTIONS 11
r. on compulsion	ARGUMENT 9
Theirs not to r. why	ARMED FORCES 30
Through r. Russia can't	RUSSIA 4
ultimate r. of things	SCIENCE AND RELIG 5
woman's r.	LOGIC 7
reasonable rather be right than be r.	WOMEN 47
r. man adapts himself	PROGRESS 13
reasonably r. be expected to do	EFFORT 16
reasoning consecutive r.	LOGIC 10
reasons finding of bad r.	PHILOSOPHY 14
R. are not like garments	LOGIC 8
r. for having children	PREGNANCY 9
r. will be wrong	JUSTICE 28
reassurance ritual of r.	LEISURE 16
reassures science r.	ARTS AND SCI 11
rebel like a true-blue r.	REVOLUTION 20
What is a r.	REVOLUTION 23
rebellion little r. now and then	REVOLUTION 11
R. to tyrants	REVOLUTION 7
sensuality, r. and revivalism	WALES 11
rebuild attempting to r.	SOCIETY 12
recall word takes wing beyond r.	WORDS 6
recalled past cannot be r.	PAST 5
receive give than r.	GIFTS 5
give than to r.	GIFTS 11
receiver r. off the hook	GOD 36
receivers If there were no r.	CRIME 5
recession r. when your neighbour	ECONOMICS 11
recherche r. du temps perdu	MEMORY 4
recipes r. in a cookbook	LIFE SCI 30
reckless because they are r.	STRENGTH 21
r. middle age	GENERATION GAP 10
reckonings r. make long friends	DEBT 8
recks r. not his own rede	WORDS AND DEEDS 12
recognize r. one's own faults	SELF-KNOWLEDGE 16
recommendation Self-praise is no r.	SELF-ESTEEM 3
reconciles Custom r. us	CUSTOM 13
feasting r.	COOKING 16
reconciliation bridge of r.	MOURNING 23
r. does not consist	FORGIVENESS 28
reconstruction road of r.	PROGRESS 18
reconvened hereby r.	SCOTLAND 22
record r. of the past	REPUTATION 7
r. or control	PAST 36
recovers from which he never r.	NAMES 13
recovery green shoots of r.	ECONOMICS 20
recreate r. it and yet keep	PAINTING 31
rectum one in the r.	MEDICINE 23
red because my skin is r.	AMERICA 21
Better r. than dead	CAPITALISM 3
keep the r. flag flying	POLITICAL PART 22
like a r., red rose	LOVE 41
not even r. brick	UNIVERSITIES 24
r. in my mind	SENSES 12
r. in the face	CORRUPTION 15
r. in tooth	NATURE 12
r. in tooth and claw	NATURE 4
r. letter day	FESTIVALS 48
r. men scalped each other	INTERNAT REL 17

right (*cont.*)
r. words, battles won | WORDS 24
Roundheads (R. but Repulsive) | WARS 22
scientists are probably r. | HYPOTHESIS 29
that they are r. | CERTAINTY 22
To do the r. deed | MORALITY 16
Ulster will be r. | IRELAND 14
Whatever IS, is R. | CIRCUMSTANCE 16
what thy r. hand doeth | CHARITY 11
wrongs don't make a r. | GOOD 8
wrongs don't make a r. | GOOD 42
your r. to say it | CENSORSHIP 4
righteous r. are bold as a lion | COURAGE 11
r. man regardeth the life | ANIMALS 11
rights about equal r. | HUMAN RIGHTS 16
championing human r. | HUMAN RIGHTS 17
dignity and r. | HUMAN RIGHTS 14
Natural r. is nonsense | HUMAN RIGHTS 9
possess their equal r. | DEMOCRACY 9
r. of man | HUMAN RIGHTS 3
r. of man | HUMAN RIGHTS 8
unalienable r. | HUMAN RIGHTS 6
wicked folly of 'Woman's R.' | WOMAN'S ROLE 21
right-wing r., like nature | POLITICAL PART 45
Rimmon house of R. | SELF-INTEREST 10
ring devil's gold r. | GIFTS 3
R. out the old | FESTIVALS 63
They now r. the bells | WARS 7
With this R. I thee wed | WEDDINGS 7
ringleaders fling the r. | CRIME 29
riot read the R. Act | CRIME 14
r. is at bottom the language | VIOLENCE 15
ripe r. and ripe | MATURITY 14
Soon r. | MATURITY 2
ripper no female Jack the R. | WOMEN 60
rise carcasses, which are to r. again | BODY 16
early to r. | HEALTH 4
his unfailing r. | NATURE 6
maketh his sun to r. | EQUALITY 4
r. above its source | CHARACTER 12
r. above principle | POLITICS 1
r. at five | IDLENESS 13
r. by other's fall | SELF-INTEREST 20
this world to r. above | NATURE 18
rising All r. to great place | POWER 15
land of the r. sun | COUNTRIES 8
r. tide lifts all | SUCCESS 9
risk Where there is no r. | ACHIEVEMENT 30
risking in r. life | MEN AND WOMEN 22
risks We took r. | DANGER 28
Ritz like the R. Hotel | JUSTICE 33
river didn't write 'Ol' Man R.' | SINGING 13
Even the weariest r. | RIVERS 10
Fame is like a r. | FAME 6
Old Man R. | RIVERS 4
Ol' man r. | RIVERS 13
r. in the tree | SENSES 12
r. Is a strong brown god | RIVERS 14
r. of white | PUBLISHING 2
R. Tiber foaming with blood | RACE 28
rook-racked, r.-rounded | BRITISH TOWNS 31
sea refuses no r. | GREED 3
sell down the r. | TRUST 13
tried to cross the r. | PARANORMAL 18
twice into the same r. | CHANGE 26
rivers r. ancient as the world | RIVERS 12
r. dry up | POLLUTION 13
r. run into the sea | RIVERS 1
road Don't leave them on the r. | EMOTIONS 16
end of the r. | DETERMINATION 41
Golden R. to Samarkand | KNOWLEDGE 45
high r. that leads him | SCOTLAND 8
midddle of the r. | EXCESS 32
middle of the r. | EXCESS 30
r. of excess | EXCESS 25
r. to En-dor | SUPERNATURAL 21
r. to hell | ACTION 9

r. to learning | EDUCATION 7
r. towards freedom | ORDER 17
r. up and the road down | SIMILARITY 14
royal r. | DREAMS 13
royal r. to geometry | MATHS 8
roads All r. lead to Rome | TOWNS 1
How many r. | MATURITY 14
Two r. diverged | CHOICE 21
roaming always r. with a hungry heart | TRAVEL 23
roar die of the r. | INSIGHT 12
to give the r. | SPEECHES 17
roaring r. forties | SEA 6
r. twenties | PAST 13
roast R. beef and Yorkshire | MURDER 22
r. their eggs | SELF 11
roasting r. of eggs | LOGIC 1
rob r. Peter | DEBT 10
robbed We was r. | SPORTS 15
robber ties the r.'s bundle | ROYALTY 23
robbers apply to Great Train R. | CRIME 54
robber-state vast parasite r. | AUSTRALIA 19
robbery exchange is no r. | JUSTICE 3
robbing r. a bank | MONEY 35
r. of a foe | DECEPTION 16
Robespierre R. was nothing but | REVOLUTION 16
robin r. and the wren | BIRDS 3
R. Hood could brave all weathers | WEATHER 15
r. red breast | BIRDS 9
round R. Hood's barn | TRAVEL 10
robs r. Peter to pay Paul | GOVERNMENT 36
rock R. journalism | JOURNALISM 29
ruled by the r. | CAUSES 9
upon this r. | CHRISTIAN CH 13
rock and roll Gardening is the new r. | GARDENS 24
rocked R. in the cradle | SEA 16
r. the system | ELECTIONS 19
rocket rose like a r. | SUCCESS 27
Up like a r. | SUCCESS 11
rockets Once the r. are up | DUTY 25
rocking r. a grown man | PROGRESS 10
Worry is like a r. chair | WORRY 6
rocks fossils in the r. | LIFE SCI 16
r. remain | STRENGTH 24
r. the cradle | PARENTS 11
rod Spare the r. | CHILD CARE 2
spareth his r. | CRIME 18
rogation R. Sunday | FESTIVALS 50
rogue r. and villain | INSULTS 4
rogues couple of r. | ACTING 4
Roland R. for an Oliver | JUSTICE 15
role not yet found a r. | BRITAIN 13
roll R. up that map | EUROPE 6
rolled bottoms of my trousers r. | OLD AGE 20
rolling He jus' keeps r. along | RIVERS 13
Like a r. stone | SOLITUDE 23
r. stone | CONSTANCY 3
rolls R. body | EXCELLENCE 15
Roman fall of the R. empire | SPORTS 10
ghost of the deceased R. Empire | CHRISTIAN CH 19
neither holy, nor R. | COUNTRIES 13
R. holiday | CRUELTY 3
r. holiday | CRUELTY 8
romance fine r. | KISSING 11
love and r. | DANCE 14
Romans Friends, R., countrymen | SPEECHES 7
R. ever done for us | GRATITUDE 19
To whom the R. pray | RIVERS 7
romantic Cavaliers (Wrong but R.) | WARS 22
r. places | MEMORY 23
romantics We were the last r. | IDEALISM 11
Rome All roads lead to R. | TOWNS 1
church of R. | CHRISTIAN CH 18
grandeur that was R. | PAST 23
loved R. more | PATRIOTISM 7
R.—at a price | CORRUPTION 7
R. shall stand | TOWNS 16

schedule s. is already full	CRISES 23
schemes best-laid s.	FORESIGHT 11
s. of political improvement	POLITICS 12
schizophrenic you are a s.	MADNESS 16
Schleswig-Holstein S. question	INTERNAT REL 18
scholar s. among rakes	WRITERS 14
s.'s life assail	EDUCATION 18
scholars Saints and S.	IRELAND 5
school at the head of s.	SCHOOLS 3
English public s.	CRIME 43
Example is the s.	EDUCATION 20
good things about s.	SCHOOLS 13
head against the s. house	EDUCATION 2
keeps a dear s.	EXPERIENCE 6
knocked out of them at s.	UNIVERSITIES 17
s. of Stratford atte Bowe	LANGUAGES 3
S. prayer . . . bears	PRAYER 30
sent to s. for	SCHOOLS 8
tales out of s.	SECRECY 6
unwillingly to s.	CHILDREN 9
schoolboy s., with his satchel	CHILDREN 9
schoolboys s. who educate him	SCHOOLS 9
schoolchildren what all s. learn	GOOD 38
schoolgirl s. complexion	APPEARANCE 8
schoolmaster send your child to the s.	SCHOOLS 9
schoolmasters s. of ever after	WRITING 18
s. puzzle their brain	ALCOHOL 11
schoolrooms s. for 'the boy'	CRIME 34
schools Public s. are the nurseries	SCHOOLS 4
S. are for schooling	SCHOOLS 17
Schrödinger S.'s cat	PHYSICAL 7
science aim of all s.	HYPOTHESIS 22
beginning of s.	SCIENCE AND RELIG 5
creation s.	SCIENCE AND RELIG 1
dismal s.	ECONOMICS 3
gay s.	POETRY 1
How s. dwindles	CRITICISM 6
it is not s.	SCIENCE 11
Kissing is not like s.	KISSING 16
Much s., much sorrow	SCIENCE 1
orderly fact of every s.	HYPOTHESIS 19
plundered this new s.	ARTS AND SCI 17
redefined the task of s.	SCIENCE 26
s. can supersede poetry	ARTS AND SCI 10
s. fiction scenario	POLLUTION 27
S. finds	TECHNOLOGY 2
S. has no enemy	SCIENCE 2
S. is for the cultivation	SCIENCE AND RELIG 3
s. is ourselves	ARTS AND SCI 6
s. is strong	MEDICINE 27
S. must begin with myths	ARTS AND SCI 13
s., read, by preference	ARTS AND SCI 5
s. reassures	ARTS AND SCI 11
S., which proceeds	NATURE 20
S. without religion	SCIENCE AND RELIG 12
Shakespeare of s. fiction	WRITERS 32
Success is a s.	SUCCESS 32
tragedy of S.	HYPOTHESIS 18
sciences Books must follow s.	SCIENCE 6
scientific as if they were s.	SCIENCE AND RELIG 10
endears it to the really s. mind	VALUE 29
importance of a s.	SCIENCE 22
new s. truth	SCIENCE 23
S. truth should be	SCIENCE 10
scientist s. says that something	HYPOTHESIS 28
s. thinks of a method	SCIENCE 27
s. to discard	HYPOTHESIS 25
s. were to cut his ear	ARTS AND SCI 16
scientists company of s.	ARTS AND SCI 15
S. are explorers	ARTS AND SCI 18
s. are probably right	HYPOTHESIS 29
scissors end up using s.	TECHNOLOGY 27
score no matter what the s.	FOOTBALL 12
Tenors get women by the s.	SINGING 8
time required to s. 500	CRICKET 15
woman keeps s.	GIFTS 23
scorer One Great S.	SPORTS 16
scorn expression of s.	INSULTS 9
S. not the sonnet	SHAKESPEARE 10
scorned like a woman s.	WOMEN 4
woman s.	REVENGE 16
scornful s. tickling	HUMOUR 5
scorpions chastise you with s.	CRIME 19
lash of s.	CRIME 13
scot s. and lot	TAXES 4
Scotch S. banker	CANADA 18
Scotland curse of S.	SCOTLAND 1
flower of S.	SCOTLAND 15
inferior sort of S.	COUNTRIES 15
rose of S.	FLOWERS 12
S. in Ireland	IRELAND 11
S. small	SCOTLAND 18
S.'s rightful heritage	SCOTLAND 21
Stands S. where	SCOTLAND 5
Scots S., wha hae	SCOTLAND 10
Scotsman S. on the make	SCOTLAND 13
S. with a grievance	SCOTLAND 14
Scottish S. play	SHAKESPEARE 1
scoundrel forty is a s.	MEN 2
plea of the s.	GOOD 31
refuge of a s.	PATRIOTISM 11
scourge S. of God	PEOPLE 20
scrabble 'Bop' is like s.	JAZZ 6
scrap just for a s. of paper	INTERNAT REL 24
s. of paper	TRUST 12
scratch S. a lover	ENEMIES 18
S. a Russian	RUSSIA 1
S. the Christian	CHRISTIAN CH 28
scratching s. of my finger	SELF 13
scream s. for help in dreams	DREAMS 17
screw But s. your courage	SUCCESS 24
to seek the right s.	DETERMINATION 47
scribble Always s., scribble, scribble	WRITING 23
we all s. poems	POETRY 5
scribbler academic s.	IDEAS 15
scribendi cacoethes s.	WRITING 3
scripture devil can cite S.	BIBLE 11
devil can quote S.	QUOTATIONS 1
Holy S. and nature	SCIENCE AND RELIG 4
scriptures look at the s.	BIBLE 13
scrotumtightening s. sea	SEA 4
scroungy all s. and bearded	WEDDINGS 14
scruples because they have s.	STRENGTH 21
sculpture austere, like that of s.	MATHS 20
scum glittering s.	CULTURE 19
Okie means you're s.	INSULTS 11
s. of the earth	ARMED FORCES 28
s. on the teeth	LIFE SCI 8
They are s.	UNIVERSITIES 23
sea afraid of the s.	SEA 19
all the s. were ink	WRITING 12
can see nothing but s.	EXPLORATION 5
down to the s. in ships	SEA 8
fish in the s.	LOVE 12
foe and s. room	ARMED FORCES 9
go down to the s. again	SEA 18
having been at s.	ARMED FORCES 21
nor s. innavigable	EXPLORATION 4
ploughed the s.	REVOLUTION 15
rivers run into the s.	RIVERS 1
rush across the s.	TRAVEL 14
sailor home from the s.	EPITAPHS 19
s. change	CHANGE 24
s. hates a coward	SEA 22
s. is not within sight	MARRIAGE 27
s. is the universal sewer	POLLUTION 21
S. of Faith	FAITH 9
s. refuses no river	GREED 3
s. to shining sea	AMERICA 24
serpent-haunted s.	SEA 20
snotgreen s.	SEA 21
steady than an ebbing s.	CONSTANCY 7
thousand furlongs of s.	SEA 10
To s. for nothing	LOVE 30

self-made (*cont.*)
s. man — SELF-ESTEEM 17
self-praise s. is no recommendation — SELF-ESTEEM 3
self-preservation s. in the other — CRISES 13
S. is the first — SELF-INTEREST 9
self-respect starves your s. — PARLIAMENT 30
self-sacrifice S. enables us — SELF-SACRIFICE 8
S. is the exception — SELF-INTEREST 8
sell I s. here, Sir — TECHNOLOGY 6
mind to s. his house — BUYING 5
precious as the Goods they s. — BUYING 6
s. down the river — TRUST 13
S. honestly — HONESTY 6
S. in May — BUSINESS 14
s. in the dearest — ECONOMICS 1
s. it cheap — BUSINESS 13
s. or deny — JUSTICE 21
s. the bear's skin — OPTIMISM 14
s. their souls — CONSCIENCE 17
we s. hope — BUSINESS 45
sell-by long s. date — SUCCESS 49
selling lives by s. something — BUYING 7
old firm is s. out — DISILLUSION 20
s. the family silver — ECONOMICS 17
Selsdon S. man — POLITICAL PART 9
semen No frozen packet of s. — PREGNANCY 18
semper *Sic s. tyrannis* — REVENGE 18
senator S., and a Democrat — POLITICAL PART 31
senators I look at the s. — POLITICIANS 17
send s. to Coventry — SOLITUDE 4
sensations life of s. — SENSES 9
s. and cheap appeals — EDUCATION 28
what are his s. — IMAGINATION 7
sense all her rays from s. — PRACTICALITY 8
good s. and good taste — TASTE 4
like a sixth s. — MONEY 33
men of s. are really — RELIGION 12
motions of the s. — EMOTIONS 9
Much fruit of s. — WORDS 11
pleasures of s. — SENSES 5
s. of being good — GOOD 44
s. out of the nonsense — DEBT 26
Shadwell never deviates into s. — FOOLS 15
something makes s. — HOPE 24
Take care of the s. — SPEECH 21
to his own s. doth smell — SELF 7
want of s. — CONSTANCY 8
want of s. — MANNERS 10
senseless kind of s. wit — MIND 19
senses five s. — SENSES 2
Parson lost his s. — ANIMALS 25
power of our s. — SENSES 8
sensible No opera plot can be s. — SINGING 15
sensual Catholic and s. — TRAVEL 31
sensuality s., rebellion and revivalism — WALES 11
sentence it's a s. — MARRIAGE 37
s. he manages to utter — LANGUAGE 29
S. structure is innate — SPEECH 30
sentenced s. to death in my absence — ABSENCE 17
sentiment corrupted by s. — EMOTIONS 22
sentimental s. passion — ARTS 16
sentimentality S. is the emotional promiscuity — EMOTIONS 25

separately man can s. do — HUMAN RIGHTS 7
We shall all hang s. — COOPERATION 23
sept that damnable s. — SCOTLAND 6
September S. blow soft — WEATHER 17
sepulchre whited s. — HYPOCRISY 6
sepulchres whited s. — HYPOCRISY 10
seraglio s. of eunuchs — PARLIAMENT 25
Serbs S. out, Nato in — WARS 32
serenity s. of age — OLD AGE 31
s. to accept — CHANGE 48
serf another man's s. — DEATH 17
serfdom abolish s. — REVOLUTION 19
sergeant s. is the army — ARMED FORCES 44
'S. Pepper'—a decisive — CULTURE 27

serial kind of s. monogamist — CONSTANCY 20
obituary in s. form — BIOGRAPHY 20
serious Gershwin a s. composer — MUSICIANS 14
it is much more s. — FOOTBALL 9
Murder is a s. business — MURDER 19
s. house — CHRISTIAN CH 34
too s. a matter — POLITICS 29
War is too s. a matter — WARFARE 40
You cannot be s. — SPORTS 28
seriously S., though — ACHIEVEMENT 5
serious-minded s. activity — CHILDREN 8
sermon honest and painful s. — RELIGION 10
S. on the Mount — CHRISTIAN CH 12
S. on the Mount — SCIENCE AND RELIG 13
sermons S. and soda-water — PLEASURE 18
S. in stones — NATURE 8
serpent s.-haunted sea — SEA 20
s. subtlest beast — ANIMALS 14
sharper than a s. tooth — GRATITUDE 8
servant become the s. of a man — WOMAN'S ROLE 23
good s. but a bad master — WAYS 4
s. is worth a thousand gadgets — TECHNOLOGY 14
well enough for a s. — UNIVERSITIES 7
servants from a family of s. — CLASS 30
s. are treated as human — EMPLOYMENT 17
s. to read — CENSORSHIP 14
serve No man can s. — CHOICE 5
s. a well-bred lion — DEMOCRACY 7
s. God and Mammon — MONEY 14
s. in heaven — AMBITION 13
s. our country — PATRIOTISM 9
s. two masters — MONEY 23
s. your captives' need — DUTY 17
They also s. — ACTION 20
served first come, first s. — PUNCTUALITY 3
Had I but s. God — DUTY 8
never well s. — BUSINESS 12
would be well s. — SELF-INTEREST 5
Youth must be s. — YOUTH 3
service no-future job in the s. sector — EMPLOYMENT 32
s. of my love — PATRIOTISM 21
s. of the nation — POLITICIANS 31
s. ranks the same — GOD 25
What is s. — GIFTS 18
serviettes crumpled the s. — MANNERS 22
serving-men six honest s. — KNOWLEDGE 43
servitude s. is at once — LIBERTY 16
sesame Open S. — PROBLEMS 7
sessions s. of sweet silent thought — MEMORY 8
sets sun never s. — COUNTRIES 10
settled People who wish to be s. — CUSTOM 16
seven City of the S. Hills — TOWNS 5
for the first s. years — EDUCATION 3
Keep a thing s. years — POSSESSIONS 3
Rain before s. — WEATHER 12
s. ages — LIFE 18
s. deadly sins — SIN 5
s. feet of English ground — DEFIANCE 10
S. Last Words — LAST WORDS 2
s.-league boots — TRANSPORT 5
s. of anything — MEMORY 9
s. seas — SEA 7
s. stars — SKIES 7
s.-stone weakling — HEALTH 6
seventy times s. — FORGIVENESS 11
s. wealthy towns — FAME 9
S. Wonders of the World — ARCHITECTURE 4
seventy Oh, to be s. again — OLD AGE 21
s. times seven — FORGIVENESS 11
s. years old — HUMAN RACE 27
s. year young — OLD AGE 17
severity S. breedeth fear — CRIME 21
sewage s. and refuse — PROGRESS 21
sewer crawl through a sewer — DRUGS 6
Life is like a s. — LIFE 47
midst of this putrid s. — BRITISH TOWNS 29
sea is the universal s. — POLLUTION 21

sewers s. annoy the air — COUNTRY AND TOWN 8
sewing s. on a button — MEN 14
sex conceal its s. — ANIMALS 26
  darling after s. — LOVE 72
  emotion without s. — SEX 46
  exactly like s. — MONEY 38
  fair s. — WOMEN 11
  have money, it's s. — SATISFACTION 34
  He has had a s. change — GOD 41
  Is s. dirty — SEX 35
  make s. less secretive — SEX 36
  Mind has no s. — MIND 9
  mostly about having s. — CHILDREN 23
  Nobody dies from lack of s. — SINGLE 12
  only unnatural s. act — SEX 29
  passion or even s. — MARRIAGE 50
  Reading about s. — PAST 41
  S. and taxes — SEX 47
  s. at its conclusion — COURTSHIP 16
  s. in the mind — SEX 23
  s. object if you're pretty — BODY 29
  s. that brings forth — MEN AND WOMEN 41
  s. with someone I love — SEX 41
  s., work, food — RELATIONSHIPS 21
  to insult s. — SEX 25
  weaker s., to piety more prone — WOMEN 21
sexes difference within the s. — MEN AND WOMEN 23
  stronger, of the two s. — MEN AND WOMEN 6
  there are three s. — CLERGY 18
sexual car crash as a s. event — TRANSPORT 27
  like s. relations — EMPLOYMENT 28
  S. fidelity is more important — CONSTANCY 17
  S. intercourse began — SEX 37
  s. lives of their parents — PARENTS 25
  strong as s. desire — SEX 7
sexuality s. in the movies — CINEMA 24
sexually s. transmitted disease — LIFE 2
shackles Memories are not s. — MEMORY 28
shade farewell to the s. — TREES 8
  thought in a green s. — GARDENS 11
shades S. of the prison-house — YOUTH 12
shadow also casts a s. — RANK 16
  but a walking s. — LIFE 19
  dispossess him of his s. — LOVE 71
  events cast their s. — FUTURE 1
  Falls the S. — REALITY 11
  s. of death — DANGER 20
  s. will be shown — GOD 29
shadowing employ any depth of s. — INSULTS 4
shadows less liquid than their s. — CATS 10
  sins cast long s. — PAST 2
shaft s. at random sent — CHANCE 24
shake s. The catsup bottle — FOOD 25
shaken S. and not stirred — ALCOHOL 18
  s. me by the hand — OLD AGE 13
  s., not stirred — ALCOHOL 7
shaker mover and s. — CHANGE 22
shakers movers and s. — MUSICIANS 7
Shakespeare Brush up your S. — SHAKESPEARE 14
  entire works of S. — COMPUTERS 17
  I could be S. — ARTS AND SCI 9
  like reading S. — ACTING 6
  read a work of S.'s — ARTS AND SCI 14
  S. had not written *Hamlet* — ARTS AND SCI 14
  S. of science fiction — WRITERS 32
  S. would have grasped — ARTS AND SCI 17
  tongue that S. spake — ENGLAND 12
shaking fall without s. — EFFORT 15
  start s. them — SPEECHES 19
shall picked the was of s. — LOGIC 19
shallow s. brooks murmur most — SILENCE 7
  s. murmur — EMOTIONS 10
shalt Thou s. not kill — MURDER 8
shame fool me twice, s. on me — DECEPTION 3
  glory is in their s. — GREED 8
  secret s. destroyed my peace — WRITERS 29
  s. and humiliation — REPUTATION 29

  s. on you — JAZZ 9
  s. the devil — TRUTH 4
  s. unto him — BODY 10
shameful s. to doubt one's friends — FRIENDSHIP 13
shape our buildings s. us — ARCHITECTURE 14
  s. and definition — LIFESTYLES 34
  s. of things to come — FUTURE 8
  you might be any s. — NAMES 9
share s. God — GOD 38
  s. in two revolutions — REVOLUTION 14
  s. no one's ideas — IDEAS 8
shared s. anguish — MOURNING 23
  trouble s. — COOPERATION 16
sharing intimate s. between friends — PRAYER 11
shark bitten in half by a s. — CHOICE 32
sharks We are all s. — POLITICIANS 35
sharp short s. shock — CRIME 15
  short, s. shock — CRIME 38
sharper s. than a serpent's tooth — GRATITUDE 8
  s. the storm — OPTIMISM 11
shaved s. head — STRENGTH 28
shaves s. and takes a train — TRANSPORT 31
shaving s. of a morning — POETRY 29
she Does she . . . or doesn't she — CERTAINTY 1
shears resembles a pair of s. — MARRIAGE 25
shed Burke under a s. — PEOPLE 33
  prepare to s. them now — SORROW 9
sheep bleating s. loses — OPPORTUNITY 3
  hanged for a s. — THOROUGHNESS 5
  hundred years like a s. — HEROES 7
  Let us return to these s. — DETERMINATION 11
  like lost s. — SIN 18
  lone s. is in danger — SOLITUDE 3
  savaged by a dead s. — INSULTS 13
  s. from the goats — GOOD 13
  s. on its hind-legs — CONFORMITY 9
  s.'s clothing — HYPOCRISY 9
  s. to pass resolutions — ARGUMENT 18
  thousand years as a s. — HEROES 1
  to his s. he yaf — BEHAVIOUR 15
  wolf in s.'s clothing — DECEPTION 8
  writer to eat a whole s. — WRITING 43
sheet wet s. and a flowing sea — SEA 15
sheets kindliness of s. — SLEEP 16
shelf s. life of the modern hardback writer — WRITING 51
shell fired a 15-inch s. — SURPRISE 13
shelter s. for the other — WEDDINGS 4
shelves your bookcases and your s. — LIBRARIES 4
shepherd Lord is my s. — GOD 6
  s.'s delight — WEATHER 14
shepherds s. and butchers — GOVERNMENT 15
shibboleth Say now S. — SPEECH 7
shield s. of British fair play — JUSTICE 40
shieling s. of the misty island — SCOTLAND 12
shift s. an old tree — CUSTOM 5
shillings can do for ten s. — TECHNOLOGY 16
shimmy s. like my sister — DANCE 11
shines hay while the sun s. — OPPORTUNITY 7
shining improve the s. hour — EFFORT 10
  s. intellectual — LEADERSHIP 16
  s. morning face — CHILDREN 9
ship desert a sinking s. — INDECISION 13
  Do not spoil the s. — THOROUGHNESS 1
  one for the s. — SEA 3
  one leak will sink a s. — CAUSES 19
  s. but a prison — SEA 12
  s. of fools — HUMAN RACE 5
  s. of state — GOVERNMENT 6
  s. of the desert — ANIMALS 9
  s. without ballast — COURAGE 4
  vineyard and a s. — COUNTRIES 37
  woman and a s. ever want mending — WOMEN 8
ships down to the sea in s. — SEA 8
  launched a thousand s. — BEAUTY 10
  Loose lips sink s. — GOSSIP 7
  s. empty of men — ARMED FORCES 15
  s. that pass — MEETING 5

ships (*cont.*)
S. that pass in the night | RELATIONSHIPS 7
sunken and damaged s. | WORLD W II 19
We've got the s. | PATRIOTISM 18
shipshape s. and Bristol fashion | ORDER 8
shipwreck s. of time | PAST 19
shire s. which we the Heart | BRITISH TOWNS 23
shirt Near is my s. | SELF-INTEREST 7
s. of Nessus | MISFORTUNES 13
shirtsleeves From s. to | SUCCESS 3
shit ocean of s. | JUSTICE 37
shock-proof s. detector | WRITING 47
shiver praised and left to s. | HONESTY 7
shivering hungry s. self | SATISFACTION 28
s. human soul | SELF 21
shock future s. | PROGRESS 2
s. of joy | OLD AGE 31
short sharp s. | CRIME 15
short, sharp s. | CRIME 38
shocked s. by this subject | PHYSICAL 19
shocking looked on as something s. | MORALITY 15
shocks s. the magistrate | LAW 33
s. the mind of a child | RELIGION 19
shoddier no s. than what they peddle | WORDS 26
shoe If the s. fits | NAMES 3
other s. to drop | AUSTRALIA 24
shoemaker s.'s son always goes barefoot | FAMILY 7
shoes call for his old s. | FAMILIARITY 15
dead men's s. | AMBITION 3
dead men's s. | POSSESSIONS 8
dressed in cheap s. | DRESS 27
I had no s. | MISFORTUNES 3
mind it wipes its s. | HOUSEWORK 12
more than dancing s. | DANCE 2
want of s. | MISFORTUNES 16
shoot he shall s. higher | AMBITION 8
s. me in my absence | ABSENCE 17
s. the pianist | MUSICIANS 8
s. your murderer | HEROES 20
shout and they s. | LIBERTY 30
young idea how to s. | TEACHING 8
shooting s. as a sport | HUNTING 14
s. without aim | ACTION 3
shoots green s. of recovery | ECONOMICS 20
shop Keep your own s. | BUSINESS 8
Women are people who s. | BUYING 13
shopkeepers nation of s. | BUSINESS 29
nation of s. | ENGLAND 14
shopping main thing today is—s. | BUYING 8
Now we build s. malls | BUSINESS 50
s. days to Christmas | CHRISTMAS 1
shoreline s. of knowledge | KNOWLEDGE 6
shorn come home s. | AMBITION 4
grass kept finely s. | GARDENS 10
to the s. lamb | SYMPATHY 2
short brutish and s. | LIFE 20
life is s. | ARTS 2
Life is s. | MEDICINE 7
Life is too s. to | PRACTICALITY 16
lyf so s. | EDUCATION 14
moment of victory is much too s. | WINNING 26
s. and the tall | ARMED FORCES 39
s., brutal lives | MEN AND WOMEN 31
s. horse is soon curried | WORK 7
s. in the story itself | WRITING 5
s. notice, soon past | WEATHER 8
s. sharp shock | CRIME 15
s., sharp shock | CRIME 38
s. time to live | LIFE 22
Take s. views | LIFESTYLES 23
shortage s. of coal and fish | ADMINISTRATION 16
shorter Cleopatra's nose been s. | PEOPLE 28
time to make it s. | LETTERS 9
shortest s.-lived professions | HEROES 13
s. night | FESTIVALS 1
s. way home | PATIENCE 8
s. way is commonly the foulest | WAYS 19

shots but of the best s. | WARFARE 20
people will take pot s. | CHARACTER 51
should not what s. be | CIRCUMSTANCE 24
shoulder looking over his s. | POLITICIANS 26
wearing a s. pad | SYMPATHY 28
shoulder-blade s. that is a miracle | BEAUTY 25
shoulders City of the Big S. | AMERICAN CITIES 51
head on young s. | EXPERIENCE 12
s. of giants | PROGRESS 7
s. of giants | PROGRESS 8
shout make room for men who s. | VIOLENCE 19
s. and they shoot | LIBERTY 30
S. with the largest | CONFORMITY 5
shouting s. fire | LIBERTY 25
thunder of the captains, and the s. | WARFARE 10
show make a s. of themselves | FASHION 4
no business like s. business | THEATRE 16
one thing to s. a man | TRUTH 20
s. business with blood | SPORTS 33
S. me a hero | HEROES 16
s. *more* affection | COURTSHIP 8
s. must go on | DETERMINATION 12
s. that you have one | EDUCATION 17
shower sweetness of a s. | FLOWERS 11
showers After sharpest s. | WEATHER 30
April s. bring forth | WEATHER 1
April with his s. soote | SEASONS 13
pleads for s. | RIVERS 5
showery S., Flowery, Bowery | SEASONS 17
shreds s. and patches | CHARACTER 25
shrimp s. learns to whistle | HASTE 22
shrines thy mouldering s. removed | SCULPTURE 4
shrouds S. have no pockets | MONEY 11
shrove S. Tuesday | FESTIVALS 53
shuffled pack is s. | UNIVERSITIES 26
s. off this mortal coil | DEATH 27
shut keep your mouth s. | FOOLS 25
s. mouth catches | SILENCE 1
s. or open | CHOICE 2
s. the stable door | MISTAKES 9
shuts When one door s. | OPPORTUNITY 17
shutter click the s. | PHOTOGRAPHY 14
shutters keep the s. up | SECRECY 24
shy nervous and s. | MATURITY 11
twice s. | EXPERIENCE 8
shyness S. is egotism | SELF-ESTEEM 28
sick be at when he is s. | SICKNESS 28
denies a s. person | SICKNESS 27
Devil was s. | GRATITUDE 1
do the s. no harm | MEDICINE 18
I'll be s. tonight | GREED 14
makes the heart s. | HOPE 3
maketh the heart s. | HOPE 9
Never s., never old | LOVE 34
s. and wicked | PERFECTION 6
s. man of Europe | COUNTRIES 11
s. you shouldn't take it | HEALTH 17
to make him s. | LOVE 30
sickness falling s. | SICKNESS 5
in s. and in health | MARRIAGE 21
s. suffered by dogs | GRATITUDE 17
Sidcup I could get down to S. | OPPORTUNITY 33
side at the other s. of the hill | WARFARE 29
God is on my s. | GOD 40
Hear the other s. | PREJUDICE 7
on the other s. | CHARITY 12
see one s. of things | OPINION 10
thorn in one's s. | ADVERSITY 7
two s. by side | RELATIONSHIPS 11
which side do they cheer for | PATRIOTISM 30
sides everyone changes s. | GENERATION GAP 15
holding on to the s. | CHARACTER 49
life from both s. | EXPERIENCE 36
said on both s. | PREJUDICE 8
s. to every question | JUSTICE 8
sideways We think s. | IRELAND 25
Siegfried washing on the S. Line | WORLD W II 7

songless s. bird in a cage	BELIEF 2
songs In writing s. I've learned	SINGING 17
s. are sad	IRELAND 15
sonnet Scorn not the s.	SHAKESPEARE 10
sonnets passably effective s.	ADVERTISING 8
written s. all his life	FAMILIARITY 17
sons Clergymen's s.	CLERGY 1
My s. ought to study mathematics	CULTURE 9
s. and daughters of Life	PARENTS 16
s. and your daughters	GENERATION GAP 16
soon S. ripe	MATURITY 2
sooner end the s.	HASTE 15
s. begun	BEGINNING 10
s. every party	ENTERTAINING 14
s. it's over	OPTIMISM 11
sop s. to Cerberus	APOLOGY 9
sophistication Hip is the s.	FASHION 9
sophistry s. and affectation	UNIVERSITIES 6
sops s. in wine	FLOWERS 3
sorcerer s.'s apprentice	PROBLEMS 11
sorriness s. underlying the grandest things	WRITING 32
sorrow beguile thy s.	LIBRARIES 3
Common s.	MOURNING 23
exciting laughter and s.	SHAKESPEARE 8
first great s.	DESPAIR 12
forgather wi' S.	SATISFACTION 21
help you to s.	MISFORTUNES 2
increaseth s.	KNOWLEDGE 18
In s. thou shalt bring	PREGNANCY 4
Labour without s. is base	WORK 32
Much science, much s.	SCIENCE 1
One for s.	BIRDS 2
selfish is s.	SORROW 25
s. and silence	SUFFERING 18
s. in store	SUPERNATURAL 21
s. of the mothers	FAMILY 28
s. thereof, and what cometh	LOVE 26
s. to the grave	OLD AGE 6
such sweet s.	MEETING 8
There is s. enough	DOGS 9
sorrowing goes a s.	DEBT 3
sorrows Half the s. of women	SPEECH 22
Man of S.	SORROW 4
remedy for the s.	SYMPATHY 26
Small s. speak	SORROW 7
sorry having to say you're s.	LOVE 68
safe than s.	CAUTION 1
Very s. can't come	APOLOGY 18
sort not at all the s. of person	CHARACTER 33
sorts It takes all s.	CHARACTER 7
sought s. it with thimbles	WAYS 2
soul adventures of his s.	CRITICISM 14
All S.' Day	FESTIVALS 6
awakened my s.	LANGUAGE 17
beauty of one's s. shine	APPEARANCE 30
captain of my s.	SELF 16
casket of my s.	SLEEP 14
composed in the s.	POETRY 23
dark night of the s.	DESPAIR 2
dark night of the s.	DESPAIR 15
engineers of the s.	ARTS 29
engineers of the s.	ARTS 33
fine point of his s.	LIFESTYLES 22
flow of s.	CONVERSATION 3
French s. is stronger	FRANCE 13
give his s. for the whole world	WALES 10
giving life to an immortal s.	PREGNANCY 7
good for the s.	HONESTY 3
hidden language of the s.	DANCE 17
his eager s.	APPEARANCE 15
if I have a s.	PRAYER 18
I owe my s.	DEBT 23
iron entered into his s.	ADVERSITY 4
like an infant's s.	BOOKS 7
lose his own s.	SUCCESS 22
most surely, on the s.	ARCHITECTURE 13
No coward s. is mine	COURAGE 25

Russian literature saved my s.	BOOKS 28
shed light on the human s.	CINEMA 21
shivering human s.	SELF 21
s. above buttons	AMBITION 14
s. be blasted	SWEARING 9
S. City	AMERICAN CITIES 40
S. clap its hands	OLD AGE 22
s. inhabiting two bodies	FRIENDSHIP 10
s. is his own	CONSCIENCE 11
s. may belong to God	ARMED FORCES 11
s. of any civilization	CULTURE 25
s. of Rabelais	WRITERS 10
s. so much a giant	SELF-KNOWLEDGE 4
s. through My lips	KISSING 7
than that one s.	SIN 25
when it has no s.	BUSINESS 30
window of the s.	BODY 2
with s. so dead	PATRIOTISM 14
soulless when work is s.	WORK 39
souls keep fat s. from sleep	DOGS 10
letters mingle s.	LETTERS 6
only in men's s.	SCIENCE AND RELIG 14
sell their s.	CONSCIENCE 17
s. with but a single	LOVE 47
they have no s.	BUSINESS 24
try men's s.	PATRIOTISM 13
windows into men's s.	SECRECY 21
sound full of s. and fury	LIFE 19
make the most s.	FOOLS 2
mind in a s. body	HEALTH 12
s. and original ideas	POLITICAL PART 34
s. of a great Amen	MUSIC 13
s. of music	MUSIC 28
s. of silence	SILENCE 14
s. of the single hand	COOPERATION 21
soundbite s. and slogan	LANGUAGE 31
substance from s.	HONESTY 17
unlike a s.	QUOTATIONS 14
sounds better than it s.	MUSICIANS 9
by s. and smells	CHILDREN 2
having similar s.	POETRY 37
s. will take care	SPEECH 21
soup blossom s.	TREES 2
cannot make a good s.	COOKING 21
sour s. grapes	SATISFACTION 11
source rise above its s.	CHARACTER 12
s. and origin	BEGINNING 14
south full of the warm S.	ALCOHOL 14
S. is avenged	REVENGE 18
South African S. police would leave	LAW 43
sovereign anger of the s.	ROYALTY 10
change for a s.	PARENTS 17
he will have no s.	HUMAN RIGHTS 5
subject and s.	ROYALTY 15
sovereigns what s. are doing	GOSSIP 21
Soviet Communism is S. power	CAPITALISM 16
Soviets power to the S.	CAPITALISM 1
sow out of a s.'s ear	FUTILITY 7
right s. by the ear	PRACTICALITY 3
S. an act	CAUSES 21
s. by the ear	KNOWLEDGE 12
s. dry	GARDENS 6
s. in tears	SUFFERING 4
s. may whistle	ACHIEVEMENT 6
s. one's wild oats	LIFESTYLES 7
s., so you reap	CAUSES 4
s. that eats her farrow	IRELAND 16
s. the wind	CAUSES 8
soweth Whatsoever a man s.	CAUSES 17
sowing time of s.	SEASONS 31
sown s. the wind	CAUSES 15
sows He s. hurry	COOKING 26
space filling the s.	JOURNALISM 19
how to waste s.	ARCHITECTURE 18
king of infinite s.	DREAMS 7
more than time and s.	WORRY 10
not putting people into s.	FASHION 12

star (cont.)
unreachable s.	IDEALISM 13
wagon to a s.	IDEALISM 6
with one bright s.	SKIES 16
star-crossed s. lovers	LOVE 18
stare stand and s.	LEISURE 8
s. at them	PHOTOGRAPHY 12
stark or Molly S.'s a widow	WARS 10
starry-eyed s.	IDEALISM 2
stars erratik s.	SKIES 9
heaventree of s.	SKIES 23
importance of fading s.	FAME 22
journey-work of the s.	NATURE 13
knowledge of the s.	SCIENCE 18
looking at the s.	IDEALISM 7
Look up at the s.	SKIES 19
loved the s. too fondly	SKIES 22
Man aspires to the s.	PROGRESS 21
melt the s.	SPEECH 20
mistake each other for s.	AMERICAN CITIES 58
ready to mount to the s.	VIRTUE 17
seven s.	SKIES 7
S. and Bars	AMERICA 8
S. and Stripes	AMERICA 9
s. rush out	DAY 9
s.' tennis-balls	FATE 16
s. to flight	DAY 13
s. where no human race is	FEAR 14
sun and the other s.	LOVE 25
with mites of s.	UNIVERSE 9
star-spangled s. banner	AMERICA 14
start S. all over again	DETERMINATION 44
s. together	MUSICIANS 15
s. where people are	CLERGY 23
started arrive where we s.	EXPLORATION 13
s. so I'll finish	BEGINNING 8
starve let his wife s.	ARTS 23
Let not poor Nelly s.	LAST WORDS 13
let our people s.	DEBT 24
s. a fever	SICKNESS 3
would sooner s.	FOOD 24
starves s. starves	ACHIEVEMENT 9
starving s. population	IRELAND 12
working or s.	LIBERTY 11
state bosom of a single s.	CANADA 7
carry a s.	GOVERNMENT 16
faithful to the s.	POLITICIANS 4
I am the S.	GOVERNMENT 13
little from a s. of things	CIRCUMSTANCE 22
Only in the s.	SOCIETY 9
ship of s.	GOVERNMENT 6
S. business a cruel trade	POLITICS 11
S. for every Star	AMERICA 20
s. has no place in	CENSORSHIP 16
S. is an instrument	CAPITALISM 17
s. is like the human body	GOVERNMENT 33
S. is not 'abolished'	GOVERNMENT 32
s. with the prettiest name	AMERICAN CITIES 54
such thing as the S.	SOCIETY 15
While the S. exists	GOVERNMENT 35
stately s. homes of England	RANK 10
S. Homes of England	RANK 15
statement black s. of pistons	TRANSPORT 17
s. is like a cheque	MEANING 13
states mental s.	LIBERTY 32
statesman gift of any s.	POLITICIANS 12
s. is a politician	POLITICIANS 25
s. is a politician	POLITICIANS 31
s. is in general	POLITICIANS 14
stations know our proper s.	CLASS 12
statistic million deaths a s.	DEATH 68
statistical s. improbability	LIFE SCI 26
statistics damned lies and s.	STATISTICS 7
experiment needs s.	STATISTICS 11
give plenty of s.	STATISTICS 5
uses s. as	STATISTICS 9
vital s.	STATISTICS 2

We are just s.	STATISTICS 3
statue s. has never been set up	CRITICISM 21
statues Most s. seem sad	SCULPTURE 10
s. are so constrained	SCULPTURE 5
stature Malice is of a low s.	ENVY 12
status source of s. is no longer	BUYING 11
status quo restored the s.	SCIENCE 17
stay Here I am, and here I s.	WARS 16
S. a little	HASTE 15
s. as they are	CHANGE 49
steadfast s. as thou art	CONSTANCY 12
steady Slow and s.	DETERMINATION 13
S., boys, steady	ARMED FORCES 20
thought more s.	CONSTANCY 7
steak he wanted s.	FRIENDSHIP 27
meat of the s.	AMERICA 38
steaks smell of s.	DAY 16
steal mature poets s.	ORIGINALITY 13
may s. a horse	REPUTATION 10
not poverty lest I s.	POVERTY 18
s. a pin	HONESTY 5
s. from many	ORIGINALITY 14
s. more than a hundred	LAW 42
s. someone's thunder	STRENGTH 11
they s. my thunder	THEATRE 9
Thou shalt not s.	CRIME 35
stealing For de little s.	CRIME 42
hanged for s. horses	CRIME 24
s. no chickens	ANIMALS 2
steals s. my purse steals trash	REPUTATION 19
stealth Do good by s.	VIRTUE 29
good action by s.	PLEASURE 19
steamers little holiday s.	WORLD W II 9
steaming wealth of s. phrases	ECONOMICS 8
steed s. starves	ACHIEVEMENT 9
steel Give them the cold s.	WARS 19
hard s. canisters	TRANSPORT 30
Is s. good or bad	TECHNOLOGY 28
more than complete s.	JUSTICE 26
rest of rubber, s., and granite	CHILD CARE 16
surgeon plies the s.	MEDICINE 24
worthy of their s.	ENEMIES 13
steeple lone religious s.	ANIMALS 28
steer s. their courses	POETRY 9
stencilled s. off the real	PHOTOGRAPHY 10
step begins with a single s.	BEGINNING 9
first s.	BEGINNING 6
one small s.	ACHIEVEMENT 29
One s. at a time	PATIENCE 10
One s. forward	PROGRESS 14
you s. on somebody's foot	APOLOGY 20
steps hears the s. of God	POLITICS 19
Knowledge advances by s.	KNOWLEDGE 35
same s. as the author	EXPERIENCE 22
sterility victory of s. and death	STATISTICS 12
stern lantern on the s.	EXPERIENCE 23
s. chase	DETERMINATION 14
sterner made of s. stuff	AMBITION 9
stick barb that makes it s.	WIT 1
carry a big s.	DIPLOMACY 9
coat upon a s.	OLD AGE 22
down like a s.	SUCCESS 11
fell like the s.	SUCCESS 27
fist holds a s.	HATRED 16
some with s.	REPUTATION 11
s. inside a swill bucket	ADVERTISING 12
s. that he seizes	CAPITALISM 9
s. to beat a dog	APOLOGY 6
Work was like a s.	WORK 41
sticking-place to the s.	SUCCESS 24
sticks Land of the Little S.	CANADA 3
S. and stones may break my bones	WORDS 5
sticky s. wicket	CRICKET 3
stigma s., as the old saying	ARGUMENT 19
stiles Essex s.	BRITISH TOWNS 1
still Because they liked me 's.'	WRITING 31
Be s. and cool	PRAYER 16

s., sad music — NATURE 10
s. tongue makes — SILENCE 5
S. waters run deep — CHARACTER 11
ye rin sae s. — RIVERS 2
stillness achieved that s. — POETS 21
stilts nonsense upon s. — HUMAN RIGHTS 9
puny demigods on s. — UNIVERSITIES 21
stimulate s. the phagoytes — MEDICINE 21
sting bitter a s. to thee — CONSCIENCE 10
death, where is thy s. — DEATH 22
it is a s. — LOVE 27
s. like a bee — SPORTS 24
sting-a-ling-a-ling where is thy s. — WORLD W I 20
stings s. and motions — EMOTIONS 9
s. you for your pains — COURAGE 18
What s. is justice — JUSTICE 34
stink Fish and s. stink — ENTERTAINING 3
stinks s. from the head — LEADERSHIP 1
worse it s. — CAUTION 15
stir more you s. it — CAUTION 15
S.-up Sunday — FESTIVALS 54
stirred Shaken and not s. — ALCOHOL 28
shaken, not s. — ALCOHOL 7
stirrup s. and the ground — EPITAPHS 7
stitch s. in time — CAUTION 19
stitching s. and unstitching — POETRY 24
stockholders working for my s. — BUSINESS 32
stocking glimpse of s. — MORALITY 15
stolen generation was s. — AUSTRALIA 31
S. fruit is sweet — TEMPTATION 2
s. generation — AUSTRALIA 8
s. his wits — COUNTRIES 23
S. waters are sweet — TEMPTATION 3
stomach Finance is the s. — ECONOMICS 4
for thy s.'s sake — ALCOHOL 10
healthy s. is nothing — COOKING 27
heart and s. — ROYALTY 11
marches on its s. — ARMED FORCES 27
think rationally on empty s. — LOGIC 20
through his s. — MEN 3
stomach-ache if you have a s. — MEDICINE 30
stone blood from a s. — FUTILITY 5
blood out of a s. — CHARITY 6
bomb them back into the S. Age — WARS 24
cast a s. — GUILT 7
cast the first s. — CRITICISM 3
give them the s. — ENEMIES 11
In the first s. — CAPITALISM 9
Like a rolling s. — SOLITUDE 23
mark with a white s. — FESTIVALS 36
once shuddering s. — SCULPTURE 10
philosopher's s. — PROBLEMS 9
rolling s. — CONSTANCY 3
standing like a s. wall — WARS 17
s. out of the heart — SUFFERING 26
s. that the devil — NAMES 8
S. walls do not — LIBERTY 9
sword out of this s. — ROYALTY 9
through a piece of s. — SCULPTURE 7
Virtue is like a rich s. — VIRTUE 23
wears away a s. — DETERMINATION 1
stone-dead S. hath no fellows — DEATH 7
stones house is built of s. — SCIENCE 14
Sermons in s. — NATURE 8
shouldn't throw s. — GOSSIP 9
spares these s. — EPITAPHS 8
Sticks and s. may break my bones — WORDS 5
thy cold grey s. — SEA 17
you buy s. — BUYING 3
stools Between two s. — INDECISION 1
necessity invented s. — INVENTIONS 8
stop come to the end: then s. — BEGINNING 20
full s. put just — STYLE 18
going to s. them — SPORTS 29
kissing had to s. — KISSING 8
kissing has to s. — ENDING 11
s. everyone from doing it — ADMINISTRATION 12

S.-look-and-listen — CAUTION 20
S. me and buy one — PLEASURE 2
Stopes book by Marie S. — PREGNANCY 2
stops buck s. here — DUTY 24
stories No s. — FICTION 20
S. to rede ar delitabill — FICTION 6
storm After a s. — PEACE 1
pilot of the s. — LEADERSHIP 10
port in a s. — NECESSITY 1
sharper the s. — OPTIMISM 11
stormy dark and s. night — BEGINNING 7
story cock and bull s. — FICTION 3
novel tells a s. — FICTION 16
One s. is good — HYPOTHESIS 4
picture tells a s. — MEANING 1
read Richardson for the s. — WRITERS 7
short in the s. itself — WRITING 5
s. and a byword — AMERICA 10
S. is just the spoiled child — FICTION 15
stout collapse of S. Party — HUMOUR 1
stove ice on a hot s. — CREATIVITY 11
no better than her s. — COOKING 4
St Paul's ruins of S. — FUTURE 15
S. had come down — ARCHITECTURE 9
straight ever ran quite s. — BEAUTY 30
makes a s.-cut ditch — EDUCATION 21
no s. thing — HUMAN RACE 10
sufficient to keep him s. — CONSCIENCE 18
unflexible as s. — MISTAKES 14
strain train take the s. — TRANSPORT 2
Words s., Crack — WORDS 23
strait S. is the gate — VIRTUE 16
strand never alone with a S. — SMOKING 3
strange something rich and s. — SEA 9
'S. friend,' I said — FUTILITY 20
strangeness s. in the proportion — BEAUTY 3
stranger cuddled by a complete s. — CHILD CARE 19
s. than fiction — FICTION 1
s. than fiction — TRUTH 5
S. than fiction — TRUTH 28
s. to one of your parents — CHOICE 16
s. to trouble — ADVERSITY 9
Who's 'im, Bill? A s. — PREJUDICE 13
wiles of a s. — FAMILY 21
You may see a s. — MEETING 24
you would be a total s. — FRIENDSHIP 1
strangers entertain s. — ENTERTAINING 8
I spy s. — PARLIAMENT 1
kindness of s. — CHARITY 22
strangled s. with the guts — REVOLUTION 9
Stratford scole of S. atte Bowe — LANGUAGES 3
S. trades on Shakespeare — TOWNS 27
straw bricks without s. — FUTILITY 6
but as s. dogs — SYMPATHY 9
clutch at a s. — HOPE 1
final s. — CRISES 6
Headpiece filled with s. — FUTILITY 22
last s. — EXCESS 3
make bricks without s. — PROBLEMS 6
pad in the s. — DANGER 15
seems like s. — INSIGHT 6
s. in the wind — FUTURE 9
s. vote — ELECTIONS 2
tickled with a s. — CHILDREN 12
strawberry Like s. wives — DECEPTION 13
on the s. — FOOD 11
straws Errors, like s. — MISTAKES 13
S. tell which way — MEANING 2
stream s. cannot rise — CHARACTER 12
swim with the s. — CONFORMITY 13
Time, like an ever-rolling s. — TIME 30
street bald s. breaks — DAY 12
don't do it in the s. — SEX 28
fighting in the s. — REVOLUTION 28
Life is a One Way S. — EXPERIENCE 35
sunny side of the s. — OPTIMISM 28
streets S. FLOODED — TOWNS 23

s. in life	SUCCESS 43
S. is a science	SUCCESS 32
s. is like fresh fruit	SUCCESS 49
s. is only a delayed	SUCCESS 44
S. is relative	SUCCESS 40
to command s.	SUCCESS 25
You cannot be a s.	BUSINESS 40
successful country be always s.	PATRIOTISM 16
famous poisoner or a s. poisoner	CRIME 54
s. is good	SUCCESS 48
successively hear the parts s.	CREATIVITY 5
such S. is life	LAST WORDS 19
suck s. melancholy	SINGING 3
sucked s. into the brain	TEACHING 19
sucker s. an even break	FOOLS 26
s. born every minute	FOOLS 24
sudden splendour of a s. thought	THINKING 16
suddenly s. became depraved	SIN 12
sue S. a beggar	FUTILITY 3
sued publish and be s.	JOURNALISM 26
suffer better to s. wrong	TRUST 26
can tell what I s.	SYMPATHY 19
Can they s.	ANIMALS 16
endure to s.	PATIENCE 1
prepared to s.	IDEALISM 9
s. fools gladly	FOOLS 11
S. the little children	CHILDREN 5
sufferance s. is the badge	PATIENCE 23
suffered s. and be healed	DESPAIR 12
suffering About s. they were	SUFFERING 28
not a hopeless s.	HEAVEN 17
put me to s.	SELF-SACRIFICE 4
S. is permanent	SUFFERING 17
s. makes men petty	SUFFERING 25
sufferings s. of my fellow-creatures	SYMPATHY 20
s. which thou art spared	SUFFERING 9
suffers inform us of what he s.	IMAGINATION 7
suffices God alone s.	PATIENCE 22
sufficient s. to finish it	FORESIGHT 8
s. to keep him straight	CONSCIENCE 18
S. unto the day	PRESENT 4
S. unto the day	WORRY 4
suffocated s. in its own wax	DEATH 72
suicide alter the s. rate	DRUGS 10
assisted s.	SUICIDE 1
longest s. note	POLITICAL PART 42
s. kills two people	SUICIDE 10
s. to avoid assassination	CENSORSHIP 12
thought of s.	SUICIDE 7
where they commit s.	COUNTRIES 34
suit come in a pinstripe s.	STRENGTH 27
suits men in s.	ADMINISTRATION 2
sum Cogito, ergo s.	THINKING 12
s. of all the choices	CHOICE 29
s. of matter remains	SCIENCE 5
s. of them all	CAUSES 16
s. of the parts	QUANTITIES 10
summer autumn follows s.	MOURNING 19
does not make a s.	SEASONS 4
ensure s. in England	SEASONS 16
Eternal s. gilds them	COUNTRIES 16
Folowen ful ofte a myrie s.'s day	WEATHER 31
if it takes all s.	DETERMINATION 39
In a s. seson	SEASONS 12
Indian s.	OLD AGE 4
Indian s.	WEATHER 25
like a s. birdcage	SATISFACTION 17
rich man has his ice in the s.	WEALTH 5
St Luke's s.	WEATHER 28
St Martin's s.	WEATHER 29
S. is icumen in	SEASONS 11
S. set lip	FLOWERS 8
s. that I was ten	CHILDREN 21
S. time an' the livin'	SEASONS 26
summits touch at their s.	INTERNAT REL 19
sun before you let the s. in	HOUSEWORK 12
best s. we have	WEATHER 37

bride that the s. shines on	WEDDINGS 2
candle in the s.	FUTILITY 16
candle to the s.	CRITICISM 6
except their s. is set	COUNTRIES 16
going down of the s.	EPITAPHS 21
Go out in the midday s.	ENGLAND 20
hay while the s. shines	OPPORTUNITY 7
kiss of the s.	GARDENS 17
land of the midnight s.	COUNTRIES 7
land of the rising s.	COUNTRIES 8
let not the s. go down	ANGER 6
love that moves the s.	LOVE 25
maketh his s. to rise	EQUALITY 4
most shene is the s.	WEATHER 30
new under the s.	FAMILIARITY 10
no new thing under the s.	PROGRESS 5
ordered the s. to stand	SKIES 10
place in the s.	INTERNAT REL 23
place in the s.	SUCCESS 16
prayer at sinking of the s.	PRAYER 9
shoots at the mid-day s.	AMBITION 8
S.-girt city	TOWNS 15
s. go down on your anger	FORGIVENESS 4
s. has gone in	WEATHER 51
s. is always setting	COUNTRIES 36
s. loses nothing	GOOD 6
s. never sets	COUNTRIES 10
S.'s rim dips	DAY 9
tired the s.	MOURNING 16
unruly s.	SKIES 13
whan softe was the s.	SEASONS 12
sunbeam s. in a winter's day	TRANSIENCE 9
Sunday Hot on S.	COOKING 33
Low S.	FESTIVALS 33
Mothering S.	FESTIVALS 42
my S. rest	MOURNING 12
Palm S.	FESTIVALS 45
rainy S. afternoon	BOREDOM 7
Rogation S.	FESTIVALS 50
Stir-up S.	FESTIVALS 54
this is S. morning	LEISURE 13
Trinity S.	FESTIVALS 57
Whit S.	FESTIVALS 59
Sundays begin a journey on S.	TRAVEL 19
sunflower S. State	AMERICAN CITIES 41
s. turns on her god	CONSTANCY 11
sunlight s. on the garden	TRANSIENCE 16
sunny If Candlemas day be s.	WEATHER 6
s. side of the street	OPTIMISM 28
sunset make a fine s.	BELIEF 24
sunsets horror of s.	DAY 17
sunshine Digressions are the s.	READING 11
ray of s.	SCOTLAND 14
s. and with applause	RELIGION 11
s. patriot	PATRIOTISM 13
superfluous nothing is s.	NATURE 7
not only with the s.	AUSTRALIA 10
s., a necessary thing	NECESSITY 22
superhuman struggle for s. beauty	BEAUTY 34
superior embarrass the s.	RANK 12
superman I teach you the s.	HUMAN RACE 23
It's S.	HEROES 17
supermarket walk around the s.	FAME 24
supermarkets s. that buy things	POLLUTION 22
supernatural s. source of evil	GOOD 34
superseded not been s.	PRIDE 14
superstar Define s.	FAME 24
superstate s. exercising a new	EUROPE 20
superstition avoiding s.	SUPERNATURAL 13
S. is the poetry	SUPERNATURAL 17
S. sets the whole world	PHILOSOPHY 9
s. to enslave	RELIGION 25
superstitions end as s.	TRUTH 30
supper after s. walk	COOKING 1
bad s.	HOPE 4
sing for one's s.	WORK 17
support men who will s. me	POLITICIANS 11

when the son s.	CHILD CARE 4
sworn only need to be s. at	SWEARING 10
swots various s., bulies	SCHOOLS 13
Sydney of S.	TOWNS 28
Satan made S.	TOWNS 21
syllable last s. of recorded time	TIME 26
syllables S. govern the world	LANGUAGE 7
symbolic s. expression	SCIENCE 10
symmetry fearful s.	ANIMALS 17
sympathy give or take s.	SYMPATHY 22
s. is cold	SYMPATHY 17
tea and s.	SYMPATHY 8
symphony s. must be like the world	MUSIC 16
symptoms hundred good s.	SICKNESS 10
syne auld land s.	PAST 8
auld lang s.	MEMORY 10
Syrens song the S. sang	KNOWLEDGE 27
syrup being covered with s.	GRATITUDE 20
system Ptolemaic s.	UNIVERSE 3
rocked the s.	ELECTIONS 19
t cross the t's	HYPOTHESIS 8
ta saying 'T.' to God	PAINTING 20
table etherized upon a t.	DAY 15
head of the t.	RANK 3
made you a bad t.	CRITICISM 8
tablet keep taking The T.	PREGNANCY 20
tablets Keep taking the t.	MEDICINE 3
tabula rasa tablet (a *t.*)	MIND 25
tactful t. in audacity	BEHAVIOUR 27
taffeta changeable t.	INDECISION 8
tail choke on the t.	DETERMINATION 6
likerous t.	SEX 9
shows his t.	AMBITION 2
such a little t. behind	ANIMALS 22
ties a kettle to a dog's t.	WRITERS 18
twist the lion's t.	BRITAIN 5
verb chasing its own t.	LANGUAGE 29
tailors Nine t. make a man	DRESS 5
tails t. you lose	WINNING 2
take Give and t.	JUSTICE 5
no longer anything to t. away	PERFECTION 12
t. a thing	GIFTS 3
t. away everything you have	GOVERNMENT 38
T. away these baubles	PARLIAMENT 14
t. it away all at a swoop	CHANCE 20
T. me to your leader	LEADERSHIP 4
t. who have the power	POWER 20
taken Lord hath t. away	PATIENCE 20
t. more out of alcohol	ALCOHOL 31
takes blesseth him that t.	JUSTICE 24
taking t. the tablets	MEDICINE 3
tale bodies must tell the t.	COURAGE 27
Canterbury t.	FICTION 2
t. never loses	GOSSIP 8
t. of a tub	FICTION 4
t. told by an idiot	LIFE 19
t. which holdeth children	FICTION 7
thereby hangs a t.	MATURITY 4
Trust the t.	CRITICISM 19
talent t. at twenty-five	GENIUS 13
T. develops in quiet places	CHARACTER 31
T. does what it can	GENIUS 9
t. to see clearly	INTELLIGENCE 20
that one t.	SENSES 7
tomb of a mediocre t.	BOOKS 19
works is my t.	LIFESTYLES 25
talents All the T.	PARLIAMENT 3
If you have great t.	WORK 26
open to the t.	OPPORTUNITY 30
tales Dead men tell no t.	SECRECY 1
t. out of school	SECRECY 6
talk Can they t.	ANIMALS 16
Careless t.	GOSSIP 1
first t. is of the weather	WEATHER 36

fun of t.	CONVERSATION 13
good to t.	CONVERSATION 1
gotta use words when I t.	WORDS 22
he made others t.	CONVERSATION 6
how much my Ministers t.	LEADERSHIP 17
If you t. to God	MADNESS 16
let the people t.	GOSSIP 16
Money doesn't t.	MONEY 40
much to t. about	ENTERTAINING 6
people don't t.	ENTERTAINING 16
people who can't t.	JOURNALISM 29
t. about things	BOOKS 8
T. is cheap	WORDS AND DEEDS 8
t. like a lady	SPEECH 23
t. of hereafter	ACHIEVEMENT 18
t. of many things	CONVERSATION 14
T. of the Devil	MEETING 3
t. the less	SPEECH 8
t. to the plants	GARDENS 22
t. well but not too wisely	ENTERTAINING 17
Two may t.	CONVERSATION 12
ways of making you t.	POWER 10
we had a good t.	CONVERSATION 7
while you t. to yourself	ADVICE 23
wished him to t. on	CONVERSATION 11
talked least t. about by men	WOMEN 16
not being t. about	GOSSIP 24
t. for a hundred years	HUMAN RIGHTS 16
talking Enough of t.—it is time now to do	WORDS AND DEEDS 21
if you ain't t. about him	ACTING 11
nation to itself	JOURNALISM 21
never done t. of Man	EUROPE 15
opposite of t.	CONVERSATION 20
stop people t.	DEMOCRACY 23
t. about it is deadly dull	ALCOHOL 33
T. to Buncombe	SPEECHES 4
t. to him like a priest	ENEMIES 22
t. without speaking	SILENCE 14
tired the sun with t.	MOURNING 16
what we are t. about	MATHS 21
you's doin' all the t.	CONVERSATION 19
talks Licker t.	DRUNKENNESS 10
Money t.	MONEY 10
Now a man t. frankly	FEAR 15
tall short and the t.	ARMED FORCES 39
t. poppy	FAME 3
taller t. than other men	DEFIANCE 10
Tallis T. is dead	MUSICIANS 3
tan put on fake t.	MIDDLE AGE 10
tangle odours t.	SENSES 12
tango two to t.	COOPERATION 10
tank tiger in one's t.	STRENGTH 12
tiger in your t.	TRANSPORT 3
tanks Get your t. off my lawn	ARGUMENT 23
tantum T. religio	RELIGION 5
tape t. we play	ADMINISTRATION 3
tapes t. we play	MORALITY 23
tapestry wrong side of a Turkey tapestry	TRANSLATION 5
tar for a ha'porth of t.	THOROUGHNESS 1
Tara T.'s halls	IRELAND 10
Tar-baby T. ain't sayin' nuthin'	CAUTION 26
tares t. of mine own brain	ORIGINALITY 7
tarheel T. State	AMERICAN CITIES 42
tarry t. the wheels	HASTE 11
You may for ever t.	MARRIAGE 19
tartar find a T.	RUSSIA 1
tartest t. vinegar	SIMILARITY 5
Tarzan Me T., you Jane	MEN AND WOMEN 20
task what he reads as a t.	READING 10
taste arbiter of t.	TASTE 2
bad t. is better than	TASTE 14
bad t. of the smoker	GOSSIP 23
better than t.	ALCOHOL 27
common sense and good t.	CHARACTER 37
create the t.	ORIGINALITY 10
difference of t. in jokes	TASTE 9

taste (*cont.*)
Every man to his t.	LIKES 1
good sense and good t.	TASTE 4
nowhere worse t.	TASTE 12
t. and humour	HUMOUR 19
t., and style	MANNERS 26
t. for them but themselves	ENGLAND 9
T. is the feminine	TASTE 11
teach t. or genius	TASTE 6
thing is in good t.	TASTE 15

tasted books are to be t. — BOOKS 5
tasteless become very t. — TASTE 16
tastes No accounting for t. — LIKES 4
Our t. greatly alter	TASTE 5
T. differ	LIKES 3
t. good, it's bad for you	HEALTH 21
t. may not be the same	LIKES 13
t. we have swallowed	DEATH 77

tasty something a little bit 't.' — FOOD 24
tattered t. coat upon a stick — OLD AGE 22
t. his ears	CATS 14

taught afterward he t. — BEHAVIOUR 15
Men must be t.	TEACHING 7
t. to any purpose	TEACHING 10
T. to be afraid	RACE 18
t. to love	HATRED 18
worth knowing can be t.	EDUCATION 24

tawse lost my leather t. — SCHOOLS 14
tax convenient time to t. rich people — TAXES 16
poll t.	TAXES 3
soon be able to t. it	INVENTIONS 12
To t. and to please	TAXES 10

taxation art of t. consists — TAXES 7
t. that can be imposed	ECONOMICS 16
T. without representation	TAXES 9

taxes All t. must, at last, fall — TAXES 13
certain, except death and t.	TAXES 14
death and t.	CERTAINTY 3
Death and t. and childbirth	PREGNANCY 10
no new t.	TAXES 19
Only the little people pay t.	TAXES 18
peace, easy t.	GOVERNMENT 16
people overlaid with t.	TAXES 6
Sex and t.	SEX 47

taxing more or less of a t. machine — TAXES 15
Tchaikovsky If I play T. — MUSICIANS 16
tea ain't going to be no t. — WRITERS 17
honey still for t.	PAST 29
Lunch, and T.	COOKING 29
sweeteners of t.	GOSSIP 20
T., although an Oriental	FOOD 20
t. and sympathy	SYMPATHY 8
t., then I wish for coffee	FOOD 19

teabag woman is like a t. — ADVERSITY 18
teach lerne and gladly t. — EDUCATION 13
no matter what you t.	TEACHING 9
people who t.	BOOKS 30
person who wants to t.	TEACHING 15
qualified to t. others	TEACHING 4
t. an old dog	CUSTOM 4
t. his son a craft	EMPLOYMENT 7
t. taste or genius	TASTE 6
t. the torches to burn	BEAUTY 12
t. the young idea	TEACHING 8
t. you more of man	GOOD 30
t. your grandmother	ADVICE 2
while they t., men learn	TEACHING 5
years t. much	EXPERIENCE 24

teacher Experience is the best t. — EXPERIENCE 4
Nobody forgets a good t.	TEACHING 3
t. affects eternity	TEACHING 14

teachers been their own t. — TEACHING 10
good t. make the best of	TEACHING 17
We t. can only help	TEACHING 16

teaches experience t. — EXPERIENCE 17
He that t. himself	TEACHING 2
He who cannot, t.	TEACHING 13

t. ill who teaches all	TEACHING 1

teaching t. nations how to live — ENGLAND 7
wouldn't wish t. on	TEACHING 20

team supporting the wrong t. — PARENTS 27
teapot further than warming the t. — WRITERS 17
t., used daily	PAST 36

tear t. is an intellectual thing — SORROW 15
Who can I t. to pieces	FRIENDSHIP 30

tears blood, toil, t. — SELF-SACRIFICE 13
crocodile t.	HYPOCRISY 5
frequent t. have run	SUFFERING 19
heart in t.	POETS 18
If you have t.	SORROW 9
kiss again with t.	FORGIVENESS 20
Nothing is here for t.	SORROW 13
sow in t.	SUFFERING 4
t. dripping out of either eye	EMOTIONS 29
T., idle tears	SORROW 17
t. shed for things	SORROW 6
t. wash out a word	PAST 25
unavenged t.	GOOD 33
waste of T.	WARFARE 39

teases he knows it t. — BEHAVIOUR 22
technically something that is t. sweet — TECHNOLOGY 15
technology Progress through t. — TECHNOLOGY 23
sufficiently advanced t.	TECHNOLOGY 24
T. happens	TECHNOLOGY 28
white heat of t.	TECHNOLOGY 4

teddy t. bears' picnic — PLEASURE 8
tedious t. season they await — SEASONS 19
teenager as a t. you are at the last stage — YOUTH 26
teeth between tongue and t. — POETRY 40
gnashing of t.	HEAVEN 7
graves with our t.	COOKING 25
he's got iron t.	PEOPLE 61
morals are like its t.	MORALITY 11
skin of my t.	DANGER 21
strike out his t.	HISTORY 9
those who have no t.	OLD AGE 1
women have fewer t.	HYPOTHESIS 23

teetotaller beer t. — ALCOHOL 21
hate to be a t.	ALCOHOL 32

Teflon T.-coated Presidency — PRESIDENCY 19
telegram visual t. — ADVERTISING 16
telegrams t. and anger — RELATIONSHIPS 9
telegraph bush t. — GOSSIP 11
t. pole in an earthquake	SEA 26

telephones Tudor monarchy plus t. — PRESIDENCY 17
television I hate t. — BROADCASTING 7
no plain women on t.	BROADCASTING 13
Radio and t.	BROADCASTING 9
stay at home and see bad t.	CINEMA 15
T. brought the brutality	BROADCASTING 12
T. contracts the imagination	BROADCASTING 15
T. has brought back murder	MURDER 23
T. has made dictatorship	BROADCASTING 17
T. is simultaneously blamed	BROADCASTING 14
T.? The word is half Greek	BROADCASTING 6
T. . . . . thrives on unreason	BROADCASTING 16
T. today has replaced	CULTURE 35

tell Blood will t. — FAMILY 3
Don't ask, don't t.	SECRECY 2
friends won't t. you	HEALTH 5
Go t. the Spartans	EPITAPHS 4
I'll t. you what I want	AMBITION 23
not going to t. you something	WARS 31
t. everything	BOREDOM 2
t. her she mustn't	BEHAVIOUR 23
T. it not in Gath	NEWS 3
T. me what you eat	COOKING 19
t. me who I am	SELF 9
t. one's beads	PRAYER 5
t. them of us	EPITAPHS 22
Time will t.	TIME 6
too bad not to t.	SECRECY 10

telling loses in the t. — GOSSIP 8
telly *you* watched it on the telly — WORDS AND DEEDS 22

things (*cont.*)

interested in t.	SCIENCE 13
people don't do such t.	HUMAN NATURE 14
rich in t.	POSSESSIONS 25
such t. to be	FUTURE 17
tears shed for t.	SORROW 6
T. ain't what	PAST 32
T. are in the saddle	POSSESSIONS 18
t. are the sons of heaven	WORDS 12
T. can only get better	PROGRESS 23
T. fall apart	ORDER 16
t. they didn't know	HISTORY 23
t. with their names	BELIEF 29
think on these t.	THINKING 8
wonderful t.	INVENTIONS 16

think able to t. isn't defeated — WINNING 25

always t. what is true	VIRTUE 40
can't t. without his hat	THINKING 24
capacity to t.	VIRTUE 20
comedy to those that t.	LIFE 25
could ever be said to t.	THINKING 28
don't even *t.* about tomorrow	PHILOSOPHY 22
don't t. much of it	LAST WORDS 26
don't t. twice	FORGIVENESS 25
do what you t. best	ADVICE 18
easier to act than to t.	ACTION 25
have time to t.	SPEECH 17
I t., therefore I am	THINKING 12
I t., therefore I am is	THINKING 29
I t. with my hands	BODY 34
know what I t.	MEANING 12
might very well t. that	OPINION 26
more clearly than you t.	SPEECH 29
not to t. much but	THINKING 10
not whether machines t.	THINKING 27
tell what I t.	THINKING 20
t. as you drunk I am	DRUNKENNESS 11
T. before you speak	CREATIVITY 12
t. for two minutes	THINKING 15
T. globally	POLLUTION 3
t. just with our wombs	WOMAN'S ROLE 27
t. like other people	CONFORMITY 7
t. of England	SEX 20
t. of yourself one way	SELF-KNOWLEDGE 17
t. only this of me	PATRIOTISM 19
t. on these things	THINKING 9
t. rationally on empty stomach	LOGIC 20
t. yourself above others	SELF-ESTEEM 15
we've got to t.	PROBLEMS 20
What will Mrs Grundy t.	BEHAVIOUR 19

thinker murder the t. — CENSORSHIP 20

thinking dignity of t. beings — SENSES 8

hear God t.	PROBLEMS 25
he is a t. reed	HUMAN RACE 14
high t.	LIFESTYLES 5
high t.	SATISFACTION 22
lateral t.	THINKING 5
not merely what we are t.	TRUTH 41
positive t.	THINKING 6
saves original t.	QUOTATIONS 11
song for t. hearts	STYLE 12
t. about themselves	YOUTH 22
t. for myself	POLITICAL PART 18
t. hand	SENSES 17
t. makes it so	GOOD 25
t. what nobody has thought	INVENTIONS 19

thinks drinks beer, t. beer — DRUNKENNESS 2

He t. too much	THINKING 11
Sometimes I sits and t.	THINKING 19
t. he knows everything	POLITICIANS 16
unhappy as one t.	HAPPINESS 11
what a man really t.	CONVERSATION 13

third It is the t. thing — KISSING 16

t. eye	INSIGHT 3
T. time lucky	CHANCE 14
t. time pays	DETERMINATION 15
t. way	POLITICS 8

T. World	INTERNAT REL 8

third-rate what in the world *is* t. — EXCELLENCE 17

Third World T. is an artificial — COUNTRIES 36

T. never sold a newspaper	JOURNALISM 27

thirsty t., give him water — ENEMIES 5

thirties dating in your t. — COURTSHIP 17

Nothing I wrote in the t.	WRITING 50

thirty I am past t. — MIDDLE AGE 7

over the age of t.	SUCCESS 36
T. days hath September	POETRY 38
t. pieces of silver	TRUST 14
t., the wit	MATURITY 7
t. who don't want to learn	TEACHING 15
Women over t.	MIDDLE AGE 18

thirty-five remained t. for years — MIDDLE AGE 23

Thomas doubting T. — BELIEF 6

T. the Divine	FARMING 3

thorn creep under the t. — TREES 1

Oak, and Ash, and T.	TREES 11
t. in one's side	ADVERSITY 7

thorns crackling of t. — FOOLS 9

thoroughfare t. for all thoughts — MIND 10

thou loaf of bread—and T. — SATISFACTION 29

Through the T.	SELF 19

thought Action without t. — ACTION 3

dress of t.	LANGUAGE 11
dress of t.	STYLE 9
enemy of t.	ACTION 24
father to the t.	OPINION 5
feel a t.	SINGING 16
forced into a state of t.	THINKING 22
form Of every t.	SCULPTURE 3
History is not what you t.	HISTORY 22
how to photograph t.	CINEMA 16
I t. so once	EPITAPHS 10
life-blood of t.	STYLE 13
Ministers of t.	DREAMS 11
murder the t.	CENSORSHIP 20
One single grateful t.	PRAYER 19
Perish the t.	THINKING 2
rear the tender t.	TEACHING 8
Religion is the frozen t.	RELIGION 27
seem a moment's t.	POETRY 24
splendour of a sudden t.	THINKING 16
sweet silent t.	MEMORY 8
t. and resolution	TEMPTATION 12
t. for the morrow	PRESENT 4
t. in one man's mind	REVOLUTION 1
T. is free	OPINION 4
t. is vicious	MEANING 11
t. more steady	CONSTANCY 7
T. shall be the harder	DETERMINATION 26
t., word, and deed	SIN 14
To a green t.	GARDENS 11
troubled seas of t.	THINKING 25
What oft was t.	STYLE 10
What was once t.	THINKING 26
where a t. is lacking	WORDS 13

thoughtcrime t. literally impossible — CENSORSHIP 11

thoughtlessness t. is the weapon — MEN AND WOMEN 21

thoughts control our t. — MORALITY 8

misleading t.	THINKING 17
My t. became persons	PARANORMAL 18
rather than of t.	SENSES 9
Second t. are best	CAUTION 18
thoroughfare for all t.	MIND 10
t. of a prisoner	CRIME 49
t. of other men	KNOWLEDGE 32
t. that arise in me	SEA 17
t. that think	MARRIAGE 46
Words without t. never	PRAYER 12

thousand dying for four t. years — THEATRE 20

forty t. men	LEADERSHIP 9
Give me a t. kisses	KISSING 3
night has a t. eyes	SKIES 20
sixty-four t. dollar question	PROBLEMS 10
t. doors open	DEATH 24

Tom Fool people know T.   FAME 1
tomorrow all be unequal t.   EQUALITY 10
  Boast not thyself of t.   FUTURE 11
  don't even *think* about t.   PHILOSOPHY 22
  Jam t.   PRESENT 2
  jam t.   PRESENT 9
  Live till t.   CAUTION 23
  put off till t.   HASTE 8
  put off until t.   IDLENESS 20
  rest of England says t.   BRITISH TOWNS 11
  T., and to-morrow, and to-morrow   TIME 26
  T. for the young   PRESENT 10
  T. is another day   FUTURE 5
  t. is another day   HOPE 21
  t. me   FUTURE 4
  T. never comes   FUTURE 6
  Unborn T.   PRESENT 8
  word for doing things t.   FUTURE 21
  you ain't still drunk t.   DRUNKENNESS 13
tomorrows For your t.   EPITAPHS 22
tone t. of the company   BEHAVIOUR 17
tongue between t. and teeth   POETRY 40
  fallen by the t.   GOSSIP 15
  grow a second t.   LANGUAGES 17
  my t. could utter   SEA 17
  My t. swore   HYPOCRISY 8
  Not a wimbling t. admit   KISSING 5
  obnoxious to each carping t.   WOMAN'S ROLE 8
  silver t.   SPEECH 5
  still t. makes   SILENCE 5
  t. can no man tame   SPEECH 9
  t. not understood   LANGUAGES 5
  t. of him that makes it   HUMOUR 6
  t. that Shakespeare spake   ENGLAND 12
  t. to persuade   PEOPLE 29
  t. to speak   PARLIAMENT 12
  use of my oracular t.   WIT 10
  voice and t.   READING 4
tongues full of t.   GOSSIP 17
  gift of t.   LANGUAGES 1
  pies of lawyers' t.   LAW 1
  time in the t.   EDUCATION 15
  t. in trees   NATURE 8
tonight I'll be sick t.   GREED 14
  Not t., Josephine   SEX 18
tonnage swallowing the t.   AMERICAN CITIES 60
tons Sixteen t.   DEBT 23
took person you and I t. me for   CHARACTER 33
tool Man is a t.-using animal   TECHNOLOGY 7
tool-making t. animal   HUMAN RACE 18
tools blames his t.   APOLOGY 3
  destine for their t.   MANAGEMENT 7
  Give us the t.   ACHIEVEMENT 5
  know *which* t.   SUICIDE 11
  secrets are edged t.   SECRECY 22
  t. to him   OPPORTUNITY 1
tooth dog's t.   ANIMALS 5
  dog's t. is truly worshipped   RELIGION 30
  each t.-point goes   SUFFERING 21
  red in t.   NATURE 4
  red in t.   NATURE 12
  sharper than a serpent's t.   GRATITUDE 8
  t. for tooth   JUSTICE 16
toothache helps not the t.   MUSIC 2
  Venerable Mother T.   SICKNESS 17
toothaches intellectual who underrates t.   THINKING 29
toothpaste t. is out of the tube   SECRECY 28
top room at the t.   AMBITION 5
  room at the t.   OPPORTUNITY 20
  T. End   AUSTRALIA 9
  T. people take *The Times*   JOURNALISM 2
toper Lo! the poor t.   DRUNKENNESS 6
topography T. displays no favourites   EARTH 10
torch pass on the t.   CUSTOM 5
torches t. to burn bright   BEAUTY 12
Tories T. remember their friends   POLITICAL PART 23
torment more grievous t.   LOVE 44

tormenting just t. the people   QUANTITIES 22
torments Our t. also   SUFFERING 12
tornado t. in Texas   CHANCE 35
Toronto T. is a kind   TOWNS 29
torrent t. of change   CHANGE 43
torso remain a t.   EUROPE 17
tortoise hare and t.   DETERMINATION 21
torture So does t.   BELIEF 31
  t. to death   GOOD 33
tortured t. who turn into   CRUELTY 13
torturers turn into t.   CRUELTY 13
Tory always be a T.   POLITICAL PART 17
  T. because William Hague   POLITICAL PART 46
  T.'s secret weapon   POLITICAL PART 35
tossed t. and gored   CONVERSATION 7
total t. solution   RACE 17
totalitarianism under the name of t.   WARFARE 50
totter t. into vogue   FASHION 5
touch Midas t.   WEALTH 10
  Nelson t.   LEADERSHIP 5
  '*Nelson t.*'   LEADERSHIP 8
  puts it not unto the t.   COURAGE 15
  T. not the cat   CATS 2
  t. of greatness   GREATNESS 8
  t. of nature   HUMAN NATURE 9
touched t. the face of God   TRANSPORT 20
touches Each of us t. one place   INSIGHT 5
  He that t. pitch   GOOD 2
toucheth He that t. pitch   GOOD 14
tough acted t.   STRENGTH 28
  T. on crime   CRIME 53
  When the going gets t.   CHARACTER 17
toughness T. doesn't have to   STRENGTH 27
tour unless you made the European t.   EUROPE 21
tourism t. is their religion   TRAVEL 38
tourist American t. abroad   DRESS 23
  loathsome is the British t.   TRAVEL 26
  t. in other people's reality   REALITY 16
tourists philosophers are t.   ARTS AND SCI 18
  T. look at themselves   TRAVEL 40
tout T. passe   LIFE 7
tower build a t.   FORESIGHT 8
  T. of Babel   LANGUAGES 2
  t. of nine storeys   BEGINNING 18
  t. of strength   STRENGTH 13
towery T. city and branchy between towers
       BRITISH TOWNS 31
town destroy the t. to save it   WARS 25
  every t. or city   SELF-ESTEEM 13
  haunted. it is to me   BRITISH TOWNS 32
  Kirton was a borough t.   BRITISH TOWNS 4
  man made the t.   COUNTRY AND TOWN 2
  man made the t.   COUNTRY AND TOWN 10
  t. and gown   UNIVERSITIES 4
  t. mouse   COUNTRY AND TOWN 7
towns seven wealthy t.   FAME 9
toy sells eternity to get a t.   CAUSES 18
toys boys with t.   DECEPTION 10
trade all is seared with t.   WORK 33
  autocrat: that's my t.   POWER 39
  cruel t.   POLITICS 11
  Every man to his t.   WORK 2
  it is His t.   FORGIVENESS 21
  People of the same t.   BUSINESS 28
  T. follows the flag   BUSINESS 16
  t. to make tables   CRITICISM 8
  t. will always be attended   BUSINESS 27
  tricks in every t.   BUSINESS 15
  Two of a t.   SIMILARITY 9
  wheels of t.   MONEY 30
trades called a jack of all t.   EXCELLENCE 18
  Jack of all t.   EXCELLENCE 3
trade unionism T. of the married   VIRTUE 43
trade unionist British T.   EMPLOYMENT 22
trade unionists came for the t.   INDIFFERENCE 15
trade unions snarl of the t.   PARLIAMENT 23
trading make t. much easier   MONEY 31

talks to the v. cleaner	BROADCASTING 19
v. is a hell of a lot	NATURE 19
vae *V. victis*	WINNING 10
vague Don't be v.	CERTAINTY 2
vagueness v., my two *bêtes noires*	MATHS 16
vain In v. the net is spread	FUTILITY 2
vale ave atque v.	MEETING 6
Valentine St V.'s day	FESTIVALS 52
vales sweet are thy hills and v.	WALES 5
valet hero to his v.	FAMILIARITY 9
hero to his v.	HEROES 5
v. seemed a hero	HEROES 9
valiant become v. and martial	TAXES 6
v. never taste of death	COURAGE 13
valley All in the v. of Death	WARS 15
bicker down a v.	RIVERS 9
great things from the v.	INSIGHT 13
v. of the shadow	DANGER 20
Vallombrosa strew the brooks in V.	QUANTITIES 20
valorous childish v.	MATURITY 3
valour better part of v.	CAUTION 5
much care and v. in this Welshman	WALES 4
v. is certainly going	COURAGE 20
valuable most v. thing we have	TRUTH 32
value little v. of fortune	WEALTH 20
nothing has v.	FUTILITY 21
v. depends on what is there	MEANING 13
v. of nothing	DISILLUSION 15
valued not merely tolerated but v.	MEN AND WOMEN 35
values not of facts but of v.	EDUCATION 25
V. are tapes	MORALITY 23
Victorian v.	VIRTUE 14
Victorian v.	VIRTUE 51
valuing v. myself according to the job	EMPLOYMENT 34
vampires stand against the v.	SUPERNATURAL 26
Vanbrugh V.'s house of clay	EPITAPHS 13
vanitas v. vanitatum	DISILLUSION 5
vanities pomps and v.	TEMPTATION 4
vanity beauty without v.	ANIMALS 30
MP feeds your v.	PARLIAMENT 30
pomps and v.	SIN 17
v. of human hopes	LIBRARIES 5
v. of vanities	DISILLUSION 5
V. of vanities	FUTILITY 14
vapours congregation of v.	POLLUTION 6
variety it admits v.	DEMOCRACY 22
v. about the New England weather	WEATHER 43
V. is the spice	CHANGE 15
V.'s the very spice	CHANGE 3
variorum Life is all a v.	LIFESTYLES 21
various things being v.	SIMILARITY 23
varlet v.'s a varlet	CHARACTER 1
vase child is not a v.	CHILDREN 7
Sevres v. in the hands	POETS 26
shatter the v.	MEMORY 11
vat doing your V. return	PRACTICALITY 17
vegetable v., and mineral	LIFE SCI 1
v. fashion	ARTS 16
vegetarianism in favour of v.	ARGUMENT 18
veil beyond the v.	DEATH 12
vein giving v.	GIFTS 14
velvet gentleman in black v.	ANIMALS 8
venal v. city	CORRUPTION 6
vengeance gods forbade v.	REVENGE 19
V. is mine	REVENGE 10
veni V., *vidi, vici*	SUCCESS 21
Venice V. is like eating an entire	TOWNS 26
V. of the North	TOWNS 12
venture Nothing v., nothing gain	THOROUGHNESS 3
Nothing v., nothing have	THOROUGHNESS 4
Venus V. entire	LOVE 37
women are from V.	MEN AND WOMEN 34
veracity heard and saw with v.	WRITING 9
verb v. chasing its own tail	LANGUAGE 29
v. not a noun	GOD 34
Waiting for the German v.	LANGUAGES 16
verba Nullius in v.	HYPOTHESIS 3

verbal v. contract	LAW 36
verbosity exuberance of his own v.	PEOPLE 39
not crude v.	STYLE 5
verbs those irregular v.	SECRECY 29
verify v. your references	KNOWLEDGE 37
verisimilitude artistic v.	FICTION 12
veritas *in vino v.*	DRUNKENNESS 3
Vermont so goes V.	ELECTIONS 10
vernal impulse from a v. wood	GOOD 30
vero Se non e v.	TRUTH 3
verse chapter and v.	HYPOTHESIS 7
died to make v. free	PUBLISHING 12
No v. can give pleasure	ALCOHOL 9
v. is a measured speech	DANCE 7
v. is prose	POETRY 11
write free v.	POETRY 33
verses cap v.	QUOTATIONS 2
version Authorized V.	BIBLE 1
vessel weaker v.	MARRIAGE 13
vessels Empty v.	FOOLS 2
vestry I will see you in the v.	CLERGY 19
vibrated better not be v.	EMOTIONS 15
vicar V. of Bray	SELF-INTEREST 22
vicariously vice enjoyed v.	GOSSIP 5
vice Art is v.	ARTS 26
best discover v.	ADVERSITY 11
between virtue and v.	GOOD 28
bullied out of v.	VIRTUE 37
from v. to virtue	POSSESSIONS 29
Gossip is v.	GOSSIP 5
in a private man a v.	AMBITION 12
lashed the v.	CRITICISM 7
liberty is no v.	EXCESS 31
lost by not having been v.	VIRTUE 33
nerve-racking v.	HYPOCRISY 19
nurseries of all v.	SCHOOLS 4
Obstinacy is a great v.	DETERMINATION 33
render v. serviceable	POLITICIANS 7
V. came in always	SIN 21
V. is detestable	SIN 23
v. of chastity	SINGLE 5
v. pays to virtue	HYPOCRISY 13
vice-presidency v. isn't worth a pitcher	PRESIDENCY 13
vices ladder of our v.	SIN 13
v. may be committed	MANNERS 13
v. which it does not have	PRESENT 12
vicissitudes v. of fortune	MISFORTUNES 16
victim Any v. demands allegiance	SYMPATHY 25
thou shalt not be a v.	INDIFFERENCE 17
victims I hate v.	CRIME 48
little v. play	CHILDREN 13
victis *Vae v.*	WINNING 10
victor to the v. belong the spoils	WINNING 14
whichever side may call itself the v.	WARFARE 46
Victorian V. values	VIRTUE 14
V. values	VIRTUE 51
victories Peace hath her v.	PEACE 11
victory Dig for V.	GARDENS 18
grave, where is thy v.	DEATH 22
how to gain a v.	ARMED FORCES 1
In v.: magnanimity	WARFARE 54
In v. unbearable	PEOPLE 56
It smells like v.	WARFARE 63
moment of v. is much too short	WINNING 26
not the v. but the contest	WINNING 17
One more such v.	WINNING 6
Pyrrhic v.	WINNING 5
v. at all costs	WINNING 20
V. has a hundred fathers	SUCCESS 41
v. in him	ORIGINALITY 8
v. over oneself	SELF 4
Vienna V. is nothing	ROYALTY 26
Viet Cong no quarrel with the V.	ENEMIES 20
Vietnam peace to V.	PEACE 29
V. was lost	BROADCASTING 12
view enchantment to the v.	COUNTRY AND TOWN 11
you get a v.	AMERICAN CITIES 63

world (*cont.*)
w., the flesh, and the devil	TEMPTATION 10
w. we will never understand	JOURNALISM 24
w. will end in fire	ENDING 18
w. without end	TIME 17
worsening the w.	BROADCASTING 14
worlds all possible w.	OPTIMISM 1
all possible w.	OPTIMISM 17
best of all possible w.	OPTIMISM 27
crack between the w.	SUPERNATURAL 25
destroyer of w.	PHYSICAL 13
number of w. is infinite	UNIVERSE 4
what w. away	SATISFACTION 26
w. of wanwood	SORROW 18
worm catches the w.	PREPARATION 3
w. at one end	HUNTING 7
w. i' the bud	SECRECY 20
w., the canker	MIDDLE AGE 6
w. will turn	NECESSITY 4
worms nor w. forget	INSULTS 7
set on me in W.	DEFIANCE 11
We are all w.	CHARACTER 45
wormwood gall and w.	ADVERSITY 3
worried w. into being	CREATIVITY 11
worry not work, but w.	WORRY 3
W. is interest paid	WORRY 5
W. is like a rocking chair	WORRY 6
w. on the doorstep	OPTIMISM 28
w.'s worst enemy	ACTION 1
worrying show their love by not w.	WORRY 16
What's the use of w.	WORRY 11
worse books had been any w.	CINEMA 11
fare w.	SATISFACTION 3
finding something w.	MISFORTUNES 23
for better for w.	MARRIAGE 21
from w. to better	CHANGE 33
I don't feel w.	GUILT 18
might have been w.	SYMPATHY 4
More will mean w.	UNIVERSITIES 25
w. appear The better	SPEECHES 8
w. than a crime	MISTAKES 16
worsening w. the world	BROADCASTING 14
worship find someone to w.	RELIGION 23
w. God in his own way	HUMAN RIGHTS 13
w. of the bitch-goddess	SUCCESS 34
Your w. is your furnaces	TECHNOLOGY 10
worshipped dog's tooth is truly w.	RELIGION 30
worst full look at the w.	OPTIMISM 23
knowing the w.	HUMAN RACE 31
prepare for the w.	PREPARATION 8
put the w. to death	CRIME 33
rape actually isn't the w. thing	VIOLENCE 22
things are at the w.	OPTIMISM 12
told the w.	BRITAIN 11
w. are full of passionate	EXCELLENCE 14
w. form of Government	DEMOCRACY 20
w. is not	SUFFERING 11
w. is yet to come	OPTIMISM 26
w. of both worlds	DIPLOMACY 10
w. of times	CIRCUMSTANCE 20
worth Because I'm w. it	SELF-ESTEEM 1
calculate the w. of a man	VALUE 26
If a thing's w. doing	EFFORT 5
makes life w. living	CULTURE 22
man's w. something	SELF-KNOWLEDGE 12
more w. than his chambermaid	CRISES 11
nothing that is w. knowing	EDUCATION 24
not w. going to see	TRAVEL 21
Ode on a Grecian Urn is w.	WRITING 46
that which is w. having	SELF-SACRIFICE 15
what is w. reading	EDUCATION 28
w. doing badly	WOMEN 39
w. forty thousand of you	VALUE 34
w. more than the price of the paint	VALUE 30
w. of a thing is what	VALUE 8
w. the paper	LAW 36
your flattery is w.	PRAISE 12

Worthington on the stage, Mrs W.	ACTING 8
worthy Lord I am not w.	SELF-ESTEEM 9
nameless in w. deeds	FAME 8
w. of his hire	EMPLOYMENT 1
w. of their steel	ENEMIES 13
would He w.	SELF-INTEREST 27
w. not, that I do	GOOD 18
wound never felt a w.	SUFFERING 10
world's worst w.	EPITAPHS 24
w., not the bandage	RELIGION 31
wounded w. by what other men	PAST 39
wounds keeps his own w. green	REVENGE 15
rubbed into their w.	SUFFERING 27
wrath down upon your w.	ANGER 6
grapes of w.	GOD 26
soft answer turneth away w.	DIPLOMACY 1
turneth away w.	ANGER 4
tygers of w.	ANGER 9
wren robin and the w.	BIRDS 3
wrench with a rusty monkey w.	DETERMINATION 2
wrestle w. not against flesh	SUPERNATURAL 9
w. with words	MEANING 14
wrestles He that w. with us	ENEMIES 12
wretched knows that I am w.	SUFFERING 16
w. people upon earth	AUSTRALIA 10
wretcheder w. one is	SMOKING 12
wring they will soon w. their hands	WARS 7
w. the withers	EMOTIONS 6
wrinkle without any spot or w.	VIRTUE 15
with the first w.	MIDDLE AGE 4
wrinkles magically take away your w.	APPEARANCE 35
writ w. in water	EPITAPHS 15
write could not w. the words	WORDS 19
didn't w. 'Ol' Man River'	SINGING 13
I will w. for Antiquity	WRITING 27
I w. the truth	HONESTY 16
Learn to w. well	WRITING 17
nothing to w. about	LETTERS 5
people who can't w.	JOURNALISM 29
such an effort to w.	LETTERS 17
such as cannot w.	TRANSLATION 3
things I w. about	MADNESS 12
Though an angel should w.	PUBLISHING 8
would write and can't w.	WRITING 2
w. all the books	CHANCE 32
w. every other day	LETTERS 15
w. for the fire	WRITING 10
w. the life of a man	BIOGRAPHY 4
w. the next chapter	HUMAN RIGHTS 16
writer best fame is a w.'s	FAME 23
great and original w.	ORIGINALITY 10
original w. is not	ORIGINALITY 9
still want to be a w.	WRITERS 25
understand a w.'s ignorance	WRITING 25
w. has to rob his mother	WRITING 46
w. to eat a whole sheep	WRITING 43
writers full of fourth-rate w.	READING 20
W., like teeth, are divided	WRITING 30
writes Happiness w. white	HAPPINESS 30
moving finger w.	PAST 25
writing art of w. silence	BROADCASTING 20
Beware of w. to me	LETTERS 20
easy w.'s vile hard reading	WRITING 20
fine w. is next to fine doing	WRITING 26
If w. did not exist	WRITING 8
incurable disease of w.	WRITING 7
In w. songs I've learned	SINGING 17
This w. business	WRITING 37
w. is on the wall	HUMOUR 22
w. on the wall	FUTURE 10
written anything may be w.	BOOKS 7
Books are well w.	BOOKS 15
w. about in their lifetime	BIOGRAPHY 23
W. English is now inert	LANGUAGES 17
w. seems like straw	INSIGHT 6
w. word as unlike	STYLE 20
wrong all was w.	SATISFACTION 23

What's new in Quotations Dictionaries?

The Oxford Dictionary
of
Modern Quotations

2nd edition

edited by Elizabeth Knowles

Landmark voices of past and present:

Norman Mailer
The world stood like a playing card on edge.—
Cuban Missile Crisis, 1961

Rudolph Giuliani
We're just being tested one more time.—*autumn 2001*

A Quotations Dictionary for the 21st century, perfect for answering the questions, 'Who said that...,and when...and why?'

OXFORD
UNIVERSITY PRESS

September 2002

www.oxford.com

ISBN 0-19-866275-0